T0320012

Harvard Studies in Business History, 43

Published with the support of the Harvard Business School
Edited by Thomas K. McCraw
Isidor Straus Professor of Business History
Graduate School of Business Administration
George F. Baker Foundation
Harvard University

The History of Foreign Investment in the United States, 1914–1945

Mira Wilkins

Harvard University Press
Cambridge, Massachusetts
London, England
2004

Copyright © 2004 by the President and Fellows of Harvard College
All rights reserved
Printed in the United States of America

Library of Congress Cataloging-in-Publication Data

Wilkins, Mira.
The history of foreign investment in the United States, 1914–1945 / Mira Wilkins.
p. cm.—(Harvard studies in business history ; 43)
Includes bibliographical references and index.
ISBN 0-674-01308-5 (alk. paper)
1. Investments, Foreign—United States—History—20th century. I. Title. II. Series.

HG4910.W428 2004
332.67'3'097309041—dc22 2003067782

Contents

Tables and Figures

Tables

Figures

Preface

Today Americans take for granted the presence within our national boundaries of foreign-owned enterprises (we often do not realize that they are foreign-owned). Industries are international. We read about the role of foreign investors in our stock markets and accept this as ordinary. "Global" is an overused term. In the late 1980s, America became a "debtor nation" in world accounts, attracting more inward foreign investments than we had outward foreign investments. Virtually overnight, the world's largest creditor nation became the world's largest debtor nation. Then, that change had seemed dramatic.

It was, however, no less dramatic and no less rapid than the transformation from debtor to creditor that occurred between 1914 and 1918. In 1914, the United States had been the world's largest debtor nation—a debtor since it attracted greater inward than it had outward foreign investments, the largest debtor since it had attracted greater inward foreign investments than any other single nation. The world economy at the start of 1914 was well integrated. Major nations were on the gold standard. Foreign investors bought American securities, new issues and traded ones. Foreign multinational enterprises had invested on an international scale, including large investments in the United States. Capital controls were virtually nonexistent. The dollar was as good as gold. There was a global economy. Yet globalization creates vulnerability. And this book to a great extent deals with that vulnerability.

In 1914, war began in Europe. The world economy was at risk. Between 1914 and 1918, as America changed from being the world's largest debtor to a creditor nation, it became a key and then the key creditor nation in the altered conditions in the aftermath of the First World War. In the decades during which America was a creditor nation, inward investments continued on. Many economists thought this inward investment was "abnormal." This book will show that while the United States was a creditor nation, foreign investment was always a two-way street; inward foreign investments never disappeared. The book will analyze the path and nature of that inward foreign investment. I reject the idea that there was anything "abnormal" about what occurred.

My book covers the years 1914 to 1945, the time of the transformation of the United States from debtor to creditor to 1945, when the United States was indisputably the world's most important creditor nation bar none. It is the sequel to my *History of Foreign Investment in the United States to 1914,* published by Harvard University Press in 1989. As in that volume, I include all long-term inward foreign investments in the United States: portfolio investments (by individuals and institutions) and direct investments (by multinational enterprises). The distinction lies between financial investments where the investor's intent was financial returns combined with safety, and those investments where the investor's intent was associated with business strategy and the return was to be derived from the business package. An appendix is included herein that provides more precise definitions on how I use the terms; as the book unfolds, I will look at these investments together and separately—as the evidence guides me.

Indeed, this book is unique in its careful combined treatment of both foreign long-term portfolio investment (FPI) and foreign direct investment (FDI), 1914–1945. Although earlier I had covered both in the pre-1914 years, others had followed that approach. For these years, however, some authors have explored certain interconnections, but most have focused on either FPI or FDI. In preparing this book, I figured out why. FPI and FDI were very different: the actors were different, and their behavior differed systematically; yet, at times, as I will show, there was convergence, overlap, and intertwining. Public policies and wars in many (but not all) cases had distinct consequences for FPI and FDI; on both, however, the impacts were profound. Despite great frustrations, I have attempted to offer my reader coherent statistical series designed to buttress my story line. Two appendixes bear witness to the fragility of the statistics, providing detailed source information for the specialist. An appendix also contains a summary of the principal U.S. laws, 1914–1945, affecting the course of foreign investments in the United States.

The fundamental separation in motivation and characteristics between FPI and FDI, while revealed clearly in the chapters covering 1914 to 1929, becomes stark in 1929–1933; and in Chapter 6, which covers these years of crisis, I take time to elaborate on the nuances of the responses by foreign portfolio investors and how in very specific terms they differed from those of direct investors (multinational enterprises). In Chapter 7, I show that during the New Deal, separate branches within the U.S. government began to pay attention to monitoring and evaluating the consequences of FPI and FDI.

For the reader who is au courant with the literature on the history of multinational enterprise, much of the material presented herein on FPI will be very new. I pay substantial attention to inward long term FPI, because throughout the years the frail statistics seem to indicate that the level of such investment always exceeded that of inward FDI. The available figures, in my view, however, underestimate the amounts of inward FDI and do not appropriately reflect the considerable activities of foreign multinational enterprises within the U.S. economy. Thus, in documenting the history of multinational enterprise, I hope macroeconomists and other students of international capital flows will find what I offer greatly enriches their thinking. Hopefully, I will be contributing to a start in reconciling what for too long a time had been very separate bodies of writings on FPI and FDI. (The literatures diverged early and then most sharply after the 1960s, as many students of multinational enterprise had deep dissatisfaction with the inability of the then standard theories of capital movements to explain multinational enterprise.)

The chapters in this volume trace the uneven course of inward long-term FPI and FDI from 1914 to 1945 while at the same time investigating the effects of general political and economic conditions on such investments, as well as the emerging public policies. I cover the alliances, joint ventures, and cooperative and competitive strategies of firms during the entire period. The book contains a lot of detail, albeit I try never to lose sight of the patterns and generalizations. I believe that the detail is required in order to arrive at my conclusions. This combined narrative and analytic examination is drawn from extensive evidence. The approach is chronological, based on the proposition that there were major changes during these years, and this volume needs to place the inward foreign investments in their evolving contextual setting. A reader who wishes to document a particular company's history can do so easily, using the book's index. Chapter 10, which covers the "old and the new," includes a comparison of the inward foreign investments in 1914 and 1945.

While the volume concludes with comparisons between the profile of inward foreign investment in 1914 and 1945, we should never forget how consequential the transformations were during the interim and how jagged was the course of those changes. Hopefully, with this book, there is no need to jump from 1914 to 1945 (as some scholars have done); now there is a full study of these critical intervening years. While it appears that the United States was the largest host to foreign investment in 1945 (as in 1914), this turned out to be an almost incidental finding—for what mattered most was that by 1945 the place of inward foreign investment within the U.S. economy was substantially different from what it had been in 1914.

This is an economic, business, financial, technological, legal, and diplomatic history. Specifically, it should enhance our knowledge of U.S. economic and business history. Too often the latter has been written divorced from the international context. This is more, however, than U.S. history. The story of foreign investment in the United States is a subset of world economic history—for the unfolding events on a global scale were mirrored in the inward foreign investments in this nation.

In *The History of Foreign Investment in the United States to 1914,* I argued that foreign investment was far more significant in U.S. economic growth and development than had been previously recognized. In this book, I maintain that although as a percentage of U.S. gross national product inward foreign investment in 1945 was far smaller and by all other measures less notable than in 1914, nonetheless its role was extremely important in the years between 1914 and 1945; that both continuities and discontinuities existed; and that if we are to understand the internationalization of today's American economy (and the broader trends in globalization), it is vital to analyze, know about, and understand the historical course of foreign investments in the United States. This is a long book because its subject matter is complex, because the story as a unity has never before been told, and because I want it to be both definitive and comprehensive. A third volume—to follow—will cover the years 1945 to the present.

Acknowledgments

This book has taken a long time to write, and so many individuals have helped in so many ways. My thanks are boundless. Part of the shaping of an intellectual experience is having people to talk with and to try out ideas. I have never been shy about asking questions, and since my research topic has been so large, I have called on many scholars, librarians, archivists, and others to help me fill in gaps and forward my efforts. My method is often that of a detective. I set a frame. I ask, "Why?" And then I search out answers in published and unpublished material. One discovery prompts the next set of queries and the next set of discoveries. I explore theories. Do they help me understand the empirical evidence? None of this can be done alone. As I have over the years spent time trying to decipher the contours of the history of foreign investments, a group of men who were doing research on the development of multinational enterprise provided me with incomparable advice and assistance. Leading among them has been my good friend Geoff Jones, whom I have known for more than two decades and who has written wisely on many topics germane to my interests; I have discussed this book with him on multiple occasions and have greatly cherished his suggestions, the conferences that he has invited me to, and his pushing me to look at corporate performance along with international corporate expansion. So, too, Patrick Fridenson has come to my rescue in dozens of ways—from helping on matters related to the automobile industry, to introducing me to French scholars, to aiding me in gaining access to French archives. Peter Hertner has kept me current on the history of German multinational enterprise (mailing me important material by young German scholars that I would otherwise have missed). Harm Schröter has supplied advice, from that on theory, to that on German business documents, to German cartels, to Swiss multinationals. Tetsuo Abo motivated me to probe more deeply into the history of Japanese multinational enterprise. Another friend and onetime colleague, Jean-François Hennart, has animated my thinking for decades; I have tremendously enjoyed my lengthy conversations with him that have taken place in France, the United States (Florida, Pennsylvania, Illinois), and Holland, as his career has conveyed him from one side of the Atlantic to the other. Ben Gomes-Casseres read this entire book in manuscript form and made splendid and much appreciated suggestions on the penultimate draft.

A crucial group of more senior scholars have throughout my career been an inspiration to me and of so much assistance in so many ways. I have truly cherished my friendships with Al Chandler, John Dunning, Bob Aliber, the late Ray Vernon, the late Rondo Cameron, the late Edith Penrose, the late Vince Carosso, the late Allan Nevins, and the late Frank Ernest Hill. Al Chandler has over many years shared with me his ideas about the nature of business development, encouraging me to consider what management means in the international context. He has had a profound influence on my thinking. I am so indebted. John Dunning opened to me with great generosity his valuable files on British direct investments in manufacturing in the United States (which were extraordinarily useful in my research, as my frequent citations reveal); his OLI (Ownership, Location, and Internalization) paradigm—in its many renditions—has prompted me to examine more carefully my unfolding evidence; his work pressed me to try to develop appropriate tables and measures of the inward foreign investments, particularly the foreign direct investments. I have known Bob Aliber for more than forty years, longer than I have known Al Chandler (I first met Al in 1962) and longer than I have known John Dunning (whom I did not meet until the 1970s). Bob Aliber is one of the very few students of multinational enterprise who for decades has sought to reconcile the literatures of FPI and FDI. I have treasured all of these individuals' brilliance, and their inspiring me to venture into new directions and to formulate my own distinctive contributions.

In addition, I have asked favors of and countless times quizzed many, many more individuals and so welcomed the helpfulness of these friends, acquaintances, and even (some) strangers. Specifically (in alphabetical order) the following were wonderfully gracious in sharing their expertise. My thanks go to each of them: Susan Becker (Metallgesellschaft); I. J. Blanken (Philips); Michael Bordo (capital flows and the gold standard; government securities); Geoffrey Bowker (Schlumberger); Wayne Broehl (from grain trade to general issues of foreign multinational enterprise); G. A. Burchett (Glaxo Wellcome); the late Marianne Burge (taxes, transfer pricing, and foreign investment); John

Cantwell (patents); Youssef Cassis (Swiss banking); Mark Casson (thoughts on multinational enterprise); Pierre Cayez (foreign silk companies in America); Emmett D. Chisum (American Heritage Center Archives); Roy Church (British business); Tony Corley (Beecham, and many other thoughts); Phil Cottrell (banking); Richard P. T. Davenport-Hines (Glaxo); Donald F. Davis (shareholdings in Studebaker); Barry Eichengreen (interwar monetary policies); Wilfried Feldenkirchen (German business); Gerry Feldman (Pilot Insurance, German business, and added contributions); Michael Geyer (Krupp); Elisabeth Glaser-Schmidt (material from the Bayer archives, Leverkusen); Gene M. Gressley (frontier investments and Wyoming connections); Les Hannah (British business history); Paul J. Hauser (Daiwa Securities); Will Hausman (public utilities and general wisdom); the late Gunnar Hedlund (Swedish multinationals); J. Heim (Bally shoes); Y. Homma (Japanese banks in the United States); Hans Ch. Johansen (shipping); Joost Jonker (Dutch investments); Birgit Karlsson (SKF); J. D. Keir (Unilever); Frank King (Hongkong and Shanghai Bank); Chris Kobrak (Schering); Even Lange (Norwegian investments in the United States); John Lesch (German pharmaceuticals); Jin-Mieung Li (L'Air Liquide); Jonathan Liebenau (Salvarsan); Bob Lipsey (FDI and FPI and splendid conceptual insights); Ragnhild Lundström (Swedish multinationals); Tom McCraw (who invited me to talk at Harvard Business School and pushed me to clarify many vague ideas); Harry McGhin (Loncala Phosphate); Dwight Miller (Hoover Papers); Mike Nash (Du Pont records); Viv Nelles (Canadian investments); Steve Nicholas (British multinationals); Janice Scott Person (Delta and Pine Land Company); Giandomenico Piluso (Italian banks); the late Bill Reader (lots of sage advice); the late Bob Roosa (foreign currency-denominated bonds); Stephen Schuker (Siemens Archives and German interests in the United States); Luciano Segreto (Swiss companies in America); Keetie Sluyterman (Dutch investments); Maureen Staniforth (Unilever); Patrick Stoffel (Stoffel & Co.); Dick Sylla (who kept me focused on finance); Tamás Szmrecsányi (many ideas); Graham Taylor (valuable ideas and data); Alice Teichova (East European banking); Adrian Tschoegl (foreign banking in the United States); Guus Veenendaal (Dutch investments, especially in U.S. railroads); Ben Wall (oil matters); Dick Williams (Du Pont records); Noel Workman (Delta and Pine Land Company); and Tsunehiko Yui (Japanese business). In a more general manner, the writings of the late Charles Kindleberger, Michael Edelstein, and Lance Davis influenced my first volume and this one as well. As I write all these names down, I realize how fortunate I have been to have had over the many years such a wide and splendid academic circle, or circles, or networks, to use the more "modern" term.

The John Simon Guggenheim Foundation awarded me a much valued fellowship, which I used to research the first volume, this second volume, and also the third one, which is still forthcoming. I am very honored to rank among the prestigious list of Guggenheim Fellows. The research on this book has been done as I have served on the faculty of Florida International University, in Miami. I have appreciated the support of my university: the awards bestowed upon me; my exemplary department chair, Panos Liossatos (to whom my thanks are legion), the Dean of Arts and Sciences, Art Herriott (who has had confidence in me over the many years); and the entire library staff, who have been extraordinary (Marge Beary, Debbie Safford, Doug Hasty, Andy Grof, Sherry Carrillo, Sherry Mosley, Patricia Iannuzzi, Steve Morris, Mercedes Sanchez, Salvador Miranda, and Larry Miller stand out, as do the newer staff members Tony Schwartz and Valerie Edwards). My two Ph.D. students, Giyas Gokkent and Pablo Toral, have helped in countless ways, while at the last stages my student assistant Fabian Murgo gave much appreciated aid. And then there is my delight with my present and past colleagues, especially Howard Rock, Gerry Bierwag, Maria Willumsen, Ken Lipartito, Costas Syropolous, Devishish Mitra, Cem Karalycin, Alan Gummerson, John Boyd, Richard Chisik, and Santanu Roy, who have in numerous ways assisted this endeavor and always furnished sound advice. "Extension 2284, Computer Services," saved the day time and time again. Mariela Delgado, Teresita Cardenas, and Charles Flores were there for me when I needed them. At Harvard University Press, Kathleen McDermott furnished invaluable suggestions and encouragement; the outcome is a far better book as a consequence of her expert touch.

Finally, last but far from least, on a sad note, my late husband, George Simmons, is ever in my mind and heart. Alas, his contribution to this volume will never be known to him; I hope he would have taken pride in this book. I dedicate it to him, as well as to my many dear friends who are no longer living. How I miss all of you. Know how I would love to share my pleasure in this publication.

August 15, 2003

Abbreviations

AAC	Anglo-American Chemicals, Ltd.
ABC	American Bosch Corporation
AB-SKF	Aktiebolaget Svenska Kullagerfabriken
ACC	American & Continental Corporation
AEA	American Economic Association
AEF	Archives Economiques et Financieres
AEG	Allgemeine Elektrizitäts-Gesellschaft
AESC	American European Securities Company
AG	Aktiengesellschaft (joint-stock company)
Agfa (or AGFA)	Aktiengesellschaft für Anilin-Fabrikation, Berlin
AGUT	Aktiengesellschaft für Unternehmungen der Textilindustrie
AHC	American Hyalsol Corporation
AIC	American International Corporation
AKU	Algemeene Kunstzijde Unie NV
Alcoa	Aluminum Company of America
AMC	American Magnesium Company
AMH	Ayerst, McKenna & Harrison
ANC	Atmospheric Nitrogen Corporation
ANOTP	Alabama, New Orleans, Texas, and Pacific Junction Railways Co., Ltd.
APC	Alien Property Custodian
APCC	American Potash & Chemical Corporation
ARC	Associated Rayon Corporation
ASCC	Advance Solvents & Chemical Corporation
AT&T	American Telephone and Telegraph Corporation
AVC	American Viscose Company (1910–1915); became

	The Viscose Company (1915–1937); American Viscose Corporation (1937–); see also TVC
Badische	Badische Anilin und Soda Fabrik, Ludwigshafen
Basf (or BASF)	Badische (Badische Anilin und Soda Fabrik, Ludwigshafen)
BAT	British American Tobacco Company
Bayer (in Germany)	Farbenfabriken vorm. Friedrich Bayer & Co.
BBE	Banque Belge pour l'Etranger
BBNA	Bank of British North America
BCI	Banca Commerciale Italiana
BCIT	Banca Commerciale Italiana Trust Company, New York (or in other cities as specified)
BDC	British Dyestuffs Corporation
Berlin Aniline	AGFA or Aktiengesellschaft für Anilin-Fabrikation, Berlin
BEW	Board of Economic Warfare
Bezit	Gemeenschappelijk Bezit van Aandelen Philips' Gloeilampenfabrieken, NV
BMC	British Metal Corporation
BOLSA	Bank of London and South America
CCA	Celanese Corporation of America
CED	*Current Economic Developments,* as in *Foreign Relations of the United States: Current Economic Developments 1945–1954, Current Economic Developments*
CEO	Chief executive officer
CFB	Corporation of Foreign Bondholders
CFP	Compagnie Française des Pétroles
CFR	Code of the Federal Regulations (the codified FR, *Federal Register*)
Chepha	Chemical and Pharmaceutical Enterprises Ltd.
CID	The Clearing Industrial District Inc.
CIL	Canadian Industries Ltd.
CMBA	Chase Manhattan Bank Archives
CNEP	Comptoir National d'Escompte de Paris
CPA	Calico Printers' Association
CPR	Canadian Pacific Railway
CRA	Catalytic Research Associates
CSF	Compagnie Générale de Télégraphie sans Fil
CTA	Comptoir des Textiles Artificiels
CUTT	Compagnie Universelle de Téléphonie et Télégraphique sans Fil

CXL	Canadian Explosives, Ltd.
DCA	Dyestuffs Corporation of America
DCD	Distillers Company Limited, Delaware
DCL	Distillers Company Limited, Edinburgh
DCO (or DC&O)	Dominion, Colonial & Overseas, as in Barclays (DCO)
DC SL	Distillers Corporation-Seagrams Ltd., Montreal
Degussa	Deutsche Gold- und Silber-Scheideanstadt
Dept.-Justice	Department of Justice
DND Calif.	District Court, Northern District, California
DNJ	District Court of New Jersey
DPF	Du Pont Pathe Film Manufacturing Corporation
DPFC	Du Pont Fibersilk Company
DPLC	Delta and Pine Land Company
DWF	Deutsche Waffen-und Munitions Fabriken
EAC	East Asiatic Company (Denmark)
EALM	Edinburgh American Land Mortgage Co.
EBC	Electric Boat Company
EDB	Economic Defense Board
Elektrobank	Bank für Elektrische Unternehmungen
EMI	Electrical and Musical Industries
Exh.	Exhibit
FABC	French American Banking Corporation
FBI	Federal Bureau of Investigation
FCSDA	Fine Cotton Spinners' and Doublers' Association
FDI	Foreign direct investment
FDIC	Federal Deposit Insurance Corporation
FDIUS	Foreign Direct Investment in the United States
FEA	Foreign Economic Administration
FIUS	Foreign Investment in the United States
FO	Foreign Office
FOC	Foreign Operations Committee
FPI	Foreign portfolio investment
FPOB	Foreign Petroleum Operating Board
FR	Federal Register
FRBNY	Federal Reserve Bank of New York
FRC	Federal Radio Commission
FRUS	*Foreign Relations of the United States*
FTC	Federal Trade Commission
GAF	General Aniline & Film Corporation
GAW	General Aniline Works
GDC	General Dyestuff Corporation
GE	General Electric

GFADC	Gold Fields American Development Co.
GM	General Motors
GmbH	Gesellschaft mit beschränkter Haftung (limited company)
GNP	Gross national product
Hapag (or HAPAG)	Hamburg-American Line
HESC	Hydro-Electric Securities Corp.
Hoechst	Farbwerke vorm. Meister Lucius & Brüning, Hoechst am Main
Homag	Hochfrequenz Maschinen Aktiengesellschaft für Drahtlöse Telegraphie
HSBC	Hongkong and Shanghai Banking Corporation
IAB	International Acceptance Bank
IARA	Inter-Allied Reparations Agency
IBSC	Investment Bond and Share Corporation
ICC	Interstate Commerce Commission
ICI	Imperial Chemical Industries
IFI	International Finance & Investment Corporation
IG Chemie	Internationale Gesellschaft für Chemische Unternehmungen AG, Basle
IGEC	International General Electric Company
IHP	International Hydrogenation Patent Company
IMCO	International Match Corporation
IMF	International Monetary Fund
IMM	International Mercantile Marine Company
Interhandel	Internationale Gesellschaft für Handels- und Industriebeteiligungen AG, Basle (successor to IG Chemie)
IPC	Industrial Potash Corporation
IRS	Internal Revenue Service
JN & Co.	Joseph Nathan & Co.
K & M	Keasbey & Mattison
KPAC	Kidder Peabody Acceptance Corporation
LGAI (or LGA)	London Guarantee and Accident Insurance Co.
LRD	Library and Records Department of the Foreign and Commonwealth Office, London
MDC	Magnesium Development Corporation
MEW	Ministry of Economic Warfare
Mij.	Maatschappij
MNC	Multinational corporation
MNE	Multinational enterprise
MSK	Mitsubishi Shoji Kaisha

Multinationals	Multinational enterprises
NA	National Archives
NACC	National Aniline & Chemical Company
NAPC	North American Philips Company
NARA	National Archives and Records Administration
NBER	National Bureau of Economic Research
NCC	National Credit Corporation
NECC	Niagara Electro Chemical Company
NECY	New England Cotton Yarn Company
NEHA	Nederlandsch Economisch-Historisch Archief
NFTC	National Foreign Trade Council
NI	Nazi Industrialists (as in the Nuremberg investigations of Nazi Industrialists)
NICB	National Industrial Conference Board
NIRA	National Industrial Recovery Act
NOT	Nederlandsche Overzee Trustmaatschappij
NRA	National Recovery Administration
NV	Naamloze Vennootschap (limited liability company)
NVNC	NV Nederlandsche Crediet-en Financiering-Maatschappij
NYK	Nippon Yusen Kaisha
NYSE	New York Stock Exchange
OAPC	Office of Alien Property Custodian (World War II)
OCC	Ore & Chemical Corporation
OSK	Osaka Shosen Kaisha
OSS	Office of Strategic Services
P & G	Procter & Gamble
PIC	Potash Importing Corporation
PRO	Public Record Office
R & H	Roessler & Hasslacher Chemical Company
RCA	Radio Corporation of America
Rev.	Revised
RFC	Reconstruction Finance Corporation
RG	Record Group
Rpt.	Reprint
RTZ	Rio Tinto-Zinc
SAC	Southern Aluminium Company
SAIC	Solvay American Investment Corporation (renamed Solvay American Corporation, June 1937)
SASTIG	Schweizerisch-Americanischen Stickerei-Industrie-Gesellschaft
SBC	Swiss Bank Corporation

Schrobanco	J. Henry Schroder Banking Corporation, New York (1923–1977)
Schroder, London	J. Henry Schroder & Co. (1940–1957)
Schröder, London	J. Henry Schröder & Co. (1818–1939)
SCUR	Société Chimique des Usines du Rhône
SDNY	Southern District Court of New York
SEC	Securities and Exchange Commission
Sidac	Société Industrielle de la Cellulose
SKF	Svenska Kullagerfabriken, or AB-SKF (Aktiebolaget Svenska Kullagerfabriken)
SKF-US	SKF Industries, an affiliate of AB-SKF (Aktiebolaget Svenska Kullagerfabriken)
Sofina	Société Financière de Transports et d'Entreprises Industrielles
SONJ	Standard Oil Company (New Jersey) or Standard Oil of New Jersey (renamed Exxon in 1972; became Exxon-Mobil in 1999)
SPC	Solvay Process Company
Stat.	Statutes
TEA	Trading with the Enemy Act
TNEC	Temporary National Economic Committee
TTC	Transatlantic Trust Company
TVC	The Viscose Company (1915–1937); the successor and predecessor of AVC, see above
UA	Unilever Archives, London
UABC	United American Bosch Corporation
UCC	United Continental Corporation
UFC	United Financial Corporation
U.K.	United Kingdom
UMC	United Molasses Co., Ltd.,
USMSC	United States Mail Steamship Company
USSB	United States Shipping Board
US-SKF (or SKF-US)	SKF Industries
UTC	Universal Trading Corporation
VGF	Vereinigte Glanzstoff-Fabriken
VYB	Vivian, Younger, and Bond
WARF	Wisconsin Alumni Research Foundation
WHIC	Western and Hawaiian Investment Co.
WRCIS	Western Range Cattle Industry Study
YSB	Yokohama Specie Bank

1.

The First World War, 1914–1918

World financial markets were in turmoil in the summer of 1914 when the European war began. Stock exchanges were closed. The *New York Times* predicted (on August 5, 1914) that when the exchanges reopened, "The United States will become less of a debtor . . . No nation in the world is better prepared for such a liquidation [of foreign holdings of American securities], because no nation in the world has such an immense stock of wealth." The *Times* continued, "No doubt the transition period will be one of strain, but its results will be worth the cost to us." It now seemed possible to end America's status as an international debtor—a position long resented by Americans. The United States had been a debtor in world accounts throughout its entire history. In the summer of 1914, it was the world's greatest debtor nation.[1]

The Austrian heir apparent Archduke Francis Ferdinand had been assassinated at Sarajevo on Sunday, June 28, 1914. European armies had been built up; the murder is considered to be the spark that ignited the First World War. Yet in the initial three weeks of July, the effects on the world economy appeared slight, although prices did slump on the Berlin and Paris Bourses. On July 4, the *New York Times* ran a story about a new French tax on income from outward foreign investments; it was front-page news, since it would have an impact on prominent Americans living in Paris who held U.S. investments; one result of the new tax was, however, *French* divestment of American securities.[2] On Monday, July 13, stock prices fell by over 10 percent on the Vienna Bourse. The following day, July 14, Europeans made "unusually large" sales on the New York Stock Market, which the *New York Times* attributed to a report from the Interstate Commerce Commission condemning the former management of the New York, New Haven and Hartford Railroad; the *New York Times* believed Europeans were disposing of their stocks and bonds because of these U.S. "official denunciations." The newspaper made no reference to any connection with political conditions in Europe, nor with the coincident mounting anxieties on European stock markets.[3]

Not until early in the fourth week of July did Americans start to pay serious attention to the growing political and economic tensions on the other side of the Atlantic. The *New York Times* reported that on Tuesday, July 21, prices had dropped sharply on the Berlin Bourse. Then, on July 23, Austria gave an ultimatum to the Serbs, accusing them of complicity in the murder of Archduke Francis Ferdinand. Serbia mobilized her army. The next day, Europeans sold heavily on the New York Stock Exchange; the price of sterling increased to $4.88 (the gold parity was $4.86); U.S. gold exports began. In the gold standard era, when the exchange rate rose to roughly $4.88 (the so-called gold export point), rather than buy sterling, transactions would be completed with the export of gold. At last, it dawned on *New York Times* correspondents that the foreign sales of American securities on July 24 were a result of European "war scares."[4] In the week beginning July 25, Europeans' selling of American securities mounted. The following excerpts—most from the *New York Times*—reflect the intensifying crisis (the days listed relate to the events, not when they were reported). Note that in 1914 stock markets were typically open on Saturday mornings.

Saturday morning, July 25:

"The bottom is dropping out of things on the [Paris] Bourse."
"The blackest Saturday in German financial history."
"Black Saturday" in London. Heavy selling there of American railroad securities especially the Union Pacific and Southern Pacific.[5]

Saturday, 6 P.M.:
Austria-Hungary severed diplomatic relations with Serbia.[6]

Sunday, July 26:
Russia announced she would defend Serbia.[7]

Monday, July 27:
Austrian troops invaded Serbia.
"Prices Crumbling on Foreign Bourses."
"War Scare Draws American Gold to Europe."
Panic stricken conditions caused the closing of the Vienna, Brussels, and Budapest Bourses.
Heavy selling of securities by foreigners in New York continued.

"Sterling cables" rose to $4.94 (sterling cables were the quoted price of sterling).[8]

Tuesday, July 28:
Austria-Hungary declared war against Serbia.
"Stock Prices Slump" in New York and abroad.
New American gold outflow.
Dollar quotations ("sterling cables") were so high as to prohibit dealings in foreign exchange. At the quoted figure (£1 = $4.95), gold could be exported to any part of the world at a profit.
Extraordinary European liquidation of securities in New York.[9]

Wednesday, July 29:
Amsterdam Bourse closed; Frankfurt and Hamburg Bourses suspended dealings; Bourse committee in Berlin deliberated shutting that Exchange.
Trading restrictions imposed in London.
Stock prices slightly *higher* in New York, despite heavy selling by foreigners.
Sterling cables now $5.02.
Russian troops mobilized along the Austrian border.[10]

Thursday, July 30:
"Business paralyzed on London 'Change."
The Paris Bourse opened, "but there was no business." All settlements for July were postponed until August 31.
Heavy foreign selling on the New York Stock Market; stock prices fell; bankers and Stock Exchange officials contemplated but decided against closing the New York Stock Exchange; Americans purchased the securities at the new lower prices.
Sterling cables rose to $5.20, probably the highest figure ever paid.
U.S. gold exports rose.[11]

Friday, July 31:
Germany warned Russia to halt military preparations.
The London Stock Exchange closed until further notice; this was without precedent and caused by the heavy selling.
British bank rate rose from 4 to 8 percent.
The New York Stock Exchange did not open, for the third time in its history. The Exchange was shut to stop Europeans' dumping their securities and to restrain gold exports to Europe to pay for these stocks and bonds. Bankers in America worried that gold exports would deplete U.S. gold reserves.

Sterling cables sold at up to $6.75.
"The Bank of France, the Bank of England, and the Imperial Bank of Germany have practically suspended specie payments."[12]

Saturday, August 1:
Germany declared war on Russia.
British bank rate went from 8 to 10 percent.
Sterling cables sold at $7.00.
Reports of about $100 to $150 million of American stocks and bonds "thrown on this [the New York] market, for whatever they would bring European holders," even though the New York Stock Exchange remained closed.[13]

Monday, August 3:
The New York Stock Exchange stayed shut down, as did stock markets in all the major cities in Europe.

By Tuesday, August 4, 1914, England, France, and Russia (the Entente) were at war with Germany and Austria-Hungary (the Central Powers). That day, the president of the National City Bank, Frank A. Vanderlip, wrote his vacationing wife, "You can not possibly have any conception of what has happened to the world. Civilization has broken down, and there is the most absolute derangement of a great part of our affairs." As a consequence of the outbreak of war, stock exchanges in Europe and the United States no longer functioned. The international economy hung in suspense. America was poised to reverse its position as the world's largest debtor nation.[14]

The Setting

The United States was, in the summer of 1914, deeply involved in the global economy. By the turn of the century, the country had become the world's foremost industrial giant. Since the late nineteenth century, it had consistently had trade surpluses (goods exports exceeded goods imports). But in mid-1914, the United States remained a net debtor in international accounts, that is, foreign investments in America exceeded U.S. investments abroad (Table 1.1). U.S. economic growth had been assisted over the many decades by the sizable contributions of foreign investors, and on the eve of World War I, foreign (principally European) investors had roughly $7.1 billion in long-term stakes in this nation. Inward foreign portfolio investments—mainly securities traded on the New York and London (and possibly Amsterdam and

Table 1.1. Creditors and debtors, July 1, 1914 (in billions of U.S. dollars)

Principal sources of capital		Principal recipients of capital	
Home country	Amount	Host country	Amount
United Kingdom	18.0	**United States**	7.1
France	9.0	Russia	3.8
Germany	7.3	Canada	3.7
United States	3.5	Argentina	3.0
Netherlands	2.0	Austria-Hungary	2.5
Belgium	1.5	Spain	2.5
Switzerland	1.5	Brazil	2.2
		Mexico	2.0
		India and Ceylon	2.0
		South Africa	1.7
		Australia	1.7
		China	1.6
Other	2.2	Other	11.2
Total	45.0	Total	45.0

Source: Mira Wilkins, *The History of Foreign Investment in the United States to 1914* (Cambridge, Mass.: Harvard University Press, 1989), 145. These are long-term obligations. Wilkins based these estimates on compilations of data by the United Nations, Arthur Lewis, William Woodruff, Herbert Feis, Douglass North, Rondo Cameron, Raymond Goldsmith, F. Bartsche, Olga Crisp, and others, along with her own research.

Note: All the figures on the table are "gross." No country is included that had long-term foreign "credits" or "debts" of less than $1.5 billion (the terms "credits" and "debts" include both equity and debt—bonds and loans). The home country is that of the "creditor"; it may not be the ultimate source of the capital. The "Other" in column 1 includes Japan and Russia (with investments especially in China), Portugal (especially in Brazil), Sweden (especially in Russia), and Canada (especially in the United States and the Caribbean), as examples. The figure for "Other" in column 4 includes the residual, *not* separately itemized: $4.7 billion for the rest of Europe, including the Ottoman Empire; $2.3 billion for the rest of Asia; $1.8 billion for the rest of Latin America, including the Caribbean; $2.3 billion for all of Africa except South Africa; and $.1 billion for the rest of Oceania.

Paris) stock exchanges—exceeded inward foreign direct investments made by multinational enterprises. Both were, however, of great significance. At the time, few Americans were aware of either the size or the importance of the investments from abroad. The amount was equal to almost 20 percent of the U.S. gross national product. No country in the world had attracted greater foreign investment.[15]

In mid-1914, U.S. federal government bonds held outside the country were minimal, as were overall state and local government borrowings. New York City had, however, relied on London and Paris money markets, and certain New York obligations would be maturing in the fall of 1914. Far more important were the huge long-term foreign investments in the private sector.[16] While the foreign investments in federal, state, and local government securities were all of a portfolio nature, those in the private sector can be divided into two categories: portfolio ones, that is, financial assets (bonds and stocks), and direct ones, that is, foreign business investments that carried with them ownership and the potentials for control (investments made as part of a business's operating strategy). The large size of the foreign portfolio holdings was reflected in the events of late July to early August 1914, that is, the concerns over the divestments of European securities' holdings.[17]

The portfolio investments in America's private sector activities comprised those in the bonds and stock of America's giant corporations—railroads, industrial enterprises, public utilities, as well as national retailers.[18] The vast U.S. railroad system had depended on foreign capital contributions. In the main, the securities of all these American corporations were denominated in dollars; but in the nineteenth and early twentieth centuries, a number of railroads and some other corporations had issued bonds payable in pounds sterling (and less often in other currencies); some were payable (principal and interest) in dollars, pounds, *and* francs. Foreigners had in years past acquired new issues of American securities, and they also bought and sold already issued bonds and shares. In the days of the gold standard, international trade in American securities was not difficult. This was especially true of the dollar-denominated securities that were traded in the United States and on foreign exchanges—London, Amsterdam, Berlin, Frankfurt, and Paris, for example. By contrast, foreign currency-denominated American securities had typically been designed for foreign markets, and transactions in them took place almost exclusively abroad. Some of the bonds issued by American companies and owned by foreign investors had maturities in 1914–1918, others in the more distant future, and there were certain ones coming due as late as the 1980s or even into the twenty-first century.[19] Portfolio investors from abroad held more bonds than shares. Bank loans existed, but these constituted a negligible portion of the long-term foreign portfolio investments in the United States.[20]

With the dollar-denominated traded securities, in practically all instances Americans joined in investing. There was a well-developed securities market in New York—*in the capital-recipient country,* which was for 1914 a unique feature of the United States as a debtor nation. In other large debtor countries (from Russia to Canada to Argentina to Australia), nationals also shared in the investments made by western Europeans, yet in no other one was there any institution approximating the size and breadth of the New York Stock Exchange. There was, in addition, in New York, the Consolidated Exchange (the "Little Board") and the New York Curb Agency. As Harvard economist O. M. W. Sprague wrote, "When, therefore, at the approach of the war European security holders frantically endeavored to convert [their foreign] investments into cash, selling pressures almost entirely concentrated on American stocks and bonds." American securities had a liquidity in the United States, available to the investor from abroad. Sprague could also have noted that because of the ease of investment and America's economic growth, in no other foreign nation—worldwide—had Europeans invested so much of their savings.[21]

Foreign direct investments in the United States were, likewise, abundant. At the same time as international markets for securities were integrated and active, many businesses also were extending over borders into the United States. Branches, subsidiaries, and affiliates of foreign enterprises participated to varying degrees in a broad range of sectors within the U.S. economy—in agriculture, mining, manufacturing, and services. Some foreign direct investments were "resource-based," but already foreign-owned companies were in the then "high tech" sectors—from rayon (by a British company) to communications (by British and German companies). The science-based German chemical enterprises had important direct investments in the United States. Foreign multinational enterprises had affiliates in America that manufactured and distributed consumer and producer goods. They sold brand-name products and also had an important presence in providing a range of services, including those in shipping, export-import trade, insurance, and international banking.[22] The foreign direct investments were geographically dispersed throughout the nation. While some of the direct investors (insurance companies' branches and affiliates, for instance) held financial assets, that is, American securities, most owned plant and equipment, real estate, patents, trademarks, and other tangible and intangible properties. Although foreign direct investors' financial assets were liquid, their far greater nonfinancial ones tended not to be. And, as it turned out, the financial assets of the sizable U.S. affiliates and branches of foreign insurance companies proved not to be liquid internationally, since they were pledged against potential losses. Domestic securities sales had to be accompanied by domestic purchases. Thus, short of going out of business, foreign-owned insurance companies operating in the United States could *not* provide returns (could not remit) to their parents after selling U.S. financial assets.[23]

Since 1879 the United States had been on a de facto, and since 1900 on a de jure, gold standard. Nonetheless, some securities denominated in dollars had "gold clauses" or defined foreign exchange parities.

Most foreign investors assumed that dollars (and dollar securities) could be converted into gold. The securities were believed to be as good as gold. Foreign investors in America in the early twentieth century had paid little attention to the small foreign exchange fluctuations. In the United States and abroad, a well-developed network of financial intermediaries existed to aid international transactions of a portfolio nature. It was simple for European or Canadian individuals (or companies) to buy and sell American securities within their own nation's boundaries with no worries over the complexities of handling a foreign currency.[24] There were also institutional investors in Europe and Canada—particularly investment trusts in Britain and Canada—with expertise in selecting portfolios of American securities.[25] As for foreign direct investors, stable foreign exchange rates reduced the inevitable uncertainties of investing abroad. Thus, for many years, foreign exchange considerations had been of little consequence in the decision making of either foreign portfolio or direct investors in the United States.[26] There were close transatlantic connections. Information moved by cable in a few minutes. Travel by ship across the Atlantic took about six days.[27] The world in 1914 was smaller than ever in history.

Of the roughly $7.1 billion long-term foreign investments in the United States at the start of July 1914 (of which some 75 percent was portfolio and the remainder direct investment), the British were the largest participants, followed by the Germans.[28] Table 1.2 gives a crude estimate by nationality of the distribution of long-term foreign portfolio and direct investments in America. Both foreign portfolio and direct investors saw the United States as a prosperous, expanding, and safe country, a land of opportunity where excellent returns could be anticipated. What "safe" meant in this context was a nation where political upheavals did not threaten investment and contracts were respected (upheld in the courts). "Safe" did not mean exemption from bankruptcy, commercial risks, or fraud—for these had long been part of the international investment scene.

The European liquidations of American securities (portfolio investments) in the first three weeks of July 1914, as noted, attracted little attention in the United States, since Europeans were in and out of the stock market on a regular basis and the trades in those weeks did not appear out of the ordinary. Even as late as July 30, the *New York Times* was reporting calm on the American stock markets.[29] No one, however, was complacent when on Friday, July 31, the British bank rate doubled and the New York Stock Exchange did not open; nor the next day, August 1, with the German declaration of war on Russia and the British bank rate up to 10 percent. Interest rate-sensitive investments were bound to be affected. When that Saturday, August 1, sterling cables

Table 1.2. Long-term foreign portfolio and direct investments in the United States, by nationality, July 1, 1914 (in millions of U.S. dollars)

Source of capital	Total	Portfolio investments	Direct investments
British	4,250	3,575	675
German	1,100	575	525
Dutch	650	525	125
French	480	400	80
Swiss	70	50	20
Belgian	30	10	20
Other European	180	100	80
Canadian	275	143	132
Japanese	25	1	24
All others	30	27	3
Total	7,090	5,406	1,684

Source: Mira Wilkins, *The History of Foreign Investment in the United States to 1914* (Cambridge, Mass.: Harvard University Press, 1989), 159 (totals). Figures reflect the level of foreign investment in the United States as of July 1, 1914. The portfolio and direct investment components of this table are my own best estimates, but they should be accepted with great caution. They modify earlier estimates made by Cleona Lewis and John Dunning.

escalated to $7.00, the financial communities in New York and London—and Paris and Berlin—were traumatized. The New York Stock Exchange had closed on Friday, July 31, for one reason only: *foreign selling.*[30]

Uncertain Times (August–December 1914)

With the advent of war in Europe, President Woodrow Wilson proclaimed America neutral.[31] Immediately, a coterie of difficulties surfaced that affected (and reflected the importance of) the large foreign investment in this country. The last five months of 1914 were a time of great economic uncertainty in the United States. I have identified seven sets of problems that represent a spectrum of challenges associated with long-term foreign investment in the United States.

The first set related to foreign portfolio investors, to stock market transactions, to desires by these investors for liquidity, to the corresponding gold exports, and to American obligations to foreigners that had to be met.[32] The New York Stock Exchange, which shut on July 31, did not reopen until November 28, and then only for restricted business; completely normal trading would not resume until April 1915. As the president of the New York Stock Exchange (H. G. S. Noble) explained, there had been "an unexpected run on Uncle Sam's Bank and the Stock Exchange was the paying teller's window through which the money was to be drawn out, so the window was closed to gain time." He later wrote, "How to reopen this window in such a way as not to pay out any more money to the foreign creditor than would suit our convenience was the problem which soon began to agitate many ingenious minds."[33] In short, foreign investors' withdrawals had been important enough to stop the New York Stock Exchange's normal operations for nearly nine months. (The London Stock Exchange would remain closed until January 4, 1915.)[34]

On August 5, 1914, a boatload of $25 million in American stock and bond certificates arrived from London for deliveries on sales made in the "days of great liquidation last week."[35] Foreign sales (and settlements on earlier sales) continued; an "outlaw" stock market developed in New York to digest the returned foreign-held securities.[36] With the perils of wartime shipments, insurance rates on gold exports soared. How would international payments be made?[37] In the first week in August, gold exports had continued. On August 8, the British bank rate dropped to 5 percent, where it would stay for the next two years.[38] This calmed the gold outflow—but there was still a problem.

Linked with the difficulties of international payments was the realization that more than $80 million of New York City securities, payable in London and Paris, in pounds sterling and francs, would be maturing between September 1914 and January 1915.[39] Sterling, which had reached $7.00 on August 1, 1914, had dropped in price in subsequent days but remained at a prohibitively high premium (well above the gold export point). To ship gold was hazardous and costly (with insurance rates soaring). To cope, on August 12, the Bank of England opened a depository in Ottawa to receive gold.[40] (Canada had followed Britain and at once declared war on Germany.) With the Canadian depository, Americans had no excuse not to remit in gold to Ottawa—although they were not eager to do so (it was fear of a gold drain that had forced the closing of the New York Stock Exchange). Would the country have adequate gold reserves to meet its obligations and maintain its domestic banking system? No one knew.

By early September, New York bankers had arranged to satisfy New York City's foreign obligations. J. P. Morgan & Co. and Kuhn, Loeb & Co. organized a syndicate and agreed to buy $100 million of the city's debt and to provide $80,243,940 in gold to meet the pound and franc requirements.[41] Gold could be dispatched, as required, for British account, to be held in Ottawa.[42] Gold deposits in Canada would then be credited to the Bank of England for the account of Morgan, Grenfell & Co. (Morgan's London house), which in turn could use the credit in

London to acquire the New York City notes as they came due; the maturities in Paris were met by purchasing exchange on Paris or by authorizing Morgan's Paris house (Morgan, Harjes & Co.) to draw on London.[43] Because the New York banks had arranged payments on New York City's liabilities, earlier plans for a gold fund to protect American bank reserves were revised; the leading New York banks placed in Ottawa $10 million in gold, while a gold fund was set up of $100 million.[44]

An added question was that as Europeans sold their railroad and other securities, would Americans buy them? The Interstate Commerce Commission's report on the New York, New Haven and Hartford Railroad and an ICC group of decisions on eastern freight rates had depressed prices of all railroad securities; the new Federal Trade Commission and Clayton antitrust legislation worried businessmen. J. P. Morgan, Jr., had written President Wilson on September 4, 1914, predicting that "urgent sellers abroad, and frightened holders here [in the United States] will flood the Stock Exchanges with selling orders" when the latter reopened, as "they must endeavour to re-open as soon as possible."[45]

By late September 1914, however, tensions had eased; the pound was down to $5.02.[46] Nonetheless, even in late October, bankers recognized that until "the exchanges [the exchange rate] have turned in our favor, any discussion bearing on the opening of the New York Stock Exchange to a free and unrestricted market for American securities owned abroad would be premature."[47] At last, by mid-November, sterling had fallen to the gold parity of $4.86; and the franc (which had gone through a similar cycle) was at par by January 1915.[48]

The New York Stock Exchange reopened for limited trading in listed bonds on Saturday, November 28. Gradually, exchange officials allowed more trading. To everyone's pleasure and surprise, foreigners did not flood Wall Street with American securities, and Americans comfortably absorbed those stocks and bonds that were repatriated.[49] New York City (aided by J. P. Morgan & Co., Kuhn, Loeb & Co., and other bankers in the syndicate) paid, as the city's obligations came due, the approximately $80 million that it owed in London and Paris.[50] The arrangements worked well. The system functioned. Stock prices did not collapse. By December 1914, U.S. gold exports had ceased.[51] The domestic banking system was out of jeopardy. When all restrictions on securities trading were finally lifted from New York Stock Exchange transactions in April 1915, no negative repercussions were evident.

While the recently established Federal Reserve Bank of New York and its first governor, Benjamin Strong (who took office in October 1914), monitored the situation and gave approvals, and while the same could be said for the new members of the Federal Reserve Board in

Washington (who took the oath of office on August 10, 1914) and of the U.S. secretary of the treasury, William G. McAdoo, the principal decisions on the operations of the New York Stock Exchange and on New York City securities were not those of governmental authorities but of "Wall Street" (stock exchange officials and bankers).[52]

In the last five months of 1914, German investors found it more difficult to cash in on their American securities than did Britishers or Frenchmen. Here the problem lay in British government policies. After Britain had entered the war, its government published a list of absolute and conditional contraband. Contraband goods were those that a belligerent forbids to be sent to the enemy because they could be employed to advance the latter's war-making ability. Absolute contraband were arms and munitions; conditional contraband were articles that had both military and peacetime use. The British roster placed foodstuffs and gold in this last category.[53] Under international law, a belligerent warship was allowed to stop neutral vessels on the high sea to inspect for both absolute and conditional contraband. In the case of the former, destination to the enemy country was sufficient for the seizure of the cargo; as for the latter, there had to be proof that the goods were going to be used for military purposes for the cargo of neutral ships to be taken over.[54] Because the British controlled the seas and wanted the blockade of Germany to work, they frequently forced neutral merchant ships into port for inspection. On August 28, 1914, the U.S. ambassador to Germany (James Watson Gerard) wrote to U.S. Secretary of State William Jennings Bryan that British naval forces had seized (as conditional contraband) gold from America sent to German private banks on the Dutch vessel *Tubania,* bound for Amsterdam; these shipments on a neutral carrier, Gerard insisted, should be released, since they were for private parties and not for the German armed forces.[55] On October 23, a vice president of the National City Bank, New York, informed the U.S. State Department that "some of our German correspondents have approached us with the suggestion that, without naming a particular security, we sell securities to increase their cash account with us." The letter writer did not indicate what the bank intended to do, nor did he see any difficulty with this transaction even though the New York Stock Exchange remained closed. What he wanted to report to the State Department was that "we have little doubt that this is indirectly for the purposes of the German government."[56] The Deutsche Bank, which did act for the German state in the period of U.S. neutrality, was a correspondent of the National City Bank at this time.[57] The Deutsche Bank had long participated in moving American securities into German hands, and this step might also have involved gaining liquidity for such investors in these troubled times.[58] Shortly after the outbreak of war in Europe, for all practical purposes the Deutsche Bank had replaced its longtime American representative (Edward D. Adams) with a man dispatched from Germany, Hugo Schmidt; the effect was to tighten Deutsche Bank's administrative control over its American business.[59] Published data do not reveal whether the British naval forces eventually released the gold on the *Tubania* (probably not), or whether the National City Bank carried forth this transaction (it probably did). I include both as indicators of the difficulties of German portfolio investors in American transactions in these months after the outbreak of war. If gold would be seized, Germans would obviously be wary of shipping it. An added problem Germans faced was that some of their American securities were physically held in London; these certificates were confiscated by the British when they took over enemy assets.[60] Yet, just as British and French (and other European) investors could sell American securities and get returns back home, it does appear that the Germans also managed to dispose of at least some of their holdings and remit at least some of the proceeds.[61] In short, the closing of the New York Stock Exchange probably slowed but clearly did not halt foreign sales of American securities; the perils of gold exports were dealt with in various ways. Americans met their foreign obligations. Thus were handled the first set of problems.

A second, and closely connected, set of concerns was later discussed by Walter E. Sachs, of the banking house Goldman, Sachs: "We used to make available funds for lending money on the New York Stock Exchange, against securities." With the war, "our clients and ourselves had large amounts of foreign exchange to cover, for maturities." Since these short-term bills of exchange—sterling credits—were coming due, Goldman, Sachs' customers "had to buy pounds to meet their obligations." Only two clients "refused to meet their obligations." Both were German direct investors in America: Forstmann & Huffmann, woolen manufacturers in Passaic, New Jersey, and the Susquehanna Silk Mills, with factories in Pennsylvania and Ohio. Neither German subsidiary's chief executive felt it appropriate to "aid the British" by purchasing pounds at the inflated rate or by being party to the shipment of gold to London (or Ottawa).[62]

A third set of problems affecting foreign investors was associated with international communications. On August 5, 1914, Wilson had issued an executive order to prevent radio stations under U.S. jurisdiction from becoming the instrument through which "unneutral" messages could be sent to ships at sea or other radio stations.[63] The U.S. government began to examine international radio messages. Reluctantly, the British affiliate, the Marconi Wireless Telegraph Company of America, allowed its long-distance and coastal stations to be monitored by navy inspectors.[64] Marconi of America was the giant in the field of radio communications. In September, the government took over the high-powered radio station at Tuckerton, New Jersey, which had been built by the German company Hochfrequenz Maschinen Aktiengesellschaft für Drahtlöse Telegraphie (known as Homag) under contract for a French wireless firm. At the outbreak of the war in Europe, the Germans had not yet transferred this station to its French owners, nor had the station obtained a license to operate in the United States (as required under the Radio Act of 1912). The takeover by the U.S. government met two needs: (1) Washington's desire for extra capacity to send neutral messages and (2) policy makers' uncertainty as to the radio station's status; with Germany and France at war, could a German company in neutral America convey an asset to the French enemy?[65]

Meanwhile, at the start of the war, the British had cut the direct U.S.-German cable connections and were intercepting other cable messages; the British were preeminent in cables.[66] The historians of M. M. Warburg and Co., Hamburg, write that on July 28 (just before the outbreak of the war) that German banking house had transferred its London representative to Amsterdam, "from which point he was able to maintain cable communications with America when, on declaring war, the British government severed the German cable link to New York." I do not know how many other German banks were able to follow a similar strategy. In any case, the Germans still had radio communication through Telefunken's facility at Saville, Long Island—and it seems they could send "unneutral messages in cypher."[67]

A fourth set of difficulties vis-à-vis long-term inward foreign investment came as a result of wartime transportation and trade interruptions. When war broke out in Europe, a large portion of American trade was being carried on foreign ships. With the war, British ships—which dominated the seas—were diverted to wartime needs. On August 7, 1914, Secretary of the Treasury McAdoo announced that the United States must provide sufficient ships to transport U.S. exports (cotton and grain were piling up). On August 18, U.S. shipping laws were liberalized, allowing foreign-built ships to fly under the U.S. flag (the goal was to "reflag" foreign ships and use them for American purposes).[68]

When war began, some fifty-four German ships were in U.S. ports.[69] Philip A. S. Franklin, vice-president of the International Mercantile Marine Co., proposed that his company buy fifteen of these ships that belonged to the Hamburg-American Line (Hapag), which would give Americans more tonnage for overseas trade. Franklin asked the U.S. government to aid in financing the acquisition. The U.S. government, which in September had assumed control of the Tuckerton, New Jersey, radio station, thought about buying these and other German ships for

U.S. government needs. In both cases, they would be reregistered as neutral American shipping. But the British and French governments objected, opposing the enhancement of American shipping—and the German government also objected to the reflagging. Thus, neither an IMM nor a U.S. government takeover of German ships occurred at this time, nor at any time during the period of American neutrality. Nearly all the German vessels lay idle, trapped in U.S. ports by the British blockade. The U.S. government was, however, committed to enlarging both U.S. shipping and shipbuilding; our dependency on foreign shipping seemed worrisome.[70]

Major problems in shipping during wartime lay in the dangers of submarine warfare—and also the perils of being stopped or delayed by the British blockade. When war began, foreign firms provided more than two-thirds of U.S. war risk insurance. The British government forbade British insurers to cover capture by the Royal Navy. Many U.S. cargoes were refused insurance by private insurers (foreign and domestic). To cope with the absence of adequate facilities for insurance of American vessels and their cargoes against the risk of war, Congress passed legislation that authorized the setting up within the U.S. Treasury the Bureau of War Risk Insurance. The law was signed, and the bureau opened September 2, 1914; the bureau would have close dealings with foreign insurance companies in the United States. Its formation represented an enlargement of U.S. government functions and an attempt to liberate Americans from reliance on foreign business (foreign-owned insurance providers).[71]

Questions of strategic imports and exports occupied U.S. policy makers' attention. Essential U.S. imports curtailed by wartime conditions included dyestuffs, potash, and tin. On August 12, 1914, U.S.-born Herman A. Metz, representative for decades of the German Hoechst company in America (and from 1913 to 1915, a congressman from Brooklyn), contacted the U.S. State Department.[72] Metz dictated a memorandum, indicating that if imports of dyestuffs from Germany ceased, within sixty days

> at least half the mills in the United States manufacturing cotton and woolen goods will have to shut down for lack of raw material. The paper trade, paper manufacturers, leather manufacturers, printing ink manufacturing, and all industries requiring colors will be similarly affected . . . Another serious item is the pharmaceutical supplies which practically all come from the works at Hoeschst [*sic*] and Leverkusen. They include antipyrin [*sic*], asperin [*sic*], 606, in fact all synthetic products.[73]

In a follow-up (August 20), Metz declared, "All theorizing as to making these products here [in the United States] is simply ridiculous. It would take years to establish plants and after they were established, they would be in competition again with the German manufacturers unless the tariff was raised to allow them to work against foreign competition." He asked for U.S. government help, since "individual communication with [the German] plants is impossible. I haven't been able to get a word from the [Hoechst] works since August 4th."[74] In October, with full knowledge of the U.S. State Department, Metz chartered the steamer SS *Matanzas* to import German colors and chemicals and to pick them up at the neutral port of Rotterdam.[75] Subsidiaries of German companies in America (foreign direct investors) received supplies from Germany on this vessel.[76] The solution was a stopgap; no one had any inkling of how long the war would last, or whether further shipments could be arranged or could get through.[77]

Potash was another critical import; it was used in fertilizers and also came from Germany. The price soared. The SS *Matanzas* brought potash to America. At once, in this case, with the ballooning prices, attention turned to possible U.S. production. Foreign direct investors (principally affiliates of British companies) would take on a major role in developing this American industry.[78]

Tin posed another trade headache. The United States was the world's premier importer of tin. None was mined or smelted within the nation. Before the outbreak of war, Bolivian tin had been exported to Hamburg, smelted there, and then reexported to the United States. Could Bolivian tin be smelted in America? Ladenburg, Thalmann & Co., New York (an affiliate of a German private bank) early in October 1914 offered to serve as agent for the Bolivian government to establish a U.S. smelter. This plan did not materialize, but the problem did not vanish, and in time, British and Bolivian direct investors would smelt tin in America.[79]

U.S. exports, as well as imports, faced wartime disruptions. Most attention was paid to cotton and grain. In the early nineteenth century, American cotton trade had been dominated by British traders; by the early twentieth century, Americans administered this trade—and this was only peripherally an issue related to foreign direct investment in the United States. Much of American grain was handled by foreign traders. The government-provided war risk insurance helped in facilitating the disrupted trade in American agricultural products.

Just as imports faced the British blockade, so did U.S. exports. In December 1914, U.S. Secretary of State William Jennings Bryan protested to the British ambassador over the many "vessels laden with American goods destined to neutral ports in Europe, which have been seized on the high seas, taken to British ports and detained sometimes for weeks by British authorities." Copper, a significant U.S. export, was especially affected; the British labeled it absolute contraband.[80] Moreover, in 1914, two of the leading U.S. copper exporters were German multinational enterprises, and a large share of America's copper output in the prewar years had gone to Germany.[81] At the start of the war, German-owned firms in America sought to maintain their exports of copper by routing the commodity through neutral European countries, especially Holland; the British quickly became wise to this maneuver.[82] The British wanted to retain America's friendship and sought ways of "crippling Krupp," without offending U.S. copper mining interests that depended on the exports.[83] On November 23, 1914, the Nederlandsche Overzee Trustmaatschappij (NOT) came into being, a private company with close links to the Dutch government and the Dutch central bank (Nederlandsche Bank). NOT's purpose was to enable the Dutch to maintain neutrality while conducting business with both the Entente and the Central Powers. NOT became an arbitrator in transactions between neutral America and Germany—when goods passed through Holland—providing guarantees that the requirements of the Allied blockade had been met.[84]

A further international trade matter involving German multinational enterprises in the United States lay in the German desire to get wool, cotton, and jute imports through the British blockade. In the last months of 1914, a German plan was drawn up that apparently worked for more than two years. Hugo Schmidt at the Deutsche Bank, from his New York office, arranged German wool purchases from the United States, South Africa, and Australia, raw cotton from the United States, and jute from India. Wool from South Africa and Australia was shipped to two German direct investors in the United States, Forstmann & Huffmann and Botany Worsted Mills, which companies would reexport the wool through a Scandinavian port to Germany.[85] Later, Forstmann & Huffmann explained that in November 1914, the firm had been contacted by Metz, who told its chief executive of the critical need for dyestuffs and that, in exchange, wool and cotton would be exported from the United States—with the approval of Secretary of State Bryan.[86]

Still another wartime problem involved U.S.-Canadian trade relations (as noted, Canada had declared war on the side of its mother country in August 1914). Sizable Canadian investments in the United States existed, including direct investments in railroads. In November 1914, the general agent for one of these foreign direct investors, the Grand Trunk Railway System (which spread over the border), asked the U.S. State Department whether the road could "be permitted to handle contraband from the Dominion of Canada across United States territory into Canadian territory." The reply was affirmative, as long as the transactions were in the ordinary pattern of trade. Again, neutrality had its limits.[87]

Fifth, several foreign direct investors in the United States had joint British-German parentage. With Britain and Germany at war, this was untenable. American Metal Company—with interests in U.S. lead, zinc, and copper refineries—was controlled by two family-united firms, Henry R. Merton & Co. in the United Kingdom and Metallgesellschaft in Germany. The British government decided Henry R. Merton & Co. was German and reorganized the British business, "eliminating alien ownership."[88] The German stakes in American Metal Company continued. With Speyer & Co., New York, which had both British and German family members as partners, Sir Edgar Speyer, a British subject and head of Speyer Brothers, London, temporarily (in October 1914) withdrew as a partner of Speyer & Co., New York, in compliance with British government rules that prohibited British bankers and businessmen from taking part in transactions with persons in Germany.[89] Speyer & Co., New York, like American Metal Company, retained its German connections.

Sixth, in July and August 1914, Andrew Weir (later Lord Inverforth) and his team of British investors were poised to obtain control over roughly one-third of California's oil production; by November 1914, these prewar plans had collapsed.[90] So, too, Heinrich Koppers, with a subsidiary in the United States, decided immediately at the start of war in Europe, that it would be futile to attempt to run his American business from Essen, Germany. He sold the controlling interest in his U.S. subsidiary to an American group, headed by Andrew Mellon (Koppers retained a 20 percent interest).[91]

Other important projects that had depended on foreign moneys were interrupted, some only temporarily. On August 1, 1914, the "infant Alabama Power Company had to discontinue all construction work" for lack of funding. At a London meeting on October 21, 1914, the English bondholders in the parent company, the Alabama Traction, Light and Power Company Ltd., agreed to waive interest on their bonds for three years. Alabama Power then was able to sell newly issued bonds in the United States.[92] Southern Aluminium, a new and large French direct investor that was building a huge complex in North Carolina, suspended work in October 1914 and sought, with no success, additional U.S. capital.[93] New moneys for projects in process were not available in European countries, which were channeling their resources into the war effort.

A seventh significant issue surfaced in the fall of 1914. By October 1914, it had become evident that Britishers (and Frenchmen) would want to purchase vast quantities of war materiel in the United States.

That month, the British Treasury dispatched across the Atlantic Sir George Paish and Basil Blackett to cope with the many problems that were bound to arise.[94] Questions followed: Would the new war-related U.S. exports compromise America's neutrality? And, more relevant to this book: How would Britain pay for these supplies? The British were well aware that a readily available source of dollars was present in British companies' and individuals' financial holdings in the United States. And it occurred to Americans (and to the British) that perhaps by supplying goods to Britain and France, the United States could rid itself of much of its international "debt," not upset exchange rates as the British and French divested American securities, not need to export gold, and, at the same time, enlarge the sale of U.S. products abroad.[95] The Germans, likewise, desired to purchase war supplies in the United States and to use for this purpose the proceeds from the liquidation of German securities held in America.[96]

In the waning months of 1914, U.S. neutrality notwithstanding, most Americans were taking sides; bankers involved in international business would have to make decisions on their dealings with belligerents. Certain ones were very partial to the Allied cause, notably the Morgan house.[97] On December 30, 1914, Frank A. Vanderlip, president of National City Bank, wrote to the bank's chairman (James Stillman) that the British were pushing hard for "very strict partisanship." America was, however, neutral. "I have no disposition to put on an English uniform in order to conduct the banking business . . . That we should continue our relationships with our German correspondents seems to me undebateable [*sic*]." Vanderlip added that "we must be diplomatic" and noted that English censors read cables.[98] Kuhn, Loeb & Co.—with intimate and long-standing German associations—straddled the fence, favoring measures to maintain the gold standard and to sustain American credit and, like National City Bank, participating in available business.[99] Other New York banks, Speyer & Co. and Goldman, Sachs, for example, had some actively pro-German partners.[100]

In short, as 1914 came to an end, the United States had (1) experienced the attempts by Europeans to divest their American stocks and bonds, forcing New York Stock Exchange officials to close the exchange. The panic transactions had, however, rapidly abated. Bankers' arrangements had avoided large gold shipments. Clearly, the country was able to absorb the continuing sales by Europeans of American securities; New York City had, with the bankers' assistance, paid off its foreign debt as the obligations had come due; by mid-November sterling was back to gold parity, and by December gold exports had ceased.[101] (2) German foreign direct investors in the United States encountered special wartime problems; they did not wish to do anything to aid the British. (3) The war gave the opportunity for the U.S. government to take over the operations of the German-owned high-power radio station at Tuckerton, New Jersey, preventing its nonneutral use (the Germans still operated another important radio station at Sayville, Long Island); radio communication remained dominated by the British affiliate, Marconi of America, albeit now being monitored by U.S. Navy inspectors. (4) The U.S. government had also contemplated buying German ships, but no purchases were made. It did act to help insure cargoes. The war disrupted normal trade, including that of foreign direct investors. (5) The war fractured certain foreign ownership connections—when owners were on both sides of the conflict. (6) Several important British, German, and French investors found their U.S. plans in jeopardy. And (7) European belligerent governments wanted to buy war supplies in the United States; dollars would be required; perhaps the sale of existing securities holdings of their nationals would provide the source of dollars.

America was seeking to determine what neutrality entailed. As 1914 came to a close, as some foreign investors retreated from or reduced their U.S. investments (this was particularly true of the portfolio holdings), American domestic investors took their place. There were no long-run negative ramifications in the United States associated with the withdrawal of existing and the absence of new foreign investments, albeit there was substantial temporary uneasiness and strain. The United States—as a participant in the world economy—was vulnerable.[102]

Before American Entry (January 1915–April 1917)

By 1915, the uncertainties present in the American economy in the last months of 1914 had for the most part been resolved, and the United States entered a war boom. Because Europeans required American goods and moneys, U.S. production expanded, and American bankers became more sophisticated, filling more of America's needs and foreign ones as well. All the while, pro-Allied sentiments in the United States rose. Nonetheless, many German businessmen (employed by German-headquartered enterprises) and certain bankers of German heritage remained in touch with families back home and sympathetic to the German side of the conflict. The United States had large numbers of citizens with German backgrounds.

The German sinking of the British passenger ships *Lusitania* (May 7, 1915) and *Arabic* (August 19, 1915) galvanized anti-German public opinion in America. Robert Lansing became secretary of state in June 1915, and despite U.S. neutrality, he allowed American bankers to extend long-term loans to the British and French.[103] German submarines made trade (and passenger travel) perilous, which intensified U.S. antagonisms. Finally, on September 1, 1915, the Germans announced no more passenger liners would be sunk without warning, but then on February 21, 1916, the Germans renewed unrestricted submarine attacks. President Wilson responded, informing the U.S. Congress—on April 18—that if Germany did not abandon its "present methods of submarine warfare," the United States would sever diplomatic relations. Germany restrained its submarines on May 10, 1916, for the next nine months. In the interim, Wilson was reelected president on a plank of having kept his country out of war. The United States finally became a belligerent in April 1917, after Germany, anxious to defeat Britain, had in February of that year once more resumed unrestricted submarine attacks.[104]

Some commentators have suggested that the large foreign investments in the United States influenced U.S. foreign policy and "dragged" America into the conflict. Clearly, the existence of the sizable inward foreign investments acted to integrate the country into the world economy; unquestionably, leading New York (and to a lesser extent Boston) bankers with intimate international connections were in contrast with the insularity of much of the nation; British (and to a lesser extent French) securities holdings did provide cash for war purchases and collateral for borrowings.[105] Likewise, both British- and German-owned assets were employed in ways that compromised U.S. neutrality. These circumstances notwithstanding, my research leads me to conclude that the alleged *causal* connections between the sizable inward foreign investments and the events that propelled America into war were so tenuous as to be deemed absent. Foreign investment in this country without doubt played important and varied roles during the period of American neutrality, but it had negligible impact (positive or negative) on the U.S. decision to become a belligerent.[106]

Here I will consider the volume, variety, and specific behavior of inward foreign investors (and, where relevant, their governments and the U.S. government) between January 1915 and April 1917, when the United States entered the war. The war abroad had impact on both inward portfolio and direct investments. In this prosperous period, in net, foreign investment in the United States continued to decline—as it had during the last five months of 1914; American investment substituted for the retreating foreign contribution. Yet now, in certain instances, there was an upswing, and were I to study only foreign direct investments, the evidence shows an enlargement in those stakes, mainly due to the expansion of foreign companies already in business in America and their reinvested earnings. Although the growth was, to be sure, frequently encouraged by the wartime boom, no cause-effect link exists between the well-being of these investors and the nation's *decision* to go to war.

Foreign Direct Investment in America before U.S. Entry

Key foreign multinational enterprises in the United States expanded. Lever Brothers, the British soap maker, for example, saw its revenues and profits in America rising.[107] In 1916, the firm's founder, William H. Lever, decided to extend the capacity of his existing Cambridge, Massachusetts, plant (which was always called the "Boston Works"), "to keep up with the present demand for Lifebuoy and Lux." Lever, who had acquired this American factory in 1897, wanted to be certain there was adequate production "to supply the appetite."[108] U.S. profits could be reinvested to finance the expansion.

Another British multinational, Courtaulds, had begun making rayon at Marcus Hook, Pennsylvania, in 1911. The output of its subsidiary, American Viscose Company (as of 1915 The Viscose Company [TVC]) soared. In 1916, the flourishing U.S. affiliate was contributing more than half of its parent's gross income. The Viscose Company was the sole U.S. manufacturer of rayon (the first synthetic textile). In 1914, the quantity of U.S. imports of rayon—mainly from the European continent—had exceeded U.S. domestic output (all of it by Courtaulds); by contrast, in 1916, TVC's production was more than double that of U.S. imports. Courtaulds' historian explained that "the circumstances of war gradually dried up continental European exports."[109]

Business also boomed at the U.S. thread plants of the Scottish J. & P. Coats. By 1917, its Pawtucket, Rhode Island, facility (acquired in 1869) ran 105,000 spindles and employed 2,500 workers. The firm's Rhode Island plant was the largest single-site textile producer in that state.[110] A fourth British enterprise, Marconi Wireless Telegraph Company of America, an affiliate of Marconi's Wireless Telegraph Company Ltd., London, also augmented its operations. It had started business in the United States in 1899, set up radio facilities, gotten a major boost from publicity surrounding the sinking of the *Titanic,* and in 1914 was manufacturing "marine wireless equipment and [equipment for] transoceanic stations in moderate quantities." Massive wartime demand for its services pushed it to add to its New Jersey factory, and for the first time (according to the parent company's historian) it became an important *manufacturing* company in America. Marconi of America already was the U.S. leader in radio communications.[111] In 1915, Marconi of America opened discussions with General Electric, proposing specialization, whereby GE would make the wireless machinery and Marconi of America would administer the communication systems.[112] Yet how would Marconi of America, in wartime, pay for the equipment it purchased from GE (it had no backlog of profits to rely upon)? Its dilemma was resolved in relation to alternators, when, as an expedient, in January 1917, GE and Marconi of America agreed that the latter would install and test the former's innovative Alexanderson alternators at Marconi's new long-distance New Brunswick, New Jersey, radio station.[113] GE remained the owner of the equipment. In short, Marconi of America, the dominant firm in the United States in the burgeoning new field of radio communication, could expand without the need for financing from abroad.[114] Marconi, like Lever, Courtaulds, and Coats, was able to grow and flourish without added capital imports.

Other British affiliates in America helped replace the three critical German imports: dyestuffs, potash, and refined tin. In dyestuffs, the British role was minor (when—early in 1917—Du Pont started to build its first dyestuff plant, it made a technical assistance agreement with the British enterprise Levinstein Ltd.).[115] In potash, the part played was more substantial. As German imports dropped and U.S. potash prices soared, the American Trona Corporation (a subsidiary of the English-controlled Consolidated Gold Fields of South Africa, Ltd., Cecil Rhodes' company) took the lead in developing newly discovered—identified not long before the war—resources at Searles Lake in California. Pacific Coast Borax (a subsidiary of another British multinational, Borax Consolidated) joined in exploiting this deposit, which became the biggest single source of potash in the United States.[116] As for tin, the domestically owned American Smelting and Refining Company took the initiative in smelting and refining Bolivian tin in the United States in March 1916. It was followed in early 1917 by a joint venture between the British firm Williams, Harvey & Co. (the largest smelters of tin in Europe), National Lead Company (the largest consumer of tin in America), and Simon Patiño (the largest miner of tin in Bolivia); the smelting technology came from the United Kingdom.[117] The British role in dyestuffs, potash, and tin in each instance assisted the United States in substituting domestic output for imports.[118]

British direct investors in America also supplied U.K. needs—which grew as wartime demands rose. The direct investors do not appear to have been involved in the British efforts to obtain major cotton imports—and to stop German imports. They did, however, participate in the British imports of grain. Two experienced Liverpool grain traders (Ross T. Smyth & Co. and Samuel Sanday & Co.), which had offices in London and New York, were central to the British government's wheat purchasing program—and were said to be effective in forcing down wheat prices.[119] Once Britishers had had major stakes in U.S. meatpacking; by 1915, the only remaining British-owned enterprise was Morrell & Co. Ltd., which had sizable packing plants at Ottumwa, Iowa, and Sioux Falls, South Dakota.[120] As British wartime purchases of foodstuffs in America rose, Morrell & Co. Ltd. (which had been in business in the United States since 1871) witnessed "a phenomenal increase in exports."[121]

Other British direct investors assisted their home nation's cause. United Alkali Company's U.S. subsidiary, North American Chemical Company, in Bay City, Michigan (a producer there since 1898), had a greater output of potassium chlorate in 1915 than ever in its history. By 1916, some 60 percent of its electrolytic capacity was devoted to producing sodium chlorate, which it shipped to Liverpool as fast as it could do so.[122] Even more important to the British war effort, in 1900 Electric Boat Company (EBC) and the British Vickers had made a twenty-five-year licensing agreement, under which the latter used the American firm's technology to build submarines. In the early twentieth century, Vickers had obtained a controlling interest in EBC; Vickers seems to have retained that substantial stake all during World War I. This was a rare case for the prewar years, where a British company had invested in the United States to utilize U.S. technology.[123] With American neutrality, the State Department had opposed U.S. construction of submarines for British war needs. Because the British required more submarines than their own shipyards could provide, Vickers arranged for EBC to provide the *Canadian* Vickers with technical assistance and other resources to manufacture the submarines.[124] Charles Schwab, head of Bethlehem Steel, served as the intermediary in these arrangements. By the summer of 1915, ten submarines, made in Montreal with U.S. know-how, were already in active service for the British cause.[125] In late 1916, to serve its war needs, the British government itself acquired several U.S. rifle plants; the U.S. government had no objection. (This direct investment proved brief; after America entered the war, the U.S. government paid $9 million to acquire the facilities.)[126]

British insurance companies with operations in the United States expanded. Early in 1917, two of America's oldest insurers—Newark Fire Insurance Co., founded in 1811, and Pennsylvania Fire Insurance Co., established in 1825—were taken over, respectively, by the Royal Insurance Co., Ltd., of Liverpool, and by the North British and Mercantile Insurance Co., London and Edinburgh. Both giant British insurers had existing business in America, as well as profits available to finance their new acquisitions.[127]

In 1915, the British government was urging the liquidation of British overseas investments (to provide dollars for British war purchases)—

and all during 1916 and 1917 British defense regulations made illegal the export of capital from the United Kingdom.[128] Thus, when British private sector firms enlarged their U.S. businesses, they typically managed to do so with moneys obtained in the United States. Good profits as well as the ability to borrow on the U.S. side of the Atlantic meant that most British direct investors in this country built up rather than contracted their business in the period of U.S. neutrality. British government's injunctions to liquidate foreign investments excluded all viable direct investments.[129]

The Belgian Solvay & Cie. and its British affiliate, Brunner, Mond, had since the 1880s interests in America in the Solvay Process Company and, later, in its spin-off, Semet-Solvay Company. Semet-Solvay, in particular, became a major producer of war materiel at its factories in Syracuse and Split Rock, New York; at Marcus Hook, Pennsylvania, in 1915 it built a plant for its affiliate, Benzol Products, to manufacture anilines and other coal tar intermediates. It constructed additional facilities in Steelton, Pennsylvania, and Ashland, Kentucky, to make yellow prussiate of soda—used in paints and dry colors.[130] Solvay Process Company also grew, albeit not as rapidly. It cooperated with Pacific Coast Borax in the potash developments at Searles Lake, California. It also acquired (in 1916) properties in Salduro, Utah, installing facilities to recover potash salts by solar evaporation.[131] While there were Belgian (and indirectly British) investments in Semet-Solvay, the latter's management acted independently. Likewise, Solvay Process Company's executives rarely consulted with men at the Belgian and British parents; in January 1917, the Belgian entrepreneur Armand Solvay lamented that Solvay Process Company was trying to "free itself from all European influence." He was right to be alarmed.[132]

The British-Dutch enterprise the Royal Dutch Shell Group, which had first moved into America in 1912, greatly added to its U.S. involvements during 1915–1917.[133] The group's Shell Oil Company of California produced 3,186,800 barrels of crude in 1915 and 4,809,403 barrels in 1916. It completed a major pipeline in California, and, most crucial, in December 1914 the first unit of its new, modern refinery at Martinez on San Francisco Bay had gone onstream. The group's California operations became fully integrated from well to consumer (the firm owned gas stations on the West Coast). The group also had three oil tankers, launched late in 1915 and early 1916 for American business. In Oklahoma, the Royal Dutch Shell Group's Roxana Petroleum Company produced 1,784,000 barrels of crude in 1915 and 4,684,000 in 1916. The Royal Dutch Shell Group acquired more Oklahoma oil properties, installed pipelines, and finished the construction of a new refinery at the Cushing fields in March 1917; in April, it started to build a sizable refinery in St. Louis.[134] Royal Dutch Shell's expansion in California and in the midcontinental fields was formidable; to finance it, the group used reinvested profits, and in 1916 it sold Royal Dutch Company (parent company) shares in America.[135] It also arranged that the Roxana Petroleum Company borrow from the Shell Company of California—essentially an intraenterprise loan.[136] The group had become a major participant in America's oil industry. Its U.S. crude oil output in 1916 reached 3.2 percent of the nation's total, up from 2 percent in 1914.[137]

Dutch direct investments in America were not confined to petroleum. Anton Jurgens' Margarine Fabrieken decided to manufacture in the United States for the first time. Early in 1917, at the initiative of the American Spencer Kellogg, Jurgens' went into a fifty-fifty joint venture with Kellogg, in Kellogg Products, Inc. The new company was floated in the United States (raising its capital in America); it began production in 1917 in Buffalo, New York.[138] Before the war, more than a dozen Dutch-owned mortgage banks had served many American communities; these expanded their lending.[139]

The French-owned Michelin Tire Company raised its U.S. output at Milltown, New Jersey, and in 1916 introduced the new "Michelin Universal Tread Tire." Michelin had begun producing in America in 1907.[140] So, too, French woolen mill owners (which had started operations in Woonsocket, Rhode Island, 1899–1910), added to their facilities.[141] And there was the new French entry into U.S. business, L'Air Liquide, which obtained a sizable minority stake (in exchange for Claude process patents) in the Air Reduction Company, formed on November 26, 1915. Air Reduction Company built factories in Philadelphia, Jersey City, Cleveland, Detroit, and Buffalo. Its oxygen plants had to be near customers, since freight costs could "eat up profits."[142] Renault's sales office (for automobiles) in New York took on a new role, serving as purchaser of American machine tools that were exported (in 1916) to Renault's Russian factories.[143] Pathé Frères, the great French multinational moviemaker, had had a sizable U.S. business before the war. The war jeopardized its outlook, but the firm's founder, Charles Pathé, was not deterred. On December 28, 1914, he formed a new American subsidiary, Pathé Exchange, Inc., and through an American lawyer (Paul Fuller of the law firm Coudert Brothers), Pathé would bring in Charles E. Merrill and Edmund Lynch of Merrill, Lynch & Co. He arranged that they be paid generous salaries, and they provided for the continuance of Pathé's flourishing movie distribution business.[144]

Swiss companies in America prospered, with Nestlé & Anglo-Swiss Condensed Milk Company in the vanguard. Its U.S. subsidiary was Nestlé's Food Company, which at the advent of the First World War had a small plant in Fulton, New York, making baby food. This Swiss firm had withdrawn from the U.S. condensed milk trade in 1905, conceding to Borden exclusive rights in this sphere.[145] With the war in Europe, however, Nestlé's Swiss parent agreed to supply the British government with condensed milk and deputized its U.S. subsidiary to obtain the milk in America. Nestlé's Food Company made sizable advances to three U.S. firms, Hires Condensed Milk Company, the International Milk Products Company, and the John Wildi Company, and during 1915 Nestlé's Food Company arranged the purchase of 1 million cases of canned milk; in 1916, 3 million; and in 1917, 5 million.[146] All of this meant Nestlé's Food Company, although not yet a canner itself, was in the canned milk business in America on a substantial scale. Its parent would need to revise its 1905 accord with Borden, which occurred in January 1918 (see later discussion). Other Swiss companies with American direct investments also expanded, including Hoffmann-La Roche, which for the first time started to manufacture in the United States. It made Digalen—a heart medicine. Uncertainties over transport moved it from exports to production across the Atlantic. In addition, Sandoz—early in 1917—began manufacturing medicines in America, its initial entry into U.S. manufacturing.[147]

The Swedish firm Svenska Kullagerfabriken (SKF) had exported to the United States and by 1910 had a U.S. sales subsidiary. With hazardous transportation, in 1916, SKF inaugurated the manufacture of bearings in America (in Hartford, Connecticut, and then in Philadelphia). Its production was financed principally in the United States; SKF thrived; soon most of its sales would go to the U.S. war effort.[148] More Scandinavian firms went into business in America, for example, Norwegian and Danish insurance companies. Two Norwegian insurers arrived during the period of U.S. neutrality, and three others after U.S. entry; one Danish company came in while the United States was still neutral, and another did subsequently.[149] Before the First World War, not a single Norwegian or Danish insurance company had direct investments in America.[150] Some of these companies handled reinsurance.

New Canadian enterprises embarked on manufacturing in the United States. The Canadian Car and Foundry Company Ltd. had received a $83 million Russian contract for munitions; by March 1915, it had subcontracted $23 million under this order to twenty-seven steel and powder manufacturers in the United States. In addition, the Canadian Car and Foundry Company acquired a plant near Kingsland, New Jersey, only to have the $16 million facility destroyed in an explosion (caused by German sabotage) in January 1917; for the two years that this Canadian-owned New Jersey factory was in production, it had run three shifts a day with 1,400 workers.[151] So, too, Canada Foundries and Forging, Ltd., built a plant in Buffalo, for pig iron production.[152]

In shipping services, with the opening of the Panama Canal (August 1914) and the LaFollette Seamen's Act (March 1915) that raised the costs to U.S.-registered shippers, there was a marked transfer of *Pacific Ocean* shipping into foreign hands. U.S. shipping, in the main, shifted from the Pacific to the more profitable North Atlantic trade. One historian found that by early 1917 every major U.S. West Coast shipping enterprise had either sold out to the Japanese or reregistered under a foreign flag (the Robert Dollar Line became Canadian); Japanese shipping interests in the United States greatly expanded.[153] (The Japanese had declared war against Germany on August 23, 1914.)

Not only direct investors from Allied and neutral nations enlarged their U.S. business; so did most German-owned subsidiaries in this country. In August 1916, the leading chemical companies *in Germany* had organized a loose community of interests; all of these companies had affiliates in America, which continued their separate operations.[154] Notwithstanding Herman Metz's comments cited earlier in this chapter about the inability of American manufacturing to fill basic dyestuffs requirements, once it became evident that the European war would be prolonged, that U.S. imports from Germany would continue to be curtailed, and, still worse in the view of the Germans, that American (and possibly British) companies would be producing dyestuffs in the United States, German firms responded and resolved to defend what had been their captive markets. Thus, they started to make on this side of the Atlantic products they had previously imported from Germany. On September 8, 1916, Congress passed an emergency tariff to assist the domestic "infant" industry. This tariff, which encouraged Du Pont to enter dyestuff production, also protected German-owned companies in the United States—as the latter added to their manufacturing.

The output of Bayer's plant in Rensselaer (near Albany, New York) spurted upward. Metz (the principal Hoechst representative in New York) acquired a half interest in Central Dyestuffs and Chemical Company in 1915, which raised its dyestuff manufacturing, as did Hoechst's Newark, New Jersey, factory (that of the Consolidated Color and Chemical Company). The German Cassella company organized a new affiliate, Century Color Company, to manufacture in America.[155] For the Germans, their dyestuffs operations in America became a delicate balancing act. On the one hand, they did not want to be left behind as American rivals emerged; on the other hand, they did not desire to help create a new U.S. industry that would substitute for the expected (and to them desired) U.S. imports from Germany once the war was over.[156] Two of the most remarkable happenings of 1916 were the arrivals in July (at Baltimore) and in November (at New London, Connecticut) of the German merchant submarine *Deutschland,* carrying basic dyestuffs from Germany.[157]

Such imports were, however, only an interim solution, and as the war continued to cut off normal trade, the Germans recognized that dyestuff manufacture in America was destined to rise, which was exactly what happened (see Table 1.3). Between 1914 and 1917, U.S. domestic dyestuffs output jumped twenty-three-fold measured in dollars and sevenfold measured by weight. Imports recorded in dollars remained about stable (despite the soaring prices of dyestuffs), but recorded by weight, they dropped sevenfold.[158] The hesitant Germans had decided to take part in the emerging U.S. dyestuffs industry.

Connected with the rise in dyestuffs manufacture in 1915–1917 was the growing output of aspirin at Bayer's plant in Rensselaer, New York. There were four reasons for this expansion: first, the difficulties in obtaining imports; second, the new availability of U.S.-made intermediates, as the dyestuff industry expanded; third, the price of aspirin advanced sharply, and profits could be made; and, fourth, on February 27, 1917, Bayer's U.S. patent for aspirin would expire. As that date approached, Bayer's American affiliate launched a $100,000 newspaper advertising campaign, stating that Bayer Aspirin was protected by a trademark and that the name could not be put on any product not made by Bayer. Several American firms prepared tablets and sold aspirins; Bayer filed suit against one, the United Drug Company.[159] After October 1915, Bayer advertised to American consumers, not merely to physicians (or to the "trade"), as had been its prior practice.[160] All this meant a sizable enlargement of Bayer business in America.

Salvarsan, a German miracle drug used to treat syphilis, was marketed in the United States under the "absolute control" of Farbwerke-Hoechst Co. in New York. With the war and trade disruption, the availability of this only known cure for syphilis became "insufficient and precarious." In 1915, an American professor (J. Frank Schamberg) in a Philadelphia laboratory began to manufacture Salvarsan "at the sufferance" of the German patent holders. Hoechst's U.S. representative,

Table 1.3. U.S. dyestuffs production and trade, 1914, 1917 (in millions)

			U.S. trade		
	U.S. production		Exports	Imports	
Year	Value ($)	Weight (lbs.)	Value ($)	Value ($)	Weight (lbs.)
1914	2.5	6.6	.4	7.5	42.2
1917	57.8	46.0	11.7	8.0	6.1

Source: Data from the U.S. Tariff Commission in U.S. Senate, Committee on the Judiciary, *Alleged Dye Monopoly,* 67th Cong. (1922), 68.

Metz, obtained a license to manufacture from the German patent owners and dispatched his brother to the Hoechst German plant (in January 1916) to learn how to do so. Reluctantly, Metz began to build an American plant. While it was under construction to fill the needs of his American customers, he purchased the drug from Schamberg.[161] In March 1917, Metz sent out a circular letter addressed "to the medical profession": "Owing to the uncertainty of obtaining further supplies of Salvarsan . . . from Europe . . . I have begun the construction of a plant for the manufacture of Salvarsan by the original Ehrlich process as carried out by Farbwerke vormals Meister Lucius & Brüning, of Hoechst a/Main, under existing patents. I hope to be able to have the product from this plant in the near future."[162] Metz, who had brought in Salvarsan on the submarine the *Deutschland* in July and November 1916, had believed he would receive added imported dyestuffs and Salvarsan in early 1917, carried in, as in 1916, by the *Deutschland,* but the merchant submarine never made it to America.[163] Thus Metz was "forced" to produce in America.

In June 1914, Du Pont had made an agreement with Norsk Hydro-Elektrisk Kvalstofaktieselskab A/S to obtain "the inventions and secret processes" of that Norwegian firm in connection with nitrate acid. Du Pont had formed in Canada (on April 13, 1915) the American Nitrogen Company, Ltd., in which Norsk Hydro came to hold debenture stock. Samuel Eyde of the Norwegian company became a director of American Nitrogen.[164] Du Pont's plans were, however, put on hold as news reached the United States on the German Haber process. In December 1916, Adolf Kuttroff, the longtime Badische representative in the United States, brought to the attention of the U.S. War Department the Haber process of obtaining nitrogen. He had received this information from Badische, which he transmitted to Washington. He cooperated with the American government in getting nitrogen production started at U.S. government facilities.[165]

The sales and profits of the German-controlled American Metal Company, New York, soared during 1915–1916 as the company expanded into new business ventures.[166] Some German-owned firms in America in 1915 and 1916 were openly pro-German. When, for example, the British blacklist (firms with which British subjects were forbidden to associate) included Orenstein-Arthur Koppel Company, this German affiliate's manager haughtily responded, "We have never tried to do business with Great Britain or her confederates and would never have made such an attempt even if there was no blacklist." That German-owned company enlarged its already substantial U.S. manufacturing facilities, making light railroad equipment that it marketed in the United States.[167]

Not all the growth of German business in America in 1915–1916 was to fill U.S. domestic requirements. By 1915, when German diplomat Heinrich Albert accidentally left his briefcase on New York City's Sixth Avenue El, the public began to learn of German sabotage.[168] Later the German ambassador to the United States, Count Bernstorff, summarized the efforts by Albert during 1915 and 1916 to circumvent the British blockade and blacklist. Albert engaged Danish firms and founded nominally "American" export companies, which when they came under English suspicion he replaced with others. According to Count Bernstorff, in 1915 the Germans started the Bridgeport Projectile Company, set up to pass "as entirely American." It bought up special machinery for the manufacture of shrapnel, seeking to limit *American* shrapnel output. Albert arranged the financing of this German government-owned company; funds were provided by the Deutsche Bank, undoubtedly using moneys made available through the sale of American securities and liquidation of the Deutsche Bank's U.S. lending. Hans Tauscher, Krupp's U.S. representative, was involved.[169]

In 1915, men from the German embassy offered Charles Schwab $100 million for his controlling interest in Bethlehem Steel, which was already heavily engaged in war work for the British and in shipbuilding. Schwab turned the Germans down.[170] Meanwhile, in 1915, the Lehigh Coke Company—a prewar German-owned firm in which the Deutsche Bank had an interest—built a U.S. plant to produce benzol and toluol for the German war ministry. The strategy was to foreclose the manufacture of these vital materials for explosives by Bethlehem Steel and to avoid their sale to the Allies. This project came to light, and the Deutsche Bank, before America entered the war, arranged for the sale of the Lehigh company to Bethlehem Steel.[171] Apparently, other plans, which did not materialize, included the acquisition and use of the Wright Aeroplane Company and its patents in German interests.[172]

Thomas Edison was making phenol (used for phonograph records) from benzol and had an excess of the latter, which his jobber sold to the Chemical Exchange Association, a firm set up by the Germans; the Germans then, in turn, sold the benzol to the German-owned Heyden Chemical Works that transformed it in the United States into salicylic acid that the German-owned Bayer subsidiary utilized to make aspirin. The "deal" was reported as having brought sizable profits to the German Imperial Treasury while converting the benzol into a harmless medicinal chemical (marketed primarily in America) instead of into a military explosive.[173]

Count Bernstorff recalled one German scheme that backfired: the German-controlled Bosch Magneto Company had a large U.S. factory in Springfield, Massachusetts, that was called on by the Allies to manufacture for their requirements; Bosch Magneto pretended to agree, at the same time conniving to delay production. When word reached Germany that this U.S. subsidiary would supply "the enemy," German public opinion turned against the parent Bosch works in Stuttgart. Like the German plan to buy Bethlehem Steel, the intention to use Lehigh Coke for German purposes, and the projected purchase of the Wright Aeroplane Company, this "plot" failed. Bosch Magneto expanded in America and provided products for British and French needs during the period of U.S. neutrality. Contemporary correspondence reveals that Bosch Magneto faced some of the same dilemmas as the German dye makers. *If* they did not meet demand in the United States, U.S. competitors would emerge to fill the orders. Bosch Magneto sought to preserve its business.[174]

An anti-German pamphlet on their plots in neutral America documented the machinations of Franz von Rintelen, who sought to stir up labor discontent in U.S. munitions plants and did so, financing the agitation with moneys deposited at the Transatlantic Trust Company, New York, a bank owned by three large Hungarian banks.[175] The Transatlantic Trust Company during 1914–1917 was said to have "vigorously pushed the sale [in the United States] of the war bonds of the Central Powers."[176] In 1915, the German government—through an agent—acquired control of the *New York Evening Mail.* The motive was propaganda. Control of this English-language newspaper remained in German hands until 1917.[177]

In sum, many foreign-controlled enterprises of different nationalities increased their U.S. business in 1915, 1916, and early 1917—some to meet U.S. domestic demand, some to export, and some (German ones) with political goals. Most found financing in America. Both the British and the Germans hoped to use direct investments to assist their respective war efforts, albeit it would be an error to judge the entire expansion solely in political terms. There were economic opportunities to be met, and the many foreign direct investors in America were prepared to satisfy the demand.

While, in net, foreign *direct* investment appears to have grown in the period January 1915 to April 1917, certain foreign direct investors did exit, and others reduced their U.S. involvements. Throughout the history of foreign business in America, entries and exits coexisted, as did expansions and contractions. The French principals in the Southern Aluminium Company continued to search in vain for funds in the United States or Europe to develop their U.S. business. By August 1915, the SAC board concluded that the company's shareholders could lose everything invested; its directors voted to sell the company's assets to the Aluminum Company of America (Alcoa) for $6,990,627, the exact sum the foreign owners had invested.[178] Alcoa would develop an important hydropower and smelter complex at Badin, North Carolina (the town kept the name of the French president of SAC and managing director of l'Aluminium Français, Adrien Badin). The project was now American owned.[179] In addition, I cannot establish that any of the prewar French automobile producers continued on as makers of cars in America.[180]

Whereas most British direct investments in America expanded, a handful did come to an end.[181] Often, however, the retreats were part of a "clearing the decks"—that is, formally closing out what were already virtually moribund, "shell," corporations.[182] In this context, economist Cleona Lewis noted the receivership of the San Antonio Land and Irrigation Co., Ltd.; well before 1914, it was a failure.[183] The Capitol Freehold Land and Investment Company, Ltd., which owned the huge XIT Ranch in Texas, was liquidated in 1915, and the British investors were paid off.[184] So, too, Stratton's Independence Ltd., whose mine was sold to a Colorado company, submitted its last shareholders list to the Companies' Registration Office, London, in 1915 (a liquidator would be appointed in 1918).[185] Most British investments in U.S. railroads had been portfolio ones (and those investments will be considered later in this chapter). There was an important exception: the British-owned and British-managed railroads associated with the Alabama Great Southern—including the New Orleans and Northeastern Railroad (which was separately owned and controlled by the Alabama, New Orleans, Texas, and Pacific Junction Railways Co., Ltd. [ANOTP]). In 1916, nearly all of the direct investment aspects of the British interest had ended; in 1917, ANOTP was transformed into Sterling Trust Ltd., an investment trust.[186] Every British direct investment that economist Cleona Lewis listed as having ended during the First World War could be classified as what I have called "free-standing companies"—companies with no related British home company operations and often weak administrative direction from the U.K. head office.[187]

The British-controlled Edgar Allen Manganese Steel Company was not in that category. Established in the United States in 1910, it had manufactured manganese steel in Chicago Heights, Illinois, and also operated a small foundry in Delaware.[188] Even though, like its parent, it was an innovative enterprise, apparently it had not been a financial success; by 1916, its facilities had been acquired by the American Manganese Steel Company.[189] British mortgage companies in America—while remaining in business—curtailed new mortgage lending (the British Treasury sought to get these companies to repatriate dollars and invest in British war loans).[190] As an example, as of March 31, 1915, the Texas Land and Mortgage Company had £798,928 invested in loans on mortgages in Texas and £4,734 in British war loans; as of March 31,

1917, this same company had £752,459 in loans on mortgages in Texas and £47,200 in British war loans.[191]

Some German and Austrian direct investors pulled back (and others sought to do so), but none for want of adequate financing, to erase past failures, for lack of decent profits, or under home government pressure. Instead, the more perceptive German and Austrian businessmen forecast America's eventual entry into the war on the side of the Entente and felt it prudent to divest their holdings before the United States became an enemy. Thus, the German Zeiss enterprise sold its 25 percent equity in its U.S. optical affiliate, Bausch & Lomb, to Americans in 1915. The German Zeiss had been upset because during 1914 and 1915 Bausch & Lomb supplied the Allies with critical optical glass; its complaints ignored, the parent succeeded in selling its holdings.[192] Perhaps Zeiss should not have been upset; the British found Bausch & Lomb's goods of poor quality; the firm refused to conform to British needs, and in time the contract was canceled.[193] The German Th. Goldschmidt was the largest individual shareholder in the Goldschmidt Detinning Company, which manufactured in Wyandotte, Michigan; Chrome, New Jersey; and East Chicago, Indiana. In 1916, the German parent disposed of the detinning company shares to American buyers.[194] Niagara Alkali Company (whose parent was Kaliwerke Aschersleben, which German potash company was beneficially Austrian owned) changed ownership in the fall of 1915 when it was acquired by the American firm Electro Bleaching Gas Company.[195] The Deutsche Bank arranged the sale of Lehigh Coke Co. to Bethlehem Steel before U.S. entry into the war.[196] On occasion, German firms sold their U.S. assets to *foreign* investors in neutral European countries (Switzerland and Sweden, for example), reducing German interests in America, but not diminishing the total foreign investment in this country.[197]

In July 1915, the U.S. Navy took over the operations of the German-owned (Telefunken's) Sayville, Long Island, radio station because "unneutral" messages were being transmitted.[198] The U.S. government believed that German wireless messages on ship movements provided German submarines with targets.[199] After the Germans lost control, Karl G. Frank, the U.S. representative of the German parent, Telefunken, sought in 1916 to sell the majority of German ownership in the Atlantic Communication Company (the corporate affiliate of Telefunken and owner of the Sayville radio station) to the neutral Swedish government, a futile effort to camouflage and safeguard the German property.[200] Frank was not alone in such *unsuccessful* attempts to divest.[201]

Frequently German businessmen sought the best of both worlds: to retain their holdings while disguising them so that should America enter the war, their assets would be protected. Later the Alien Property

Custodian and the courts would have to decide whether "sales" of German investments to Americans or to companies in European neutral countries were real or merely an opportunistic step to veil the true continuing German ownership and control.[202] If the "sale" was made in early 1917, the Alien Property Custodian would often conclude that it was not legitimate.[203] As we have seen, however, most German investors accepted (or at least acquiesced in) the advice of their U.S. representatives and expanded their American operations, 1915–1917.[204]

The Decline in Foreign Portfolio Investment in America before U.S. Entry

By far the most significant change in the pattern of foreign investment in America, 1915–1917, was the dramatic reduction in what had been the huge European portfolio holdings—a liquidation begun in 1914; this decline greatly offset the net rise in foreign direct investments.[205] After the New York Stock Exchange reopened, it became easier for foreign investors to sell their securities. On March 21, 1916, the U.S. Commissioner of Internal Revenue ruled that "under the decision of the Supreme Court of the United States in the case of Brushaber v. Union Pacific Railway Company, decided January 24, 1916, it is hereby held that income accruing to nonresident aliens in the form of interest from bonds and dividends on the stock of domestic corporations, is subject to the income tax imposed by the Act of October 13, 1913." This IRS ruling reversed a prior U.S. Treasury Department decision, which had exempted interest on bonds and dividends on stock of domestic corporations owned by nonresident aliens from U.S. income tax. The standard tax of 1 percent would be withheld at the source.[206] The threat of a higher tax was present. Table 1.4 reveals the sharp (and typical) decline in foreign holdings in United States Steel Corporation's common and preferred shares (measured by numbers of shares held). Note that the steepest attrition—at least in common share holdings—was during 1915 (before the Supreme Court decision).[207] Table 1.5 gives the breakdown in common share holdings in U.S. Steel by nationality. The most marked drop (by number of shares and by specified nationality) was in the English holdings, and by December 31, 1916, Dutch stakes exceeded those of the English.[208] Table 1.6 provides the par value of certain American railroad securities held abroad; the documented January 31, 1915, to January 31, 1917, reduction in the par value of these holdings was in excess of $1.5 billion.[209] Prewar railroad regulations had slowed railroad rate increases; lines had deteriorated; and by 1916, fully a sixth of the nation's railroad network was in receivership; part of the drop in foreign interest in U.S. railroads can be attributed to the distressed state of American railroads.[210]

Table 1.4. Foreign holdings in the United States Steel Corporation, 1914–1917 (number and percent of shares)

	Common shares		Preferred shares	
Date	Number	%	Number	%
Mar. 31, 1914	1,285,636	25.29	312,311	8.67
June 30, 1914	1,274,247	25.07	312,832	8.68
Dec. 31, 1914	1,193,064	23.47	309,457	8.59
Dec. 31, 1915	696,631	13.70	274,588	7.62
Dec. 31, 1916	502,632	9.89	156,412	4.34
Mar. 31, 1917	494,338	9.72	151,757	4.21

Source: Commercial and Financial Chronicle, Oct. 20, 1923, 1740.

Table 1.5. Foreign holdings of common shares in United States Steel Corporation, by nationality, 1914–1917

	Number of common shares						
Date	England[a]	Holland	France	Canada	Other foreign	Total foreign	Percent foreign
Mar. 31, 1914	801,497	357,293	68,269	42,390	16,187	1,285,636	25.29
Dec. 31, 1914	710,621	342,645	64,537	54,259	21,002	1,193,064	23.47
Dec. 31, 1915	355,088	238,617	50,193	38,011	14,722	696,631	13.70
Dec. 31, 1916	192,250	234,365	34,328	31,662	10,027	502,632	9.89[b]
Mar. 31, 1917	188,146	231,745	30,420	39,777	4,250	494,338	9.72

Source: Commercial and Financial Chronicle, Apr. 21, 1917, 1548. I could not locate a breakdown by nationality for June 30, 1914

a. Scotland included in "other foreign"; the amounts were not large.

b. I have corrected an error in the original.

Table 1.6. American railroad securities held abroad, 1915–1917 (par value in millions of U.S. dollars)

Date	Amount
Jan. 31, 1915	2,704.4
July 31, 1915	2,223.5
July 31, 1916	1,415.6
Jan. 31, 1917	1,185.8

Source: Figures of L. F. Loree, as given in the *Commercial and Financial Chronicle,* Mar. 31, 1917, 1217. See also *Annalist,* June 28, 1915, 674; Gordon Blythe Anderson in *Annals,* 67 (Nov. 1916): 121; and Cleona Lewis, *America's Stake in International Investments* (Washington, D.C.: Brookings Institution, 1938), 532.

Much of the decline in foreign holdings was by the British—and was a result of British government policies. With a mounting negative trade balance and rising domestic wartime needs, in February 1915, British Chancellor of the Exchequer Lloyd George declared that British overseas investments "must be liquidated." The *New York Times* commented that for the British "there are only United States investments that can be liquidated. There is no market for South American or Balkan or African or Asiatic, nor for Canadian investments. And neither Russian bonds nor Belgian nor Austrian will be taken in this market."[211] The item about Canadian investments was perhaps too extreme, but were the British "to liquidate" their overseas investments, clearly the most promising place to do so was in the United States; the reason for the desire to liquidate was that the British needed dollars to buy supplies from America.

Table 1.7 indicates how far the divestment process had gone by December 1915. The repatriations continued in 1916 and 1917. There was sufficient wealth in America to absorb the sales; domestic buyers acquired the securities.[212] There were two basic routes in the significant reduction of foreign portfolio investments. One path was that of private sales; the second involved government or government-induced selling. Private sales took place for a number of reasons, including the poor financial performance of American railroad securities, the possibilities of higher returns in Europe, and, as some American securities rose in value with the "war boom," the desire to take advantage of the capital gains. When the British government issued a war loan in June 1915, many Britishers sold American stocks and bonds to buy their home bonds.[213] On June 25, Henry P. Davison (a partner in J. P. Morgan & Co.) cabled from London that the "new war loan is having marked effect increasing sale of American securities."[214] In July, such British divestment became particularly heavy.[215] On a visit to the

Table 1.7. American securities sold by Europeans from the outbreak of war in Europe to December 1915 (in millions of U.S. dollars)

Residence of seller	Amount
Great Britain	950
Germany	300
France	150
Holland	100
Switzerland and other countries	50
Total	1,550

Source: New York Times, Dec. 18, 1915.

United States in September, Robert Fleming, who for years had participated in acquiring American securities, especially railroad bonds—on his own behalf, on behalf of his firm Robert Fleming & Co., and on behalf of a group of British trust companies—was reported to be looking after the sale of "American bonds."[216] On November 18, Jacob Schiff of Kuhn, Loeb & Co. wrote of the "enormous return of American securities held abroad."[217] All during 1916 and into 1917, private sales by European investors continued. Britishers, Frenchmen, Germans, the Dutch, and other Europeans as well made such sales. Particularly sizable private repatriations of French holdings in America occurred in 1915 and 1916.[218] The cream of German portfolio investments were divested (mainly private sales), obstacles to the transactions notwithstanding.[219] Some of these divestments took place in early 1917: Rothschild Frères, Paris, learned from August Belmont & Co., on February 7, 1917, that U.S. markets were "nervous . . . there has been considerable liquidation at the Stock exchange for foreign account . . . presumably for Germany and Austria."[220] Dutch investors similarly disposed of securities through private channels, sometimes acting on behalf of German principals.[221]

The second path by which America repatriated foreign-held securities is far better documented. It related to the need by the British government, and to a far lesser extent the French and German governments, to obtain dollars and the recognition that the securities held by their nationals provided an excellent source of the required foreign exchange. The British government sought dollar securities that were liquid and could be sold to acquire dollars and/or were acceptable as collateral for dollar borrowing. Except for certain British direct investors in mortgage-granting companies that, as we have seen, were pressured to reduce their lending and invest in British war loans, otherwise none of the British government policies served in any manner to reduce foreign *direct* investment in America. The impact of the mobilization policies was on foreign portfolio investments.

In October 1914, the British Treasury had dispatched Basil P. Blackett and Sir George Paish across the Atlantic to handle problems associated with British government purchases of American goods.[222] They discussed using American securities held by Britishers as a means of obtaining dollars to pay for the goods.[223] In January 1915, the British War Office and the Admiralty (and in May 1915 the French government) appointed J. P. Morgan & Co. their commercial agent. The Morgan house became adviser to the British and French governments and soon would be offering financial assistance.[224] Morgan in New York, in London (Morgan, Grenfell), and in Paris (Morgan, Harjes) had the expertise to take on this crucial role.[225] By May 1915, after Reginald McKenna replaced Lloyd George as Chancellor of the Exchequer in Herbert Asquith's new Liberal coalition government, the British earnestly set out to find ways to finance their ever-growing purchases of supplies in the United States.

In the summer of 1915, British government officials were becoming alarmed about the foreign exchange situation. In 1914, the dollar's depreciation had been everyone's concern. In 1915, with the war boom and the giant British purchases in America, demand for dollars pushed up their value. Thus, British authorities faced two associated problems: (1) the need for dollars to pay for the supplies acquired in America, and (2) the need to stabilize the exchange rate, since the depreciating pound (appreciating dollar) was making the British imports more expensive.

To cope with both difficulties, on June 3, 1915, Morgan partner Henry P. Davison suggested that the British government borrow American securities "from your trust companies or other holders of American securities, such holders lending these securities and being secured by British securities, also receiving small premium as compensation for lending their securities."[226] Davison's cable to Morgan's London house planted an idea, which influenced future events.

To assist the governor of the Bank of England, Lord Cunliffe, in providing foreign exchange for British government purchases in America, Chancellor of the Exchequer McKenna summoned—on July 22—Sir Thomas Dewey, A. C. Thompson, Sir Joseph Burn, and Sir George May of the Prudential Assurance Company and asked them how much their insurance office owned in American securities. The response was $40 million. McKenna asked, "'Will you give it to me and let me settle later?' . . . The directors [of Prudential Assurance] instantly replied they would . . . The Bank of England supplied another £5,000,000 in gold. The whole 65,000,000 dollars was promptly paid into the Morgan house in London." The $65 million in securities and gold became the collateral for a $50 million loan from J. P. Morgan, New York, the proceeds of which could be applied to British purchases in America.[227]

That summer of 1915, the British government began to encourage its residents to sell to *it* their foreign securities in exchange for British government bonds. On July 25, Prime Minister Asquith wrote to McKenna "that the process of acquiring and collecting American securities here for export should be conducted as quietly and unostentatiously as possible"; the initial operations went forward in secrecy. The British Treasury instructed the Bank of England to buy American dollar-denominated securities in London and transmit them to New York for sale.[228] The British cabinet met on August 18, ratified the earlier steps, and agreed that American securities would be bought by the British government from their British owners for resale in New York.[229] The dollars acquired would be used to buy war materiel in the United States. J. P. Morgan & Co. would handle all the transactions.[230] Soon the British were doing additional borrowing in the United States to pay for supplies.

When in September an Anglo-French delegation traveled to America to negotiate a loan on behalf of the Allied powers, the delegation did not pledge securities as collateral but did—with Morgan's aid—raise a large ($500 million) Anglo-French loan.[231] Yet, to protect the rate of exchange and as collateral for subsequent borrowings in New York, the Bank of England continued to buy (and now to borrow as well) from U.K. holders sizable amounts of American securities.[232] On November 15, McKenna set up an Exchange Committee to handle Britain's exchange requirements and attempt to stabilize exchange rates.[233] By the end of 1915, the Chief Cashier's office at the Bank of England had purchased $233 million in dollar-denominated securities.[234]

The efforts of the British government to buy and borrow American securities had accelerated when, on December 15, the British Treasury Department dispatched a circular letter to British insurance and trust companies asking them to submit lists of American dollar securities that they were willing to sell or to deposit on loan with the Treasury. A notice appeared in the *London Gazette,* December 17, defining suitable types of securities, and on December 31, 1915, a circular went out to the British general public requesting such securities.[235] George May, the secretary of Prudential Assurance Company (which had been so helpful in July 1915), became the manager of the American Dollar Securities Committee, which was organized at the end of 1915 to collect the mobilized dollar securities, sell them to provide dollar exchange, and hold them to serve as collateral for British borrowings.[236]

From January 1916 to April 1917, British government purchases of supplies in the United States continued to climb, with the need for dollars growing ever more urgent. In January 1916, the American Dollar Securities Committee provided the British public with a list of 54 American dollar securities that it wanted to buy or borrow. By May 16, the list was enlarged to include 909 different securities. To encourage Britishers to sell or to loan such securities to their government, on May 29 an extra British income tax of two shillings per pound was imposed.[237] Meanwhile, on March 21, in the United States, the IRS had reversed a prior ruling and held that dividends and interest paid to nonresident aliens could be subject to U.S. income tax.[238]

The British tax (added to the potential American one) resulted in a flood of securities being delivered to the British government.[239] In June 1916, Sir Brien Cokayne (later Lord Cullen), then deputy governor of the Bank of England, wrote to Benjamin Strong at the New York Federal Reserve Bank on the effect of the British surtax: "It is wonderful how the patriotism of our holders of Americans has been stimulated by a little fillip of additional taxation." Sir Brien noted, with amazement, that despite the earlier sales of American securities, "there seem . . . to be plenty of them left here." In a similar vein, Montagu Norman from the Bank of England wrote to Strong: the stream of American securities "has been almost too great for easy handling."[240] The submissions were of vital importance in providing the British Exchange Committee with "cover" to deposit with Morgan and other New York lenders.[241] Between January 1, 1916, and March 31, 1916, the British Treasury obtained about $270 million from reselling American securities. In the next year, April 1, 1916, to March 31, 1917, British government *sales* of American securities added an extra $532 million.[242] The American market had no difficulty in absorbing the influx.[243]

From September 1916, the Exchange Committee had suspended the sale of British government-owned dollar securities; henceforth, according to Bank of England historian R. E. Sayers, all American dollar securities, whether bought or borrowed by the American Dollar Securities Committee, were held to be used as collateral (this is very doubtful, for the records show that resales in New York continued, albeit at a much diminished pace).[244] That September 1916, the U.S. federal government started to collect the income tax of 1 percent on dividends and interest paid on American securities to nonresident aliens and announced that the tax would be raised to 2 percent from January 1, 1917.[245] Once the U.S. tax was a reality, Britishers felt more prone to turn over their securities to their government. It was not until January 1917, however, that the British Treasury was given the power to requisition securities.[246]

Three large loans to the British government were issued in New York, on September 1, 1916 ($250 million), October 30, 1916 ($300 million), and January 18, 1917 ($250 million); the mobilized American securities served as collateral for these loans. The Morgans arranged the loans and the collateral.[247] Britain had become dependent on the United States for war finance.[248] In April 1917, America entered the war. On April 26, 1917, for the first time, the U.S. *government* became a lender to Great Britain.[249]

In 1915 and 1916, British investment trusts—that had been large holders of American securities—had made private sales of these securities and also cooperated with their government in its effort to mobilize dollar securities that were acceptable for American credit.[250] The British investment trusts made no new American investments in wartime. They reduced their American holdings. Not only British restrictions on capital exports were a deterrent; the new American income tax meant double taxation for British investment trusts and encouraged divestment. Likewise, managers reported that the relative returns on American holdings no longer merited retaining the large stakes of earlier years.[251]

British insurance companies also had for many decades accumulated substantial U.S. holdings—separate and distinct from their direct investments in America. Aside from Prudential, many others cooperated with the British government and the American Dollar Securities Committee. British insurance companies had two types of U.S. investments: (1) those that were part of a *British* company's portfolio, and (2) those that were made by branches and subsidiaries in America (as of December 31, 1913, forty-two British branches and subsidiaries of fire and marine insurance companies had some $116 million U.S. "admitted assets"—the bulk of which was in American securities).[252] Only the first category of investments could be mobilized by the British government. The second category—associated with the direct investments in selling insurance—could not be mobilized. Since the "admitted assets" were held against liabilities (against possible loss claims), they could not be divested and not replaced, short of discontinuing the American business.[253] As of December 31, 1918, U.S. branches and subsidiaries of British fire and marine insurance companies had "admitted assets" of $202 million; their U.S. assets rose rather than declined in the war years.[254] It was the portfolio holdings in America (mainly American railroad bonds) of the British *parent* firms *and* those of British insurance companies with no business in America that were reduced as a consequence of the British government mobilization.

Table 1.8 indicates the *resales* by the British Treasury of over $800 million of securities in New York from January 1, 1916, to March 31, 1917. Remember, the British Treasury did not sell all the securities that it bought, and it sold none that it borrowed from British investors.

The French and German government mobilizations of American securities were on a far smaller scale than that of the British. In June 1915, J. P. Morgan & Co. and two other New York banks (the First National Bank and National City Bank) agreed to lend Rothschild Frères, Paris, $30 million, to be secured by deposit as collateral of franc bonds of the Chicago, Milwaukee and St. Paul Railroad. These franc-denominated American railroad securities were acquired by the French government from French nationals in exchange for the new French National Defense Bonds. The "Rothschild Frères loan" would be for French government purchases in America.[255] The French acted similarly to their British allies in mobilizing dollar securities; there were French government resales of these securities in America, as well as

Table 1.8. Resales in New York of securities purchased by the British Treasury under the auspices of the American Dollar Securities Committee, Jan. 1, 1916–Mar. 31, 1919

Year ending March 31	(1) Dollars received (in millions)	(2) Average rate of exchange ($/£)	(3) Sterling equivalent (in millions)	(4) Sterling received (in millions)	(5) Total sterling equivalent (in millions) (3) + (4)
1916 (3 mos. only)	270.84	4.72	57.38	.10	57.48
1917	531.13	4.76 7/16	111.48	.05	111.53
Total, Jan. 1, 1916–Mar. 31, 1917	801.97		168.86	.15	169.01
1918	116.93	4.76 7/16	24.54	.01	24.55
1919	65.65	4.76 7/16	13.78	3.31	17.09
Total, Mar. 31, 1917–Mar. 31, 1919	182.58		38.32	3.32	41.64

Source: Final Report upon American Dollar Securities Loaned to the Government and Purchased by the Government, Sept. 30, 1922. Reprinted in U.S. Senate, Special Committee Investigating the Munitions Industry, *The Munitions Industry, Hearings,* 74th Cong., 2nd sess. (1936), pt. 35 (Exhibit 4252), 11813.

French government use of the securities as collateral for borrowing in America.

The best source on the French government's efforts during 1915 and 1916 to realize dollars on franc obligations issued by American corporations and held in France is Robert T. Swaine, *The Cravath Firm;* this law firm handled many of the transactions. Americans were delighted to comply with the French government wishes, for American railroads now had the opportunity to retire the franc bonds at a profit and avoid the newly imposed French taxes on interest payments. The Southern Pacific, which had guaranteed the 250 million franc, thirty-five-year, 4 percent bonds of 1911 of the Central Pacific, repatriated about two-thirds of these. Kuhn, Loeb & Co. arranged that the Chicago, Milwaukee & St. Paul and the Pennsylvania Company franc-denominated bonds were replaced with dollar obligations.[256] The U.S. banking house J. & W. Seligman & Co. in 1916 made a $13.8 million one-year 6 percent dollar loan to the French government, secured by St. Louis and San Francisco Railroad bonds and coupons held in France (the latter were deposited under a railroad reorganization plan, and new securities were issued and sold to liquidate the loan).[257] In July 1916, J. P. Morgan & Co. arranged a $100 million French loan; the collateral included bonds and stocks of American corporations, plus other securities.[258] French holdings in America were nowhere near as great as those of the British (and French investors had learned to disguise their holdings); thus, the French government transactions were much less extensive than those of the British.[259]

As for the German government, it used the dollars obtained by its nationals' selling securities in America to make U.S. purchases, to finance German propaganda in the United States, and, in some instances, to encourage the "plots" of German direct investors.[260] Like the British and the French, it, too, tried to raise money in the United States to support its war effort. Some 32,000 subscribers in the United States to German and Austrian war loans were later identified from Deutsche Bank files;[261] some of these subscribers were nonresident German investors in the United States who utilized dollars previously invested in American securities. The Germans, however, came to be very dissatisfied in their efforts to market German war bonds in the United States.[262]

In short, from January 1915 to April 1917, sizable private sales (repatriations) by Europeans of American securities took place. I do not know what proportion of the sales went through private channels.[263] There were also sales by Britishers, Frenchmen, and Germans of American securities *to* their respective governments; these securities were, in turn, sometimes resold in the United States or used (in the case of the British and French) as collateral for U.S. loans. For the Germans, dollars appear to have been utilized to buy German war bonds in the United States or to support German "plots." In addition, the British and French government borrowed American dollar securities from British investors and placed them as collateral for U.S. loans. Overall, the result of British government policy was that many U.K. banks, other financial intermediaries, and private investors that over the years had acquired and held American stocks and bonds were "forced out of them into war loans, Treasury bills, exchequer bonds or some other form of government credit."[264] A similar reduction in holdings occurred by French, German, and other European investors. By my calculations, whether through private sales or through government channels, between July 1, 1914, and April 1917, some $3.1 billion in American securities returned to domestic U.S. ownership.[265]

The New Nationalism

As the Allies and the Central Powers fought in Europe, as American lending to belligerents (principally to the Allies) rose, Americans turned their attention to a domestic agenda. The 1916 U.S. tariff was a protectionist measure by a Democratic administration that had earlier pledged to lower duties on imports. Americans became concerned that their economy should be under *national* control and not at the mercy of international influences. Strong arguments were put forth for U.S. government aid to shipbuilding and shipping, with Treasury Secretary William G. McAdoo urging that "our economic dependence on Europe . . . be . . . removed."[266] Since 1817, foreign participation in American coastal shipping had been prohibited, but there had been loopholes.[267] In the Shipping Act of 1916, the Jones-White Act (designed to encourage *American* shipping), the term "citizens" was explicitly extended so as to exclude from coastal shipping *corporations* controlled by non-U.S. citizens.[268] The law authorized a new Shipping Board, giving the U.S. government the right to purchase and to construct merchant vessels.[269]

Americans were also uneasy about foreign hegemony over international communications. Once more, there was precedent for their nervousness. The dominance over the nation's nascent radio industry by the British-controlled Marconi company had long troubled U.S. Navy Department officials.[270] The misgivings had intensified when in 1914 Marconi of America had the audacity to question President Wilson's policy on unneutral messages; the British affiliate had not been pleased that the U.S. Navy insisted on monitoring its transmissions. In 1914 and 1915, the U.S. government had taken over the operations of the German-constructed Tuckerton, New Jersey, and Sayville, Long Island, radio stations, actions that had, however, the unwanted consequence of enhancing the premier position of Marconi of America in the private sector. Early in 1917, Congress held hearings on radio communication regulation legislation, but at this time it did not change the policies laid down under the 1912 law (which required licensing of radio communication yet did not impede foreign-owned corporations from obtaining such a license).[271]

As indicated, the U.S. federal government in September 1916 started to collect a 1 percent income tax on dividends and interest paid to nonresident aliens, a tax raised to 2 percent on January 1, 1917. Americans could not care less if the new tax angered foreign investors; there was no particular wish for inward foreign investment.

The higher tariff, the Shipping Act of 1916, the congressional hearings on the radio industry, and the taxes imposed on foreign investors were harbingers of a more intense postwar nationalism. "America for Americans"—once a populist motto—had a wide appeal. Paradoxically, even before the United States became a combatant, many Americans responded to events in Europe by becoming more insular.

The United States at War, April 1917–November 1918

In retrospect, it seems strange how long—from August 1914 to April 1917—the United States clung to neutrality. In part, the reason lay in the history of U.S. detachment from European quarrels; in part, its roots were in the rising nationalism just described. Finally, on April 2, 1917, Wilson—condemning German submarine activity—asked Congress for a declaration of war. Four days later, April 6, the president signed a joint congressional resolution declaring war on Germany.

That day Hugo Schmidt—the U.S. representative of the Deutsche Bank—was arrested. In the next forty-eight hours, there was a further roundup of German "spies," and the group including personnel of German-owned businesses in America. Among those detained was Karl G. Frank, head of the Atlantic Communication Company, which had controlled the Sayville, Long Island, radio station that the navy had been operating since July 1915; Frank was in April 1917—as in earlier years—the Siemens representative in America.[272] Because he was an American citizen, he was soon released.[273] Schmidt, however, remained in jail for the duration of the war.[274] Others imprisoned at the start of hostilities included former employees at the Tuckerton transatlantic wireless station and two American citizens who worked for the Hamburg-American Line.[275]

On April 6, the day war was declared, customs officials had commandeered the ninety-seven German and Austrian ships present in U.S. ports. The new United States Shipping Board (USSB)—authorized under the Shipping Act of 1916—would take charge. By the summer of 1917 most of the freighters and tankers had been put to use, supplying Allied needs, and the great German passenger liners were carrying American forces to fight in Europe.[276] On April 7, 1917, the navy took control of the operations of the nation's fifty-three commercial radio stations, practically all owned by the British firm Marconi of America.[277] The U.S. government was assuming an unprecedented role in these vital sectors.

German-owned businesses, in general, became the target of U.S. government takeovers, but on the same day that war was declared a rather remarkable exception was made. On April 6, Wilson issued a proclamation authorizing the *continuance* in business in the United States of existing branch establishments of German insurance companies, "subject to certain limitations as to the transmission of their funds . . . and subject to state regulation." Wilson did this in response to an April 5 letter from New York, Massachusetts, and Connecticut state regulators.

These insurance regulators had recommended that the federal government protect the interests of Americans who held insurance written by the German companies, which the regulators estimated at "not less than" $3.5 billion, representing premiums of $37 million paid by over 2 million holders. Over 8,000 agents were involved and several thousand office employees—practically all American citizens. "A very large part of this insurance," the state insurance supervisors wrote, "cannot be satisfactorily absorbed by other companies now transacting insurance business in this country."[278] Others disagreed, and on July 13, 1917, the president issued a supplementary proclamation, prohibiting German insurance companies from continuing transactions in marine and war risk insurance but still allowing them to go on writing fire insurance.[279] Many Americans wondered at this special privilege.

Meanwhile, in June 1917 (with the Espionage Act), the right of Americans to export gold was restricted, and soon all foreign exchange transactions came under federal government regulation.[280] On October 6, 1917, President Wilson signed the Trading with the Enemy Act, setting up the position of Alien Property Custodian (APC). The APC was authorized to sequester the properties of German and other enemy investors.[281] The first APC, A. Mitchell Palmer, hired Francis P. Garvan (1875–1937), an energetic attorney, to head the APC's Bureau of Investigation; Garvan would figure importantly in dealing with foreign investment in America for the rest of his life.[282] By January 1, 1918, Garvan's staff had gathered 11,170 reports on property held for the account of an enemy; as a result, the bureau mailed 50,000 letters of inquiries.

Garvan called on the nation's law firms, interrogating them on their knowledge of enemy assets. He asked American bankers for help in tracing enemy money and properties. He wrote letters to building and loan associations. Postmasters were requested to provide information on enemy property, as were internal revenue collectors and bank examiners. From Military Intelligence, Naval Intelligence, the Department of Justice, the Cable Censor's Office, the War Trade Board, the Internal Revenue Service, and the Department of State, Garvan collected voluminous data. His bureau enlisted the assistance of the British embassy, the French High Commission, and other friendly embassies in Washington. His employees examined copies of some 250,000 intercepted radiograms that had passed to and from Germany and Austria and the United States between January 1, 1915, and April 6, 1917.[283] By February 15, 1919 (the Armistice was, of course, November 11, 1918), the APC had obtained 35,400 reports on enemy assets in the United States.[284]

Garvan's information contained details on the sizable enemy stakes, notably German ones, that were present in this country. He learned about portfolio investments, although the best of such securities had already been sold before U.S. entry into the war. But, for example, the American banking house Kuhn, Loeb surrendered to the APC bonds held for such German banks as Disconto-Gesellschaft.[285] The copious files of the New York office of the Deutsche Bank were combed and found to include valuable data on both portfolio and direct investments.[286] The extent of the German direct investments astonished the APC. In every state of the union there were nonresident German-owned properties. The APC predicted (in February 1919) that when the valuations were completed, the total would come to $700 million.[287] Years later (in 1943, in the midst of the Second World War), the amount of German property subject to U.S. government control *during the First World War,* was estimated to have "exceeded $600,000,000."[288]

Special U.S. government attention turned to transactions with neutral nations, lest the latter offer a cloak for enemy activity.[289] While U.S. Secretary of State Robert Lansing was interested in trade and investment matters, while Secretary of the Treasury William G. McAdoo paid special attention to the activities of German business, particularly in shipping and insurance, while the Federal Reserve Board kept vigilant, it was the APC that led in the takeovers of enemy assets.[290]

Whenever possible, the APC put enemy enterprises to work on behalf of the American war effort. By the time of the Armistice, the APC "was supplying the [U.S.] Government with magnetos for aeroplane and automobile motors, with cloth to make the uniforms for soldiers and the dyes with which the cloth was dyed, with medicines, surgical instruments and dressings, with musical instruments, with ball bearings, telescopes, optical instruments and engineering instruments, with coconut charcoal for making of gas masks, with glycerin for the making of high explosives, and a large number of other and varied products," all made in the confiscated German factories in America.[291] Some of the acquired German companies that the APC administered to assist the U.S. war effort are listed in Table 1.9.

The APC became impressed that the principal properties taken over were those of "Germany's great industrial army."[292] Before the war, no one had any conception of the extent of German direct investment in the United States.[293] In taking over German assets, a large number of issues related to German patents arose. By the time of the Armistice, it was unclear how these matters would be handled. The Federal Trade Commission was given authority to license certain German patents. In the fall of 1918, the APC set out to sell the German assets to Americans; prior to the Armistice it had started "the sale and liquidation of the enemy interests in the great American metal, textile, chemical, electrical, and other industries." The APC wanted to be sure that the properties "would be separated from their former enemy owners forever" and that Americans would have access to German technology.[294]

The German-owned Bayer affiliates would be sold for $5.31 million to the American-owned Sterling Products, which kept the pharmaceutical business, including the rights to the Bayer name and logo, while at once selling the dye facilities and dyestuff patents to the American-owned Grasselli Chemical Company.[295] The American-owned National Aniline & Chemical Company—a dyestuff producer formed in May 1917—would acquire other German dyestuff properties.[296] Merck & Co.'s securities would be sold for over $3 million to a group headed by Goldman, Sachs and Lehman Brothers; George Merck—an American citizen—retained control.[297] Most of the APC sales occurred after the Armistice. However, on September 12, 1918, the Orenstein–Arthur Koppel Company's business—with U.S. assets of $2.3 million—went

Table 1.9. Formerly German-owned companies engaged in U.S. war work (World War I) (in millions of U.S. dollars)

Company	Value of war work
New Jersey Worsted Spinning Co., yarn	8.6
Gera Mills, yarn and woven goods	8.0
Botany Worsted Mills, yarn and woven goods	6.0
Bosch Magneto Co., magnetos	2.6
Knys-Scheerer Corp., surgical instruments	2.1
Passaic Worsted Spinning Co., yarn	1.8
Bayer Co., aspirins and dyes	1.2
Norma Co., ball bearings	1.1

Source: Alien Property Custodian Report 1918–1919, 10.

to Pressed Steel Car Co., Pittsburgh.[298] By April 1917, the Koppers Company (before 1914 a small German-controlled firm) had sold 80 percent of its stock to Americans. This company had expanded greatly during 1914–1917, reaching the rank of 112 among all U.S. industrials. After U.S. entry in the war, the major American shareholders reported that Heinrich Koppers owned 20 percent of the stock. The APC auctioned the stock off "at bargain basement prices"; the buyers were the existing American shareholders, including members of the Mellon family.[299] The standard pattern vis-à-vis the German industrial firms was one of acquisition by the APC and then sale of the once enemy-owned properties to American companies or American citizens. The process was just beginning to take shape at the time of the Armistice.

Initially, under the October 1917 Trading with the Enemy Act, enemy insurance and reinsurance companies were given special treatment. They could apply to the secretary of the treasury for a license to remain in business and pending further action could continue writing insurance policies.[300] *The Standard*—a weekly insurance industry newspaper—on August 4, 1917 (before the passage of the Trading with the Enemy Act) had blasted the U.S. policy of permitting German fire insurance companies to go on writing insurance, insisting that the nation had no need for such firms. In a front-page story, it had editorialized that while the German fire insurers had—by year end 1916—$3.56 billion insurance in force in the United States, two U.S. companies each had over $3 billion, and "a dozen American and British companies had twenty-three billion." Thus, existing companies in the United States could absorb the German business. And, in a reference to the views of the state regulators (which I noted earlier), the insurance industry paper argued, "the representation that German fire insurance is indispensable to the protection of the American property owner is ridiculous." The *Standard* insisted it was improper that we were at war with Germany and yet allowed German fire companies to write policies and to collect information on our vital industries.[301]

The policy toward enemy, German, insurers was revised. On November 26, 1917, the secretary of the treasury announced that all insurance companies existing under the laws of enemy or ally of enemy countries, other than life insurance companies, must liquidate their U.S. business under the supervision of the secretary of the treasury and the APC.[302] In the months that followed, most of the thirteen German fire and marine and life insurance companies in the United States that had been active in insurance and reinsurance were liquidated. Two Bulgarian companies and one Austrian company were also affected. In four cases, the business of the U.S. branches of the German insurers was reinsured by American companies (the two German life insurance companies were reinsured by Metropolitan Life Insurance). The Tokio Marine and Fire Insurance Company reinsured the business of the Aachen and Munich Fire Insurance Company's U.S. branch. In addition, a Swiss company (Swiss National Insurance Company, Basle) that was beneficially owned by the Munich Reinsurance Company would be liquidated.[303] The U.S. Shipping Board continued during the war to utilize the "commandeered" German and Austrian ships; in 1918, the board acquired from the APC the docks at Hoboken, New Jersey, previously owned by the two principal German-controlled steamship lines—the Hamburg-American Line and the North German Lloyd Line.[304] So effective were the APC's activities, and those of other sections of the government that cooperated with it, it is fair to say that by the time the fighting stopped, there were zero German-owned assets in the United States.[305]

Did the presence of the large and important German direct investments in America in any way slow the U.S. war effort? What was their impact on the American economy? In the period of neutrality, good evidence exists of German attempts to impede U.S. support of the Allied cause. Yet in those months, German companies had also introduced new technologies into the country. After the United States entered the war and after the formerly German-owned facilities became American directed, these plants provided assistance to the American side. There seems to have been sufficient technological transfer to the U.S. affiliates so that once divorced from their parents, most (but not all) of these satellite firms could continue to manufacture for the American war effort.[306] The one major exception was that with dyestuff imports cut off, there was inadequate knowledge within the United States to replicate the formerly imported products. These limitations did not prove serious to the war effort, but the U.S. consumer was not well served. As Metz (the prewar representative of the German Hoechst) later—in 1922—reminded a U.S. senator, "During the war . . . when your wife bought a pair of stockings they would be brown in daylight, green at night, and pink when they came back from the laundry."[307] Mastery of the German dye-making skills by the former German affiliates and by American-owned manufacturers was not easily achieved. The earlier concerns of the state regulators that the U.S. public would suffer as a consequence of the liquidation of German insurance services proved, however, to be unwarranted.

There were far smaller interests in the United States by other than German enemies, and these too were taken over. Three Hungarian banks had large interests in the Transatlantic Trust Company; the APC ordered the TTC to be dissolved.[308] In the conclusion to this particular investment, there was no material impact on the U.S. war effort, or on most Americans, although there was considerable inconvenience to many Hungarian-Americans, who had used the TTC as a conduit for remitting savings to their families in Hungary.[309] In sum, a major drop in the size of foreign assets in the United States, 1917–1918, resulted from the end to German direct investments, while the end to other enemies' investments made little mark in terms of the overall decline.

In the year and a half that America was at war, portfolio investments in the United States from Allied and neutral countries also fell, often more now in value than in quantity of securities held. There had been the very substantial holdings abroad of railway securities; those amounts had declined from 1914 to 1917. Yet there remained investments, and it was these securities that lost value, particularly after December 26, 1917, when the U.S. railroad system was placed under government operations.[310] The drop in the foreign portfolio equity ownership in U.S. Steel, measured by numbers of shares held, continued, albeit the largest reduction had occurred before U.S. entry into the war.[311] The American Dollar Securities Committee, set up by the British government, went on selling securities in New York (see Table 1.8), but that process had slowed.[312] By war's end the American Dollar Securities Committee had purchased or borrowed 1,421 different dollar bonds and 389 different dollar shares. Its largest purchases and borrowings had been of railroad bonds and shares.[313]

Before America had entered the war, J. P. Morgan & Co. had been instrumental in the lending to the British and French governments, with much of the borrowing backed by British-owned American securities. After American entry into the war, the U.S. government became the source of funding for the Allied powers. In February 1917, the British government had gotten a "demand loan" from J. P. Morgan & Co., secured by American securities that the British government had borrowed from its subjects. When part of this demand loan came due in February 1918, U.S. government moneys paid off the obligation to Morgan, and the U.S. government assumed control over the collateral. A similar pattern was maintained during the rest of the war and its immediate aftermath (by August 1, 1919, the Morgan demand loan had been entirely repaid). None of the securities that the British government "borrowed" from its subjects appears to have been sold.[314]

It seems clear that the bulk of the liquidation of portfolio investments of both British and continental Europeans (Allies and neutrals) occurred before the United States became a belligerent and while the repatriations went forward, the decrease in the amount of stocks and bonds held abroad—April 1917 to November 1918—was not great, albeit the fall in the *price* of railroad securities lowered the market value of these holdings. Dutch interests in American securities in net seem to have gone down in the eighteen months that America was at war, but contrary to the overall trend, three American companies—Union Pacific, Cities Service, and American Telephone & Telegraph—actually raised moneys in Holland during 1918.[315] There is no indication that the new U.S. exchange controls had any appreciable effect on the behavior of foreign portfolio investors in the United States.[316]

As for foreign direct investors from Allied and neutral countries, there were few retreats during the period the United States was at war. To be sure, Fiat's automobile plant in Poughkeepsie, New York, where the Italian cars had been made since 1910, was acquired in 1918 by the American firm Duesenberg Motor Company—a rare wartime divestment of a small foreign stake.[317] Whereas before U.S. entry into the war, the British Treasury had urged British mortgage lenders in the United States (which were direct investors) to reduce their business and remit dollars, the idea of encouraging "calling up loans" to American farmers who were producing food for victory seemed inappropriate. It was not only food; the British needed raw cotton as well. Accordingly, in October 1917, the British Treasury issued a circular withdrawing prior restrictions and stating that British mortgage companies in America could continue on normal lines (but permitting no increases in American advances).[318] The United States Mortgage Company and the Oregon Mortgage Company—both Scottish investors—announced in mid-1918 that the downward course in their investments in the United States had stopped.[319] To adjust to changing circumstances, in April 1918 the Scottish American Mortgage Company made plans to acquire the American Mortgage Company of Scotland; there appear to have been other such mergers.[320] Over time, there would be fewer British mortgage lenders in America.

Mortgage lenders aside, all other foreign direct investors in the United States were totally excluded from the British asset repatriation policies. Indeed, typically, U.S. affiliates of foreign companies with headquarters in Allied and neutral countries built up their business in America in the eighteen months that the United States was directly involved in the war. This was true, for example, of Lever Brothers, which British firm added Pears' Soap to its American production of Lifebuoy and Lux.[321] The subsidiary of Courtaulds, The Viscose Company, flourished. This British-owned business completed construction of its second plant, in Roanoke, Virginia, that began spinning operations in the summer of 1917; this was the pioneer synthetic fiber plant in the American South (and the second—both belonging to Courtaulds—in the entire nation).[322] In 1918, The Viscose Company's sales and before-tax profits reached a new peak; U.S. taxes, however, lowered its net income. In 1914, Courtaulds' American taxes (federal and state) had taken a mere .5 percent of the British subsidiary's U.S. earnings; in 1916, that figure was still only 1.2 percent. With U.S. entry into the war, this changed. In 1917, Courtaulds' U.S. taxes soared to 48.5 percent of its U.S. earnings, and in 1918, with the excess profits tax, the share went to 67.7 percent.[323] It was a sign of the times; for the first time in American history, income taxes mattered.

During 1917, another important British investor in America, J. & P. Coats, Ltd., rationalized its large multiplant, multifunctional U.S. business (merging its already owned Clark Mile-End Spool Cotton Company and George A. Clark & Brothers—both of which manufactured in New Jersey—into Clark Thread Company). It raised the capital of this New Jersey affiliate (Clark Thread Company) from $750,000 to $12.5 million and enlarged its thread output; its separate affiliate in Rhode Island also increased production. In 1917, J. & P. Coats, Ltd., decided to sell the plant of its Florida affiliate, "which is no longer of value to us as a source of supply." In 1918, it dissolved the Florida Manufacturing Company; this southern venture was but a small part of its total operation, and overall during the war period there was expansion, not contraction.[324]

Many other foreign-owned companies in America built up their production to fill rising demands. By 1917, the partly Belgian-owned Semet-Solvay ranked among the top 150 corporations in the country.[325] The British-Belgian Solvay Process Company, the British firm United Alkali Company (its subsidiary was North American Chemical Company), and the other affiliates and subsidiaries of foreign enterprises prospered, producing to meet wartime needs.[326] Firth Sterling Steel Company, a subsidiary of an English firm, manufactured stainless steel for airplane valves and naval shells.[327] Michelin, the French tire maker, in Milltown, New Jersey, made gas masks as well as tires.[328] American Trona Corporation, the U.S. subsidiary of the British Consolidated Gold Fields, greatly enhanced its potash output.[329] In 1917–1918, National Lead, in a joint venture with the British firm Williams, Harvey & Co., Ltd., and the Bolivian entrepreneur Simon Patiño, put into operation a smelter and refinery at Jamaica Bay, New York, processing Bolivian tin.[330] C. E. Johansson, a Swedish company, started a U.S. manufacturing subsidiary, making precision gauges, employed in American weapon production.[331] In 1918, the American Cellulose & Chemical Manufacturing Co., Ltd., was organized; financed by British capital, it began construction of a plant in Cumberland, Maryland, to supply the U.S. army with cellulose acetate.[332]

A spectacularly fast-growing Swiss enterprise in America was Nestlé & Anglo-Swiss Condensed Milk Company, which in January 1918 renegotiated its restrictive prewar agreement with Borden. After doing so, Nestlé & Anglo-Swiss Company bought an interest in John Wildi Evaporated Milk Company of Columbus, Ohio, and the Hires Condensed Milk Company of Philadelphia. The Swiss company, which in 1917 had produced neither condensed nor evaporated milk in America, with its acquisitions during 1918 became second only to Borden and that year provided 12.9 percent of U.S. canned milk output. (Borden accounted for 19 percent; Carnation, in third place, 12.5 percent; Helvetia—later Pet Milk—9.8 percent.) According to the Nestlé historian, at the beginning of 1919, the firm's U.S. subsidiary controlled forty-two canned milk factories in the United States. To finance this formidable expansion, the Swiss parent raised the capital of Nestlé's Food Company, New York, from $250,000 to $15 million.[333] In 1917, another Swiss company, the Wander firm, started to manufacture its branded product, Ovaltine, in Villa Park, Illinois (in metropolitan Chicago)—both for export and for the U.S. market. Ovaltine, made of milk, eggs, barley, and malt extract, was used in Allied hospitals in Europe to meet soldiers' nutritional needs.[334]

The Brompton Pulp and Paper Company, a Quebec papermaker, acquired in 1918 four New Hampshire paper companies (Claremont Paper Company, Wyman Flint & Sons Paper Company, Odell Manufacturing Company, and Groveton Paper Company). Probably with wartime transportation the U.S. markets of this Canadian firm had been disrupted, hence the need to cross over the border.[335]

In addition to all these ventures (and they are but a representative sample), it is important to note the marked growth in the business of foreign affiliates and branches of fire and marine insurance companies and the new arrivals, especially of Norwegian and Danish firms. Prior to February 1, 1918, only enemy or ally of enemy insurance companies had been required to obtain a license from the U.S. secretary of the treasury to do business; in late November 1917, the decision had been made—as indicated previously—to liquidate the enemy firms. On December 7, 1917 (to be effective February 1, 1918), the president had issued an executive order, under the Trading with the Enemy Act, that extended the licensing to all foreign insurance companies. The British embassy immediately argued that different provisions should apply to the British, since Great Britain had its own laws to prevent trading with the enemy (and thus did not need U.S. government monitoring). A blanket license was granted on January 28, 1918, to all British insurance companies, albeit each had to apply for that license. That same day, a similar general license was given to those French insurance companies that applied and on January 29, 1918, to all applicants from neutral countries.[336] Insurance companies that had been regulated by state governments for the first time had to get licenses from the federal government.

Table 1.10 indicates (by nationality) the change in numbers, net premium income, and admitted assets of foreign companies in fire and marine insurance in the United States as of December 31, 1913, and December 31, 1918. The increase in the business of the companies from Allied and neutral countries is impressive, considering the U.S. takeover of the important well-established German firms, which takeovers were more than offset in number by new insurers from neutral nations.[337] A good part of the rise in business occurred in the period 1917–1918. The four largest British insurers in America in fire and marine insurance ranked in the top eight in America (measured in admitted assets).[338] Wartime meant additional business for all these firms. *Best's Insurance* directories intermingled insurers and reinsurers. Both were included on the December 1913 and December 1918 lists. Concern arose in Washington as to whether the new Norwegian entries were German firms in disguise, but nothing was established.[339]

Virtually all the foreign direct investments in the United States were from Europe and Canada. There was also, however, an enlargement of the far smaller Japanese inward direct investments, which were concentrated in shipping, insurance, trade, and banking. I have already noted expansion of Japanese shipping and the investments related to it (after American entry, additional growth occurred) and the extension of Tokio Marine and Fire Insurance Company's existing business. There was a similar expansion of Japanese trading companies: Mitsubishi Goshi Kaisha opened new offices in New York and Seattle, joining Mitsui and other trading companies with U.S. representation.[340] Mitsubishi Goshi's Seattle branch, set up in 1918, expedited shipments of American steel to Japan, where at the Mitsubishi shipyards work went forward on the construction of cargo vessels for the U.S. Shipping Board.[341] America was purchasing more from Japan than vice versa, and when restrictions had been placed on U.S. gold exports in 1917, the business press commented that "practically the only trade balance running against the United States and being paid in gold is Japan's."[342] Since the purpose of the restrictions was to stop gold from passing to the enemy, licenses seem to have been issued for the Japanese transactions.[343] Thus, the restrictions did not impede the growth of Japanese trading companies' activities with the United States. Likewise, Japanese banks increased their U.S. presence. The Bank of Taiwan and the Sumitomo Bank established new "agencies" in New York, while the Yokohama Specie Bank, which had had a New York agency since 1880 and had long been present in San Francisco and Honolulu, and which in 1915 had opened a branch in Los Angeles, in September 1917 inaugurated a Seattle branch to provide financing for the expanded U.S.-Japanese trade associated with that West Coast city.[344]

Table 1.10. Foreign insurance companies in fire and marine insurance in the United States, 1913, 1918, by nationality (year end; includes branches and affiliates)

	Total present				Net premium income				Admitted assets			
	Number		% of total		In million U.S. dollars		% of total		In million U.S. dollars		% of total	
Nationality	1913	1918	1913	1918	1913	1918	1913	1918	1913	1918	1913	1918
British	42	51	47	57	68	126	56	60	116	202	63	67
Russian[a]	9	9	10	10	18	32	15	15	19	33	10	11
French	9	9	10	10	4	12	3	6	7	14	4	5
Norwegian	0	5	0	6	0	14	0	7	0	16	0	5
Swiss	3	3	3	3	3	4	2	2	3	6	2	2
Danish	0	2	0	2	0	7	0	3	0	7	0	2
Canadian	2	2	2	2	3	5	2	2	4	7	2	2
Swedish	2	2	2	2	2	3	2	1	3	5	2	2
German	13	0	15	0	18	0	15	0	24	0	13	0
Bulgarian	2	0	2	0	3	0	3	0	3	0	2	0
Six others[b]	7	7	8	8	2	6	2	3	5	12	3	4
Total[c]	89	90	100	100	121	209	100	100	184	302	100	100

Sources: Tabulations based on data in *Best's Insurance Reports, Fire and Marine, 1914,* and *Best's Insurance Reports, Fire and Marine, 1919.*

a. *Best's Insurance Reports* explained that on December 1, 1918, the Soviet government of Russia had decreed the dissolution of all private insurance companies and the confiscation of their assets by the state on Apr. 11, 1919. It was assumed that this would "terminate the authority of their U.S. representatives," but that the assets in the United States could only be used to liquidate obligations incurred in America. See Chapter 2 herein for more details.

b. The others in 1913 included those from China (with two branches) and Spain, Holland, New Zealand, Austria, and Japan (with one branch each); the others in 1918 excluded the Austrian branch, included those from China (with two branches) and from Spain, Holland, New Zealand, Japan, and Cuba.

c. Totals may be off because of rounding. Net premium income and admitted assets percentages were derived before rounding.

In 1917–1918, not only were there more Japanese banks involved in America, but changes occurred in the status of foreign financial institutions in the United States, which were associated with the new rules under the Federal Reserve System. Prior to the passage of the Federal Reserve Act in December 1913, U.S. federal law, as interpreted by the courts, denied national banks the use of acceptances to finance international trade.[345] U.S. trade typically had been financed in sterling and, to a lesser extent, reichsmarks or francs. The new legislation (along with wartime conditions) opened the way for *American* banks to use dollar acceptances. Once this occurred, some British financial institutions that had long financed U.S. trade with sterling acceptances felt they had to meet the new competition. Thus, Frederick Huth & Co., a British merchant bank, which had participated in American business for nearly a century, for the first time in 1917 started its own New York house, Huth & Co., which would handle dollar acceptances, mainly in connection with the growing U.S.–South American trade.[346] Another British merchant bank, Baring Brothers (its American interests dated back to the eighteenth century) cooperated with Kidder Peabody, Boston, in a firm, newly named the New England Investment Company.[347] Other banks from Allied nations (including the two from Japan) established new agencies in New York.

What was truly new in these war years was the role of the federal government; never in U.S. history had the federal government been so much a participant in American economic life—and this involvement spread over to affect all aspects of foreign investment within the country. New U.S. government regulations affected enemy properties. They had impact on the properties of companies and citizens from Allied and neutral nations as well. There was the excess profits tax. Restrictions existed on commodity and gold exports. All foreign insurance companies had to get federal government licenses. The U.S. Navy took over the operations (but not the ownership) of the British affiliate Marconi of America, with its high-powered radio stations in Massachusetts, New Jersey, California, and Hawaii; it integrated Marconi's shore-to-ship coastal stations into the navy's system. The U.S. Shipping Board had taken command of building up U.S. shipping capacity. In 1918, when the Shipping Board ordered the purchase from Marconi of America of all the leased radio transmitters on vessels owned and controlled by the board, Marconi had to sell.[348] Most significant, in 1918 the navy took steps to prevent Marconi of America from obtaining important arc patents. At Marconi's New Brunswick, New Jersey, station (which the navy operated), where the two newly installed Alexanderson alternators continued to be owned by General Electric, the navy made plans to see to it that when the fighting stopped, the alternators would not be acquired by Marconi.[349]

The U.S. Shipping Board supervised all facets of American shipping and shipbuilding; it took control over all shipyards and ships being built in these yards (even those under contract to foreign shipowners). It encouraged a spectacular growth of American shipping. It requisitioned all American ships afloat, including those of the newly reorganized International Mercantile Marine Company (an enterprise that still had sizable Allied and neutral country ownership).[350] In addition, the Shipping Board requisitioned neutral ships. It chartered some ships of Allied nations (by March 1918 the United States was chartering Japanese ships for the Atlantic war effort).[351] New banking rules gave American banks more ability to finance American trade with dollar acceptances.

The War Industries Board took charge of the economy. Within the country, from oil to meat, new regulations multiplied. Royal Dutch Shell's American affiliates had to conform.[352] On November 1, 1917, the U.S. government put all meatpacking concerns in America under the watch of the Food Administration, limiting their profits and requiring quarterly reports. The U.S. operations of the British-owned meatpacking firm Morrell & Co. were, thus, subject to U.S. government mandates.[353] Wherever there were U.S. government involvements, and that was virtually everywhere, foreign-owned businesses were impacted. None of the controls by the U.S. government of Allied or neutral companies' properties (or operations), however, resulted in this period in retreats or reductions in foreign assets in America; the regulations did not impede the increase in direct investments. Nevertheless, the U.S. government takeover of the railroads, given the poor state of the facilities, did have as an outcome lower portfolio investments in this sector.

While most of the growth in U.S. foreign obligations in 1917–1918 related to the rise in direct investments of companies from Allied and neutral countries, one unique governmental transaction served to increase America's foreign liabilities. In June 1918, U.S. expeditionary forces in Europe were purchasing supplies in Spain. The peseta was at a premium. A representative of the U.S. Treasury Department in August 1918 arranged for U.S. borrowings in pesetas; the U.S. Treasury sold certificates of indebtedness, payable in pesetas.[354] The authority for these Spanish "peseta bonds" was the Trading with the Enemy Act of 1917.[355] As best as I can determine, these were the first foreign currency-denominated U.S. federal government borrowings since 1795; by 1810, the U.S. government foreign currency-denominated debt had been entirely extinguished.[356] The peseta debt was very short-lived and paid off rapidly as Spanish exchange began to drop.[357] Not until the Roosa bonds of 1962, the Carter bonds of the 1970s, and some 1980s borrowings would the U.S. government again assume foreign currency-denominated obligations.[358]

In sum, in the period from America's entry into the war to the Armistice (November 11, 1918), while German investments and the smaller stakes of other enemies were sequestered, while overall portfolio holdings continued to decline (the Spanish peseta bonds—an oddity—in no way compensated for the reduction), foreign direct investments of companies from neutral and Allied countries grew. Government controls (including new taxes) were extensive but in these years did not hinder that rise in inward foreign direct investments, albeit they probably did have a negative impact on the inward foreign portfolio ones. The decrease in the amount of overall foreign investment (portfolio investments plus enemy direct investments) more than offset the growth in foreign direct investments, so that the ongoing decline in America's foreign obligations was not reversed, and the country's "debt" to the rest of the world was lower in November 1918 than it had been in April 1917.

The Outcome (1914–1918)

In November 1918, when the Armistice was signed, the United States was no longer a debtor nation in world accounts. W. P. G. Harding (appointed to the Federal Reserve Board in 1914 and since 1916 its governor) had written in 1915, "It is quite possible that this war . . . will . . . work an unlooked for miracle and transform the United States from a debtor nation into the world's commanding creditor nation."[359] The miracle had occurred.

During the entire period, 1914–1918, American bankers expanded their international lending; there were new securities issued to meet Latin American countries' as well as general worldwide requirements. So, too, U.S. outward foreign direct investment rose. Once America entered the war, the U.S. government provided huge loans to its allies. U.S. government inter-Allied credit soared past the expanding U.S. private foreign lending and foreign direct investments.[360] As outward American foreign investments mounted, in absolute amounts foreign investments in this country fell.

At war's end, in 1918, inward foreign portfolio and direct investments did, nonetheless, remain, although at a much diminished level. As for the inward portfolio stakes, some British investors continued to hold American stocks and bonds, the mobilization notwithstanding.[361] In addition, the British government retained dollar securities, some of which had been sold to it, and some of which it had borrowed from its subjects (by 1922 it had returned to British "depositors" some £332 million in securities, principally American ones).[362] In 1919, Bankers Trust Company would dispatch to France securities (mainly French and foreign, but some American ones as well) that it had held as collateral on French loans.[363] It seems that the remaining collateral required by private lenders for Allied borrowings (1915–1917) would be returned, including the collateral turned over to the U.S. Treasury when the latter purchased Morgan's demand loan.[364] Many Dutch and Swiss portfolio investors had kept (and some investors even increased) their U.S. securities holdings, 1914–1918. German owners of American stocks and bonds had, when possible, transferred securities to Dutch or Swiss or Scandinavian "friends" (and an unknown quantity of American bearer bonds—perhaps once owned by Germans—floated about in Europe at the end of 1918).[365] Investors of other nationalities still held American securities.[366] This said, overall there had clearly been a steep decline between July 1, 1914, and December 31, 1918, in the once giant foreign portfolio investments in the United States.

At the start of the European war, some foreign direct investments (most noticeably those of Andrew Weir and Southern Aluminium) had been nipped in the bud; others had come to an end; still others had been reduced, although not discontinued; likewise, during the period of U.S. involvement in the war, the takeover of enemy properties had resulted in a sizable reduction in inward foreign direct investments. By contrast, many foreign direct investors from Allied and neutral nations had enlarged their American interests.[367] Indeed, the sharp decline in foreign investments in the United States from 1914 to 1918 was much more the consequence of the substantial retreats from portfolio holdings (and the lower value of railroad securities) than the result of a reduction in foreign direct investments, despite the end to the large German direct investments. British mortgage companies excepted, no British direct investments were touched in the British governmental efforts to gain dollars through the liquidation of British holdings in America.

As the First World War marked the U.S. transition from debtor to creditor, as foreign investments in the United States had declined, Americans had also responded to other related symbols of "dependency." During the war, the U.S. government had encouraged the buildup of American shipping. Whereas in 1913, merely 14 percent of the country's international trade had been carried on American-flag ships, during the war American domestic investments in shipping had resulted in an almost eightfold increase in the country's shipping tonnage, so that by war's end the country was second only to Great Britain on a global scale and by 1918, American-flag ships carried more than 40 percent of U.S. foreign trade.[368]

Whereas early in 1914, U.S. foreign insurers wrote over two-thirds of the insurance policies covering American shipping, during the war, aided by the U.S. government-sponsored war risk insurance program,

American-owned insurance coverage greatly expanded.[369] At the start of 1914, America's commerce with the rest of the world had been financed in great part with sterling acceptances; by 1918, the use of dollar acceptances had grown by leaps and bounds, and the potentials for the further extension of American finance and dollar acceptances were manifest. Early in 1914, transatlantic communications—cables and radio—had been almost completely under foreign control. At war's end, the British still dominated cables and radio; however, in the interim the navy had taken over the administration of radio communications, and although ownership remained primarily in the hands of the British-controlled Marconi of America, the navy had become convinced that it did not desire Marconi of America (because of the British control) to have any future in this vital industry.

Before the war, railroad securities (especially bonds) had represented the single greatest attraction for foreign portfolio investors. In 1914–1918, it was these securities in particular that were repatriated. If bonds had matured, in most cases foreign moneys had not been reinvested in new U.S. railroad bonds. Years later the U.S. Department of Commerce tried to document the drop in foreign holdings during World War I of a selection of common and preferred shares of U.S. railroads (see Table 1.11). The downward trend it charted reflected the lower holdings of bonds as well as stock. Economist Cleona Lewis believed that foreign holdings (at par value) of all U.S. railway bonds and stock slipped from $4.17 billion to $1.28 billion between June 30, 1914, and December 31, 1919 (the December 31, 1919, figure appears to have been smaller than the December 31, 1918, one).[370] As a portion of the total

Table 1.11. Index showing decline in number of common and preferred shares held by foreigners in sample of U.S. railroads, 1914–1918 (Dec. 31, 1914 = 100)

	Index showing decline in foreign holdings	
Year end	Number of common shares	Number of preferred shares
1914	100	100
1915	94	90
1916	32	38
1917	28	34
1918	26	34

Source: U.S. Department of Commerce, Bureau of Foreign and Domestic Commerce, *Foreign Investments in the United States* (Washington, D.C., 1937), 74, 103. I have corrected what appears to have been a typographical error on page 74.

Table 1.12. Income on foreign investment in the United States, 1913–1918 (in millions of U.S. dollars)

Year	Income
1913	210
1914	200
1915	136
1916	118
1917	100
1918	100

Source: U.S. Department of Commerce, Bureau of the Census, *Historical Statistics of the United States* (Washington, D.C., 1975), II, 864 (figures are those of Raymond Goldsmith).

Table 1.13. Long-term foreign investment in the United States, by nationality, July 1, 1914, and Dec. 31, 1918 (in millions of U.S. dollars)

Nationality	July 1, 1914	Change	Dec. 31, 1918
British	4,250	−2,400	1,850
German	1,100	−1,100	0
Dutch	650	−110	540
French	480	−350	130
Swiss	70	+10	80
Belgian	30	0	30
Other European	180	−100	80
Canadian	275	0	275
Japanese	25	+10	35
All other	30	−10	20
Total	7,090	−4,050	3,040

Source: 1914 figures are from Table 1.2. 1918 figures are based on data presented in this chapter. These figures include both portfolio and direct investments.

outstanding, foreign holdings in U.S. Steel common stock (measured by numbers of shares) dropped from 25 percent on June 30, 1914, to 9.7 percent on December 31, 1918.[371] Raymond Goldsmith sought to calculate the income paid to foreign investors on their American stakes. His figures, presented in Table 1.12, show the effects on foreign income of the lower foreign investments in the United States. I have grave doubts about the amounts, but the trend is undoubtedly accurate.

Under its wartime monitoring of foreign exchange transactions, the Federal Reserve Board assembled information on securities held in the United States for foreign account. As of December 31, 1918, it verified that $1,640,754,000 in American securities were held in the United

Table 1.14. Estimated long-term foreign investment position of the United States, June 30, 1914, and Dec. 31, 1918 (in billions of U.S. dollars)

	U.S. investments abroad					Foreign investments in U.S.				
			Private accounts					Private obligations		
Date	(A) Total	(B) Government lending	(C) Total	(D) Portfolio investments	(E) Direct investments	(F) Total	(G) Government borrowings	(H) Total	(I) Portfolio investments	(J) Direct investments
June 30, 1914	3.5	0	3.5	0.8	2.7	7.1	0.1	7.0	5.3	1.7
Dec. 31, 1918	13.7	7.6	6.1	2.5	3.6	3.0	0.1	2.9	1.9	1.0

Sources: This table differs from the one I provided in Mira Wilkins, *The Maturing of Multinational Enterprise: American Business Abroad from 1914 to 1970* (Cambridge, Mass.: Harvard University Press, 1974), 30, in three ways: (1) the end date is Dec. 31, *1918*, not Dec. 31, 1919 (thus I revised the figures accordingly). (2) The foreign investment in the United States figures have been revised based on my own research for the present book and for Mira Wilkins, *The History of Foreign Investment in the United States to 1914* (Cambridge, Mass.: Harvard University Press, 1989). And, (3) the data in Wilkins, *Maturing*, were based on information provided in the U.S. Department of Commerce, Bureau of the Census, *Historical Statistics of the United States* (Washington, D.C., 1960), 565, which in turn was based on Cleona Lewis, *America's Stake in International Investments* (Washington, D.C.: Brookings Institution, 1938), 447. These figures excluded the foreign obligations *to* the U.S. government. See ibid., 361–362, 375, 420–421, 447. These obligations represented wartime intergovernmental lending. The Liberty Loan acts set a maximum of $10 billion; the lending (which eventually came close to $10 billion) continued to May 29, 1922. The 1918 figure in column B in the above table is based on ibid., 362, 447, and on Charles Bullock, John H. Williams, and Rufus S. Tucker, "The Balance of Trade of the United States," *Review of Economic Statistics*, 1 (July 1919), 247. For symmetry, I added column G. Lewis, *America's Stake*, 447, gives *U.S.* government obligations as $0.4 billion on Dec. 31, 1919, but a large part of this seems to have been short-term trade credits. My figures cover only long-term obligations and are for Dec. 31, 1918.

States for the British government or other foreign account.[372] This amount would be a bare minimum (a floor figure) for inward foreign investment: it excludes most foreign direct investment in the United States and all foreign portfolio investment where the securities were physically held abroad. In Table 1.13, based on the data presented in this chapter, I provide estimates of the size of foreign investment in the United States, by nationality, as of July 1, 1914, and December 31, 1918. I estimate a drop of $4.1 billion in foreign long-term assets in the United States in this period.

America's creditor/debtor nation position in 1914 and 1918 is summarized in Table 1.14, which contrasts the dramatic rise in outward U.S. foreign investments with the fall in the inward stakes. Symptomatic of the "revolution" in America's role are the estimates from a 1919 study of the U.S. balance of payments. It found that between 1896 and 1914, "interest payments on total foreign capital invested in the United States" had been five times "the interest payments on American capital invested abroad"; by contrast, in the period between July 1, 1914, and December 31, 1918, the "interest on American capital abroad" equaled 2.8 times that paid on foreign capital in the United States. Servicing America's foreign obligations had not been a major strain before 1914; now it was no burden at all.[373] In fact, the nation was already reaping the returns on its creditor position.

In short, the transformation was dramatic. Not only had the United States rid itself of its debtor nation status and become a creditor nation in world accounts, but by war's end the earnings on U.S. capital invested abroad already surpassed foreigners' earnings on their U.S. investments. The $3 billion invested by foreigners in the United States at year end 1918 was, by my estimate, a bare 43 percent of their holdings at the beginning of the European war. The United States was in a new position in the global economy.

2.

America's New Role, 1919–1923

The United States emerged after the First World War as an important creditor nation, a position it would maintain until abruptly in the late 1980s it once again became an international debtor.[1] In the meantime, long-term foreign investments in this country persisted—those retained from earlier years, coexisting with fresh investments, including reentries of investors that had exited in times past. Despite America's new status as a net creditor, its prominence as "the world's financial rentier," and its businesses' vast expansion abroad, the country remained attractive to inward foreign portfolio and direct investments.[2] Indeed, economist William Adams Brown wrote of the United States in the interwar years in the context of "the dilemma of a capital importing creditor nation."[3] Foreign investment was always a two-way street—with, however, an asymmetry in the lanes.

Before I turn to the immediate postwar period, as a setting I will provide a brief profile of the long-term foreign investments in the United States between the two world wars. The course of inward foreign investment was not linear; it was complex, involving throughout an admixture of foreign portfolio and foreign direct investments, with the proportions varying over time. Thus, for 1919 and 1920 the decline in inward foreign investments that had characterized the 1914–1918 years continued. Thereafter, there was an uneven rise in overall inward investments until 1939, whereupon there appears to have been a fall in the level of inward investment, 1939–1941, as a consequence of the war in Europe. Table 2.1 documents—as best I can establish—the overall growth of inward investments, 1919–1941, based on a variety of American sources. The story lines from different collators are not always consistent. The figures presented are in current dollars, that is, they are not corrected for price changes.

Table 2.1. Level of long-term foreign portfolio and foreign direct investments in the United States, 1919–1941 (in millions of U.S. dollars)

	Foreign portfolio investment							Foreign direct investment						Total foreign investment						
Year end	1	2	4	5	6	7	8	1	4	5	6	7	8	1	3	4	5	6	7	8
1919	1,624							899						2,523						
1924	1,933							975						2,908						
1927		3,700														3,700				
1929	4,259					4,325		1,400				1,485		5,659		4,700			5,810	
1931															2,250					
1933	2,565							1,518						4,083						
1934			2,839	3,143					1,518	1,800						4,357	4,943			
1935			3,529						1,580							5,109				
1936			4,468						1,640							6,108				
1937				4,229						1,883							6,112			
1938				4,575						1,895							6,470			
1939				4,312	4,312	5,815				1,935	1,978	2,875					6,247	6,290	8,690	
1940					3,797						2,004							5,801		
1941[a]							5,761						2,438							8,199
							3,566						2,438							6,004

Sources: The U.S. Department of Commerce collected figures on foreign investments in the United States. Its level of foreign investment figures (position at year end figures)—from various Commerce Department sources—are included in columns 2 through 6. In 1938, Cleona Lewis presented her own figures for 1919 through 1933 (see columns 1); her data for 1934–1936 were identical with those of the Commerce Department (columns 4). Robert Sammons in 1950—who was then with the Commerce Department—revised the latter's 1929 *and* 1939 figures (see columns 7). Meanwhile, in 1945, the U.S. Treasury had published the results of a *1941 Census* (columns 8). Most other U.S. figures (e.g., the oft-cited ones of Hal Lary, data in *Historical Statistics of the United States,* and data of Raymond Goldsmith) appear to be derived from one of the above sources. In some secondary works, 1929 figures are occasionally given as 1930 ones. All the figures are in current dollars. See Appendix 3 for details on the sources by column.

a. June 14, 1941.

They show the long-term inward foreign investment *position* at year end (except for the 1941 data that are as of June 14 of that year). The statistics, although the most reliable available, are fragile.[4]

The data suggest that during the interwar era, as in times past, inward foreign portfolio investment (FPI) always exceeded inward foreign direct investment (FDI), ranging from highs of 75 and 74 percent of the total in 1929 and 1936, respectively, to a low of 63 percent of the total in 1933—if the figures are to be trusted (a low of 59 percent appears with the second set of 1941 figures). FPI probably (in very rough terms) wobbled around two-thirds of the total, within the 63–75 percent band, in most of these years (1941 possibly excluded). The upward course of FPI was not steady, and the numbers in Table 2.1 show a sharp decline in FPI in 1929–1933, albeit not to the 1919 nor even to the 1924 level. I interpret (in Chapter 8) the figures for 1939–1941 as indicating a drop in FPI. Over the years, America—as creditor—had, if we exclude the obligations created by the huge U.S. government intergovernmental wartime lending, far higher ratios of outward FDI to outward FPI compared with the inward FDI/FPI ratios.[5]

The figures on FPI include financial assets—stocks and bonds—and some "miscellaneous long-term" claims. The size of the latter in the numbers supplied in Table 2.1 are small, until 1939 and 1941 (in Column 8, the second set of figures omits these "miscellaneous" assets). The level of FPI was measured in part at par value and in part at market values (used for common shares, sometimes for preferred shares, and rarely with bonds); since a sizable portion was measured by market values, figures on the level of America's inward FPI were affected by stock market fluctuations.[6] Most inward FPI was denominated in dollars; the FPI that was not so denominated was altered by the value of the dollar, which in the early 1920s and again in the 1930s varied greatly in relation to different foreign currencies.[7]

Little information exists on inward foreign investments in American national, state, and local government securities during most of the interwar years. In its census of foreign-owned assets in the United States as of June 1941, the U.S. Treasury Department noted the absence of prior estimates on such holdings. Of the $5.8 billion in long-term FPI in the United States in June 1941 identified in the census, a mere $306 million was in such government obligations (or roughly 5 percent of the total long-term FPI in the United States).[8]

With the FPI in stocks and bonds, foreign investments in American-issued securities did not necessarily represent investments in the United States. As the country became a creditor nation, as New York became a significant international securities market, and as securities were issued for U.S. outward foreign investments, investors from abroad frequently bought these securities in America. A "recycling" of foreign moneys occurred, as foreigners acquired such U.S.-issued "foreign" securities. It is possible (particularly after 1934) to differentiate between foreign purchases in the United States of "domestic securities" and of dollar-denominated "foreign securities." Acquisitions by foreign investors of the former were always more important than of the latter, although both occurred.[9] Also, foreign investments in American-issued securities were not necessarily in new issues; as before and during the First World War, foreign investors bought and sold existing securities. The trade in securities was into and out of the United States, but there were also markets for American securities abroad, that is, one foreign investor could buy from another (changing the nationality of ownership, with no modification in the "level of foreign investment in the United States"). A large part of the FPI in the United States in the interwar period comprised purchases of traded securities. There was a sizable flight of private capital to the United States, designed to circumvent exchange controls and other restrictions on free capital movements.[10]

As for the stocks and bonds, in the interwar years, significant trends occurred in inward FPI. Whereas outward FPI throughout these years appears to have been mainly in bonds (including government bonds), inward FPI in domestic securities went increasingly into corporate equities—preferred and common shares. By the 1920s, the move from corporate bonds to shares was already apparent. The shift started long before the stock market crash of 1929 and continued in its aftermath.[11] A second trend was from the more conservative preferred shares to common shares. Economist Cleona Lewis concluded (based on 1934 data) that "foreigners have lost their pre-war [World War I] predilection for American bonds and have greatly increased their purchases of common shares."[12] A U.S. Department of Commerce study using 1937 statistics found that with bonds measured at par *and* common and preferred shares at market, foreigners' holdings of equities were 6.5 times their holdings of bonds.[13] In 1939, the U.S. Securities and Exchange Commission estimated that about 90 percent of the foreign trading in American securities was in common stock.[14]

Paralleling this trend from corporate bonds to equity and from preferred shares to common shares, there was a marked swing away from investments in U.S. railroads. Despite foreign investors' divestments during the First World War, in 1919 roughly two-thirds of the inward FPI was still in railroad securities. But by 1941, the portion was minor.[15] Table 2.2 reveals the pattern in 1919–1935; there is evidence of an even greater acceleration of this trend in 1935–1941.[16]

Although inward FPI predominated over inward FDI throughout interwar years, there was considerable FDI in America.[17] In the col-

Table 2.2. Percentage of foreign portfolio investments in the United States in railway securities, 1919–1935

Year end	Percentage
1919	66
1924	47
1929	19
1935	14

Source: Percentages calculated from data provided in Cleona Lewis, *America's Stake in International Investments* (Washington, D.C.: Brookings Institution, 1938), 558.

lected statistics for 1919–1939, FDI was always measured by "book value," which may mean such investments were undervalued.[18] During 1919–1939, FDI in the United States increased gradually and steadily, according to most of the figures in Table 2.1 (although the crudity of the data masks some important retreats—especially during the early 1930s). The figures on the path of FDI from 1939 to 1941 are inconclusive.[19] All the inward FDI figures do not take into account business abroad by foreign affiliates in the United States.

At times, there are conceptual difficulties in distinguishing FDI and FPI. As I monitored the data collection procedures and went to primary sources, I realized that the amount of FDI (as presented in Table 2.1) is an underestimate.[20] Nonetheless, in these years, I still believe (as stated earlier) that total inward long-term FPI probably always exceeded the total inward FDI.

The United States remained throughout the interwar period a creditor nation, and not until 1939 did the amount of inward long-term foreign investment in the United States (FPI plus FDI) finally surpass the 1914 level.[21] And, in 1939, the size of the U.S. gross domestic product was two and a half times that in 1914—so the relative impact of the inward foreign investments was much less than it had been in 1914.

Table 2.3 offers figures on the income of foreign investors from their American holdings, 1913–1941. By 1926, income on foreign investment in the United States was (if the figures are accurate) in current dollars up to the 1914 amounts, while in the same period inflation had occurred (thus, in constant dollars the figure was nowhere near the 1914 returns).[22] For the interwar years, the income paid (or credited) peaked in 1929, mirroring the national prosperity. The 1930–1933 reductions reflect both the depression divestments (including business failures), low or no profits, as well as defaults on interest payments. The 1933–1937 figures show increasing income, which is consistent with the rising size of foreign investment in the United States and the improving economy; the lower 1938 number coincided with the recession that year. The 1939–1941 figures were influenced by the war in Europe and the decrease in FPI in the United States.

From where did the inward foreign investment come in the interwar years? Table 2.4 provides information, although all the figures (especially those for 1918 and 1929) should be viewed with caution.[23] Data for 1941 will be presented in Chapter 8. The table shows that Britain continued, as before the First World War, to be the largest single source of foreign investment in the United States.[24] At the close of the First World War, however, because of the heavy wartime intergovernmental borrowings, Britain was the debtor to the United States rather than vice versa. During the interwar years, British capital exports were substantially less than before 1914.[25] And, whereas in 1914 and probably still at year end 1918, the United States had ranked first in the world among the countries drawing in British capital, by 1929–1930 Australia, India, Canada, Argentina, and South Africa *apparently* each individually recorded more U.K. obligations than the United States.[26] The same *may have been* true all during the 1930s. Yet the evidence for 1929–1930 and

Table 2.3. Income on foreign investment in the United States, 1913–1941 (in millions of U.S. dollars)

Year	Income	Year	Income
1913	210	1928	275
1914	200	1929	330
1915	136	1930	295
1916	118	1931	220
1917	100	1932	135
1918	100	1933	115
1919	130	1934	135
1920	120	1935	155
1921	105	1936	270
1922	105	1937	295
1923	130	1938	200
1924	140	1939	230
1925	170	1940	210
1926	200	1941	187
1927	240		

Sources: 1913–1918: Table 1.12 herein. 1919–1941: *Survey of Current Business,* July 1954, 14–15. The 1913–1918 series is not strictly comparable to the 1919–1941 series. The figures are similarly combined in U.S. Department of Commerce, Bureau of the Census, *Historical Statistics of the United States* (Washington, D.C., 1975), II, 864.

Table 2.4. Long-term foreign investment in the United States by nationality, 1918, 1929, 1934, 1937, 1938, 1939 (in millions of U.S. dollars)

Nationality	1918	1929	1934	1937	1938	1939
United Kingdom[a]	1,850	1,560	1,935	2,388	2,500	2,348
Canada	275	935	1,075	1,085	1,190	1,060
Holland	540	400	685	823	875	888
Switzerland	[b]	200	380	635	705	746
France	130	400	255	452[c]	440[c]	436[c]
Belgium	[b]	75	105	132	142	152
Germany	0	400[d]	125	125	115	100
Italy	[b]	52	40	45	45	40
Latin America	[b]	[b]	75	110	115	120
Rest of world[e]	245	678	268	317	343	357
Total	3,040	4,700	4,943	6,112	6,470	6,247

Source: 1918: Table 1.13 herein. 1929: U.S. Department of Commerce, Bureau of Foreign and Domestic Commerce, *The Balance of International Payments of the United States in 1929,* by Ray Hall (Washington, D.C., 1930), 11–13, 32; of the 1929 data, Hall wrote, "Least certain of all are estimates by countries of foreign investments in the United States. Some of them are hardly more than guesses." His 1929 figures were based on the estimated capitalized value of earnings. 1934–1939: U.S. Department of Commerce, Bureau of Foreign and Domestic Commerce, *Foreign Long-Term Investments in the United States, 1937–39,* by Paul D. Dickens (Washington, D.C., 1940), 10.

Note: Figures are year end.

a. This is given in the source for 1929 as "England," but it is probably the figure for the United Kingdom. The other figures are for the United Kingdom.

b. Included in "Rest of world."

c. Includes $100 million in foreign holdings of U.S. government bonds thought by the U.S. Department of Commerce to belong to French investors and possibly some other nationalities.

d. "Much . . . is still in the charge of our Alien Property Custodian," according to the U.S. Department of Commerce. Yet it was classified as German investment.

e. Includes countries not separately itemized.

for the 1930s is not conclusive, which is why I have italicized "apparently" and "may have been." American economist Cleona Lewis believed that as of 1938 the United States held first place as a recipient of British capital.[27]

In this connection, Tables 2.5 and 2.6 are instructive on FPI. They chart the portion invested in American securities of portfolios of different samples of British investment trusts. These investment trusts had long histories of American investment. Table 2.5 covers 1914–1935; comparable data for 1935–1939 are not available. Table 2.5 demonstrates the diversification *away* from American securities. Yet if one juxtaposes that table with Table 2.6 (which spans 1923–1939 and is based on different sources), the suggestion is that while the overall trend away from American securities was reversed after 1935, the high 1914 much less the early post–World War I percentages (1922–1923) were not reestablished; the data on this table reveal relatively more British investment trust involvement in American securities in the early 1920s (a residue from times past) than in the late 1930s.[28] When the U.S. Federal Reserve monitored the rising foreign investments in American domestic securities in the 1930s (traded securities), its data indicated that about 37 percent of the sizable inward flow of capital into American domestic securities came from the United Kingdom.[29]

Table 2.5. British investment trust companies, selected firms: percentage of total investments in American securities, 1914, 1922, 1934, 1935

Investment trust	Ca. 1914	1922	1934	1935
Alliance Trust	83[a]	16[b]	n.a.	n.a.
American Investment and General Trust Co. (pre-1919: American Investment Trust Co.)	100	n.a.	11	n.a.
Anglo American Debenture Corp.	60–70	25	8	n.a.
British Assets Trust	81	n.a.	40	30
Industrial and General Trust	24	6	6	n.a.
Merchants Trust	51	31	20	11
Northern American Trust Co.	71	n.a.	6	n.a.
Railway Debenture and General Trust Co.	60–70	25	4	4
Railway Share Trust and Agency Co.	60–70	25	3	3
Scottish American Investment Co.	ca. 95	55[c]	46	n.a.
Scottish Northern Investment Trust	50	12	9	8
Second Scottish Northern Investment Trust	60	12	8	n.a.
Third Scottish American Trust Co.	76	n.a.	12	n.a.
Average (excluding Scottish American Investment Co.)[d]	65	19	11	11

Source: Mira Wilkins, *The History of Foreign Investment in the United States to 1914* (Cambridge, Mass.: Harvard University Press, 1989), 500 (1914 data). U.S. Department of Commerce, Bureau of Foreign and Domestic Commerce, *British Investment Trusts,* Trade Information Bulletin No. 88 (Washington, D.C., 1923), 29–30; George Glasgow, *Glasgow's Guide to Investment Trust Companies* (London: Eyre & Spottiswoode, 1935), passim; J. C. Gilbert, *A History of Investment Trusts in Dundee 1873–1938* (London: P. S. King & Son, 1939), 121; and Ronald B. Weir, *A History of the Scottish American Investment Co., Ltd., 1873–1973* (Edinburgh: Scottish American Investment Co., 1973), 18 (1923), 20 (1925).

n.a. = not available.

a. Includes mortgages as well as stocks and bonds.

b. Bonds and stocks only.

c. 1923.

d. Average is total—excluding Scottish American—divided by number of companies recorded (i.e., 1914, 12; 1922, 8; 1934, 11; 1935, 5). I excluded Scottish American Investment Co., since it remained more deeply involved than any other trust and because the 1923 percentage was probably higher than the 1922 one, thus, creating a further distortion (by 1925, its U.S. share was up to 67 percent of its portfolio).

Table 2.6. British investment trust companies: percentage of total investments (book value) in the United States, 1923, 1929, 1933, 1939

Area	1923	1929	1933	1939
United States	18	10	8	14
United Kingdom	34	37	42	56
Rest of world	48	53	50	30
Total	100	100	100	100

Sources: Economist, Feb. 15, 1930, 347; Dec. 1, 1934, 8; Aug. 12, 1939, 305. Youssef Cassis, "The Emergence of a New Financial Institution: Investment Trusts in Britain, 1870–1939," in *Capitalism in a Mature Economy,* ed. J. J. van Helten and Y. Cassis (Aldershot: Edward Elgar, 1990), 147. (The figures for 1923 and 1929 are for 26 companies; for 1933, 20 companies; and for 1939, 61 companies.)

As for British direct investments in the United States, although many pre–World War I companies persisted and new ones entered, although British fire and marine insurance companies—joined by casualty ones—stayed very much involved in America, overall the number and variety of British participants in U.S. business activities in the interwar period failed to measure up to the involvements in the years before 1914. Moreover, there were in the immediate post–World War I years some significant retreats.

Clearly, in the 1920s, more British savings stayed at home or flowed into continental European and Empire investments than went to the United States. There appears to have been some redirection to the United States in the 1930s (and a major drop in investments—particularly portfolio ones—in continental Europe), but this did not offset the trend toward Britishers' investing more at home (and within the Empire) rather than in the United States and other foreign countries. Put in different terms, between 1875 and 1914, at a minimum about 20 percent of U.K. capital invested overseas was in the United States; a set of estimates that may exaggerate, but certainly highlights, the difference puts the share at 5.4 percent for 1930 and 7.5 percent for 1938.[30]

While Britain kept its status as a creditor nation on an international scale from the end of World War I to the start of World War II, Germany, which had been number two after Britain as a foreign investor in the United States in 1914, was throughout the interwar years a debtor to the United States and also in world accounts, because of its major reparation obligations and its formidable borrowings of the 1920s. Germany became, in the first postwar decade, the world's largest debtor nation.[31] This said, German multinational enterprises gradually resumed their business in the United States. By contrast, German prewar portfolio holdings were not restored; no financial surpluses existed in Germany in the 1920s and 1930s; there were, however, periodic episodes of German capital flight to the United States that took the form of FPI.

Some uncertainty exists on the international investment position of the Dutch in the interwar years. Although the Dutch had heavy losses in their pre–World War I Russian and eastern European securities, although other Dutch stakes abroad declined during 1914–1918, and although the Dutch borrowed heavily in 1918, the nation emerged from the First World War in a position of strength.[32] Table 2.4 suggests that at year end 1918 the Dutch were second only to the British in their investments in America; much of this was FPI, and part could be cloaking for German investors. In the aftermath of the war, the Dutch appear to have reallocated their savings, placing more capital at home and in the Netherlands East Indies. Until the 1970s, all the literature had characterized Holland as a creditor nation throughout the interwar era.[33] But economic historian Johan de Vries indicates that by 1930, if not earlier, the Dutch had become a net importer of capital.[34] If the figures are to be trusted, Table 2.4 suggests that, like the British, Dutch stakes in the United States were smaller at year end 1929 than at year end 1918.[35] In the interwar period, Holland continued to import German capital and reinvest some of it in the United States (and this might explain the sizable increase in Dutch investment in the United States indicated in Table 2.4 from 1929 to 1934). German investors frequently came to use Dutch financial intermediaries for both FPI and FDI. The controversy on Holland's international status aside, in 1929 and throughout the 1930s, the Dutch appear to have ranked third among foreign investors in the United States. Yet whereas before the war, the Dutch had more invested in the United States than they had in any other country outside of Holland, by 1938 (at least according to Lewis' figures), the Netherlands East Indies far surpassed the United States as a host to Dutch investment abroad.[36]

France was a net creditor in international accounts during the 1920s and 1930s.[37] With wartime borrowing, it was (like Britain) at war's end a net debtor *to* the United States. The French had never been giant investors in America, and after the First World War, with some notable exceptions, they paid scant attention to making new U.S. investments in this country.[38] Table 2.4 shows, however, a rise in French stakes in the United States in 1918–1929, a sharp drop in 1929–1934, and then an increase in 1934–1937.

According to the U.S. Department of Commerce, by the mid-1930s the Swiss—also a creditor nation in world accounts—had moved ahead of the French, having larger stakes in the United States than their European neighbor. By 1934 the Swiss were said to rank fourth as foreign investors in America (see Table 2.4). However, for tax and other reasons, French and German investors often employed Swiss intermediaries for their U.S. investments; thus the place of Switzerland (in terms of Swiss beneficial ownership) is inflated on these rosters. Nonetheless, during the First World War and thereafter, identifiable Swiss investments—especially direct investments—grew in the United States.[39] Lewis, considering the worldwide stakes of the Swiss in 1938, found no single country attracted more Swiss investments abroad than did the United States.[40] By 1938 the winds of war in Europe, swelling socialist sentiments in France, and fascism in Germany had made neutral, conservative Swiss investors and intermediaries conscious of the need to send their capital far from the madness in nearby lands.[41]

As in times past, the United States continued to be the largest host to Canadian foreign investors.[42] The ties between Canada and the United States multiplied, for as British capital exports were curtailed, Canada came to depend more on its neighbor to the south.[43] Still, as on a global scale, so with Canadian-American investments, both FPI and FDI were a two-way street. In the interwar years, Canada, remaining a net debtor in international accounts, would move from its 1914 fifth place (after Britain, Germany, Holland, and France) to a 1918 third rank (after Britain and Holland) and then to a 1929 second rank (after Britain) as a foreign investor in the United States; it held that number two position throughout the entire 1930s.[44] Unlike British and Dutch investments, Canadian ones in the United States grew substantially in the 1920s.[45] However, it must be emphasized that the relative significance of the Canadians during the interwar period was more because of the preoccupation elsewhere of European investors and continental European capital shortages than because of any fiercely overall aggressive Canadian behavior in the United States.[46] This said, whereas in 1929 British and the identifiable and measured German investments in the United States were barely more than one-third of their 1914 totals, recorded Canadian holdings in this country were more than triple their prewar ones. Geographic, cultural, and economic proximity, along with the relative European indifference to U.S. investments, in much of the 1920s in large part explain the high Canadian standing.[47] For Canadians resident in Toronto and Montreal, Chicago and Buffalo were much closer than Vancouver (indeed, so was New York). Canadians made both FPI and FDI in the United States in the 1920s and 1930s: opportunities across their southern border often seemed more promising than those in the Dominion, with the larger population in the United States providing the more sizable market. In 1936, measured as a proportion of source country national wealth and population, Canadian direct investments in the United States were greater than the truly ubiquitous U.S. direct investments in Canada.[48] FPI and FDI from other countries—Italy, Sweden, Japan, China—and from Latin America, for example, were also in evidence in the United States and appear to have risen in the interwar years.

A Bird's-Eye View of the Immediate Postwar Years

The 1914–1918 years were a watershed. In the aftermath, the world economy was in disarray. The war devastated most of Europe. There had been the Russian Revolution in 1917. The old order was replaced in 1918 in Germany, and famine spread over much of eastern and central Europe that year. The flu epidemic in 1918–1919 was a disaster. In March 1919 the Communist "Third International" was organized; communist demonstrations in Germany (in Bavaria) and Hungary stirred American and western European anxieties that the Bolshevik Revolution would not be contained. Practically everywhere governments enlarged their roles—at least in comparison with earlier peacetime periods. There had been during the war a vast redistribution of long-term foreign assets and liabilities. Participants in the international economy at the start of 1919 faced a new, and unsettling, instability.

The difficulties encountered by Europeans in 1919–1923 were awesome. The peace treaty signed at Versailles (1919) left a resentful Germany. Capital for European recovery was inadequate. The prewar global system—based on the gold standard—had been torn apart. International investing was no longer simple. Restrictions abounded. Wartime taxes continued. Currencies fluctuated.[49] Britain and France chafed under burdensome war debts to the United States and thought it unreasonable that the United States insisted on being repaid.[50] In 1922–1923, hyperinflation swept through central Europe, destroying savings and shattering confidence in the future.[51] French and Belgian troops occupied the Ruhr on January 11, 1923, since Germany was not meeting its reparation obligations.

Separated from the chaos in Europe, the United States emerged from the war a mighty power, seemingly unscathed. It was stronger in relative as well as in absolute terms. There was no physical destruction on this side of the Atlantic. The country had held to the gold standard during the war (even though from June 1917 through June 1919 licenses were required for gold exports).[52] The postwar dollar was strong. A New Yorker in Europe in August 1919 found his nation had "immense prestige" and that everywhere in Europe, men in positions of authority were turning to America for aid in reconstruction.[53] Canadians, who had depended on Britain for finance, called on the United States, as did Latin Americans. For the first time in its history, the United States had to be included as a (possibly even "the") dominant nation in the world economy.

The immediate postwar years (1919 to early 1920) saw an economic boom in the United States, as purchases for European recovery placed heavy demands on American producers. The strong dollar notwithstanding, U.S. exports soared to unprecedented heights in 1920 (not to surpass that peak again until 1943).[54] Trade finance was often with dollar acceptances, something very new. In 1920, over half of American trade was on U.S.-flag ships.[55] At the end of 1920 and during 1921, the United States experienced a severe, but brief, recession. Although Woodrow Wilson had gone to Versailles, the United States never ratified the treaty made there. Thus, the United States remained technically at war until July 2, 1921, when with the Knox-Porter resolution Congress formally and finally concluded the conflict with Germany and Austria-Hungary (the peace treaties were ratified in October 1921).

By 1922–1923, with the war formally as well as actually over, and its economy having weathered the short economic downturn, the United States seemed poised for prosperity. Throughout 1919–1923, the United States exported capital, filling the requirements of Europe, Canada, Latin America, and the rest of the world. The United States was the only major country in the world on the gold standard. Britishers marveled at America's new international stature: a rapid transformation that "would ordinarily have taken generations to accomplish."[56]

Yet within the United States, there was an ambivalence about the nation's new position. In 1918, Congress had passed the Webb-Pomerene Act, allowing U.S. businesses to act in unison to spur exports (the act gave participants in Webb-Pomerene associations exemptions from U.S. antitrust laws); in 1919, the Edge Act authorized federally chartered corporations for foreign banking and investments. These two acts were measures designed to aid U.S. businesses in their future role within the world economy. At the same time, in 1918 Americans had elected a Republican-controlled Congress that turned to domestic issues. In 1919, Americans were concerned lest "bolshevism" spreading from Europe infect the United States.[57] In 1921, Republican Warren Harding replaced Democrat Woodrow Wilson as president. Whereas Wilson had proposed the League of Nations, the United States never joined. "The League of Nations," populist Senator William E. Borah of Idaho proclaimed in 1919, "makes it necessary for America to give back to George V what it took away from George III."[58] Once the war was over, many Americans wanted no entangling alliances with foreign powers. This was true of most Democrats as well as Republicans. Occurrences abroad seemed "alien"—un-American. Within the United States there was a mounting distrust of "foreigners," which was reflected in calls for (and the introduction of) new restrictions on immigration and higher tariffs.

Historians, economists, and political scientists have deliberated at great length on the political posture of the United States in 1919–1923, usually agreeing that policies coming from Washington combined internationalism with insularity, but vigorously dividing on the weight appropriate to each stance and disagreeing on what constituted "internationalism."[59] Toward inward foreign investors, especially direct investors in America, with few exceptions U.S. policies tended to be insular and nationalistic.[60] And, of course, herein lay the paradox. Never before had the United States been economically stronger in absolute terms and relative to other nations. There was the commitment to aid U.S. business in world markets (as witnessed by the Webb-Pomerene and Edge Acts and other measures as well). Yet federal government policies more often than not failed to rise to the challenges of world economic leadership. There remained a desire to separate the nation from a perceived economic dependency in a number of sectors and also to distance the United States from a Europe where prevailing ideas and ideologies seemed to clash with American values. Indeed, the Webb-Pomerene Act was a response to cartels in Europe that blocked U.S. exports, while the Edge Act attempted to liberate U.S. international trade finance from reliance on British sterling acceptances.

Foreign Portfolio Investments in the United States, 1919–1923

With the postwar uncertainties, FPI in the United States was less in 1920 than in 1918.[61] Despite lingering wartime and new postwar European exchange restrictions, American securities continued to be bought and sold by foreign investors, and initially there were more sales than purchases. In 1921, with the relaxation of British controls on capital exports, the pattern was reversed. During 1921–1923, the existing British restraints on capital flows had virtually no impact on constraining British long-term investments in the United States.[62]

Cleona Lewis' data (see Table 2.1, Column 1) indicate that FPI in the United States was greater at year end 1924 than at year end 1919. We do not know the composition by nationality, but evidence suggests a broad revival of interest in American securities. No general U.S. controls existed on capital imports—albeit there were certain sectoral restrictions and public policies that affected FDI but *not* FPI. Some of these measures, as I will show later in this chapter, had the effect of transforming what had been FDI (that is, investment that carried control) into FPI (passive financial investments). Table 2.7 indicates that

Table 2.7. Comparison of foreign and American domestic bond yields, 1920–1924

Year	Weighted average of yield index of new foreign bonds	Index of yields on sixty high-grade domestic bonds	Excess of average yield on new foreign bonds
1920	7.69	5.88	1.81
1921	7.54	5.79	1.75
1922	6.63	4.94	1.69
1923	6.42	4.98	1.44
1924	6.56	4.85	1.71

Source: John T. Madden, Marcus Nadler and Harry C. Sauvain, *America's Experience as a Creditor Nation* (New York: Prentice-Hall, 1937), 14.

foreign bonds had higher yields than American domestic bonds, 1920–1924. This suggests that foreign investors would tend to turn away from American bonds; it also reveals the attraction of foreign bonds for U.S. investors. At the same time, U.S. income tax law resulted in higher taxes on foreigners' holding American securities than on U.S. residents; British investors were, for example, subject to double taxation—in the United States and in Britain.[63]

Given the economic malaise in Europe and the need for capital there, the strong U.S. dollar that raised the cost of American securities to the foreign investor and encouraged sales of existing investments, the relatively low American bond yields vis-à-vis foreign bonds, along with the tax penalty that persisted all during the years 1918–1923, why did any foreign investor keep or put his money in American securities? Why was there in net the apparent rise in inward FPI?

Before I answer this question, it is important to consider the characteristics of FPI in the United States and of the transactions. FPI in this country in 1919–1923 was overwhelmingly in the private, not the public, sector. By mid-1920, all the U.S. government "peseta bonds" (see Chapter 1) had been redeemed.[64] A small amount of U.S. government liberty bonds (issued to finance the war) were still owned outside the country or had in these years drifted abroad. There is, however, no evidence of any significant interest in foreign countries in this period in U.S. federal government issues, although U.S. government bonds were bought by foreign governments and used to pay their inter-Allied war debts (the bonds would then be redeemed; it is doubtful foreign governments held the bonds for long).[65] As for state and local government financing in America, this took place at home.[66] In short, sovereign debt, that is, American government securities, does not stand out in the inward FPI story, 1919–1923.[67] Instead, long-term FPI in the United States continued to be—as it had been for decades—predominantly in stocks and bonds of large corporations established in America, securities denominated in dollars. What occurred with FPI were *sales* (liquidations of existing securities holdings), *continuities* (prior investments retained), and *purchases* (new acquisitions of stocks and bonds of American corporations—new issues, but much more often traded securities). In addition, foreigners bought in the United States not only outstanding American domestic securities but also the new *U.S.-issued* "foreign" securities and existing foreign securities. The foreign securities—typically denominated in dollars—were sometimes foreign-government issues and sometimes corporate issues.[68]

First, the sales (the divestments): the strong dollar in 1919–1920 encouraged the sale by Europeans of their existing dollar-denominated securities. U.S. Secretary of the Treasury Carter Glass attributed the "depression" in the price of high-grade securities in 1920 to liquidations by overseas investors, who expected to gain in the exchange transaction.[69] Recorded sales by Dutch investors of American securities during the first seven months of 1919 came to f58,729,805—more than in the entire period from mid-1916 through 1918; these sales were offset by the transfer to Holland in that same seven-month period of the equivalent of f28,780,007 in American securities—representing a net recorded divestment of f29,949,798 (or merely $12 million).[70] Three important Dutch investment funds that had specialized in American securities—Vereenigde Amerikaansche Fondsen, Vereenigd Bezit van Amerikaansche Fondsen, and Syndicaat van Amerikaansche Industrieele Aandeelen—were, however, dissolved during 1920–1922, since they had no further plans for U.S. investments.[71]

At the same time, other foreign investors made different choices, retaining their American holdings. The Scot William Mackenzie, for instance, who had over the decades acquired a sizable personal portfolio of American investments (particularly in railroads) and who worried about his Pennsylvania Railroad common stock, did nothing. On August 21, 1921, he wrote a friend, "I have not done anything on this [my Pennsylvania Railroad shares] or any other [American] investment and perhaps it is just as well to let things simmer for a while."[72] Three and a half years later, Mackenzie noted the improvement in the value of the pound and added (once more in a private letter) that it did not matter: "Some years ago I made up my mind to keep as much money in American Dollars as possible and was not tempted by low sterling to bring money home."[73] Similarly, when another large British investor, Lord Mount Stephen, died in December 1921, his estate showed giant American railroad investments, remnants (like Mackenzie's) of his important prewar involvements.[74] In August 1922, a director of Baring Brothers & Co., London, Gaspard Farrer, wrote, "There are still a good many holders in this country [of Great Northern and Northern Pacific shares] and some in considerable amounts."[75] What Mackenzie was describing, what Lord Mount Stephen's estate revealed, and what Farrer observed can best be understood as lethargy. Why not continue as an investor in America? The United States was on the gold standard; Britain was not; perhaps it was prudent to keep as "good as gold" securities. Some Dutch investors made similar evaluations. During World War I, a number of U.S. railroads (the St. Louis and San Francisco; the Chicago, Rock Island, and Pacific; and the Missouri, Kansas and Texas, for example), which had attracted large Dutch investments, had been reorganized and issued new bonds to replace the old ones. There appears to have been no sizable drop in these Dutch railroad holdings from 1919 to 1923. Some of the "Dutch" holdings may have been former German ones that had been divested during the First World War and in its immediate aftermath (that is, sold by Germans to Dutch investors on Dutch or Danish exchanges).[76]

This said, overall, American railroad securities had lost their luster as *new* acquisitions. During the war the railroads had been taken over by the U.S. government; when they reverted to private ownership and control on March 1, 1920, they were "in a sorry condition of undermaintenance and with the efficiency of railroad labor impaired"; their fares and profits were now regulated by the Interstate Commerce Commission.[77] Railroads had difficulty raising new moneys. Before the First World War, in 1914 the best American railroads could issue bonds with 4.5 percent and 5 percent coupons, which was now impossible. In 1920, the rate was 7 percent for ten-year secured bonds of the Pennsylvania Railroad and Union Pacific equipment trust certificates; the higher interest meant some few of these U.S. -issued securities became salable abroad. Just as during the First World War, on occasion in the postwar period, foreign bondholders got new issues in exchange for old ones: for example, in 1922 the New York, New Haven and Hartford Railroad could not cover its maturing 145 million French franc ($27,985,000) fifteen-year, 4 percent European loan of 1907; holders of these debentures received 10 percent in cash and 90 percent in new three-year, 7 percent bonds.[78] Other than such securities substitutions, new acquisitions of railroad bonds and shares were few and far between. The overall pattern from 1919 to 1923 appears to have been a reduction in foreign holdings in American railroad securities. Indeed, many of the foreign divestments of "high-grade" securities in 1920 were railroad issues, and the drop in FPI in U.S. railroads—begun in the war years—proceeded.[79] But we should take care not to overestimate the decline, nor should we ignore the enduring (lethargic) interest by some foreign investors in American rails. The *Stock Exchange Official Intelligence*, published annually in London, retained its special section devoted to American railroads, as did the Dutch *Van Oss' Effectenboek,* indicating a continuing interest in obtaining information on these securities.[80] British investment trusts, once heavily involved in U.S. railroad securities, seem to offer a mirror of the overall process. In 1922, these trusts maintained U.S. holdings (securities they had deposited with the British government during the war, which were now returned), but typically as a far smaller percentage of their portfolio than in prewar times (see Table 2.5). There seems to have been some shift in their portfolios from railroad bonds to shares and from railroads to other securities. Cleona Lewis' figures indicate that foreign investors held $814 million in American railroad securities in 1924 (or 47 percent of FPI, down from 66 percent at year end 1919).[81]

Inward FPI in American corporate securities, aside from railroads, probably dropped in 1919–1921, and then appears to have risen. This was not true, however, of U.S. Steel Corporation securities; if corporate records are a guide, total foreign holdings of both common stock (see Table 2.8) and preferred stock of U.S. Steel continued to decline.[82] At the outbreak of World War I, 25 percent of the common shares of U.S. Steel, still America's largest industrial, had been owned abroad; at the time of the Armistice, the figure was 9.7 percent; by December 1923, it was less than 4 percent.[83] Note that 62 percent of the drop from 1919 to 1923 was attributable to Dutch holdings, whereas 25 percent related to the English investments.

In 1919, the American investment banking firm William Saloman & Co. purchased from British holders approximately 75 percent of Otis Steel Company preferred and common stock (securities first intro-

Table 2.8. Foreign holdings of common shares of United States Steel Corporation by nationality, 1918–1923 (year end)

	Number of common shares						
Date	England[a]	Holland	France	Canada	Other foreign	Total foreign	Percent foreign
1918	172,453	229,285	29,700	45,613	14,529	491,580	9.68
1919	166,387	124,558	28,607	35,686	13,657	368,895	7.26
1920	159,613	73,861	13,939	31,311	14,111	292,835	5.76
1921	167,752	50,741	13,210	30,885	17,438	280,026	5.50
1922	160,876	48,827	10,499	24,948	16,618	261,768	5.15
1923	101,118	51,054	11,203	23,422	16,312	203,109	3.99

Source: Commercial and Financial Chronicle, July 19, 1924, 285–286.

a. Scotland included in "other foreign"; the amounts were not large.

duced in Britain in 1889). Otis Steel Company reverted to American ownership.[84] Historian Donald Davis found that in December 1919, the Nederlandsch Administratieen Trustkantoor held 7,700 of 300,000 common shares outstanding (2.6 percent) and 3,070 of the 150,000 preferred shares outstanding (2.0 percent) of the Studebaker Corporation. Its total of 10,770 shares was almost as large as that of the Studebaker family (which owned 10,784 shares).[85] The initial Dutch investment had been made before the war.[86] It seems likely in 1923 that these securities were still held in Holland.[87]

Some foreign portfolio investors paid special attention to U.S. public utilities. The Société financière pour entreprises électrique aux États-Unis, founded in Geneva in 1910, with a capital of 7 million francs, invested in American light and power companies. It kept its holdings all during the war and into the postwar era.[88] Likewise, the Canadian insurance company Sun Life Assurance Company was ready to invest in the securities of American public utilities.[89]

But to what extent was there new FPI? There is evidence of German capital flight to the United States right after the war. The Germans passed a law on December 24, 1920, against capital exports. This attempted to strengthen earlier laws. The new measure, like the prior ones, did little good, for as the mark depreciated and inflation mounted, and as new taxes were imposed, sophisticated Germans moved their moneys into foreign assets; German-Americans were reported to have assisted their former countrymen in investing in American corporate securities.[90]

By the summer of 1923, the National City Company (an affiliate of the National City Bank) had men in London, seeking to sell American securities there.[91] Kathleen Burk found that by 1923, Morgan Grenfell, the Morgan house in Britain, was investing in American securities "on some scale."[92] Herman Harjes (a Morgan partner in its Paris firm) in 1923 asked Edward Stettinius (a Morgan partner in New York and a director of General Electric) about purchasing General Electric shares.[93] Rufus S. Tucker of the U.S. Department of Commerce, in his report on the balance of payments in 1923, found "instances of American concerns borrowing money in the Netherlands and elsewhere." The amount of these borrowings was put at about $32 million.[94] By 1924, American corporate securities owned abroad seem to have risen above the level at year end 1919. The holdings appear to have been concentrated in U.S. market leaders to facilitate reselling.

In 1929, the National Industrial Conference Board (NICB)—with the aid of the U.S. Department of Commerce—compiled figures on outstanding American securities moving internationally (Table 2.9). The NICB explained the repatriations of 1920 as due to good U.S. prices (and foreign exchange gains) and those of 1921–1923 as due to depressed

Table 2.9. International movements of outstanding American securities, 1919–1923 (in millions of U.S. dollars)

Activity	1919	1920	1921	1922	1923
1. Repatriation by foreigners of American securities	n.a.	258	26	213	212
2. American securities sold to foreigners	n.a.	n.a.	42	285	492
3. Net decrease (−) or net increase (+) in foreign holdings of American domestic securities	−195*	−258*	+16	+72	+280

Sources: All figures, except those marked with an asterisk, are from the National Industrial Conference Board, *The International Financial Position of the United States* (New York: National Industrial Conference Board, 1929), 64. The 1919 and 1920 figures marked with the asterisk are presented as "net stock and bond transactions" of foreign investors; they are in U.S. Department of Commerce, Bureau of Foreign and Domestic Commerce, *Foreign Investments in the United States* (Washington, D.C., 1937), 27. I know, however, of American securities sold to foreigners in 1920, so for 1920, if row 1 is right, row 3 must be wrong and vice versa. The Federal Reserve monitored for January to June 1919 "foreign exchange" transactions and found $236.2 million in repatriation by foreigners of American securities *and* $200.6 million in American securities sold to foreigners in those six months. *Federal Reserve Bulletin,* May 1922, 544. The figures provided for 1922 and 1923 on this table do *not* correspond to ones given in Hal Lary, *The United States in the World Economy* (Washington, D.C., 1943), 107, nor do they correspond to the balance of payments figures published earlier (in 1924) by the U.S. Department of Commerce. In all cases, however, the direction of the activity is identical.

n.a. = not available.

business conditions in European markets and "normal readjustments . . . by individual investors, insurance companies, and investment trusts, especially in Europe and Canada."[95] The purchases—the new inward investments in 1921, 1922, and 1923—the NICB attributed to monetary instability in Europe ("flight capital").[96] Perhaps it should have added that the prosperity in America by 1923 was an attraction. All during America's years as a creditor nation, a major motive for the entry of FPI into this country lay in the search for a secure haven, "risk avoidance." In the early 1920s, some foreigners wished to place their savings in dollar securities; the dollar was backed by gold; the dollar seemed likely to appreciate in terms of most other currencies in Europe; and America had recovered rapidly from the sharp downturn in late 1920–1921. The U.S. Department of Commerce called the influx into the United States of flight capital during 1923 from countries with instable currencies "a rather anomalous movement."[97] The characterization of inward FPI as "anomalous" or "abnormal" would recur frequently in the interwar period. In the early 1920s, as in subsequent years, the assumption was that America's positive trade balance "should" be matched with capital outflows. There were capital outflows, but at the same time foreign capital came to America. Portfolio diversification to a safe and promising nation seemed a sound practice.[98]

Thus, even while Europe desperately needed capital, while the dollar was strong (and therefore expensive for foreigners to acquire), while returns—nominal and real—were in 1919–1923 usually lower in the United States than abroad, while there existed concerns over double taxation, and while Americans were making large investments abroad, there were those in foreign lands who viewed the United States as a country with a good future and excellent growth prospects, and American-based corporations as safe and desirable investments.[99] Those foreigners who looked for safety purchased U.S. corporate securities even during the late 1920–1921 downturn. There was no absence of financial intermediaries (American and European) to assist in these transactions and to aid the investors in avoiding existing restrictions imposed by their governments on capital exports. A sophisticated international banking and brokerage community emerged to facilitate such capital movements.

Yet unlike in the years before 1914, when American railroad and industrial companies went to Britain, Holland, and France with numerous new issues (and German banks took large participations in and distributed newly issued American stocks and bonds to their German and other European customers), what occurred in 1919–1923 was typically the trade in (the exchange of) existing American securities or, to a far lesser extent, new American issues, where European banks' allotments existed but were limited. Stocks and bonds of many of the largest American corporations were by now regularly traded in London and Amsterdam. Bonds that reached maturity were redeemed or exchanged for other securities.

Although most American companies that required new capital relied on domestic capital markets, on occasion they went overseas to "friends," or possibly interested parties, for funding. Under very special circumstances, as I will show in Chapter 3, General Motors obtained capital in Great Britain in 1920, but *not* through a new issue there. The head of the Industrial Potash Corporation (IPC) of Salt Lake City, Utah, wrote the president of the Tokyo Chamber of Commerce in March 1922, seeking $500,000 to $2 million in Japan to finance his company. Japan was an importer of potash; perhaps Japanese companies might want to invest. Nothing came of this idea, and the U.S. Bureau of Foreign and Domestic Commerce (whose help was solicited by IPC) was far from enthusiastic: "We do not think it is the function of this office to interest itself in the possibilities of securing foreign capital for development of industries in the United States."[100] When, in August 1923, the National City Company was attempting to market American securities in Britain, it met strong opposition from London newspapers. The *Telegraph* declared, quite sanctimoniously—reflecting a now common view—that savings available in Britain ought to be invested at home.[101]

In addition, there was the category of foreign purchases of "foreign securities" in the United States: in 1921, 1922, and 1923, foreigners bought dollar-denominated foreign securities in the United States to the extent of $32 million, $206 million, and $125 million, respectively. These sums were much smaller than foreign acquisitions of American domestic securities (see line 2, Table 2.9).[102] What existed here was often a "recycling" of foreign moneys through New York.[103] A writer in the *London New Statesman* of February 10, 1923, noted that because the U.S. public was new to foreign lending, American loans to foreign governments had a superior yield to those marketed in London. He explained that a British investor would do better purchasing the dollar bonds rather than sterling ones. "He [the British investor] can keep them in his bank in this country [Great Britain] and cash coupons here with just the same facility as if they belonged to the British issue." National City Company—the securities affiliate of National City Bank—reprinted the article, as it sought to market these foreign securities in Britain.[104]

In 1923, the National City Company obtained control of the United Financial Corporation (UFC), Montreal, one of Canada's largest investment houses—that is, this was an American direct investment abroad. But National City Company used UFC to sell American issues in Canada, as well as to underwrite Canadian issues in New York. Canadian issues in New York would be sold in the United States and in Canada.[105]

In short, in the years 1919–1923, while FPI divestments occurred, FPI remained and grew, based in part on holdings that were retained from earlier days, new investments, some FDI transformed into FPI, as well as certain efforts of U.S. industrial and financial institutions to seek out foreign finance and to try to place foreigners in American stocks and bonds. Most of the rise in FPI was the result of foreigners buying traded issues—both domestic and foreign ones.

Foreign Direct Investments, 1919–1923

FDI in the United States followed a different course from FPI, yet here, too, retreats coexisted with new involvements. The differences lay in investors' motivations. A number of investments of foreign multinational enterprises (MNEs) that survived and even flourished during the war years came to an end in peacetime, some for strictly business reasons, some as a result of *foreign* government action, and others owing to *U.S.* government policies. Some that entered during the war exited at its close. Many of the FDIs that ended for business reasons were part of the ever-present entry and exit patterns characteristic of FDI in general and, of course, of all business activities.

Retreats Based on Economic Considerations

Although FDI was typically less liquid than FPI, this did not stop withdrawals. In 1919, for example, an American firm, Tobacco Products Corporation, bought the U.S. investments of the British enterprise Philip Morris & Co., in the process acquiring the valuable trademarks Philip Morris and Marlboro.[106] Another withdrawal from FDI occurred in 1920 when Americans purchased from the Sheffield (England) firm William Jessop & Sons a small works to make saw steel that the latter had built near Pittsburgh, Pennsylvania, in 1901; the rationale behind this divestment was based on the parent firm's managerial priorities.[107] Roughly two years later, in 1922, the British-born, U.S.-resident representative (and joint-venture investor in) H & B American Machine Company took over one-half of the 60 percent English controlling interest in this textile machinery maker (established in Attleboro, Massachusetts, in 1894). Because of the entrepreneurial initiatives taken on the *American* side of the business, control moved across the Atlantic.[108]

The British-owned Rollin Chemical Company in West Virginia went into receivership in 1923, and on recovery the British interest does not seem to have survived.[109] Two long-standing British direct investments in copper also came to a conclusion. Scottish investors had organized the Arizona Copper Company, Ltd., in 1882, which had become a highly successful venture, remaining profitable through the war years. The company expanded in 1919, only to encounter major difficulties when primary product prices collapsed in the recession of 1920–1921. In response, in 1921, the Scots sold the mine and smelter to the American firm Phelps Dodge Corporation. The British investors were paid with stock with a book value of $18.2 million and became passive portfolio investors in the large Phelps Dodge.[110] In Tennessee, the English-owned Ducktown Sulphur, Copper and Iron Co., Ltd. (established in 1891), went into receivership with the 1920–1921 downturn. Eventually, in 1925, a group of businessmen from Chattanooga, Tennessee, and New York City reorganized it as the Ducktown Chemical and Iron Company—and, in the process, it became American controlled.[111] During World War I, a British company (in a joint venture) had built a tin smelter and refinery at Jamaica Bay, New York. With the high cost of operations, the British investor, Williams, Harvey & Co., Ltd., closed the smelter and refinery in 1923.[112] As in the cases of Rollin Chemical, Arizona Copper, and the Ducktown enterprise, the bad times of 1920–1921 prompted this exit.

During the war years, British mortgage companies had curtailed their business, and for some recovery was impossible. Thus, the sizable Land Mortgage Bank of Texas, Ltd. (registered in the United Kingdom in 1886) was liquidated in 1922; once it had had an excellent performance record.[113] Larry McFarlane reports that four Scottish and three English firms withdrew from lending in North and South Dakota in 1920–1921 because higher returns were available elsewhere—outside the United States.[114] Balfour Williamson's once-flourishing Pacific Loan and Investment Company found mortgage lending on the West Coast no longer lucrative; in January 1923, the British trading enterprise resolved to liquidate this mortgage and securities company, which had been organized in 1878. In 1922, Balfour Williamson had also closed out its Pacific Trust Association, for the same reason: lack of adequate profits.[115]

In 1923, another long-lived British direct investment came to a final conclusion. In 1889, America's leading flour maker, the Pillsbury company, had become British owned; in 1908, Pillsbury Flour Mills Company had taken over the operations, while the British parent, Pillsbury-Washburn Flour Mills Company, Ltd., had been transformed into a financial "shell."[116] Subsequently, the American operating company had gone its own way, but not until 1923 did the Pillsbury-Washburn Flour Mills Company, Ltd., finally sell out entirely to Americans. In its July 4, 1923, issue, the Minneapolis trade journal *Northwestern Miller* joyfully proclaimed Pillsbury's independence: the properties were now "completely American." To be sure, some minor British portfolio holdings lingered; it was, however, the Pillsbury family and "native Minneapolis interests" who were totally in charge. Decades later—a century after this company had first become British owned—in 1989 Pillsbury would once again move back into British ownership.[117]

Not only British companies departed from or reduced their U.S. involvements in the years 1919–1923. Pathe Freres Phonograph Company—a French manufacturing subsidiary established in 1912—went into receivership in 1921.[118] Far more important, its onetime French parent, Pathé Frères, was also involved in the American movie business. Pathe Exchange—the American subsidiary of Pathé Frères (as of 1918 Pathé Cinéma)—was a major producer and wholesaler of movies in the United States; from September 1920 to January 1921, Pathe Exchange released eighteen full-length feature films. In 1921 Pathe Exchange was acquired by Merrill, Lynch & Co., the stockbrokers.[119] Pathé Cinéma may have retained a small minority interest in Pathe Exchange; it made an agreement to transfer its technology to Pathe Exchange, and Charles Pathé stayed on as a director of the American company.[120]

In 1923 the Dutch firm Anton Jurgens' Magarine Fabrieken ended its 1917 joint venture in Buffalo, New York, selling out to its partner, Spencer Kellogg, after unsatisfactory experiences.[121] L. M. Ericsson, a Swedish enterprise that had been manufacturing also in Buffalo (but since 1907), shut down in 1920, unable to compete; it sold its U.S. assets in 1923.[122] Three more Swedish manufacturing investments came to an end: (1) AB Baltic's Empire Cream Separator Company faced financial difficulties and went into liquidation in 1921; (2) in April 1920, a certificate of dissolution was filed in New York State for the American Lux Light Company; and (3) the company established by C. E. Johansson during World War I to make precision gauges was sold by its Swedish founder to Ford Motor Company in 1923.[123] Even more significant, a number of the Norwegian insurance companies that had entered during the First World War and some that came in right after the Armistice had by 1923 left the American market. The Norwegian insurers appear to have retreated because of large loan losses in 1919–1922 on their marine business.[124]

A leading Canadian pork packer, the William Davies Co., invested $750,000 in its own packing plant in Chicago in 1918 and made ambitious plans for the postwar years. The 1920–1921 downturn made the project unworkable, and the brief U.S. operations came to a stop.[125] A more important Canadian divestment was that of Sun Life Assurance Company, which in 1923 sold (for the tidy sum of $30.9 million) its investment in the Illinois Traction Company, made before the First World War. This sizable holding had been in part FDI and in part FPI.[126] The insurance company's historian states that all the dollar proceeds were "reinvested on the same day received." Data in the company's archives suggest that a large share of the receipts went into U.S. FPI.[127]

In sum, in the years after the war, a number of foreign direct investors disposed of their businesses in the United States. On occasion, however, the size of the inward foreign investment in America did not drop, since investors did not repatriate their moneys but instead substituted FPI in American-run enterprises. Moreover, whether or not any foreign interests were sustained, productive activity in most cases continued—under Americans' management and control. In at least one instance (that of Philip Morris), ultimately a major U.S. enterprise would emerge, based on the acquired British assets. So, too, the takeover by Phelps Dodge of the Scottish-controlled mine contributed materially to that American company's subsequent prominent role in U.S. mining history. The Pillsbury company flourished under its domestic ownership and was a strong and healthy enterprise when, two generations later (in 1989), it would be subject to a $5.75 billion acquisition by another British company. The successor to Pathe Exchange (Metro-Goldwyn-Mayer) went back to French ownership in 1992, albeit only for a brief interlude. When L. M. Ericsson reentered the United States after the Second World War, there was no continuity with its earlier U.S. business "flop."

In the years 1919–1923, some foreign direct investors did not leave the United States, yet their role was sharply "downsized." This was true of a number of mortgage lenders, which stayed on—providing fewer mortgages than in prior years. The Scottish-controlled Texas Land and Mortgage Company apparently sold its office building in Dallas in 1920 or early 1921; in 1922, for the first time, its balance sheet contained entries for "securities foreclosed—in Texas."[128] The Scottish American Mortgage Company, Edinburgh, like the Texas Land and Mortgage Company, stayed in business but curtailed its American lending, placing more of its resources into investments in the United Kingdom. Increasingly, Scottish firms continued their transformation from mortgage companies to investment companies; in the process, they often diversified their portfolios, making new investments outside the United States.[129] Dutch mortgage banks in America also reduced their U.S. lending, even though most persisted in business from 1919 to 1923.[130] Another foreign firm that cut back its business was the Mountain Copper Company, Ltd., in California; with the slump in 1920, it had shut down its copper operations, resuming them in 1923 on a smaller scale. The company remained British owned and became more important in pyrite ores than in copper.[131]

Nestlé & Anglo-Swiss, which had enlarged its U.S. business in a formidable manner during the First World War, in 1919 continued this expansion. In 1920, directly or indirectly, it took over eleven additional plants, principally in California and Wisconsin, bringing its total to fifty-three American factories. In terms of *number of establishments,* it had undoubtedly, for the moment, become the largest foreign investor in America. But its management had been too optimistic. For the first time in its long history, in 1921 the Swiss *parent* company lost money. By December 1921, of its fifty-three U.S. factories, only twenty were producing canned milk (eight were distributing fresh milk; twenty were idle; and five had been sold). The chastened Swiss company stayed on. For many years, it was, however, a conservative (and modest) direct investor in America.[132] This sample of retreats offers an insight into the ebb and flow of foreign direct investors' experiences with economic adversity.

Retreats Due to Foreign Government Policies: The Russian Case

Before the 1917 Russian Revolution, there had been FPI and some FDI in the United States by Russian individuals and firms, most notably Russian insurance companies. Many of the individually held small portfolio holdings of wealthy Russian investors had been sold between 1914 and 1917. By contrast, at year end 1918, nine Russian insurance firms in the United States had greater "admitted assets" than at year end 1914 (see Table 2.10 for their admitted assets at year end 1918).

Table 2.10. "Russian" insurance companies in the United States, Dec. 31, 1918

Company	Date of entry into the United States	Admitted assets (000s of U.S. dollars)
The Petrograd group		
1. Rossia Insurance Co.	1904	11,468
2. Salamandra Insurance Co.	1899	4,185
3. Second Russian Insurance Co.	1913	2,876
4. First Russian Insurance Co.	1907	2,699
5. Russian Reinsurance Co.	1907	2,457
The Moscow group		
6. Jakor Insurance Co.	1908	3,993
7. Moscow Fire Insurance Co.	1900	3,162
8. Northern Insurance Co.	1910	1,424
The Warsaw Company		
9. Warsaw Fire Insurance Co.	1911	1,087
Total admitted assets		33,351

Source: Based on *Best's Insurance Report, Fire and Marine, 1919.*

"Admitted assets" were those assets listed on the books of these companies and published in *Best's Insurance Reports.* These firms handled fire reinsurance. The Russian insurance companies in the United States had maintained business despite a decree by the revolutionary government of December 1, 1918, that dissolved their *parent* companies.

The fate of these "orphan" Russian insurance companies in the United States varied. The largest, Rossia Insurance Company, established a new Rossia Insurance Company of Hartford, Connecticut. Effective April 1, 1919, the U.S. branch of the Rossia Insurance Company transferred its surplus to the new American company, which remained in business with no foreign parent. The parent of the second largest, the Salamandra Insurance Company, had in April 1918 set up a holding company in Denmark, named Reinsurance Company Salamandra, to conduct business outside Russia; by 1923, that Danish holding company had taken over the entire business of the U.S. branch of Salamandra Insurance Company. An American firm, the Anchor Insurance Company, organized by an "attorney-in-fact" of the Jakor Insurance Company, Moscow, in 1922 acquired the assets of the American branch of that company, the third ranking of the Russian enterprises. Other Russian insurers ceased business in 1923 and reinsured their outstanding liabilities. The manager of the Warsaw Company declared that the firm was a "Polish company"—outside "Bolshevik control." For all practical purposes, by 1919–1923 not one of these ex-Russian companies was under Soviet control.[133]

In connection with U.S. recognition of the Soviet Union a decade later, in 1933 the Soviets agreed to waive all claims to "Russian" properties in the United States, assigning such assets to the U.S. government (the so-called Litvinov Assignment) to be used to pay the claims by *American* companies against the Soviet Union. The U.S. government eventually realized roughly $9 million from the Litvinov Assignment, representing in the main pre-1917 Russian bank deposits in the United States and money orders held by the U.S. Post Office. Only $1.69 million was obtained from the former Russian insurance companies, none of which came from the three largest enterprises.[134] Considering that the admitted assets of the Russian insurance companies on December 31, 1918, had been $33.35 million (see Table 2.10), the $1.69 million was a paltry sum, in no way reflective of the earlier Russian presence.

In sum, even though there continued to be Soviet claims against these insurance assets and other "Russian properties" in the United States until 1933, and the final disposition of these investments was not clear until many years later, it is legitimate to conclude that between 1919 and 1923, for all practical purposes, there were no Soviet insurance company investments in the United States and indeed no Soviet FDI of any sort.[135] Amtorg, the Soviet state trading company, would open an office in America in 1924 to try to encourage trade; at a much later date (in the 1970s), there would be other small Soviet investments in America; the pre–World War I Russian interests can, however, be considered as ended in the years 1919–1923.[136] They ceased because of the Russian Revolution and because of the Soviet Union's policy of nationalizing the parent enterprises.

Retreats Due to Foreign and U.S. Government Policies

Foreign government taxes—resulting in double taxation—had an impact on inward FDI. Sometimes there was a corporate restructuring of the investments to minimize taxes. There is, however, little evidence of major changes in operations, owing to the new foreign government taxes. One case where taxes did have significant consequences lay in the real estate sector (real estate is considered as FDI, since the foreign investor is able to exercise control). Waldorf Astor (the 2nd Viscount) and his brother, John Jacob Astor V (Baron Astor of Hever), inherited large amounts of Manhattan real estate from their father, William Waldorf Astor, who died in 1919 (the latter had moved to England from the United States in the 1890s and been elevated to the peerage in 1916). There was double taxation of the rents from the brothers' New York real estate; in 1919, the siblings, who lived in England, paid $1,680,000 in taxes to the British government and $1,134,000 to the U.S. government—or a total of $2,814,000—on rental income of $2,500,000. As a result of the tax burden, the brothers decided to reduce their U.S. property holdings. By 1924, they had sold over $20 million in New York apartment houses, hotels, office buildings, and some lots (they retained some $20 million in New York properties after these sales).[137] Their real estate holdings were by far the largest by individual foreign investors; there is, in addition, evidence of divestments by other investors for the identical tax reasons.

Retreats (and Constraints) Due to U.S. Government Policies

Significant retirements from FDI in the United States, 1919–1923, were the consequence of *American* federal government policies. In the case of Prohibition, U.S. law affected foreign and domestic investors alike. In all the other major instances, FDI was the specific target of what were nationalistic measures. I will begin with Prohibition and then look at the range of federal (and, where appropriate, state) government policies that led to exits from FDI.

Large British direct investments had been made in 1889–1892, which had often been takeovers of U.S. manufacturing facilities, including breweries.[138] Over time, most of these 1889–1892 British stakes in manufacturing had fallen by the wayside; some that persisted finally ended in 1919–1923 for purely economic reasons (the British interests in the Pillsbury company and in Otis Steel are two examples). Those made in breweries had been unique in that the majority had continued, despite their far from satisfactory performance.[139] In wartime, the American Dollar Securities Committee had ignored the British companies' brewery investments—just as the committee had ignored virtually all FDI.[140]

During 1914–1918, Americans' opposition to alcoholic beverage consumption had grown, as German-Americans were disparaged as "drinkers." Anti-German sentiment, along with the temperance movement, prompted state legislators to ratify the Eighteenth Amendment (the "Prohibition" amendment) to the U.S. Constitution. In October 1919, Congress passed the Volstead Act, which—as of January 16, 1920—made illegal the manufacture, sale, and transport of alcoholic beverages to and within the United States. Yet it was not German investors who suffered as an outcome of Prohibition; instead, British (and American) ones saw, as one angry Britisher put it, their "trade stopped without compensation."[141] Although some small Canadian direct investment in the United States existed in alcoholic beverages and was affected by the legislation, the big foreign losers were British investors. One estimate put asset losses of U.K. firms at $150 million. The Volstead Act ended the large British brewery investments, even though the law was not prejudicially aimed at alien interests.[142]

By contrast, U.S. public policies in four other sectors—(1) communications (radio and cables), (2) transportation (principally shipping), (3) energy (mainly oil), and (4) banking—did mark FDI for special treatment. In each of these four sectors, the federal government sought to safeguard and to promote domestic interests at the expense of foreign ones. In some instances, the nationalistic federal government policies were supplemented by new restrictions imposed by state governments. These four strategic sectors were associated directly or indirectly with "national defense"—with the defense of national sovereignty.[143] These were sectors "affected with a public interest," wherein Americans saw themselves as still excessively "dependent," at least in some aspects.[144] The United States was not alone in protecting such activities from alien domination.[145] Also, in certain of these sectors, federal government policies sought to use U.S. power over foreign business in the United States not only to protect American business at home but also to obtain leverage to assist U.S. companies abroad through "reciprocity" requirements. In some cases there were inward FDI retreats and in others the keeping of new inward FDI at bay. In some of these sectors, earlier public policies were now bolstered with new measures. I will consider each sector separately.[146]

First, in international communications—radio and cables—the British seemed supreme over all nationalities on a global basis. At war's end, the leading firm in America's infant radio industry was the Marconi Wireless Telegraph Company of America, an affiliate of the British enterprise Marconi's Wireless Telegraph Company. There were no American-owned rivals, and Americans (especially U.S. Navy personnel) feared a dangerous monopoly by the British of U.S. and global radio transmissions.[147]

For years, men in the U.S. Navy Department had perceived a peril to national security in foreign domination over radio communication. While America was in the war, the navy had operated the country's radio stations and campaigned for postwar U.S. government ownership. After the Armistice, on November 30, 1918, the navy purchased from Marconi Wireless Telegraph Company of America for $1.45 million 45 coastal radio stations as well as 330 ship stations; this, however, left the British-controlled enterprise with ownership of the principal high-powered radio stations (although they remained under navy operations).[148] The prewar German-owned stations, at Tuckerton, New Jersey, and Sayville, Long Island, had been taken over by the navy in

September 1914 and July 1915, respectively. In the summer of 1919, the U.S. government paid a French company (the prospective owner of the Tuckerton station) $400,000 for its use of the station during the war years and transferred it to French ownership, while at the same time retaining it under navy operations. The navy acquired from the Alien Property Custodian the ownership of the Sayville station.[149]

These steps, while important, did not address the broader question of postwar control. By early 1919, key navy officials recognized that their hope for U.S. government ownership of all U.S.-based radio facilities was not going to be an acceptable public policy in a postwar America committed to reducing the bloated governmental wartime involvements and to returning control over economic activities as fast as possible to the private sector. Yet the navy did not abandon its view that radio communication should be in American hands. Thus, encouraged by the navy, in the summer of 1919, Owen Young (then vice-president of General Electric) started to craft a strategy for an American-owned (nongovernmental) radio company.

The U.S.-born Edward J. Nally (vice-president and general manager of Marconi of America) faced a not atypical dilemma for a manager of an affiliate of a multinational enterprise. On the one hand, Nally represented a British parent; on the other hand, he was an American citizen, doing business in his own country.[150] As economic historian Hugh Aitken has recognized, Nally had his own personal agenda that in many ways came to coincide with Young's; Nally's goal was to maintain the survival of the business within the constraints of U.S. political reality.

On July 11, 1919, President Woodrow Wilson signed a resolution (passed by Congress) ordering the return to private ownership and control of telephones, telegraph, and cables. The expectation was that an order on the relinquishment of government control over radio stations would follow. In September 1919, Marconi of America acquired ownership of the Tuckerton station from the French Marconi affiliate.[151] This station continued to be operated by the navy, as were the rest of Marconi of America's facilities. That September, Young and Nally (and Nally's British superiors) finalized arrangements for an American radio company, with *no* ownership by the British Marconi enterprise. Table 2.11 shows the ownership of Marconi of America in September–October 1919, before the new plans were put into effect. As is evident, Marconi of America was more than 60 percent owned from abroad, although the British parent held only 364,826 shares, that is, an 18 percent interest.

On October 17, 1919, the Radio Corporation of America (RCA) was incorporated in Delaware. Before it took over the assets of Marconi of America, General Electric purchased the British Marconi's 364,826 shares. Next, in exchange for the transfer of Marconi of America's assets to RCA, all the then existing shareholders in Marconi of America

Table 2.11. Stock holdings in the Marconi Wireless Telegraph Company of America, September–October 1919

Residence of stockholders	Number of shares held	% of total
England and Scotland	1,053,809	52.7
Shares held by British Marconi	**(364,826)**	**(18.2)**
Ireland	116,513	5.8
Canada	16,925	.8
Belgium	12,125	.6
Holland	7,600	.4
France	5,571	.3
Switzerland	1,550	.1
Italy	1,206	.1
Germany	1,100	.1
Portugal	700	[a]
Other foreign countries	880	[a]
Total shares held by foreign residents	**1,217,979**	**(60.9)**
United States	650,918	32.5
Unknown[b]	131,103	6.6
Total	2,000,000	100.0

Source: Based on Hugh Aitken, *The Continuous Wave: Technology and American Radio, 1900–1932* (Princeton, N.J.: Princeton University Press, 1985), 42. I have corrected an addition error.

a. Less than .05 percent.

b. Lots of 50 shares or less, the majority of which was believed to be in the United States.

received, for each share they owned, one preferred share ($5 par value) and one common share (no par value) in RCA. These transactions ended the involvement of the multinational enterprise, the British Marconi Company, although based on the data in Table 2.11, foreign individuals would still have held at least 853,153 preferred shares in RCA of $4,265,765 par value and an equal number of common shares at no par value. RCA's total capital was made up of 5 million preferred shares (par value $5) and 5 million common shares (no par value). With the elimination of the British Marconi holding and the enlarged capital, foreign ownership of the new company was reduced to about 17 percent of the total shares (compared with more than 60 percent of the old Marconi of America). The charter of RCA stated that no more than 20 percent of the stock could be voted by foreigners, and to enforce this, stockholders resident abroad received so-called foreign share certificates.[152] Another provision in the charter prohibited the appointment or election of an officer or director who was not a U.S. citizen.[153]

RCA obtained most of the assets of Marconi of America (the only significant property excluded was the New Jersey factory, which Marconi of America leased to General Electric; Marconi of America was not dissolved; it persisted as a corporate shell). At origin, RCA entered into an agreement with the British Marconi to divide world markets, including those in South America.[154] Most important, in the transactions, RCA received Marconi of America's entire staff, with their skills and knowledge; David Sarnoff, who would soon become the principal figure in the development of American radio, was part of the "acquisition." RCA's first chairman of the board was GE's Owen Young; its first president was Nally.[155] Apparently, the managing director of the British Marconi, Geoffrey Isaacs, had insisted on Nally's becoming president before Isaacs would recommend to the European shareholders that they ratify the arrangements (the overseas shareholders had to approve the transfer of the assets from Marconi of America to RCA).[156]

Nally's appointment to the presidency of RCA did not, however, please navy officials, and in December 1922 Nally resigned to become RCA's managing director of international relations; he was replaced by Major General James G. Harbord. In his new position, Nally would be based in Europe, which provoked the snide remark from Commander Stanford C. Hooper (a staunch advocate of the "all-American company") that this would put Nally closer to "his master's voice." Navy men's suspicions died hard.[157] It seems that all GE's crucial negotiations with the British Marconi in the establishment of RCA were with Isaacs. Guglielmo Marconi held the title of chairman of the British company. Born in 1874, in 1919 the inventor was forty-five years old; he would live until 1937. He had visited the United States some forty times between 1897 and 1917, yet his name never appears in the reports on the transatlantic discussions. Undoubtedly, he personally owned some of the 17 percent foreign interest in RCA that persisted after the establishment of the American-controlled company, but I can find no evidence that he (or Isaacs, for that matter) had any subsequent involvement in the American business.[158]

Thus, in the fall of 1919, Radio Corporation of America had been born, and the navy's desire for domestic ownership-control had been realized. On March 1, 1920, RCA received from the U.S. Navy the right to operate its newly acquired facilities, which included practically all the high-powered radio stations in the United States (the only exception was the formerly German-owned radio station at Sayville, Long Island; the navy retained the ownership it had obtained from the Alien Property Custodian). RCA still had foreign (principally British) shareholders, but the equity ownership from abroad was now so diluted that overseas control had ended; the holdings were all FPI—passive foreign investments. And so there came to a close a major, innovative FDI in the United States. The British Marconi company's stake in the United States had lasted two decades (1899–1919); foreign technology had been transferred; and now the new U.S. company could function, expand, and flourish without British assistance.[159] Seventy years later (in 1989), two students of FDI in the United States would insist that it was "virtually impossible to conceive of a scenario," excluding war conditions, whereby nationalist sentiment in the United States would "interfere with a [foreign] corporation's activities in any fundamental way"—yet in 1919, in peacetime, when the FDI of the British Marconi was divested, U.S. nationalism *was* responsible.[160] During the Harding administration, the president favored federal government regulation of all "radio stations transmitting and receiving international traffic," and also the establishment of "rules and regulations necessary to prevent chaos on the domestic airwaves." When a law was finally passed years later (in 1927), it would contain restrictions on foreign investment in this industry.[161]

American insistence on domestic control over the nascent radio communications industry was associated with a national perception of British hegemony over worldwide communications, including cables—although (unlike in radio) it was recognized that the British did not have a U.S. cable monopoly. At the Paris Peace Conference in 1919, Americans argued with British delegates over the disposition of prewar German cables, fearing a further extension of British influence. But, unlike in the case of Marconi, in the United States no pressures existed for any repatriation of ownership and control of the U.S. assets of existing British, or French, cable companies.[162] Instead, following a strategy—which as I will show was applied in 1920 in the oil sector—in 1921 Congress passed the Kellogg Cable Landing Act that gave the president authority to withhold or to revoke a U.S. license for landing cables from a foreign country, *if* "such action will assist in securing rights for the landing or operation of cables in foreign countries, or in maintaining the rights or interests of the United States or its citizens in foreign countries." This U.S. policy related to landing rights (and thus to foreign direct investments in cables in America) was identified with reciprocity, with assisting American business abroad.[163] In 1921, Secretary of State Charles Evans Hughes asked the U.S. ambassador in France to remind the French Foreign Office of the French cable company's seven offices in New York; Hughes wanted U.S. cable companies to be allowed to have such offices in France.[164] In short, in cables as well as radio, Americans asserted their interests.

Second, in transportation, mainly shipping, U.S. government policies sought to challenge foreign—basically British—mastery, while at the same time pursuing American advantage. Here, as in radio communications, the navy took the initiative, insisting that since the United States was intending to build up a great merchant marine, the country would require a powerful navy to keep trading routes secure.[165] The Merchant Marine Act of 1920 (the Jones Act), which provided for the return of the fleet of the U.S. government's Shipping Board to private ownership, reiterated what had long been U.S. policy. The Jones Act forbade the coastwise transportation of merchandise "by water . . . between points in the United States . . . either directly or via a foreign port . . . in any other vessel than a vessel built in and documented under the laws of the United States and owned by persons who are citizens of the United States."[166] The act went beyond (and amended) the Shipping Act of 1916 in defining "citizens of the United States"; it specifically excluded from the prohibited practices corporations that were not at least 75 percent owned by citizens of the United States.[167] In addition, the law extended the coastwise bans to the Philippines, allowed preferential rail rates for shippers that used U.S. vessels, and authorized the president to abrogate treaties that *did not allow* discrimination in favor of U.S. shipping. The law's sponsor, Senator Wesley Jones, applauded the new legislation as a declaration of war against foreign shipping: "They say it will drive foreign shipping from our ports. Granted; I want it to do it."[168] During the First World War, the British-Dutch Shell company in the United States had built three vessels for its coastal oil trade; the 1920 law precluded the foreign-owned Shell company from using its new tankers in this manner. The multinational enterprise did not sell the vessels; instead, it deployed the ships to other routes.[169]

The Jones Act did permit the Shipping Board in the privatization process to sell its ships to aliens, but only those "unnecessary" to national shipping.[170] The law also sought to encourage American maritime insurance, and in June 1920 Admiral William S. Benson, head of the Shipping Board, announced the formation of the American Marine Insurance Syndicate. So strong, however, were the foreign insurers that this government-sponsored American syndicate accepted one-third participation by foreign insurance companies with branches in the United States.[171]

In transatlantic shipping, Americans tried to maintain the momentum of the wartime expansion. The British Cunard had been—and was still—the world's largest passenger line. International Mercantile Marine Company (IMM), the "American" challenger of the prewar era, had gone into receivership in 1915 to reemerge in 1916. IMM had over the years attracted substantial British and Dutch investments.[172] By 1917, all its ships had been requisitioned for U.S. (or British) wartime use. Once the war was over, IMM aimed at rebuilding its passenger and freight service. Yet its plans were not viewed with favor in Washington, since its historic associations with the British had been far too intimate. In Washington, the American president of IMM (Philip A. S. Franklin) was perceived as a figurehead, standing in for Harold A. Sanderson of the White Star Line, Liverpool (Sanderson had, in fact, been Franklin's predecessor as president of the IMM); for Lord Pirrie, chairman of the Royal Mail Group of shipping lines and head of the Belfast shipbuilders Harland & Wolff; and for Edward C. Grenfell of Morgan's British house. Accordingly, in its postwar plans for a domestic shipping industry, the Shipping Board increasingly sought to bypass IMM.[173] Even though the Shipping Board was selling off its vessels to existing companies and was promoting the founding of new ones, the board retained a number of ships and through its control of the newly formed United States Lines endeavored to provide added—and fully *American*—competition on transatlantic and other routes.[174] The board's aim was to fashion a worthy U.S. shipping industry so as to gain "maritime control of the world."[175] Initially, a spectacular success seemed in the offing. Yet the expectations would not be realized, although for a brief interval, before the late 1920–1921 economic downturn buried the dream, it had seemed possible.[176]

In transportation, as in communications, U.S. public policy makers paid little heed to FPI. Thus, no one proposed a divestment of the British and Dutch ownership of IMM securities.[177] The minority interest of British insurers in the new American Marine Insurance Syndicate would bestow, it was believed, little power, albeit these were direct investments. The ongoing European holdings of bonds and shares of the country's railroads evoked no negative responses, for the reduced stakes gave foreign investors little leverage, much less control over U.S. railroad management. National security considerations vis-à-vis transportation were, moreover, confined to businesses from across the oceans—across the Atlantic and to a far lesser extent the Pacific.[178] Canadian railroads, which were FDI, crossed the border as they had for many years, but they troubled no one.[179] There were as yet no laws on possible foreign interests in airplane travel. That would come—in 1926—and would follow the example of the shipping legislation. At this point, Americans had no concern about foreign influence over U.S. airlines (the Post Office had in May 1918 opened the first scheduled airmail service).[180]

Third, energy—specifically, oil—epitomized a sensitive sector where foreign business in America was in the spotlight.[181] Here, as with communications and transportation, U.S. postwar policies focused on European direct investments and exempted Canadian ones, for the latter constituted no conceivable challenge to the emerging global role of the United States. During the First World War, anxieties had surfaced as to whether U.S. domestic oil resources would be adequate to meet the nation's expanding future needs; U.S. companies were encouraged to invest abroad to locate additional oil resources.[182] Here again, as in radio communications and shipping policies, the navy, which had converted to oil-powered ships, was particularly outspoken—and the issue was once more framed in terms of national security.

On February 25, 1920, the president signed the Mineral Lands Leasing Act, covering the leasing of U.S. public lands to oil companies.[183] The law had a reciprocity clause:

> Citizens of another country, the laws, customs, or regulations of which *deny similar or like privileges to citizens or corporations of this country,* shall not by stock ownership, stock holding, or stock control, own any interest in any lease acquired under the provisions of this Act [my italics].[184]

The law did not forbid foreign investment in U.S. oil production and applied only to public lands (but some of these contained the best-known potential oil deposits on U.S. soil). As with U.S. cable policies, this act was designed to give the State Department leverage to pressure foreign governments to open the door to U.S. businesses that wished to expand abroad.[185]

In 1919, Verner Z. Reed, who had placed foreign capital in the Wyoming oil industry, died.[186] This seems to have led to a reduction in European investments there (some earlier divestments had been made during the First World War). Franco Wyoming Oil Company (founded in 1909 and headquartered in Paris) had attracted French, Dutch, and Belgian investors to the Wyoming oil industry.[187] In 1919, Franco Wyoming cut back its direct involvements in that state's oil developments.[188] In 1920–1921, the Dutch firm Petroleum Maatschappij Salt Creek sold its important Wyoming holding.[189] In 1921, Franco Wyoming made further moves to withdraw from active participation.[190] It stayed involved in Wyoming, however, and became principally a "royalty company," with wells, land, and securities.[191] Meanwhile, in August 1920, Standard Oil Company (Indiana) acquired roughly a third of the outstanding shares of Midwest Refining Company in Wyoming; and by July 1921, Standard Oil (Indiana) had obtained majority ownership of this once foreign-owned and foreign-controlled refining and oil producing firm.[192] In a complex set of transactions relating to Franco Wyoming's divestments and Standard Oil (Indiana)'s acquisitions, French and other foreign investors obtained portfolio interests in Standard Oil (Indiana).[193] Before the First World War, representatives of the French investors had taken on a managerial role in the development of the Salt

Creek oil properties in Wyoming; by 1923 this was no longer true. There may have been a limited connection between the Lands Leasing Act of 1920 and the pulling back of foreign business from Wyoming.[194] In the early 1920s, European investors' financial holdings in Standard Oil (Indiana) were too small to be of consequence.

In the immediate postwar years, the French company Union des Pétroles d'Oklahoma became American controlled. This firm had invested in the United States in 1911.[195] In 1918, it had transferred its properties to the Oklahoma Producing and Refining Corporation in exchange for the latter's stock.[196] In 1920, Ohio Cities Gas Company (soon to be acquired by Pure Oil Company) seems to have purchased control of the parent French company (Union des Pétroles d'Oklahoma), resulting in the Americanization of these assets.[197] Once more, the passage of the 1920 law may have had influence on the domestication process. I do not, however, believe that the Lands Leasing Act was the fundamental cause for the retreats of foreign companies from active foreign investments in either Wyoming or Oklahoma.[198]

Of all the foreign oil interests in the United States in 1920, those of the Royal Dutch Shell Group were the greatest; in this case, evidence exists on the adverse impact of the 1920 Lands Leasing Act. This group had entered the United States in 1912 and subsequently had expanded dramatically. When Congress had debated the lands leasing bill, U.S. representatives of the group visited Washington to oppose its enactment. Several years later, a legal adviser of Shell in New York would regret the tactic, believing this kind of lobbying had been contrary to explicit headquarters policy of not interfering in a host country's political affairs, but worse still, the effort had been counterproductive, for the law had passed.[199]

Early in 1920, Shell had identified a promising tract of U.S. government land, and on the very day that the president signed the Mineral Lands Leasing Act, the Shell Company of California applied for a permit (the so-called Woodside Permit) to drill on public land in Utah. Not long thereafter, an American—C. P. Trasker—also filed for a lease on the same tract. For a time nothing happened on either application. Warren Harding became president in March 1921, and on April 21 Trasker lodged a protest with the U.S. Interior Department, opposing the grant of the Woodside Permit to Shell because that company was not in compliance with the reciprocity clause in the Lands Leasing Act.[200]

Between February 25, 1920, and April 21, 1921, between the date of Shell's filing and Trasker's protest, no action had been taken on the two applications, but a considerable amount of behind-the-scenes diplomatic jockeying had occurred on related oil matters. The American consul general in London, Robert P. Skinner, wrote the U.S. State Department of his personal concerns over British ownership of American oil resources; Skinner pointed to the many British restrictions on expansion in the British Empire by U.S. companies.[201] He reported on the proposed operations of two British firms: (1) the British Motor Spirit Company, Ltd., capital £1 million (which owned all of the Anglo-Texas Oil Company, Inc., and the preferred shares of the Louisiana Petroleum Products Company, Inc.) and (2) the United Oil and Refinery Company, Ltd. (formed to acquire the property and assets of the Kansas Oklahoma Oil and Refinery Company, Ltd.).[202] Both British companies had properties in Oklahoma, a state with alien land laws.[203]

The then U.S. Secretary of the Interior John Barton Payne did not believe that the federal government could do anything under the Oklahoma law, but rather that the newly enacted Lands Leasing Law would be the appropriate club to bargain for an end to British restrictions on U.S. business abroad.[204] Arthur C. Millspaugh from the U.S. Office of the Foreign Trade Adviser disagreed, recommending that the State Department *not* move against foreign oil companies in the United States.[205]

Skinner from London countered, warning that British investors in the United States would deplete the dwindling U.S. oil resources: the State Department should take action to clear the way for American oil companies not only in the British Empire but in Persia, Mesopotamia, and the Near East, in general, since the United States would soon be dependent on oil imports.[206] The U.S. ambassador to Great Britain, John W. Davis, thought the Lands Leasing Act of 1920 gave "a valid reason" to pursue wide-ranging U.S.-British discussions on oil policy.[207] When the San Remo agreement of April 24, 1920, became known, many Americans saw the British and French governments as greedily dividing up world oil supplies and blatantly excluding U.S. business.[208] The U.S. Navy expressed a fear lest U.S. warships become hostage to British-controlled fuel.[209]

As the policy debates went forward, as worries over the possible exhaustion of domestic oil resources fed the controversy, and as U.S. companies' exclusion from foreign oil-producing sites became apparent, a Canadian-owned American corporation (the Vancouver Midway Oil Company) applied for a lease on public land. The Interior Department decided in December 1920 that Canadians were not to be treated in the same manner as citizens of other parts of the British Empire. Canada was a "reciprocating country" under the terms of the act (American enterprises could explore and produce in Canada). The lease was granted.[210] This clarification notwithstanding, uncertainty persisted on how the reciprocity provisions of the law would be enforced, and in the case of Shell's Utah application nothing had been settled when Harding took office as president and Albert B. Fall became his new secretary of the interior.

Fall's sympathies lay with his nation's oil companies, and it was Fall who received Trasker's April 1921 protest against the foreign-owned Shell company's obtaining the Woodside lease in Utah. As Shell's legal adviser, Avery Andrews, would later recall, Fall began a campaign against Royal Dutch Shell, based on the erroneous assumption that the group was owned and controlled by the British *government*.[211] The British ambassador to the United States, Sir Auckland Geddes, denied this, as did the Royal Dutch Shell Group.[212]

Meanwhile, the Royal Dutch Shell Group had continued to enlarge its U.S. business. Already in 1918, its U.S. oil output had been 27,500 barrels daily compared with Standard Oil of New Jersey's 18,800 barrels.[213] It also expanded in Mexico and Venezuela with an eye to serving the U.S. market. In April 1921, the group arranged to merge most of its substantial U.S. assets (the Shell Company of California and the Roxana Petroleum Corporation were its principal American affiliates) with the Union Oil Company of Delaware. The result would be the giant Shell Union Oil Corporation, to be formed on February 7, 1922.[214] The new company would have assets of about $180 million.[215] It would be by far the largest foreign investor in the United States.

As the group added to its American and worldwide operations and made plans for the sizable U.S. merger, it received an avalanche of negative U.S. press coverage. On December 15, 1921, Andrews wrote in a private and confidential letter to the group's home office that the firm had been too passive, that while it had publicized (in self-defense) its insistence that it was not controlled by the British government, other than that it was now following the group's policy of noninvolvement in host country political affairs. Yet with its much expanded interests in America, perhaps it should not ignore the power of the press. Andrews advised that the group allocate funds to improve the firm's image. His words fell on deaf ears; his recommendation was vetoed in London and the Hague, the home offices of the group.[216]

That December, Sir John Cadman of the British-owned Anglo-Persian Oil Company (a company that was in part British government owned; it was the predecessor of British Petroleum) was visiting the United States; on the twenty-third of the month Cadman was in Washington and dropped by at the State Department. F. M. Dearing (in the office of the assistant secretary) recorded the comments of this respected British oil executive:

> Sir John said he had been tremendously shocked and surprised when he came to America to discover how hostile and antagonistic the atmosphere was to the British Government in petroleum matters.
>
> Sir John referred to the Royal Dutch and accused them of all sorts of bad practices . . . He said the Royal Dutch was now ruled by a Jewish Camarilla,

and seem to think them thoroughly unprincipled. He maintained stoutly that the British Government had nothing whatsoever to do with the Company.[217]

The poison offered by Cadman did not help matters for the Royal Dutch Shell Group, which filed a few additional applications for leases on U.S. public land without pressing them, since the interpretation of the reciprocity clause remained unresolved.[218] In June 1922, with the lease applications still pending, a Senate resolution directed the Federal Trade Commission to study foreign ownership in the U.S. petroleum industry. The resolution had been provoked by the formation of the giant Shell Union Oil Corporation.[219]

As the FTC investigation went forward, Secretary of the Interior Fall (on September 12, 1922) wrote to Shell's attorney, requesting that the firm provide evidence that it was qualified under the Lands Leasing Act to hold public land. On September 19, Adrian Corbett, president of Shell Union Oil Corporation, met with Fall; Corbett asked for and received an extension of time (to March 1, 1923) for submission of the evidence on eligibility.[220] Fall told Corbett that certain parts of the British Empire denied American oil companies entry, which meant that Britain was a nonreciprocating country, and this would disqualify Shell from obtaining the lease. The secretary also said that even though the Royal Dutch Shell Group was not owned by the British government, he (Fall) believed it carried out British government policies and, thus, was controlled by the "British Government in fact but not in form."[221]

Then, in December 1922, Fall dropped a new bombshell. He decided to apply, by regulation, the reciprocity clause in the Lands Leasing Act to leases of *Indian lands.*[222] This terrified Shell officials. In March of that year, Fall had amended the regulations on the leasing of Indian lands to forbid the making or renewing of any leases to aliens, and now the Interior Department was instructing superintendents and field officials in the Indian Service not to approve the assignment of *Indian* leases to "corporations in which foreigners or non-citizens own a controlling interest in the stock of said Corporation."[223]

And if this were not bad enough for Shell interests, the Oklahoma legislature was debating a new alien land bill (the Ferrall bill) targeted specifically at foreign oil companies and particularly at the Royal Dutch Shell Group.[224] After the Ferrall bill came the Glasser one (also in Oklahoma), considered by the group's legal adviser to be even more dangerous.[225] Meanwhile, an alien land bill (aimed at resident Japanese landowners) had become law in Texas in 1921.[226] Next, on February 12, 1923, the FTC issued its report documenting the vast U.S. holdings of the group.[227] The handwriting was on the wall, and on February 21 (before Fall's March 1 deadline), the group formally withdrew its original application for the lease on the Utah land.[228] Earlier, Fall had announced that he would resign as secretary of the interior as of March 4, 1923, but just before doing so, he issued an adverse decision in the Roxana *Indian* lease case (the Roxana company—a subsidiary of the Shell Union Oil Corporation—had applied for leases on Indian land that were now denied).[229]

By mid-March 1923, the Royal Dutch Shell Group faced an unprecedented rush of truly bitter U.S. newspaper coverage. Andrews was convinced that the press was trying to make it politically impossible for Hubert Work (the newly appointed secretary of the interior) to rescind Fall's decision in the Roxana case. Temporarily, Andrews believed, the group might obtain a reversal of Fall's decisions on the Indian leases and might be able to prevent the passage of the damaging bills proposed in Oklahoma; in the long run Andrews predicted that there would be worse legislation and more punitive regulations.[230] He told his superiors in Europe that he did not think the group's property would be confiscated; however, unless the reciprocity matter was resolved—as he explained in a private letter—he believed that the company might be compelled to liquidate and withdraw from the United States. In sum, this was serious.[231]

The solutions lay, Andrews advised the parent enterprise on March 23, 1923, in pressing both the British and the Dutch governments to provide the reciprocity that the Americans desired. Andrews wrote that the British embassy had indicated to him that the remaining restrictions in the British Empire could and should be removed, while the Netherlands already claimed to be a reciprocating nation (Standard Oil of New Jersey had gotten a concession sought in the Dutch East Indies).[232] Andrews urged the home office officials of Royal Dutch Shell—Sir Henri Deterding and J. B. Aug. Kessler—to have their most able men in London and in the Hague take up the matter with the British and Dutch foreign offices and demand speedy, comprehensive action in giving public proof of reciprocity. He once again recommended that the group participate in educating Americans on the value of Shell's contribution to the American economy.[233]

On April 17, 1923, a rehearing took place on the Roxana Indian leases before Secretary of the Interior Work; and on May 16, Work revoked Fall's decision and approved the transfer of these leases to Roxana; he ruled that the Lands Leasing Act of 1920 applied only to the public domain and not to Indian lands, which the Indians owned in fee.[234]

Meanwhile, in London, Robert Waley Cohen, a talented high-level executive in the group, wrote officials at the British Board of Trade that it would be to the British advantage to remove restrictions in the Empire against foreign capital. His argument, put forth in a May 15, 1923, letter was as follows:

> So long as British Companies [and in this communication he presented the Royal Dutch Shell Group as a "British company"] are in control of large oil

> production, whether in British or foreign territories, they can quickly and secretly make such arrangements as the Government may desire for the supply of any kind of oil products in any part of the world. If, however, they are dependent upon purchases from outside foreign organisations they may have great difficulty in providing the requirements at all, and the knowledge of their purchases and of the places of delivery will be common property.[235]

The Royal Dutch Shell Group wanted the support of the British government in its expansion in the United States.

As 1923 came to an end, the Lands Leasing Act remained the law of the land. On October 23, 1923, hearings had begun before the Senate Committee on Public Lands and Surveys, and soon the American public turned its attention to the Teapot Dome Scandal.[236] The subject of foreign ownership of American oil leases, once top news, faded into the shadows as the drama of corruption in the Interior Department unfolded. Even so, the efforts of the State Department to obtain an open door for U.S. business abroad remained a high priority. By late 1923, at the same time as the Netherlands authorities were prepared to let foreign oil companies into the Dutch overseas empire, it became clear that the British government was unlikely to do so for the British Empire. The government of India, a Shell official concluded, was very stubborn.[237] At the close of 1923, although the matter had receded from the U.S. limelight, Shell Union Oil Corporation appeared ineligible to lease U.S. public land.[238]

In 1919, Royal Dutch Shell had acquired—in connection with its international expansion and in its desire for more crude oil to supply the U.S. market—Lord Cowdray's interests in the important Mexican Eagle Company.[239] Lord Cowdray, with Thomas Ryder (the former head of Mexican Eagle), organized a new firm, Amerada Petroleum Corporation (1919), which took possession of oil wells in the United States that Ryder and his associates had obtained earlier.[240] This British newcomer, Amerada, was a small player compared with the towering Royal Dutch Shell; since it had no plans to lease public land, its management did not believe that the Lands Leasing Act would matter. Yet when it appeared that the law might be extended to cover native Indian lands, Amerada's executives grew apprehensive, and early in 1923 Lord Cowdray joined the Royal Dutch Shell Group in lobbying the British government to open the doors to U.S. capital in the Empire.[241] Amerada saw itself as the "proverbial innocent bystander" in what seemed to its managers an assault on the huge Royal Dutch Shell.[242] When in May 1923 Interior Secretary Work decided that Indian leases were not subject to the 1920 act, the alarm of Amerada's management subsided; the company did, however, restructure its Texas business in response to the Texas anti-alien land law.[243]

But for the Royal Dutch Shell Group, its pressure politics in London and the Hague would continue. Andrews' comments in the spring of 1923 that unless the reciprocity issue were favorably resolved, the group might be compelled to withdraw from the United States was perhaps extreme. Six more years would pass before there was a solution to the group's American difficulties. There is no question, however, that the Lands Leasing Act of 1920 had a profound impact on Royal Dutch Shell's American business, even though the group went on enlarging its exploration on land that was not public property. In 1922, for the first time, the United States had become the foremost producing country in the Royal Dutch Shell's global business (with 38 percent of the group's output).[244] Royal Dutch Shell's position in the United States was pivotal in the group's international strategies.

In a second energy sector, in 1920 Congress passed the Federal Water Power Act, authorizing the creation of the Federal Power Commission, which would grant licenses for the building of facilities at federally controlled water power sites. These licenses were restricted to Americans: states or municipalities, U.S. citizens, associations of citizens, or corporations organized under U.S. or state laws.[245] The legislation had the older, broad formulation in relation to U.S. citizens and corporations, including nothing about the ownership of the corporation; thus it had no impact on foreign investments in the United States.[246] The insertion on licenses to "Americans only" seems to have been more pro forma than material.

If communications, transportation, and energy captured policy makers' attention, the fourth set of public policies on FDI that got special post–World War I notice related to banking. The new postwar federal and state government policies were forged to assure a sound domestic banking system and (in the case of the federal government) to encourage American business expansion abroad. Since 1864, federal law had required U.S. citizenship for directors of national banks.[247] This did not change with the Federal Reserve Act of 1913. In 1919, Congress passed the Edge Act, seeking to stimulate U.S. financing of international trade. "Edge Act banks" set up under this legislation were off-limits for foreign direct investors, since not only a majority of their directors had to be U.S. citizens, but a majority of the shares had to be owned by U.S. citizens or by companies controlled by U.S. citizens.[248]

Foreign banks that wished to do business in the United States were—as in past years—subject to regulation under federal and state laws.[249] Federal law gave no authorization for foreign banks to carry on branch banking in the United States.[250] Each state had its separate rules. New York State did not permit foreign bank branches: no foreign bank could through a branch take deposits in that state.[251] In 1920–1923, attempts to lift this long-standing restriction made no progress.[252] In New York State, however, foreign-owned trust companies could take deposits. Likewise, in New York State, no ownership restrictions existed on "international banking organizations," formed under state law. In the state of Washington, a 1919 act allowed foreign banking corporations established within the state to loan money on mortgage securities and to buy and sell exchange, coin, bullion, or securities, but they could not engage in commercial banking within the state (entries before the passage of the 1919 law could persist). An Illinois law—effective at the close of 1920—prevented foreign banks from opening branches in Illinois (it "grandfathered in" those operating prior to that time).[253] A 1920 Massachusetts law imposed new rules for rigorous annual bank examinations, which had the effect of deterring new foreign entries.[254] These statutes and other existing state laws notwithstanding, foreign banks were able to expand in the United States. Foreign banks, however, had to structure their business so as to conform with the rules in this highly regulated sector; both the government-imposed restrictions that were general to domestic and foreign participants and those that were specific to foreign investors had pronounced impact on the type, size, and, most particularly, forms of banking operations. While the new state laws tended to be *more* constraining than those of prior years, I know of no foreign bank withdrawals in this period as a result. Although the Bank of Montreal did close its Spokane, Washington, branch in 1924, I found no evidence that this was prompted by the adverse state rules.[255] The federal government's confining the use of Edge Act corporations to U.S. banks was discriminatory (yet foreign banks had the perfectly viable option of participating in similar types of organizations, incorporated in New York State). An inadvertent consequence of the development of federal and state regulations was that foreign banks could conduct business in more than one state (a privilege not available to American banks).[256] Did the rules and regulations bar new entries that might otherwise have occurred? It is hard to say; I have seen isolated evidence that this might have been the case.

Two additional categories of government policies need to be briefly covered: first, those on alien land ownership. By 1919–1923, these were all state government measures, and although they alarmed foreign direct investors and sometimes the rhetoric was anti-British, with the aid of a good local attorney they seem to have been relatively easy to circumvent. Thus, as far as I can gather, none of the multitude of alien property laws appears to have caused pullouts from FDI.[257]

Insurance was also a regulated sector, traditionally regulated by state laws. During the First World War, all foreign-owned insurance companies had to be licensed by the federal government. While foreign-owned insurance companies played a major role in the United States, no effort was made to rid Americans of dependence on foreign insurers, although there was—in connection with the promotion of shipping—an eagerness to expand the provision of American marine insurance. There was discussion about extending the federal insurance licensing rules into peacetime, but this was only talk; after the war's end (with the Knox-Porter resolution in 1921), the brief experience with federal regulation concluded.[258] Foreign firms continued to operate under state laws with no difficulty. Unlike in banking, a domestic insurance company (as well as a foreign one) could be registered to do business in many states. Although occasionally there were special provisions in state laws applying to foreign-owned companies, these were designed to assure the safety of American customers.

In short, even though foreign direct investors met few obstacles from state alien land laws and state insurance regulations, these investors in America did face public policies with important effects on their existing (and future) business operations. To summarize: the Volstead Act of 1919 (inaugurating Prohibition) was the cause of the liquidation of the sizable British brewery assets in this country. The navy's insistence resulted in the formation of Radio Corporation of America, the end to the direct role of Marconi's Wireless Telegraph Company that had held a near-monopoly position, and a national commitment to a public policy that broadcasting should be confined to Americans. The Kellogg Act of 1921 sought to use new foreign entries in cables to Americans' negotiating advantage. The Merchant Marine Act of 1920 prompted a redeployment of the Shell Company's tankers and aimed to augment American shipping (to the exclusion of foreign shipping). The Mineral Lands Leasing Law of 1920 may have scared off certain oil industry investors; it did stop the Royal Dutch Shell Group from leasing promising public oil lands (Shell was, however, able to expand its overall operations in America). The Federal Water Power Act, by contrast, had no impact on foreign stakes. The 1919 Edge Act prohibited foreign investors from taking advantage of a newly available (to American banks) form of international banking, while certain state laws closed off some potential new entries of foreign-owned banks. All the federal legislation passed in 1919 through 1921 (and the state laws in banking) targeted toward restricting foreign direct investment—the Federal Water Power Act excepted—applied to both individuals and corporations, defining "alien" status by stock ownership.[259] A number of measures aimed at using foreign business in America, with the "reciprocity clause," to assist American business abroad. The agenda was "America first." The policies were reflections of postwar nationalism.

In each of the specific sectors covered here—the Telefunken property and those of the German insurance companies aside—the foreign investors affected were America's Allies or neutrals in the First World War. Most under fire were the British, the largest foreign investors in the United States. After a period of wartime cooperation, America and Britain clashed in the immediate postwar years over many other matters, including future payments on Allied wartime debts to the U.S. government and questions linked with naval parity. The United States was the humbled Britain's sole rival on the global stage. Heightened British-American discord was a short-lived outcome of the war.[260] The U.S. legislation and policies endorsed in 1919–1921 were *not,* however, in most instances temporary. Much of their substance became embodied in U.S. public policy for decades (in certain cases to the 1990s). Enforcement ebbed and flowed, as did interpretations of the laws.

The Germans

U.S. government policies also shaped German direct investors' tentative efforts to resume or to start new business in America. During the First World War, German investments in the United States had been taken over by the Alien Property Custodian (APC), and prior to the Armistice the APC had just begun to sell these properties to Americans. In the immediate postwar period, under APC A. Mitchell Palmer and then Francis Garvan, these sales accelerated.[261] And as they did so, German business leaders regrouped and formulated their postwar strategies.

Not long after the Armistice, German-Americans (along with American-born prewar representatives of German firms) restored the contacts that had been virtually severed when the United States became a combatant. In 1919 German industrialists and bankers met with Americans, typically in Paris, Zurich, or Amsterdam, but occasionally in Germany; by 1920, more often the meetings took place in Germany.[262] In this section, I consider the general and immediate postwar issues associated with German business in America, reserving the chemical and pharmaceutical story for the next section.

As of March 4, 1919, Garvan became the Alien Property Custodian. Earlier, as head of the agency's Bureau of Investigation, he had been aggressive in the takeover and disposition of German assets; as APC he maintained a fervent belief that the Germans should never be permitted to resume their prewar importance in American industry.[263] The U.S. Congress on July 11, 1919, and June 5, 1920, amended the 1917 Trading with the Enemy Act and allowed any person other than an enemy to file claims against the APC; a number of suits were initiated.[264] Technically, America was still at war, since the U.S. Senate had refused to ratify the Treaty of Versailles.

After Harding became president in March 1921, he replaced Garvan with Thomas W. Miller. The new APC had no deep-seated antagonism toward Germans; in addition, Miller seems to have personally disliked Garvan, in part because the latter was a Wilsonian Democrat.[265] In the Treaty of Versailles (which the United States never ratified), Germany gave up possession of properties confiscated by the Allies during the war. By contrast, the American Knox-Porter resolution that formally ended U.S. participation in the war (on July 2, 1921) was vague on this subject and did not explicitly validate the wartime takeovers. In August 1922 a Mixed Claims Commission (United States and Germany) was organized to deal with American claims against Germany for U.S. assets commandeered there. The latter were far smaller than German properties in the United States.[266] During 1922, Miller began publicly to criticize the measures taken by the APC under Palmer and Garvan's leadership.[267]

In January 1923, Miller endorsed the passage of a bill to return to their owners all "alien trusts" with a value of less than $10,000. There were 30,368 such trusts held by the APC, involving some $44 million (or an average of less than $1,500 per trust). Section 5 of the Knox-Porter resolution had provided that the APC should retain the former enemy assets until the German and other former enemy governments had made satisfactory settlements on the claims of American citizens (based on U.S. business abroad). Miller responded that there would be ample property left for this purpose and that administering the thousands of small trusts was a nightmare.[268] Accordingly, on March 4, 1923, Congress passed the Winslow Act, allowing the return of property or the proceeds of the sales of such enemy property by the APC if the amounts were less than $10,000; the law excluded any moneys obtained from the sale of patents.[269] In what follows, I will omit consideration of the properties in the 30,368 trusts, for the small dollar amounts (none more than $10,000) offered little opportunity for significant German reentries. Instead, I will focus on major developments, beginning with the best known, indeed most notorious, case of the American Metal Company.

Late in 1919, the German holdings in American Metal had been sold by the APC for about $6 million to a syndicate that included the naturalized American Berthold Hochschild (the company's prewar president). In the syndicate was Carl M. Loeb, who had started his career with Metallgesellschaft and who had followed Hochschild in May 1917 as president of American Metal. Like Hochschild, Loeb was a naturalized American.[270] The Merton family of London and Frankfurt (principals in Metallgesellschaft) argued that the alleged German interest in American Metal had been confiscated illegally during wartime, since

Metallgesellschaft before the APC takeover had sold its shares to a Swiss holding company, Société Suisse pour Valeurs de Metaux, and the Swiss were not enemies. In 1921, after Harding had become U.S. president and Miller APC, and after the Knox-Porter resolution, Richard Merton traveled to Washington and donated $441,000 to the Republican National Committee. Then Merton filed a claim (on September 20, 1921) for the moneys received by the APC in the sale of the "illegally seized" assets. Three days later, Miller as APC *refunded* Merton the approximately $6 million that its office had received by selling the stock in American Metal. The latter remained American owned, with the friends of the Mertons in charge.

These transactions became public knowledge when, on October 30, 1925, a grand jury would indict Miller, the brothers Richard and Alfred Merton (Alfred was head of Metallgesellschaft), Metallgesellschaft, and Société Suisse pour Valeurs de Metaux on charges of bribery. Richard Merton agreed to testify before the grand jury. On May 7, 1926, the grand jury issued a new indictment, now excluding the Mertons, Metallgesellschaft, and the Swiss defendant. After a trial Miller, found guilty of taking a bribe from Merton, went to jail for eighteen months. (The U.S. attorney general, Harry M. Daugherty, was also said to have benefited from Merton's "gift" to the Republican National Committee, but nothing was proved.)[271] Meanwhile, American Metal under Loeb's leadership (he was president from May 1917 to June 1929) resumed its trading relations with the German Metallgesellschaft group. And, as early as 1923, Metallgesellschaft was back in the United States, with a patent-holding company, American Lurgi Corporation.[272]

The story of American Metal and the U.S. corruption case was widely publicized. Where this story differed from the experiences of other ex-German companies was the size of the sum paid to Merton for his former holdings and that American Metal was singled out in the bribery charges against APC Miller and Attorney General Daugherty.[273] Where it was not distinctive was that often the prewar German-owned properties moved into the hands of naturalized U.S. citizens of German background. This was true, for example, of another important once German-owned metal trading company, L. Vogelstein & Co. Ludwig Vogelstein, a naturalized American, had also joined in the Hochschild syndicate that had bought American Metal, and then Vogelstein merged his company into the now "domestic" American Metal.[274]

The same pattern was there with certain key German wool and worsted enterprises. Naturalized German-Americans continued the once nonresident German-owned businesses. When, for example, the large Botany Worsted Mills was advertised (on December 2, 1918) as for sale by the APC, the sale was postponed to await the outcome of litigation initiated by Max Wilhelm Stoehr, a naturalized American citizen and the son of Eduard Stoehr of Leipzig, Germany, head of the former parent company, Stoehr & Co.[275] Max Stoehr maintained that a New York corporation, in which he was a shareholder, had acquired the German parent's shares in Botany Worsted Company; accordingly, the APC's sequestration of the formerly German-owned shares was illegal. In February 1921, the U.S. Supreme Court ruled against Max Stoehr, describing the New York corporation's acquisition as "a mere cover to avoid the inconveniences of a state of war."[276] This decision came before Merton had been rewarded in his quest.

Max Stoehr persisted, trying a slightly different legal tactic. In January 1923, Judge Learned Hand of the Southern District Court of New York refused to dismiss Stoehr's new suit, stating, "I take it that the United States was not looking for plunder, but to prevent enemies from owning property within its borders."[277] Next a lower court ruled against Stoehr; the circuit court, in December 1923, however, disagreed, accepting that the intent of the father, Eduard Stoehr, had been to transfer the American side of the business to his son Max. This court decided that the APC had had no authority to seize the shares that were really (by intention) those of the American Max Stoehr.[278] The government did not appeal; the political climate by 1923 had changed. In 1924, Botany Consolidated Mills, Inc., was organized under Delaware law. It took over the business and property of the Botany Worsted Mills of Passaic, New Jersey, and of the Garfield Worsted Mills of Garfield, New Jersey (another prewar German-controlled business). The president of the new Botany Consolidated Mills was Max Stoehr. His brother, Georg Stoehr, of Liepzig, was openly listed as a director.[279]

Forstmann & Huffmann, Passaic, New Jersey, had been 31 percent German owned before the war.[280] Now the German immigrant founder took full charge, and this firm persisted in the interwar years as a highly prosperous producer of woolens.[281] In still another example of "domestication" that affected two prewar German-owned woolen makers in Passaic, Danish-born Christian Bahnsen, who had emigrated first to Germany and then to the United States and had been instrumental in the founding of the Gera Mills and the New Jersey Worsted Spinning Co., headed a syndicate that acquired and then in 1922 merged the Gera Mills and New Jersey Worsted. Bahnsen, a naturalized American, became president of the resulting New Jersey Worsted Mills.[282]

So, too, the Susquehanna Silk Mills, a large multiplant silk manufacturer that was German owned before 1917, reemerged after the war with Henry Schniewind, Jr., the American son of the former German owners, as the new president. On February 14, 1919, Henry Schniewind, Jr. purchased from the APC the property once held by the German family firm of H. E. Schniewind, Elberfeld.[283] The only case where there was not domestication of the prewar German-owned textile plants in America was that of the Passaic Worsted Company. In this exceptional situation, control passed to the Gaunt interests in England.[284]

German immigrant Frederick August Otto Schwarz had opened the first F. A. O. Schwarz store in Baltimore in 1862. The business remained in the family and, in 1917, had been 25 percent nonresident German owned. Members of the American side of the family bought the German stake; the toy store thus became fully American and stayed in the family (until 1963).[285]

In 1919 the American-owned American Bosch Magneto Corporation was organized to take over the manufacturing and distribution business of the Bosch Magneto Company, the formerly German-owned and German-controlled enterprise that had been seized by the APC. Two years later, Robert Bosch AG, Stuttgart, founded the Robert Bosch Magneto Company, Inc., a sales company to promote German imports. At once, there were suits and countersuits to determine which of the two enterprises in the United States had rights to the Bosch name; the sale of the Bosch company by the APC was criticized by Republicans as part of the general attack on Miller's predecessors; the litigation was not resolved until 1929–1930.[286]

In electrical equipment and supplies, the American companies General Electric (GE) and Westinghouse had dominated the prewar domestic market, although the principal German enterprises had made short-lived and in large part unsuccessful forays into U.S. direct investments.[287] By 1920 both of the leading German electrical manufacturers, Allgemeine Elektrizitäts-Gesellschaft (AEG) and Siemens, had individuals in the United States, carefully scrutinizing "every action taken by GE and Westinghouse." Siemens' man in this country was Karl G. Frank, the firm's prewar representative.[288] Frank, a naturalized U.S. citizen, had stayed in America during the war period; 1919–1920 found him reporting back to his former (and now present) German superiors.[289]

When Frank wrote to Carl Friedrich von Siemens, on June 25, 1920, that Gerald Swope, head of International General Electric Company (and in 1922 to become president of IGEC's parent, General Electric), wanted to discuss with von Siemens the "reconstruction of the prewar [light] bulb cartel [and a] general understanding with AEG and Siemens, including the 'exchange of all patents and experience of a scientific and technical nature, allocation of the world market, etc.,'" von Siemens endorsed "an understanding" rather than "open competition," if the Germans were given a satisfactory share of world markets.[290] In 1921 Siemens desired to resume exports to the United States. After talking with Swope, Frank wrote von Siemens that GE had no objection "as long as Siemens respected GE's price level."[291]

That year, European lamp manufacturers (including Osram GmbH, controlled by Siemens and AEG, as well as seven other lamp makers) organized a price cartel; the European affiliates of International General Electric Company participated.[292] In January 1922, GE and AEG revived their 1903 accord on the exchange of patents and the allocation of markets.[293] In 1924 Siemens-Schuckertwerke GmbH would make a similar pact with Westinghouse.[294] Although the 1921 lamp arrangements collapsed in 1924, they were at once replaced by the so-called Phoebus Agreement that (as Harm Schröter has put it) created for "the world light bulb industry" an "efficient" cartel.[295]

Data in the Siemens Archives show that at the same time as these cartel arrangements were being negotiated, there was a restoration on a very modest basis of a Siemens presence in America. In September 1919, Frank visited Germany, explaining to Siemens officials what had occurred during the war and thereafter: Frank had been appointed the liquidator of the tiny Siemens prewar office in the United States. In May 1919, he had personally hired three of the four members of the latter's office staff, paying them from his own companies' accounts (Frank had formed the American Precision Works and the Techno-Service Corporation). As of May 1, 1919, no Siemens office existed in the United States, only Frank's own corporations, which, as he told the Germans, had nothing but an American character.[296] In September 1919, Frank organized the Concord Finance Corporation (authorized capital $1 million) as a holding company for his Techno-Service Corporation. Concord Finance Corporation was to promote American-German economic relations.[297] In October 1919, Siemens & Halske and Siemens-Schuckertwerke formally engaged Frank's services for 1920–1922, as Siemens' U.S. representative.[298]

When in 1922 GE and AEG revived their postwar associations (see previous discussion), Frank kept Siemens current. As early as 1920, he had advocated a Siemens-Westinghouse pact.[299] In Germany, in 1920, Siemens and Hugo Stinnes joined in a cooperative venture—the Siemens-Rheinelbe-Schuckert-Union, a vertical combination that did everything from mine coal to make electric lightbulbs.[300] Like the Siemens group, Hugo Stinnes had an interest in American business.[301] In 1921, Frank suggested that Carl von Siemens, Hugo Stinnes, or Otto Henrich (managing director of Siemens) should become shareholders in a new American sales company to encourage German trade with the United States.[302] With this goal, Frank formed the Adlanco Industrial Products Corporation, which began business in October (but was considered operative as of May 1921). This sales company, majority owned by Siemens and Stinnes interests, served its German parent, in both electrical and steel products.[303] Adlanco was not profitable.[304] As German hyperinflation occurred, German exports were not competitive.

Adlanco's activities were sharply curtailed in 1923; Frank resigned as its managing director to concentrate on being the Siemens and Stinnes representative in the United States for information and negotiations (rather than sales).[305] Nonetheless, in the years 1921–1923 there were small German investments in the new sales company (Adlanco), and Frank had been reinstated in his role as the Siemens (and also as the Stinnes) man in the United States.[306]

Stinnes was not alone among the leaders in the German steel industry who desired to do business in America. Krupp managers in 1920 made similar overtures, through different channels. In 1920, Krupp men in Germany were discussing with Lieutenant Colonel Edward Davis, the American military observer in Berlin, plans to sell Krupp "secrets" to Americans. As Davis reported, "On account of the Peace Treaty and the decline of Germany as a military power, Krupps believe that they must go abroad to seek a field for the exercise of their mechanical skill and organizing ability and for the perpetuation of their many important secret processes."[307] The Krupps proposed to "transfer their technical engineering staff to some great manufacturing plant in the United States, on a private commercial basis to be arranged by them." Davis saw "enormous advantage to the United States should such a plan materialize."[308]

In October 1920, Krupp offered—for $2.75 million—to sell to the U.S. military plans for a long-range gun.[309] Neither this sale nor any other suggestion from Krupp came to fruition even though negotiations continued into 1922.[310] That year, Hans Tauscher, who had before U.S. entry into the war lived in the United States and had represented Krupp, returned to America, seeking, with no success, to sell Krupp output and secrets to the U.S. military.[311]

The Treaty of Versailles prohibited German production of military aircraft. The Aeronautical Commission of the peace conference concluded that civilian airplanes were easily convertible to war purposes and, thus, initially forbade their development within Germany. To evade the sanctions, German aircraft manufacture started up in factories abroad.[312] The Fokker firm went to the Netherlands. Anthony Fokker was Dutch by origin and had produced planes in Germany during the war years.[313] The U.S. Army had tested some captured German-built Fokker aircraft and later purchased several of Fokker's Dutch-made planes. The army urged Fokker to manufacture in America, which he started to do in 1924.[314]

According to Cleona Lewis, in 1923 Germans "joined with" Americans in the Goodyear-Zeppelin Corporation.[315] This company would, in time, introduce the Goodyear blimp. Before World War I, Count Ferdinand von Zeppelin had built the first rigid airship, an all-metal plane.[316] In 1922, the Allies ordered the Zeppelin firm to dismantle its German plant.[317] The newly formed Goodyear-Zeppelin Corporation filled the gap, using German technology and employing former Zeppelin personnel, with its existence sponsored by the U.S. Navy Bureau of Aeronautics.[318] The U.S. government had apparently obtained a Zeppelin as part of German reparations and wanted such products made in America.[319] Goodyear controlled the Goodyear-Zeppelin Corporation.[320]

The Carl Zeiss Works at Jena, in Germany, which had until 1915 interests in Bausch & Lomb (an American company), in 1920 set up its own unincorporated sales outlet in New York to handle German exports of its specialized optical glass. Its goal was to compete with the American "renegade," Bausch & Lomb.[321] The competition did not last; in 1921, Zeiss and Bausch & Lomb signed a technical exchange agreement.[322]

In the regulated American banking sector, German bankers also made plans to resume U.S. business connections. None of the new rules provided earlier in this chapter, however, seem to have had major effect on the form (or substance) of German involvements, since much of the revival was informal. Thus, the prewar family business ties of M. M. Warburg & Co., Hamburg, with Kuhn, Loeb & Co. recommenced quite naturally after the war was over. Max M. Warburg, the senior partner of M. M. Warburg & Co., went to Switzerland in July and August 1919 to discuss with Swiss bankers the possibilities of creating an international acceptance bank to help in the financing of postwar German trade.[323] Max's brother Paul M. Warburg joined them in Saint Moritz in August.[324] Before he served on the Federal Reserve Board (1914–1918), Paul Warburg had been a partner of Kuhn, Loeb & Co. as well as in M. M. Warburg & Co. After the war and after he left the Federal Reserve, Paul Warburg did not rejoin either banking house as a partner or with any formal arrangement; nonetheless, he had brothers who were partners at the American and German firms (gone were the German-U.S. interlocking partnerships, but family associations remained). In 1921 Paul Warburg formed (in New York) the International Acceptance Bank (IAB). Although M. M. Warburg & Co., Hamburg, was not a founding shareholder in IAB, Max Warburg was included in the planning.[325] IAB would be able to benefit from M. M. Warburg & Co.'s well-established prewar network of European correspondent banks.[326]

Another firm with close U.S.-German affiliations was Speyer & Co., New York. Before America had become a belligerent, Speyer & Co., New York, had had interlocking partnerships with the long-established Frankfurt firm Lazard Speyer-Ellissen. Soon after the Armistice, James

Speyer in New York was again in touch with his brother-in-law Eduard Beit von Speyer, who headed the Frankfurt bank. Beit von Speyer would, in time, once more be a partner in Speyer & Co., New York. Like the Warburgs, the Speyers were in an excellent position to take part in postwar U.S.-German finance.[327] Moreover, in addition to his brother-in-law, James Speyer had other important German family, for his cousin Anna Speyer was married to the Deutsche Bank's Arthur von Gwinner.[328] These personal ties are essential to an understanding of the international business relationships of the 1920s.

Less is known about the New York house Knauth, Nachod & Kuhne, which had prewar German connections.[329] By 1923, however, when it was bankrupt, a large number of its creditors were described as "European banking and commercial houses, mostly Germans."[330] The big Berlin banks sent men to New York as representatives. After Congress formally ended the war (July 2, 1921), the Disconto Gesellschaft, Berlin, appointed Adolf Koehn as its New York "representative."[331] When Knauth, Nachod & Kuhne was in difficulty, Koehn joined its Creditors' Committee.[332] Hugo Schmidt, who had replaced Edward Adams in 1914 as the Deutsche Bank's man in New York, was considered a "dangerous enemy alien" and spent 1917–1918 in a prison camp, near Fort Ogelthorpe, Georgia. On his release from jail after the Armistice, he resumed his position as the Deutsche Bank man in New York, and in time he became an American citizen.[333]

In shipping the Germans sought to restore their prewar connections. Prior to the war, Germany had been a major power in shipping, with "shipping tonnage" more than double that of the United States.[334] This was now no longer true; the war losses took their toll. On March 17, 1919, before the Treaty of Versailles had been signed (June 28, 1919), the victors agreed that the United States could retain the German ships seized after U.S. entry into the war, ships which the United States Shipping Board (USSB) had put into commercial trade.[335] The USSB, fearful over British hegemony, paradoxically was prepared to assist the postwar revival of German shipping. The U.S. government had been hesitant to deal with International Mercantile Marine Company, concerned lest it open the way to continued British superiority. W. Averell Harriman carried no such stigma.

Harriman (the son of the railroad leader E. H. Harriman) had during the war started building ships and now intended to enter shipping for the first time.[336] In April 1920, Harriman visited Europe for talks with officials of the Hamburg-American Line (Hapag). The banker Max Warburg, in Hamburg, facilitated the discussions out of which came a preliminary alliance between Harriman and Hapag announced on June 6, 1920. Some articulated public dismay in the United States about dealings with the "enemy" notwithstanding, encouraged by the USSB, Harriman had in August 1920 finalized an agreement with Hapag.[337] That same year, the second of the giant German shipping lines, the North German Lloyd Line of Bremen, initialed a cooperative arrangement with the United States Mail Steamship Company (USMSC; soon—in 1921—to be taken over by the United States Lines), an accord that involved the USMSC's leasing from the USSB eleven former German passenger vessels.[338] In 1923, Harriman's United American Lines entered into a new joint activity with Hapag to provide regular service from Europe to the American Pacific Coast via the Panama Canal.[339] All of these arrangements cleared the path for a revival of German shipping.[340] The door was also opened for Harriman to participate in German finance.

Thus, by 1923, some prewar German enterprises were slowly reestablishing American alliances. Others would never return—nor provide a basis for a successful postwar U.S. business. The formerly prosperous chocolate company Stollwerck, for example, was sold to Americans (and did badly under domestic ownership).[341] Likewise, the important German firm Orenstein & Koppel was never able to reinstate its operations—but not for lack of trying.[342] In broadcasting (and telecommunications in general), the Americanization process that had pushed out British Marconi left no room for the return of the Germans, that is, Telefunken. In a few situations, that of Krupp for one, ambitious German postwar U.S. plans went unrealized.

In many instances, what happened was that American citizens, who were members of the families of prior German owners (or had been longtime employees of formerly German-owned firms) domesticated the once nonresident FDI. In the cases of American Metal, Botany Worsted, and Susquehanna Silk Mills, for example, nonresident German direct investments in the operating U.S. firm would not be restored. Yet in general, when Americans of German heritage retained control, prewar business contacts were revived (even when FDI was absent). And on some occasions, the initial forays of 1919–1923 heralded future significant German direct investments. What is basic is that prior to the close of 1923, already small stakes existed by German-headquartered firms in America (in American Lurgi, in Robert Bosch, in Adlanco, possibly in Goodyear-Zeppelin, and certainly in the unincorporated Carl Zeiss sales outlet). The Disconto-Gesellschaft and the Deutsche Bank had men in New York. The principal German shipping companies were back in service. In the electrical industry, cartel relations were being reinstated and new ones introduced. A far more impressive German reentry would come about in 1924–1929, with new firms joining the prewar participants.

The Chemical and Pharmaceutical Industries, 1919–1923

Before the First World War the chemical industry in the United States had drawn in sizable, European, particularly German, direct investments; the foreign-owned businesses had often served to encourage large U.S. imports of both intermediates and final products; in wartime, the German direct investments had been acquired by the Alien Property Custodian. The APC takeovers paved the way for a formidable rise in U.S. domestic production that substituted for the German imports. A new patent-intensive, science-based American industry emerged. In the process of acquiring German properties, the APC had taken over roughly 6,000 German patents, a large percentage of which were in chemical products and processes. Under the authority of the Trading with the Enemy Act, the Federal Trade Commission had licensed American companies to manufacture under these patents.[343]

Before the war, the American company Du Pont had been a maker of explosives—with agreements with the Anglo-German Nobel group. During the war, Du Pont had maintained its ties with the British Nobels, and in January 1920 Du Pont made a new patents and process accord with the latter that divided world markets and effectively precluded the British Nobel firm from undertaking U.S. direct investments.[344] Possibly at this time, the latter may have purchased (through a nominee) a small amount of Du Pont stock.[345]

Far more important, during wartime Du Pont had diversified, emerging in 1918–1919 as a large multiproduct chemical enterprise.[346] It innovated and, in addition, sought technology from others. In synthetic ammonia and dyestuffs, new fields for Du Pont, the American enterprise had looked abroad for ideas. It held off on synthetic ammonia, but in 1917 Du Pont had begun to manufacture dyestuffs, under a license from the British company Levinstein Ltd.[347] In 1918 Du Pont filed a suit against Edgar Levinstein, who largely owned and ran I. Levinstein & Co., Inc., its British namesake's U.S. sales outlet.[348] As Du Pont sought to develop its own dye-making and marketing competence, its friction with Edgar Levinstein persisted into 1919–1920. In the United Kingdom, the British Dyestuffs Corporation Ltd. (established in 1919) took shape as a holding company for Levinstein Ltd. and its competitor, British Dyes Ltd.[349] Du Pont had hired men from the prewar U.S. Badische organization (in particular Morris Poucher); had obtained rights to various dye-making processes from British, French, and Italian companies (including British Dyes Ltd.); had in May 1918 bought the Lodi, New Jersey, plant of the United Piece Dye Works (an enterprise that in times past had attracted French direct investments); and had licenses—under the Trading with the Enemy Act—to use certain sequestered German patents.[350] Despite all this, Du Pont still faced severe technical difficulties in preparing dyes.[351] Du Pont had put in a losing bid for the German Bayer business in America. Instead, the APC had sold the Bayer assets to Sterling Products.[352]

Meanwhile, in May 1917, the National Aniline & Chemical Company (NACC) had been formed by a group that included the American-born individuals—William J. Matheson and Robert Shaw—who in the prewar years had represented the German Cassella Company. Matheson would become president of the NACC. In October 1917, Matheson had attempted to transfer Cassella's German patents to NACC, but the APC had refused to permit that to occur and made the patents available to all American companies, under license from the Federal Trade Commission.[353]

When Sterling Products had acquired the Bayer facilities as well as some 1,200 Bayer patents in December 1918, anxiety grew among other U.S. enterprises, especially Du Pont and NACC: Would all the valuable German chemical patents and trademarks in the future be transferred into private hands? Would existing American companies be excluded from using them? Early in 1919, Francis Garvan of the Alien Property Custodian's office (as of March 4 the APC) suggested the formation of a nonprofit corporation, The Chemical Foundation, Inc., to take possession of the remaining German patents. It was organized on February 16, 1919, and owned by all the major U.S. chemical companies. Du Pont played a leading role in advising Garvan. By executive order (February 26, 1919), President Wilson authorized the sale to The Chemical Foundation by APC of its holdings of the confiscated German patents and trademarks (since the Bayer properties had already been sold, Bayer trademarks and patents were not part of what The Chemical Foundation purchased). The Chemical Foundation would make available, under license, the German patents. It received some 4,500 patents.

From the start Garvan was president of The Chemical Foundation, which immediately licensed U.S. firms (including Du Pont). Garvan declared that the import of any chemicals for which American manufacturing licenses had been granted had to be halted and the importer subjected to prosecution for patent infringement. The Chemical Foundation would eliminate the possibility that American companies—especially those in the new domestic dyestuffs industry—would be excluded (because of the monopoly granted to patent holders) from benefiting from the German patents. Its certificate of incorporation indicated that only American firms could be licensed—natural persons, copartnerships all of the partners being U.S. citizens, and corporations, where at least 75 percent of the capital stock was American owned.[354]

Coincidentally, in Paris in 1919 before and after the signing of the Treaty of Versailles discussions on that treaty were occurring.[355] As these went forward, American, British, and French businessmen sought news on Germany's wartime research accomplishments. Since Germany was the Mecca for advanced chemical processes—particularly in dyes and nitrates—Americans (and their Allies) were eager to catch up on what had happened during the war period, when contacts had been virtually nil. What they learned was that executives of the German chemical companies anticipated a complete resumption of the status quo ante bellum—that is, of German global hegemony in this industry.[356]

In the United States, the extensive prewar German business activity in this industry had been disrupted; not only had the properties been sequestered, but Germans had been interned. Seven top Bayer executives had been arrested for espionage in 1918, including Bayer's former U.S. president, Emanuel von Salis, corporate vice-president Hermann C. A. Seebohm (who was the brother-in-law of German Bayer leader Carl Duisberg), Dr. Christian Stamm, Dr. Rudolf Hütz, Dr. Arthur Mothwurf, and Dr. R. J. Pabst. Von Salis and soon Stamm had been quickly released from jail, since someone had to run the Rensselaer plant, as the Bayer company in America produced for the American war effort—under the authority of the Alien Property Custodian. The other men were interned for the duration of the conflict.[357] When Sterling Products had purchased the Bayer properties, the American company had immediately sold the dyestuff part of the business to the Grasselli Chemical Company. Now, in the aftermath of the war, both Sterling Products and Grasselli Chemical needed German know-how and personnel so as to utilize successfully their new acquisitions. Thus, in May 1919, Sterling Products had sent an emissary to Holland to meet with Carl Duisberg of the German Bayer.[358] In August, Grasselli Chemical was also in contact with German businessmen.[359] In October, Sterling Products' chief executive, American-born William E. Weiss, met with Duisberg in Baden-Baden, Germany.[360] Hütz, once out of jail, went to work for Grasselli Chemical.[361] The ownership of Bayer assets had moved to American hands—but key personnel remained German, as did the technology.

The winners of the war worried lest the German chemical industry recapture its former supremacy. There were ominous signs that this might happen. The victors, who sought large reparations from Germany, believed a revitalized chemical industry could help pay that levy. In the Treaty of Versailles, signed on June 28, 1919, Annex VI to Part 8 covered "every kind of dyestuff and chemical drug" but left the particulars on the dyestuff reparations to be arranged.[362]

For the infant American dyestuffs industry, especially Du Pont, any talk of resumption of German dyestuff exports to the United States was terrifying. A flood of imported reparation dyes could easily wipe out the fledgling U.S. industry. In October 1919, the Textile Alliance obtained from the U.S. War Trade Board the exclusive right to import into America reparation dyes.[363] Since Du Pont and other new U.S. dyestuffs makers continued to have technical problems, many U.S. textile plants wanted to purchase the superior imported German dyes.[364] Yet the president of the Textile Alliance was Garvan's friend.[365] Morris Poucher (once with the prewar Badische group but now a loyal Du Pont employee) had become a director of the Textile Alliance. As a later biographical sketch put it, Poucher was active in seeing to it that American textile manufacturers got only those German dyes "not produced in this country."[366] Most significant, hovering over all the transactions was Garvan's newly formed Chemical Foundation, poised to sue if any dyes covered by its (once German) patents were imported without its permission.[367]

As German chemical company managers prepared to resurrect their prewar preeminence in the U.S. dyestuffs industry, Charles Meade of Du Pont was in Europe, lecturing the Germans on how much had changed. On November 29, 1919, Meade wrote home from Paris that he had spent "the last two months making it clear to the Germans that the U.S. market is not free for them to use as they will."[368] Meade informed the German chemical makers about the sale of their patents to The Chemical Foundation, which (as he reported home) the Germans found "a very startling thing . . . and this evidence of America's power has been a great factor in making it possible to deal with them."[369]

And, make no mistake, Meade desired "to deal with them." Just as Sterling Products and Grasselli Chemical had required help from Germany, Du Pont also wanted and needed it. Meade was in Europe that fall of 1919 to obtain German cooperation in the production of nitrates of ammonia (with the new Haber-Bosch process) and dyestuffs in the United States. In both product groups, U.S. (and also British, Belgian, and French) chemical enterprises desired German aid while at the same time dreading a rebuilt German industry. International conversations on ammonia and dyestuffs became intertwined and linked with a possible resumption of German direct investments in the United States.

In November 1919, Du Pont executives met in Zurich with men from the German Badische, the British Brunner, Mond, and the Belgian Solvay & Cie., negotiating arrangements on postwar exchanges of technology in nitrates of ammonia. Early in 1920, Carl Bosch (of Badische) was set to cross the Atlantic for further discussions, but he failed to get a U.S. visa.[370] Bosch did, however, sign a draft contract with Du Pont, dated February 23, 1920, for a Badische–Du Pont joint venture in manufacturing in the United States, a plant that would employ the Haber-

Bosch process. The contract was never finalized—and the joint venture never came about.[371]

Meanwhile, in 1919–1920, as Du Pont and German Badische executives talked, businessmen at Brunner, Mond and Solvay & Cie. were uneasy. They realized that Du Pont was becoming a strong diversified enterprise. At the same time, Orlando Weber, the new president of National Aniline & Chemical Company (NACC), was putting together another U.S. chemical giant, comprising NACC, as well as the U.S. affiliate of Brunner, Mond and Solvay & Cie.—Solvay Process Company (SPC)—and Solvay & Cie.'s U.S. affiliate Semet-Solvay. NACC, like Du Pont, had become a key player in the infant U.S. dyestuffs industry. Even though the British and Belgian firms held a majority of the stock in SPC, and Solvay had an interest in Semet-Solvay, both Brunner, Mond and Solvay & Cie. recognized they would have no say in Weber's proposed large multiproduct chemical enterprise that would soon be competing with Du Pont.[372] Atmospheric Nitrogen Corporation (ANC), in Syracuse, New York, was building a synthetic ammonia plant; and ANC was to be absorbed in Weber's new big business.[373] Brunner, Mond and Solvay & Cie., like Du Pont, were deep in negotiations with Badische over nitrates of ammonia. It was all awkward, tangled, and somewhat incestuous.[374]

Early in 1920, Du Pont and the Germans began to part ways. The curtailing of reparation dye imports into America was influenced by Du Pont (through Poucher and Garvan), and the Germans were furious. Bosch threatened a Du Pont manager (toward the end of January 1920) that "he [Bosch] would at once break off all negotiations with us [Du Pont]" on the matter of the Haber-Bosch process, "if we [Du Pont] have anything to do with the difficulties raised against the German dyes in America."[375] The Textile Alliance was importing only those German dyes not made in America, thus supporting the new U.S. industry.[376]

In April 1920, Weiss of Sterling Products was back in Germany, renewing his conversations with Duisberg at the Bayer Company; at that time, Duisberg told him of arrangements made between Grasselli Chemical and the German Bayer.[377] After lengthy deliberations, on October 28, 1920, Sterling Products and the German Bayer agreed to a division of profits in the *Latin American* aspirin trade; the accord was limited and contained nothing on U.S. domestic business, but U.S.-German collaboration had begun.[378]

In June 1920, American-born Herman Metz (long identified with the German Hoechst in the United States) and several men employed by Kuttroff, Pickhardt & Co. (for years the Badische representative in America) were in Germany, where they told Bosch that Poucher (who before the war had been a vice-president of the U.S. Badische affiliate and who had been close to the Kuttroff and Pickhardt families for about three decades) was—in his new position at Du Pont—actively thwarting the restoration of German business in America. Based on their reports, Bosch assumed Poucher had been personally responsible for his (Bosch's) failure to obtain a U.S. visa in February 1920.[379]

During the meetings in Zurich back in November 1919, Du Pont executives had invited the Badische company to work with them in the United States in the ammonia project and also in dyestuffs. At that time Poucher had told the German Badische managers that Du Pont had invested "millions of dollars" in dyestuff manufacture (since no German dyes had been available during the war); Du Pont had no intention of abandoning this investment. By June 1920, Eysten Berg of Du Pont was informing the German Badische that an association in dyestuffs and ammonia remained possible, but if the Germans did not wish it, Du Pont would proceed alone—in both activities.[380] Although the Germans were very agreeable to a joint venture in ammonia in America, they did not want Du Pont in the sector where they held an immense lead and foresaw a major postwar role, that is, in dyestuffs. According to Berg, because of Du Pont's "dyestuff policy," the plans for the joint venture in ammonia fell into oblivion.[381]

In the summer and fall of 1920, Du Pont sought to learn German dyestuff methods without the cooperation of German companies. When Du Pont began to hire German chemists, Bosch was outraged, accusing Du Pont of "stealing" German employees. Bosch warned that as soon as peace had been officially restored between the United States and Germany, Badische and Bayer would reenter America (and put Du Pont out of business).[382] In February 1921, the German press reported that four chemists, trained at Bayer & Co., Leverkusen, Germany, had—while still under contract with Bayer—agreed to join Du Pont in America and to provide Du Pont their experience and knowledge. The German Bayer Company saw this as a breach of contract, and the German police issued arrest warrants for the men. Two had already left for America, but two were arrested; the latter were eventually released and made it to Du Pont headquarters in Wilmington.[383]

Du Pont defended its hiring, considering it appropriate, since the German chemical enterprises were intending an offensive against the American dyestuff makers. Irénée du Pont—president of Du Pont—felt "many needless experiments could be avoided if there were available in this country men who had practical experience in the dye industry"—that is, the German chemists. He recognized that the German threat to reenter America was inevitable: "It is self-evident that they must endeavor to do so. On the other hand, it seems wise to me that the U.S. should have a dye industry."[384]

Congress agreed and in May 1921 passed the Emergency Tariff Act, extending the protection of domestic industry.[385] In the fall of that year, Sir William Alexander, a director of the British Dyestuffs Corporation (BDC), was in the United States, seeking to settle the litigation between Du Pont and Edgar Levinstein; Sir William noted the "futility of America and Great Britain setting out to best the Germans when the closest cooperation and harmony [between the two English-speaking companies] were absent." Du Pont and BDC reached an understanding, covering world markets; Levinstein and Read Holliday's American sales units remained, but with the U.S. tariff, their business would be minimal.[386] Even though imports of certain dyestuffs persisted, henceforth an increasing number of dyestuffs would be made in America—either by domestic companies or by foreign direct investors.

As for the ammonia process, when commodity prices fell in late 1920–1921, this matter became less urgent. Du Pont concluded that there was overcapacity in existing nitrogen fixation plants and no need for new facilities, so it was not at all dismayed at the collapse of the plans for the joint venture with the Germans in U.S. ammonia production.[387]

In December 1920, Weber had organized the holding company Allied Chemical & Dye Corporation, which acquired five large chemical producers, one of which (Solvay Process Company) had the majority of its stock held abroad and a second of which (Semet-Solvay) had some Belgian ownership. Included was the major U.S. dye maker, National Aniline & Chemical Company, which Weber had headed, and which had acquired the German prewar Cassella properties, as well as much of the latter's personnel. Weber hailed Allied Chemical as contributing to the growing dynamic, multiproduct *American* chemical industry, "free from foreign domination."[388] At origin, the Belgian Solvay & Cie. and the British Brunner, Mond and related individuals owned roughly 20 percent of Allied Chemical's shares and were represented on its board of directors by Armand Solvay, Emmanuel Janssen, and Roscoe Brunner, yet Weber scorned these men, refusing "utterly to co-operate with them in the manner of the old [pre–World War I] Solvay group." As for the Germans, Weber hoped to use German talents but had no intention of allowing German influence, much less control.[389] Finally and reluctantly, however, in August 1921, Weber did sign a "tripartite agreement," delineating the relationships between Allied's subsidiary, Solvay Process Company, Brunner, Mond, and Solvay & Cie., and eliminating competition among the three.[390] At its start, Allied Chemical's assets were $282.7 million; Du Pont's in 1920 were $253.4 million.[391]

There were numerous other participants with past or ongoing foreign associations in the vibrant postwar U.S. chemical and pharmaceutical industries. Union Carbide and Carbon Corporation had come into existence in October 1917. It had acquired Linde Air Products, which had some prewar German ownership. No foreign investment in Union Carbide, however, appeared to be present in 1919–1921. Eighty percent of the stock of Merck & Co. had been taken over by the APC, and the securities were sold to a group friendly to the naturalized American George Merck; a ten-year trustee arrangement was set up to guarantee that the enterprise remain American. After the war, there were no non-resident German interests in the U.S. Merck.[392]

American citizens had purchased the German shares in The Roessler & Hasslacher Chemical Company (R & H) in February 1917 (before the United States entered the war). The APC believed the transaction was a sham and had sequestered the "German" securities. After delivering the stock, the attorney for R & H had in May 1919 initiated a court action to enjoin the APC from selling, assigning, or voting the shares until after suits were heard to determine whether the stock should be returned to ownership of the American purchasers. For two years, the securities of R & H had lain, unendorsed, in a trust company vault. Early in September 1921, after Congress resolved to end the war with Germany, a lawyer for R & H "suggested that an effort be made to induce the Alien Property Custodian [now Thomas Miller] to reconsider the decision he [actually a predecessor] had reached [in taking over the Americans' securities in the first place] . . . with a view of obviating the necessity of trying ten actions which had been brought" to have the securities returned to the American owners. September 23, 1921, had seen the settlement of American Metal's claim. In an agreement dated October 3, 1921, "the ownership of the stock [in R & H] was admitted as claimed by the respective *Americans*" (my italics); the suits were dropped.[393]

Late in 1920, Otto Antrick of the Schering company, Berlin, traveled to the United States to find out what had happened during the war. He resumed contact with Schering & Glatz, the firm's prewar distributor. Given tariffs and the uncertain status of its patents and trademarks, Antrick decided to start Alyco Manufacturing Co., a joint venture with Schering & Glatz that would manufacture the pharmaceutical tradenamed Atophan, using the Berlin company's know-how. Manufacturing began in 1923 and went forward all during the 1920s, in Bloomfield, New Jersey. The German Schering's role was kept secret.[394]

In January 1919, the French Société Chimique des Usines du Rhône—SCUR—(as of 1928 Rhône-Poulenc) started a joint venture with Americans in Rhodia Chemical Company, which acquired a New Brunswick, New Jersey, factory, that had been owned by SCUR's prewar American representative. Rhodia Chemical was a small firm, making aromatics, medicines, and coal tar–based photographic chemicals.

A French manufacturer of cosmetics in 1922 formed an American subsidiary, Coty, Inc.[395]

Of key importance were the new U.S. activities of the leading Swiss chemical firms (Geigy, Sandoz, and Ciba). Before the First World War, these Basle-headquartered dyestuff makers had had close ties with the German producers. In 1918, the three had established a "community of interest agreement" in Switzerland.[396] In the United States, J. R. Geigy & Co. had had a joint venture (Geigy-Ter-Meer Company), which had invested in minor manufacturing in 1903; the Swiss parent had bought out the German stake, and this subsidiary had become The Geigy Company.[397] In 1919 Sandoz set up a U.S. sales unit, Sandoz Chemical Works, Inc. (earlier, in 1917, it had started to make medicinal products in America).[398] In 1920, Geigy, Sandoz, and the third Basle firm, Ciba, purchased for $2.5 million the dyestuff factories of Ault & Wiborg Company, Cincinnati (an American maker of printing ink), and in June of that year the Swiss trio had organized the Cincinnati Chemical Works, Inc., to operate these facilities.[399] In addition, on February 1, 1921, Ciba took over the U.S.-owned Aniline Dyes and Chemicals, Inc., renaming it Ciba Company, Inc.—a sales, production, and research firm.[400] Thus, by 1921, the three principal Basle dye makers—sometimes called the Basler I.G.—had separate U.S. companies, basically for sales (but with some manufacturing), and together the parent enterprises owned the Cincinnati Chemical Works, Inc., a dyestuff producer. All three Swiss companies were involved in both chemicals and pharmaceutical products in the United States. Ault & Wiborg Company obtained a pledge from them that no German money would ever be used in the Cincinnati venture; Ault & Wiborg had left this business because it lacked sufficient technical expertise in dyestuffs.[401] One additional Basle firm, Hoffmann-La Roche, deserves mention. In 1922, it had forty-seven employees in New York City: twenty-two in administration and twenty-five in production (both shared the same facilities).[402]

Some British chemical companies in the United States maintained businesses as holdovers from prewar times: United Alkali's subsidiary, North American Chemical Company, in Bay City, Michigan, and Albright & Wilson's Oldbury Electro Chemical Company at Niagara Falls. Castner-Kellner Alkali Company Ltd. (as of 1920 controlled by Brunner, Mond) probably retained a small minority stake in Mathieson Alkali Works and certainly had a more sizable minority one (a 27 percent interest) in the Niagara Electro Chemical Company, also at Niagara Falls.[403] The British drug company Burroughs, Wellcome & Co. continued to be active in America.[404] In short, in 1919–1921, the U.S. chemical industry was highly international.

As a response to protests from the prewar importers of German dyes (the representatives of the German chemical companies) and given the changed views of the administration in Washington toward Germany, on December 14, 1921, the U.S. State Department ended the Textile Alliance's exclusive right to import reparation dyes.[405] Most important, as an I. G. Farben official would later explain to the Reich Ministry of Economics, Herman Metz (before the war, Hoechst's "man in America") had

> staked his entire private property without being asked to and without any legal obligation—in order to buy the assets, in particular the patents belonging to the Hoeschter Farbwerke, from the American sequestrator [the APC], and after the war, in return for his expenses, placed them again at the disposal of our constituent Company. Personality alone was the decisive factor in that situation, when, according to English and American laws of war, all contractual relations with the enemy were automatically severed by entry into the war.[406]

By 1922, Kuttroff, Pickhardt & Co. (the Badische representatives) had resumed imports of German dyes, paying royalties to The Chemical Foundation for a license to do so under the former German patents held by the foundation.[407]

In September 1922, Congress enacted the Fordney-McCumber Tariff, which gave good protection to the U.S. organic chemical industry. The law introduced rates on coal tar products based on the "American selling price" (and if there was no such price, on estimated U.S. value).[408] The high duties encouraged and sheltered domestic production. Foreign chemical companies would have to manufacture in the United States if they wished to reach this large, attractive market. During 1922, the prewar U.S. representatives of the German chemical companies—particularly Metz and Adolf Kuttroff—once more formally became the designated "eyes and ears" of Hoechst and Badische, even though there was no actual equity participation in their business from the Germans. Germans and German-Americans were employed at Sterling Products and Grasselli Chemical. This was also the case at Allied Chemical's subsidiary, NACC.

In 1922, the Justice Department initiated an investigation as to whether The Chemical Foundation had bought in 1919 the APC's holdings of the seized German patents and trademarks at a ridiculously low price (the price was $250,000). When in 1921 Miller had become APC, Garvan had invited him to become a director of The Chemical Foundation, but Miller had refused, "owing to the demands on his time." In June 1922, The Chemical Foundation had filed suits against various Federal Trade Commission licensees of patent rights (these were patents licensed *before* the foundation bought the patents). In July APC Miller countered and, citing instructions from President Harding, demanded The Chemical Foundation return the German patents and trademarks *to the APC.* Garvan refused, whereupon the U.S. government sued The Chemical Foundation for the return of the patents and trademarks, challenging the legality of President Wilson's 1919 executive order that had authorized the APC to sell these intangible properties to The Chemical Foundation. In the suit, Metz testified on behalf of the U.S. government. On January 3, 1924, the court would decide in favor of the Foundation; the government appealed, and eventually (in 1926) the U.S. Supreme Court ruled unanimously in favor of the Foundation. The Germans would lose this round.[409]

But they won others. Not only did the APC Miller have none of Garvan's bitterly anti-German feelings, as noted Miller was—along with others in the Harding administration—very corrupt. What increasingly transpired (accompanied by, in at least some instances, side payments to ease the process) was not the return of the securities of prewar German companies to overseas German ownership; rather—as, for example, in the American Metal, Botany Worsted, Merck, and Roessler & Hasslacher cases given earlier—the assets often went to Americans who had been closely identified with the Germans before the war. These men, in turn, especially in the U.S. chemical industry, were comfortable in cooperating with the Germans, and through time various new arrangements evolved that became, in many instances, tantamount to the reentry of German business. The relationships with the Germans were part of a network of international alliances involving British, Belgian, French, and Swiss companies as well.

Some of the individuals who managed former German properties were sons or brothers of Germans; some were not but instead were part of a German "business family," immersed in the culture of German business. Metz (born in New York in 1867), for example, had at age fifteen joined a dyestuff-importing firm; from age seventeen on (from 1884), he was with a series of firms that acted as importers of Hoechst dyes.[410] Similarly, Adolf Kuttroff, who at age fourteen had migrated to America (in 1860), who was naturalized in 1867, and who began importing Badische dyes in 1870, was very much a part of the Badische "family."[411] Rudolf Hütz, who joined Grasselli Chemical, was "a thoroughgoing Bayer man," born in Elberfeld, Germany, in 1877, and with the Bayer organization since receiving his Ph.D. in 1901; he had come to the United States in 1909 as manager of Bayer's Boston office.[412] These men (and others like them) remained active during the 1920s. Those who were German born became naturalized U.S. citizens.

Aside from the existence of representatives and the clandestine Schering interest in Alyco, the first of the key German chemical companies' resumption of FDI in the United States did not occur until 1923. That year, Chemische Fabrik Griesheim-Elektron A.G. organized a U.S.

subsidiary, Elektron Metals Corporation, to develop its interests in magnesium; this subsidiary never got under way (its activities were suspended in 1924).[413] Also in 1923, in photographic goods, Agfa Products Inc. was set up in New York, a modest venture, basically to import German film.[414] Most momentous was Bayer's 1923 renewal of business. Carl Duisberg of the German Bayer had from 1919 been in touch with the two American owners of Bayer's prewar U.S. assets—Sterling Products and Grasselli Chemical. In 1923, the American William Weiss of Sterling Products made an agreement with the German Bayer, whereby the latter would provide Sterling Products' subsidiary, Winthrop Chemical Company, with know-how and new patents; in exchange, Bayer got a half interest in the profits of Winthrop Chemical. The German Bayer was back in business in the United States.[415]

Bayer's reentry had been preceded by a major setback. Before the United States had gone to war, the U.S. Bayer unit had sued the United Drug Company that was selling aspirins, labeled "U.D.Co." Bayer had argued that Aspirin was its trademark, which United Drug was violating. When Sterling Products acquired the Bayer assets, it continued the trademark suit against United Drug. On April 14, 1921, Judge Learned Hand declared that for consumers aspirin had become a descriptive name of the product. The judge stated that because prior to 1915, Bayer had advertised to physicians and the trade rather than to the general consuming public, the word "aspirin" for the latter was now in the public domain.[416] This defeat notwithstanding, by 1923 Bayer had returned to business in the United States, with Sterling Products offering the gateway.[417] By 1923, Bayer was also in conversations with Grasselli Chemical.[418] In 1923, with hyperinflation in Germany, one would not expect capital to be available for any German moves abroad. Yet the expansion occurred. Bayer's comeback involved no capital export; Bayer's position in America was assured by its provision of scientific and technical knowledge.

In 1923, Du Pont made an agreement with Comptoir de Textiles Artificiels of France for a joint venture (52 percent Du Pont, 48 percent Comptoir des Textiles) to make a new product, cellophane.[419] By that year, nothing had arisen from Du Pont's lengthy negotiations with the Germans. Du Pont was their adversary in the marketplace. The Germans deeply resented Du Pont, and the latter's management felt more at ease in alliances with French and British companies than with the German ones. Allied Chemical was also seeking to pursue its own independent course in the American chemical industry—despite the sizable foreign ownership, its tripartite agreement with Brunner, Mond and Solvay & Cie., and NACC's association with former German interests.

In sum, by 1923, the United States had a dynamic, diversified, yet new and highly insecure chemical industry at home. International agreements were made during 1920–1923, some reinstating—or at least based on—prewar relationships: the accords included Du Pont with the British Nobels and the British Dyestuffs Corporation; Allied Chemical with the British Brunner, Mond and the Belgian Solvay & Cie.; and Sterling Products with the German Bayer. A number of British, Swiss, Belgian, and French direct investments were present in the U.S. chemical (including the pharmaceutical) industry; and by 1923, obstacles notwithstanding, German firms had begun to return to America. Much of the FDI and the arrangements with European enterprises were what today are called "strategic alliances." In England, in November 1923, a Heads of Agreement was drawn up and initialed, providing the basis for a cooperative relationship between British Dyestuffs and the leading German dye makers. British Dyestuffs agreed to share its profits with the Germans in return for technical assistance. Even earlier, the Germans had resumed their associations with the principal French dyestuff producer.[420] By the end of 1923 the stage was set for the reopening of America to the German chemical companies.

An Interim Summing-Up, 1919–1923

After a short period, amid the postwar uncertainties, inward foreign portfolio investment had risen. The growth had been modest, following a jagged course. Capital did not flow freely. Nonetheless, lethargy and then eventual new interests meant renewed FPI involvements—basically in traded stocks and bonds. As for foreign direct investments, there were retreats and retrenchments caused by economic and political conditions. Dozens of foreign companies in the United States failed to survive the sharp 1920–1921 economic downturn. In some instances, the exits of foreign direct investors left in their wake viable domestically owned U.S. enterprises (on occasion with FPI interests remaining).

Before the war, political influences (foreign and domestic) had played a relatively minor role in shaping the overall strategies of foreign multinationals' doing business in the United States; during the war, political matters were focused on war-related preoccupations. For certain foreign multinational enterprises, in the immediate postwar years, political considerations had become uppermost; politics took precedent over economics. This was true of the adjustments required by the sizable Russian insurance companies in the United States, whose parent enterprises were expropriated. High wartime taxes were not cut back substantially, and another influential role of the state arose in relation to taxation. Double taxation caused withdrawals from U.S.

investments. Prohibition, a political measure, terminated the major British direct investments in U.S. breweries.

The U.S. federal government, in highly nationalist policies, sought to encourage U.S. business abroad and to counterbalance feared foreign domination of the U.S. economy. Steps were taken to assure that radio communications were domestic; the outcome was the conclusion to the near-monopoly position of the British-owned Marconi of America. This was an extreme case, but other U.S. measures tried to use foreign multinationals already in the United States to force open markets to American companies or, in the same spirit, gave advantages to American businesses over foreign ones (as in the Edge Act legislation). Americans remained insecure and felt a need to confront perceived foreign economic power. Thus, in cables, the policy was to pressure foreign governments to allow U.S. cable companies to have landing rights and to have offices in foreign countries. Foreign cable companies stayed on in the United States. In shipping, the United States had a long history of protection. The policies were sustained and made more adverse to foreign shippers. Yet here, too, foreign shipping persisted and would, after a brief pause, even increase in relative importance. In oil, with the anxieties over future dependency on imports, as the once rich U.S. resources seemed to dwindle, the United States wanted to encourage U.S. investments abroad; in this context, there was the use of foreign oil companies in the United States to prod foreign states into allowing U.S. companies to explore in their territories. This was done by not permitting the leasing of public land in the United States by companies from nonreciprocating countries. Another key concern was dependence on foreign finance. U.S. policies were crafted to help the country's banks become more competitive in financing international trade; it was hoped that dollar finance would substitute for sterling acceptances. Banking and insurance were regulated industries, and some of the rules and regulations specifically targeted foreign firms.

Then there were the policies and attitudes toward the German multinational enterprises; what would their future be in America? The initial hope, immediately after the Armistice, was that all the enemy investments would become American. Important steps were taken to make German technology (German patents) available to American industry. Early postwar policies sheltered the infant domestic chemical industry that had emerged during the war. The policies toward Prohibition excepted (and some might not exempt them), the U.S. public policies covered in this chapter endeavored to build a strong America. They were designed to free the nation of actual, or sensed, economic dependence; their pursuit had significant impact on specific foreign multinationals in the United States.

3.

Survival, Expansion, and New Arrivals, 1919–1923

From 1919 to 1923, a number of British, French, Dutch, Belgian, Swiss, Swedish, Italian, Canadian, and Japanese direct investors in the United States maintained and increased their American presence. In certain sectors, new firms arrived from these and several other countries. Unlike a large number of the companies surveyed in the last chapter, these investors tended to be influenced more by economic than by political considerations. Often their pattern was expansion in 1919–1920; contraction with the recession of 1921; and then sometimes (but not always, depending on how searing the experience was in 1921) a resumption of growth in 1923. I omit, herein, the developments in the oil and chemical industries covered in the prior chapter. Likewise, this chapter is not concerned (except in passing) with German investors, whose strategies were deeply affected by postwar politics and whose activities I have already documented in Chapter 2. I do, however, discuss the enlargement of all the foreign involvements in insurance, banking, and finance, taking care not to repeat what was included earlier and assuming the constraints set forth by the laws and regulations. If a foreign company was known to be controlled from the United States and that firm had, in turn, *inward* U.S. direct investments (e.g., "Canadian" firms such as International Nickel and Algoma Steel), I have in general excluded them from my coverage herein.[1]

My aim is not to chronicle all the enterprises that survived (and there were many), nor to list all the newcomers. Table 3.1 offers a tabulation of new entries in this period. I hesitated in presenting this table, for the information is flawed and incomplete; there were far more than thirty new entries into foreign direct investment (FDI).[2] The tabulation offers no sense of the size or significance of an investment. Problems notwithstanding, I found it useful as a starting point. My goal in this

Table 3.1. New entries: number of foreign direct investments in the United States (exclusive of insurance companies), 1919–1923

	Country of company							Sector					
Date	Canada	U.K.	France	Holland	Switzerland	Other Europe	Total	Manufacturing	Distribution	Oil & mining	Banking	Transportation	Misc.
1919	4	3	1	—	1	—	9	7	1	—	[illegible]	—	—
1920	—	4	3	—	2	1	10	6	3	—	—	—	1
1921	—	1	—	—	1	—	2	2	—	—	—	—	—
1922	—	1	1	—	—	—	2	1	1	—	—	—	—
1923	1	3	—	—	2	1	7	3	1	—	2	1	—
	5	12	5	0	6	2	30	19	6	0	3	1	1

Source: U.S. Department of Commerce, Bureau of Foreign and Domestic Commerce, *Foreign Investments in the United States* (Washington, D.C., 1937), 41. This table includes *only* those foreign direct investments remaining in the United States in 1934. A "new" entry was an "incorporation" or "acquisition."

chapter is to focus on those inward foreign direct investments that mattered: Was the investment prominent in a particular sector? Was it representative of a particular nationality's investments? Was the investor a technological innovator? Did the investment provide a sample of a type or form of foreign-owned business that was or became prevalent?[3] There was more FDI than has been recognized, and it was extremely uneven in national origins and sectoral characteristics.

Railroads

Although the bulk of foreign investments in American railroads continued to be portfolio ones (FPI), among the largest FDIs in the United States to survive the First World War were those of the Canadian railroads that spread over America's northern border. Canadian railroads had coped with wartime demands. If, however, they *operated* smoothly, this was not true of their financial condition, and between 1917 and 1923 in Canada, a nationalized government-owned railroad system took over much of that country's railroad network, under the name Canadian National Railway. The Canadian Pacific Railway was not included in the nationalization.[4] Both the Canadian National (based on its predecessors' operations) and the Canadian Pacific retained railroad mileage in the United States; the railway extensions were mainly "tie-ups" to terminals, ports, and other facilities in the United States.[5] In 1919–1923 (and subsequently), Canadian railroads made new investments in the United States solely for upkeep. The same was true of the only other FDI in railroads on U.S. soil—the National Railways of Mexico (a stake much smaller than that of the Canadian roads).[6] As best I can determine, the Mexican railroads had been the first *foreign government-owned* business that invested in the United States; the Canadian National was probably the second.[7]

Land and Real Estate

Foreign investment in land and real estate had, before the First World War, been in both rural and urban properties. Once nonresident foreigners owned substantial agricultural tracts in the American West and South, but by 1914 the amounts had already declined.[8] The downward trend had continued during the war, although there persisted some foreign stakes in cotton growing, cattle raising, and other farmland. British and Dutch mortgage lenders (temporarily) acquired farmlands when there were mortgage defaults.[9] Ivan Wright found it "strange" that "European investors consider the American farm mortgage a good security upon which to loan money."[10] By the time his book appeared in 1923, it was already out-of-date. With defaults (especially in 1921–1922), the security was often not the farm mortgage but the farm itself, and that was not good backing. After 1921 (and through the rest of the decade), agricultural commodity prices were depressed. No major new investments were made by foreign investors in land in rural America. It was low prices of farm products (i.e., the market), not the alien land laws (which could be relatively easily circumvented), that deterred new foreign investments.

As for urban real estate, at war's end, the most sizable overseas holdings were in New York City by the British branch of the Astor family: Waldorf Astor (the 2nd Viscount Astor) and his brother John Jacob Astor V. These were properties inherited from their father, William Waldorf Astor. As noted in Chapter 2, because of heavy taxation, the siblings sold about half of their holdings, yet they held on to Manhattan real estate valued in the early 1920s at about $20 million, thus continuing on as large foreign investors.[11] A small assortment of such foreign investments existed in New York City and other urban areas, principally Chicago, Denver, Seattle, and Spokane. There were also (temporary—as a consequence of foreclosures) holdings by foreign mortgage companies in office buildings and hotels, mainly in western cities.[12]

Primary Product Production and Purchasing

Foreign-owned companies participating in the production of U.S. farm and forest products in 1919–1923 were few, especially when measured by the size of this U.S. sector. Two prewar stakes in cotton plantations in the Mississippi Delta remained, only one of which was substantial. The first and smaller of the two, that of the Scottish firm Deltic Investment Co., Ltd., had long been and continued to be unprofitable.[13] The second set of investments was, however, important: the plantations of Fine Cotton Spinners' and Doublers' Association (FCSDA), of Manchester, England. The latter had acquired these properties in 1911 in what was then described as the "biggest sale" (some 38,000 acres) ever seen in the Yazoo Delta.

Very quickly, however, FCSDA had problems with its plantations; it discovered that the cotton produced in Mississippi was not suitable for its U.K. purposes. It decided that the crop would be sold domestically in the United States, not exported. Memphis promoter Lant K. Salsbury, who had negotiated the sale of the land to FCSDA, managed the operations for the British owners. During World War I, Salsbury had hired a prominent plant geneticist, whose efforts placed the plantations on the leading edge of research. In addition, Salsbury had installed as general manager Jesse Fox, who had run the agricultural experimental stations in Greenville, Mississippi, and was an expert on land husbandry. In 1919, the principal plantation, headquartered in Scott, Mississippi, took over an existing corporate charter, the Delta and Pine Land Company (DPLC). A second plantation of some 8,800 acres (Delta Farms, later Delta Planting) was about forty miles north of Scott, at Deeson, Mississippi. Although the corporate structure was distinct, both properties appear to have been jointly managed.

DPLC's plantation, often described as the largest in the United States, certainly the largest in Mississippi, did corporate farming. Its early years had been difficult due to floods and the boll weevil, but in 1915 profits had been forthcoming, and with good prices during the war years, the company had anticipated a promising future. When cotton prices soared in 1919, Salsbury miscalculated; he stored cotton, gambling on still higher prices, and was instead left with huge inventories when prices collapsed in 1920–1921. Thus, with no interest in using the cotton in Britain, in the early 1920s FCSDA was all set to sell; Mitsui Bussan (the Japanese trading company) and others expressed interest, yet no buyer was found; as a consequence, FCSDA stayed on as the largest corporate cotton farmer in Mississippi.[14]

Before the First World War, especially in the 1880s, British cattle companies had fenced the ranges. Many had failed in the late 1880s and 1890s; few persisted up to World War I.[15] By the early 1920s, of the numerous giant ranches, only those of the Matador Land and Cattle Company, Ltd., in Texas, and the Swan Land and Cattle Company in Wyoming had survived as foreign owned.[16] The latter had added sheep to its holdings in the early twentieth century (and with the heavy demand for wool had prospered during the war years); but its performance at the start of the 1920s had been deplorable.[17] Riverside Orange Co., Ltd., a British enterprise established in 1890, was still growing oranges in California. As for other agricultural products, existing foreign participation in production was trivial.[18]

The limited FDI in farming and stock raising was not indicative of an absence of interest by foreign investors in American crops. There were a number of international trade-related investments. Even though the United States became in the 1920s a net importer of farm produce,[19] foreign investors still desired to purchase and export from the United States certain agricultural and processed farm commodities. Thus, foreign-owned trading firms, principally Japanese, played a vital role in handling America's raw cotton exports. Two years excepted, all during the twentieth century until 1937, raw cotton was America's largest single export.[20]

British, French, Belgian/Argentine, and Japanese firms took on a significant role in U.S. wheat and flour exports. Balfour, Williamson—a

British merchant house with a lengthy U.S. history—not only was in the grain trade but also owned a flour mill in Portland, Oregon (Crown Mills).[21] Foreign-owned trading companies stationed representatives within the United States, maintaining close associations with shippers, bankers, and insurers. I will return later in this chapter to the important activities of foreign-owned export houses in the grain trade.

Foreign investors were also active in leaf tobacco and tobacco products export, although just as in grain, so in tobacco, there was little, if any, FDI in the cultivation of these crops.[22] In tobacco British cigarette companies (rather than merchants) were the major foreign-owned buyers of U.S. leaf tobacco; they had investments in purchasing and, in one case, also the manufacture of cigarettes for export. Three principal British-based enterprises were involved: Imperial Tobacco Company, Gallaher, and British American Tobacco Company (BAT). For many years, the first two had had U.S. direct investments to buy and process American leaf tobacco for export to Great Britain, where these companies manufactured cigarettes for sale in that domestic market. These investments continued.[23]

BAT was different. American Tobacco and Imperial Tobacco had in 1902 organized BAT for business outside the United States and Great Britain. From its origins, BAT was a multinational enterprise with its U.S. investments designed to supply its worldwide needs. When formed, BAT had been two-thirds owned by American Tobacco and one-third by Imperial Tobacco. It had taken over the existing international business of its two parent companies. Although headquartered in London, it was an American multinational enterprise. After a 1911 U.S. antitrust case, American Tobacco had been required to divest its shares in BAT; it distributed the securities to its own shareholders and sold some to outsiders. The most prominent American tobacco entrepreneur, James B. Duke, became chairman of the board of BAT.[24] From 1911 on, Imperial Tobacco raised its holdings in BAT stock and became the biggest single owner of BAT shares.[25] Although BAT (with its own management and London head office) remained independent of Imperial Tobacco, BAT and Imperial Tobacco were allies, and the two enterprises continued to divide markets. Not until 1972 (to comply with European Community trading rules) did the 1902 BAT "territorial agreement" with Imperial Tobacco finally end; the equity links between Imperial Tobacco and BAT persisted until March 1980, when Imperial Tobacco sold its last holdings in BAT (it had made large divestments of the company's stock in 1975 and 1979).[26]

From BAT's origin in 1902, Hugo Cunliffe-Owen (1879–1947)—the brother-in-law of H. H. Wills (W. D. and H. O. Wills Ltd. was the key predecessor company to Imperial Tobacco)—played a major role in

BAT affairs. Cunliffe-Owen became BAT's vice-chairman in 1906. In 1912, he had moved to New York to represent BAT.[27] He stayed in that city during most of the war years, developing BAT's cigarette and leaf tobacco exports to Latin America and elsewhere.[28] BAT enlarged its U.S. manufacturing in Virginia to fill export market needs (in 1916 it built a new factory in Richmond, Virginia, principally for cigarette exports to China; this export factory operated in tandem with BAT's existing ones in Petersburg, Virginia). Its Export Leaf Tobacco Co. subsidiary was headquartered in Danville, Virginia, and also had a branch in Greenville, North Carolina, for purchasing, redrying, and shipping leaf tobacco. Duke, who as chairman of BAT may have planned to reside in Britain, with the outbreak of war in 1914 had returned to the United States. Increasingly, as time went by, BAT became a British-dominated and British-run multinational enterprise.[29] Toward the beginning of 1918, Cunliffe-Owen had returned to London, and from there he took over the management of BAT's worldwide business, although Duke retained the nominal title of chairman until 1923, when both the title and the functions were assumed by Cunliffe-Owen.[30] By 1923, if not 1919, BAT could definitely be described as a British-headquartered multinational. During these years, it had maintained and expanded its prewar and wartime U.S. direct investments in leaf purchasing, processing, and cigarette manufacturing for export. It still honored its 1902 arrangements with American Tobacco and made no attempt to compete in the United States. BAT did, in 1919, launch a short-lived joint-production venture with R. J. Reynolds Tobacco Company, in a tinfoil and waxed paper firm—United States Foil Company (later in the 1920s, it apparently divested its interest in this firm).[31] In time, BAT would decide to compete in the United States and become a major British investor in this country; even though in 1923 it already had sizable U.S. interests, it was not a contender in the American domestic market. Its sales were global—outside the United States and Great Britain. Thus far its investments in the United States were to serve markets abroad.

In the timber and timber-related industry (including paper and pulp) foreign direct investors were present, with scattered miscellaneous properties. Foreign-owned stakes in timberland tended to be associated with other activities.[32] Brompton Pulp & Paper, a Canadian firm, had paper mills in New Hampshire.[33] A Norwegian enterprise (Aktieselskapet Borregaard)—through a British subsidiary, Kellner Partington Paper Pulp Company, Ltd.—controlled the Waterfall Paper Company in Maine.[34] J. & P. Coats (the Scottish thread company) provided financing for companies in Maine that supplied the Coats group with wooden spools; BAT owned a small paper company in Lee,

Massachusetts.[35] A subsidiary of the British-owned Forestal Land, Timber, and Railways Co. continued to process quebracho logs and to manufacture various tanning extracts at a plant in Brooklyn, New York.[36] Some of the same Japanese trading companies that exported grain also sold U.S. forest products in Asia; for example, Mitsubishi Shoji Kaisha's Seattle office exported from the United States lumber, logs, and other wood products.[37]

As for mining, in the early 1920s roughly 5 percent of U.S. gold output was foreign, principally British, owned.[38] The Tomboy Gold Mines, Ltd. (part of the British-French Rothschild group of companies) was, for example, a carryover from earlier times, as were most of the other investments.[39] In silver, minimal FDI existed. By the end of the First World War, the U.S. copper, lead, and zinc industry was attracting only isolated FDI. Some Canadian steel companies integrated backward into American iron ore and coal mining: the Steel Company of Canada, for example, in 1918–1919 had purchased U.S. iron ore properties in the Lake Superior region and coal fields in Pennsylvania.[40] In April 1920, the British firm Andrew Weir & Co. set up Loncala Phosphate Company, which bought some 30,000 acres of Florida land. Over the years, this land would be used more for timber than for phosphate mining. Andrew Weir (later Lord Inverforth) was heavily involved in shipping and earlier had been interested in an oil project in California that never materialized.[41] His FDI in phosphates was not alone, although the sizable prewar foreign interests in U.S. phosphate mining do not appear to have been sustained in the 1920s.[42]

The high price of potash during the war years had attracted new interest by foreign (and domestic) investors. In 1919, Consolidated Goldfields of South Africa, Ltd., headquartered in London, which already had U.S. gold mining interests, elaborated bold, far-reaching plans for investments in U.S. mineral resources, none of which came to pass (wiped away in the 1921 downturn). At the same time, despite adversity, Consolidated Goldfields of South Africa, Ltd., continued on as an important player in developing potash resources at Searles Lake, in California. Its U.S. subsidiary, American Trona Corporation, was at war's end the largest potash producer in the United States.[43]

Before the war, Germany had had a near monopoly in potash output and global sales. The postwar settlements, however, gave Alsace to France, and with that territory went seventeen valuable potash mines. The redrawing of the borders eliminated German hegemony.[44] Once the war was over, exports from Germany and from the newly French-owned mines resumed. As a consequence, U.S. potash prices plummeted. Since farmers used potash in fertilizers, they loved the lower costs, and the infant American industry got no tariff protection. With the competition from imports, many of the new American-owned potash producers—established and sheltered during the war years—went bankrupt. Of the 128 potash companies in America in 1918, by 1922 only three remained active, with American Trona by far the front-runner. Between 1919 and 1922, American Trona wrote off substantial investments and applied scientific and technical advances to reduce its costs. It became a high-technology, efficient producer of potash and also, as a by-product, borax. First in potash, the British-controlled American Trona ranked second in the U.S. borax industry.[45]

The preeminent company in borax output was another British multinational, Borax Consolidated Ltd.'s U.S. subsidiary, Pacific Coast Borax Company.[46] Interestingly, borax was sold to American consumers by the two British companies under the trade names "20-Mule Team" (Borax Consolidated) and "Three Elephant" (American Trona).[47] In 1923, potash and borax were the only American mineral resources in which the leading producers were foreign owned. America was once again becoming a major importer of potash; it was self-sufficient in borax. It exported neither mineral.[48]

Food, Beverages, Soap, and Matches

Foreign direct investment in processed foods and beverages included a highly diverse collection of companies in meat products, flour mills, candies, and tea. Morrell & Co.—a British-owned meat packer—was the sole remaining British participant in an industry that had once attracted prominent British involvements.[49] As noted, there were British stakes in flour milling, principally those of Crown Mills. The British producer of Mackintosh Toffee decided in 1922 to seek to reach U.S. consumers. John Mackintosh, the candy company's founder, had died in 1920; his firm's early twentieth-century venture in America had failed and been discontinued before the First World War. The new generation in this family firm, using modern packaging, was prepared to try once more, and in 1922 the Mackintosh firm began anew to manufacture in America to sell to Americans.[50] I find no evidence of the firm's success. Indeed, when in 1924 the British candy maker Rowntree (a future partner of Mackintosh) considered investing in the United States, its board noted that many British firms in America had lost money, probably including the Mackintosh venture.[51]

The best-known direct investment in candy in this period was not by the British (who never made any significant headway in this U.S. market for reasons that are not entirely clear) but rather by the Swiss, with the Nestlé interest in Lamont, Corliss & Co. Nestlé & Anglo-Swiss, through its Swiss investment in Peter, Caillers, Kohler had an indirect stake in making and selling Nestlé bars and other Swiss chocolates in the United States. The chocolate business of Nestlé & Anglo Swiss, which was separate from its troubled milk business, was promoted by Lamont, Corliss, an expert in the sale of branded products.[52]

Probably the most successful of the British food and beverage companies in America was Thomas J. Lipton, Inc., with its extensive U.S. domestic wholesale trade. During the war years, this firm had enlarged its U.S. sales, and in August 1919 it moved its packing plant and main office to a large eleven-story building in Hoboken, New Jersey, on the Hudson River, where, posted in giant letters, the Lipton name could be viewed by passengers of ocean liners that docked in Manhattan. Several months earlier (in January 1919), Lipton had opened a new tea-packing factory in San Francisco to handle its western distribution. Lipton Tea was the best-selling tea brand in the country. The U.S. Lipton was owned not by Lipton, Ltd. (a British company), but directly by the British company's founder, Thomas Lipton.[53] Another British firm, Tetley Tea, had a sizable American market share.[54] Salada Tea Company (founded in Toronto in 1892) also marketed in the United States.[55] In addition, three British trading companies took part through representative offices in tea distribution in the United States: Harrison & Crosfield, which in the United Kingdom in 1916 had become associated with the established tea importer Twining, became one of the largest tea importers in the United States in the interwar years. The trading firm in the Finlay group, Anglo-American Direct Tea Trading Company, in the early 1920s was in New York and poised for expansion throughout the country. A third British trader, Dodwell & Co., with offices in New York and on the West Coast, specialized in importing teas from China, Japan, and Ceylon.[56] Whereas the Twining brand became well known in the United States, typically these British traders sold to American stores that often used their own brand names.

Soap was a branded product, retailed in groceries. The British investor Lever Brothers Company had an impressive market share. The company's expansion in the United States during the First World War continued, with its Cambridge, Massachusetts, factory making laundry and toilet soaps; its sales and profits rose, only minimally affected by the 1921 downturn (see Table 3.2).[57] This manufacturing operation, begun before the turn of the century to produce behind the high U.S. tariff, was still protected from imports by that tariff. Lever's American business was managed by American-born Francis A. Countway, who had been with the U.S. company for many years. The British parent had introduced Lifebuoy as a laundry soap, but, as its chief executive and founder, William H. Lever, would write (in 1921), "The public in America have decided that Lifebuoy is a toilet soap."[58] Lever thought

Table 3.2. Lever Brothers Company sales, profits, after-tax profits, 1918–1923

Year	(A) Sales (in millions of U.S. dollars)	(B) Profits (in thousands of U.S. dollars)	(C) After-tax profits (in thousands of U.S. dollars)
1918	9.7	482	378
1919	11.0	709	534
1920	12.5	945	762
1921	12.3	1,772	460
1922	12.8	1,338	1,139
1923	14.7	1,841	1,653

Sources: Moody's 1928, 2674 (columns A and B) and data from Unilever, PLC (A and C). I am not sure why in 1921 the firm's after-tax profits were so much lower than the pretax profits.

it was "extraordinary the trade" in Lifebuoy soap that Countway had obtained.[59] In these years, Lever Brothers' main brands in America became Lifebuoy, Lux Flakes, and Rinso soap powder.[60] Countway advertised lavishly. And, in Britain, the parent company's management was in awe: Countway's advertising request was (in 1923) "getting very close to as much as the whole rest of the world added together." Yet, as Lever explained, "On the other hand, Mr. Countway gets results and meets competition without injury to the business which we must bear in mind."[61] When Lever put Ernest Walls in charge of the Lever Brothers Ltd.'s advertising *in Britain* in the summer of 1923, he sent him to America with the following instructions: "You will want . . . to get a grasp of our American advertising because I am rather ashamed that the parent company is not leading as parents ought to do, their offspring, but their offspring . . . are setting a good example to the parent."[62] It was not the first time, nor the last, that foreign directors in America learned from their subsidiaries.

Countway created a vast sales network within the United States. Until 1919, Lever Brothers had handled its marketing in New England, while the rest of the United States had been covered by an independent agent. In 1919 Countway integrated forward and opened ten sales offices throughout the country.[63] By 1923 so satisfactory was the U.S. business and its future prospects that the subsidiary acquired a second manufacturing premise, at Edgewater, New Jersey.[64] Although no market share figures are available, qualitative data make it clear that by 1923 Lever Brothers was a leading competitor in the American soap industry, probably already in the nation's top three.

In matches, a Swedish entrepreneur, and his company, became newly conspicuous. Matches in this period were an extremely important product, used in every household to light cigarettes, gas stoves, and candles. In 1917, the principal match producers in Sweden had merged to form the Swedish Match Company, with Ivar Kreuger the managing director.[65] In the 1920s Kreuger would become a high-profile businessman in America—and worldwide. He was a remarkable individual, nimble with figures, ambitious, enthusiastic, and able to instill confidence. Swedish Match Company was central to his vision. Kreuger was a match producer, but, in addition, and more significant, he was a speculator and wizard at creative finance. Whereas in tea and soap individual entrepreneurs (Thomas Lipton and William Lever) stood out, these business leaders differed in style from Kreuger. Although Kreuger was identified with a cheap everyday type of consumer good, he was much more than a match producer; his far-reaching multinational ventures spread over into the arena of international finance. In 1908, in Sweden, Kreuger had formed Kreuger & Toll (a partnership); in 1911, it had become Kreuger & Toll A/B; and in 1917, it was the financial holding company for Swedish Match Company securities. The strategies of Kreuger & Toll A/B were under Kreuger's sole command.

Late in 1919, Kreuger visited the United States to enlarge his American interests in matches and also in finance. Kreuger established a subsidiary of Kreuger & Toll A/B, called American Kreuger & Toll, which began buying into a number of American businesses, including a cigarette packaging concern and a real estate brokerage house.[66] On this 1919–1920 trip, Kreuger told his colleagues that he had secretly obtained more than one-third of the stock of Diamond Match (America's foremost company in the match industry); Kreuger claimed to have an option to purchase, before 1923, additional shares that would provide him with a majority.[67] At this time, Diamond Match was serving as Swedish Match's "representative" in the United States. Diamond Match had decided in 1919 to manufacture safety matches in America, and it anticipated that this product would be protected by a future tariff.[68] The new production and the customs duties would threaten Swedish exports to the United States; Swedish Match took steps to challenge its competitor. At the start of 1920, coincidentally with Kreuger's American trip, Swedish Match publicized the organization of its own sales subsidiary, Vulcan Match Company, to take charge of Swedish Match's exports to America.[69] Next Swedish Match announced plans to buy Minnesota Match Company, a small U.S. match manufacturer (price, $2 million).

This was bluster. The Minnesota Match purchase never occurred. Instead, in December 1920, Diamond Match and Swedish Match entered into a comprehensive division-of-markets agreement.[70] In Kreuger's scheme, Diamond Match was allocated the match markets of the United States and Canada, while Swedish Match had the rest of the world.[71] But this accord did not mean a retreat by Kreuger from direct participation in American affairs. In 1923, Kreuger established a U.S. subsidiary of the Swedish Match Company, International Match Corporation (IMCO)—a holding company with an initial capital of almost $30 million.[72] IMCO issued preferred stock and debentures in the United States to finance its international endeavors: Swedish Match Company's *Annual Report for 1923* stated that IMCO's resources were "intended for investment in North and South America and East Asia."[73] That year Kreuger was telling his colleagues that he owned a majority of the stock of Diamond Match.[74] A decade later (in 1932, after Kreuger's death), the accounting firm Price Waterhouse found no evidence that Kreuger, or any Kreuger-associated company, owned either one-third in 1920 or a majority in 1923 of Diamond Match equity.[75] Yet Kreuger behaved as though he held these securities, and, more important, IMCO became Kreuger's vehicle for raising money in the capital-rich American market—for his numerous projects in the United States and abroad.

As part of the "corporate architecture," before Kreuger had formed IMCO, he had set up the Continental Investment Corporation in Vaduz, Liechtenstein. To avoid taxes in America and Sweden, the Vaduz company was to be the repository for the joint profits of IMCO and Swedish Match. Also, some of IMCO's assets were to be held by Continental, which was, in turn, reported to have become a wholly owned subsidiary of IMCO.[76] In short, during 1919–1923, Kreuger had (1) finessed a division-of-markets agreement between Swedish Match and Diamond Match, (2) led his associates and others to believe that he owned a substantial portion of Diamond Match stock and thus presumably could dictate the policies of that company, and (3) formed two financial intermediaries in the United States—American Kreuger & Toll and IMCO—as well as a tax-haven company in Liechtenstein. His plans for America had barely begun, but already they extended far beyond the match business.

Textiles

In textiles there were a number of foreign stakes–both continuities from the past and significant new entries in manufacturing. British, French, Swiss, Belgian, and Italian firms participated. Most of the ongoing facilities had been set up or acquired originally because U.S. tariffs (which remained) had cut the possibilities of exporting to America. Foreign interests in the U.S. textile industry involved natural fibers and synthetics.

In the natural fibers, foreign investors in textiles were highly specialized producers. The nature and characteristics of these FDIs differed little from before the First World War, except (1) the German wool and woolen producers and the German silk makers were no longer present, and (2) most of the other investors had expanded in the course of the war years.[77] In thread making, the Scottish firm J. & P. Coats (operating under the Coats name in Pawtucket, Rhode Island, and with the Clark name in the Newark, New Jersey, area) built up its business after the war. In 1922, J. & P. Coats demolished its original "Mill No. 1" in Pawtucket, where Hezekiah Conant had started the business in 1868; in its place it had erected a new finishing mill. In 1919 it constructed in Pawtucket two more mills for spinning and twisting; in 1923 it added still another mill, making eight in all at this Rhode Island site. In New Jersey, where the Scottish firm's Clark subsidiary operated, in 1921 it increased its manufacturing capacity, putting up a new bleaching and dyeing plant in Bloomfield. In sum, the J. & P. Coats group expanded greatly in this period. So, too, the New England mills of the American Thread Company (the subsidiary of English Sewing Cotton) raised their capacity. Likewise, the Linen Thread Company, Ltd.—a multiplant producer—remained in business. Just as before the First World War, these British-owned enterprises led in thread making in the United States.[78]

In fine woolen worsted products, in Woonsocket, Rhode Island, the three prewar French-owned manufacturers flourished and were joined by other French-owned participants.[79] The so-called French process of production was becoming the norm in U.S. fine woolens. A newcomer in the postwar years was the Verdun Worsted Company, founded in 1920 and owned by the Lepoutre family in France; between 1920 and 1922, this company erected in Rhode Island fully integrated mills, which carried on all phases of woolen textile manufacture, including weaving; Verdun Worsted Company was the only French-owned textile maker in Woonsocket to weave cloth.[80] The second new French entry came after the March 1923 visit of Jean Prouvost of Roubaix, France, who represented the Prouvost LeFebvre interests. Jean Prouvost selected a location near Woonsocket, arranged for the formation of the Branch River Wool Combing Company, and started to erect a plant (which was completed in 1924 and in operation in 1925).[81] The third French newcomer arrived in 1924, the Masurels of Tourcoing.[82] Accordingly, by 1924, Woonsocket had six French-headquartered family firms, all of which were from the same region in northwest France near the Belgian border. They hired French-Canadian labor that had migrated to Woonsocket and were large employers in this Rhode Island textile town. In the American woolen and worsted industry (which comprised numerous producers), their share of the national market was small, but these companies were well known for their high-quality output, and in Woonsocket they stood out as key businesses.

In silk, several prewar French investments persisted: the Duplan Silk Company in Hazelton, Pennsylvania (part of the Tissages de Vizille group), and J. B. Martin, in Norwich, Connecticut (a subsidiary of J. B. Martin, Lyon).[83] In 1919, the Société Anonyme de la Schappe, a large Lyon-based enterprise, entered a joint venture in the United States with the Société Industrielle de la Schappe (of Basle) and the Société Italienne Novare. These three firms (one French, one Swiss, one Italian) formed the New England Spinning Silk Company, purchased an existing mill from the American Silk Company, Providence, Rhode Island, and also constructed a new factory.[84] Another silk firm from Lyon (Bianchini Férier) acquired a weaving mill in Port Jervis (in Orange County, New York) in 1921 and soon added a dyeing and finishing works. It had sales offices in the United States, as did other Lyon silk manufacturers.[85]

Sizable Swiss investments in the United States—begun before World War I—were in silk and embroidery. Aktiengesellschaft für Unternehmungen der Textilindustrie (AGUT) had an interest in Schwarzenbach, Huber & Co., which had a chain of silk plants in four states (New Jersey, Pennsylvania, Connecticut, and Virginia).[86] The Schweizerisch-Amerikanischen Stickerei-Industrie-Gesellschaft (SASTIG) owned the New York embroidery firm Loeb & Schoenfeld Company, the Camden Curtain and Embroidery Company in Camden, New Jersey, and the Glenham Embroidery Company in Fishkill, New York. This multiplant venture, using imported high-technology Swiss embroidery machinery, filled a very specialized U.S. market.[87]

Although the most prominent British investments in natural textile products were in thread, other British textile-related and textile investments existed. A plant of the large Bradford Dyers' Association finished textile piece goods in Bradford (Westerly), Rhode Island; by 1922, for the first time since it started operations in 1912, this venture had adequate revenues to overcome the high costs of doing business and began to show profits.[88] Smaller British manufacturers in the U.S. Northeast included J. & J. Cash (which made name tags in South Norwalk, Connecticut); Sir Titus Salt, Bart., Sons & Co., Ltd. (which produced plushes in Bridgeport, Connecticut, through Salt's Textile Company); and Winterbottom Book Cloth Company, Ltd. (which—through Interlaken Mills—manufactured book cloth in Rhode Island). In 1921, the Winterbottom Book Cloth Company, Ltd., started a second venture (also in Rhode Island), the Arkwright Finishing Mills, which made tracing cloth. Each of these British textile makers, which almost seem too incidental to document, filled a "niche" market.[89]

In sum, in the natural fiber textile and textile-related industries, foreign direct investors from Britain, France, Switzerland, and Italy (only one) participated. Several of these firms had multiplant establishments in the United States. Other than American Thread, none ranked on Alfred Chandler's lists of America's big businesses, although the British parents of some of these firms made Chandler's British big business lists. Most of the U.S. affiliates of foreign firms in natural fibers were specialty producers.[90]

In the early 1920s, the far more dynamic story of FDI in textiles was that in rayon. Before and during the war, the British-owned Courtaulds' American subsidiary (in the 1920s known as The Viscose Company and later the American Viscose Corporation) had been the sole manufacturer in the United States of artificial silk; the name "rayon" was not adopted by the industry until 1924, and then largely through the efforts of Samuel A. Salvage, president of The Viscose Company.[91]

Courtaulds' U.S. subsidiary spun rayon yarn with the viscose process, which throughout the interwar period dominated American industry. There were, however, other technologies: the nitrocellulose, the cuprammonium, and the cellulose acetate processes—and since Courtaulds' U.S. viscose patents expired in 1920, the viscose process also became available to competitors. All four methods would contribute to the rayon "gold rush" to the United States in the 1920s.[92]

This was a high-technology activity. The principal challenger to Courtaulds in America came to be the U.S. company Du Pont, which as we have seen was becoming a diversified, multiproduct concern. Du Pont lacked the technical skills to enter the rayon industry on its own. In 1918 Du Pont had purchased the United Piece Dye Works, which had put Du Pont managers in contact with Edmond Gillet and, through him, with the preeminent French rayon producer Comptoir des Textiles Artificiels (CTA). In 1920, CFA became Du Pont's partner in rayon production, owning 40 percent of the shares in the newly formed Du Pont Fibersilk Company (DPFC). This sixty-forty (U.S.-French) joint venture used French know-how. DPFC built a plant (virtually a replica of a similar facility in France) in Buffalo, New York; it made its first viscose yarn in 1921. DPFC then constructed an additional, larger factory some forty miles from Nashville, in Old Hickory, Tennessee; it, too, used the viscose process.[93]

The second postwar entry into rayon making in America was the Tubize Artificial Silk Company, formed in 1920. Its new plant was in Hopewell, Virginia. This firm had a close working relationship with the Belgian-headquartered Fabrique de Soie Artificielle de Tubize and operated under the latter's nitrocellulose patents, in exchange for which Fabrique de Soie Artificielle acquired a substantial stock interest in the American enterprise.[94] The third new arrival, in 1920, was the Industrial Fibre Corporation of America, an affiliate of the giant Italian firm Snia Viscosa. Its factory in Cleveland, Ohio, employed the viscose process.[95]

Notwithstanding these three new rivals—all involving foreign business and foreign technology—Courtaulds' The Viscose Company maintained its lead in this U.S. industry. By 1923, it had American factories at Marcus Hook, Pennsylvania (established in 1910); Roanoke, Virginia (1916); Lewistown, Pennsylvania (1920); as well as a plant at Nitro, West Virginia, to produce and process cotton linters for textile use.[96] In 1923 every rayon company in the United States included the participation of a European (British, French, Belgian, Italian) multinational enterprise. Under the aegis of these businesses from abroad, the United States had become the world's largest manufacturer of rayon.[97] Rayon, the first synthetic textile, was an American industry that foreign-based multinationals created.

Leather Goods and Leather-Related Products

In 1923, Bally in Switzerland opened a U.S. sales office in New York City for ladies', men's, and children's shoes. This would be the springboard for Bally's later (early 1930s) investment in manufacturing. As in the case of many other European manufacturers before it, the sales unit preceded the FDI in manufacturing. Bally's New York office also acted as a purchasing agent for U.S. leather and shoe "findings" for the Bally factories in Switzerland.[98] The French leather goods firm Revillon Frères set up a subsidiary in New York in the early 1920s, probably for sales.[99] One other foreign participant in the U.S. leather goods industry was the Liverpool merchant Booth & Co., which maintained its prewar leather manufacturing facilities in Philadelphia, Pennsylvania, and in Gloversville, New York.[100]

Automobiles and Automotive Equipment

By the 1920s, in automobiles and automotive equipment, the United States led the world. Before the First World War, a number of European (French, German, Italian) companies had had direct investments in America, in selling and even manufacturing cars. Aside from the sales outlet of the French car producer Renault, none of the prewar stakes survived (or was revived) in America in the immediate postwar years.[101] The French Citroen in 1923 considered but rejected the idea of building a U.S. assembly plant.[102] There was, however, one new arrival from abroad: in 1919, Rolls Royce became the first British enterprise to decide to make cars in America.

Luxury car imports into United States faced a 45 percent tariff.[103] Accordingly, Rolls Royce formed an American company, Rolls-Royce of America, Inc., to manufacture behind the tariff barrier. The financing was American, obtained before the recession of 1920–1921. The British firm received an interest in the venture in exchange for its know-how, its designs, and the use of the Rolls Royce name. Rolls-Royce of America acquired the factory of the Wire Wheel Company in Springfield, Massachusetts, and planned an output of about 380 chassis per year for a product identical with that produced in Britain. Not until January 1921 was the first American Rolls built, by which time the affiliate was facing financial woes. A profit in 1923 failed to offset the earlier losses, nor by 1923 had the numerous other administrative and technical problems of this company been solved. Nonetheless, Rolls Royces were being made in America.[104]

A much larger British interest in the U.S. automobile industry that arose in an entirely different manner provides a case where the line between FDI and FPI is muddy. Its genesis arose out of the needs of Du Pont to find financing for General Motors (GM). By the end of 1919, Du Pont had acquired a 28.7 percent holding (an investment of roughly $49 million) in GM, America's second-largest car maker (in 1919 Ford Motor Company was the industry leader).[105] Pierre du Pont had become chairman of the board of GM. In 1919, GM sold 344,000 cars and was expanding rapidly.[106] GM required for its projected growth a large commitment of capital, and the new chairman turned to his friends at British Nobels (Nobel Industries, Ltd., as of November 1920).[107]

On March 19, 1920, J. J. Raskob—a close associate of Pierre du Pont in GM and Du Pont management—had written the Du Pont Finance Committee about the car company's outlook: "Due to the investment conditions existing in the world and particularly in this country it is felt impossible to raise this new capital through the sale of debenture stock . . . We are in the fortunate position of having Nobels keenly interested in this matter. Sir Harry McGowen [of Nobel Explosives Company, Ltd.] is here now and we have discussed the matter with him." Raskob's proposal was that GM would offer added stock to existing shareholders; then William C. Durant (GM's founder) and Du Pont's share in the new offering would be sold to the Nobels, with the understanding that the British investors would hold the securities "as an investment."[108] Although the Nobels did not provide as much financing as Raskob desired, their contribution was substantial.[109] In May 1920 the British Nobels agreed to purchase 609,425 shares of GM (the book value in these shares in British Nobels' records was £3,460,899).[110]

With its investment, Nobel Industries acquired roughly 4 percent of GM stock, much less than that owned by the Du Pont Company. Sir Harry McGowan and Arthur Chamberlain (both from the British Nobel firm) joined the board of directors of GM.[111] There is, however, no evidence that the Nobel Industries directors had control over or even influence on the strategies of GM. Indeed, Alfred Sloan's *My Years with General Motors,* which chronicled important happenings at that company, never mentions McGowan or Chamberlain.[112] In 1922, Nobel Industries raised its interests in General Motors stock to 809,425 shares, with a book value of £4,099,508.[113]

Should this multimillion-dollar investment be classified as FPI or FDI? Even with the extra holdings in 1922, the Nobels' percentage of the equity fell far short of the 10 percent "cutoff" used today by the U.S. Department of Commerce to define FDI; the Nobels did not seem to have even the potential to exercise control of GM; moreover, their main reason for investing appears to have been financial—for "investment purposes." Given these circumstances, it could be argued that this was a FPI made by a multinational enterprise. Yet this interest was not arm's length; it was closely associated with Nobel Industries' American strategies; the investor did get board representation; the large size of the interest could mean possible influence (if not control); on matters of tires, there were reasons why the Nobels might wish to affect GM policies; most important, however, the investment would not have been made had it not been for the ongoing relationships between Du Pont and the British Nobels. Thus, this investment has aspects of FDI. Definitions aside, the Britishers' capital contributed materially to assisting GM through a difficult period.

Rubber Tires

The growth of U.S. automobile sales stimulated the output of numerous other industries, among them rubber tires. The Du Pont–British Nobels' friendly ties were once more associated with a foreign investment in America. Here, there is no ambiguity. The Dunlop Rubber Company was a FDI in America. The story is complex. The British Nobel company in 1918 had obtained a substantial block of shares in the British-headquartered Dunlop Rubber Company and in The Tyre Investment Trust Company, Dunlop's intermediary for overseas investments.[114]

When Dunlop considered producing in America, Sir Harry McGowan of the British Nobel firm had discussed the subject with his allies at Du Pont. In July 1919—before the Nobels had invested in General Motors—McGowan had tried, in vain, to convince GM to make a commitment to buy tires from Dunlop's projected U.S. factory.[115] GM's principal original equipment supplier was the U.S. business Goodyear, in which GM had a half million dollars invested.[116]

During 1919, GM was expanding abroad.[117] Early in 1920, it considered the acquisition of the British carmaker Austin, an investment that was never made; Harvey du Cros, Jr.—of Dunlop—was a large shareholder in Austin.[118] Apparently, in 1919 GM had bought a sizable interest in the *British* Dunlop Rubber Company, with a twofold goal: (1) to aid GM's *British* expansion and (2) to monitor Dunlop Rubber Company's *American* expansion plans.[119]

The British Dunlop in 1919 moved forward with its proposed U.S. factory. It acquired from the Du Pont company a large site in Buffalo, New York, on which to build the new facility. In the fall of 1919, it issued securities in London for Dunlop America, Ltd.[120] In January 1920, the American affiliate took over the Utica Spinning Company in Utica, New York, to obtain its own supply of cotton fabrics for its made-in-America tires.[121] It was in May 1920 that the Nobels had agreed to buy the GM shares. According to Alfred Chandler and Stephen Salsbury, as a consequence of GM's investment in the Dunlop Rubber Company, on August 13, 1920, Pierre du Pont was elected to the board of directors at Dunlop's *American* subsidiary, which at the same meeting changed its name to Dunlop Tire and Rubber Company of America.[122] At that board meeting, the directors learned that tire production in Buffalo would begin in January 1921 and that the new Buffalo plant would be in full production by the end of 1921.[123] This did not happen.

By mid-December 1920, Dunlop in America was in a "serious financial condition." In desperation, McGowan cabled Pierre du Pont, who was by this time president as well as chairman of the board of GM, asking him "to consider whether G M C [General Motors] cannot advance to Dunlop America six hundred thousand dollars weekly for next seven weeks principal and interest to be repaid first week February stop Leading British Bank will guarantee principal and interest stop I need not emphasis serious position and hope G M C can help us out stop." The money would be used "to avoid closing factory down."[124]

In reply, du Pont cabled a rejection of McGowan's request and, in a follow-up letter, explained that "the financial situation in General Motors is not such as will warrant cash commitments of any kind unless absolutely necessary for General Motors own business . . . With Dunlop I should think it best not to proceed until financing is thoroughly well assured. The financial situation in this country is not good and I should be fearful of over commitment to banks."[125] Thus, even though

McGowan was by this time on the board of GM, he still could not get his way. The entire tire industry in America was in trouble in late 1920–1921.[126]

Dunlop postponed its start-up of its tire factory in America. Nobel Industries remained an investor in GM and did not reallocate its resources to the new Dunlop project. During 1922, with the U.S. economy recovering from the sharp 1921 downturn, Dunlop in America was able to obtain adequate financing and resumed factory construction. Finally, in 1923, Dunlop began to manufacture tires in Buffalo, New York.[127]

This was a reentry into U.S. business for Dunlop. The British Dunlop had had investments in manufacturing in the United States for roughly five years in the 1890s. It had sold these facilities, along with rights to its name, before it had become aware of the immense potential for tire sales in the United States; as automobile consumption had risen in the early 1900s, Dunlop had regrets about its divestment and had desired to return to America.[128] Tariffs, the presence of rival tire producers in the United States, along with the sale of its name made reaching the U.S. market through exports impossible. After much effort, Dunlop reacquired rights to use its own name in 1916; now in 1923, four years after it had become committed to the Buffalo site and just as the U.S. automobile industry was reentering a boom, Dunlop was poised to fill the high demand for made-in-America tires. It was not alone; many other manufacturers had exactly the same idea, and competition would prove intense (there were 129 firms operating 160 tire-making factories in the United States in 1923).[129] The price of tires fell. Dunlop completed its first year of production (1923) with a loss of £392,781 (roughly $1.6 million).[130] Even though Pierre du Pont was president of GM and McGowan was on the GM board, even though GM had an interest in the parent Dunlop Rubber Company, even though in 1923 Dunlop did a good business with GM, GM did not make Dunlop its preferred, much less principal, supplier.[131] Nonetheless, Dunlop's arrival in America was that of a significant British direct investor. Dunlop joined Lever Brothers, J. & P. Coats, English Sewing Cotton, Courtaulds, and Shell as an important British multinational in the United States.

Among Dunlop's many competitors was a second substantial foreign direct investor. Since 1907, France's foremost tire maker, Michelin, had manufactured in Milltown, New Jersey. Michelin advertised widely, picturing a man with rubber ribs—beating the Michelin drum and announcing that "the 1923 MICHELIN CORD is some tire"; the advertisements reminded the public of the quality and dependability of the Michelin brand.[132] Advertising aside (and Michelin's advertising was much more impressive than Dunlop's in 1923), by 1923–1924 neither Dunlop nor Michelin ranked in the top five in U.S. tire output. Both do appear, however, to have been in the leading ten.[133]

Iron and Steel

Framerican Industrial Development Corporation, controlled by the French steel group Schneider, was incorporated in New York in 1917 to handle its U.S. business. By 1920–1921, Framerican was investing on behalf of Schneider in the Union Européenne Industrielle et Financière, which had major investments in central Europe.[134] In January 1922, Framerican issued in the United States $10 million in gold debentures, offered by leading American underwriters J. P. Morgan, Guaranty Company, National City Company, Bankers Trust Company, Harris Forbes & Co., Lee Higginson & Co., and Halsey Stuart & Co. Then it purchased from Schneider certain coal, iron, and metallurgical facilities in France.[135] This type of finance was in line with an emerging pattern whereby a foreign-controlled American-incorporated company would raise money in the United States for business abroad. What occurred was an inward FDI—that is, the use of a company in the United States—to finance outward international business. The process in this case bore a striking resemblance to that used by Kreuger's International Match Corporation. Far more of this way of tapping American capital markets would occur in the late 1920s in iron and steel as well as other industries—well beyond matches. The ventures can be appropriately labeled "cosmopolitan finance."

More conventional inward FDIs in iron and steel were those in crucible steel—the only branch of the U.S. steel industry where foreign investors were of any consequence. In this sector, investors from Sheffield, England, had long made foreign direct investments. Crucible steel was used for cutlery and a variety of tools.[136] In the early 1920s, one British firm—William Jessop & Sons—exited (see Chapter 2), one remained, and one arrived anew. The continuing producer was the highly successful Firth Sterling Steel Co., a small, innovative enterprise. The new entry was Hadfields Ltd., an important maker in Sheffield of manganese steel. In 1919, Hadfields invested over $1 million and furnished technological know-how in exchange for a 40 percent holding in the newly organized Hadfield-Penfield Co. of Bucyrus, Ohio.

Hadfield-Penfield anticipated large U.S. government orders for weapons, which with the war over never came. It also planned to sell to the U.S. automobile industry, but the 1920–1921 recession cut sharply into these orders. Nonetheless, its optimistic British parent, Hatfields Ltd., offered the fledgling affiliate additional support, raising in 1922 the British portion of the equity to 75 percent. The problem was not, however, absence of capital. Rather, it lay in the lack of U.S. government orders, the 1920–1921 recession, overcapacity in the American manganese steel industry, and, most serious for the future, bad management of the Ohio enterprise. As other British companies in America discovered, doing business on this side of the Atlantic was anything but routine. Hadfields Ltd. sent almost $3 million to this never profitable endeavor (by 1927, it was in receivership).[137] That left Firth Sterling Steel Co. as the one healthy British crucible steelmaker in America. The British contribution, even in this specialized market niche, would become peripheral. The formidable U.S. iron and steel industry was domestic.

Nonelectrical Machinery and Related Products

The national character of the nonelectrical machinery industry was also manifest. To be sure, a handful of new (and miscellaneous) FDIs were undertaken by British firms in the United States in this industry, basically to get within U.S. tariff barriers and to meet U.S. demand. Thus, for example, in 1920, the British firm Baker Perkins began to manufacture food and chemical machinery in Saginaw, Michigan.[138] Cambridge Instruments Co., Ltd., London, opened a small plant in Ossining, New York, in 1922, to produce medical instruments.[139] The Hoffmann Manufacturing Company, Ltd., of Chelmsford, Essex, England, obtained a controlling interest in the Norma Company of America, a onetime German-owned enterprise that manufactured bearings in America (the latter was renamed the Norma-Hoffmann Bearing Company).[140] Much more important, SKF—the Swedish bearings company—increased its U.S. business.[141] Several additional Swedish firms had stakes in machinery. In farm equipment, the Canadian enterprise Massey-Harris continued as a manufacturer in Batavia, New York, although its business was sharply curtailed in the 1920–1921 downturn.[142] When one compares all these investments to the global expansion of International Harvester, Singer Sewing Machine, and National Cash Register (as cases in point), the asymmetries in FDI are apparent. Bearings possibly excepted, in no nonelectrical machinery industry did foreign investors take on a notable role in the United States. And, in bearings, there were sizable "cross-investments": the American-owned Timken Roller Bearing Company was a large multinational enterprise.[143]

Electrical Manufacturing

The absence of foreign direct investors in U.S. electrical machinery and equipment was even more pronounced. The exits of Marconi (which, as noted, had moved into manufacturing during World War I), Pathe Freres Phonograph, and Ericsson, as well as the Germans, left the U.S. domestic industry—for a brief interlude—unchallenged at home by international competition (the German reentry forays were very modest). American enterprise in the electrical manufacturing industry was aggressive in its global expansion, combining outward FDI with cartel alliances.[144]

Other Manufacturing

A Canadian investor in printing and publishing deserves notice. Samuel J. Moore of Toronto was well established in Canada as a manufacturer of sales books and business forms. Since the 1880s, he had made a variety of direct investments in the United States.[145] All four of the new Canadian investments in 1919 shown in Table 3.1 could be those of Moore. That year Moore interests acquired three New York City companies, the Beardsley Press, New York Cash Book Sales Co., and Eastern Book Co., as well as the Pacific Manifolding Book Co. of San Francisco. Add these to Moore's existing properties, which already included the numerous U.S. plants of the American Sales Book Company. By 1923 the entrepreneur controlled a collection of multiplant U.S. businesses that operated across the continent, from the Atlantic to the Pacific Coast.[146] He was one of the most significant Canadian investors in the United States.

Accounting, Trade, and Shipping Services

Foreign-owned companies continued to provide a range of services—in accounting, trade, shipping, insurance, finance, and banking. British accountants had by the start of the 1920s become an established part of the U.S. profession.[147] Typically, the "ownership" ties with their British parent consisted of interlocking partners. The American side of their business had assumed a life of its own, although these firms were well qualified to handle international business problems. Thus, during World War I, Price Waterhouse in the United States—which for many years had provided accounting services to the House of Morgan—was able to help that American bank as it assisted in Allied finance.[148]

In the period 1919–1923, British accounting firms in this country took on an increasingly U.S.-driven orientation. Relationships once directed from overseas were so no longer, although the associations between the British parents and their American affiliates remained strong; George O. May of Price Waterhouse, for example, made annual pilgrimages to London.[149] When the transactions that the British accounting firms in America monitored were international, more often than not they now involved the export of U.S. capital. (Once these accounting firms had been especially active in examining British investments in the United States—inward investments; now the new position of the United States as a creditor nation was reflected in their business activities, as their concerns were with outward FDI—with assisting American businesses that were operating abroad). The British accounting firms stayed on as active participants in business in this country, with their role much in evidence. It should be noted that the British accounting firms came to be very much associated with British investment trusts—and some of the associations would come to be extended into America.

Foreign-owned trading companies were crucial in linking America to the rest of the world. It is possible to distinguish two types of foreign-owned trading houses that did business in the United States—dedicated and general trading ones. There is now a new recognition of the significance of foreign-owned trading institutions in the United States in these years.[150] Many were family firms, varying in size from several individuals to giant enterprises.[151] Sizable foreign-owned dedicated (or specialized) trading companies were present in the grain, cotton, and metals trade. In a number of commodities (coffee, sugar, and rubber, for example), there were also specialized foreign-owned merchant firms. Then there were the general trading houses that dealt with a wide assortment of diverse products, some of which were traded by specialist firms, and some of which were not (cotton and silk, for instance, were traded by both specialist and general trading houses). The largest general trading companies might have departments that handled particular commodities. Certain trading firms had a specialized regional concentration (i.e., they emphasized Latin American or Asian trade). By contrast, numerous foreign and U.S. industrials—multinational corporations—had by the interwar period bypassed trading firms and were conducting their own intrafirm international trade. Some of the merchants (the trading houses) were merchant bankers—handling the trade that they financed.

Although there were a multitude of U.S. export-import houses, foreign-owned businesses played a prominent role in arranging American commerce. The foreign-owned firms handled exports from and to the United States, depending on the commodity. These firms were global or regional traders; rarely was their business simply bilateral. In U.S. grain exports, for example, foreign-owned companies were highly significant.[152] Included was the Paris-based grain trader Louis Dreyfus & Co. that had long had a New York office.[153] The Argentine-Belgian Bunge & Co. (Bunge & Born), whose New York "agent" in 1919 was Maclaren & Gentles, in 1920 became associated with the New York and Chicago business of P. N. Gray & Co.[154] In 1923, the trading house organized the Bunge Corporation in the United States, which appears to have acquired P. N. Gray & Co. and merged it into Bunge Corporation.[155] A newcomer in these postwar years in New York City (in 1921) was the French-headquartered Continental Grain Company, established by Jules and René Fribourg.[156] Additional foreign-directed grain traders included the extremely important British Samuel Sanday & Co. (alone it handled 15 percent of U.S. wheat exports in 1921).[157] The three—Dreyfus, Bunge (Bunge & Born), and Continental Grain—would, however, come to tower over the rest and become sizable investors in the United States. Specialized Japanese cotton trading companies maintained branches in Texas to buy raw cotton and facilitate its delivery to Japan.[158] Various metal traders—particularly British and French ones—had New York representatives.[159]

Brazilian Warrant—a British-owned coffee trader with a large Brazilian business—had offices in New York and New Orleans to sell its Brazilian coffee to American importers and roasters.[160] The British were key in U.S. tea imports. There were Japanese and French silk trading firms with New York offices; Jardine Matheson, the great British China trader, had a New York branch to sell Chinese tea and silk.[161] A number of merchant firms specialized in U.S. rubber imports.[162]

Foreign-owned general trading houses had New York City outlets. The London merchants (qua merchant banks) Balfour, Williamson & Co. and Antony Gibbs & Co., deeply involved in Latin American commerce, had New York offices; E. R. Kenzel (deputy governor of the Federal Reserve Bank) learned from them informally ("in strict confidence") information that came from their London principals.[163] Balfour, Williamson's New York office was at 43 Exchange Place, in the heart of the financial district.[164] Although Gibbs was known as a specialist in nitrates, the firm handled other commodities as well as the financing of them.

Although there were Japanese specialist enterprises in cotton and silk, none was in the grain trade; grain was one of the many commodities handled by the Japanese general trading companies.[165] Mitsui & Co. was the largest of these general trading companies. It had had an office in New York City for decades, and by 1919 it had 105 employees located there, while 60 more employees staffed other Mitsui & Co. offices in San Francisco, Dallas, Seattle, and Portland.[166] In 1919, the transactions undertaken by Mitsui & Co.'s New York office exceeded those of any one of Mitsui & Co.'s branches worldwide.[167] Mitsubishi, another prominent Japanese general trading company, opened its first New York office in 1916.[168] In 1920, its New York City branch had 69 employees, and it imported into the United States huge quantities of silk, along with a range of other products.[169] From its Seattle office, Mitsubishi participated in the export of wheat, flour, lumber, timber, and scrap metal.[170] The large Japanese general trading companies had representatives in New York City, and most also had offices on the American West Coast. The opening of the Panama Canal had resulted in a sizable enlargement of Japanese-American commerce—and much of that trade came to be handled by Japanese trading firms.

As Americans sought to expand exports in the aftermath of the First World War, foreign-owned trading companies assumed importance, for often Americans lacked experience in the complexities of international commerce. Because of the size of the domestic market, typically U.S. companies had concentrated first on sales at home. Foreign-owned trading companies—whether dedicated or general ones—were often more knowledgeable in the pricing of international transactions, coping with the paperwork of moving goods over borders, dealing with foreign exchange, arranging for shipping and insurance, locating financing for the trade, and matching producers and customers. Most managed remarkably well to weather the adversities of the downturn of 1920–1921, when many U.S. firms engaged in international trade stumbled.[171] Foreign-owned trading houses filled a crucial gap in handling exports and imports, typically in primary products and processed undifferentiated products, as well as small-volume commerce in differentiated manufactured goods.

Foreign-owned shipping companies (particularly British, Norwegian, and Japanese) enlarged their U.S. service after the conclusion of World War I, the prohibitions of the Jones Act of 1920 notwithstanding. Despite wartime and the immediate postwar efforts by Americans to develop a strong, competitive merchant fleet, now as before the war (although not to as great an extent), much of the country's foreign trade would once again come to be carried on foreign ships. By 1923 German shipping had resumed. The American merchant marine reached its peak share in U.S. foreign trade in 1920, after which foreign-owned and foreign flag vessels reemerged to resume significance.[172] The foreign participation was exclusively in international trade. Coastal shipping was domestic, because of U.S. law.[173]

Insurance Services

One of the most important sectors to attract FDI was insurance and the British were the leaders. They excelled in mercantile marine insurance. Foreign investors in the United States offered not only marine but also fire and casualty coverage. Canadian firms were the only ones to offer life insurance to Americans. Insurance companies (foreign and domestic) were licensed to operate under state laws but could do business in any number of individual states.[174]

In fire and marine insurance, foreign-owned companies continued—as they had before the First World War—to play a significant role. *Best's Insurance Reports* regularly listed foreign-owned companies in the United States.[175] There were ninety foreign fire and marine insurers in the United States in 1918. By 1923, with the exits, which included all the nine Russian insurers, and the new entries, by my count, the number was up to ninety-seven (see Table 3.3). Many foreign insurers handled reinsurance as well; some specialized in reinsurance.

British insurers sustained their lead; indeed, their role became relatively more important. They operated through subsidiaries and branches. Royal Insurance Co. (Liverpool), Commercial Union Assurance Co. (London), Liverpool & London & Globe (Liverpool), North British & Mercantile Insurance Co. (London and Edinburgh), and Phoe-

Table 3.3. Foreign insurance companies in fire and marine insurance in the United States, number and percentage, by leading nationalities, 1918, 1923 (year end; includes branches and affiliates)

	Number		% of total	
Nationality	1918	1923	1918	1923
British	51	58	57	60
French	9	9	10	9
Japanese	1	4	1	4
Norwegian	5	4	6	4
Danish	2	4	2	4
Swedish	2	3	2	3
Swiss	3	3	3	3
Canadian	2	2	2	2
Chinese	2	2	2	2
Indian	0	2	0	2
New Zealand	1	2	1	2
Russian[a]	9	0	10	0
Others[b]	3	4	3	4
Total[c]	90	97	100	100

Source: Tabulations based on data in *Best's Insurance Reports, Fire and Marine, 1919,* and *Best's Insurance Reports, Fire and Marine, 1924.*

a. *Best's Insurance Reports* explained that on Dec. 1, 1918, the Soviet government of Russia had decreed the dissolution of all private insurance companies and the confiscation of their assets by the state on Apr. 11, 1919. It was assumed that this would "terminate the authority of their U.S. representatives," but that the assets in the United States could only be used to liquidate obligations incurred in America. See Chapter 2 herein for more details.

b. The others in 1918 included one branch each from Spain, Holland, and Cuba; others in 1923 included these same three, plus one from Australia.

c. Percentages are off because of rounding.

nix Assurance Co. (London) were among the most prominent. (In Britain, Liverpool & London & Globe came to be owned by Royal Insurance Company in 1919; in the United States, the two insurers kept their separate organizations.)[176] Three of these five leading firms had started writing insurance in the United States before the Civil War; the other two began in the late 1860s.[177] Thus, these British enterprises were an integral part of the American insurance scene. Some existing British companies expanded in these years by taking over U.S. insurers. Three examples are (1) Atlas Assurance Co., London, which had its own New York branch, in addition purchased in 1922 Albany Insurance Co. (an American firm, founded in 1811); (2) Norwich Union Fire Insurance Society, Norwich, England, with its own New York branch, acquired in 1923 the charter of a dormant New York company, Eagle Fire Co. (originally founded in 1806); and (3) London Guarantee and Accident Insurance Co. (LGAI) bought United Firemen's Insurance Co. of Philadelphia (the latter, in 1923, passed to Phoenix Assurance, London, when it, in turn, acquired LGAI).

British-owned insurers also started up new companies or branches. Four such cases are (1) Employers' Liability Assurance Corporation, which had a branch in Boston and first entered the United States in 1886, organized in 1921 an American fire insurance "running mate," the Employers Fire Insurance Co., Boston; (2) Scottish Union and National Insurance Co. of Edinburgh, which had a U.S. branch in Hartford, Connecticut, and another branch in New York that did maritime insurance, organized in 1923 the American Union Insurance Co., a separate subsidiary; (3) London and Provincial Marine and General Insurance, controlled by Yorkshire Insurance Co., York, England (which had a New York branch), established its own U.S. branch in New York in 1920; and (4) British General Insurance Co., London, inaugurated a U.S. branch in New York in 1920.

A new British arrival was Prudential Assurance Co., which had long had an important U.S. portfolio of securities but had never conducted operations (i.e., had FDI) in America. In 1922, for the first time, it set up a U.S. subsidiary (Prudential Insurance Company of Great Britain, located in New York), which provided fire reinsurance.[178] What seems evident is that although the war years had resulted in a cutback of British activities in some sectors in America and British portfolio investments had shrunk, this was not true with British insurance, where the growth of new British business in the United States was impressive. The expansion, moreover, was not only in fire and marine insurance but also in a wide range of other insurance coverage.

As of December 1918, nine French fire and marine insurance companies were operating in America; the number was the same five years later (year end 1923), although some of the firms had been reorganized, and some would exit in 1924–1926 because of unsatisfactory performance in the immediate postwar years. The three sizable Swiss fire and marine insurance companies doing business in the United States in 1923 were all headquartered in Zurich (Prudentia Re- and Co-Insurance Co., New York Branch; Swiss Re-insurance Co., New York Branch; and Switzerland General Insurance Co., New York Branch). The first two did reinsurance and were under the identical management.

The First World War years had seen a dramatic rise in new entries of Scandinavian, particularly Norwegian, insurance companies. After the war's end, there was a sorting out of these investments. In 1914, in the United States there had been only two insurers from a Scandinavian country (both Swedish); by the end of 1918, there were nine (Norwegians, Danes, and Swedes), and by the end of 1923, eleven Scandinavian insurers. The most remarkable postwar change was the continuing arrival and then the swift exodus of new Norwegian investors: at year end 1918, there were five Norwegian fire and marine insurers doing business in the United States; by the end of the next year, the number had soared to eight; by year end 1923, only four were left; and by the end of the 1920s, only one would still have a U.S. presence, and that one, Christiana General (Storebrand) Insurance Company, Oslo, was managed in the United States by a group associated with the Swedish company Svea Fire and Life Insurance of Göteborg.[179] In 1923, four Danish and three Swedish companies offered fire and marine coverage. There was a conspicuous difference in the business experience of the Norwegians, Swedes, and Danes. Swedish and Danish firms (with one exception) did not have the difficulties of their Norwegian counterparts and in fact modestly increased their business in America in these years. Was it, as one scholar suggested, Norway's "colonial," dependent, background that rendered its insurers incapable of effective management abroad?[180] Could the problems lie in the postwar difficulties with Norwegian shipping?[181]

In 1919–1923, at least three new Japanese marine and fire insurance companies opened U.S. operations, making four in total. Yet two of the three new entries would depart rapidly (since their parent companies were harmed by the 1923 earthquake). Two Indian marine and fire insurers entered in these years; one was short-lived, but the other—New India Assurance Co., Bombay, linked with the Tata family interests—persisted. It started business in the United States in 1921 and provided fire insurance. As for the two "Chinese" companies, one was known to be established by British interests.[182]

In the past the role of foreign-owned insurers had been principally to provide fire and marine insurance, although British insurers, in particular, had not confined themselves to these sectors. Some British companies set up separate subsidiaries to handle automobile, workmen's compensation, accident, health, and other non-life insurance.[183] The large British insurers in America, such as Royal Insurance Co., Liverpool, and Commercial Union Assurance Co., London, for example, had or newly established subsidiaries in the United States to transact various types of non-life insurance.[184] In addition, there was one major British insurance company in the United States not affiliated with a fire and marine company giant: Employers' Liability Assurance Corp., London (but, as noted previously, it had in these years set up a separate fire insurance subsidiary). In 1919–1923, the only key foreign-owned *casualty* insurance company in America that was not British was the Zurich General Accident and Liability Co. Ltd., with its U.S. branch in Chicago. As for life insurance, Canada Life Assurance Co. (Toronto), Great-West Life Assurance Co. (Winnipeg), and Sun Life Assurance Co. (Montreal) were licensed to do business in various American states.

Investment Trusts, Mortgage Companies, and Mortgage Banks

Usually British investment trusts did not have their own men in the United States; they did not make FDI; their portfolio investments could be undertaken easily from their U.K. locations. Often they had arrangements with New York banks to hold their American securities and aid them in their U.S. transactions. Some of these investment trusts had contacts with brokers in Chicago, Philadelphia, and Boston.[185] A few had more extensive associations. By contrast, foreign-owned mortgage companies (many of the British ones were being metamorphosed into investment trusts), as long as they continued mortgage lending, did require men on the spot to supervise the lending and the collection of interest.[186] A number of exits and cutbacks in such business had occurred from 1914 to 1923 (as noted earlier); by 1919–1923, surviving mortgage companies included the Texas Land and Mortgage Company, the Alliance Trust, the Scottish American Mortgage Company, and the Oregon Mortgage Company.[187] Dutch-owned mortgage banks in Washington, Minnesota, and Texas also remained, continuities from the pre–World War I era.[188]

Foreign Banks

By 1919, New York City had become a major financial center, vying with London for the premier rank in the world economy; American banks looked to global business as never before.[189] Immediately after the fighting ceased, and for the next few years, among foreign and domestic banking elites there was a heightened sense of excitement as American banks competed for business abroad—and foreign banks wanted to be part of "the scene" in New York City.[190] The period 1919–1923 saw foreign bank entries along with the enlarged participation of foreign banks already there. In New York City, there emerged a truly vibrant international banking community with numerous domestic and foreign banks.

Because of the new U.S. role as creditor in world accounts, the activities of both U.S. and foreign banks were not what they had been before the war. More of the initiative came from the U.S. side of the Atlantic. The house of Morgan, for example, had changed. J. P. Morgan had died in 1913, and his son (with a strong group of partners) carried on the international banking tradition, retaining close relationships with Morgan Grenfell, London, and Morgan, Harjes et Cie., Paris. During World War I, the direction in international banking within the house of Morgan increasingly came from New York; this would set the future tone.[191] Kuhn, Loeb remained a prominent U.S. investment banking house, but the senior prewar and wartime partner, Jacob Schiff, died in 1920; the new generation that took over at Kuhn, Loeb (as described in Chapter 2) reinstated their Warburg family associations—those with M. M. Warburg & Co., Hamburg. Sir Ernest Cassel, Schiff's close friend and a prewar British leader in facilitating capital transfers from Europe to America, died in 1921; no comparable British figure of stature came to be associated with Kuhn, Loeb in the 1920s.[192]

In the international banking picture, one of the sharpest discontinuities was the reduced role in the United States of the British and French Rothschilds. August Belmont (son of the longtime U.S. representative of the British and French Rothschilds) lived until 1924; there is correspondence between his firm and the French Rothschilds that goes to 1926, but it becomes increasingly sparse.[193] Lord Rothschild (Nathaniel Meyer Rothschild) of the British Rothschilds had died in 1915.[194] His important U.S. contact, Henry Lee Higginson, of Lee, Higginson & Co., passed away in 1919; I have seen no evidence of an ongoing relationship between Higginson's Boston firm and the British Rothschilds.[195] Thus, while both the British and the French Rothschild houses continued to participate in U.S. banking business after the First World War, their presence in the United States was a shadow of an earlier era.[196]

Sir Edgar Speyer of Speyer Brothers, London, who had gone through an abysmal experience during the war years (as a target of anti-German animus), closed down his British house in 1919 and migrated to America. After the war, the American Speyer house resumed its interlocking-partnership relations with its German counterpart; there was, however, no British house remaining, only a representative there.[197]

In sum, as New York emerged as a major global banking hub, a new set of foreign and American bankers would take advantage of the promise. Although there were many continuities from before the war, there were also key changes in the "actors" in international banking; even more important, the nature of the business changed in this altered postwar environment.

Since 1911, New York State had licensed foreign bank agencies. Foreign banks that wanted to be in New York City could operate there as a state "licensed agency." Such an agency (owned by a foreign bank) was under state law not permitted to take deposits.[198] Between the time of the Armistice and the end of 1923, the number of foreign (out-of-country) banks with licensed agencies in New York City soared from twenty-four at year end 1918 to thirty-eight at year end 1923, the peak number for the entire interwar period.[199] Table 3.4 gives an alphabetical roster of foreign banks, at year end 1918 and 1923, with agencies licensed under New York State law. At year end 1918 (as before the First World War), London-headquartered overseas banks were the principal users of this business form. They had ten agencies. Canadian banks had six. At the close of that year, 1918, there were eighteen U.K., Canadian, and other British Empire—Hong Kong and South African—bank agencies out of the twenty-four (or 75 percent of the total). By the end of 1923, there were nine London-headquartered overseas bank agencies, six Canadian ones, three from Hong Kong, and one from Pretoria, South Africa, adding up to nineteen U.K., Canadian, and other British Empire bank agencies; however, since the total out-of-country New York agencies had risen to thirty-eight, the "British" share in the representation had fallen to 50 percent of the total.[200]

And, in 1923, two of the "Hong Kong banks" were Chinese run and not really British, even though domiciled in British Hong Kong (the third was the very British, long-standing Hongkong and Shanghai Banking Corporation). The Chinese Merchants Bank, Ltd., of Hong Kong, which opened in New York in 1921, advertised that it was the first "Chinese" bank in New York and one of the largest, most influential financial institutions in China. It offered to provide American manufacturers with "the proper channels so necessary to all successful transactions," presumably when the latter wanted to develop U.S. business with or within China. Lo N. Lau (who after his graduation from Cornell University in 1919 had briefly been employed at the head office of the bank) ran the New York agency. Four of his cousins had earlier participated in the founding of the parent Chinese Merchants Bank, Ltd., which had branches in Canton, Shanghai, and Saigon.[201] The

Table 3.4. Foreign (out-of-country) banks with agencies licensed under New York State banking law, 1918, 1923

No.	In existence Dec. 31, 1918	Date started[a]	Date ended[b]	In existence Dec. 31, 1923	No.
1.	African Banking Corp., London	Early 1900s(?)[c]	1920[d]	[See Standard Bank of South Africa][d]	
2.	Anglo-South American Bank, London	1907	—	Yes	1.
	—	1921	—	Banca Chrissoveloni, S.A., Bucharest, Roumania	2.
3.	Banca Commerciale Italiana, Milan, Italy	1918	—	Yes	3.
	—	1920	—	Banca Marmorosch, Blank & Co., Bucharest, Roumania	4.
4.	Banco di Napoli, Naples, Italy	[e]	—	Yes	5.
	—	1922	—	Banco di Roma, Rome, Italy	6.
	—	1920	—	Banco Nacional Ultramarino, Lisbon, Portugal	7.
	—	1922	—	Bank of Athens, Athens, Greece	8.
5.	Bank of British North America, London	Mid-1850s	1919[f]	[See Bank of Montreal][f]	
6.	Bank of British West Africa, London	Early 1900s(?)[c]	—	Yes	9.
	—	1922	—	Bank of Canton, Ltd., Hong Kong	10.
	—	1919	—	Bank of Chosen, Seoul (Korea), Japan	11.
7.	Bank of Montreal, Montreal	1859[g]	—	Yes	12.
8.	Bank of Nova Scotia, Nova Scotia	1907[h]	—	Yes	13.

Table 3.4 *(continued)*

No.	In existence Dec. 31, 1918	Date started[a]	Date ended[b]	In existence Dec. 31, 1923	No.
9.	Bank of Taiwan, Taiwan, Japan	1917	—	Yes	14.
	—	1921	—	Banque Belge pour l'Etranger, Brussels, Belgium	15.
	—	1921	—	Bohemia, Czechoslovak Foreign Banking Corp., Prague, Czechoslovakia	16.
10.	Canadian Bank of Commerce, Toronto	1872	—	Yes	17.
11.	Chartered Bank of India, Australia and China, London	1902[i]	—	Yes	18.
	—	1921	—	Chinese Merchants Bank, Ltd. Hong Kong	19.
12.	Colonial Bank, London	1890	—	Yes	20.
13.	Commercial Bank of Spanish America, London	1912	—	Yes	21.
	—	1923	—	Credit Commercial de France, Paris, France	22.
	—	1920	—	Credito Italiano, Genoa and Milan, Italy	23.
	—	1920	—	Dominion Bank, Toronto	24.
14.	Hongkong and Shanghai Banking Corp., Hong Kong	1880	—	Yes	25.
15.	London and Brazilian Bank, London	1886[c]	—	Yes	26.
16.	London and River Plate Bank, London	1891[c]	—	Yes	27.
	—	1920	—	Mercantile Bank of India, Ltd., London	28.

17.	Merchants Bank of Canada, Montreal	Mid-1870s	1922[j]	[See Bank of Montreal][j]	
	—	1920	—	Mitsubishi Bank, Ltd., Tokyo, Japan	29.
	—	1921	—	Mitsui Bank, Ltd., Tokyo, Japan	30.
18.	National Bank of South Africa, Ltd., Pretoria, South Africa	1915	—	Yes	31.
19.	Philippine National Bank, Manila, Philippines	1916	—	Yes	32.
20.	Royal Bank of Canada, Montreal	1899	—	Yes	33.
21.	Standard Bank of South Africa, London	1905	—	Yes	34.
22.	Sumitomo Bank, Osaka, Japan	1918	—	Yes	35.
23.	Union Bank of Canada, Winnipeg	1917	—	Yes	36.
	—	1920	—	Union Bank of the Cooperative Societies of Poland, Posen, Poland	37.
24.	Yokohama Specie Bank, Yokohama, Japan	1880	—	Yes	38.

Sources: New York State, Banking Department, *Annual Reports*, 1918–1923, and Mira Wilkins, *The History of Foreign Investment in the United States to 1914* (Cambridge: Harvard University Press, 1989), 464–465—except where otherwise indicated in the notes.

a. A number of these New York agencies started before the 1911 act that required licensing of the agency.

b. This column is confined to dates before Dec. 31, 1923.

c. In existence before 1911. Date of start-up in New York from Geoffrey Jones.

d. The African Banking Corporation went into voluntary liquidation in 1920 in order to amalgamate with the Standard Bank of South Africa, London. Geoffrey Jones, *British Multinational Banking 1830–1990* (Oxford: Oxford University Press, 1993), 403.

e. Between 1906 and 1911; second New York agency started in 1919.

f. The Bank of British North America was acquired by the Bank of Montreal in October 1918. Merrill Denison, *Canada's First Bank: A History of the Bank of Montreal*, 2 vols. (New York: Dodd, Mead & Co., 1967), II, 331.

g. There was an earlier independent agent, 1818–1841.

h. The date is from Joseph Schull and J. Douglas Gibson, *The Scotiabank Story* (Toronto: Macmillan of Canada, 1982), 309. The bank had had an independent agent in New York as early as 1832, the year the bank was founded. Then there was a long period with no New York agency.

i. In 1881, this bank already had some kind of New York office.

j. The Merchants Bank of Canada, Montreal, was taken over by the Bank of Montreal, Apr. 1, 1922. *Stock Exchange Official Intelligence, 1923*, 382.

second new Chinese bank was the Bank of Canton, Ltd., Hong Kong. Its New York agency (set up in 1922) was under the direction of Ginarn Lao (also a recent U.S. college graduate, from Lehigh University) and Hew Fan Un, a shareholder in the Bank of Canton, Ltd., who had arrived in New York in 1922 to be the principal man in charge.[202]

As in trade, shipping, and insurance, in banking the Japanese had far more activity in the United States than the Chinese.[203] Since 1880, the Yokohama Specie Bank had carried on business in New York; in 1914, it had the only Japanese bank agency in New York City. By 1923, six Japanese bank agencies were present, having arrived in a speedy sequence: the Bank of Taiwan (1917), the Sumitomo Bank, Osaka (1918), the Bank of Chosen (1919), the Mitsubishi Bank, Tokyo (1920), and the Mitsui Bank, Tokyo (1921). All six would remain in New York until the attack on Pearl Harbor, in striking contrast to the ephemeral stay of many of the other new entries of these years.[204] In number of bank agencies, by 1923 the Japanese were second only to the London-headquartered group (and equal to the well-established Canadian contingent). This was a remarkable change.

Four Italian banks had agencies in New York in 1923. Like Japan, Italy had been an ally of the United States during the First World War. The Banco di Napoli had been in New York from before the First World War. In 1918, prior to the Armistice, the Banca Commerciale Italiana (BCI), Milan, had opened a New York agency. BCI was Italy's largest bank and the main institution involved in financing industry in northern Italy. It had been founded by German banks, but by 1914 the German role was small, and Banque de Paris et des Pays-Bas, Paris, had become the principal influence. Italy's second-largest bank, Credito Italiano, Genoa and Milan, opened a New York agency in 1920. The fourth bank agency was that of Banco di Roma, which inaugurated its New York agency in 1922.[205]

Other nationalities with newly organized New York agencies included two Bucharest (Roumania) banks and one each from Brussels (Belgium), Paris (France), Lisbon (Portugal), Athens (Greece), Prague (Czechoslovakia), and Posen (Poland).[206] No German, Austrian, or Turkish banks had agencies in New York at year end 1923—nor were there any Dutch, Swiss, or Swedish bank agencies.

The wide geographic diversity of the homelands of the New York foreign bank agencies relates to their functions. Some served as conduits for emigrant remittances. Thus, a second agency of the Banco di Napoli opened an office at 355 East 149th Street, in the midst of an Italian neighborhood. Banco di Napoli was exceptional in this location; typically, the bank agencies had their offices in New York's downtown financial district. Some of the new ones seemed to have been less associated with immigrant needs than with their parent country's borrowing requirements. These banks sought to help in moving U.S. capital to their home nations. Another important function of the bank agencies (new and old ones alike) involved trade finance. Now, unlike in the prewar years, they often handled dollar acceptances. All these agencies had expertise in foreign exchange transactions. Most helped out travelers or foreign direct investors (in fields other than banking) that required assistance. All provided information to their parents on what was happening in New York.

As in years past, the important British and British Empire banks were specialists in financing British and U.S. international trade. During the war, dollar acceptances had begun to be used to an unprecedented extent. Beginning about 1917, the Federal Reserve System had started to rediscount bankers acceptances. From almost nothing, by 1920 bankers dollar acceptances had catapulted to about $1 billion.[207]

In May 1919, A. G. Stephen (in Shanghai) wrote to N. J. Stabb, chief manager of the Hongkong and Shanghai Banking Corporation, on that bank's U.S. business: "As this Gold Dollar business has apparently come to stay it appears to me very important that some means should be devised to eliminate the London transfer as much as possible if we are to compete on even terms with American banks." Stabb had agreed: since commercial and financial relations with the United States were bound to increase, the Hongkong Bank's position in America had to be improved to meet the inevitable new competition. Stabb envisaged a larger Hongkong Bank role in both New York and San Francisco.[208] Other British overseas bank managers made similar ambitious postwar plans in 1919 and early 1920.

But by the fall of 1920, some British bankers in New York had become wary of dollar acceptances. The New York agency of the Anglo-South American Bank refused, for example, to purchase dollar drafts on India, indicating that "they would buy bills if drawn in sterling."[209] Similarly, the New York agency of the Chartered Bank of India, Australia and China showed a preference for sterling rather than dollar drafts on India. British banks preferred sterling bills, since their resources were in sterling and the purchase of dollar bills left them open to exchange risks.[210] They had the same concerns on the South American as well as Indian trade.[211] As one observer noted in December 1920, "There was some grounds for the report that sterling credits were again being preferred by shippers in foreign countries but that it was because of the greater convenience in dealing with granters of credit who had a century of experience back of them."[212] This notwithstanding, dollar acceptances would continue to be used in the 1920s, although they had not pushed out sterling bills.[213]

The expansion (and in some cases the new presence) in the United States of foreign banks did not always bring satisfactory results. Newcomers were particularly at risk. The National Bank of South Africa (a South African-owned bank), for example, found its "reserve was wiped out" after the 1921 failure of an unidentified New York firm "with liabilities of two million sterling"; only temporarily could the National Bank of South Africa survive as an independent entity.[214] Yet in the period 1918–1923, exits from banking by New York agencies were few, entries numerous.[215]

Since under New York State law the agencies were not permitted to take deposits, foreign banks that wished to do so could adopt another approach to conducting business, which was the use of the "trust company" form. Trust companies in New York (under New York State law) were allowed to serve as commercial banks, as well as having the added privilege of conducting a fiduciary business.[216] The Banca Commerciale Italiana before World War I (in 1913 or 1914) had obtained an equity interest in the Lincoln Trust Co., New York, which it sold in 1922 (two years later it would set up its own trust company).[217] An early foreign-owned trust company, formed in New York, was the Italian Discount and Trust Company (authorized to do business, November 9, 1918); it proved to be short-lived and was put in liquidation by the New York State Banking Department when in 1921 its parent, Banca Italiana di Sconto, was shut.[218] The Anglo-South American Bank, London, which had a licensed New York agency, organized (in addition) on November 27, 1923, the Anglo-South American Trust Company, which allowed it to carry on a full banking business, including the receipt of deposits.[219] By the end of 1923, it was the only remaining foreign-owned trust company in New York; nonetheless, the form had been tried and would subsequently be used by foreign banks.

Some foreign banks had neither licensed agencies nor trust companies in New York; they had a "representative." By the end of 1923, this was true of the British clearinghouse bank the Westminster Bank Ltd., London; the Bank Nationale Français du Commerce Exterieur, Paris; and the Disconto-Gesellschaft, Berlin.[220] These are just a few examples; no list exists, but clearly a number of foreign banks had men in New York who were paid employees and acted for the bank.

Still an additional way for foreign banks to structure their U.S. business was to set up, under New York State law, an international banking organization. Whereas international banking units formed under the federal Edge Act of 1919 were restricted to U.S. citizens and had to be controlled by U.S. capital, no similar taboo existed on those established under New York State law.[221] Included in this category was the

American Foreign Banking Corporation, formed in 1917 by about three dozen U.S. and one (unspecified) Canadian bank; it opened branches abroad.[222] It had a short existence, reduced its capital in 1920, closed many of its overseas branches in 1922–1923, and sold the remainder to Chase National Bank in 1925.[223] A second New York corporation for foreign banking with Canadian involvement was formed in 1919: the Park Union Foreign Banking Corporation, a joint venture between the National Park Bank of New York and the Union Bank of Canada. By year end 1919, it had foreign branches in Yokohama, Tokyo, Shanghai, and Paris.[224] It, too, lacked longevity (in 1922 it merged with the Asia Banking Corporation, which had a brief life; and there is no indication that the Union Bank of Canada remained a participant after the merger); Union Bank of Canada did, however, continue its *agency* in New York, but only through 1924.[225]

Although the New York–incorporated international banking organizations with Canadian equity interests were transitory, others that involved the participation of European banks as shareholders proved successful and long-lasting. One of the most prominent was the French American Banking Corporation (FABC), set up under New York State law on May 21, 1919; half of its stock was owned by Comptoir National d'Escompte de Paris (CNEP) and half by the First National Bank of Boston and the National Bank of Commerce of New York. FABC was to encourage the development of trade relations between the United States and France; it advertised that "we solicit deposit accounts in foreign currencies and offer our services for foreign and commercial banking of every description."[226] The bank provided a means by which its two American parents could do business in the French colonial empire.[227] The French shareholder, CNEP, had about 200 branches in France, as well as branches in Spain, England, Belgium, Australia, New Zealand, and India; CNEP also had close working relationships with French colonial banks in Algeria, Egypt, East Africa, Madagascar, Martinique, and Indo-China. The customers of FABC would have all these facilities available.[228]

Of great importance, with even stronger backing, was Paul M. Warburg's creation, the International Acceptance Bank (IAB), formed in New York in April 1921.[229] Total capital of its American shareholder banks came to $276 million, while that of its foreign shareholder banks equaled $271 million.[230] As in the FABC, First National Bank of Boston was among its founding owners, which also included the American International Corporation (New York), as well as the many foreign banks.[231] Although M. M. Warburg & Co., Hamburg, was not a stockholder until 1925, the German banking house was intimately involved from the start in IAB activities. Kuhn, Loeb & Co. (closely linked with

M. M. Warburg) was a stockholder in IAB—and had very special connections with the new bank.[232]

In 1922, the participating foreign stockholding banks and firms in IAB were from Belgium (Banque de Bruxelles, Brussels, and Banque Centrale Anversoise, Antwerp); Canada (Bank of Montreal, Montreal); Denmark (R. Henriques, Jr., Copenhagen); England (National Provincial and Union Bank, London, and N. M. Rothschild & Sons, London); France (Banque de Paris et des Pays-Bas, Paris); Netherlands (Hope & Co. and Nederlandsche Handel-Maatschappij, both of Amsterdam); Norway (Den Norske Creditbank, Christiana); Sweden (AB Svenska Handelsbanken and Skandinaviska Kreditaktiebolaget, both of Stockholm); and Switzerland (Crédit Suisse, Zurich, and Swiss Bank Corporation, Basle). In addition, there were twenty-two banks and firms in the United States that held shares; these were located in sixteen cities across the nation.[233]

IAB's policy was "to co-operate with stockholding banks and banking houses in the important countries abroad where we extend credit."[234] Paul Warburg (and members of the Warburg family) became leaders in the United States in international finance in the 1920s. By July 1921, IAB was financing grain shipments to Germany. It would soon be engaged in a far broader range of transactions involving trade finance.[235] In the fall of 1921, Paul Warburg's son, James, was in Europe seeking business for IAB. One company he considered to be a good prospect was the Swedish SKF, which James Warburg reported was "manufacturing extensively" in the United States and was not "wedded to Brown Bros."[236] Likewise, James Warburg suggested it would be possible to do business with the Danish East Asiatic Company, which had an office in New York and imported rubber and additional products from the Far East.[237] In Germany, James Warburg contacted the leading metal traders and Siemens & Halske. The latter told Warburg that they had bank connections in New York and saw no reason for a change.[238] IAB would specialize in banking transactions with Germany and other continental European nations.[239]

British merchant banks obtained beachheads in New York and used similar international banking structures to pursue their strategies. The most energetic newcomer was J. Henry Schröder & Co., a leading British acceptance house that had long participated in American business but had never had its own presence in New York.[240] Heading the British house in the 1920s were Baron Bruno von Schröder and Frank C. Tiarks.[241] The Schröder family had German connections: Baron Bruno, born in Hamburg in 1867, became a naturalized British subject only in August 1914, after war was declared.[242] In the 1920s, Baron Bruno's brother was the senior partner in Schröder Gebrüder, Hamburg, a private banking house. In 1921, Baron Bruno's cousin, Kurt von Schröder, became a partner in J. H. Stein, a Cologne bank.[243] Tiarks, a director of the Bank of England, was on the latter's Committee of the Treasury that was "consulted by [the governor, Montagu] Norman at every stage."[244] Given the German associations of the Schröders, it was unsurprising that Tiarks became deeply involved in postwar Anglo-German business; from 1921 onward, Tiarks advised Norman in dealing with the Reichbank.[245] It was Tiarks who in 1923 was responsible for setting up the J. Henry Schroder Banking Corporation in New York; its balance sheet showed assets of $10.7 million at the end of that year. While in New York, Tiarks explained to E. R. Kenzel, deputy governor of the Federal Reserve Bank of New York, that his bank was opening in Manhattan because he and his partners were "looking forward to the time, possibly ten or fifteen years hence, when they anticipated New York would be more important financially even than it is now and when dollar and dollar credits would be in essential demand in financing overseas trade, especially South American trade." Schroder's aspired to be among the leading "dollar bankers in New York."[246]

Other British merchant banks also became engaged in the new dollar acceptance business, including those mentioned earlier in this chapter, under the rubric of trading companies, that is, Balfour, Williamson & Co. and Antony Gibbs & Co., both of which were deeply engaged in the financing of South American trade. The British merchant bank Frederick Huth & Co. had (as indicated in Chapter 1) started a New York firm, Huth & Co., in 1917. Like some other of its British compatriots that felt they had to be in New York City, Frederick Huth & Co.'s regional interest was in South America. This British house had long had a director on the board of the Bank of England, and its paper was thought of in the market as "substantially guaranteed" by the Bank of England. In 1920, the assets of Huth & Co., New York, were $4.1 million.[247] In 1922, after Frederick Huth Jackson's death in December 1921, the Bank of England had intervened to assist the financially imperiled parent firm, Frederick Huth & Co. In his rescue proposal of July 1922, the Bank of England's governor, Montagu Norman, insisted that the firm close its New York house. This did not occur.[248] In October 1922, Huth & Co., New York, was advertising in *Bankers Magazine* that it handled foreign bonds and investment securities, commercial credits, deposit accounts, and foreign exchange.[249] It remained a partnership, not an incorporated company under New York law.

During 1919–1923, as many foreign banks and financial intermediaries sought visibility in the New York City banking community, some had (or continued to have) representation elsewhere in the United States. Typically, the other place or places were in addition to the New

York location. Thus, the Bank of Nova Scotia, which had a licensed agency in New York, also kept its Boston branch (organized in 1899).[250] Since 1886, the British merchant banking house Baring Brothers & Co., Ltd., had been closely allied with Kidder, Peabody & Co., Boston. On April 1, 1922, when the Kidder Peabody Acceptance Corporation came into being (as the successor to the New England Investment Company), Barings had a total investment of $2,499,950, on which Kidder, Peabody guaranteed an 8.5 percent return for six and a half years.[251] Kidder Peabody Acceptance Corporation was important in handling dollar acceptances, along with the French American Banking Corporation, the International Acceptance Bank, and J. Henry Schroder Banking Corporation.[252] Although its head office was in Boston, Kidder, Peabody, & Co. had had a Wall Street address since 1891.[253]

In the Midwest, the pre–World War I Chicago branches of the Bank of Montreal and the Bank of Nova Scotia remained open; when, in 1920, the Banco di Napoli was organized in Chicago, it was set up as a separate bank.[254] All three of these banks had a larger presence in New York than in Chicago. On the West Coast, foreign banks included the Bank of Montreal, the Canadian Bank of Commerce, the Hongkong and Shanghai Banking Corporation, the Commercial Bank of Spanish America, the Yokohama Specie Bank, the Sumitomo Bank, and the Fujimoto Bill Broker Bank, Ltd. The configuration of subsidiary banks, agencies, and branches varied, although each of these foreign participants had a presence in San Francisco. In the immediate post–World War I years, the Bank of Montreal had a bank and an agency in San Francisco, as well as a branch in Spokane.[255] The Canadian Bank of Commerce had branches in San Francisco, Seattle, and Portland (Oregon).[256] The Hongkong and Shanghai Banking Corporation expanded its long-existing business in San Francisco, benefiting from the growing U.S. trade with the Far East.[257] A newcomer was the Commercial Bank of Spanish America, a British overseas bank, which opened in San Francisco in December 1918, attracted to the possibilities of financing Latin American trade from a West Coast outpost.[258] The key and well-established Japanese bank in the West was the Yokohama Specie Bank, in San Francisco and Los Angeles, as well as in Seattle (where its branch had opened on September 24, 1917).[259] On August 11, 1916, even before it started its New York agency, the Sumitomo Bank, Osaka, had incorporated a new branch bank in San Francisco, and in 1919 the Sumitomo Bank of Seattle was incorporated under the laws of the state of Washington.[260] Fujimoto Bill Broker Bank Ltd. inaugurated a San Francisco securities trading office in 1923 (that year it was the sole foreign financial institution that was on the West Coast but not in New York, and soon thereafter it opened in New York City).[261]

The banking and securities activities of foreign banks in Boston,

Chicago, and on the West Coast (San Francisco, Los Angeles, Seattle, Spokane, and Portland) notwithstanding, by far the most significant postwar developments lay in the proliferation of and the diversity of foreign bank activity in New York, America's financial metropolis. Table 3.5 attempts to provide a summary and reveals the preeminent position of that city. The table profiles the status of foreign banking

Table 3.5. Foreign banks in the United States, by type of representation, location, and nationality, 1923 (year end)

Type of representation	No.	Nationalities of investing banks
New York (New York)		
Licensed agencies	38	British / Canadian / Chinese / Japanese / Italian / Roumanian / Portuguese / Greek / Belgian / French / Czech / Polish
Trust companies	1	British
Representative office	?[a]	British / French / German / other?
International banking corporations	4	Canadian / French / Swiss / British / Swedish / Dutch / German / Austrian / Argentine
Merchant banking houses[b]	3+	British
Massachusetts (Boston)		
Branch	1	Canadian
Acceptance company	1	British
Illinois (Chicago)		
Banks and branches	3	Canadian / Italian
California (San Francisco, Los Angeles)		
Banks and branches	7	Canadian / Japanese / British
Agency	1	Canadian
Securities offices	1	Japanese
Washington (Seattle, Spokane)		
Branches	3	Canadian / Japanese
Bank	1	Japanese
Oregon (Portland)		
Branch	1	Canadian

Sources: See text and notes for names of banks and sources. The table excludes the Dutch mortgage banks in Washington, Minnesota, and Texas. Whereas licensed agencies, representative offices, branches, and the one trust company were "wholly owned," the other forms might involve shared ownership—that is, an individual foreign bank did not wholly own the U.S. affiliate.

a. More than a dozen.

b. This includes merchants, where the line between merchant and merchant banking was ambiguous.

in the United States as of the end of 1923. The numbers are not very meaningful. What is fundamental is that every important bank (worldwide) had some kind of association in New York, if only a correspondent relationship. I have not listed the number of correspondents because I have no idea how many there were; and they were not foreign direct investments, whereas all the forms on the roster involved FDI, however small. All the foreign banks were engaged in some aspect of international banking. None (with the possible exception of one or two in Chicago) took part in routine domestic banking in the United States, which was handled by the thousands of national, state, and private banks existing in the country. The foreign banks' U.S. involvements could be best described as important albeit shallow rather than deep, a vital connecting link with the global economy but not serving the average American in his or her banking needs, which were fully met through the American banking system.

Conclusion

In summary, World War I had reduced, although far from eliminated, foreign investment in the United States; the downturn of 1920–1921 discouraged some foreign investors, but foreign investment in this country persisted and survived the stream of postwar nationalistic U.S. legislation. In Chapter 2, I showed that inward FPI in the United States had risen in the period 1919–1923—and so did inward FDI. Many of the foreign multinational enterprises that participated in American business financed their investments within the United States. Often they contributed technology in exchange for equity investments. A large number of businesses of different nationalities took part in the inward FDI.

The British remained active in differentiated trademarked products, such as tea, soap, and thread, but also in the "high-tech" rayon industry, in mining, and in oil (interestingly, in all of these last three categories, the British had brand names for some of the goods sold in America). The British were particularly evident in the service sector—in trade, accounting, insurance, and international banking (especially in trade finance). With the Canadians, proximity was critical; Canadian businesses that invested in the United States did so fundamentally because the United States was nearby. There appears to have been little, if any, Canadian FDI in the United States south of New York City (on the East Coast) or south of San Francisco (on the West Coast). Virtually all the Canadian FDI in the United States appears to have been concentrated north of an arbitrary line drawn across the continent from just south of New York to just south of San Francisco. One is struck by the long-term continued involvement of the Bank of Montreal. The French stood out in fine woolens, silk, perfumes, and cosmetics, and also in rayon, cellophane, and high-performance rubber tires; there were, in addition, some important French banking interests. The Swiss had significant FDI in condensed milk, chocolates, embroidery, dyestuffs, insurance, and banking. Japanese FDI was concentrated in trade, shipping, insurance, and banking services. The German reentry was as yet very small. That the mix of investments differed markedly by nationality was not surprising; it reflected the fact that economic growth followed separate paths in different countries.[262]

In the immediate postwar years the new involvements of foreign direct investors in manufacturing were far from an avalanche, albeit the flawed U.S. Department of Commerce figures (see Table 3.1) suggest that more than half the new inward direct investments were in manufacturing. Often the rationale behind foreign manufacturing in America was to vault tariff walls (or expected tariff barriers); practically all the manufacturing investments were to reach U.S. customers in the large domestic market (there were a few ongoing manufacturing investments for export where this generalization does not apply). New activities that are particularly notable were those of the French wool makers in Woonsocket, Rhode Island; Dunlop in tire production; S. J. Moore in printing; and, as discussed in Chapter 2, the Swiss companies in dyestuffs and related products. In 1923, rayon was the sole truly significant (fundamentally innovative) U.S. industry where foreign direct investors—the existing ones and newcomers—held a dominant position, assuming Kreuger's claim of control over Diamond Match was not legitimate. Foreign investors also held first place in the thread industry and in the potash and borax ones.[263]

In most sectors where there was FDI, continuities prevailed over new establishments or acquisitions. With the ongoing firms, some success stories existed: in mining, for example, the British-owned American Trona and Pacific Borax; in manufacturing (and processing), Lipton, Lever, the Coats group, and, of course, The Viscose Company. The expansion of the Royal Dutch Shell Group, adversities aside, was spectacular. In accounting, trade, shipping, insurance, and mortgage finance, the chronicle of foreign business involvements lacks drama, although the reader should not underestimate the importance of British firms in providing insurance coverage to U.S. producers and consumers, as well as for international commerce. Another highlight—in the service sector—was the establishment on American shores of the major foreign grain traders; indeed, it seems likely that by the early 1920s, they were handling a substantial portion of America's international trade in grain.

In banking, a veritable burst of new activities occurred, far more than in other sectors. What had begun to emerge were financial intermediaries set up (some wholly, others partly, foreign owned) for international trade and finance—and to facilitate the *outward* movement of U.S. capital. During World War I, foreign direct investors in the United States had on a sizable scale started to finance their U.S. business in America; this continued. Now, not only were foreign enterprises coming to this country to sell in a huge market where per capita income was the world's highest, and some fewer in number had interests in the United States for export purposes—the tobacco companies, for example—but foreign enterprises were also making FDI to gain from America's financial prowess, to raise short-term credits and long-term capital in the United States for their U.S. business and for their business around the globe. Foreign banks set up joint ventures in New York to work with American banks and to share in and to help the latter develop worldwide business. And, of course, this is what being a creditor nation is all about.

4.

Prosperity, 1924–1929

The United States prospered in the late 1920s. No nation was richer. Urban homes became electrified. Sales of consumer durables, particularly automobiles, escalated. America became the world's first true consumer society.[1] By 1926–1929, the nation manufactured more than 42 percent of total global output.[2] Americans invested at home and abroad. U.S. lending financed governments and enterprises in Canada, Europe (especially Germany), Latin America, Asia, and farther afield.[3] At the same time, U.S. business invested internationally on an unprecedented scale; virtually all of America's giant enterprises were multinational.[4] As U.S. foreign portfolio and foreign direct investment (FPI and FDI) flowed out to six continents, a far more modest rise occurred in the long-term FPI and FDI in the United States. The outward and inward capital movements, although disproportionate, were frequently interlaced. With both FPI and FDI there were "cross-investments"; thus, as American capital went abroad, foreign capital came to the United States.

By year end 1929, the estimated level of long-term foreign investments in the United States was $5.8 billion compared with outward U.S. long-term investments abroad of $27.1 billion (see Table 4.1). Foreign portfolio investments in the United States were $4.3 billion—columns I plus G (compared with $7.8 billion representing outward private U.S. portfolio stakes—column D); estimates have put foreign direct investments in the United States at a mere $1.5 billion (compared with $7.6 billion of outward U.S. direct investments). These figures are vulnerable; there were no census data, only approximations. Nonetheless, if the figures are not to be read as carved in stone and are recognized as rough, the story line portrayed in these numbers does appear to be fundamentally sound.

Table 4.1. Estimated long-term foreign investment position of the United States, 1918, 1929 (in billions of U.S. dollars)

	U.S. investments abroad					Foreign investments in U.S.				
			Private accounts					Private obligations		
Date	(A) Total	(B) Government lending	(C) Total	(D) Portfolio investments	(E) Direct investments	(F) Total	(G) Government borrowings	(H) Total	(I) Portfolio investments	(J) Direct investments
Dec. 31, 1918	13.7	7.6	6.1	2.5	3.6	3.0	0.1	2.9	1.9	1.0
Dec. 31, 1929	27.1	11.7	15.4	7.8	7.6	5.8	0.1	5.7	4.2	1.5

Sources: 1918 figures are from Table 1.14 herein. The 1929 figures on U.S. investments abroad are from Cleona Lewis, *America's Stake in International Investments* (Washington, D.C.: Brookings Institution, 1938), 450, 605–606 (columns B, D, E), and Mira Wilkins, *The Maturing of Multinational Enterprise: American Business Abroad from 1914 to 1970* (Cambridge, Mass.: Harvard University Press, 1974), 55 (column E). The 1929 figures on foreign investment in the United States are based on the column 7 entries in Table 2.1 herein; in that table portfolio investments in the United States are given as $4.3 billion, which is the sum of columns G and I in this table (column G consists of foreign portfolio investments in American government securities). Note that these figures differ from the 1929 one given in Table 2.4, which was based on the total provided in column 4, Table 2.1.

The significant asymmetry in the inward versus the outward foreign investment at year end 1929 lay not only in the matter of the sizes of each (the high ratio of outward to inward stakes) but also in the role of governments. Foreign governments were debtors to the U.S. government (to the extent of $11.7 billion—column B) and to American private investors (a sizable portion of the outward nongovernmental portfolio investments of $7.8 billion column D—represented loans to foreign governments).[5] By contrast, governments *abroad* had little in the way of long-term holdings in American securities.[6] To be sure, during the 1920s, under the funding agreement with Great Britain of 1923 (and subsequent debt funding arrangements with other countries), foreign government debtors to the U.S. government had the right to pay the principal and interest on their U.S. government obligations in any U.S. government bonds issued since April 6, 1917 (valued at par plus accrued interest). This meant that if the U.S. bonds could be acquired by the foreign government debtors below par, it was worthwhile for them to do so. The U.S. Treasury saw this as a market stabilizer *and* a way of reducing the national debt, for the bonds were retired when used as payment.[7] Over the years, foreign governments followed this procedure; there is no indication, however, that the foreign governments *held* the U.S. bonds; they seem to have purchased and then immediately turned them in.[8] Although a few government-owned companies had direct investments in the United States (the Canadian National Railway and the National Railways of Mexico are the most prominent examples), this was atypical.[9] Basically, the inward investment story of the 1920s is of American obligations to private investors abroad.

Dividend and interest payments to foreign investors in the United States on their inward portfolio and direct investments reached an interwar peak in 1929 of $414 million (or $330 million, according to another source). By contrast, some $979 or $982 million was paid by foreigners to the United States as income on U.S. private investments abroad.[10] The 1929 peak in income going to foreign investors (as a result of their inward investments in the United States) was due to large dividend and interest payments by American corporations in the prosperous 1920s, along with the overall rise in foreign holdings of American securities, particularly during the summer of 1929.

Britain and Holland went back to the gold standard in 1925. With strong currencies, outward foreign investment from these countries once more was appealing.[11] The Dawes Plan (1924) stabilized the German currency and appeared to set Germany on a path to recovery. By contrast, the French economy, governed by a left-wing coalition from May 1924 to July 1926, seemed temporarily in peril, causing capital flight.[12] Paradoxically, inward investment into the United States resulted from both strength *and* weakness abroad.

In the United States, Secretary of the Treasury Andrew Mellon in November 1925 put forth plans to compensate Germans for properties that the United States had taken over during the First World War. By 1927, Mellon was stating that the confiscation of property of private citizens was "repugnant to the American sense of justice. . . . There may not be a legal duty to return the property to the alien owners, but there certainly is a moral duty."[13] The Settlement of War Claims Act of 1928 set down procedures to meet the big claims of the prewar German shipping companies and radio station owners.[14]

By the last years of the 1920s, much of the world community looked like there was a return to "normal" times.[15] The French adopted a gold exchange standard in 1926 and the gold standard in 1928. The Young Plan—announced in 1929—sought a lasting resolution on the payment of German reparations. Although everywhere mountains of economic and political problems cast a shadow on the horizon, and although there was far from the ease of international transactions characteristic of the pre–World War I years, nevertheless, there was during 1924–1928 and well into 1929 a resumption of large international capital flows, including long-term foreign portfolio and direct investment flows into the United States. In 1928 and during the first half of 1929, the upward trend in U.S. stock market prices made equities tempting to Americans and foreigners alike. In fact, in the last half of the 1920s, as the United States stood tall as a creditor nation, its prosperity at home came to pull in investors from abroad. During most of 1929 a sense of well-being existed in the United States and, to a lesser extent, in western Europe.

Like London in the last decades of the nineteenth century and in the early twentieth century, New York City had become a key "financial entrepôt," a magnet, attracting moneys from abroad (*inward* foreign investment) but then frequently reexporting such funds around the world (*outward* foreign investments).[16] Table 4.2 reveals the sharp rise in the total of new domestic and foreign securities issues in the United States. A "domestic" issue was for an American company; a "foreign" issue was for a foreign borrower. Both were generally denominated in dollars. The larger domestic issues always appealed more than the foreign ones to inward foreign investors, but the latter purchased both.[17] In addition, and as important as the new issues, foreign investors in the United States—like their American counterparts—bought and sold (i.e., traded in) existing stock market securities as well as the new issues. Both the new issues and the traded ones combined to attract new portfolio investments in the United States.

Table 4.2. Capital issues (domestic and foreign) in the United States, exclusive of refunding issues, 1919–1929 (in millions of dollars)

Year	Total domestic and foreign	Domestic issues	Foreign issues	Foreign issues as percent of total
1919	3,626	3,234	392	10.8
1920	3,732	3,235	497	13.3
1921	3,644	3,021	623	17.1
1922	4,391	3,627	764	17.4
1923	4,437	4,016	421	9.5
1924	5,557	4,588	969	17.4
1925	6,201	5,125	1,076	17.4
1926	6,314	5,189	1,125	17.8
1927	7,556	6,219	1,337	17.7
1928	8,040	6,789	1,251	15.6
1929	10,091	9,420	671	6.6

Source: Federal Reserve Board, *Annual Report 1931,* 199.

Taxes influenced how inward (and outward) foreign portfolio (and also some direct) investments were structured. By this I mean that the conduits were often shaped by tax considerations. World War I had introduced the highest tax rates in U.S. history, and in spite of the immediate postwar reductions, all during the 1920s taxes remained above the prewar levels. Abroad, everywhere, national governments sought new sources of revenues. In the 1920s there was a commitment on the part of governments to play a role in restoring their domestic economies, which led to more government spending, more taxes, and more borrowing. Countries began to negotiate treaties to avoid double taxation in international transactions; during the 1920s the United States did not enter into any double-taxation treaties, but economists and government policy makers participated in discussions on this vital subject.[18] Businessmen and bankers had always desired secrecy for competitive reasons, yet the enlarged role of tax collectors in the United States and abroad made concealment for the preservation of assets seem more urgent. To government officials, investors, counselors, and many observers, international transactions often were seen as a means of avoiding taxes.[19] Later a *Fortune* article described America in the 1920s: "Tax laws like the prohibition laws were laws you dodged if you could."[20] This was true of foreign investors in the United States as well as Americans.[21] It made the monitoring of such international transactions extremely difficult (which contributed to the weaknesses in available statistics).

In the late 1920s in the United States, domestic private debt mounted. Everyone borrowed, with credit readily available. American lending abroad was associated with the expanding private obligations. Bankers offered credit abroad just as they did at home, facilitating the export (and also the import) of capital. There was, however, an aspect of debt at home in which foreign investors played no role: consumer debt—from financing a car to a college education—was purely domestic. By contrast, in this decade, as more Americans than ever in history invested in stocks and bonds, many of the same bankers, securities dealers, and brokers who reached out to the average American to woo him to stock exchange purchases also went abroad to bring in additional investors—foreign ones. In 1928, for the first time, the total value of American stock issues surpassed that of bonds, and in 1929 the New York Stock Exchange had its first billion-share year in trading. Investment trusts and holding companies proliferated in the United States, particularly new public utility holding companies.[22] Foreign investors—like their domestic counterparts—perceived profitable opportunities in the stock market boom. Foreign investors participated not only in buying securities but also in the underwriting and financing of these purchases.

Inward foreign investments blended in with those made by Americans in the vibrant 1920s securities markets. Frequently the same stock brokers handled domestic and foreigners' investments and might keep both in a "street name." Banks played a "custodial" role, holding and trading in securities on behalf of the foreign investors. Most of the long-term foreign portfolio investments in the United States were in the form of purchases of traded stocks and bonds (new issues and existing ones) in American corporations—and increasingly more in stocks more than in bonds. Virtually all the American securities acquired by foreigners were by 1929 denominated in dollars.[23] Many bonds were explicitly gold backed.

In 1928 and a large part of 1929, as prices of common stock on the New York Stock Market soared, so did the value of foreign-owned shares, for the domestic and foreign buyers took part in the same financial markets. Then, in October to December 1929, stock prices tumbled, precipitously after the October stock market crash. The year end 1929 figures on long-term portfolio investments in the United States (the $4.3 billion total, cited earlier) put common stock at market and preferred shares and bonds at par. At year end 1929, their drop in value notwithstanding, common stocks represented 54 percent of the foreign portfolio investments in the United States.[24] It is not clear whether the 1929 portfolio investment figures captured the FPI in "foreign securities" as well as the FPI in domestic ones; the inward FPI figures may not reflect the sizable foreign interest in American securities. Table 4.1

gives an estimate for year end 1929 inward direct investment in the United States of $1.5 billion; I have no doubt that number understates the amount of inward FDI, since I have identified numerous stakes unknown to the compilers. Moreover, the compilers used a "book value" figure, which is usually considered to be low, if the investment has had any longevity.[25]

Blemished statistics aside, it is evident that despite the rise in foreign investment in America in the last years of the 1920s, the estimated $5.8 billion level of inward foreign investments at year end 1929 (see Table 4.1) remained well below the $7.1 billion level of June 30, 1914, on the eve of World War I.[26] Americans could and did finance their own economic activity in the 1920s—and some of the economic activity worldwide as well. The level of foreign investment in the United States before the First World War had equaled almost 20 percent of the U.S. gross national product.[27] For year end 1929, with the growth of the American economy, similar calculations come up with a mere 5.6 percent.[28] Tax disguises, the attrition in the value of stock holdings in late 1929, the possible omission in the FPI figures of foreign investments in "foreign" securities, along with the tabulators' likely underestimation of FDI cannot account for the dramatic difference in percentages. The lower involvement was both absolute and relative and is explained by America's wealth and its new role as a major creditor nation in the world economy. Also, prior to 1914 within Europe there had been abundant savings available to meet global investment opportunities. By contrast, in the late 1920s, British industries were requiring rationalization, and German ones rebuilding; central and eastern European economies cried out for new capital. Thus, within capital-starved Europe, these and other calls for investment presented competing demands. The 1924–1929 international capital flows (particularly those *from* the United States) aimed at meeting European and global requirements. At the same time, with America's new riches, investors from abroad perceived relatively lower returns in the United States than elsewhere, returns seemingly further reduced by a U.S. tax structure that discouraged (or at least was not conducive to) inward foreign investments.[29] Thus, even though foreign investment in the United States was on the rise in the late 1920s, I do not want to overemphasize its importance relative to America as a creditor nation—as a supplier of capital to the rest of the world.

Cosmopolitan Finance

A careful look is needed at the emerging intricate networks of "cosmopolitan finance," by which I mean the intertwining of inward and outward U.S. foreign investments—the mingling of the U.S. role as both recipient and source of long-term capital. Insights into this truly international setting are essential as a background for an understanding of the role of foreign investment in the United States in the late 1920s. Aspects of this brew of inward and outward investment and of FPI and FDI were not unique to the late 1920s, yet never before had the United States been such an important capital exporter, and that altered the picture. Also, never before had New York been so pivotal within the world economy. Overnight, New York had come of age as an active, free-wheeling global financial center—which it had not been in the 1914 world economy.[30] The blending of the inward and outward investments involved both external capital markets *and* internal allocations of capital within the firm. With the complications in the melding of inward and outward long-term foreign investments, it is not surprising that when analysts (and policy makers) have considered the process, they frequently fell into the trap of confusing the inward and outward foreign investments.

Combinations of inward and outward long-term foreign investments during 1924–1929 took on a variety of forms that involved both FDI and FPI. In Table 4.3 I have tried to simplify (perhaps oversimplify) some of the complexities, mapping certain of the combinations and permutations present in the late 1920s. The schema seeks to help steer us through the tangled international maze. The classifications in Table 4.3 should not be seen as rigid, for there were many overlaps. Rather, the scenario aims to throw light on the labyrinth of international capital transactions in this era.

Table 4.3, Part A, looks at outward foreign investment from the United States that resulted in or was linked with inward investment into the United States. Row 1, Part A, covers outward FDI from the United States in a company that then made or facilitated direct investments into the United States: U.S.-controlled companies in Canada (outward U.S. FDI), for example, International Nickel, owned properties in the United States, inward FDI.[31] Because the securities of the U.S.-controlled, Canadian-incorporated International Nickel were traded in the United States, Canada, and England, Americans, Britishers, and Canadians (and very likely investors of other nationalities) acquired securities of this Canadian corporation as portfolio investments; the enterprise (International Nickel) had, in turn, FDI in the United States. To the extent that the FPI (the investments in the securities of a Canadian company) were U.S. outward ones, this would fit in Row 2, Part A (outward FPI, inward FDI). A second example of the situation in Row 2, Part A, existed in the late 1920s, when the management of the Canadian-headquartered and Canadian-controlled Sun Life Assurance Company feared the acquisition of its shares by Americans (outward U.S. portfolio investments),

Table 4.3. Foreign investments: outward and inward; inward and outward

A. Outward and then inward		
Outward investments *from* the United States	Country X	Inward investments *to* the United States
1. U.S. direct investment abroad	in a company that makes	direct investments in U.S.
2. U.S. portfolio investments abroad	in a company that makes	direct and portfolio investments in U.S.
3. Banks and securities dealers make direct investments abroad	in offices that intermediate	portfolio investments into American securities.
B. Inward and then outward		
Inward investments *from* Country X	United States	Outward investments *from* the United States
1. Portfolio investments (stocks or bonds)	in a U.S. corporation that makes	direct investments abroad.
		portfolio investments abroad.
2. Portfolio investments (stocks or bonds)	in U.S. corporations that	foreigner uses as collateral to borrow in America.
3. Direct investments	in a U.S. affiliate that makes or facilitates	portfolio investments in Country X or in a third country.
		direct investments in Country X and / or in a third country (countries).
4. Portfolio investments	in dollar-denominated foreign securities issued	to finance a government or a corporation abroad in Country X or in a third country (countries).

Note: "Country X" is a foreign country (not the United States); "third country (or countries)" designates a country that is neither the United States nor Country X.

at the same time, as Sun Life was making large investments in the United States, both portfolio investments in American securities and direct investment in the insurance business (which constituted inward FPI and FDI in the United States).[32]

On Row 3, Part A, a third variation of the outward and then inward pattern is shown—as many American banks and securities dealers set up operations abroad (outward FDI), eager to develop business abroad *and* as a part of that business to sell American securities to foreigners (resulting in inward FPI). In all the examples presented in Part A, outward U.S. investments were combined with inward ones (FDI and FPI); in Rows 1 and 3, Part A, the outward investments were direct investments; in Row 2, the outward ones were portfolio investments.

Table 4.3, Part B, offers a profile of the flip side of the "blend," starting now with inward long-term foreign investments in the United States that served as the basis for the outward long-term investments from the United States. In Row 1, inward portfolio investments were made in securities of a firm established in the United States. This was the simplest of the patterns. Often, because information was abundant, such inward portfolio investments were in prominent American-headquartered giant enterprises, such as General Motors, which, in turn, were expanding internationally. Thus, the inward FPI was in the securities of General Motors, which as a U.S. multinational enterprise was undertaking outward direct investments. There was also FPI in U.S. companies, which were lending abroad.

Row 2, Part B, gives a different mode, wherein a foreign investor might purchase American domestic securities (inward FPI in the stocks or bonds of an American company or companies) and then use those securities as collateral for short-term or long-term borrowing in the United States, thus creating an American credit to the foreign investor (an equivalent to an outward investment).[33]

Row 3, Part B, offers still another variant of the inward and outward interconnections: here a foreign firm (or sometimes a group of foreign individuals) would set up or become owner or part owner of a company in the United States (inward direct investments), and this company would engage in or facilitate the export of American capital (outward foreign investments). The inward foreign direct investment would result in outward portfolio and/or direct investments. This occurred frequently. Thus, Yokohama Specie Bank's New York agency (an inward direct investment) had for many years arranged payments of interest on Japanese government borrowings in the United States and continued to do so; it was, accordingly, facilitating the export of American capital to Japan. Other foreign banks with direct investments in New York agencies played a similar role—and by the 1920s were assisting U.S. lending abroad as well as U.S. direct investments in their homelands.[34] What emerged in the early 1920s and subsequently accelerated (and seems to be new to this decade) was the formation of a sizable number of foreign-controlled companies in the United States designed to dispatch long-term capital to Europe (and to a lesser extent elsewhere), and not on a modest but on a vast scale. Most of these companies (e.g., International Match, Hugo Stinnes Corporation, Solvay American Investment Company) did some U.S. business or had U.S. investments, but in addition, they expedited the export of American capital to projects typically in Europe, but also farther afield.

In Row 4, Part B, I provide still a fourth case of linked inward and outward international investments. In this instance, inward portfolio investments were made in "foreign" securities, typically dollar-denominated foreign securities. Inward foreign portfolio investors not only bought stocks and bonds of American companies (as in Rows 1 and 2, Part B) but also purchased securities issued in the United States by foreign governments and foreign corporations, when the foreign entities were raising money in America (outward investments). For example, foreign investors bought Kreuger & Toll securities in the United States, and German investors purchased the Dawes Plan loan on the New York Stock Exchange.

In short, Part B focuses on inward investments (Rows 1, 2, and 4, portfolio investments in the United States; Row 3, direct investments in the United States) and indicates that these might be associated with the export of American capital (FDI or FPI). It is perhaps worthwhile to recapitulate rapidly and to elaborate a little more on Rows 1 and 2, and especially Rows 3 and 4. In Row 1, the largest inward foreign portfolio investments were in *domestic* stocks and bonds. For the foreign investors, in their choices, information was crucial: foreign investors often bought securities with familiar names, such as General Motors shares; GM was known abroad because it was a multinational enterprise. In Row 2, inward foreign portfolio investors could borrow against their American securities' holdings. Some of the borrowings were for outward foreign investments; some (brokerage loans) seem to have been used to finance more purchases of American securities.

In Row 3, inward foreign direct investors facilitated the export of American capital. This became very important in the 1920s, and nowhere was it more significant than in the activities of the Swedish financier Ivar Krueger. His inward investments in America were part and parcel of a global business. As already indicated in Chapter 3, in Sweden Kreuger had established at the pinnacle of his "empire" Kreuger & Toll, which controlled Swedish Match Company. He had set up in the United States in 1923 the huge International Match Corporation and even earlier the American Kreuger & Toll (the latter's 1925 successor was the Swedish American Investment Corporation). In addition, Kreuger & Toll (the Swedish company) was traded in New York. It is impossible to determine which investment company did what. Kreuger juggled assets, and the public and bankers trusted him. The assumption was that his secrecy would serve to minimize taxes. On the one hand, Kreuger had the core match business, and on the other, his foreign direct investments in the United States provided for his worldwide speculations and his foreign government loans; all the activities were interrelated.[35]

During the 1920s, *if* Kreuger ever had an interest in Diamond Match Company, he seems to have sold it.[36] In July 1928, the president of Diamond Match, W. A. Fairburn, met with Kreuger, and they agreed to cooperate in a joint fifty-fifty purchase of Ohio Match Company, Diamond Match's most important U.S. rival. The purchase occurred later that year.[37] This looked like a typical inward direct investment with an eye to obtaining market share in the match industry. The rest of Kreuger's ventures were far from ordinary. Kreuger & Toll set up the Swedish American Investment Corporation (1925)—an inward direct investment; its board interlocked with that of International Match Corporation—another inward direct investment; between 1925 and 1928, Swedish American raised some $15 million in the United States in issues that were bought principally (but not exclusively) by Americans. It siphoned this money out of the United States through a Dutch subsidiary of Kreuger & Toll (the dollars would vanish).[38]

Swedish American was a modest conduit for capital exports when compared with International Match Corporation (IMCO), also fully controlled by Kreuger, which assembled far larger sums in the United States, leaving only a small part in this country. *Moody's* rated its bonds Aa. On November 1, 1927, it had a $50 million bond issue. The money it raised went to loans to France and to many other governments to set up match monopolies in Poland, Estonia, Latvia, Yugoslavia, Roumania, Ecuador, and elsewhere.[39] Between 1923 and the end of 1927, IMCO's offerings of securities in the United States reached almost $97 million.[40] In addition, Kreuger & Toll obtained funds in America, which once again were used to meet the needs of Kreuger's international adventures; in 1928–1929, Kreuger & Toll raised more than $98 million.[41] Here, it is worthwhile to turn briefly to Row 4, Part B, in Table 4.3: foreign portfolio investors—as well as Americans—speculated in Kreuger & Toll's American securities.[42] In all, between 1923 and 1929, Kreuger companies collected from Americans (and foreign investors in the United States) in excess of $210 million.[43]

Returning to Row 3, Part B, although the Kreuger companies were the largest of such financial intermediaries of the 1920s (direct investors in the United States that sent moneys abroad), other foreign businessmen took similar steps to tap American capital markets for their own requirements. German steelmaker Hugo Stinnes died in 1924, and in 1926 two companies, Hugo Stinnes Corporation and its wholly owned subsidiary Hugo Stinnes Industries, Inc., were incorporated in Maryland to take over the assets, principally in Germany, of the Stinnes estate and to redeem claims of German banks against these assets. The two Maryland companies raised $21 million by selling in the United States ten- and twenty-year gold notes and debentures, which sum was paid to German banks that held claims against the Stinnes estate. Stinnes' widow (Claere Stinnes) turned over her inherited equity in the Stinnes assets in exchange for a 50 percent interest in the shares of Hugo Stinnes Corporation (which shares she placed in a Stinnes holding company). In short, the two Maryland-registered companies, Hugo Stinnes Corporation and Hugo Stinnes Industries Inc., controlled from Germany, held *German* assets, principally coal mines and coal reserves. The two firms' negligible U.S. assets related to the sale of German coal in America.[44] Once again (Row 3, Part B), what is present here is inward direct investments serving as a means of directing American moneys outward—toward German needs.

This approach to the financing of German industry differed from the 1925 loans to Krupp and Thyssen and the 1926–1927 loans to Vereinigte Stahlwerke (United Steel Works).[45] In these instances, there was no U.S. company; the issues floated were for the foreign firms. Yet here, too, foreign direct investors in the United States helped to facilitate the process. Thus, J. Henry Schroder Banking Corporation—established in New York in 1923 by the British merchant banking house J. Henry Schröder & Co. (an inward direct investment)—took part in the banking and selling syndicate led by the American firm Dillon, Read & Co. that underwrote the $64.2 million in loans to Vereinigte Stahlwerke. (It also participated in many other bond-issuing syndicates.) The British banking house intended to sell the bonds (American-issued "foreign" securities) through its British parent house. (There would then be portfolio investments from abroad in dollar-denominated foreign securities, as in Row 4, Part B.)[46]

By contrast, Framerican Industrial Development Corporation (see Chapter 3) seems to have been the counterpart of (perhaps the model for) the Hugo Stinnes companies, serving a similar function for the French steel company Schneider-Creusot. It operated at a loss in 1926, 1927, and 1928; nonetheless, in 1929 *Moody's* still gave its gold debentures that had been issued in 1922 an A rating.[47] In a like manner, in

1924, Simon I. Patiño, the Bolivian tin magnate, set up in the United States Patino Mines and Enterprises Consolidated, capital $50 million. Control was apparently in the hands of Patiño. The aim of forming an American-incorporated company was to obtain money in the United States for business abroad. Once again, these cases represent the pattern seen in Row 3, Part B.[48] So, too, the International Acceptance Bank (which had American and European banks as owners) involved inward direct investments that provided the basis for aiding the outflow of capital.

For foreign public utilities, reliance on U.S. financial markets was frequent. As an example of the inward/outward investment conjunction, in 1928 the Italian Superpower Corporation was formed in the United States by a group of Italian banks (Banca Commerciale, Credito Italiano, Banco di Roma, Banca Nazionale di Credito), some Italian electrical manufacturers, and American specialists in public utilities finance. Italian Superpower issued bonds in the United States that were sold to the American public. It owned stock in a long list of Italian public utilities.[49] Of the four Italian banks participating in Italian Superpower, three had direct investments in licensed agencies in New York.

In the late 1920s in the United States, new investment companies proliferated to manage the investments of small savers—and large investors. The Securities and Exchange Commission identified only 161 investment companies in the United States at the end of 1926, and then almost 600 formed in the United States from 1927 through 1929.[50] British investment trusts that had long histories serving the same functions provided the models for these companies.[51] Yet whereas the latter were often conservative, the new U.S. investment companies were not. Later the SEC estimated that in 1929 investment company issues accounted for 30 percent of all U.S. corporate financing.[52] Many of the new U.S.-based financial intermediaries were American owned and run (and invested exclusively in the United States); however, a good number were established by, or in cooperation with, foreign investors (inward FDI); then they raised money in the United States for investment in this country and abroad (outward FPI). As an example, in 1928 the United States and British International Company, Ltd., organized under Maryland law, issued preferred stock in America; it advertised that it was associated with the "best [investment] management groups in Great Britain."[53]

Among the foreign-owned companies that issued bonds in the United States were, in August and September 1929, Solvay American Investment Corporation (Belgian owned, through a Swiss intermediary) and Anglo-American Shares, Inc., a Delaware corporation with the Marquess of Carisbrooke and the president of the Royal Aeronautical Society, London, Colonel, the Master of Sempill, as directors.[54] Often, in the mind of the public, "investment companies" were the same as "holding companies."[55] Thus, a Hamburg insurance firm, H. Mutzenbecher, Jr.—through New York Hamburg Corporation (organized in 1928)—controlled the Hamburg American Insurance Company in New York. The New York Hamburg Corporation, in keeping with most of these new holding company structures, issued stock in New York. Its president was F. F. Mutzenbecher of Hamburg.[56] All the cash raised did not stay in the United States.

The preceding examples of the blending of inward direct investments and outward portfolio and direct investments conform, with some noted exceptions (that fit into Row 4, Part B), to what is described in Row 3, Part B. Turning now to Row 4, Part B, of Table 4.3, a foreign investor could (and did) invest in securities that provided financing to the government or to firms in his own nation (i.e., the purchase of foreign securities). Thus, a German investor would buy in New York securities that represented loans to Germany. Alternatively, a foreign investor could acquire "foreign" securities that furnished financing for a third country; this was the case when a British investor bought loans to Chile that had been issued in New York. In both situations an inward foreign portfolio investment in the "foreign" securities was associated with an outward one. When discussing Row 3, Part B, I noted that foreign investors purchased the American-issued securities of the Swedish firm Kreuger & Toll (inward portfolio investments), and that provided the basis for financing the Swedish firm. So, too, when, for example, J. Henry Schroder Banking Corporation participated with Dillon, Read & Co. in issues for German securities, it often sent its tranche to Europe, for it had no network for distributing securities in the United States; the consequence was the attraction of foreign portfolio investment to foreign issues in America. Foreign portfolio investors purchased foreign issues within the United States and also traded the foreign securities.

The purchase of foreign securities in New York was not new to the 1920s. In the past, foreign investors had, for convenience, bought Canadian Pacific stock, for example, on the New York Stock Exchange, where it had been traded for many decades. When foreign investors acquired the securities of Canadian Pacific in the United States, their investment was made in a foreign-headquartered company that did its principal business outside America. The inward foreign investments in new foreign issues and traded foreign securities increased in importance during the 1920s. As the United States became the financier for the world, there were many more such securities available.

Moving on from the inward/outward, FDI/FPI, story presented in Table 4.3, we need to consider more examples of the complexities of cosmopolitan finance. Certain foreign-owned financial intermediaries were set up in the United States principally to mobilize moneys for investment there. Instead of combining inward and outward investments, these combined inward direct and inward portfolio investments. Thus, the Société financière pour entreprises électriques aux Etats-Unis, formed in Geneva in 1910, to invest in American power and light companies, decided in 1925 that it could best function with its "nominal" head office in New York. It created the American European Securities Company (AESC), an investment trust company that took over the U.S. assets of the Swiss firm.[57] The chairman of AESC was Frédéric Dominicé of Geneva. Dominicé (1868–1938) was managing director of Union Financière de Geneva, a firm active in promoting investment trust–type companies, such as AESC, that operated outside Switzerland.[58] Six of AESC's eleven directors listed Geneva as their place of residence; their family names are well known to students of Swiss banking activities in the United States. Aside from Dominicé, the other five directors were Edmond Aubert, R. L. Hentsch, Jean Lombard, Aymond Pictet, and Albert Lullin.[59] The founding chairman (in 1910) of the Société financière pour entreprises électrique aux Etats-Unis had been Guillaume Pictet.[60] The newly restructured AESC acquired stock in a wide variety of public utilities across the United States. By 1920s standards, it was not a giant enterprise: as of November 30, 1927, its assets were a mere $7.9 million.[61] Yet I include it, because it was in keeping with the various ways in which foreign investors were participating in American securities markets—as part and parcel of the networks of global finance.

An even better case of cosmopolitan finance is evidenced in the activities of the Belgian entrepreneur Alfred Loewenstein (1877–1928), who was a Kreuger-type character, a master of intricate financial "deals" involving rayon companies and public utilities.[62] Edward Peacock of Baring Brothers & Co., London, described Loewenstein in 1926 as "a market operator and splendid at that."[63] Loewenstein played a major role in the formation in 1926 in Canada of Hydro-Electric Securities Corporation, which would acquire interests in public utilities, principally in the United States. Loewenstein made his first trip to America in April 1928, by which time he already had sizable U.S. investments (as well as large U.S. borrowings).[64] His host in New York was Prentiss Gray of the J. Henry Schroder Banking Corporation (in Britain, Loewenstein had close ties with the parent London Schröder house).[65] Through Canadian holding companies, set up mainly for tax reasons, Loewenstein held such American securities as Allied Chemical, Atchison Topeka Railroads, Buffalo Niagara, Commonwealth Edison, Consolidated Gas of New York, Missouri Pacific Railroad, Pennsylvania

Railroad, Standard Gas and Electric, and possibly Middle West Utilities.[66] At the time of his death in 1928, he was contemplating pledging his American stocks and bonds against additional American borrowings.[67] In August 1929, after Loewenstein's death, *The Economist* noted that the Canadian-incorporated Hydro-Electric Securities Corporation had interests in Spanish, Italian, Belgian, Brazilian, and Mexican utility companies, but about 90 percent of its investments were in the United States; whereas its stockholders were mainly American and Canadian, there had been recent speculative British buying.[68]

There were other tiers in the holdings of American assets, for instance, those involving German-Dutch-German-American ownership relationships. Clusters and layers of financial units with complex webs of international linkages became common in the late 1920s. By the mid-1920s, M. M. Warburg & Co., Hamburg (along with other European banks), for example, had interests in the International Acceptance Bank (IAB), New York.[69] In London, M. M. Warburg & Co. formed the Industrial Finance & Investment Corporation (IFI). In Amsterdam, in 1928 it set up (along with Mendelssohn & Co., the Nederlandsche Handel-Maatschappij, and other Dutch, Swiss, Austrian, German, English, and American banks) the NV Nederlandsche Crediet-en Financiering-Maatschappij (NVNC). This Dutch investment corporation was modeled on the American & Continental Corporation (ACC), New York (established earlier by IAB for outward U.S. international investments), and on the Industrial Finance & Investment Corporation, London. All three companies, IFI, NVNC, and ACC, acted together to intermediate long-term foreign capital to German industry.[70]

Partly or wholly foreign-owned financial intermediaries that operated in New York were by the late 1920s working intimately with the now very international American-headquartered private investment banks (Morgan; Dillon, Read; Kuhn, Loeb; Lee, Higginson—to mention a few), as well as with the internationally oriented New York commercial banks (National City, Chase National, for example) that had underwriting subsidiaries.[71] These and many more American financial intermediaries were by the late 1920s global in their lending. In addition, U.S.-headquartered brokerage houses such as Hallgarten and A. Iselin (which at times functioned as investment bankers) had extensive international connections. Foreign investors in the United States found all these institutions helpful partners.[72] Lee, Higginson, Boston and New York, for instance, was the lead American banker for Kreuger.

Corporate pyramids and international financial alliances multiplied in the late 1920s. In the foregoing rendition, I have combined discussions of legitimate and sham operations. In the flamboyant finance of the late 1920s, the two were frequently indistinguishable. Investors and speculators were often one and the same. In the main, markets were not regulated.[73] These new and complicated institutional structures moved large quantities of capital internationally. There were (under U.S. law) withholding taxes on dividends and interest, and taxes on capital gains of nonresident foreign investors in the United States. Yet the taxes were not conscientiously collected; the various new corporate arrangements were not easy to decipher or to tax. Indeed, in 1929 the U.S. Department of Commerce concluded that no estimate could be made of foreign investments in the United States based on data from the commissioner of Internal Revenue.[74]

What was the reason for such complex cosmopolitan corporate structures? Why were there often so many different national corporations involved? Was tax the sole motivating factor? Taxes were clearly important, but there was more to it. The answer to the first two questions lies in the financial roles of cities in the world economy of the late 1920s. New York was paramount, because the United States had the wealth. London remained central, with its long experience as a financial center. Amsterdam shared that advantage along with others (namely, close German connections; a tradition of secrecy in financial transactions; and lenient Dutch tax authorities). For similar reasons, Basle, Zurich, and Geneva banks were engaged in the new international financial arena in the 1920s in an unprecedented manner.[75] Swiss holding companies were often used for tax reasons. Stockholm took on a curious role, enhanced by Kreuger's dynamism but also associated with the very international Wallenberg family's Stockholms Enskilda Bank. The German international banking connections were personal and long-standing and survived the war to reconstitute themselves. Brussels- and Paris-headquartered financial intermediaries were numerous (and experienced). Milan banks—in particular—sought to attract moneys to Italian economic development. Toronto and Montreal were locales for holding companies, owing to lax monitoring, minimal taxes, and special expertise in public utilities finance; in the 1920s, global public utility finance was of great importance in the global spread of electrification.[76] International finance—of which foreign investment in the United States was an integral part—became a jungle of corporate complexities, based both on the core competencies of financial intermediaries in particular nations and on the vast demand for capital.[77] The late 1920s labyrinthine international associations and transactions of cosmopolitan finance set the fundamentals in the story of foreign investments in the United States. Relationships were not bilateral but truly multicountry ones. The tangled strands make the picture hard to paint. Yet hopefully this crude rendition offers an opening to the more specific discussion of FPI and, in Chapter 5, FDI in the United States.

Foreign Portfolio Investments in the United States, 1924–1929

Foreign portfolio investors in the United States could buy new issues or outstanding ones. If they bought outstanding ones, these would usually be traded on the New York Stock Exchange, the Curb Exchange, and/or an exchange abroad. Foreigners might make the purchase of the securities within the United States or outside the country (often in this case through American banks or brokers located abroad). The securities bought could be physically held in the United States (by American banks or brokers) or could be held outside the country. Foreigners acquired domestic and foreign dollar-denominated securities. Despite the attraction of higher nominal yields abroad, in this period, FPI in the United States in domestic securities increased. Table 4.4 shows the excess of average yields on new foreign bonds over domestic bonds narrowed during the late 1920s; economists would predict increasing purchases of the high-grade domestic bonds over the foreign ones after 1926. The statistics are not good enough to establish this. There is, however, clear evidence of more investments in equities rather than in bonds—to take advantage of stock appreciation.

Table 4.2 showed the rapid rise of new domestic issues in the United States in the late 1920s. These securities were sold mainly to Americans, although a small portion went abroad. I do not have any numbers on the exact amounts that were sold outside the United States. Table 4.5 offers estimates on the movement of outstanding American domestic securities, 1924–1928.[78] The information is comparable to that given in Table 2.9 for earlier years. Table 4.6 uses Cleona Lewis' figures on the composition of inward long-term portfolio investments in the United States. Whereas Table 4.5 monitored the trade in existing securities, Table 4.6 deals with the level of long-term FPI in the United States at year end 1924 and 1929.[79]

Table 4.4. Comparison of foreign and American domestic bond yields, 1924–1929

Year	Weighted average of yield index of new foreign bonds	Index of yields on sixty high-grade domestic bonds	Excess of average yield on new foreign bonds
1924	6.56	4.85	1.71
1925	6.51	4.72	1.79
1926	6.51	4.60	1.91
1927	6.14	4.47	1.67
1928	6.09	4.49	1.60
1929	5.81	4.69	1.12

Source: John T. Madden, Marcus Nadler, and Harry C. Sauvain, *America's Experience as a Creditor Nation* (New York: Prentice-Hall, 1937), 14.

Table 4.5. International movements of outstanding American (domestic) securities, 1924–1928 (in millions of U.S. dollars)

Activity	1924	1925	1926	1927	1928
1. Repatriation by foreigners of American securities	351	307	485	661	1,153
2. American securities sold to foreigners	397	530	665	861	1,634
3. Net increase in foreign holdings of American domestic securities	46	223	180	200	481

Source: National Industrial Conference Board, *The International Financial Position of the United States* (New York: National Industrial Conference Board, 1929), 64. I am unable to reconcile these figures with the ones given in Hal Lary, *The United States in the World Economy* (Washington, D.C., 1943), 107.

Table 4.6. Foreign portfolio investments in the United States, by type, 1924, 1929

	Year end 1924		Year end 1929	
Investments	In millions of dollars	Percent of total	In millions of dollars	Percent of total
Foreign holdings in railroads				
Common stock (at market)	255	13.2	335	7.9
Preferred stock (at par)	68	3.5	74	1.7
Bonds (at par)	580	30.0	405	9.5
Total railroads	903	46.7	814	19.1
Other foreign holdings				
Common stock (at market)	500	25.9	1,985	46.6
Preferred stock (at par)	140	7.2	540	12.7
Bonds (at par)	140	7.2	170	4.0
Miscellaneous portfolio stakes	250	12.9	750	17.6
Total other foreign holdings	1,030	53.3[a]	3,445	80.9
Total portfolio investments	1,933	100.0	4,259	100.0

Source: Based on Cleona Lewis, *America's Stake in International Investments* (Washington, D.C.: Brookings Institution, 1938), 558; see also U.S. Department of Commerce, Bureau of Foreign and Domestic Commerce, *Foreign Investments in the United States* (Washington, D.C., 1937) for more specifics.

a. The percentages do not add up due to rounding.

Between 1924 and 1929, as foreign portfolio investors in this country increased their holdings, it is clear that they moved away from preferred shares and bonds to common shares (in 1924, common shares at market constituted 39 percent of the foreign portfolio investment in the United States, compared with 54 percent at year end 1929).[80] Investors became more ready to take risks, shifting from the presumably assured (albeit low) returns of preferred stock and bonds to the seemingly bound-to-appreciate—at least until the October crash—corporate shares. Domestic shares provided alternatives to domestic bonds. The pattern was similar to that of American buyers of their own securities.[81]

Table 4.2 showed that between 1924 and 1927 new "foreign issues" as well as domestic ones mounted in the United States. The new foreign issues involved the export of capital. I have no statistical information on how many of the new foreign issues were purchased by non-U.S. residents. There was also trade in existing foreign securities. Table 4.7 indicates the sale abroad of outstanding foreign securities, that is, the purchase by foreigners of foreign securities. When outstanding foreign securities owned by Americans were acquired by foreigners, this involved an inward flow of capital. It might mean the repatriation of a foreign debt (the reduction of outward foreign investment), or, alternatively, it might mean that foreign holders were buying dollar-denominated, U.S.-issued foreign securities as investments. There is no way to tell from these figures. We have no figures for 1929 on foreign holdings of U.S.-issued foreign securities, much less as to whether foreign investors were buying their own securities (Germans buying German bonds) or whether foreign investors were buying third-country securities (Britishers buying German bonds in New York).[82]

When domestic (or foreign) securities were purchased by foreign investors, it did not necessarily mean that the actual securities were exported. The securities could be, and frequently were, physically held in the United States, in custodial accounts, by banks and brokers.[83] The securities could be in the name of a nominee, rather than the ultimate investor. Banks and brokers would purchase and sell securities on behalf of foreign investors, reinvesting capital gains. Thus, the purchase of securities did not require a corresponding import of capital to buy

Table 4.7. Foreign investors' purchase of foreign securities, 1924–1928 (in millions of U.S. dollars)

Activity	1924	1925	1926	1927	1928
Outstanding "foreign" securities sold to foreigners	177	216	299	398	442

Source: National Industrial Conference Board, *The International Financial Position of the United States* (New York: National Industrial Conference Board, 1929), 64. I do not on this table give a net figure because it is not meaningful. When Americans bought outstanding "foreign" securities that had been held by foreigners, the Americans were making an outward foreign investment.

the stocks and bonds. This was also the case, since such securities could be purchased on margin.[84] So, too, since the value of the securities fluctuated, the levels varied with stock market valuations. Accordingly, a recorded increase in portfolio investments in domestic and foreign securities did not correspond to an equal capital flow into the United States.

Foreign investors had before the First World War bought American securities; they had, as we have seen, resumed their acquisitions in the immediate postwar period. There existed well-established conduits for such purchases. American investment bankers and brokers typically offered their European associates a tranche in new issues and made it relatively easy for foreign investors to buy traded securities. Financial institutions abroad served the same functions.

There is no evidence of any special interest by foreign investors in U.S., state, or local government securities. This is important, since much of global lending in these years went to governments (including U.S. outward investments).[85] Yet within the United States, governments borrowed at home. They did not have to go outside the country for financing. Some U.S. Treasury bonds and some New York City bonds were held abroad, but the amounts were small.[86] Every year, however, the reports of the Corporation of Foreign Bondholders, London, would harp on the long-standing debt defaults by American southern states—particularly Mississippi (its debts went back to the 1830s and defaults to the early 1840s). After protracted negotiations, in 1920 West Virginia had repaid its outstanding debt. For a half century that state had refused to recognize its obligations; the U.S. Supreme Court had given a judgment against the state in 1915, and, finally in 1920, it had settled. That did not create a precedent. In the late 1920s there remained eight southern states in default (Alabama, Arkansas, Florida, Georgia, Louisiana, Mississippi, North Carolina, and South Carolina). Annually, the Corporation of Foreign Bondholders argued that the United States—now a creditor—should take responsibility for the debts of the states. The corporation likened the worst case—the Mississippi default—to the behavior of Russia. Its and others' efforts notwithstanding, after 1920 there were no further settlements.[87] States found adequate financing at home, so the opprobrium made no difference.

Branches and affiliates of foreign insurance companies that provided insurance coverage within the United States held securities, including U.S., state, and local government securities.[88] We must beware of double counting. These insurers were (and should be considered) direct investors in America; the assets held by them were those of the branches and affiliates.

Table 4.6 showed the continuing relative (and absolute) decline in foreign portfolio investments in railroads. Railroads lost their luster for investors. Nonetheless, important foreign investments in railroad securities were sustained, and some new ones were made.[89] Unquestionably, however, particularly by the end of the decade, the shift had been to shares of industrial and power, light, and telephone companies. By year end 1929, the bulk of foreign portfolio investments in the United States was in major American industrials and public utilities.

For most of the decade, U.S. Steel continued carefully to monitor the investments from abroad in its common and preferred shares. By year end 1927, its records showed foreign shareholdings at a mere 2.5 percent. It then stopped tracing these trivial numbers. While it seems likely that the amounts held abroad rose slightly in 1928 and more in 1929, U.S. Steel officials did not perceive the holdings as significant. It could be that because of the withholding tax, foreign investors used nominees—and thus the records of U.S. Steel fail to capture the extent of the foreign investments.[90] Perhaps, more important, the lack of interest reflected the maturity of the American steel industry.[91] Foreign investors, like their American counterparts, wanted to invest in the more vibrant sectors within the economy.

By contrast, for advertising purposes General Motors boasted in 1924 that it had more than 68,000 investors, who lived in every state in America, in Canada, and in sixteen other foreign lands.[92] Early in 1926, Dillon, Read & Co. announced an underwriting of 1.1 million shares of National Cash Register (another U.S. multinational enterprise). The investment banker noted an "unusual aspect" of the underwriting was that the shares would be offered simultaneously in Switzerland, the Netherlands, the United Kingdom, and Canada—in response to "popular demand."[93] In the years 1927–1929 such broad foreign offerings of new issues of U.S. industrials were no longer unusual. Securities of the principal American industrial corporations became widely available abroad.

The financial needs of U.S. public utilities were formidable. Within the United States, new issues were the norm. By the end of the 1920s, American Telephone and Telegraph (AT&T) provided all but a minor part of the U.S. telephone services, ten groups of "systems" sold roughly 75 percent of the nation's electric power, and sixteen gas groups had control over 45 percent of the nation's gas output.[94] Foreigners invested directly and through intermediaries in the securities of many of these public utilities, both new issues and outstanding ones. AT&T had long gone to foreign markets for financing.[95] There continued to be an abiding interest abroad in the American telephone giant. By 1929 the three largest electric and gas system holding companies—United Corporation, Electric Bond and Share, and the Insull Utility Group—had all attracted foreign investments (FPI). In January 1929, when J. P. Morgan & Co. issued shares of the United Corporation, it reserved—as was its usual practice—securities for Morgan, Grenfell & Co, London, and for Morgan & Cie., Paris.[96] Electric Bond and Share securities appeared in foreign portfolios.[97] Forrest McDonald's book on Samuel Insull suggests that both before and after the First World War, Insull had turned to the British for financing, particularly to Robert Benson & Co. and Robert Fleming & Co. These British merchant banks were closely associated with investments trusts that acquired interests in Insull's companies. In the late 1920s, Insull had a London firm marketing his securities (Insull, Son & Co.).[98] Insull also relied heavily on Sun Life Assurance Company of Canada, which had long and close ties in the Chicago area.[99] Data in the archives of Sun Life Assurance Company indicate that the latter's president, T. B. Macaulay, was especially committed to buying securities in Insull companies. In April 1924, he wrote Insull, "I appreciate very much the amount of personal attention you have given to our purchases of securities in your companies."[100]

Included among the other major U.S. public utilities that were especially appealing to foreign investors was Cities Service Co., which from its origins in 1910 had (and continued to have) foreign investors.[101] In 1929, it had an assistant secretary in London, a London office in the City, and one British director (Thomas St. John Bashford).[102] Likewise, there were sizable foreign investments in Consolidated Gas Company of New York and Standard Gas & Electric. Foreign investments existed not only in the largest holding companies but in their affiliates as well—for example, in Detroit Edison and Public Service Corporation of New Jersey.[103] My research uncovered no pattern as to whether foreign investments went to the holding companies or to the operating ones (typically holding companies did not own all the stock in the operating utilities, and thus outsiders could invest or retain earlier investments).

James Bonbright and Gardiner Means' 1932 classic on holding companies, which covers all the major public utilities holding companies, has nothing on foreign investment.[104] One wonders why. Two reasons emerge: (1) the sums contributed by foreign investors, although large in absolute amounts, seem relatively small compared with the total capitalization of these entities, and (2) the foreign holdings blended with domestic ones and presented no unique problems. These were FPIs and posed no "threat" of control. Clearly, the principal, formidable financing required by U.S. public utilities (and by U.S. industrials) was American. The foreign contribution was marginal. It is not hard, however, to explain the rising foreign investments in these domestic securities. Investors from abroad were lured by what seemed to be a healthy American economy.

What is more complicated is the foreign investors' participation in *foreign* securities. Transactions in new foreign issues and in outstanding securities went through the identical institutional channels as domestic securities. Thus, when Morgan, for example, had a foreign bond issue, the banking house shared it with its friends abroad, just as it did with the domestic issues. Donald Moggridge found evidence in British Treasury Department records that on many occasions underwriters of new foreign issues in New York reserved substantial blocks of securities for European sales.[105] Why did the investment bankers (and securities dealers), through their transatlantic contacts, market the foreign issues outside the United States? One answer to this question is that American underwriters and securities dealers desired to enlarge the demand for their securities; they had a domestic market but wanted a larger one. Thomas Lamont, a partner in the Morgan bank, insisted that continental European "markets" take a set tranche in the Dawes loan in October 1924. He claimed that this was required by American investors, which was perhaps a euphemism for the wish by the Morgan house to involve foreign bankers; when the latter participated in the foreign loans, it was assumed that they would take steps to secure responsibility by the borrowers and thus minimize the possibility of defaults.[106] Often foreign borrowers, who had once gone to London, now turned to the United States, where issuing costs had declined as a result of competition between issuing houses. When that occurred, British and other foreign investors purchased the foreign securities in New York.[107] One New York broker noted that his firm had done £7 million of such business in 1924 to 1927.[108] Moggridge writes of a joint London–New York issue of Australian bonds in July 1925 where "a large portion of the New York *tranche* . . . found its way almost immediately to London." He added that the reverse rarely, if ever, occurred.[109] It is likely that Americans were not ready to absorb Australian bonds that were easily salable in London. Indeed, it was said that because Americans were unfamiliar with foreign securities, American financial institutions had pushed the sale of these particular issues in London.[110]

Foreigners bought foreign securities issued and sold in the United States and denominated in dollars for a number of reasons: (1) Sometimes foreign issues to the identical foreign borrower carried a higher coupon rate when the issue was done in New York rather than London (this was particularly true in the mid-1920s and less so later); the coupon rate was superior in New York because American bankers had insisted that to sell the bond to Americans, who were new to foreign issues, the interest rate had to be greater. This argument had reduced cogency as the decade progressed, but in the mid-1920s, foreign investors purchasing the foreign issue could take advantage of the larger returns.[111] (2) Certain investors (Germans, for example) were more confident about German securities bought through New York; moreover, they could evade turnover taxes and income taxes in the international transactions.[112] (3) The Dawes loan was offered in nine countries simultaneously—with dollar-denominated bonds in the United States, sterling-denominated bonds in Great Britain and elsewhere—except for Italy, where the bonds were lire denominated, and Sweden, where they were denominated in kroners.[113] Yet foreigners still considered it convenient to buy the dollar-denominated issues. (4) When Britain returned to the gold standard in 1925, restrictions were imposed on foreign issues but not on the purchase of outstanding securities traded in New York.[114] Thus, Britishers (and others), much to the annoyance of contemporaries, bought on Wall Street, and the commissions and fees went to Americans. (5) There was also arbitrage—buying an internationally traded security in New York and selling it in London or Amsterdam; but in the 1920s, with the speed of information (by cable), markets quickly adjusted, and these possibilities, although continuing, had narrowed.[115] And (6) foreigners had a sense of confidence in buying a dollar-denominated foreign security; there was some "flight capital" to the safe haven in America.

No satisfactory statistics—by source country—exist on FPI in the United States in the late 1920s. Making international portfolio investments varied in difficulty, by nationality. U.S. investments were probably easiest for a Canadian who lived in Toronto or Montreal. By 1929 in all probability Canadians ranked second only to the British in portfolio investments in the United States. Many Canadians believed U.S. opportunities were better than those within their homeland and were not timid about investments south of the border. Indeed, Canadian brokers would boast when they were able to convince their Canadian customers to switch *from* American to Canadian securities.[116] Wealthy individuals and also Canadian financial intermediaries (on their own behalf and on behalf of clients) made large portfolio investments in the United States. Canadian investors were reported to be particularly adept at interexchange arbitrage.[117] Their investments were mainly in market leaders (on Wall Street) and particularly in public utilities. Many Canadians were in the U.S. market not for speculative purposes but for long-term investments.

In 1923, National City Company (the securities affiliate of National City Bank) had purchased control of one of Canada's largest investment houses, the United Financial Corporation, Montreal; UFC marketed American issues in Canada, as well as underwriting Canadian issues in New York.[118] There emerged in Canada in the late 1920s a coterie of Canadian-owned financial intermediaries. The principal ones were associated with (1) A. E. Ames & Co., Toronto; (2) Dominion Securities, Toronto; (3) Royal Securities, Montreal; (4) Nesbitt, Thomson & Co., Ltd., Montreal; (5) Wood, Gundy & Co., Ltd. (home office in Toronto but connected with investment companies in Montreal); and (6) Arthur Meighen, Toronto.[119] Each was involved in international business, not only bringing in foreign (outside of Canada) capital but also undertaking and intermediating outward investments—including those in the United States.

The first three executed on a regular basis American investments on behalf of clients. E. R. Wood, president of Dominion Securities, also served as a director of the Tubize Artificial Silk Co., a Belgian enterprise in the United States.[120] Royal Securities was headed by I. W. Killiam, who followed William Maxwell Aitken (the future Lord Beaverbrook) when the latter moved to England in 1910; it apparently held as well as dealt in American securities.[121] In the Nesbitt, Thomson group was the Power Corporation of Canada, Ltd., organized in 1925, which invested in public utilities in Canada and the United States.[122] The Wood, Gundy group had a collection of investment companies, including Investment Bond and Share Corporation (IBSC), formed in 1927 and involving A. Iselin & Co., New York (which had British, Swiss, and French associations); the president of IBSC was Herbert S. Holt, president of the Royal Bank of Canada, by 1929 Canada's largest bank.[123] Several trusts linked with Wood, Gundy also made U.S. investments. As for the Meighen group (Arthur Meighen was Canadian prime minister in 1920–1921, and 1925–1926), it included the General Investment Trust, Ltd., set up in late 1926 and with a portfolio at decade's end that contained American as well as Canadian and a small amount of European securities.[124] Canadian securities companies and investment trusts collected savings from individual Canadians and made investments abroad, a large share of which went to the United States.[125]

Other Canadian institutional investors in the United States comprised the insurance companies. Sun Life Assurance Company of Canada's president, T. B. Macaulay, in November 1926, wrote of "the bright future opening before us in the United States. Our development of the next quarter of the century should be chiefly in that country, and I certainly am expecting great things."[126] Macaulay was referring both to his investment plans (portfolio investments) and to the expansion of the insurance business (direct investments). By December 31, 1928, the market value of that insurance company's American stocks and bonds was $293.9 million, or 75 percent of its entire portfolio of bonds and stocks listed at market values in its *1928 Annual Report*.[127] Sun Life

Assurance Company of Canada in May 1929 had 18.73 percent of its investment portfolio in electric power, light, and gas companies, principally in the United States.[128]

If the Canadian FPI in the United States was substantial, it seems clear that British FPI was larger; the United Kingdom remained in first place among foreign portfolio investors in the United States. Certain of the stakes were "lethargic" ones; long-established investment patterns were not easily broken. British-headquartered investment trust companies and insurance offices held U.S. investments—although, in most cases, on nowhere near the scale of past years. Indeed, as a proportion of their overall holdings, there was a reduction in British investment trust percentages over the last part of the decade as British investment trusts paid more attention to home investments and to those on the European continent; what is truly striking is the 1920s shift away from the United States toward continental Europe.[129]

The British (like the Canadians) engaged in substantial trade in American securities, purchases and also sales. Donald Moggridge suggests that because of "the unattractiveness of American securities [to the British investor] for other than short-term speculation during the years 1919–1925 when sterling was expected to rise in value," there had been a pent-up demand. When Britain went back to the gold standard (in 1925) and at the same time took steps to limit foreign issues in London, this "might have induced a [the] more rapid rebuilding of American portfolios."[130] Moggridge found that between 1926 and 1929 British "life insurance companies, with National Mutual in the vanguard, became more adventurous in their portfolios and in some respect 'discovered' the New York market."[131]

Between 1925 and 1929, eighty-two investment trusts were formed in Great Britain.[132] These new trusts concentrated on industrial securities, unlike many of the earlier ones that had invested heavily in railroads. One study of British investment trusts showed that in 1929 the newer ones had a larger percentage of their portfolios in the United States than did those founded before World War I. For most old and new British investment trusts, it seems evident that the United States was not the primary locale for their investments in the late 1920s.[133] Yet the Bensons and Flemings group of trusts kept substantial investments in America.[134]

Other British investment trusts were even more involved. Thus, for example, the Scottish American Investment Co., Ltd., Edinburgh, in 1925 still had 67 percent of its portfolio in American securities.[135] It had advisers in the United States. In the fall of 1928, its manager, Charles Munro, after a visit to the United States, recommended "increasing our Railroad list," so as to be in a better position when the speculation in the market cooled; on the other hand, as he had traveled from New York to San Francisco, he commented on the "signs of solid prosperity . . . I begin to feel that no outside influence could arrest the expansion for any length of time. That there must be ups and downs in trade I admit, but my experience here for almost twenty years, and the progress witnessed, makes me as bullish as ever on things American." He was not alone in this view, and while Scottish American would curtail its U.S. holdings in the late summer of 1929 before the stock market crash, that fall it continued to have the majority of its assets in American securities.[136]

Another sizable British holder of American securities was Nobel Industries and its 1926 successor, Imperial Chemical Industries (ICI). Du Pont had gotten Nobel Industries involved in FPI in General Motors shares. At various times between 1922 and 1926, Nobel Industries had bought and sold GM stock, and when, in 1926, Nobel Industries became part of ICI, it transferred to the latter 750,000 GM shares. During 1927 and 1928, ICI sold 375,000 GM shares (half its holding) for the dollar equivalent of £3,466,436 ($16.8 million). It did so in three transactions, seeking to profit from the rising market, and reinvested these moneys in England. At the end of 1929, ICI retained 375,000 shares; Sir Harry McGowan of ICI kept a seat on the GM board, albeit he apparently had no influence on GM decision making.[137]

Certain of the largest British institutional investors maintained close contacts in America and obtained guidance and information from representatives there. This was true of the principal Scottish investment trusts. Other sizable investors had "friends"—that is, bankers in New York and Chicago—who handled their accounts. Most Britishers, however, purchased American securities through (1) British banks (commercial banks and merchant banks, including those such as Morgan, Grenfell with its long-standing U.S. associations, and J. Henry Schröder & Co., with its active New York subsidiary); (2) London branches of American banks, especially, Guaranty Trust Company, National City Bank, Chase National Bank, and Bankers Trust; (3) British stockbrokers; and (4) in particular, a small coterie of London stockbrokers who specialized in American securities.[138] In addition, before 1926, the New York Stock Exchange had been represented in London by the firm Pynchon & Co. That year, Gerald Maxwell, a onetime Chrysler salesman in England, opened a London office for the New York Stock Exchange firm G. M.-P. Murphy & Co.[139] Other New York Stock Exchange members had branches in London: Baker, Weeks & Harden; Dominick & Dominick; Frazier Jelke & Co.; Hallgarten & Co.; Hirsch, Lilienthal & Co.; A. Iselin & Co; Post & Flagg; L. F. Rothschild & Co.; Shields & Co.; and Spencer Trask & Co.[140] For a few years, 1927–1930,

Gordon Leith, who lived in London, was a partner in Kuhn, Loeb, which New York investment banking house paid Leith's London office expenses. Leith, an experienced banker (who had been with Speyer Brothers, London, 1900–1919, and subsequently had represented Speyer & Co., New York, in England), served as an officer or director of more than a dozen British companies (all except two were trust companies) that held American securities.[141] As noted earlier, Samuel Insull in 1924 had established Insull, Son & Co., Ltd., London, to distribute securities of various Insull public utilities.[142] On August 5, 1929, Samuel Insull wrote Insull, Son & Co., Ltd. that there would be a large syndicate formed for the refinancing of the Middle West Utilities Company. Insull, Son & Co. Ltd. would assume "the primary obligation" and form the syndicate. Participants would include Robert Fleming & Co., Robert Benson & Sons, Kitcat & Aitken, and possibly the Boissevain firm. Insull expected nobody would get much stock, "as there will be such a demand for this underwriting."[143] By the summer of 1929, U.S. underwriters of securities assumed participation from Britain. The bevy of Americans in the City provided one of many conduits, easing the investment process.

A few of the American houses active in London—Kuhn, Loeb, Hallgarten, and A. Iselin—had for decades taken part in intermediating foreign moneys into America.[144] L. F. Rothschild & Co. (no relation to N. M. Rothschild) concentrated on arbitrage.[145] Others of these brokerage houses–qua–investment banking houses were fresh to the international intermediation process and actively "cultivated accounts of London brokers." London was literally next door to New York: the average buying or selling time for an order was thirty seconds.[146] A May 1928 publication of the U.S. Department of Commerce reported that British investors had reverted to their prewar practice of investing in American securities.[147] This was obvious by the summer of 1929.

By decade's end, a study found that the most popular American securities for Britishers were U.S. Steel, American Telephone and Telegraph, and the Pennsylvania Railroad—securities well known before the First World War.[148] The marketing of securities by British and American firms in London consisted of both American and foreign securities. At the same time, American brokers and bankers in London (and their British counterparts) eagerly sought to line up European borrowers and European securities for sale in the United States.[149]

By 1928–1929, in Britain there arose an interest by the general public in investing in securities of all kinds. A contest was won in 1928 by a man who advised Britons to invest equally in the stock of Courtaulds, Kreuger & Toll, General Motors, and Woolworth.[150] The list is revealing. Woolworth and General Motors were, of course, American companies. The Swedish Kreuger & Toll was traded in New York (as well as in London). And a substantial part of the British Courtaulds' gross income came from its U.S. direct investments.[151] The average Britisher probably did not buy American securities (at least in large amounts), but institutions did—companies, investment trusts, and insurance offices—as did the well-to-do. Some companies and individuals were, as I earlier quoted Moggridge, "discovering" the American market, and particularly for new investors enthusiasm mounted in early and mid-1929, as values on the New York Stock Exchange soared. Added to the prospects of gain were the British Labour Party victory in the general election on May 30, 1929 (which upset some affluent Britishers), and also a flat British stock market; thus, British individuals were motivated to shift more of their liquid assets into American stocks and to a lesser extent bonds.[152] Winston Churchill was far from alone when in 1929 he had invested in American shares.[153]

Not only Canadians and Britons bought new and traded in existing American securities. Hallgarten & Co., mentioned previously as having an office in London, was among the most active of U.S. financial houses abroad. It participated in "general banking, financing new securities, forming underwriting syndicates, reorganizing old concerns, buying and selling foreign exchange and transacting a general stock and bond business." Its salesmen were in London and also in Berlin, Geneva, Paris, and Amsterdam. In January 1926, it appears to have acquired Boisevain & Co., a Dutch firm that had participated in intermediating moneys into American business since the nineteenth century. Hallgarten & Co. created a vast international network through which it moved both American and foreign securities.[154] So, too, Kuhn, Loeb retained its long-standing ties with leading continental European banks and clients.[155]

In the late 1920s, Dutch long-term investments in the United States climbed rapidly from an estimated $300 million (in 1927) to $450 million (in 1929)—at least according to one estimate.[156] Part of the increase was direct investment; much of it, however, was associated with Dutch purchases of American securities. The earlier mentioned U.S. Department of Commerce report (published in May 1928) that noted British investors were raising their purchases of American securities found the same to be true of the Dutch.[157] *Van Oss' Effectenboek* reveals new listings in Amsterdam of American stocks and to a lesser extent bonds and renewed attention to American securities.[158] A later Royal Institute of International Affairs study of international investment identified "fairly considerable purchases" of American securities by Frenchmen in the years 1928–1929.[159] Morgan's house in Paris had a tranche in all Morgan's issues—domestic and foreign. The French and American

Lazard Frères houses cooperated in providing moneys to France but also in bringing French investments to the United States.

There were also purchases of American and foreign securities by other Europeans, including Germans. Germans apparently bought mainly American-issued "German" securities. Historian Stephen Schuker uncovered evidence that Germans purchased "units in the Dutch or Swiss *tranches* of American loans" to Germany, and also that they "invested funds directly in such issues on Wall Street." Dillon, Read, a major participant in American underwriting for German loans in the 1920s, carried out a survey in 1929 on where the bond coupons were presented for payments and learned that by then about two-thirds of some of its earlier high-interest German loans had moved to German ownership.[160] Speyer & Co., New York, underwrote German issues in the United States, while the German Speyer house—Lazard Speyer-Elissen, Frankfurt and after 1926 in Berlin as well—aided in selling them in Germany. When the German rayon companies set up subsidiaries in America (see Chapter 5), the Speyers assisted in the transactions (as did Teixeira de Mattos, Amsterdam). Networks of finance were ubiquitous. Eduard Beit von Speyer was in 1929 on the board of directors of the Deutsche Bank.[161] These were merely a few of the many participants in American-German business. After the Second World War, the Swedish government would argue that German state property in Sweden should be used to meet the obligations of the German state to Swedish nationals who held bonds issued in the 1920s in connection with the Dawes and Young loans.[162] Swedish banks had participated in the cosmopolitan finance.

In 1924 the Fujimoto Securities Company, Ltd., affiliated with Fujimoto Bill Broker Bank, Osaka, opened a New York office to buy and to sell Japanese and foreign investment securities on behalf of its Japanese clients.[163] Fujimoto was the pioneer Japanese securities dealer in New York.[164] In March 1927, a second Japanese securities firm, Nomura Securities Co., Ltd., joined Fujimoto in New York.[165] There was the expectation in 1927 that the Japanese government would repeal the embargo on the export of gold (which, in fact, did not occur until January 1930). Nomura's Wall Street office (at 120 Broadway) was established—according to a company history—primarily as an agent for the head office in "processing dollar-denominated bond transactions."[166] The Japanese government was floating dollar loans in the 1920s.[167] In Japan, Nomura's parent firm concentrated on bond issue placements.[168] Initially, at least, with the gold embargo and Japanese supplies of dollars limited, it seems obvious that Fujimoto and Nomura would not have been important in investing Japanese moneys in the United States, yet they did sell some U.S. loans in Japan.[169]

Numerous other nationalities bought and sold American-issued and American-traded securities. There were recipients of American foreign lending in Latin America and to a lesser extent in other third world countries who, in turn, invested the "skimmed" moneys in the United States.[170] With the portfolio holdings, there was a substantial amount of trading—purchases and sales. The trading was also true of Americans and in no way was distinctive to the inward foreign investors. Indeed, perhaps the only distinctive aspect about the FPI was the location of the residence of the buyer. New issues bought by foreigners in New York could be traded abroad, in London, for example, maintaining the foreign investment, albeit changing the individual investor. Or the security could be sold back to Americans, domesticating the investment.

In the years from 1924 to roughly mid-1928, the U.S. government and public were, in the main, indifferent to the foreign moneys invested in stocks and, to a lesser extent, bonds. In June 1924, Rufus Taylor, acting chief of the Finance and Investment Division of the U.S. Bureau of Foreign and Domestic Commerce, wrote, "On the whole, at the present time, we are more interested in finding opportunities for American capital abroad than in encouraging the sale of American securities to foreigners; nevertheless, it is desirable that foreigners should hold American securities, as in that case they will be more interested in the welfare of this country."[171] Beginning in June 1928, however, when more sizable amounts of moneys flowed into the United States, principally to purchase stocks on the rising market (experiencing the appreciation and contributing to it), there did surface some concern over and attention to the influx.[172] The capital inflow was substantial, but not when it was compared with the size of the United States or with the rising volume of New York Stock Market transactions.

Moreover, there was no individual sector in the U.S. economy wherein long-term foreign portfolio investments seemed to make an appreciable difference. Foreign investors had interests in many sectors, but their contributions were absorbed in the vast amount of new U.S. activity. America could finance its industry and infrastructure at home. The country was, after all, the world's greatest industrial and financial power. In the late 1920s, Americans and foreigners alike perceived U.S. prosperity as enduring. America was now the capital exporter par excellence. Capital exports greatly overshadowed the growing inward foreign investments. In the late 1920s, Americans were convinced that the nation's role as a global lender would go on forever.

Yet in the summer of 1928, American foreign lending had slowed, partly as a result of increasingly stringent Federal Reserve monetary policy and partly as a consequence of good alternative domestic opportunities (Americans wanted to invest at home in the spiraling stock market).[173] American capital had aided European recovery, helped stabilize European currencies, assisted Britain in returning to gold at the prewar rate, and, in general, served to stimulate the world economy.[174] In addition, American portfolio and direct investment had gone to Canada, Latin America, and Asia.

In late 1928 through the summer of 1929, however, Americans reallocated resources and channeled far more moneys into domestic investments, contributing to the upward course of the Dow Jones—and as a complement, as I have indicated, foreign moneys also arrived, attracted by the same possibilities in the stock market, as well as by the increases in domestic interest rates. As one author put it, U.S. financial institutions involved in foreign lending enlarged their "European investor base for U.S. dollar securities."[175] Stocks could be bought on margin; U.S. and foreign banks provided brokers' loans.[176] Stock market purchases—domestic and, to a lesser extent, foreign—created the boom, which added to the glow of prosperity in America.

5.

The Foreign Multinationals, 1924–1929

From 1924 to 1929, many companies from abroad made new or raised existing direct investments in the United States. There were, to be sure, retreats in the late 1920s, but far fewer than those in 1919–1923. Sometimes, moreover, as in the earlier period, the pullbacks meant a shift of predominant foreign ownership to minority or no ownership from abroad, yet the ongoing productive activity continued under domestic ownership and control. Overall new participation along with enlargement of existing businesses characterized the activities of foreign multinational enterprises in the late 1920s. The U.S. Department of Commerce (and most other contemporaries) had little clue on the extent of the foreign enterprises operating in the United States. American tariffs went up in 1922, and at decade's end it seemed likely that they would again be increased. A number of foreign companies vaulted the tariff barrier to invest in manufacturing in America, the largest market in the world, as measured by the number of people with high per capita incomes (relative to the rest of the world).

Frank A. Southard, writing on U.S. industry in Europe (in a book published in 1931 but reflecting developments at the close of the 1920s), commented casually that "there is a reverse process of some magnitude taking place," that is, European firms were establishing themselves in the United States. He did not elaborate, yet he was right. Foreign direct investment (FDI) continued to be both outward *and* inward. In certain cases, there were "preemptive" investments in the United States: European companies responded to the vast push of American business abroad. In other cases, it was the opposite: European companies came to America, and U.S. companies countered with investments in the particular European country.[1] Some foreign-headquartered enterprises used their direct investments in the United States as a negotiating tool in agreements to divide world markets. Partial entries, cartel relationships, and licensing of processes created complex networks in the international business arena that paralleled the cosmopolitan finance described in Chapter 4. Joint ventures in the United States between foreign and American firms were ubiquitous. Foreign multinationals did not have to rely on their parent firm for finance; frequently the financing of a foreign-controlled venture would be done within the United States, where capital was cheap and abundant. The late 1920s saw a combination in many industries of cooperation and competition. Numerous foreign firms invested in the United States—in a wide variety of sectors (see the incomplete Table 5.1, covering only new entries).[2]

It is difficult to generalize about foreign-owned firms in America in the late 1920s. A few performed brilliantly, for example, Courtaulds, but many foreign-owned companies found investments in the United States more a burden than a delight. Often, however, they persisted, for the U.S. market seemed too promising to exit. Frequently foreign companies had more than one factory in the United States. These multiplant operations were both "horizontal" (i.e., factories making the same product in different locations) and "vertical" (i.e., factories making inputs for a final product that would be made elsewhere in the United States). Some of the multinational enterprises had long had multiplant establishments; others added new facilities in the late 1920s.

The size of the foreign-owned business ranged from small offices with fewer than a handful of employees to major corporations. Prior to the First World War, the largest foreign-owned enterprises in America employed roughly 6,000; very few had workforces of more than 2,000.[3] Now, still exceptional foreign-owned businesses—Shell Union Oil Corporation and The Viscose Company (Courtaulds' American subsidiary)—had as many as 35,000 and 20,000 employees, respectively. A number of foreign-owned firms—in thread, rayon, chemicals, and tires—employed more than 2,000 individuals.

By the end of the 1920s, classifying foreign-owned companies by industry had become problematic, for many were not only multiplant but also multifunctional and multiproduct units in their U.S. business. Thus, under agriculture and forestry I include most of those foreign investors in primary production, storage facilities, and trade; I, however, defer consideration of a large foreign-owned cigarette manufacturer (that did a sizable amount of tobacco handling and purchasing) and the Canadian paper mill proprietors (that also owned forestland in America), and place these later under the rubric "manufacturing." Under oil production, I mention briefly the largest foreign-owned crude oil producer, reserving commentary on this giant for subsequent sections on the chemical industry and on integrated oil enterprises.

Table 5.1. New entries: number of foreign direct investments in the United States (exclusive of insurance companies), 1924–1929

	Country of company							Sector				
Date	Canada	U.K.	France	Holland	Switzerland	Other Europe[a]	Total	Manufacturing	Distribution	Oil & mining	Banking	Misc.
1924	2	2	2	—	3	3	12	7	3	1	1	—
1925	4	1	—	—	—	4	9	3	3	1	1	1
1926	3	2	—	—	—	4	9	7	—	—	1	1
1927	1	2	1	1	2	—	6[b]	6	—	—	—	—
1928	4	3	—	2	1	—	10	9	1	—	—	—
1929	7	—	—	1	3	5	15[b]	5	3	1	3	3
Total	21	10	3	4	9	16	61[c]	37	10	3	6	5

Source: U.S. Department of Commerce, Bureau of Foreign and Domestic Commerce, *Foreign Investments in the United States* (Washington, D.C., 1937), 41. This table includes *only* those foreign direct investments remaining in the United States in 1934. A "new" entry was an "incorporation" or "acquisition."

a. Includes German, Belgian, Norwegian, and other European enterprises.

b. A joint enterprise, involving two foreign countries, makes the total of the country of company short by one.

c. The two joint enterprises (in 1927 and 1929), involving two foreign countries, make the total of the country of company short by two.

Multiproduct businesses that invested in the United States included companies in laundry products and mustard, textiles and chemicals, as well as chemicals and oil. Service companies proved, in some cases, hard to classify, and I made cavalier decisions. It is, however, useful to give an overview of foreign multinationals by industry. Where there were no new developments, I will be brief; only when changes of consequence occurred will I offer details.

Transportation, Land and Real Estate, Agriculture, Trade in Agricultural Products

Existing Canadian and Mexican railroad systems stretched over the borders; there was nothing new in the late 1920s. No major foreign investments were made in either farmland or urban real estate, although some foreign-owned mortgage banks did acquire substantial amounts of real estate, principally through foreclosures. Foreign-owned insurance companies owned or had long-term leases on buildings—some of which were seen as "white elephants."[4] Toward the end of the 1920s, urban real estate prices began to soar; however, I have found no evidence that this sector attracted significant new foreign investments.[5]

Probably the most consequential development affecting foreign business involvements in the U.S. farm sector was the spread of the leading foreign-owned grain traders into the American interior. The trend, barely started in the early 1920s, accelerated toward the end of the decade. By 1929, both Bunge and Dreyfus (Louis Dreyfus & Co.) had their own men in Duluth, Minnesota. The Fribourgs' Continental Grain Corporation operated grain elevators in St. Louis, Missouri; had people in Chicago, Duluth, Kansas City, New Orleans, and Galveston (Texas); and seems to have been the most aggressive of this emerging group of "Big Three" international grain traders. In the late 1920s Jules Fribourg, from Paris, had instructed his representative in New York: "Don't bother to look at them [grain elevators in the interior]—just buy them."[6] As yet, none of these large grain merchants invested in growing U.S. crops.[7]

As these three enlarged their stakes, the British role in the U.S. grain trade was dwarfed, in both absolute and relative terms. As of 1921 the Federal Trade Commission had found that three houses, the British firm Sanday & Co., Louis Dreyfus, and Bunge, led in U.S. wheat exports, handling more than 30 percent of the U.S. export trade.[8] Sanday and other British trading firms, such as Ross T. Smyth & Co., lost ground in the 1920s. Historian Dan Morgan suggests that powerful British millers, such as Rank, took a direct role in grain purchases.[9] Balfour, Guthrie—the U.S. arm of the trading company Balfour,

Williamson—continued as a grain trader, based on the West Coast; it did not, however, follow Louis Dreyfus, Bunge, and the assertive newcomer, Continental Grain, into the American interior. It did keep its earlier investment in milling. In fact, Balfour, Williamson's historian refers to Balfour, Guthrie's stake in the Crown flour mills (in Portland, Oregon) as the "brightest star" in its firmament in the late 1920s.[10] By the late 1920s, Balfour, Guthrie seems to have been the only foreign-owned grain trader with an interest in flour mills. (Balfour, Guthrie also had investments in California Packing Corporation, a firm engaged in canning and packing fruits and vegetables).[11] Large Japanese trading companies (in particular Mitsui and Mitsubishi) handled grain and flour exports from their West Coast offices.[12] By 1929, however, Louis Dreyfus, Bunge, and Fribourg's Continental Grain dominated U.S. grain exports.

A new foreign-owned, substantial specialized trader in the United States was United Molasses Co., Ltd. (UMC), formed in Britain in 1926 to acquire the business of two British molasses merchants (molasses, which is derived from sugarcane and beet sugar, is used principally in cattle feed, in commercial alcohols, and by distillers of alcoholic beverages). After stiff competition with the American-owned Dunbar Molasses Co., New York, the "struggle" ended in May 1928, when UMC obtained "on most favorable terms" an interest in its rival. In June of the next year, UMC bought the molasses business of the National Distillers Product Corporation (the old "Distillers Trust," which with Prohibition was now confined to commercial alcohols); in exchange, National Distillers obtained a small interest in the British trader. Then, in July 1929, UMC formed Pacific Molasses Co., San Francisco, which subsidiary took over the West Coast molasses distribution activities and facilities of the California and Hawaiian Sugar Refining Co. By the end of the 1920s, United Molasses, through its U.S. affiliates, had become the clear leader in the American molasses trade (it operated on a global basis).[13]

Little change occurred in the foreign investors' role in the U.S. cotton export trade. Japanese trading companies maintained their offices in and trade from Texas. The British firm Fine Cotton Spinners' and Doublers' Association (FCSDA) reluctantly kept its Mississippi cotton plantations; as in the past, its cotton output was sold in America (not exported). Low cotton prices meant its plantations were unprofitable. The U.S. government badgered the company to pay back taxes. FCSDA wanted to sell the plantations yet could find no buyer. In 1927, a flood destroyed much of the company's crop and put a substantial part of its properties under water. That year, FCSDA reduced the capital stock of Delta and Pine Land Co. (the corporate owner of the principal plantation), wrote off $1 million, and announced the delay of the redemption of a first mortgage gold bond that had come due. The parent installed a new chief executive officer, an American who had been with the company, not someone from the United Kingdom. Finally, in 1928 and 1929, after years of losses, FCSDA's cotton plantations were making profits; it would be only a brief respite.[14] The other long-standing foreign-owned stake in cotton growing, that of the Deltic Investment Company, was retained, although this Scottish firm also tried without success to dispose of its loss-producing venture (it would finally shed these properties in 1940–1941).[15]

In 1924, the British-owned Imperial Tobacco, a large purchaser and exporter of American tobacco, opened a new headquarters in Richmond, Virginia, for its American Leaf Organization.[16] The British independent cigarette producer Gallaher was reported to have in 1929 nearly £500,000 ($2.4 million) in U.S. investments associated with its "buying policy."[17] British American Tobacco Co., with sizable U.S. investments in buying, processing, and exporting leaf and manufacturing for export, in a major strategy change, for the first time in its history, expanded into cigarette making to sell to Americans (its new ventures will be discussed later).

The Matador Land and Cattle Co., Ltd., in Texas remained British owned; it had a short interlude of "good times" from 1927 to 1929.[18] By 1924, the directors of the other large continuing British owned cattle ranch, the Swan Land and Cattle Company, Ltd., in Wyoming, had become obsessed with the "millstone of double taxation." The U.S. tax was "2s 6d in the pound," to which shareholders had to add a British tax of 4s 6d per pound—or 7 shillings total, about 35 percent of the company's profits. The Swan company's British chairman thought this "intolerable." To deal with the double taxation, the Swan company was, in 1926, reestablished with a Delaware incorporation, and shareholders of the Scottish company became shareholders of the Delaware entity. The control was maintained from Scotland.[19] Such reorganizations for tax reasons were common and had no impact on operations.

Some Canadian enterprises purchased American forestlands; there were also other miscellaneous foreign stakes in timberland.[20] Of more consequence was the trade in U.S. forest products. In 1925, a British Columbia–based lumber exporter, H. R. MacMillan Export Co., opened a New York office to handle its growing U.S. East Coast business. Under the Jones Act of 1920 (and earlier laws), foreign vessels were not allowed to ship goods from one U.S. port to a second. The U.S. coastal trade monopoly enabled U.S. shippers to charge high prices. The vessels of H. R. MacMillan's Canadian Transport Co. could carry lumber from Vancouver to the U.S. East Coast at lower rates and still make good profits. Thus, much of British Columbian lumber went on Canadian ships, through the Panama Canal, to the U.S. East Coast, with the transactions arranged by H. R. MacMillan Export Co. Other Canadians followed H. R. MacMillan Export Co. to form lumber trading houses, installing representatives in New York—to meet U.S. import requirements. Meanwhile, in 1926, H. R. Macmillan Export Co. opened offices in Portland, Oregon, and in Seattle, Washington, to export American lumber, principally to the Far East.[21] Japanese trading companies also transported American lumber across the Pacific, from outposts on the American West Coast.[22]

The British-owned Balfour, Guthrie had some long-standing interests in Alaska (in Alaska Packers Association); the trading company exported large quantities of canned salmon on behalf of Alaska Packers.[23] Balfour, Guthrie was virtually alone as a foreign investor in U.S. fisheries and seafood processing. I have no evidence of Canadian or Japanese involvements at this time.

Mining, Processing, and Trade

The Canadian Pacific Railroad had an interest in a coal mine in Ohio. The Steel Corporation of Canada owned several iron ore mines in the Lake Superior region and coal mines in Pennsylvania.[24] The Canadian-headquartered Algoma Steel Corporation (with U.S.-British-Canadian ownership, but which in the late 1920s came under the control of Canadian-born London resident Sir James Dunn) owned U.S. coal mines and limestone quarries.[25] In addition, other Canadian firms owned a handful of coal mining properties.[26] Canadian enterprises were unique among foreign investors in their U.S. stakes in coal and iron ore mining in this decade. In another mineral, linked with steel production, a British direct investor in the United States (Firth Sterling Steel Co.) integrated backward, investing in the principal U.S. company that mined tungsten ores (probably a minority holding).[27]

U.S. gold and silver mines attracted little new attention from foreign multinationals in the late 1920s, although scattered FDIs persisted, including that in Camp Bird Ltd. (with a gold mine in Colorado). In 1929 Camp Bird Ltd. became associated with the London-headquartered Consolidated Gold Fields of South Africa, Ltd., which had some additional U.S. gold mining interests.[28] A study of U.S. domestic silver mining and refining concluded that output in 1929 was 100 percent under American control.[29] I have no comparable 1929 data on gold, but a likely guess would be 98 to 99 percent U.S. control. In short, even through there remained some foreign interests in gold mining, they were not of great consequence.

So, too, foreign multinationals made no new entries in copper, lead, or zinc mining or processing, albeit some existing mineral properties continued to be owned and operated by foreign investors (Mountain Copper Co., Ltd., for example).[30] International trade in these three principal nonferrous minerals saw important developments. Copper Exporters Inc., formed on October 11, 1926, to promote U.S. exports, had European "associates," including British Metal Corporation (London), Metallgesellschaft (Frankfurt), Rio Tinto Co. (London), Henry Gardner & Co. (London), and Aron Hirsch & Söhn (Halberstadt, Germany).[31] Most of the latter also took part in encouraging U.S. lead and zinc (as well as the copper) exports. Metallgesellschaft became the leading non-U.S. associate in Copper Exporters Inc.[32] At least three of the foreign associates in Copper Exporters Inc. had further U.S. direct investments. Thus, British Metal Corporation had an interest in C. Tennant Sons & Co.'s New York City office; C. Tennant Sons & Co. were traders in ores and concentrates as well as metal products.[33]

The two other associates had investments in phosphates in America. Metallgesellschaft made new investments in trade in the United States as well as in the Florida phosphate industry, while Rio Tinto had a 20 percent stake in Davison Chemical Co., which, in turn, had as a subsidiary (as of 1928) Southern Phosphate Corporation, with modern phosphate facilities at Bartow and Lakeland, Florida.[34] There were some additional foreign investments in Florida phosphates.

The only two minerals in the United States where foreign direct investors were able to control U.S. production (and trade) continued to be potash and borax. This was true in 1923 and in 1929. By 1929, foreign investors participated in the mining of 100 percent of the small U.S. potash output (in 1929, U.S. production was roughly 2.3 percent of the world total).[35] The story of FDI in the American potash industry is highly significant, this low global market share notwithstanding. As recounted earlier, with imports curtailed during World War I, U.S. potash output had grown, but the tariff act of 1922 had offered no protection to this infant industry, since farmers desired cheap potash (used in fertilizers); thus, the way was opened for renewed German and now, also, French exports to America (the French had acquired German territory in the postwar settlements and with that domain large potash mines).

In 1923, the Potash Importing Corporation (PIC) was incorporated in Delaware to serve as agent for German potash imports. In August 1924, the German Kali (Potash) Syndicate and the French Société Commerciale des Potasses d'Alsace (SCPA) formed a cartel to share world markets, including the U.S. one.[36] When in 1925 the German Potash Syndicate sought to raise money in the United States, the U.S. State and Commerce Departments objected, fearing that the support of the

German syndicate would mean higher prices to U.S. farmers.[37] By 1926 a U.S. congressional committee found the German-French potash combination to be an illegal cartel, and in 1927 the Justice Department indicted sixteen defendants, including the German Potash Syndicate, the French SCPA, and the PIC.[38] That year, in the aftermath of the indictment, the Germans and the French organized a jointly owned sales company, NV Potash Export Mij., Amsterdam and New York.[39] A 1929 State Department memorandum indicated that a modus vivendi was worked out between this Dutch firm and the Justice Department; U.S. import prices of potash were to be lowered.[40] Meanwhile, the litigation against the German-French cartel had proceeded slowly. Questions arose on sovereign immunity; the French government owned many of the Alsace potash mines and argued that for this reason the U.S. courts had no jurisdiction. This defense was disallowed in January 1929. The case ended with a consent decree on February 28, 1929.[41] (A consent decree is a negotiated settlement of a complaint.) Charles C. Concannon, chief of the Chemical Division of the Commerce Department, applauded the decree as a victory for the American farmer.[42] When the State Department received a protest that the decree failed to protect U.S. farmers from being "mulcted by the Franco-German potash control," its response in March 1929 was that "the present price [of potash] is fair."[43]

Yet, unbeknownst to the Commerce or State Departments (or to anyone else in the U.S. government), that year the Germans effectively acquired dominance over U.S. domestic potash output. Therein lies a separate behind-the-scenes tale, involving not trade but inward FDI. The principal survivor of America's war-created domestic potash industry had been the American Trona Corporation (ATC), a subsidiary of the British-owned and London-headquartered Consolidated Gold Fields of South Africa. By 1924, the innovative ATC could produce potassium chloride at a cost competitive with imports. Undoubtedly, this—along with the U.S. government pressure—made the German-French cartel ready toward the end of the 1920s to lower prices of potash exported to the United States. In 1926, ATC's potash properties were acquired by a new corporation, American Potash & Chemical Corporation (capital: $1 million), still owned by Consolidated Gold Fields. In 1928, American Potash & Chemical supplied roughly 15 percent of the U.S. potash market, with most of the remainder served by imports from Germany and France. In 1929, Hope & Co., Amsterdam, bought a controlling interest in American Potash & Chemical. Hope & Co.'s denials notwithstanding, the Dutch banking house was acting on behalf of Salzdetfurth AG and Wintershall AG, the two leading potash companies *in Germany*. More than a decade and a half later, when information on the German ownership was published, it was said that the concealment had been so effective that even the top management of American Potash & Chemical had no knowledge of the beneficial owners. Be that as it may, in 1929 the premier potash mining company in the United States had passed from British to German beneficial ownership.[44] What had happened by 1929 was that key German potash producers through a complex network dominated both the export trade to the United States and U.S. production. FDI was part and parcel of the strategy.

American Potash & Chemical (and its predecessor) had developed new domestic potash output by a process of separating potash from borax, working with the Searles Lake, California, brine; the company had, accordingly, moved into the by-product borax industry. In California it built the world's largest borax plant and in 1927 began to manufacture boric acid. Thus, it became a formidable rival of the Pacific Coast Borax Company (the subsidiary of the British firm Borax Consolidated, Ltd.), long the undisputed leader in U.S. borax. Now the U.S. borax industry had two giant producers—both foreign investors. Borax Consolidated rose to the challenge; it abandoned its Chilean borax mines (they were not as low cost as its California output); it made giant new U.S. commitments. Thus, in borax, as in potash production, foreign-owned firms consolidated their leadership.[45] Potash and borax (and possibly phosphates) aside, otherwise, by 1929 American mining was under domestic ownership and control. There was, however, the substantial foreign involvement in the metal trades.

Oil Production and Services

In 1929 the United States continued as the world's largest producer of crude oil, and in U.S. crude oil extraction the British-Dutch Royal Dutch Shell was a giant. It was not the only foreign direct investor in U.S. crude oil extraction. Of the British companies, Kern River Oilfields of California, Ltd. (registered in England in 1910) had by the late 1920s an output in California of some 1 million barrels annually.[46] In 1926, Lord Cowdray's successful Amerada Corporation, which produced 5.6 million barrels of crude that year, was reorganized with a majority of its shareholders U.S. citizens. Cowdray died in 1927, and the Pearson family firm, Whitehall Petroleum Corporation, retained a 23 percent holding in Amerada after the reorganization.[47] There were additional foreign-owned oil producers.[48]

A new entry into services related to oil production was the French engineering firm Schlumberger, which in 1921 had introduced into the United States unique methods of prospecting, using electrical measurements.[49] That year, its U.S. engagements had been short missions, and with the recession, its business had evaporated.[50] It resumed U.S. operations in 1925, and in 1925–1927 fulfilled a major prospecting contract on behalf of one of Royal Dutch Shell's American affiliates, Roxana Petroleum. Schlumberger opened an office in Dallas. In 1926, it made a contract with Shell Oil in California.[51] By spring 1927, if not before, Schlumberger had a New York office, at 25 Broadway, near the headquarters of Shell Union Oil Corporation (the latter was at 65 Broadway) and across the street from Standard Oil of New Jersey's head office (at 26 Broadway).[52] Early in 1929, Schlumberger started "electric coring" in Venezuela; its first U.S. tests of this technologically advanced measurement method were conducted at the end of August 1929 at a Shell oil well in California.[53]

Paper

In paper and pulp products, the largest foreign investors in the United States were Canadian: Brompton Paper and Pulp in New Hampshire, Fraser Companies, Ltd. in Maine, and Westminister Paper Co. across the continent, in Washington.[54] A Norwegian firm had a paper mill in Maine.[55] F. O. Fernstrom, Fernstrom & Co., Sweden, and members of the Fernstrom family in 1926 established the California Fruit Wrapping Mills, Inc., as a manufacturer in Pomona, California, of paper wraps for fruit.[56] In a range of specialty papers (including sales books, sales slips, and printed business forms), the Canadian firm Moore Corporation extended and rationalized its sizable multiplant U.S. operations.[57]

Food, Beverages, Soap, Toiletries, Matches, and Cigarettes

John Morrell & Co., a large meat packer (although not of the rank of Swift or Armour), had for decades been an affiliate of a British-headquartered multinational enterprise. Since 1871, it had expanded in the United States to become a multiplant firm, and its growth had continued during and after World War I. Increasingly, the center of its activity had shifted to the United States, and in 1928 the U.S. company became the parent; in effect, this multinational enterprise was now and would from this point on be U.S. based. This was, to use Geoffrey Jones' apt phrase, a case of a "migrating multinational." It was the last of the British-owned meat packers in America.[58]

By contrast, other British companies expanded in the United States, supplying many branded grocery store products. Crosse & Blackwell, Ltd., which since the 1840s had sold to U.S. consumers through exports, found that with the U.S. tariff, its high-quality specialty food items were not competitive. Yet affluent Americans liked its delicacies. The market familiar, in 1925 the British company decided to can and bottle its offerings in America; early in 1927, it made its first investment in U.S. manufacturing, opening a plant in Baltimore, Maryland.[59]

Reckitt and Sons, Ltd.—for many years a manufacturer in the United States of laundry products (starch and whitening agents), with a factory in New Brunswick, New Jersey, had in the 1920s also assisted another British family firm, J. & J. Colman, in the latter's mustard exports to America from the United Kingdom. In 1926, Reckitt, together with Colman, acquired the largest U.S. mustard company, R. T. French Co., Rochester, New York; Colman took over the management. In time, Reckitt's New Jersey factory would be shut and the equipment transferred to Rochester. In 1928, Colman, Reckitt, and R. T. French organized the Atlantis Sales Corporation to unify the wholesaling for the three firms' grocery products in the United States.[60] Added British businesses in branded grocery store articles included Lipton's Tea and Tetley Tea.[61] The British Cantrell and Cochrane sold a ginger ale with the brand name C & C.[62]

The most successful British enterprise in making, marketing, and advertising branded grocery store goods in America was Lever Brothers Co.[63] During the late 1920s its revenues (and profits) continued to soar. By 1929, it had 2,180 employees and ranked third in the U.S. soap market, after Procter & Gamble and the newly combined Colgate-Palmolive-Peet. It had within the United States a research and development division, which by the late 1920s had a laboratory staff of 100. In 1929, it made plans for a new factory in Hammond, Indiana, to serve its growing midwestern and western markets, a plant that would be financed largely through profits made in America.[64] Lever Brothers Co.'s principal brands were Rinso (a granulated soap), Lux Flakes (for delicate garments), Lifebuoy, and Lux Toilet Soap. Introduced in 1924, Lux Toilet Soap was "the first white, milled, perfumed soap to be made and sold in America at a popular price."[65] In September 1929, Lever Brothers Co.'s parent agreed to merge with the Dutch Margarine Unie. The result was Unilever, a British-Dutch giant, which became the parent to the prospering U.S. subsidiary.[66]

A new, related—albeit far smaller—British entry was Yardley & Co., Ltd., London, makers of men's perfumes, toilet soaps, and toilet preparations, which opened a factory in Union City, New Jersey, in 1928.[67] With the tariff reducing its exports and with high demand for its offerings, Yardley had decided to manufacture in America. Its products were probably sold through drugstores and department stores rather than grocery stores. Yet all these British branded goods, from Crosse & Blackwell condiments and other specialties, to Lux soap, to Yardley's vanity items, seem very much identified with America's affluent consumer society of the late 1920s. Among foreign direct investors, the British stood out in such offerings.

Fewer than a handful of Canadian firms' making or selling branded, packaged goods had a presence in America. George Weston, Ltd., Toronto, a baker of biscuits, in 1928 sold its U.S. rights to George Weston Biscuit Co., Inc., which would manufacture in Watertown, Massachusetts. The Canadian head office, in exchange for the rights, received a 22 percent interest in its New England affiliate.[68] Salada Tea Company, a Canadian-owned enterprise, actively promoted its packaged and advertised product in the United States.[69] Another Canadian company with a branded good was J. J. McLaughlin Ltd., Toronto, which had developed a drink called Canada Dry Ginger Ale. In 1923, this Toronto company dispatched a representative to New York to visit its ailing U.S. subsidiary. The man moved to New York and personally bought the subsidiary *and* its parent (in 1924); the company (and the ownership of the brand) became U.S. headquartered—another migrating multinational.[70]

The Dutch had some American interests in margarine and, apparently, some marketing stakes in selling cocoa.[71] Much more important in branded foods were the Swiss. In its well-advertised canned milk lines, the subsidiary of the Nestlé & Anglo-Swiss Condensed Milk Company, Nestlé's Food Company, had, however, seen a slimming of its business since the early 1920s. For a while, it had retained its shuttered factories, hoping for better sales, but competition, especially in evaporated milk, proved intense. In 1925, the parent company decided to sell a number of its U.S. plants.[72] In the late 1920s, Nestlé appears to have ranked in the top four in the U.S. canned milk industry, with Borden, Pet Milk, and Carnation; it had, however, lost its onetime status as second only to Borden's. Nestlé's original Fulton, New York, factory, which had in the past made Nestlé's baby food, after 1925 made only chocolate and cocoa products.[73] In 1929, in Switzerland, Nestlé & Anglo-Swiss merged with Peter, Cailler, Kohler—the Swiss chocolate maker, and the merger had ramifications in the United States. Lamont, Corliss—which produced and distributed Nestlé's chocolates in America—became 37 percent owned by Nestlé & Anglo-Swiss.[74] Lamont, Corliss by 1929 was one of the principal makers of chocolates in America, and Nestlé's chocolates provided keen competition to Hershey's. Another Swiss branded milk drink, Ovaltine, was made in Illinois; the Swiss parent was the Wander company.[75] In matches, the Swede Ivar Kreuger sought to expand greatly Swedish Match's activities in the United States, and in 1928 in a joint venture with the U.S. industry leader, Diamond Match, had acquired Ohio Match Company.[76]

Of all the branded products that foreign-owned companies made and sold to Americans, probably the most far-reaching developments in the late 1920s took place in the cigarette industry: British American Tobacco Company (BAT), for the first time, began to manufacture cigarettes for sale in the United States. BAT had from its formation in 1902 done business in the United States as an exporter of tobacco and cigarettes from America. In 1923, James B. Duke had stepped down as BAT chairman and was replaced by Sir Hugo Cunliffe-Owen, who would remain in that position until 1945. Cunliffe-Owen's title as BAT chairman symbolized the completion of the shift of BAT from its pre-1911 status as an American-controlled multinational to its now being without question fully British controlled.

In 1923, BAT had in the United States a New York office, sizable leaf purchasing and processing operations for export (in Virginia and North Carolina), and factories in Petersburg, Virginia (acquired in 1903–1904), and in nearby Richmond, Virginia (a new one was built in 1916), to manufacture cigarettes for overseas markets.[77] It was a substantial investor in the United States. By far, BAT's largest sales were in China, with India and Malaya in second and third place. During the First World War and in the early 1920s, the firm had enlarged its role in Latin America.[78] When it was formed in 1902, it had acquired the brand names of American Tobacco and Imperial Tobacco, for use outside the United States and Great Britain.

Because of growing anti-British sentiment in China and, to a lesser extent, India, in 1927 BAT decided it would be prudent to reduce its still heavy reliance on Asian markets. That year, breaking with its past, it purchased for $3.3 million a small, nearly bankrupt, American firm, Brown & Williamson that had in 1925–1926 made certain strategic investments (in 1925 Brown & Williamson had acquired J. G. Flynt Tobacco Co., which produced a pipe tobacco called Sir Walter Raleigh). Brown & Williamson had its headquarters in the heart of tobacco country, Winston-Salem, North Carolina. BAT had decided to sell cigarettes in the United States, using Brown & Williamson as its means of entry. Since none of the brands that BAT had obtained at origin in 1902 was available for its use in the United States, to enter into the American market, it believed that it had to take the acquisition route. At once, American Tobacco counterattacked, buying J. Wix & Son, an English cigarette maker, competing, however, not with BAT, since BAT was not allowed to sell in the United Kingdom, but with its British associate Imperial Tobacco.[79]

BAT's beachhead in the U.S. market was further extended in 1929, when its U.S. subsidiary, Brown & Williamson, inaugurated a newly constructed modern factory in Louisville, Kentucky, to manufacture Raleigh cigarettes (positioned as a high-priced prestige brand). Raleigh was the brand name that BAT acquired with the purchase of Brown & Williamson. In 1929, Raleigh cigarettes captured a mere 0.5 percent of the U.S. market, but the change in strategy had been made, and BAT (through its subsidiary Brown & Williamson) was now a contender in the U.S. market.[80]

In sum, British, Canadian, Dutch, Swiss, and Swedish businesses offered a variety of branded "convenience" goods in America. From mustard to soap to matches to cigarettes, foreign direct investors manufactured in the United States to sell to U.S. consumers. Some of the foreign-owned firms had only minority interests in their affiliates; others had 100 percent control. Heavily advertised brands such as Lifebuoy, Lux Flakes, Lipton's Tea, Nestlé's chocolates, and Ovaltine were by the late 1920s household names in America.

Textiles, Leather Goods, and Floor Coverings

British, French, Swiss, and other foreign investors went on making textiles in America, as had long been the case. The British investors in cotton thread (Coats and English Sewing Cotton) and in linen thread (Linen Thread Ltd.) retained their leadership in the U.S. thread industry. J. & P. Coats sold branded thread from its multiplant operations. In the late 1920s, the primary development in the U.S. thread industry was the start of the relocation of plants from the North to the South. American Thread Company (controlled by English Sewing Cotton) set the pace, with its first southern factory in Dalton, Georgia, in 1925.[81] Like the rest of U.S. domestic cotton manufacturing, the attraction of Georgia lay in a lower-cost, more passive workforce.

The wool makers stayed in the North. The large British plant of Bradford Dyers' Association, in Westerly, Rhode Island, persisted.[82] Gaunt interests from Britain operated the formerly German Passaic Worsted Company in Passaic, New Jersey.[83] The key foreign investments in woolens and worsted were, however, by French family firms in Woonsocket, Rhode Island, which produced high-quality worsted goods. The Germans, important before the war in the American woolens industry, never returned. Their factories were now (with the one British exception) under domestic ownership.

A handful of British firms maintained production in specialized, miscellaneous branches of the textile industry: thus, the Winterbottom Book Cloth Co., Ltd., London, made bookbinding cloth at its Interlaken Mills and tracing cloth at the Arkwright Finishing Mills in Rhode Island, while J. & J. Cash manufactured cotton name tapes in Connecticut.[84] A Canadian firm, Woods Manufacturing Company, had a jute and cotton mill in Ogdensburg, New York.[85] So, too, in the late 1920s, the French and Swiss silk and the Swiss embroidery investments persevered.[86]

One long-standing investor in America was the Liverpool trading house Alfred Booth & Co. that had a tannery in Gloversville, New York, which it shut down because of absence of profits, 1924–1929; it also operated a large leather tanning factory in Philadelphia. Booth had facilities in America to make glazed leather and felt for shoes. In 1926, it agreed to prepare skins for the giant International Shoe Company—providing it with a sizable new market.[87]

The British-owned Forestal Land, Timber & Railway Co., Ltd., with its factory in Brooklyn, New York, that made liquid extract used in leather tanning from quebraco logs imported from Argentina, was important. In the mid-1920s, it restructured its U.S. business operations (probably for tax reasons): in 1927 The Tannin Corporation sold the Brooklyn properties and built a modern plant in Wilmington, Delaware; it also operated "liquefying and powder plants" at Newark (N.J.), Boston, and Chicago. The Tannin Corporation was the successor to the New York Quebraco Extract Co. and the New York Tannin Corp. A complex corporate structure notwithstanding, the British Forestal company continued to dominate (and control) the provision of quebraco in the American market.[88]

In carpets and floor coverings, the Canadian-owned Toronto Carpet had two manufacturing facilities in the United States.[89] More important in floor coverings in 1924, an American firm, the Congoleum Co., merged with its chief rival, the Nairn Linoleum Co., the U.S. affiliate of the eponymous Scottish enterprise. The Nairn Linoleum Co., established in New Jersey in 1886, had begun production in Kearny (East Newark), New Jersey, in 1888, where some thirty-six years later it had a fifty-acre site with thirty-three principal buildings. When, in 1924, Congoleum-Nairn Inc. was formed, the Scottish Nairn company (or its principals) maintained a minority interest in the combined unit.[90] At origin, Congoleum-Nairn had fifteen directors, five of whom were from the Nairn side of the business. The five included three men from Scotland (two of whom were the sons of Michael Baker Nairn, the Scottish firm's founder: Sir Michael Nairn and Robert Spencer Nairn) and two men from Newark (from Nairn's U.S. affiliate: Peter Campbell and his son Robert). In 1886, the founder, Michael Baker Nairn (who died in 1915), had dispatched Peter Campbell to the United States to start and manage the U.S. business. Campbell had remained in New Jersey, and his son, Robert, was American-born. At origin, Congoleum-Nairn was the largest linoleum company in the United States. It was American managed (Robert Campbell was a vice-president).[91] According to a Scottish Nairn company history, the principal reason that the Scots had favored the merger was that J. & W. Sloane, Nairn's sole selling agents in America, had been unable to handle the rapidly expanding output of Nairn's New Jersey plants. Thus, Peter Campbell had proposed the combination with the Congoleum Co. to gain access to the latter's extensive sales organization.[92]

The activities of foreign-owned firms in natural textiles, leather products, and floor coverings were small when compared with the truly formidable involvements by foreign-owned enterprises in synthetic textiles. In this branch of the textile industry, foreign firms were innovative and, with few exceptions, very profitable. Rayon was the world's first synthetic textile, and as in the early 1920s, so in the last half of the decade, there were significant foreign arrivals into business in the United States. Now most of the new factories were built in the South, in Virginia, Maryland, Tennessee, North Carolina, Georgia, and West Virginia (prior to 1925, only two states in the South—Virginia and Tennessee—had had any commercial rayon manufacture).[93]

Economists predict that when there are high profits, if barriers to entry are not too steep, companies will go into an industry. By the late 1920s, most of the basic rayon patents had expired. Accordingly, foreign-based multinational corporations invested in the United States—challenging but remaining far behind the leader, the British-owned first-mover Courtaulds' subsidiary, The Viscose Company. In 1928 the estimated share of U.S. production with some foreign ownership involvement was 95 to 98 percent (see Table 5.2).

The earliest and most significant rival to the British front-runner was Du Pont with its joint venture with the French Comptoir des Textiles Artificiels (CTA): Du Pont Fibersilk Company (renamed in 1924 Du Pont Rayon Company).[94] In 1929 Du Pont bought out its French partner's share for approximately $62 million, retaining the cross-licensing agreements. The domestication of Du Pont's rayon business does not appear to have been a cash transaction; instead, CTA obtained a very small minority shareholding in Du Pont itself, and in May 1929 Edmond Gillet of CTA was elected to the Du Pont board of directors.[95] In the interim (1924–1929), although Du Pont Rayon Company expanded its Buffalo, New York, and its Old Hickory, Tennessee, facilities and constructed additional plants, it failed to catch up with The Viscose Company (the latter's U.S. output in 1928 was about triple that of Du Pont Rayon).[96] In 1929, at a new plant in Waynesboro, Virginia, Du Pont had started to make acetate rayon (all its previous output had been by the viscose process). Its relations with CTA led it to buy U.S. rights to the acetate yarn process of the Société pour la Fabrication de la Soie "Rhodiaceta."[97]

The second newcomer of the 1920–1923 years, Tubize Artificial Silk

Table 5.2. U.S. production of rayon, by leading companies, 1928 (production measured by weight—in pounds)

		Foreign ownership			
Rank	Company	Nationality	Extent	Production	% of total
1	The Viscose Co.	British	a	54,000,000	55
2	Du Pont Rayon Co.	French	b	18,161,000	18
3	Tubize Artificial Silk	Belgian	b	8,500,000	9
4	Celanese Corp. of America	British	c	5,000,000	5
5	Industrial Rayon Co.	Italian	b	4,250,000	4
6	American Bemberg Corp.	German	a	2,100,000	2
7	Belamose	Belgian	b	1,650,000	2
8	Delaware Rayon	French	d	1,500,000	2
9	Skenandoa	French	d	1,150,000	1
10	Acme Rayon	—	none	740,250	1
11	American Glanzstoff	German	a	350,000	*
12	All others	—	d	500,000	1
	Total			97,901,250	100

Source: Mois H. Avram, *The Rayon Industry,* 2nd ed. (New York: Van Nostrand, 1929), 53, 71 (Celanese Corp. of America).
a = majority. b = minority. c = "control." d = if any foreign ownership, *very* small.
* less than .5 percent; plant was just starting up in 1928.

Company, found the nitrocellulose process not competitive with the viscose one. Although this Belgian affiliate maintained its output at its Hopewell, Virginia, plant, its market share slipped, while other firms expanded; yet, in 1928, it ranked third in U.S. production—following The Viscose Co. and Du Pont Rayon.[98] During the 1920s, in large part, American replaced the Belgian ownership.[99]

The third new arrival of the early 1920s, the affiliate of Snia Viscosa (of Turin, Italy), the Industrial Fibre Corporation, failed to flourish; in 1925, a new Industrial Rayon Corporation replaced it. The Italian holdings in this successor firm—some 394,000 shares—constituted a minority stake; the management was American.[100] In sum, by decade's end, of the four firms making rayon on a commercial basis in the United States in 1924, two (The Viscose Co. and Du Pont Rayon) were performing brilliantly and two (the affiliates of the Belgian and Italian enterprises) had lagged behind.[101] Du Pont Rayon was 100 percent American owned by the close of 1929. In the case of both the Belgian and Italian parents, their financial control over their American units had diminished over the course of the decade.

Yet what happened to this first wave of rayon producers did not mean less foreign influence (at least during the 1920s), since from 1925 to 1929, a new batch of European enterprises—from Britain, Belgium, Germany, Holland, and Italy—began commercial production in the United States, employing the cellulose acetate, viscose, and cuprammonium processes to manufacture rayon.[102] During the First World War, the cellulose acetate process had been developed in Great Britain, and the successor to the original company, British Celanese Ltd. (organized in 1923), using this process to make rayon, became a competitor to Courtaulds, Ltd., in the United Kingdom; Courtaulds used the viscose process.[103] In 1918 the British-controlled American Cellulose & Chemical Manufacturing Co. Ltd. (ACCM) had begun construction of a plant in Cumberland, Maryland, to make cellulose acetate for military purposes. This facility had not started production until late in 1921, after the war was over.[104] ACCM became a subsidiary of British Celanese Ltd., and in 1925 ACCM (from 1927 renamed Celanese Corporation of America) started commercial output of rayon at the Cumberland, Maryland, plant (actually in Amcelle, Maryland). This factory used its parent's cellulose acetate processes to make rayon.[105] Courtaulds' U.S. management was alarmed at this new competition in the American market, and in response The Viscose Company broadened its product line, building in 1928 a plant in Meadville, Pennsylvania, for acetate yarn manufacture while at the same time it continued its far larger output of viscose yarn.[106]

In 1925, the Belamose Corporation—owned by American and Belgian interests—started production of viscose yarn at Rocky Hill, Connecticut.[107] Much more important, 1925 saw the initial German drive into the U.S. rayon industry.[108] The German rayon companies were new participants in America, not the return of prewar firms.[109] They did, however, hire at least one manager, who had been associated with a prewar German chemical company in the United States.[110] The first of the German firms—in 1925—was J. P. Bemberg, AG, of Barman, Germany, which in a joint venture with the premier German rayon producer, Vereinigte Glanzstoff-Fabriken, AG, of Elberfeld (VGF), organized the American Bemberg Corporation. In October 1926, at its newly built plant near Elizabethton, Tennessee (some nine miles from Johnson City), American Bemberg Corporation began to make rayon, using the cuprammonium process. Nearby, in the fall of 1928, the American Glanzstoff Corporation (a wholly owned subsidiary of VGF) embarked on rayon manufacture, utilizing the viscose process. The two factories in Elizabethton had the same German management.[111] By 1929, the two German firms had some 5,000 employees.[112] Still another new arrival was the Dutch firm NV Nederlandsche Kunstzijdefabriek "Enka," which in 1928 organized the American Enka Corporation and in 1929 commenced rayon production in Asheville, North Carolina, using the viscose process.[113]

Meanwhile, late in November 1928, the Associated Rayon Corporation (ARC), incorporated in Maryland, issued a prospectus to sell $20 million 6 percent cumulative convertible preferred stock and 100,000 shares of common stock (no par value). This was the type of holding company described in Chapter 4 under the rubric "cosmopolitan finance." The president of ARC, Dr. Fritz Blüthgen, was a managing director of VGF. Its board of directors had men from the banking houses Speyer & Co. and Lehman Brothers (New York), Teixeira de Mattos Brothers (Amsterdam), and Lazard Speyer-Ellissen (Berlin and Frankfurt). The bankers sold its securities in Holland and Germany, as well as in the United States. ARC was controlled through stock ownership by VGF. In turn, it owned shares valued (at the 1928 market price) at $45 million—in two German companies (in its parent, VGF, and J. P. Bemberg, AG), as well as in the Austrian Erste Oesterreichische Glanzstoff-Fabrik AG; in the Italian Snia Viscosa; in the Japanese Asahi Kenshoku Kabushiki Kaisha; in Enka and another Dutch firm; and in the United States in American Bemberg Corporation, the American Glanzstoff Corporation, and the American Enka Corporation. Independently, VGF also continued to hold stock in all these same companies.[114] In 1929, in Holland, the Algemeene Kunstzijde Unie NV (AKU) was organized by the Dutch Enka firm and the German VGF. One author has explained the formation of AKU as a "result of the unfavorable German taxation conditions."[115] These American (ARC) and European (AKU) combinations were, however, more than financial wizardry. In effect, they placed the American Bemberg Corporation, the American Glanzstoff Corporation, *and* the American Enka Corporation under common management.[116]

One added significant entry into the U.S. rayon industry (in 1928) was a second Italian firm, La Soie de Chatillon, which with American partners set up the American Chatillon Corporation and built a plant in Rome, Georgia, to manufacture both viscose and acetate yarn.[117] Some smaller, basically domestic companies also started rayon production, often under the direction of foreign technical staffs.[118] And in the late 1920s, with high demand, rayon imports began to rise.[119]

In short, by 1929, The Viscose Company, still by far outdistancing its rivals, was facing substantial competition in the United States. Its initial response had been to seek price-maintenance arrangements, obtaining Du Pont's acquiescence to "an informal [joint] policy."[120] At decade's end, despite the many new producers and the rising imports, demand for rayon seemed insatiable.[121] Thus, in the fall of 1928, Dr. Arthur Mothwurf, president of the American Bemberg Corporation, announced that his firm would expand way beyond its original plans.[122]

While The Viscose Company's first strategy had been to cooperate with competitors to keep prices up, with heightening competition, in 1929 it altered its approach and dropped its prices.[123] It had built new factories to meet the upswing in demand (a viscose plant at Parkersburg, West Virginia, in 1926 and the acetate plant at Meadville, Pennsylvania, in 1928); it also had enlarged its output at its existing viscose facilities at Marcus Hook, Pennsylvania, at Roanoke, Virginia (its biggest plant), and at Lewistown, Pennsylvania. In addition, it had a cotton linters plant at Nitro, West Virginia. The Viscose Company made splendid profits. Its net return on its average investment in the rayon business, 1925–1929, ranged from a high of 72.6 percent (in 1925) to a low of 44.6 percent (1929).[124] The British subsidiary was a giant. Notwithstanding the new rivalry in the industry, its share of total U.S. rayon production in 1928 was at least 55 percent.[125] Its historian does not provide employment figures for the late 1920s, but by 1929 they seem to have been in the vicinity of 20,000.[126] The book value of Courtaulds' assets in America in 1929 was $122.9 million.[127] The Viscose Company was the largest rayon producer in the world, with an output greater than that of its British parent.[128]

In sum, by the start of 1929, British, Belgian, French, Italian, German, and Dutch businesses were making rayon in America and in fact excelled in this industry. Technical skills and experience had been transferred across the Atlantic, and as a result rayon had become among the most spectacular U.S. growth industries of the 1920s. The industry leader, The Viscose Company, owned by British Courtaulds Ltd., no longer had (as prior to the First World War) a monopoly position; yet it was a substantial, prosperous, and aggressive enterprise. At the end of 1929, this important "high-tech" industry continued to be dominated by foreign multinationals (with the newly 100 percent American-owned Du Pont Rayon the only major totally domestically owned producer).[129]

Glass

French and Belgian companies participated in America's glass industry. Three glassmakers—the French Saint Gobain, the Belgian Saint-Roch, and the American Corning Glass Works—organized the Blue Ridge Glass Corporation in 1925, which reopened a shuttered Corning Glass Works in Kingsport, Tennessee, and began to make glass in 1927. This was a significant but short-lived venture. Production ended in 1929, when Saint Gobain made an agreement to divide markets with the U.S. industry leader, Pittsburgh Plate Glass.[130] Meanwhile, Solvay &

Cie., the Belgian chemical firm, also invested in the American glass industry (the glass industry was a major purchaser of Solvay & Cie.'s principal product). So, too, there were German investments related to optical glass.

Chemicals

In the late 1920s most aspects of the U.S. chemical industry were deeply and materially affected by European investors, who were a major source of technological innovations. The associations were apparent in the new synthetic textile industry (in rayon). The rest of the story is frightfully complicated, for the chemical industry comprised numerous products with diverse international network alliances. I will begin with the most important European actor in the 1920s global chemical industry. In November-December 1925, I. G. Farben came into being in Germany, uniting the principal participants in that nation's chemical industry: Badische Anilin und Soda Fabrik (Badische, now called BASF); Farbenfabriken vorm. Friedrich Bayer & Co. (Bayer); Farbwerke vorm. Meister Lucius & Brüning, Hoechst am Main (Hoechst); Aktiengesellschaft für Anilin-Fabrikation (Agfa); Chemische Fabrik Griesheim Elektron (Griesheim); and Chemische Fabriken vormals Weiler-ter-Meer (Weiler-ter Meer); as well as Leopold Cassella, GmbH, and Kalle & Co., AG. In a reaction to the German combination, in 1926 Imperial Chemical Industries (ICI) brought together Britain's leading chemical enterprises: Brunner, Mond & Co.; Nobel Industries; United Alkali Company; and British Dyestuffs Corporation.[131] The two formidable mergers in Germany (in 1925) and Britain (in 1926) had profound transatlantic ramifications.

By 1923 I. G. Farben's precursors, all of which had had direct investments in America before World War I, had barely begun to reenter the United States. There had been the renewal of ties with the prewar importers, Agfa's new subsidiary (in 1923), and Bayer's 1923 arrangements to share profits with Sterling Products in Winthrop Chemical Company. I. G. Farben inherited and built on these and on some additional 1924–1925 foundations (in 1926, for example, I. G. Farben and Sterling Products arranged to share fifty-fifty ownership of Winthrop Chemical; Winthrop Chemical had acquired H. A. Metz Laboratories with all the long-standing Hoechst pharmaceutical experience related to Salvarsan, Novocaine, and other products).[132]

When in 1918 the Alien Property Custodian had sold Bayer's prewar U.S. assets to Sterling Products, the latter had retained only the medicine lines and had resold the dyestuff portion of its purchase to an American firm, Grasselli Chemical Company. In 1924 Grasselli Chemical separated its dyestuff manufacture and sales and put them in a new Grasselli Dyestuff Corporation, which also became the U.S. sales agent for Bayer's German-made, imported dyestuffs; Grasselli Chemical and the German Bayer shared fifty-fifty in the profits of this new joint venture.[133] The pattern was one that Bayer had established in 1923 with Winthrop Chemical, for pharmaceuticals.[134] Thus, Bayer resumed its interests in all facets of its prewar dyestuffs business. Grasselli Dyestuff, with a capital of $4 million, operated Bayer's prewar Rensselaer, New York, plant and another factory in Linden, New Jersey.[135]

The next move in the German chemical companies' reentry began to take shape just prior to the November–December 1925 formation of I. G. Farben. Herman Metz, the pre- and postwar representative of Hoechst interests in the United States, proposed the combination of the American *sales* representatives of the German dyestuff makers, and on July 1, 1925, Metz formed the General Dyestuff Corporation (GDC).[136] In sequence GDC acquired (1) most of the "Metz businesses" in the United States: H. A. Metz & Co. (American sales agent for Hoechst), as well as the Consolidated Color and Chemical Company and the Central Dyestuff and Chemical Company (small dyestuff manufacturers); (2) the sales agency for Cassella dyes: B. A. Ludwig, who not long before had been appointed sole importer of Cassella dyes, brought that sales agency into GDC; (3) Grasselli Dyestuff's sales unit for Bayer dyestuff (in October 1925); and (4) the Badische dyes sales agency: on January 1, 1926, Kuttroff, Pickhardt & Co. transferred its exclusive selling agency for Badische dyes to GDC.[137] One source described GDC as being financed one-third by Metz-Ludwig, one-third by Grasselli-Bayer, and one-third by Kuttroff-Pickhardt (the latter, however, billed its main contribution back to Badische in Germany).[138] GDC united and rationalized the importers' branch offices and warehouses in Boston, Providence, Philadelphia, Charlotte (N.C.), Chicago, and San Francisco. It placed under one management the previously separate sales organizations of the importers of German dyes. Metz became its first president; Adolf Kuttroff was chairman of the board.[139] I. G. Farben explained that "our superiority over our competitors in other countries is based not only on the higher quality of our products, but above all on the well-organized and excellently trained sales staff and on the technical service to our customers."[140] GDC provided such services in the United States.[141]

Early in 1926 Jaspar Crane of Du Pont wrote Irénée du Pont that I. G. Farben was "particularly seeking to establish itself in the United States."[142] Rumors circulated that I. G. Farben would build a synthetic ammonia plant in America; in spring 1927, its Synthetic Nitrogen Products Corporation was incorporated in Delaware.[143] The futile negotiations of 1919–1920 between Badische—now part of I. G. Farben—and Du Pont resumed, discussing a possible joint venture in the United States in ammonia production. Yet by November 1927 these talks had collapsed.[144] Du Pont charted its own path.[145] I. G. Farben did not, however, construct an ammonia plant in America. Synthetic Nitrogen Products Corporation, with its head office in New York, became the U.S. sales representative of the Stickstoff Syndikat, I. G. Farben's fertilizer subsidiary.[146]

At about the same time in 1926, Carl Bosch of I. G. Farben proposed an exchange of shares between his company and Allied Chemical & Dye Corporation; Orlando Weber, president of Allied Chemical, rejected Bosch's overtures.[147] Relations between Weber and Bosch cooled further, as Allied Chemical's subsidiary, National Aniline & Chemical Co. (NACC), began dumping dyes in European markets.[148] Another Allied Chemical subsidiary started production of synthetic nitrates at Hopewell, Virginia.[149]

In contrast with its temporary friction with Du Pont and Allied Chemical, on September 27, 1927, I. G. Farben and Standard Oil of New Jersey (SONJ) made a significant hydrogenation agreement that provided the giant American oil company with access to German technology on the hydrogenation of crude oil (a new technology to raise gasoline yields).[150] A June 21, 1928, SONJ memorandum made it clear that Du Pont executives were aware of the SONJ–I. G. Farben arrangements; the oil company wanted Du Pont to know "that our backing of the I. G. in the chemical business in the United States is not directed against them." SONJ wished to be in a position "to serve" both I. G. Farben and Du Pont in the business that would later be called petrochemicals.[151]

In March 1928, Agfa-Ansco Corporation, Inc., was organized, joining an existing weak American film manufacturer and Agfa, an I. G. Farben subsidiary, which had a sales unit in America. In the film industry, I. G. Farben's American initiative was a reaction to Eastman Kodak's German expansion. Agfa-Ansco had a paper and camera plant in Binghamton, New York, and employed more than 1,000 persons there.[152] That same year, Du Pont acquired the Grasselli Chemical Company, at which time I. G. Farben raised its interest (obtained through Bayer) in Grasselli Dyestuff Corporation to 100 percent and changed that firm's name to General Aniline Works. General Aniline Works had two large American dyestuff factories.[153]

Then, at the beginning of 1929, I. G. Farben took a big step to enlarge, to consolidate, and to rationalize its U.S. business, setting up a holding company that would combine and finance the principal *manufacturing* facilities of I. G. Farben affiliates in America, the plant of the Agfa-Ansco Corporation and more important those of General Aniline

Works. Thus, in April 1929, the American I. G. Chemical Corporation was established (incorporated in Delaware but headquartered in New York City).[154] It was listed in *Moody's Industrials* as being "affiliated with" I. G. Farben, which guaranteed "unconditionally" the $30 million in bonds that the new enterprise offered to the American public. I. G. Farben's interest in this company would in time be held through a Swiss holding company, known as I. G. Chemie.[155] As was the case of many foreign companies in America, I. G. Farben went to U.S. capital markets for financing. The American I. G. had a star-studded board of directors that came to include Carl Bosch, Walter Duisberg, Fritz ter Meer, Hermann Schmitz, Max Ilgner, and Wilfrid Greif (all from I. G. Farben). Also serving as directors were Herman Metz and Adolf Kuttroff, the longtime importers for Hoechst and Badische in the United States, and William Erhard Weiss, of Drug Inc., a holding company that had acquired Sterling Products in 1928 (recall that in 1926 I. G. Farben and Sterling Products had the fifty-fifty joint venture Winthrop Chemical, which handled both Bayer and Hoechst pharmaceuticals). In addition, on the board of American I. G. were Charles E. Mitchell, head of National City Bank, New York, and Paul M. Warburg, who was by December 1929 chairman of the board of The Manhattan Company that had just acquired his International Acceptance Bank. Rounding out the roster of directors were Edsel Ford, president of Ford Motor Company, and Walter Teagle, president of Standard Oil of New Jersey (SONJ).[156]

The president of American I. G. Chemical Corporation was Schmitz, the first vice-president, Greif. Since Schmitz resided in Germany, Greif was I. G. Farben's main representative in New York.[157] Metz was vice-president and treasurer. The American bankers and industrialists brought prestige to the new venture: Mitchell and Warburg ranked among the nation's most prominent investment bankers; National City Company and the International Manhattan Company (respectively, securities affiliates of National City Bank and the Manhattan Bank) were the lead underwriters of the May 1, 1929, $30 million bond offering of American I. G.[158] Ford Motor Company had sought national representation on the boards of its European affiliates, and Bosch had agreed to join the German Ford board only if Edsel Ford would reciprocate and be a director of the new American I. G.[159]

As for Teagle, SONJ and I. G. Farben had made the 1927 hydrogenation agreement (see earlier discussion); SONJ saw I. G. Farben as a splendid source of information on advanced technologies and a potential source of competition (if synthetic fuels could be produced cheaply from coal). On November 9, 1929, SONJ and I. G. Farben would finalize a series of accords that brought the two companies into even closer harmony.[160] The first of these agreements—known as the Four-Party Agreement—set the framework. It covered the hydrogenation of oil and coal (and superseded the 1927 agreement), providing for a new U.S. joint venture to be named the Standard-I. G. Company—80 percent owned by SONJ and 20 percent by the Germans. Standard-I. G. was a patent holding company, with worldwide rights, outside of Germany, to the hydrogenation process.[161] The second was a "division of fields agreement"; I. G. Farben recognized the "preferred position" of SONJ in oil and natural gas, while SONJ acknowledged the "preferred position" of I. G. Farben in the chemical industry. A third accord allocated world oil product markets (except those in Germany) to SONJ, while a separate fourth agreement covered the German market. A fifth set up the approach for dealing with "future eventualities."[162] In return for the benefits SONJ received (use of patents, technological know-how, and field and territorial rights), SONJ agreed to pay I. G. Farben $35 million in shares of SONJ. When the arrangements were completed—on November 9, 1929—the market price per SONJ share was $65.00; accordingly, I. G. Farben received 546,011 shares in SONJ—or about 2 percent of SONJ's outstanding stock. The transaction made I. G. Farben second only to the Rockefellers as the largest single shareholder in the world's biggest oil company.[163] After the group of agreements were ratified, Bosch had achieved his goal—"a marriage" of I. G. Farben and SONJ.[164] Indeed, with Teagle on the board of the American I. G., with the joint venture Standard-I. G., and with I. G. Farben's owning 2 percent of the stock of SONJ, Teagle and Bosch could watch over one another in America. The two men held each other in the highest esteem.[165] The arrangements pleased both corporate leaders.

The new American I. G. Chemical Corporation was not mere financial architecture. It provided the basis for a concerted invasion of the U.S. market by Germany's chemical colossus. American I.G's. balance sheet, as of May 21, 1929, showed $61 million in assets. It was a holding company; its subsidiaries Agfa-Ansco Corporation and General Aniline Works (GAW) continued to operate under those names.[166] American I. G. also acquired I. G. Farben's interests in Winthrop Chemical.[167]

While Standard Oil of New Jersey and I. G. Farben's businesses were complementary (the potential competition in oil products and chemicals had been regulated by the 1929 accord), Du Pont and I. G. Farben were both chemical companies and frequently at odds. All during this period, they were in conversations. I. G. Farben and Du Pont discussed possible friendly arrangements on ammonia, dyestuffs, and other goods. Near decade's end, I. G. Farben and Du Pont had considered a merger of I. G. Farben's U.S. dyestuff business with that of Du Pont's in a joint enterprise. But the Germans were still superior to Du Pont in dyestuffs and saw little to gain (and much to lose) from such an alliance.[168] Moreover, Du Pont insisted on control, and I. G. Farben refused; throughout, I. G. Farben's management felt Du Pont remained "singularly independent."[169] The only joint venture between I. G. Farben and Du Pont to emerge in the 1920s was in a small seed disinfectant firm, Bayer Semesan Company, entered into in 1928, with 50 percent of the stock owned by Du Pont and 50 percent by Winthrop Chemical Company (which in turn was in that year 50 percent owned by I. G. Farben).[170] On the other hand, by 1929, Du Pont appears to have purchased a small quantity of shares in I. G. Farben and in the latter's Swiss holding company, I. G. Chemie.[171] Both I. G. Farben and Du Pont wanted to know exactly what the other was up to, in technology, product strategies, and market penetration.

Thus, as the 1920s came to a close, I. G. Farben was fully committed to an active and direct involvement in the U.S. chemical industry.[172] Through General Dyestuff (the dyestuff sales company) and American I. G., I. G. Farben had reacquired an interest in or complete ownership of virtually all the properties its predecessor firms had lost during World War I. I. G. Farben was in a far stronger position in 1929 (had much larger U.S. assets) than its precursors had had before the war, although the German monopoly in dyestuffs no longer existed. There were by 1929 viable American companies able to compete in the U.S. dyestuff industry (indeed, the German presence may well have spurred American competitiveness). In addition, as it began to move at home in Germany into synthetic oil products, I. G. Farben had acquired the sizable shareholding in the premier international oil company, Standard Oil of New Jersey (and had a joint venture with that company in the Standard-I. G. Company). With Du Pont, it had the small joint venture Bayer-Semesan and an uneasy combination of cooperation and competition.

Most notable about I. G. Farben's U.S. march was that there had been little, if any, new capital introduced by the Germans. Practically all I. G. Farben's sizable investment at year end 1929 was based on the German giant's technical edge (its technological contribution); it used moneys raised in the United States. There is no question, however, that in I. G. Farben's chemical investments in the United States control (and direction) came from Germany.[173] The new activities occurred at the same time as Bosch was stating (in 1929) that I. G. Farben "did not wish to go into competition in the United States with the U.S. chemical industry."[174] Bosch wanted to hold Americans at bay worldwide.[175] I. G. Farben's role in America was a balancing act of aggression and of coopting its rivals. In 1929 Bosch declared that "it was the policy of the

I. G. not to go into old fields already occupied but to create new industries and new fields."[176] I. G. Farben was energetic in its U.S. strategies, advancing new frontiers.[177] Its approach was in sharp contrast with that of its British counterpart, Imperial Chemical Industries.

As I. G. Farben proceeded in its U.S. endeavors, ICI retreated from active involvement in the United States. At the time of its formation in 1926, ICI had a large number of existing interests in the United States and was already in a close relationship with Du Pont, based on the long history of cooperation between Nobel interests and Du Pont. At origin, ICI obtained (through its acquisition of Nobel Industries) a sizable investment in General Motors, which it reduced in 1927 and 1928.[178] United Alkali, which had become an ICI subsidiary, had a plant in Bay City, Michigan, which ICI shut down in 1928. This Michigan facility had been in existence for three decades, but low prices of chlorates made operations unprofitable; ICI made no effort to lower costs and become competitive.[179] British Dyestuffs Corporation (BDC), another of the companies that had been merged into ICI, had in 1922 set up a U.S. subsidiary, Dyestuffs Corporation of America (DCA). In 1924, DCA had combined the U.S. sales outlets of the predecessor firms of BDC: I. Levinstein & Co. and Read Holliday & Sons. This combination may have been the incentive for the formation in 1925 by the Germans of the General Dyestuff Corporation, but whereas the latter became an effective marketing unit, DCA was inconsequential (although it did distribute in the United States certain colors manufactured by BDC and selected Du Pont dyes, based on Du Pont's prior arrangements with Levinstein).[180]

Brunner, Mond, another member of the ICI group, had brought into ICI its £1.6 million (1925 value) stake in Allied Chemical & Dye Corporation, which had its genesis in Brunner, Mond's 1880s investment in Solvay Process Company.[181] The management of Brunner, Mond had never liked Orlando Weber, president of Allied Chemical; Brunner, Mond became particularly irritated when Weber in 1926 voided a 1921 division-of-markets agreement in the alkali business. Yet in 1926, through Brunner, Mond, ICI had a sizable investment (about 5.3 percent of the stock) in Allied Chemical, which like Du Pont was a giant in the U.S. chemical industry.[182] ICI, through Brunner, Mond's subsidiary, Castner-Kellner Alkali Company, also had acquired a minority interest (4,320 shares, equal to 8.9 percent of the shares outstanding) in the much smaller Roessler & Hasslacher Chemical Company.[183]

In March 1927, Sir Harry McGowan (of ICI) proposed that he sell ICI's holdings in GM shares and buy 45,000 Du Pont shares; Du Pont officials vetoed that idea.[184] Nonetheless, given the close relations between Du Pont and ICI, Du Pont officials were nervous about ICI's sizable shareholdings in Allied Chemical.[185] To satisfy its American friends, in November 1928 ICI sold 105,600 shares of Allied Chemical to Solvay & Cie.—its Belgian partner in Allied Chemical. This left ICI with 10,316 shares in Allied Chemical, enough to gain information but not enough to exercise any kind of influence or control.[186]

In short, in 1929, ICI held a mere 5,000 shares in Du Pont, 10,316 shares in Allied Chemical, and, through Castner-Kellner, 4,320 shares in Roessler & Hasslacher Chemical Company. These interests were too small for anything except "keeping in touch." Du Pont would take over the Roessler & Hasslacher Chemical Company in 1930—and ICI would in the process obtain some added Du Pont shares (not a substantial amount).[187] DCA still existed in 1929—controlled by ICI (it would be acquired by Du Pont in 1931).[188] After ICI had sold the bulk of its shares in Allied Chemical, it entered into a comprehensive 1929 Patents and Process Agreement with Du Pont, which, for all practical purposes, barred ICI from any future significant FDI role in America.[189] In effect, ICI left the U.S. market to Du Pont. Its continuing U.S. investments were business related but entirely passive; it was bound by the agreement not to compete with Du Pont.[190]

If I. G. Farben and ICI took divergent paths, the Belgian Solvay & Cie. followed still a third route. Solvay & Cie. was not nearly as large as I. G. Farben or ICI, nor did it have such a diversified product line. Unlike ICI, but not to the extent of I. G. Farben, it expanded its U.S. presence in the late 1920s. Like other European firms with good connections, Solvay & Cie. in 1924 had raised $10 million in a U.S. bond offering (led by Lee, Higginson & Co.).[191] In January 1927, Solvay & Cie.—through a Swiss intermediary—formed Solvay American Investment Corporation (SAIC) to acquire, hold, and sell securities. SAIC immediately had a $15 million U.S. bond offering (also by Lee, Higginson & Co.), the proceeds of which were used to lend $10.5 million to Solvay & Cie., in Belgium, and also to acquire shares in the American Libbey-Owens Sheet Glass Co. (soon to be Libbey Owens Ford Glass Company).[192] Even though SIAC's holdings in the glass company were not controlling, the purchase was strategically designed to harmonize the interests of the U.S. Libbey-Owens with key Belgian glass interests; Solvay & Cie. was at the same time a large stockholder in Libbey-Owens' European affiliates.[193] In July 1927, Emmanuel Janssen of Solvay & Cie. met with an executive from the French glass company Saint Gobain to discuss how Libbey-Owens might cooperate in the United States with its American rivals; this set the stage for the accord in the U.S. glass industry, whereby Saint Gobain stopped producing in Tennessee.[194] Thus, some of Solvay & Cie.'s U.S. investments related to the allocation of international glass production.

More crucial, as of January 1, 1928, SAIC owned 366,488 shares of Allied Chemical stock with a market value of more than $48 million.[195] Then, according to ICI records, after the November 1928 sale by the latter of its shares in Allied Chemical to Solvay & Cie., the Belgian firm—through SAIC—raised its holdings to 457,195 shares in Allied Chemical, or 20.9 percent of Allied Chemical's issued capital.[196] Solvay & Cie. had two representatives (Emmanuel Janssen and Armand Solvay) on the Allied Chemical board of directors.[197] The Belgian firm—through SAIC—held the largest single block of Allied Chemical stock.[198] In August 1929, SAIC offered the U.S. public $25 million in SAIC preferred stock (all the common stock of SAIC continued to be owned by Solvay & Cie.—through a Swiss intermediary).[199] The 20.9 percent interest would (by today's U.S. Department of Commerce standards) define this as a direct investment. It poses questions on ownership and control. Clearly, Allied Chemical was American run and American controlled; in a subsequent chapter, I will show that Solvay's interest was *not* passive (the concept of "control" in this case, and in others, was often fraught with ambiguity).

Aside from the U.S. involvements of I. G. Farben, ICI, and Solvay & Cie. and the U.S. stakes of foreign-owned rayon and drug companies, the additional European interests in America's chemical industry in 1929 constituted an assortment of typically product-specific endeavors, although some of these would have a certain amount of diversification in chemical lines; and some assisted Du Pont in its growth as a leader in the American chemical industry.

In this second collection of investments, the largest new commitments in chemicals were those by the Royal Dutch Shell Group. In 1928 The Shell Union Oil Corporation organized the Shell Development Company, which, in turn, started important laboratories in Emeryville, California, to do research on chemicals derived from petroleum products. The following year, in 1929, Shell Union formed Shell Chemical Company to manufacture and market the new chemicals developed by the research arm. In 1929, Shell Chemical began to construct the first West Coast ammonia plant (in California).[200] Shell Union's entry into the U.S. chemical industry must be understood in an international context. Its parent, Royal Dutch Shell, had entered the chemical industry right after the First World War.[201] In 1927–1929, when Standard Oil of New Jersey was making its arrangements with I. G. Farben, ICI had considered as a response an alliance with Royal Dutch Shell and had approached the latter in London, offering to sell to the oil enterprise a process of cracking heavy oils by hydrogenation. Royal Dutch Shell had an ammonia process it thought might interest ICI. ICI and Royal Dutch Shell discussed a U.S. joint venture. ICI told Du Pont, which turned thumbs down on that idea, considering an ICI–Royal Dutch Shell linkup most undesirable.[202] Accordingly, Shell Chemical was not a joint venture. ICI managers believed Royal Dutch Shell "was not on very good terms with IG [Farben]."[203] Yet it was not that simple; even though I. G. Farben had agreements with Standard Oil of New Jersey, it also had ongoing negotiations in Europe with Royal Dutch Shell; and, by 1928–1929, Royal Dutch Shell and Standard Oil of New Jersey had developed reasonably amicable relations on *oil policies*.[204] Global strategic interrelationships were mirrored in all these multinational enterprises' U.S. business.

Certain German chemical companies that had been active in America before 1914, for example, Deutsche Gold- und Silber-Scheideanstalt (Degussa), did not seek to reenter with FDI in the chemical industry, but Degussa did maintain close connections with Th. Goldschmidt's former American affiliate, now renamed Metal & Thermit Corporation.[205] In 1926, the Buffalo Electro-Chemical Company began (at Tonawanda, New York) the electrolytic manufacture of hydrogen peroxide under a license from The Chemical Foundation. It became the largest manufacturer of hydrogen peroxide in the United States. During World War II, it was found to be partly German owned.[206] Other German enterprises reentered in alternative ways. Otto Haas (the American partner of Rohm & Haas) had visited Germany in 1920 and while there had promised his partner, Otto Röhm, that he, Haas, would attempt to recover the German's prewar holdings. In 1925–1926, Haas bought the stock once held by Röhm, placing it in a beneficial trust for Röhm and his heirs. Röhm obtained dividend income on this stock (representing a 40 percent interest in Rohm & Haas). The U.S. and German firms shared technological information and divided markets. In 1924, while on a trip to Germany, Haas met Drs. Kurt Albert and August Amann of Chemische Fabrik Dr. Kurt Albert. Albert and Amann had invented certain synthetic resins, and in 1927, Haas and the Albert firm formed a joint venture (seventy-thirty) to make and sell the resins in the United States. The Albert firm received its 30 percent interest in exchange for its American patent rights, know-how, and trademarks. The new Resinous Products and Chemical Company was an immediate success.[207]

In aromatic chemicals the German firm Schimmel & Co. worked closely with Fritzsche Brothers; I do not know whether the prewar German investment was resumed. In another case, also in fine chemicals, there was also a revival of prewar connections: Heyden Chemical Works, an important German direct investment in prewar America, was sold to Americans by the Alien Property Custodian. In 1925, the American-owned Heyden Chemical Works acquired Norvell Chemical Corporation, which had employed George W. Simon (the founder of the prewar German Heyden subsidiary in the United States); Simon quickly restored communications with the ex-German parent. If the "foreign direct investment" aspects of Schimmel/Fritzsche Brothers and Heyden-Germany/Heyden-US are unclear, the interconnections were obvious.[208]

Beyond ICI and the British-Dutch Shell, other British companies in the U.S. chemical industry included Oldbury Electro-Chemical Company (a subsidiary of Albright & Wilson), at Niagara Falls, New York, which met "ruinous competition" from imports but survived, primarily through extending its product line and providing chemicals used in a new weed killer. F. Austin Lidbury of Oldbury Electro-Chemical became a spokesman for higher U.S. tariffs to shelter the British investment in the United States.[209] Another British participant in several U.S. chemical endeavors was the Rio Tinto Company (its principal business was mining in Spain). It had a U.S. subsidiary, Pyrites Company, which during the First World War had been the largest American importer of pyrites. In 1926, Rio Tinto's management decided to modernize and to enlarge the Pyrites Company's cinder treatment operations in Wilmington, Delaware. The latter's best customer was the Davison Chemical Company, which in 1926 was the fourth-ranking producer of fertilizer in the United States with more than sixty plants. In 1927, Rio Tinto acquired a 20 percent holding in Davison's ordinary shares (cost £420,000). Its capital injection aided Davison's expansion and, thus, assisted Rio Tinto sales. In 1929, Rio Tinto and Davison participated in a joint venture to produce silica gel (a new product used for air-conditioning and refrigeration).[210] Another British venture was American-British Chemical Supplies, Inc. (ABCS), formed in 1924 as a trading subsidiary to handle the U.S. chemical business of Charles Tennant & Co., Ltd., Glasgow; in the late 1920s, ABCS invested in two small American chemical manufacturers, Kay Laboratories in West Nyack, New York, and Fries & Fries in Cincinnati, Ohio.[211]

French enterprises also contributed to developments in the U.S. chemical industry, typically with short-lived, minority investments. In the 1920s, Du Pont had three (not counting the one in rayon) joint ventures with French firms, all designed to attract new technologies to the United States. However, by the end of 1929, the French equity interest in each of these joint ventures was past history. The first of the three, started in 1923, was in cellophane; in 1929, at the same time as it ended its joint venture with Comptoir des Textiles Artificiels in rayon, Du Pont bought out the latter's minority holding in Du Pont Cellophane Company—for $12 million.[212] Du Pont retained close relations with CTA. Although CTA had a small minority interest in Du Pont and Edmond Gillet of CTA was on the Du Pont board, Gillet did not attend the directors' meetings.[213]

Du Pont's second joint venture in chemicals with a French business was in 1924 in Du Pont Pathe Film Manufacturing Corporation (DPF), set up to facilitate Du Pont's diversification into film production. The 1922 U.S. tariff, which protected dyestuffs, also shielded film manufacturers from import competition. When in 1921 Merrill, Lynch had acquired control of Pathe Exchange, Inc., the latter had obtained rights to use certain patents and processes developed by its former parent, Pathé Cinéma S.A. In exchange for 49 percent of the common stock in DPF, early in 1925 Pathe Exchange, Inc., transferred to DPF the rights it had acquired from Pathé Cinéma. (Du Pont held 51 percent of the common stock of DPF.) At this time, Pathé Cinéma—the French company—received 5,000 "founders" shares in DPF. Before embarking on this venture, Du Pont had considered cooperation with the German Agfa, which spurned Du Pont's advances (Agfa would join with Ansco in the United States in 1928). As DPF prospered, Eastman Kodak became alarmed; it did not want Du Pont as a competitor. In 1927, Kodak arranged a joint venture (later to be 100 percent) in France with Pathé Cinéma (in Kodak-Pathé S.A.); Pathé Cinéma retained its French movie distribution and exhibition facilities. As a result of Kodak's French activities, DPF did not compete in the United States with Kodak. Instead, DPF manufactured various types of film not made in the United States by Kodak. In the late 1920s, DPF "redeemed" the founders' shares, ending forever the French Pathé Cinéma's equity participation in DPF.[214]

Du Pont's third joint venture with a French enterprise (like the second, inaugurated in 1924) was in Lazote Inc.; this was with L'Air Liquide interests and offered a basis for Du Pont's move into ammonia production (Du Pont sought out the technology of Georges Claude). Here again, Du Pont tried to make arrangements with the Germans (before, and after, its association with L'Air Liquide). In 1929, Du Pont bought out L'Air Liquide's holdings in Lazote Inc.[215] Separately, L'Air Liquide retained an interest (initially acquired in 1915) in Air Reduction Company, a major participant in the U.S. oxygen market.[216] Société Chimique des Usines du Rhône (SCUR)—a predecessor to Rhône-Poulenc—found its participation in Rhodia Chemical Company a source of frustration and no profits; after six years of involvement, it divested in 1925, although Rhodia Chemical Company remained as the French firm's "agent" in America. When, in 1927–1928, Du Pont had bought rights to the acetate processes and had in 1929 started to make acetate rayon, it dealt with the parent and with Rhône-Poulenc's former U.S. subsidiary. In 1929 Newport Chemical Company would acquire the Rhodia Chemical; and Du Pont would in 1931 take over Newport Chemical.[217]

Solvay & Cie. was not the only Belgian chemical company in America. Belgian investors seem to have paralleled the French in some product lines, where there were U.S. investments: in rayon with the Tubize firm, in cellophane, and in film. In 1929, Société Industrielle de la Cellulose (Sidac) set up a subsidiary, Sylvania Industrial Corporation, to make cellophane in Fredericksburg, Virginia. Sidac had started by exporting to the United States; when in 1929 U.S. duties on cellophane were raised from 25 to 60 percent ad valorem, this prompted the Belgian firm to invest in manufacturing in the United States.[218] The Belgian film producer Gevaert had a sales subsidiary in New York; it did not yet manufacture in this country.[219]

The Swiss role in the U.S. chemical industry came to be principally in pharmaceuticals, albeit the Swiss-owned Cincinnati Chemical Works carried on as a significant dye maker.[220] In 1924, L. Givaudan & Cie., Geneva, obtained an interest that it soon raised to 100 percent in the former U.S. aromatic chemical subsidiary of the French Antoine Chiris. Initially, Givaudan's U.S. manufacturing company appears to have been called Burton T. Bush, Inc. A separate sales subsidiary, organized in 1926, was named Givaudan-Delawanna. L. Givaudan & Cie. provided its "American branch" with financial and technical assistance, along with aid in purchasing, manufacturing, and selling.[221]

A lone Canadian investor in the U.S. chemical industry was Canadian Electro Products Company. This subsidiary of the Shawinigan Water and Power Company of Montreal had developed synthetic acetic acid, an important heavy chemical used in the manufacture of cellulose acetate. Canadian Electro Products had exported to the United States through a sales subsidiary, but with import duties and growing U.S. demand, an American plant seemed necessary. In 1925, Canadian Electro Products, Union Carbide, and Roessler & Hasslacher formed Niacet Chemicals Corporation, which built a factory at Niagara Falls, New York, where production of synthetic acetic acid began in 1927.[222]

In sum, although the foremost U.S. chemical companies, Du Pont and Allied Chemical, were American controlled and managed, each had numerous associations with foreign investors. The U.S. domestic chemical industry was thoroughly international. The foreign stakes in Du Pont (and Du Pont affiliates) and in Allied Chemical were intimately linked in networks of relationships. Of the three major U.S. chemical companies in the late 1920s, Union Carbide and Carbon Corporation (formed in 1917) seems to have been the least influenced in its behavior by foreign multinationals, although it did have the U.S. joint venture in Niacet Chemicals with Canadian Electro Products and Roessler & Hasslacher. New to the U.S. chemical industry in this decade were the international oil companies (Standard Oil of New Jersey and Shell Union); and they were closely connected with the existing foreign-owned chemical giants. Alliances and agreements crisscrossed in a complicated web. Many (but by no means all) of the foreign investments in the U.S. chemical industry in the 1920s were minority stakes. Product-specific joint ventures and collaborations were the norm. Cooperation and competition were intermixed. Tariffs impeded imports and protected domestic production, encouraging foreign investments behind the tariff walls.[223] The foreign involvements in the United States assisted the ongoing transfer of technology from Europe across the Atlantic and the development of a diversified and innovative domestic American chemical manufacturing industry. In chemicals, foreign business was much more active in the United States than U.S. business was abroad.[224]

Pharmaceuticals

Parts of the pharmaceutical branch of the chemical industry were closely tied with the rest of that industry (same companies, even same plants); other segments were quite separate. Thus, neither Allied Chemical nor Union Carbide ever became a manufacturer of medicines. Du Pont considered diversifying into this sector in the 1920s but chose not to do so.[225] By contrast, I. G. Farben and the Swiss firms Ciba, Geigy, and Sandoz were chemical companies that had pharmaceutical lines. Leadership in the pharmaceutical industry came from Europe.[226] Subsidiaries and affiliates manufactured in the United States, and a very few were starting U.S. research laboratories.

I. G. Farben's Bayer was deeply involved in pharmaceuticals; Winthrop Chemical Company was its vehicle for operations in the American market; in the arrangements after the First World War, Winthrop Chemical Company obtained Bayer's U.S. pharmaceutical patents. I. G. Farben's Hoechst had been the innovator in Salvarsan, the antisyphilis drug; and, in 1926, after the formation of I. G. Farben, Winthrop acquired H. A. Metz Laboratories (and the preserved Hoechst assets). Since Sterling Products (the 50 percent owner of Winthrop with I. G. Farben) was ill equipped to pursue the required advanced science, an I. G. Farben chemist was dispatched to Rensselaer, New York, to manage the plant, and Winthrop Chemical Company embarked on a limited research program. Then, in 1928, Sterling Products had become part of Drug, Inc., a holding company that included United Drug Company, Bristol Myers, Vick Chemical, and Life Savers Inc. The combination did not last (it ended in 1933, with the component parts restored); Winthrop Chemical Company remained intact throughout the corporate reorganizations.[227]

The Swiss dyemakers Ciba, Sandoz, and J. R. Geigy (all three participants in Cincinnati Chemical Works) had during the 1920s separate

U.S. sales and production companies, with increasing interests in prescription drugs; in the main their activities were in marketing, with minor production of medicinal products. The parents were science-based companies. The Swiss F. Hoffmann-La Roche & Co. (as of 1929 the U.S. subsidiary was Hoffmann-La Roche, Inc.) in 1926 employed in its New York City business merely 116 employees (38 in administration and 78 in production), up, however, from the 47 total in 1922; its business was mainly filling, tableting, and packaging, using bulk ingredients imported from Basle, as well as the full production of a small number of drugs. In 1929, however, it completed its first buildings at Roche Park in Nutley, New Jersey, where it made barbiturates and strychnine (used for pest control), as well as other fine chemicals and pharmaceutical specialities, and that year it laid out plans for research and development facilities in the United States.[228]

A new German participant in U.S. pharmaceuticals was C. F. Boehringer & Söhne of Mannheim. It owned 50 percent of Rare Chemicals, Inc., organized in 1927, which had a plant near Yonkers, New York; Merck & Co. acted as sales agent for this firm.[229] As for Merck itself, it remained separate (in terms of ownership) from its prewar German parent, E. Merck, Darmstadt, yet, friendly family contacts had resumed. The U.S. and German Merck firms did not compete; they shared knowledge of products.[230] On December 27, 1928, Schering-Kahlbaum, AG, Berlin, set up the Schering Corporation, New York, a sales subsidiary, which did packaging and distribution of its parent's medicines.[231]

Burroughs Wellcome & Co. expanded in the United States in the late 1920s and was important in the U.S. market, with its trademarked "Tabloid" lines. In 1925–1926, it moved its American manufacturing facilities from New York City to a ten-acre site in Tuckahoe, New York, a suburban Westchester town, where in 1928 Burroughs Wellcome added a research laboratory; at the same time, it also continued to sell patent medicines.[232] Still another pre–First World War British company in America, A. J. White Ltd.—and its subsidiary, Menley & James Ltd.—developed in 1927 arrangements with the U.S. company Smith Kline & French. Unlike Burroughs Wellcome, neither White nor Menley & James was a major factor in the American market. White was in patent medicines; Menley & James in prescription drugs.[233]

In 1924, the United States passed the Heroin Prohibition Act, forbidding the import of opium and the selling of heroin.[234] Several foreign-owned firms were affected by this ban; international concerns over narcotics prompted German and Swiss enterprises to develop alternative medicinal products, which, in turn, were introduced in the United States through these firms' subsidiaries.[235]

In short, there were harbingers of the highly significant role that European companies would come to play in the U.S. domestic pharmaceutical industry. As in the chemical industry in general, so particularly in pharmaceuticals, in the late 1920s research laboratories of foreign companies emerged in the United States. In pharmaceuticals, U.S. research by foreign affiliates was, as of 1929, still very limited.

Over-the-Counter Drugs

While some British drug companies (Burroughs Wellcome, for example) had a line of over-the-counter medicines, others confined themselves to patent medicines. This was the case with Beecham's, which sold pills to cure a variety of ailments. Changes at Beecham's parent in Britain resulted in a neglect of the U.S. business.[236] Sometime between 1924 and 1928, Beecham disposed of its Brooklyn, New York, factory, and in 1926 it moved its U.S. manufacture of pills to a plant at Niagara Falls, New York, where it united the management of its U.S. and Canadian subsidiaries and continued producing for several years before stopping all output in the United States.[237] Beecham's major post–World War II activities in the United States would stem from completely different roots, that is, from the business of the Canadian Harold F. Ritchie, who in Canada in 1928 had formed International Proprietaries, Ltd., which, in turn, acquired the entire capital of the English firm J. C. Eno, Ltd. The latter, founded in 1868, made Eno's Fruit Salt, marketed over-the-counter. When, in 1928, Ritchie obtained control over J. C. Eno, Ltd., that English firm was already a multinational enterprise, with plants in England, Canada, France, Germany, Spain, and the United States (in Buffalo).[238] In his expansion, Ritchie also bought a controlling interest in Scott & Browne, Inc., obtaining rights to sell in the United States cod liver oil, under the brand name Scott's Emulsion.[239] Ritchie would die in 1933, and in 1938 the British Beecham would buy his international business, by then mainly reorganized under the "Eno" name. Many years later, Beecham's would become an ethical drug company; in the 1920s its products and those of Eno were closer in type to the offerings of the many British branded-goods enterprises than to the chemically based pharmaceutical companies that marketed principally through doctors.[240]

Farm Equipment

Whereas there was an immense economic and technological impact in the United States of foreign chemical and pharmaceutical companies (and a far smaller one on patent medicines), when we turn to other industries, for example, the farm equipment industry, the presence of FDI was minimal. Massey-Harris Company, Ltd., was Canada's largest farm equipment producer. Its U.S. subsidiary failed to make headway in the U.S. market, while the parent met stiff competition from large U.S. firms that crossed into Canada.[241] To improve its position in the *Canadian* market, the parent company arranged in 1926 to obtain from J. I. Case Plow Company, Racine, Wisconsin, the exclusive rights to market in Canada (and parts of the United States) the Wallis tractor made by that enterprise. Then, in 1928, Massey-Harris purchased the physical assets of J. I. Case Plow Company, along with all rights to the Wallis tractor, for $1.3 million in cash and the guarantee of $1 million in bonds outstanding (in the transaction, Massey-Harris sold the Case name to the J. I. Case Threshing Machine Company, for $700,000).

This 1928 acquisition marked a renewed commitment by the Canadian farm equipment company to U.S. business. A subsidiary, The Massey-Harris Company (capital $8 million), was formed to unify under common management its existing Batavia, New York, implement factory and its Racine, Wisconsin, tractor plant. The head office for the U.S. operations was transferred to Racine, and Massey-Harris' U.S. subsidiary opened branches in the leading agricultural distribution centers in the United States, adding new product lines. In 1928–1929, Massey-Harris was among the half dozen world leaders in farm equipment; it was actively engaged in international expansion, including the United States. In 1928, its U.S. factories employed 1,900 (a high for the 1920s, but not up to its 2,500 employees in the United States in 1914).[242] By 1929, its U.S. assets came to $12.5 million.[243] Yet compared with the giant International Harvester (assets in 1930, $383.8 million), Massey-Harris was a small player in the United States (and worldwide).[244] Its U.S. market share in 1929 was 1.7 percent; by contrast, International Harvester captured 28.3 percent of the U.S. farm machinery market.[245] At least in 1929, after a long period of losses, Massey-Harris was again a profitable enterprise in the United States.[246]

Another foreign participant in farm equipment was De Laval Separator Company (Lavalco), a subsidiary of the Swedish firm AB Separator (later Alfa-Laval). Lavalco specialized in dairy equipment and was highly innovative. When during the First World War it had met competition in the United States from another Swedish company, A. B. Baltic with its "Empire Milker," Lavalco developed a superior milking machine. A. B. Baltic did not survive in the United States (it went out of business in 1921). By contrast, for a time, Lavalco flourished. In 1921, its Swedish parent acquired rights to the subsidiary's milking machines. During the course of the 1920s, Lavalco came to be affected by the difficulties in U.S. agriculture, and this once extremely profitable subsidiary found by the late 1920s that its profits, although still forthcoming, were sharply curtailed.[247] It had a niche market but nothing more.

Automobiles and Automobile Parts

In the middle and late 1920s, the U.S. automobile industry came of age. In 1929, U.S. factory sales of passenger cars soared to 4.5 million vehicles.[248] Ford and General Motors led in the industry. As for FDI, the Rolls Royce plant in Springfield, Massachusetts, was a rarity. After a precarious start, by 1925 the works had 1,000 employees and in 1926 was finally profitable. In January 1926, Rolls-Royce of America bought control of Brewster & Co., Inc., a builder of coaches and bodies with a plant in Long Island City. But the multiplant output of Rolls-Royce's U.S. facilities was not—or so customers believed—up to the quality of the British-made product. The British parent was not pleased with its affiliate's performance. The company's historian believes that the reason that Rolls-Royce was not successful in America was that the British parent was inflexible: "the rigid conception which English management held of American market requirements."[249] No matter the reason, Rolls-Royce, although a well-known name, was not growing as fast as the American car market.

The second British carmaker to attempt to manufacture vehicles in America targeted an entirely different segment of the market. In 1922, Sir Herbert Austin had introduced in England the Austin Seven—a small, mass-produced automobile. Sir Herbert began to make the car in Germany in 1927 (where the product was called the Dixi) and soon thereafter in France (the Rosengart). In 1929, Sir Herbert resolved to pursue U.S. sales. His arrangements with an American group were that "for a directorship and the usual two percent fee he would grant a license and supply designs as well as a team of experts to guide the new enterprise into production."[250] On February 28, 1929, the American Austin Car Company was incorporated in Delaware. Its capital consisted of 1 million shares; Sir Herbert and his British company had an option on 50,000 shares, and another 100,000 were "reserved" for British investors. Most of the issued shares were acquired by Americans. The plant would be in Butler, Pennsylvania (the new firm bought an idle factory). By the end of 1929, automobile production had not yet begun.[251] Rolls-Royce and Austin represented the sum total of FDI in U.S. car manufacturing, a minor footnote in the formidable expansion of this industry. American carmakers supplied the domestic market; imports were negligible. American business was expanding worldwide.[252]

As for automobile parts, in the magneto industry, the U.S. sales subsidiary of the German firm Robert Bosch competed with the American-owned American Bosch Magneto Corporation, which had acquired the pre–World War I Bosch assets in the United States, including the factory at Springfield, Massachusetts. In 1929, the disputes between the two rivals were resolved in a way that opened the path for the German Bosch's reentry into manufacturing in America.[253] In Germany, Bosch's magneto for cars, its spark plugs, its electrical systems for cars, and its diesel injection pump (first made in 1927) put it in the forefront of technological progress. In bearings, some of which were sold to the automobile industry and some bought by other industries, the Swedish firm's manufacturing affiliate SKF excelled, while Norma-Hoffmann Bearing Company (a British investment in manufacturing) was a smaller contender in this market. Aside from Bosch and the manufacturers of bearings, the nation's automobile parts industry was virtually entirely American.

Aircraft

The new U.S. aircraft industry—like the farm equipment, automobile, and automobile parts industries—was dominated by domestic participants. The two modest postwar foreign entries' operations in the United States were American controlled. One was the Goodyear-Zeppelin Corporation, controlled by Goodyear, which became for all practical purposes an American company. The second was that of Anthony Fokker—who maintained his factory in the Netherlands—and went into a series of joint ventures in America, first with Frank Ford and George Davis of the engineering firm Ford, Bacon & Davis, and then, in May 1929, General Motors acquired a 40 percent interest in Fokker's U.S. business, by this time named the Fokker Aircraft Corporation of America. General Motors paid $7.8 million for its holdings and became the largest shareholder in the enterprise. (It is not clear how the other 60 percent was held, but it is very unlikely that Fokker himself or his Dutch company owned a major part of that amount.) In May 1929, Fokker of America had two small leased plants, one in Hasbrouck Heights, New Jersey, and one in Glendale, West Virginia. Its main business lay in sales to the U.S. government. Certificates representing common shares were offered to Dutch investors. Other American investors, aside from General Motors, also held shares. As the largest single shareholder, GM had effective control. General Motors bypassed the firm's founder, deciding that the "dependency on Dutch designs for the American market would have to go"; GM signed an agreement with the German Claude Dornier, and on October 22, 1929,

GM formed the Dornier Corporation of America. Anthony Fokker was ignored within his own company (in 1929 he still had some sharehold-ings but clearly had no control over the company, much less the designs of the planes built by the company that bore his name).[254]

Rubber Tires

With the booming U.S. domestic automobile industry in the late 1920s, demand for rubber tires soared. Michelin enlarged its output at Milltown, New Jersey. At its peak, probably in the late 1920s, this French-owned firm had more than 2,000 employees and made some 4,500 tires and 15,000 tubes daily. Milltown was a company town: "Practically every family in Milltown had somebody on the [Michelin] company payroll." The plant had fifteen large buildings, including a large tire testing facility.[255]

Dunlop—the only other foreign investor in the U.S. tire industry—also expanded; its manufacturing was in Buffalo, New York. Pierre du Pont remained on the board of the American Dunlop company; General Motors was a customer but not a sizable one.[256] For financing, Dunlop, like many other foreign direct investors in America, raised moneys in this country.[257] By 1926–1929, Dunlop was obtaining less than 1 percent (.8–.9 percent) of U.S. tire sales.[258] Its costs were high because of unused capacity: in July 1929, it was producing 17,000 tires *a week,* while its facilities were built to turn out 10,000 tires *a day.*[259] Thus, its daily output was less than that of Michelin. Its Du Pont connection gave it no special advantage. Moreover, Du Pont had in 1927 acquired control of U.S. Rubber, one of the industry's "Big Four," and had little interest in providing support for Dunlop.[260]

In the late 1920s, the U.S. tire industry had become highly competitive, and as a consequence, prices of tires had fallen rapidly. In 1923 there had been 129 firms with 160 plants in the United States; in 1929, only 62 firms with 91 factories survived. In those six years, tire output had surged from 44 million to 66.5 million per year. Excess capacity plagued not only Dunlop but also the entire industry. I have failed to locate data on Michelin's financial performance. Dunlop, however, had only one profitable year (1926) in the entire late 1920s, and its profits that year came nowhere near offsetting its losses during 1923–1925 and 1927–1929. Its accumulated loss (1923–1929)—net of the small profit in 1926—was £2,558,760 (about $12 million).[261] Despite its Du Pont–General Motors connections, Dunlop was unable to penetrate the original equipment market.[262] It had to depend on replacement sales. It was not the prosperous twenties for this British firm in America.

The U.S. tire industry in the 1920s had an added problem. In 1922 the British Stevenson plan had pushed up crude rubber prices. The parent companies of both Dunlop and Michelin owned rubber plantations in the East that partly insulated them from the higher rubber prices. Like the large American companies, they were not protected when crude rubber prices collapsed in 1929.[263] Both Dunlop and Michelin were second-rank rubber tire companies in the United States, far behind the American industry leaders, Goodyear, Firestone, B. F. Goodrich, and U.S. Rubber.

Steel and Steel Alloys

In steel and steel alloys, foreign multinationals occupied small niche positions. The Firth Sterling Steel Company, at McKeesport, Pennsylvania, a British-owned enterprise, made stainless steel and tungsten carbide cutting alloys.[264] It was the last of what had once been a collection of British crucible steelmakers in America. In the late 1920s, the Germans began to participate in America in specialty steels. Krupp had three U.S. affiliates: Krupp Nirosta, Carboloy, and Nitralloy.[265] Krupp Nirosta Corporation, New York, established in 1928, was a patent holding and licensing company.[266] Carboloy Company, set up that same year, manufactured (under Krupp patents) tungsten carbide and other hard metal compositions along with some tools and dies made from these materials; its ownership, at origin, is obscure, albeit Krupp appears to have had an interest. Later it would become a wholly owned subsidiary of General Electric. Carboloy Company licensed other firms (including the British-owned Firth Sterling Steel) to use certain Krupp patents.[267] I have been unable to determine the functions of the Nitralloy Company. Of the three, Krupp Nirosta Corporation—with its important weldable stainless steel patents—was the only one in which Krupp would retain an equity interest (it was from the start and in subsequent interwar years continued to be 51 percent owned by the German firm).[268] J. A. Henckels, the well-known German cutlery company, with its famous "twin" trademark, had had a 50 percent interest in a U.S. marketing company before the First World War. Between the wars, probably in the late 1920s, it reentered the United States, gaining control over the sales outlets: the Fifth Avenue Cutlery Shop, Inc., and Graef & Schmidt, Inc.[269] There was no significant FDI in America's huge basic iron and steel industry.[270]

Miscellaneous Nonelectric Machinery, Equipment, and Instruments

The two foreign-owned bearing makers, SKF and Norma-Hoffmann, and Bosch magnetos had broader markets than those in the car industry. A British company, Baker-Perkins (a producer of food processing, chemical processing, and mixing equipment), had since 1920 manufactured machinery in Saginaw, Michigan.[271] Another "food machinery" maker in America was the Dutch Van Berkel's Patent, with a slicing machine.[272] There may have been some Swiss manufacturing in America in textile machinery (although I think the Swiss investments, which appear to have been discontinued in 1929 or 1930, were in sales outlets).[273] A few Swedish companies (beyond those mentioned earlier, SKF and AB Separator) fit in this sector: AB Gasaccumulator (often called AGA) made light beacons; the De Laval Steam Turbine Co. manufactured turbines; both these companies had started in the United States before World War I and continued on.[274] These and some other miscellaneous foreign machinery makers were isolated cases; Americans excelled at home and abroad in practically all branches of the nonelectrical machinery and equipment industries.[275]

As for instruments, precision equipment, and optical goods, a small number of foreign multinationals had a U.S. presence. There was the British firm Cambridge Instrument Co.[276] The German Aktien Gesellschaft für Fein Mechanik, which before the war had owned Kny-Scheerer Corp., started in 1929 a new U.S. subsidiary, Jetter & Scheerer Products Inc.[277] The German firm Carl Zeiss (specialists in optical instruments) incorporated a sales subsidiary in New York in December 1925, seeking to reenter the U.S. market.[278] It never reacquired its prewar equity stake in Bausch & Lomb Optical Co., Rochester, New York. Initially, however, the Americanized Rochester company appears to have benefited greatly from technology obtained from Zeiss, under contractual relationships. Zeiss did not on its own restart its U.S. manufacturing but did set up repair shops for its "high-tech" optical instruments. By the late 1920s and early 1930s, in certain products, the German Zeiss and American-owned Bausch & Lomb were competitors.[279]

Electrical Equipment

The German Siemens (along with Hugo Stinnes' steel complex) was represented in the United States in the early 1920s by Adlanco and by Karl Frank. U.S. sales were negligible. After Stinnes died in 1924, Siemens withdrew from the German combine.[280] In 1926, Siemens & Halske AG and Siemens-Schuckertwerke GmbH issued $24 million in twenty-five-year 6½ percent debentures; this was to support the parent organization.[281] Frank continued to represent Siemens in America; he became a salaried employee in 1929.[282] In the late 1920s, neither Siemens nor the other German electrical industry giant, Allgemeine Elektrizitäts Gesellschaft, made any plans to invest in business in America. Indeed, General Electric was expanding internationally and, as economist

Frank Southard wrote, "coupled with the contracts of earlier years, there remains [in 1929] no single German electrical manufacturing company of importance in which, remotely or directly, General Electric influence is not felt."[283] The principal German electrical manufacturers did not intend to compete in America.[284]

In the 1920s International General Electric Company acquired a substantial minority interest in NV Philips' Gloeilampenfabrieken. In 1924, IGEC executives feared the "serious danger" of a Philips invasion of the U.S. market in incandescent lamps. Anton Philips was aggressively enlarging the business of his company. In December of that year, the Dutch firm, however, became a party to the so-called Phoebus Agreement, which effectively halted any plans Philips might have had to provide competition. Once again, GE's influence was felt.[285]

By contrast with the Germans and the Dutch, in the fall of 1925 the Swiss Brown, Boveri & Co. declared its intent to invest in the United States and become "the third great electrical manufacturing company in this country," a rival to General Electric and Westinghouse.[286] As a first step, Brown, Boveri acquired the facilities of the New York Shipbuilding Corporation, with its impressive shipbuilding installation at Camden, New Jersey.[287] With the war over, demand for ships had fallen; New York Shipbuilding had diversified, but in 1924 this American company was operating at a loss. Its major stockholders had, therefore, happily agreed—in August 1925—to sell out to Brown, Boveri.[288] The latter changed the shipbuilding company's name to American Brown Boveri Electric Corporation and sent over Swiss management from the parent along with its own patents and technology. It furnished new production equipment to manufacture electric transformers, circuit breakers, and locomotives. The principal planned market for Brown, Boveri's U.S. output was to be U.S. public utilities, which a Brown, Boveri spokesman declared were spending about $1 billion annually on equipment.[289] American Brown Boveri would also continue in shipbuilding.[290]

Even before these arrangements were completed, Brown, Boveri announced added expansion: it would purchase the Condit Electrical Manufacturing Company of Boston, a maker of electrical switches, switch gears, and other electrical apparatus. To finance its U.S. business, Brown, Boveri issued stock in its American affiliate, which it sold in the United States in a heavily oversubscribed offering.[291] Before the end of 1925, the new American Brown Boveri Electric Corporation was reporting that it would take over the Moloney Electric Corporation of St. Louis, one of the largest manufacturers of electrical transformers in the United States.[292] At the close of 1925, Brown, Boveri's U.S. investments were estimated at $35 million.[293]

During 1926, the company moved forward with sizable additional new investments in its electrical business at its main plant site in Camden, New Jersey. It built more facilities and adapted the existing ones to its special requirements. Yet that year, according to its *Annual Report,* it made practically no deliveries of electrical equipment; however, it claimed to have orders totaling $4 million for 1927–1928 delivery.[294] But by the summer of 1927, American Brown Boveri's management recognized that it could not proceed as anticipated, since its "existing financial resources" did not "justify" further expansion.[295] During 1927, "the fundamental contract" between the American affiliate and its Swiss parent, "having proven to be burdensome and unworkable under the conditions of the American market, was canceled," and after a few months a "more equitable" contract was prepared under which the American Brown Boveri secured the benefits of "the engineering, design, and background of experience of the Swiss company."[296] By this time, American Brown Boveri was in full retreat.[297] A 1927 publication of the British Electrical & Allied Manufacturers' Association was more forthright than the firm's annual reports. It called Brown Boveri's operations in the United States "practically moribund."[298] In June 1928, American Brown Boveri sold off its controlling interest in Moloney Electrical Company.[299] It was the beginning of the end.

All during the 1920s, General Electric—the leader in America's electrical manufacturing—retained and cemented close ties and made new patent agreements with all the major electrical companies around the world, bar one—Brown, Boveri.[300] The evidence is weak, but GE could not have been pleased with Brown, Boveri's U.S. direct investments. In the 1920s, GE would acquire a minority interest in the parent Brown, Boveri, undoubtedly with the goal of obtaining leverage to tame its rival.[301] Many years later, W. R. Herod (in 1929 the assistant to the president of International General Electric) would recollect, "Brown, Boveri (in Switzerland) didn't trust G.E.; they were always afraid that we would do something unpredictable; we might limit their latitude, might want to operate their operations, and they wanted independence."[302]

Yet, in the U.S. market, Brown, Boveri—its efforts notwithstanding—failed to achieve its ambitious goals. Its optimistic foray had dissipated with extraordinary rapidity. By 1929, there were two diversified giants in the U.S. market—General Electric and Westinghouse—and both were U.S. owned; Brown, Boveri retained its manufacturing subsidiary, but its first four years in America were, to say the least, a disaster.[303]

Brown, Boveri was not the only European enterprise to participate in the dynamic U.S. electrical industry. The other entries were, however, less daring and aimed to fill highly specialized market needs. Bosch, which I discussed under the rubric automotive parts, had certain products that were clearly part of the electrical industry. In 1924, two senior executives in the Okonite Company (a U.S. firm that before the First World War had been British controlled) visited London to explore the possibilities of a joint venture in the United States with the large British enterprise Callender's Cable and Construction Company. As a result, the two businesses joined in the new Okonite-Callender Company to take over Okonite's existing U.S. facilities and to equip a Paterson, New Jersey, plant to make Callender's products in America. Almost immediately, the British parent found the new venture a burden and regretted its participation. The financial arrangements had been poorly prepared and executed; the British managers had greatly underestimated the amount of new moneys needed (like many other firms in which foreign investors were involved, Okonite-Callender raised added capital by selling preference shares in America). And there were technical problems at the U.S. manufacturing facilities; Callender dispatched a production supervisor from Britain to troubleshoot. Every year, the financial requirements rose, although the losses of 1924–1926 finally turned to three years of modest profits, 1927–1929.[304]

In still another distinct market in the electrical industry, a record company, Columbia Graphophone Co., Ltd. (established in Britain as a U.S. business abroad but now British-headquartered), in 1925 acquired 93 percent of the stock of its former U.S. parent, Columbia Phonograph Record Company—to help out that ailing firm. Yet its role as a British direct investor in America proved episodic, and by late 1929 reports indicated that the U.S. Columbia company had repurchased most of its own shares (and indeed may have repurchased some of the parent British enterprise's shares as well).[305]

One more specialized entry into American business was the Swedish multinational AB Electrolux, a manufacturer of vacuum cleaners. In the 1920s, it purchased a Swedish patent for refrigerators and became internationally important as a maker of household appliances.[306] In 1929, Electrolux made a contract with a firm in the United States for the latter to produce its refrigerators; in exchange, Electrolux received cash and shares in the American company along with a royalty on all sales.[307]

Thus, Dutch, Swiss, German, British, and Swedish businesses eyed the American electrical equipment and machinery market and aspired to take advantage of its potential. U.S. companies, however, towered over their European counterparts. The U.S. companies were too well entrenched and too technologically superior for the Europeans to make any headway in this sector. European involvements, with the exception of certain specialized niches (Bosch's role and perhaps Electrolux's with its licensing arrangements), were unimpressive. Brown, Boveri—the only truly large investor—made no headway whatsoever.

Other Manufacturing

There were additional assorted foreign manufacturing firms in the United States. For example, the British firm Crittall Manufacturing Company, in 1929, made "considerable additions" to its U.S. investments. It had long been involved in attempting to convert users of wooden window frames to metal ones.[308] In 1926, Henry Hope & Son, Ltd., bought the International Casement Co. (a firm founded in 1912 by a British immigrant to America). It also made metal window frames.[309] In publishing, Oxford University Press, which had founded its New York branch in 1896 and had for two and a half decades sold books printed in Britain, began in the 1920s to publish general nonfiction books on its own account and in 1927 started to publish college textbooks.[310] Many other miscellaneous FDIs in manufacturing existed, mostly small, inconsequential operations. Those covered in the foregoing were designed to show the overall variety, not to be all-inclusive.

Integrated Oil Companies

In 1924 Shell Union Oil Corporation probably represented the largest FDI in the United States. It was a major actor in the American oil industry, but it was a company "under siege." In the 1922 consolidation, Shell Union Oil had acquired 26 percent of the Union Oil Company of California, which firm resented the alliance—and for that reason, along with antitrust ones, in 1924, Shell Union had divested its holdings in that California company. (The name Shell Union had come from the 1922 merger with Union Oil Company *of Delaware* and would be retained until 1949, when the now familiar name, Shell Oil Company, was adopted.) The 1924 divestment of Union Oil of California was exceptional; Shell Union raised $30 million with this "downsizing," which was promptly reinvested in the U.S. business.[311] The Shell Union course in the 1920s was typified by an active, energetic expansion.

Yet in 1924–1925, owing to its British-Dutch ownership, Shell Union still remained ineligible, under the 1920 Mineral Lands Leasing Law, to lease U.S. government land.[312] By the end of 1925, Shell Union had reluctantly rejected an Oklahoma proposition "of considerable magnitude," since it involved public lands; so, too, Shell Union wanted to explore in Alaska, but for the identical reasons, it could not participate. It was, in addition, losing out on good opportunities in California.[313] A stream of intracompany correspondence crisscrossed the Atlantic on how the company would cope with these obstacles to expansion. By January 1927, Royal Dutch Shell officials believed it was imperative to establish Shell Union's right to hold U.S. government leases. Yet the U.S. State Department did not consider either the Dutch or the British "reciprocating nations" under the terms of the 1920 Mineral Lands Leasing Law. However, by 1927, the Netherlands government had given concessions to Standard Oil Company (New Jersey) in the Dutch East Indies and was prepared to grant even larger ones. The British Foreign Office also agreed to allow U.S. oil companies to participate in the Turkish Petroleum Company—as one British government official put it—"to tranquilize the U.S. government."[314]

In the summer of 1927, Standard Oil of New Jersey's Walter Teagle was in Europe, seeking further leases in the Dutch East Indies. Royal Dutch Shell knew Teagle was going to get his leases, and the group felt that "S.O.C. of New Jersey should now help to get things improved for us in the U.S." In the fall of 1927, J. B. Aug. Kessler of Royal Dutch Shell wanted to know what Standard Oil of New Jersey was actually doing.[315] J. C. van Eck of Shell Union met with George H. Jones, chairman of the board of Standard Oil of New Jersey, who indicated that "they will not put any obstacle in our way," but Jones told the Shell Union executive that it would not be "wise" for Jersey Standard to approach the State Department.[316] Shell Union's plan by early 1928 was to have the U.S. State Department declare the Dutch government a reciprocating country—and to use Dutch diplomatic channels. The Dutch were able to threaten to withhold concessions in the Dutch East Indies, if "they did not get a satisfactory reply at once."[317] Shell Union argued that it was in reality Dutch controlled. In short, through the Dutch government, Royal Dutch Shell had bargaining power.

In the summer of 1928, as a result of what had become a worldwide oil glut, a number of new arrangements were made in the international oil industry that brought Royal Dutch Shell and Standard Oil of New Jersey into closer harmony. On July 31, 1928, negotiations on Iraqi oil were completed with the Red Line Agreement; on August 31, Teagle stated that he favored the status quo in the French market; and on September 17, with the Achnacarry Accord, Jersey Standard, Royal Dutch Shell, and Anglo-Persian agreed to end "ruinous" competition.[318] That same day, September 17, 1928—by coincidence (?)—the State Department recognized Holland as a "reciprocating country" under the terms of the 1920 U.S. Mineral Lands Leasing Act.[319]

But just when everything seemed all set for Shell Union to obtain

U.S. government leases, early in 1929 the U.S. Department of the Interior sent back to Shell Union, without approval, the so-called Ralph Permit, a lease application for drilling oil on government lands in California.[320] Henri Deterding, Royal Dutch Shell's chief executive officer, was furious—and believed there had been "bad faith." Teagle was to be told that this action "was bound to have adverse effect on [the] Dutch Government's consideration [of] further concessions" in the Dutch East Indies. Deterding called on the Dutch government to ask the Dutch ambassador to protest.[321] Meanwhile, Royal Dutch Shell's management learned that the British Colonial Office was interfering with Gulf Oil's expansion plans in the Near East and that Gulf Oil was looking into Texas laws with an eye to retaliating against Shell Union. A top Royal Dutch Shell official suggested that Shell Union's management "see Mellon," advising him that the group was willing to contact British officials on Gulf Oil's behalf.[322] The "Mellon" in question could have been William L. Mellon, chief executive of Gulf Oil, or William's uncle, Andrew Mellon, secretary of the treasury and the true head of the family. Andrew Agnew (of Shell in London) wrote the British Foreign Office on May 7, 1929—pushing as he had many times before for an unequivocal end to all restrictions in the British Empire.[323] It was, however, Teagle who came through with what the group desired. Teagle wrote Deterding on June 20, 1929, that the U.S. Department of the Interior was issuing the Ralph permit "today."[324] Finally, Shell Union could start drilling on U.S. government land. Thus ended roughly nine years of exclusion. Shell Union had won.

In 1929, Shell Union completed a pipeline connection from its west Texas oil fields to its new refinery in Houston; it took over various distributing organizations in New England and extended its marketing facilities.[325] By decade's end, it conducted business in all forty-eight states; it operated nine refineries and had 35,000 employees in America.[326] To finance its huge capital expenditure, in 1929 Shell Union issued $40 million in 5½ percent preference shares in June and in September $50 million 5½ percent sinking fund gold debentures.[327] Shell Union ranked eleventh in asset size among all "American industrials." It was fifth in asset size (with assets of $677 million) among U.S. oil companies, following Standard Oil of New Jersey, Standard Oil of Indiana, Gulf Oil, and Standard Oil of New York, but ahead of Standard Oil (California) and Texaco.[328] After Shell Union was allowed to drill on public lands, further significant applications by the U.S. government of the Mineral Lands Leasing Act would be suspended for more than five decades.[329] The relationships between Standard Oil of New Jersey and Royal Dutch Shell executives grew closer after the Achnacarry Agreement and the settlement of Shell Union's problems in the United

States. In 1934, Deterding would write, "One of my best personal friends in America has long been Mr. Walter C. Teagle" of Standard Oil of New Jersey.[330]

Shell Union was the only important integrated foreign oil company in the United States, albeit there were other smaller ones. In the 1920s, British American Oil Company had emerged as the largest Canadian-owned oil enterprise. It established within Canada two refineries in Toronto and a domestic distribution system; according to historian Michael Bliss, it also imported into Canada gasoline from refineries that it owned in the United States.[331] Other sources indicate that British American owned wells and pipelines in Texas and Oklahoma and shipped *crude oil* to Canada, where it refined and distributed the output.[332] It also may have had investments in the Bennett Pump Corporation in Muskegon, Michigan.[333]

Lord Inverforth and Franco Wyoming had investments in Standard Oil Company (Indiana), which were insufficient for any appreciable influence.[334] Lord Cowdray's Amerada Corporation participated in refining as well as production (in 1926, as noted earlier, control of Amerada passed to Americans). I. G. Farben's 1929 acquisition of 2 percent of the shares of Standard Oil of New Jersey had no impact on that giant's domestic oil operations, although the accompanying division-of-market arrangements gave I. G. Farben opportunities to pursue synthetic oil production in Germany.

In 1929, Anglo-Persian Oil Company (the predecessor of British Petroleum) dispatched Basil Jackson to open an office in New York.[335] In the 1920s Anglo-Persian had embarked on a worldwide oil exploration effort—practically everywhere except in the United States.[336] The reasons for its skipping the United States are never explained by its historians. They could lie in its knowledge of Royal Dutch Shell's experiences with the Mineral Lands Leasing Act, or in its perception of anti-British sentiment in this country, or in the structure and strength of the U.S. oil industry, and Anglo-Persian management's wariness to enter into competition with companies already well established.[337] Its New York office was inaugurated after the Red Line Agreement and the Achnacarry Accord (see earlier discussion); Jackson would stay in contact with Standard Oil of New Jersey and Shell Union officials in the United States. Apparently, the New York office was also used to purchase American oil equipment but, most important, to keep Anglo-Persian posted on the latest occurrences in the United States.[338] The United States remained by far the largest oil producer in the world, accounting for 68 percent of the world's crude oil production in 1929; it was the world's largest oil market, with the growth of the automobile industry. It was the center of the world's oil industry.[339]

Services

In the 1920s, in the United States there was a formidable expansion of telephone service as well as gas and electrical utilities. There was, however, no noteworthy inward foreign *direct* investment in communications or in power and light services in the decade.[340] Yet it was not only in primary production and manufacturing that foreign direct investors were present in the United States. Integrated cross-border enterprises did participate in services from research and development, to advertising, to distribution. In the 1920s, foreign-owned oil, chemical, and pharmaceutical enterprises, in particular, had begun to establish research laboratories in America as an integral part of their business operations. So, too, integrated foreign-owned companies advertised, as they had done for decades. There were, however, no separate foreign-owned research laboratories or foreign-owned advertising agencies set up in America. Foreign-owned companies' activities in domestic wholesaling, likewise, were typically related to the forward integration of foreign manufacturers (those that reached the U.S. market through exports *and* those that manufactured in America) and certain foreign trading companies' domestic sales. Most foreign trading companies participated principally in international transactions rather than extensive domestic trading. Foreign traders also served to aid American companies abroad (thus, the New York branch of the Japanese trading firm Morimura Brothers assisted IBM in its entry into the Japanese market).[341]

Very few foreign companies integrated forward into retailing. In retailing there were investments associated with horizontal rather than vertical integration. For example, three Canadian chains extended into the United States: T. P. Loblaw, with "groceterias" in Canada, spread over the border, opening stores in Chicago, Buffalo, and elsewhere in western New York State; Honey Dew, Ltd., had sandwich restaurants and stretched its Canadian chain southward; and the Canadian Laura Secord Candy Shops Ltd. participated in the 1919 organization and subsequent expansion of Fanny Farmer outlets in the United States.[342]

Another retail chain of an entirely different character was that of T & A Bata, a Czech company, which at home manufactured shoes; it operated some 1,000 retail shoe stores in Czechoslovakia and abroad, "a number" of which were in the United States. A unique retailer in the United States was a Japanese-owned enterprise with stores that sold Chinese art treasures (its New York store was set up around 1900).[343] The 1920s was for America the first great age of chain stores and restaurants; the American retailing sector was immense; foreign companies' participation was idiosyncratic and trivial when viewed in an overall context.

America in the 1920s saw the rise of the movie and the spread of motion picture theaters. From the movie industry's beginnings, there had been an active European film industry, and French, British, and German companies had looked to American sales. Charles Pathé—who has been called France's leading media industrialist—continued as a director of Pathe Exchange (after it became American owned in 1921); his presence on its board suggests that perhaps there may have persisted a lingering albeit very limited French minority interest. By 1929, Pathe Exchange had branch offices throughout the United States and served 13,000 motion picture theaters. In the late 1920s, the French Pathé Cinéma ended its involvement with Du Pont *in manufacturing* movie films; in 1929, in France, Charles Pathé sold Pathé Cinéma to a group headed by Bernard Natan. After 1929 there is no indication of any French FDI involvement in the movie industry in America—at least for more than six decades.[344] Gaumont was another French film company that became international. The Gaumont-British Corporation, with a large number of theaters in the United Kingdom, leased one on Broadway, which proved to be an unsuccessful venture and did not survive the 1920s; before the end of the decade, the premier German movie company, Universum Film AG, with theaters in Germany, had leased that same Broadway theater.[345] By 1929, the American movie business abroad was of far greater importance than foreign moviemakers in the United States.

Accounting Services

The major accounting firms in America had grown out of British direct investments. Before World War I, firms such as Price Waterhouse, Deloitte, and Touche had taken root in this country.[346] Sir William B. Peat in 1919–1925 had temporarily cut off his relations with the American accountants Marwick, Mitchell, but these associations were revived with the formation in 1925 of Peat, Marwick, Mitchell & Co.[347] Accounting firms in America were increasingly called on in the 1920s to deal with tax matters, the growth of the new public companies, mergers, and American business abroad. The international accounting firms were deeply involved; their activities merged the domestic U.S. business with those involving international business.

Insurance Services

The last half of the 1920s saw further expansion of British fire and marine insurers in America (see Table 5.3). There were more British affiliates and branches, in absolute numbers; also, relative to other nationalities, the British became more important. In 1913, British fire and marine insurers represented less than half the total number of foreign insurers in this sector in America; in 1918, their share was 57 percent, and in 1929, 67 percent.[348] Most of the British firms did greater business than in earlier years and provided over the course of the decade a broader range of insurance products.[349] The British set up new companies to furnish motor vehicle and workmen's compensation insurance—along with a collection of other non-life policies.[350] The five largest British insurers in America, including their branches and affiliates, continued to be Royal Insurance Co. (Liverpool); Commercial Union Assurance Co. (London); Liverpool & London & Globe (Liverpool), which was part of the Royal Insurance Co. group; North British & Mercantile Insurance Co. (London and Edinburgh); and Phoenix Assurance Co. (London).[351]

As British insurers expanded, there was also a rise in importance of the Swiss (all from Zurich). By contrast, several French insurance companies exited in 1924, "because of weakness of the franc."[352] Table 5.3 shows four fewer French companies in America in 1929 than in 1923. The Swedes increased business, but the Norwegian retreat of the early 1920s accelerated in the later part of the decade.

Table 5.3 lists only two German insurers that I identified as "foreign owned," based on material from *Best's Insurance Reports:* The Hamburg American Insurance Company (licensed in 1925 to do business by the New York State Insurance Department) and The Assecuranz-Union of 1865, Hamburg (which in 1929 acquired a substantial interest in Metropolitan Fire Insurance Co., New York).[353] However, from its foundation in 1925, Pilot Reinsurance Company, New York, was associated with Munich Reinsurance Company, a major German insurer, which had sizable U.S. assets before the First World War.[354] The president of Pilot Reinsurance was German-born Carl Schreiner, who had been the prewar manager of the U.S. branch of Munich Reinsurance, in Hartford, Connecticut; all the officers of Pilot Reinsurance had German connections. Material from the archives of Munich Reinsurance shows that at origin Munich Reinsurance owned 40 percent of Pilot Reinsurance shares; Union Reinsurance, Zurich, 24 percent; Assicurazioni Generali, Trieste, 20 percent; and Allianz, Berlin, 16 percent. Together Munich Reinsurance and Allianz held the controlling interest.[355]

Tokio Marine & Fire survived the 1923 earthquake that bankrupted many other Japanese fire insurers and continued its business in the United States. Fuso Marine & Fire Co., Tokyo, which had entered the United States in 1920, ceased writing fire insurance in 1923 but stayed on in the marine insurance business. A third Japanese company in America in 1929 was Kyoto Fire Insurance Co. of Osaka, which in 1926 was licensed to do business in New York.[356]

What is striking about Table 5.3 is that even though there were more

Table 5.3. Foreign insurance companies in fire and marine insurance in the United States, number by leading nationality, 1918, 1923, 1929; net premiums and admitted assets, 1918, 1929 (year end; includes branches and affiliates)

	Firms						Net premiums				Admitted assets			
	Number			%			Amount in millions of dollars		%		Amount in millions of dollars		%	
Nationality	1918	1923	1929	1918	1923	1929	1918	1929	1918	1929	1918	1929	1918	1929
British	51	58	66	57	60	67	126	161	60	78	202	366	67	78
French	9	9	5	10	9	5	12	10	6	5	14	16	5	3
Swiss	3	3	4	3	3	4	4	11	2	5	6	21	2	4
Danish	2	4	4	2	2	4	7	7	3	4	7	15	2	3
Swedish	2	3	3	2	3	3	3	5	1	2	5	10	2	2
Japanese	1	4	3	1	4	3	2	4	1	2	3	15	1	3
Canadian	2	2	2	2	2	2	5	1	2	1	7	6	2	1
German	0	0	2	0	0	2	0	2	0	1	0	4	0	1

New Zealand	1	2	2	1	2	2	1	1	a	a	1	3	a	1
Indian	0	2	2	0	2	2	0	1	0	a	0	2	0	1
Chinese[b]	2	2	2	2	2	2	1	1	1	a	2	2	1	a
Norwegian	5	4	1	6	4	1	14	1	7	1	16	4	5	1
Russian	9	0	0	10	0	0	32	0	15	0	33	0	11	0
Others[c]	3	4	3	3	4	3	4	2	2	1	5	6	2	1
Total	90	97	99	100[d]	100[d]	100	211[e]	207	100	100	301[e]	470	100	100[d]

Sources: 1918 and 1923 figures are from Tables 1.10 and 3.3 herein, supplemented by data in *Best's Insurance Reports, Fire and Marine, 1919.* 1929 figures are my tabulations based on data in ibid., *1930/1931.*

a. less than .49 percent.

b. one of the "Chinese" companies, the North China Insurance Co., Ltd., Shanghai, was organized by British interests and incorporated in 1928 under Hong Kong law.

c. The others in 1918 included one each from Spain, Holland, and Cuba; in 1923, the others included the same three plus Australia; in 1929 the others were from Spain, Holland, and Australia.

d. Totals are off because of rounding; net premium income and admitted asset percentages were derived before rounding

e. This number does not tally with that in Table 1.10 because of rounding (in Table 1.10, there were six "others," and in this table three "others"; I adjusted the figures accordingly).

foreign-owned companies involved in writing fire and marine insurance in America in 1929 than in 1918, and even though their admitted assets were greater at the end of the twenties than at the end of World War I, the net premiums collected by these firms had not risen; indeed, the figure was slightly lower in 1929 than in 1918. The reason lay mainly in the withdrawal of the substantial Russian companies (that were still included in 1918) and the sharp decline in the business of the Norwegian ones.[357]

As in the past, foreign-owned insurance companies remained concentrated in the fire and marine business, but the big British insurers were extending their business to offer far broader coverage. The three largest U.K. insurers in the U.S. casualty business were Employers' Liability Assurance Co., Ocean Accident & Guarantee Corp. (owned by Commercial Union Assurance Co.), and London Guarantee and Accident Insurance (acquired by Phoenix Assurance in 1922).[358] Most of the non-life, non-fire and marine foreign insurers in America were British.[359] An exception was Standard Surety and Casualty Company, New York, incorporated in 1928 and controlled by Tokio Marine and Fire Company. The other important exception was Zurich General Accident and Liability Insurance Company, Ltd.[360] With life insurance, the only international participants in the U.S. market were Canadians.[361]

In fact, one of the leading foreign insurance companies in the United States was Sun Life Assurance Company of Canada. By 1927, its president was writing to the Canadian superintendent of insurance (G. D. Finlayson), "Our business in the United States is growing so rapidly that our Canadian business, large though it is, will soon be less than ten per cent of the total . . . The Company's profits are being earned by Canadian brains and Canadian enterprise, but not from Canadian premiums."[362]

In sum, during the late 1920s, British participation in the U.S. insurance industry rose. Insurance became an ever greater portion of the total British direct investment in the United States. Other nationalities stayed involved and had new entries, but their role was dwarfed by the British. Insurance was, however, a sector of great interest to foreign investors in the United States.

Shipping

By the late 1920s, U.S. transatlantic and transpacific shipping was once again dominated by foreign shippers, although not to as great an extent as before the First World War. All the foreign shipping companies had American representatives in the key ports where they discharged passengers and cargo. Table 5.4 indicates the change during the 1920s: the

Table 5.4. Shipping in America's foreign trade, by nationality, 1920, 1929 (entrances and clearances, measured in tonnage)

Nationality of tonnage	1920 (%)	1929 (%)
British	29.1	30.2
Norwegian	4.5	6.7
German	0	4.7
Japanese	2.7	4.2
Other foreign	12.9	16.6
Total foreign	49.2	62.4
American	50.8	37.6

Source: Adapted from S. G. Sturmey, *British Shipping and World Competition* (London: Athlone Press, 1962), 130.

supremacy U.S. shipping had assumed in the country's international trade right after the First World War had proved ephemeral. By the end of the 1920s, although American ships had more entrances and clearances than any other single nationality, only 37.6 percent of these entrances and clearances were American (compared with 50.8 percent in 1920). British shipping remained significant, and the British role improved marginally in the course of the decade. In 1927, the International Mercantile Marine sold the White Star Line (which it had owned since 1902) to the Royal Mail Steam Packet Company, a sale symbolic of the declining importance of U.S. shipping.[363] Norwegian shippers raised their market share, even while retreating from their involvements in insurance.[364]

German vessels resumed a notable role in America's international commerce. As one observer put it, "Hapag [Hamburg-American Line] rose like a Phoenix from the ashes after the World War."[365] In December 1925, it raised $6.5 million on the New York market.[366] Early in 1926, W. Averell Harriman ended his almost six-year alliance with Hapag. For $5.5 million in cash, bonds, and securities, plus 10 million reichsmarks' worth of Hapag stock, Harriman sold three passenger lines, the stock of his United American Lines, and three shipping subsidiaries to the German enterprise.[367] As for the North German Lloyd Line—the other major German shipping firm—its relations with U.S. Lines were sustained, but it, too, developed its own separate and substantial business. In November 1927, it raised a $20 million loan in the United States.[368] With the Settlement of War Claims Act (1928), both Hapag and the North German Lloyd Line anticipated a sizable sum in compensation for their World War I losses.[369]

Japanese shipping, which had expanded greatly during and after

World War I, went on growing. With the Panama Canal open, raw silk could be shipped directly from Yokohama to New York, avoiding transhipment from ship to train at a West Coast port. Nonetheless, some silk (still Japan's largest export to the United States) continued to be transhipped; this was faster than direct shipping. Japanese shipping became thoroughly international. Thus, for example, Osaka Shosen Kaisha (OSK) would load coffee at Santos in Brazil, deliver it to New Orleans, pick up raw cotton there, and return to Japan via the Panama Canal. The Mitsui Line transported raw silk, chinaware, and other Japanese products to the U.S. Northwest, returning with American wheat and lumber to be shipped to China and Japan. Nippon Yusen Kaisha (NYK) also did a large U.S. business, carrying a wide variety of cargoes.[370]

Banking

If foreign-owned companies were important in providing trading, accounting, insurance, and shipping services to Americans, they were also in banking—typically as related to providing for America's international transactions, albeit to the extent that some of these banks got involved in the New York money market, in short-term and call lending, they engaged in "domestic" business. Foreign banks and financial institutions continued to use a variety of forms in doing business in the United States, forms that were selected under the constraints of federal and, even more important, state banking laws.

Foreign banks could be present in the United States through a licensed New York agency (remember that New York State law did not allow foreign banks to set up branches; since 1911, they could have licensed agencies that were forbidden to take deposits). The number of such foreign bank agencies in New York declined from a peak of thirty-eight at year end 1923 to twenty-six at year end 1929 (see Table 5.5). The attrition was caused by (1) the retreat from New York of Roumanian, Czech, and Polish agencies (the reason for these pullbacks seems to have been that the agencies were superfluous; U.S. and western European financial institutions could handle the central European business); (2) one Portuguese and one Greek bank would alter their form of New York operations—from agency to trust company—so this was not, in fact, a real withdrawal; (3) changes in the control of the bank, changes in name, and mergers of existing parent banks (this restructuring of British overseas banks reduced the nominal number of British overseas banks in the United States, but not their presence); (4) the Chinese Merchants Bank, Ltd., Hong Kong, exited in 1925 (it was listed as in liquidation in 1924); and (5) the Union Bank of Canada,

Table 5.5. Foreign (out-of-country) banks with agencies licensed under New York State banking law, 1923, 1929

		Activity, 1923–1929			
No.	In existence Dec. 31, 1923	Subtractions	Additions	In existence Dec. 31, 1929	No.
1.	Anglo-South American Bank, London			Yes	1.
2.	Banca Chrissoveloni, S.A., Bucharest, Roumania	1928			
3.	Banca Commerciale Italiana, Milan, Italy			Yes	2.
4.	Banca Marmorosch, Blank & Co., Bucharest, Roumania	1924			
5.	Banco di Napoli, Naples, Italy			Yes (2 agencies)	3.
6.	Banco di Roma, Rome, Italy			Yes	4.
7.	Banco Nacional Ultramarino, Lisbon, Portugal	1924 as agency		[Set up New York trust company in 1924]	
8.	Bank of Athens, Athens, Greece	1928 as agency		[Set up New York trust company in 1926]	
9.	Bank of British West Africa, London	1924[a]			
10.	Bank of Canton, Ltd., Hong Kong			Yes	5.
11.	Bank of Chosen, Seoul, Korea (Japan)			Yes	6.
	—		1924	Bank of London and South America, London[b]	7.
12.	Bank of Montreal, Montreal			Yes	8.
13.	Bank of Nova Scotia, Nova Scotia			Yes	9.
14.	Bank of Taiwan, Taiwan (Japan)			Yes	10.

Table 5.5 *(continued)*

No.	In existence Dec. 31, 1923	Activity, 1923–1929		In existence Dec. 31, 1929	No.
		Subtractions	Additions		
15.	Banque Belge pour l'Etranger, Brussels, Belgium			Yes	11.
	—		1925[c]	Barclay's Bank (Dominion, Colonial and Overseas)[c]	12.
16.	Bohemia, Czechoslovak Foreign Banking Corp., Prague, Czechoslovakia	1924			
17.	Canadian Bank of Commerce, Toronto			Yes	13.
18.	Chartered Bank of India, Australia and China, London			Yes	14.
19.	Chinese Merchants Bank, Ltd. Hong Kong	1925			
20.	Colonial Bank, London	c			
21.	Commercial Bank of Spanish America, London	1928[d]			
22.	Credit Commercial de France, Paris, France	1925			
23.	Credito Italiano, Genoa and Milan, Italy			Yes	15.
24.	Dominion Bank, Toronto			Yes	16.
25.	Hongkong and Shanghai Banking Corp., Hong Kong			Yes	17.
26.	London and Brazilian Bank, London	1924[b]			
27.	London and River Plate Bank, London	1924[b]			

28.	Mercantile Bank of India, Ltd., London			Yes	18.
29.	Mitsubishi Bank, Ltd., Tokyo, Japan			Yes	19.
30.	Mitsui Bank, Ltd., Tokyo, Japan			Yes	20.
	—		1925	National Bank of Greece, Athens	21.
31.	National Bank of South Africa, Ltd., Pretoria, South Africa	1926[c]			
32.	Philippine National Bank, Manila, Philippines			Yes	22.
33.	Royal Bank of Canada, Montreal			Yes	23.
34.	Standard Bank of South Africa, London			Yes	24.
35.	Sumitomo Bank, Osaka, Japan			Yes	25.
36.	Union Bank of Canada, Winnipeg	1925			
37.	Union Bank of the Cooperative Societies of Poland, Posen, Poland	1926			
38.	Yokohama Specie Bank, Yokohama, Japan			Yes	26.

Sources: New York State Banking Department, *Annual Reports*, 1923–1929.

a. The Bank of British West Africa came to be controlled by the Standard Bank of South Africa, London.

b. The London and Brazilian Bank and the London River Plate Bank, London, were merged into the Bank of London and South America (BOLSA). As of June 30, 1928, Lloyd's Bank held 56 percent of the stock of BOLSA. *Stock Exchange Official Intelligence, 1929*, 381.

c. The Colonial Bank in 1925 was still listed, but with the explanation, "name changed to Barclay's Bank (Dominion, Colonial and Overseas)"; it was not listed in 1926. The National Bank of South Africa became part of Barclay's Bank (Dominion, Colonial and Overseas).

d. By 1928, the Commercial Bank of Spanish America was 99 percent owned by the Anglo-South American Bank Ltd.

Winnipeg, was in deep difficulty at home in 1924, the last year of its New York agency.[371] The drop in the count of New York agencies, 1924–1929, did not in any way signify a smaller role for New York as a global emporium; the remaining foreign banks were part and parcel of a vibrant and vital international financial hub.

By now well established among the New York agencies were the principal Canadian commercial banks—the Royal Bank of Canada, the Bank of Montreal, the Canadian Bank of Commerce, and the Bank of Nova Scotia. All had long had New York agencies, and these took part in the call and short loan markets in New York. These bank agencies (direct investments) were intermediaries in placing short-term portfolio investments. There was no call market of importance in Canada, so these banks' call loans were usually made in New York. The amounts these banks loaned outside of Canada (mainly in the United States) peaked in the summer of 1929 at about $333 million.[372] Canadian firms were active in Latin America and the Caribbean; and the financing of this trade was done by Canadian financial institutions through New York. Thus, the Royal Bank of Canada—by 1929 Canada's largest bank—became especially prominent in Cuba as well as other countries in Latin America; much of its New York agency's business related to the Cuban trade.[373] So, too, the Caribbean (Cuba, in particular) took up a substantial proportion of managers' time at the New York agency of the Bank of Nova Scotia.[374] Of the twenty-six bank agencies in New York in 1929, five were Canadian (the previously mentioned four plus the smaller Dominion Bank, Toronto). The representatives of these banks had become an integral part of the Wall Street community.

In 1929, six major London-headquartered "overseas banks" had New York agencies: (1) the Anglo-South American Bank, often labeled the "nitrate bank," because of its significance in the Chilean nitrate trade; (2) the Bank of London and South America, otherwise known as BOLSA—a 1923 merger of the London and River Plate Bank with the London and Brazilian Bank, both of which had had New York agencies; BOLSA was controlled by Lloyd's Bank, London; (3) Barclay's Bank (Dominion, Colonial & Overseas), formed in 1925, a combination of existing British overseas banks, including the Colonial Bank; (4) the Chartered Bank of India, Australia, and China; (5) the Mercantile Bank of India; and (6) the Standard Bank of South Africa.[375]

In addition, the large Hongkong and Shanghai Banking Corporation, a British overseas bank with a Hong Kong registration, maintained its New York agency. The Bank of Canton, Ltd., also of Hong Kong, survived in New York (unlike the Hongkong and Shanghai Banking Corporation, it was a "Chinese" bank, with ownership from the mainland—and by 1929 the only one with a licensed New York agency).[376]

In contrast with the limited representation from China, all six Japanese banks that had earlier set up agencies in New York actively enlarged their business.

Some of the British and Japanese banks—like their Canadian counterparts—participated in placing call and short loans in New York; for these bank agencies, their principal functions lay in trade finance—in handling acceptances. The British and Japanese bank agencies were also extremely important as channels of information, a broad function, ranging from reporting to the home office on what was happening in the United States to providing for the needs of visiting bank officials and businessmen from abroad (arranging contacts and appointments and, in the Japanese case, aiding with translations).

The New York agency of the Banque Belge pour l'Etranger, Brussels, had in the spring of 1926 sizable dollar-denominated deposits with the Austrian bank Wiener Bank-Verein, which the latter used to finance eastern European credits.[377] Many of the New York agencies of foreign banks played an important role in moving dollars abroad to support international trade expansion, imports, and exports (and often financing trade that did not necessarily include the United States).

In addition, foreign bank agencies in New York frequently served their compatriots as correspondent banks or "agents" ("agents," as distinct from "agencies," were not owned by a parent abroad). Thus, as an example, the Yamaguchi Bank, Ltd., in Osaka, Japan, had six independent New York "agents," four of which were American commercial banks; its other two "agents" were the New York agencies of the Bank of Taiwan and the Yokohama Specie Bank.[378]

A second way for a foreign bank to do business in New York was to organize a trust company. By 1929, at least six foreign banks had trust companies in New York (most as a means of getting around the New York state rule that agencies were not permitted to take deposits). Some banks had both New York agencies and trust companies, and some one or the other. Anglo-South American Bank had opened the Anglo-South American Trust Company in 1923 (this British bank had both an agency and a trust company). Two Italian banks established trust companies: Banca Commerciale Italiana (BCI) set up Banca Commerciale Italiana Trust Company in 1924, while Banco di Sicilia formed Banco di Sicilia Trust Company the next year. (BCI had a New York agency; the Sicilian bank did not and was new to the United States with this trust company.)[379]

The Banca Commerciale Italiana Trust Company (BCIT) opened five New York branch offices to take deposits, two in lower Manhattan, one in Brooklyn, one on Long Island, and one on Second Avenue and 116th Street—all in Italian neighborhoods.[380] Both BCIT and the Banco di Sicilia Trust Company sent remittances home for Italian immigrants. BCIT was also an underwriter in the 1928 American bond issue of Italian Superpower Corporation; Siro Fusi, president of BCIT, was vice-president of Italian Superpower Corporation.[381] In addition, Fusi represented other Italian business interests in America. Thus, he served on the board of directors of the American Chatillon Corporation, a direct investment of the Milan rayon company La Soie de Châtillon.[382]

The fourth and fifth trust companies were those of a Portuguese bank (Banco National Ultramarino), which founded the Trust Company of North America in 1924, and a Greek bank (Banque d'Athenes), which formed the Bank of Athens Trust Company in 1926 (as noted earlier, both of these foreign banks would close their New York agencies; their trust companies were substitutes). Like the Italian trust companies, these "banks" held the savings of immigrants in New York and helped the latter transfer moneys to families back in their native land. The sixth foreign-owned trust company, J. Henry Schroder Trust Company, was established in April 1929 to conduct a general banking and trust business; it was controlled by the J. Henry Schroder Banking Corporation, New York, which in turn had been inaugurated in 1923 by the eponymous London merchant banking house.[383] The Schroder trust company coexisted with the banking corporation.

"Banking corporations" were yet another mode of doing business in New York. In the late 1920s, J. Henry Schroder Banking Corporation handled dollar acceptances, dealt in foreign exchange, and took part in underwriting securities (between 1925 and 1930, it participated in fifty-seven foreign bond issues, many for central European and Latin American clients of its British parent). Its banking clientele was predominantly foreign, with Europeans, mainly Germans, receiving 70 percent of its credits, Latin Americans about 10 percent, and U.S. firms some 20 percent (of which a large part went to the sugar broker Czarnikow-Rionda, with which firm the London Schroder house had had a long association).[384] J. Henry Schroder Banking Corporation also served as a correspondent for other foreign banks; in 1929, for example, the State Bank of the U.S.S.R., Moscow, listed it as one of the latter's New York correspondents.[385]

Aside from Schroder's, a variety of other foreign (and "quasi-foreign") firms took part in investment banking in the United States; for many of them the type of operation was an office or a partnership association.[386] The principal Canadian investment bankers, really stock brokers, active in American securities, as well as bringing U.S. funds to Canada (including A. E. Ames & Co., Ltd.; Wood, Gundy; and Dominion Securities), had their own New York offices.[387] Eduard Beit von Speyer, head of Lazard Speyer–Ellissen, Berlin and Frankfurt (now joined by his son, Herbert Beit von Speyer), was once again a partner in Speyer & Co., New York, while James Speyer, in New York, was (in turn) a partner in the German house, headed by the senior Beit von Speyer (his brother-in-law). The U.S. and German Speyer houses cooperated in American overseas lending.[388] Lazard Frères, New York, was closely associated with Lazard Frères & Cie., Paris.[389] Two Japanese securities companies—Fujimoto Securities Co., Ltd. (the precursor to Daiwa Securities), and Nomura Securities Co. Ltd.—had New York offices.[390]

Some foreign banks, jointly with American ones, held shares in banking corporations. Paul Warburg's International Acceptance Bank (in the late 1920s in part owned by a number of European—German, Austrian, Dutch, Swiss, English, French, Belgian, and Swedish—banks) flourished. Its average annual earnings, which had been about $1 million in 1922 and 1923, rose to $1.8 million in 1924 and 1925 and increased still further to average $2.1 million in 1926, 1927, and 1928.[391] It successfully used its parent company banks to obtain information on European banking and credit conditions.[392]

In 1924, IAB organized the American & Continental Corporation (ACC) to provide assistance to German borrowers. In ACC, leading New York banks were allied with a European group that served as adviser and partner in the advances. The European group—some of its participants became stockholders in ACC—included the Deutsche Bank (Berlin); M. M. Warburg & Co. (Hamburg); A. Levy, Sal. Oppenheim & Cie., and J. H. Stein (all three from Cologne); Hope & Co. (Amsterdam); Société Financière de Transports et d'Enterprises Industrielles (Brussels); Skandinaviska Kreditaktiebolaget and Svenska Handelsbanken (both from Stockholm); and Österreichische Creditanstalt für Handel & Gewerbe (Vienna).[393]

Companies similar to ACC multiplied in the financial whirl of New York City. For central European finance, for example, a number of companies were established, usually including both American and foreign banking houses. Thus, the European Mortgage and Investment Corporation, formed in 1925, was backed by the British-owned J. Henry Schroder Banking Corporation, New York, as well as by the Boston and New York house Lee, Higginson. In 1926, the American, British and Continental Corporation was organized by J. Henry Schroder Banking Corporation; Blyth, Witter (a New York firm); and the Hungarian Commercial Bank of Pest.[394] A similar enterprise was the Central European Investment Corporation, set up in New York in 1927, with a capital of $4 million. Shareholders included W. Averell Harriman interests, Niederösterreichische Escompte-Gesellschaft, Banque de Bruxelles, Comptoir d'Escompte (Geneva), and Union Européenne Industrielle et Financière (Paris).[395] Harriman was also a director of the ACC, not surprising given his close connections with the Warburg family.[396] In December 1926, to enhance "head-office security operations," the Bank of Montreal established the Montreal Company of New York, a wholly owned subsidiary, to engage "in the underwriting and distribution of investment securities" in the United States.[397] All these new companies (and there were many, many more) were part of the cosmopolitan financial architecture described in Chapter 4. They represented direct investments by foreign banks in the United States in order to facilitate U.S. capital exports.

Foreign financial houses along with American ones that attracted the participation of foreign banks ranked high among the top 100 U.S. "accepting institutions," furnishing acceptances for foreign trade. Indeed, each of three principal specialized acceptance institutions in the United States had foreign banks as investors: International Acceptance Bank; J. Henry Schroder Banking Corporation; and Kidder, Peabody Acceptance Corporation (with Baring Brothers' interest). During the years 1925–1929, these three held between 9.3 percent (year end 1928) and 11.4 percent (year end 1926) of all American acceptance liabilities outstanding. Nine New York agencies of foreign banks, including the four agencies of the main Canadian commercial banks, were also heavily involved in acceptances. According to a Japanese source, the Yokohama Specie Bank's New York agency accounted for fully 3.2 percent of the total outstanding bank acceptances in the New York money market at year end 1928. In addition, the French American Banking Corporation (half of its stock was owned by Comptoir National d'Escompte de Paris) was very active in handling dollar acceptances.[398] At the end of 1929, bankers acceptances outstanding reached a record high of $1,732,436,000. Of this total, foreign banks bought up as short-term investments 51.4 percent ($891,132,000). This was volatile short-term money.[399]

The files of the International Acceptance Bank (IAB) show its customers and the formidable variety of trade financing in which it engaged. It financed the sale of coffee from South America to Norway; zinc ore from Belgium to Germany; cotton, copper, and wheat from the United States to Europe; diamonds from Europe to the United States; linen from Belgium and Germany to the United States; and numerous other products. Often M. M. Warburg & Co., Hamburg, shared in IAB risks.[400] A large part of IAB's business involved future exchange contracts, which it bought and sold. As of June 16, 1928 (a date for which information is available), its customers' liability on these contracts totaled $182.3 million, compared with $54.1 million liability in dollar acceptances.[401]

A number of foreign banks had representatives in New York, who did not engage in "banking" but arranged for their banks' participation in European borrowings and kept au courant on what was happening in New York money markets. The Deutsche Bank, for example, had no New York licensed agency or bank, but had a New York representative (Hugo Schmidt).[402] The Dresdner Bank had a brother of Henry Nathan (of the parent bank) as its man in New York.[403] The German private banking house Gebüder Arnhold, Dresden, opened a New York office in 1928.[404] Comptoir National d'Escompte de Paris (in addition to its 50 percent interest in the French American Banking Corporation) had a New York representative, as did the French banking firm Louis Dreyfus & Cie.[405] The largest English *domestic* banks had individuals resident in New York.[406] This is but a sample.

Many foreign banks, however, settled for New York correspondents, although a bank might have both a representative and a correspondent bank (or banks). Dresdner Bank had both. More typically, The Disconto-Gesellschaft and the Danat Bank (the Darmstädter und Nationalbank)—with no New York representatives—had correspondent banks. Thus, as an example, the Danat Bank in 1928 had sixteen correspondent banks—including National City Bank, Hallgarten & Co. (with which it had had intimate prewar interconnections), International Acceptance Bank, Bank of the Manhattan Company, National Bank of Commerce, and J. Henry Schroder Banking Corporation.[407] In fact, by far the most used form of business in New York by foreign banks was the engagement of one or more New York correspondent banks. Banks from about forty-five countries had correspondents in New York City in 1929.[408] The correspondent bank approach was particularly popular with German, French, and Belgian banks.[409]

In December 1928, the Bank of the Manhattan Company, New York (often called The Manhattan Company), agreed to acquire the assets of the International Acceptance Bank. It would exchange one share of its stock for two shares of IAB common stock.[410] The arrangements were completed in 1929.[411] IAB remained a separate institution and continued to handle foreign acceptances. A newly formed International Manhattan Company would deal in issues and general securities.[412] At the time of the merger, the stock of IAB was closely held by a group consisting of the Warburg family and their "friends and business associates," including the European banks. Twenty-five different foreign stockholders owned 37.6 percent of the stock in IAB.[413] The foreign shareholders in IAB would become (through the exchange of common stock) stockholders in The Manhattan Company.[414] The Swiss Bank Corporation, for instance, perceived its new interests as a means of strengthening its American position.[415] The Bank of the Manhattan

Company had Stephen Baker as chairman and Paul M. Warburg as associate chairman. The International Acceptance Bank (foreign banking facilities) and the new International Manhattan Company (investment securities) were affiliated companies. Subsequently, but still in 1929 (in November and December), a holding company structure was established, with Paul Warburg, chairman of the board of the holding company, The Manhattan Company.[416] With the union of IAB and the Bank of the Manhattan Company, for the first time in the 1920s, foreign banks had become involved in an important, full-service deposit-taking American bank—with a domestic commercial and investment banking business as well as a sizable foreign business. It seemed to all involved an ideal combination of domestic strengths on the part of the Bank of the Manhattan Company and international ones from IAB.[417]

By 1929 all the large New York banks (in varying degrees) participated in international lending and had connections with foreign banking institutions. The involvements of the big New York banks during the 1920s typically related to joint issues and syndications, along with correspondent relationships. After the acquisition of IAB, The Manhattan Company group seems to have been exceptional among the major New York banks in its having the equity participation by European banks. But even when such equity stakes were absent (as was usually the case), the presence of the many foreign banks in New York with agencies, trust companies, banking houses, representatives, and numerous correspondents materially contributed to the dynamic Wall Street role in global finance.

Outside New York City, foreign banks (including merchant banks)—as in the past—were far less evident. They were present only in Boston, Philadelphia, and Chicago and on the West Coast. Kidder, Peabody, which had a New York office, retained its Boston headquarters; its long experience in banking and foreign exchange meant that it had attracted sizable foreign deposits.[418] Kidder, Peabody continued its close association with Baring Brothers but had no partners from Barings. Barings did, however, continue to participate with Kidder, Peabody in the Kidder, Peabody Acceptance Corporation, which by 1928–1929 not only handled acceptances but also served as an underwriter and investor in Kidder, Peabody's promotions.[419] Lee, Higginson was a Boston house with a vast international business but no foreign partners; like Kidder, Peabody, it too had an important Wall Street office. The Bank of Nova Scotia kept its long-standing Boston branch office.[420] In addition, the Bank of Athens had a Boston subsidiary, Athens Bankers' Corp.[421]

Banca Commerciale Italiana, Milan, in 1929, established the Banca Commerciale Italiana Trust Company in Boston and Philadelphia—to cater to the Italian immigrant communities. These were deposit-taking institutions.[422] As far as I can tell, BCIT was the sole foreign-owned bank in Philadelphia. Chicago, in 1929, had three foreign banks (the branches of Bank of Montreal and the Bank of Nova Scotia, as well as the separately incorporated Banco di Napoli).[423]

On the West Coast, in 1929, a half dozen foreign-owned banks did business (see Table 5.6).[424] Two were Canadian, the Bank of Montreal and the Canadian Bank of Commerce, Toronto; in 1929 the latter, to strengthen its position, organized itself under California law as a state bank—The Canadian Bank of Commerce (California)—to take over its existing "branch."[425] There were two Japanese banks: of these, the Yokohama Specie Bank was the larger, but the Sumitomo Bank assumed new prominence when in 1925 it acquired the already existing Nippon Bank of Sacramento, California, and became a full-service commercial and savings bank in that city.[426] The other two banks were from Hong Kong. One was the important branch of the Hongkong and Shanghai Banking Corporation—a British bank—that had been in San Francisco since 1875 and with its New York agency played a significant role in financing U.S.–Far Eastern trade; it advertised that it was prepared to serve "the financial requirements of American interests in the East."[427] The other, the Bank of Canton, was a Chinese bank and new to San Francisco (it opened in 1924).

All six of these banks were in San Francisco (all six also had agencies in New York). The two Japanese banks had branches in Los Angeles and banks in Seattle, Washington. The Canadian Bank of Commerce was in Seattle, Washington, and Portland, Oregon, as well as San Francisco. The Canadian and Japanese banks in Seattle and Portland were involved in financing the lumber trade. In addition, serving a different function, the Fujimoto Securities Co., affiliated with the Fujimoto Bill Broker Bank, Osaka, continued to do business in San Francisco.[428]

Beyond the foreign banks already discussed, in the West, Midwest, and Texas there were foreign-owned mortgage lending institutions. Some of the prewar Dutch mortgage banks stayed on, a shadow of times past. By 1929, their number was smaller than in prior years, with the decline the result of poor performance. Between 1923 and 1929, two of these banks had gone into liquidation; one bank was in default of its obligations to the Dutch investors; two more went into bankruptcy and were replaced in 1928 and 1929 by reorganized new companies. The eight remaining in 1929—located in St. Paul (Minnesota), Spokane and Seattle (Washington), and Port Arthur (Texas)—are listed in Table 5.7. The troubled condition of American farmers in the 1920s could be read in these banks' balance sheets. The banks made fewer loans than in the peak times before and during World War I; more serious, they had come to own sizable amounts of real estate, undoubtedly acquired

Table 5.6. Principal foreign-owned banks on the West Coast, 1929 (excludes Dutch mortgage banks and other mortgage lenders)

Name of bank and headquarters	West Coast city (entry date)	Agency in N.Y.
Bank of Canton, Ltd., Hong Kong	San Francisco (1924)	Yes
Bank of Montreal, Montreal	San Francisco (1918)[a]	Yes
Canadian Bank of Commerce, Toronto	San Francisco (1864);[b] Seattle, Wash. (1900); Portland, Ore. (1901)[c]	Yes
Hongkong and Shanghai Banking Corporation, Hong Kong	San Francisco (1875)	Yes
Sumitomo Bank, Osaka	San Francisco (1916); Los Angeles (1924); Sacramento (1925); Seattle (1919)	Yes
Yokohama Specie Bank, Yokohama	San Francisco (1899);[d] Los Angeles (1913); Seattle (1917)[e]	Yes

Sources: Superintendent of Banks (California), *Annual Reports;* Mira Wilkins, *The History of Foreign Investment in the United States to 1914* (Cambridge, Mass.: Harvard University Press, 1989), 106. 459–461, 852n.52; Ira Cross, *Financing an Empire,* 4 vols. (Chicago: S. J. Clarke, 1927); Merrill Denison, *Canada's First Bank: A History of the Bank of Montreal* (New York: Dodd, Mead & Co., 1967), II, 332, 353; Victor Ross, *A History of the Canadian Bank of Commerce* (Toronto: Oxford University Press, 1922), II, 558.

Note: I have also excluded Fujimoto Securities Co., San Francisco, which was an affiliate of Fujimoto Bill Broker Bank, since it seems to fit into a different category.

a. In 1918, when the Bank of Montreal took over the Bank of British North America, it established a bank in San Francisco, the British American Bank, which in 1927 was renamed the Bank of Montreal, San Francisco. It also (in 1919) opened an agency in San Francisco. The Bank of British North America had set up in California in 1864.

b. The Bank of British Columbia was set up in San Francisco in 1864; it was acquired by the Canadian Bank of Commerce in 1901; there was a direct continuity from the 1864 entity.

c. According to Herbert Marshall, Frank A. Southard, and Kenneth W. Taylor, *Canadian-American Industry* (New Haven, Conn.: Yale University Press, 1936), 197, in 1925 "the Portland branch absorbed the business of the Pacific Bank of Portland." The Canadian Bank of Commerce did a general commercial banking business in California and Oregon.

d. In 1886, the Yokohama Specie Bank set up a representative office or agency in San Francisco; the office became a branch bank in 1899.

e. September 24, 1917, is the date provided in the inventory of Yokohama Specie Bank, RG 131, National Archives.

through foreclosures. Aside from the two reorganized firms, no new Dutch mortgage banks had been established in America since 1912.[429]

Similarly, the mortgage lending of British firms such as Scottish American Mortgage Company, Ltd., and Texas Land and Mortgage Company, Ltd., went on, but at a reduced pace; here, too, it was the condition of the American farmer that made the business so problematic.[430] The Scottish American Mortgage Co.'s annual reports regularly

Table 5.7. Dutch mortgage banks in America, 1929

Name	Year founded in the U.S.	Headquarters in Holland	U.S. center
Nederlandsch-Amerikaansche Hypotheekbank—Reorganized as Nieue Nederlandsch-Amerikaansche Hypotheekbank (1929)	1893	Groningen Groningen	St. Paul, Minn. St. Paul, Minn.
First Northwestern and Pacific Hypotheekbank	1889	Amsterdam	Spokane, Wash.
Holland Bank	1896	Amsterdam	Spokane, Wash.
Internationale Hypotheekbank—Reorganized as Nieue Internationale Hypotheekbank (1929)	1909	Deventer Groningen	Spokane, Wash. Spokane, Wash.
Second Northwestern and Pacific Hypotheekbank	1910	Amsterdam	Spokane, Wash.
Vereenigde Transatlantische Hypotheekbank	1912[a]	Rotterdam	Seattle, Wash.
Holland-Noord-Amerika Hypotheekbank	1912	Gorinchem	Seattle, Wash.
Holland-Texas Hypotheekbank	1911	Amsterdam	Port Arthur, Tex.

Sources: Mira Wilkins, *Foreign Investment in the United States to 1914* (Cambridge, Mass.: Harvard University Press, 1989), 514–515; and *Van Oss' Effectenboek 1929* and *1934.* I am indebted to Guus Veenendaal for assistance on these mortgage banks.

a. Predecessor companies.

recorded the company's difficulties in conducting its mortgage business. Table 5.8 reflects this one company's gradual withdrawal from the U.S. mortgage lending and its turn to alternative uses of its assets. Throughout the 1920s, the company's annual reports noted disbursements for salaries of "trustee and inspector in America" and for other expenses in the United States. Throughout, its auditor recorded that the American accounts had been verified.[431]

In 1928, the Alliance Trust Company of Dundee, Scotland, told its shareholders that it had resolved to withdraw entirely from the American mortgage business.[432] The Alliance Trust Co. had 25 percent of its funds in American mortgages in 1927; by 1929, the share was down to 18 percent.[433] Another Scottish firm, The Oregon Mortgage Company, compared the situation in the 1920s with that of the agricultural depression of the 1890s. It, too, decided to withdraw from mortgage lending (and as late as 1927 began to move its financial resources from mortgages to securities).[434] In 1925, the Edinburgh American Land Mortgage Co. (EALM) changed its name to the Second British Assets Trust Ltd. Founded in 1878, for its first forty years, EALM had been almost exclu-

Table 5.8. Investments in the U.S. mortgage business of Scottish American Mortgage Co., 1925–1930 (as a percentage of the total Scottish American Mortgage Co. investment portfolio)

Year end, May 31	Percent
1925	56
1926	48
1927	42
1928	32
1929	25
1930	22

Source: Based on data in Scottish American Mortgage Co., *Annual Reports,* Film Z-G2, Reel 55, Bancroft Library Archives, University of California, Berkeley.

sively involved in the U.S. mortgage business; it was now leaving that behind.[435] The same pattern was evident when, in 1928, the United States Mortgage Company of Scotland, Edinburgh, restyled itself as the United States Trust Company of Scotland, reflecting its altered business.[436] What was happening was clear. The Scottish mortgage companies were becoming transformed into investment companies; they were investing in American but also British and other securities.

The English firm The Trust and Mortgage Company of Iowa, Ltd., and its subsidiary Iowa Land Company apparently continued lending in the American West. Its resident American "agent" was C. W. Benson & Co., with a central office in St. Paul, Minnesota. The Benson merchant bank in London was involved in investment trusts and securities, not mortgage lending.[437] In sum, British companies still provided mortgages to American farmers, but there were fewer lenders and a far reduced volume of mortgage lending than in times past. However, many of these same firms were participating in the stock market and purchasing American securities (as portfolio investments). Thus, the retreat from mortgage lending was not a full retreat from U.S. investments.

Public Policy, Public Sentiments, and Conclusions

By mid-1929, superficially it seemed that a world economy, not unlike that of 1914, was being re-created. Britain was back on the gold standard. British multinational enterprises were investing in the United States. German ones, with reasonable confidence, were resuming their international role and anticipating sizable further U.S. investments. Other nationalities participated.

But there were many elements unlike in 1914. Foremost among them was the altered role of the United States, with its pivotal place as a creditor nation: its bankers and businessmen were deeply involved in international lending and outward foreign direct investments; for the United States the extent was unprecedented. Also, unlike in 1914, everywhere governments were greater participants in national economic life. To be sure, their wartime involvement had been reduced but not to 1914 levels. Government tax policies and monetary ones were far more in evidence than in 1914. The government role in Russia was at the extreme. And, unlike in 1914, in 1929 Russia was no longer a truly integral part of the world economy. In 1914 it had been a magnet for inward foreign investment. In 1929 it was not. Paradoxically, Russia's unavailability as a place for sizable inward investment put the United States in an even more strategic position. At the same time as the United States was a creditor nation, inward foreign investment remained attractive. After all, the United States had the largest domestic market in the world. Inward foreign portfolio investment and inward foreign direct investment, reduced during World War I, had by 1929 revived.

This chapter has given abundant details on the development of foreign multinational enterprises in the United States in the late 1920s. In most activities, there was a substantial enlargement of foreign direct investments. The arrivals and growth were in a wide variety of sectors. What stands out are the activities in branded products, in rayon, in chemicals, in oil, and in insurance. There were new entries into manufacturing of branded consumer goods (from Crosse & Blackwell's specialty condiments to Yardley's vanity items); British American Tobacco began to market in the United States for the first time, with its newly acquired Raleigh cigarette brand, made in America for the American market (before it had manufactured in America, but only for exports). Lever, already a manufacturer in the United States, broadened its line of consumer goods to include Lux Soap. There were also a set of new and expanded "high-tech" investments, principally in rayon and chemicals. Although foreign companies no longer held a monopoly position in rayon, they still represented the bulk of production in this new product. In chemicals, novel products and processes proliferated. Shell Union Oil Corporation had become a major actor in the U.S. domestic oil industry and was a new participant in the chemical industry. One should, moreover, not underestimate the role of foreign companies in supplying insurance coverage.

Along with the overall expansion of foreign multinationals, there were retreats. A number of exits (e.g., the British divestment of John Morrell's meatpacking operations and the French departures from their joint ventures with Du Pont) were based not so much on bad performance but on the attractiveness of the assets to the acquiring American investors. Whereas the general malaise in American agriculture created opportunities for foreign grain traders who built up their direct investments in trading facilities, other investors in agriculture-related sectors performed badly; this was particularly true of those British and Dutch enterprises that were providing farm mortgages; foreign offerings of farm mortgages dropped sharply. Some foreign companies were not competitive in the U.S. market. Brown, Boveri is a prime example. It came and went. Other retreats because of poor performance included Imperial Chemical Industries's United Alkali. Yet some companies with low profits or losses persisted and changed management (e.g., Delta and Pine Land Company). Others did badly and coped by diversifying (e.g., Oldbury Electro-Chemical). Still others, for instance, Massey-Harris, acquired new facilities and tried to restructure their business. The U.S. market was not easy to penetrate, as many foreign multinationals discovered.

In the late 1920s, complex international cooperative agreements governed the way foreign direct investors behaved in industries ranging from potash to linoleum to rayon to glass to chemicals to electrical goods and to oil. Some of these agreements stopped inward foreign direct investments; others did not, only setting the rules of the game. American companies that joined in these arrangements sought to structure them to avoid possible future antitrust vulnerability.

Despite certain retreats and despite certain sectors that were barely touched by foreign multinationals, clearly in the late 1920s there was a considerable presence of foreign direct investors in the United States. Yet measured relative to the size of the domestic economy, the amounts are far less impressive. And, whereas in the immediate postwar years, there had been many nationalistic public policy measures targeted toward foreign multinationals that had investments in this country, none of this intensity in policy making existed by the late 1920s.

In the late 1920s, although there were additions to the existing body of legislation affecting foreign investors in this country, in the main scant attention was paid toward the inward FDI, and few new policies surfaced. Where policy matters were aired, they were broad in nature or typically addressed prior unresolved issues or represented a perpetuation of, or application of, approaches defined in earlier years. Yet there were policies that affected inward direct investors, and it is useful to summarize some of them. There were the concerns over taxes, on the part of both policy makers and investors (foreign investors developed means to reduce tax burdens). Tariffs, as in prior years, often encouraged inward foreign direct investors to jump over them and to invest in the United States. The Heroin Prohibition Act of 1924, which prohibited the import of opium, prompted Swiss and German investors in pharmaceuticals to develop other products—in the United States (and abroad).

Major steps were taken toward the resolution of war claims with the 1928 Settlement of War Claims Act. Throughout the late 1920s substantial litigation persisted over the activities of the Alien Property Custodian on how it handled German properties; that wartime-created agency had remained in existence into peacetime and did not come to an end until 1934.[438] So, too, there was in the late 1920s the lingering matter of whether Royal Dutch Shell was eligible to lease public lands, eventually resolved in the foreign firm's favor in 1929. The State Department maintained its advocacy of reciprocity, an open door for American business abroad (and Royal Dutch Shell had been a pawn in this overall policy).

That American federal and state legislation represented an overall "lack of hospitality in welcoming foreign banks to our shores" was no harbinger for reform.[439] In 1924 there was discussion on using federal and state policies toward inward investments by foreign banks as leverage for more openness toward U.S. multinational enterprises, yet no substantive changes were made in banking law—at either a federal or a state level—with this goal in mind. Suggestions notwithstanding, reciprocity considerations had no legislative impact in the banking sector.[440]

State government insurance departments, as they had for years, regulated all insurers, and on occasion special attention was directed toward certain foreign enterprises; on the whole, however, the insurance regulations were applied evenly to domestic and foreign insurance companies alike. The regulations were designed to protect policy holders by making certain that insurers had adequate reserves and did not charge excessive premiums.[441]

In aviation and radio regulation there were new laws: what had been "talk" at the beginning of the 1920s now was translated into legislation. The first federal statute on aviation (aside from that on postal subsidies) was the Air Commerce Act of 1926; it was modeled on the long-standing legislation that restricted foreign participation in shipping (the most recent antecedent measure was the 1920 Jones Act). Under the Air Commerce Act of 1926, aircraft registry in the United States was allowed only to "American citizens" (individuals or corporations). Foreign aircraft had to have U.S. permission to fly over the country. Commercial traffic between any two points in the United States was confined to aircraft of U.S. registry. In the more relaxed regulatory environment of the late 1920s, the definition of citizenship was based not on the 1920 but instead on the 1916 Shipping Act (a corporation organized in the United States, with at least a majority of its stock owned by American citizens). The 75 percent U.S. ownership requirement (in the 1920 Shipping Act) would be subsequently imposed—in the Civil Aeronautics Act of 1938. The 1926 Air Commerce Law did specify, however, that an American airline had to have an American citizen as president, and at least two-thirds of its board of directors were required to be American citizens.[442] The Jones-White Act of 1928 (to encourage the development of an American merchant marine) did not revise the rules in the 1920 Jones Act vis-à-vis foreign involvement in U.S. shipping (it did offer lucrative postal subsidies available only to American shipping companies).[443] In both air travel and shipping, U.S. law sought to stimulate the domestic provision of these vital services.[444]

In contrast with the Air Commerce Act of 1926, the Air Corps Act passed later that same year, and designed to foster a U.S. aircraft *manufacturing* industry, stipulated that the U.S. Air Corps could award construction contracts only to U.S. citizens and corporations at least 75 percent owned by U.S. citizens, which had 100 percent of the directors as U.S. citizens; manufacturing plants had to be in the United States. But the act also stated (and this dealt with the difficulties in determining corporate ownership) that a U.S. government contract could be made with a "domestic corporation" listed on a stock exchange, unless the secretary of war or the secretary of the navy knew that a majority of the stock was foreign owned.[445] Earlier in this chapter, I covered airplane production by companies associated with Anthony Fokker in the United States. Since his main business was with the U.S. government, it has to be assumed that his facilities qualified under this legislation.[446]

The Radio Act of 1927 created the Federal Radio Commission (FRC), which had the authority to license radio stations. This act forbade the FRC from licensing aliens, foreign governments, companies organized under foreign law, or any company with an officer or director who was an alien, or a company where more than one-fifth of its capital stock could be voted by aliens.[447] Although the law was new (and long set the basis for U.S. policies in this sphere), the principles on which it was grounded had been embedded in the 1919 arrangements made when Radio Corporation of America was organized. Indeed, later, in 1932, the then secretary of the navy would explain that the passage of the 1927 Radio Act had been "intended to preclude foreign dominance of American radio" and had arisen from "the lessons that the United States had learned from the foreign dominance of cables and the dangers from espionage and propaganda disseminated through foreign-owned radio stations in the United States prior to and during the [First] World War."[448] The restrictions on foreign involvement that were in the Radio Act of 1927 were not introduced to preserve American culture from outsiders; rather, legislators believed that for national security reasons, foreigners should not be permitted to control domestic broadcasting.[449]

The issue of "sovereign immunity" in its relation to FDI in the United States surfaced in several contexts in the 1920s, with miscellaneous and inconclusive court findings. In one case, *Oliver American Trading Company v. Government of Mexico* (1924), the plaintiff had a claim against the Mexican government-owned Mexican National Railways, and the targeted property was in the United States. The court ruled that because the railroad was owned by the Mexican government, its U.S. assets were immune from attachment.[450] On the other hand, even though the French government had an interest in the potash syndicate (through its holdings in the potash mining companies), this did not impede the U.S. government's antitrust case against the cartel, notwithstanding protests from the French ambassador.[451]

To improve the preparation of balance of payment statistics, in the late 1920s economists paid new attention to charting foreign investments—both outgoing and incoming. The first "official" (government-prepared) international balance of payments statement had been in 1922; thereafter this became an annual rite of the U.S. Department of Commerce. The 1927 balance of payment report included more than its predecessors on foreign investment in the United States, noting the difficulties in deriving good figures.[452] Despite efforts of the Commerce Department, throughout the 1920s there was no effective monitoring of foreign investments (portfolio or direct); no mandatory reporting requirements existed.

Moreover, by the late 1920s, how "American ownership" (or, conversely, "foreign ownership") was defined in U.S. laws depended on the sector: in shipping, 75 percent U.S. equity ownership was required; for aircraft registry, 51 percent; for radio broadcasting, 80 percent. The Commerce Department, while recognizing the category "direct investment" and associating it with "control," did not yet specify what percentage of the equity ownership constituted that control.[453] The percentages that defined "foreign" would, over time, in some cases be altered; they continued to lack uniformity. By the 1920s, however, it had been firmly established that equity ownership of a corporation defined its nationality, not its place of registration (thus, a company incorporated in the United States was not excluded from a "foreign" classification). This was true despite the difficulty in determining the "nationality" of owners (in addition, in some cases "residence" established nationality, and in others there was a "citizenship" requirement).[454]

Likewise, since it was assumed that directors controlled the conduct of corporations, rules had emerged in U.S. law on the nationality of the directors (and sometimes officers as well). These, too, lacked consistency: national banks (banks chartered under federal law) could be 100 percent owned by foreign individuals, but all the directors had to be U.S. citizens. Under the Air Commerce Act of 1926, two-thirds of the directors had to be U.S. citizens; in the Air Corps Act of 1926, all directors of companies obtaining U.S. government contracts were required to be U.S. citizens; in the Radio Act of 1927, the board had to be 100 percent U.S. citizens.

The reasons why in "vital sectors" (shipping, airlines, and radio broadcasting, for example) 100 percent U.S. *ownership* was not compulsory were several: (1) the attention was to control; law makers did not perceive foreign investors with small interests as a problem; (2) in some cases foreign money was desired, absent control; and (3) if the shares of a company were widely traded, it was likely that some might drift into foreign hands; administratively this would be hard to follow; moreover, with the aim of sustaining the transferability of securities and protecting property rights, there was the benefit (with no offsetting harm) in allowing limited amounts of foreign ownership.[455] Where the letter of the law seemed to require no alien ownership (as in the statement in the Mineral Lands Leasing Act of 1920 on foreigners from nonreciprocating countries), implementation related to the "spirit" of the law.[456] Laws requiring U.S. nationality for directors focused specifically on the matter of control.

In sum, all during the late 1920s there continued to be support for the preservation of what were by this time established norms in U.S. law. The navy retained its strong distrust of foreign "intervention." Occasionally concerns surfaced about the "tribute" going to European multinationals that had invested in and, indeed, created the prosperous rayon industry in the United States. America, it was defensively suggested, was fully capable of "financing and engineering" its own rayon factories.[457] This discussion was part of the late 1920s tariff debates. The press, at times, ran exposés on international cartels (and there were court cases); mention would then be made—in a derogatory manner—of foreign businesses in the United States that participated in these restraint-of-trade arrangements; the critique was more "anticartel" and "antiforeign" than specifically targeted at existing FDI in the United States.[458]

So, too, populist sentiment remained, and the "formula" vocabulary of popular discourse in the West and South was antagonistic to both eastern and British capital. State alien land laws stayed on the books, a vestige from a long-past era, and now and then they were invoked.[459] Amerada Corporation, some thought, decided to become "Americanized" to conform with Texas statutes.[460] On the whole, however, most Americans were relatively blasé toward the inward FDI.

When in May 1929 some 5,000 workers struck the two German-owned rayon plants at Elizabethton, Tennessee, the public policy response to the labor strife had nothing to do with foreign ownership. The German companies got court orders to enjoin the strikers from picketing, and the governor of Tennessee sent in 800 federally armed state militia to enforce the orders.[461] The policy would have been identical had the plants been American owned, although there was some antiforeign rhetoric by the defenders of the strikers.[462]

The one significant articulate exception to the rather general indifference to the foreign ownership in America was embodied in the views of Francis P. Garvan, president of The Chemical Foundation and formerly Alien Property Custodian. Whereas populist sentiment was antiforeign, mainly anti-British, Garvan was and remained disturbed over German business involvements in America. Whereas populist sentiment was general and nativistic, Garvan was specific and dealt with threats to America's competitive vigor. During all of the 1920s, The Chemical Foundation—through its ownership of key onetime German patents—had a major impact on chemical imports and at the same time encouraged research and manufacture by American enterprises. Data in Garvan's papers show his great dismay in the late 1920s over the reentry of German multinational enterprises, concerns that he publicized when the American I. G. Chemical Corporation was organized in 1929.[463] At that time, Garvan lashed out at its "purpose of cutting the throat of our chemical independence and safety in national defense." "The health of our children" was at peril. I. G. Farben, Garvan insisted, had been brought to America by a "group of our commission-mad bankers." The *New York Times* and others reported Garvan's German-bashing rhetoric.[464]

Garvan's papers contain a draft of a letter he wrote to Charles Mitchell, Walter Teagle, Edsel Ford, and Paul Warburg. I cannot establish whether this remarkable letter was actually mailed; if so, it had no impact on the recipients, at least none resigned as a director of the American I. G. There was no investigation at this time of American I. G., as Garvan proposed.[465] Yet, his May 1929 draft letter is of immense interest—for it dealt directly with foreign multinational companies and America's competitive position, and it defined some of the principal anxieties over intrusions by outsiders. Moreover, most of Garvan's arguments would resurface in subsequent years at numerous congressional hearings. Garvan predicted, in 1929, that the German multinational I. G. Farben would act to retard American economic progress.

He addressed each American director of American I. G. Chemical Corporation as follows: "As you may know, I am deeply concerned in furthering industrial development in our country, through the promotion of scientific research. For that reason, believing, on the basis of experience, that the admission of the German Dye Trust to this country, under the aegis of yourselves and the other distinguished gentlemen associated with you on the board of the American I. G., constitutes a threat to sustain the research of a purely national character, I cannot—in the absence of assurances that you have taken precautions to prevent the Germans making use of your position in their plan to obstruct industrial research in this country—allow their program to proceed without challenge.

"I am sure that you cannot be aware of the record of the German I. G. in the matter of hampering and obstructing scientific research in this and other countries. The Germans have allocated to themselves a monopoly of industrial progress through scientific research; their assumptions of superiority are warranted, at least in this respect—they know that leadership in the industrial progress of the future will belong to the nations whose scientists lead in the race for new knowledge of the nature and synthesis of matter, and have known it for a long time. Before the war they did not hesitate to use every and any means to block and discourage research in other countries. Is it, or is it not, significant that practically all of the progress made in this and other countries in the field of scientific research has been made in the last few years—all, or nearly all since the war and the breaking of the German grip on the chemical and related industries of the world."

After briefly cataloguing the pre–World War I German "crimes"—"everything, from theft of ideas to the use of every known device for the throttling of competition, price-cutting, bribery, tying-contracts, rebates, subsidies, and all the rest"—Garvan continued to expound on the German's "most powerful weapon," that of the propaganda of superiority: "The Germans can make purer medicine, more brilliant dyes and more destructive explosives than any other people on earth. Which, of course, is mere rot." Now, Garvan claimed, "This propaganda has reappeared. It was the meat of the newspaper stories covering your announcement of the formation of the American I. G." The reports said the combination is one of "German brains and American capital." "It is the old story."

Garvan then explained if "all were otherwise right with research in our country, it might be that we would have nothing to fear from this new invasion by the Germans. But all is not right . . . pure or fundamental science is making little or no progress in this country, and, furthermore, is being gradually undermined by the drafts that are being made upon it by industrial research . . . Industry is concerned with the application of known scientific principles to the production of goods. The little pure research that is done in our universities" was too small. Garvan noted that Americans were not making the progress of the Germans.

> I hope that none of us are credulous or naive enough to believe that the Germans will even consider sharing the knowledge gained in their laboratories with the rest of us. In a competitive world, such as we live in, they would be foolish if they did make their secrets known to other countries. Their survival as a nation, perhaps, depends upon their ability to command markets that must be won through superior technology. For the sake of immediate needs they may consent to the production and sale in this country of goods made with their processes and under their direction and control, but even now I venture that their associates in this country know nothing whatever about the fundamental secrets of the German processes.

Garvan complained about dependence on Germany, a nation "with which we must inevitably come in conflict in the field of commerce, and perhaps even of war." He told the directors that "but for your consenting to serve on the board of the American I. G., the German trust would never have dared to attempt to reenter this country . . . it knew that it needed a Greek horse to enter the citadel from which it had been expelled in disgrace, and you gentlemen have innocently, perhaps, consented to represent the horse."

After criticizing the Germans for striving for world power "through a monopoly of science," Garvan urged the directors to tell him that "my fears are groundless." Then he threatened: "In the absence of such assurances I feel it my duty to appeal to the Government for an investigation of the situation that has been created."[466]

I. G. Farben managers may have seen this letter (if it was sent); they certainly read the news reports on Garvan's views. So unsettling did the attack seem, American I. G. retained the nation's premier public relations man, Ivy Lee (recommended by director Walter Teagle of Standard Oil of New Jersey), to calm the opposition.[467] Lee had, for many years, done public relations work for John D. Rockefeller, Jr.[468] The fury Garvan sought to generate did not spark a reaction—at least in the summer of 1929. There were in the late 1920s other matters on the minds of Americans. FDI in the United States was not a top priority.

6.

A Time of Anguish, October 1929–March 1933

Newspapers in the United States in August 1929 ran stories on British and German purchases of American securities. One investment banking house noted more than $20 million in sales abroad of securities of a single U.S. company.[1] Reports from Amsterdam indicated that buying of American stocks was occurring with an enthusiasm comparable to prewar demand. As European acquisitions of American railroad shares rose, a banker forecast that should this continue, foreign holdings in U.S. railroads would reach as high as before the war. Canadian investors were also being drawn to Wall Street.[2]

In contrast, in the summer of 1929, managers of certain Scottish investment trusts were said to have read a circular for the Blue Ridge Corporation and found it preposterous: if Americans could "swallow this," then the "country has surely gone mad." The time to divest had come.[3] Such sales countered the general trend. During the summer and early fall of 1929, foreign purchases of American securities far exceeded selling.[4]

Ramsay MacDonald had become British prime minister in June 1929, and after the general elections, wealthy Britishers had been uneasy about the Labour leader. In the third quarter of 1929, British common stocks fell in value; the slide became particularly evident after the "Hatry failure." Clarence Charles Hatry, a British company promoter and financier, had participated in the late 1920s in a number of high-wire financial dealings through his Austin Friars Trust Ltd. and his Corporation and General Securities Ltd.; it was his pyramided empire that had crumbled. Beginning on Thursday, September 19, 1929, the Hatry scandal became public knowledge.[5] The next day, there was a sharp decline on the New York Stock Market. The latter was affected, since the British, to meet their home obligations, sold their high-priced liquid American securities. Several years later, in 1933, *Fortune* would call the Hatry bankruptcy "the Sarajevo of the Depression."[6]

New York Stock Market values had peaked on September 3, 1929; the attrition, for a while, had been orderly. The first major break in the New York Stock Market occurred after the "large withdrawal of funds to London"—stimulated by the Hatry crisis—and the slump in stock values in New York continued thereafter, encouraged even more by the increase from 5.5 to 6.5 percent in the British Bank Rate (on September 26).[7] The historian of the Bank of England R. S. Sayers believes that the "Bank Rate was raised in the shadow of, but not because of the Hatry crash. It was raised to deal with [British speculation on] Wall Street."[8]

Among the many contemporary explanations for the New York Stock Market plunge in October 1929 was that it was triggered by the withdrawal of foreign, especially British, money.[9] A *Fortune* writer summed up contemporary views: "It is a quite tenable thesis that the British [sales of securities] precipitated the New York Stock Exchange Crisis of 1929. A relatively small amount of real cash definitely withdrawn from a paper market can cause results out of all proportion to its volume."[10]

In the same spirit (and barely a week after Black Thursday, October 24, 1929), Lord Norman, governor of the Bank of England, had reported to that bank's Committee of the Treasury (on October 30, 1929) that the increase in the Bank Rate to 6.5 percent on September 26 "seemed largely to have contributed to the changes that had since taken place on the New York Stock Market."[11] It was commonly accepted that since investors went where the yields were highest, the rise in the Bank Rate meant British liquid moneys returned home. Both money in the call loan market (i.e., short-term) and that invested in equally liquid traded securities flowed from the United States. The line between "short-term" (call loans and short loans) and "long-term" (equities and bonds) blurred.[12] The Federal Reserve Board, in its *Annual Report for 1929,* stated that the exodus of gold in the closing months of the year was a result of the "liquidation of foreign holdings of American securities and the decline in money rates in the United States."[13]

In fact, how much did what occurred across the Atlantic contribute to the stock market crash in New York? How much did subsequent foreign selling perpetuate the fall in stock market values during 1929? One economist estimated that in 1928–1929, the total value of foreign purchases and sales of American securities amounted to less than 2 percent of the total value of trading on the New York Stock Exchange.[14]

This notwithstanding, at the time, many individuals were convinced of British "causes" for the crash, some choosing to emphasize the Hatry failure and others the rise in the British Bank Rate as the primary stimulus for the American debacle. Not only Lord Norman, but a number of other reputable observers offered a similar diagnosis: foreign withdrawals "precipitated" the crash in the United States in October 1929.[15] Later, Charles Kindleberger would write that the divestments by overseas investors were part of "a chain" of happenings that finally culminated in panic. In a subsequent book, he concluded, "His [Hatry's] failure led to . . . the October crash."[16]

In general, however, the explanation that foreign (or specifically British) withdrawals caused the crash has proved unattractive. Heywood Fleisig, among other authors, has noted that the actual amount of foreign investment in American securities was very small relative to the total value of listings on the New York Stock Exchange. "I suspect even the most diehard operationalist would entertain the suspicion that foreign liquidation would be insufficient to reverse a bull market sustained by domestic buying"; accordingly, he continued, "the suggestion that the stock market collapse was triggered by foreign selling . . . [is] quite unlikely."[17]

John Kenneth Galbraith went further, debunking "the lore of 1929" that "the unmasking of Hatry in London . . . struck a sharp blow to confidence in New York." Galbraith does not mention the higher British Bank Rate. He writes, "What first stirred . . . doubts [in the bull market] we do not know, but neither is it very important to know."[18] Surely, Galbraith was wrong here; it *is* useful to know whether America's involvement in the international community created an extra vulnerability and whether it had impact.

Did *subsequent* foreign selling (and foreign selling that was not only from Great Britain) in November and December 1929 accentuate the persisting downturn in stock prices? No one has suggested (much less argued) that investors from abroad behaved in a countercyclical manner. Perhaps because they had bought less on margin and had higher down payments, they may have been slower to liquidate.[19] Yet the evidence for this is not conclusive. Some foreign investors' holdings were heavily leveraged.[20] Perhaps because they had less information than Americans, foreign holders of American securities were slower to sell. This does not seem to be the case. All available data indicate that after the crash, foreign investors behaved exactly like domestic ones, that is, they were bearish, and many rid themselves of their American securities in the last months of the year. Fleisig has argued that because of sheer numbers, "domestic sales were more depressing than foreign sales," but since both domestic and foreign sales were to domestic buyers, "domestic *purchases* were more important than foreign purchases in supporting the market."[21]

My own conclusion is similar to that of Kindleberger's, that is, that the retreat of foreign investors prior to the stock market crash (and on Black Thursday October 24 and the next week) should be included as one among many factors in the bursting of the stock market bubble. Their retreat may have had a special impact, affecting the timing of crash, but I would not wish to set up the counterfactual that without the late September and October foreign withdrawals there would have been no crash; I am convinced that the highly inflated market bubble would have burst, foreign investors aside. As for the second issue, the subsequent selling in November and December, which continued the stock market slide, I think foreign liquidations had the identical overall negative consequences as those of domestic investors.[22]

The first reaction to the falling prices on Wall Street was, as one economist put it, "a feeling of relief in Europe." The boom in stock market values had diverted—it was believed—U.S. and foreign capital *to* New York, moneys that otherwise would have been lent, or so it was assumed, to Germany and other debtor nations. Thus, the initial expectations were that the effect of the Wall Street decline would mean *more* U.S. lending to Europe and the rest of the world. The opposite proved true. Since much of the bull market had been financed on margin, when stock prices tumbled, brokers sold out the speculators; there were no American "surpluses" to be reallocated for lending abroad. The Wall Street slump, in addition, made Americans distrustful of all securities, foreign and domestic alike; in fact, foreign ones seemed especially suspect (Americans had long been distrustful of what occurred outside the country). So, too, Europeans who repatriated their funds added little to their own countries' (or global) needs; many such holders of American securities took losses and found themselves in financial difficulties.[23]

The Tariff

During the 1929 U.S. tariff hearings, certain American companies had lobbied for higher duties, a regular part of the domestic political agenda. The desires for and receptivity toward greater protection were magnified in 1930 as economic malaise followed in the wake of the Wall Street crash. In bad times, American legislators have often found tariff solutions attractive, putting the onus of the bad times on "outsiders." Just as Americans had been quick to blame "foreigners" for the Wall Street crash, so, too, they were prepared to pull in the wagons and turn nationalistic. In June 1930 the U.S. Congress enacted the Smoot-Hawley Tariff, raising the tariff wall.

Included among the manufacturers in the United States that had sought protection from imports were the foreign-owned rayon producers. In the tariff debate, Senator Burton K. Wheeler, a Democrat from Montana—in a traditional populist formulation—railed that to increase rayon cloth duties would benefit foreign direct investors, who were making "huge profits in the United States and sending the money back to England and other foreign countries." The senator ridiculed those who favored the tariff as "protection of American labor." Quite the contrary, he insisted, the foreign-owned companies had "been paying the laborers . . . a most meager pittance, scarcely a living wage." And, in a specific reference to labor strife at the German-owned American Glanzstoff plant in Tennessee, Wheeler declared, "They will not permit union labor to be employed there." This would be true, of course, in 1929–1930 of practically all plants in Tennessee—foreign and domestic—but the senator's attack was directed specifically at the foreign-owned rayon producer. He next appealed to a different constituency. The tariff, he claimed, would not help the American farmer: "God help the American farmer! We ought to draw away the mask and say . . . 'we are here legislating in the interest not only of the great trusts of the country but of the Courtaulds of London, this foreign-owned and controlled American Viscose Co.,' that has for its emblem, if you please, the British crown."[24]

Wheeler stressed that for Congress to enact the projected high duties would take money away from "the people who wear rayon clothes" and put it "into the pockets of the Viscose Co." and the other foreign-owned enterprises. He repeated that the American Viscose Company's trademark was the British crown: "Why should the British crown not be the trade-mark of the American Viscose Co. when the American people are digging down in their pockets to keep it going."[25] The Montana senator's rhetoric echoed the antipathy long expressed by western farmers, an antagonism to foreign, particularly British, capital.[26] The hostility was to royalty, to the Crown, to Old World aristocracy, all of which were seen as antithetical to American democracy.

Wheeler's views failed, however, to prevail; his Senate colleagues voted for protection for the rayon companies and also the many other supplicants. Senator Royal Copeland of New York spoke up strongly on behalf of the rayon tariff, insisting that even were "the ownership . . . 100 per cent foreign . . . the plants are here . . . are operated by American workmen." Copeland added if duties were not boosted the result would be that small, nonforeign, U.S.-owned rayon companies would go out of business, "putting ourselves wholly into the hands of the foreign group."[27] These comments were a bit disingenuous, considering that by this time the leading U.S.-owned rayon producer, Du Pont, was anything but a "small" company.[28]

Senator Furnifold McL. Simmons of North Carolina accepted that "a large part of the capital invested in the rayon business here is foreign capital. I regret that it is not all American capital, but I do not think we ought to deprecate the fact that foreigners are willing to come and invest their money in this country in developing the production of a very essential commodity. The communities in which rayon factories are located benefit just as much . . . I do not see any particular difference [between foreign and American capital] so far as the effect on the community is concerned."[29] Protection, this senator believed, would keep jobs in America.[30]

The controversy over the rayon tariff, while specific to one industry where foreign investors had a notable presence, is significant in its presentation of existing attitudes toward foreign companies in America in 1930: we did not like them, but if they provided work for Americans, many felt they should be tolerated and even favored. In addition, the disagreements over this section of the tariff bill mirrored other more general concerns. While there was opposition to the Smoot-Hawley Tariff for traditional reasons (freer trade rather than higher duties was desirable, since America was a net exporter of goods; increases in tariffs would provoke retaliation and impair U.S. exports; higher tariffs were bad for the consumer, raising domestic prices), while senators from many rural states saw the raised tariffs as sheltering industry at the expense of farmers, and while there were further objections such as those voiced by Wheeler, just as the principal views expressed in this segment of the debate had favored protection of the rayon industry, so, too, across-the-board, protection had a popular appeal, which motivated congressional passage of the high Smoot-Hawley Tariff in June 1930. At the core of the support was the prevailing belief that high duties would safeguard employment.[31]

The result of the enactment of the Smoot-Hawley Act was, as everyone anticipated, lower imports. With no dollars to pay interest on their loans, foreigners defaulted. U.S. exports plummeted as countries abroad retaliated and protected their own domestic markets.[32] The new tariff, instead of aiding the ailing American economy, as intended, made matters worse. It served to detach the United States from the benefits of world trade. As a consequence, Americans became ever more parochial, more sensitive to looking after their own national interests, devoting themselves—as the isolationist Senator William Borah of Idaho put it—"to our own people."[33] On the other hand, like earlier tariffs, the high Smoot-Hawley Tariff did encourage some foreign firms to jump the tariff barrier and to invest in manufacturing in the United States. But this response was muffled by the absence of a healthy U.S. economy; there is no sense vaulting a tariff barrier if behind that wall there is not a promising market.

The Deepening Depression, 1930–1931

Economic historians have long argued over the connection between the Wall Street crash in October 1929 and the subsequent Great Depression.[34] There may have been a cause-and-effect relationship between foreign investors' behavior and what happened to stock prices, but that does not specifically address the role of foreign investors (if any) in the subsequent downturn in the American economy. Though this is not the place to review the causes of the Depression, it is important for our purposes to consider whether the latter was "almost entirely homegrown," as maintained, for example, by Gottfried Haberler and many others, or whether global relationships, particularly as associated with inward foreign investment, made a difference.[35] In this context, it is of interest to read in the U.S. Department of Commerce's study of the nation's balance of payments in 1929 (dated May 1930): "That American prosperity will continue for many years, with no protracted setbacks, is seemingly one of the few predictable things. The resulting increased yield on existing foreign investments here is an important element in any consideration of our future balance of payments."[36] Of course, the Commerce Department misunderstood the "setback." In 1930 and 1931, economic conditions worsened.

Without question the size of foreign investment in the United States was far too small to be the sole culprit for the U.S. descent into economic distress. But was it a culprit at all? Also, as Peter Temin has insisted, "purchases of shares on the stock exchange do not represent investment in the Keynesian sense. They are transfers of ownership, not allocations of real resources."[37] Thus, to the extent that foreign investors (portfolio investors) sold securities, their impact on "investment" was indirect. If the cause of the Depression was faulty monetary policy in the United States and the United Kingdom, as some economic historians have insisted, I will show where the story of foreign investors fits. The connections are not straightforward. I am not able to show that investors in the United States exercised a major influence—as inward foreign investors—on maintaining the gold standard or on central banking policy. Yet foreign investors were swept up in and part of the story line.

Foreign investors reacted to what was occurring in America; with some few and often temporary exceptions, their responses—at least during 1930, as in the last two months of 1929—coincided closely with those of U.S. domestic investors.[38] During 1931, however, there were significant divergences in the rationales behind foreign and domestic investors' behavior, which stemmed from the crises in Europe, the imposition by foreign nations of exchange controls, and particularly in September 1931 the devaluation of the pound sterling.[39] In addition, both during 1930 and 1931, notable dissimilarities surfaced in the patterns between inward foreign portfolio and direct investors in America, even though each set of foreign investors was affected by the troubled economy. Once more, I am clearly writing on "effects" rather than "causes." Foreign investors were small players in the overall macroeconomic changes.

As in times past—albeit now shaped by the special circumstances of 1930 and 1931—foreign portfolio investors in American securities were motivated to buy or sell by (1) the market price of securities (to buy if they perceived bargains; to sell if they could obtain gains or halt losses); (2) exchange rates (e.g., to buy if they anticipated a future strengthening of the dollar, or to buy if the dollar was strong and would stay strong vis-à-vis their own currency, so as to assure the value of future returns; alternatively, to sell if the dollar was strong vis-à-vis their own currency so as to register immediate gains in their own currency or, if the dollar's decline was expected, to stop losses); (3) interest rates in the United States relative to those abroad (for instance, to buy if yields seemed relatively high in the United States; to sell if interest rates seemed relatively low); (4) their existing holdings (purchases and sales were highly dependent on when securities had been acquired);[40] (5) perceived "real" value of assets (adjustments for relative prices in the United States and in their home country); (6) where present, foreign governments' exchange controls or likely ones (to buy or to hold American securities if they anticipated a future inability to buy); and (7) general expectations on (and interpretations of) the overall political and economic business environment. In addition, more specifically, the tax consequences of purchases and sales varied by country and investor and in certain cases influenced investors' decisions to buy or sell.[41] Add to these items, different foreign portfolio investors had diverse information, and since they came from separate countries, the realities were different as well. Thus there was far from uniformity in the conduct of foreign portfolio investors. None of the preceding rationales for investment was unique to or new to this period, and at times certain ones were not relevant. In 1930–1931, with the rising nervousness and based on these considerations, in net there came to be pullbacks in foreign portfolio investors' holdings in the United States, both in the quantities of securities owned and in their market value. There were purchases as well as sales, but far more sales than purchases by foreign portfolio investors.

As for foreign direct investors in 1930 and 1931, most stopped new involvements and decreased existing ones in the United States because of the general reduction of U.S. (and worldwide) demand for goods and services. Some retreated entirely from their U.S. investments. Some new arrivals were designed to jump the tariff barrier; others were differently motivated. Some, few, existing investors made new investments to cope with adversity. The cutbacks and exits offset the new entries and new investments. Overall, however, foreign direct investors' ownership of plant and equipment and their established market relationships meant they had far less liquidity than the portfolio investors. Foreign direct investors were not very sensitive to the considerations outlined here as influencing foreign holders of securities; indeed, those factors as a group were *not* predictive of foreign direct investors' strategies.

Returning to the foreign portfolio investments, it is difficult to establish any sharp differences during 1930 in the general responses of U.S. and foreign holders of American securities—in neither case was there great confidence. In May and June 1930, when public utilities entrepreneur Samuel Insull needed capital, his biographer, Forrest McDonald, writes "There was no time to go to London."[42] In this uncertain era regular channels of finance were shut off; it was hard to obtain moneys anywhere. In December 1930, the Bank of United States in New York, with its more than 400,000 depositors, failed. Its name implied a nonexistent official status. Its demise added to the existing economic woes. This was the worst bank disaster in American history and one that received global publicity and made foreign portfolio investors ever more uneasy. Bank failures multiplied.

Yet in 1930, defying the overall trend toward retrenchment in FPI, the large Bank für Elektrische Unternehmungen (Elektrobank), Zurich, made its first large purchases of securities of American public utilities—taking advantage of the low prices in New York.[43] Elektrobank invested in American Telephone and Telegraph (an old favorite on international markets), as well as in the major U.S. power and light holding companies and their most important affiliates. Thus, Elektrobank bought stock in United Corporation (Morgan's giant grouping), Middle West Utilities (a key Insull company), and American Gas & Electric Co. (a major firm in the Electric Bond and Share group).[44]

In 1931, conditions in the American economy worsened, and the economic crisis spread to Europe. Early in the year, signs of disarray became everywhere apparent, yet—as one economist put it—"until the late spring of 1931, the depression in many respects [had] followed the course of ordinary business slumps of the past."[45] The 1930 purchases in America by Elektrobank reflected such assumptions. But in May 1931 a run took place on the Austrian bank Credit-Anstalt. The Austrian government and Credit-Anstalt's foreign creditors sought to support the bank; unable to do so, the Austrian government resigned on June 16. The Bank of England lent moneys to the Austrian National Bank to prevent the entire collapse of Austrian finance. The economic plague extended across the border to Germany.

On June 20, 1931, President Herbert Hoover, aware of Germany's now precarious financial situation, proposed a one-year moratorium on German reparations and on other intergovernmental war debts.[46] Since without German reparations, World War I intergovernmental Allied debts could not be serviced, much less repaid, the moratorium had covered these huge obligations to the U.S. government; all through the 1920s, Americans had insisted that these debts had to be repaid; now the U.S. government was reluctantly making a "temporary" concession to the reality. However, there was nothing temporary in what happened. Germany never resumed payments of reparations. Except for token amounts (and Finland, which continued to pay in full), the Allies would, in turn, default on their World War I debts to the U.S. government. The $11.7 billion of U.S. government credit would evaporate.[47] What did *not* evaporate, however, was the anger of many Americans at the defaults, which would cast a dark cloud over American policies throughout the 1930s.[48]

German economic disorder was neither alleviated nor remedied by the moratorium. On July 13, 1931, the Darmstädter und Nationalbank (the Danat Bank) closed; a run on other German banks followed. That nation's financial houses shut down (not to resume normal operations until August 5). German capital that had been fleeing the country because of the adverse economic outlook now left in far greater quantities (some perhaps going to the United States). The German government imposed exchange controls, seeking to halt capital exports. Sophisticated Germans figured out means of evading the rules.[49] Anticipated and then actual controls seem to have resulted in more German portfolio investment in the United States.[50]

The August 1931 German exchange controls froze British short-term assets in Germany; the pound showed weakness; the Bank of England stepped in to support the British currency.[51] The British considered whether long-term private British assets in the United States could be mobilized to defend the pound.[52] During World War I (not that many years past and well within policy makers' memory), dollar securities of Britishers had been utilized to support the exchange rate. Was that possible now? On August 24, the British government secretly sold certain dollar securities that it owned, trying desperately to maintain the value of the pound and to hold to the gold standard.[53]

On August 31, in a front-page story, the *New York Times* reported that Prudential Assurance Company had offered its investments in the United States to the British government "to bolster up sterling." Other British insurance companies and large investment houses were said to have followed—and "in a few hours there were ample dollar securities available to back any credit the British Government might require." Some $500 million in securities were said to have been secretly mobilized in that few hours.[54] To contemporaries, the news sounded like a replay of the summer of 1915. Yet the next day the *New York Times* ran a retraction: "Wall Street bankers" denied "that such a mobilization of foreign holdings had played any part in the extension of $400,000,000 credits to the British Government by bankers here and in Paris." The article noted that whereas securities mobilization had occurred during the First World War, it was "an extreme step that was hardly warranted by the British Government's present difficulties."[55]

Several weeks later, with the suspension of the gold standard on September 21, Chancellor of the Exchequer Philip Snowden explained to the House of Commons that the subject of mobilizing American dollar securities "was one of the first points to which His Majesty's Government directed their attention" (he did not mention the August 24 sales by the British government of its own holdings). However, no plan had been developed, since "the drain" (the flight from sterling) was too rapid. Snowden held out hope that the dollar securities might well serve as a reserve for support of the exchange rate in the future.[56]

The *New York Times*, on Monday, September 21 (in two separate stories), and Wednesday, September 23, provided three different numbers on the size of British investments in the United States: (1) Great Britain had $20 billion in overseas investments, of which $3 to $4 billion were in this country; (2) Britain's total overseas investments were $25 billion, of which roughly one-third (or $8.3 billion) was in the United States! and (3) British investments in the United States were $1.5 billion. The *Times* gave no source for the first two estimates. The third, and smallest, was attributed to the U.S. Department of Commerce and contained an addendum: "in the past few months [i.e., before (and in anticipation of?) the British suspension of gold payments] this investment has been steadily growing . . . The situation is viewed [in Washington] as temporary." Clearly, no one—American or British—had any notion of the amount of short-term or long-term British holdings in the United States (the *New York Times* reports covered a range of from $1.5 billion to $8.3 billion).[57]

On September 21, the London Stock Exchange did not open. The value of the pound tumbled.[58] Even though prices of American securities were low, those British owned and purchased many years earlier (as well as those purchased in 1931 with the expectation that the pound would be devalued) showed capital gains in terms of sterling. Thus, after the British suspension of gold, the governing committee of the New York Stock Exchange predicted British (and also nervous American) sales.

So deep was the anxiety in the United States that on that day the New York Stock Exchange instituted a ban on short selling.[59] Two days later, it rescinded the order, explaining that the rule had been imposed because of the "emergency." With the London Stock Exchange closed, alarm prevailed in New York that "a sudden and demoralizing attempt would be made to liquidate American securities" on this market. By September 23, however, the London Stock Exchange had reopened. The immediate crisis had passed, but the New York Stock Exchange's governing board insisted that henceforth member firms report daily on the short positions of their customers.[60] A number of British holders of dollar securities (especially investment trusts) did divest and repatriated their capital, which contributed to a further attrition in the prices of American stocks.[61]

Early in October 1931, the New York Stock Exchange forbade short sales of stocks on the decline.[62] Hoover responded to the continuing steep fall in American stock values and the coincident rise in gold exports by arranging a series of meetings with bankers and businessmen out of which came the creation of the National Credit Corporation, which sought to strengthen the now extremely fragile American banking system.[63] Since the U.S. currency was still based on gold, frequently foreign sellers of securities would convert their dollars to gold. To halt the flight of gold abroad, the Federal Reserve raised the rediscount rate on October 9, and on October 16; as predicted, the export of gold briefly ceased.[64] The Federal Reserve, which—in the view of today's economists—should have been stimulating the troubled domestic economy, was "forced" to defend the gold standard in the United States newly threatened by the withdrawals by foreign portfolio investors.[65] At this point, even though the size of FPI in this country was unclear and probably not great,[66] it was sufficient so that foreigners' (and complementary Americans') sales after the fall in the value of the British pound did have substantial negative U.S. domestic consequences. Many economists argue that bad Federal Reserve policy was responsible for the severity of the Depression. To the extent that such policy was a response to fears of foreign divestments, there was an indirect connection between the foreign involvement and the U.S. Depression. More important, during 1930 and also 1931, neither foreign portfolio (nor foreign direct) investors contributed in any way to limiting much less reversing the tide of economic distress in the United States—and one can conclude that the presence in the market of foreign portfolio investors in 1931 probably made matters worse.[67]

The Downturn Continues

In January 1932, Congress authorized the Reconstruction Finance Corporation to help prop up the domestic economy. In February the first of the Glass-Steagall Acts passed Congress. It extended the powers of the Federal Reserve; one goal was to enable the Federal Reserve to offset further foreign withdrawals that were leading to gold exports and the contraction of domestic credit. These policies notwithstanding, 1932 saw a further deterioration in economic conditions in the United States. The stock market's nadir was reached in June 1932, when stock prices averaged less than 16 percent of their September 1929 high.[68] The American economy was in shambles. Unemployment was at an all-time peak. Late in 1932, bank failures multiplied.

During the first half of 1932, British and other foreign investors had feared the United States would not be able to maintain gold payments. As a consequence, there were—according to a November 30, 1932, memorandum prepared by the Federal Reserve Bank of New York—"periodic reports of the sale of American securities by British investment trusts and by other foreign holders" that intensified the uneasiness of policy makers.[69] The Federal Reserve still lacked the ability to counter such withdrawals—despite its new powers under the Glass-Steagall Act of 1932. Also, no one had adequate information on the size of the foreign stakes, which contributed further to the uncertainty.

To compound problems, in the spring and summer two major financial collapses shook world confidence: those of the "empires" of Ivar Kreuger (after his March 12 suicide) and of Samuel Insull (the unraveling began April 7; he resigned from his executive and directors' positions on June 6). Both bankruptcies hurt foreign (as well as domestic) investors in the United States. Both had international ramifications, affecting inward FPI and FDI. To the public in 1930 and 1931, Kreuger and Insull had seemed strong and invulnerable.

During 1930 and 1931, the "Swedish Match King," as Kreuger was called, had enlarged his business in America. In its 1929 director's report, Swedish Match Company noted that since it was likely U.S. customs duties would rise (that the Smoot-Hawley Tariff would be enacted), "The International Match Corporation has therefore been making arrangements to manufacture in the United States."[70] International Match Corporation was Kreuger's principal U.S. holding company. By the end of 1929, Kreuger already had a fifty-fifty joint venture (in the Ohio Match Company) with the U.S. match industry giant Diamond Match Company. In 1930, when his "partner" was in financial distress, Kreuger came to the rescue. In January 1931 he acquired 350,000 shares (for $13 million) in a reorganized Diamond Match, which gave the Swede a one-third interest in America's largest match producer. In March 1931, Kreuger bought a majority of the shares in Federal Match Corporation (an independent U.S. match manufacturer), as well as control over several smaller U.S. producers of matches and raw materials used in match making.[71] By mid-1931, with these acquisitions, Kreuger had FDI in businesses representing 92 percent of U.S. match output, a commanding position in the American market (see Table 6.1). Today the match industry is relatively insignificant; in 1931, when most Americans smoked and many Americans had gas stoves, the match industry was central. No American home was without matches. But the match business and these FDIs were only a part of Kreuger's activities; he was also deeply involved in using American moneys to lend to foreign governments.

Many foreign (as well as domestic) investors had purchased International Match Corporation and Kreuger & Toll securities. In January 1931, in the midst of the Depression, International Match Corporation could offer successfully, in New York, a $45.6 million new securities issue, such was the confidence in this enterprise.[72] All during 1930 and 1931 and even immediately after Kreuger's suicide on March 12, 1932, his sprawling enterprises appeared prosperous. Reporting on his death, the press heaped praise on this financial "genius." Less than a month later, however, the public heard about fictitious assets, auda-

Table 6.1. The Swedish Match Group's percentage of total U.S. production, June 1931 (percent of U.S. production by the specified company provided in parenthesis)

Principal U.S. producers	% U.S. output
I. Swedish Match Group—Controlled companies[a] (Federal Match, 8%; Ohio Match, 17%)	25
II. Swedish Match Group—Large minority holding[b] (Diamond Match, 67%)	67
III. Outsiders	8
Total U.S. production	100

Source: Håkan Lindgren, *Corporate Growth: The Swedish Match Industry in Its Global Setting* (Stockholm: LiberFörlag, 1979), 356, 421n.18.

a. 50 percent ownership or greater.

b. Less than 49 percent ownership.

cious forgeries, and massive fraud.[73] Innocent, unsuspecting investors had been duped. Naively, they had accepted secrecy. There had been no effective monitoring of Kreuger's corporate architecture.

As the exposures multiplied on Kreuger's misdeeds, the public became more wary of the networks of international banks, which had endorsed Kreuger's securities. Donald Durant, a partner of Lee, Higginson & Co. (Kreuger's bankers, brought down with the fall of his empire), told a Senate committee in January 1933 how well-established financial institutions throughout Europe, and he provided a roster of great banks, had had full confidence in Kreuger.[74] Who now was to be trusted? George O. May, of the accounting firm Price, Waterhouse, which was investigating and documenting the dimensions of the scandal, groaned, "I do not suppose there has been anything to compare with it since the South Sea Bubble [of 1720]."[75]

Samuel Insull's bankruptcy in 1932 also involved foreign investors in the United States, but in a different manner. Kreuger himself was a foreign investor, and to Americans he tainted all foreign investors by his fleecing of Americans and Europeans alike. Insull was born in England, although his long years in America made him very much of a "U.S." success story. As an entrepreneur, Insull had built up and found financing for public utilities throughout the American Midwest. His headquarters was Chicago. Forrest McDonald explains how Insull had avoided "Wall Street," turning instead principally to American individual investors throughout the country (and also to London financial institutions, Canadians, and other foreign investors). In 1930, however, Insull had (of necessity) turned to New York City financial institutions for capital.[76] To outsiders, during 1930–1931, his public utilities seemed in fine condition.

Insull was in New York on April 7, 1932, to discuss the refinancing of a $10 million note (soon to come due) of one of his companies, Middle West Utilities. In New York, he visited with representatives of Robert Fleming & Co., London, and Sun Life Assurance Co. of Canada; they discussed a syndicate to refinance the note, arrangements that failed to materialize. Insull's loyal friends from Britain and Canada were not able to help him out, and New York banks would not. As McDonald put it, "For the want of ten million dollars, a billion and a half dollar corporation went under."[77] Insull's public utilities empire toppled, and on June 6, 1932, Insull resigned from his chairmanships, presidencies, and the receiverships of roughly 60 corporations.[78] A few years later, Insull would write in his memoirs, with bitterness and regret, that had he paid less attention to London bankers and more to New York ones, when "the troubles came in 1932," he would have been better off.[79] Foreign portfolio investors (and they were numerous) in Insull companies saw a major drop in the value of their U.S. holdings.

Indeed, with dismal economic conditions in the United States, many foreign (along with domestic) investors saw the value of their American stocks and bonds plummet. This was true of Robert Fleming's Investment Trust Corporation and of the Montreal-headquartered Sun Life Assurance Co. and explains why they were unable to come to Insull's aid.[80] His collapse had adverse consequences for foreign institutional investors in his securities.

The Kreuger and the Insull bankruptcies had both real and symbolic impacts on foreign (and domestic) investors' views of America, reinforcing the economic gloom. Nothing seemed sacrosanct any longer. If Kreuger and Insull could fail, where was the hope? Even so, in the summer of 1932 and again in early 1933, so depressed were the prices of American securities that some foreign portfolio investors concluded that they could fall no further and made purchases.[81]

With the election of Franklin Delano Roosevelt in November 1932 and particularly before his inauguration in March 1933, many foreign investors forecast that unlike Hoover, Roosevelt would not support the dollar. In anticipation of a devaluation, early in 1933 these investors sold much of their remaining dollar securities, the low prices notwithstanding; their sales contributed to the continuing fall in the Dow Jones indicator.[82] In addition, British and other foreign direct investors in the United States bought gold. Thus, the British American Tobacco Company acquired $7 million in gold, while the U.S. subsidiary of the Swiss Nestlé in early February 1933 "had recently borrowed between $2 and $3 million—an amount equivalent to their total quick assets in America, which they promptly withdrew and which he [W. P. Conway of Guaranty Trust Company] has every reason to believe was used for the purchase of gold." George Harrison at the New York Federal Reserve thought that such loans were nothing but speculation, "gambling on our going off gold."[83] Foreign direct investors in the United States—with their presence in the country—were using their on-the-spot information for financial gain.

The London Stock Exchange, Institutional Investors, and Financial Conduits, Fall 1929–Spring 1933

When the British bought American securities, they typically did so on Wall Street. American railways continued to be quoted on the London Stock Exchange, although the nominal value quoted was down substantially from earlier years.[84] A collection of New York brokerage houses in London went on handling such transactions; some present in the late 1920s exited; but newcomers arrived in 1932. For example, that year the New York broker Fenner, Beane & Ungerleider opened an office in London (it also had one in Paris).[85]

By 1929 much of the FPI in the United States appears to have become "institutional investments." There had long been institutional holdings in the United States by foreign-owned investment trusts and insurance companies, as well as other financial institutions. Also, British industrial corporations had in years past typically parked their surpluses in U.S. railroad securities.[86] Nonetheless, the evidence indicates that a sizable share of the pre-1914 inward FPI in the United States was held by individuals. My research suggests that after World War I, at least until the speculative boom of 1928–1929, individual foreign investors (as well as institutions) had paid less attention than before the war to American investments. Despite the new interest by individuals in 1928–1929, in relative terms in the 1920s institutional portfolio investments seem to have grown vis-à-vis those of individuals. To the extent that there were investments in the United States by individual European residents, the holdings were, with some exceptions, by the very wealthy or the very well connected.[87] Family investors (encouraged by financial advisers) set up personal investment trusts for their American securities, and these became "institutional" investors.[88] The one sizable exception to the apparent trend toward institutional investments and concentration in inward FPI related to Canadian investors. Canadian brokers traded easily in New York. Here, too, important institutional investors and some very wealthy Canadian individuals participated.[89]

As stock market values in the United States had declined after the October 1929 crash, individuals were often the first to unload their shares—unable to sustain losses. By contrast, some foreign institutional investors with geographically diversified holdings saw opportunities with the lower prices. With the institutional investors, while some retreated, others had staying power. During 1929–1933, the trend toward foreign institutional investment over foreign individuals' investment seems to have increased.

The foreign financial intermediaries that had long taken part in transatlantic transactions faced the economic downturn, which typically did not destroy but often weakened the parent. For example, Baring Brothers & Co.'s American business floundered. As early as 1928, the Barings had a bad setback: the New York trading house of L. C. Gillespie & Sons, a client of Barings for many years (since before the First World War), had gone bankrupt, leaving Barings with a £300,000 loss.[90] Much more damaging were the problems arising from Barings' association with Kidder, Peabody in the joint venture Kidder Peabody Acceptance Corporation (KPAC). Since its formation in 1922, KPAC's business in joint account acceptances had boomed—only to fall sharply in 1930. KPAC's American parent, Kidder, Peabody, was in such a financial morass that it would be reorganized under new management in March 1931.[91] Barings contributed $600,000 to help revive its longtime ally.[92] By the spring of 1931, KPAC had withdrawn from participation in the acceptance market.[93] From this point on, Barings, in effect, exited from American business, paying ever less attention to what was happening on the U.S. side of the Atlantic and marking the end of more than a century of truly intimate U.S. involvements.

N. M. Rothschild & Sons had sharply limited its role in American affairs. It—along with the French Rothschilds—was the principal investor in the Rio Tinto Company. When that British mining company had acquired shares in Davison Chemical Company, the Rothschilds had been "party to all the negotiations" and independently had obtained their own holdings—amounting by January 1931 to 14 percent of the shares in the Davison company; by 1932, the latter was bankrupt.[94] The Rothschilds had a small stake in the 1920s in Paul Warburg's International Acceptance Bank (IAB); there is no evidence of linkages after 1932 with the Manhattan Bank, the acquirer of IAB.[95] By 1933 the French Rothschilds were completely out of American securities investments.[96]

Robert Fleming, who had been actively engaged for more than six decades in American securities markets and had put his numerous trust companies into U.S. railroads and then public utilities, died in 1933. It must have been sad for him to see so many of the securities he had endorsed selling at such paltry prices. He had conducted business in America through the panics of 1873, 1893, 1907, and 1921 and had seen recoveries, which undoubtedly was for him a cause for some optimism. Unlike the Barings and the Rothschilds, the Fleming group (and its new generation of leaders) retained a specialist, Maurice Hely-Hutchinson, who was devoted to the "American side of the business." The Fleming group had direct or indirect influence over some fifty-six British investment trusts, many of which had U.S. holdings in their portfolios.[97]

Another British investment trust leader with long experience in American securities was Robert Benson & Co. Ltd. Robert (Robin) Benson, who died in 1929, had delegated substantial responsibility for U.S. and other investments to his associate Henry Vernet, who in turn died in November 1932. A new generation of Bensons (sons of Robin) took charge, and according to the company's historian, in the 1930s the sons tried to stay au courant with developments in American securities markets.[98]

During 1929–1933, the Fleming and Benson investment trusts along with other clusters of British investment trusts took part in both buying and selling in American securities markets. Most of the more experienced British investment trusts kept involved, even as the value of their holdings sunk; and with the devaluation of the pound, in September 1931, the rewards were higher values vis-à-vis sterling. The evidence suggests that the overall pattern for British investment trusts was to move away from continental European investments far more than from U.S. ones—as a share of their portfolios. A study of the geographic distribution of securities held by fourteen British trusts showed little attrition in the U.S. portion of their portfolios (from 13.3 percent in 1929 to 13.1 percent in 1933).[99] Yet the size of the portfolios was smaller; the market value in pound sterling of the investments in the United States of these fourteen trusts in 1933 was 58 percent of what it had been in 1929.[100]

In June 1932, some Scottish investment trusts were buying American securities, hoping to take advantage of the low prices. In that month, British buying was reported to represent roughly 20 percent of the New York Stock Exchange volume.[101] This was an erratic business. Investment trusts, such as the Scottish American Investment Co. Ltd., which in the mid-1920s had had as much as 67 percent of its portfolio in American securities (an exceptionally high percentage), was down to 61 percent in December 1931 and 45 percent in December 1932.[102] In early 1933, in anticipation of Roosevelt's abandonment of support of the dollar, British investment trusts seem to have done the same as all non-U.S. portfolio investors, that is, sell.

In 1929–1933, with the German economy in a sorry condition, even the very limited renewal of German portfolio investments in the United States that had occurred in the 1920s was over, all except a dribble of flight capital, avoiding exchange controls. The Speyer houses, having survived the 1919 end of Speyer Brothers, London, and having resumed the interlocking partnerships between Speyer & Co., New York, and the Frankfurt and Berlin Lazard Speyer-Ellissen, had been active in the flamboyant international financial world of the 1920s; the Frankfurt and Berlin Speyer house had been involved in the promotion of Associated Rayon Company and had major losses in that connection. The German Speyer also showed red ink on other U.S. (and non-U.S.) endeavors. In the early 1930s, Speyer & Co., New York, tried to bail out the near-ruined German partnership, and when the head of Lazard Speyer-Ellissen, Eduard Beit von Speyer, died in 1933, Speyer & Co. "acquiesced" in the liquidation of its onetime parent—a firm that had been in German-American business almost since its formation in 1836.[103]

An equally dismal transatlantic depression tale was that of the once proud M. M. Warburg & Co., Hamburg. Like the Speyers, the Warburgs had been associated in numerous international undertakings during the 1920s. Even though M. M. Warburg & Co. had little in the way of U.S. investments, its head, Max Warburg, had cooperated with his brother Paul in the formation of the International Acceptance Bank; another brother (Felix) was a partner in Kuhn, Loeb. At the start of the 1930s, M. M. Warburg & Co. was heavily in debt to the Manhattan Company (after the latter had acquired the assets, and liabilities, of IAB). By 1931, the Hamburg bank's financial problems were so acute that it seemed unlikely to be able to meet its obligations. Max's American brothers, Paul and Felix, personally lent the German bank some $9 million. Paul Warburg died in January 1932; the Bank of the Manhattan Company was reorganized, and the IAB was liquidated.[104] Subsequently, M. M. Warburg & Co. would play no role in American finance, although Max Warburg's nephew (James), who was an American citizen, stayed on at the Manhattan Bank, and Felix Warburg at Kuhn, Loeb maintained the family ties.[105]

J. Henry Schroder Banking Corporation—the New York affiliate of J. Henry Schröder, London—had, like the Speyers and Warburgs (and often jointly with them), been deeply involved in the 1920s in German loans. It and its London parent survived. But Deichmann & Co., the Cologne bank of Baron Bruno Schröder's wife's family, failed. As for the New York banking corporation (a British direct investment in America), while it had in the late 1920s been an active intermediary in bringing foreign moneys to America, this was no longer true.[106]

The 1934 edition of *Van Oss' Effectenboek,* the Dutch stock exchange manual, gave details on the amounts of common and preferred shares in American railroads held by the principal Dutch Administratiekantoors (see Table 6.2). The total value of the investments came to less than $17 million. How meager this seems when one realizes that in 1909 Dutch interests in the common and preferred shares of the Kansas City Southern alone came to $17.7 million. This table does not capture all Dutch institutional investments in America (nor all Dutch investment in general), but it reveals how the once huge U.S. railroad holdings by these investment funds had shrunk.[107]

Elektrobank, which had become a new owner of American securities in 1930, continued throughout this period to list American public utilities in its securities portfolio. It did not publish the market value of these particular securities in its *Annual Reports,* clearly uneasy about revealing to its shareholders the declines in the value of its holdings. Its behavior as a new entry and as a significant ongoing investor was a rarity; Elektrobank in these depression years did undertake new involvements in American public utilities; it believed that these were solid stocks that would in time rise in price, and all it needed to do was wait.[108]

Table 6.2. Holdings of Dutch Administratiekantoors in American railroads, 1932–1934

Railroad	Type of shares	Value (in U.S. dollars)	Year
Chicago Great Western	Common	129,500	1934
Chicago, Milwaukee, St. Paul & Pacific	Common	52,588[a]	1934
	Preferred	542,000	1934
Kansas City Southern	Common	33,136[a]	1934
	Preferred	708,576[a]	1934
New York, Ontario & Western	Common	1,474,000	1932
Norfolk & Western	Preferred	180,900	1933
St. Louis & San Francisco	Common	1,318,300	1933
	Preferred	605,400	1933
Union Pacific	Common	5,230,000	1933
	Preferred	2,890,000	1933
Wabash	Common	3,299,300	1933
	Preferred	485,000	1933
Total		16,948,700	

Source: Van Oss' Effectenboek 1934, courtesy of Dr. Augustus J. Veenendaal.

a. The source left blank the value of Chicago, Milwaukee, St. Paul & Pacific common shares but did give the total number held as 12,020; it also left blank the value of the common and the preferred shares of the Kansas City Southern but gave the number of common shares held as 2,705 and the number of preferred shares as 44,286. I calculated the dollar amounts in the third column based on the closing "bid" as of June 29, 1934.

In Japan in January 1930, the nation's embargo on gold exports (imposed in 1917) was lifted, and belatedly Japan restored the gold standard. When, in September 1931, Britain went off gold, most Japanese institutional investors knew Japan would soon follow. The Mitsui Bank and Mitsui & Co.—along with other Japanese firms—rushed to buy dollars.[109] When the Bank of Japan allowed the Yokohama Specie Bank to sell dollars, seven of the ten largest buyers (between September 1931 and March 1932) were Japanese.[110]

The New York office of the Osaka securities house Nomura Securities Ltd. at once got orders from its head office: "Buy at Market."[111] Japan's interlude with fully convertible currency proved brief. On December 14, 1931, Japan suspended the gold standard, "after having lost a large amount of gold as a result of flight capital to the United States."[112] From January 1930 to December 1931, Nomura Securities Ltd. had been a buyer not only of dollars but also of dollar-denominated bonds. Its company history reports that the Japanese Capital Outflow Prevention Act of 1932, along with the foreign exchange laws that became effective in May 1933, "made Nomura's dealings in New York increasingly difficult. As a result, [the firm's] foreign bond deals decreased to such a level that the [New York] office became unviable." It would close on December 31, 1936.[113] The experience of the other Japanese securities house in New York, Fujimoto Securities Ltd., seems to have been similar. Apparently, it shut down its New York office even earlier, in about 1933.[114] By 1932–1933, Nomura and Fujimoto were no longer buying, and were probably selling, American domestic and dollar-denominated foreign securities. Their transactions were not material in relation to the U.S. market.

Some of the largest foreign institutional participants were Canadians. Companies such as Dominion Securities and Sun Life Assurance saw the value of their U.S. holdings fall sharply. They did not retreat entirely, weathering the American downturn. These were conservative investors who stayed the course.

A later reconstructed index suggests that inward foreign portfolio investors were harder hit by the stock market decline than their American counterparts (see Table 6.3). This finding would not be surprising, since foreign investors as a group had less information than their domestic counterparts, and, also, their decisions were affected by exchange rates and other considerations outside the United States, making them less attuned to the U.S. market and more vulnerable to loss. (The argument here is that investors who are motivated only by domestic market considerations will be, by definition, more able to engage in prudent strategies than ones who have to take into account a number of additional exogenous elements.) Some new purchases by the foreign institutional investors (and foreign individuals) notwithstanding, there seems no question that between October 1929 and March 1933, FPI in the United States was reduced—measured by both price and quantity.

Table 6.3. Average year end prices of foreign-held common and preferred shares of American corporations compared with average prices of all issues listed on the New York Stock Exchange, 1929, 1932, 1933 (in dollars with index numbers in parenthesis)

Type of shares	1929	1932	1933
Foreign-held stocks listed on New York Stock Exchange			
Common shares	87.00 (100)	21.00 (24)	28.00 (32)
Preferred shares	94.00 (100)	34.00 (36)	42.00 (45)
All stocks listed on New York Stock Exchange			
Common shares	55.25 (100)	16.04 (29)	24.33 (44)
Preferred shares	77.50 (100)	35.28 (46)	41.81 (54)

Source: U.S. Department of Commerce, Bureau of Foreign and Domestic Commerce, *Foreign Investments in the United States* (Washington, D.C., 1937), 100.

Foreign Direct Investments, October 1929–March 1933

The economic malaise in America was more profound than in any other major nation. At the end of 1932, U.S. manufacturing activity was a little more than half its 1929 level (see Table 6.4). The country's large agricultural sector was in desperation as farm product prices plunged. The prices of minerals also dropped, along with the general deterioration in commodity prices. Profits evaporated. Many businesses failed. Foreign direct investors are attracted by opportunities that were now sharply curtailed throughout virtually all of the U.S. economy. Nonetheless, there were new foreign direct investments.

While some foreign firms in the United States retreated, others tried to reposition themselves for what they believed would inevitably be better times. Many had losses in all these years, but they continued, hopeful about the future and recognizing the importance of participating in what was still a large American market (moreover, at times exit with a satisfactory return proved impossible, given the unfavorable conditions). More firms stayed than left, and those that remained were generally ones with sufficient resources to take a long view. A few foreign companies were able to take advantage of U.S. adversities and buy bankrupt U.S. businesses. In certain instances the Smoot-Hawley Tariff prompted foreign-owned firms that had been exporters (and already had established markets and sales branches or affiliates) to invest behind the tariff wall, limited immediate prospects notwithstanding. Sometimes the investments made were in "screwdriver plants" that did nominal finishing and benefited from using imports that could be valued for customs purposes at a reduced price and subject to a lower tariff rate classification. Thus, even though retrenchment was the norm among the foreign direct investors, there were exceptions. What follows is an overview by sector of the principal developments in FDI in the United States, 1929–1933. What seems apparent are the varieties of rationales (and domestic and international considerations) associated with the dynamics of the inward foreign direct investors' strategies.

Table 6.4. Indexes of manufacturing activity, United States, United Kingdom, Germany, France, world, 1929–1932 (1913 = 100)

Year	U.S.	U.K.	Germany	France	World
1929	181	100	117	143	153
1930	140	91	102	140	138
1931	122	82	85	123	122
1932	94	82	70	105	108

Source: League of Nations, *Industrialization and Foreign Trade* (Geneva: League of Nations, 1945), 134.

Agriculture

Agricultural prices collapsed. Foreign investors in farming and cattle raising lost money. The subsidiary of Fine Cotton Spinners' and Doublers', Delta and Pine Land Co., with its large cotton plantations in Mississippi, had losses in 1930–1932 that more than offset its profits in 1928–1929.[115] Imperial Tobacco, the big leaf tobacco buyer, acquired in England in 1932 a 51 percent interest in Gallaher, a heretofore independent cigarette manufacturer; in the United States, the two British firms combined forces as purchasers of American leaf tobacco, cutting the costs of their purchasing and providing the combined group with more market power that pushed down further the already depressed tobacco prices.[116]

Mining and Metals

Heterogeneous changes took place in the profile of foreign investors in the mining and processing sectors. Near its principal operations in northern California, the British firm Mountain Copper Company, Ltd., owned a gold mining property with low-grade gossan ore, which it had never developed. By 1930, this company was a producer of pyritic ore and fertilizer; its copper resources were virtually exhausted; with the economic downturn, demand for all its existing products evaporated. Thus, in 1930 it built a mill and cyanide plant to be able to use the gold ore; this was in anticipation of a new demand for gold.[117]

An entirely different route in establishing new inward foreign investment occurred in the case of American Metal Company, which before the First World War had been German owned, which in the 1920s was fully American, and which had expanded abroad during that decade and been tempted by mining prospects in Northern Rhodesia. In 1930, London-based promoter and mining engineer Alfred Chester Beatty (1876–1968) sold his *African* holdings to American Metal Company, propelling the latter into a prominent position in the Northern Rhodesian copper industry. In exchange, Beatty's investment firm, Selection Trust, Ltd., London, acquired (according to Beatty's biographer) a roughly 25 percent share holding in the American Metal Company.[118] The result of this transaction was a new British direct investment in the United States. Selection Trust became the largest single shareholder in American Metal Company.[119]

In the potash industry, where inward foreign investment was already dominant, there were new developments. The American Potash Company (in 1929 renamed United States Potash Company) had explored for potash in New Mexico during the 1920s; it was virtually alone as a domestically owned firm in this mining sector. Based on its 1929–1930 discoveries, it sought capital to begin New Mexico production (the earlier domestic potash industry had been in California). In 1930, Borax Consolidated Ltd.'s American subsidiary (Pacific Coast Borax) acquired a 50 percent interest in U.S. Potash. The London-headquartered Borax Consolidated was the largest borax producer in the United States (and in the world). This acquisition was part and parcel of its competition with the German-controlled American Potash & Chemical Corporation, the front-runner in American potash mining, which was also a producer of borax in California. Borax Consolidated had responded to the competition in its principal industry by strengthening its U.S. borax activities; now it was poised to challenge its rival in American Potash & Chemical's principal activity, potash. With its interests in U.S. Potash, Borax Consolidated was set to counterattack and to develop the new Carlsbad potash deposits in New Mexico. Borax Consolidated's investment proved a good one, and by 1932, U.S. Potash's exploration had identified a large, high-quality ore body. On June 1, 1932, U.S. Potash began to produce in New Mexico; it constructed a refinery to manufacture muriate of potash. Its low-cost potash output was competitive with imports and with American Potash & Chemical's California production.[120] Thus, as in the case of Mountain Copper Ltd. and American Metal, so too with Borax Consolidated, there was a depression-time expansion of an inward British direct investment. In this case, one large foreign-owned company (Borax Consolidated) matched its competition, which was another large foreign-owned company (the German-controlled American Potash & Chemical), a behavior pattern that fits well with a theory of oligopolistic responses.

The Consolidated Gold Fields of South Africa—through New Consolidated Goldfields—maintained its interests in America, including those in Gold Fields American Development Company, American Potash & Chemical, and Missouri Mining Company. It also became an investor in the Celanese Corporation of America. New Consolidated Goldfields had a three-man American advisory committee, with an office at 233 Broadway.[121] There is no evidence that it expanded, but also no sign of retreat.

Johnson Matthey & Company, one of the world's leading producers of platinum, had a sales office in New York, opened in 1920, to import and to sell platinum and platinum products. In 1931 this British enterprise bought J. Bishop & Co., a small and nearly bankrupt platinum manufacturer in Malvern, Pennsylvania. This was a new direct investment, probably based on import duties (and on the failure of a customer).[122]

Oil

When in 1928 the three leading international oil companies had met at Achnacarry to agree to "as is" conditions in world oil markets, they had acted in response to the "glut" in world oil supplies, a situation made far worse by the huge east Texas oil discoveries in 1930. The three giants in the oil industry—Standard Oil of New Jersey, Royal Dutch Shell, and Anglo-Persian—continued to try to stabilize and to raise oil prices, a proposition made far more difficult with the economic downturn. Royal Dutch Shell's American company, Shell Union Oil Corporation, remained an important participant in the U.S. market. With the economic distress, in 1930 Shell Union paid no dividends on its common stock.[123] It "systematically pursued" a policy of conservation in the United States, seeking to hold back production to prevent the further fall in oil prices. At the same time, it complained of "unprecedented low prices."[124] Neither it nor the other big companies were able to stem the decline in oil prices. Shell Union lost money in 1930 through 1933.[125]

In October 1931, Royal Dutch Shell's managing director, J. B. Aug. Kessler, proposed an international organization to cartelize the entire oil industry. Almost immediately, it became apparent that such a plan would conflict with American antitrust laws. Undeterred, Kessler put forth a revised set of suggestions in March 1932.[126] In Royal Dutch's *Annual Report for 1932,* the oil company complained that "efficient cooperation" to control oil output in the United States had not been achieved—despite "steps in the right direction." Its management applauded the U.S. Supreme Court's upholding of the Oklahoma Proration Statute, the Texas Law regulating crude oil production, and the proposals of the new Oil States Advisory Committee to govern oil output. At the same time, the company warned (and worried) that other measures in California, Oklahoma, and Texas did not bode well for the production controls advocated by Royal Dutch Shell's management.[127] In December 1932, with the altered worldwide economic conditions, the major oil companies revised the 1928 Achnacarry Agreement. The new arrangement, in which more oil companies participated, was (like its precursor) unsuccessful in controlling global oil markets.[128]

No oil company could afford to "stand still," as was the plan. Indeed, at the same time as the Royal Dutch Shell Group was seeking to have others limit output and was trying to raise prices, it was aggressively acquiring new American oil fields and greatly enlarging its own oil reserves (in California, Texas, Louisiana, and Kansas). Losses notwithstanding, it was too large even to consider exiting from the United States. Instead, it restructured its U.S. distribution organization to

Table 6.5. Market ranking of the five leading gasoline marketers in the United States, 1933 (% share of U.S. gasoline market)

Company	Market share (%)
Socony-Vacuum Oil Co.	9.3
Standard Oil Co. (Indiana)	8.7
The Texas Company	7.7
Shell	6.4
Standard Oil Co. (New Jersey)	6.1

Source: John G. McLean and Robert W. Haigh, *The Growth of Integrated Oil Companies* (Boston: Division of Research, Graduate School of Business Administration, Harvard University, 1954), 104. Later Socony-Vacuum became Mobil, Standard Oil Co. (Indiana) became Amoco, while Standard Oil Co. (New Jersey) would be renamed Exxon. (The Texas Company came to be known as Texaco.) Subsequent mergers created Exxon-Mobil, BP Amoco, and the absorption of Texaco into the old Standard Oil of California, Chevron.

make it more effective. Shell Union sought successfully to strengthen its competitive position in the American market (see Table 6.5).[129] It was a fully integrated company in the United States.

By contrast, Anglo-Persian Oil Company, with only a New York office, made no attempt to enter into U.S. business operations. Indeed, when Standard Oil Co. (Indiana) lowered its crude oil prices in January 1933, Basil Jackson, Anglo-Persian Oil Company's representative in New York, reported to his London home office that this created a situation "charged with dynamite."[130] Jackson wanted American companies' help in pushing up world oil prices. The major international oil companies watched carefully the trends in the price of crude—seeking to prevent a further deterioration. They had no reservations about cooperating in this regard, U.S. antitrust laws notwithstanding. Yet they failed to control the price of oil, which continued to fall.

Food, Beverages, Soap, and Cigarettes

The three largest foreign-owned food and beverage companies in the United States in 1929–1933 were the Swiss Nestlé, the British Lipton's Tea, and the British-Dutch Unilever (its forte in the United States was in soap products rather than in food or beverages). Nestlé's Food Company Inc. changed its name to Nestlé Milk Products Company Inc. in 1930; its sales remained steady, although Nestlé chocolate sales (handled by Lamont, Corliss & Co.) encountered some "sales resistance" as a result of depression conditions.[131] Entrepreneur Thomas J. Lipton, who had personally controlled the U.S. Lipton company (Thomas J. Lipton Inc.), died in 1931, at which point his estate became the British owner of this highly successful enterprise, the leading tea company in the United States. In

December 1931, Lord Inverforth (formerly Andrew Weir), representing the estate, became president of the American Lipton company.[132] Roughly a dozen other British, Canadian, and Swiss branded food and drink makers had U.S. investments, in niche markets; very few had a noteworthy market share; they did stay on through the bad times.[133]

The Depression notwithstanding, the expansion of Unilever's U.S. subsidiary, Lever Brothers Co., Boston, accelerated. In 1930, Procter & Gamble (P & G) had 40 percent of the U.S. soap market; Colgate-Palmolive-Peet, 24 percent; and Lever Brothers, 14 percent.[134] Lever Brothers was, thus, the smallest of the "Big Three," but it did rank in that top tier. That year, Lever Brothers started producing at its newly built facilities at Hammond, Indiana—described as "the most modern soap plant in the world."[135] The capital of the Boston company was raised to $20 million.[136] In 1930–1931, the firm began radio advertising.[137] In 1930 and early 1931, P & G attempted to acquire Lever Brothers, yet the extensive negotiations came to naught.[138]

The "Big Three" in the U.S. soap industry all had "sideline" businesses. For P & G it was lard replacements; for Colgate, shaving cream and toothpaste; for Unilever, margarine.[139] In April 1930, Unilever concluded that in the United States its existing margarine trade should be folded into its far more important Lever organization.[140] With the breakdown of its U.S. merger discussions with P & G, a special committee of Unilever decided (in April 1931) that its subsidiary would need to make a product in the United States to compete with P & G's Crisco; the strategy was to build a factory, on Lever Brothers' property on the Hudson River, at Edgewater, New Jersey, and to enter into the "edible trade." In 1932, Lever Brothers completed the Edgewater plant for the manufacture of shortening. Its new product was called Zesta (which in 1936 would be renamed Spry).[141] Thus, for Lever Brothers, the years of the Depression saw new plants, new product lines, and a renewed strong commitment to the American market. Lever Brothers was surely exceptional in that every year from 1930 to 1932 its net profits after taxes rose and were higher than ever in the subsidiary's history. The parent company attributed the success to Lever Brothers' American management.[142]

Another foreign multinational enterprise with branded products, British American Tobacco Co. (BAT), also invigorated its U.S. business while taking cost-cutting steps. As a consequence of the sharp drop in its U.S. sales abroad, in 1931 BAT shut down its main export plant in Petersburg, Virginia.[143] Worse, BAT's U.S. subsidiary, Brown & Williamson, with its Raleigh cigarettes, had positioned itself at the expensive end of the American domestic market; depression conditions meant that Raleigh sales fell sharply. Accordingly, at the start of the 1930s, the decision of BAT's chief executive, Sir Hugo Cunliffe-Owen, to enter the U.S. domestic market in 1926 now encountered sharp criticism from his directors, since the results had been major losses, and the losses continued to mount. (Prior to 1926, BAT had large U.S. operations for the export of leaf tobacco and cigarettes, but no U.S. domestic sales.) Cunliffe-Owen kept, however, to BAT's new strategy of seeking to sell in the United States. Its U.S. subsidiary, Brown & Williamson, introduced low-priced brands, Wings and Avalon. In 1932, Brown & Williamson reduced the price of Raleighs and of Wings and Avalon. For a brief interlude, Wings was the cheapest cigarette on the U.S. market. U.S. companies reacted swiftly to the competition.[144] Brown & Williamson was, however, aggressive, presenting in February 1933 Kool, a mentholated cigarette. Virtually overnight, BAT became a serious contender in the U.S. domestic market. In 1931 it moved its U.S. head office from New York to Louisville, Kentucky, reaffirming its pursuit of U.S. domestic sales as central to its plans. The domestic business had risen rapidly in 1932 and 1933 with the low-priced cigarettes (see Table 6.6). Thus, in 1932 BAT reopened its shuttered Petersburg, Virginia, plant to meet American domestic demand. By 1932, Brown & Williamson's domestic sales exceeded P. Lorillard's, and the British-controlled company assumed fourth place in the highly competitive American market (after American Tobacco, Liggett & Myers, and R. J. Reynolds).[145] It was still far behind the three American-owned leaders. As Table 6.6 shows, U.S. consumers were, however, becoming of increasing importance in BAT's far greater global sales. By 1933, the United States had become second (albeit a distant second) to China as a BAT market (7.4 billion sticks versus 39.7 billion sticks).[146] BAT's investments in the United States were closely linked with its global plans.

Textiles and Leather Goods

The J. & P. Coats group, which had long manufactured in the North (in Rhode Island and New Jersey), had discussed starting up new facili-

Table 6.6. British American Tobacco Co.'s U.S. cigarette sales, 1929–1933 (number of sticks and percentage of BAT's worldwide sales)

Year	Number of sticks (in millions)	Percentage of BAT's sales worldwide
1929	434	0.4
1930	259	0.3
1931	224	0.2
1932	4,578	5.1
1933	7,455	7.9

Source: Howard Cox, "The Global Cigarette," Ph.D. diss., University of London, 1990, 377.

ties in the American South in 1922 and again in 1929, but it did not build its first southern plant until the early 1930s, when it selected a site two miles from the town of Austell in rural northern Georgia, near the South Carolina border. There, its Clarkdale mill (as it was called) began operations in September 1932, a complete manufacturing unit with more than 40,000 spindles. Coats cut back but did not close its operations in New Jersey; its Rhode Island facilities remained.[147] In 1932 two existing spool-producing companies that had long been suppliers to the Coats group merged, forming the Stowell-McGregor Corporation, with headquarters in Dixfield, Maine. The predecessor firms had been "financially beholden" to the J. & P. Coats group. John B. Clark—president of Clark Thread Co. (a Coats subsidiary in the United States)—became chairman of Stowell-McGregor at the time of the merger. In 1931, the Coats group's New York headquarters was in the newly opened Empire State Building.[148]

Although the Coats group's product line included embroidery thread, it seems likely that in the early 1930s the last of the Swiss-owned embroidery-making subsidiaries in America shut down. The Swiss Stoffel & Co. had a New York office, set up in the late 1920s, to sell "fashion fabrics"; in the early 1930s, it was a "converter," contracting with U.S. printing mills to have the designs made in accord with its specifications. Some Swiss-owned silk makers continued in business in America.[149]

In addition, there was a new British entry into textile making and a new Swiss one in leather goods (both designed to manufacture behind the U.S. tariff wall). The British investor was the hosiery firm Hollins & Co., which produced Viyella cloth yarns and had since 1919 a sales subsidiary in the United States. During the 1920s, U.S. customs authorities had queried the declared price of its imports. After litigation, which Hollins & Co. lost, and given the 1930 passage of the Smoot-Hawley Tariff, in 1932 the British firm acquired mills in Forestdale, Rhode Island (renaming them Viyella Mills).[150] Bally Shoes of Switzerland had exported to America and had an existing sales subsidiary; in the early 1930s it bought J. Edwards & Co., Philadelphia, a manufacturer of children's shoes.[151]

The Czech shoe manufacturer Bata, which had also been selling imported footwear in the United States and had a chain of retail stores principally in the Chicago area, in 1933 purchased 2,000 acres of acres of land in Maryland, about twenty-five miles from Baltimore, intending to establish a major production facility. It postponed its plan to build the factory (until late in 1938), owing to the parent firm's unwillingness to commit large financial and human resources to the project.[152]

The new investments and others remaining from earlier times notwithstanding, the most prominent and biggest foreign investments in textiles continued to be those in rayon, in which industry foreign investors still held leadership. With the elevated 1930 tariff, as predicted, rayon imports had fallen sharply. The drop in imports was, however, more than offset by the rise in domestic output, based on the new plants that started up in 1929.[153] The rayon "rush" of the 1920s was over; in the early 1930s no new foreign firms entered the United States. And, on March 12, 1930, in response to the intense competition in the industry, the Belgian firm Tubize Artificial Silk Company of America merged with the Italian one American Chatillon Corporation to form Tubize Chatillon Corporation.[154]

The front-runner in the rayon industry, Courtaulds' U.S. subsidiary, The Viscose Company, had sharply reduced profits and kept losing market share. Its on-and-off efforts to enlist cooperation from its competitors failed to boost prices. All in all, 1930–1933 was not a happy time for this once seemingly blessed enterprise, nor for this once profit-coining industry.[155] Yet, principally because of the large foreign involvement in rayon, Commerce Department figures suggest that in 1933 the level of FDI in textiles was greater than in any other manufacturing sector in the United States.[156]

Glass

The French glassmaker Saint Gobain had retreated from U.S. manufacturing in 1929, prepared to divide world markets. In 1932 a small independent American glassmaker, Standard Plate Glass Company, was about to fail; Eugène Gentil of Saint Gobain, after getting permission from the International Convention (the glassmakers' cartel), bought that company's factory in Butler, Pennsylvania, for $406,000. Saint Gobain and Saint-Roch (a Belgian glass enterprise) had in 1927 organized the Franklin Glass Corporation, a commercial and financial firm, which now acquired the Butler plant that began to produce under its new ownership in 1933 (Pittsburgh Plate Glass and Libbey Owens Ford, the two American giants, had raised no objection).[157] In 1933, Saint Gobain made a new market-division arrangement with its American competitors.[158]

Chemicals

In the early 1930s, foreign firms in the U.S. chemical industry restructured many of their international alliances. Imperial Chemical Industries became more committed to its 1920s strategy of quiescence in the U.S. market, and, consistent with that pattern, in 1931 it sold to Du Pont its equity interest in its U.S. sales agency, the Dyestuffs Corporation of

America—the last remaining U.S. business in which it held a controlling interest.[159] ICI retained, however, a sizable, although entirely passive, stock holding in General Motors and its far smaller, also passive, ones in Du Pont and Allied Chemical & Dye Corporation. The value of these stock market–traded securities (especially those in General Motors) fell dramatically. Sir Harry McGowan told the group gathering at the ICI annual meeting in April 1932, "My colleagues and I have been convinced believers in the long-range wisdom of international agreements as instruments of world rationalization of industry."[160] In keeping with this approach, McGowan was often back and forth across the Atlantic—staying informed on what was happening in America.[161]

In contrast with ICI, the Belgian Solvay & Cie., the largest single shareholder—through Solvay American Investment Corporation—in Allied Chemical, became more involved in the American business. Like ICI, its management endorsed international cartels; indeed, for years Solvay & Cie. had resented Allied Chemical's independent president, Orlando Weber, who sought to set his own agenda. In 1930, the International Nitrogen Cartel had been organized, headed by Hermann Schmitz of I. G. Farben, which included Solvay & Cie. and ICI.[162] Weber, however, had built a huge nitrogen-fixation plant in Hopewell, Virginia, and had insisted on enlarging it in the early 1930s. Worse still, the plant began to export when worldwide demand was at a new low.[163] Weber's defiance of these cartel arrangements snapped the patience of Solvay & Cie. executives, who soon would start intervening to change the leadership and to force the rogue Allied Chemical into compliance with the "negotiated environment."[164]

In 1929–1933, Royal Dutch Shell was a relative newcomer to the U.S. *chemical* industry, having in the late 1920s embarked on chemical research and production in America. In 1930, it began building a new synthetic ammonia plant in California.[165] During the economic downturn, Shell Union became for the first time important in oil- and gas-related chemicals.[166] As it did so, other firms in the international chemical industry paid heed. They sought (successfully) to bring Shell Union into their cooperative accords; the parent, Royal Dutch Shell, was amenable.

Of all the European big businesses in chemicals, I. G. Farben was the most innovative, with multiple roles in the U.S. chemical industry. At the heart of its U.S. business was the American I. G. Chemical Corporation (organized in April 1929), a holding company with two principal subsidiaries: (1) Agfa-Ansco Corporation, the film manufacturer, and (2) General Aniline Works, the dye maker; General Aniline, in turn, held a 50 percent interest in Winthrop Chemical Company, a producer of pharmaceuticals. At the depth of the Depression, Agfa-Ansco Corporation, which had never been financially strong, hovered on the brink of bankruptcy; in 1932 I. G. Farben considered shutting it down, but instead the German giant reorganized and strengthened Agfa-Ansco.[167] It did so at a time when the German economy was in deep trouble, yet it was able to find the resources to aid its American business. Unlike Agfa-Ansco, General Aniline had no comparable problems. Aided by the protection granted by the 1930 Smoot-Hawley Tariff, technologically at the cutting edge, General Aniline was able to gain market share and to prosper.[168] General Dyestuff Corporation—a separate firm—did all the U.S. marketing for I. G. Farben's imported as well as for its domestically produced (by General Aniline) dyes. The ratio of I. G. Farben's sales of made-in-America to imported dyestuff rose as General Aniline expanded its manufacturing and import substitution occurred.[169] I. G. Farben kept its earlier joint venture with Sterling Drug in Winthrop Chemical Company.[170] To all of these businesses, I. G. Farben dispatched German chemists and chemical engineers, who transferred skills and new technologies on a regular basis; other highly trained German immigrants found these companies a congenial place for employment.[171]

As for I. G. Farben's ties with Standard Oil Company of New Jersey (SONJ), the two companies came into closer harmony. The two recognized that the 1929 division-of-fields arrangements were unrealistic and decided to organize in the United States a fifty-fifty joint venture to develop so-called borderline processes (those in both the oil and chemical industries). In 1930 they formed Jasco, Inc., the Joint American Study Company. I. G. Farben "lodged" in Jasco its worldwide rights (outside of Germany) to numerous patents, including some on synthetic rubber. Each project that Jasco undertook was separate, and the company (I. G. Farben or SONJ) "turning over an invention would retain control of it as well as a five-eighths financial interest."[172] Jasco undertook research on synthetic rubber and other products, with I. G. Farben and SONJ sharing the costs.[173] In 1931 Jasco got involved with Procter & Gamble in developing a method of synthesizing fats from petroleum.[174] Jasco was I. G. Farben's second "high-tech" joint venture with SONJ (the first had been in 1929, with the Standard-I. G. Company).

Jasco's plans for synthetic rubber research took form when the price of this commodity was at a new low. SONJ, I. G. Farben, and Du Pont had begun considering the prospects for synthetic rubber in the middle of the 1920s, when crude rubber prices had soared under the impact of the 1922 Stevenson Plan (a cartel designed to help crude rubber producers).[175] By the end of the 1920s and early 1930s, as rubber prices had tumbled, for Americans there was no urgency in creating an alternative for the cheap and abundant natural rubber. Despite this, after its 1929 hydrogenation agreement with I. G. Farben, a SONJ affiliate had embarked on building facilities at Baton Rouge, Louisiana, for various new processes and products, including synthetic rubber.[176]

In 1930, I. G. Farben organized the United States & Transatlantic Service Corporation, to be renamed in April 1931 Chemnyco, Inc. This company was deputized to act through "appropriate" legal channels to obtain the return of I. G. Farben properties still held by the World War I Alien Property Custodian and to seek compensation under the 1928 Settlement of War Claims Act for its World War I losses. Indeed, according to the research of Kathryn Steen, on January 23, 1931, the War Claims Arbiter (appointed under the 1928 legislation) issued his final decision granting I. G. Farben an award of $537,555.69, which with interest since 1921 (the date of the official end of the war between the United States and Germany) came to $739,175.89. In May 1931, I. G. Farben received one-quarter of the award, but with the Hoover Moratorium (June 1931) and the breakdown of international exchanges, there were no further payments.

However, Chemnyco remained and served as a liaison office for I. G. Farben and negotiator with many American firms; it provided I. G. Farben with a window on "financial and industrial conditions in the U.S.A." Chemists from I. G. Farben, who came to America for short stays, would work out of Chemnyco's New York office at 521 Fifth Avenue or, alternatively, would be dispatched from there to SONJ's new hydrogenation operations at Baton Rouge or to other locales. Chemnyco, supported by a retainer fee from I. G. Farben, handled the U.S. expenses of I. G. Farben employees on their brief visits to this country; it acted as "a kind of traveling [travelers'] office." This became ever more important as foreign exchange restrictions were imposed by Germany. Chemnyco also took charge of the correspondence from various U.S. companies to I. G. Farben in Germany—and vice versa. Thus, in the numerous negotiations between American enterprises and I. G. Farben, someone at 521 Fifth Avenue was available to facilitate the communications (and translations) and field whatever queries (legal or technical) might arise. Chemnyco became an information-gathering firm. The retainer paid to it was approved by the German government, so as foreign exchange controls impeded travel and discussions, this office would cope with the complications. Chemnyco became and continued on through the 1930s a hub for the development of I. G. Farben's U.S. business.[177]

On June 23, 1930, at the annual meeting in London of The "Shell" Transport and Trading Company (the British counterpart of Royal Dutch and joint owner with the latter of the American affiliate, Shell

Union Oil), Lord Bearsted reported that the Royal Dutch Shell Group had been "giving great attention to processes for the manufacture of synthetic benzine" from coal or oil: "We have now arranged to join hands with the Standard Oil Company of New Jersey and the great German chemical company known as the I. G." Experience and patents on hydrogenation would be shared and "worked out conjointly."[178] On April 10, 1931, ICI joined the alliance—and an "international treaty" known as the Hydrogenation Cartel came into being. Although these arrangements (covering business only outside of the United States, for antitrust reasons) technically did not involve the new I. G. Farben joint ventures in the United States or I. G. Farben's new service company, they had broad implications for Standard-I. G. and Jasco, as well as Chemnyco.[179]

In addition, I. G. Farben in the early 1930s made further "connections" in the United States. Since Jasco would be generating new products, I. G. Farben wanted to be sure that those related to chemicals were commercially developed by the Germans' own existing (or newly established) U.S. domestic sales organizations. Thus, for example, as output of acetic acid (used as a solvent) went up at SONJ's pilot plant in Baton Rouge, I. G. Farben organized the Advance Solvents & Chemical Corporation (ASCC) to handle the sale of imports and the American-made (by SONJ) solvents as well as other organic and inorganic chemicals. Herman Metz—still active in the I. G. Farben "family" in America—was president of ASCC.[180] In 1933, Metz was writing The Chemical Foundation that Advance Solvents desired to import certain vinyl products covered by a Chemical Foundation patent. The goods were not made in the United States, and "Our customers assure us that they cannot use the products which have been offered by domestic manufacturers." Metz asked for confirmation that "we are at liberty to import these materials, subject to a royalty to you of 10 per cent."[181] When the SONJ Baton Rouge plant started production, Union Carbide (as one-third owner of the Niacet Chemical Corporation—see Chapter 5) was informed by William vom Rath of American I. G. Chemical that the Baton Rouge plant would be making acetic acid.[182] It was all very cozy and would get even cozier.[183]

In 1931, I. G. Farben formed with Pennsylvania Salt Company a fifty-fifty joint venture sales company, Pen-Chlor, Inc., to distribute within the United States a bleaching concentrate known as Perchloron. Because of high U.S. tariffs, Pen-Chlor began to manufacture in America in 1933.[184] Meanwhile, in March 1932, I. G. Farben and Aluminum Company of America (Alcoa) set up a fifty-fifty joint venture, the Magnesium Development Corporation (MDC). It was to develop and exploit processes in the magnesium and electrometal field. Alcoa had in 1919 purchased the stock of the American Magnesium Company (Alcoa was the largest U.S. consumer of magnesium used to make hard aluminum alloys). On a worldwide basis, I. G. Farben was the greatest producer of magnesium, having obtained its interest in magnesium when Griesheim-Elektron joined the group in 1925. With Metallgesellschaft, I. G. Farben shared a half interest in an aluminum plant in Germany. I. G. Farben had substantial technological know-how that it offered to MDC. In February 1933, I. G. Farben also became the fifty-fifty partner of Alcoa in American Magnesium Company (AMC), now a processing company that received its inputs from Dow Chemical Company.[185]

With Jasco, Pen-Chlor, MDC, and AMC, I. G. Farben had during 1930–1933 entered into four important U.S. joint ventures, enlarging the German enterprise's role in America. Beyond this, it had formed the new Chemnyco and the Advance Solvents & Chemical Corporation. In February 1931, Hermann Schmitz, Wilfrid Greif, and Max Ilgner (all I. G. Farben directors on the board of American I. G. Chemical) visited Wilmington, Delaware, to meet with Irénée du Pont, Lammot du Pont, and Jasper Crane. Nothing special came of this gathering, although undoubtedly the Germans briefed Du Pont officials on their conversations earlier in the month with Walter Teagle and Frank A. Howard of SONJ and on their general U.S. plans.[186]

On this trip to America Hermann Schmitz stopped by the White House and talked (on February 25) with Hoover.[187] (This was when reparation negotiations were going forth, and American bankers were warning that if Berlin refused further reparations payments, German credit would be in trouble.)[188] What is important about this meeting is not what Schmitz told Hoover (I do not know), but that it took place at all—that I. G. Farben officials had such access.[189]

In the late 1920s, to avoid taxes, like many other companies, I. G. Farben had used foreign (Dutch and Swiss) holding companies for its international business. After 1931, as German restrictions on foreign exchange transactions multiplied, it became increasingly difficult for German firms to engage in business abroad. I. G. Farben (like other German concerns) used these same holding companies in Holland, Switzerland, and elsewhere to circumvent foreign exchange controls.[190] The holding companies were financial architecture with no impact on the way international business operations were conducted. Legal structures notwithstanding, I. G. Farben managers treated their American companies as part of a multinational enterprise. Francis Garvan—the longtime critic of I. G. Farben—in 1932 had a translation prepared of Helmut Wickel's book, *I. G. Deutschland. Ein Staat im Staate* (I. G. Germany. A State within a State). He read the contents carefully, underlining key passages.[191] Americans, who knew the pre–World War I role of the German chemical industry in the United States, watched nervously as I. G. Farben's activities in America grew. I. G. Farben was by far the most significant foreign enterprise in the American chemical industry. It made major technological contributions. Its investments combined knowledge-providing and knowledge-seeking. In this time of economic hardship in Germany and the United States, its American presence expanded.

There seems little to report on the Swiss affiliates in the U.S. chemical industry in these years; Ciba, Geigy, and Sandoz remained involved in dyestuffs and a range of other products. There was at least one new German entry, the soap company Henkel & Co., which in 1932 (along with two of its German subsidiaries, Deutsche Hydrierwerke, AG, and Boehme Fett Chemie, GmbH) formed a patent holding company, the American Hyalsol Corporation (AHC). The patents were for "soapless soaps," and this prefaced the introduction of the new age of detergents and soapless shampoo. In the 1930s, AHC would license Procter & Gamble, National Aniline & Chemical Co. (a subsidiary of Allied Chemical), and Du Pont to produce under its patents.[192] Procter & Gamble boasted of its many new products that were emerging: synthetic detergents, shampoos, and liquid dentifrices.[193] Charles Tennant & Co., Ltd., Glasgow, through its subsidiary American-British Chemical Supplies Company, combined two late 1920s investments into the newly formed (1930) Kay Fries Chemicals Inc., which built a modern plant at West Haverstraw, New York (Fries' Cincinnati plant was shut down).[194]

A retreat from the U.S. chemical industry was that of the London headquartered Rio Tinto Company, which had over the years 1925–1931 invested £678,000 ($3.3 million) in its own Wilmington, Delaware, plant; the Davison Chemical Company; and the Silica Gel Company. None of these projects prospered. Rio Tinto shut down the Wilmington factory in January 1932. Davison Chemical was bankrupt by 1932; and when it reemerged from the receivership in December 1935 as the Davison Chemical Corporation, I have no evidence of any Rio Tinto (or other foreign) participation. As for the highly innovative Silica Gel Company, in 1930 Rio Tinto's management decided to withdraw, convinced that it "should not have entered the business."[195]

What is remarkable, however, was the almost complete disappearance of French interests from the U.S. chemical industry. In the early 1930s, the principal French chemical enterprises—Rhône-Poulenc and Kuhlmann—had no branches, subsidiaries, or affiliates in America. Saint Gobain had a minor role in glass, but none in chemicals. The once important Comptoir des Textiles Artificiels (CTA) no longer had any direct investments in the United States: Edmond Gillet, president of

CTA, who was a director of Du Pont, died in Paris on October 14, 1931; he had been the channel whereby Du Pont had obtained its initial rayon and cellophane processes, and probably Du Pont's link with the French Pathé. Some of Du Pont's French connections continued on, but the intimacy of the days when Gillet was active were gone forever.[196] L'Air Liquide retained a small stake in Air Reduction Company, with little say in that company's strategies.

In sum, in the years 1929–1933, certain foreign participants in the U.S. chemical industry—those of the Germans, Royal Dutch Shell, and Solvay & Cie.—raised their direct involvements; the Swiss continued on; the French, ICI, and Rio Tinto either played little part or were in retreat. The U.S.—and the world—chemical industry was characterized by an extensive network of cartels and related complex strategic alliances that had been formed over the many years and now multiplied, and that were continually being redefined. Numerous exciting new technological prospects arose within these information exchange webs. Patents were fundamental in this industry. By 1933, there were literally hundreds of international agreements in the chemical industry, involving products, processes, and companies in a range of different configurations.[197]

Pharmaceuticals

In 1928 Drug Inc. had been formed in the United States and had acquired Sterling Products (and its part of the joint venture with I. G. Farben, Winthrop Chemical Company); Drug Inc. also merged United Drug Company, Life Savers, and Bristol-Myers. But Drug Inc. failed to survive the Depression, and in 1933, Sterling Products had resumed its independence.[198] During this period, 1928–1933, there was no discontinuity in the role of William Weiss, chief executive of Sterling Products, nor in his relationship with I. G. Farben.

The newly established German-owned Schering Corporation, which had begun as a sales affiliate importing pharmaceuticals (and bulk chemicals), enlarged its innovative product lines and spent heavily on advertising. It lost money. By 1933, its management recognized that it would have to manufacture in America to reach the U.S. market. In Ampere, New Jersey, it started to produce Saraka, a laxative. Soon it would be expanding.[199] Another pharmaceutical company, the Swiss Hoffmann-La Roche, which had started manufacturing at Nutley, New Jersey, in 1929, extended its facilities there, at the same time encountering low depression prices.[200] (The American affiliates of the Swiss chemical companies Ciba, Geigy, and Sandoz all had pharmaceutical offerings.)

Farm Equipment

The books of Massey-Harris Company, Ltd. (the largest foreign-owned farm equipment maker in the United States), showed red ink in 1930 of $1.5 million—triple its 1929 profits. The next years for this Canadian firm were awful. Massey-Harris thought seriously of abandoning its entire American business.[201] The Swedish-owned De Laval Separator Co. (Lavalco) had an equally poor performance. Farmers had no purchasing power in these years. De Laval's turnover of $7 million in 1929 was down to $2 million in 1933. It stopped sending remittances home to its parent.[202]

Automobiles and Aircraft

The Rolls Royce company in America had from its origins been a source of frustration to its British parent, which decided on October 21, 1929, to stop building cars in Massachusetts, on the completion of the 2,900th U.S.-produced Rolls Royce. Rolls Royce's management thought that were the 1930 tariff high enough, output might resume. The 1930 Smoot-Hawley Tariff provided protection, but with deteriorating economic conditions, demand for luxury automobiles evaporated. By late 1930, sections of the Rolls Royce Springfield, Massachusetts, factory were being dismantled. The Massachusetts Rolls Royce company passed to total American control; finally, on August 29, 1934, under pressure from its ex-British parent, the company changed its name to the Springfield Manufacturing Company.[203] The Rolls Royce car was no longer made in America.

Meanwhile, the British small-car maker Sir Herbert Austin was in 1929–1930 temporarily optimistic about his plans for the American Austin, a narrower and shorter vehicle than any existing made-in-America model.[204] Although 80 percent of the stock of the American Austin Car Company was in the hands of U.S. citizens, close cooperation existed between the U.S. and British factories in getting production under way, and Austin Motor Co., Ltd., always referred to this venture as "its American plant."[205] On May 21, 1930, production of the Austin began at the Butler, Pennsylvania, factory. To outsiders, the car seemed a success, so much so that William C. Durant made a similar arrangement with E. E. C. Mathis, the French small, light car manufacturer. Durant organized the American Mathis Inc., with the intention of making this French automobile in America (American Mathis never functioned).[206]

Initially, the American Austin Car Company was aggressive, advertising widely, appointing dealers, and organizing a distribution network. Yet sales were not up to its managers' expectations. By the end of 1930, the company had sold 8,558 cars, far fewer than had been forecast. In the depression year of 1931, only 1,279 Austins were built in Pennsylvania. In 1932, the American Austin Car Company went into receivership. It was revived, but with no assistance from abroad; in 1933, the British investment was nominal—if any.[207] In 1934, the new American management once more filed for bankruptcy; Sir Herbert Austin had "long since lost interest."[208]

Thus, by 1933 not a single foreign company had a direct investment in assembling, much less manufacturing, either cars or trucks in America. Of the 1.6 million cars sold in the domestic market in this depression year, 88 percent were produced by General Motors, Ford, and Chrysler; the remainder came from other domestic car companies; imports were trivial.[209] A generation would pass before foreign firms would once more play a role in car production in America.

In May 1929, as noted in an earlier chapter, General Motors had acquired a sufficient stake in the Fokker Aircraft Corporation of America to exercise control; GM managers had increasingly pushed out the firm's Dutch founder, Anthony Fokker, planning to substitute the German designs of Claude Dornier for those of the Dutchman. With this in mind, GM had set up Dornier Corporation of America in October 1929. Economic conditions altered the plans, and GM went its own way. In May 1930, GM folded the "production units" of the Fokker and Dornier corporations into a newly formed GM-controlled holding company, General Aviation Corporation. Then GM resolved to drop the names Fokker and Dornier from all General Aviation products, and finally, in July 1931, General Aviation returned to Anthony Fokker all the manufacturing and marketing rights to as well as the brand name Fokker. At this point, the Dutch entrepreneur and aircraft designer announced that he would start a new U.S. company to build Fokker planes in America. That never occurred. As a historian of Anthony Fokker's ventures put it, in July 1931 "his career as an aeronautical constructor in the U.S. was over." Fokker went back to Holland.[210] The U.S. aviation industry was—and would be subsequently—totally American owned and controlled.

Tires and Automotive Parts

The experience of foreign direct investors in U.S. rubber tire making reflected the woes of depression times. Michelin, which had inaugurated manufacturing in Milltown, New Jersey, in 1907, announced on April 25, 1930, that its plant would close—with a reopening date uncertain. By April 1930, it had reduced its labor force to a skeleton group of 300. Michelin never resumed production at the New Jersey plant and in September 1930 put its buildings there up for sale.[211] When Michelin returned to the United States, forty-five years later, it would be with new tire products and a group of managers most of whom had not been born when Michelin had been in America—"round one."

The British firm Dunlop continued to operate its Buffalo, New York, tire plant, but every year from 1929 through 1933 it experienced huge losses. Because it was unable to penetrate the original equipment market, it sought to develop retail sales of replacement tires; in the early 1930s Dunlop created a network of chain stores to sell its branded product (in 1929 and 1930 it had 20 stores; by 1932, over 400; and by 1934, it led in the United States in this industry in the number of its retail outlets). Although the low depression prices combined with the reduced sales volumes went on bringing red ink to the company's income statements, with many competitors (including Michelin) going out of business and with Dunlop's vigorous retailing strategy, its U.S. market share rose from a mere .9 percent in 1929 to 1.4 percent in 1933. Thus, it stayed on as a minor participant in this American industry (in 1933 the leading four U.S.-owned tire makers captured more than 72 percent of domestic consumption, up from 62 percent in 1929).[212] In tire production and sales, domestically owned companies had no serious competitors. Unlike Michelin, however, Dunlop would maintain operations, uninterrupted, as a tire maker and marketer in America—until 1986, when its U.S. business would be acquired by another foreign-owned company, Sumitomo Rubber Industries.[213]

Bosch was the only top-ranking foreign-owned automotive parts and accessories producer in the United States.[214] In 1929, Robert Bosch Magneto Co., Inc. (a sales subsidiary of its namesake German parent), had settled its conflict with the American Bosch Magneto Corporation, which had acquired the pre–World War I U.S. Bosch business, including the sizable Springfield, Massachusetts, manufacturing plant. In 1930, the two U.S. Bosch companies merged into the United American Bosch Corporation (UABC), which at once (in 1930 and 1931) made agreements with Bosch in Stuttgart on "reciprocal sales agencies, trademarks, and patents." Prior to the 1930 merger, the American Bosch company had greatly enlarged the Springfield factory's manufacturing activities. In 1919, American Bosch had had only one product, a line of high-tension magnetos; it had started to make a variety of automotive parts; and in 1925, it began making radios, including car radios. Accordingly, in the early 1930s, UABC, the now German-controlled Bosch enterprise in the United States, was far more significant than it had been before the First World War.[215]

Electrical and Other Equipment

In 1931, Allis-Chalmers Manufacturing Company acquired from American Brown Boveri all the latter's assets related to the electrical business—including patents, patent rights, and the entire stock of the Conduit Electrical Manufacturing Corporation. Allis-Chalmers became the licensee in the United States of Brown, Boveri. Separately, and earlier, the American Brown Boveri divested its shipbuilding facilities at Camden. Brown, Boveri's direct investments in America came to a formal end—not to be resumed for many years.[216]

By 1933, all the leading European electrical manufacturers were bound with General Electric and/or Westinghouse in cartel accords that effectively precluded their making direct investments in operations in the United States. Siemens maintained a small "liaison office" in New York, but it was only that; the office kept the large German firm au courant on what was happening in America.[217] In 1931, Electrical and Musical Industries (EMI) was formed in Britain, a merger of existing companies, including the British Columbia company; in the process, the new EMI obtained a small holding in the American firm Columbia Phonograph Record Company. In 1932, EMI sold these shares, which left it with no direct investments in the United States.[218] It would reenter U.S. business after the Second World War.

In 1933, the sum total of FDI in the U.S. electrical industry included the German firm Robert Bosch, Okonite-Callender's Cable in cable construction, Electrolux in refrigerator manufacture, and the small office of Siemens. These investments, and perhaps some few others, did not add up to much; American business had complete hegemony in the large and dynamic U.S. electrical industry.

As for other equipment, there was a true paucity of new investments. One such was the Sandviken Steel Works Co., of Sweden, which in the early 1930s started subsidiaries in several countries, including the United States, to bypass high tariff charges.[219] In the United States, its new Sandvik Conveyor Manufacturing Company imported products from its Swedish parent, made certain parts in this country, and installed the completed units.[220]

Foreign-Owned Industrials

For 1930, Alfred D. Chandler compiled a list of America's top industrial companies, ranked by assets.[221] That year, of the largest hundred "U.S." companies, at least five involved inward FDI: Allied Chemical & Dye Corporation, American Metal Company, International Match Corporation, Shell Union Oil Corporation, and The Viscose Company. The first two (Allied Chemical and American Metal) were American controlled (with the foreign direct investors in a minority role). The third (International Match) would have to be dropped from the list by 1933, with the collapse of the Kreuger empire. The biggest foreign-controlled company was Shell Union, which ranked eleventh on Chandler's roster Courtaulds' subsidiary, The Viscose Company, was not on Chandler's roster but should have been, for it ranked in the top hundred by his criterion.[222] The nationalities involved in these leading foreign businesses in America are of interest. The principal foreign direct investor in Allied Chemical was Belgian; in International Match was Swedish; in Shell Union, British-Dutch; and British direct investors took part in American Metal Company and The Viscose Company. The absence of a German-, Canadian-, or French-owned industrial enterprise in the group is worth noting.

Services

In numerous service sector activities from retailing to trading to shipping to insurance to banking (including mortgage lending), foreign companies had a visibility of varying importance. In food sales, by the start of 1932, Loblaw Groceterias Company—a Canadian self-service chain—had 132 retail stores in the United States, 77 of which were in Chicago and the rest in upstate New York, making it the largest foreign-owned food chain in the United States. Yet depression conditions so adversely affected its business that in March 1932, it sold (for cash and preferred shares) its Chicago stores to the American-owned Jewel Tea Company. It continued a much reduced business, confined to upstate New York.[223]

During 1929–1932, America's foreign trade (merchandise exports plus imports) declined from $9.6 billion in 1929 to $2.9 billion in 1932.[224] With this attrition, most traders—whether foreign or domestically owned—saw the sharp contraction reflected in their balance sheets. Among the inward foreign direct investors encountering difficulties was the British trading house Balfour, Williamson. Over the decades it (and its California house) not only had participated in America's foreign trade but also had invested in a number of U.S. firms (in some case firms whose products it had handled). With low commodity prices, it was financially strapped. The Bank of Montreal gave it aid, requiring as collateral shares in the Crown Mills (the firm's California flour mills); Alaska Packers (in which it had a minority stake); California Packing Corporation (Del Monte brand of canned fruits and vegetables, in which it had a small interest); and United States Steel (for many foreign investors over the years, this had been a typical portfolio holding).[225] Problems notwithstanding, Balfour, Williamson (and its California house) stayed on in America.

The trading firm United Molasses Co., Ltd., which in the late 1920s had become well established in the American market, early in 1931 sold off Eastern Alcohol Corp. (which it had purchased as recently as 1929 from National Distillers Products Corp.). By 1931, American Solvents and Chemical Corp., in which United Molasses had obtained an interest, was bankrupt. This left United Molasses in mid-1931 with four U.S. subsidiaries: Anglo-American Mill Co. (with a mill in Owensboro, Kentucky); Dunbar Molasses Co.; Old Time Molasses Co. (the leader in U.S.-Cuban molasses commerce); and Pacific Molasses Co., San Francisco. Not long thereafter, United Molasses seems to have divested Anglo-American Mill Co., and in 1933 it disposed of Dunbar Molasses and Old Time Molasses, retaining only Pacific Molasses Co. It was a shadow of its earlier prominence.[226]

Antony Gibbs & Co., Inc., the New York affiliate of the eponymous British firm, witnessed heavy losses in 1929–1934 yet persisted in what had become a highly diversified trading business. Other British traders found that direct representation in the United States involved costs far exceeding the benefits. Thus, in the early 1930s, Dodwells (the big tea exporter from China and India and, by the early 1930s, a participant in exporting many other products from Asia into America) "withdrew from general trading" through its U.S. branches and closed them. The important British trader Jardine Matheson shut down its New York office in 1931. Key among its U.S. imports had been silk; it was thus acutely affected by the disappearance of demand for this luxury item. The remaining Jardine Matheson's U.S. business came to be handled by the weakened but still active Balfour, Williamson.[227]

Japanese trading companies were particularly hard hit during 1929–1930 (with the low U.S. silk imports); they readjusted and diversified their product lines to cope with the new circumstances (I did not find exits).[228] In contrast, a very few, rare, trading houses obtained profits from the low agricultural prices, or so it seems. In the late 1920s, the French Fribourgs' Continental Grain had expanded into the American interior; now Continental Grain enlarged its activities, leasing in 1930 a terminal in Galveston owned by the Southern Pacific Railroad and in 1931 buying well-placed grain elevators in Kansas City, Toledo, and Nashville.[229] Its goal was to be positioned to buy grain when prices were depressed and store the product, awaiting higher prices.[230]

The decline in U.S. (and world) trade had a dire effect on international shipping, with the British particularly hard hit.[231] In 1930 the German Hamburg-American Line and the North German Lloyd Line (which were experiencing sizable depression losses) formed a pool. To make matters worse for these shippers, the German lines had gone through a recent big expansion on the assumption that they would be reimbursed for their World War I losses; as it turned out, neither was ever fully reimbursed, since the Hoover Moratorium (of June 1931) affected all intergovernmental payments. Because Germany was not paying reparations and other inter-Allied debts were in limbo, the United States did not feel obligated to complete most of its promised payments to the Germans. The German shipping industry was especially hurt by the breakdown in the 1928 war settlements agreement.[232] Nevertheless, the German government had made a major commitment to its shippers and in 1932 had inaugurated a "scrap-and-build" program in ship construction. Thus, despite the adversities, by 1933 German ships were obtaining a larger portion of U.S. entrances and clearances than in 1929. So, too, between 1929 and 1933, Norwegian ships enlarged their market share.[233]

Under the unsatisfactory circumstances of 1929–1933, the Japanese response was truly innovative. In the late 1920s, the Japanese had started producing modern diesel-powered ships. In 1930, Osaka Shosen Kasha (OSK) introduced an "express line" to the U.S. East Coast through the Panama Canal, cutting the time from Yokohama to New York from thirty-five to twenty-six days. In 1932, the Japanese government, like the German state, initiated a "scrap-and-rebuild" program that would greatly enhance Japanese shipping.[234] By 1933, 63.2 percent of shipping in U.S. international trade was on foreign-registered ships: 26.8 percent was British; 7.3 percent, Norwegian; 6.5 percent, German; and 4.7 percent, Japanese.[235]

Insurance Services

By 1929–1933, foreign-owned insurance companies in the United States had only a small portion of their business in marine insurance, although in relative terms they remained important in this segment of the insurance business. Most of the insurance coverage by foreign companies involved fire and now also casualty coverage; foreign companies (especially British ones) were very significant. Only Canadians took part in life insurance, as had been the case in prior years. The effects of the economic downturn on all the foreign insurers were serious; the U.S. insurance industry (and the foreign participants in it) felt the brunt of the bad economic conditions, as prices of their assets collapsed.[236]

Sun Life Assurance Company of Canada, for example, had appeared to do well during 1930 and near the close of that year had secured a group life, health, and accident policy covering the employees of the entire Illinois Central Railroad system, the largest policy the Canadian insurer had ever issued.[237] Yet in 1930 and 1931, the assets of Sun Life had dived with the slide in stock market prices. The firm's income evaporated as Canadian and U.S. companies passed dividends and defaulted on interest payments. According to its historian, Sun Life's surplus of $60 million in 1929, after reevaluation of its portfolio, had dwindled to $31 million in 1930, $16 million in 1931, and, by the end of 1932, after the Insull failure, to $6 million.[238] Individuals who had exhausted their other savings often borrowed on their life insurance policies. At the same time, many holders of policies stopped paying premiums, eliminating the insurer's income stream.[239] The failure of the Insull group was thus only partially responsible for the woes of this Canadian insurer, albeit it made the troubles far more severe. This longtime ally of Insull was deeply injured, and when Insull needed support, Sun Life could not provide it.

Despite horrendous problems, in the main the vast bulk of foreign-owned insurers appear to have survived, including Sun Life. Exceptions included one Australian insurer in the United States and one Danish reinsurer that exited from U.S. business in 1931 and 1932, respectively.[240] Two short-lived late 1920s German entries departed in 1930 and 1932.[241] The German-controlled Pilot Reinsurance, however, remained.[242]

The experienced British participants in American fire, casualty, and other insurance markets weathered the difficult times. Of the numerous British insurers listed as offering casualty insurance in 1929, there were only two fewer in 1933 (and the dropouts were small, relatively recent arrivals). All those remaining were rated A or A+ by *Best Reports,* covering 1933.[243]

According to the U.S. Department of Commerce for year end 1934, no single sector in the United States had attracted more inward FDI than insurance; I do not believe the conclusion would be substantially different for 1932 or 1933 (although no figures are available for those years).[244] The British were the leaders among the foreign participants in this sector, but many other nationalities took part. The firms were in both insurance and reinsurance.

Banking Services

At year end 1929, twenty-six bank agencies of foreign banks were licensed to do business in New York; by the end of 1933, the number was twenty-five, with newcomers two, departures three (Table 5.5 gave the year end 1929 list; Table 7.10 has the year end 1933 tally). The new participants were the Banco National de Mexico, Mexico City, and Thomas Cook & Sons, London. The Banco National de Mexico appears to have been the first bank headquartered in a Latin American country to open a New York agency. No longer on the list in 1933 were the Bank of Canton, Hong Kong; the Mercantile Bank of India, Ltd., London; and the National Bank of Greece.[245] The National Bank of Greece was not a "real" exit, for in 1930 it set up the Hellenic Bank Trust Company, chartered in New York, so it was just changing the form of operation.[246] In 1931–1932, the Anglo-South American Bank, London, hovered near the brink of failure, but it went on doing business, as did the greatly debilitated Bank of London and South America.[247] In 1930, the Banco di Napoli founded the Banco di Napoli Trust Co. in New York (it retained its New York agency—and joined two other Italian banks, Banca Commerciale Italiana and Banco di Sicilia, in adopting the trust company form); in addition, on December 31, 1930, it incorporated (under Illinois law) the Banco di Napoli Trust Co. of Chicago, the successor to its earlier Chicago bank (Banco di Napoli).[248]

Foreign banks in the United States were heavily engaged in international transactions (which were far more significant for them than purely U.S. business); as world trade and investment dropped and as the world economy became ever more fractured, these bankers saw their prospects sharply curtailed; at the same time, however, banking became more complicated with the devaluation of sterling in 1931 and the general unpredictability in global conditions. The New York agencies of foreign banks had the appropriate expertise. Many of the banking houses mentioned earlier in this chapter as foreign institutional investors, including Barings and Rothschilds, had long taken part in FPI in the United States and also in the 1920s in the complex financial structures that moved U.S. moneys abroad. In the past, their FDI in the United States had been limited. Now the ties were entirely cut: thus, Barings' association with Kidder, Peabody ended, as did its links with Kidder Peabody Acceptance Corporation (the latter was merged into Consolidated Investment Trust in 1932).[249]

The most dramatic change in these years of the Depression vis-à-vis foreign banks in the United States was reflected in the complete collapse of the enthusiastic international dreams envisaged when in 1929 the Bank of the Manhattan Company had merged with (acquired) the International Acceptance Bank. Paul Warburg had worked out the details of the foreign banks' equity interests. His vision for the future was, however, shattered by the deterioration of world economic conditions, and with his death in January 1932, not only did the group's special relations with M. M. Warburg & Co., Hamburg, create monumental difficulties as described earlier, but the entire international program of the new bank and its affiliates crumbled. After his death, the Bank of the Manhattan Company reverted to its old name (the one it had held from 1799 to 1929, before the acquisition of IAB); its business was totally restructured.[250] Warburg's son (James) remained involved, and many foreign banks kept their equity interests in the reorganized Bank of the Manhattan Company, but the exciting cooperative arrangements envisioned in the late 1920s were history.[251]

With the devaluation of sterling in 1931 and the proliferation of exchange controls in many countries, international banking grew more in need of specialized knowledge, calling on the services and experience of the foreign banks that had agencies, trust companies, banking corporations, or partnerships in New York. With numerous bank failures in the United States and abroad, bankers needed "insider information," which they obtained through their Wall Street contacts. Whereas abroad foreign banks met formidable crises, those that did business in the United States tended to be in a separate category. Except for the trust companies, they did not take deposits in the United States, and then principally in relation to international transactions, so they were not particularly vulnerable to American runs on banks.[252] Those that had been involved in broker loans and acceptances faced losses as well as some bankruptcies. Canadian banks, as historians have noted, survived better than their U.S. counterparts, and this was reflected in their business south of the border.[253] This was a trying time for all banks in America.

British mortgage lenders were in an especially perilous position; in the 1920s they had already been reducing their participation in U.S. farm mortgages; now they pulled back even further as farmers faced sinking prices, lacked collateral for borrowing, and had inadequate revenues to cover their existing mortgage loans. The impact of these conditions on the Alliance Trust portfolio was typical. In 1929, 18 percent of its funds were still employed in the U.S. mortgage business; by 1933, that share was down to 12.5 percent. As an indication of how bad matters were, in 1933 some 64 percent of Alliance Trust's investments in the U.S. mortgage field were in loans on which no interest was being paid and in real estate on which it had foreclosed.[254] Since there were no buyers for real estate, Alliance Trust, like many mortgage lenders (foreign and domestic), often saw no sense in foreclosing on loans in default; in addition, a number of state governments enacted foreclosure moratoriums.[255] Alliance Trust could only hope for better times, when borrowers could bring their loans current. In short, the involvement of the British in mortgage lending in the United States continued to shrink.

Conclusion

In conclusion, during 1929–1933, FPI declined—measured by quantity of securities held and also by their price. The purchases of securities made by foreign investors were more than outweighed by the far greater securities sales. The lower FPI reduced the total inward foreign investment—FPI plus FDI (see Table 2.1). As for FDI, according to the figures of Cleona Lewis, the book value of inward FDI at year end 1933 was slightly higher than at year end 1929.[256] She supplies no figures for year end 1932, and her 1933 FDI figures are identical with those FDI figures given by the U.S. Department of Commerce (and by Lewis herself) for year end 1934.[257] With the FDI there had been some new entries to jump the tariff wall and for other reasons as well, but there were also exits in reaction to the adverse economic conditions.

If, however, Lewis' figures on FDI are accepted, one might infer that in 1929–1933, FPI and FDI moved in divergent directions (one set falling and the other rising). I am not comfortable with such a conclusion.[258] The data do, however, strongly support the proposition that FPI and FDI actors took into account different considerations as they formulated their strategies. This finding, long apparent in our historical discussions, was highlighted in the crisis years of 1929–1933. FPI decisions were always financially focused. With FPI there was volatility. By contrast, FDI choices were more broadly connected with distinctive economic (and political) conditions along with the particular investor's historical experience within a defined business sector. Moreover, the decisions of individual investors in the case of FPI and FDI were far from uniform or predetermined; different portfolio investors made dissimilar choices, and the same was true of foreign direct investors, even within an identical industrial sector (thus, Michelin, after twenty-three years in America, closed down; Dunlop, with a decade of bad performance, made new investments in distribution outlets).

Depending on the home country, there were clear differences in FPI patterns, reflecting the economic (and sometimes political) conditions within that country. There is less evidence of systematic variations by nationality in the behavior of foreign direct investors. With British direct investments, for example, Rio Tinto exited under adversity, as did both British car manufacturers (Rolls Royce and Austin); ICI continued to opt for divided markets and retreated from its one remaining FDI. By contrast, British American Tobacco, Dunlop, and J. & P. Coats responded aggressively with new strategies, the first with new products (Wings and Avalon), the second with new functions (expanded retailing), and the third with a new low-cost plant (in the American South). Hollins & Co. vaulted the tariff barrier and acquired its first textile mill in the United States; Beatty's Selection Trust became a new investor in American Metal to aid his African expansion plans. It seems self-evident that home nation considerations were highly relevant in affecting the decision making of foreign-owned firms in America, but responses to conditions at home were not alike, and such considerations must be viewed in the context of those tailored by corporate, industry, and U.S. economic and political conditions. Unilever was a rarity in its subsidiary's rising U.S. profits in 1930 to 1932.

With neither FPI nor FDI were the amounts of the investments (or the changes in the amounts) large enough to affect in any material manner the general macroeconomic conditions within the United States. The presence and dynamics of FPI and FDI were not countercyclical. Instead, the course of FPI contributed to the stock market decline (along with responding to the ongoing decline), while those new investments by foreign multinationals were insufficient to offset the concurrent pullbacks and exits.

It seems evident that in March 1933, when Franklin Delano Roosevelt took office as president, overall foreign long-term investment in America was smaller and less significant than it had been in the late 1920s. The reduction had (albeit only marginally) contributed to but was, more important, a response to the economic malaise in the United States. The attractiveness of the country as a place for both foreign portfolio and direct investors (and domestic investors as well) had temporarily dimmed.

7.

A World at Risk, 1933–1939

America in the 1930s was for the most part a somber place. The downturn of 1929–1933 left deep scars. The New Deal's increasing commitment to government intervention and government-stimulated recovery shaped the path of national development. America's role in the world economy went through a metamorphosis. When on Saturday, March 4, 1933, Franklin Delano Roosevelt assumed the presidency, most of the nation's banks were closed. On Monday the president declared a four-day bank holiday "to save" the system. That same measure forbade (except with the permission of the U.S. Treasury) bank transactions in gold, including gold exports. Contemporaries perceived this as a stopgap solution. It was, however, the first step in the devaluation of the dollar and the abandonment of the gold standard. Hoover had considered the dollar, backed by gold, to be the bedrock of the international order: the gold standard was sacrosanct. By contrast, Roosevelt saw in the depreciation in the value of the dollar (the raising of the dollar price of gold) a means of aiding the weak U.S. economy. The devaluation, he thought, would revive flagging U.S. exports, end the plunge in commodity prices, and have what he believed to be the desirable outcome of boosting U.S. domestic prices.[1]

With a set of executive orders in April 1933, Roosevelt took the country off the gold standard. The Treasury Department announced it would no longer issue (except under very special circumstances) gold export licenses. No U.S. person or institution, other than the Federal Reserve, could hold gold or gold certificates; only gold for artistic purposes or as a collector's item was exempted. As anticipated, the value of the dollar fell. On June 5, 1933, a congressional resolution canceled the gold clause in public and private contracts: from this point on, all existing gold obligations were payable in legal tender, that is, in dollars. Often bonds owned by foreign investors had a "gold clause" (i.e., they were payable in dollars or gold), which was now repudiated.

In June 1933 a world economic conference convened in London. On July 3, Roosevelt shocked the delegates when he rejected any responsibility for exchange stabilization and, instead, put U.S. domestic recovery as his top priority.[2] The dollar continued to lose value. Finally, on January 30, 1934, after Congress passed the Gold Reserve Act, the Treasury Department set the gold price at $35.00 an ounce (up from $20.67 an ounce before Roosevelt became president). The U.S. government would buy gold at $35.00 an ounce. It would sell gold at $35.00 an ounce, but only to foreign central banks and governments. The act put the United States on a gold standard internationally and on an irredeemable paper standard domestically. With this new higher price of gold, the Roosevelt administration had formally devalued the dollar.[3]

During the 1930s, the world economy witnessed competitive devaluations, exchange controls, and fluctuating exchange rates.[4] As war clouds came to darken the global landscape and as nowhere looked safe, the United States appeared as an oasis in a deeply troubled international environment, and this despite the 1933–1934 devaluation of the dollar, the 1933 repudiation of the gold clause in contractual obligations, and the subsequent inadequate recovery from the depth of the Depression.[5] In the years 1933–1939, to be sure, there were episodic times of euphoria: in November 1936, for example, investors seemed "eager to share in the great prosperity which they are convinced *lies ahead* of the United States."[6] Increasingly, however, the Atlantic and the Pacific Oceans formed a moat—seemingly separating and protecting the American nation from the ever more awful follies in Europe and Asia. Everywhere abroad property rights appeared in jeopardy, whereas they seemed less at risk in America. It was a matter of degree, for many at the time believed the New Deal was destroying such rights. Yet investors made comparisons, and the result was from 1934 to 1939 a flood of gold and foreign capital flowed into the United States, motivated mainly (but not exclusively) by a search for safety and security. Investors desired to transfer their savings to what they saw as a stronger and more reliable currency than their own. Also—the generally anemic economy notwithstanding—the U.S. standard of living remained the highest in the world (see Table 7.1). It is possible that in the late 1930s, the United States was the world's largest recipient of capital (see Table 7.2).[7]

As early as December 1934, economist Arthur Feiler, addressing the Annual Meeting of the American Economic Association, was commenting on the movement of capital from debtors to a creditor country, that is, to the United States. He thought this was associated with the disintegration of the world economy. Writers labeled the subsequent

Table 7.1. Nonmonetary indicators of national consumption levels, 1934–1938 (United States = 100)

Nation	Relative position
United States	100
United Kingdom	76
Germany	62
France	58

Source: M. K. Bennett, "International Disparities in Consumption Levels," *American Economic Review*, 41 (Sept. 1951): 648. The composite index of the nonmonetary indicators includes food, tobacco, medical and sanitary services, education, transportation, and communication.

and rising heavy influx of moneys into America as "abnormal." Capital was "supposed" to flow from wealthy to poor countries, from older industrial to newer nations. Now it was moving from rich (but impoverished) lands to a richer (but depressed) country; it was going from industrial to industrial nation—and on some occasions from less developed countries to the leading industrial one.[8] By decade's end, American economists were complaining about the influx, the "golden avalanche," yet long before that economists were thinking about policy alternatives in the face of what they judged to be serious problems arising from foreign purchases of American securities.[9]

In the 1930s, the America First isolationist movement had major political, social, and economic consequences. Isolationists joined the many alarmed economists in diagnosing the inflow of capital from abroad as "contaminating." Americans in this decade heard little that was positive about the rest of the world: Japanese aggression in Manchuria and China; the alarming speeches and actions of Hitler; the Italo-Ethiopian crisis; and the Spanish civil war. Conflict was ubiquitous. Dictatorships challenged democratic beliefs. The ailing domestic economy notwithstanding, outside the country everything seemed far worse.[10] During the entire period 1933–1939, the overarching views in the United States toward inward foreign investment—both portfolio and direct investments—were negative, in line with the notion that "foreign" could only be bad. Before I provide the details on the inward foreign investments, I will survey the potpourri of attitudes, policies, court decisions, and laws that emerged out of both the general climate of opinion and the more specific circumstances of the growing inward foreign portfolio and direct investments.

Reactions to and Policies toward Inward Foreign Portfolio Investments, 1933–1939

Of the escalating FPI economist Arthur Bloomfield wrote: "Foreign purchases of American securities raised a variety of important policy problems centering around the feasibility of restricting this category of capital inflow which, far from conferring any positive benefit on the United States . . . accentuated the upswing in the stock market in 1935–37, increased the amount of potential selling pressure that could suddenly arise as a result of developments abroad, and above all contributed significantly to the unwanted inflow of gold."[11]

Table 7.2. Creditors and debtors, ca. 1938

Principal sources of capital[a]		Principal recipients of capital[b]	
Home country	Level (in billions of U.S. dollars)	Host country	Level (in billions of U.S. dollars)
United Kingdom[c]	22.9	**United States**	7.0
United States	**11.5**	Canada	6.6
Netherlands	4.8	Australia	3.7
France	3.9	Argentina	3.2
Canada	1.9	India	2.8
Switzerland	1.6	Germany	2.7
Belgium	1.3	China	2.6
Japan	1.2	Dutch East Indies	2.4
		Brazil	2.0
		Mexico	1.8
		South Africa & Rhodesia	1.4
		Chile	1.3
		United Kingdom	1.2
		Rest of Europe[d]	6.3
		Rest of Latin America[e]	4.3
Others	5.9	Others	5.7
Total	55.0[f]	Total	55.0

Source: Cleona Lewis, *Debtor and Creditor Countries: 1938, 1944* (Washington, D.C., Brookings Institution, 1945), 4–12, 48–53. No country is included on the above table that had long-term "credits" or "debts" of less than $1.0 billion (I am using the terms "credits" and "debts" to include both equity and debt—bonds and loans). The home country is that of the "creditor"; it may not be the ultimate source of the capital.

Note: Lewis gave these figures as of 1938; however, her U.S. inward estimate is from the U.S. Commerce Department for mid-1937, *not* the one that the U.S. Commerce Department gave for year end 1938 (see Tables 2.4 and 7.3 herein). The difference is sufficient to change the ranking of the United States as a "debtor" from first to second place, after Canada.

a. Gross long-term outward foreign investments.

b. Gross long-term inward foreign investments.

c. Lewis converted the number to dollars at $5 = £1, with bonds at par.

d. Except for Germany and the United Kingdom.

e. Except for Argentina, Brazil, Mexico, and Chile.

f. I raised Lewis' figure to correspond to the capital recipient totals.

His statement (published in 1950) embraced opinions from the middle and late 1930s. From the start of the Roosevelt administration, Americans expressed anxieties over foreign holdings of American securities. Frequently, the nervousness was more amorphous and more politically tinged than the Bloomfield quotation suggests, but certainly just as disapproving. The concerns were evident in an exchange that occurred during a June 1933 session of the U.S. Senate Committee on Banking and Currency (hearings that became known as the Pecora investigation), when Senator Robert R. Reynolds questioned George Whitney, a partner of J. P. Morgan & Co. The North Carolina senator's approach mirrored the prevailing isolationism blended with American populist sentiments that had long been tinged with a distrust of foreign investors. On learning that in 1929 J. P. Morgan & Co. had allocated part of its share offerings of United Corporation (the largest American public utilities holding company) to Great Britain and France, Reynolds asked Whitney, "Don't you think, in view of turbulent conditions abroad . . . that it is unwise to give to Europeans stock [in American companies]?" To Whitney's response that conditions were very different in 1929 from 1933, the senator retorted that in 1929 as in 1933 there existed a huge European debt to the United States. Whitney agreed there was indeed a giant *intergovernmental* debt, but he pointed out that the shares to which the senator referred went to Morgan houses—Morgan, Grenfell, London, and Morgan & Cie., Paris—and had nothing whatsoever to do with the obligations of European governments to the United States. The senator was unconvinced: "Don't you believe [that providing American securities to your firms abroad] tends to line up favored Europeans behind projects in which J. P. Morgan & Co. are interested to the detriment of American public welfare?" Whitney replied that the 1929 arrangement was in no way harmful to America. In a populist manner (and with the complete, but not atypical, mix-up of private and public sector transactions), Reynolds probed further: "Have you heard that the family of King George, or that King George himself, was one of the individuals who participated in this allotment to London?" Whitney: "I have never heard it suggested . . . I very seriously doubt it." Earlier in the hearings, it had come out that Giovanni Fummi, Morgan's Italian representative, had been the underwriter for a small amount of shares of another American issue. Reynolds inquired, had Mussolini gotten shares? Whitney: "No, I have not heard, I am sure, anything of that kind." The point the senator belabored was that having American securities in European hands placed the nation at risk. The senator assumed that the securities must be owned by European royalty or leading politicians (which he equated with European governments and their unpaid World War I debts).[12]

These Senate hearings took place in the same month (June 1933) that Congress abrogated the gold clause in American public and private obligations. Foreign holders of American bonds with gold clauses litigated, and in February 1935 the U.S. Supreme Court upheld Congress' right to regulate the value of American money, including the right to cancel the gold clause in contracts with private parties and with state and local governments, but not in U.S. federal government obligations; the U.S. government then formally repudiated the gold clause in U.S. federal government bonds, completing the process.[13]

Despite this violation of what many foreign (and domestic) critics deemed fundamental property rights, capital continued to flow into America, since the economic and political situation in the rest of the world seemed so much more adverse, since the establishment of the gold-exchange standard (even if the domestically held dollar was inconvertible into gold) did seem to provide monetary stability in the United States, and since the price the U.S. government would pay for gold was high ($35.00 an ounce was seen as high).[14]

Neither was the capital inflow deterred when, in another perceived assault on private property, in May 1934 the U.S. Supreme Court did not allow the Principality of Monaco to sue the sovereign state of Mississippi over bonds in default from 1841 (these were bonds Monaco had received as a gift from the heirs of the original owners); this matter was truly part of a very distant American past; foreign investors had years earlier concluded that this almost century-old reneging on debt was a sunk cost and should not (and did not) affect future investments. The month before, in April 1934, the Johnson Act had forbidden American loans to foreign governments in default, and aside from many foreigners' noting the contradictory nature of U.S. policies, the court decision had no effect on slowing inward flows of foreign investment.[15] Thus, during 1935–1937, as the stock market resumed its ascent, foreign buyers participated. For the most part, foreign buyers of American securities were not in the 1930s interested in state government bonds (or bonds in general); rather typically they purchased corporate securities, principally equities.

In the literature of the time and later, often gold and capital flows were (correctly) analyzed together. Gold dispatched to the United States had to be converted into dollars and thus became part of the influx of moneys into the country. The dollars could be used to purchase goods. They could be placed in bank deposits or other short-term assets. Or they could be employed in buying stocks, bonds, or other U.S. long-term assets. If used in this last manner, the gold flow to the United States was identical to a long-term capital inflow. Accordingly, U.S. policies toward gold in 1933–1939 had direct impact on long-term inward foreign investments. The opposite was also true. A *New York Times* editorial of November 25, 1936, explained that the change in U.S. gold policy (all gold exports would be conducted through the U.S. government) might be based on "specific fears of a sudden withdrawal of the large foreign funds here."[16] U.S. gold policies were shaped with purely domestic considerations uppermost; that foreign capital inflows came *as a result* was not the intention (gold policies were framed so that capital outflows taking the form of gold outflows would not injure the nation's fragile recovery from the Depression).

Similarly, and also not by design, America's silver policies had the effect of encouraging inward foreign portfolio investments. On June 19, 1934, Congress attempted to aid western silver mining interests and passed the Silver Purchase Act. Later on, U.S. government buying of silver pushed up its price, which resulted in an influx of silver, especially from China.[17] And some of the income from the precious metal sales became the basis for long-term inward foreign portfolio investments.

In the discourse of many Americans, international creditor-debtor relationships grew increasingly blurred. America was a creditor nation, and as we have seen in the 1920s, there had been a blending of outward and inward foreign investments in complex interrelationships. Now the United States *as creditor* was in a predicament as "unreliable Europeans" repudiated (or at least refused to pay interest on) their World War I debts and many other foreign borrowers defaulted. In October 1933 isolationist Senator Hiram Johnson (of California) echoed a common lament, complaining that international bankers were "driving us deeper and deeper into the European maelstrom."[18]

Rhetoric attacking international bankers reached a high pitch. Try as the bankers would to separate governmental loans from commercial transactions, the bankers were increasingly tarred.[19] In April 1934, Congress had passed the Johnson Act that forbade American lending to governments in default on war debts. That "foreigners," who were terrible credit risks, were purchasing American securities (inward investment—the other side of the coin) seemed suspect; how could they afford to buy American securities at the same time as they were defaulting on American loans?[20] The identical group of bankers were intermediaries in outward lending and the attracting of inward stakes in American securities. New Deal critiques of the bankers were extended to hostility toward inward portfolio foreign investments.

After the stock market crash of 1929, in the investigations of bankers and brokers, lawmakers had sought out information on securities markets. Regulation of these markets became a 1933–1934 priority. In 1934 Congress passed a law that established the Securities and Exchange

Commission (SEC), whose regulations came to require that whenever an investor or group of investors (domestic or foreign) acquired 5 percent or more of the voting stock of a traded U.S. company, there had to be disclosure. This gave the SEC the opportunity to monitor some of the rising foreign investments in American securities.

From the start of the New Deal years, from the Pecora investigations of stock exchange transactions to the Nye Committee hearings on munitions (1934–1936), bankers were political targets. No group was more denigrated as internationalists than the private bankers, especially the House of Morgan.[21] The term "internationalist" took on pejorative connotations. When these bankers fretted about U.S. economic nationalism—when Morgan partner Russell C. Leffingwell wrote, "Everything we are and have today is because Europeans believed in us and invested money in us"—these were voices in the wilderness.[22] The more generally accepted view was articulated in the 1936 Democratic platform, which vowed to guard against Americans being dragged into war by international bankers. And it was not only Democrats: Chicago Republican William H. Stuart, writing in 1935, quoted approvingly a comment on why Americans entered World War I: "Because America and the American people were helplessly, hopelessly in the grip of the International Bankers." In 1935, 1936, and 1937, Congress passed neutrality acts aimed at keeping Americans out of "impending wars."[23]

The general attack on the bankers blended easily with discussions of tainted international capital and tax evasion. Throughout the New Deal era, attention was paid to how government efforts could encourage economic recovery; and when questions arose as to whether the presence of inward foreign investments compromised this endeavor, policy makers looked at tax issues. As New Deal spending rose, more government revenues had to be located; the New Deal's mantra was that "the rich" could pay. Yet lawyers for the wealthy, including those acting on behalf of foreign investors (as in the 1920s), devised ways of helping their clients lessen the impact of each new round of taxes. U.S. Treasury officials found that well-to-do *Americans* set up companies in foreign countries to reduce or eliminate their tax obligations. One New Yorker, for example, whose 1936 tax return showed no taxable income, owned a Canadian holding company with an income of more than $1.5 million from its U.S. investments.[24]

The subject of the use of foreign corporate intermediaries by America's wealthy fused with that of foreigners' ability to evade U.S. taxes. The two (outward/inward investment and solely inward investment) often seemed indistinguishable to Treasury Department tax officials. Under U.S. law, nonresident aliens were taxed—at the source—on dividends and interest paid on their American securities. Nonresident aliens were also expected to pay capital gains tax, but in the past little effort had been made to collect this tax. In the search for new revenues, in 1934 the Treasury Department began "investigating and dunning foreigners for back taxes due under the capital gains provision."[25] This seemed a painless way to raise extra needed moneys without burdening Americans. Then, in 1936–1937, the federal government started to consider using taxation not only to increase revenues but coincidentally to discourage inward foreign investments, that is, foreign speculation in American bonds and shares.[26] The Roosevelt administration discussed placing a prohibitive tax on speculative moneys from abroad. It failed to do so, however, since it found that it was impossible to distinguish between those foreign investments that might just conceivably be helpful in coping with the nation's ills and the undesirable so-called speculative funds.[27] In addition, the State Department strongly opposed any such plan, fearing retaliation by foreign governments on U.S. business abroad.[28]

Nonetheless, the 1936 Revenue Act did modify the tax treatment of nonresident aliens. Economists Roy and Gladys Blakey believed the revisions were more administrative (designed to improve tax collection) than policy oriented.[29] In the 1936 act, the liability of nonresident aliens for future capital gains taxes on the sale of assets within the United States was eliminated because it had been found "administratively impossible to assess and collect this tax."[30] Secretary of the Treasury Henry Morgenthau's analysis was different from that of the Blakeys. Morgenthau felt the result of the 1936 act was to grant "relative freedom from taxation" to nonresident aliens and, thus, to encourage added foreign investment in the United States and, more important in his view, more tax evasion, through foreign intermediaries, by rich Americans.[31] To deter inward foreign investment, the Treasury Department then weighed the idea of raising the rate of income tax to be levied on interest and dividends paid to foreign holders of American securities and the reimposition of the capital gains tax.[32]

The Revenue Act of 1937 removed many of the loopholes in the tax code; it "radically altered the treatment of foreign personal holding companies and removed a differential favoring nonresident taxpayers."[33] Whereas the 1936 law had imposed a 10 percent tax on income from U.S. sources received by nonresident aliens (except where there was a prior tax treaty), the 1937 act said the tax would be no less than 10 percent.[34] Foreign investors were a group that no one wished to favor; framers thought this revision in the tax law might impede the influx of foreign capital. In the 1937 law, the tax on foreigners' capital gains was not reimposed, but that year the Treasury accelerated its efforts to collect back taxes (those due before the 1936 removal of the capital gains tax on foreign investors).[35] The reforms in the Revenue Act of 1937 were addressed more at American tax evaders who used foreign holding companies than at foreign investors in the United States. The changes had, however, that extra effect of hiking taxes on the true investors from abroad. The increases were not material and did not slow investments coming from abroad, since, in the main, the search for safety offset the lower (after the new tax) rate of return. Still, tax policies clearly did matter. Thus, in the 1930s (and 1920s), foreign investors did not typically invest in state and municipal bonds, and the reason appears to have been connected with tax considerations; these had tax advantages for American investors and not for those investors from abroad.[36]

In 1935–1937, much of gold and capital inflow went into short-term assets. Fears mounted that the short-term (and long-term) money, seeking safety in the United States, was "hot" money, extremely volatile and dangerous.[37] A week after his election to a second term, in November 1936, Roosevelt at a press conference called the influx of "hot" money a "potential danger."[38] At the U.S. Treasury and at the Federal Reserve, there was uneasiness as to whether the inflow affected America's ability to determine its own monetary policy. Should Americans' use of monetary policy instruments be constrained by foreigners' "speculations"? Figure 7.1 indicates the volatility in foreign purchases (and sales) of domestic securities.[39] At the end of 1936, a Treasury plan was implemented to sterilize the gold influx, so that gold coming from outside the country would not affect the size of U.S. gold reserves and domestic monetary policy could remain independent.[40]

By 1937–1938, however, Morgenthau began to have reservations on the sterilization of gold. After mid-1937 (as Figure 7.1 shows), the volatility of foreign capital inflows into American securities was subsiding. As the U.S. economic expansion of 1933–1937 faltered, Morgenthau wondered whether perhaps the inflow of gold could be used to expand reserves and to stimulate the economy. In February 1938, Morgenthau (and Chairman Marriner Eccles at the Federal Reserve) announced that the Treasury would no longer sterilize gold imports or gold production, unless the level exceeded a set limit. In April 1938, sterilization was entirely discontinued in an effort to expand credit.[41] Resources from abroad were now (albeit temporarily) being incorporated into a program for domestic recovery.

Yet the negative image of foreign investments in the United States by those both in and outside of government did not dissipate; concerns persisted lest the perceived volatility of foreign moneys (leaving aside the matter of gold policy) might undermine the economy. Specifically, the chairman of the Securities and Exchange Commission, William O. Douglas, wrote in January 1938 that any rise in foreign holdings of

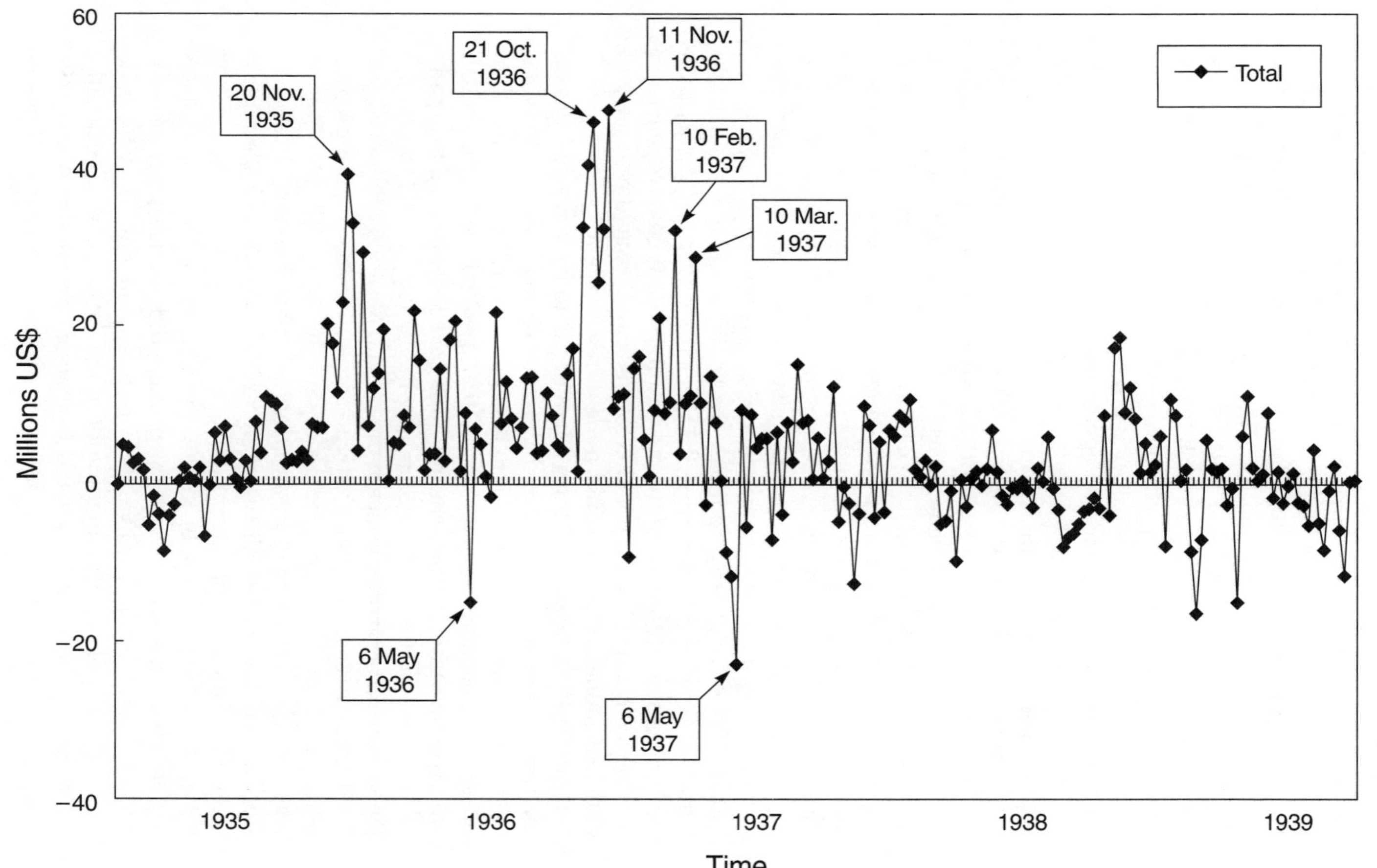
Total
Millions US$
60
40
20
0
−20
−40
1935
1936
1937
1938
1939
Time
20 Nov. 1935
6 May 1936
21 Oct. 1936
11 Nov. 1936
10 Feb. 1937
10 Mar. 1937
6 May 1937

American securities was not in the public interest.[42] Moreover, with the so-called hot money, the line between short-term and long-term capital was often obscure, since foreign moneys on deposit or in short-term bills could be easily shifted into (and out of) equally liquid American stocks and bonds that were by the definitions typically used "long-term" investments. Always in the background lay the haunting fears that the U.S. economy would be imperiled were the influx to cease and become an outflow—and to confirm the worries there were weeks when such outflows did occur (see Figure 7.1).[43] It was far better, most U.S. policy makers concluded, not to have the unpredictable outsiders' money in the American securities markets.

Officials at the Federal Reserve monitored stock market transactions. Eccles agreed with others' assessment of the impact of foreign moneys, stating in February 1938 that the flow of foreign funds into the stock market in recent years had proved not to be constructive. He believed that foreign investors had accentuated stock market booms and done little to check declines. Their "speculative tendencies" were, he wrote, a "disorganizing influence on the entire economy."[44]

Meanwhile, from a different, but equally negative perspective, in a February 1937 pamphlet, Francis P. Garvan (the onetime Alien Property Custodian) sounded an alarm against foreign investment in America—both FPI and FDI—suggesting that no one knew the size of such stakes, that the U.S. government based its figures on information furnished voluntarily (a "wretched method" of collection), and that the amounts were dangerously large. "Are we not, in truth and in fact, a debtor nation?" Garvan asked.[45]

Garvan felt that European investors in the United States had a vast financial hold over American industry, more than before World War I. That condition in 1917, in Garvan's opinion, "created [an] economic suction sufficient to draw us into war." James Powers, foreign editor of the *Boston Globe,* in June 1937 forwarded a statement of Garvan's to Senator David I. Walsh of Massachusetts, warning of "the danger ahead of us, in case of a European fracas."[46]

Economic historian Christina Romer has suggested that the gold influx of the 1930s played a positive role in ending the Great Depression.[47] She may well be right. When, in April 1938, the sterilization of

Figure 7.1. Inflow of foreign capital into the United States, domestic securities, weekly data. Week ending Jan. 9, 1935–Aug. 30, 1939. Source: Prepared by G. Gokkent from data in Board of Governors, Federal Reserve System, *Banking and Monetary Statistics* (Washington, D.C., 1943), 620–623, 626–629. Cumulative purchases came to $1,177.5 million. Cumulative data are the sum of weekly transactions Jan. 2, 1935–Aug. 30, 1939. Net movement from the United States is minus (−).

gold was entirely discontinued, this idea was tentatively endorsed in Washington. Yet Romer's favorable retrospective conclusions are out of keeping with those of most contemporaries, who for economic, political, and (in great part) emotional reasons saw the influx as fraught with peril; most economists (analysts and policy makers alike) as well as the general public would have been happier without the "contribution" from abroad.

Reactions to and Policies toward Inward Foreign Direct Investments, 1933–1939

During the 1930s, the preponderance of policy makers' attention was directed toward the large inward foreign portfolio investment flows. This said, inward foreign direct investment was not neglected, and the hostile attitudes described earlier in relationship to FPI washed over to inward FDI. Indeed, for policy makers not only were the distinctions between FPI and FDI—inward *and* outward—frequently ignored, but when in 1934 a special committee of the House of Representatives held hearings on un-American activities, there continued to be a blurring between private and public sector activities. American public relations man Ivy Lee, who had as a client the American affiliate of I. G. Farben, and in 1933–1934 the German parent as well, had a terrible time convincing the congressional committee that he was working for a company with large U.S. interests rather than for the German government.[48]

On June 24, 1934, Congress passed the Harrison Resolution (Public Resolution 53), which stated that with German bond defaults and until the president said otherwise, no further payments were to go to compensate Germans for their losses of properties in the United States during the First World War. These properties were primarily direct investments. Edwin Borchard, an expert on international law, commented in 1936 that "if European affairs can be restored to any kind of balance," ways should be worked out so that foreign (read German) investors who in good faith invested in this country could be compensated.[49] The Supreme Court disagreed and, on February 1, 1937, upheld Public Resolution 53. The German investors in the United States were never fully reimbursed for their World War I losses.[50]

During 1933–1939, existing U.S. federal laws restricting FDI in critical sectors—radio, shipping, and aviation—were reaffirmed, more strictly enforced, and extended. The Communications Act of 1934, which created the Federal Communications Commission to regulate interstate and foreign commerce by wire and radio, reiterated (and expanded) the rules set down in the Radio Act of 1927 that forbade the granting of broadcasting licenses to foreign owners.[51] The longstanding bans on foreign ownership of coastal shipping were more scrupulously implemented. The Central Vermont Transportation Company, incorporated in Maine and beneficially owned by the Canadian National Railway Company, was moving freight by water within the United States; a U.S. customs officer confiscated the goods being transported on the grounds that under the Merchant Marine Act of 1920, Central Vermont, as a "foreign company," was not allowed to participate in such trade. In 1935 the U.S. Supreme Court upheld the action of the customs officer. In the 1936 Merchant Marine Act there was a "codification of the prohibition against ownership of foreign-flag ships by subsidized U.S. lines." In the newly emerging international aviation industry, a regulatory regime emerged comparable to that applied to shipping. The Civil Aeronautics Act of 1938 (which supplemented the Air Commerce Act of 1926) set up the Civil Aeronautics Board. Under the 1938 law, as in the 1926 one and as in shipping, only "domestic" businesses could engage in carrying passengers from one place to the next within the borders of the United States. As in 1926 the president of the airline and two-thirds of the board members had to be American citizens, but now a domestic company was defined as 75 percent or more owned by U.S. citizens (the 1926 act had required only majority ownership).[52]

By 1938 William O. Douglas of the SEC had strong reservations about FDI in America. Douglas, whose concerns over foreign ownership of American securities have already been noted, wrote that European holdings could grow large enough "to become an important factor in the conduct of the affairs of some American corporations. . . . We do not view such outside pressure on management as making for sound national policy."[53]

In 1938, Congress passed the Foreign Agents Registration Act, seeking to prevent foreign governments from pulling the United States into any new European war (years later, this act would be applied to ferret out foreign direct investors' influence on U.S. government policies in war and peace). At this time, it was merely a part of the general "antiforeign" nationalistic mood.[54]

American tax policies affected FDI. When after 1934 there materialized a new vigilance in tracking down past-due back taxes (and not only those related to capital gains), this put many foreign multinationals that did business in the United States on the defensive.[55] Under the 1936 Revenue Act, the U.S. income of foreign banks was taxed at a higher rate than that of domestic banks, while foreign insurance companies were treated in exactly the same manner as their domestic counterparts.[56] Foreign multinational enterprises, in all sectors, adjusted their ownership relationships to alleviate the mounting tax burdens under changing U.S. (and foreign) tax laws.[57]

U.S. trade policies had an impact on FDI. In some cases, high tariffs continued to encourage new inward FDI (an inadvertent consequence of protection). If any inputs were imported, elevated tariffs raised the costs for existing foreign investors in America.[58] The 1934 Reciprocal Trade Agreements Act sought to press foreign governments into relaxing their restrictions on trade, and, in a reciprocal manner, the United States would lower its duties. In the deliberations on the 1934 act (and in its implementation), I have found no discussions of inward FDI, nor did I find that this legislation had any specific effects on the strategies of foreign multinationals in the United States.

On occasion in other contexts, however, U.S. commercial policies did become interwoven with FDI matters. Thus, in the 1930s Americans paid attention to foreign dumping of goods on the U.S. market, that is, selling in America below "fair value" (home domestic prices or home costs). U.S. Treasury agents visited Germany to examine dumping practices. I. G. Farben's commercial committee met (August 20, 1937) to consider how to react. The giant German chemical enterprise resolved to try "to settle the matter amicably with the [U.S. Treasury] agent without informing him of any details of our business." By 1937 I. G. Farben was insisting that it had no U.S. direct investments; thus, its management concluded it was "inappropriate at the present time, to suggest to the German authorities that a general decree prohibiting [the providing of] information should be issued."[59] The U.S. Treasury frequently investigated foreign companies' trade practices and their use of American-based sales affiliates in dumping.[60]

The reciprocity program fundamental to the 1934 trade legislation did have an earlier inward FDI legislation counterpart in the laws affecting cables and the leasing of mineral lands (see Chapters 2 and 5). When in 1934 and 1935, Great Britain passed new petroleum laws, Standard Oil of New Jersey's British affiliate, Anglo-American Oil Co., Ltd., was apparently uneasy lest these laws affect its obtaining prospecting licenses *in the United Kingdom.* Accordingly, the reciprocity clause in the 1920 Mineral Lands Leasing Act was briefly reactivated—to aid U.S. business abroad. The result was a British interpretation favorable to Anglo-American Oil Co.; and, for the first time, in 1936, the United States (rather reluctantly) designated Britain as a "reciprocating nation" under the terms of the 1920 Lands Leasing Act.[61]

The New Deal's "green light" to trade unions with the 1935 Wagner Act was in no way targeted at inward foreign multinationals, yet it had spillovers, as many foreign multinationals, especially those in the textile industry, faced labor unrest. The New Deal's endorsement of collective bargaining was seen by domestic and foreign-owned corporations as part of the offensive against big business.

By far the most significant overall U.S. public policies in the 1930s that affected inward FDI were those associated with the implementation of antitrust measures. These were general policies, but they had a differential impact on foreign multinational enterprises. In the early years of the New Deal, with the National Industrial Recovery Act, there had been a relaxation of antitrust enforcement with the aim of encouraging business involvement in economic revival.[62] This notwithstanding, in 1934 the Federal Trade Commission had begun formulating restraint-of-trade charges against foreign multinationals in the rayon industry. By 1938, the New Deal had come full circle on antitrust matters. Congress on June 16, 1938, set up the Temporary National Economic Committee (TNEC); investigations of domestic and international corporations and their connections with one another multiplied. Within the Roosevelt administration there was no longer any acceptance of a compromise with agreements that restrained trade or with "monopolies"; instead, there was a crusade against such practices. Before the outbreak of World War II in Europe, this late New Deal wave of antitrust fervor had already resulted in indictments of foreign multinational enterprises, and everything was in place for the charges and court cases to escalate. U.S. and foreign businesses would face major run-ins with America's antitrust authorities.[63] In this context, it is important that prominent among the allegedly evil internationalists of the 1930s were not only the bankers but also the largest U.S.-headquartered industrial corporations. These businesses, along with the bankers, were pilloried. Reflecting prevailing sentiments in the 1930s, historian Walter LaFeber would write, "Some firms, led by Du Pont, Standard Oil, General Motors, and Union Carbide, even worked closely—sometimes secretly and illegally—with German firms until the late 1930s, or in some cases, even to 1941."[64] The language of condemnation echoed existing U.S. attitudes toward big business in the 1930s. Du Pont, Standard Oil of New Jersey, and Union Carbide had alliances with I. G. Farben.

By contrast, as will be shown later in this chapter, several foreign direct investors had "friends" in Washington. Curiously, the cases that stand out are in agriculture: Fine Cotton Spinners' and Doublers' Association's Mississippi cotton plantations appear to have benefited greatly from New Deal agricultural subsidies, while in the grain trade, the French Fribourgs developed special Washington connections.[65]

The Search for Information

The enlarged and more active U.S. federal government meant a demand for information on international transactions and numerous new inquiries. This was true in the Treasury Department, which monitored the inflow of both short- and long-term foreign moneys as well as gold flows. On a weekly basis, beginning January 1, 1935, Federal Reserve banks gathered statistics on foreign purchases and sales of securities and shared their findings with the Treasury Department. This meant that data on inward investment from the Treasury and Federal Reserve were identical. The Federal Reserve banks relied on reports from banks, brokers, and dealers. They recognized that there were "unreported capital movements which may at some periods have been fairly substantial."[66] The Securities and Exchange Commission (established in 1934) was concerned with inward foreign capital flows, principally as they affected stock markets, although the SEC would toward the decade's end broaden its interests to matters of corporate "control," thus examining inward FDI.[67]

Meanwhile, all during the 1930s, the U.S. Commerce Department's coverage of the nation's balance of payments improved, and in 1937 the Commerce Department published a major report on inward foreign investments—direct and portfolio—followed by another in 1940.[68] The Commerce Department tracked both FPI and FDI but increasingly concentrated its attention on FDI. It did not have primary interest in European trading in American stocks, which, it believed, fell under the bailiwick of the Treasury Department, the Federal Reserve Board, and the Securities and Exchange Commission.[69] This separation in responsibility in monitoring foreign investments would, in the future, cause profound confusion.

Seeking incomes subject to tax and assuming that U.S. individuals used foreign intermediaries to evade U.S. taxes, the Bureau of Internal Revenue (within the Treasury Department) investigated inward foreign investments. Treasury Department tax forms contained information on income payments on foreign investments.[70] A number of congressional committees held hearings that touched on the behavior of foreign investors in the United States, dealing with topics from national security to the size of monopoly "rents." Thus, inward foreign investment became the subject of much study in Washington.

This was mirrored in research outside government, where outstanding scholarly contributions included Cleona Lewis' classic *America's Stake in International Investments* (1938). Lewis wrote on FPI and FDI inward into the United States and outward from the United States to the rest of the world.[71] Two years earlier, Herbert Marshall, Frank A. Southard, Jr., and Kenneth W. Taylor's *Canadian-American Industry* had appeared. It likewise dealt with "cross-investments," but only FDI: American business in Canada and Canadian enterprise in the United States.[72] Indeed, in the 1930s, foreign investment in the United States started to be documented as never before. Whereas many of the publications contained historical as well as current materials, all looked backward principally with the aim of understanding the contemporary situation.[73] Economists in this decade were well aware of the cross-investments, in both FPI and FDI.[74]

Foreign Investors by Nationality

For nearly all of the nation's history (except in the very earliest years), the largest inward foreign investments have come from the United Kingdom.[75] In the 1930s, the estimated inward foreign investment from Britain equaled just under 40 percent of the total.[76] Table 7.3, Column C, gives mid-1937 ratios, by nationality. After Roosevelt had let the dollar depreciate, American securities, already depressed by years of free fall, became still cheaper. Some British investors perceived bargains; indeed, so worrisome did the buying of American securities become to the British government that on May 17 and June 12, 1933,

Table 7.3. Estimates of long-term foreign investment in the United States, by nationality, mid-1937, portfolio and direct investment (in millions of U.S. dollars)

(A) Nationality	(B) Total	(C) (%)	(D) Foreign direct investment	(E) Foreign direct investment as % of total (D ÷ B)
United Kingdom	2,743	(39)	833	30
Canada	1,180	(17)	463	39
Netherlands	970	(14)	179	18
Switzerland	743	(11)	74	10
France	408	(6)	57	14
Belgium	142	(2)	71	50
Germany	124	(2)	55	44
China	58	(1)	5	9
Sweden	51	(1)	30	59
Italy	48	(1)	12	25
Japan	48	(1)	41	85
Rest of world	372	(5)	63	17
U.S. national, state, and municipal bonds not identified by nationality	100	(1)	—	—
Total	7,007	(100)[a]	1,883	27

Source: U.S. Department of Commerce, Bureau of Foreign and Domestic Commerce, *Foreign Long-Term Investments in the United States, 1937–39* (Washington, D.C., 1940), 21–22.

a. Total is off because of rounding.

Chancellor of the Exchequer Neville Chamberlain requested London stockbrokers to refrain from large block purchases.[77]

Four years later, economist A. T. K. Grant wrote, "Britain is now in a state of economic semi-insulation in relation to a large part of the world, and even countries in the sterling group are likely to be less sensitive to movements of [interest] rates in London . . . Any changes of rates in Great Britain will then affect internal conditions rather than international conditions." However, Grant qualified the statement to note that "flows of British funds for investment in New York may be affected [by changes in British interest rates]." Earlier in the same book, he wrote, "The most significant form of capital exports [from the United Kingdom] is the purchase of securities in New York—a case of one creditor country speculating in the stock markets of another."[78] All during the 1930s, American securities retained their special place in the portfolios of British investors.[79] British scholars continued to see the British flows to the United States as unlike other overseas investments. In 1933–1939, the purchases (and sales) were typically of traded securities, not of new issues.

As in times past, British purchases of American securities could be executed on the London or New York exchanges. Some transactions involved arbitrage, trading in the same security in different markets to take advantage of the price differentials. As the 1930s progressed, Americans worried about trades that occurred in London, thus avoiding the new U.S. regulation of securities markets.[80] By contrast, economic historian Ranald Michie has argued that whereas once London had been an important place of trade for American securities, by 1938 American securities were "really a New York market." Michie shows that the nominal value of American railroad securities *in the London Stock Exchange Official List* was £1,418.9 million in 1933; this was reduced to £865.4 million in 1939.[81] As noted earlier, railroads were not the main American securities of interest to foreign investors by this time. On the other hand, Michie points out that whereas in 1927 there were ten members of the New York Stock Exchange with offices in London, by 1937 that number had climbed to twenty-five (the number increased at the end of the 1920s; there were some exits of firms after the stock market crash; and then the new entries). In the 1930s these New York Stock Exchange brokers and dealers "focused exclusively on the transatlantic trading of dollar securities"; they could rapidly buy or sell American securities for clients in England at the existing New York prices.[82]

Figure 7.2 gives weekly purchases (negative purchases are sales) by British residents of American domestic securities, compared with the activities of all foreigners, based on transactions made through U.S. banks, brokers, and dealers from January 1935 through the week ending August 30, 1939, as monitored by Americans.[83] The Federal Reserve also followed the smaller British trade in dollar-denominated "foreign securities."[84] Clearly, a sizable percentage of the inward foreign investments in American securities, as recorded by the Federal Reserve, was British. Because of heavy British trading in late 1936 and early 1937, in 1937 the British government once again attempted to restrain capital exports that went into purchases of American stock exchange securities.[85] Within Britain, most economists believed that the capital outflow substituted for needed investment at home and was not desirable.

By the 1930s, much of the British ownership of American securities was by institutions, mainly British investment trusts and insurance companies.[86] As the 1930s progressed, British investment trusts were in and out of American securities, and to the extent that they resumed interest, it was with nowhere near the involvements of the pre–World War I era. Now their investments were mainly in equities rather than in bonds.[87] For 1934, George Glasgow identified 35 British investment trusts with more than 15 percent of their securities portfolio in the United States (see Table 7.4). One estimate, for 1938, based on market values, put the U.S. share of a sample of British investment trust portfolios at 19.5 percent of the total. Based on market value, the *Economist,* scrutinizing the accounts of 144 British investment trusts, found that in 1939 about 17 percent of their portfolios was in American securities. Apparently, a number of investment trusts, particularly Scottish investment trusts (25 out of the 35 identified by Glasgow), retained (and may have even increased during the 1930s) their long-established involvements in the United States, with the percentages fluctuating over the years. The trusts often were in clusters, and the Fleming and Robert Benson groups kept their American contacts.[88]

Some British holdings of American stocks had been purchased long before the 1930s.[89] Some were outcomes of what had once been British direct investments in America, but the assets were no longer British controlled.[90] Often U.S. businesses with direct investments in Britain, which were familiar to Britishers, found that the American parent's securities had, to a small extent, migrated into British hands.[91]

As for the British direct investments, these were more numerous than most Britishers (and Americans) realized. It is true that not many British enterprises entered anew in the years 1933–1939, and those that started to manufacture were primarily motivated to get behind U.S. tariffs and other barriers to trade. Likewise, basically for tax reasons, gone in the main as investors in the United States were the free-standing companies so prevalent in the pre–World War I capital-rich Britain. British overseas banks in New York (banks that had started as free-standing firms) were no longer in that category; these banks were

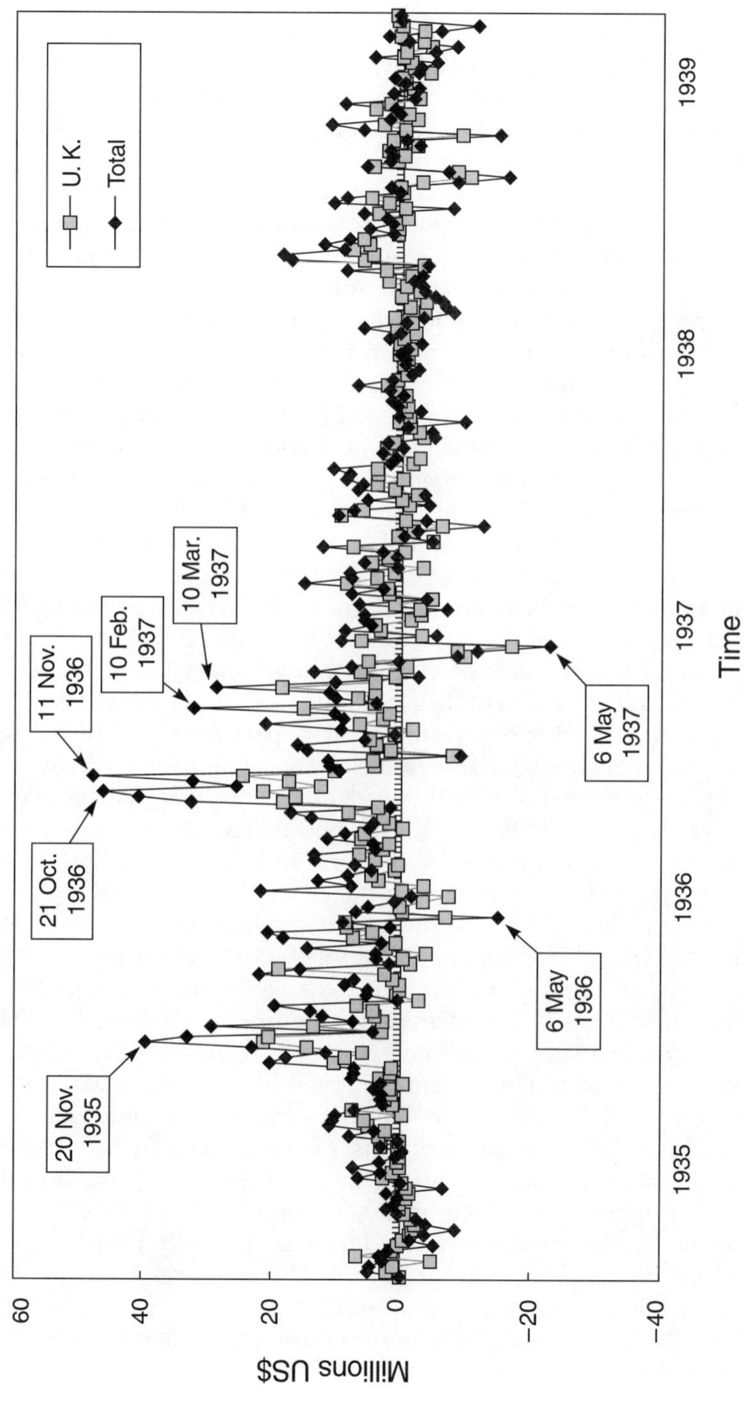
U. K.
Total
20 Nov. 1935
6 May 1936
21 Oct. 1936
11 Nov. 1936
10 Feb. 1937
10 Mar. 1937
6 May 1937
Millions US$
60
40
20
0
−20
−40
1935
1936
1937
1938
1939
Time

multinational enterprises with their own internalized core competencies.[92] A small number of British direct investors of long duration found the U.S. environment too competitive and retreated; other British companies, which periodically (over the years) had explored the idea of investing in the United States, gave up the effort, since America in depression times seemed to offer few good opportunities. So, too, certain British giants acquiesced in division-of-market and licensing arrangements—strategic alliances—and these businesses kept merely a nominal presence or no "operations" in the United States: important firms in this category were Imperial Chemical Industries and Pilkington (which in 1934 joined with Pittsburgh Plate Glass and Libbey Owens Ford to divide markets).[93] By contrast, many British enterprises, with insurance companies in the vanguard, stayed on as direct investors; in this category were highly successful affiliates (both in terms of profitability and with substantial market penetration) along with less successful participants. As of 1941, the U.S. census would identify more than 600 branches and subsidiaries of British firms in the United States.[94]

Canada ranked in second place after Britain as the largest source for foreign investment in the United States, with about 20 percent of the total.[95] In the 1930s, the U.S. Commerce Department always adjusted its Canadian data downward, seeking not only to eliminate U.S. residents (who used Canadian intermediaries for tax purposes) but also to account for French, U.K., Dutch, Swiss, and Belgian investment through Canadian companies. The figures given on Table 2.4, earlier in this volume, suggest little change from 1934 to 1939 in the overall size of Canadian investments in the United States, which hovered at about $1.1 billion; these Commerce Department data (covering both direct and portfolio investments) mask retreats and also the new involvements. On a regular basis, Canadian investors continued to buy and sell stock in American corporations (portfolio investments). Figure 7.3, which shows Canadian activity in American domestic securities, is unremarkable. It indicates a small increase in purchases over sales. As a 1939 Dominion Bureau of Statistics report concluded, "A considerable

Figure 7.2. Inflow of British capital into the United States compared with all foreign inflows, domestic securities, weekly data. Week ending Jan. 9, 1935–Aug. 30, 1939. Source: Prepared by G. Gokkent from data in Board of Governors, Federal Reserve System, *Banking and Monetary Statistics* (Washington, D.C., 1943), 620–623, 626–629. Cumulative British purchases came to $433.5 million; all foreign, to $1,177.5 million. Cumulative data are the sum of weekly transactions Jan. 2, 1935–Aug. 30, 1939. Net movement from the United States is minus (−).

Table 7.4. Thirty-five British investment trust companies' U.S. portfolios, 1934

Company	U.S. holdings as % of total holdings
Scottish American Investment Co., Ltd., Edinburgh	41.3
Independent Investment Trust Co., Ltd., London	41.3
British Asset Trust Ltd., Edinburgh	40.4
Scottish and Dominion Trust Ltd., Edinburgh	31.0
Second Clydesdale Investment Co., Glasgow	26.0
Second Scottish Investment Trust Co., Ltd., Glasgow	25.9
Third Caledonian Trust Co., Ltd., Glasgow	25.2
London and Clydesdale Trust Ltd., London	24.4
Scottish Investment Trust Co., Ltd., Edinburgh	24.3
London and Holyrood Trust Co., Ltd., London	23.9
Scottish Capital Investment Co., Ltd., Edinburgh	21.6
Nineteen-Twenty-Nine Investment Trust, London	21.2
United States Trust Co. of Scotland, Edinburgh	20.7
Scottish Mortgage and Trust Co., Ltd., Edinburgh	20.5
Third Scottish Western Investment Co., Ltd., Glasgow	20.2
London Stockholders Investment Trust, Ltd., London	20.0
Merchants Trust, London	19.6
Scottish Western Investment Trust Co., Ltd., Glasgow	19.5
Caledonian Trust Co., Glasgow	19.1
English and New York Trust Co., London	18.7
Melville Trust Ltd., Edinburgh	17.8
London and Provincial Trust Co., London	17.8
Second Edinburgh and Dundee Investment Co., Edinburgh	17.3
Second Scottish National Trust Co., Glasgow	17.0
Winterbottom Trust, Manchester	17.0
Third Scottish National Trust Co., Glasgow	16.9
Scottish National Trust Co., Ltd., Glasgow	16.8
Friars Investment Trust Ltd., London	16.4
American Trust Co., Ltd., Edinburgh	16.4
Second Scottish Western Investment Co., Glasgow	16.4
Clydesdale Investment Co., Ltd., Glasgow	16.2
Edinburgh Investment Trust, Edinburgh	16.0
Scottish Eastern Investment Trust, Ltd., Edinburgh	15.7
Third Edinburgh Investment Trust Ltd., Edinburgh	15.4
Pentland Investment Ltd., Edinburgh	15.2

Source: George Glasgow, *Glasgow's Guide to Investment Trust Companies* (London: Eyre and Spottiswoode, 1935). In addition, Glasgow indicated that in 1934 the Alliance Trust Co., Ltd., Dundee, had 56 percent of its securities portfolio outside Great Britain; it is likely that more than 15 percent of its total securities holdings was in the United States.

amount of trade in stocks between Canada and the United States" resembled internal stock exchange trading; "its international character is only incidental."[96] Figure 7.4, however, is more interesting. It covers Canadian trade in foreign securities, as reported by American banks, brokers, and dealers. Whereas overall, January 2, 1935, to August 30, 1939, foreign purchases of foreign securities traded in the United States rose, Canadians—by contrast—sold such securities (indeed, in net, they had sold far more than they bought of American domestic securities). With one exception, every major downward spike on Figure 7.4 was pushed down by Canadian transactions. Before mid-March 1937, upward spikes were also Canadian driven; afterward, only one was (the week ending January 4, 1939). A Canadian report explaining the sales noted that during the 1920s, Canadians had made large purchases of dollar bonds of Latin American governments, "parts of which were distributed in Canada along with the main flotations in the United States." It was these bonds ("foreign securities") and some other dollar-denominated foreign bonds that were sold by Canadians in the 1930s.[97] Canadians were accustomed to buying and selling American dollar-denominated (domestic and foreign) securities in New York; it was easy for them to do so. A Canadian report indicated that in 1939 a great variety of U.S. domestic securities were held, "although holdings of a relatively small number of issues of prominent United States corporations constitute a large part of the total."[98] Canadian direct investments in the United States during the New Deal years declined in the U.S. railroad sector. In contrast, a dramatic rise took place in Canadian direct investments in manufacturing in the United States, principally in alcoholic beverages. In this sector, Canadians were well prepared to respond rapidly at the end of Prohibition.[99]

Dutch and Swiss investments in America mounted during the decade, associated with the desire of investors to flee European uncertainties (and also reflecting certain readjustments in corporate arrangements): in 1934, Dutch and Swiss investments had represented just over 20 percent of the total foreign investments in the United States; in 1939, their share was in excess of 25 percent.[100] Often Dutch and Swiss intermediaries were used to channel German capital flows to America; thus, some of the nominally Dutch and Swiss stakes were beneficially those of Germans. European investors of other nationalities as well, for tax and secrecy reasons, invested in the United States through Holland and Switzerland. And there were the arbitrage dealers. Dutch investors were savvy in arbitrage between New York, London, and Amsterdam. The Swiss Banking Law of 1934, which strongly reinforced bank secrecy, encouraged third-country investors to move their moneys to the United States through Switzerland, under a shield of privacy.[101]

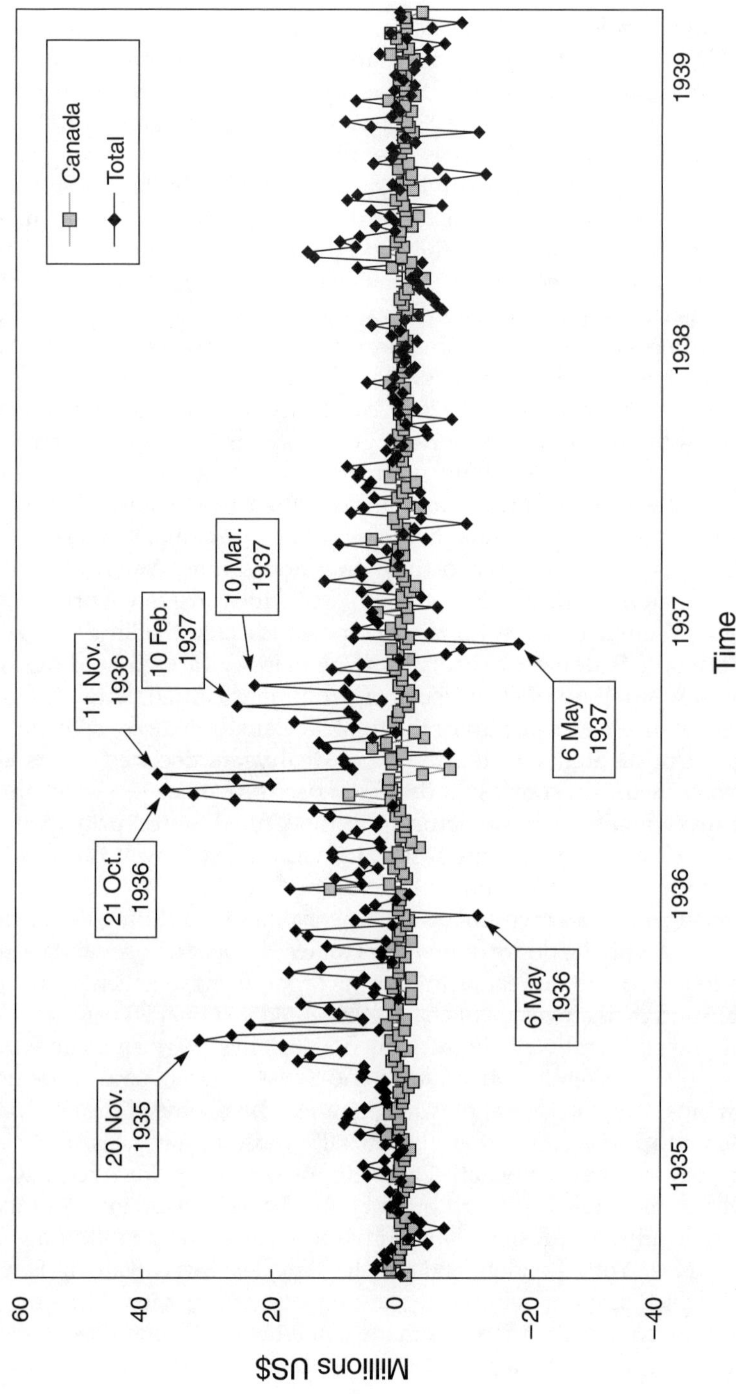
Canada
Total
20 Nov.
1935
21 Oct.
1936
11 Nov.
1936
10 Feb.
1937
10 Mar.
1937
6 May
1936
6 May
1937
Millions US$
60
40
20
0
−20
−40
1935
1936
1937
1938
1939
Time

At the same time, other "Dutch" and "Swiss" portfolio investments in the United States came from (rather than through) Holland and Switzerland. It was by no means clear that either country would be able to stay neutral were a war to occur; thus, nationals of both countries sought safety in America. Frequently, it is impossible to separate the moneys sent to the United States that originated in the Netherlands and Switzerland from those investments by other Europeans that filtered through Amsterdam, Zurich, Basle, and Geneva en route to America. In addition, there were existing U.S. assets held by foreign investors that were transferred to Dutch (and Swiss) ownership, without new capital flows.[102]

In the mid-1930s, Commerce Department studies were commenting on the comparatively heavy Dutch holdings in American railroad bonds, a remnant of the past. In December 1937, the American investment bank Dillon Read, in association with Mendelssohn & Co., Amsterdam, and Nederlandsche Handel- Maatschappij, was arranging the introduction of more American securities on the Amsterdam stock exchange, and early in 1938, the *Midland Bank Monthly Review* reported that shares of American companies represented a large portion of the business on the Amsterdam exchange.[103] Data from *Van Oss' Effectenboek* (the Dutch stock exchange manual) confirm this and show the formation of new Dutch publicly traded financial intermediaries with sizable holdings of American securities.[104] Throughout the 1930s, *Van Oss' Effectenboek* listed numerous American industrial, public utilities, and railroad securities.[105] Toward the end of the 1930s, there was a heightened interest coming from Switzerland in American stocks and bonds. Here, too, much of the investment was institutional rather than by individuals. The large Zurich-headquartered public utilities holding company, Bank für Elektrische Unternehmungen (Elektrobank), for example, acquired a sizable portfolio of American public utilities; by 1939, about 25 percent of its securities were American.[106] Figures 7.5 and 7.6 give Federal Reserve data on the Dutch and Swiss purchases of American domestic securities on U.S. stock exchanges (these numbers appear to exclude Dutch trading in American securities on the Amsterdam or London market, so they would underestimate the extent of Dutch involvements).

Figure 7.3. Inflow of Canadian capital into the United States compared with all foreign inflows, domestic securities, weekly data. Week ending Jan. 9, 1935–Aug. 30, 1939. Source: Prepared by G. Gokkent from data in Board of Governors, Federal Reserve System, *Banking and Monetary Statistics* (Washington, D.C., 1943), 620–623, 626–629. Cumulative Canadian purchases came to $13 million; all foreign, to $1,177.5 million. Cumulative data are the sum of weekly transactions Jan. 2, 1935–Aug. 30, 1939. Net movement from the United States is minus (−).

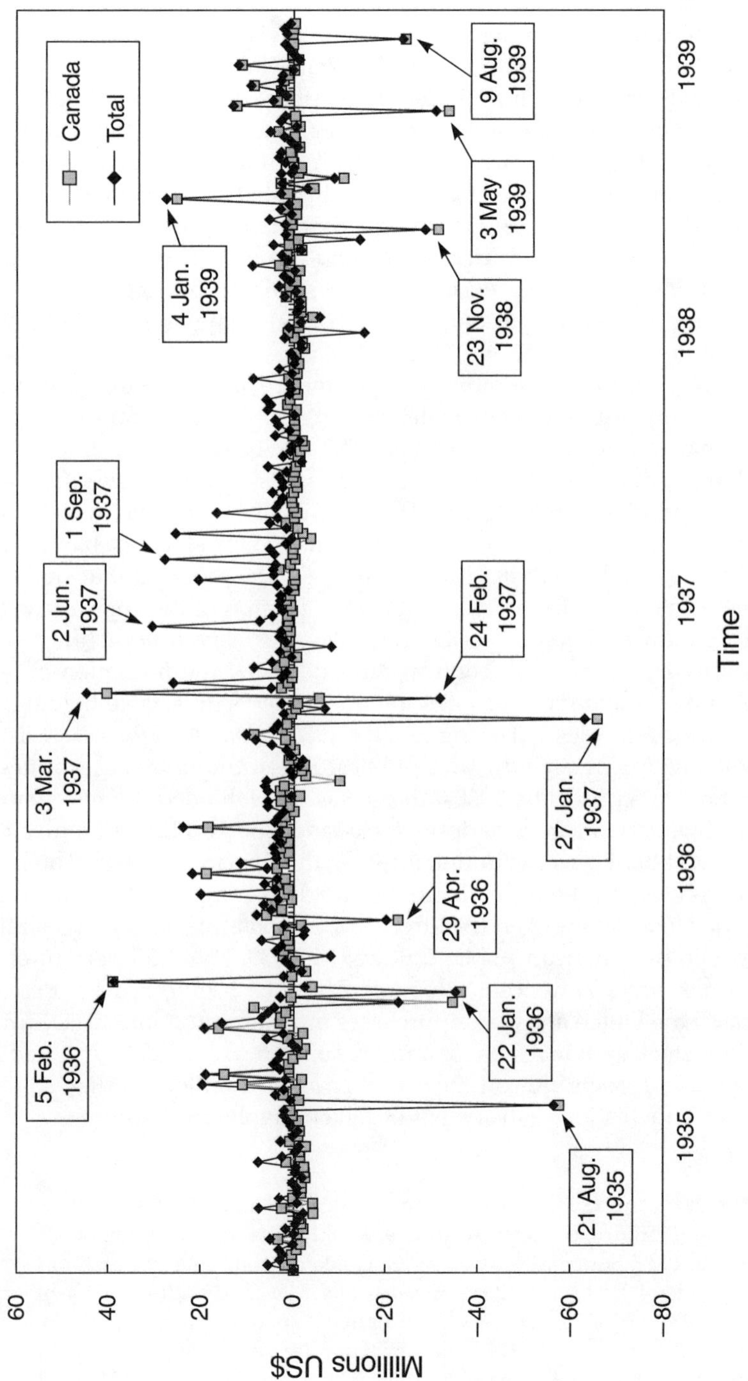

Canada
Total
Millions US$
60
40
20
0
−20
−40
−60
−80
Time
1935
1936
1937
1938
1939
21 Aug. 1935
5 Feb. 1936
22 Jan. 1936
29 Apr. 1936
27 Jan. 1937
3 Mar. 1937
24 Feb. 1937
2 Jun. 1937
1 Sep. 1937
23 Nov. 1938
4 Jan. 1939
3 May 1939
9 Aug. 1939

The Netherlands and Switzerland not only provided conduits for portfolio investors from those countries and from other nations for their U.S. interests; this was also the case with direct investors. Thus, the British-Dutch enterprise Unilever in 1937 and 1938 placed its U.S. business under Dutch rather than British ownership, even though the "head office" for the U.S. business remained in London. A historian for Unilever refers to its American business from the late 1930s as "technically" Dutch owned.[107] I. G. Farben used Dutch and Swiss intermediaries as "owners of" its U.S. interests (and had done so even before the period 1933–1939).

There appears to have been substantial concentration in Dutch direct investments in the United States with the German-Dutch rayon maker Algemeene Kunstzijde Unie NV (AKU), the British-Dutch Shell, and, after 1937, Unilever, together representing some 95 percent of the total. The large Dutch enterprise NV Philips had very small investments in the United States.[108] Swiss direct investments consisted of many more participants, but with none in either rayon or oil—and none directly in competition with Unilever's product lines; there were also no stakes that were competitive with NV Philips. Swiss direct investments were in food products (different ones from those of Unilever), in textiles (excluding rayon), and importantly in chemicals and pharmaceuticals. Although some of the "Swiss" chemical industry direct investments were beneficially German, many of those in the United States by Swiss chemical and pharmaceutical enterprises had "genuine" Swiss parents.

In the 1930s, by Commerce Department calculations, more than 80 percent of both inward foreign investment in general and FDI in particular came from four nations—the United Kingdom, Canada, Holland, and Switzerland.[109] In point of fact, individuals and enterprises from a wide range of nations around the globe had investments in America. Some of these investments passed through the four key nations. Just as with the four leading nationalities, so with the others, the relative importance of portfolio and direct investments varied substantially by source nation (see Table 7.3).

Figure 7.4. Inflow of Canadian capital into the United States compared with all foreign inflows, foreign securities, weekly data. Week ending Jan. 9, 1935–Aug. 30, 1939. Source: Prepared by G. Gokkent from data in Board of Governors, Federal Reserve System, *Banking and Monetary Statistics* (Washington, D.C., 1943), 620–623, 626–629. Cumulative Canadian purchases came to $−41.5 million; all foreign, to $657.8 million. Cumulative data are the sum of weekly transactions Jan. 2, 1935–Aug. 30, 1939. Net movement from the United States is minus (−).

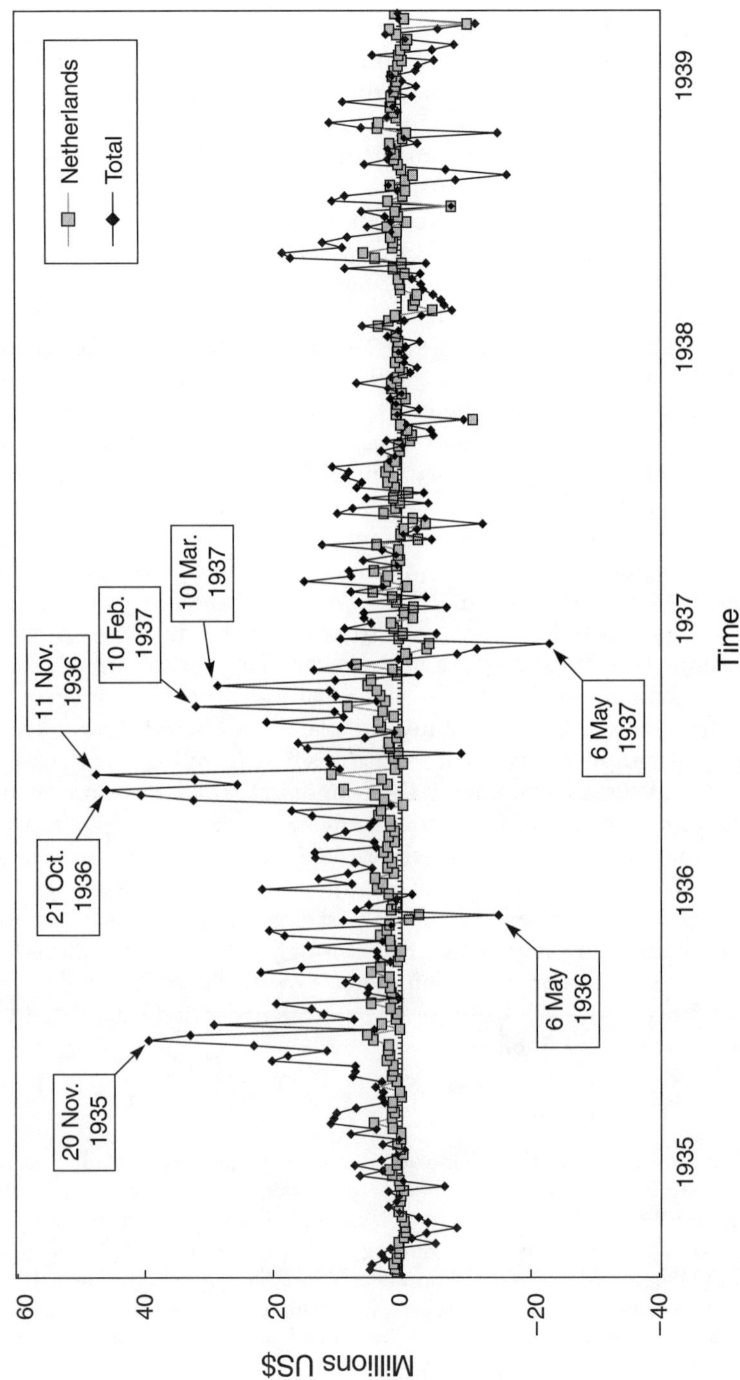
Netherlands
Total
20 Nov. 1935
6 May 1936
21 Oct. 1936
11 Nov. 1936
10 Feb. 1937
10 Mar. 1937
6 May 1937
60
40
20
0
−20
−40
Millions US$
1935
1936
1937
1938
1939
Time

According to Commerce Department figures, France was in fifth place in terms of foreign investors in the United States. The same securities J. P. Morgan & Co. dealt with in New York and Morgan, Grenfell handled in London were often picked up in France (and elsewhere in Europe) through Morgan & Cie., Paris. Despite the Glass-Steagall Act of 1933 and the formation of Morgan Stanley in 1935, J. P. Morgan & Co. continued to offer advice on the buying and selling of American securities in Europe. Also, Morgan Stanley after 1935 seems to have, at least initially, offered new issues to the French and British Morgan houses.[110] The Commerce Department probably underestimates French investment, for British banks and brokers and Swiss private banks bought American securities on behalf of French clients.[111] France, like the United Kingdom, the Netherlands, Switzerland, and Belgium, maintained "free exchange markets" in 1934 to 1939; thus, it is possible that French intermediaries could have been used to export moneys to the United States from other countries subject to controls. In 1935–1936 (before France devalued the franc, September 25, 1936), there was a flight from the franc—some of which went into dollars; on various occasions, in 1935 and 1936, reports circulated that the French were large buyers of dollars and investors in securities in the United States.[112] French direct investments in the United States existed but were relatively small—that is, relative to other nationalities and to the total French holdings in the United States.[113]

There had never been giant Belgian investments in America, although by the decade's end, according to Commerce Department records, Belgian investment exceeded that of the Germans. Belgian stakes in the United States were highly concentrated. More than half the amount indicated in Table 7.3 could be from a single investor (Solvay & Cie.). One large Belgian public utility holding company (Sofina) had by 1937 greatly expanded its U.S. interests.[114]

By contrast to most nationalities, as suggested by data from both the Federal Reserve and the Commerce Department, German investments in the United States declined in the 1930s. Between 1935 and the last week of August 1939, in net Germans sold $27.1 million in American

Figure 7.5. Inflow of Dutch capital into the United States compared with all foreign inflows, domestic securities, weekly data. Week ending Jan. 9, 1935–Aug. 30, 1939. Source: Prepared by G. Gokkent from data in Board of Governors, Federal Reserve System, *Banking and Monetary Statistics* (Washington, D.C., 1943), 620–623, 626–629. Cumulative Dutch purchases came to $220.6 million; all foreign, to $1,177.5 million. Cumulative data are the sum of weekly transactions Jan. 2, 1935–Aug. 30, 1939. Net movement from the United States is minus (−).

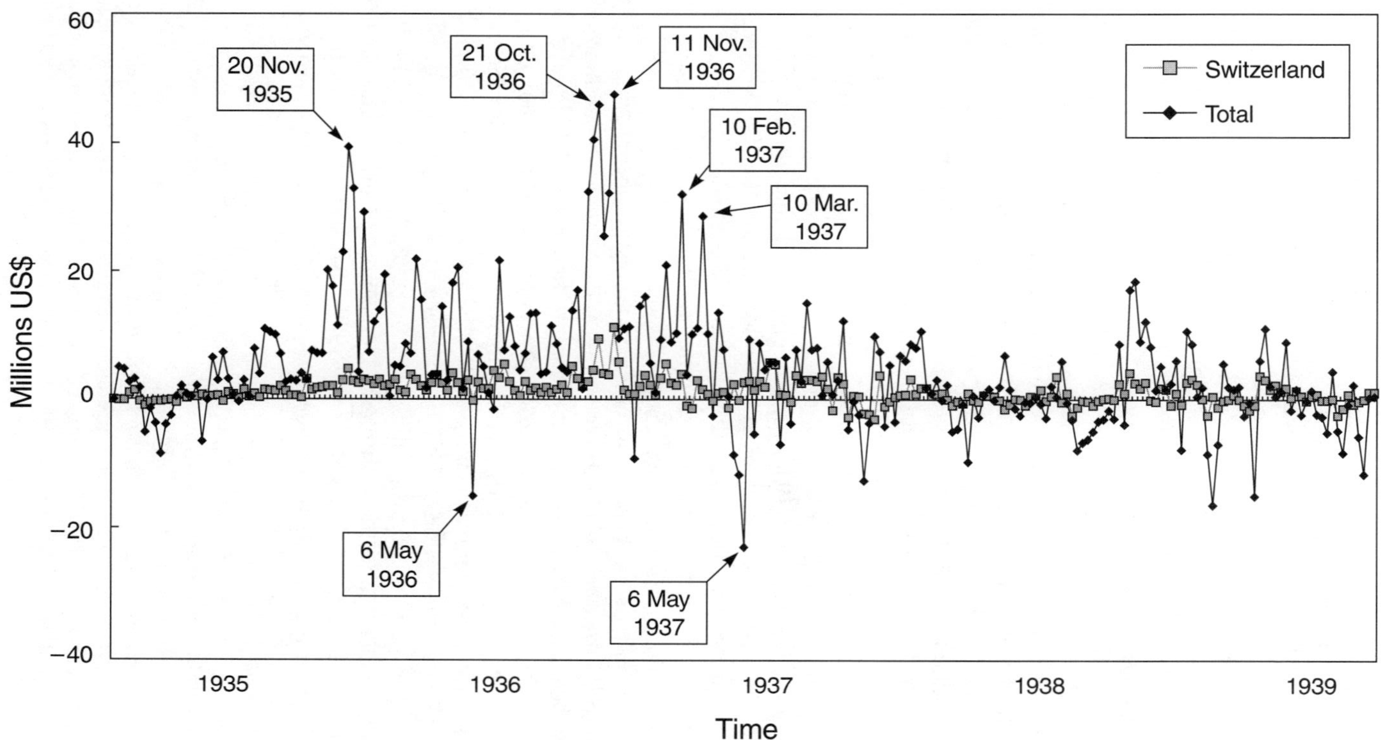

Switzerland
Total
20 Nov. 1935
21 Oct. 1936
11 Nov. 1936
10 Feb. 1937
10 Mar. 1937
6 May 1936
6 May 1937
Millions US$
60
40
20
0
−20
−40
1935
1936
1937
1938
1939
Time

domestic securities (yet in the same period they purchased $36.4 million in "foreign securities," very likely involving the repatriation, or "buybacks," of American investments in Germany rather than German investments in the United States).[115] Data from the Commerce Department indicate that at year end 1934 German investments in America totaled a mere 2.5 percent of all foreign investments in this country, while at year end 1939 they were a trivial 1.6 percent.[116] With stringent restrictions on German capital exports from 1933 to 1939, the remaining German investors in America (especially German direct investors) "cloaked" their holdings. On December 1, 1936, a German law stipulated that "a German citizen who, knowingly and unscrupulously, from motives of gross self-interest or other motives, . . . leaves property abroad, thereby causing gross injury to the German economic system, will be punished by death."[117] By this time, the methods for hiding foreign assets were well honed by sophisticated Germans. During the First World War, to protect their U.S. properties against the Alien Property Custodian takeovers (and then after the takeovers), Germans had devised subterfuges. Subsequent to the Armistice, they had crafted further schemes to circumvent Treaty of Versailles requirements and German restrictions on capital exports. In the late 1920s, German businesses developed complex ownership pyramids to avoid German (and possibly U.S.) taxes. The camouflage techniques were valuable in the early 1930s to get around the German exchange controls. By the Nazi period, the management of large German enterprises (and prominent Germans) knew exactly how to use American "nominees" as well as Dutch, Swiss, Swedish, and Danish conduits to achieve business confidentiality. In the years 1933–1939, German multinationals continued to do business in the United States (and took further steps to conceal, cloak, and preserve their U.S. properties). Thus, technically little German investment existed in the United States in 1933, 1937, or 1939. The figures fail, however, to reflect the profound impact of German multinational enterprises in America. Moreover, frequently German firms would combine negligible direct investments with the licensing of German patents, giving German parents substantial "control" and

Figure 7.6. Inflow of Swiss capital into the United States compared with all foreign inflows, domestic securities, weekly data. Week ending Jan. 9, 1935–Aug. 30, 1939. Source: Prepared by G. Gokkent from data in Board of Governors, Federal Reserve System, *Banking and Monetary Statistics* (Washington, D.C., 1943), 620–623, 626–629. Cumulative Swiss purchases came to $313.4 million; all foreign, to $1,177.5 million. Cumulative data are the sum of weekly transactions Jan. 2, 1935–Aug. 30, 1939. Net movement from the United States is minus (−).

influence within the United States. Indeed, much of the German "investment" had grown through technological rather than financial exports and so had not been subject to the "capital export" restrictions—albeit after 1936 Germans had to defend with vigor such investments.[118] The Germans, more than any other nationality, undertook licensing, which was far from arm's length. German patterns of licensing and German technological exchanges differed sharply from those of the British. Political conditions in Germany had immense impact on the *form,* if not the substance, of the operations.

Swedish and Italian investors had various stakes in America.[119] So, too, wealthy elites from the rest of Europe, Latin America, and China, for example, dispatched their savings to America in the 1930s, seeking a secure haven for their moneys in a nation not subject to exchange restrictions. Theirs were principally (but not exclusively) portfolio investments. More specifically, the rest of Europe added only a minimal amount to U.S. capital inflows (with the main contributions probably from Austria and Czechoslovakia), principally motivated by fears of war, but there were also investments arising from the "cosmopolitan finance" of the 1920s. Economist Barbara Stallings, writing on U.S. portfolio investments *in* Latin America, found the flows in 1933–1939 were negative ($290 million), comprising repayment of debt and Latin American outward capital flight (inward investment in the United States).[120] Figure 7.7 is revealing in this regard. More than one-quarter (27.2 percent) of all net foreign purchases of "foreign" securities in America, 1935–1939 (coming to $178.8 million), were made by Latin Americans.[121]

Chinese investments in the United States involved another illustration of wealthy elites' capital flight. These interests were directly stimulated by U.S. silver policies. China was on a silver standard (to November 1935); as U.S. purchases raised silver prices in late 1934 and 1935, leading Chinese businessmen, bankers, and government officials exported silver to America, leaving the sales proceeds there and building up personal nest eggs in the United States.[122] These Chinese bought American shares on Wall Street, and their American holdings later served as collateral for loans from American bank branches and other foreign banks *in China.*[123] Members of the Soong family, for instance,

Figure 7.7. Inflow of Latin American capital into the United States compared with all foreign inflows, foreign securities, weekly data. Week ending Jan. 9, 1935–Aug. 30, 1939. Source: Prepared by G. Gokkent from data in Board of Governors, Federal Reserve System, *Banking and Monetary Statistics* (Washington, D.C., 1943), 620–623, 626–629. Cumulative Latin American purchases came to $178.8 million; all foreign, to $657.8 million. Cumulative data are the sum of weekly transactions Jan. 2, 1935–Aug. 30, 1939. Net movement from the United States is minus (−).

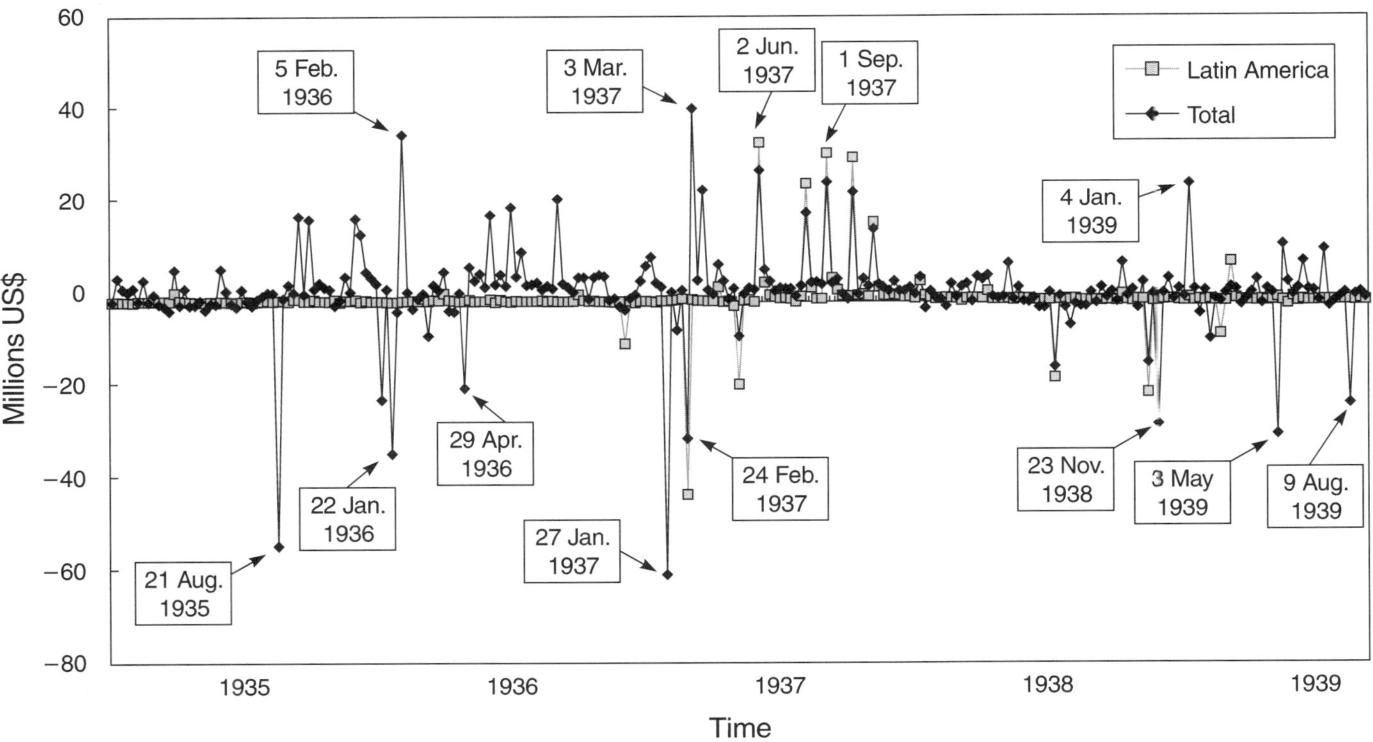
Latin America
Total
Millions US$
60
40
20
0
−20
−40
−60
−80
1935
1936
1937
1938
1939
Time
5 Feb. 1936
3 Mar. 1937
2 Jun. 1937
1 Sep. 1937
4 Jan. 1939
29 Apr. 1936
22 Jan. 1936
21 Aug. 1935
27 Jan. 1937
24 Feb. 1937
23 Nov. 1938
3 May 1939
9 Aug. 1939

acquired sizable holdings of American securities (Chiang Kai-shek was married to May-Ling Soong; her sister was the wife of H. H. Kung, China's minister of finance; T. V. Soong, as of 1935 chairman of the board of the Bank of China, was May-Ling's brother).[124] Japanese investments in the United States had different characteristics. The Japanese were present in America mainly with banks, trading companies, and insurance providers (service sector multinational enterprises).[125] Table 7.3 suggests that 85 percent of Japanese investment in the United States by mid-1937 was FDI.

As in times past, European (and not only British and German) businesses in America partook in licensing agreements and had "assets in the United States" reflected in these licensing contracts; the licensing practices involved both large and relatively small European firms.[126] The Commerce Department collected 1937 data on royalties for the use of patents paid by subsidiaries and affiliates to their *parent* companies, noting that these royalties were "more common in cases of partial [foreign] ownership than in cases of complete ownership." I calculated the royalty payments by nationality as a percent of each country's mid-1937 direct investment position, hoping the figures would be indicative of technological contributions. The results showed the Swedes with 3.0 percent and the Germans with 1.3 percent in the clear lead; followed by the Swiss (0.4 percent) and the Dutch (0.179 percent); then the French (0.028 percent), British (0.018 percent), Italians (0.012 percent), and Canadians (0.005 percent).[127] Sometimes licensing accompanied production joint ventures, and sometimes not.[128] The 1941 Census of foreign assets in the United States uncovered "more than 60,000 patents and cross-licensing and other patent agreements," about 40 percent by German nationals, 15 percent by U.K., 12 percent by Dutch, and 8 percent by Swiss nationals.[129] The lack of coincidence between these percentages and the 1937 returns (provided earlier) seems to result from the following: (1) the first set of figures deal with returns to *parent* firms as distinct from returns to licensors, and (2) numerators and denominators are completely asymmetrical.

Cosmopolitan Finance

The flamboyant financial architecture of the 1920s—the Kreuger-type endeavors—often became casualties of the Depression, as pyramids collapsed and regulators looked unkindly on such artifacts. Yet some companies owned fully or in part by foreign investors and set up in the United States to hold properties overseas persisted—for example, the two Stinnes companies (see Chapter 4). Also in this category was the United Continental Corporation (UCC), New York, formed in 1929 as a holding company for the German properties of the Czech

Julius Petschek group.[130] It reflects the complexities of some of the foreign holdings in the United States, particularly those involving 1930s refugees from fascism. UCC's first president was John Foster Dulles; its second, Dulles' close friend George Murnane. Sullivan & Cromwell, Dulles' law firm in the 1930s (as well as in the 1920s), acted on behalf of many European investors in the United States. In the 1930s, Murnane frequently assisted the law firms' clients, including the Belgian, Solvay & Cie. and the German firm, Robert Bosch. He would aid the Czechs.

Murnane was once a partner in the American banking house Lee Higginson & Co., which he left after its 1932 reorganization. Dulles introduced Murnane to Jean Monnet (who would later be the inspiration for European unification). They established in 1935 a New York–headquartered investment banking firm, Monnet Murnane & Co. Murnane, as president of the UCC, participated in negotiations between the Julius Petschek family (who were Jewish) and the Nazis who wanted them out of Germany.[131] The Petschek properties in Germany were lignite coal mines, which German industrialist Frederick Flick desired to acquire.[132] At one point in the discussions (in January 1938), Murnane suggested that UCC's assets in Germany be swapped for I. G. Farben's chemical plants in the United States. Murnane pointed out that since he was a member of the board of Allied Chemical, he could facilitate the arrangements. Flick responded that "under no circumstances could the Reich government be expected to agree to such an exchange."[133] Murnane insisted that two-thirds of the stock of UCC was owned by Americans, who were Aryans.[134] In May 1938, he sold the Petschek properties and got foreign exchange.[135] Paul Petschek, who had managed the German mines of the Julius Petschek group, would emigrate to Toronto; his foreign investment in UCC became Canadian; other family members moved to New York (and there would be no more "foreign" investment in the United States).[136]

Perhaps more typical of the cosmopolitan finance were the continuing pyramided ownership structures of many foreign portfolio investments in the United States. For tax, foreign exchange control, and other political reasons, even more frequently than in the 1920s, the nominal foreign owner of American securities was not the beneficial owner. Foreign buyers of securities often acted on behalf of individuals in third countries. Complications of ownership again and again made the classification by nationality of investors extremely difficult to define, much less determine.

Portfolio Investments

In the years 1933–1939, the majority of long-term foreign portfolio investments in the United States were in traded securities, domestic and foreign. The level was affected by immigration. Refugees tried and often succeeded in expatriating their moneys before arriving in the United States. Once they became U.S. residents, by definition, there was no longer foreign investment. Trade in foreign securities continued to be problematic: it was never clear whether it represented a repatriation of earlier holdings or, alternatively, a change from domestic (U.S.) to third-country foreign ownership of dollar-denominated foreign securities. One estimate indicated that by the end of 1935 at least 40 percent of all foreign dollar bonds outstanding had been repurchased without cancellation and were actually owned outside the United States. Figure 7.8 shows the trade in the United States in foreign securities *by* foreign investors. The cumulative net purchases of these foreign securities that the Federal Reserve tracked (between January 1935 and the end of August 1939) came to $657.8 million. Qualitative evidence lends support to the view that a sizable portion of the "cumulative net purchases" were *not* to acquire U.S. holdings but instead the return to the source country of discounted outstanding U.S. dollar-denominated bonds.[137] In its studies of foreign capital in the United States in the 1930s, the Commerce Department does not discuss the foreign holdings of dollar-denominated foreign securities.

By contrast, a great deal of attention was paid to the rising investments by foreigners in American domestic securities. The net cumulative purchases from January 1935 to the end of August 1939 came to $1,177.5 million, according to Federal Reserve Bank figures. The pace of this investment was motivated by a variety of economic and political considerations. The particularly high peaks in foreign buying in November 1935 and in October–November 1936 recorded in Figure 7.1 seem to coincide with political events: the first with the Italian invasion of Ethiopia in October 1935 (which frightened Europeans and resulted in capital flight across the Atlantic), and the second in the aftermath of the Tripartite Monetary Agreement between the United States, the United Kingdom, and France in late September 1936 (which by October had the effect of stimulating "investments of idle funds in all of the principal stock markets of the world").[138] The Tripartite Agreement banned competitive exchange depreciations and endorsed the easing

Figure 7.8. Inflow of foreign capital into the United States, foreign securities, weekly data. Week ending Jan. 9, 1935–Aug. 30, 1939. Source: Prepared by G. Gokkent from data in Board of Governors, Federal Reserve System, *Banking and Monetary Statistics* (Washington, D.C., 1943), 620–623, 626–629. Cumulative purchases came to $657.8 million. Cumulative data are the sum of weekly transactions Jan. 2, 1935–Aug. 30, 1939. Net movement from the United States is minus (−).

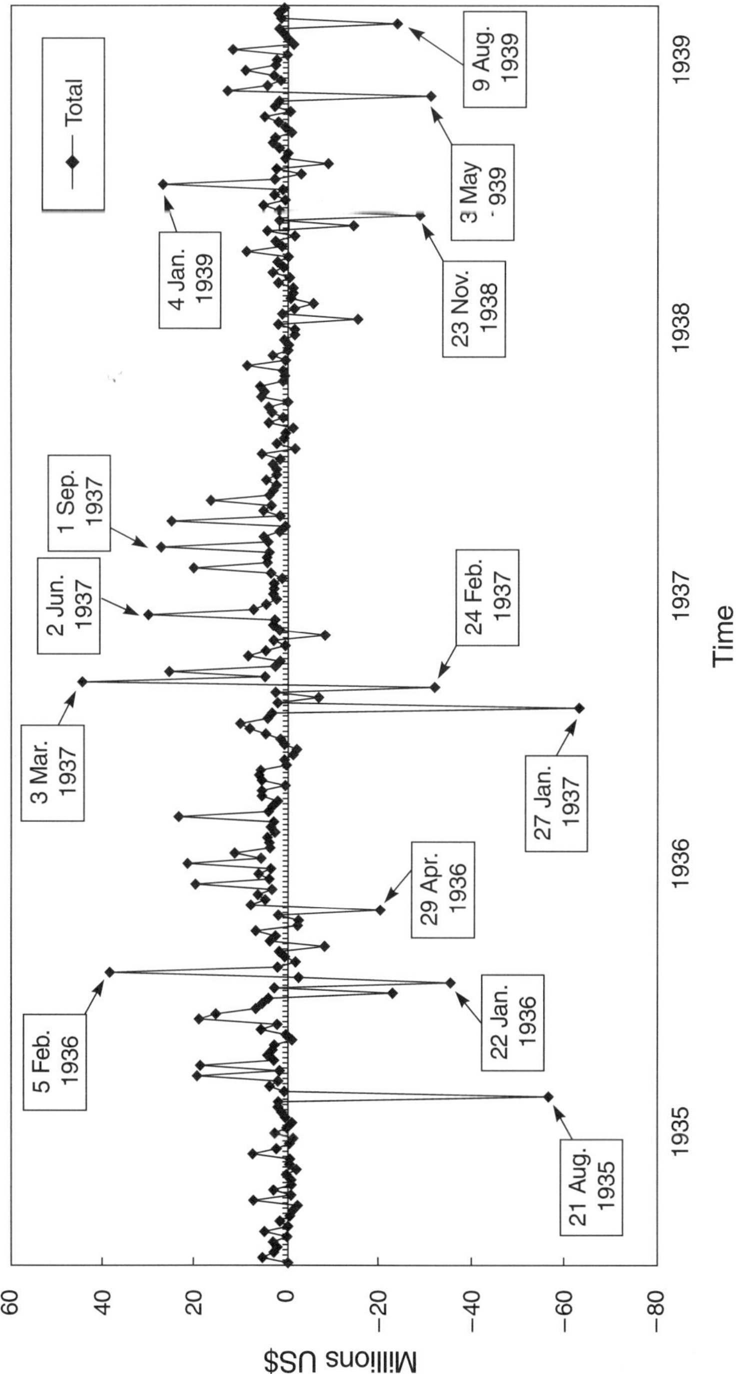
Total
9 Aug. 1939
3 May
4 Jan. 1939
23 Nov. 1938
1 Sep. 1937
2 Jun. 1937
24 Feb. 1937
3 Mar. 1937
27 Jan. 1937
29 Apr. 1936
5 Feb. 1936
22 Jan. 1936
21 Aug. 1935
1935
1936
1937
1938
1939
Time
60
40
20
0
−20
−40
−60
−80
Millions US$

of trade and exchange restrictions; some have called it a precursor of the postwar International Monetary Fund.[139] The sizable foreign acquisition of American securities in early 1937 was probably a response to rising prices on American stock exchanges.[140]

Sparse details exist on foreign holdings of U.S., state, and local government securities in the 1930s.[141] Foreign-owned insurance companies doing business in the United States and other foreign financial institutions with business in this country often had such securities in their portfolios.[142] Other foreign investors seem not to have been especially interested in such investments.[143] Foreign investors chose stock in the big (well-known) American industrials and public utilities; common shares, not bonds or preferred stock, were most attractive to investors from abroad.[144] FPI in the United States through most of the decade came primarily from foreign individuals, financial institutions, and corporations; there are, however, some indications that foreign governments did park limited surpluses in American securities, in part for currency stabilization purposes. A September 1940 report indicated that in the spring and summer of 1939, "foreign governments and central banks began to build up balances on a large scale in this country." The report was not clear as to whether these balances were short-term deposits in American banks or were invested in securities (probably both).[145]

Foreign Direct Investments

As in past years, the path of FDI differed from that of FPI. Both attracted attention and grew during the New Deal period. As one views the entries and exits of affiliates of foreign multinational enterprises in the 1930s, insights from the research on network approaches to such businesses seem highly germane. Within the United States, especially in the chemical industry, "multifaceted long-term and cooperative" international connections were "competitive and complementary" as well as "cumulative and changing."[146] The intricate webs had evolved from relationships formed originally in many cases before the First World War. At the same time, certain FDI was straightforward, involving additions to existing investments and some new arrivals. What follows is a review—by key sectors—of FDI in the United States, 1933—1939. Tables 7.5, 7.6, and 7.7 give the Commerce Department findings for year end 1934 and mid-1937.[147]

Railroads

Whereas most of the foreign investments in U.S. railroads had been FPI, the Canadian Pacific Railway (CPR) had over the years made sizable direct investments across the border, investments that had not fared well. Much of the Soo Line (the Minneapolis, St. Paul and Sault Ste. Marie Railway—with more than 4,000 miles of track) had been financed by the sale of securities guaranteed by its parent, CPR, which assumed these obligations when the Soo Line was unable to do so. The Soo Line's serious difficulties had begun in 1932, when the Wisconsin Central, which it controlled, went into receivership. Likewise, another of CPR's U.S. subsidiaries, the Spokane International Railway, was taken over by a trustee in the early 1930s. Then, in 1936, the Duluth, South Shore and Atlantic (also a CPR line) went into bankruptcy; finally, in 1937, so did the Soo Line itself. In May 1938, CPR's president, E. W. Beatty, concluded that since the late nineteenth century, CPR's total investment in its railway system in the United States had amounted to $61.2 million; it had received interest and dividends totaling $33.7 million; and it had built up a reserve of $23.5 million against capital losses. A year later, in 1939, the CPR used $15.6 million of this reserve to write off its remaining stock holdings in the Soo Line, the Spokane International Railway, and the Duluth, South Shore and Atlantic.[148] There is no evidence that the American affiliates of the other large Canadian railway system, the Canadian National Railway Company, did better.

Agriculture

No new foreign investments emerged in the American farm sector. Perhaps the most remarkable events affecting FDI in agriculture occurred in Mississippi, where the British firm Fine Cotton Spinners' and Doublers' Association (FCSDA), had huge cotton plantations. In 1927 FCSDA had hired a new chief executive for its Delta and Pine Land Co. (DPLC), the corporate owner of its principal cotton plantation. The man was Oscar Johnston, a small-town Mississippi lawyer and banker with contacts in Washington, D.C. After losses in 1930–1932, he had DPLC back to making operating profits during the 1930s. The corporation adopted advanced management methods. It had high productivity—relative to other plantations in the area. It had an experimental station and participated in plant breeding. Its raw cotton sales were all domestic, but its cotton *seed* sales became international (in fact, it came to be the largest seller of cotton seed in the world); it sold cotton seed to planters throughout the American South, as well as to those in India, Argentina, China, and Greece. Its plant-breeding activity resulted in "an enormous body of scientific knowledge about cotton, its nature, and production which ante-bellum planters, who crowned the crop king, never suspected." By the late 1930s, DPLC's revenues from cotton seed sales were roughly a

Table 7.5. Foreign direct investment in the United States, by industries, year end 1934, mid-1937 (book value in millions U.S. dollars and percentages)

Sector	1934		1937	
	FDI (in millions of dollars)	%	FDI (in millions of dollars)	%
Transportation, incl. railroads	246	16.2	257	13.6
Agriculture			13	0.7
Mining	35	2.3	24	1.3
Petroleum[a]	207	13.6	283	15.0
Manufacturing	565	37.2	729	38.7
Distribution[b]	86	5.7	119	6.3
Finance, incl. insurance	360	23.7	412	21.9
Miscellaneous[c]	20	1.3	45	2.0
Total	1,519	100.0	1,883	100.0

Manufacturing				
Chemicals	129	22.8	220	30.2
Textiles	209	36.5	217	29.8
Foodstuffs, beverages, and tobacco	77	13.6	116	15.9
Other manufacturing	153	27.1	176	24.1
Total	565	100.0	729	100.0
Finance, incl. insurance				
Banks, trust companies[d]	47	13.0	61	14.8
Insurance	313	87.0	351	85.2
Total	360	100.0	412	100.0

Sources: U.S. Department of Commerce, Bureau of Foreign and Domestic Commerce, *Foreign Investments in the United States* (Washington, D.C., 1937), 32 (1934); and U.S. Department of Commerce, Bureau of Foreign and Domestic Commerce, *Foreign Long-Term Investments in the United States, 1937–39* (Washington, D.C., 1940), 37 (1937). Totals may be off because of rounding. The number of companies covered in 1934 is not specified; for 1937 the data are based on 1,172 companies.

a. Petroleum covers production, pipelines, refining, distribution, and so forth.

b. Distribution covers trading companies, as well as all wholesaling and retailing *not* associated with manufacturing.

c. Miscellaneous includes $8 million for public utilities in 1934 and $9 million for public utilities in 1937; in 1934, it includes an unspecified sum for agriculture.

d. This is designation in 1934; in 1937 it was given as "banking, securities."

Table 7.6. Foreign direct investment in the United States, by nationality and industry, year end 1934 (book value in millions of U.S. dollars)

Country / region	Manufacturing	Distribution[b]	Transportation[c]	Public Utility	Petroleum[d]	Mining	Finance[e]	Misc.[f]	Total
Europe	484.9	52.0	41.3	0.1	192.2	26.3	277.8	10.9	1,085.5
United Kingdom	305.1	37.4	32.0		25.7	26.2	241.7	10.2	678.3
Netherlands	61.8	0.6	1.1		159.0		1.2	0.3	224.0
Switzerland	69.3	4.6	0.5		3.9		12.5		90.8
France	10.0	1.9	1.5	0.1	2.8		8.2		24.4
Other Europe	38.7	7.5	6.2		0.8	0.1	14.2	0.4	67.9
Canada[a]	76.8	10.0	201.1	8.0	11.5	8.5	50.3	0.5	366.7
Latin America	0.4	4.7	0.3		0.6	*	0.2	*	6.2
Rest of world	2.7	19.6	3.1		2.6		31.4	0.7	60.0
Total	564.8	86.4	245.6	8.0	207.0	34.8	359.7	12.2	1,518.4

Source: U.S. Department of Commerce, Bureau of Foreign and Domestic Commerce, *Foreign Investments in the United States* (Washington, D.C., 1937), 32. Totals may be off because of rounding. The number of companies covered is not specified. "Direct investments include all foreign investments in those American corporations or enterprises which are controlled by a person or small group of persons (corporate or natural) domiciled in a foreign country." Some miscellaneous investments in foreign-controlled enterprises were also included. *Less than $49,000.

a. Canada appears to include Newfoundland, although this is not specified.

b. Distribution covers trading companies, as well as all wholesaling and retailing not associated with a direct investment in manufacturing or petroleum.

c. Transportation includes railroads.

d. Petroleum covers production, pipelines, refining, distribution, and so forth.

e. Finance includes insurance.

f. Miscellaneous includes agriculture.

Table 7.7. Foreign direct investment in the United States, by nationality and industry, mid-1937 (book value in millions of U.S. dollars)

Country / region	Manufacturing	Distribution[b]	Transportation[c]	Public Utility	Petroleum[d]	Mining	Finance[e]	Misc.[f]	Total
Europe	591.1	69.7	39.1	0.9	247.9	13.6	334.9	40.2	1,337.4
United Kingdom	366.5	29.7	30.3	0.9	92.9	13.1	277.1	22.8	833.3
Netherlands	27.8	5.0	1.0		142.5	0.3	1.3	0.5	178.5
Belgium	65.7	3.6	0.1		*	0.1	1.1	0.6	71.2
Germany	45.8	6.3	2.5				0.1	0.3	55.0
Switzerland	24.2	12.9	0.2		2.3		28.0	6.4	73.9
France	24.1	7.4	1.5		10.1		11.7	1.8	56.5
Sweden	25.0	1.4	0.7				2.6		29.7
Other Europe	11.9	3.4	2.8				13.1	7.9	39.2
Canada[a]	130.9	11.0	215.6	8.1	35.0	10.2	45.7	6.2	462.7
Latin America	2.2	14.0	*	0.2	0.1	0.1	1.5	0.3	18.4
Africa, Asia, Oceania	2.8	24.5	1.8				30.2	1.1	60.4
Japan	0.9	16.5	1.8				21.8	*	41.0
Other	1.9	7.9	*				8.4	1.1	19.3
Country unknown	1.7	*	0.4		0.4	0.1	*	1.1	3.8
Total	728.7	119.2	257.0	9.2	283.4	23.9	412.4	48.9	1,882.6

Source: U.S. Department of Commerce, Bureau of Foreign and Domestic Commerce, *Foreign Long-Term Investments in the United States, 1937–39* (Washington, D.C., 1940), 34. Totals may be off because of rounding. The data are based on 1,172 companies. Direct investment is defined as controlling ownership of the common stock ("no arbitrary percentage" was used). Once defined, it includes other forms of investment. *Less than $49,000.

a. Canada includes $102 million for Newfoundland ($2 million in mining and $100 million in miscellaneous).

b. Distribution covers trading companies, as well as all wholesaling and retailing not associated with a direct investment in manufacturing or petroleum.

c. Transportation includes railroads.

d. Petroleum covers production, pipelines, refining, distribution, and so forth.

e. Finance includes insurance.

f. Miscellaneous includes $12.7 million for agriculture, not specified by country.

quarter of its revenues from cotton sales (later it would specialize in plant breeding and cotton seed production).

In the 1930s, its raw cotton growing was not mechanized. The company's labor force consisted of black sharecroppers (about 1,000 families); the company provided the seeds, mules, and minimal equipment (everything was handpicked), housing for the tenants, and credit facilities at the company store. The crop was shared, half to the tenant farmer, half to the company. Johnston combined sharecropping with an organized managerial structure. He became adept in his cotton sales strategies, hedging on cotton futures.

Of the greatest importance, Johnston's Washington, D.C., contacts meant that with the New Deal he was appointed finance director of the Agricultural Adjustment Administration in 1933, became a vice-president of the Commodity Credit Corporation later that year, and served as manager of the New Deal–sponsored cotton pool (1934–1936). DPLC became a major recipient of "plowing under benefits"—that is, subsidies for removing acreage from production, with an eye to raising prices. It also became the target of populist critics, who saw New Deal farm benefits going to British corporate farming rather than to the American family farm. The British had found excellent American management; there is no evidence that any of the entrepreneurial initiative came from the United Kingdom.[149]

In agriculture-related activities, there was foreign ownership in inputs such as fertilizers, certain agricultural chemicals, and farm equipment. There were changes in FDI in some processed agricultural outputs. Foreign investors also continued to participate in international trade in agricultural products. In farm mortgages the foreign investors' role was sharply reduced. Foreign direct investors were significant players in fertilizers and in U.S. agricultural exports. In fertilizers, they took part in phosphate mining and trade, were leaders in potash production and trade, and had impact on developments in synthetic nitrates. I have no figures on the share of U.S. agricultural products exported by foreign-owned multinationals, yet the qualitative materials make it evident that in grain, tobacco, and to a far lesser extent cotton, foreign-owned trading companies had a leading role in facilitating U.S. agricultural exports.[150]

Minerals

There were some new foreign multinational enterprise activities in gold. Mountain Copper Company, Ltd., in California, which turned to gold production when demand for its other output slumped, became the biggest producer of gold in northern California. Its output peaked in 1936 and then began to decline. Consolidated Golds Fields also enlarged its gold mining activities in California.[151] Far more important were the ongoing activities by foreign multinationals in phosphates, potash, and borax.

In the phosphate industry, in 1933 the German trading company Metallgesellschaft merged its Florida phosphate holdings into the newly formed and sizable Pembroke Chemical Corporation and obtained 49 percent ownership (the British Albright & Wilson's U.S. subsidiary, Oldbury Electro-Chemical Company, held the other 51 percent); Ore & Chemical Corporation (a trading affiliate of Metallgesellschaft) would come to hold the 49 percent interest on behalf of its German parent.[152] In Germany, Metallgesellschaft developed new processes of manufacturing phosphates, which apparently were introduced in the United States.[153] In addition, other foreign stakes in Florida phosphates seem to have persisted during the 1930s.[154] According to a Canadian source, a subsidiary of the Canadian Pacific Railway, Consolidated Mining and Smelting Co. (renamed in 1966 Cominco), had started to mine phosphates in Montana; this Canadian mining company would years later become important in U.S. mining.[155]

Of much greater consequence were the FDIs in potash. During the years 1933–1939, the innovative American Potash & Chemical Corporation (APCC) continued to be the premier potash producer in the United States; it was, through a Dutch intermediary, secretly controlled by two big German potash firms, Salzdetfurth AG and Wintershall AG. In the first half of 1938, when the Germans made arrangements to take over the Czech Julius Petschek's lignite assets in Germany held by United Continental Corporation (see earlier discussion), the two German potash companies provided $5 million in foreign exchange. They did so "independent of their normal export."[156] Obviously, these financial resources were available from their "cloaked" American business.

Whereas in 1929 APCC, which mined potash at Searles Lake, California, had been virtually alone as an efficient U.S. potash producer, United States Potash Company (as of 1930, 50 percent owned by the British-owned Pacific Coast Borax, a subsidiary of Borax Consolidated Ltd.) had in 1932 begun potash extraction in New Mexico. U.S. Potash improved its mining and refining methods, based on research at Carlsbad, New Mexico, at the Missouri School of Mines, as well as at the Pacific Coast Borax's California laboratories. Its share of the American potash market rose.[157]

In 1935, the German-controlled APCC, the British-run U.S. Potash, and the Potash Company of America (the one new U.S.-owned potash enterprise), along with NV Potash Export Mij. (the Amsterdam-based trading firm of the German Potash Syndicate and the French Société Commerciale des Potasses d'Alsace) set up the American Potash Institute for agricultural research. By 1939, U.S. potash output (the bulk of it foreign owned) furnished roughly three-quarters of the country's requirements, with the rest imported.[158] Foreign ownership transformed this industry, replacing imports with domestic output. The potash affiliates were very profitable.[159] On May 26, 1939, the three potash producers and NV Potash Export Mij. were indicted, accused of a conspiracy to fix prices and to eliminate competition, a part of the late New Deal wave of antitrust litigation.[160] Borax was the only other U.S. mineral resource under foreign control. The dominance lay with the identical firms that were in the potash industry: Borax Consolidated Ltd.'s Pacific Coast Borax and American Potash & Chemical Corporation.[161]

Consolidated Gold Fields of South Africa, London, was not merely involved in U.S. gold mining. It retained a diverse U.S. presence.[162] Another noteworthy British investor was Chester Beatty's Selection Trust, Ltd., London, which persisted as the largest shareholder in the sizable American Metal Company.[163] In 1934, Turner & Newall, Ltd., of Manchester, England, wanted to buy a Canadian asbestos mine owned by the American asbestos building products firm Keasbey & Mattison (K & M) of Ambler, Pennsylvania. Turner & Newall ended up acquiring K & M and its U.S. plant facilities along with the Canadian mine.[164] It did no mining in the United States.

As one looks at the collection of FDI in America's mineral industries, one is struck by the variations in motivations. The new interests in gold were to meet the rising price of gold. This was not the case with the phosphate, potash, and borax commitments. The investments in potash and borax fit into a theoretical structure that emphasizes oligopolistic behavior. Consolidated Goldfields' strategies are those of an investment group. Selection Trust and Turner & Newall became involved in the United States not because of U.S. business but because of third-country interests (in the case of Selection Trust it was Beatty's interest in mining in Northern Rhodesia, and with Turner & Newall it was a mine in Canada).

Oil

Shell Union Oil Corporation continued as by far the most prominent foreign-owned integrated oil company. Other foreign-owned firms had investments in oil production and in refining, but none was as important as Shell Union. Every year in its annual reports, its parent Royal Dutch Shell documented U.S. developments: new oil wells drilled, new reserves discovered, superior grades of gasoline introduced, lubricating oils "of exceptional qualities" produced with new processes, modernization of refineries, new pipelines, and constantly increasing scientific research. Shell Union had a new aviation department. In addition, the affiliate took strides forward in chemistry.[165]

In 1933–1934, the Royal Dutch Shell Group complained of heavy U.S. taxation. Annually, it put forth its views on how output should be controlled to raise prices. Yet to stop outsiders' draining its reserves and to drill before leases expired, from 1933 to 1937 the firm's production in America rose steadily (with only a minor decline in 1938 with the recession).[166] In 1934, Shell Union had a $1.4 million loss, but by 1935–1939 the corporation was back to profitability.[167] It rationalized its business and in June 1938 began the process of abandoning marketing in most states between the Rockies and the Mississippi. That year it decided to close two of its older refineries, and its operations were "reoriented around arteries of cheap transportation." It looked toward consolidation, competitiveness, and efficiency.[168]

The predecessor of British Petroleum, Anglo-Persian Oil Co. (Anglo-Iranian as of 1935), had nothing comparable in the United States, only a New York office. Staff of the London-headquartered parent company did, however, travel frequently to America to seek out information and to make contacts. The firm's historian writes that in the 1930s "it was primarily by acquisition from the USA rather than by its own inventions that the Company kept up with some of the most important developments in refining."[169] It could do so through its New York office. There was no parallel with Royal Dutch Shell, which had a far larger research establishment in the United States than Anglo-Iranian had in Britain.

During the middle and late 1930s, the French engineering firm Schlumberger was active in the United States, providing "high-technology" oil drilling and exploration services to Shell Union and other oil companies as well. Its measurements offered the basis for discoveries in and managing of American oil fields.[170]

Manufacturing

In mid-1937, by U.S. Department of Commerce estimates, FDI in U.S. manufacturing came to $729 million and was the greatest single sector attracting FDI, representing almost 40 percent of the total; the chemical industry drew in the most FDI, barely exceeding that in textiles, which had been in a comfortable first place in 1934 (see Table 7.5). In the years 1933–1939, manufacturing in America attracted a number of foreign participants—with innovative processes and trademarked products.

All the food, beverage, cigarette, soap, and match products of foreign multinational enterprises had brand names. In each category, except for matches, foreign multinationals expanded. In food, British, British-Dutch, and Swiss firms participated; in beverages, British (British-Dutch), Swiss, and Canadians were involved; in cigarettes, one British enterprise took on increasing importance; in soap, there was a single giant foreign investor. In matches, the Swedish goliath retreated.

Food specialty items included the offerings of the British firm Crosse & Blackwell, which had started to produce in Baltimore in 1927. The depression years took their toll on this marketer of premium-priced brands; by 1935, however, conditions had improved, and in 1937 Crosse & Blackwell was introducing its first advertisements in national U.S. magazines, featuring a packaged date and nut bread. Reckitt & Colman Holdings Ltd., Hull, England, captured a sizable portion of a niche market through R. T. French, manufacturers of mustard and condiments, its subsidiary based in Rochester, New York.[171] Unilever became important for the first time in branded cooking products. And, in food, the Swiss Nestlé had its interests in chocolates, through Lamont, Corliss & Co.[172]

In addition, Nestlé's American subsidiary, Nestlé's Milk Products Co. (formed in 1930 as the successor to Nestlé's Food Co.), in 1934 had fourteen and in 1939 sixteen factories in the United States, canning sweetened condensed milk; Nestlé trailed a good distance after the U.S.-owned Pet and Carnation milk companies in the American market. In 1938, in Switzerland, Nestlé had introduced Nescafé, its first nonmilk product; the next year, it began to manufacture Nescafé in the United States.[173] Another branded Swiss "drink" (made in Illinois) was Ovaltine.[174] The British tea packer Thomas J. Lipton, Inc., became associated in May 1937 with the Unilever group (earlier the American unit had been owned by Lipton himself and then, after his 1931 death, by his estate; "technically" in the process of affiliation with Unilever, Lipton became mainly Dutch owned, albeit the managerial direction came from the United Kingdom).[175] Lipton remained the key tea enterprise in the United States (it innovated, developing the market for its tea bag brand).[176] Two other foreign-owned tea companies had sizable market shares in the United States: the British Tetley tea company and the Canadian Salada tea firm. The British Cantrell & Cochrane (with its C & C Ginger Ale and its factory in Long Island) was an exceptional foreign multinational in the U.S. "soft drink" industry; its market penetration was not substantial.[177]

Truly striking in these years was the new foreign, overwhelmingly Canadian, role in the U.S. alcoholic beverage industry. The Commerce Department estimated that in mid-1937, of the $116 million invested by foreign companies in food, beverage, and tobacco manufacture, fully $65 million (or more than half) was in "beverages," with the lion's share in alcoholic beverages.[178] Early in December 1933, after the states ratified the repeal of the Prohibition amendment, alcoholic drinks were once more legal in the United States. The Federal Alcohol Control Administration, created on December 4, 1933, set up a permit system for distillers and importers—granting permits to companies (and individuals) that had not been convicted of bootlegging.[179]

During Prohibition (1920–1933), across America's northern border Canadian businesses had flourished. Some Canadian firms had bought American machinery; many engaged in smuggling, but most had avoided bootlegging convictions. Thus, they qualified for permits—and were prepared to do business in the United States. They had clear advantages over Americans, for they had been legally making alcoholic beverages for years.[180] With trade restrictions, many found FDI within the United States was required.

The most important Canadian enterprise to benefit from the new opportunities was the Distillers Corporation-Seagrams Ltd. (DC-SL), Montreal. DC-SL had been organized in 1928 as an affiliate of the giant Distillers Company Limited (DCL), Edinburgh. The Canadian holding company brought under one corporate umbrella the Waterloo, Ontario, distillery business originally built up by Joseph Seagram (he died in 1919) and the Montreal distillery enterprise of Samuel Bronfman. DCL had had interests in both prior to the formation of DC-SL, but Bronfman was the prime mover in DC-SL.[181] Late in December 1933, Samuel Bronfman and his brother Allan traveled to Scotland to discuss with DCL their plans for selling in the United States. Historian Peter Newman writes that the Bronfmans were surprised to learn that DCL had its own agenda and did not want them as partners in the United States.[182] At this point, the Bronfmans raised $4 million and in 1934 acquired DCL's interest in DC-SL.[183] The now independent, fully Canadian DC-SL moved rapidly and aggressively. The Bronfmans realized that they could not reach the huge U.S. market through exports, and before the end of 1933 (before they completed the purchase of DC-SL), DC-SL had bought the Rossville Union Distillery in Lawrenceburg, Indiana, and established a U.S. subsidiary, Joseph E. Seagram and Sons, Inc., to administer that distillery.[184]

The Bronfmans opened a New York City office to manage their U.S. business, arranged banking connections with the Manufacturers Trust Company, and in 1934 acquired a second facility, the Calvert distillery in Relay, Maryland.[185] Samuel Bronfman later recalled, "I was long accustomed to a totally integrated operation . . . distilling, maturing, blending, quality control and bottling, and also . . . marketing. I was determined that as American distillers we would follow the same procedure."[186]

In August 1934, the Bronfmans introduced their Seagram Five Crown and Seagram Seven Crown brands, and advertised heavily. The Bronfmans had equally skillful campaigns to promote Lord Calvert whiskey.[187] Soon, however, the new entry met obstacles in the United States. The Treasury Department, which administered alcohol controls and taxation of alcoholic beverages, went after the firm for back taxes—which it collected in May 1936.[188]

In addition, the Bronfmans encountered antitrust problems. As part of their sales strategy, they insisted that retailers sell the firm's branded goods at a price fixed by the distiller. Samuel Bronfman would later refer to the company's philosophy of "a fair profit to the wholesaler, a fair profit to the retailer, and a fair price to the consumer."[189] Before the 1930s, retail price maintenance agreements had been, in the main, rejected by U.S. courts as illegal under antitrust statutes. However, in the early 1930s, the code provisions of the National Industrial Recovery Act had seemed to permit price fixing, and certain states (including Illinois) passed "fair trade laws," specifically allowing manufacturers to determine retail prices. In the initial years of the New Deal, the Justice Department had (as noted earlier) a relaxed antitrust posture.[190] Nonetheless, a large Chicago retailer challenged the Illinois Fair Trade Act and took Seagram to court when the latter sought to set retail prices on its brands.[191] In *Old Dearborn Distributing Co. v. Seagram Distillers Corp.* (1936), the U.S. Supreme Court upheld the Illinois law and the validity of price maintenance. Seagram, the Judge wrote, had made a substantial investment in advertising its whiskey and should be allowed to profit from the results of the goodwill obtained. It was a complete victory for the Canadian enterprise.[192]

With the favorable Court ruling, and these particular obstacles overcome, the Bronfmans pushed forward: they invested $5 million to build a new distillery in Louisville, Kentucky, opened during Derby week in 1937. The Canadian firm specialized in well-aged, carefully blended whiskeys. Its business in the United States soared past that in Canada.[193] The Bronfmans proved adept in reaching American consumers. Their firm had experience, trademarked beverages, and a sophisticated marketing strategy.[194] By 1937, Seagram's Crown whiskeys were the clear sales leader in the United States.[195]

Other Canadian companies also invested in the United States to satisfy the thirst of drinking Americans; they also found it desirable to distill their whiskey within the United States. The newcomers included the combination run by Canadian entrepreneur Harry Hatch, Hiram Walker-Gooderham & Worts (with its Canadian Club rye), and, of less importance, the Canadian Industrial Alcohol Co. Ltd. (with its Corby's and Wiser's brands).[196] Hiram Walker-Gooderham & Worts became one of the top four in the U.S. distilling industry.[197] At a cost of more than $5.7 million, it erected a new distillery in Peoria, Illinois, producing Canadian Club. When the plant opened in July 1934, the Peoria distillery was said to be the largest in the world. In 1936, Hiram Walker-Gooderham & Worts bought the Scotch whisky maker Ballantine & Son, Ltd., and using its U.S. marketing outlets it imported and sold Ballantine Scotch.[198]

Meanwhile, before Roosevelt's 1932 election, the Edinburgh-headquartered Distillers Company Limited (DCL) had organized a subsidiary, Distillers Company Limited, Delaware (DCD).[199] In June 1933, Thomas Herd of DCL had visited the United States to explore the post-Prohibition opportunities. DCL had long had connections through its industrial alcohol and chemical interests with the National Distillers Products Corporation and with U.S. Industrial Alcohol Co. Herd renewed the contacts with the American companies.[200] DCL's plans for the U.S. market were already taking shape when, as noted, DCL divested its interests in the Bronfmans' Canadian enterprise.[201] Accordingly, on its own, DCL invested in the United States, building a new plant in Linden, New Jersey, opened in 1934, where it produced Gordon's gin.[202] The Edinburgh company continued as an exporter to the United States of Scotch and did not distill in this country (or elsewhere) bourbon or rye, leaving that immense market to the subsidiaries of the Canadian businesses and to Americans.[203] Gordon's gin, however, became the best-selling gin in the United States.[204] Other foreign entries into the U.S. market included W. A. Gilbey, Ltd. (of Britain), and deKuyper & Zoon (of Holland), which two companies licensed the American firm National Distillers Products Corporation to make their gin and cordials.[205]

One added foreign direct investor making alcoholic drinks in America was the Cuban-based Bacardi Company. Founded in 1862, Bacardi (unlike most Caribbean rum producers) had developed trademarked and advertised products.[206] Before Prohibition, Bacardi had exported to the United States; with repeal, it appointed the American-owned Schenley Distillers Company as its U.S. distributor. In 1934, Schenley and Bacardi, in a joint venture, invested in a small plant in Philadelphia to produce rum. This business was discontinued in 1936 when the machinery and equipment were transferred to a new Bacardi facility in Puerto Rico.[207] For the rum maker, Puerto Rico became its locale for expanding U.S. sales.

Prior to Prohibition, a number of breweries in the United States had been British controlled.[208] As the legal alcoholic beverages industry reemerged in the 1930s, all the principal beer producers resurfaced as American owned.[209] The sole remaining British-owned brewer to survive the Prohibition years was F. W. Cook Co., Evansville, Indiana.[210] In 1933–1934, three Canadian enterprises purchased from a third to full interest in seven U.S. breweries on the West Coast and in Montana. A fourth Canadian brewer (which made Carling beer) acquired a minority stake in a U.S. company with plans to enter brewing. This meant there came to be Canadian interests in eight U.S. breweries; none of them, however, ranked among the most prominent in the U.S. market.[211] So, too, the German von Opel family—through Ubersee Finanz-Korporation, AG, a Swiss holding company—owned and operated one of the largest breweries in New England (that of the Harvard Brewing Company, in Lowell, Massachusetts).[212] In 1935, there were in the United States 703 breweries; thus, the 10 foreign-owned ones had little overall impact.[213] What occurred in beer contrasted sharply with the whiskey industry, where the Canadians—particularly DC-SL and Hiram Walker-Gooderham & Worts—ranked as leaders in the United States.

One estimate was that at the decade's end roughly 37 percent of U.S. whiskey production was foreign controlled.[214] The Canadian-owned Distillers Corporation-Seagrams Ltd. maintained its first place in American sales. Hiram Walker-Gooderham & Worts' Canadian Club was a major brand. The best-selling gin in America was Gordon's—made in America by a subsidiary of Britain's largest distiller (Distillers Company Limited). For a short period, the Cuban Bacardi enterprise had an interest in a Philadelphia plant and then owned a big Puerto Rican rum distillery. In sum, during the 1930s, there was a surge in foreign, especially Canadian, direct investments in making and selling alcoholic beverages in the United States.[215]

In cigarettes, there were significant developments by a foreign multinational enterprise. In the 1930s, Brown & Williamson, the subsidiary of British American Tobacco (BAT), for the first time became a contender in the highly concentrated U.S. cigarette market. In 1933, its best-seller was the economy brand Wings (with U.S. sales of 5.1 billion sticks compared with 36.7 billion for American Tobacco's Lucky Strike, 29.3 billion for Liggett & Myer's Chesterfield, and 25.6 billion for Reynolds' Camels).[216] With all its brands, in 1933 Brown & Williamson produced 5.5 percent of total U.S. output.[217] Brown & Williamson pioneered the mentholated Kool brand in 1933 and then, in 1936, the filter-tipped Viceroy, in each case a "first" in America.[218] During the decade, domestic sales of its Raleigh brand pushed upward, so that in 1938 and 1939, Raleigh sales passed those of Wings, becoming the firm's leading brand.[219] Table 7.8 indicates Brown & Williamson's portion of U.S. cigarette production almost doubled, from 5.5 percent in 1933 to 10.6 percent in 1939. In both 1933 and 1939 it was in fourth place, but while still trailing the three front-runners (the successors of the old tobacco combination), it was gaining ground.[220] The U.S. market represented merely 8 percent of BAT's worldwide sales in 1933; the figure had risen to 13 percent in 1939 (China remained BAT's largest market in the 1930s).[221] By 1933–1939, BAT was apparently increasingly serving its

Table 7.8. U.S. cigarette production, 1933, 1939 (percentages)

Company	1933	1939
Reynolds	22.8	23.6
American	33.0	22.9
Liggett & Myers	28.1	21.6
Brown & Williamson	5.5	10.6
Philip Morris	0.8	7.1
Lorillard	4.7	5.8
Others	5.1	8.4
Total	100.0	100.0

Source: American Tobacco et al. v. U.S., 328 U.S. 781, at 794 (1946).

worldwide cigarette markets with exports from the United Kingdom rather than from the United States (it also produced in many markets abroad); it persisted, however, as an important exporter of raw tobacco and to a lesser extent cigarettes from the United States.[222]

Among the most successful foreign firms in America was Lever Brothers Co.—Unilever's U.S. subsidiary—which had a multiproduct line. When the Commerce Department assembled its industry statistics, it is not clear where it placed the firm's soap and laundry offerings. Yet these branded goods were similar to those in the food, drink, and cigarette category (Lever also had branded food products). Lever's U.S. sales in 1933 were $46.3 million; in every year from 1933 to 1939, they mounted, reaching $91.3 million in 1939. The company's after-tax profits were $5 million in 1933 and $7.3 million in 1939.[223]

Uneasy that its capital was low relative to its earnings (and fearful over the Roosevelt administration's hostility toward big business and "profiteers"), in 1933 Lever had enlarged its U.S. capital from $20 million to $28 million.[224] By 1939, Spry—its shortening (introduced in 1936)—captured 7.5 percent of the very competitive market for "edible fats"; Procter & Gamble's Crisco had 10 percent.[225] In its traditional soap products, by 1939, Lever sold more in America than its parent did in all its other non-European markets combined. In 1940, Lever's estimated share of the U.S. laundry soap market came to roughly 30 percent, neck and neck with Procter & Gamble at 34 percent.[226]

As for matches, in the wake of the collapse of the Kreuger empire, there was a "fundamental re-direction" of Swedish Match's U.S. strategies. The outcome was an agreement in 1934 between Swedish Match and America's key player, Diamond Match, whereby the latter "was conceded a leading position in the United States." Thereafter, Swedish Match left the U.S. market to Americans.[227]

Textiles

Textiles continued to be extremely appealing to inward foreign investors in manufacturing. This sector had been in first place in 1934, and it ranked a close second to chemicals in 1937. The principal foreign investments were in thread, fine woolens, and, most important, rayon.[228] British investors remained—as throughout the twentieth century—the top companies in U.S. thread production. The thread industry attracted three of the largest British investors in America: the J. & P. Coats group, American Thread (still controlled by English Sewing Cotton), and Linen Thread Company.

American Thread had been the first of the set to start a southern textile mill (in 1925 in Dalton, Georgia, just south of Chattanooga, Tennessee). J. & P. Coats had followed with Georgia plants in Clarkdale in 1932 and a larger one in Toccoa in 1937. Both of J. & P. Coats's Georgia plants were located near the South Carolina border. Northern plants were not shuttered in these investors' move to the South, although employment was reduced as southern output substituted for that in the older plants. The advantages of the southern locations were cheaper and initially nonunion labor, as well as closeness to the source of raw cotton.[229] The handful of French wool and worsted manufacturers did not migrate south; they continued to manufacture in Woonsocket, Rhode Island, where their mills became "hotbeds" of union organization.[230]

The foreign-owned thread and wool makers were by the 1930s less important than the major stakes by foreign investors in rayon. Courtaulds' U.S. subsidiary, after 1937 (and sometimes before 1937) known as the American Viscose Company (AVC), maintained its premier rank in the U.S. rayon industry, although competitors (foreign and American) cut into its market share.[231] Nonetheless, in the late 1930s, Courtaulds' investment in AVC was probably the largest wholly British-owned direct investment in the United States.[232] Because of its leadership in the still new rayon industry, the company was highly conspicuous. Like many other big enterprises in this decade, it came under fire. In 1934, the Federal Trade Commission started antitrust investigations against the rayon producers. The FTC entered a complaint against AVC and nine other viscose yarn producers (six of the ten involved FDI). The ten defendants were charged with having conspired to maintain prices and restrict production; in July 1937, the FTC issued a cease and desist order against the viscose yarn makers.[233] Meanwhile, AVC was also the object of an investigation by the Internal Revenue Service, a dispute over back taxes that lasted from 1934 to April 1939.[234] To compound matters, when the head of the Justice Department's antitrust division, Thurman Arnold, and the Temporary National

Economic Committee in the late 1930s began the new inquiries on "monopoly power," AVC once more became a target. Because of its market lead, of all the foreign-owned (and domestically owned) rayon enterprises, AVC drew the most attention. It became more cautious and not only lost market share but also neglected to invest in new research and development.[235]

The Depression notwithstanding, industry-wide rayon sales in the United States had grown steadily, a rise that reflected the activities of the many other foreign-owned affiliates.[236] For obvious public relations purposes, in 1934 the German-controlled (via Holland) American Glanzstoff adopted a new corporate name, North American Rayon. At decade's end, the British (AVC and American Celanese), the German (North American Rayon, American Bemberg), and the Dutch (American Enka) multinationals were all key players in the U.S. rayon industry.[237]

In Chapter 5, I noted the organization of Associated Rayon Co. in the United States and Algemeene Kunstzijde Unie in Holland and the tangled international ownership (legal) structures that had evolved in 1928–1929. Initially, the Germans had found the Dutch "cloak" was useful for tax and financing purposes. By the 1930s, the Dutch shelter was helpful to the Germans for other reasons. The story is complex, as was true of all the camouflaging experiences. AKU purchased Vereinigte Glanzstoff-Fabriken (VGF) bonds that had been issued and owned in the United States and had been used to finance VGF's American rayon plants. On December 21, 1936, the stockholders (principally AKU) approved the liquidation of Associated Rayon, the holding company set up in the United States in 1928. After this, nominally, North American Rayon, American Bemberg, and American Enka were directly owned by the Dutch AKU. When in 1937 the German government wanted VGF to take over its parent (the Dutch AKU), VGF insisted that to safeguard its U.S. subsidiaries, AKU had to appear as non-German owned with a majority of Dutch participation.[238] A masking structure to come to terms with the rise of Nazism in Germany was emerging. In 1939, North American Rayon and American Bemberg (in Elizabethtown, Tennessee) had some 4,600 employees, while American Enka (in Enka, near Asheville, North Carolina) had 2,850.[239] *Moody's Manual 1940* still listed E. G. von Stauss, a principal in the Deutsche Bank, as a director of all three "German-Dutch" rayon companies in Tennessee and North Carolina, although he probably resigned from the boards in May 1939.[240]

Rayon was the first synthetic fiber; others followed. In 1939, Du Pont licensed I. G. Farben, Rhône-Poulenc's subsidiary Rhodiaceta, and Imperial Chemical Industries to produce its new discovery nylon in Germany, France, and Britain, respectively.[241] It was the start of a new age in textiles. Over the subsequent decade, rayon would become a second-string product, dwarfed in the vast array of new synthetic textiles. The 1930s was rayon's last decade of glory. With the nylon and later the polyester fabrics, superiority in synthetic textiles would move from Europe to America.[242] Yet in the time of Europe's technological supremacy, there had been the transatlantic transfer of rayon research and development.

Chemicals and Medicines

Chemicals ranked first in FDI in U.S. manufacturing in 1937 (see Table 7.5).[243] By 1933–1934, the leading European chemical enterprises had created a tangled net of agreements with American firms, covering numerous products and processes, along with the licensing of the latest technological advances.[244] In the 1930s, these private treaty alliances persisted and became more elaborate. Typically, they restrained U.S. business investment and sales abroad, as well as foreign business activities in America.[245] The agreements addressed allocations of markets, prices, and technological interchanges (including the licensing of patents). Some involved production and research joint ventures. Patent accords between European and U.S. companies were formal written documents.[246] Agreements on prices and orderly marketing were typically "understandings," given the taboos in U.S. antitrust law (and the warnings from foreign firms' American legal staffs). The thicket of arrangements did not impede and, indeed, in many cases seem to have stimulated technological advances.[247] Raymond Vernon, describing alliances of the 1980s, has written that part of the motivation was "an effort of each of the participating firms to reduce the risks associated with lumpy commitments to new research and development projects and to ensure that they are abreast of their competitors in their research resources."[248] He could have been writing of the chemical industry—fifty years earlier.

Imperial Chemical Industries (ICI), one of the largest European enterprises with global business, was completely passive in the United States. By the beginnings of the 1930s, ICI's strategy had come to rely entirely on the rules of the game set down by its many international agreements; its historian has written of ICI's "distaste for competition."[249] Although it retained through most, and probably all, of the 1930s its purely financial holdings in General Motors and its minor interests in Du Pont and Allied Chemical shares and held other American securities in small amounts, it had no U.S. "operations" and "did no trade in the USA." Its New York office served an "ambassadorial function," closely observing industry developments to assure other firms conformed in the United States to the various pacts to which ICI was party and to keep current on what was happening in America.

By the decade's end, ICI's global business was governed by some 800 agreements, the most significant ones being those in nitrogen, dyestuffs, alkalies, and hydrogenation-related products along with its broad 1929 Patents and Processes Agreement with Du Pont (renewed in 1939). ICI's three principal allies in its international transactions were Du Pont in the United States, Solvay in Belgium, and I. G. Farben in Germany.[250] Because of U.S. antitrust law, no American companies were signatories to the important European nitrogen and dyestuff cartels, yet ICI's New York office saw to it that U.S. businesses kept to the cartel rules. As of the late 1930s, ICI continued to be content with its passive role. The man in charge of its New York office explained to the parent company in Britain (in November 1938) in connection with nitrogen matters: no records were kept of activities, American producers did not bind themselves, "the whole thing is in the form of a loose conversation," transmitted by transatlantic telephone, and "so far as the Nitrogen Cartel is concerned it works perfectly."[251] In an internal review of the comprehensive 1929 Du Pont–ICI technology exchange agreement (in connection with the negotiations for its 1939 renewal), Du Pont officials also expressed their pleasure with the arrangements. From ICI, Du Pont obtained vital technical know-how. Du Pont managers believed that access to the results of ICI research had brought large savings to the American company. The Du Pont study concluded that after nine years' experience with the 1929 agreement, "no disadvantage whatever has been found."[252]

When in the late 1930s the Roosevelt administration embarked on its vigorous antitrust crusade, the U.S. attorney general (in June 1939) subpoenaed ICI officials in New York, requiring them to appear before a grand jury to determine "whether ICI's relations with American nitrogenous fertilizer companies in the United States" violated U.S. antitrust regulations. ICI cooperated.[253] This was one harbinger of future formidable litigation involving the international chemical industry as a whole.

Meanwhile, the Belgian Solvay & Cie. enlarged its U.S. investments and its U.S. role. In the early part of the 1930s, the New York Stock Exchange (NYSE)—in an attempt to clean house—began to require more reporting from listed companies, and in 1933 it removed Allied Chemical & Dye Corporation from trading after that giant failed to supply the solicited financial data.[254] Solvay & Cie. used this as an excuse to try to discipline Allied Chemical's independent president, Orlando Weber, who was defying the nitrogen cartel restrictions. Weber responded, bitterly lashing out over the domination of *his* enterprise "by powerful foreign chemical industries." Solvay & Cie. defended its intervention: after all, it was the biggest single owner of Allied Chemical shares and had an interest in the latter's well-being.[255] Acting on

Solvay & Cie.'s behalf, the New York law firm Sullivan and Cromwell took steps to remove Weber, who resigned as president of Allied Chemical in 1934 and as chairman in 1935 (at the age of only fifty-seven). Henry F. Atherton, Weber's successor, proved more amenable to directives from abroad, and Allied Chemical came to conform with the rules of the International Nitrogen Cartel.[256] As of March 31, 1934, Solvay & Cie.'s U.S. holding company—Solvay American Investment Corporation (SAIC)—owned 500,000 shares of Allied Chemical, valued (according to the NYSE quotation) at $76.5 million. Four years later, as of March 31, 1938, Solvay American Corporation (named SAIC until June 1937) reported that it held the same 500,000 shares.[257] In the late 1930s, the "tamed" Allied Chemical lost rank in the U.S. industry.

Solvay & Cie.—through Solvay American Corporation—not only had equity ownership in Allied Chemical but also had a sizable (albeit smaller) stake in America's third major interwar chemical company, Union Carbide and Carbon Corporation, which firm—by contrast with Allied Chemical—was expanding in the 1930s in an impressive manner. Solvay & Cie.'s interest in Union Carbide seems to have been more for information and financial returns than for technological transfer (in either direction), control over prices, production limitations, restraints on exports, or other purposes.[258]

Within the chemical industry, far and away the most dramatic story of a foreign multinational was that of I. G. Farben, which by 1933 was engaged in the United States in a wide range of products, including dyestuffs, film, pharmaceuticals, synthetic rubber, bleaching compounds, and magnesium. It had interests in and a role in the U.S. holding company American I. G. Chemical Corporation (and through the latter in General Aniline Works, Agfa-Ansco Corporation, and Winthrop Chemical Company), the General Dyestuff Corporation, Standard Oil Company (New Jersey), Standard-I.G. Co., Jasco Inc., Pen-Chlor, Magnesium Development Corp., and American Magnesium Corp., as well as other firms. Its multitude of direct investments and alliances were at the same time accompanied by a robust technological dynamism. I. G. Farben's U.S. strategies combined cooperation with fierce competition. It was reported that I. G. Farben's cartel agreements numbered over 2,000.[259]

With Adolf Hitler in power in Germany after 1933, I. G. Farben's operations were constantly proctored by the German state. After 1936, as German rearmament accelerated, regulations were ubiquitous. Germany had no colonies, and the government was keenly aware that the nation's access to critical raw materials could be blocked in a future war. I. G. Farben's product lines—chemical substitutes for natural resources—coincided with Hitler's military needs. Synthetic nitrates, synthetic rubber, gasoline derived from coal, and high-octane aviation fuel were fundamental for a Germany preparing for war. With military goals paramount, the German state subsidized I. G. Farben.

I. G. Farben's many U.S. involvements in the 1920s and the beginning of the 1930s had been created in large part through technology transfer rather than through a German injection of financial capital. Long before it received state subsidies, the German chemical giant had been at the leading edge in research and development. It had entered into contractual obligations with companies in the United States to provide its know-how. As the 1930s progressed, the German government became increasingly wary about such technological outflows. At the same time, I. G. Farben was often quick to blame the German state when (for competitive reasons) it did not desire to share its proprietary knowledge. Evidence exists that for business reasons I. G. Farben had ambivalence over certain technological transfers, including those required under its U.S. contracts. Business strategy and technological sharing (or not sharing) were intertwined with German politics.[260]

In August 1933, before George von Schnitzler, commercial director of I. G. Farben in charge of dyestuffs, traveled to America, he wrote Erwin Selck of I. G. Farben's Berlin office, "We have up to now, without exception, acted according to the rule that in foreign countries we represented only our firms and not the Reich or the interests of the entire industry." Yet this was changing. Max Ilgner (a director of American I. G. Chemical and in I. G. Farben's Berlin office) had visited Scandinavia, seeking to improve Hitler's image. In the United States, Ilgner had seen to it that I. G. Farben's American public relations man, Ivy Lee, boost National Socialism. "We now appear," von Schnitzler recounted, "as the champions of the German cause in general and also appear as auxiliary government agents." Von Schnitzler detested this new role.[261] Like it or not, I. G. Farben managers came to realize that business and politics in fascist Germany were closely bound—and that this was particularly true in the chemical industry. In 1933, when Americans boycotted German products to protest Hitler's treatment of Jews, I. G. Farben's affiliates in the United States were affected, and the company became alarmed at the potential loss of U.S. business.[262]

One response to the convergence of politics and business was a further cloaking of German business in America. An internal I. G. Farben document from 1939 would explain that "because of (1) tax laws, (2) national sales propaganda ('buy in your own country'), (3) the desire to avoid boycotts, [and] (4) the desire to avoid special controls applicable to foreign companies," I. G. Farben's foreign sales affiliates had been "organized, as a matter of principle," to appear that I. G. Farben was *not* the owner.[263] In 1933 the German government began an inquiry on what was concealed, assuming German tax evasion; I. G. Farben rapidly negotiated a settlement of the tax matters, while at the same time it did not abandon but rather increased its cloaking practices.[264]

In the mid-1930s, I. G. Farben's camouflaging became more elaborate, dictated by conditions in both Germany and the United States. Its disguises involved the careful use of Dutch and Swiss firms. Central to the scheme of things for I. G. Farben in the United States was its Swiss holding company, I. G. Chemie, Basle, which had been organized in 1928 by Hermann Schmitz (who was second only to Carl Bosch in the management of I. G. Farben). In 1935, Schmitz resigned as president of the American I. G. to avoid that explicit connection between American I. G. and the German I. G. Farben, although he remained a director of American I. G. until 1939.[265] I. G. Farben's Fritz ter Meer and von Schnitzler "repeatedly and unreservedly" told a legitimately incredulous Walter Carpenter of Du Pont in the fall of 1935 "that the German IG did not own directly or indirectly the General Aniline Works or [the holding company] American IG."[266] The denials persisted. When the Securities and Exchange Commission requested that corporations disclose their "parents," the American I. G. replied on May 15, 1935 (and then repeated annually for the fiscal years ending March 31, 1936, 1937, and 1938, as well) that it had no parent. After persistent SEC inquiries, finally in American I. G.'s report covering the year ending March 31, 1939, that company indicated it "did not know whether it had a parent." After the European war started in September 1939, the company would alter its response to the SEC query.[267]

Notwithstanding the repeated I. G. Farben statements, despite the legal and verbal cloaking that occurred in 1933 to 1939, the evidence is conclusive that throughout this period close operating associations existed between I. G. Farben and its various U.S. affiliates.[268] Managers and chemical engineers from I. G. Farben made numerous trips to the United States; correspondence abounds. There is no question but that I. G. Farben's multiproduct American business was part and parcel of a German-headquartered multinational enterprise. Dietrich A. Schmitz (who was a naturalized American citizen since 1909) took over in 1936 as president of American I. G., after his brother Hermann Schmitz resigned from that position.[269] Walter Duisberg (son of one of the founders of I. G. Farben—Carl Duisberg—and an American citizen since 1933) held the post of first vice-president.[270] In 1932, Rudolf Hütz had become and continued in the role of president of General Aniline Works (GAW), the dye-producing subsidiary of American I. G. Like Dietrich Schmitz and Walter Duisberg, the naturalized American Hütz was a man I. G. Farben personnel knew well and trusted. Under Hütz's direction, GAW greatly enlarged its intermediate dye plant at Linden, New Jersey, as well as its dye and chemical plants at Grasselli, New Jersey, and Rensselaar, New York.[271] Indeed, all the top management of American I. G. had intimate, long-duration ties with the German parent.

The General Dyestuff Corporation (GDC)—I. G. Farben's separate U.S. dye sales company—had from its origin been technically owned by Americans. Apparently, Dietrich Schmitz held voting control of GDC from 1931 to 1939. During the 1930s, GDC was managed by another member of the I. G. Farben "family," Philadelphia-born Ernest K. Halbach, whose connections with Badische went back to 1899. Chemical industry historian Williams Haynes has called Halbach "the recognized dean of the [U.S.] dyestuff industry." GDC marketed both imports and American-made dyestuffs (those produced by GAW). In the mid-1930s, so large were GDC's imports from I. G. Farben that GDC required sizable credits from American banks; I. G. Farben dispatched a representative to New York to arrange the financing. By 1936, GDC had "outlived its second executive headquarters" and built a nine-story structure at 435 Hudson Street in downtown Manhattan, where it had executive and clerical offices and also stored, mixed, and shipped products; the top floor of the new building had an "application laboratory." GDC, in addition, had sales outlets located throughout the United States.[272] Together, GAW and GDC were major participants in the U.S. dyestuff industry, with thousands of employees.[273]

In New York, another I. G. Farben company, Chemnyco Inc., had a small staff of roughly thirty, led by Dietrich Schmitz, Walter Duisberg, and Rudolf W. Ilgner (brother of I. G. Farben's Max Ilgner); it continued to be the "technical service agency" for I. G. Farben's numerous U.S. business activities. Rudolf Ilgner compiled U.S. chemical industry statistics and other economic data, for example, on U.S. customs duties and freight rates. Chemnyco collected information for I. G. Farben (and its American affiliates) on American patents, processes, and inventions. It was the center for communications between I. G. Farben and American businesses (affiliates and nonaffiliates of the German giant).[274]

As in dyestuffs, so in many other products, I. G. Farben's U.S. operations grew and prospered in the 1930s. Unyte Corporation, a subsidiary of American I. G., which in 1932 had begun producing plastic moldings at Grasselli, New Jersey, merged with Plaskon Company in 1936 (adopting the latter's name); American I. G. retained an interest in the highly innovative Plaskon Company.[275] After recovering from its depression losses, in 1937 Agfa-Ansco (a subsidiary of American I. G.) introduced a new film that impressed the industry. Agfa-Ansco was second to Eastman Kodak as a manufacturer of photographic materials in the United States, although it lagged far behind its U.S. rival.[276] Winthrop Chemical Company (yet another enterprise in the American I. G. Farben cluster) was a key player in U.S. pharmaceuticals. It launched in the United States the German-developed Atabrine, a drug greatly superior to quinine for the treatment and suppression of malaria.[277] Winthrop Chemical's German associations led it to its offering of the first sulfa drugs, Prontosil and Prontylin. Prontosil saved the life of President Roosevelt's son, who in 1936 had a severe streptococcal infection.[278] As was true of all I. G. Farben's affiliates in America, visitors and correspondents from the German company maintained "a close exchange of experiences in the scientific and business field" with executives at Winthrop Chemical.[279]

Although I. G. Farben did not manufacture synthetic nitrogen in the United States, its Leuna plant in Germany was the world's largest. I. G. Farben watched carefully the activities in America in this product line; its Synthetic Nitrogen Products Corporation (formed in the 1920s) sold imports, and its managers discussed controls over output with U.S. producers, notably Allied Chemical, whose Hopewell, Virginia, facility was America's biggest (Du Pont also had an important synthetic nitrate plant at Belle, West Virginia).[280]

In still other products, American I. G. and Union Carbide managers had talks on their common interests, principally in acetic acid. In early 1934, Joseph G. Davidson of Carbide and Carbon Chemicals Corporation, a Union Carbide subsidiary, met in Frankfurt with I. G. Farben officials, where arrangements were made for the "orderly marketing" of acetic acid. Participants in the conversations included U.S. affiliates of I. G. Farben (Advance Solvents & Chemical Company) and of Union Carbide (Niacet Chemical Corporation).[281] In the fall of 1935, Carl Krauch of I. G. Farben reported to the latter's central committee on a contract made with Union Carbide.[282] Thus, Union Carbide not only was attracting investments from Solvay & Cie. but also had entered into direct associations with I. G. Farben. During the 1930s, Union Carbide's subsidiary Carbide and Carbon Chemicals Corporation became the undisputed leader in the United States in the field of chemicals derived from aliphatic hydrocarbons.[283]

Throughout the 1930s, both independently and with ICI, Du Pont had sought, in vain, to negotiate a general patents and process agreement with I. G. Farben (comparable to the one it had with ICI). Du Pont and I. G. Farben had only one U.S. joint venture, which was in agricultural chemicals (the Bayer-Semesan Company, started in 1928). In 1934 Du Pont owned shares in I. G. Farben and in the latter's Swiss holding company, I. G. Chemie, Basle—shares it was seeking to sell; the manager of Du Pont's foreign exchange division wrote that year to Du Pont's vice-president, J. E. Crane, that "we could not feel that our disposing of these shares would in any way affect the very pleasant relations existing between" I. G. Farben and Du Pont.[284] Apparently, Du Pont did divest its interest in I. G. Chemie but continued (in 1936) to hold stock in I. G. Farben.[285] In turn, American I. G. had a small amount of Du Pont stock.[286] In addition, I. G. Farben had a very tiny stake in Hercules Power and Atlas Power.[287] Yet the relations between I. G. Farben and Du Pont were not always pleasant. By 1936, Du Pont was not happy with its one joint venture with I. G. Farben: "Information and research results have gone on to I. G. via Bayer-Semesan and Winthrop whereas Bayer-Semesan has received nothing in return." Du Pont learned that I. G. was "deliberately holding back information" lest it go through Bayer-Semesan to Du Pont.[288] Much more important than this joint venture and these cross–share holdings, Du Pont and I. G. Farben had a number of product-specific cross-licensing agreements as well as informal arrangements. These substituted for the unattainable general agreement. In 1936, when Du Pont evaluated the outlook for closer relations with I. G. Farben, it concluded (in an internal company report), "The I. G. is open to the suspicion of not cooperating or observing the stipulations of a contract when it does not appear to its advantage. It is worthwhile to bear this in mind in adjusting our expectations between the theoretical advantages of a general technology agreement with the I. G. and the realities of their psychology."[289]

I. G. Farben and Du Pont were both research-oriented firms; each was highly competitive; each had a wide range of product lines; and each saw clear advantages in alliances—but only if the cooperation did not hamper each one's own business growth. Whereas Du Pont did not completely trust I. G. Farben, the latter continued to view Du Pont as an "upstart"; at the same time, I. G. Farben became aware that the American firm was making major strides forward in chemistry. During the 1930s, discussions at the highest levels of management between the U.S. and German giants were frequent, on general issues and on particular products and processes, even though there never was a comprehensive accord.[290]

One subject of conversation between I. G. Farben and Du Pont was synthetic rubber. As German rearmament had built up in the 1930s, the Reich Economic Ministry and the army knew that with war, Germany would have difficulty obtaining natural rubber. In addition, foreign exchange scarcity made German domestic output of synthetic rubber desirable. Years earlier, I. G. Farben's predecessors had done research on synthetic rubber. Now the German government pressed I. G. Farben to put forth renewed effort in this regard. When I. G. Farben officials demurred, explaining the unlikeliness of profits, the German state guaranteed the company against losses and urged I. G. Farben not only to do research but also to draw on available U.S. expertise.[291]

Principally because the price of natural rubber was low and because Americans did not anticipate that their supply might be cut off (the United States was not preparing for war), neither U.S. businesses nor the U.S. federal government was devoting substantial resources to research on synthetic rubber. Thus, in the 1930s, Du Pont (which had an interested research group and a synthetic rubber product viable for specialized uses), Standard Oil Company of New Jersey (which had been doing research on synthetic rubber), and the U.S. tire makers (which had access to cheap natural rubber) did not undertake intensive research on a synthetic substitute. The U.S. government (unlike the German one) had no inclination to sponsor, much less subsidize, such pursuits. Nonetheless, I. G. Farben—through its American affiliates, especially Jasco, Inc. (its joint venture with Standard Oil of New Jersey) and through its chemists who regularly visited America—kept abreast on the technological progress in the United States, while Americans sought to keep current on what was happening in Germany.[292]

By the late 1930s, however, there were no longer two-way technological exchanges on synthetic rubber. I. G. Farben in Germany, with its government aid, had moved ahead rapidly, and the German firm was not releasing information to its American friends, as it was bound to do by contract.[293] In 1938, Standard Oil Company of New Jersey, by contrast, provided full data to the Germans on its studies of butyl rubber. Later, at U.S. congressional hearings and in court cases, there would be accusations that I. G. Farben had "stolen" American technology and thus greatly slowed the U.S. war effort.[294]

Similar allegations on "theft" of American technology would be made on the matter of magnesium. Here I. G. Farben's American partner was Alcoa; Dow Chemical had been brought into the arrangements. The resulting alliance would later be denounced by critics as having impeded the growth of a domestic U.S. magnesium industry.[295] So, too, I. G. Farben's laboratories did advanced work on synthetic gasoline, once more spurred on by the German state. With low oil prices in the 1930s, and what were seen as adequate U.S. oil reserves, American companies were little concerned with substitutes for the natural product. Synthetic gasoline research in Germany was sponsored by the German government as necessary to that nation's rearmament. Again, subsequently it would be assumed that the connections between American and German companies in the 1930s had retarded American research.

As the 1930s progressed, I. G. Farben came under mounting pressure in Nazi Germany to act as an instrument of national goals. In 1936, with German firms (and the German economy) desperate for foreign exchange, as noted earlier, a German decree had prohibited German firms' investing abroad the income of their foreign subsidiaries. This had been a principal means of financing German business abroad in the 1930s. That year the German government had adopted the policy of "forcing its nationals to sell their foreign holdings of stocks and other assets."[296] I. G. Farben, however, retained its multifaceted business in the United States within the constraints of German rules and regulations.

By early 1939, I. G. Farben's management was well aware that war was imminent and that when it occurred the United States was likely to become an enemy. Memories of its predecessors' losses in World War I were still fresh, and I. G. Farben's lawyers wanted to secure the firm's U.S. assets. "Cloaking" had taken place much earlier, but in March 1939, I. G. Farben's legal committee considered further ways of protecting the enterprise's foreign assets.[297] In July, I. G. Farben calculated that its claims against the Consolidated Dyestuff Corporation (in Montreal), General Aniline Works, and General Dyestuff Corporation came to $2,850,000. The three firms issued bills of exchange amounting to $1,200,000, which bills were handed over to National City Bank "as securities for the credits of about 2 million USA $ which National City Bank has allowed I. G." I. G. Farben put out an "irrevocable order to the three firms stating that payments on I. G. claims are to be paid into National City Bank." After these transactions, I. G. Farben figured its exposure (re: such claims) was only $850,000.[298] Soon, however, it would worry that its vulnerability was much greater and would attempt to fine-tune the means by which it would attempt to preserve its U.S. assets.

Other foreign-owned chemical companies in the United States maintained and enlarged their businesses in the 1930s. Shell Union Oil Corporation—controlled by Royal Dutch Shell—increased its participation in oil-related chemicals. Another Royal Dutch Shell company in the United States, Shell Development Company—with research laboratories near the campuses of the University of California (Berkeley) and Stanford University—doubled its staff from more than 200 by 1935 to more than 400 in 1938. It engaged in pioneering research. Its twin, Shell Chemical Company, was the producing unit; it manufactured synthetic ammonia and fertilizers, a range of petrochemicals (involving alcohols from olefins), and many other chemical products. In 1934 Shell Chemical—based on innovations emerging from research on hydrogenation (in which Shell Development cooperated with Standard Oil of New Jersey and I. G. Farben) made the first commercial shipments of 100-octane gasoline to the U.S. Army Air Corps. Shell Development also undertook cutting-edge research on butadiene, an important ingredient in synthetic rubber.[299]

I. G. Farben's relations with the parent Royal Dutch Shell, and with both Shell Development and Shell Chemical in the United States, were always tempered by I. G. Farben's friendly associations with Standard Oil of New Jersey and Du Pont. On one occasion, for example, in January 1938, Royal Dutch Shell and I. G. Farben were negotiating a license from I. G. Farben to Shell Chemical on sulfuric ester salts from olefins. The

German enterprise decided that "we can grant Shell a license only with Standard's consent since this process affects the Jasco agreement . . . And, even if this process should not technically come within the Jasco agreement, we still would need Standard's consent for reasons of fairness because the process is competitive in a sense with the process for the manufacture of acetic acid from acetylene which has been brought into Jasco." At this time, I. G. Farben had pending discussions with Du Pont on this same process, but it intended "to limit Du Pont's license to fields outside raw materials of the oil industry." I. G. Farben wrote to its New York office (Chemnyco) that if Standard Oil of New Jersey had no objection, it would like to license Shell Chemical on the process—since "that might make it possible for us to come to an understanding with the same company [Royal Dutch Shell] in another very *important* field."[300]

At a London meeting in October 1938, representatives of Standard Oil of New Jersey, Standard-I. G. Co., I. G. Farben, M. W. Kellogg Co., and Standard Oil of Indiana formed the Catalytic Research Associates (CRA). They were soon joined by Royal Dutch Shell, Anglo-Iranian Oil Co., The Texas Co., and Universal Oil Products Co. CRA's purpose was to develop catalytic cracking and achieve high-octane fuels. Standard Oil of New Jersey took the lead.[301]

Principally but not exclusively in dyestuffs and pharmaceuticals, Swiss multinationals were key investors in the United States. This group of enterprises was also enmeshed in the web of international agreements and joint ventures, so characteristic of the chemical industry. Ciba, Sandoz, and Geigy (the so-called Basler I. G.) kept their post–World War I shared ownership of the Cincinnati Chemical Works, which was by the 1930s a sizable American dyestuffs manufacturer. All three companies (parents and affiliates) were active in taking out patents in the United States.[302] Beyond the joint venture in the Cincinnati Chemical Works, each had separate business. Ciba had the largest. On its own Ciba was a distributor of dyes (its Ciba Co. Inc. had branches in all the principal U.S. textile centers, where it engaged in research and development on dyestuff applications).[303] In still another, and major, involvement, in 1937, Ciba Pharmaceutical Products, Inc., opened a production and research facility on an eighty-acre site in Summit, New Jersey; Ciba became a leader in synthetic hormones, among other products.[304]

As for Sandoz, it had a U.S. sales organization (Sandoz Chemical Works Inc.) that was a distributor of dyestuffs, various chemical products, and pharmaceuticals; it had offices across the country, which undertook minor manufacturing; its head office and "manufacturing" was in New York City; it also had a factory in Paterson, New Jersey.[305] The third of the group, Geigy, in 1933–1934, had closed its old factory and warehouse in Jersey City and rebuilt anew for its own use the shuttered Bayonne, New Jersey, plant of Duryea Manufacturing Company. Geigy's product lines comprised textile finishes, mothproofing agents, bactericides, and insecticides. In 1938, in Basle, its parent organized a pharmaceutical division, which as part of its broader business pursued markets in ethical drugs in the United States.[306]

The Swiss-owned Hoffmann La Roche (like Ciba, Sandoz, and Geigy, headquartered in Basle) concentrated on pharmaceuticals. It increased its output at its huge Nutley, New Jersey, facility, adding new products and new buildings. Hoffmann-La Roche pursued a research agenda at its Nutley laboratories, which became the locale for pathbreaking work in synthetic vitamins. The company was manufacturing vitamin C by the mid-1930s and vitamin B_2 by the end of the decade.[307] In addition, in 1937, Hoffmann-La Roche cooperated with NV Organon (a subsidiary of Zwijnenburg's Vleesfabrieken of Oss, Holland) in a U.S. joint venture production unit, Roche-Organon, to make and distribute hormone products in the United States.[308]

Rounding out the Swiss collection of firms were three more, in fine chemicals, perfumes, and flavors. The parent firms were L. Givaudan & Co., Firmenich & Co., and Usines de l'Allondon, S.A. The first was involved in Givaudan-Delawanna, Inc.; the second in Firmenich & Co., Inc., New York; and the third in Allon-Bayonne Co., New York. Givaudan-Delawanna (by the 1930s a manufacturer in the United States) introduced in 1933 a new synthetic musk, Moskene; it also was a producer of vanillin.[309]

A handful of British manufacturers of medicine were present in the United States in the late 1930s, but only one, Burroughs, Wellcome & Co., had any stature. When Henry Wellcome (a founding partner) died in 1936, he left all his shares in the British parent to The Wellcome Trust, which was required to apply profits to medical research. Burroughs, Wellcome's American subsidiary (with its sizable Tuckahoe, New York, plant and research facilities) was a vibrant, multiproduct pharmaceutical enterprise.[310]

As for two other British firms that would in later years become prominent in America, one, the predecessor of Glaxo Laboratories, Joseph Nathan & Co., in 1934 went into a U.S. joint venture with the Montreal-headquartered Ayerst, McKenna & Harrison.[311] The second, Beecham's, had in the late 1930s merely a skeletal presence in the United States (it had stopped its earlier manufacturing). In 1932, Beecham's had briefly sought to rekindle its American business without success. Then, in 1938, in the United Kingdom Beecham's acquired Eno Proprietaries Ltd. and, with it, the latter's U.S. affiliates, which manufactured Eno's Fruit Salt and Scott's Emulsion (a cod liver oil product). Thus, Beecham's remained in America, a far cry from what it had been or would become.[312]

By contrast, in 1933 the German-owned Schering Corporation had transformed its U.S. business from one in sales to manufacturing, at first making Saraka (a branded laxative). In 1934, this subsidiary purchased a building in Bloomfield, New Jersey, and moved its production there; soon it was adding new products and operating research and development laboratories. In 1939, it erected a second factory, in Union, New Jersey. Schering innovated in synthetic sex hormones. Julius Weltzien, who had been with the Berlin firm since 1913, serving on its board (1922–1937), handling the setting up of international subsidiaries around the world, had on his mother's side a Jewish great-grandparent. In 1937 Weltzien left Germany, and in 1938 he took over the management of the Schering Corporation in Bloomfield, which maintained intimate links with its German parent (after 1937, Schering AG). According to Weltzien, in 1937 Hermann Goering's office had ordered Schering AG to sell its U.S. subsidiary but only under conditions whereby the latter continued to supply as much foreign exchange to Germany as before. Schering AG cooperated with the Swiss Bank Corporation to achieve that goal. Late in 1937, following the cloaking process common among German enterprises, Schering AG formed a Swiss holding company, Chemical and Pharmaceutical Enterprises Ltd. (Chepha). The majority of the stock in Chepha was, ostensibly, owned by the Swiss Bank Corporation. In February 1938, Schering AG entered into a royalty agreement with its "former" U.S. subsidiary. The U.S. offspring of Schering AG—still completely coupled in all its operations with the German firm—made proprietary products (the laxative, a cosmetic depilatory, and a sunburn preventive) but was also significant in the pharmaceutical industry. It had the line of hormones and, in addition, sold diagnostic products, an important sulfa drug, medicines used to treat arthritic conditions, and an antacid. In the late 1930s, the Stockholms Enskilda Bank assisted the German parent, Schering AG, in the further cloaking of the U.S. firm.[313]

By the end of the 1930s, Rare Chemicals, Inc., another producer of hormones and other pharmaceuticals (which at origin was 50 percent owned by C. F. Boehringer & Söhne, Mannheim) had come to be 100 percent owned by the "American" son of the president of its "ex-German parent."[314] Heyden Chemical Corporation (before World War I a subsidiary of the German Chemische Fabrik von Heyden) also expanded in the 1930s; its subsidiary, Norvell Chemical Corporation (an offshoot of the drug company McKesson & Robbins), branched into new fine chemicals and medicines. Although the German ownership relationships are obscure (and probably were nonexistent), Heyden Chemical had "amicable" ties with its onetime (pre–World War I) German owner.[315]

A number of added British, Belgian, French, and German multinationals were involved in making and/or selling various specialized chemical products in America.[316] Not only were the leading foreign enterprises in the chemical industry interconnected with U.S. chemical companies through licensing and market-control arrangements of various kinds; most other foreign direct investors in U.S. chemicals also had licensing agreements with the giants and with one another. Thus, the parents of Ciba, Sandoz, and Geigy (the Basler I. G.) were bound in a cartel with I. G. Farben, relating to the international dyestuff business.[317] In the United States, Roche-Organon, Ciba, Schering, and Rare Chemicals (each with foreign "parents" or close foreign connections) cooperated in the U.S. hormone trade—exchanging patents and processes, fixing prices, and attempting to bar entries of outsiders.[318] A pact between the Belgian Société Industrielle de la Cellulose and Du Pont governed the cellophane market.[319]

Whereas in the 1920s the principal foreign investors in the U.S. chemical industry had been to a great extent the providers of technology, by the 1930s not only Du Pont but also the entire American industry had matured. Frequently, now, foreign companies sought to acquire U.S.-generated technology. An impressive technological vitality existed, based on industrial research in the United States and abroad. Foreign-owned companies began to develop R and D capabilities within the United States, drawing not only on foreign but on domestic U.S. expertise as well. Cartels in the chemical industry, by dividing markets and maintaining prices, offered an umbrella, protecting and encouraging creative energies rather than (as is usually assumed) suppressing scientific achievements. In retrospect, although certainly not in the eyes of 1930s, 1940s, or 1950s policy makers, the U.S. economy was a sizable beneficiary from the interaction between foreign multinationals, their American affiliates, and domestic companies.

Other Manufacturing

In the 1930s, America's basic iron and steel production was completely domestic. FDI existed only in small fringe markets; Firth Sterling was the only remaining British investor in crucible steel, where once there had been a group of British firms.[320] The major British, French, Belgian, and Luxembourg steelmakers had no FDI in America. Some German steel companies had U.S. assets: Krupp, for example, had a patent holding and licensing company, Krupp-Nirosta Corporation, organized in 1928; its forte was in stainless steel.[321] On February 1, 1937, because of German foreign exchange controls, Krupp had been unable to redeem certain bonds that were part of the Young Plan loan from American investors. Fearful that American bondholders would attach the Krupp holdings in Krupp-Nirosta, in May 1937 Krupp transferred the ownership of that firm to a Dutch banking house (H. Albert de Bary & Co., Amsterdam). The ploy did not work, and the bondholders pursued Krupp assets.[322] In September 1938, Krupp believed war was imminent and tried to minimize its British and U.S. exposure (it was more concerned about its properties in England than its far smaller ones in the United States). It sought to cede its foreign assets to its foreign creditors as security for their claims. The goal was to see to it that Krupp's assets were not confiscated, while its foreign debts endured. Krupp then had de Bary & Co. sell its interests in Krupp-Nirosta to Wolframerz, AG, a Swiss firm.[323] All during the 1930s, Krupp retained a handful of independent sales agents in New York.[324] It also participated in a variety of licensing arrangements. J. A. Henckels, the German stainless steel company, known for its branded, famous "twin" trademark, had by the 1930s resumed its pre–World War I business in the United States. It had a small factory (owned by Graef & Schmidt) that made scissors, knives, and manicure instruments, which were sold through another of its subsidiaries, the Fifth Avenue Cutlery Shop.[325]

Three foreign-owned firms did stand out in U.S. manufacturing in this decade. One was the Swedish SKF, whose large Philadelphia factory ranked among the top producers of bearings in the United States. The British-controlled Norma–Hoffmann Bearing was also among the leading manufacturers in the United States in this industry (its plant was in Stamford, Connecticut).[326] The third firm was the multidivisional German-controlled United American Bosch Corporation (UABC), which was renamed American Bosch Corporation in 1938. UABC manufactured, assembled, and sold automotive equipment and accessories, diesel fuel-injection equipment, and gas-fired water heaters. Its radio division made, assembled, and marketed Bosch radios for use in homes and automobiles (including police cars); on average, in 1933–1937, this division accounted for roughly 35 percent of UABC business. However, UABC concluded the division was unprofitable, and in 1938 it discontinued the radio production. Thus, it concentrated on producer goods. Aside from the radio business, UABC's main customers throughout the decade were other manufacturers. It excelled in production of magnetos, which it sold mainly to the automobile industry. The company had begun marketing diesel engine equipment in 1931 (first importing from the German Bosch); it started manufacturing such equipment at its Springfield, Massachusetts, plant in 1934. Meanwhile, in 1933, it acquired a maker of gas-fired water heaters and embarked on this new line of activity. In 1938, the newly renamed American Bosch Corporation employed 800 persons. Like other German affiliates in America, UABC was put under a "camouflage." In this case, the disguise came to be through a Dutch intermediary; in 1935–1939, Mendelssohn & Co., Amsterdam, held the controlling interest; in 1935, the foreign owners appointed George Murnane as chairman of the U.S. company's board of directors. The "cloaking" scheme went awry, however, when after some large-scale speculation, on August 9, 1939, Fritz Mannheimer, the head of Mendelssohn & Co., Amsterdam, committed suicide. Mannheimer's death meant the Germans needed a new veil; the new "cover" had no impact on the ongoing operations of the American Bosch Corporation.[327]

One participant in America's immense "machinery" industry was Massey-Harris, the Canadian company, which remained as a supplier of farm equipment, although the depressed state of the U.S. farm sector in the 1930s did not prompt new investments; in any case, Massey-Harris' business was dwarfed by that of International Harvester.[328] The Swedish dairy products company AB Separator also persisted in a defined niche market. AGA (AB Gasaccumulator), another Swedish longtime investor in the United States, sold lighthouse and signal equipment; in the 1930s it had seven acetylene plants (to provide gas for the lighthouse beacons).[329]

The huge U.S. automobile and truck industry had become virtually wholly domestic by the 1930s (except for fewer than a handful of suppliers, such as the Bosch company). Car and truck imports had almost evaporated, leaving the scattered remaining sales outlets of European vehicle producers nearly dormant. In 1933–1939, no foreign company assembled or manufactured cars or trucks in the United States.[330] Imperial Chemical Industries, to be sure, continued to hold a large block of General Motors shares but, as in the past, played no role whatsoever in the management of the American giant. As for rubber tires, with the closing in 1930 of the Michelin plant, Dunlop was the sole foreign-owned tire maker in America. And, year after year Dunlop experienced losses, despite its introduction of a chain of U.S. retail stores and new tire brands. The only compensating feature was that Dunlop's experiences in America apparently led to certain efficiencies that could be adopted by the *parent* factory in Britain.[331]

During the New Deal years, the U.S. electrical industry was almost completely domestic. As in chemicals, so too in the electrical industry, a maze of agreements divided up the world. But whereas in chemicals, many foreign multinationals participated in the U.S. market in an important fashion, this was not the case in the electrical industry. The single aggressive foreign company in America in the 1920s—Brown, Boveri—had by the 1930s exited, having failed to penetrate the U.S. market. Siemens & Halske maintained a liaison office in America and affiliates (Siemens, Inc., Adlanco X-Ray Corp., and Roentgen Supplies Inc.), none of which was a substantial player in the United States.[332] As in chemicals, so too in the electrical industry, the complex international alliances tended to be process and product specific. Most of the time, Siemens & Halske dealt with the U.S. industry leaders in its discussions, especially Westinghouse, but also General Electric. When, however, Siemens & Halske had patents on new processes in beryllium manufacture, its licensing negotiations were with Metal & Thermit Co., the postwar successor to Th. Goldschmidt's American interests. Metal & Thermit Co. was managed in the interwar period by Dr. Franz Hirschland, a naturalized American, and represented Deutsche Gold- und Silber-Scheideanstadt (Degussa) in the United States. Through Metal & Thermit Co., Siemens & Halske sought to keep American "outsiders, like the Beryllium Corporation, the General Electric Co., etc." from "the realm of the beryllium heavy metal industry."[333]

The miscellaneous FDIs in America in electrical equipment and related products were all in specialized activities. The Swedish AB Electrolux appears to have kept its earlier stake (likely a minority one) in a U.S. producer of its goods.[334] In 1934 the Dutch NV Philips had set up a small subsidiary to make X-ray equipment, not a profitable venture.[335] Also in 1934 the British enterprise Decca Record Co. Ltd. participated in the formation of Decca Records, Inc., New York, which manufactured Decca records in the United States and distributed them in North and South America. As of March 31, 1939, the British company listed its investment in the New York company at £72,909.[336]

There were numerous other assorted stakes in U.S. manufacturing by foreign investors, ordinarily small, more continuations from times past than new interests, although some foreign manufacturers did start sales affiliates that would later be the basis for expansion into U.S. manufacturing. Carl Zeiss, Inc., fits in this category. It imported optical goods and scientific instruments from Carl Zeiss, Jena, Germany. In addition, it repaired products in use.[337] Other German-owned companies in machine tools and precision instruments included J. M. Lehmann Co., Inc., and E. Leitz. The German-owned Arabol Manufacturing Company made adhesives and glues.[338] In an entirely different activity, some Swiss watchmakers, to evade U.S. duties on 21 jewel watches, were reported by 1939 to have "screwdriver plants" in the United States that existed solely to add extra jewels and thus avoid the high tariff.[339]

Construction and Real Estate Development Services

A new British investor in the United States in the late 1930s was Taylor Woodrow Homes Ltd. Founded in 1921 as a construction company, in

1935 Taylor Woodrow started one of the early housing complexes on Long Island (New York). The development became known for its curvilinear streets and garden-style row houses.[340] It was a precursor for the many post–World War II projects by foreign investors in the United States. In years past, foreign direct investors had acquired agricultural and urban land and real estate. Taylor Woodrow's stake in suburban real estate was new but then so was suburbia, which had emerged in America in the 1920s (only to be, temporarily, stalled by the Depression).

Trading Companies

Typical foreign investments in services were those in trade, shipping, insurance, and banking—and these continued to be abundant. Despite the reduced level of international commerce in the 1930s, foreign-owned trading companies (with their specialized knowledge) for the most part persisted in their business, and there were new arrivals. In the grain trade, several important novelties surfaced. In 1937, Frederic Hediger immigrated to the United States from Switzerland and founded Garnac, which became a key U.S.-based grain trading company linked financially with the Swiss André company. This appears to have been the start of the André company's extensive U.S. business; André became one of the "Big Five" in the world grain trade.[341] Another of this quintet, the French Fribourgs (Continental Grain), had entered U.S. business much earlier and stood out as an energetic participant in U.S. commerce. In 1933, Jules Fribourg arranged the purchase and export to Europe of a million tons of wheat from the Federal Farm Board. The Roosevelt administration was delighted (an exceptional case of pleasure over the behavior of a foreign multinational). Subsequently, the Fribourgs were reported to have friends in high places.[342] It is not obvious how Continental Grain took advantage of its political connections, but clearly by the 1930s this Paris-based firm was well entrenched as a major player in the U.S. grain trade.[343] In addition, both the Paris-headquartered Louis Dreyfus firm and Bunge & Born (which had become Buenos Aires based) retained their pivotal roles in this trade, with the former probably more important than the latter.[344] Only one (Cargill) of the "Big Five" in the world's grain trade was American.[345]

In the U.S. leaf tobacco export trade, there was a separate group of significant traders: two British-headquartered enterprises, Imperial Tobacco and British American Tobacco, apparently were the largest exporters of tobacco from the United States.[346] The activities of BAT's American-based leaf tobacco purchasing organization (Export Leaf

Tobacco Co.) were coordinated from London, as was the case with Imperial Tobacco's procurement group.[347] In raw cotton, there was no similar foreign dominance of international trade, although data suggest that large Japanese trading houses handled much of this commodity that moved to Japan and elsewhere in the Orient; apparently, they and other foreign traders also handled some transatlantic raw cotton exports.[348]

In the 1930s a sizable number of foreign-owned trading firms in America dealt with a variety of exports and/or imports. Some of these firms were commodity specific, others not. Thus, United Molasses Co., Ltd. (UMC), for instance, towered above all other traders in the U.S. commerce in molasses. After recovering from its bad years, 1930–1933, its U.S. subsidiary, Pacific Molasses Co., became "one of the brightest jewels" in UMC's "crown."[349] The Finlay group's Anglo-American Direct Tea Company specialized in tea imports from the East; it had outlets in New York, Chicago, Philadelphia, and San Francisco (it also owned three tea estates in south India).[350]

Balfour, Williamson's American house, Balfour, Guthrie, conducted import-export trade in a range of products. Balfour, Guthrie's capital was restructured in 1935, as a consequence of bad times.[351] Japanese trading firms enlarged their U.S. business during the 1930s, selling a diversified line of goods in America, from cotton textiles to tuna fish. By 1939, the four principal Japanese general trading companies (Mitsui & Co., Mitsubishi Shoji, Okura Shoji, and Asano Bussan) moved more than 44 percent of Japanese exports to the United States—and much of the rest of U.S. imports from Japan were handled by other Japanese trading houses (including the specialized silk traders). From 1933 to 1939, Japan ranked third (after the United Kingdom and Canada) as a market for U.S. exports, and the four leading Japanese trading companies arranged fully 57 percent of these U.S. exports to Japan.[352] The Japanese trading companies not only took part in Japanese-U.S. trade but also engaged in a broader commerce involving U.S. imports from and exports to third countries.[353]

Late in 1938, the Universal Trading Corporation (UTC)—owned by the Chinese government—was founded in New York to facilitate Chinese exports, such as tungsten, tung oil, and tin, to pay for Chinese imports of American machinery, equipment, and raw materials. The Export-Import Bank (established in 1934 to encourage American trade) provided credit to the UTC.[354] Here the activities may have been more politically motivated than commercial, as the Chinese faced the Japanese invasion of 1937.

There seems little doubt but that foreign-owned companies had a significant role in expediting America's international trade. The qualitative data are lean and the quantitative data nonexistent. Although there needs to be more study of the role in U.S. imports and exports by foreign companies, I can conclude here with comfort that the impact of the foreign-owned trading enterprises in America on the nation's international trade far surpassed the size of these firms' inward FDI.

By contrast, in *domestic* trade—wholesale and retail—foreign multinationals' place was trivial. To be sure, a number of foreign manufacturers (with or without factories in the United States) did integrate into U.S. distribution, typically at a wholesale level (foreign dyestuff producers owned outlets in textile centers). Very few multinationals had FDI in retailing chains (Dunlop, with its tire marketing, and Bata, with its shoe stores, were exceptional). The Japanese luxury stores of Yamanaka and Co., which sold imported Chinese artworks, catered to an elite clientele. Seagram controlled retail pricing but owned no retail stores. Some trading houses had investments in American sales offices. There were other very limited investments (horizontal integration) by foreign retailers in the United States. All of this was, however, a mere drop in the bucket in the U.S.'s huge wholesaling and retailing sector.

Shipping Services

A significant portion of America's international commerce seems to have been handled by foreign-owned trading companies, but it is even more clear that a large share of U.S. imports and exports was shipped on foreign carriers. Between 1933 and 1938, U.S. shipping steadily lost out to that of other nations, particularly Great Britain, Norway, and Japan (see Table 7.9). By 1938, using tonnage as a measure, there were

Table 7.9. Shipping in America's foreign trade by nationality, 1933, 1936, 1938 (entrances and clearances, measured in tonnage) (percentages)

Nationality	1933	1936	1938
American	36.8	31.2	26.6
British	26.8	27.4	27.5
Norwegian	7.3	10.3	12.5
German	6.5	6.0	6.0
Japanese	4.7	5.2	5.1
All others	17.9	19.9	22.3
Total foreign	63.2	68.8	73.4

Source: Adapted from S. G. Sturmey, *British Shipping and World Competition* (London: Athlone Press, 1962), 130. The "all others" category included numerous different nationalities, none of which individually constituted more than 5 percent of U.S. entrances and clearances.

more British than American ships entering and clearing U.S. ports for the first time in the entire interwar period. That year, by this same measure, 73.4 percent of America's international shipping was foreign. While in 1938, German shipping still represented a higher percentage of America's foreign trade than that of the Japanese, the latter's share had grown from 1933 to 1936, which had not been true of the German portion.[355] Foreign shipping companies, particularly those of the British, Norwegians, Germans, and Japanese, had representatives within the United States, comprising small amounts of foreign direct investment.

Insurance Services

Some of the insurance services offered by foreign investors related to international trade, but many foreign insurance offices also handled insurance needs inside the U.S. domestic market. Canadian life insurance companies did a sizable domestic U.S. business over the border, with Sun Life Assurance Co., Ltd., Montreal, in the lead. Of Sun Life's total insurance in force in 1933 ($2.8 billion), $1.3 billion was payable in U.S. dollars. Of its total assets that year ($624.4 million), $386.4 million were denominated in U.S. dollars.[356] And, if this was impressive, even more striking and more numerous were the British insurance companies; these offered fire, marine, and casualty insurance and had long histories in America. Five large groups of British insurance companies continued to stand out: in alphabetical order, Commercial Union, London & Lancashire, North British & Mercantile, Phoenix, and Royal.[357] British insurance companies constituted a major segment of the British direct investment in the United States.[358]

The British insurers were more prominent than all the others, but French, Swiss, Danish, Swedish, Japanese, and German insurers offered their services, in both direct insurance and also, in some instances, reinsurance. Three Japanese insurance companies—Tokyo Marine and Fire Insurance Co., the Sumitomo Marine and Fire Insurance Co., and the Meiji Fire Insurance Co.—did business in California, New York, and Illinois.[359] Their business appears to have been principally to assist Japanese trading companies and shipping firms. Goods that were warehoused prior to shipping required fire insurance protection. Goods moving in international trade needed marine insurance.

The Pilot Reinsurance Company seems to have been the only important German insurer in the United States in the 1930s. An early 1939 memorandum in the archives of Munich Reinsurance indicated that the latter owned 49.98 percent of the shares of Pilot Reinsurance with the other owners: the German, Allianz (14.93 percent), the Italian, Assicurazioni Generali (18.67 percent), the Swiss, Union Reinsurance (7.47

percent), and the U.S. directors (6.31 percent). Munich Reinsurance in April 1939 began to arrange Swedish "cloaking."[360] Table 7.5, provided earlier in this chapter, suggests that in mid-1937 out of $1,883 million total FDI in the United States, $351 million was in insurance.[361]

Banking Services

At year end 1933, there were twenty-five New York State–licensed agencies of foreign banks in New York City. In the years to 1939, only one was dropped from the roster: Anglo-South American Bank, whose business was acquired by the Bank of London and South America in 1936.[362] (Anglo-South American had both a New York agency and The Anglo-South American Trust Company; the latter changed its name in 1937 to the Bank of Montreal Trust Company.)[363] Five new agencies of foreign banks were added to the list, so the final tally as of December 31, 1939, reached twenty-nine (see Table 7.10): the entries included four from the European continent, a Prague bank, a Polish bank domiciled in Paris, a Swiss bank, and a French one, along with the Bank of China.[364] In November 1935, China had abandoned the silver standard. The Bank of China opened its New York agency in 1936 with the purpose of aiding in Chinese currency stabilization.[365] Agencies of the Czech and Polish banks started up in New York in 1938.[366] In 1939, the first Swiss and French banks to use the licensed agency form of doing business obtained licenses from the New York State Banking Department. The Swiss Bank Corporation applied for a New York agency license in July 1939 (it would not actually begin operations until October 16, 1939).[367] The French bank was the important Société Générale, founded in 1864, which had long participated in U.S. business.[368] It did not apply for permission to set up a licensed New York agency until after the war had started in Europe, although Julien Chadenet (head of the bank's foreign department) indicated that the plans had been made prior to the outbreak of war.[369] Political conditions in Europe were obviously the underlying reason for both the Swiss and the French banks' formal licensing, as was the case with the Czech and Polish banks. During the New Deal period, there was no change in the law governing these state-licensed foreign bank agencies; they were still forbidden to take deposits.[370]

In the 1930s, the by now well-established core of foreign banks with licensed New York agencies maintained their sizable business. The first set comprised the Canadian group: the Bank of Montreal, Royal Bank of Canada, the Bank of Nova Scotia, the Canadian Bank of Commerce, and the Dominion Bank. This coterie of Montreal (the first two) and Toronto (the next three) banks had by this time become an integral

Table 7.10. Foreign (out-of-country) banks with agencies licensed under New York State banking law, 1933, 1939

		Activity, 1933–1939			
No.	In existence Dec. 31, 1933	Subtractions	Additions	In existence Dec. 31, 1939	No.
1.	Anglo-South American Bank, London	1936		No	
	—		1938	Anglo Prague Credit Bank, Prague	1.
2.	Banca Commerciale Italiana, Milan, Italy			Yes	2.
3.	Banco di Napoli, Naples, Italy			Yes (2 agencies)	3.
4.	Banco di Roma, Rome, Italy			Yes	4.
5.	Banco National de Mexico, Mexico City			Yes	5.
	—		1936	Bank of China, Kum-ming [*sic*], China	6.
6.	Bank of Chosen, Seoul, Korea (Japan)			Yes	7.
7.	Bank of London & South America, London			Yes	8.
8.	Bank of Montreal, Montreal			Yes	9.
9.	Bank of Nova Scotia, Halifax, Nova Scotia			Yes	10.
10.	Bank of Taiwan, Taiwan (Japan)			Yes	11.
	—		1938	Bank Polska Kasa Opieki Spolka Akcyjna, Paris	12.
11.	Banque Belge pour l'Etranger, Brussels, Belgium			Yes	13.
12.	Barclay's Bank (Dominion, Colonial & Overseas)			Yes	14.
13.	Canadian Bank of Commerce, Toronto			Yes	15.

14.	Chartered Bank of India, Australia and China, London		Yes	16.
15.	Cook, Thomas, & Sons		Yes	17.
16.	Credito Italiano, Genoa and Milan, Italy		Yes	18.
17.	Dominion Bank, Toronto		Yes	19.
18.	Hongkong and Shanghai Banking Corp., Hong Kong		Yes	20.
19.	Mitsubishi Bank, Ltd., Tokyo, Japan		Yes	21.
20.	Mitsui Bank, Ltd., Tokyo, Japan		Yes	22.
21.	Philippine National Bank, Manila, Philippines		Yes	23.
22.	Royal Bank of Canada, Montreal		Yes	24.
	—	1939	Société Générale pour favoriser le Développement du Commerce et de l'Industrie en France, Paris	25.
23.	Standard Bank of South Africa, London		Yes	26.
24.	Sumitomo Bank, Osaka, Japan		Yes	27.
	—	1939	Swiss Bank Corporation, Basle	28.
25.	Yokohama Specie Bank, Yokohama, Japan		Yes	29.

Sources: New York State, Banking Department, *Annual Reports*, 1933–1939.

part of the New York banking community, handling foreign exchange transactions and trade finance.[371] A large amount of their business appears to have continued to be linked with Latin America—relating to both trade and investments.[372]

The second set consisted of the British overseas banks: Bank of London and South America; Barclay's (DCO); the Chartered Bank of India, Australia, and China; the Hongkong and Shanghai Banking Corporation; and the Standard Bank of South Africa. These five participated in trade finance, typically between the regions where they were specialists and the United States, albeit they also arranged the financing of trade within their specialized regions that did not involve the movement of goods to or from the United States. Their New York offices were part of elaborate networks. Like all the foreign bank agencies, without exception, these banks were also in New York for information purposes. Interestingly, for these banks, there does not seem to have been much attention to their American earnings; rather, their purpose was to serve their affiliated financial outlets in the particular regions where they operated.[373] In addition to these British "overseas banks," Thomas Cook & Sons, London, had a licensed New York agency that catered specifically to the requirements of British visitors to America, providing foreign exchange, travelers checks, and the like.

The third set of banks, the four from Italy—Banca Commerciale Italiana, Banco di Napoli, Banco di Roma, and Credito Italiano, from Milan, Naples, Rome, and Genoa—were there to meet the special needs of the large Italian immigrant community in New York City; these agencies specialized in helping immigrants send remittances back home. Finally, the fourth set of banks were the six Japanese ones—the Bank of Chosen, Bank of Taiwan, Mitsubishi Bank, Mitsui Bank, Sumitomo Bank, and Yokohama Specie Bank—that financed U.S.-Japanese and U.S.–Japanese–third country trade, acted on behalf of Japanese interests in New York (and, to a lesser extent, elsewhere in the United States), and in the case of Yokohama Specie Bank arranged remittances on Japanese government debt.[374]

Beyond the bank agencies, there remained in New York representatives and correspondents of all the major foreign banks.[375] In 1933 there were also eight foreign-owned trust companies in New York; by the summer of 1939, this number was down to six (see Table 7.11). Trust companies could take deposits. Whereas in 1933 there had been three Italian trust companies, by the summer of 1939 only one remained: the Banco di Napoli Trust Co. The latter, which had acquired the Bank of Sicily Trust Co. in 1936, in 1939 operated five branches in New York City and was a member of the Federal Deposit Insurance Corporation (FDIC).[376] The FDIC had been established under the Banking Act of

Table 7.11. Foreign-owned trust companies in New York in the 1930s (in boldface, those present in the summer of 1939)

Present in 1933	Year founded	Changes, 1933–1939
Anglo-South American Trust Co.	1923	Renamed **Bank of Montreal Trust Co.,** 1937
Banca Commerciale Italiana Trust Co.	1924	Assets and liabilities acquired by Manufacturers Trust Co., New York, Feb. 1939; after this BCIT was liquidated
Banco di Napoli Trust Co.	1930	Acquires the Bank of Sicily Trust Co., 1936
Bank of Athens Trust Co.	1926	
Bank of Sicily Trust Co (renamed 1929; originally Banco di Sicilia Trust Co.)	1925	Acquired by the Banco di Napoli Trust Co., 1936, and merged into Banco di Napoli Trust Co.
Hellenic Bank Trust Co.	1930	
J. Henry Schroder Trust Co.	1929	Renamed **Schroder Trust Co.,** 1937
Trust Company of North America	1924	At origin, the Banco Nacional Ultramarino (Portugal) had an interest in the Trust Company of North America; I do not know how long that interest was sustained

Sources: Text and notes of present book; specifically on Schroders: Richard Roberts, *Schroders* (Houndmills: Macmillan, 1992), 228; on the Banco Nacional Ultramarino: Clyde William Phelps, *The Foreign Expansion of American Banks* (New York: Ronald Press, 1927), 201. In general, see Web site of the Banking Department of New York State: http://banking.state.ny.us/histba.txt and *Moody's Banks, 1939.*

1933 to provide insurance coverage to depositors; Banco di Napoli Trust Co. deposits were insured. The Banca Commerciale Italiana Trust Co. (BCIT), New York, the first of the Italian banks to set up a New York trust company, had flourished during the late 1920s, but after 1932 it had paid no further dividends. When the FDIC was formed, it too became a member. However, on February 11, 1939, its assets and liabilities were acquired by the American-owned Manufacturers Trust Co., New York, and the BCIT was liquidated.[377]

In addition, fewer than a handful of affiliates of foreign financial institutions stayed on in New York as "banking corporations." This group included the French American Banking Corporation, established in 1919 and 50 percent owned by Comptoir National d'Escompte de Paris. Its principal activities were financing export and import transactions and making and receiving transfers of funds for the account of its foreign customers.[378] And then there was the J. Henry Schroder Banking Corporation (Schrobanco). Because of its experience with German business, this British-owned American bank had opened an office in Berlin in the summer of 1933 to try to unscramble problems with frozen German credits. Schrobanco was also a participant in brokerage activities in American securities in Europe and helped channel portfolio capital westward across the Atlantic. It provided dollar acceptance credits and advances to U.S. commodity importers and European traders and in the late 1930s built up a sizable Latin American banking business. It was affected by the passage of the federal Banking Act of 1933 (the Glass-Steagall Act), which required a separation of commercial and investment banking. Schrobanco's historian explains that when in the mid-1930s there was a revival (after the nadir of the Depression) of the securities issuing business, Schrobanco decided to organize a separate investment banking company: on July 8, 1936, Schroder, Rockefeller & Co., Inc. came into existence to acquire the underwriting and general securities business formerly done by Schrobanco. This new firm, a joint venture between the British Schroder partners and Avery Rockefeller, was active in underwriting syndicates for subsidiary companies of Standard Gas and Electric Corporation and other U.S. enterprises. Ownership of some of (perhaps a large portion of) the securities it handled moved to Europe to go into the hands of its foreign customers.[379]

Lazard Frères was also affected by the Glass-Steagall Act, separating commercial and investment banking; it selected the investment banking route.[380] A newcomer, on July 11, 1939, Crédit Suisse organized a New York subsidiary, the Swiss American Corporation, to take part in the investment security business. Swiss American began with resources of $3 million and had Daniel Norton, president of the U.S. Nestlé company, as its chairman of the board.[381] The Swiss Bank Corporation (see earlier discussion) and the Crédit Suisse resolved to enter the United States within days of one another, owing to the threats of war in Europe (Crédit Suisse would soon establish a New York–licensed agency, as well as continuing on with Swiss American). By 1938–1939, refugees from Europe were arriving in New York; the French and Swiss banks served that clientele, who frequently had been their customers in Europe.

Recall that when in 1929 the Bank of the Manhattan Company had acquired the International Acceptance Bank, foreign banks had become stockholders in the Manhattan Company, and in 1932 the International Acceptance Bank had been dissolved. I have sought without success to determine exactly what happened to the foreign banks' equity interests in the Bank of the Manhattan Company during the remainder of the 1930s. A number of foreign banks stayed on as passive investors, as the Bank of the Manhattan Company returned to its focus on domestic banking activities. It did have some international business, and there is evidence that it provided assistance to certain foreign multinationals investing in the United States. The equity holdings of each individual foreign bank had always been small. It is very likely, however, that the contacts of the foreign banks might have helped in handling certain sideline foreign exchange problems that the Bank of the Manhattan Company may have encountered; foreign banks probably referred their clients to the Bank of the Manhattan Company; the bank kept in contact with foreign banks and foreign customers. However, for the years after 1933, I found no evidence that any individual foreign bank had a strategic impact on the Bank of the Manhattan Company.[382]

Throughout the 1930s, foreign banks and international banking came to be increasingly confined to New York City. On the West Coast in San Francisco, Sacramento, Los Angeles, Seattle, and Portland, a small coterie of Canadian and Japanese banks, along with the Hongkong and Shanghai Banking Corporation, did keep up their activities established in prior years. When the Bank of Canton Ltd., Hong Kong, was in financial difficulties in 1935, it was rescued by T. V. Soong and reorganized; in 1937, its San Francisco branch was transformed into a new Bank of Canton, San Francisco.[383] Most of the foreign-owned banking activity on the West Coast involved the financing of foreign trade and dealings with foreign exchange and, in the case of the two Hong Kong banks (one British, one Chinese) and the Japanese banks, providing services, respectively, for the Chinese and Japanese residents on the West Coast.

In Chicago, the Bank of Montreal and the Bank of Nova Scotia retained their long-standing branches, while Banco di Napoli Trust Co. of Chicago undertook general banking (it became a member of the FDIC); controlled by Banco di Napoli, it handled immigrant accounts.[384] The Banca Commerciale Italiana Trust Co., incorporated in Pennsylvania in 1929, had undertaken a general banking business and in the 1930s had become a member of the FDIC. In December 1938 (less than two months before the BCIT, New York, would divest), BCIT, Philadelphia, was acquired by the Liberty Title & Trust Co. (Philadelphia).[385] Banca Commerciale Italiana (which had set up a Boston trust company in 1929 when it established itself in Philadelphia) "wound up" BCIT, Boston, in 1937–1938.[386] In Boston, the branch of the Bank of Nova Scotia lingered on.

Mortgage Lenders

During the 1930s, some British (principally Scottish) mortgage lenders—adverse conditions notwithstanding—still offered their services to Americans as they had for generations. Table 7.12, on the Scottish

Table 7.12. American investments of the Scottish American Mortgage Co., 1933–1939 (in £s)

Year end, May 31	Mortgages and real estate in America[a]	American securities owned[b]				Total securities owned[c]	American securities as % of total securities[d]
		Bonds	Preferred & guaranteed shares	Common stock	Total		
1933	503,736	6,531	41,156	100,155	147,842	1,387,771	10.6
1934	472,311	6,331	54,261	90,852	151,444	1,640,462	9.2
1935	427,207	4,091	62,091	89,453	155,635	1,764,665	8.8
1936	403,576	—	149,707	169,503	319,210	2,213,628	14.4
1937	373,936	—	140,486	301,499	441,985	2,480,124	17.8
1938	356,331	1,439	102,700	180,894	285,033	1,991,841	14.3
1939	330,924	6,114	143,404	239,284	388,802	2,104,443	18.5

Source: Scottish American Mortgage Co., *Annual Reports,* Film Z-G2, Reel 55, Bancroft Library, University of California, Berkeley

a. Mortgages and real estate are "at or under cost" and entered at $4.90 to £.

b. At market and entered at $4.90 to £.

c. The figures in this column are the total of marketable securities owned by the Scottish American Mortgage Co., including American, U.K., and other securities. The figures are at market. They exclude mortgages and real estate owned in America.

d. The percentage is obtained by dividing the total American securities owned (as given in the table) by the total securities owned (as given in the table). The percentage excludes the investments in mortgages and real estate owned in America.

American Mortgage Company's investments, is of particular interest. Note that in 1933, the company's investments in American mortgages (and real estate) were still substantially larger than its interest in American securities. Over the years, it had diversified away from U.S. involvements and had become more of an investment trust than a mortgage company.[387] From 1933 to 1939, its investments in American mortgages (and real estate) steadily declined, so that by 1939 its stake in the mortgage business was less than that in American stocks and bonds. Its portfolio of American securities is also of interest: the market values rose rapidly to 1937, witnessed a sharp decline in the 1938 market downturn, and then once more moved upward. Throughout, its U.S. common stock holdings were larger than those in American bonds and preferred and guaranteed shares combined. Its American bond portfolio was small and disappeared entirely in 1936 and 1937; when its holdings of bonds resumed, they remained very limited. As indicated in the last column of Table 7.12, the portion of American securities in the company's overall (worldwide) securities total declined annually to 1935, rose to 17.8 percent in 1937, but by 1939 was at an all-time high for the decade (18.5 percent).[388] Another Scottish mortgage lender, the Alliance Trust, Dundee, followed the identical pattern. In 1933, its investments in the U.S. mortgage field had been 12.5 percent of its entire investment portfolio, and in 1937 this was down to 8.6 percent. It substituted stocks and bonds for mortgages and real estate. In 1938, of its worldwide portfolio of stocks and bonds, 17 percent was invested in America.[389]

The Texas Land and Mortgage Co., once a major British-owned mortgage lender in Texas, also shifted from mortgage lending to investing in securities, some of which were in the United States. With the devaluation of the dollar, it wrote down its "loans on mortgages on real estate in Texas" from £636,793 (March 31, 1933) to £386,197 (March 31, 1934). It then stopped lending in Texas. A new manager (B. F. Brewer) was dispatched from the United Kingdom to Texas in July 1933. The company had sold its office building in Dallas in the early 1920s. In 1933, it transferred its Texas office from Dallas to Lubbock. Its outstanding Texas mortgage loans fell from £386,197 (March 1934) to £22,776 (March 1939). Its "securities foreclosed and real estate in Texas" mounted, so that by 1935 that sum exceeded its outstanding mortgages; that year, for the first time, its "investments"—some in the United States, but mostly in the United Kingdom—surpassed its loans on mortgages on real estate in Texas. By 1937, its "securities foreclosed and real estate" peaked at £328,535. In 1939, this figure was down to £270,560. This firm was liquidating its mortgage business and being transformed into an investment trust.[390]

In short, as British mortgage lenders came to be investment trusts, some stayed on as portfolio investors in America in securities. The Dutch mortgage lenders, faced with depression conditions in the 1930s, also sharply reduced their mortgage portfolios; nonetheless (according to one source) the Holland-Texas Hypotheekbank, Amsterdam in 1938 still had almost $1 million in real estate mortgages outstanding in Port Arthur, Texas.[391] As the Dutch pulled back from mortgage lending, most of the Dutch firms do not seem to have reinvested in the United States. Overall, the long-term trend away from mortgage lending by foreign investors in the United States accelerated sharply in the 1930s. Indeed, by 1939, in aggregate, the role of foreign direct investors in providing U.S. farm (and urban) mortgages had become inconsequential.

Conclusions

Foreign investment in the United States in the years 1933–1939 gradually assumed new characteristics, shaped by economic and political occurrences at home and abroad. Although the breakdown in the international economy reduced international trade and turned nations to their own needs, this did not mean a halt to international investment. The rising FPI in American stock market securities (especially in common stock) captured the most attention; usually, these were investments not in new issues but in traded securities. The inward FPI increased from 1933 to 1939 as war clouds darkened the global outlook. These inward investments were sufficient to be the object of considerable public policy concern within the United States. The anxieties over FPI ebbed and flowed, with policy makers' concerns stemming from the experience of the stock market crash of 1929 and a dread of its repetition. FPI seemed less amenable to national regulatory solutions than domestic investments. FPI often went into the securities of well-known traded American domestic corporations. These were frequently in sectors different from those dominated by inward FDI or even of interest to foreign multinationals. Thus, American Telephone and Telegraph was a favored stock, and there was no FDI in the U.S. telephone industry. In contrast, there was considerable inward FPI in companies in the oil industry, a sector where there was also substantial inward FDI. Most critical, none of the public policy considerations vis-à-vis FPI seems to have been industry driven.[392]

FDI, where the story line was different from FPI, also rose over the years 1933–1939. Abroad, foreign multinationals that invested in the United States responded to exchange controls, increased government regulations, and mounting taxes and altered their American business activities to meet these changing circumstances, as well as to deal with the evolving conditions and laws in the United States. High U.S. tariffs meant some additional FDI in manufacturing to reach American customers. A big surge in new FDI came with the end of Prohibition. In general, in the United States, foreign businesses encountered the same problems of depression malaise and expanding government intervention as their U.S. counterparts. Although they met with labor unrest, particularly in the textile industry, they may have run into less sweeping labor difficulties than U.S. industry in general, since foreign multinationals were not in iron and steel, automobiles, or the electrical industry, which had such serious labor strife in these years and where the National Labor Relations Act of 1935 had profound impact. There remained in place within the United States the historical restrictions on foreign businesses' participation in certain crucial sectors (and no inclination on the part of any Americans to bend or rewrite the rules; in fact, at times they were more rigorously enforced); yet foreign affiliates were eligible for some government assistance offered by the New Deal (farm subsidies, for example). Indeed, and overall, the legal environment for foreign multinationals in America was (the long-standing excluded sectors apart) nearly identical to that for domestic enterprises. Opportunities opened for U.S. companies as well as foreign ones with the end of Prohibition. And, just as U.S. companies faced a barrage of new taxes, new regulations, and, as the 1930s progressed, the revival of antitrust investigations and litigation, so too the outsiders were subjected to the same U.S. public policies, although the applications to foreign multinationals might be accompanied with substantial antiforeign rhetoric. However, foreign parents' lack of familiarity with the regulations and the need to depend on the advice of American lawyers and bankers as well as managers at the corporate affiliate may have resulted in differential effects of U.S. rules on the foreign multinationals.

By contrast with FPI, industry mattered greatly in the case of FDI. Not only were public policies affecting FDI often industry specific, throughout 1933–1939 FDI's significance was confined to certain industries. In roughly a dozen, in particular in oil, potash, borax, soap, whiskey, thread, rayon, and a handful of chemical and pharmaceutical lines, foreign multinationals were highly innovative and extremely important. A number of foreign-owned firms operated industrial research laboratories in the United States. In borax, soap, whiskey, thread, and pharmaceuticals, they offered trademarked products and advertised heavily. By contrast, America's principal heavy industries, the great industrial establishments of Pittsburgh, Detroit, and Schenectady—steel, automobiles, and electrical equipment—were in the New Deal years virtually untouched by businesses from abroad. There was by the end of the 1930s only one foreign multinational in the rubber tire industry (and it was not in the industry leadership group). So, too, FDI in public utilities—power and light as well telephone service—has not even been mentioned in this chapter, for it was virtually nonexistent. Foreign insurance companies continued to do sizable business in fire and casualty coverage. But in the vast retailing sector, the presence of foreign multinationals was practically nil. There is weak evidence that a large (how large is unknown) share of U.S. international commerce was handled by foreign multinationals (industrial enterprises and trading firms), and certainly a great portion of it was transported on foreign ships and insured by foreign-owned insurance companies. Foreign banks that had agencies in New York City provided foreign trade finance, and with fluctuating exchange rates and foreign exchange restrictions their specialized expertise was in demand. By contrast, there was little or perhaps no impact of foreign banks on domestic retail banking.

New government participation in every facet of the U.S. economy and new complexities in doing business notwithstanding, because of the dismal state of the international economy (the general lack of opportunities outside the United States), there seems no question but that in 1939, on the eve of the outbreak of war in Europe, total long-term foreign investment in the United States (both FPI and FDI) was larger than it had been when Roosevelt took office in 1933.[393]

8.

War Abroad, 1939–1941

On September 3, 1939, Britain and France declared war on Germany after its invasion of Poland. The United States did not enter the conflict until December 7, 1941, when the Japanese bombed Pearl Harbor. In November 1939 the U.S. Congress rewrote the Neutrality Act of 1937: Americans could sell munitions to belligerents but only on a "cash-and-carry basis," yet throughout 1939–1941 strong isolationist sentiments prevailed within the country, while at the same time the nation's sympathies became increasingly aligned with those of Great Britain.[1] In the closing months of 1939 and during 1940–1941, foreign investors in the United States (and U.S. policies affecting them) were deeply impacted by what was occurring abroad.

When the war in Europe began, the initial fears in the United States associated with the inward foreign investment focused on the stock market. Would the situation resemble 1914, with massive liquidations by foreigners? There had been much nervousness over the influx of foreign moneys in the 1930s; would there now be a destabilizing exit? A second set of immediate anxieties related to how dependent the United States was on imports that would be curtailed by the war and the coincident disruption of U.S. exports and shipping (concerns intimately linked with the behavior of foreign direct investors in the United States).

Between September 1939 and April 1940, apart from the hostilities between Russia and Finland, there was no fighting in Europe. Then, in the spring of 1940, as the Germans swept through Denmark, Norway, Holland, Belgium, and France, Americans became frightened that the Germans would invade Britain. What would be the U.S. role? And how would this affect U.S. outward as well as inward foreign investments? Many citizens worried lest foreign investments (outward or inward) propel Americans into the war. The German bombing of Britain began in August 1940. When Japan joined with Germany and Italy in the Tripartite Pact on September 27, 1940, debates in the United States on the nation's international role intensified.

The vast majority of Americans favored the British cause, which presented obvious difficulties for German investors in the United States. Americans did not want the U.S. assets of residents of German-occupied countries to be used by the Germans. During 1941, Americans were becoming ever more alarmed by Japanese aggression in East Asia along with the German-Japanese Axis. To guarantee that the U.S. assets of residents in and companies in German-occupied territories, Germany, and Japan, as well as in selected other countries, were not utilized in manners contrary to American national security goals, the U.S. Treasury Department put in place a "Foreign Funds Control" program, and in this context, in 1941, a census was undertaken to determine the amounts of all foreign assets in the United States.[2]

Throughout most of the period 1939–1941, the general disquiet over inward foreign investment in the United States, so evident during the prior years of the New Deal, heightened. Previously inaugurated (and new) antitrust investigations of international cartels and of foreign businesses' U.S. involvements intensified. These inquiries now carried with them an ever more hostile political rhetoric. As one law professor put it, I. G. Farben was "the villain in most of the foreign monopoly cases."[3] Questions proliferated on the effects of corporate international networks on national security, defense, and economic well-being accompanied by the more narrowly construed issues of the safeguarding of free and open competition. Were European businesses—especially German ones—with their cartel practices retarding the progress of American industry? Had they undermined the nation's competitive vitality, draining Americans of essential technologies? Had the Germans done this damage through their direct investments in the United States? The answers came forth readily and were not kind to the foreign investors.

Other matters pertinent to foreign investment in the United States surfaced: Were foreign-owned multinational enterprises in the United States serving nefarious political ends on behalf of their mother countries? Were foreign insurance offices, for example, engaged in espionage? And, with the war in Europe, as U.S. commerce with Latin America expanded, were German companies in the United States taking advantages of these opportunities for their own unsavory purposes? German influence in Latin America became a subject closely tied to the sweep of scrutinies of German business in the United States. Managers of German companies, reading the writing on the wall, responded with frantic efforts to insulate themselves from future asset losses.

In the meanwhile, British firms (and the British government) wanted to be sure that they had nothing to do with enemy enterprises through neutral America. As in the First World War, the British government invested in the United States in building its own munitions plants. Canada had joined Britain in declaring war in September 1939; it imposed foreign exchange controls. These controls notwithstanding, Canadian companies in the United States continued as before; in fact, their numbers increased. In 1939–1941, European enterprises (notably NV Philips and Nestlé) set up temporary (wartime) U.S. headquarters—away from the battle zones. French investors made adjustments, first to the potential of invasion, and after Hitler crossed the border into France, some French companies managed to transfer their personnel to safety in the United States. Jewish refugees from many parts of Europe came with their businesses to America. Japanese enterprises in this country, faced with the deterioration of U.S.-Japanese relationships, responded, frequently if possible repatriating their assets.

Of all nations, in 1939–1941, the United Kingdom and Canada had the greatest interests in the United States. The Canadians were supplying part of their ally's wartime needs. How did their U.S. investments fit into that equation? The British were purchasing military supplies in Canada, but they depended far more on the United States. The U.S. Neutrality Act of 1937 had hampered British buying in America, but after the new Neutrality Act of November 1939, Britain (and its French partner) could obtain goods on a "cash-and-carry" basis. How were they to pay? How were adequate dollars to be found? Throughout practically all the period 1939 to 1941, for the British (virtually alone after the defeat of France in June 1940), this was a major concern, affecting British inward investments in the United States. By the spring of 1941 the answers to these questions dominated the discourse on foreign investment in the United States, since an obvious source of dollars was British assets in the United States. In early 1941, as Americans debated lend-lease legislation, a spotlight beamed on British dollar holdings within the United States—both British-owned stock market securities and direct investments. Many Americans wondered whether the United States should be lending to Britain, when the British had their own financial resources within this country. In March 1941, Congress passed the Lend-Lease Act, committing the United States to aid the Allies. Prior to and closely linked with the act's passage, many measures were taken vis-à-vis U.K. investments in this nation.

On August 14, 1941, Roosevelt and Britain's Prime Minister Winston Churchill issued a joint statement—the Atlantic Charter—endorsing the goal of postwar international economic cooperation. Nothing in the charter dealt with capital movements, yet its global perspective would herald a more open world economy for the future. By the summer of 1941, U.S. isolationism was in retreat. Indeed, before U.S. direct involvement in the war, numerous significant matters connected with inward foreign investments in this country came to the forefront. Although most of the U.S. responses toward the inward foreign investments from September 1939 to December 1941 were negative, now and then a tolerance and even receptivity toward the inward foreign investments crept into the public discourse.

In the 1941 Census (published in 1945), the Treasury Department tried to determine the level of foreign investment in the United States. Table 8.1 summarizes its findings on FPI in domestic securities. The census also included foreign direct investments, conducting a far more comprehensive survey than had the U.S. Department of Commerce in past years. The census discovered that the number of foreign-owned firms ("U.S. enterprises controlled from abroad") within the United States was larger than anyone at the time had recognized. The census found 2,816 U.S. enterprises controlled from abroad—1,616 more than the 1,200 foreign direct investments on the Commerce Department lists. Table 8.2 provides the Treasury Department data on foreign-owned enterprises. Comparing Tables 8.1 and 8.2, the value of inward long-term FPI in securities, as in earlier years (at least according to the best available data), exceeded the inward FDI, but now by a very narrow margin.[4] Table 8.3, also from the census, gives an overall profile of long-term foreign investment in the United States, ranked by leading source countries, based on "reported address." Two figures are presented for each country: the first is the total; the second is confined to "citizens" of that particular country. This suggests that a sizable portion of foreign investment in the United States was by citizens of another country whose foreign assets were included in the country total.[5] Table 8.3 contains a category of long-term foreign investments entitled "trusts and estates," which investments were closely associated with Americans abroad, immigration, and family connections.[6] As of June 1941, according to the U.S. Treasury Department census, inward FPI in American securities came to $2.7 billion, whereas FDI in the United States was $2.3 billion.

I will hold the important story of British (and initially French) military purchasing needs and the dramatic effects on foreign investments in the United States to the last part of this chapter, so as to cover this story as a unity. Here it should be emphasized that, with some very few exceptions, from September 1939 to December 7, 1941, it was the war abroad that offered the stage for the basic trends in foreign investments in the United States.

Table 8.1. Long-term foreign portfolio investments in American domestic securities, June 14, 1941 (market value in millions of U.S. dollars, on the basis of reported address)

	Type of security							
Country/region	U.S. govt.	State & local govt.	Corporate bonds	Common stock	Preferred stock	Other securities	Total[a]	Rank by country
Canada and Newfoundland	32.2	4.9	43.0	388.9	66.9	6.9	542.9	
of which								
Canada	32.0	4.8	41.8	379.0	66.4	6.9	530.9	2
South America	9.0	1.7	8.2	70.7	10.0	.4	100.1	
of which								
Argentina	5.4	.6	4.4	35.4	5.4	.2	51.4	9
Brazil	.8	.7	1.6	9.0	1.5	.1	13.6	14
Mexico and Central America	5.1	1.2	6.8	66.4	10.3	.2	89.9	
of which								
Mexico	2.5	.3	2.7	18.8	3.3	.2	27.6	13
Panama	1.4	.4	3.3	41.7	6.6	[b]	53.3	8
The Caribbean	21.8	5.6	12.0	55.7	7.3	.2	102.5	
of which								
Cuba	17.6	2.7	8.3	34.5	3.0	.2	66.2	6
Europe	116.0	76.9	132.9	1,159.3	196.1	15.9	1,697.1	
of which								
United Kingdom	18.9	38.4	41.5	403.0	84.5	1.2	587.5	1
Switzerland	64.4	7.4	42.5	259.3	42.9	.7	417.2	3

Table 8.1 *(continued)*

	Type of security							
Country/region	U.S. govt.	State & local govt.	Corporate bonds	Common stock	Preferred stock	Other securities	Total[a]	Rank by country
Netherlands	3.0	.4	15.1	268.7	31.2	1.3	319.8	4
France	15.6	19.0	18.3	115.1	18.0	.2	186.4	5
Sweden	.6	.2	.9	22.7	1.4	10.1	35.9	10
Belgium	1.5	0.1	2.3	26.5	2.9	1.6	34.9	11
Italy	2.0	8.9	2.9	16.3	2.6	.3	33.0	12
Germany	.8	.6	2.4	6.2	2.2	.1	12.4	15
Africa	.7	.2	1.2	12.9	1.2	[b]	16.3	
Asia	24.4	2.2	14.4	82.9	13.9	.8	140.8	
of which								
China	11.2	.4	5.9	30.2	5.5	.5	53.7	7
Japan	7.2	[b]	.2	4.0	.2	.1	11.7	16
Oceania	1.2	.1	.7	4.8	.9	.1	7.8	
Unknown[c]	.2	.1	.3	1.1	.1	[b]	1.8	
Total (all areas)[a]	213.7	92.7	219.4	1,842.6	306.1	24.5	2,699.1	

Source: U.S. Department of the Treasury, *Census of Foreign-Owned Assets in the United States* (Washington, D.C., 1945), 18 and 24 (totals); 22 and 24 (regional totals); 78–88 (country detail). The census was as of June 14, 1941.

Note: This excludes foreign direct investments in the securities of American companies. U.S. citizens who were residing abroad were included as foreign investors. This would have particular impact on the high ranking of Cuba, for example. The investments in securities are exclusively "domestic securities."

a. The figures are rounded and will not necessarily add to the total.

b. Less than $50,000.

c. Includes some bearer securities (primarily bonds), which were "in general, only reported [in the census] when held by custodians and nominees."

Table 8.2. Number of U.S. enterprises controlled from abroad and value of foreign investments therein, June 14, 1941 (values in millions of U.S. dollars)

Country/Region	No. of enterprises		Value of foreign direct investment		Country Rank	
					Number	Value
Canada and Newfoundland	241		529.8			
of which						
Canada		238		518.5	5	2
South America	41		61.4			
of which						
Argentina		a		19.7		11
Uruguay		a		14.7		14
Bolivia		a		14.2		15
Mexico and Central America	36		39.1			
of which						
Panama		a		28.6		10
Mexico		a		9.4		17/18
The Caribbean and Bermuda	41		22.3			
of which						
Cuba		a		15.9		13
Europe	1,985		1,569.4			
of which						
United Kingdom		623		711.5	1	1
Netherlands		179		336.0	6	3
Switzerland		245		137.8	4	4
Germany[b]		171		105.1	7	5
France		250		99.6	3	6
Belgium		59		82.9	8	7
Sweden		a		34.4		9
Italy		a		10.0		16
USSR		a		9.4		17/18
Africa	19			9.4		
of which						
South Africa		a		4.7		20
Asia	444		74.2			
of which						
Japan		360		35.1	2	8
China		47		16.7	9	12
Philippines			a	8.0		19

Table 8.2 *(continued)*

Country/Region	No. of enterprises	Value of foreign direct investment	Country Rank	
			Number	Value
Oceania	9	5.3		
of which				
Australia			a	2.9	21
New Zealand			a	2.4	22
Unknown		1.7		
Total (all areas)	2,816[c]	2,312.6		

Source: U.S. Department of the Treasury, *Census of Foreign-Owned Assets in the United States* (Washington, D.C., 1945), 29–30, 64–65. The census was as of June 14, 1941.

Note: "Control" is defined as 25 percent or more of voting stock. Values were if possible those in the market and if not possible book value. "Because interests in these enterprises which are not actually associated with the controlling persons are included in this table, it sometimes happens that substantial investments are reported in countries where control does not exist" (*1941 Census,* 29). U.S. citizens who were residing abroad were included as foreign direct investors if they controlled more than 25 percent of the voting stock of a U.S. enterprise; this may have materially affected the investments from Latin America, the Philippines, China, South Africa, and perhaps elsewhere as well. "Enterprises" include branches, sole proprietorships, corporations, and other organizations.

a. Information not available.

b. Of the 171 "German enterprises" included here with a value of $105 million, 43 with a value of $88 million were reported as held by Swiss, Dutch, or other nonenemy investors, sometimes involving more than one country. (The German figures were compared with the subsequent vesting orders of the Alien Property Custodian.) *1941 Census,* 30.

c. The total number of enterprises includes 39 nonprofit organizations.

The Stock Market

On Friday, September 1, 1939, the German army attacked Poland. The London stock market did not open that day, and officials announced it would remain closed for an indefinite time.[7] Before the New York Stock Exchange started trading that Friday (at the normal hour of 10:00 A.M.), members of the administration in Washington were in telephone contact with exchange officials, who were well aware of events across the Atlantic.[8]

Less than five months earlier, Secretary of the Treasury Henry Morgenthau had discussed with men at the State Department, the Securities and Exchange Commission, and the Federal Reserve, as well as the chairman of the board of governors of the New York Stock Exchange, "what we would do in the case of world war, as far as stocks were concerned."[9] The group had recalled the closing of the New York Stock Exchange in 1914. Jerome Frank and William O. Douglas of the SEC had at the April

Table 8.3. Summary of long-term foreign investments in the United States, June 14, 1941 (in millions of U.S. dollars)

Country	Total[a]	Type of security								Miscellaneous		
		U.S. govt.	State & local govt.	Corp. bonds	Com. stock	Pref'd stock	Other securities	Total[b]	Controlled enterprises[c]	Real estate	Real estate mortgages	Trusts & estates[d]
United Kingdom	1,745.5	18.9	38.4	41.5	403.0	84.5	1.2	587.5	711.5	32.4	9.8	404.3
of which citizens[e]	1,471.9	11.5	7.6	30.4	320.3	70.1	1.0	441.0	677.6	21.9	8.3	323.1
Canada	1,100.3	32.0	4.7	41.8	379.0	66.4	6.9	530.9	518.5	10.3	6.3	34.4
of which citizens	979.3	23.8	4.3	33.8	321.9	54.1	6.8	444.6	505.5	6.8	5.4	17.0
Netherlands	667.5	3.0	.4	15.1	268.7	31.2	1.3	319.8	336.0	1.1	.1	10.5
of which citizens	618.0	2.6	.4	14.0	256.2	30.3	1.3	304.8	303.4	.8	.1	8.9
Switzerland	627.0	64.4	7.4	42.5	259.3	42.9	.7	417.2	137.8	7.5	2.5	62.0
of which citizens	451.2	23.8	2.6	34.5	219.0	36.3	.6	342.7	88.3	1.9	1.1	17.2
France	418.3	15.6	19.0	18.3	115.1	18.0	.2	186.4	99.6	6.3	3.2	122.3
of which citizens	233.9	5.8	1.8	6.5	65.1	8.2	.1	87.4	94.1	3.0	1.0	47.9
Germany	172.4	.8	.6	2.4	6.2	2.2	.1	12.4	105.1	3.0	1.8	50.1
of which citizens	147.4	.5	.5	1.9	4.3	1.4	.1	8.7	96.3	2.1	1.2	39.1
Belgium	124.5	1.5	.1	2.3	26.5	2.9	1.6	34.9	82.9	.3	.2	6.2
of which citizens	98.1	1.1	f	1.9	20.7	2.3	1.6	27.6	67.7	.2	.1	2.5
Italy	95.7	2.0	8.9	2.9	16.3	2.6	.3	33.0	10.0	3.2	1.6	47.9
of which citizens	43.4	.6	.5	.8	3.0	.4	.2	5.5	9.3	.9	.7	27.0

Table 8.3 *(continued)*

Country	Total[a]	Type of security: U.S. govt.	State & local govt.	Corp. bonds	Com. stock	Pref'd stock	Other securities	Total[b]	Controlled enterprises[c]	Miscellaneous: Real estate	Real estate mortgages	Trusts & estates[d]
Cuba	90.1	17.6	2.7	8.3	34.5	3.0	.2	66.2	15.9	.2	.6	7.1
of which citizens	64.5	13.6	2.4	6.1	28.3	1.9	.1	52.4	6.5	.1	.6	4.9
Panama	87.6	1.4	.4	3.3	41.7	6.6	f	53.3	28.6	—	5.6	.1
of which citizens	86.6	1.4	.4	3.3	41.0	6.5	—	52.6	28.4	—	5.6	f
Sweden	78.0	.6	.2	.9	22.7	1.4	10.1	35.9	34.4	.5	.1	7.1
of which citizens	70.9	.2	.2	.8	20.8	.8	10.1	33.0	34.3	.2	.1	3.3
Argentina	74.8	5.4	.6	4.4	35.4	5.4	.2	51.4	19.7	.4	.1	3.2
of which citizens	55.1	4.1	.4	2.8	24.9	4.1	.2	36.1	18.2	f	f	f
China	72.6	11.2	.4	5.9	30.2	5.5	.5	53.7	16.7	.4	.3	1.5
of which citizens	32.5	5.1	.3	2.8	14.8	2.5	.4	26.0	6.1	f	.1	.3
Japan	49.4	7.2	f	.2	4.0	.2	.1	11.7	35.1	1.5	.3	.7
of which citizens	45.7	6.8	—	f	2.1	.1	f	9.0	34.6	1.3	.3	.5
Rest of world[g]	600.1	32.1	8.9	29.6	200.0	33.3	1.1	304.8	160.8	18.6	6.1	109.9
Total (all areas)[h]	6,003.8	213.7	92.7	219.4	1,842.6	306.1	24.5	2,699.1	2,312.6	86.2	38.6	867.3

Source: U.S. Department of the Treasury, *Census of Foreign-Owned Assets in the United States* (Washington, D.C., 1945), 78–88 (country detail), 18 (totals); 16 (the U.K. citizen line includes $700,000,000 collateral). For explanations on "citizenship" see ibid., 78; for definitions on trusts and estates, ibid., 13–14.

Note: For general note and notes a–h, see Appendix 3, Notes to Table 8.3.

1939 meeting forecast that foreign owners of American securities would sell; U.S. holders would follow; and the result could be a panic downturn. The SEC wanted to stop trading should this occur. Morgenthau had agreed it was wise to be prepared and told those gathered that he was in talks with the British and French governments and was encouraging them to take over American securities held by their nationals and to hold them; later, such securities could be disposed of in an orderly manner, thus avoiding panic selling. Short of that, Morgenthau suggested he would—if need be—impose exchange controls, that is, freeze foreign accounts to prevent foreign divestments.[10]

Late in August, in anticipation of war, the British had placed controls on the sale of foreign securities, but on September 1, American policy makers were nonetheless uneasy.[11] They decided, however, to allow the New York Stock Exchange to open as usual, and (to their surprise) their fears of massive foreign selling turned out to be for naught. Trading in New York showed no sign of panic. On Saturday (the market was open), instead of the forecasted foreign and domestic liquidations, war stocks boomed, raising overall market values. In Washington and New York, policy makers were relieved. Unlike in 1914, there had been no European rush to sell. The New York Stock Exchange was closed on Monday for the Labor Day holiday. When it reopened on Tuesday, September 5, Britain and France were at war with Germany. The New York Federal Reserve announced it would lend at par on U.S. government obligations. Again, U.S. policy makers' worries over a major sell-off proved unwarranted. War stocks "raced upward."[12] What were the dissimilarities from 1914, and why?

The motivations for European investments in American securities before World War I had been different from those in the 1930s. In the pre-1914 years, the capital flows to the United States had been in pursuit of new opportunities. The so-called abnormal flows of the thirties had been in large part a search for a secure haven; accordingly, with the war in Europe in 1939, the United States became even more attractive for a foreign investor in American securities. Moreover, because much of the 1930s inward investment in the United States was for safety, it was not especially responsive to changes in interest rates; thus, higher rates, and the prospect of even higher ones in Europe, did not pull moneys back there.

In addition, there were, relative to the size of the U.S. economy, lesser amounts invested from abroad than in 1914. This meant European liquidations—had they occurred—would have had less impact. So, too, the long period of uncertainty before the actual declaration of war moderated the reaction when the war actually came (there had been a widespread expectation of a European war). Thus, unlike in 1914, the war's start was no great shock. Indeed, ever since the Germans had moved into Austria in March 1938, many observers saw war as inevitable.[13] It had, they thought, only been postponed by the Munich agreement of September 1938. After Hitler annexed the remaining Czech lands in March 1939 and the British and French governments announced they would guarantee Polish borders, war had seemed close at hand, even imminent with the Nazi-Soviet Pact (August 23, 1939).

On August 24, as Bank of England historian R. S. Sayers writes, "the final stage of the long run-up to war was reached"; the British abandoned defense of sterling at $4.68 but raised the British Bank Rate from 2 to 4 percent.[14] The financial press in England recollected that the advance in the Bank Rate from 4 to 8 percent on July 31, 1914, and to 10 percent on August 1, 1914, had resulted in £4 million of gold shipped from America to London. A similar movement, "or its equivalent—that is the sale of dollars . . . to the Exchange [Equalisation] Account," the *Financial Times* noted on August 25, "cannot be expected at this time."[15] There was no such reaction principally because of the motivations for British investments in the United States, perhaps because the British hike in interest rates was not great enough to move moneys and, some have suggested, because of the small quantities of securities involved. But Americans had taken no chances; officials at the Federal Reserve were in constant touch with their British counterparts, monitoring the potential effects.

Thus, on August 25, George L. Harrison, president of the Federal Reserve Bank of New York, had established a foreign exchange committee to cope with foreign currency problems in case of war; the committee members included a representative from the New York Stock Exchange along with leading commercial and private bankers, one of whom was an experienced foreign banker located in New York, C. J. Stephenson of the Canadian Bank of Commerce.[16] On August 26, the British Treasury prohibited British owners of American securities from selling or transferring them without permission from the British Treasury.[17]

By September 1, the British government had allowed the sale of about $1 million of British-owned American securities (not enough to generate any alarm); the Bank of England told the Federal Reserve Bank of New York that such transactions in the future were not likely to be on a large scale.[18] By September 5, the pound had been stabilized at $4.03.[19] No wild fluctuations in its value occurred, as in the summer of 1914. The situation was under control.

Perhaps of most importance, the formidable influx of gold into the United States in the late 1930s meant U.S. gold reserves were at an all-time high. American financial experts realized that even if Europeans were to liquidate their U.S. investments and foreign governments were to sell their dollars for gold, Americans had abundant gold. The U.S. financial system was not at risk. Harrison, in a telephone call to a U.S. Treasury official in Washington, had assured the latter that the key New York banks had "enormous excess reserves. They are all liquid. Nothing to put them in embarrassing position."[20] The situation in 1939 was entirely different from that of 1914.[21]

In early September 1939, since there had been no panic moves into foreign exchange, no depreciation of the dollar occurred as in 1914. The New York Stock Exchange continued open. The London Stock Exchange reopened on September 7.[22] The orderliness of financial markets impressed everyone. Americans had been prepared for the worst, which did not occur. Most crucial, throughout, officials from the Treasury Department, the SEC, and the Federal Reserve watched the international economic and political situation, well aware that events in Europe mattered in America.

Imports, Exports, and Shipping

On September 12, 1939, Lammot du Pont, speaking at the spectacular New York World's Fair, boasted of domestic accomplishments, contrasting the chemical industry's present status with that before the First World War. Now, he told his audience, the United States had adequate synthetic nitrogen capacity; practically all its dye needs could be met through production at home; the nation no longer relied on Germany for potash; and his own company had developed a new synthetic rubber, neoprene, that was superior to the natural product. Du Pont, however, neglected to note that an international cartel limited U.S. output and held up the price of synthetic nitrates. Nor did he tell his listeners that a sizable share of the dyes made in America were manufactured by affiliates of German and Swiss multinational enterprises. He may not have known that the principal "domestic" potash producers had German and British parents. And, while he bragged that his company's neoprene was better than natural rubber, the material had not yet been adapted for use in tire making and was, moreover, very costly to produce. Du Pont had no inkling of the bitter barrage of criticisms that his company and other firms on the frontier of U.S. chemistry would soon encounter. But America had, to a great extent, liberated itself from its pre–World War I *import* dependency on chemicals. This was a great success of the interwar years, one achieved through the interaction of U.S. and foreign technology (and through the presence of FDI in the United States).[23]

Even so, in the United States concerns persisted over the adequacy of supplies of crucial raw materials. In June 1939, in anticipation of war, Congress had passed the Strategic Materials Act, under which, in June 1940, two subsidiaries of the Reconstruction Finance Corporation (the Metal Reserve Company and the Rubber Reserve Company) were organized, the first to deal with strategic and critical metals and the second to stockpile rubber. This legislation and its implementation had an impact on both U.S. business abroad and foreign enterprise in this country.[24] The U.S. government sought to encourage domestic output and substitutes for imports, whenever possible. There was attention to tin, based on World War I experiences. The United States neither produced nor smelted tin. The smelters built during the First World War had closed down. American companies had no expertise in this field; and just as before 1914, so now Americans depended on imported smelted tin. In 1940, the occupation of Holland by the Germans notwithstanding, the U.S. government negotiated with the Dutch-owned NV Billiton, which had tin mining operations in the Dutch East Indies and operated a smelter in Holland. That year, the Tin Processing Corporation, a subsidiary of NV Billiton, agreed to design, build, and run a smelter in Texas on behalf of the U.S. government. Construction began in Texas City in March 1941; the first furnace would not go into production until April 1942. The smelter would process Bolivian tin. The German occupation of Holland and the Japanese push into the Dutch East Indies did not disrupt the plans; NV Billiton's subsidiary would manage the Texas City smelter, which would operate all during the war. The U.S. government owned the smelter. There arose no criticisms of this project at its origins or subsequently. Indeed, Americans were able to limit tin use, find substitutes for tin (aluminum and plastics in some cases), and use "recovered" tin, so tin did not present a serious bottleneck.[25] On the other hand, in 1942, after the Japanese had occupied Malaya and the Dutch East Indies and cut off 90 percent of U.S. rubber imports, congressional investigators would condemn the 1940–1941 rubber programs as "woefully inadequate"; Lammot du Pont's pride in his firm's abilities in synthetic rubber would be disparaged as Du Pont's and other U.S. companies' earlier relations with I. G. Farben would be blamed for American shortages.

In September 1939, the war disrupted shipping. The Germans began submarine attacks on vessels approaching Allied ports. In the months that followed, the British imposed new trade restrictions, including a complete blockade on seaborne German exports and controls over German imports. The British made up a blacklist (the so-called Statutory List) of shipping companies, trading houses, and other firms suspected of dealings with the Germans. No British firm was allowed to carry on transactions with companies on the blacklist.[26] As a neutral, the United States sought to shape its own course amid the new impediments to trade. On September 12, 1939, the *New York Times* reported that the Hamburg-American and the North German Lloyd steamship lines were discharging their U.S. employees—effective September 30. The two German lines, which operated under a single management in the United States, had 200 employees in New York City (all except 25 of whom were U.S. citizens). The German steamship companies closed their office at Rockefeller Center and announced they would retain only a skeleton staff at their 57 Broadway office.[27] The British blockade would keep German ships off the high seas. As at the start of the First World War, German ships that were in American ports stayed put. In 1939 Britain was still the global leader in shipping, with command of the seas; but whereas the British merchant fleet had 42.4 percent of the world's registered tonnage in 1913–1914, in 1939 its share was reduced to 31.0. The United States, with a mere 9.8 percent of world merchant shipping in 1913–1914, in 1939 had a 14.4 percent share. With Europe at war, Americans recognized the need to devote resources to strengthening the nation's merchant fleet.[28] The 1939 U.S. Neutrality Act set the rules on what was permissible in U.S. trade and shipping. To circumvent restraints, American owners often transferred their vessels to Panamanian registry—with the approval of the U.S. Maritime Commission.[29]

Finance, Frozen Funds, and Other Worries

From the outbreak of war in Europe, the Treasury Department and the Federal Reserve proctored the financial impacts as they affected the U.S. economy, including those related to inward foreign investment and not only apropos the effects on the stock market. In 1914, when the Federal Reserve System was new, J. P. Morgan & Co. and the British government had cooperated one-on-one in handling foreign exchange, war finance, and, more broadly, matters related to British investments in the United States. That was no longer acceptable. Now such matters were definitely a U.S. *government* prerogative, albeit the Morgans were involved (as I will show later). The House of Morgan knew more about British inward investments—especially portfolio ones—than anyone in the U.S. government.

During the 1930s, Washington's intrusions within the American economy had risen steadily—as had the national debt. The European war would mean much larger U.S. federal government economic participation, along with a greatly expanding debt. The U.S. gross public debt outstanding stood at $25.5 billion on June 30, 1919; by June 30,

1930, it had been reduced to $16.1 billion; in the thirties, with the New Deal programs, it had burgeoned, reaching $43.0 billion by year end 1940.[30] Despite the often-expressed alarm over inward foreign investment, for the interwar years I never uncovered concerns over foreign holdings of U.S. publicly issued debt. All U.S. federal debt was dollar denominated. By the start of the 1940s, however, with the soaring national debt, scattered questions did surface on who held these U.S. securities. Sidney Ratner, commenting on the economic significance of the growth in the U.S. debt, concluded, "The public debt . . . does raise a problem when a transfer of wealth or income from the country [the United States] is made possible by large foreign investments in national debt."[31] There was nothing more in Ratner's 1942 book on externally held debt, only the implicit, unstated hint that American policy makers should be wary.[32] Ratner's casual reference undoubtedly flowed from the general, enhanced attention in 1941 to foreign moneys in America. The Treasury Department census would report that as of June 14, 1941, foreigners owned merely $214 million in U.S. federal government obligations (see Table 8.1).[33]

Other foreign investments in the United States attracted more notice. In the spring of 1940 Hitler began his sweep through Europe, conquering Denmark and Norway in April; Belgium, Holland, and Luxembourg in May; and France in June. Policy makers in Washington became troubled lest Germans obtain access to the U.S. assets of citizens and companies from occupied countries, moneys that had been dispatched across the Atlantic for safekeeping. The Trading with the Enemy Act, passed in 1917, gave the president broad economic powers over international financial transactions; in 1933, during the banking crisis, Congress had expanded presidential powers under this law to cover times of "national emergency" as well as those of war. In 1940–1941, these powers were used to set up Foreign Funds Controls to protect the U.S. assets of nationals of countries that had been invaded by Hitler's armies (preventing the forced repatriation and confiscation of such assets).[34]

The Treasury Department administered the nation's Foreign Funds Control regulations.[35] From April 1940, President Roosevelt issued a series of executive orders that blocked—that is, "froze"—the U.S. assets of nationals of the designated country. Table 8.4 provides the sequence. The first controls were imposed on April 10, after the German moves into Denmark and Norway. These were followed on May 10 by new freeze orders, covering Holland and Belgium. In the week ending Saturday, May 18, 1940, the New York Stock Market dropped 15.45 points, the largest weekly decline in almost a decade.[36] Thomas Lamont—a partner in J. P. Morgan & Co.—spoke to Roosevelt on May 19, telling

Table 8.4. Foreign Funds Control and related measures, Apr. 10, 1940–Dec. 7, 1941

Date	Measure
1940	
April 10	Executive Order 8389: U.S. assets of Danes and Norwegians frozen to safeguard their assets after the German invasion
May 10	* : Freezes U.S. assets of nationals of the Netherlands, Belgium, Luxembourg
June 17	* : Freezes U.S. assets of nationals of France (including Monaco)
July 15	* : Freezes U.S. assets of nationals of Latvia, Estonia, and Lithuania
Oct. 10	* : Freezes U.S. assets of nationals of Romania
1941	
Mar. 4	* : Freezes U.S. assets of nationals of Bulgaria
Mar. 13	* : Freezes U.S. assets of nationals of Hungary
Mar. 24	* : Freezes U.S. assets of nationals of Yugoslavia
Apr. 28	* : Freezes U.S. assets of nationals of Greece
June 14	* By Executive Order 8785 U.S. assets of nationals of the following European countries are frozen: Albania, Andorra, Austria, Czechoslovakia, Danzig, Finland, Germany, Italy, Liechtenstein, Poland, Portugal, San Marino, Spain, Sweden, Switzerland, and USSR
June 14	* : Census of Foreign Assets in the United States on Form TFR-300
July 17	Presidential Proclamation authorizing a list of "certain blocked nationals and controlling certain exports" (the so-called American "blacklist")
July 26	Executive Order 8832: Freezes Japanese assets in the United States "in the same manner" in which European assets were frozen on June 14, 1941. Also extends freezing control to China. The freeze was "effective" as of June 14, 1941.

Sources: U.S. Department of the Treasury, *Census of Foreign-Owned Assets in the United States,* (Washington, D.C., 1945); and U.S. Department of the Treasury, *Documents Pertaining to Foreign Funds Control* (Washington, D.C., 1945).

*Amended Executive Order 8389.

the president there were "no British sales."[37] Apparently, the May 10 freezing controls notwithstanding, there was "some selling for the account of Netherlands and Belgian sources largely because of the inability of brokerage firms to make contact with those sources, so that they decided, as a protective measure, to dispose of their holdings." Yet, as the *New York Times* reported on May 19, 1940, "at no time had foreign selling appeared in large volume."[38]

The blocking of Danish, Norwegian, Dutch, Belgian, and Luxembourg assets was succeeded, on June 17, 1940, by the blocking of French assets, after the Germans invaded France. In July, Latvian, Estonian, and Lithuanian assets were blocked when these countries were absorbed into the Soviet Union. In October, Roumanian assets were blocked (Roumania had allowed German troops "to protect" its oil fields). By November, subsequent to Roosevelt's reelection to a third term in office, concerns emerged among Germans that the "pro-British" Roosevelt would soon be freezing the U.S. assets of German residents. Gordon Rentschler, chairman of National City Bank, telephoned Harrison at the New York Federal Reserve bank on November 27 to inform him that the National City Bank had just received cable instructions from the Reichsbank to close out its account and to transfer the entire balance (about $480,000) to the Swiss Bank Corporation at Zurich. Rentschler added "that their Japanese friends were getting nervous about their funds in New York lest they too might be frozen." Harrison thought that a "recent court decision on attachment of Reichsbank funds, and new attachment of such funds with us [the Federal Reserve Bank of New York] partially a contributing factor also."[39]

German funds were not blocked until June 14, 1941. A press release issued that day noted, "In view of the unlimited national emergency declared by the president, he has today issued an Executive Order freezing immediately all German and Italian assets in the United States. At the same time the Order also freezes the assets of all invaded or occupied European countries not previously frozen. These include Albania, Austria, Czechoslovakia, Danzig, and Poland." Because of the "interrelationship of international financial transactions," the executive order was also extended to the remaining countries in continental Europe. On July 26, 1941 (but effective June 14, 1941) Japanese and Chinese funds would also be blocked.[40] In addition, the June 14, 1941, "freeze" included the assets of neutral countries, such as Switzerland and Sweden. The initial press release stated that it was intended "through the medium of general licenses" that the freezing controls would be lifted, given adequate assurances "from the governments of such countries that the general licenses will not be employed by them or their nationals to evade the purposes of this Order."[41] In June 1941 the Foreign Funds Control program changed from "a defensive weapon primarily intended to protect the property of invaded countries, to a frankly aggressive weapon against the Axis."[42]

Because the foreign assets in the United States had been "blocked," licenses were required to release the assets. Licenses were issued, allowing foreign-owned enterprises to continue to operate. Throughout, problems existed in determining which assets should be frozen.[43] With the broad extension of the span of the blocked asset program in June 1941, it became evident how little was known about the foreign investment in this country. Accordingly, the census of foreign assets in the United States was ordered by Roosevelt, to be conducted by the Treasury Department. By the date of the census (June 14, 1941), U.S. assets of residents in continental Europe were blocked. On June 22, the Germans invaded the Soviet Union, and a modification of the freeze was made.[44]

On July 23, Americans got news that Japanese troops were penetrating southern Indo-China, moving into a position to cross into Thailand and Burma—and possibly to continue into Malaya and the Dutch East Indies. This precipitated the freezing of Japanese and Chinese assets in the United States on July 26, but effective June 14. China was included in the freeze order at the specific request of Chiang Kai-shek—with the goal of shielding Chinese assets in the United States against their use by the Japanese invaders.[45]

From the time of the first freezing order until June 14, 1941, some $4.5 billion of foreign assets had been put under the authority of the Treasury Department.[46] In December 1941, a Treasury Department report stated that the "Control" covered more than $7 billion in foreign assets; later this total would be estimated at "almost $8 billion."[47] Two items must be noted here. First, on July 17, 1941, in connection with the Foreign Funds Control program, the president issued a proclamation "authorizing a proclaimed list of certain blocked nationals and controlling certain exports." This so-called American blacklist (or Proclaimed List) included "certain persons deemed to be acting for the benefit of Germany or Italy or nationals of those countries, and persons to whom the exportation, directly or indirectly, of various articles or materials is deemed to be detrimental to the interests of national defense." More than 1,800 persons and business institutions in "other American republics" were on the Proclaimed List issued that same day. This inaugurated a new scrutiny of business dealings. Second, it should be repeated that when the assets of an ongoing business were "frozen," usually a Treasury Department license would be issued, allowing the firm to continue in business. Thus, in the main, even when assets were "blocked," foreign-owned businesses could carry on their "normal" operations. By December 1941, according to a contemporary Treasury Department report, roughly 2,500 business enterprises in the United States were operating under licenses issued by the Control.[48]

Separate rules emerged on shipping. When war broke out in Europe, the United States had turned its attention to building up new national shipping capacity, and to where foreign firms fit in the planned scenario. A small number of German and Italian ships in U.S. ports remained there, essentially trapped. When the Germans moved into Denmark, Danish ships at sea headed toward neutral locations. Those in the United States stayed there, protected by the freeze order. As for Norwegian ships (which were among the most modern), when the Germans attacked, those at sea sailed for Allied and neutral ports. The Norwegian government in exile in London arranged for the British to use Norwegian ships in Allied ports. In time, Norwegian ships in the United States went into service for the Allied cause.[49] Early in 1941, Italian crews began to sabotage Italian ships in U.S. ports (the crews feared that the ships would be appropriated and put to Allied use). When it seemed possible that the Germans and Danes might behave in a similar manner in relation to their nations' vessels, on March 30, 1941, the Coast Guard "took under protective custody the ships of the German, Italian, and Danish merchant fleets" docked in U.S. ports.[50] In May, the U.S. Maritime Commission formed a "shipping pool" to be operated under its supervision (500,000 of the 2 million deadweight tons would come from "Axis ships interned in U.S. ports and under government custody").[51] Congress passed, on June 6, the U.S. Ship Requisition Act, and under Executive Order 8771, the U.S. Maritime Commission was authorized to take over certain foreign merchant vessels. This included forty-one Danish ships. Most of these ships were reregistered under a Panama flag and a few as U.S. ships, given new names, and started sailing thereafter, carrying goods for the Allied cause.[52] In July, the U.S. Navy began to provide convoy services for U.S. merchant vessels going to Iceland, and in August for those bound for Britain; on September 11, the escorts were permitted "to shoot first" *if* American ships were threatened.[53] The United States was clearly no longer "neutral." When Japanese assets in the United States were frozen, Edward Foley, undersecretary of the treasury, explained that the order technically froze the title of Japanese ships in U.S. harbors; the ships could not leave without permission, but this did not mean that they would be "seized." On August 5, the Japanese government announced the withdrawal of its merchant marine from U.S. trade.[54]

At the same time as the Foreign Funds Control regulations were being implemented and the United States strengthened its own shipping capabilities, new concerns arose in the United States over German business influence in Latin America—and the relationships between German-controlled firms in the United States and those to the south. The U.S. blacklist of July 17, 1941, comprised companies and individuals, mainly in Latin America.[55] The measure affected some German and other European affiliates in the United States engaged in exports and operating under Treasury Department licenses. It enlarged the authority of Foreign Funds Control administrators.[56] The British blacklist (or Statutory List) had been introduced in September 1939; the American one (the Proclaimed List) of 1941 mirrored the erosion of U.S. neutrality.

Other steps were undertaken that affected foreign business in America. Late in May 1941 the president had set up the Office of Petroleum Coordinator for National Defense, with Harold Ickes in charge.[57] On July 30, Roosevelt appointed Vice President Henry Wallace to head the new Economic Defense Board (EDB) with authority—shared with the Treasury Department—over international economic matters, foreign exchange, and international trade. The board included representatives from the State, War, and Navy Departments.[58] America prepared for war.

Foreign Business under Fire

Meanwhile, spurred on by Assistant Attorney General Thurman Arnold, the Temporary National Economic Committee and the Justice Department intensified their investigations of international cartels. In early April 1941, they were joined by the Truman Committee, a Senate committee on national defense.[59] The Treasury Department, as administrator of the Foreign Funds Control regulations, cooperated with the Justice Department in its inquiries.[60] Henry Wallace's Economic Defense Board took part. When the operations of the First World War's Alien Property Custodian (APC) had concluded in 1934, the Justice Department had inherited the APC files and remaining residual responsibilities; the Justice Department's Alien Property Bureau was now reactivated.[61] The State Department was deeply involved.[62] So, too, the Federal Bureau of Investigation began to delve into the behavior of German businessmen, pursuing not only possible German espionage in the United States but also German business influence in Latin America (in the course of these inquiries, it obtained information on German affiliates in the United States).[63] The Securities and Exchange Commission pressed forward with its examination of investment holding companies, including those set up by foreign investors in the United States.[64] Behind the scenes, British intelligence was intercepting correspondence and ferreting out German business in America.[65]

During 1940–1941, a torrent of revelations unfolded on what Thurman Arnold would call "the great national and international patent cartels."[66]

For years Francis P. Garvan had warned of the economic and political dangers of German business penetration within the American economy (he died in 1937). Now Arnold took up the mantle, passionately denouncing "foreign control of United States production." Like Garvan before him, Arnold was deeply disturbed by the role of patents in "turning over control" of U.S. industry to "foreign potentially enemy firms."[67] In the same spirit, Wyoming senator Joseph C. O'Mahoney—chairman of the Temporary National Economic Committee—denounced the international chemical, iron and steel, metal, electrical, and shipping cartels for "their part in the growth of Hitler's power."[68] He, too, would seek to ferret out their U.S. interests. Hostility to foreign enterprise was further fueled by American isolationists, who warned that foreign-controlled businesses would not hesitate to betray U.S. interests.[69] The isolationists continued to perceive the involvements of all foreign investors (including the British) as contaminating.

The topic of international cartels, more often than not, focused on the role of German firms, even though other "foreigners" were also caught up in the denunciations. Cartel arrangements were seen as restraint of trade, and since Britain and Germany were at war, not only were the prewar contracts challenged on those grounds, but looming in the background was the subject of the morality and legality of the dubious dealings between enemies that in some (often not very well defined) manner encompassed U.S. business. U.S. court cases (with some resolutions) snowballed. In the investigations of the nitrogen cartel, Imperial Chemical Industries (ICI) in New York and London provided information to the Justice Department. ICI believed it was not engaged in wrongdoing.[70] Yet early in September 1939 a federal grand jury had returned an indictment against Allied Chemical & Dye Corporation, naming as coconspirators I. G. Farben and forty-one other foreign firms (including ICI and the International Nitrogen Cartel). This particular case on the nitrogen cartel, *U.S. v. Allied Chemical & Dye Corp., et al.*, was settled with a consent decree on May 29, 1941. But neither I. G. Farben nor ICI was a party to that decree. A separate case, involving Synthetic Nitrogen Products Corp. (a U.S. affiliate of I. G. Farben), would end in September 1941 with a consent decree; the defendant was ordered to report to the attorney general on international agreements in nitrates and nitrogen products. A nitrate case against ICI would be resolved in 1942.[71]

Meanwhile, in May 1940 the earlier-initiated potash cartel case concluded. On May 15, 1940, the Justice Department would substitute a civil complaint for the criminal one and drop the charges against NV Potash Export Mij. (the latter stopped operations once Germany and France went to war). On May 21, 1940, the three potash producers in the United States (the two largest of them affiliates of foreign firms) would sign a consent decree forbidding price setting.[72] A suit, filed by the United States against Bausch and Lomb Optical Co., ended on July 8, 1940, with a consent decree that found specified agreements between Bausch and Lomb and Carl Zeiss, of Germany, to be unlawful and enjoined the U.S. company from complying with them.[73] After the British affiliate Firth Sterling Steel Co. complained of unfair pricing practices by Carboloy (a General Electric subsidiary), General Electric, Carboloy, *and Krupp* were indicted on August 30, 1940.[74] (The British Firth Sterling was the "good guy" in this episode, a rare instance of a foreign investor on the "side of virtue.") On January 27, 1941, a complaint was issued against General Electric in the incandescent lamp case; NV Philips' Gloeilampenfabrieken was also a defendant.[75] The antitrust bombardments accelerated as 1941 went forward—covering foreign parents and affiliates alike.

On January 30, 1941, I. G. Farben was indicted along with Aluminum Company of America, Dow Chemical Co., and American Magnesium Corp.; the group was charged with monopolizing the magnesium sector to the detriment of U.S. industry.[76] In April 1941, the *New York Times* reported there were federal subpoenas for the books of General Aniline & Film Corp. (the successor to American I. G. Chemical Corp.), Sterling Products, Winthrop Chemical, Schering Corp., and the Swiss Bank Corp.; these "foreign-controlled" firms were requested to explain their relationships with 100 companies in the United States and abroad. The listed corporations, as the *New York Times* put it, "read like a 'Who's Who' in the drug and chemical industry."[77]

In September 1941, the United States settled its restraint-of-trade suit against the Alba Pharmaceutical Co., Bayer Co., Sterling Products, and Winthrop Chemical, which firms were said to have had illegal relationships with I. G. Farben: a consent decree enjoined each of these defendants from combining with I. G. Farben to restrain trade.[78] A companion consent decree specifically covered the American Bayer Co.'s links with I. G. Farben.[79] Then, a month before Pearl Harbor, in November 1941, the Department of Justice filed charges against Standard Oil Company (New Jersey) (SONJ), based on the latter's alliances with I. G. Farben.[80] This wave of 1941 cases—some criminal and some civil—placed German business in particular under fire. U.S. press coverage was extensive, and uniformly the reports condemned the heinous behavior of the German and German-controlled participants in the international cartels; the Americans who took part were also tarred.[81]

A few antitrust targets were foreign-owned corporations, but outside of the context of the war in Europe. Thus, antitrust litigation against American Tobacco and the other leading domestic cigarette producers cast its net to include British American Tobacco (BAT) along with two of its U.S. subsidiaries—Brown & Williamson and Export Leaf Tobacco Company. Imperial Tobacco was also a defendant (it was a purchaser of tobacco, not a cigarette producer in the United States). Although BAT, its two subsidiaries, and Imperial Tobacco were defendants, this was essentially a domestic antitrust case, and in contrast with most of the international cartel investigations, the indictment did not, in the words of historian Nannie M. Tilley, "attract the attention of a citizenry preoccupied with the country's probable entry into another world war."[82] The suit was, however, significant; it began on July 24, 1940, when the United States charged the tobacco companies with restraint-of-trade violations. A jury trial in Kentucky from June to October 1941 found the defendants guilty. While the three U.S. cigarette companies—American Tobacco, Reynolds, and Liggett & Myers—"fought the case," the foreign parents and their American subsidiaries acquiesced in the verdict and did not take part in the appeal.[83]

As part of the bevy of activity, on September 30, 1940, the attorney general had filed an antitrust suit against the American Petroleum Institute, dozens of small oil companies, and twenty-two major ones, including Shell Union Oil Corporation. This comprehensive case (with sixty-nine charges)—the so-called Mother Hubbard suit—covered conspiracy to maintain crude oil prices, monopoly over crude oil available for refining, and excessively high prices, which allegedly emerged from the domination by large companies over wholesale and retail outlets.[84] Once Ickes, as Petroleum Coordinator for National Defense, began in the second half of 1941 to work with the oil industry, the Justice Department promised "to go slow" in pursuing these defendants.[85]

Aside from the storm of antitrust litigation, in April and May 1941, Japanese (and other) insurance companies in the United States became subject to attention; were these insurers conduits for information reaching Germany that could be used to sink American and British vessels? In a June 6, 1941, report Admiral Emory S. Land, chairman of the U.S. Maritime Commission, exonerated the Japanese: their U.S. representatives were Americans; "no 'leaks' on U.S. and British shipping were reaching German submarines or surface raiders through Japanese marine insurance here."[86] It may have been otherwise with German and Swiss insurers; subsequently, Treasury Department officials would conclude that in 1940 and 1941, ships leaving U.S. ports were frequently sunk by German submarines because their sailing dates and destinations were familiar to German and Swiss insurance and reinsurance companies.[87] There were other anxieties over information held by foreign-owned insurance companies. Attorney General Robert Jackson reported in January 1941 that to obtain domestic insurance some U.S.

companies were delivering complete drawings of their plants to foreign providers of insurance, thus sharing American "secrets."[88] The allegations, suits, and investigations of 1940–1941 put foreign (and especially German) business at the center of public discourse—and very much on the defensive.

The German Firms

What, in fact, was occurring with German affiliates in the United States? In September 1939, at the outbreak of war in Europe, I. G. Farben took added precautions to cloak its U.S. interests, for which it required a green light from the German government. On September 9, a little more than a week after German troops invaded Poland, Gustav Schlotterer of the German Economics Ministry sent a top secret dispatch to the chief of finance in the foreign currency section on "safeguarding foreign assets," a message that endorsed the camouflaging of remaining German firms abroad.[89] In the last week of September, Friedrich Ringer (an assistant to August von Knieriem, I. G. Farben's general counsel) and Frank A. Howard (of the SONJ) met in Holland to initial the so-called Hague Memorandum on the transfer to the American oil company of I. G. Farben's 20 percent interest in the Standard-I. G. Corporation (soon to be renamed the Standard Catalytic Co.), its 50 percent interest in the Joint American Study Co. (Jasco), and its rights to some 2,000 patents. The quid pro quo for I. G. Farben's divestment was an assignment to I. G. Farben of all Jasco's patent rights outside of the United States and the British and French empires. According to the historians of SONJ, its executives believed their company had obtained full ownership of Jasco and Standard-I. G. and of the patents for the United States and the British and French empires. Arrangements for a periodic review of royalty receipts so as to make adjustments in accord with the original Jasco formula would later bring the delivery of I. G. Farben's shares and its patents rights into question. More important, a supplementary agreement (discovered in I. G. Farben files after the war) authorized the German giant to cancel all these arrangements and get its U.S. assets back, when it was safe to do so.[90] This obviously suggested a sham transaction.

In its filing with the Securities and Exchange Commission for the period ending December 31, 1939, American I. G. Chemical Corp. (in October 1939 for public relations purposes restyled as General Aniline & Film Corp.) indicated that Internationale Gesellschaft für Chemische Unternehmungen AG (I. G. Chemie), Basle, Switzerland, was its parent, "by virtue of its being the beneficial owner of a majority of the stock of this corporation."[91] Its previous response (before the outbreak of war) had been that it did not know whether it had a parent.

In July 1939, the management of I. G. Farben in Germany had decided that "real protection" of its foreign companies "against the danger of sequestration in wartime can only be obtained by our renouncing all legal ties of a direct or indirect nature between the stockholders and ourselves." The German enterprise would rely on its friends—on "personal connections of many years standing"—in the United States and Switzerland. I. G. Farben was confident these loyal men would "never dispose of these [I. G. Farben's] assets otherwise than in a manner entirely in accordance with our interests."[92] In August 1939, I. G. Farben had assured the German Ministry of Economics that "we shall have unrestricted influence upon the foreign companies, even after the carrying out of the measures arrived at."[93] Schlotterer's top secret dispatch was the ministry's response to I. G. Farben's proposal. In June 1940, "having persuaded the German Economics Ministry that I. G.'s real possession of the Swiss firm—I. G. Chemie—remained unimpaired," I. G. Farben completed its divestiture of its interests in I. G. Chemie.[94] On June 29, 1940, Hermann Schmitz, by then chief executive officer of I. G. Farben, resigned as chairman of the board and as a board member of the Swiss I. G. Chemie.[95] In 1939, he had resigned from the board of I. G. Chemie's "American subsidiary," General Aniline & Film.[96]

The German consul in Basle reported to the German Foreign Office on September 7, 1940, his views on what had happened: I. G. Chemie, Basle, had discontinued its agreement on the guarantee of dividends with I. G. Farben. For 25 million Swiss francs "nominal value," I. G. Chemie had bought back from I. G. Farben its own shares, so that "seemingly every link between the two corporations had been severed by this operation." The "divorce" was, the German consul noted, in anticipation of the possible U.S. entry in the war. I. G. Farben desired to avoid any repetition of its predecessor companies' losses in World War I. "I. G. Farben," wrote the German consul, "hopes to maintain in the future close personal, financial and operational contacts with its former [U.S.] affiliate."[97] As noted, I. G. Chemie was "the parent" of General Aniline & Film.

Meanwhile, Standard Oil Company (New Jersey) had a problem related to its own sizable direct investments in Germany and its desire to protect its assets there. Its management approached General Aniline & Film (GAF), proposing an exchange. I. G. Farben would buy SONJ's German business and pay for it with GAF. A meeting was held in Basle in March 1940 to discuss the matter. But I. G. Farben officials piously denied that they had any interest in GAF. GAF executives then suggested that SONJ acquire GAF from I. G. Chemie (the Swiss owner of record); this did not solve SONJ's German asset problem, so the American oil company was uninterested.[98]

In May 1940, I. G. Farben sold the rest of its U.S. patents to GAF (those not covered by the Hague Memorandum) and arranged for GAF to absorb the Ozalid Corporation, which since 1935 had been producing in the United States machines to make sensitized paper (and the paper itself) on the basis of licenses from I. G. Farben's Kalle & Co.[99] The Ozalid Corporation leased and serviced blueprinting and other copying machines.[100] In June 1940, Libbey-Owens-Ford acquired the majority interest in Plaskon Co., Inc., a subsidiary of GAF.[101]

From its predecessor's 1929 origins, Carl Bosch of I. G. Farben had been a director of GAF; he died in April 1940. Bosch had for years been a close friend of Walter Teagle of SONJ. He had also brought Edsel Ford to the American I. G. board. His death marked the passing of the personal ties between I. G. Farben and the German affiliate's most prestigious American supporters.

By the autumn of 1940, the management at GAF was in chaos, with the secretary of the company, William H. Vom Rath, telling an FBI informant of the "silly mess." Vom Rath denounced the "treachery and double dealings" of Dietrich A. Schmitz, president of GAF, who, unknown to the company's board members, had earlier acquired an option to buy GAF shares from the Swiss I. G. Chemie. The FBI informant noted that Vom Rath hoped to "help cook the goose of D. A. Schmitz."[102]

In its 1941 SEC filing for the year ending December 31, 1940, GAF once again stated that the Swiss I. G. Chemie was its parent. The SEC expressed displeasure, seeing the response as evasive. In March 1941, the German consul in Basle reported to the German Foreign Office that "U.S. authorities" doubted the Swiss character of I. G. Chemie, but the Swiss embassy in Washington had intervened successfully on behalf of I. G. Chemie.[103]

During 1941 GAF took more protective measures to distance itself from its German associations. In February (after the initiation of one antitrust suit against I. G. Farben and intensely hostile press coverage), GAF sold to Aluminum Company of America (Alcoa) its 50 percent interest in American Magnesium Corporation. Alcoa pledged to increase U.S. output of magnesium, vital to the U.S. aircraft industry.[104]

In June, the Securities and Exchange Commission reported to Congress on how "foreign interests"—namely, Germans—had control over GAF and its predecessor, American I. G. Chemical Corporation. The SEC argued the alleged Swiss ownership of GAF was a ruse.[105] And, once more, the SEC wrote to GAF management, complaining that in its filings it had not stated whether the "Swiss" I. G. Chemie had a parent. The SEC asked the "registrant" (GAF) to inquire of its directors and officers whether any "person or persons," directly or through intermediaries, had power "to direct or cause the direction of management" from April 1, 1934, to May 1940 (the period when American I. G. Chemical Corporation had claimed to have no parent—or that it did not know whether it had a parent). And did the directors know the *parent to I. G. Chemie* on December 31, 1939, and December 31, 1940 (when GAF had reported I. G. Chemie was the parent to GAF)?[106] On September 3, 1941, the secretary of GAF (William H. Vom Rath) forwarded the SEC's queries to all the present and past directors. Apparently, no director—past or present—indicated that he knew I. G. Farben was ever the "parent."[107]

In June 1941, after the U.S. assets of German and Swiss companies were frozen (see Table 8.4), GAF operated under a Treasury Department license, while the latter pursued a full-fledged investigation.[108] By this time, GAF's directors had become desperate to identify an American buyer for I. G. Chemie's holdings.[109] Edsel Ford—a director of GAF—had been approached in May 1941 to purchase the stock owned by I. G. Chemie. Ford rejected the proposition and resigned from the GAF board.[110] Months earlier, in 1940, Teagle had stepped down.[111] Sosthenes Behn of International Telephone and Telegraph Corporation showed some interest in making the acquisition, hoping to exchange his enterprise's blocked assets in Germany for the chemical company's properties in the United States, but the Germans, insisting GAF was not in any manner owned by I. G. Farben, would not (could not) accept this proposition.[112]

The U.S. public had some inkling of what was occurring. On July 28, 1941, *Time* magazine ran a story that the Swiss owners were trying to sell the $62 million General Aniline & Film. According to *Time,* GAF was the second-largest U.S. manufacturer of photographic equipment (after Eastman Kodak) and tied for third place with American Cyanamid (after Allied Chemical and Du Pont) in making dyestuffs.[113] Its earnings in 1940 had been $4 million, much of which came from defense business; it was America's largest producer of khaki.[114] Table 8.5—based on later information—gives 1940 figures on the U.S. production and sales of dyestuffs; by all four measures, GAF ranked well above American Cyanamid, and by two measures of value, above the National Aniline and Chemical Company division of Allied Chemical. Du Pont ranked first by three of the four measures, but GAF exceeded Du Pont in the value of domestic sales, including imports (some imports were apparently getting through in 1940, despite the British blockade).[115] *Time* pointed out that while I. G. Chemie was the owner of record of GAF, GAF's president, Dietrich A. Schmitz, was

Table 8.5. U.S. production and sales of dyestuffs, 1940 (percentage share by major companies)

	Sales of domestic production including exports, excluding imports		Domestic sales excluding exports, including imports	
Firm	By quantity	By value	By quantity	By value
Du Pont	27.6	31.9	27.2	27.1
Allied Chemical & Dye (National Aniline & Chemical)	27.6	20.5	21.9	14.7
General Aniline & Film	13.1	20.7	16.5	27.9
American Cyanamid (Calco Chemical)	10.7	9.0	9.7	7.7
Cincinnati Chemical Works (owned by Ciba, Sandoz, Geigy)	8.8	7.8	11.3	14.5
All others	12.2	10.1	13.4	8.1
Total	100.0	100.0	100.0	100.0

Source: Based on data collected by the U.S. Tariff Commission and presented in U.S. Senate, Committee on Patents, *Patents Hearings,* 77th Cong., 2nd sess. (1942), Exhibits, pt. 5, p. 2481. National Aniline & Chemical and Calco Chemical were the dyestuff subsidiary and division of the listed American companies; Cincinnati Chemical Works was owned by the three Swiss companies Ciba, Sandoz, and Geigy.

the brother of the chairman of the board of I. G. Farben (Hermann Schmitz) and the father of its secretary, William H. Vom Rath, had been a high official in the German I. G. Farben.[116] *Time* did not note that Walter Duisberg, also active in GAF, was the son of Carl Duisberg—one of the principal founders of I. G. Farben.[117] Dietrich Schmitz, William H. Vom Rath, and Walter Duisberg were naturalized American citizens.

I. G. Chemie proposed the sale of GAF to General Dyestuff Corporation (i.e., to the friendly American-born Ernest Halbach). In the United States, GAF directors were sharply divided, most recognizing that the Treasury Department would never permit such a sale, for Halbach had over many years been identified with the German interests; since Swiss and German assets were "blocked" and GAF was operating under a Treasury Department license, the Treasury Department would have to approve such a transaction. In September 1941, to become more American, the majority of the GAF board of directors voted to oust Dietrich Schmitz. In frustration, and opposition, Felix Iselin, chairman of I. G. Chemie, cabled from Basle, demanding the resignation of the "rebellious" majority of the GAF board. Iselin prepared to travel to the United States to assert his authority, but he was refused a British transit visa. On October 2, as anticipated by the majority of the GAF directors, the Treasury

Department formally vetoed the proposed GAF sale to General Dyestuff. The GAF directors, having ignored Iselin's call for their resignations, on October 31 elected a longtime friend of Roosevelt, John E. Mack, to replace Dietrich Schmitz as GAF president. Subsequently, on December 5, they elected to the board William C. Bullitt—onetime U.S. ambassador to the Soviet Union (1933–1936) and, more recently, to France (1936–1940). Bullitt was also a confidant of Roosevelt's. After Pearl Harbor, Bullitt would become chairman of the GAF board. As the German consul in Basle reported to the German Foreign Office, the reorganization occurred in defiance of the expressed wishes of I. G. Chemie. The consul added that the installation of "the notorious war mongerer Ambassador Bullitt" was "at the request of the U.S. government."[118] Actually, Mack had recruited Bullitt; clearly, the majority of the GAF directors wanted the company as "American" as possible; the Treasury and Justice Departments would have concurred.[119] In 1941, GAF, along with other chemical companies, had been investigated by Assistant Attorney General Thurman Arnold—at the same time as the Treasury Department and the SEC were scrutinizing GAF's behavior. Three criminal indictments would be issued against the company on December 19, 1941—not long after America entered the war.[120] GAF, with more than 6,000 employees, was a sizable enterprise.[121]

As for the rest of I. G. Farben interests in the United States, the stock of General Dyestuff Corporation (GDC) was entirely in the hands of Americans. Until 1939, Dietrich Schmitz (a naturalized American) had held controlling interest; then the control was transferred to the loyal American-born Halbach. In 1940, Schmitz and Halbach had—according to Vom Rath—used GDC to evade the British blockade and blacklist.[122] In May 1941, GDC had 670 employees; all except 15 were U.S. citizens; of those, 12 had applied for citizenship, leaving only 3 noncitizens (two Germans and a Canadian). GDC was managed by Halbach, who had been associated with the company from its origin.[123]

I. G. Farben's affiliate Winthrop Chemical Co. (owned through GAF) took steps to develop independence; it engaged in import substitution, making in America pharmaceuticals that it had once imported from Germany.[124] It enlarged its U.S. research capacity. It had ten employees with Ph.D.s in 1939; by the end of 1941, the number was fifteen (up from five in 1936).[125] American-born William Erhard Weiss of Sterling Products, I. G. Farben's U.S. partner in Winthrop Chemical, in November 1940 promised I. G. Farben he would continue to act as best he could in its interests and aid the German company in Latin America in circumventing the British blacklist. When Weiss' commitments became publicly known and after the issuance of the U.S. blacklist (July 17, 1941), on August 29, 1941, Sterling Products—under pressure from the

Justice, State, and Treasury Departments—ousted Weiss from the management of the company he had founded. A new leadership team, headed by Edward S. Rogers and James Hill, took over at Sterling Products (and Winthrop Chemical); their strategy was to make Sterling Products a strong competitor of I. G. Farben in Latin America. On September 5, 1941, in *U.S. v. Alba Pharmaceutical Co.,* Sterling Products signed the consent decree, severing all ties with I. G. Farben.[126]

When I. G. Farben ignored Justice Department demands that it respond to charges in the Magnesium Case, in May 1941 Attorney General Robert H. Jackson sequestered I. G. Farben's "credits with the General Dyestuff Corporation, and with National City Bank"—but only temporarily (the sequester was soon canceled). Then, with the blocking of German assets in the United States, a mere $25,000 account with the National City Bank was frozen. By July 1941, the English banker Kleinwort Sons & Co. (as compensation for earlier loans to I. G. Farben) "seized" I. G. Farben's claims against SONJ; I. G. Farben made efforts to invalidate this action.[127]

As late as July 21, 1941, I. G. Farben was applying to the German Ministry of Economics for foreign exchange to pay a monthly retainer of $20,000 to Chemnyco Inc., New York, which it described as a firm with which "we have no financial connection." The fee was to enable Chemnyco's staff to supply I. G. Farben with "information pertaining to our spheres of interest" and to "support us in negotiations for contracts concerning the utilization of our American patents, and notify us of unfair competition and patent infringements."[128]

In its September 1939 arrangements with SONJ, I. G. Farben had assigned its buna rubber patents to the U.S. oil company, which in 1940 was prepared to license the four major U.S. tire companies. Firestone and U.S. Rubber accepted the license terms, but Goodyear and Goodrich did not—and in October 1941, the oil company sued Goodrich for patent infringement, requesting I. G. Farben's aid in the suit.[129] Earlier, in April 1941, Du Pont suggested to I. G. Farben (and the German giant agreed in June) that they discontinue the exchange of technical information "until the present emergency has past [*sic*]."[130]

In addition to these U.S. activities, during 1940–1941 I. G. Farben kept in contact with the Basle dye makers (Ciba, Sandoz, and Geigy) that had operations in America. I. G. Farben thought it prudent to keep its links with these firms "informal," insisting that the Swiss companies follow a "general business routine" (I. G. Farben was, however, party to decisions on the size of Swiss dyestuff exports to the United States).[131] The Swiss companies were in an awkward position of being put on the British blacklist (and subsequently the American one) if they did business with the Germans. Links had to be informal.

In sum, although "technically" by 1941 I. G. Farben had zero direct investments in America, in point of fact its U.S. interests were many; and as a multinational enterprise it continued to be an important influence in America's chemical industry. The absence of *formal* direct investments was its means of protecting its U.S. business. Strategic informal alliances and social networks substituted for explicit equity control. By the summer and fall of 1941, there were concerted efforts on the U.S. side of the Atlantic to sever even the informal relationships.

The German rayon producers in the United States were nominally controlled by the Dutch Algemeene Kunstzijde Unie NV (AKU). The Germans apparently felt this cloak was sufficient, and when "Dutch" assets in the United States were frozen (May 10, 1940), these affiliates continued to operate under Treasury Department license.[132] Other German companies in America, however, scampered to shelter their U.S. assets. The Schering Corporation of Bloomfield, New Jersey—nominally owned by the Swiss Chemical and Pharmaceutical Enterprises Ltd. (Chepha)—took over intracompany exports to the Latin American subsidiaries of the German Schering enterprise, Schering, AG. The U.S. Schering acted, as had Sterling Products, to circumvent the British blacklist. It sold in Latin America through Atlantis SA, a shell corporation incorporated in Panama, and then remitted profits to a German Schering-controlled Swiss firm.[133] On May 28, 1940, the Swiss Ciba exercised an option and bought from the Stockholms Enskilda Bank (through a Panamanian company) the Swedish bank's 49 percent interest in Chepha. Ciba saw this as an opportunity to get "hold of a key position in the U.S. hormone business."[134] But some Ciba officials fretted that the German connections might hurt the good standing of Ciba. "'This damned Chepha affair,' Schering," wrote the president of Ciba-Basle, James Brodbeck, to his son in America on December 5, 1941. The Swiss Bank Corporation held the other 51 percent of Chepha.[135]

A key German business in America was that of Robert Bosch. Its camouflage had been principally through the Mendelssohn bank, Amsterdam, which had gone bankrupt in August 1939. On behalf of the German Bosch the Stockholms Enskilda Bank acquired the shares of American Bosch (May 7, 1940), shares with a market value of about $10 million. When the Germans invaded Holland on May 10, Dutch assets in the United States were frozen. On May 20, American Bosch announced that 535,000 shares of its stock, formerly owned by Mendelssohn & Co., had been acquired by interests identified with the Stockholms Enskilda Bank and that no change in management was planned. In November the Enskilda bank appointed the American George Murnane "voting trustee" for its shares. Murnane had been chairman of the board of American Bosch since 1935; William L. Batt (president of the Swedish-owned American SKF), who had become a director of American Bosch in 1938, now became president of American Bosch.[136] In June 1941, Swedish assets in the United States were blocked, and American Bosch obtained a license to continue to operate.

Krupp-Nirosta Corporation, nominally owned by a Swiss company, shortened its name in January 1940 to the Nirosta Corporation. Its U.S. management recommended a transfer from Swiss to American ownership, but Krupp rejected the idea in July 1940, convinced that Germany would win the war and the Swiss ownership cover would be adequate to shield its assets.[137] Another German firm, Henkel, transferred its U.S. patent-holding company, American Hyalsol Corporation, from German to Swiss company ownership.[138] In September 1939, Metallgesellschaft took added steps to disguise its U.S. assets: its shares in Ore and Chemical Corporation went to three firms, Rotopulsor (Switzerland), the Luxembourg Union Bank, and NV Hollandsche Koopmansbank, Amsterdam, while its shares in Pembroke Chemical Corporation were held by Rotopulsor (Switzerland).[139]

Indeed, every enterprise in the United States with German "ownership" reviewed its cloaking in the years 1939–1941, with an eye to safeguarding its assets. New provisions were made related to ownership, contracts, and technological interchanges.[140] All these arrangements aimed at minimizing German exposure, with the Germans trying to protect their U.S. properties using Dutch, Luxembourg, Swedish, and particularly Swiss intermediaries. One expert on Swiss economic history has written that "from June 1940 on, following the collapse of France, Swiss ruling circles virtually integrated the Swiss economic and financial apparatus within the economic sphere of the Axis powers."[141] The Foreign Funds Control policies of the Treasury Department made European holding companies' strategies ever more precarious for the German affiliates in America, since once the assets were blocked, the Treasury Department would conduct investigations. Accordingly, the German goal shifted—in many instances—to seeking U.S. "ownership," often by nominees, which did not serve as an effective shelter, or by hyphenated German-Americans, loyal to their former homeland enterprise if not necessarily to their former homeland.

In operations (as distinct from formal corporate structures) the facts of war meant that German businesses in the United States tended to do more production (substituting for imports), undertake more research, and partake in greater exports. The Germans did not like the growing independence of their American affiliates, but they had little choice. In 1939–1941, most German businessmen assumed the war would be short, Germany would be victorious, and the parent German enterprise would reemerge triumphant.

British Firms

In September 1939, Britain, at war with Germany, at once forbade its enterprises' dealing with the enemy through U.S. companies. British direct investments in the United States were larger than those of any other nationality. Because of the maze of international agreements and connections made in the interwar years, the new British restrictions posed more problems than they had in America's period of neutrality during the First World War when similar prohibitions had been instituted. Thus, Standard Oil Company of New Jersey and I. G. Farben had in the 1930s cooperated in research, including developing new methods of catalytic refining to obtain high-octane aviation fuels; Royal Dutch Shell and Anglo-Iranian Oil Company had shared the outcomes. The British government did not want royalties paid by the British enterprises for the technology to end up in Germany. Anglo-Iranian's New York representative, Basil Jackson, got from SONJ qualified, albeit apparently acceptable, assurances that there would not be payments for research transmitted to the Germans.[142]

At least in 1939, certain executives at SONJ believed that "the war introduced quite a number of complications. How we are going to make these belligerent parties [the British and Germans] lie down in the same bed isn't quite clear as yet . . . Technology has to carry on—war or no war—so we must find some solution to these last problems."[143] Initially, at least, the war was perceived by some American business leaders as an "inconvenience." Many German industrialists had a similar view. The commitment was to their business; "we are businessmen and politics are a nuisance." This was not so much a mentality of "profits über alles" (although obviously the German firms did not expect to produce or sell without profits); instead, what emerges from the records was a pride in enterprise accomplishments and a desire to continue what they had been doing.[144]

I. G. Farben officials wrote Du Pont on October 4, 1939, "You advise us that for the duration of the war, you will not pass the experiences and applications which you receive from one licensee on to another [i.e., I. G. Farben technology would *not* go to Imperial Chemical Industries]. We thank you for having quickly taken the necessary steps for meeting the altered condition."[145] It was little wonder that the British were concerned.

In many ways the relationship between the Royal Dutch Shell Group and I. G. Farben was the most troubling. The United States was not a belligerent until 1941. Yet during the very time that Britain and Germany were at war, there is ample evidence of correspondence on the business associations between Shell in the United States and I. G. Farben. Only after the Germans invaded Holland did Shell Union Oil Corporation (on May 13, 1940) write politely—albeit crisply—to Chemnyco (I. G. Farben's New York representative) that "because of the recent political development," discussions on the licensing arrangements and the markets served on the oxidation of ketones "would have to cease."[146] Royal Dutch Shell was odd when it came to "nationality." At times it insisted it was British; at other times, it emphasized its Dutch character.

Some managers of U.S. affiliates of British companies in late May 1940 were in what one parent firm called an "exaggeratedly hysterical state of mind to which members of that great country are regrettably prone." Americans, the British chairman of Macmillan & Co. Ltd., wrote "labour under the delusion that we are in our last gasp." Macmillan & Co. Ltd. owned 52 percent of the stock of Macmillan Co., a New York corporation. The latter's president, George Brett, felt that were Britain to fall, the Germans would capture control of the American affiliate; to avoid that he wanted to move the physical possession of the stock to New York. The British parent saw no need to do so.[147] By contrast, in some cases Americans did acquire what had been British assets. Thus, Decca Record Co. Ltd. had an interest in its American affiliate of £72,909 as of March 31, 1939; a year later the investment was listed at £1. The divestment occurred before the Germans invaded Denmark, Norway, Holland, and Belgium and so was probably not motivated by fear of British defeat but rather by general "prudence" and British government pressure.[148]

Because American domestic companies were cautious in developing output to meet wartime conditions, in the spring and summer of 1940 the British government provided capital to finance such production. New plants actually owned by the British government were established in the United States. Thus, in April 1940, Du Pont agreed to build and to operate a facility for the Tennessee Powder Company; the latter was owned by the British (and initially the French) government.[149]

The British-Dutch Shell Union Oil Corporation was the largest foreign-owned firm in the United States. In the period 1939–1941, it sustained its innovative role. It produced 100 octane aviation fuel—a new product. It took part in supplying butadiene for synthetic rubber. It developed a process of toluene (for explosives) production from petroleum.[150] Thus, despite its 1939 questionable relationships with the Germans, by 1940–1941 it had become deeply involved in activities fundamental for British and crucial for subsequent U.S. wartime needs.

Some British affiliates enlarged their U.S. business, using reinvested earnings. More research capabilities and knowledge crossed westward over the Atlantic. The British pharmaceutical company Burroughs Wellcome, for example, built up its research staff at its Tuckahoe, New York, complex.[151] In an entirely different activity, new British involvements in America occurred. In the summer of 1939, the Britisher Ian Ballantine and the American Betty Ballantine had started the U.S. branch of the paperback house Penguin Books, which had been founded in Britain in 1935; the U.S. sales affiliate was 51 percent owned by the British parent and 49 percent owned by the Ballantines. With its new Pocket Books, Penguin became a pioneer in what became the "paperback revolution" in America. The U.S. firm had planned to handle only exports from the United Kingdom, but with war in Europe (and shipments curtailed), the company began to produce books in America. Everything was financed in the United States.[152] Penguin Books joined Macmillan and Oxford University Press—long-established British publishers—in America.

The U.S. Foreign Funds Control regulations did not apply to British companies. Most British businesses in America in the period 1939–1941 were, however, affected by the British blockade and blacklist and then, after July 17, 1941, by the U.S. blacklist. Thus, Schroders' U.S. subsidiary, J. Henry Schroder Banking Corporation, at once announced it would not do business with any firm on the British blacklist. This bank had been a sizable participant in German business transactions in the interwar years.[153] Some British businesses (ICI and BAT, in particular) were under fire in America as antitrust litigation intensified. All those that engaged in international trade were hampered by the dislocation of Atlantic shipping. Isolationists in the United States remained particularly hostile, wary that British business would propel America into the war. Most important, however, all the British investments in this country were affected by the British government's growing need for dollars to buy war materiel in the United States.

The Canadians

Canada joined Britain in declaring war in September 1939. A few days later, the Canadian government set up the Foreign Exchange Control Board, seeking to prevent the outflow of Canadian (and non-Canadian) capital. The Canadians also issued controls over enemy property in the Dominion. Canadians had in the 1930s been net purchasers of American domestic securities and even larger net sellers of American issues of foreign securities. The reverse took place in 1939–1941: Canadians became net sellers of domestic securities ($57.7 million) but were even larger net buyers of foreign securities ($76.9 million).[154] Canadian portfolio investments in American domestic securities were mainly in American equities, purchased before Canada entered the war; these had appreciated in value; the Canadian government encouraged but did not require such sales. The sales of domestic securities were to be expected. The sizable Canadian purchases of foreign securities in the U.S. market recorded by the U.S. Federal Reserve Board (and reversing the trend of January 1935 to September 1939) are not easy to explain, and I remain uncertain on what was happening here. The Dominion Bureau of Statistics indicated that after the introduction of foreign exchange controls there was a marked tendency to sell American securities (which was reflected in the reduction in domestic securities). It also noted a "considerable turnover in the Canadian holdings of foreign securities arising through permitted switching and trading." Clearly, the purchases of "foreign securities" in New York fit under this category. The latter might well represent repatriations of Canadian stakes held in the United States; they perhaps related to the activities of refugees in Canada.[155]

As for Canadian direct investments, at the start of the First World War (when Canada was a participant and the United States still neutral), Canadians had built munitions plants across the border in the United States; at the advent of the Second World War, this did not happen. Now Canadians purchased machine tools in the United States and expanded their own Canadian output. There was, however, a rise in Canadian direct investments in the United States from 1939 to 1941, and on at least one occasion a Canadian direct investment substituted for a U.K. one (in Glaxo Laboratories' joint venture in the United States).[156] The effect of the new Canadian capital export controls on the direct investments appears to have been inconsequential.

Existing Canadian direct investments in America blended comfortably with others in the United States. The principal ones remained in the branch railroad lines, in the U.S. liquor industry, and those by the life insurance companies. After a dismal time in the early and mid-1930s, Massey-Harris agricultural equipment factories in the United States were once again viable.[157] By 1941, by one measure, Canadian-controlled enterprises (i.e., direct investments) exceeded Canadian long-term portfolio stakes in domestic securities in the United States.[158] Canadian companies had been less involved than British ones in the intricate cartel structures associated with German firms, and there was little indication that Canadian affiliates in neutral America were trading with the German enemy.[159]

The Dutch, Belgians, Swiss, and Swedes

During the First World War, the Dutch had remained neutral. When war broke out, there was some Dutch capital flight into American securities.[160] In the 1930s, Dutch businessmen had recognized that in a future war, they might be vulnerable, and well before the German army overran Holland in May 1940, some Dutch firms had taken precautionary measures that embraced a U.S. presence. Thus, the innovative electrical enterprise NV Philips, headquartered in Eindhoven, Holland, had minor operations in the United States (one small factory making X-ray equipment), yet its activities were multinational—in Europe and Latin America—and it had routinely filed for U.S. patents on its inventions.[161] In anticipation of a possible German invasion of Holland, NV Philips had formed Bezit, a holding company in Curaçao, in the Dutch West Indies. Bezit assumed control over NV Philips' Gloeilampenfabriken, which on April 26, 1940, transferred its registered office to Curaçao. Earlier, NV Philips had made a trust agreement whereby the Hartford National Bank and Trust Co., Hartford, Connecticut, came to have "control" over Philips' business in the United States and South America (and Portugal). Key Philips executives moved to New York. The arrangements were to protect Philips' assets for the duration of the war.[162]

Philips was not the only Dutch company to shift its place of business to the Dutch West Indies. The head office of Royal Dutch was also set up in Curaçao.[163] So, too, the Dutch parent of the U.S. firm Roche-Organon Co. formed NV Organon in Curaçao, while at the same time it managed Organon's international business from London.[164] Océ-Van der Grinten, a small Dutch maker of specialized chemicals and copy paper, sent an employee to the United States in 1939 to make chemicals in this country—just in case the Germans occupied Holland; that Dutch firm arranged to supervise its licensees from the United States.[165] Despite the Dutch ownership of Lever Brothers Co., the parent for administrative purposes was in London, and this U.S. affiliate made no major changes in the way its business was conducted.[166] As for Thomas J. Lipton, Inc., which was by 1940 in large part technically Dutch owned, it expanded in the United States, in September 1940 acquiring 100 percent of Continental Foods, Inc., a manufacturer and seller of dried soups. This was the initial diversification of Lipton beyond the tea business.[167] Despite the sixty-forty Dutch ownership of Shell Union Oil Corporation and despite Royal Dutch's new head office in Curaçao, British-American "administration" went on running the operations when the Germans occupied Holland.[168] When Dutch assets were frozen after the Germans invaded Holland, the U.S. Treasury permitted all of these Dutch operations to continue their activities under its licenses. The Nederlandsche Handel-Maatschappij NV at once established an organization in London to manage its East India and British Empire branches. As a result of Dutch funds in New York being blocked, it seemed likely that the East India and British Empire branches of this trading company/bank would default. Arrangements were made with the Foreign Funds Control authority, and Nederlandsche Handel-Maatschappij NV opened a licensed bank agency in New York in January 1941.[169]

Solvay & Cie., the Belgian glass interests, and some rayon involvements aside, Belgian stakes in the United States had been limited. Société Financière de Transports et d'Entreprises Industrielles (Sofina), Brussels, the great Belgian public utilities holding company, had over the years made small U.S. investments. That pattern seemed to change when, in October 1936, Sofina had bought a large block of common shares of Middle West Corporation (this firm, formed in 1935, was the reorganized Middle West Utilities Company, one of the Insull companies that had gone bankrupt in 1932).[170] Although Sofina maintained its head office in Brussels all during the war, before the Germans invaded Belgium the public utilities holding company had removed part of its administration, its books, and its principal personnel to Lisbon and to New York. Dannie Heineman, born in North Carolina but raised in and trained as an engineer in Germany, was the genius behind Sofina (he had become its head in 1905). In the late 1930s, he was still Sofina's managing director. He was Jewish. Naturally, he was active in relocating Sofina's business to neutral locales. Sofina's principal bank was Crédit Suisse, Zurich, associations that undoubtedly crossed the Atlantic in tandem. After the Germans' invasion of Belgium, the occupiers tried to prevent Sofina from shifting more of its assets to the United States, yet by then it was too late, for there was little left in Belgium for the Nazis to take over.[171]

Banque Belge pour l'Etranger (BBE)—controlled by Société Générale de Belgique—had had a New York agency since 1921, which had been set up through London. When, in May 1940, Belgian assets in the United States were frozen, George Bolton of the Bank of England informed the Federal Reserve "that this bank was a British institution, registered in England [and] that full control was in London." Subsequently, the agency's assets were unfrozen.[172] According to Harold James, historian of the Deutsche Bank, by the summer of 1940, the Société Générale de Belgique had transferred the management of its holdings in Africa to London and New York.[173] A new Belgian investment in the United States in these years was that of the Banque Diamantaire Anversoise, SA, which opened a New York State–licensed bank agency, probably early in 1940.[174] It operated under a U.S. Treasury Department license after the freezing of Belgian assets in the United States.

The Belgian photographic paper and film company Gevaert had had a U.S. sales subsidiary since 1920 and by 1939 had sales offices in New York, Boston, Chicago, Philadelphia, and Los Angeles. With the war imminent, the U.S. affiliate of this Antwerp-headquartered company acquired a vacant textile mill in Williamstown, Massachusetts, where in 1941 it began to manufacture paper and film coating.[175] For a time, Gevaert had tried to supply its U.S. market from London, with materials made by the British Ilford. Once manufacturing began at Williamstown, the U.S. sales branches were served from the factory there.[176] A Treasury Department license allowed its operation.

While the Dutch frequently used the Dutch West Indies for offshore corporate shelters, and while the Belgians relied on London, New York, and Lisbon, many Swiss investors favored Panamanian intermediaries for their Western Hemisphere business. As of June 1941, forty-three Swiss-owned Panamanian companies had U.S. investments.[177] As early as the mid-1930s, Nestlé's management had wondered if Switzerland would be able to maintain neutrality should there be a war. In 1936, Nestlé had organized Unilac, Inc., incorporated in Panama. It served initially as the holding company for Nestlé's activities in Latin America. With war in Europe, Nestlé shifted all its properties not under German domination to Unilac ownership. In addition, Nestlé/Unilac set up a voting trust. Unilac opened an executive office in Stamford, Connecticut, and from there Nestlé's top leadership, Edouard Muller and Gustave Huguenin, managed the international business. Joined by Indiana-born Daniel F. Norton, president of Nestlé's Milk Products Co. (the U.S. subsidiary), the two Swiss executives ran all Nestlé operations outside German-occupied territories.[178] In 1939 Nestlé began to manufacture in the United States its first nonmilk product, Nescafé; in July 1940, it launched an impressive sales campaign to market the instant coffee.[179] A new Swiss manufacturer in America was Fabrique de Produits Maggi, SA, Zurich; it inaugurated a U.S. factory in New Milford, Connecticut, in 1940—making dried soups and seasonings. It had long been an exporter to America and obviously worried lest trade be cut off in wartime.[180]

The chief executive of the Swiss pharmaceutical company Hoffmann–La Roche moved to the United States, bringing along a number of key scientists.[181] Earlier, in 1938, this company (with its sizable synthetic vitamins plant in New Jersey and its joint venture with the Dutch Organon company) had organized a Panamanian subsidiary, Sapac Corporation, for its North and South American and British Commonwealth interests.[182]

Unlike Nestlé and Hoffmann-La Roche and the other forty-one Swiss companies that used Panamanian corporations, the Swiss dyestuff and pharmaceutical company Ciba adopted a different strategy for protecting its principal U.S. assets. In 1937–1939, this Basle-based company had transferred many of its U.S. holdings to a company organized in Canada, Anglo-American Chemicals, Ltd. (AAC). The process was only half completed when the European war began. In the fall of 1940, Ciba decided to set up two trusts—in Canada and the United States—to which it transferred AAC along with Ciba's other U.S. holdings (those not owned by AAC). The trusts were established irrevocably for a twenty-one-year period, with Ciba-Basle the beneficiary.[183] Apparently, Geigy and Sandoz did not do anything similar, but their U.S. interests were not as extensive as those of Ciba.[184] In 1939–1941, Ciba's manufacturing and exports from the United States escalated (in 1939, Ciba's U.S. pharmaceutical exports had been a mere 2.5 percent of its output; in 1941, its exports, principally to South America, came to 21.5 percent of sales).[185] Stoffel & Co., the Swiss organdy producer, was on the British blacklist because it delivered fabrics to the Germans in exchange for cellulose fiber raw material. On the advice of its Swiss lawyer, for the war's duration, the stock of Stoffel & Co.'s American affiliate was conveyed to its New York manager (a Swiss-born U.S. citizen).[186]

On October 16, 1939, the Swiss Bank Corporation, Basle, opened its first New York agency. SBC had about $50 million of its funds in the American market (in November 1939) and planned gradually to increase, even double, that amount. The men in charge of SBC explained that their U.S. expansion plans were "due to Switzerland's favorable balance of payments, the exchange market and safety requirements." They expected to become an acceptor and have bills outstanding in New York. In addition, SBC would execute securities orders for its clients and provide them with information on conditions in the United States. Early in 1940, Crédit Suisse, Zurich, followed the SBC, also starting its first New York agency. In July 1939, Crédit Suisse had organized the Swiss American Corporation, New York, to take part in the investment security business.[187] As one historian has put it, "When [in 1939–1940] the United States became a major zone of Swiss financial interests, the two biggest [Swiss] banks established themselves in New York."[188] On September 18, 1940, the Swiss central bank (Banque Nationale Suisse) shifted its sizable holdings of American securities from the new New York agency of Crédit Suisse and from several New York banks to an account at the New York Federal Reserve.[189] On June 14, 1941, the United States froze Swiss assets (see Table 8.4); at that time, Swiss public and private assets in the country were estimated at $1.5 billion, "considerably beyond what Switzerland might be expected to carry legitimately for herself and nationals," or so the *New York Times* editorialized.[190] Later, the Treasury Department would calculate that Swiss long-term and short-term assets in the United States came to $1.2 billion: long-term assets, $627 million (see Table 8.3) and such short-term assets as bullion, currency, and deposits, $495 million.[191]

On June 20, less than a week after the freezing of Swiss assets in the United States, the Swiss consul general in New York, Victor Nef, met in that city with roughly seventy Swiss businessmen and bankers, representing fifty Swiss firms doing business in the United States. Present were men from Unilac/Nestlé, Maggi, Hoffmann-La Roche, Sandoz, Geigy, the Swiss Bank Corporation, and Crédit Suisse, as well as individuals from Swiss insurance companies (Winterthur, Société Suisse de Réassurance); equipment manufacturers (Sulzer, Brown, Boveri & Co., Landis & Gyr, Tavaro); a watchmaker (Roland Gsell & Co.); a shoe company (Bally); silk and textile firms (Schwarzenbach, Huber & Co., Stoffel & Co.); and banking (Union de Banques Suisses, Lombard, Odier & Cie., and Pictet & Cie.).[192] The private Geneva banks (especially Lombard, Odier but also Pictet) had invested their Swiss, French, and other clients' moneys in the United States since the nineteenth century.[193]

As it had since 1935, the Federal Reserve kept track of the purchases and sales of American securities by foreign investors; overall, from September 1939 to December 1941 (from the outbreak of the Second World War in Europe to Pearl Harbor), by its calculations, there had been a $550.8 million net reduction in foreign holdings of American securities (i.e., sales by foreign investors); the Swiss, however, countered the trend: Swiss net purchases came to $23 million, practically all concentrated in late 1939 and early 1940.[194] Swiss portfolio investments in the United States far exceeded direct investments (see Table 8.3).

Swedish interests in the United States were less than those of the Dutch, the Belgians, or the Swiss, yet in 1939 the Swedes shared with these other investors the same anxieties over what might happen in Europe. Like the Swiss, the Swedes would remain neutral during the entire war, but no one knew that for sure in 1939–1941. Indeed, in 1940, Marcus Wallenberg of the Stockholms Enskilda Bank was in the United States, organizing a voting trust that conveyed control over SKF's American business to the latter's U.S. president, William L. Batt. In the spring of 1941, AB-SKF (the parent firm) exchanged its shares in its U.S. affiliate, SKF Industries, for the trust certificates; after five years the shares were to revert to the Swedish parent. SKF Industries, which made ball bearings, was probably the largest Swedish direct investment in the United States; its Swedish parent also had a plant in Germany, which would attract substantial attention.[195] Because the Stockholms Enskilda Bank participated in a set of transactions involving U.S. assets of German investors, American observers were uneasy whenever this bank seemed involved. Swedish assets in the United States were frozen on June 14, 1941.[196]

The French

In November 1939, Société Générale, Paris, applied for permission from the New York State Banking Department to open a licensed agency in

New York City.[197] By the end of 1939, it had opened for business. Its formal representation meant that it joined in New York the French American Banking Corporation, which was 50 percent owned by Comptoir National d'Escompte de Paris.[198] When French assets were frozen (June 17, 1940), the amounts would be estimated at $1.6 billion (mostly gold and securities). Data on French investments in American securities are poor. The French were exceedingly secretive in their transactions and often went through Swiss and other intermediaries (e.g., American nominees). I view with caution all valuations of French stakes in American securities.[199] As of June 14, 1941, the U.S. Treasury census identified 250 enterprises in the United States controlled by French "persons," with the total amount less than $100 million (two-thirds of which sum was categorized as in the finance and the "public utility and transportation" sectors).[200] The census recorded another $186 million in securities.[201] Even given large French gold holdings, the discrepancy between $1.6 billion and $286 million seems huge.[202]

Two significant French-owned firms in the United States keenly affected by the situation in Europe were the giant grain traders the Fribourgs' Continental Grain Co. and the Louis-Dreyfus company. Before the fall of France, several Continental Grain Co. officials arranged the transfer of that company's head office from Paris to New York.[203] The Louis-Dreyfus family also came to live in New York after the German invasion and after French assets in America had been frozen. That firm's New York partners were by then U.S. citizens, and the cousins in Europe arranged for the New Yorkers to take charge of the Louis-Dreyfus holdings in a fifteen-year trust. By the summer of 1940, Louis Dreyfus & Co. claimed to have $8 million in U.S. assets, while family members were said to have additional large U.S. holdings.[204] Other Frenchmen turned up in New York after the German invasion of France and the "Aryanization" of Jewish banks by the Vichy government.[205] Thus, partners in the Paris Rothschild Bank took up residence in New York, but they did not reestablish the Rothschild business in America.[206] By contrast, two of the principal French partners of Lazard Frères et Cie., André Meyer and Pierre David-Weill, installed themselves in New York and would, in 1943, take charge of the firm's New York house.[207]

One key French business in America was Schlumberger. In 1939–1941, the demand for its oil services expanded rapidly; it was "logging" (using its sophisticated electrical measurement techniques) on fully a quarter of all oil wells drilled in the United States.[208] Another group of French investors were those in the wool factories in Rhode Island. Charles Tiberghien arrived in the United States in 1940 to administer his firm's U.S. affiliate.[209] In the case of both the Schlumberger and

Tiberghien ventures, family members stayed on in France and collaborated with the Germans to preserve their French assets.[210]

The Japanese

There was little Japanese portfolio investment in the United States in 1939–1941 (see Table 8.1). Japanese-controlled enterprises in the United States consisted primarily of banks, insurance companies, trading firms, and shipping lines. Table 8.2 indicated that as of June 14, 1941 there were 360 Japanese branches and subsidiaries within the United States (a number that seems large compared with the $35 million "value" of the investments).[211] With certain exceptions, these important service sector affiliates were located in New York City and on the West Coast.[212] Over the years, these businesses had built up sizable operations, and by this time much of U.S.-Japanese trade (imports and exports) was financed, insured, arranged, and shipped by Japanese enterprises.[213] The largest Japanese investor in the United States was the Yokohama Specie Bank (YSB). Between June and December 1941, blocked assets notwithstanding, the Japanese government repatriated $27 million held for it by the New York agency of YSB, an amount equal to nearly half the agency's assets. It seems that before the Pearl Harbor attack, YSB was not unusual, and "many of the [Japanese] companies had parts of their assets withdrawn by the foreign owners or depositors."[214]

A Czech Firm

The large multinational Czech shoe manufacturer Bata had, given U.S. tariffs in the 1930s, contemplated manufacturing behind them and had purchased a plot of land in Belcamp, Maryland, some twenty-five miles from Baltimore. Its postponed plans for the factory had taken form in 1938–1939, but as the political environment in Europe worsened, the Bata management decided as a priority to develop its business in Canada, where it set up a new corporate headquarters. As of September 1939, Bata's U.S. plant had not yet been built, for Bata seems to have had difficulties finding financing. When the brother of the company's founder tried to import into the United States gold from Canada that the Bata group had transferred there, he met with the Canadian government's enemy alien restrictions. In the United States, he was accused of being a Nazi sympathizer, and early in 1941, with his visitor's visa not renewed, he set sail for Brazil, where he lived during the war years. Bata's Maryland business (under the management of a longtime Bata employee who was a naturalized U.S. citizen) eventually obtained authorization from the Canadian government to transfer the gold and to build up the U.S. business. It seems as if these moneys from Canada were not affected when Czech assets in the United States were frozen in June 1941.[215]

The Effects of the Blocked Assets

By 1941 all foreign business in America was under public scrutiny. British and Canadian investors excepted, by the last half of 1941, the other most important foreign assets in the United States were "blocked."[216] As in the interwar years, and as in the future, the Treasury Department in its collection of data on foreign investment worked closely with the New York Federal Reserve. A department set up at the New York Federal Reserve processed the Foreign Funds Control license applications, which were readily granted; foreign direct investors continued in operation.[217]

The efforts of the Foreign Funds Control group grew, with the behavior of German business closely monitored. Swiss investments, in particular, were subjected to scrutiny, as numerous questions were addressed on German-Swiss links. So, too, Swedish enterprise became a topic of study. Investigations multiplied into continental European companies that were using Panamanian, Netherlands Antilles, and other intermediaries (including trust companies and American nominees) to protect their assets. The Japanese did not use such devices but were reducing their exposure by repatriating assets.[218]

Canadian-British, Australian-British Relationships

British and Canadian investors in America—the two largest—did not have their assets frozen, yet their investments in America were also under a spotlight. The British government required the sales of many of its nationals' assets in Canada to finance British wartime purchases there.[219] The British lacked, however, the leverage to mobilize or to use *Canadian* investments in the United States to finance British purchases in America, even though they would have liked to have done so. Right after the outbreak of the European war, the British government had sent a purchasing mission to Ottawa to buy munitions from its ally. As British buying in Canada rose, Britain's capacity to pay lagged. In addition, Canada faced deficits in its trade balance with the United States, since a sizable share of the inputs for Canadian industrial output were imported from across its southern border. How was Canada to finance its U.S. trade? Canadians did sell some dollar securities.[220] After the Lend-Lease bill passed the U.S. Congress in March 1941, providing for the financing of U.K. purchases in the United States, Canadians feared their mother country would buy directly from the United States, bypassing the Dominion. The Canadian government hesitated to apply for U.S. lend-lease aid, apprehensive lest "this might create pressures from the American side for liquidation of all Canadian assets in the United States." (London diplomats believed that insofar as Canada had an adverse trade balance with the United States, the Canadian government should be insisting that its citizens sell their American securities to obtain the needed U.S. dollars; the Canadian government had little inclination to press such sales.) Finally, on April 20, 1941, with the Hyde Park Declaration, made by Roosevelt and Canadian prime minister Mackenzie King, a portion of the British lend-lease allocations could be used by Canadians to buy goods and services in the United States, and to their relief, Canadians would *not* be required by the United States (or by Great Britain) to divest their U.S. assets.[221] The reasons Canadians were so fearful that they might be forced to sell lay in the experiences of the United Kingdom.

Although U.K. assets in the United States were never blocked, they were in great jeopardy—indeed, in far greater jeopardy than most of the blocked assets in 1940–1941. The British were desperate for dollars to purchase military supplies in the United States, and as they sought dollar resources, they had put pressure on the Canadians and also on their Australian allies. In May 1940, the Foreign Office was in touch with the Australian government about the possible mobilization of American securities held by Australian nationals. In the Australian case (unlike that of the Canadians), the amounts were small, especially when allowances were made for Australian government dollar bonds and the stakes of Australian insurance companies, which the British government believed were "off bounds." Nonetheless, the British did try to convince Australians to sell their other negligible U.S. interests to obtain dollars for British wartime purchases.[222]

British Purchases and Lend Lease

The most far-reaching impact on foreign investments in the United States, 1939–1941, related to the British need to find a way to pay for U.S. wartime supplies. From the start of the war, it was evident that the British and their French allies would desire to acquire large amounts of goods in the United States and would require dollars to do so. Constraints on such purchases existed that had been absent in 1914. The 1934 Johnson Act prohibited U.S. bankers from lending to governments in default on their World War I obligations (and this included Britain and France). A congressional resolution of February 1936 had banned

U.S. lending to any belligerent. And the 1937 U.S. Neutrality Act had reaffirmed a 1935 congressional arms embargo, forbidding U.S. exports of arms and munitions to any warring nation. These measures had reflected widely held sentiments that Americans did not want to be drawn into another European conflict. The policies had emerged as scholars and legislators alike had stridently sought to blame American bankers and businessmen for the U.S. involvement in the First World War.

However, the November 1939 Neutrality Act had permitted belligerent nations to buy arms and munitions in the United States if they paid cash; no credit was to be extended. Almost at once the British sought to raise that cash by arranging the sales of British-owned American dollar-denominated securities. The British tried to get the French to share with them the costs of fighting the Germans, and the French government tried to assemble dollar securities. The French purchasing commission cooperated with the British to obtain and use the dollars to buy military materiel in America. In December the Anglo-French Purchasing Commission was set up in Washington. Yet French securities in the United States were not plentiful (and because of the long tradition of secrecy were extremely hard for the French government to identify); and then, with the defeat of France in June 1940, the British had to cope on their own.

Thus, it is important to concentrate on the British story. That nation's efforts to obtain dollars focused on U.K. assets in America. There was great uncertainty regarding how much these investments would bring in. Anticipating the outbreak of war, the British government had issued an order dated August 26, 1939, that prohibited British owners of American securities from selling them without prior approval from the British Treasury. That same order required British owners to register their American securities with the Bank of England. Based on these registrations, the British Treasury estimated that about $1 billion of dollar securities were in British hands (other British estimates were lower).[223] Owners were allowed to sell their American securities to Americans, but the dollar proceeds had to be surrendered to the British Treasury—at the rate of $4.04.[224] At this time, the U.S. Treasury Department had an entirely different perception of the amounts of British assets in the United States. It calculated that British and Frenchmen together held some $15 billion of gold, American securities, and American properties—with half of the $15 billion (or about $7 billion) owned in the United Kingdom, one-quarter in the British dominions, and the remainder in France.[225]

As the dispute over the size (and the composition) of British assets in America remained unresolved, in September 1939 the British Treasury determined gradually to "vest [i.e., assume] title to the [British-held American] securities itself"—reimbursing its nationals at $4.04 to the pound. It planned in an orderly fashion to sell these securities on the U.S. market, obtaining the needed dollars to buy American supplies.[226] British Defence Regulations mandated that all investment trusts and mortgage lenders place their American investments at the disposal of the British Treasury. The Scottish Investment Trust Company, Edinburgh, for example, instructed J. P. Morgan & Co., which held American securities on its behalf, to sell—being careful not to upset the market (the dollars were then passed on to the British government).[227] The Scottish American Mortgage Company announced that in compliance with the wishes of the Treasury, the directors were continuing to bring back to Britain "all available collections" in the United States.[228] Table 8.6 shows the drastic reduction of U.S. holdings of this firm from May 31, 1939 to May 31, 1941. By May 31, 1940, this company's American securities portfolio was about 28 percent of what it had been a year earlier. By May 31, 1941, it would fall to a mere 10 percent of the figure of two years before.[229]

Late in September 1939, the governor of the Bank of England, Montagu Norman, had made plans to form a small committee to advise the British Treasury on British holdings of foreign securities. Toward the end of October, as the passage of the U.S. Neutrality Act of 1939 seemed assured, the Bank of England and the British Treasury decided to send Walter K. Whigham across the Atlantic to oversee the disposal of American securities for the needed cash.[230] Whigham—a director of the Bank of England—was a principal figure in Robert Fleming & Co., Ltd. (the merchant banking house that had once been the premier specialist in American securities and still was highly knowledgeable on the subject).[231] Although well informed, Whigham was not an authority on American securities. British trust companies, once deeply involved in the U.S. market, had over the years invested relatively more at home. Whigham assumed that what would now be available for sale by the British government was a bare fraction of the amount attainable at the time of the First World War.[232]

With the "phony war" in the winter of 1939, the British government postponed vesting American securities, meeting its initial cash requirements by selling gold reserves and encouraging voluntary divestments.[233] Certain private sales of American securities were made, and the dollars went to the British government. Whigham returned to Britain in December 1939, and in mid-January 1940, T. J. Carlyle Gifford—an Edinburgh solicitor who was chairman of a collection of investment trusts (including the Scottish Investment Trust Company) and who had done business with the

Table 8.6. American investments of the Scottish American Mortgage Co., 1939–1941 (in £s)

Year end, May 31	Mortgages and real estate in America[a]	American securities owned[b]				Total securities owned[c]	American securities as % of total[d]
		Bonds	Pref'd. & guaranteed shares	Common shares	Total securities		
1939	330,924	6,114	143,404	239,284	388,802	2,104,443	18.5
1940	282,197	—	57,906	51,905	109,811	1,882,036	5.8
1941	243,926	—	27,484	13,027	40,511	2,020,852	2.0

Source: Scottish American Mortgage Co., *Annual Reports*, Film Z-G2, Reel 55, Bancroft Library, University of California, Berkeley

a. Mortgages and real estate are "at or under cost" and entered at $4.90 to the £.

b. At market and entered at $4.90 to the £.

c. This figure is the total of marketable securities, including American, U.K., and other securities. It is at market. It excludes the investment in mortgages and real estate.

d. This figure was obtained by dividing the total American securities owned (as given in the table) by the total securities owned (as given in the table). It excludes the investments in mortgages and real estate.

Morgans for many years—traveled to the United States, deputized by the Bank of England to take charge in America of the requisitioning and realization of the dollar securities. Once again, the British had chosen an experienced trust company man. Except for a short holiday in Edinburgh in the fall of 1940, Gifford remained in the United States until August 1941. His letters home, which were privately published, provide an invaluable record of British policies.[234]

Throughout, J. P. Morgan & Co. assisted the British in selling the dollar securities, although Gifford was told bluntly by the British ambassador that he had to have an office separate from the Morgans, and while the "great bulk of his real work would be done in Morgans," he must keep his distance. This "maintenance of distance" from the Morgans had been at the insistence of the White House from the start of the war and would be reiterated as time went on. The Roosevelt administration feared that if the British had too visible a contact with the Morgan partners, this would be grist to the mill of isolationists in Congress.[235]

By January 1940, British gold sales had come to $125 million, and private sales of American securities equaled $112 million. Not until the start of February 1940 did the first British government requisitions of American securities begin; a second set of requisitions followed in April. These covered 177 securities, with a value of $310 million.[236] The British also continued to sell gold. In April the Germans invaded Denmark and Norway. Added vesting orders were announced so that eventually the British government acquired its countrymen's interests in 484 different American stocks and bonds, through a total of five separate vesting orders, issued between February 1940 and April 1941.[237]

In April 1940, the Alliance Trust directors—at the Scottish trust's annual meeting—indicated that they expected the requisition process would accelerate until virtually all American stocks and bonds had been acquired by the British government; this firm's portfolio of dollar securities was at that time more than 20 percent of its total assets.[238] At the end of May 1940, after the German sweep into Holland, Belgium, and Luxembourg, the Bank of England informed the Federal Reserve Bank of New York that new British regulations were being introduced

> to place current payments between the sterling area and the U.S.A. . . . on the basis of the official rate of 4.02½ to 4.03½ [and] . . . the following New York agencies of United Kingdom banks
>
> Standard Bank of South Africa Ltd.
> Chartered Bank of India, Australia and China
> Hongkong & Shanghai Banking Corporation
> Barclays Bank (D.C. & O)
>
> are being given exchange by us at 4.02½ to enable them to negotiate sterling bills covering U.S.A. exports to Empire destinations.[239]

British controls multiplied, as did British requirements. On May 11, 1940 (the day after Dutch assets in America had been frozen), the head of British purchasing in the United States, Arthur Purvis, reported to London on $600 million worth of American dollar securities "held by investment houses in Holland, which, if saved from the German invader, could be used for the purchase of Allied supplies in the United States."[240]

After the war began, a few British direct investors divested small holdings in their American affiliates (Decca Record Co. Ltd. and Glaxo Laboratories were examples). In some cases in the interest of "patriotism," British properties in America that were "white elephants" were sold. Thus, the Deltic Investment Company (in which Alliance Trust held a major interest) finally found a buyer for its Louisiana cotton plantations (it had wanted to sell them for many years).[241] In addition, the Alliance Trust had owned land in New Mexico since 1881, the so-called Chavez Land Grant. The U.S. government wished to extend the Pueblo Indian reservation. In 1940, the Alliance Trust sold its remaining 47,000 acres for $67,350, reserving for fifty years oil rights on the land. This last was a relatively modest sale; by the spring of 1941, the British government had requisitioned $4 million of Alliance Trust's dollar securities; beyond that, the trust obtained from sales, interest, dividends, and collections from its mortgage business a further $5 million, which it transferred to the British Treasury.[242]

Before the German invasion of France, J. P. Morgan & Co. and Lazard Frères together had helped sell French-owned American securities to raise moneys for the French war effort.[243] The new licensed New York agency of the French bank, Société Générale, was reported to be working with the French purchasing commission in buying war supplies.[244] When, in June 1940, the Germans moved into France, the British took over the French supply contracts and managed to gain control of French frozen assets in the United States for use for Allied purposes.[245] By this time, the British were becoming more desperate to find dollars to meet their wartime programs. In June they raised their U.S. orders for war materiel—putting financial concerns "on the lap of the Eternal Gods."[246] As the Germans began the bombing of Britain, British needs catapulted upward and its resources seemed increasingly limited.

By the start of 1941 the British Treasury reported that the British government had spent "a very great proportion" of its gold reserves and was steadily selling off the remaining requisitioned American securities. In 1941, the Cravath law firm in New York represented Kuhn, Loeb & Co. in the purchase and distribution of sizable blocks of Union Pacific, Pennsylvania, and Southern Pacific stock, securities that the British government had taken over and wanted to sell for

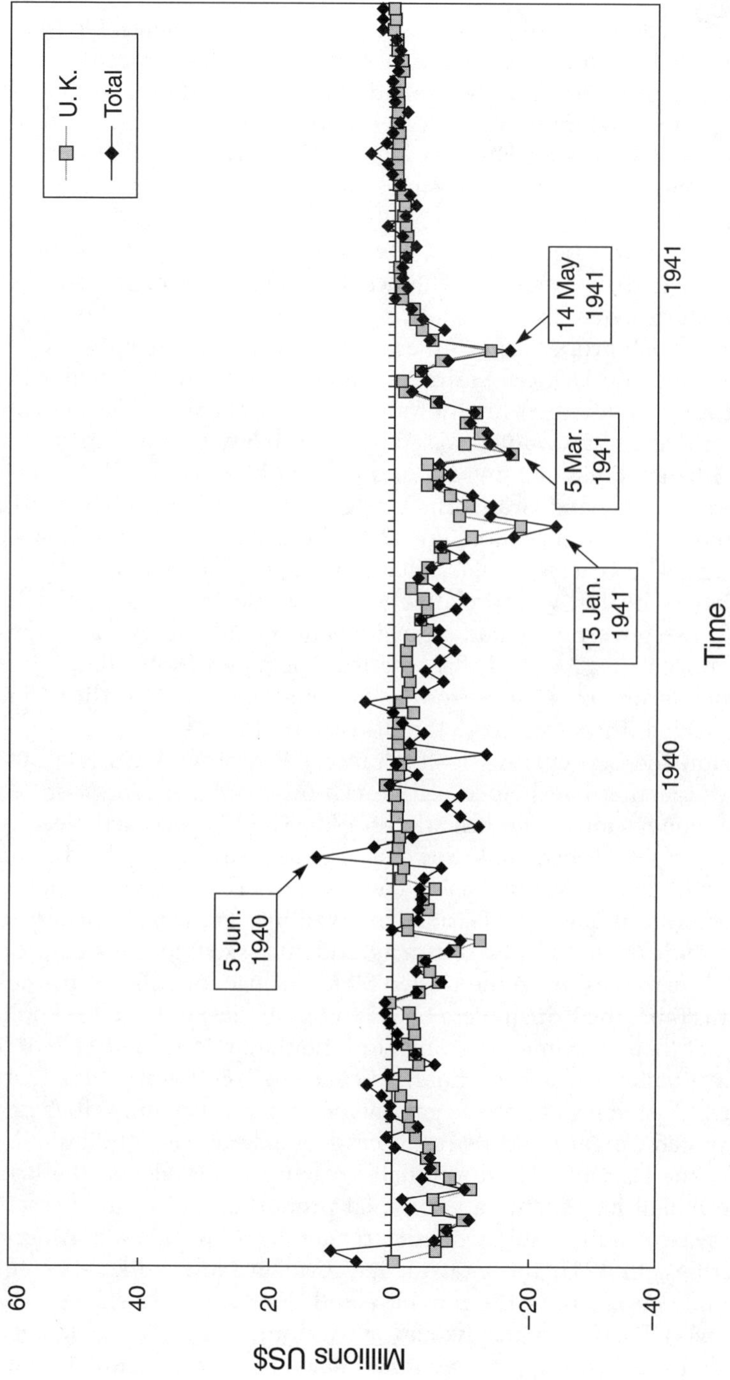
U.K.
Total
14 May 1941
5 Mar. 1941
15 Jan. 1941
5 Jun. 1940
1940
1941
Time
Millions US$
60
40
20
0
−20
−40

dollars.[247] J. P. Morgan & Co. was never the exclusive seller of dollar securities on behalf of the British.

Figure 8.1 summarizes the course of U.K. divestments of American domestic securities (as compared with overall foreign sales of domestic securities) from August 30, 1939, to December 31, 1941. There would be net British sales in the stock market over this period of more than $503.6 million of traded domestic securities, which represented a sizable portion of the entire retreat from American domestic securities in this period (net sales of $550.8 million).[248]

Early in 1941, British sales of securities had intensified, but by that time the British believed they had sold the most salable American securities, and for the first time the British government—under intense American pressures—considered seriously the sale of British-owned and -controlled business enterprises that operated in the United States.[249] This had not been done during the First World War, when only securities traded on the stock market had been mobilized. Now, under U.S. government prodding to liquidate British direct investments to raise cash, Sir Edward Peacock—a close associate of the governor of the Bank of England and a director of the bank—traveled to the United States.

Canadian-born Sir Edward Peacock had in 1924 joined Baring Brothers, as a director. Gaspard Farrer, who over the years had been very much a participant in Barings' North American business, had retired in 1925; Lord Revelstoke had died in 1929, at which time Peacock became the principal partner in Barings and a director of the Bank of England. At Barings—Peacock's Canadian background notwithstanding—he had concentrated on U.K. business and corporate finance, along with restructuring and rationalizing domestic industry. After Barings' abysmal experience with Kidder Peabody in 1931–1932, the merchant bank had taken only a trivial part in U.S. transactions during the 1930s.[250]

British bankers and trust company officials (and the British Treasury) knew little about most British direct investments in the United States. During the 1930s, British overseas investments had been monitored by Lord Kindersley, a Bank of England director from Lazard Brothers &

Figure 8.1. Flow of British capital to and from the United States compared with all foreign capital, domestic securities, weekly data. Week ending Sept. 6, 1939–Dec. 31 1941. Source: Prepared by G. Gokkent from data in Board of Governors Federal Reserve System, *Banking and Monetary Statistics* (Washington, D.C., 1943), 620–623 626–629. Cumulative British purchases came to $-503.6 million; all foreign, to $-550.8 million. Cumulative data are the sum of weekly transactions Aug. 30, 1939–Dec. 31, 1941. Net movement from the United States is minus (−).

Co.; his collection methods excluded most of the overseas investments by British multinational enterprises. In January 1941, a British Treasury spokesman stated there was no way to estimate the value of British direct investments in the United States, and "probably the owners themselves do not know what they are worth at market."[251] Gifford wrote home in February 1941, "these 'direct investments' involve far more difficult questions than do my Stock Exchange investments."[252]

By contrast, U.S. Secretary of the Treasury Henry Morgenthau insisted he knew everything about British direct investments in America.[253] Arthur Purvis, the head of British purchasing in the United States, was also well informed.[254] When Sir Frederick Phillips from the British Treasury had been in Washington in July 1940, seeking U.S. loans and trying to devise means of getting around the Neutrality Act restrictions, Morgenthau had lectured him on the large "British-owned" companies in the United States, according to Morgenthau, American Viscose, Shell Oil, Lever Brothers, Dunlop Tire and Rubber, and Brown & Williamson Tobacco. Morgenthau argued that the value of such investments equaled $833 million; later the American press would place a $900 million figure for the size of British direct investments in America in 1940.[255] That July 1940 Morgenthau had asked Phillips what was then a rhetorical question: How could Americans justify providing assistance to the British when the latter had such important assets in the United States? Phillips had not taken the query seriously.

After the November 1940 U.S. elections, the 1934 Johnson Act and the 1939 Neutrality Act notwithstanding, Roosevelt had become openly committed to helping the British cause. "Lend lease" became the formula: lending *goods* instead of money, thus circumventing the legal prohibitions.[256] If there was to be such American aid, Morgenthau insisted that the British must show good faith—that is, he believed they must part with their companies' direct investments as well as their nationals' dollar securities, using the proceeds to help pay for their purchases. In December 1940, Phillips had crossed the Atlantic once again, with specific instructions from the British government to resist all American pressure to divest the U.S. assets of British multinational enterprises. But Phillips found Morgenthau (and Roosevelt as well) adamant; having gotten a full commitment on the sale of British portfolio investments, Morgenthau had become bent on gaining a similar agreement from the British on the sale of British direct investments in America. Phillips had stalled. Morgenthau countered that he had to demonstrate to a still-isolationist U.S. public and Congress that Britain was not asking for funds from Americans while it had its own sizable resources in this country. By December 28, 1940, an exasperated Winston Churchill was describing the U.S. insistence as that of "a sheriff collecting the last assets of a hapless debtor." The British were indignant, seeing pure U.S. greed. The day before, Phillips had cabled the British Treasury that much of the targeting of British direct investments was "inspired and paid for by United States insurance companies who are exceedingly anxious to obtain the [British] properties." Phillips worried lest the many British insurers in America be put out of business; the large British insurers had a major (and long-standing) presence in the United States—and in the United Kingdom, British insurance companies had political clout. Phillips was determined not "to sacrifice" these investments.[257]

The direct investments (and not only those in insurance but in all sectors) were unlike "listed" American dollar securities. As a later commentator explained:

> A subsidiary existing by virtue of its connections with an old firm with world-wide interests and reputation would stand to lose much of its value [if put up for sale]. Severance would mean loss of goodwill, of technical assistance, of patent rights, trade names and other assets. In the view of the British Government these businesses were in a different category from market securities. They were going concerns, resulting from decades of healthy competitive effort. They were part of the living tissue uniting the British and American economies, which could only be cut at the risk of hurting both.

More narrowly, John Maynard Keynes saw direct investments as "part of Britain's exporting capacity."[258]

Yet Morgenthau—to British dismay—in January 1941, at a hearing of the U.S. Senate Foreign Relations Committee, reported that the British had agreed to sell "every dollar of property, real property or securities that any English citizen owns in the United States" to obtain foreign exchange to pay for the British orders already placed in the United States.[259] Jesse H. Jones, U.S. secretary of commerce and federal loan administrator, added on February 12 that U.S. loans could be made available to Americans "who might wish to purchase British holdings in this country which are to be liquidated by the British Government to obtain dollar exchange for war purposes."[260] In the United Kingdom, a committee of insurance offices was organized, which held "worried discussions with the Governor of the Bank of England in February 1941."[261]

This, then, was the dreadfully uncomfortable context for Peacock's late January–February 1941 visit to America, which extended into March. The British government was extremely reluctant to order its nationals' companies to sell; U.S. government officials were not inclined to budge.[262] Initially, Peacock had dallied, claiming that a forced liquidation of British direct investments would bring small returns, since a subsidiary separated from its parent had reduced value, and there were problems of technical assistance, patents, and trade names.[263] As he hemmed and hawed, Senator Burton K. Wheeler, an isolationist who had previously taken a dim view of the behavior of the British direct investor American Viscose Corporation, denounced the warlike New Deal's "triple A foreign policy; it will plow under every fourth American boy"; Senator D. W. Clark of Idaho sputtered that England was fighting for "gold, trade, commerce, and the maintenance of their ruling class."[264]

Such anti-British oratory got wide press coverage as the U.S. Congress debated the Lend-Lease bill. With isolationist voices stirring up discontent, Morgenthau grew ever more angry, insisting that the British were not demonstrating the "proper attitude."[265] Peacock knew that Shell and Lever—with British-Dutch and Dutch parentage—would be very complicated to sell. On March 8, after the Senate approved the Lend-Lease bill, Morgenthau delivered to Peacock an ultimatum. Morgenthau was going to testify on the appropriation bill. The British must stop procrastinating.[266] On March 11, Roosevelt signed the Lend-Lease bill. The British recognized that none of the lend-lease appropriation would be available to pay for the large existing British orders, since Morgenthau was confident the British had adequate dollar resources to cover them, and such dollars could (and should) come from the sale of the remaining British assets in America.[267]

On Saturday, March 15, the Defense Plant Corporation (a subsidiary of the Reconstruction Finance Corporation) agreed to buy five munitions plants in the United States that had been financed by the British government. The price was $46 million. The goal was to make dollars available to the British purchasing board.[268] The next day came the announcement by Peacock and Harold Stanley (president of Morgan, Stanley & Co., the spin-off from J. P. Morgan & Co.) that a group of American investment bankers, led by Morgan, Stanley & Co. and Dillon, Read & Co., had bought American Viscose Corporation, the Courtaulds subsidiary. The sale of this British rayon company affiliate, Peacock stated, would be the forerunner of other sales of British direct investments to obtain dollars. The price paid for the giant American Viscose (with its seven U.S. plants and 18,000 American employees) would depend on the amount realized in the bankers' subsequent resale.[269] Estimates in the press of American Viscose's value ran in excess of $100 million. The British negotiators believed the American Viscose transaction would bring in more than $80 million.[270]

When the bankers' acquisition was made, Peacock spoke "of the goodwill and mutual trust" on both sides.[271] His courteous remarks were totally at odds with the reality. Courtaulds' management was furious. John C. Hanbury-Williams of the British parent company called it a "frame-up" and felt "Viscose had been sold down the river."[272] One historian has called the process an "unanaesthetized amputation."[273] Another historian writes of American Viscose as "a victim."[274] The insider's account by Gifford shows that there were cables to London for authority "if necessary to force Courtaulds to sell and to arrange what terms we [the British government representatives] liked."[275]

After some futile attempts to abort the transaction, on May 26, 1941, the stock of American Viscose was resold by the bankers to the U.S. public; only $62,295,546 was raised; and after commissions to the intermediaries, the British government obtained about £13,500,000 in dollars, or roughly $54 million at the then current rate of exchange. Courtaulds' reimbursement, by a British arbitration commission in July 1942, came to £27,125,000 plus interest at 3 percent.[276]

Peacock's March 16 declaration notwithstanding, American Viscose Corporation was the *only* British direct investment to be sold under these pressures. Had Courtaulds' management been wiser, had the British government known more about the nature of British direct investments, this might never have happened.[277] Two days after the sale to the investment bankers, the *New York Times* (on March 18) editorialized that the transaction

> should convince the most determined skeptic of the dire financial straits in which Great Britain stands . . . It should silence those cynics who would have us believe that Britain is prepared to accept American aid under the lease-lend [*sic*] bill without making every financial sacrifice within her power . . . Britain must import to live, and she pays for her imports by the proceeds of her trade, her shipping, her financial services, and her income from foreign investments . . . If Britain is to throw all these investments on the auction block she may emerge from the war victorious over the Nazis but incapable of supporting herself in the days to follow.
>
> Great Britain's direct investments in this country fill a role in her economy out of all proportion to the amount of money that can be raised by selling them. Many American subsidiaries of British companies would have little or no value once they were separated from their parent. In other cases, parent organizations in Britain would be greatly weakened by the loss of their American affiliates. This is especially true of the British insurance companies whose American subsidiaries make up probably half of Britain's direct investments here . . . We have pledged our all-out aid to preserve Britain as a free and democratic nation. That means preserving Britain, not as a bankrupt nation but as a going concern.[278]

Over the months that followed this editorial, many Britishers and Americans had further doubts about the wisdom of the sale of British direct investments and also of the remaining British securities at "distress prices." The low value received by the British government on the bankers' resale of the American Viscose Corporation at the end of May 1941 strengthened the British Treasury's long-standing resolve not to capitulate to U.S. pressures.[279] Also, at once, as can be imagined, English and Scottish multinationals with interests in the United States became extremely nervous. Their managers rushed to formulate creative means to avoid losing their U.S. affiliates. At the same time, Americans were anxious lest continuing sales of British securities depress prices on the New York Stock Exchange.

The Lend-Lease Act of March 1941 gave the president the power to spend an initial $7 billion to aid the Allies (later the amounts would climb).[280] Meanwhile, British American Tobacco feared that its subsidiary, Brown & Williamson Tobacco Company, would be the next "sacrificial lamb." Like American Viscose, Brown & Williamson had been under attack by the U.S. government. As noted earlier, along with its British parent, it had been indicted for antitrust violations in July 1940; the trial was scheduled to begin in June 1941. BAT dreaded the adverse publicity. Unlike American Viscose, which was in first place in U.S. rayon production, Brown & Williamson ranked fourth in U.S. cigarette output.[281] Nonetheless, BAT's management was very uneasy. BAT officials had prepaid British taxes to get in the good graces of the British Treasury.[282] On March 28, they had a long meeting in New York with Gifford to explore the available options.[283] BAT's management would propose that—while it continued to administer its U.S. business—the common stock of Brown & Williamson would be pledged as collateral for a Reconstruction Finance Corporation (RFC) loan *to* Brown & Williamson; BAT would then arrange that the greater part of the dollars borrowed from the RFC would go to the British government. The loan—for $40 million—was negotiated and announced on April 17.[284] No one mentioned the pending antitrust case. The dollars the British government received ($25 million) would be used to pay for the already existing British orders, not covered under the lend-lease legislation.[285]

The BAT arrangements set the stage for more RFC involvement in aid to Britain.[286] John Maynard Keynes went to Washington for talks in mid-May.[287] In June, Congress authorized the RFC to make collateralized loans directly to belligerents.[288] Immediately, Jesse Jones, Federal Loan Administrator, told reporters that an RFC loan to the British government would be provided "secured by the remaining British investment in this country," which Jones estimated at about $900 million to $1 billion (current value). This would give the British dollars to pay off much of the "pre-lend-lease commitments." The later 1941 census report put the approximate value of the collateral at about $700 million.[289] The loan agreement between the United Kingdom and the RFC was made on July 21, 1941; and by the week of the attack on Pearl Harbor, $350 million had been disbursed on the $425 million RFC loan, which was collateralized by British-owned assets deposited with the Federal Reserve Bank of New York.[290] The collateral provides a partial profile of British long-term investments in the United States. Lists on the collateral are contained in the schedules in the agreement.[291] The collateral involved three categories of British investors in the United States: (1) British direct investors (excluding the insurance companies); (2) two separate groups of British insurance companies, one involving subsidiaries and the second branches; and (3) British-held American corporate securities, most of which were traded or were marketable. Table 8.7 provides an alphabetical list of the affected British direct investors, excluding the insurance companies. Among the direct investors, the most significant were the J. & P. Coats group; American Thread Co.; Linen Thread Co.; Dunlop Tire & Rubber Corp.; Oldbury Electro-Chemical Co.; Distillers Co. Ltd. (Del.); United States Potash Co.; and Firth Sterling Steel Co.

British-owned U.S. insurance companies and branches of British insurers supplied a second set of collateral (the branches were not technically collateral; instead, their earnings were to be applied to the interest on and reduction of the loan). Table 8.8 lists the eighty-two British insurance subsidiaries and branches involved, as given in the agreement schedules. Table 8.9 contains the major insurance branch and subsidiary clusters. By far the most prominent groupings were the Royal Insurance Co., its associated Liverpool & London & Globe Insurance Co., the Commercial Union Assurance Co., the Phoenix Assurance Co. Ltd., and the North British & Mercantile Insurance Co. The historian of the Phoenix writes that in connection with this transaction in August 1941 the company "transferred $3.4 million worth of shares in its American subsidiaries as a loan to the British government"; the $3.4 million consisted of $993,500 worth of shares in Columbia Insurance, $912,000 of shares in the Imperial Assurance, $397,508 of shares in United Fireman's Insurance, and $1.1 million in Phoenix Indemnity capital stock. In addition Phoenix would subsequently make available to the British government its U.S. branch earnings.[292]

As the third contribution to the collateral, a wide range of other preferred and common stock of leading American companies was deposited; this included large blocks of Shell Union Oil and General Motors shares. Table 8.10 indicates the traded and marketable securities put up as collateral.[293]

All the direct investments (including those of the insurance company subsidiaries) were "pledged," that is, the British companies maintained ownership but lent their assets to the British government until the RFC

Table 8.7. British direct investments used to collateralize $425 million RFC loan, July 1941 (excluding insurance companies)

Company	Notes
A. J. White Ltd.	Patent medicine[a]
American Association, Inc.	Owned land
American Thread Co.	Thread; parent English Sewing Cotton
Arkwright Finishing Co.	Tracing cloth; parent Winterbottom[b]
Atlantis Sales Co.	Sales; parents Reckett & Sons and J. & J. Coleman[c]
B. Priestley & Co. Inc.	
Baker Perkins Inc.	Food and chemical machinery; parent Baker Perkins Ltd.
C. Tennant Sons & Co. of New York	Wire strapping; associated with Glasgow Tennant group, metal traders; partly owned by British Metal Corp.
Clark Thread Co.	Thread; parent J. & P. Coats[d]
Clark Thread Co. of Georgia	Thread; parent J. & P. Coats[d]
Crown Mills Inc.	Flour mill; parent Balfour, Williamson
Delta Planting Co.	Cotton plantation; parent Fine Cotton Spinners' and Doublers' Association[e]
Delta and Pine Land Co. of Mississippi	Associated with Delta Planting; cotton plantation; parent Fine Cotton Spinners' and Doublers' Association[e]
Dentists Supply of New York*	Sales company; affiliate of Amalgamated Dental Co. Ltd.
Distillers Co. Ltd. (Del.)	Gin; parent Distillers Co.
Dunlop Tire & Rubber Corp.	Rubber tires; parent Dunlop Rubber Co.
Ensign-Bickford Co.*	Explosives, fuses
F. W. Berk & Co. Inc.	Medicines
F. W. Cook Co.*	Brewery
Ferguson-Sherman Mfg. Corp.	Distributor of Ford tractor/Ferguson system
Firth Sterling Steel Co.	Stainless steel, tool steel; parent Firth Brown
Funch, Edye & Co. Inc.	Shipping company
Hecht, Levis & Kahn Inc.	Rubber merchants
Interlaken Mills	Book cloth; parent Winterbottom[b]
J. & P. Coats (R.I.) Inc.	Thread; parent J. & P. Coats[d]
Jonas Brook & Bros. (U.S.A.)	Thread; parent J. & P. Coats[d]
Joseph Tetley & Co. Inc.	Tea; parent Tetley & Co.
Josiah Wedgwood & Sons Inc. of America*	Sales company; parent Josiah Wedgwood
Keasbey & Mattison Co.	Asbestos building products; parent Turner & Newall

Table 8.7 *(continued)*

Company	Notes
Lea & Perrins Inc.	Worcestershire sauce; parent Lea & Perrins
Linen Thread Co. Inc.	Linen thread; parent Linen Thread
Menley & James Ltd.	Medicines; ointments; parent A. J. White Ltd.[a]
Mica Insulator Co.	Building products; parent Associated Insulation Products
Morganite Brush Co. Inc.	Carbon brushes; parent Morgan Crucible
Norma-Hoffmann Bearings Corp.*	Bearings; parent Hoffmann Manufacturing Co.
North Georgia Processing Co. Inc.	Thread related; parent J. & P. Coats[d]
Okonite-Callender Cable Co. Inc.*	Cables; parent Callender Cable
Oldbury Electro-Chemical Co.	Chemicals; phosphorous compounds; parent Albright & Wilson[f]
Pacific Molasses Co. Ltd.	Molasses-related businesses; parent United Molasses
Pembroke Chemical Corp.*	Chemicals; phosphorous related; parent Albright & Wilson[f]
R. T. French Co.	Mustard; parents Reckitt & Sons and J. & J. Coleman[c]
Spool Cotton Co.	Sales company; parent J. & P. Coats[d]
Stowell-MacGregor Corp.	Spools for cotton thread; J. & P. Coats group[d]
Twenty-five Broadway Corp.	Real estate company?
United States Potash Co. Inc.	Potash; parent Borax Consolidated
Yardley of London Inc.	Toilet preparations; parent Yardley & Co.

Sources: The list of companies, which I have alphabetized, comes directly from the Agreement between the United Kingdom of Great Britain and Northern Ireland and Reconstruction Finance Corporation, July 21, 1941, Schedules B-2 (a) and B-2 (b), London 1941, Cmd. 6295, "Loans: RFC," FO 115/3431, Public Record Office. The schedules are on pp. 17–18 of the agreement; p. 5 of the agreement explains the characteristics of the companies listed in Schedules B-2 (a) and B-2 (b). The above table excludes British direct investments in the insurance sector. The notes, which include the British parents, are based on a variety of sources, including information from T. A. B. Corley, Lance Davis, Tab Lewis (National Archives), John Dunning files (University of Reading), Coats Archives (University of Glasgow), as well as a myriad of published company, bank, and industry histories. Only one note cell is left blank, which is because I failed to identify either the product line or the parent company.

Key to multiple companies of a single British parent or set of British parents:

a. Owned by A. J. White.
b. Owned by Winterbottom Book Cloth Co..
c. Owned or partly owned by Reckitt & Sons and J. & J. Coleman.
d. Part of the J. & P. Coats group.
e. Owned by Fine Cotton Spinners' and Doublers' Association.
f. Owned or partly owned by Albright & Wilson.

* In these companies—listed on Schedule B-2 (b)—the British ownership was "substantial." In all the others—listed on Schedule B-2 (a)—the British ownership was said to be "controlling." Schedules B-2 (a) and B-2 (b) provide details on the actual holdings (common stock, "capital stock," and also preferred stock, class of stock, bonds, and so forth that were put up for collateral). No dollar amounts are specified.

Table 8.8. Branches and subsidiaries of British insurance companies used to collateralize $425 million RFC loan, July 1941

No.	Company/branch
1	Albany Insurance Co.
2	Alliance Assurance Co., Ltd.*
3	American & Foreign Insurance Co.
4	American Central Insurance Co.
5	American Union Insurance Co. of New York
6	Atlas Assurance Co., Ltd.*
7	British General Insurance Co., Ltd.*
8	British & Foreign Marine Insurance Co., Ltd.*
9	Caledonian Insurance Co., Ltd.*
10	Caledonian-American Insurance Co.
11	California Insurance Co.
12	Capital Fire Insurance Co. of California
13	Car & General Insurance Co., Ltd.*
14	Central Union Insurance Co.
15	Century Insurance Co., Ltd.*
16	Columbia Insurance Co. of New York
17	Columbia Casualty Co.
18	Commercial Union Fire Insurance Co. of New York
19	Commercial Union Assurance Co., Ltd.*
20	Commonwealth Insurance Co. of New York
21	Eagle Indemnity Co.
22	Eagle Fire Co. of New York
23	Eagle Star Insurance Co., Ltd.*
24	Employers' Liability Assurance Corp., Ltd.*
25	Eureka-Security Fire & Marine Insurance Co.
26	Federal Union Insurance Co.
27	General Accident Fire & Life Assurance Corp., Ltd.*
28	Globe Indemnity Co.
29	Homeland Insurance Co. of America
30	Imperial Assurance Co.
31	Indemnity Marine Assurance Co., Ltd.*
32	Law Union & Rock Insurance Co., Ltd.*
33	Liverpool & London & Globe Insurance Co.*
34	London & Lancashire Indemnity Co. of America
35	London & Lancashire Insurance Co., Ltd.*
36	London & Provincial Marine & General Insurance Co., Ltd.*

Table 8.8 *(continued)*

No.	Company / branch
37	London & Scottish Assurance Corp. Ltd.*
38	London Assurance*
39	London Guarantee & Accident Co. Ltd.*
40	Manhattan Fire & Marine Insurance Co.
41	Marine Insurance Co., Ltd.*
42	Maritime Insurance Co., Ltd.*
43	Mercantile Insurance Co.
44	Monarch Fire Insurance Co.
45	Newark Fire Insurance Co.
46	North British & Mercantile Insurance Co. Ltd.*
47	Northern Assurance Co., Ltd.*
48	Norwich Union Fire Insurance Society, Ltd.*
49	Norwich Union Indemnity Co.
50	Ocean Accident & Guarantee Corporation, Ltd.*
51	Ocean Marine Insurance Co., Ltd.*
52	Orient Insurance Co.
53	Palatine Insurance Co. Ltd.*
54	Pearl Assurance Co., Ltd.*
55	Pennsylvania Fire Insurance Co.
56	Phoenix Assurance Co. Ltd.*
57	Phoenix Indemnity Co.
58	Potomac Insurance Co. of the District of Columbia
59	Providence Fire Insurance Co.
60	Prudential Insurance Co. of Great Britain, located in New York
61	Queen Insurance Co. of America
62	Reliance Marine Insurance Co., Ltd.*
63	Royal Indemnity Co.
64	Royal Exchange Insurance Co., Ltd.*
65	Royal Insurance Co. Ltd.*
66	Safeguard Insurance Co.
67	Scottish Union & National Insurance Co. Ltd.*
68	Sea Insurance Co., Ltd.*
69	Seaboard Fire & Marine Insurance Co. of New York
70	Seaboard Insurance Co.
71	Standard Marine Insurance Co., Ltd.*
72	Star Insurance Co. of America
73	State Assurance Co., Ltd.*

Table 8.8 *(continued)*

No.	Company / branch
74	Sun Underwriters Insurance Co.
75	Sun Insurance Office, Ltd.*
76	Sun Indemnity Co. of New York
77	Thames & Mersey Marine Insurance Co., Ltd.*
78	Union Marine & General Insurance Co., Ltd.*
79	Union Assurance Society, Ltd.*
80	United Firemen's Insurance Co. of Philadelphia
81	Yorkshire Insurance Co. Ltd.*
82	Yorkshire Indemnity Co.

Source: The list, which I have alphabetized, comes from the Agreement between the United Kingdom of Great Britain and Northern Ireland and Reconstruction Finance Corporation, July 21, 1941, Schedules B-1 and C, London 1941, Cmd. 6295, "Loans: RFC," FO 115/3431, Public Record Office (Schedule B-1, containing subsidiaries, is on pp. 16–17, while Schedule C on branches is on p. 20 of the agreement; pp. 4–5 explains the characteristics of the subsidiaries and branches listed in these schedules).

* Branches, listed on Schedule C. All the others are subsidiaries and listed on Schedule B-1.

loan was repaid. By contrast, much of the investment in the "securities of other corporations" was vested, that is, the British government had already acquired ownership of the securities. Table 8.10—part 1—has the first part of the list of securities in Schedule B-3, which appear to have been vested by the British government; part 2 contains a list of securities, also in Schedule B-3, which the *Financial Times* described as nonvested (or pledged), that is, those borrowed by the British government.[294] The distinction between those securities pledged and vested was between a temporary arrangement and a permanent one (the British government borrowed the pledged securities and bought the vested ones from the owners). The returns on all these American investments would go to servicing, reducing, and ultimately paying off the loan. When the loan was repaid, the British government agreed to return all the pledged assets to the full ownership/control of their original owners. The British government had title to the vested securities, which it could hold or sell as it pleased.

Of critical importance, with the direct investments (none of which was vested), during the period that the British government borrowed these assets, no changes were to be made in the managerial control or business operations while the assets remained as collateral.[295] As the historian of one company put it, these British properties "were theoretically in pawn . . . but everything went along normally."[296] The British parent companies obtained from the British Treasury the sterling

Table 8.9. Principal British insurance groups in the United States, 1941

Insurance group
Atlas Assurance Co., Ltd.*
Albany Insurance Co.
Caledonian Insurance Co., Ltd.*
Caledonian-American Insurance Co.
Commercial Union Assurance Co., Ltd.*
American Central Insurance Co.
California Insurance Co.
Columbia Casualty Co.
Commercial Union Fire Insurance Co. of New York
General Accident Fire & Life Assurance Corp., Ltd.*
Potomac Insurance Co. of the District of Columbia
Liverpool & London & Globe Insurance Co.*
Federal Union Insurance Co.
Globe Indemnity Co.
Star Insurance Co. of America
London & Lancashire Insurance Co., Ltd.*
London & Lancashire Indemnity Co. of America
Orient Insurance Co.
Safeguard Insurance Co.
London Assurance*
Manhattan Fire & Marine Insurance Co.
Norwich Union Fire Insurance Society, Ltd.*
Eagle Fire Co. of New York
Norwich Union Indemnity Co.
North British & Mercantile Insurance Co. Ltd.*
Commonwealth Insurance Co. of New York
Homeland Insurance Co. of America
Mercantile Insurance Co.
Pennsylvania Fire Insurance Co.
Phoenix Assurance Co. Ltd.*
Columbia Insurance Co. of New York
Imperial Assurance Co.
United Firemen's Insurance Co. of Philadelphia
Phoenix Indemnity Co.
Royal Exchange Insurance Co., Ltd.*
Providence Fire Insurance Co.

Table 8.9 *(continued)*

Insurance group
Royal Insurance Co. Ltd.*
American & Foreign Insurance Co.
Capital Fire Insurance Co. of California
Eagle Indemnity Co.
Newark Fire Insurance Co.
Queen Insurance Co. of America
Royal Indemnity Co.
Scottish Union & National Insurance Co. Ltd.*
American Union Insurance Co. of New York
Central Union Insurance Co.
Sun Insurance Office, Ltd.*
Sun Indemnity Co. of New York
Sun Underwriters Insurance Co.
Yorkshire Insurance Co. Ltd.*
Seaboard Insurance Co.
Yorkshire Indemnity Co.

Source: Financial Times, July 24, 1941, and Table 8.8. This list contains only 53 branches and subsidiaries compared with the 82 listed in Table 8.8.

* Branch.

equivalent to the income that would have been received from the American subsidiaries and branches.[297] Whether pledged or vested by the British government, these assets remained as British investments in the United States.

The lists of direct investments and stock market securities put up as collateral for the RFC loan (Tables 8.7–8.10) are revealing. First, the highly significant role of the British insurance companies emerges (which had been evident as an undercurrent in the deliberations during the prior months). Although no values were assigned to these insurance assets in the agreement schedules, the year end 1940 "total U.S. assets" of the fifty-three insurance branches and subsidiaries given in Table 8.9 came to more than $805 million.[298]

Second, according to the U.S. Treasury Department census (the results of which were not available in 1941), there were, as of June 14, 1941, 623 British-controlled enterprises in the United States. Roughly 130 (including the insurance subsidiaries and branches) were listed as British direct investments on the agreement schedules (see Tables 8.7–

Table 8.10. British-owned corporate securities used to collateralize $425 million RFC loan, July 1941

Name	Type	Number of shares	Value of bonds
Part 1: Securities included in Schedule B-3 (and in *Financial Times*)			
Shares			
Allied Stores	5% cum pfd	35,000	
Allis-Chalmers Manufacturing Co.	com	19,000	
Amerada Corp.	capital	133,000	
American & Foreign Power	$7 1st cum pfd	100,000	
American Locomotive	7% cum pfd	4,800	
American News Co.	capital	10,000	
American Rolling Mill Co.	com	133,000	
American Smelting & Refining Co.	com	56,000	
American Sugar Refining Co.	7% cum pfd	4,000	
American Telephone & Telegraph Co.	capital	70,000	
American Tobacco	B com	34,000	
Arkansas Power & Light	$7 cum pfd	6,000	
Barnsdall Oil Co.	capital	50,000	
Briggs Manufacturing Co.	capital	35,000	
Chrysler Corp.	com	36,000	
Columbia Gas & Electric	A 6% cum pfd	19,000	
Commercial Investment Trust Corp.	com	59,000	
Commonwealth & Southern Corp.	6% cum pfd	50,000	
Cons'd Gas & Electric—Baltimore	com	11,000	
Continental Baking Co.	8% cum pfd	12,000	
Eastman Kodak Co.	com	57,000	
Electric Power & Light Corp.	$6 cum pfd	15,000	
Flintkote Co.	com	27,000	
First National Bank City of N.Y.	capital	1,500	
General American Transportation Corp.	com	10,000	
General Motors Corp.	com	434,000	
Gillette Safety Razor Co.	$5 cum conv pf	30,000	
Grant (W. T.) Co.	com	11,800	
Great Northern Railway Co.	pfd	44,000	
Ingersoll-Rand Corp.	com	54,000	
Loew's, Inc.	com	34,000	
Lorillard (P.) Co.	com	12,500	

Table 8.10 *(continued)*

Name	Type	Number of shares	Value of bonds
Marlin-Rockwell Corp.	com	7,000	
McGraw Electric Co.	com	22,000	
Monsanto Chemical Co.	com	53,000	
National Biscuit Co.	com	60,000	
New York Air Brake Co.	com	8,500	
Oxford Paper Co.	\$5 cum pf	25,000	
Public Service Corp. of New Jersey	com	24,000	
Radio Corp. of America	com	177,000	
Radio Corp. of America	\$3.50 1st cum conv pfd	8,000	
St Joseph Lead Co.	capital	10,000	
Sears Roebuck & Co.	capital	47,000	
Servel, Inc.	com	30,000	
Shell Union Oil Corp.	com	900,000	
Simmons Co.	capital	17,500	
Socony-Vacuum Oil Co., Inc.	capital	130,000	
Standard Brands, Inc.	com	170,000	
Standard Oil Co. (Indiana)	capital	315,000	
Sterling Products, Inc.	capital	36,000	
Timken Roller Bearing Co.	com	19,000	
Tri-Continental Corp.	\$6 cum pfd	30,000	
United Shoe Machinery Corp.	com	15,000	
United States Steel Corp	7% cum pfd	21,000	
Vick Chemical Co.	capital	10,000	
Westinghouse Air Brake Co.	capital	40,000	
Wheeling Steel Corp.	\$5 cum conv prior pfd	7,000	
Woolworth (F. W.) Co.	capital	247,000	
Youngstown Sheet & Tube Co.	com	75,000	
Bonds			
American & Foreign Power	5% debs, Mar. 1 2023		\$2,750,000
Cities Service Power & Light	5½% debs, Nov. 1, 1952		\$350,000

Table 8.10 *(continued)*

Name	Type	Number of shares	Value of bonds
Part 2: Securities included in Schedule B-3 *and* described in the *Financial Times* as "non-vested listed securities"			
Shares			
Celanese of America	7% cum prior pfd	50,000	
Celanese of America	7% cum 1st ptg pfd	40,000	
Celanese of America	com	230,000	
Chicago Pneumatic Tool	$3 cum conv pf	30,000	
Climax Molybdenum	com	80,000	
Congoleum-Nairn	com	300,000	
Dividend Shares, Inc.	capital	3,800,000	
Grace (W. R.) & Co.	8% cum A pfd	4,700	
Grace (W. R.) & Co.	8% non-cum B pfd	4,100	
Grace (W. R.) & Co.	6% cum pfd	3,400	
Grace (W. R.) & Co.	com	26,400	
Gt Northern Iron Ore Props	certs of ben interest	70,000	
International Paper & Power	5% cum conv pfd	50,000	
Morrell (John) and Co.	com	57,000	
Pure Oil	5% cum conv pfd	9,000	
Singer Manufacturing	capital	95,000	
Standard Oil (New Jersey)	capital	180,000	
U.S. and International Securities Corp.	$5 cum 1st pfd	30,000	
Bonds			
Cities Service Power & Light	5% conv gold debs, June 1, 1950		$1,250,000
Virginian Corp.	5% serial note M Jan. 1, 1952		$1,974,000

Source: Agreement between the United Kingdom of Great Britain and Northern Ireland and Reconstruction Finance Corporation, July 21, 1941, Schedule B-3, London 1941, Cmd. 6295, "Loans: RFC," FO 115/3431, Public Record Office (Schedule B-3 with listing). *Financial Times*, July 23, 1941 (part 1); *Financial Times*, July 23, 24, and 26 (part 2). Abbreviations: ben: beneficial; certs: certificates; com: common; conv: convertible; cum: cumulative; debs: debentures; non-cum: non-cumulative; pf: preference; pfd: preferred; prior: priority; ptg: participating. A and B were classes of securities.

Notes: The securities entered in parts 1 and 2 were listed in Schedule B-3, with the second group following the first group that was in alphabetical order. The *Financial Times*, July 24, 1941 (with a correction, July 26, 1941), wrote that most of the stocks on Schedule B-3 were vested, but the list "also included the following [which I have put in part 2] securities which have not hitherto been subject of a vesting order." Schedule B-3 does not indicate whether securities were vested or pledged. The securities included in part 2 appear to have been "pledged" to the British government rather than vested. These securities were different from the ones included in Schedules B-1 and B-2 and Schedule C, since the latter were not typically traded, that is, were considered to be direct investments. These for the most part were traded, marketable securities.

8.8).[299] What can be said about the rest? Courtaulds' U.S. business was not part of the collateral, nor should it have been in the census, since it had been sold by June 14, 1941. British American Tobacco and its several affiliates were excluded from the collateral list because BAT had made the separate arrangements. Imperial Tobacco, described in the 1941 antitrust case as the largest buyer of flue tobacco in the United States, is not on the list (was that because of the size of the investment?).[300] Many of those omitted from the roster of direct investments appear to have been relatively small (properties valued under $500,000) and thus hardly worth the effort to chase down for collateral purposes. A handful were larger and simply appear to have been overlooked. Certain omissions—such as the borax interests of Borax Consolidated—are very hard to explain (the potash interests of Borax Consolidated were included).[301] Particular British businesses in America were apparently purposely excluded.[302] At least one stake was not available for collateral because it was already being used as collateral for other borrowings.[303] The sizable Lever and Lipton interests were in 1941 Dutch owned and thus not in the category of British investments (but they should not have been in the U.S. Treasury census' 623 total). Some direct investments were in companies that had securities listed on stock exchanges and can be found on another schedule (see Table 8.10) [304]

"Collateral" presumably can be realized through sales. The British (and the RFC) seem to have decided that there was no established market for certain properties, and such assets were omitted from the lists.[305] Aside from the insurance branches and subsidiaries, no British financial institutions were on the direct investment schedules. British mortgage companies with their remaining investments in mortgages and real estate were not on the lists of direct investment, probably in this case because the plan was that these assets would be gradually liquidated so as to maximize the return of dollars to Britain. Likewise, some large cattle properties were absent. In short, the forty-six companies listed in Table 8.7, along with the eighty-two insurance companies included in Table 8.8, did not by any means represent the sum total of British direct investments in America; this was, to repeat, a partial profile.

Third, the group of securities put up as collateral contained only one railroad, Great Northern Railway (44,000 preferred shares).[306] This seemed extraordinary, given the earlier immense involvements. Apparently, in 1941, Kuhn, Loeb & Co. bought large blocks of vested railway shares from the British government and fed them into the American market (see earlier discussion). The principal British holdings in American railroads, which survived the liquidation during World War I and had weathered the post-1929 downturn and the 1930s, were, it seems likely, finally disposed of in 1941.[307] Railroads had become passé as investment securities.[308] Perhaps, moreover, the remaining railroad holdings were not considered suitable collateral.[309]

Fourth, the list of traded securities (Table 8.10) has only four bonds—American and Foreign Power Company, two Cities Service Power and Light Company debentures, and the Virginian Corporation serial note. The later published 1941 census of total long-term foreign investments in the United States revealed that of the domestic American securities (portfolio investments) held in the United Kingdom, a mere 7 percent were in corporate bonds.[310] This, too, is striking. On the eve of World War I, the bulk of American securities owned in Britain had been bonds. The shift in British holdings from debt to equity had taken place gradually from 1914 to 1941 and had probably accelerated in the 1939–1941 period.[311]

Fifth, there are no surprises in the list of dollar securities given in Table 8.10, those held in the United Kingdom and considered "marketable," that is, suitable for collateral. The companies included (with very few exceptions) were well known and probably obvious choices for British investment trusts; some had been part of wealthy Britishers' portfolios for many years. The list has a wide range of industrials and public utilities, plus a few American "investment trusts," precursors of today's mutual funds: Commercial Investment Trust Corp., Dividend Shares Inc., Tri-Continental Corp., and U.S. and International Securities Corp.[312] Some securities on the roster of traded securities were associated with British direct investments in the United States of a prior era—for example, the interests in Allis-Chalmers, Amerada Corp., Radio Corporation of America, Standard Oil Co. (Ind.), W. R. Grace & Co., and John Morrell & Co.[313] The 230,000 common shares in Celanese of America represented 22.4 percent of its common shares outstanding, while the 300,000 shares in Congoleum-Nairn equaled 24.1 percent of its common shares outstanding; Celanese of America and Congoleum-Nairn securities were "pledged."[314] On the other hand, it is of interest that the large blocks of General Motors and Shell Union Oil Corp. shares were vested.[315] With Celanese of America and Congoleum-Nairn the British securities' owners obviously wanted a continuing relationship after the Second World War, while these British investors in General Motors and Shell Union Oil Corp. shares had no such commitment.

When the U.S. Treasury Department census tabulated British investments in the United States—as of June 14, 1941—it found $587.5 million in securities and $711.5 million in direct investments. Unlike the overall total of foreign investments in the United States (where investments from abroad in securities still exceeded those in direct investments), because of the sales of securities from the outbreak of war to June 1941, according to these figures, British direct investments had come to surpass those in securities.[316]

After the RFC loan collateral was arranged and before the end of 1941, there would be some, but not substantial, additional liquidations of British investments in the United States; more small divestments took place after the United States entered the war. The oft-stated proposition that the British were required to dispose of all their American investments before becoming eligible for lend lease may have been the American intention and, surely was part of the rhetoric of the era. It failed to conform with the reality.[317] American Viscose aside, none of the operations of the British manufacturing multinationals nor of the British insurers was in any way impeded because of the British dollar requirements. Although the British affiliates were used as collateral for the RFC loan, their business went forward under their existing management. Indeed, by August 14, 1941, when Roosevelt and Churchill issued the Atlantic Charter—heralding future economic cooperation—the crisis over British assets in the United States had been for all practical purposes resolved. Although the subject would resurface sporadically, the plans for future economic, political, and military Anglo-American cooperation were not further muddied by acrimony over the disposition of British assets in the United States.

Conclusions

Between the start of September 1939 and the first week of December 1941, radical changes took place in the status of much of the long-term foreign investment in the United States, shaped in a fundamental manner by the domestic ramifications of the war abroad. The assets of investors from thirty-one European and two Asian nations were frozen and put under the U.S. Treasury's Foreign Funds Control oversight. The Proclaimed List affected the trade patterns of foreign multinationals. The Justice Department indicted and charged a number of foreign companies and their U.S. affiliates with antitrust violations. German businesses in the United States scampered to fine-tune the camouflaging of their stakes and, in doing so, often ostensibly at least disposed of their U.S. interests. British affiliates in the United States sought assurance that they would not be dealing with the enemy through neutral America. There was a brief period of British government investments in munitions plants in the United States. Canadian-owned enterprises in the United States stayed in business, albeit Canadian portfolio investments in domestic securities declined, as did U.K. portfolio holdings and even more sharply. Dutch, Belgian, Swiss, Swedish, and French investors maintained business, adjusting to the asset "freeze." Corporate structures became ever more complex and arcane. All inward investments were shaped by the new rules and regulations. The

Japanese rapidly reduced their exposure, before but particularly after their assets were blocked. In March 1941, U.S. lend lease had been inaugurated; in April 1941, the Hyde Park Declaration heralded close U.S.-Canadian economic cooperation. Although it seems clear that by most measures *total* foreign investments in the United States were smaller in 1941 than in 1939, all the available statistics indicate that the amounts were larger in 1941 than they had been in 1929, much less 1933 (see Table 2.1).

British long-term assets in the United States stayed as the largest of any foreign nationality. The British would claim (in 1942) that "British assets used in the United States" to buy munitions were a "main instrument in building up American war industry."[318] Notwithstanding the decline in the level of British investments, as investments (principally portfolio ones) were liquidated to obtain dollars to purchase U.S. supplies, British investments in the United States did persist. A large part of those remaining British assets in the United States served as collateral on the Reconstruction Finance Corporation loan, announced in June 1941, and linked with the provisions of the Lend-Lease Act. Later, the U.S. Treasury would estimate that British government-induced sales of its nationals' American assets, including the sale of American Viscose along with the private divestments of portfolio interests, came to $600,000.[319]

For the first time since 1853, the U.S. Treasury in 1941 conducted a census of foreign assets in the United States. On publication in 1945, the report stated, "Never before has a full record of all types of foreign-owned United States assets been available as a point of reference for work in this field."[320] Indeed, this was far more extensive than the 1853 survey, which the authors seem to have known nothing about.[321] Table 8.3 herein, prepared from the 1941 census, supplied a summary overview of the status of inward long-term foreign investments, less than six months before U.S. entry into the global war. Given the contemporary tensions and the cloaking devices, the census results were very imperfect. Nonetheless, it is clear that on the eve of America's entry into World War II, there were substantial long-term foreign investments in the United States, far more than contemporaries had realized.

9.

World War II, 1941–1945

With the bombing of Pearl Harbor on December 7, 1941, Japan and the United States were at war; on December 11, the United States declared war on Germany and Italy. Before the shock of Pearl Harbor, Americans had made plans on how under wartime conditions they would cope with inward foreign investments. The Treasury Department's Foreign Funds Control group was cooperating with other agencies in the Treasury Department (including Customs, the National Bank Examiners, the Coast Guard, the Secret Service, and the Internal Revenue Department), as well as with the Federal Reserve, the State Department, the Justice Department, the Navy Department, the Maritime Commission, the Securities and Exchange Commission, the Federal Bureau of Investigation, the Office of Naval Intelligence, Army Intelligence—and also with the British—to hunt down Axis infiltration in the nation and "to follow the money trail." The staff of the Treasury Department was convinced that in the interwar years, German interests had reorganized themselves within the United States as "an industrial and commercial network, centered in chemicals but penetrating also the electrical and heavy goods industries." The men at Treasury saw such activities as constituting "a base of operations for carrying out Axis plans for supporting fifth-column movements and for creating an economy geared to an Axis-dominated world."[1]

Because of the existence of Foreign Funds Control, and the already blocked assets, when the United States declared itself at war, Treasury Department officials could act at once to attend to what were now "enemy" properties. On the day after the attack on Pearl Harbor, the Treasury Department—working with the New York State banking authority—"took possession of the Japanese bank agencies in New York."[2] The Treasury Department issued a press release stating, "No

Japanese bank, business enterprise, or other organization now has the status of a generally licensed national, including the Yokohama Specie Bank, Ltd. and all its branches, the Bank of Taiwan, the Sumitomo Bank of Hawaii, the Sumitomo Bank of California, the Sumitomo Bank of Seattle, and the Pacific Bank, Honolulu."[3] Two days later, Louis Pink, the New York State superintendent of insurance, filed an application to the courts on the dissolution and liquidation of the assets of the U.S. branches of three Japanese insurance companies (Tokyo Marine and Fire Insurance Co., Meiji Fire Insurance Co., and Sumitomo Marine and Fire Insurance Co.).[4] The Treasury Department took part in the takeovers of these state government-regulated banks and insurance companies.

Steps against German and Italian properties were equally swift. On December 11, the very day the United States went to war with Germany and Italy, the Treasury Department shut down the New York office of Chemnyco (I. G. Farben's liason office).[5] It also took over the assets of the four Italian bank agencies in New York, Banca Commerciale Italiana, Banco di Napoli, Banco di Roma, and Credito Italiano.[6] The next day, the Treasury Department installed five of its own men at the main New York offices of General Aniline & Film Corporation (GAF) and at each of the latter's three principal plants: its film factory at Binghampton, New York, and its dye factories at Rensselaer, New York, and Linden, New Jersey.[7] An employee at the research laboratories of GAF's photographic division in Binghampton recalled that most of the department heads were German; they were at once suspended from their positions.[8]

The same day that Treasury Department men occupied GAF facilities, they assumed control of the Harvard Brewing Company in Lowell, Massachusetts (the brewery was owned by the German von Opel family, through a Swiss intermediary).[9] That day, the Treasury Department sent guards to the Bloomfield and Union, New Jersey, facilities of the Schering Corporation.[10] On December 15, the Treasury took charge at American Bosch Corporation.[11] Germany, Italy, and Japan were "enemies"; the Treasury Department acted even before the passage of the War Powers Act of December 18, 1941, which amended the 1917 Trading with the Enemy Act (TEA).

Indeed, on December 18, Secretary of the Treasury Henry Morgenthau submitted a report to President Roosevelt on the administration of Foreign Funds Control from its inception in April 1940 to that date. Morgenthau forwarded a copy to Vice-President Henry Wallace, who was also head of the Board of Economic Warfare (the BEW was the renamed Board of Economic Defense).[12] At that time, "the Control covered $7 billion of assets and the transactions of 33 countries." The report declared that through the Control "we are taking appropriate steps to nullify or eliminate vicious and undesirable influences in business enterprises in this country owned and dominated by the Axis." The Treasury Department had built a highly flexible organization suitable for "modern economic warfare." Five hundred individuals at the New York Federal Reserve (along with a smaller group at other Federal Reserve banks) handled the daily procedures of the Control. Another 650 individuals in Washington managed other aspects. This administrative structure had enabled the Treasury Department to respond immediately once the United States had become a belligerent.[13]

The Treasury Department continued to pursue the takeover of enemy assets. On January 13, 1942, it removed five senior executives of General Aniline & Film (all naturalized American citizens).[14] One of those ousted was F. W. von Meister, head of the Ozalid Division of GAF. By leasing and servicing blueprinting machines, Ozalid employees had gained access to some 3,500 industrial plants in the United States (including defense establishments); the Treasury Department thought this was particularly dangerous.[15] On January 29, the Treasury Department fired Julius Weltzien and seven other Schering employees, barring them from the Schering premises.[16] On February 16, the secretary of the treasury sequestered more than 97 percent of the shares of GAF on the grounds that "the real interest in these shares is German" (the owner of record was the Swiss company I. G. Chemie).[17] By the spring of 1942, Foreign Funds Control had shut down certain enemy enterprises "whose activities endangered national interest and had taken over the management of more than fifty other ['enemy'] firms."[18]

On March 18, the Treasury Department in "General Ruling No. 11" made it unlawful, unless licensed under the freezing regulations, for any trade to take place or any communication to occur with an enemy national. The ruling forbade trade or communication with anyone in "enemy territory," which included Germany, Italy, and Japan and the areas under their control; "any person whose name appears on the Proclaimed List, or 'black list'"; or any representative of an enemy government (inside or outside enemy territory).[19] This ruling was very specific on particular practices: a person (which included a corporate person) could trade or communicate with anyone in Latin America, unless that person was on the black list or was known to represent an enemy. "Thus" the ruling read, "a person may deal with the Buenos Aires branch of an Italian firm so long as such branch is not placed on the black list or is not known to be acting as a cloak for a Proclaimed List national or for the Axis. Of course, a person may not trade or communicate with such Latin American branch if in fact he intends to use this as a device for actually communicating with the head office of the firm in Italy."[20] By this time, the Treasury Department was highly knowledgeable on the networks of international business contacts and sought to define what was and was not appropriate in wartime.

On April 24, the Treasury Department arranged for the sale of General Aniline & Film's then-existing holdings of 153,053 shares of the common stock of Standard Oil Company (New Jersey).[21] Back in 1929, I. G. Farben had acquired 546,011 shares of this giant, the largest American oil company. In time, some (perhaps most or all) of I. G. Farben's stock holdings had been transferred to American I. G. Chemical, the predecessor of GAF.[22] American I. G. and then GAF had gradually sold off these shareholdings in Standard Oil (New Jersey), using the dollars received to reduce the principal of American I. G.'s 1929 bond issue and to pay interest on that debt (bonds guaranteed by I. G. Farben). As of March 31, 1938, American I. G. had owned 289,225 shares of Standard Oil (New Jersey).[23] A year later, it held 220,548 shares; as of December 31, 1940, GAF's stake was reduced to 203,053 shares, and by December 31, 1941, to 153,053 shares. These were the shares that were sold to the American public on April 24, 1942, by Morgan, Stanley & Co. through a group of dealers and brokers. GAF agreed to apply the proceeds from this stock sale to the redemption of a portion of its 1929 U.S. bond issue. The debt that American I. G. had incurred was $30 million in 1929; as of April 24, there was still $18 million outstanding on the 5.5 percent bonds, due May 1, 1949, and callable at par.[24] That day the vested stock in GAF itself (vested by the Treasury Department in February 1942) was taken over by the newly established Office of Alien Property Custodian (set up March 11, 1942).[25] In short, in the early months after U.S. entry into the war, the vigilant Treasury Department was the principal U.S. government agency deputized to deal with enemy-owned enterprises in the United States; it acted aggressively, owing to its familiarity with the overall situation.

Court Cases

The Treasury Department was not alone in its pursuit of enemy businesses; it was joined by the Justice Department, which had a separate agenda. The Justice Department had embarked on an antitrust crusade, designed to reinvigorate the U.S. economy. In the aftermath of U.S. entry into the war, the department issued new indictments against international cartels, resolved certain pending cases, and in a host of instances reluctantly postponed other cases. When there were postponements, the department's intention was to revive the antitrust campaign as soon as feasible. Its antitrust program was comprehensive and in no way limited to enemy or to foreign enterprises. Yet, just as before

U.S. entry, once the United States had become a combatant, the suits involving German businesses or their U.S. affiliates were perceived as being not only associated with eliminating restrictions on competition but also identified with protecting national security.

Litigation (and solutions) barreled forward from December 1941, and the number that affected foreign enterprises and their U.S. affiliates was awesome. On December 17, in the "hormone cases," the Justice Department filed a collection of bills of complaint in criminal cases in the District Court of New Jersey against a group of foreign affiliates and their management. The defendants (which included four German- and Swiss-owned affiliates—Schering Corp., Ciba Pharmaceutical Products, Roche-Organon, and Rare Chemicals—and five of their principal executives) entered pleas of nolo contendere and were fined, thus resolving these cases.[26] In a separate civil case the same day, the identical defendants signed a consent decree, prohibiting them from further activities in violation of the antitrust laws. Schering Corp. agreed to cancel all its agreements with Schering AG.[27] In yet another related civil case that day, the Swiss Bank Corporation accepted a consent decree that ordered it to arrange the sale of its stock and that of Chemical and Pharmaceutical Enterprises Ltd. (Chepha) in the Schering Corp.[28] The goal was to dismantle what the Justice Department saw as cartel relationships.

Two days later, three separate criminal indictments were issued against General Aniline & Film, addressing its associations with I. G. Farben: the first indictment covered dyestuffs, the second photographic materials, and the third photo-printing materials.[29] These three so-called New York cases remained pending and did not go to trial during the war years.[30] After the United States joined the war, SONJ's patent infringement suit against Goodrich (related to German patents) was dismissed; under the auspices of the Rubber Reserve Company, the oil company agreed to participate in patent pooling for buna rubber technologies.[31] On February 18, 1942, a consent decree concluded one of the antitrust suits in a nitrate cartel case against Imperial Chemical Industries.[32]

On March 25, SONJ accepted a comprehensive consent decree that required it to sever all ties with I. G. Farben. The oil enterprise was enjoined from having any future relations with I. G. Farben without informing the Justice Department. It was, moreover, ordered, during the "present emergency" (the war), to license or sublicense royalty-free all the patents held by Standard Catalytic Co. and Jasco, which comprised patents it had obtained from I. G. Farben in rubber as well as other critical products and processes.[33] This decree settled the U.S. government suit, which had been initiated in November 1941.[34] On

April 15, the Justice Department obtained a consent decree in the case against the Aluminum Company of America (Alcoa), Dow Chemical, American Magnesium Corp., and Magnesium Development Corp., relating to magnesium and magnesium products; the decree forbade these defendants from making any contracts with I. G. Farben "without filing with the Department of Justice a copy of such contract within ten days after the date thereof."[35] With these decrees achieved, Assistant Attorney General Thurman Arnold, in charge of antitrust, boasted, "We compelled the Standard Oil to give their patents royalty free [these were the rubber and other patents] and we got the compulsory license out of Dow Chemical [re: magnesium]."[36] Arnold was triumphant yet still not entirely satisfied in his quest to uphold America's antitrust law.

His further campaign would, however, have to be temporarily suspended: in March 1942, the Justice Department had "agreed to postpone the trial of antitrust cases when in the opinion of the War or Navy Department immediate prosecution would interfere with war production by the defendants."[37] Thus, the trial already under way of General Electric, NV Philips, and other defendants in an incandescent lamp case was in 1942 delayed at the request of the secretaries of war and navy.[38] A case against General Electric that included Krupp and the Carboloy Company was also placed on hold.[39]

In May 1942, however, the Justice Department filed a fourth antitrust suit against General Aniline & Film (this one in the District Court of New Jersey); as in the "New York" cases, GAF was not the only defendant. The charge in this case, *U.S. v. Allied Chemical & Dye Corp.*, was restraint of trade in dyestuffs. Other corporate defendants included Du Pont, American Cyanamid, General Dyestuff Corp., Ciba Co., Sandoz Chemical Works, and Geigy Co., as well as ten individuals associated with these companies. Among the coconspirators, named but not indicted, were I. G. Farben, the parent companies of the three Swiss-owned American affiliates, and Imperial Chemical Industries. Indeed, all the important participants in the global dyestuff industry were listed, as either defendants or coconspirators. The Justice Department agreed to delay the trial, at the request of the War Department.[40] The "Mother Hubbard" suit against the oil companies, in which Shell was a defendant, was also postponed.[41] Still, as late as August 10, 1942, the Justice Department was filing new indictments of Rohm & Haas and Du Pont—followed by agreed suspensions in pursuing the litigation. In one of these cases, I. G. Farben, Imperial Chemical Industries, and Röhm and Haas, AG, Darmstadt, were named as coconspirators.[42] In the background in many of these cases was the question of whether foreign parents, or foreign firms that had licensing and other arrangements with

American ones, were within the jurisdiction of U.S. courts.[43] In 1943 and particularly in 1944, the Justice Department was once again wielding the antitrust cudgel. Indeed, antitrust, "economic democracy," and "political democracy" seemed intimately allied—at least in the view of the Justice Department. Meanwhile, in February 1942, a deputy of Thurman Arnold had brought into the Justice Department James Stewart Martin, who set up and would head within that department the Economic Warfare Section, designed to investigate international business relationships that might benefit the enemy.[44]

The Office of Alien Property Custodian

From the time that the United States had declared war, the Foreign Funds Control group within the Treasury Department—which ran the "blocked assets" program—had been the principal U.S. government agency involved in dealing with enemy properties. It lobbied to maintain its "exclusive rights" in this domain. At the same time, however, Attorney General Francis Biddle believed the Justice Department should be playing a more prominent role vis-à-vis enemy assets. Not only was the Justice Department targeting foreign-owned firms for antitrust violations (as it had for some time), but since 1934, when the World War I Alien Property Custodian's office had shut its doors, an Alien Property Bureau in the Justice Department had dealt with residual matters; then, in February 1942, it had started the Economic Warfare Section. Justice Department officials argued that the Alien Property Bureau should maintain authority over enemy property, or better still, there should be reestablished, as during the First World War, a new Alien Property Custodian. Biddle thought the World War I APC ought to be the model for the World War II administration of enemy properties.[45]

The Treasury Department demurred, insisting that the situation was different from that in 1917. For almost fifteen years before U.S. entry into the hostilities in 1941, Axis business interests had "been taking comprehensive steps to insulate themselves against an alien property custodianship with its seizure of legal title. As a result . . . only a negligible portion of Axis-influenced property would pass into the hands of a custodian whose powers are limited to the seizure of 'enemy' title." The "title" concept, it asserted, was outmoded. "The title to some of the most dangerous of the Axis-influenced enterprises is Swiss, Dutch, or Panamanian. Other enterprises are 100 percent American so far as the title is concerned." The Treasury Department insisted that often the Axis connections were to be discovered in contracts and patent licensing arrangements. Alliances frequently were "informal, based on personal fealty or family relations." Accordingly, it favored retaining "the flexible procedure of foreign funds control," claiming it had the experience, the knowledge of the subterfuges, and the ability to pierce the corporate veils.[46]

Roosevelt rejected, however, the jurisdictional arguments of Secretary of the Treasury Henry Morgenthau and authorized setting up an Office of Alien Property Custodian, under the newly passed War Powers Act of December 18, 1941. The War Powers Act effectively formalized the "flexibility" that the Treasury Department wanted.[47] On March 11, 1942, within the Office of Emergency Management, the Office of Alien Property Custodian (OAPC) came into being. Roosevelt put Leo Crowley in charge; Crowley and Morgenthau had long been at loggerheads with one another.[48]

Executive Order 9142 of April 21 spelled out the relationships between the Justice Department and the OAPC and turned over to the latter the residual World War I activities of the Justice Department's Alien Property Bureau; most Justice Department–initiated investigations of enemy properties done prior to the establishment of OAPC were transferred to the new agency.[49] On May 19, the attorney general formed within the War Division of the Justice Department the Alien Property Unit (subsequently to be renamed the Alien Property Litigation Unit), which worked closely with the OAPC, representing the latter in court cases and offering advice on legal strategies.[50] The Economic Warfare Section remained in the Justice Department. The associations between the OAPC and the Justice Department were harmonious.

This was not true between the OAPC and the Treasury Department. Not until July 1942 was there a clarification of the exact functions of OAPC and the Treasury Department and a mandate for the two agencies to put an end to their bickering. Under a new executive order, the Treasury Department would hold control over foreign-owned property subject to the authority of the OAPC until that control was formally assumed by the OAPC. The Treasury Department also continued to retain "power over" all other "blocked" foreign-owned assets not under the jurisdiction of the OAPC.[51] At last, the roles of the Justice Department, OAPC, and the Treasury Department were delineated. Thereafter, Justice and OAPC cooperated with one another, but the same could not be said for Treasury and OAPC, where the relationships continued to be fraught with conflict.[52]

Undeterred by the disputes, the Office of Alien Property Custodian had embarked on its task of taking over enemy assets. On April 18, 1942, it vested 43,994 shares of the common and 2,225 shares of the preferred stock of Schering Corp., New Jersey, a company already under the charge of the Treasury Department.[53] On April 24, it took over most of the vested stock of General Aniline & Film, once again from the Treasury Department; and on June 30, it vested all the shares of the capital stock of General Dyestuff Corp.[54] One of its earliest vesting orders involved 5,000 shares of Magnesium Development Corp.[55] On May 19, the custodian had vested 77 percent of the stock of American Bosch Co. "because after investigation he had concluded that Germans held the controlling interest in this stock."[56] In August, OAPC vested 37.6 percent of the stock of Rohm & Haas.[57] Later in 1942 it would vest 90.79 percent of the shares in American Potash & Chemical Corp., as well as an option held by the "Hope Syndicate," entitling the latter to buy 5,000 shares of American Potash held by Gold Fields American Development Co., Ltd.[58] According to economist Jesse Markham, the U.S. government assumed control over the plants of the North American Rayon Corp., the American Bemberg Corp., and American Enka and operated them during the war, under OAPC orders.[59]

From its start, the Office of Alien Property Custodian was fully aware that the identification of ownership and control of properties had "been complicated by widespread efforts which have been made by enemy nationals to conceal or cloak beneficial ownership." It found, as had the Treasury Department before it, that German firms had used complex holding company structures in neutral countries and a range of other "cloaking devices." The cloaking was of both tangible assets and patent ownership.[60] The OAPC accepted the view of the Treasury Department that because of the disguises, the enemy could not be defined by the actual title holder.[61]

In his first annual report, covering March 11, 1942, to June 30, 1943, Alien Property Custodian Crowley concluded that the enemy-owned property in the United States at the beginning of World War II was less than at the time of our entry into World War I. The report explained that between 1920 and 1939 the countries with which we were at war were not in an economic position to export substantial capital. (Moreover, unlike during World War I, when German investment in the United States was greater than U.S. investment in Germany, the opposite was true now.) Rigid controls on exchange transactions during the 1930s had "tended to keep" German and other enemy capital from migrating to the United States. This notwithstanding, Crowley concluded that the amount of enemy-owned property in the United States "was still rather substantial at the time of our entry into this war," and "much of it was of strategic importance in American industry."[62] The OAPC's goal was to eliminate any benefit to the enemy from these U.S. assets, while at the same time using the latter to promote America's war effort.

During the First World War, the Alien Property Custodian had been responsible for all enemy property. Its mandate in 1942 was not that broad. Distinctions were made between two groups of enemy assets: first, cash and investment securities, not involving "control over specific productive assets," which the OAPC left under the ongoing jurisdiction of the Treasury Department; and, second, business enterprises, patents and trademarks, and real and personal property, including estates and trusts that were under the OAPC. The OAPC would handle this second category of enemy property in three ways: (1) with vesting orders, which meant an outright transfer of the title to the OAPC; (2) with supervisory orders, that is, interim protective devices while the true beneficial ownership was being investigated (with supervisory orders, the OAPC assumed "direction, management, and supervision of the property," but not the title); and (3) with general orders, which made the property subject to regulation.[63]

In its first fifteen months of existence, the APC issued 1,792 vesting orders, but the dollar total of vested enemy interests came to merely $125 million. Only 361 vesting orders affected business enterprises (estates and trusts constituted the vast majority of the vested properties).[64] The largest corporation vested by OAPC was General Aniline & Film, with assets as of March 31, 1942, of $68.75 million.[65] Other large and important firms vested in 1942 included American Bosch, American Potash & Chemical, General Dyestuff, Schering, Mitsubishi Shoji Kaisha (U.S. branches), and Yokohama Specie Bank (U.S. branches).[66] In addition, in its first annual report, OAPC indicated it had secured supervisory control over properties valued at $20 million; it did not reveal the number or names of the properties that were subject to supervisory control.[67]

By contrast, with the relatively limited number of businesses (particularly large-scale ones) affected by vesting or supervisory orders, 36,000 patents and 5,000 patent applications were vested in the fifteen months surveyed by the first annual report. OAPC did not assign any values to these patents and patent applications, which were in most industrial sectors but were markedly concentrated in chemicals (including plastics and pharmaceuticals) and electrical equipment. There were also key patents and patent applications related to production of ordnance and aircraft. The vested patents included those of "enemy residents" (meaning companies and individuals resident in enemy countries) and also of residents of enemy-occupied countries. This inclusiveness was peculiar to patents (other properties of nationals of enemy-occupied nations, not identified as beneficially enemy owned, remained under the jurisdiction of the Treasury Department's continuing Foreign Funds Control program). The patents vested corresponded to approximately 5 percent of the total number of unexpired patents in 1942 registered with the

U.S. Patent Office.[68] As for shipping, one vesting order covered twenty-seven Italian and two German ships. (The ships, "seized" by the U.S. government early in 1942 before the OAPC was established, were under the administrative control of the Maritime Commission and the War Shipping Administration.)[69] The OAPC became "an interested" party in a bevy of court cases involving the shipping companies.[70]

The manufacturing operations and patents that the OAPC took over in its first fifteen months were principally German; the trading companies, banks, and insurance firms overwhelmingly Japanese; ships excepted, the OAPC reported Italian assets to be of minor significance; and "little or no property of consequence" was discovered belonging to nationals of Roumania, Hungary, or Bulgaria.[71] The OAPC's first annual report indicated that some 200 enterprises that it had taken over were already being liquidated; these were mainly trading companies, banks, and insurance offices. If possible, the Alien Property Custodian arranged that vested manufacturing plants would do war work for the Allies.[72] All the patents of enemy nationals not already under exclusive license to Americans were available to be licensed by the OAPC on a nonexclusive, royalty-free basis. Patents of nationals of enemy-occupied nations not already under license to Americans were to be licensed on a royalty-free basis for the duration of the war (with provision for reasonable royalty payments at war's end). The difficulty was that many (indeed most) of the vested patents were already under license to U.S. companies and, thus, not available for licensing by the OAPC. In addition, many of these licensing arrangements, as the OAPC first annual report noted, were "tied up with agreements restricting price, production, use, sale, and market area." The Justice Department, with its antitrust agenda, examined these associations. The OAPC report added that whenever possible these contracts would be modified to remove the restrictions and make the patents more generally available.[73] The aim—promoted strongly by the Justice Department—was to eliminate the cartel-type restraint-of-trade provisions that were often tied in with patents and patent licensing arrangements.

The Office of Alien Property Custodian lasted from March 11, 1942, to October 14, 1946—through the uncertainties of 1942 and 1943 (with the Axis offensives and the Allied counteroffensives), through the turn-of-the-tide in 1943 and the campaigns of 1944, through V-E Day (the victory in Europe, May 8, 1945) and V-J Day (the victory over Japan, August 14, 1945), and well into the next year. On September 3, 1943, Italy signed an armistice with the Allies, and on October 13, 1943, it joined in the war against Germany; at the request of the State Department, the OAPC stopped classifying Italy as an enemy.[74]

Table 9.1 covers the activities of the OAPC from its origins through its last fiscal year, under Crowley and his successor. On March 27, 1944,

Table 9.1. Activities of Office of Alien Property Custodian, 1942–1946

Activity	Mar. 11, 1942– June 30, 1943	Year end June 30, 1944	Year end June 30, 1945	Year end June 30, 1946
Dollar value of vested enemy properties (in millions)	$125	$212.4	$242	$368
Dollar value of properties under control of OAPC exclusively by supervisory orders (in millions)	$20	$31.6	$27.4	$2.5
Number of vested patents, patent applications, and abandoned patent applications	41,000	46,000	45,129	47,000
Number of business enterprises vested (cumulative figures)	318	387	408	413
Number of business enterprises sold to Americans (cumulative figures)	None	11	19	27
Number of business enterprises liquidated or in the process of liquidation (cumulative figures)	200	259	291	297
Licenses issued by OAPC covering number of different patents and patent applications (cumulative figures)	Not available	5,853	7,343	7,903

Source: Office of Alien Property Custodian, *Annual Report 1942–1943,* 3, 35; ibid., *1943–1944,* iii–iv, 15; ibid., *1944–1945,* 20, 28, 19, 11, 45, 49, 101; ibid., *1945–1946,* 38, 35, 95, 38, 47, 51, 98.

Crowley was succeeded as APC by his longtime deputy, James E. Markham.[75] By June 30, 1945, a total of $242 million in enemy properties had been vested ($368 million as of June 30, 1946). During each of the war years, the OAPC investigated more businesses and vested added properties, although by June 1945 the number of businesses vested had come to only 408 (and 413 in June 1946). Of the 408 vested businesses by June 1945, "the former owners" of 200 were German, 169 Japanese, 33 Italian, and 6 of other nationalities.[76] The annual reports contained aggregate dollar value figures on the vested enemy properties as well as lists of all the vesting orders, with identification of the vested properties. They provided the dollar value of properties exclusively under supervisory orders (sometimes supervisory control was linked with partial vesting): the dollar values of these properties peaked at year end June 30, 1944 (when $31.6 million in properties were under supervisory orders). The OAPC stopped issuing supervisory orders in October 1944; by June 30, 1946, only $2.5 million in assets remained under such orders.[77]

At the end of the war, Markham told a Senate committee that there were twenty-eight cases involving takeovers of German business enterprises during World War II that overlapped with "seizures" during the First World War (see Table 9.2). In many instances, these were small companies: for example, the third company on the list, the Milwaukee, Wisconsin, John Barth Co., which was in the general wine and liquor business, had been returned after the First World War to German immigrants and had resurfaced during the Second World War as being owned by John Barth & Söhn in Germany. The most significant instances of companies that reverted to German control were American Bosch and those involving I. G. Farben's predecessors (Bayer, Berlin Aniline, Badische).[78] Markham was impressed with the different ways in which German interests came back to this country, "such as the reestablishment by a German steamship company of its branch office in the United States [the reference is to the Hamburg-American and North German Lloyd Lines], the inheritance of property in business enterprises in the United States by Germans who happened to be heirs to American citizens [here he was referring to the particulars of the Haarmann & Reimer interests in Haarmann–de Laire–Schaefer and the successor arrangements related to Maywood Chemical Works], and the resumption of control by Germans over firms in the field of chemical manufacturing."[79]

By its second year of existence, the OAPC had started to sell to U.S. companies its vested interests in ongoing enemy enterprises, but by June 30, 1945, with the war in Europe over, it reported that it had sold its interests in only nineteen companies and that no single transaction had brought in more than $650,000.[80] The group of nineteen did *not* include General Aniline & Film's 50 percent interest in Winthrop Chemical Company, which was sold for cash at public auction on April 23, 1945, to the only bidder, its joint owner, Sterling Drug, Inc., for $9.5 million (Sterling Products' corporate name had been changed to Sterling Drug in 1942). That sale took place about two weeks before V-E Day and was made with a set of conditions designed to avoid these properties' once more reverting to German ownership. A ten-year voting trust was set up, which required the consent of the Alien Property Custodian (or his successor) before Winthrop or its business could be sold or reorganized. In addition, the Alien Property Custodian (with the

Table 9.2. List of enterprises vested by the Alien Property Custodian in both world wars

World War I companies		World War II companies		How Germans reestablished their interests
Name	% vested	Name	% vested	
I. Cases in which the companies and the owners are the same in the two wars				
American Platinum Works	53	American Platinum Works	30	Stock sold by APC to Americans, but partly regained by former owners in trade of patents for stock
Arabol Manufacturing Co.	25	Arabol Manufacturing Co.	30	Stock released by APC to former owners
John Barth Co.	65	John Barth & Söhn	100	Stock released by APC to former owners
Bayer Co. Berlin Aniline Badische Co.	100 100 100	General Aniline & Film Corp. and General Dyestuff Corp.	98	See text of book
Bosch Magneto	100	American Bosch Corp.	77	Original company sold to U.S. citizens; Germans started new company in competition and merged with U.S. firm
Rohm & Haas	60	Rohm & Haas	38	Enemy interests bought by U.S. interests; gift made to German interests

Table 9.2 *(continued)*

World War I companies		World War II companies		How Germans reestablished their interests
Name	% vested	Name	% vested	
II. Cases in which the owners are the same but the companies are different in the two wars				
Hamburg-American Terminal & Navigation Co. North German Lloyd Dock Co.	100	Hamburg-American Line–North German Lloyd, U.S. branch	100	New branch of German company established
International Ultramarine Works	100	The Ultra Corp.	100	Stock reacquired by German owner, who sold company to American Cyanamid in 1941; some real estate assets not in sale went to Ultra
J. A. Henckels, Inc.	50	Fifth Ave. Cutlery Shop Graef & Schmidt, Inc.	100 100	Enemy interests bought by U.S. citizens and resold to Germans
E. Leitz, Inc. (1916)	80	E. Leitz, Inc. (1916) E. Leitz, Inc. (1941)	100 100	Enemy interests bought by U.S. citizens and resold to Germans in 1930s; 1941 company formed to take over assets and business of E. Leitz, Inc. (1916)
J. M. Lehmann Co. Inc.	67	J. M. Lehmann Co. Inc	80	Enemy interests bought by U.S. citizens and resold to Germans in 1921

Markt & Hammacher Co. Markt & Schaefer Co. Hammacher, Schlemmer & Co.	43 27 16	Markt & Hammacher Co.	30	Enemy interests in Markt & Hammacher Co. stock bought by a U.S. citizen, relative of former German owners, and resold to them; other 2 companies dissolved
Muhlens & Kroppf	50	Ferd. Muhlens, Inc.	99	Original company sold to U.S. citizens; Germans started new company in competition and merged with U.S. firm
Frederick Pustet & Co.	66	Frederick Pustet & Co.	36	Enemy interests bought by U.S. interests and resold to German interests
Kny-Scheerer Corp.	100	Jetter & Scheerer Products	100	Stock sold to U.S. citizens; company absorbed in 1929 by American firm; new company started by Germans
Munich Reinsurance Co.	100	Pilot Reinsurance Co.	95	Former owners started new company
Henry Pels & Co.	100	Henry Pels & Co.	100	Former owners started new company

Table 9.2 *(continued)*

World War I companies		World War II companies		How Germans reestablished their interests
Name	% vested	Name	% vested	
Riedel & Co.	100	Riedel-de Haen Inc.	100	Riedel & Co. sold by APC to Americans; former German owners in 1929 start new company
Siemens & Halske	100	Adlanco X-Ray Corp. Roentgen Supplies Inc. Siemens Inc	100 100 100	Former owners started new companies
L. Vogelstein & Co.	100	Central Mining & Securities	100	Former owner started new company
Vogemann Shipping Co.	100	Vogemann-Goudriaan Co. owned 95% Metropolitan Stevedoring Co.	100 100	Former owner started new companies
III. Cases in which the owners are different but the company is the same in the two wars				
Dresden Lace Inc.	55	Rondak Corp. (holding company for Dresden stock)	100	Stock sold to U.S. citizen, who died and left part of his holdings to heirs in Germany (Rondak owned 40% of Dresden stock)

IV. Cases in which both the companies and owners are different in the two wars but some other connection exists				
American Draeger Co.	50	Draeger Shipping Co. Inc. Schenker & Co. Inc. Merchandise Factors Inc.	100	Former owner of American Draeger started a new company and sold it to Germans
American Refractory Co.	16	American Magnesium Metals Corp.	36	Austrian property of American Refractories Co. was purchased by AMMC; certain assets of the two firms were identical
Haarmann-de Laire-Schaefer	33⅓	Maywood Chemical Works	23	Stock sold to Americans; company eventually absorbed by Maywood Chemical Works, part of whose stock passed by inheritance to Germans

Source: This table is virtually identical to the one included with the testimony of James E. Markham, Alien Property Custodian, June 28, 1945, U.S. Senate, Committee on Military Affairs, *Elimination of German Resources for War, Hearings* 79th Cong., 1st sess. (1945), II, 588–589. The only changes made are (1) a reference to the text of the present book, (2) a correction of some typographical errors, and (3) some minor formulations. The reader will find commentary on the most important of these companies in Mira Wilkins, *The History of Foreign Investment in the United States to 1914* (Cambridge, Mass.: Harvard University Press, 1989), and in the current book (the companies that have been omitted were so because of their minor role).

concurrence of the attorney general) agreed that the 1941 consent decree against Sterling Products should be amended so as "to guard against" the future transfer of this 50 percent interest in Winthrop to "unfriendly interests"; Sterling was specifically prohibited from selling or conveying control of Winthrop to I. G. Farben; it was required "to notify the Attorney General if any non-nationals are proposed as parties to any contracts or arrangements involving Winthrop or its subsidiaries. The Attorney General may cause court review of any such proposed contracts or arrangements with non-nationals."[81] By 1945 Sterling Drug was a very different company from its prewar predecessor.[82]

When the OAPC ended (June 30, 1946), it had sold merely twenty-seven "vested" enterprises to "qualified purchasers," with just one large sale (excluding that of Winthrop stock, which was not included in the twenty-seven). The one big sale was that of American Potash & Chemical Corp., which was sold after V-E Day for $15.5 million. It was described by the Alien Property Custodian as "the first of the Custodian's larger vested enterprises to be sold."[83] Everything else remaining would be left for resolution in the subsequent postwar years.

Rather than sell the entire enemy property, in many more cases the OAPC decided to liquidate the businesses so "their assets and labor supply could be made available to other [i.e., U.S.] producers."[84] By June 1945, the OAPC had 291 enemy businesses in the process of liquidation. Those liquidated were generally in banking, insurance, wholesaling, and retailing.[85] Thus, Pilot Reinsurance Company (controlled by Munich Reinsurance) was put into liquidation. By June 30, 1945, the liquidation proceedings had progressed to the point that the total assets of that company were reduced from $4,371,087, at the time of vesting to $534,539.[86] Most of the Japanese businesses in the United States were placed in liquidation.[87] Other businesses not sold or liquidated, that is, many of the largest manufacturing enterprises, were put into war production—under the OAPC's direction.

Throughout wartime, the OAPC extended its program of licensing of patents.[88] By June 1946, the custodian had vested title to roughly 47,000 patents and patent applications (34,000 patents and patent applications of nationals of enemy countries and 13,000 of nationals of formerly enemy-occupied countries).[89] The OAPC joined with the Justice Department in seeking the removal of restrictions in existing contracts on patent use.[90] Thus, for example, on December 29, 1942, American Bosch Corporation was compelled, by a court decree, to issue licenses under all Bosch patents to American firms—royalty free.[91] The Justice Department believed that U.S. companies had "seen fit to aid I. G. Farben in attempting to prevent seizure of German-owned patents by the American Alien Property Custodian by the execution of specious patent assignments."[92] These were to be uncovered and nullified. The activities of the OAPC (and the Justice Department) in relation to the dispersal of technological knowledge embedded in foreign patents represented some of the most consequential policy measures linked with foreign assets in the United States; they set the broader precedent for compulsory licensing of patents when in the public interest.[93]

Complicating the administrative tasks of the OAPC was the fact that not all the assets of enemy-owned companies were in the United States. In the cosmopolitan finance of the 1920s, U.S. corporations had been used by foreign investors for many purposes. Enemy-owned American companies had assets in Germany and other countries. Indeed, when on September 1, 1943, the custodian vested a majority of the shares of the Hugo Stinnes Corporation, he learned that the bulk of the properties held by this company and its subsidiaries were located in Germany, beyond "the control" of the OAPC—at least during wartime.[94] The OAPC faced numerous difficulties in its attempts to take over from their former owners the control of enemy properties, no matter where those properties were located.[95]

Under Investigation

Throughout the war years, deep suspicions persisted over the activities of both U.S. and foreign-based multinational corporations, especially German-owned firms and those other multinationals that had participated in the interwar years with German businesses in patent licensing arrangements that Americans typically labeled as "cartels." For many in the United States, the intensity of the late New Deal antagonism to big business and big banks did not subside in wartime. The antitrust cases that had multiplied during 1939–1941 had shown no sign of letting up in the immediate aftermath of U.S. entry into the war, and even though major litigations had been settled or postponed during the first year after America became a combatant, still the cases "on hold" cast a dark shadow over foreign enterprise in this country and over the latter's U.S. corporate allies. Throughout the war years, Justice Department representatives continued to make strongly worded public statements on numerous occasions to the effect that U.S. companies' connections with European businesses not only had been in the past but also continued to be antithetical to U.S. national interests.[96] Within the Justice Department, the Economic Warfare Section obtained information from private international businesses to identify bombing sites abroad, but the section also warned that through the same established multinational enterprises' links the enemy knew the locations of U.S. plants that could be subjected to sabotage.[97]

The Treasury Department delved deeply into Nazi influences maintained through neutral countries. In 1943 the department went so far as to suggest that it examine the foreign customers of British banks in the United States (the accounts held by these British banks) to ferret out enemy influence. The customers it wanted to investigate were those from neutral countries. The Bank of England vehemently objected, insisting that secrecy was essential in sustaining the integrity of the British banking system; it was, moreover, concerned over the "loss of business."[98] Bank secrecy clashed with national security considerations. A British official in the embassy in Washington warned the Bank of England correspondent that to use the argument with the U.S. Treasury Department about "loss of business" would "be quite fatal," since "the recurring criticism which we [the British] have to face here [in the United States] is that when it comes to the point, we are not prepared to sacrifice our business interest to winning the war."[99] This had, of course, been the Treasury Department's contention during the debate over lend lease, when the British seemed determined to protect their subjects' direct investments in America.

Indeed, the Treasury Department made little headway in its attempt to investigate British banking transactions in the United States. It did, however, monitor carefully the behavior of Swiss and Swedish firms in this country, fearful that they were serving as stand-ins for German treachery. (The Swiss and Swedes were equally sensitive on matters of private business and banking disclosures.) It was well known in Washington that all during the war neutral Switzerland and neutral Sweden kept contacts with Germany. In the Treasury Department, intensive studies were undertaken of the Swiss pharmaceutical companies and their German associations. There were similar investigations of Swiss banks.[100] Treasury Department officials looked equally closely at the operations of Swedish firms, particularly SKF and the Stockholms Enskilda Bank [101]

William L. Batt, head of SKF Industries (SKF-US), served in Washington as vice-chairman of the War Production Board—much to the dismay of critics, who believed SKF-US (as well as its parent in Sweden) was engaged in improper activities.[102] The Office of Strategic Services (OSS) in 1944 reported that the Wallenbergs of the Stockholms Enskilda Bank were to be seen as "ruthless and lacking in public spirit." The OSS noted that the Swedish bank was associated with big banks in America—the National City Bank and J. P. Morgan & Co.—connections that in the antibusiness, antibanking context of this era had negative connotations.[103]

In September 1943 the Foreign Economic Administration (FEA) had been established, combining the Board of Economic Warfare (BEW) and the Lend-Lease Administration. In 1942, the BEW had joined in the scrutiny of U.S. firms and their ties with enemy businesses, investigations continued by the FEA.[104] Crowley was the founding head of the FEA.[105] As 1943 came to a close, Crowley was still feuding with Treasury Department personnel; the British Ministry of Economic Warfare (MEW) sought not to irritate either Crowley or the men at the Treasury Department, both of which agencies were now trying to outdo each other in the protection of U.S. security.[106]

The story of the suspicions over SKF Industries (SKF-US) is a splendid example of conflicting wartime interests. SKF-US made bearings essential to the U.S. war effort. Its Swedish parent (AB-SKF) had a giant bearings factory in Göteborg, which exported to Germany; AB-SKF also had sizable manufacturing plants in Germany and one in Great Britain (the latter was smaller than SKF's German or Swedish facilities). In 1942, the Swedish managing director of AB-SKF, Harald Hamberg, made an agreement with German government officials to increase exports of ball bearings to Germany. Key British and American diplomats were aware of the agreement.[107] Normally, SKF-US would have been put on the British and U.S. blacklist, since its parent dealt with the Germans, but both the United Kingdom and the United States required bearings for national defense. The British, moreover, wanted to import from AB-SKF; thus, the Allies treated AB-SKF with kid gloves.

Throughout 1943–1945 within the U.S. Treasury Department there were strong voices of discontent over the behavior of AB-SKF and distrust of the latter's U.S. affiliate. In November 1943, concern arose among the Allies that the "Germans do not make up for losses in production of bearings brought about by our [British] air raids [on SKF factories in Germany] through purchases in neutral countries [i.e., Sweden]." In April 1944 Allied pressures mounted to stop exports of Swedish ball bearings to Germany. The State Department and the FEA favored threats to blacklist AB-SKF, but the British resisted, since they desired to buy from the Swedes. In May 1944, the British found out that "a more energetic enquiry is being conducted [by the U.S. Treasury] into possible enemy interests in and control of the American subsidiary of SKF." In May, June, and October 1944 (under FEA sponsorship), Jean Pajus wrote reports detailing what he believed were the perfidious activities of AB-SKF and SKF-US. Pajus thought AB-SKF was German controlled and that the Office of Alien Property Custodian should vest the properties of SKF-US as enemy assets. In response to his initial report and his subsequent investigations, an internal Treasury Department and OAPC memorandum of August 26, 1944, had indicated that no reliable proof of German control of AB-SKF could be found; thus, OAPC did not vest the shares of SKF-US, but Pajus kept up his pressure.

Meanwhile, throughout Batt at the War Production Board sheltered SKF-US, with which he had long been identified. This was possible only because of the importance of bearings to the U.S. war effort. Behind the scenes, intense negotiations went forward, none of which were known to the general public at this time. The British proposed preemptive purchasing of Swedish ball bearings from AB-SKF to cut off German supplies. In December 1943, a secret Anglo-American-Swedish Economic Agreement was signed in London, whereby the Swedes agreed to limit ball bearing sales to Germany. Thereupon, the Allies offered to buy up all the Swedish-produced ball bearings, but the Swedish government rejected this, arguing it would violate Swedish-German contracts. In March 1944 the Swedish government wanted AB-SKF to honor its earlier agreements with Germany, and the British learned that the Swedish government would never allow AB-SKF to accept an Allied order for the whole of Swedish output because this would be tantamount to dishonoring their engagements with the Germans. By April 1944, U.S. military authorities were pressing Secretary of State Cordell Hull to leave no stone unturned to get AB-SKF to stop exporting to Germany. As an Allied victory began to seem likely, finally the Swedes were ready to bargain. Moreover, in the United States, the press caught wind of the Pajus investigations, and SKF-US obtained a lot of negative publicity. In May 1944 the Treasury Department and the Office of Alien Property Custodian confirmed that examinations of SKF-US were going forth but insisted that the War and Navy Departments had advised them that SKF-US had an excellent record for war production.

The parent Swedish company, AB-SKF, became party to the governmental diplomatic negotiations, which intensified during 1944. In June 1944, the U.S. War Department once more expressed its discontent that AB-SKF was still exporting to Germany. By contrast, AB-SKF complained that the Treasury Department and the FEA inquiries on SKF-US were "persecution." In October 1944, the U.S. ambassador in the United Kingdom wrote to the State Department that as a quid pro quo for AB-SKF's halting its exports to Germany, perhaps the AB-SKF could request "the U.S. to cease persecuting its subsidiaries in the U.S. and that both Governments [of the United States and of Britain] could be requested to reiterate assurances that SKF properties which might be confiscated by Germany would be restored to the company after the war." In short, the U.S. ambassador mapped the appropriate formula for the response. AB-SKF made the "suggested" request, adding a "no publicity" clause. Not until October 1944 did AB-SKF finally discontinue its exports to Germany. The United States officially denied (in diplomatic correspondence) that it was discriminating against SKF-US. The presence, however, in the United States of SKF-US gave the U.S. government leverage against AB-SKF that it would not otherwise have had.[108]

Meanwhile, testimony before several congressional committees fueled an overall climate of mistrust against big business and foreign investors in the United States. The committee hearings offered profuse details on international business practices, far beyond the accusations against SKF-US. The Truman Committee, investigating national defense preparations, which had presented its first annual report to the U.S. Senate on January 15, 1942, convened through the war years. It called up 1,798 witnesses to more than 400 sessions and presented fifty reports.[109] In a radio address in June 1942 (and on other occasions as well), Senator Harry Truman accused "Standard Oil" of supplying "the Farben Company complete control of patents in the chemical field including rubber." Standard Oil—he told the American public—in cooperation with I. G. Farben had refused to license domestic tire makers. "Needless to say," Truman went on, "I. G. Farben's position was dictated by the German government."[110] By the time of this June broadcast, Standard Oil (New Jersey) had already agreed—in its March 25, 1942, consent decree—to license royalty-free all the patents that it had acquired from I. G. Farben, but this did not quell the hostility, nor did it temper the Washington rhetoric.

Beginning in April 1942, the Truman Committee's inquiry into nefarious business practices was joined by that of Senator Homer T. Bone's Committee on Patents. Populist Senator Robert M. La Follette from Wisconsin set the tone at these hearings: the Standard Oil (New Jersey)–I. G. Farben relationships were "industrial treason"; he urged the Bone Committee to launch "a drive which will put an end to the economic penetration of America from Nazi firms." La Follette lambasted the March 1942 consent decree as insufficiently punitive. Senator Joseph C. O'Mahoney of Wyoming (who had been chairman of the Temporary National Economic Committee from June 1938 to April 1941 and in that capacity had looked into concentration of economic power in the United States) predicted that SONJ would revert to its "old ways," its noncompetitive agreements once the war was over and done: "One almost gets the impression," O'Mahoney declared, "that they [SONJ] regard this war as an annoying interruption to their Fascist economic alliances." Senator Bone, on being informed about the consent decrees signed by SONJ and Dow Chemical, agreed that they were entirely inadequate: "The sinner has not repented." La Follette echoed the committee chairman's sentiments: "He [Standard Oil (New Jersey); Dow Chemical] claims patriotism and yielded," to which Bone added, "He got religion only temporarily; he will return to sin after the crisis has passed."[111] The Bone Committee hearings lasted from April to August 1942 and, like the Truman Committee sessions, received extensive press coverage. Senator Bone was from the State of Washington. Midwesterners and westerners were especially critical of "eastern" businesses and their international outlook and connections.

The extensive hearings of Senator Harley Kilgore's Subcommittee on War Mobilization started in 1943 and went on through the rest of the war years (and beyond).[112] They supplemented and fortified the findings of the ongoing Truman and the now-completed Bone Committee hearings on the dire effects on the war effort of international cartels (and, by implication, international business in general). Kilgore was from West Virginia, but the rest of the committee was dominated by westerners. These Senate committees, with their parade of witnesses and their subpoenaed company records, documented and exposed to public scrutiny a complex of interwar cartel relationships involving American, German, British, Swiss, Dutch, French companies and those of other nationalities. The accent was, however, on German perfidy.[113] The Kilgore hearings examined international business alliances in synthetic rubber, tungsten carbide, magnesium, leather tanning, aviation fuel, dyestuffs and other chemicals, pharmaceuticals, and many additional products.[114]

In March 1942, the first of a sequence of U.S. publications on I. G. Farben's (and other German firms') "pernicious" activities appeared: John Boylan's *Sequel to the Apocalyse. The Uncensored Story: How Your Dimes and Quarters Helped Pay for Hitler's War.*[115] This well-illustrated booklet contained dialogues between the sinister I. G. Farben conspirators as they plotted their American (and other international) schemes. As in the many other books, articles, and reports of this ilk, I. G. Farben was depicted as having prepared the way for Hitler and as the principal creator of the German war economy. I found a copy of the Boylan study in the files of Francis Garvan (who by 1942 was long deceased) and later learned that its publication had been sponsored by The Chemical Foundation.[116]

In 1944, economist Corwin Edwards prepared a report for the Kilgore Committee on the economic and political aspects of international cartels. The committee chairman, Senator Kilgore, in his preface to the monograph, noted that Edwards' study "points out a number of instances where cartels and monopolies, before the war, hindered the full development of technology in the United States and jeopardized our preparedness for national defense." The senator added that although there were "indications" that cartels and monopoly restrictions had been "partly removed during the period of active fighting," the underlying thinking behind the relationships, he claimed, had continued "to thrive."[117] Edwards wrote that the arrangements that companies such as the Dutch firm NV Philips had made before U.S. entry into the war had provisions for the postwar reestablishment of the prewar associations.[118] He warned that in wartime the most dangerous aspect of international business alliances "lies in the continuance of mutual loyalties and of joint property interests which unite concerns lying on opposite sides of the battle lines." Edwards documented few special relationships that existed from the time of U.S. entry into the war to the time of the publication of his study in 1944, but he was confident that the prewar connections with enemy nationals "provide a standing incentive for qualified allegiance to one's own belligerent nation" (read: the United States) and that the existence of "established contacts with enemy concerns through concerns in neutral countries affords a constant opportunity to promote trade interests by transmitting information and even supplies which may be of value to the enemy." Edwards argued that for the multinational enterprise, it was not merely a conflict between patriotism and greed but a "natural desire to maintain property and profits."[119] NV Philips' management in the United States was outraged by the Edwards report; the group's directors denied that contact was maintained with its plant in occupied Holland.[120] Its refutation of the allegations got no publicity in the United States.[121]

Part of America's discomfort about the flood of information on international alliances lay in the nation's antitrust tradition, one not shared by European firms. The word "cartel" for Americans had long had pejorative connotations; U.S. antitrust laws made restraint-of-trade agreements illegal.[122] European business leaders held different perceptions: English, Dutch, and Swiss executives spoke openly of the desirability of cartel relations. Historian Tony Freyer quotes Imperial Chemical Industries' Lord McGowan as saying in 1943, "I see no hope of collaboration between British and American business unless the United States repeals its Sherman Antitrust Act." Americans could not fathom such a sentiment. In Washington there was a prevailing desire to strengthen the Sherman Antitrust Act. No one in the United States endorsed the repeal of the country's basic antitrust legislation.[123] In the discussion of cartels, it is important that there was little awareness on the part of the U.S. public (or public policy makers) of the differences between multinational enterprises and cartels; this absence of distinctions would carry over into the postwar years. Standard Oil (New Jersey)'s defense of its prewar international business associations got little sympathy.[124] The late 1930s attacks on big business and bankers continued to mold much of the hostile sentiment of Americans toward international businesses.[125]

Accordingly, although U.S. isolationism waned rapidly and although Americans came to recognize that the country was very much a part of the international community, nonetheless suspicions over U.S. corporations, especially in their relationships with the Germans but also extending to other nationalities, remained very much alive. And, as Americans came to favor a more open, free, and competitive world economy for the postwar era, cartels seemed totally antithetical to those plans.

As victory for the Allies came to appear inevitable, the Justice Department was poised to reinvigorate its temporarily postponed antitrust offensive. Foreign direct investors in the United States were caught up in the new sweep. Thurman Arnold left the Antitrust Division early in 1943 to become a judge, but his successors in the Justice Department followed closely his ideological approach. Attorney General Francis Biddle was fully committed to the view that private restrictive international agreements were illegal.[126] By the fall of 1943, the Justice Department claimed to have uncovered at least 162 agreements of I. G. Farben with impact on business in America.[127] On June 28, 1943, National Lead, Du Pont, and the Titan Co. had been indicted in a case that involved titanium; the trial was temporarily postponed; although Imperial Chemical Industries and I. G. Farben were not indicted in this instance, they were mentioned as parties in the alleged cartel.[128] Then, on January 6, 1944, the attorney general filed a suit against Imperial Chemical Industries, I.C.I. (New York), Du Pont, and some others, charging restraint of trade. The suit accused ICI and Du Pont of dividing markets, with the aim of eliminating competition. ICI and Du Pont's contacts with German companies had been—in the perception of the Justice Department—detrimental to the national security of the United States.[129] Other cases were also resumed or newly begun in 1944.[130] In December 1944, the Justice Department initiated an antitrust suit against SKF Industries.[131] By late 1944, the antitrust agenda was back on U.S. policy makers' front burner.

Moreover, strong anticartel beliefs were not confined to the Justice Department. In the State Department, a deep resolve emerged toward opening markets in the peaceful postwar world.[132] If, however, there seemed to be within the State Department a readiness to support under some circumstances international cooperative agreements, such views were—in the words of a memorandum in British files—obscured by those of "extremists," who condemned cartelization.[133] In these years, a distinction, moreover, came to be made between private parties in international restrictive agreements (which were always suspect) and international commodity agreements that involved governments and could possibly be used—under certain circumstances—to stabilize volatile commodity prices.[134] U.S. antitrust policies would have a profound impact on the postwar course of foreign business in America.

Financing the War Effort

During World War II the U.S. government raised roughly 41 percent of its war costs through taxation (compared with 33 percent in World War I). This meant elevated levies on both U.S. companies and foreign businesses in the United States. It also meant higher withholding taxes for foreign owners of American securities.[135] The rest of the war finance came from bond issues and was reflected in the soaring national debt. In 1945 alone nearly $60 billion in war bonds were sold. The U.S. national debt, which had gradually mounted in the 1930s with New Deal programs, skyrocketed, jumping more than fourfold between the end of 1941 and the end of 1945.[136] All the national debt was dollar denominated.

By 1942, most countries around the world had capital controls. There were, however, new foreign acquisitions of U.S. debt. In 1942, U.S. military strategy had been to build up China with U.S. loans to aid Chiang Kai-shek. In April 1942, H. H. Kung, China's minister of finance, asked the Treasury Department to deposit $200 million (of China's borrowed moneys) in an account at the New York Federal Reserve; Kung requested that the funds be invested in U.S. bonds and notes until China was ready to use them (and until through the sale of the securities to the Chinese, Kung could cover his country's earlier borrowing). Treasury Secretary Morgenthau complied with Kung's request. The Chinese loan, aimed at stabilizing Chinese currency and controlling inflation, did neither.[137] But the result, in technical terms, was a Chinese claim on U.S. government securities.

I can identify other foreign investments in U.S. government bonds by Canadians and Latin Americans—both private investors and governments. A portion of Canadian government dollar reserves was invested in U.S. government bonds. Latin American investors, who were seeking security, bought such bonds, and there seem to have been investments by Latin American government officials in reserves to stabilize currencies.[138]

J. Henry Schroder Banking Corporation, the New York subsidiary of J. Henry Schroder & Co., London, after riding out its worries over the possible sacrifice of its U.S. assets to pay for the pre-lend-lease purchases, had (like most other British-owned enterprises—bar Courtaulds' subsidiary, American Viscose) survived and flourished. Its principal wartime business became that of assisting the U.S. Treasury in marketing bills and bonds to finance the war effort. Throughout the war, its active bond trading operations were the source of much of its profits. In conducting this business, it raised its own portfolio of U.S. Treasury bills and bonds, so that by war's end, the latter accounted for some 60 percent of its U.S. assets. The holdings of J. Henry Schroder

Banking Corp. of U.S. government securities represented an indirect "British" investment in the United States. The firm's historian does not indicate where the bank marketed the U.S. federal government securities; some were undoubtedly sold to non-U.S. residents.[139] Foreign-owned insurance companies in the United States continued to hold U.S. government securities in their portfolios and appear to have increased such holdings. Of Phoenix Assurance, for example, its historian writes, "By October 1943 some 59% of all Phoenix's considerable investment in the USA (over £5 million) was in government stock and only 17% in the old American staple of railroad bonds."[140]

A 1948 U.S. Commerce Department study reported that in the years 1942 through 1944 there were net foreign purchases of some $285 million of "United States securities. From the data available, it appears that a very large part of the total represented purchases of United States Government long-term issues for official foreign account." That same report identified another $68 million net foreign purchases of U.S. government long-term issues in 1945. It estimated a rise in foreign investment in long-term U.S. government securities from $150 million at year end 1941 to $493 million at year end 1945.[141]

Other estimates differ. In total, however, it seems clear that the overall size of the foreign investments in U.S. government securities was not great, especially if viewed as a percentage of the huge national debt. The long-term U.S. wartime national debt was almost entirely domestically held; Americans had the moneys to buy the war bonds; only a small portion of the U.S. debt came to pass to foreign ownership, albeit the amounts may well be larger than those in the Commerce Department estimate. A brief flurry of U.S. concern (in 1942) about the nation's "external" debt proved a blip.[142] In sum, I uncovered little discussion of, much less anxiety over, foreign holdings of the soaring U.S. national debt. The foreign contribution to financing the American war effort through tax payments and bond purchases was trivial.

Production and Business during Wartime

Foreign direct investors did, however, assist in wartime production, add to wartime technological accomplishments in the United States, and offer vital information to intelligence services. Some of the output in the United States for military purposes was by foreign-owned (or once foreign-owned or presumed to be foreign-owned) enemy companies, which took place under the aegis of the Office of Alien Property Custodian. Other output occurred with licenses issued by the Treasury Department, covered by the Foreign Funds Control regulations. Still added manufacturing was by British companies, many of which were pledged as collateral for the Reconstruction Finance Corporation loan.

With prewar German-owned (or assumed to be German-owned) firms vested by or under the supervision of the Office of Alien Property Custodian, the OAPC appointed the U.S. top management to run the plants. Generally, the OAPC's policy was to retain the existing middle management, "wherever it is determined that complete confidence can be placed in it. To do otherwise would result in an unnecessary disturbance of management and would retard the war effort." Only "in exceptional cases" were field representatives of the OAPC stationed at the business enterprise site and required to send back daily reports.[143]

In the case of properties of affiliates of companies in occupied territories or neutral lands in Europe, where Treasury Department licenses were required, top executives who had temporarily moved across the Atlantic frequently took over command, sometimes working with and at times replacing the U.S. management of the subsidiary. Thus, for example, top executives from Europe became directly involved in the U.S. business of the Swiss firms Hoffmann-La Roche and Nestlé, the French Lazard Frères, and the Dutch Philips.[144] After the German occupation of Holland, British-Dutch enterprises in the United States (when there had been joint British-Dutch managerial direction) had shifted the "headquarters" activities to London. British firms (both those that were put up for collateral for the Reconstruction Finance Corporation loan and those that were not) continued to be administered under Anglo-American direction. The collateral status created no special issues related to the governance of the enterprise. The insurance companies that were pledged as collateral all carried on their normal functions, expanding their business during the war years.[145]

Table 9.3 indicates (as of June 30, 1944) the wartime involvements of selected "enemy enterprises" producing in the United States for the American and Allied cause. All or part of the securities of these firms had been vested by the Alien Property Custodian (or in the case of Winthrop Chemical, the securities of its parent, General Aniline & Film, had been vested).[146] Winthrop Chemical (50 percent owned by General Aniline & Film) made Atabrine—an antimalarial drug. The U.S. Armed Forces relied heavily on Atabrine after the Japanese moved into the Dutch East Indies, cutting off the main source of quinine. The OAPC informed government war agencies as well as the private sector of available patents. Winthrop Chemical licensed eleven companies to make Atabrine.[147] One of the important manufacturers of this antimalarial drug under the government-sponsored program was the National Aniline Division of Allied Chemical and Dye Corp., which in 1943 was responsible for "a substantial portion" of this production.[148]

Table 9.3. Wartime involvement of selected enemy enterprises as of June 30, 1944

Company	Products
American Bosch Corp.	Magnetos, electrical equipment, fuel injection apparatus
American Platinum Works	Platinum equipment
American Potash & Chemical Corp.	Chemicals and potash used in production of military explosives, armor plate, instrument glass used in bombsights and gunnery fire-control devices
Arabol Manufacturing Co.	Adhesives, glues, etc., used in naval crafts to prevent cracking and tearing of asbestos
Buffalo Electro-Chemical Co., Inc.	Hydrogen peroxide and potassium persulphate
Cork Foundation Co.	Vibration insulators for diesel engines, devices used to absorb explosive impacts for ships—developed for navy
General Aniline & Film Corp.	Dyes, film, photographic supplies, sensitive paper for charts
General Dyestuff Corp.	Developed formulas for textile dyestuffs used in uniforms; developed tracers to aid the location of airmen forced down at sea
Graef & Schmidt, Inc.	Surgical instruments for the army and navy
J. M. Lehmann Co., Inc.	Machine tools, optical grinding and polishing machines
E. Leitz, Inc.	Precision instruments
Maywood Chemical Works	Chemical and metal compounds
J. C. Muller, Inc.	Bilge pumps used by the navy; machined forgings for the noses of projectiles
Ore & Chemical Corp.	Lead and zinc reclaimed from mining dumps in Colorado
Resinous Products & Chemical Co.	Glue film for plywood gliders and transport aircraft
Rohm & Haas Co.	Plexiglas, used on military airplanes
Schering Corp.	Pharmaceuticals; hormone products; X-ray media
Winthrop Chemical Co.	Pharmaceuticals
Carl Zeiss, Inc.	Optical Instruments

Source: Office of Alien Property Custodian, *Annual Report 1942–1943*, 54, 63 (Winthrop Chemical); idem., *Annual Report 1943–1944*, 47–49, 64–65 (American Bosch), 66 (American Potash & Chemical), 69 (General Aniline & Film), 72 (General Dyestuff), 74–75 (Schering), 80 (Carl Zeiss). Note that all of these were German.

The largest single beneficial owner of Allied Chemical was the Belgian firm Solvay & Cie.

By June 30, 1944, the OAPC was operating 128 enterprises as going concerns, and most of them were engaged in war work. Their output included aviation magnetos, potash, armor plate, pharmaceuticals, surgical instruments, other precision instruments, coal tar dyes, and photographic supplies.[149] In some cases before the war, the operations of these enterprises had been very modest. Thus, Carl Zeiss, Inc., had only a repair shop in the United States in the 1930s; to be sure, before the firm had been vested, with added machinery and staff, the repair shop had been transformed into a small factory to manufacture certain precision instruments. Under the new management, selected by the Alien Property Custodian, the factory was further enlarged to make microscopes and micrometers for the war effort. Similarly, Graef & Schmidt, 100 percent owned by the German Henckels, had done minor manufacturing of scissors, knives, and manicure instruments; during the war, it embarked on the manufacture of surgical instruments for the army and navy.[150] Schering Corp., which before U.S. entry into the war had barely begun to develop a research and clinical presence in America, now fully separated from its German parent had sufficient talent within its organization to expand these activities on a broad scale. It introduced new products, and its research staff participated in key developments in the field of penicillin.[151] American Bosch Corp. received Army-Navy "E" (Excellence) Awards in 1943, 1944, and 1945, while American Potash & Chemical Corp. and General Aniline & Film received the "E" Awards in 1944 and 1945, in each case for their substantial wartime contributions to the Allied cause.[152]

In 1944, the OAPC considered vesting the Dutch-German rayon companies—North American Rayon, American Bemberg, and American Enka—affiliates of Algemeene Kunstzijde Unie NV (AKU).[153] All three affiliates had had their assets "frozen" under the 1940 regulations on Dutch assets in the United States, and they had subsequently received Treasury Department licenses to continue operations.[154] They maintained production throughout the war years, filling U.S. military and domestic requirements. In 1944 American Enka Corporation, which had its origins in the Dutch side of AKU, completed an extension to its Asheville, North Carolina, plant. The latter had a capacity of producing 10 million pounds per annum of "high-tenacity yarn," used in making automobile and airplane tires. As of December 31, 1944, it employed 4,250 people, up from 2,878 on December 31, 1940.[155]

A keen awareness was present in Washington of the importance of German patents to U.S. war needs. Not long after the Treasury Department and then the OAPC took over General Aniline & Film, the newly installed management at that firm organized a research division with a central laboratory at Easton, Pennsylvania; its goal was to examine and to develop for U.S. war purposes I. G. Farben patents in GAF's possession; by mid-1944 the laboratory employed sixty researchers with doctoral degrees.[156] There were 3,909 patents and 382 pending patent applications owned by GAF.[157]

To aid the U.S. war effort, the OAPC reviewed its thousands of vested patents, seeking with the help of the Justice Department to cancel or at least to modify restrictive agreements and to make the patents widely accessible on a nonexclusive basis. Since many of the vested patents were already under license to U.S. companies and "tied up" with restrictions, the OAPC's investigations aimed at removing these perceived obstacles to the diffusion of technological accomplishments.[158]

In this regard, the most visible problems had involved rubber. Pressures from the OAPC (and the Justice Department) assured that numerous once foreign-controlled or restricted rubber-related patents were effectively made available to and could be used by U.S.-owned businesses.[159] This became imperative early in 1942 because the Japanese military controlled the largest plantation rubber sources. German patents, along with American ones, greatly assisted the demanding process of creating a viable U.S. synthetic rubber industry. Difficulties notwithstanding, the growth of synthetic rubber output in the United States from 1942 to 1945 would be described by chemical industry historian Williams Haynes as "one of the most thrilling chemical achievements of World War II."[160] The Second World War did for synthetic rubber what the First World War had done for nitrates and dyes. It fostered the emergence of a new domestic U.S. industry, no longer dependent on foreign natural resources—or on German ingenuity.[161]

There has been substantial controversy as to whether the activities of I. G. Farben before America's entry into the war impeded U.S. synthetic rubber developments. This was the orthodoxy of the "suspicious" during the war years. Later scholarship has, however, suggested that "German patent barriers actually stimulated U.S. research and development on synthetic rubber during the 1930's," which research served as a foundation for the U.S. success in wartime.[162] Indeed, it seems likely that the interchange of patents and the impact of foreign multinational enterprise proved positive rather than negative. Early in the spring of 1945, Allied forces captured a synthetic rubber plant in Germany and discovered that the Germans were using a new compound that improved the quality of synthetic rubber. Samples were given by the OAPC to General Aniline & Film laboratories, and in less than a month GAF was able to deliver the compound in commercial quantities to

American tire companies.[163] This would have been impossible if GAF had not had the past knowledge and experience.

The U.S. domestic synthetic rubber success story involved oil, tire, and chemical companies; it required both imitation and innovation. In these industries there were foreign direct investments by other than German firms that contributed to the success of the synthetic rubber program, for example, the British-Dutch Shell—through its Shell Chemical and Shell Development subsidiaries. Like Standard Oil (New Jersey), the British-Dutch Shell had had prewar access to German technology. For reasons not entirely clear, Royal Dutch Shell managed to escape the scathing wartime criticisms that SONJ received. Indeed, it was a Shell chemical plant in Houston, Texas, which had gone on-stream in September 1941, that became the first full-scale facility in the United States to produce butadiene; during 1942, as more production came on line, this Houston plant supplied the largest output in the United States of this key ingredient for synthetic rubber. In addition, on behalf of the Rubber Reserve Company, Shell Chemical designed, constructed, and operated at Torrance, California, another butadiene plant, a huge facility that began production in July 1943. Shell Chemical also furnished technological assistance to other participants in the nation's synthetic rubber program.[164]

Butadiene can be manufactured from oil or alcohol. In 1942, the Canadian company Distillers Corporation–Seagrams Ltd. participated in producing alcohol for the U.S. synthetic rubber program; it also conducted research on butadiene within the United States.[165] Meanwhile, by 1941, all the leading U.S.-owned tire makers were building synthetic rubber plants; the foreign multinational enterprises' impact on their activity—aside from the foreign patents that SONJ licensed—was indirect (John Collyer, Goodrich's chief executive officer, had learned the rubber tire business at the British-owned Dunlop's Buffalo plant).[166] It is not evident how much technological assistance the American tire companies received from General Aniline & Film, but surely it had some relevant patents. Parenthetically, it should be noted that Seagrams' distilleries were put to other U.S. government purposes, to produce alcohol for war needs—not only for synthetic rubber.[167]

Critical to the war effort were the oil companies, ensuring that supplies were adequate, and handling the logistics of getting the products to where they were required. On November 28, 1941, Secretary of the Interior Harold Ickes had formed the Petroleum Industry Council for National Defense; after U.S. entry into the war, this agency became the Petroleum Industry War Council; still later (in December 1942), it was renamed the Petroleum Administration for War. Within this agency, in December 1941, the Foreign Operations Committee (FOC) had been organized.[168] So, too, that same December 1941, Henry Wallace's Board of Economic Warfare had set up the Foreign Petroleum Policy Committee, which in turn formed the Foreign Petroleum Operating Board (FPOB). Membership of FPOB comprised the leaders of the American oil industry along with Harold Wilkinson (Royal Dutch Shell Group) and Basil Jackson (in charge of the Anglo-Iranian Oil Company's New York office). These same men apparently would serve on the competing FOC.[169] In 1942, Wilkinson would become the British government petroleum representative in Washington.[170] These men from the two major foreign multinational oil enterprises contributed to the debates over the wartime and postwar international petroleum policies of the United States.

For Americans, the principal petroleum policy concern lay in the adequacy of domestic oil reserves and the growing necessity to supplement these reserves with foreign oil. Thus, a large part of U.S. oil policy deliberations focused on the means by which foreign oil resources could and would be developed. This involved considerations related to outward FDI.[171] British government policy makers (and British oil producers) viewed "oil questions" from a separate angle. They supported cooperation among private companies in the oil industry to achieve satisfactory supplies.[172] Moreover, and very urgent, both the foreign-owned oil companies and the British government were apprehensive lest the expansion of U.S. activities abroad would leave Americans with "all [the oil] that is left."[173] The British government wanted to be sure Shell and Anglo-Iranian were not excluded from oil developments in the United States and around the world. During the Second World War, as in earlier years, Anglo-Iranian Oil Company had no U.S. operations—only the office in New York, which was a window on what was happening in the industry. By contrast, Shell continued to be a major player in the U.S. oil (and chemical) business. In 1941–1945, Shell was undoubtedly the largest and most important foreign-owned enterprise in the United States. And, as in the past, it took on a British as well as Dutch identity in the diplomatic arena. In the war years, it not only aided the American rubber program but also served the Allied war effort in many other ways. It was a fully integrated multiproduct company within the United States (as well as globally). It addressed the key technological challenges in the oil industry, introducing new processes of catalytic cracking in refining as well as producing high-octane fuels for aviation needs. Shell was in the lead in research in the international oil industry. It assisted in advancing new methods in catalytic cracking and high-octane gasoline (effectively combining the use of U.S. and German patents with its own). It participated in raising U.S. domestic crude and refined oil output dramatically.[174]

Another important foreign-owned company, in a different industry, producing for the U.S. (and the Allied) war effort was the previously mentioned Swedish-owned SKF Industries (and its affiliated SKF Steel). Its contribution of steel bearings was essential for U.S. planes and had many other applications. The criticisms and investigations of SKF Industries became so intense that both the Treasury Department and the Alien Property Custodian had jointly issued a statement in May 1944, declaring that even though they were examining the ownership and control of the Swedish parent to determine whether the latter was a front for the Germans, the investigation had not been undertaken

> because of any question concerning the production of SKF Industries, Philadelphia, or of SKF Steel, New York, and should not be interpreted as any reflection upon either management or employees of these two companies. Both the War and Navy Departments have advised the Treasury Department and the Alien Property Custodian that all of the production of SKF Industries and SKF Steel contributes to the war effort of the United States and the other united and associated nations and that such production is vital to our war effort. The War and Navy Departments also confirm that SKF Industries and SKF Steel have excellent records for war production and state that any serious loss of production at those companies would have an immediate and serious effect on the production of war munitions needed for planned operations.[175]

Thus, scrutiny and suspicions aside, SKF Industries continued to manufacture in the United States for the Allied war effort. There was no (and would not be subsequently) vesting by the APC.

Other affiliates of foreign businesses were actively involved in the U.S. war effort in a range of sectors. During World War II, research in the United States on pharmaceuticals grew—and the foreign affiliates' offerings (not only those of enemy enterprises) proved to be at the leading edge. Before 1939, many of the foreign-owned units in the United States in pharmaceuticals had been essentially "branches," very much dependent on their parents for research and innovative direction, although some had already embarked on U.S. operations "separate" from those of their parent, that is, they undertook research on their own initiative, developed their own products, and formulated their own strategies. After war broke out in Europe, the companies had grown more self-reliant, and those that had done minor manufacturing now substituted domestic output for imports of key inputs. During World War II, they could build on the prior international contributions in a material manner within the United States. They copied their parents' products and processes and then went beyond their parent firms.

Many of the foreign-owned pharmaceutical producers became truly innovative in their own right.

This was the case of the Swiss enterprises Ciba, Sandoz, Geigy, and Hoffmann-La Roche, which substantially enlarged their U.S. operations, adding to American domestic technological accomplishments in hormones, vitamins, sulfa drugs, and other pharmaceuticals. Ciba, which had built a modern pharmaceutical plant in Summit, New Jersey, in 1937 expanded rapidly during the war years, while Sandoz's pharmaceutical division made vital discoveries in the United States in digitalis research, in curing epilepsy, and in laxatives.[176] Hoffmann-La Roche, at its burgeoning complex in Nutley, New Jersey, had during the war years twenty-five chemists engaged in research. A number of its highest-ranking executives and scientists came from Switzerland to spend these years in America. Under their aegis, Hoffmann-La Roche's research capacity and pharmaceutical output rose.[177] Elmer H. Bobst, an American, had over many years energized Hoffmann-La Roche's U.S. operations. After the First World War, he had been put in charge of what was then a small, troubled affiliate. As an incentive to him, his contract had given him a salary that included a remuneration of 5 percent of the American company's sales. As the latter had grown, Bobst had become a very wealthy man (according to one source, only the president of General Motors had a higher salary in 1944). When the Swiss management from the parent firm settled in the United States, they wanted to take charge. In 1944 Bobst resigned from Hoffmann-La Roche and became president of Warner Co., soon to be Warner-Lambert (in a 1950 merger). Bobst would also transform Warner-Lambert into a pharmaceutical giant, remaining active until his death in 1978 at the age of ninety-eight (his experience at Hoffmann-La Roche proved invaluable). Meanwhile, the U.S. affiliate of Hoffmann-La Roche that he had nurtured flourished under the guidance of the parent company executives present in America. The subsidiary came to be a major supplier of vitamins to the United States and its allies; at Nutley, it had begun to manufacture penicillin in 1943, under a U.S. government program. Its U.S. employment went from 669 in 1940 to 2,000 by war's end. At Nutley, it constructed new factories as well as a new laboratory building. Whereas in 1940 the parent company in Basle had employed more people than the affiliate in the United States (800 versus 669), the reverse was true in 1945 (1,200 versus 2,000).[178] Hoffmann-La Roche's joint venture with the Dutch Organon—in hormone research—was managed in the United States by Basle enterprise.[179]

So, too, the research activities in America of the longtime British investor the pharmaceutical firm Burroughs Wellcome blossomed. Its research had begun in the United States on a significant scale by 1940; but under the wartime stimulus, production as well as research escalated. The Burroughs Wellcome affiliate had general offices in the Wellcome Building at 9 and 11 East Forty-first Street in New York (across from the New York Public Library), while its research and production took place in Tuckahoe, New York (in Westchester County). It manufactured a wide range of products from Empirin (a painkiller) to digitalis (a cardiac stimulant). It had the trademark "Tabloid," which a company brochure declared "stood for the highest possible standards of Purity, Quality and Accuracy." By 1944 Burroughs Wellcome & Co. (U.S.A.) was staffed entirely by Americans. In January 1944, it received an Army-Navy "E" flag for "continued excellence in war production."[180]

Business from abroad prompted substantial U.S. research in medicines: the U.S.-owned American Home Products Company, for example, moved into prescription drugs for the first time. In the process, in March 1943, it acquired the Canadian firm Ayerst, McKenna & Harrison Ltd. (AMH) along with the latter's U.S. subsidiary, which by then was engaged in manufacturing and selling hormone, biological, vitamin, and pharmaceutical products; this small U.S. subsidiary before 1941 had been a joint venture between the Canadian AMH and Glaxo Laboratories. It was located at Rouses Point, in upstate New York, near the Canadian border. It added to the technological competence of its new American owner.[181]

In the chemical industry, aside from the pharmaceutical part, independently and together Ciba, Sandoz, and Geigy aided the Allied war effort. Since 1920 the three Swiss firms had shared in the ownership of Cincinnati Chemical Works; in 1943, this plant extended beyond its dyestuff product lines to include the manufacture of the insecticide DDT, a new product, based on the Swiss research of Geigy scientist and soon to be Nobel Prize winner Paul Müller. DDT proved highly effective in containing epidemic disease in battle zones, particularly in tropical areas.[182] Independently, Ciba innovated in dyestuffs.[183]

The Belgian Solvay & Cie. remained the largest single beneficial owner of the multiproduct Allied Chemical & Dye Corporation. The latter's National Aniline Division contributed dyestuff goods of various sorts to the war effort. After the attack on Pearl Harbor (and before the completion of U.S. government-owned ammonia plants), the Solvay Process Company, a wholly owned subsidiary of Allied Chemical, provided the main source of synthetic nitrogen products from its Hopewell, Virginia, plant.[184] Although the Belgian Solvay & Cie. was a key shareholder in Allied Chemical, it is doubtful that by the time of World War II it had much—if any—impact on new technologies at the giant U.S. chemical corporation. Nonetheless, historically there had been substantial influence, and the linkages (including past technological transfers) among the global chemical companies had clearly been encouraged by the Belgian investor. Early in 1945, Baron Boël of Solvay & Cie. told Du Pont officials that he attached "great importance to technical cooperation with ICI and if possible, with Du Pont." Given the antitrust environment and Solvay & Cie.'s links with Allied Chemical, Du Pont could not contemplate such an alliance.[185]

Other foreign multinationals developed their business in the United States. The Swiss firm Nestlé—with its fifteen U.S. plants—tripled its output of canned and powdered milk, with about 60 percent of production going to the U.S. and Allied armed forces. Its joint venture in chocolates prospered. As for its new product, Nescafé—introduced in 1939—the entire American output was commandeered by the U.S. armed forces.[186] British FDI expanded. Climax Molybdenum and American Metal would receive U.S. government awards for their superior wartime service (1941–1945).[187] The thread companies—the J. & P. Coats group, American Thread, and Linen Thread—all enlarged their multiplant operations, and the first two added new mills in the American South (Coats in Georgia and American Thread in South Carolina), confirming their commitment to this region.[188] American Thread won an Army-Navy "E" Award for excellence in war production, and its output rose sharply at its Dalton, Georgia, plant.[189]

Although Dunlop Tire Company did no research for the U.S. synthetic rubber program, its Buffalo factory did manufacture tires and tubes—as well as blimps—for war purposes.[190] Two manufacturing companies on the RFC list of British affiliates put up for collateral, Ensign-Bickford and J. W. Berk & Co., produced in the United States for war purposes, the first making prima cord in Avon, Connecticut, and fuses in Simsbury, Connecticut, the second manufacturing calomel (a white powder used as a purgative and fungicide).[191] British American Tobacco's U.S. subsidiary Brown & Williamson sold a sizable portion of its cigarette output to the American military.[192]

In June 1944, Unilever's American subsidiary, Lever Brothers Co., purchased the Pepsodent Company, Chicago, a leader in toothpastes and toothbrushes. Wartime profits were used to finance the acquisition. Lever Brothers flourished, advertising its products with great acumen. Lux Soap was the soap of movie stars: "9 out of 10 Screen Stars use it." Rita Hayworth, Claudette Colbert, and Shirley Temple were featured in its advertisements, as were romances with soldiers. And there were calls for patriotism: "Don't Waste Soap." Lever Brothers was during the war years a very profitable and successful company.[193]

NV Philips had made a trust agreement under which the Hartford National Bank and Trust Co., Hartford, Connecticut, came to have "control" over Philips' business in the United States. On January 9, 1942, North American Philips Company (NAPC) was founded, incorporated in Delaware, to handle Philips' U.S. business. NAPC's shares were held and voted by the Hartford trust.[194] NAPC embarked on war production, supplementing its small existing X-ray plant in Mount Vernon, New York, with a January 1942 purchase of a factory building in Dobbs Ferry, New York; later that same year (in June), NAPC took over the business of the American Electro Metal Corporation, in Lewiston, Maine, producers of molybdenum and tungsten rods. In 1944, NAPC acquired Amperex (with a factory in Brooklyn, New York), a supplier of valves to the U.S. Navy's Signal Corps. It got U.S. government security clearance to continue as a supplier of the military. In addition, NAPC established a research laboratory in Irvington, New York, in 1944. Its executive group in America set out plans for how the U.S. affiliate would develop in the post–World War II years. Its vision was not to compete with General Electric or Radio Corporation of America, its prewar associates, but rather to emphasize other sectors. Its strategies were shaped by the cloud of possible antitrust litigation. Its historian writes that "the agreements between Philips and GE/RCA . . . had been terminated in 1942 for practical reasons." Philips' management thought, however, that this was temporary and initially at least expected that after the war, the agreements would be renewed, antitrust considerations notwithstanding.[195] Like many other European multinationals, the management from NV Philips had blinders and failed to understand either the intent or the seriousness of American policy makers' commitments to an antitrust agenda. But postponement was the order of the day on antitrust matters during most of the war years; meanwhile, Philips produced in the United States for the Allied cause and built up and diversified its previously negligible American operations.

The preceding examples of production in wartime by foreign-owned companies in the United States are far from inclusive. They should, however, give an indication of the ongoing role of foreign business in the vast and expanding American economy. Indeed, what happened with the foreign direct investors during the period that the United States was engaged in the war as a belligerent was that the affiliates usually raised levels of output and became more detached from their parents and more self-reliant in terms of production and research. A number of the ones that had been in the United States for many years started new and impressive research and development facilities, as well as introducing new products not necessarily derived from their parent company's home operations. All the producing affiliates cooperated in the Allied war effort. Although typically no new capital came from abroad, reinvested earnings and domestic borrowings within the

United States proved adequate to finance corporate expansion, albeit in some cases there did seem to exist financial restraints (in the case of Philips, for example, a loan granted by the U.S. government to stimulate war production aided the firm in its U.S. expansion).[196] As had become typical of multinational enterprise, a sizable number of American affiliates within the U.S. market were far from mere "branch" plants, but instead functioned as viable, strong enterprises in their own right. This is important, for it seems quite clear that over the course of time separate large units within giant international businesses take on lives of their own. This was particularly apparent in the cases of Shell Oil and Lever Brothers, for example, but true of a number of other foreign-owned affiliates as well.

Foreign Banks, Insurance Companies, and Shipping Services

Throughout the war, the large Canadian banks retained their agencies in New York City, and Canadian bankers stayed on as an integral part of the Wall Street community. Economic ties between the United States and Canada grew ever closer, and experienced Canadian bankers in New York were able to handle the mounting transactions.[197] When America entered the war, Japanese and Italian banking operations in the United States ceased, taken over first by the Department of the Treasury (and state regulators) and then by the Office of Alien Property Custodian; by war's end, these financial institutions' outlets in the United States were in various states of liquidation.[198] German banks' pre–World War II role in the United States had been very limited; there were no German bank agencies to liquidate.

British banks and other foreign banks in New York supplied vital intelligence. Shortly after Pearl Harbor, for example, the British Foreign Office asked the British embassy in Washington "to keep directly in contact with A. G. Kellogg," manager of the New York agency of the Hongkong and Shanghai Bank. Like many of the New York personnel at foreign banks, he was a highly knowledgeable international banker.[199] Generally, foreign banks had sent top people to serve in New York; they thrived on being well informed—and not only about banking.

The banks that had been headquartered in enemy-occupied territories typically maintained their U.S. operations, often under the aegis of bankers who fled to the United States to escape the Germans. They received licenses to operate. It was Dutch bankers who explained to the Office of Alien Property Custodian many of the details of the cloaking processes.[200] The French American Banking Corporation (FABC), New York—50 percent owned by the Comptoir National d'Escompte de Paris—acted as a financial intermediary for the Western Hemisphere colonies of France, "using Vichy Government funds under the supervision of the U.S. Treasury. It ordered and supervised the printing of currency for nearly all the French colonies."[201] In March 1942, it reported to the Federal Reserve that its domestic accounts had increased substantially over the last few years because "many customers of long standing in various parts of the world have now come to reside in this country [the United States]. In most instances our bank was the only financial institution within the United States with which these people had any connection. Furthermore, their establishment in this country has in general nothing permanent about it nor can it have any quality of permanency until each one finds out what his position is after the war." By contrast, "foreign" transactions had gone down, due to the "blocking of practically all our foreign accounts."[202] French executives of the Banque de l'Indo-Chine temporarily stationed themselves in New York to protect that bank's interests.[203] Jewish arrivals Pierre David-Weill and André Meyer from the French Lazard Frères et Cie. transformed their American investment banking house; they ousted its principal partner, Frank Altshull, and exercised French "control" (during wartime from New York rather than Paris).[204] The British-owned J. Henry Schroder Banking Corporation marketed U.S. government bonds; its executives also provided intelligence services to the U.S. government, using its prewar German contacts. Over the years this British firm had grown larger than its parent.[205]

In short, in New York a coterie of talented foreign bankers and banks offered a range of international banking services. None supplied basic retail banking for American consumers; all participated in "international banking," broadly defined. Interestingly, whereas with the manufacturing affiliates, the tendency during the war had been to set the basis for more independence from their parent organizations, in the case of Lazard Frères it was the opposite: when the French partners settled in New York, they took control and would maintain it in the postwar era.

The war years meant that foreign banks tended to be more than ever concentrated in New York City. The one foreign bank in Boston, Bank of Nova Scotia, closed its branch in 1942.[206] In Chicago, the Bank of Montreal did retain its long-standing branch. On the West Coast, the takeovers of the Japanese banks sharply reduced the foreign banking presence, although the Hongkong and Shanghai Banking Corporation kept its longtime San Francisco agency, and the Canadians remained, as did the Bank of Canton, San Francisco.[207] But New York was the hub for foreign banks and international banking.

Foreign (particularly British) insurance companies were far more numerous than the foreign banks. Unlike the foreign banks, they served mainly domestic (American) clients. The ranks of these insurance companies were only slightly depleted with the OAPC takeover of Pilot Reinsurance Co., the only major German, or for that matter "enemy," investment in insurance (the Japanese and the one Italian insurance companies were small by comparison).[208] British insurers prospered. So, too, Swiss reinsurance companies came to play an ever larger and more important role.[209]

Perhaps the biggest change in these service sector investments during the war years was in the revival of American shipping and the consequent reduction in the relative importance of foreign shipping. As in World War I, the U.S. government invested heavily in boosting its nation's shipping capacity and proved highly successful in doing so. By war's end, as historian René De La Pedraja has put it, "for the first and last time in history," U.S. shipping represented "a majority of the world's ocean trade . . . the United States emerged [from World War II] with the world's largest merchant fleet and a majority of the world's tonnage." It was an astonishing accomplishment. Yet it was not enduring. The U.S. ships were almost immediately obsolete. In the postwar period, U.S. shipping would once again go into decline, in both absolute and relative terms.[210]

The Special Anglo-American Relationship

Throughout the war years, British investment in the United States persisted as the largest of any single nationality. When in 1939–1941 the United States had not yet become a combatant, substantial attention from Washington and the rest of America—as well as within Britain—had focused on the plans to decrease British assets in America so as to obtain dollars to cover the costs of British and Allied purchases of supplies. Discussions had reached a high pitch when Congress had debated lend lease (passed March 1941), when Courtaulds' U.S. properties had been sold, and when the Reconstruction Finance Corporation loan had been negotiated.

Finally, roughly three months after the attack on Pearl Harbor, on February 23, 1942, the United States and Britain signed the so-called Mutual Aid Agreement, elaborating the principles for lend lease. Article 7 of the agreement set forth the legal framework for postwar economic planning.[211] In the context of the still-unresolved topic of lend-lease repayments, over the course of 1942–1945 there were further, although decidedly toned-down and sporadic, discussions on British assets in the United States. While the attention to British holdings in this country ebbed and flowed, it never at any time approximated the ferocity or visibility that had been evident early in 1941.[212] The major sales of British-owned

American securities took place before December 1941, albeit there continued to be a steady stream of sales. The British companies that were put up as collateral for the Reconstruction Finance Corporation loan went on doing business in the United States, as did others not so committed. The authorized RFC loan had been $425 million; the British drew only $390 million and did this by the end of the third quarter of 1942.[213] The collateral was more than adequate. No one in the United States championed additional major British sales of private holdings. As British economist D. F. McCurrach pointed out (in 1948), with direct investments "their earning power depended, not only upon the trading link, but upon the very reputation and goodwill of the British owners. Divested of these ties their sale meant the grossest sacrifice. Moreover, they were an integral part of the British trading and financial economy. It was widely recognized later in America [after the Courtaulds sale] that they should never have been treated as available for sale."[214]

Nonetheless, on occasion, concerns over British assets in America were rekindled in the discourse on Britain's postwar obligations under lend lease and in the context of designing an appropriate international monetary regime for the postwar era. Throughout the British insisted they had given up all there was to offer in the way of their nationals' U.S. assets, and America should take care not to leave its ally as a helpless destroyed economy; the British argued that they needed income from overseas investments to cope with the dire state of their country's balance of payments and to provide for postwar recovery.[215] When, however, the British were worried in 1943 and subsequently about the sentiment in Washington that "we are not entitled to lend-lease as long as we have a dollar in the till," the focus moved away from British stock market securities and British direct investments to "British gold and dollar reserves"—which after 1943 had begun to rise as a consequence of British exports, South African gold production, and the spending of U.S. troops.[216] In addition, there continued to be many Anglo-American diplomatic exchanges on oil policies (and a planned Anglo-American Petroleum Agreement, which never came to pass).[217]

In 1942–1945, a slow (now very limited) attrition in certain existing British investments in America went forward. The British government liquidated some added American securities that it had vested from British subjects in 1939–1940 and had not been pledged against the RFC loan. Scottish mortgage companies that were still in the U.S. mortgage business in 1942, "in accord with the wishes" of the British Treasury, "continued to bring home [from the United States] all available collections."[218] By 1945, the Scottish American Mortgage Co., for example, was entirely out of U.S. mortgage lending. Its 1942 annual report—presented July 29, 1942—had shown £194,716 in U.S. mortgages and real estate. The 1945 report (August 11, 1945) revealed zero such investments. The company did, however, list £62,105 in American securities (actually up from £36,094 in 1942). As it closed off the mortgage business, it put some of the paybacks into securities.[219] The Texas Land and Mortgage Company, Ltd., another firm with strong Scottish connections, revealed in its year end March 1943 annual report for the first time in its history no loans on mortgages; it still had some real estate holdings based on foreclosures. It invested in securities, albeit it is not clear how large a portion of these securities was in the United States.[220] Other British companies closed out their mortgage lending.[221] The process of Scottish and English withdrawal from American mortgage lending was ongoing during the war and nearly completed by war's end.

The Liverpool merchant house Booth & Co. had a factory in Gloversville, New York, opened in 1877; it had been periodically shut down (in 1920 to modernize, in 1924–1929 and 1931–1933 because of an absence of possibilities of profit, and for the last time, in 1938, owing to the lack of demand for its output). The factory was finally sold to Americans in 1942. The company did, however, keep its Philadelphia manufacturing plant.[222] In 1941, shortly after the outbreak of war, to conserve shipping space, the U.S. government had barred the import of quebracho logs, allowing, however, the import of solid extract. Since the Forestal Land, Timber & Railway Company's plant in Wilmington, Delaware, was built (in 1927) to obtain liquid quebracho extract from the logs, in 1942 the British firm sold this plant to Americans.[223] Once again this was only a partial retreat: Forestal's affiliate the Tannin Corporation continued to handle about 70 percent of U.S. imports of quebracho extract. Indeed, Seymour D. Lewis of the Antitrust Department of the Justice Department testified at a 1943 hearing that Forestal controlled "this material from the tree [in Argentina] to the United States consumer."[224]

One British divestment was the Firth Sterling crucible steel plant (a manufacturing involvement that dated back to 1896); for some time, its British parent had ceased to play a managerial role in the activities of this affiliate; although the parent retained a majority of the shares, the investment when sold to Americans in 1944 had for all practical purposes become a passive one.[225] That year, 1944, the Anglo-American Direct Tea Trading Company sold its U.S. subsidiary (incorporated in 1912) to the latter's U.S. management.[226]

So, too, Balfour, Guthrie—the affiliate of the British Balfour, Williamson—curtailed its activities. Its flour milling investment (Crown Mills) had been put up for collateral on the RFC loan; it was apparently released as collateral and sold; this had also been the case with Firth Sterling.[227] There was also the spin-off of the Delta Planting Co., Deeson, Mississippi (another firm put up as collateral on the RFC loan); it owned a cotton plantation and was in turn majority owned by Fine Cotton Spinners' and Doublers' Association (FCSDA) and jointly managed with the latter's far larger and more important cotton plantations (which were owned by the affiliated company, Delta and Pine Land Company, Scott, Mississippi). DPLC, with its huge cotton plantations, remained British owned, by FCSDA.[228]

In sum, the exits from U.S. investments represented a very small portion of British stakes in America. Most British multinational enterprises stayed on and expanded. In fact, although in the years 1942–1945 there may have been a net reduction in British portfolio holdings in America (this is not clear because of the appreciation of some of the remaining holdings), it appears that the few departures by British direct investors during 1942–1945 were more than offset by the reinvested earnings of ongoing British companies (while some remitted dollars to England, many apparently built up their U.S. business).[229]

In July 1944, meetings were held at Bretton Woods, New Hampshire, to plan for the International Monetary Fund and the World Bank, and to shape the course of the world economy. Delegates from forty-five nations participated, but Americans and British took the lead.[230] Discussions arose on how enemies and their collaborators were transferring assets to and through neutral countries in order to conceal them. An attempt was made to develop internationally consistent policies on enemy and neutral countries' assets that had been "blocked" during the war (not only in the United States but in many countries). Under Resolution VI at Bretton Woods, the so-called Safehaven Program was formulated, which aimed to track down enemy assets hidden outside the enemy lands. The British were particularly eager to see to it that the United States did not gain these assets at British expense.[231]

At the Bretton Woods meetings the roles of governments were charted in the creation of a proposed new international monetary order and in the plans for the revival of international trade and investment. The dollar would be central to the international system. Issues of monetary stability, convertibility, national recovery, and reconstruction and development were foremost. Foreign investment in the United States was barely at the margin in the deliberations; it only sneaked in the side door when the British balance of payments was discussed, when inter-Allied obligations were pondered, and when there was the ongoing dialogue about the treatment of "looted" property—property that Germans had spirited (or might spirit) out of Germany or had accumulated in occupied and neutral lands. Interestingly, although everyone at Bretton Woods was hoping for future more open markets and for the reduction and elimination of barriers to trade, there was a general acceptance of the view that in the postwar era sustained capital controls might be necessary. Nothing in the charters of the new Bretton Woods institutions provided for the free flows of capital. Capital controls were seen as a requisite tool in monetary policy.[232]

In April 1945, when Roosevelt died, Harry Truman replaced him as president of the United States. V-E Day was May 8 and V-J Day, August 14. As the war drew to a close, British postwar obligations were still ill defined. The British insisted that their economy was in ruin, and their assets in America were minimal and should be left alone.[233] The British had drawn only $390 million of the $425 million Reconstruction Finance Corporation loan, and by August 31, 1945, the principal on that loan was down to $272 million as a result of the contributions of some sales of collateral ($17.5 million) and income in excess of the interest requirements on the loan.[234] In the main, the operations of British firms in the United States had gone forward—affected by war conditions, regulations, and taxes—but not hobbled by the international politics of Allied war finance. The pre–U.S. entry sacrifice by the British of the Courtaulds business proved a painful exception. During the years of U.S. participation in the war, most British direct investments (whether or not put up as collateral) had continued and appreciated in value, as did most of the other British vested and pledged investments in this country. As planning for the peace occurred, British investment assets in America were no longer a priority topic for debate. Much more serious for the British was the changing U.S.-U.K. relationship. Britain was steadily losing prestige in international finance, humiliating to the once great power.[235]

The Special Canadian-U.S. Relationships

As of June 1941, Canadian investments in the United States were second only to those of the United Kingdom. During the war years, a number of new issues of Canadian government and corporate securities were acquired by U.S. investors (outward foreign portfolio investments). There was substantial trade in these and existing Canadian securities on Wall Street, but also on Canadian exchanges; the trade was by both Americans and Canadians.[236] For the Canadians, all transactions in securities and other properties required a license from the Canadian Foreign Exchange Control Board. Data collected by the Canadians indicated a large increase in U.S. holdings of Canadian securities (outward U.S. investments); to the extent that these were U.S. issues and formerly held by Canadians, this would reduce Canadian investments in the United States.[237] As in times past, there was considerable trade in U.S. domestic securities over the border, the foreign exchange controls notwithstanding. One study of international transactions by foreigners in American securities noted that Canadians had purchased U.S. government bonds in large amounts in 1944 and then sold these same securities in 1945.[238] The Canadian trading in American securities was easily done through well-established channels in the United States and in Canada. At war's end, private sector Canadian portfolio investments in the United States appear to have been smaller than in December 1941. At year's end 1945, however, the Canadian government's international reserve assets in the United States came to $1.3 billion, a remarkable wartime increase. Canadians were active producing for war at home, and their business activities in the United States seem to have been subordinated to the task of winning the war. Nonetheless, Canadian direct investments increased in the United States from December 1941 to December 1945, probably mainly through reinvested earnings. While a substantial part of the Canadian direct investments in the United States continued to be in railroads, all the rise was in "industrial and commercial" direct investments. Canadian statistics for year end 1945 indicate that by then Canadian direct investments exceeded private sector Canadian portfolio investments in the United States, with FDI rising 1939–1945 and FPI declining 1939–1945.[239]

Performance

Throughout this volume I have said little about the performance of foreign investment in the United States (owing to the sparseness of data). For the 1920s, I noted the prevailing view (and overall measures) indicating that rates of return were greater on U.S. outward than on inward investments. For the 1930s, with the many defaults on outward investments, it was hard to find appropriate gauges on rewards to outward versus inward investments, albeit I did comment on the diverse performance of foreign multinational enterprises within the United States—the very successful ones and others that had difficulties (above and beyond those of comparable domestic enterprises in the same industries). For the war years, after more care in measurement, some striking figures exist, comparing inward foreign investment to domestic investment and comparing outward and inward foreign investments. A study (published in 1948) looked at the ratio of dividends to market values on *Moody's* series of 200 common stocks and compared it with the ratio of dividends to market values on foreign portfolio investments in corporate stock 1942–1945; the ratios corresponded closely, although the returns to foreign investors in corporate stock were slightly lower than those on the *Moody's* 200 common stocks.[240] Theory would suggest that foreign investors with less information than domestic ones might well have slightly lower returns.[241]

What was most dramatic, however, were the 1942–1945 comparisons between (1) the ratio of income paid out to the book value of U.S. outward direct investments, (2) the dividends of all U.S. corporations, and (3) the payments made by inward (into the United States) foreign direct investors. The first (the return on U.S. business abroad, running just under 5 percent to 5.5 percent) was by far the highest; the second was more or less about 1 percent below the first (ca. 4 percent); but the third (the ratio of income paid out to the book value of foreign direct investment in the United States) was consistently some 1.5 percentage points below the second (ca. 2.5 percent).[242] What does this mean? It could be interpreted as indicating that during the war years foreign business in the United States performed in a manner worse than U.S. business abroad and all American companies in the United States. Alas, it is not that simple, for there are other explanations, including the obvious one that foreign businesses in the United States reinvested earnings rather than paid them out in dividends, so "income paid out" may be an inappropriate measure of performance.[243] The Commerce Department study pointed out that there were wide differences among various groups of inward investors in rates of return, with Canadian direct investments in railroads having extremely low income, while the returns on foreign direct investments in the oil industry were substantial.[244] I include these partial, unsatisfying findings as part of the overall story of foreign investment in the United States; clearly parent companies of American business abroad got immediate financial benefits that greatly exceeded those of the parents of foreign business in the United States.

Conclusions

What, then, can we conclude about the principal changes in size and characteristics of long-term foreign investments in the United States in the period of American involvement as a belligerent in the Second World War? On the size, as a benchmark, we have the census data for June 14, 1941, with total long-term inward investment given as $6 billion, composed of $2.7 billion in securities, $2.3 billion in controlled enterprises, and $1 billion in trusts and estates, real estate mortgages, and real estate. These numbers are reproduced in the first column of "estimate 1" on Table 9.4, along with an "updating" in the second column for year end 1945. Table 9.4 also has a second set of estimates on the level of foreign investment in the United States, year end 1941 and 1945, based on different figures published in 1948.[245] Estimate 2 can be best reconciled to the first estimate if the category under private obligations labeled "other" is subtracted from both the December 31, 1941, and the 1945, figures, as is done in the second total.[246]

Table 9.4. Long-term foreign investments in the United States, 1941, 1945, two estimates (in millions of U.S. dollars)

A. Estimate 1

Investments	June 14, 1941	Dec. 31, 1945
Securities (total)	2,699	4,420
Bonds	546	1,090
Stocks	2,153	3,330
Controlled enterprises	2,313	2,400
Estates and trusts	867	800
Mortgages and real estate	125	n.a.
Total	6,004	7,620

Sources: 1941: See Table 8.3 (based on *1941 Census*). 1945: These figures were the June 14, 1941, ones carried forward by the Treasury Department "in collaboration with the International Economics Division, Office of Business Economics, Department of Commerce." They were provided for comparative purposes in U.S. Department of the Treasury, Office of the Secretary, *Census of American-Owned Assets in Foreign Countries* (Washington, D.C., 1947), 9. Securities were at market value, while controlled enterprises (i.e., direct investments) were given at book value. Bonds include government as well as corporate securities, along with some other "long-term" securities. The value of enemy property in the United States seized by the Alien Property Custodian *is not excluded* from the 1945 figures.

B. Estimate 2

Obligation	Dec. 31, 1941	Dec. 31, 1945
Private obligations		
Securities (total)	2,425	4,062
Corporate bonds	475	692
Corporate stocks	1,950	3,370
Direct investments	2,700	2,675
Estates and trusts	775	655
Other	1,300	1,110
U.S. government obligations		
Long-term	150	493
Total	7,350	8,995
Total (minus "other")	6,050	7,895

Source: 1941 and 1945: U.S. Department of Commerce, Office of Business Economics, *International Transactions of the United States during the War, 1940–1945,* Economic Series No. 65 (Washington, D.C., 1948), 110, 224–225. Securities were at market value; in both years corporate bonds included an estimate of $100 million of state and municipal obligations. Direct investments were given at book value. Personal property and real estate held by individuals for nonbusiness uses were excluded. The value of enemy property in the United States seized by the Alien Property Custodian *is excluded* from the 1945 figures. The large category of "other" is subtracted from the second total, so as to reconcile the two estimates.

The year end 1945 figures in the first estimate indicate that total long-term foreign investment had risen during the war years to $7.6 billion, composed of $4.4 billion in securities, $2.4 billion in direct investments, and the rest in trusts and estates (no figure was given on real estate and real estate mortgages). Estimate 2 (excluding the "other" category) is slightly different from the first for 1945 and gives some added precision. If we subtract the $1,100 million "other," the total comes to $7.9 billion, composed of $4.6 billion in securities ($4.1 in securities plus $.5 in U.S. government obligations), $2.7 billion in direct investments, and the rest in trusts and estates. Actually estimate 2 divides the $4.6 billion in securities into $3.4 billion in corporate stock, $.7 billion in bonds (of which $.6 billion was in corporate bonds plus $.1 billion in state and municipal bonds), and $.5 billion in U.S. government long-term bonds. It increases the amount of direct investment by $.3 billion over the first estimate.

All these figures are to be evaluated with great caution. What they do seem to demonstrate is that during the time of U.S. participation in the Second World War, while there may have been a slight decline in British investments in American securities and there certainly was a drop in British investments in real estate mortgages, while the Office of Alien Property Custodian's takeover of enemy properties should be treated as a reduction in foreign investments in the United States (as is done in estimate 2, but not in estimate 1), overall—the subtractions in foreign investment notwithstanding—there does appear to have been in net a rise in the level of inward foreign investments from December 1941 to December 1945.[247] The increase during the war years seems to be based mainly on (1) the appreciation in values in the American stock market (for portfolio investments, the level was measured by market values) and (2) new investments in traded securities from private individuals and governments, seeking safety, rising values, and in the case of governments, currency stabilization.[248] Both estimates in Table 9.4 show a growth in the value of inward foreign portfolio investments during the war; the increase in corporate stocks exceeded the rise in the Dow Jones industrial average from Pearl Harbor to V-J Day.[249] Estimate 2 suggests that a part of the upturn in foreign portfolio investments during wartime was based on an enlargement in foreign holdings of long-term U.S. government debt; other data lend credence to this.

The figures in Table 9.4 for estimate 1 (which do not take into account the vesting activities of the Office of Alien Property Custodian) suggest a growth in inward foreign direct investments, whereas estimate 2 (which has higher FDI figures for 1941 *and* 1945) records a slight decrease in foreign direct investments, apparently based mainly on the takeovers by the Alien Property Custodian; as I have detailed there were also some other small exits. There were, in addition, during the war years increases in FDI through reinvested earnings by existing foreign direct investors in the United States.

Interestingly, despite the trauma of war and the massive government interventions in the United States and abroad, the overall contours of foreign investments in the United States during the years of American involvement in the war (1942–1945) changed only slightly (a far larger change having taken place in 1939–1941). The obvious difference lies in the takeover of the German and Japanese interests, reducing these to zero. But long before U.S. entry into the war, recorded German and Japanese interests had become small, so that their elimination failed to lower in a dramatic manner the statistics on foreign investments in the United States (although their end certainly modified the nature of operations and control). Another change was the increase in foreign ownership of U.S. federal government bonds (albeit the sums were still small).

Neither the U.S. Commerce Department nor the Treasury Department provided general figures by nationality on the level of all inward long-term foreign investments in 1945, but my own research can establish a ranking with a reasonable degree of confidence.[250] When the war was over, it seems clear that the British remained the largest single nationality in terms of level of investments in the United States. The Canadians were in the second spot, with no shift in rank from 1941 (or from 1929). Swiss stakes (although "blocked" during the war, based on the 1941 Foreign Funds Control regulations) had undoubtedly grown in relative importance, a growth already evident in the years 1939–1941. Whether they or Dutch interests were in third or fourth place is not clear, albeit there is evidence that at least nominally Swiss holdings had come to exceed those of the Dutch.[251] As for the Dutch role, direct investors in the United States apparently extended their businesses principally through reinvested earnings and other financing separate from capital imports, while the blocked portfolio investments had appreciated in value. It is hard to identify any major changes in the blocked French investments in the United States. France had, of course, been an occupied country, as was Holland. Wealthy investors from other European nations, from Latin America, and from Asia (principally China) had put much of their savings in American securities. Because of the takeovers by the Alien Property Custodian, I am prepared to set the level of German, Japanese, and Italian investments in the United States in 1945 at zero.

At war's end the ratio (the mix) of inward foreign portfolio investment and inward foreign direct investment had not been radically restructured (when compared with either June 1941 or December 1941), although the doubtful figures in Table 9.4 suggest that the ratio of inward FPI to inward FDI increased. It does seem likely that overall inward FPI continued to exceed inward FDI. Some figures suggest, however, that in the case of both the British and the Canadians, at war's end FDI exceeded FPI.[252]

What about other characteristics of the foreign investments in the United States? The near end to British mortgage lending in America was significant—but not in terms of overall numbers, since the British mortgage share in 1941 was already quite tiny; also, frequently, as in earlier years, onetime mortgage lenders were becoming investment trusts. The Americanization of Courtaulds' large rayon properties had been dramatic, but this had occurred before U.S. entry into the war. The elimination of the important German influence on the U.S. chemical industry, a profound difference in inward foreign investment, did represent a break with the past, which, however, would prove temporary. German (and Swiss) direct investments had helped to set the basis for a vibrant U.S. domestic pharmaceutical industry. Affiliates of Swiss firms expanded during the war years and continued to be highly innovative. American companies had been able to absorb rapidly German technologies. An outcome of the war was more research and high-technology activities by existing foreign direct investors. All this notwithstanding, although foreign investment in the United States in current dollars appears to have grown, the rise was nowhere near that of the overall expansion of the American economy. Suspicions and criticisms aside, in the war years the foreign contributions to U.S. technological developments (through FDI) were more important than the additions to the level of U.S. investment. Foreign investors aided the U.S. war effort.

10.

American Hegemony

When the Second World War ended, America was the global leader. The United States emerged from the war with the strongest economy in the world. It was a creditor nation (see Table 10.1)—and by far the most important one. Yet creditor status did not mean the absence of foreign obligations, only that its obligations were less than those of foreigners to Americans. Unlike at the close of the First World War, when the United States was newly transformed into a creditor from its prior debtor nation position, now the nation was secure in this role and poised to assume the responsibilities of leadership. In 1945, when references were made in the United States to "foreign investment," typically it was to outward, not inward, investments.

The course of foreign investments in the United States since 1914 had been jagged. Foreign investments had dropped sharply during World War I; inward foreign investments had grown in the 1920s and even more in the 1930s, were reduced in 1939–1941, and had risen during World War II. Meanwhile, the U.S. economy (the economic downturns notwithstanding) had expanded, so that by the end of the Second World War, inward foreign investment, measured as a share of U.S. gross national product, was at a low level vis-à-vis that in 1914, or 1929, or 1939 (see Column 1, Table 10.2). Column 2 of Table 10.2 tells a similar story, but exclusively for foreign direct investments. Put another way, in 1945, in current dollars, total foreign investment in the United States was slightly more than in 1914 (foreign direct investment was roughly 1.6 times its 1914 level), while the nation's gross national product had soared almost sixfold. Although the underlying figures for these calculations are fragile (and the comparisons of level of inward investment and gross national product are of apples and oranges), the trend is unmistakable. It, of course, reflects the subordinate nature of inward foreign investment—and America's creditor nation status.

Table 10.1. One estimate of the long-term foreign investment position of the United States, 1945 (in billions of U.S. dollars)

	U.S. investments abroad					Foreign investments in U.S.				
			Private accounts					Private obligations		
Date	(A) Total	(B) Government lending	(C) Total	(D) Portfolio investments	(E) Direct investments	(F) Total	(G) Government borrowings	(H) Total	(I) Portfolio investments	(J) Direct investments
1945 (Dec. 31)	13.9	1.6	12.3	4.2	8.1	7.9	0.6	7.3	4.6	2.7

Source: This table, which is to be used with great caution, is an attempt to provide information analogous to what was presented in Table 1.14. It is based on a table on the "International Investment Position of the United States," given in U.S. Department of Commerce, Office of Business Economics, *International Transactions of the United States during the War, 1940–1945,* Economic Series No. 65 (Washington, D.C., 1948), 110. Appendix 3 provides details.

Table 10.2. Foreign investment in the United States as a percentage of gross national product, rough estimates for 1914, 1918, 1929, 1939, 1941, and 1945

Date for level of foreign investment	(1) Foreign investment in the U.S. as % of GNP (3) ÷ (5) × 100	(2) Foreign direct investment in the U.S. as % of GNP (4) ÷ (5) × 100	(3) Level of foreign investment in the U.S. (in billions of dollars)	(4) Level of foreign direct investment in the U.S. (in billions of dollars)	(5) GNP for the year (in billions of dollars)
1914 (June)	19.5	4.7	7.1	1.7	36.4
1918 (Dec.)	3.9	1.3	3.0	1.0	76.4
1929 (Dec.)	5.6	1.4	5.8	1.5	103.1
1939 (Dec.)	6.8–9.6	3.2	6.2–8.7	2.9	90.5
1941 (June)	4.8	1.8	6.0	2.3	124.5
1945 (Dec.)	3.7	1.3	7.9	2.7	211.9

Sources: Columns 1 and 2 are based on data in columns 3–5. Columns 3 and 4: Table 1.14 (1914, 1918); Table 4.1 (1929); Table 2.1 (foreign investment, 1939); Table 2.1, column 7 (foreign direct investment, 1939); Table 8.3 (1941); Table 10.1 (1945). Column 5: U.S. Department of Commerce, *Long-Term Economic Growth 1860–1965* (Washington, D.C., 1966), 167 (1914); U.S. Department of Commerce, Bureau of the Census, *Historical Statistics of the United States* (Washington, D.C., 1975), I, 224, Series F1 (1918–1945).

Caveat: The reader is warned to be wary of these estimates; they are presented merely to suggest the trends. In earlier chapters I have provided alternate estimates. Here, with the exception of 1939, I made selections of the estimate that I felt was most appropriate.

In 1945 U.S. policy makers sought to shape a peaceful world, one that would not a generation later result in a Third World War. No one desired to return to prewar conditions. Rather the goal was to craft a new order where trade could and would expand. During the 1930s and the war, around the globe current and capital account controls had proliferated.[1] In 1945 there was a broad international commitment to dismantle the former, but not the latter. Arthur I. Bloomfield (who was at the Federal Reserve Bank of New York) stated at the annual meeting of the American Economic Association (AEA) in December 1945, "It is now highly respectable doctrine, in academic and banking circles alike, that a substantial measure of *direct* control over private capital movements, especially of the so-called 'hot money' varieties, will be desirable for most countries not only in the years immediately ahead but also in the long run as well." Bloomfield included the United States in his thinking about "most countries."[2] Bloomfield cited approvingly a 1944 comment made by the British economist Joan Robinson: "It is clear enough in principle that private owners of wealth have no right to the liberty to move funds around the world according to their private convenience, and it is clear that, in the uneasy conditions of modern times, no conceivable international currency system can survive for long if that liberty is granted."[3] Bloomfield favored controls on both inward and outward capital movements.[4] But in his AEA presentation, he dealt with portfolio flows and paid no attention to direct investments. In 1945–1946, worldwide, governments had to approve capital movements. In the postwar United States the existing freezes of foreign assets imposed in 1940–1941 were restrictions on capital flows. Following the Keynesian view, government was perceived by most economists and policy makers as playing a major role in fiscal and monetary as well as foreign economic policy. If monetary policy was to be effective, John Maynard Keynes believed that governments could not be at the mercy of international forces; regulations over capital movements were appropriate.[5]

When the war ended, it left in its wake a raft of unresolved matters associated with inward foreign investments in the United States. None related to the ability of Americans to meet obligations; the country was, after all, a creditor nation. The uncertainties arose out of the circumstances of war. As the problems were addressed (and some of importance remained pending until the 1960s), inward foreign investments would once more start to grow, slowly at first, and then from the early 1970s onward in a crescendo.

The legacies of the 1914–1945 years that would influence the post–World War II experiences were not trivial. As late as 1961, just under half of the foreign-controlled enterprises operating in the United States had been established or acquired prior to 1941; even more to the point, in 1961 these historical carryovers accounted for fully 80 percent of the value of the level of inward foreign direct investment.[6] I have no comparable measure, across all nationalities, on the ongoing inward foreign portfolio investments, although scattered evidence does show important continuities, and if not of the investments themselves, then certainly of the knowledgeable institutional investors that used their accumulated information to shape their future investment strategies. By 1970 the total foreign investment into the United States remained only 5 percent of gross national product, that is, a share lower than in 1929 or 1939, much less in the heyday before the First World War.[7] Cross-investments, both FPI and FDI, persisted.

Matters to Be Resolved

What were the immediate pending problems related to inward foreign investments in the United States at war's end? One broad group was associated with the design of the international monetary system and the international trading system. Global in nature, these topics were only very tangentially joined with considerations of inward foreign investment. Most important in the shaping of overall postwar policies, the linkages that were present were not made explicit or perceived as key items on the agenda. Nonetheless, although foreign investment in the United States was not significant in the formation of such policies, the opposite was the case: these policies influenced the thinking about existing inward foreign investments.[8]

The issues associated with foreign investments in the United States derived from specific prewar and wartime developments and can be divided by source of investments: (1) those by residents of nations that had been America's wartime allies and whose assets had never been blocked—principally the inward investments from the United Kingdom and Canada; (2) those by residents of nonenemy nations (including both formerly enemy-occupied and neutral countries), the assets of which had been blocked since 1940–1941, mainly those of Dutch, French, Swiss, and Swedish investors; and (3) those of residents of enemy nations, overwhelmingly German and Japanese assets; since the takeover of these properties had been authorized during the war, these were, so to speak, no longer inward foreign investments. Under each of the three rubrics, separate public policy considerations arose. Although British assets had not been frozen, many had been put up as collateral for the Reconstruction Finance Corporation (RFC) loan. In addition, the question of repayments—if any—for lend lease had to be weighed in the context of British assets in the United States. In the second category, there were debates on the unblocking of assets, while in the third group a separate but often related set of difficulties surfaced. In addition, foreign-owned firms in all three classifications had been the targets of antitrust suits that during the war years had for the most part been held in abeyance and now would be revisited and, frequently, revived. The perceptions about and treatment of foreign assets in the United States were intimately tied in with the visions of policy makers as they formulated plans for the postwar world economy—including not only international monetary and trading relationships but also the rebuilding of a fractured British economy, the attempts to understand the consequences of the war, the questions inherent in developing appropriate occupation and postoccupation policies toward Germany and Japan, and, most critical, seeing to it that peace prevailed. Almost from the start of the postwar deliberations, reciprocity topics came into play as the U.S. government sought to encourage American outward investment worldwide.

Winston Churchill's "Iron Curtain" speech, delivered March 5, 1946, marked the start of the Cold War—and the realignments of friends and foes. The Morgenthau plan of leaving Germany totally without resources was abandoned. The United States became committed to restoring both West Germany and Japan as viable democratic nations with healthy economies. The Marshall Plan in 1947 confirmed America's leadership role in the postwar world.

British Assets and Obligations

The British government wanted to be certain that the war's victory would not be a Pyrrhic one. British Treasury and Bank of England officials insisted that their nation depended on dollar assets to obtain dollar earnings and that to deprive Britain of its overseas (in particular its remaining American) assets would prove a death knell to the British economy. British economists and diplomats continued to plead that Britain was destitute. British investors and business leaders, in addition, saw their private property in the United States as legitimately theirs. At war's conclusion, there was no need for further "sacrifice."

The British held elections in July 1945, resulting in the Labour Party's Clement Attlee replacing the Conservative Winston Churchill. It was for Attlee's government to negotiate the postwar agenda. In August President Truman approved the abrupt cancellation of lend lease. In the ongoing discussions on the Lend-Lease Settlement and the Anglo-American Financial Agreement of 1946, British investments in the United States were included in the deliberations.[9] In the Lend-Lease Settlement, the United States accepted the write-off of all claims for some $25 billion in lend-lease supplies and services provided during the war, and in the Agreement the United States would lend the United Kingdom new moneys, deferring interest payments until 1951.[10] The British were able to convince Americans that they had no important existing U.S. assets to pay back any of the lend lease, or the sales of which could substitute for the new loan. The 1946 arrangements left untouched the sizable portion of British assets in America that had been put up as collateral for the RFC loan (the collateral now greatly exceeded the principal of the loan) as well as the British assets not included in the collateral. Throughout, the British reiterated that these assets were inconsequential, and they should be allowed to retain the little that was left because of their nation's dollar requirements. In this spirit, one British economist wrote in 1948, "It is to be hoped that we shall not need to sell the relic of our marketable securities, and even more that our direct investments will be preserved."[11]

By August 31, 1945, the British debt to the RFC stood at $272 million, and by October 1951, in advance of predictions, the British government repaid the entire amount, "in no small measure due to the post-war dollar earnings of the British insurance companies" operating in the United States.[12] The collateral was released, and the British government was free to return to the original British owners the pledged securities and direct investments and do as it wished with the vested American securities it owned. It held on to the latter and in 1956 still owned much of the holdings in American securities that it had vested in 1940–1941 and used as backing for the RFC loan; the value of these securities had appreciated during the war and continued to do so thereafter; they furnished a source of dollar earnings for the British government.[13]

Once the settlement of lend lease had been determined and the Anglo-American Financial Agreement made, the matter of British assets in the United States reverted to a diplomatic back burner. There was no consideration—at least none that I have found—of British investments in the United States in the debates on Marshall Plan aid (in fact, there was an explicit decision not to have as a condition of this aid program the liquidation of any foreign assets in the United States).[14] Subsequently, in all the numerous postwar U.S.-British diplomatic interchanges on future international economic relationships, I have located no evidence that British investments in the United States figured in any critical manner.[15]

Meanwhile, in the immediate postwar years, there had been several exits of long-enduring British investments in America—direct investments that had not been tied up as collateral for the RFC loan, probably in anticipation that they would be divested. Between 1943 and 1950, The Swan Company—the successor to the Swan Land and Cattle

Company (a British investment that originated in the 1880s)—sold off its almost 375,000 acres of Wyoming land and its livestock (principally sheep), paid off its bondholders, and issued a last dividend to its stockholders. In 1951 the company was dissolved.[16] Another British investment that went back to the 1880s, The Matador Land and Cattle Company, comprised vast operations in Texas, Montana, South Dakota, and Nebraska (800,000 acres and 50,000 head of cattle). When, in December 1949, a major oil strike was made near the Matador ranch in Texas, new interest arose in these properties. A year later, Lazard Frères, New York, proposed to buy the property. The owners from Dundee, Scotland, wanted assurance from the British Treasury that they could reinvest the proceeds of the sale in other American securities; they also wanted to retain a "hefty share of the oil and mineral rights on the property." Lazard Brothers, London, aided the New York Lazard house with negotiations. The sale took place in 1951 (for $19 million), and a breakup of the properties occurred. With the end to the Swan and the Matador enterprises as such, the last of the huge British-owned cattle ranches were out of business. This marked the close of an epoch.[17]

Some of the longest-standing British investments in America had been by mortgage companies and investment trusts. Just after the Second World War, the mortgage company investments that had begun in the nineteenth century came to a final close. A late example of the long-evolving process of "mortgage company to investment trust" occurred in 1946 when the Texas Land and Mortgage Company was symbolically restyled the London and Aberdeen Investment Trust.[18]

Other retreats were slower in occurring. Two such were those of pre–World War I investors in textiles. Linen Thread Company faced severe competition and falling revenues—and finally, in 1959, it sold its multiplant U.S. operations to Americans.[19] Bradford Dyers' Association, with a large factory in Westerly, Rhode Island, had 1,250 employees in 1950, only 855 in 1960, and was sold to Americans in 1961.[20] These exits reflected declines in the U.S. textile industry.

In the main, during 1940–1941, the leading Scottish and English investment trusts had transferred their dollar securities to the British government, and most of the securities had been vested by the British government. In 1946, according to one survey sample, Scottish and English investment trusts held on average a mere 3 percent of their portfolios in American securities, compared with 19.5 percent in 1938 for this same sample.[21] Yet because the investment trusts had an extended history in America, their managers knew the country, and some had the background that would provide them a basis for reentry. These investors got back their small amounts of pledged securities, kept and resumed their American contacts, and would (as soon as the British Treasury gave them permission) return to developing new portfolios of American securities. In fact, disturbed by the programs of the Labour government in Britain, many British investment trust managers had very rapidly concluded that "profits from investments in the United States were great enough to justify paying the premium on the purchase of American dollars to re-enter the field."[22] They did so in the late 1940s, and a number would arrange to enlarge their investments in the 1950s, after the Labour Party was no longer in office. By early 1959, Alliance Trust Company, Ltd., a traditional investor in America, had 45 percent of its portfolio in American securities (it was probably exceptional in the size of its interests).[23] In the aftermath of the Second World War, despite the exits, there were substantial carryovers of British direct investments in the United States (from the released RFC collateral) and resumptions based on the prewar British investments in the United States.[24]

As for other "nonblocked" American assets of foreign investors—those of the Canadians, for example—no bones of contention emerged out of the war that required solutions. Canadian holders of American securities and direct investments persisted in postwar America. Canadians traded in American securities as in times past, with the Canadian capital controls not impeding the activities either in the securities markets or in relation to Canadian direct investments in the United States. At year end 1945, 63 percent of Canada's outward FDI and 70 percent of its nationals' FPI in corporate shares were in the United States. The high U.S. portions (in keeping with past history) reflected the ease of investment over Canada's southern border.[25] Never-blocked investments of other nationalities (Australian assets, for example) represented a negligible portion of the U.S. inward foreign investment total and posed no special problems.

Blocked Assets of Neutrals and Formerly Enemy-Occupied Countries

By the end of July 1941, before American entry into the war, the assets of thirty-one European and two East Asian countries had been frozen. After the attack on Pearl Harbor, some of these nations became enemies, some remained enemy occupied, and others stayed neutral.[26] On the postwar future of all these assets, the U.S. State and Treasury Departments (and other branches of the U.S. government) engaged in protracted international negotiations. These commenced before V-E Day, when the State Department had asked neutral countries to freeze all German assets within their borders, investigate transactions since 1939 involving Axis or Axis-controlled territory, and identify German assets. The United States wanted to be certain that when it unblocked the U.S. assets of neutrals, this was not the equivalent of unblocking enemy assets. Hopefully, enemy assets in neutral nations (or moved abroad by neutrals) would not be returned to their former owners; rather, the plan was that they should be used to meet claims against the enemy.[27] There were, however, major doubts about whether some of the assets of neutrals in the United States were those of the neutral or of an enemy.

The two neutral nations whose residents (banks, companies, and individuals) had the largest U.S. assets were Switzerland and Sweden, both of which kept close German connections before and during the war years. A U.S.-Swiss agreement (the Washington Accord), signed on May 25, 1946, provided for the unblocking of Swiss assets in the United States.[28] Less than two months later, on July 18, a comparable U.S.-Swedish agreement was signed, wherein the United States agreed to unblock Swedish holdings in the United States.[29] In both cases the understanding was that genuine Swiss and Swedish assets would be unblocked, but not the U.S. assets of enemies that had used dummy entities set up in Switzerland and Sweden to mask their American operations. Arduous efforts were made by U.S. government officials to determine what was truly Swiss or truly Swedish.

The Swiss and Swedish governments were asked to certify ownership before a particular asset would be unblocked. Initially, the United States sought a precise identification of the private assets that had passed through Switzerland to the United States. The Swiss government staunchly defended bank secrecy, and the United States gave in; assets were unfrozen with no weakening of Swiss bank secrecy.[30] With Swiss direct investments, sometimes attempts to establish ownership proved simple. Nestlé's U.S. assets, for example, were quickly unblocked, as that company allowed the scrutiny of its shareholder lists and Americans accepted the Swiss government verification that some 55 percent of Nestlé stock was held in Switzerland, 24 percent in France, and about 10 percent in foreign countries other than France (the rest of the stock holdings could not be confirmed). Another instance of a direct investment where the Swiss government certification of ownership was straightforward was Hoffmann-La Roche. Its U.S. assets were held by Sapac Corporation, based in Panama. Here, too, Americans accepted the Swiss certification that 78 percent of the shares of the parent Hoffmann-La Roche was held in Switzerland (and less than 1 percent in Germany and Japan). Hoffmann-La Roche's American assets were unblocked.[31] Similar examinations took place of Swedish assets in the United States. AGA (AB Gasaccumulator), for instance, which had manufactured in the United States since before the First World

War, sold its stock in the American Gas Accumulator Co. in 1949; these assets were apparently unblocked with no difficulty and made available for sale to Americans.[32]

Far more frequently, however, American officials had questions about the ownership and control of Swiss and Swedish assets in the United States. The Swiss and (less often) Swedish government declarations on ownership failed to satisfy American negotiators, and the unblocking process came to entail prolonged investigations that did not end with the United States' signing of the 1946 agreements with Switzerland and Sweden. The historian Mauro Cerutti located, for example, in Swiss government archives 394 boxes of documents relating to matters of "real" ownership and covering the period 1947–1951, and the controversies lasted long beyond 1951. There appears to be comparable material in Swedish government and corporate archives, although unlike in the Swiss case, the principal heated debates occurred prior to the signing of the 1946 accord. There are as well voluminous data in U.S. government archives on what was and was not disguised ownership.[33]

As for the assets of residents of onetime enemy-occupied nations, comparable queries were pursued by U.S. policy makers. Before the war was over, the governments in exile of these occupied countries had entered into conversations with U.S. State and Treasury Department representatives on the blockages and on what was known about the asset holders. After the German defeat, as legitimate governments were reconstituted, deliberations went forward on the unblocking of their nationals' assets in the United States; once again, as in the case of the neutrals, American officials wanted to be sure that German assets were not unblocked in the process. Here the largest groups of assets in the United States were those of the Dutch and the French, although all the countries affected took part in separate and ponderous negotiations. There were, for example, diplomatic discussions on Belgian and Norwegian assets. Like the governments of neutral nations, the governments of formerly enemy-occupied countries were asked to certify that the assets to be unblocked were not those of a wartime enemy.

Some French and Dutch owners of assets that had been blocked in the United States worried that because of the dire dollar shortages in Europe, their home nations might request that they sell their U.S. assets and convert their dollars at adverse official rates of exchange. It was not an idle worry. As one commentator put it, "The repatriation of blocked holdings was opposed by some foreign nationals for reasons that the various foreign governments considered selfish and unpatriotic." Owners would rather have the blocked U.S. assets than depreciated francs, for example. Thus they concealed their assets.[34]

The newly reconstituted French government was in desperate need of dollars to import wheat and other products from the United States. An obvious source was French assets in the United States. To obtain the dollars, in 1945 the French government forced L'Air Liquide to sell its shares in the Air Reduction Company and in Du Pont; the U.S. government allowed the dollars to be unblocked.[35] The opening to the unblocking of French assets in the United States occurred with General License 95, effective October 5, 1945. The process proceeded from 1945 to 1953, given the possibilities of "enemy interests" and the French difficulties in identifying hidden French assets. A French decree of July 26, 1946, provided for French requisition of American securities. Even before that, Winthrop Aldrich, president of Chase National Bank, was in Paris, offering his help to the French Ministry of Finance with the sale of French-held American securities. There was substantial correspondence on concealed French assets in the United States. The French prepared a list of American securities held by Frenchmen and attempted to identify the physical and juridical locations of the holdings. An impressive quantity was held within the United States, followed by Switzerland and Great Britain.[36] In the international diplomatic correspondence on the unblocking of French assets, there was a quid pro quo, a "reciprocity" consideration, for Americans: "It is understood that nationals of the United States holding assets in France shall be authorized to administer such assets and their income, within the framework of the controls and regulations of the French Government, without application of measures to them which would be discriminatory in relation to nationals of any other nations."[37]

The French multinational enterprises in the Rhode Island woolen textile industry that had operated through the war continued on, but in the 1950s the textile industry in this state began to shrink. Between 1952 and 1973, these French-owned mills shuttered their plants, ending a longtime group of French direct investments in America. Had the war weakened the ties? It is doubtful.[38] Rather, these later exits from America, when they finally occurred, seem more based on a structural change in U.S. industry (with synthetics replacing natural textiles) and also on the traditional New England textile industry in decline. Yet the departures would come to represent a discontinuity with the past. Some of these affiliates had been established prior to the First World War, others in the 1920s.

The Paris-headquartered, Franco-Wyoming Oil Co. (with its French, Belgian, and Dutch stockholders) survived the war and remained in business, only to be acquired by Lazard Frères, New York, in 1964 and liquidated. Lazard Frères itself persisted.[39] The French American Banking Corporation (FABC), New York, had since its origins in 1919 been owned 50 percent by Comptoir National d'Escompte de Paris (CNEP was one of the four large deposit banks in France that was nationalized in December 1945). The other 50 percent of the FABC was owned in equal amounts by two U.S. banks, Guaranty Trust Company of New York and the First National Bank of Boston. The French government was FABC's largest customer. FABC did its principal business in France and in the French colonies.[40] In December 1947, the Banque de l'Indo-China, the leading French colonial bank, bought the 50 percent share that the American banks had held, and the FABC became 100 percent French owned.[41] Here as in other cases, dollar needs did not interrupt the continuities. (In fact, the FABC undoubtedly aided the financing of French exports.)

The Dutch, similarly, were acutely short of dollars as the war came to an end. American banks agreed to assist the Dutch government in the liquidation of American securities.[42] NV Philips' management became extremely nervous lest its newly developed wartime-nourished business in the United States be sacrificed: the Dutch government might expect it to sell its U.S. operations. This was one of several reasons that Philips decided to keep the trust form of organization it had set up earlier (originally to protect itself from a German takeover of its U.S. assets).[43]

To obtain dollars, in 1946 the Dutch government "made it compulsory for private individuals and companies to sell their American securities."[44] NV Philips was exempted, possibly because of the trust arrangements and possibly for other reasons. The Maxwell Land Grant Company, a Dutch investment that had its genesis in the mid–nineteenth century, had over the many years been maintained, with the Dutch receiving income from lumber, cattle grazing, and royalties from a gold mine. In 1949, after the Dutch manager in Cimarron, New Mexico, died, the scenic Cimarron Gorge was sold to the state of New Mexico; other land sales reduced the size of the property. Mining stopped. Yet the Dutch-owned company retained mineral rights on some 200,000 acres, so there was a slim line of continuity.[45] Otherwise, no "Dutch" direct investment in the United States appears to have been reduced, much less liquidated (I use quotation marks here because some holdings were found to be German and sold to Americans). The Dutch investments in the United States of Unilever and Royal Dutch Shell went through an almost seamless transition to their prior ownership and control relationships.[46] The British government had designated a special category called "technical enemies," which included those countries occupied by Germans. In 1944, the British government signed agreements with the governments of some of these "technical enemies" (Netherlands, Belgium, and Norway) that provided for the retention of their nationals' property with the British custodian until the governments in exile resumed full control over their countries, when such property covered by the agreements would be placed at their disposal.[47] In 1945, everything went smoothly. On August 30, 1945, Unilever in London welcomed its Rotterdam colleagues back "into the fold"; the identical boards of the British and the Dutch companies were restored, as were the prewar ownership associations. The effect was that Lever Brothers Co. in the United States, which had expanded greatly during the war years, kept its prewar and wartime status as Dutch owned. In September 1946, the parent, Unilever, "completed its acquisition of the controlling interest in Lipton's U.S.A."[48] Like Unilever's affiliates, Shell Union Oil Corporation (after 1949 known as Shell Oil) appears to have had no difficulty in sorting out the wartime ownership complications, at least none that I have uncovered.[49] There were no crises in the immediate postwar changes in these British-Dutch properties, in the United Kingdom or the United States. Lever, Lipton, and Shell had evolved as "American" organizations within the United States, technically Dutch owned and technically directed from London. Lever and Lipton had long had American managers at the helm, while in 1945–1950 Shell projected "a new public image, downplaying its majority foreign ownership, declaring Shell to be an American company, with American directors, and guided by American decision-making."[50]

In June 1953 the U.S. government released the remaining blocked assets in the United States that belonged to citizens of thirteen European countries (Austria, Belgium, Denmark, France, Greece, Italy, Luxembourg, the Netherlands, Norway, Sweden, Switzerland, Liechtenstein, and West Germany) and Japan—although this did not end the debates over German properties in the United States. The release indicated that assets of citizens of Bulgaria, Hungary, Roumania, Yugoslavia, Czechoslovakia, Poland, Estonia, Latvia, and Lithuania, as well as eastern Germany, continued to be frozen.[51] In the Cold War environment, the small Eastern European assets in the United States were not unblocked as part of the postwar processes; for many more years they stayed blocked "pending settlement of claims by U.S. citizens for compensation for property confiscated by governments of these countries."[52]

Enemy Assets

As arrangements were made for the assets of neutral and formerly enemy-occupied nations to be unblocked, controversies over what were, and what were not, enemy assets flared. Some enemy assets in the United States were, to be sure, easy to ascertain. The assets of the Italian enemy were the least complicated; many had been liquidated during the war period. In August 1947 virtually all the remaining freezing regulations related to Italian assets in the United States were removed, so that when in June 1953 Italy was included in the broad release, it was pro forma.[53] Austrian, Hungarian, Roumanian, and Bulgarian assets were too small to occupy much attention; moreover, the State Department determined that properties of Austrians were not those of the Germans, and Austria constituted liberated rather than enemy territory.[54] Japanese investments in the United States had been numerous and conspicuous. Most had been vested immediately after Pearl Harbor, albeit the vesting process and, especially, the liquidation of these assets did persist once the war was over.[55] It was, however, the investigations of the cloaked German assets in the United States that absorbed the most time and energy of government officials in the United States and abroad.

During the war, U.S. policy makers had concluded that German business and the German state were one and the same. Attorney General Francis Biddle had warned the Kilgore Committee in the summer of 1944 that "when the Nazis lose, these German firms will undoubtedly announce that the war was not of their choosing and that they are only commercial enterprises." He had cautioned, "A peace with Germany that leaves these companies intact will insure another war against us."[56] After the First World War, Americans had sought to guarantee that no German assets in the United States were returned to their original ownership, a resolve that faded in the 1920s. Initially, planners wanted to be sure that the resumption of a German presence did not repeat itself in the aftermath of the Second World War.

The State Department told the Kilgore Committee in June 1945 that the department had "abundant evidence that the Nazis, in anticipation of military defeat," had hidden assets in foreign countries to rebuild a powerful Germany. The "Safehaven Program" (initiated at Bretton Woods in 1944) aimed "to forestall German attempts to hide assets outside of Germany."[57] The goal was to remove "thoroughly and permanently" Germany's potential for future war.[58]

American thinking about German assets in the United States evolved along with the more general U.S. policies on Germany's postwar direction.[59] At Yalta, in February 1945, Stalin had favored heavy reparations on Germany; Roosevelt had endorsed a Reparations Commission.[60] On January 14, 1946, eighteen nations (including the United States) signed the Paris Agreement on German Reparation, under which the Inter-Allied Reparations Agency (IARA) was established. Article 6A read: "Each Signatory Government shall, under such procedures as it may choose, hold or dispose of German enemy assets within its jurisdiction in manners designed to preclude their return to German ownership and control." Article 6C provided that the net proceeds of liquidation or disposition of enemy assets in neutral countries would be made available to the IARA for "distribution on reparation account."[61]

In the United States, the Office of Alien Property Custodian (OAPC) came to an end on October 14, 1946, its functions transferred to the Office of Alien Property, Department of Justice. But before that occurred, in the last full fiscal period of its existence, June 30, 1945, to June 30, 1946, the OAPC had expanded its vesting of enemy properties.[62] In May 1945, the secretary of state, the secretary of the treasury, and the Alien Property Custodian (APC) had recommended to Truman that "the Government vest and retain all German and Japanese enemy property without compensation to the former owners by the United States." The president had signed an order on June 8, 1945, authorizing the OAPC to vest all types of property in the United States owned by nationals of Germany and Japan, resident in those countries. This order extended the OAPC's authority to the enemy properties that had been left under the Treasury Department's jurisdiction during the war years. It did not matter that the war in Europe was over; Truman was prepared to increase the vesting powers of the OAPC and to include "cash, bank balances, credits, investment securities, insurance policies, and other kinds of property . . . that had previously been subjected . . . to the freezing controls of the Treasury Department." The custodian was authorized to return vested property to foreign nationals who had not been hostile to the United States.[63] In August 1946, a U.S. law (Public Law 671) passed that permitted the release from the control of the Alien Property Custodian assets of victims of racial, religious, or other persecution if they fulfilled certain criteria.[64] As for identifiable enemy properties, no provisions were made for the return of the assets or proceeds from the sale of these assets.

After October 1946, the Office of Alien Property in the Justice Department continued, unabated, the vesting, selling, and liquidating processes, along with the attempts to determine which assets were those of former enemies. The Foreign Funds Control Department in the Treasury Department was formally abolished (by Treasury Department Order No. 86, July 10, 1947).[65] Henry Morgenthau had resigned as secretary of the treasury in July 1945 and was followed by Fred M. Vinson and then by John W. Snyder. Neither Vinson nor Snyder had Morgenthau's passion about German assets, and as the Cold War reshaped national visions and plans for Germany, so, too, the Treasury Department's role was transformed. Morgenthau's plans for a Germany stripped of all abilities to rebuild were abandoned.[66] I do not think it was an accident that in June 1945 there had been the extension of the OAPC's authority and, subsequently, the enlargement of the Justice Department's role at the expense of the Treasury Department. With the Foreign Funds Control Department's activities curtailed and then in 1947 closed down, the assets that remained blocked had been transferred to the charge of the Office of Alien Property, Department of Justice, which did, however, prove to be very aggressive: there were more vesting orders from October 15, 1946, to April 17, 1953, than in the entire period March 11, 1942, to October 15, 1946 (the life span of the Office of Alien Property Custodian).[67]

The 1948 War Claims Act confirmed that identified enemy assets in the United States would not be returned to their prewar owners. The principal Japanese assets, those of trading, banking, and insurance enterprises, continued to be in liquidation. With the 1952 treaty that ended the U.S. occupation of Japan, the Japanese gave up all claims to any returns from their prewar assets in the United States.[68] When the Japanese resumed their investments in America, they would do so anew.[69]

As for Germany, the 1952 treaty ending the occupation of the western zones had a clause whereby West Germany agreed to abide by Allied measures with respect to German external assets, that is, the West German government accepted (at least nominally) the takeover of German properties in the United States by the Office of Alien Property Custodian and its successor Office of Alien Property, Department of Justice. As in the Japanese case, German investment in America would subsequently start up afresh. But unlike with the Japanese, before and after the end of the occupation, disputes over what were German assets in the United States did not cease.

With the German companies, because of the extensive disguises, thorough examinations were made to determine whether Swedish companies were really Swedish, Dutch firms truly Dutch, and Swiss ones genuinely Swiss. The Justice Department, like the OAPC before it, sought to establish whether the prewar (and wartime) corporate arrangements should be accepted as legitimate or, alternatively, interpreted as devices for hiding beneficial ownership and control. These inquiries delayed the unblocking of neutral and enemy-occupied country assets. Thus, investigations were made of reports that SKF Industries's Swedish parent was really German controlled. The Swedes argued this was a false accusation. SKF-US, however, felt it prudent to retain the trust company form it had established to protect its U.S. assets, which kept the parent Swedish firm aloof. The decision may, in part, have been to facilitate the unblocking of the assets; it may have been for antitrust reasons; or its later retention may have been to get defense orders. In any case, SKF Industries' assets were unblocked, but the charges had a profound impact on SKF's postwar legal and organizational structure, as well as its strategies in its U.S. business. All during the war, the Stockholms Enskilda Bank had protested (in vain) that the vesting of its shares in the American Bosch Corporation was not valid, and with the war over, the Swedish bank had filed a suit against the Alien Property Custodian for a return of the 535,000 shares vested. It claimed Swedish ownership and that the shares should be unblocked under the American-Swedish agreement of 1946. Its protests notwithstanding, the Justice Department sold the securities to an American firm. In the final settlement of the litigation in 1950, the Enskilda Bank was reimbursed $2.6 million. With the Cold War, circumstances had changed, and America wanted to assure itself of a friendly Sweden that did not have too close ties with the Soviet Union.[70]

In July 1945, members of the Kilgore Committee, at its hearings on the elimination of German resources for war, had asked the Alien Property Custodian why he had not vested the U.S. subsidiaries of the Dutch rayon company Algemeene Kunstzijde Unie, NV (AKU) in the fall of 1944, when OAPC investigators had suggested that this enterprise was a cloak for German investments. The APC replied that the OAPC had considered vesting the properties of AKU in the United States—American Enka Corporation, American Bemberg Corporation, and North American Rayon Corporation—but had recommended that the State Department be consulted, and the latter had asked the APC "not to vest the interests of AKU at that time" but to look further into the ownership and control of AKU after the liberation of the Netherlands, since the Netherlands Government in exile had "serious disagreements with certain findings in our [OAPC's] investigation report." Not until August 1947, after the OAPC had concluded its functions and turned them over to the Office of Alien Property in the Justice Department, were American Bemberg and North American Rayon vested; and in December 1948, the controlling interests in these Dutch-German companies were sold to the American-owned Beaunit Company (a small, domestically owned producer of rayon that had just entered the rayon industry). As for American Enka, after an agreement with the Dutch government, this affiliate was returned to AKU ownership. AKU was exceptional among the Dutch multinationals. As Harold James wrote, "It [AKU] was the only Dutch multinational whose management the German authorities could control. Shell, Philips and Unilever had moved their headquarters abroad, and were run under the occupation by trustees. In this way they, unlike AKU, were able at least partially to escape the grasping hand of the New Germany."[71] Unlike AKU, as indicated earlier, Shell, Philips, and Unilever were able to preserve all their U.S. properties at war's end. Yet Philips, like the Swedish SKF, had maintained the trust form set up during the war years. Although the Philips company's historian attributed the retention of the trust legal structure to fear that the Dutch government (in search of dollars) might order its divestment, it is altogether possible that among the other reasons Philips chose to retain the arm's length trustee was its desire to keep its American affiliate at an appropriate distance from the Dutch parent, which had continued in business all during the German occupation.

It is impossible to document the thousands of matters that came up related to enemy assets. A few more examples will have to suffice. On August 27, 1946, the American firm Heyden Chemical Corp. filed a complaint in the Southern District Court of New York, claiming that it had made an agreement in April 1942 before the vesting of Schering Corp. stock to purchase those shares from the Schering Corp.'s two Swiss owners of record (the Swiss Bank Corporation and the Chemical and Pharmaceutical Enterprises, Ltd.). Heyden Chemical Corp. asked the court to require the OAPC to recognize the validity of that 1942 sale. The OAPC argued that the Swiss owners were fronting for the Germans. The court agreed and dismissed Heyden Chemical Corp.'s complaint. Further disputes slowed the process, and the sale of Schering Corporation to Americans did not take place until March 6, 1952.[72] Schering AG would reenter anew in the post–World War II period.[73] Interestingly, before World War I, Heyden Chemical had been German owned.[74]

The OAPC had vested some enemy companies (the most prominent instance was the Hugo Stinnes Corporation) that held their principal properties not in the United States but in Europe. At war's end, these assets in Germany became subject to the management and control of the military authorities in the zones where they were located; other assets were under the supervision of the enemy property custodian of the governments of the respective countries. Decisions on the disposition of such properties were thus dependent on the "international arrangements . . . for the ultimate disposition of foreign assets owned by companies in which interests have been vested by the various allied custodians."[75] These arrangements were worked out through time—in demanding negotiations.

There were also awesome questions related to the ownership and use of patents. During and after the war, the Office of Alien Property Custodian had encouraged the nonexclusive licensing of enemy patents. When the OAPC came to an end, the Office of Alien Property, Justice Department, endorsed this policy, wherever possible arranging nonexclusive licensing on a "reasonable royalty basis." The Justice

Department had long been convinced that many prewar patent arrangements had been associated with cartels and probably (in the eyes of Justice Department officials) violated U.S. antitrust law. Thus, for instance, prior to the sale to Americans in 1948 of the U.S. government's ownership in the vested North American Rayon and American Bemberg, these firms had agreed to accept a provision that they license their patents on a nonexclusive basis. In July 1946, thirty-four countries had joined with the United States as parties to the London Patent Accord; each country had pledged to license on a nonexclusive basis to citizens of the signatory countries patents formerly owned by a national of Germany. Exceptions to this policy were patents not available for licensing because of exclusive licenses that had been acquired by a national of a nonenemy nation prior to August 1, 1946 (and these exclusive licenses had not been voided by consent decrees).[76] Among the patents and patent rights that had been seized by the OAPC had been those covered by the 1939 Hague Memorandum; Standard Oil of New Jersey sued for their return to the U.S. oil company. Litigation was completed in 1948, when the courts ordered a large number, but not all, of the patents to go back to the American enterprise.[77]

The ink was no sooner dry on the 1952 treaty ending the occupation of the western zones of Germany and West Germany's acquiescence in the takeovers of German properties in the United States when, in the Cold War context, new debates arose in the United States on whether there should be a return of private enemy property to the original owners.[78] The debates concerned German properties (although the phrase "enemy properties" was used, the prewar Japanese assets were never at issue.) As litigation continued, by far the most burdensome leftover from the blockages and the vesting related to General Aniline & Film Corporation (GAF), the successor to American I. G. Chemical Corporation. Americans were convinced this company had been an affiliate of I. G. Farben. The alleged Swiss ownership of GAF notwithstanding, the stock in this company had been vested immediately after U.S. entry into the war on the assumption that the Swiss were camouflaging I. G. Farben properties. The vested shares had been transferred from the Treasury Department to the OAPC, which operated the company during the war years. With the war over, the owner of record, the Swiss I. G. Chemie, renamed in December 1945 Internationale Gesellschaft für Handels- und Industriebeteiligungen, or Interhandel as it was called, sought to regain what it claimed was its prewar control over GAF. In 1946, when the U.S. government had agreed to unblock Swiss properties in the United States, the Swiss government took the view that Interhandel was Swiss, not German. The U.S. government strongly dissented. In 1948 Interhandel sued, seeking a court order to obtain the return of its shares in GAF. The legal ins and outs were tangled; throughout the litigation GAF remained in business, its directors appointed by the U.S. government.[79] In Germany, under the occupation, I. G. Farben was split into separate companies.[80] The successors to I. G. Farben (Bayer, BASF, and Hoechst) were not involved in any of the lengthy negotiations and court battles over GAF, so from the European side this was not a matter of returning "enemy" properties: the controversy was between the Swiss government representing Interhandel and the U.S. government, with the U.S. government insisting that I. G. Chemie, Interhandel's predecessor, was Swiss only in name and German in fact, whereas the Swiss government held to its defense of Interhandel as a genuinely Swiss firm. Finally, in 1965, the dispute was resolved, when in an out-of-court settlement, Interhandel received 38 percent of the equity in GAF and the U.S. government received the remainder. Immediately thereafter (as part of the settlement), the two owners put their shares in GAF on the market, with a public offering on March 9, 1965. Interhandel received $121.9 million from the sale of its stock in General Aniline & Film Corporation (which would be formally renamed GAF Corporation in 1968). It was now American owned. Meanwhile, the German companies that had emerged out of the broken-up I. G. Farben were gradually (and separately) resuming U.S. investments.[81]

The foregoing is only a hint of the multiple issues involving the verification of U.S. assets of neutrals, nationals of wartime enemy-occupied countries, and enemies. The assets involved FPI and FDI. Not until 1965—with the General Aniline & Film settlement—were the big problems of enemy assets finally resolved.[82] By then, nearly all the 1940–1941 blocked properties had been unblocked, and on May 13, 1966 (with Executive Order 11281), the negligible sums still blocked were as of June 30, transferred from the jurisdiction of the Office of Alien Property, Justice Department, to the Office of Foreign Assets Control, Treasury Department.[83]

The unblocked assets of nationals of neutral and occupied nations—those not found to be enemy assets and those not sold shortly after they were unblocked—created the foundation for the resumption of postwar activities by the identical foreign multinational enterprises; by contrast, most of the portfolio investments lacked that continuity. As for enemy properties that had been sold or liquidated, there was a sharper discontinuity. German and Japanese investors had to begin anew in business in the United States, which they did, at first cautiously and then, as time passed, in an impressive manner. At the close of the 1960s, minor litigation aside, the only blocked assets left from the 1940–1941 freezes were the small Eastern European holdings.[84] Not until 1995, subsequent to the end of the Cold War and the independence of the Baltic States, were the minimal residual activities stemming from the World War II Foreign Funds Control finally concluded.[85] By then, a new round of blocking of assets had long been under way.[86]

Antitrust

While one set of unresolved matters arising from World War II affected the ownership of assets of foreign investors in the United States, another important set affected the strategies of ongoing businesses as well as of new arrivals. From 1938 the Roosevelt administration had become pledged to a vigorous antitrust agenda, and a number of antitrust cases had put foreign-owned businesses on notice. Parent companies and their U.S. affiliates had been vulnerable. For the war's duration, many of the antitrust suits had been postponed and/or placed on temporary "hold," as new ones were regularly inaugurated or contemplated. With the war over, during the Truman administration, the Justice Department renewed its assertive antitrust posture, and many added cases were initiated.[87] The antitrust story was twofold, one of unfinished business and a second, involving a further surge of charges and indictments. Both had profound influence on the future of foreign business in America.

The postwar antitrust cases had formidable impact on U.S. enterprises abroad (outward foreign direct investment) as well as on foreign businesses in the United States. In the past, I have argued that the multiplication of cases in many instances (at least in the short term) impeded the international expansion of American companies.[88] The opposite seems true of foreign direct investment in the United States. The antitrust cases, making manifest that agreements in restraint of trade were illegal, cleared the way for businesses from abroad to enter the American market. Foreign companies that had restrained their U.S. involvements and been satisfied with a liaison office and international agreements could no longer be party to such arrangements.

In the immediate postwar years many antitrust suits were revived that involved foreign business in the United States, even though I. G. Farben (the "arch villain" of much of the previous "international" litigation) had been broken up after the war and no longer existed as an operating entity. Nonetheless, the British-owned Imperial Chemical Industries was a defendant in several cases. And many other participants in the chemical industry, with its maze of agreements, proved vulnerable as antitrust targets. But it was not only the chemical industry that was under fire. I have mentioned that SKF and Philips kept their wartime "trust" structures, in part for reasons associated with the uncertainties about the postwar disposition of blocked assets (and in part to get future defense contracts, in the SKF case and possibly the Philips one as well). For both SKF and Philips, antitrust considerations played a key role in the legal and organizational structure of their postwar business. The parents of these companies tried to keep out of bounds from antitrust penalties.[89] An uncertain matter as the war ended was how much jurisdiction American courts had over the parents of foreign affiliates in the United States. If there was the possibility of conspiracy to limit trade, could parent company records be subpoenaed? What did doing business in the United States entail? Imperial Chemical Industries had only a New York office. The same was true of Anglo-Iranian Oil Company (the predecessor to British Petroleum). And what about Shell, with its sizable U.S. operations? Could the Justice Department gain access to records abroad of parent companies to document antitrust violations? The British government thought the U.S. wish to bring parent companies into the litigation constituted a breech of sovereignty, an "unacceptable assertion of extraterritoriality." Other European governments held the same views.[90]

Implementation of antitrust policies required a new transparency. It meant judicial scrutiny of corporate behavior. In the years after the war, Americans believed that political and economic democracy were allied. If Germany and Japan were to emerge as democratic nations, they must have competition. Thus, U.S. antitrust policies were introduced during the occupation of both countries, with an eye to stimulating the creation of a more vital, competitive world. In Germany, there was the breakup of I. G. Farben and in Japan the dissolution of the *zaibatsu* (holding company) groupings. In the thoughts of U.S. Justice Department prosecutors, intramultinational enterprise arrangements were frequently not distinguished from intercompany restraint-of-trade accords. Often, the pejorative label "cartel" was loosely applied to both types of arrangements. Cartels were perceived by U.S. policy makers to be the very antithesis of the free and open society that was in their future global plans.

It would rapidly become evident to foreign multinationals (as well as to their U.S. counterparts) that restraint of trade and division of market agreements were unacceptable. Imperial Chemical Industries, for example, realized that its prewar arrangements with Du Pont were no longer possible in the postwar political climate. NV Philips' prewar strategies had been constrained by its accords with General Electric and Radio Corporation of America, and prior to its wartime expansion the firm had done little in America. During the war, Philips' management believed that the prewar networks would be restored. What happened to Philips' postwar business was materially shaped by the new reality that the old patterns of behavior could not be reintroduced, given the legal environment. In the postwar period, the heightened U.S. antitrust litigation directly affected a large number of the existing foreign firms in America as well as newcomers, and for the next fifteen years antitrust suits and their remedies would probably have more impact on foreign direct investors in America than any other U.S. governmental policies.

Already by 1945, U.S. antitrust measures had made a difference. The Standard Oil case in 1911 had paved the way for Royal Dutch Shell's first entry into investment in America in 1912. It is unlikely that this enterprise would have become the largest single foreign business in America had antitrust considerations not made it impossible for Standard Oil of New Jersey to erect barriers to the foreign firm's entry. Likewise, British American Tobacco Company (through its subsidiary Brown & Williamson) would not have become important in the American domestic cigarette market had it not been for the 1911 Tobacco case.[91] Yet in the past, antitrust had not been sufficient to clear the way for foreign competition in other industries. It had not been adequate, for example, when the French aluminum company l'Aluminium Français (with its U.S. affiliate, Southern Aluminum) had tried to maintain an entry.[92] Moreover, the relaxation of antitrust enforcement in the 1920s had made feasible the complex networking alliances. However, throughout, behind the scenes, the country's antitrust heritage was there, and when in 1938 the renewal of antitrust enforcement had taken shape, foreign companies had been particularly exposed to its extension. At war's end, the managers of most foreign multinational enterprises had little understanding of America's antitrust traditions. Antitrust would in subsequent years introduce new possibilities of competition into the U.S. domestic market and allow new foreign involvement in a wide range of industrial activities.

Other Public Policies

A collection of U.S. laws, rules, regulations, restrictions, and, in a more amorphous way, attitudes and viewpoints had influenced the course of inward foreign investment over the years. In general, in 1945, there was more acceptance of a peacetime governmental role by U.S. as well as foreign governments than ever in history. After the First World War, there had been an attempt in the United States to cut back governmental involvements; the same would be true after the Second World War, but there was less commitment to do so.

The government policies (beyond those already discussed earlier in this chapter) that affected inward foreign investment were diverse in nature, as were their post-1945 impacts. One set of policies related to patents and their licensing—and linked with antitrust—also had a separate history. Foreign direct investors were often conduits for technology transfer, and their patents were part of their investments. During the First World War enemy (principally German) patents were licensed by the Federal Trade Commission, and in that war's aftermath The Chemical Foundation (not a governmental body but initially supported by the government) had licensed American companies. During both wars, there had been an attempt to make enemy patents more widely available and to spread foreign technology to more of the nation's domestically owned enterprises. World War II policies toward licensing of patents, when in the public interest, created new precedents; the Justice Department became committed to making patented technology accessible—and, where possible, became an advocate of nonexclusive licensing. This approach had long-term consequences. It emerged in part from the policies toward foreign direct investors in the United States.[93]

A different set of government interventions targeted foreign investors in particular sectors (policies toward landownership, shipping, and banking). Such measures had a long history. In the United States between 1914 and 1945, but principally in the interwar years, new sector-specific laws hindered certain inward foreign investments, from measures in broadcasting to those in oil to those in banking. Pre-1914 sectoral restrictions had not been removed and more often were strengthened. The sector-specific laws and regulations were part of the policy heritage that continued after 1945. Often in association with the sector-specific rules, as American policy makers promoted certain outward U.S. investments, "reciprocity" rules were introduced—in the Mineral Lands Leasing Act of 1920 and the Kellogg Cable Landing Act of 1921, for example—and inward FDI was affected. America as a creditor nation would in the interwar (and also in the post–World War II) period at times use the reciprocity club against foreign direct investors in the United States to achieve advantage abroad. Indeed, it was recognized in the interwar period and subsequently that the treatment of foreign investment in the United States could and would have impacts on policies toward U.S. outward foreign investment worldwide.

And then there were the tax policies that carried over after 1945. Whereas before 1914 taxes influenced certain foreign investors' decisions, during and after the First World War, throughout the interwar period, and from that point thereafter, every inward investor in America had to take into account U.S. and foreign taxes. In the immediate post–World War I years, taxes do seem to have deterred certain investments. Double taxation (by the home country and by the United States as host country) figured in the structuring of inward foreign investments. In the interwar years, there was the initial U.S. participation in tax treaties. Tax policies (including tax treaties) would influence the strategies and structures of inward foreign investors throughout the post-1945 decades. Policy makers in the United States (and abroad) often suspected—and would continue to suspect—inward foreign investment in the United States was linked with tax evasion.[94] By 1945 both inward FPI and FDI were deeply affected by U.S. (and foreign) tax policies.

Between 1914 and 1945, new governmentally imposed impediments to capital flows had multiplied—in the United States as well as abroad. During the First World War both foreign and U.S. government restrictions had interfered with the flows of capital. The British government intervened to cut back British investments in the United States (and the U.S. government endorsed this). In the United States, as enemy assets the large German inward investments had been subject to takeover by the Alien Property Custodian. There were in the United States certain foreign exchange restrictions. If many governmental restrictions on capital flows had been cut back in the 1920s, new ones multiplied in the 1930s.

In the 1930s, there had been some attempts to try to insulate the United States from the impact of "hot money," which was seen as upsetting to the fragile stock market recovery. Indeed, in that decade, policy makers at the Treasury Department, the Federal Reserve, and the SEC considered imposing restrictions on speculative international capital flows (they did not do so). By contrast, abroad, during the 1930s, rules limiting capital movements had multiplied. With German aggression in Europe and the U.S. blocking of assets from 1940, new American regulations that applied to inward foreign investments proliferated and would do so all through World War II.

Although it was rarely articulated, throughout the years 1914–1945, U.S. (as well as foreign government) policies toward foreign portfolio and direct investments into the United States were in the main distinct. Thus, antitrust policies affected foreign direct investors, not foreign portfolio ones. Policies toward licensing of patents likewise were germane to foreign direct investors and not to foreign portfolio ones. Sectoral public policies in the United States affected FDI, not FPI. A surprising number of important exits from the United States by foreign direct investors had been U.S. federal government (rather than market) induced: for example, exits of the German companies (as a result of World War I and II); of the British breweries (with Prohibition, which affected American and foreign investors alike); of Marconi (with the sectoral policies toward broadcasting); of Courtaulds (under U.S. Treasury Department pressure); and of the Japanese investors (as a result of U.S. policies during World War II).

Tax policies had different impacts on foreign portfolio and foreign direct investments (with differing responses by the investors).[95] There were exits of portfolio investments based on U.S. government policies during wartime, but the policies toward portfolio and direct investment liquidation were separate, and during World War II the U.S. Treasury Department maintained jurisdiction over enemy foreign portfolio investments as the Office of Alien Property Custodian took charge of enemy direct investments (during World War I the Alien Property Custodian had administrative authority over both inward FPI and FDI). U.S. uneasiness over the impact of inward foreign investment on the stock market was directed toward FPI and was of little consequence in shaping either the strategies or the structures of foreign direct investors. Monetary policies affecting interest rates resulted in both withdrawals and entries of FPI but seem to have had little effect on the overall operations of foreign multinationals in the United States, albeit clearly they had impact on the financial strategies of business managers. The division in government policies between those toward inward FDI and FPI would carry over to the post–World War II years, as would the distinctive responses by each type of investor.

Many U.S. laws influenced the course of inward foreign investments; in Appendix 4, I have listed the key ones passed in 1914–1945 and discussed in this volume. The itemized summary excludes the voluminous state legislation. It also excludes regulatory measures. Some of the many restrictions that emerged on inward foreign investment would be removed in the transition to a peacetime economy (blockages of foreign assets, for example). Some were for all practical purposes ineffective, such as the multiplicity of state restrictions on alien landownership.[96] Others, such as federal laws applying to radio broadcasting, for many decades would bar foreign direct investment. Federal and state banking legislation sharply curtailed what foreign banks could do in the United States.[97] The long-standing rules on foreign involvements in shipping would limit foreign investment in this sector. Yet specific sectors exempted (and "enemy" reentry in the short-term discouraged), in the post–World War II years America was open to new foreign portfolio and direct investments. In general (once again, certain specific sectors excluded), as of 1945 foreign investors were not adversely treated compared with their domestic counterparts. No overall U.S. governmental restrictions existed on remittances of dividends or interest.[98]

If, with the exceptions just indicated, in 1945 investments from abroad were not materially deterred by American law specifically targeted at the outsiders, foreign businesses were nonetheless in many instances at a disadvantage in the United States. American companies had a familiarity with domestic conditions. To be sure, the foreign multinationals that had been in the country for decades were knowledgeable, but over time these enterprises changed management in the United States (at the affiliate) and abroad (in the parent company), which often required a relearning process. New managements abroad had to refresh (frequently from scratch) their internal corporate information. "Age effects"—that is, the assumption that experienced companies managed better than newcomers—have to be modified by adding a life cycle dimension. Experience within corporations was far from linear. In fact, the complexities of doing business in the vast U.S. domestic market under evolving national and state rules and regulations, far more than the tangling with explicit U.S. governmentally imposed antiforeign barriers to investment, presented even the most long-standing foreign investors with numerous challenges; usually the response (for better or worse) was to rely on American advice and counsel. And this, of course, involved the principal/agency problems, including a misalignment of parent and affiliate goals.

Yet in 1945 the low level of inward foreign investments in the United States was undoubtedly more due to the paucity of capital worldwide than to any political or economic conditions in the United States, or to any condition inherent in the structure of business organization. In addition, in the immediate post–World War II years, the major restrictions on flows of capital into the United States came from abroad, from foreign governmental controls, and not from the United States, where except for the sectoral restrictions, new investment entry was not deterred by governmentally imposed barriers, where profits and interest payments could in general be freely remitted, and where there were no worries over future policies that would threaten private property and, in this manner, jeopardize new stakes. In 1945, while inward foreign investors paid close attention to taxes (and possible double taxation) and made investment decisions influenced by tax policies, with appropriate legal and accounting advice they seldom found American taxes a reason to curb investments in the United States. Soon after 1945 there tended to be a relaxation, a dissipation, of many of U.S. policy makers' fears over inward foreign investments (except those related to the defense sector, which fears heightened after the advent of the Cold War); some of the apprehensions and debates that arose during the interwar years would resurface, but not for decades and then in a greatly modified manner.

Conclusions and Comparisons

In 1914 the United States was the world's largest debtor nation; in 1945 it was the world's largest creditor nation. Why is this important? How do long-term foreign portfolio and foreign direct investment in the United States fit into my story line, aside from differences in U.S. policy responses to each? My definition of debtor and creditor has not been value laden. I have used, as my reader is well aware, the word "debtor" to indicate long-term obligations to foreigners were greater than foreigners' obligations to Americans, and conversely "creditor" to denote foreigners' long-term obligations to Americans as exceeding those of Americans to them. Over the years, however, in much of the literature, the phrase "debtor nation" has evoked a negative image. Why should that be the case? We associate (in a positive manner) the Schumpeterian entrepreneur with using credit effectively (i.e., borrowing). There is nothing wrong per se with "debt" (external or internal), only debt that is inappropriately used and unable to be serviced. Indeed, one conclusion from my study is that prosperity has nothing to do with international debtor or creditor status. A debtor nation that uses funds from abroad effectively can be very prosperous, as was the United States in 1914 on the eve of the First World War (and as the nation would be subsequently after the late 1980s, when once again the country became a debtor in international accounts). As for the other side of the coin, U.S. creditor nation status was accompanied by prosperity in the 1920s, but in all likelihood it made the Great Depression of the 1930s at home worse as foreign defaults multiplied. I share the view of recent scholarship that the sizable inward FPI from 1933 to 1939 probably served as a positive element in U.S. economic recovery.[99]

This brings me to another finding: when a country is a debtor nation, there are not only inward foreign investments but outward ones as well. (This may seem obvious, but it needs emphasis.) So, too, as a creditor nation, as once again the reader of this book is well aware, the United States attracted inward foreign investments along with generating the outward ones. Some see this as a "paradox," that is, that a creditor nation should attract large inward capital flows. It is not a paradox. What is key is that both inward and outward foreign investments coexist. Net figures obscure reality. The cross-investment in both portfolio and direct investment is normal, not abnormal (as economists once believed about portfolio investments). It was also an accepted view in the past that a key element that distinguished a theory of foreign direct investments from foreign portfolio ones was cross-investment.[100] My research shows clearly that this was never a unique feature of FDI. The existence of cross-investments with both FPI and FDI was, however, in each case complex, asymmetrical, and far from uniform within time periods. My book has demonstrated that for the United States, while the transition from debtor to creditor took place rapidly in the years 1914–1918, in the period 1918–1945 as the United States was a creditor nation, inward foreign investment—both FPI and FDI—never disappeared, and at times new inward investments became substantial and influential. Continuities and discontinuities coexisted.

Considerations of inward investments in the context of debtor-creditor relationships have to be accompanied by an awareness of the extent and the characteristics of an individual nation's place in global integration. The extent involves the size of the debtor or creditor nation's position. The greater the global integration, the larger the international involvements (however measured, and there are numerous measures available), the more will be the benefits, and also the more will be the vulnerability—whether a country (the United States or another country) is a debtor or a creditor nation.

Characteristics of the inward investments also matter (and vary with the FPI and FDI "mix"). For inward investments—whether in a debtor or creditor nation—in periods when currencies fluctuate, the currency of the obligation makes an important difference. This is particularly true of FPI. Throughout America's debtor nation decades before 1914, the nation had some obligations denominated in foreign currencies.[101] In 1914, all U.S. federal government borrowings were in dollars; and with one trivial 1918 exception noted in Chapter 1, all subsequent U.S. federal government borrowings were dollar denominated (this would remain true until 1962). In 1914, however, the exclusively dollar-denominated federal government debt was not true of other borrowings. New York City had, for example, obligations in pounds and francs, while a number of railroad bonds were denominated in foreign currencies. And, there were gold clauses that insulated the lender against currency devaluation. There were also clauses that set the rate of exchange for interest and dividends. In the generation before 1914, with major nations (including the United States) on the gold standard, none of this had made a difference to the United States as a debtor nation. Yet, foreign currency-denominated inward foreign investment did create (as was explained in Chapter 1 herein) temporary vulnerability within the United States during the First World War.

After 1919, as best I can ascertain, all new foreign obligations of the United States, its state and local governments, and its businesses were dollar denominated. On the other hand, post–Civil War U.S. federal government issues had been payable in the coin standard of the United States and in gold coin after the 1890s.[102] In 1933, the United States rejected gold clauses in securities contracts, including federal government issues. In 1945 all U.S., state, and municipal government obligations were dollar denominated, and with virtually no exceptions, all other American private sector international obligations were as well.[103] Meeting obligations denominated in a country's own currency insulates the borrower from the uncertainties related to fluctuations in the value of foreign exchange. A debt denominated in a foreign currency puts the borrower at the mercy of international markets. In 1945, not only was the United States the leader in the world economy, but its public and private international obligations were in its own currency. As had been the case for many years, its private sector international obligations far exceeded its public sector international obligations. Historically, the vast bulk of American obligations had been dollar denominated. For the recipient of inward investments, this eliminated an important aspect of uncertainty. This seems to have distinguished the United States from most other host countries (and certainly from less developed countries in the post–World War II era). In the U.S. case the vulnerability was shifted to the investors from abroad.[104]

In considering the characteristics of inward investments, it is important to look at the private sector–public sector mix. Throughout the years 1914–1945, to repeat, the vast bulk of inward foreign investment in the United States did not go to governmental bodies, not to the federal, state, or local government borrowings; it was not in government-issued securities. The latter throughout constituted a very small part of the inward foreign investment. Although in the U.S. case, both FPI and FDI went primarily into the private sector, it is nonetheless crucial to accent the division between FPI and FDI in the nation's obligations. The delineation of this divide is one of the most important results from my research. The benefits and costs of inward (into the United States or into any host country, for that matter) FPI and FDI are evaluated sometimes explicitly and sometimes implicitly both by governments and by private investors through separate lenses.

Throughout the years 1914–1945 inward FPI exceeded inward FDI into the United States, so to leave out the former omits a major aspect of foreign investment. The inward FPI went in large part into traded securities and aided the viability of financial markets. Earlier in this chapter, in the summary of public policies, I indicated that policies varied toward FPI and FDI. In this book, I have documented the complicated cosmopolitan finance of the 1920s that mixed inward and outward direct and portfolio investments. FPI and FDI are different, yet at times they overlap and intersect.

In the 1920s, when outward FPI from the United States reached new heights, it went primarily into foreign government bonds. Inward FPI went principally into equities. There were also major differences between outward and inward FDI. Economist Stephen Hymer argued that with FDI cross-investment often occurred within industries (and I found this was true in a number of instances), but what was also very apparent in the U.S. case was that the inward FDI in textiles had no counterpart in outward FDI, while outward FDI in machinery had no interwar counterpart in inward FDI. So, too, there were major asymmetries in inward and outward FDI in the interwar chemical and electrical industries, as examples.[105]

Interestingly, throughout the years 1914–1945 (with the possible exception of 1929), whereas U.S. outward foreign direct investments were greater than outward private foreign portfolio ones, the opposite was true in the same years vis-à-vis inward foreign investments (with FPI exceeding FDI). In addition, as one views the inward investments into the United States by country, the ratios of inward FPI to FDI diverged sharply (and these changed by country through time). I would attribute the reasons for these asymmetries to the variations in structure of business and financial institutions in particular countries abroad as well as within the United States. National differences reflected themselves internationally. This book has traced the course of inward FPI and FDI. I am not satisfied that there is any sequencing, with one preceding or following the other; instead, FPI and FDI coexisted in highly complex interrelationships.[106] Both offered benefits and costs, which included the exposure of the source country and the recipient one to the vulnerabilities inherent in international economic interactions; yet the benefits and costs of FPI and FDI were distinct.

After World War II was over, within the United States considerable academic interest arose in what was then perceived as the end to major British (and other inward foreign) investments. Many studies were conducted of past FPI and FDI, covering railroads, cattle ranches, meatpacking, mortgage companies, and mining enterprises.[107] The frontier had long been closed, and that era of British investment was seen as long past.[108] The foreign portfolio investments in railroads, those of the British and the Dutch in particular, had been an integral part of a nineteenth-century story that had carried over into the twentieth. In 1914, foreign investments (principally portfolio ones) in American railroads were still huge. In 1945, however, little in the way of most of those earlier portfolio interests in the country's railroads remained. By contrast, the sizable long-standing Canadian direct investments in U.S. railroads persisted (taken for granted and not something that concerned Americans). There would subsequently be no renewal of foreign portfolio investments in American rails; by contrast, the Canadian-owned rail connections with U.S. cities and ports continued.[109]

So, too, in postwar America there would be no resumption of the large nineteenth-century direct investments in cattle ranches. Nor did the nineteenth-century direct investments in meatpacking return; the last important meatpacking venture (John Morrell & Co.) became American in 1928. The British mortgage lenders were also from a long-lost age (although over the post–World War II decades there would resurface inward foreign investments in mortgage finance).[110] Foreign investments on the mining frontier were identified with times past. In 1899, foreign investors had controlled some 25 percent of America's copper mining output; by 1914, however, this had already been reduced to less than 3 percent The last important British company in copper mining in this sequence, Arizona Copper Company, was acquired by Phelps Dodge in 1921.[111] In contrast, a large British investment in a Mississippi cotton plantation (initially made in 1911), which always sold its cotton in the domestic market, did continue—that of Fine Cotton Spinners' and Doublers' interest in Delta and Pine Land Co. It was a rarity as a sustained large landholdings from earlier years, but then this investment was made in the twentieth century and was not a part of the nineteenth-century frontier involvements.[112] Although it is unquestionably legitimate to conclude that foreign direct investments in mortgage companies were more significant in the last thirty years of the nineteenth century than they ever would be in the post–World War I, much less in the post–World War II, decades, it is also probably accurate to agree that in relative terms the FDIs in mining were of more consequence in the last thirty years of the nineteenth than in the last three decades of the twentieth century.[113] As for large landholdings, these were part of that other era (albeit there did come to be sizable future investments in urban real estate).

Clearly, between 1914 and 1945 the involvements of inward foreign direct investors in many sectors altered. The waves of past direct investments in the U.S. textile industry were beginning to be dwarfed by activities in more modern industries. In 1914, there existed sizable German, British, French, and Swiss direct investments in textiles in the United States. The big German wool makers had not resumed business after World War I. As for British enterprises, there had been significant British direct investments in producing thread; the largest of these continued after 1945, but the thread industry itself had relatively less import as consumers bought ready-made clothing off the store racks and sewing machines disappeared from American households. Nonetheless, in 1960 subsidiaries of two British-owned thread companies (J. & P. Coats and English Sewing Cotton) would rank in the top five in British affiliates' manufacturing employment in the United States.[114] Both of these firms had moved within the United States from the American North to the South, mirroring U.S. industry trends. In addition, thread sold to consumers was a trademarked good; and J. & P. Coats in the United States had over the years spent substantial sums in advertising and promoting its brands. In the immediate post–World War II period, this Scottish company also undertook chemical research in the

United States connected with the thread industry.[115] Thus, thread was not by any means a typical undifferentiated textile mill product. In textiles, the major French investments in manufacturing woolens lasted after 1945, but all seem to have exited by the mid-1970s. Over the years the Swiss investments in the textile industry had gradually lost their relative importance. Yet both the French and the Swiss direct investments in textiles had had specialized characteristics in terms of process technologies. And then there had been the highly innovative foreign stakes in rayon; Courtaulds, the first mover in manufacturing this pioneer synthetic fabric, had been sacrificed to the British war effort (in 1941); the company would return to U.S. investments after the war (in 1951), yet it never recovered its former glory, as rayon itself was superseded by numerous other synthetics, and as U.S. rather than foreign companies took the initiative. Already in 1937, the chemical industry had become the leading sector in manufacturing for inward FDI, barely exceeding that in textiles, which had been in an unambiguous first place in 1934. While textiles remained (and would remain) a large sector for foreign investors, chemicals and pharmaceuticals and other modern industries were the future for many more foreign multinational enterprises. Some of the harbingers of what was to come were already in evidence by the end of World War II.

If there were no ongoing inward investments in the post–World War II decades in certain activities linked with the frontier, and if there was a diminished relative role of textiles in general, key continuities do stand out. The one big British cotton plantation investment that persisted (Delta and Pine Land Co.) was in the vanguard of large-scale corporate farming in the South.[116] The principal continuities were foreign multinational enterprises with branded products and/or advanced technological know-how—Lever, Lipton, Brown & Williamson (owned by British American Tobacco), and Seagrams are prime examples in the first category, while Ciba and Hoffmann-La Roche are excellent fits for the second group (and along with their technological contributions, most of the Swiss chemical companies' drugs had brand names, a shortening of the complex name of the chemical compound). Then there were also the giant British insurance companies with a long uninterrupted history in the United States.

Because of the changes between 1914 (before the outbreak of war in Europe) and 1945 (after the end of the Second World War), the profile of foreign investment in the United States in 1945 was different from that in 1914. At the risk of some repetition, it is worthwhile to summarize the differences at these benchmark years. In 1914, the United States was bound in numerous ways to a global economy, and it was far and away the largest single recipient of capital in the entire world. In 1945, the world depended on the United States for capital. In 1914, capital flows faced few political obstacles. In my *History of Foreign Investment in the United States to 1914,* I wrote about conditions on the eve of the First World War: "The multiplicity of regulations and restrictions notwithstanding, the easy flow of capital from abroad into America is what stands out rather than the impediments."[117] In 1945, impediments to an integrated world economy were the norm rather than the exception. In 1914, inward foreign capital was contributing in a material manner to American development. Although there are no figures available for 1945 on the global dispersion of inward foreign investment, existing albeit sparse evidence suggests that in 1945, as in 1914, the United States was the greatest host to inward foreign investment. Unlike in 1914, however, it was not separated from the next largest host by a wide divide, and far more important, in 1945 foreign capital was (because of its relatively small size within the vast U.S. economy) on the margin of American economic change.[118] In 1914, the closing of the New York Stock Exchange was caused by the withdrawals of foreign investors. In 1945, the health and safety of America's financial system could in no way be affected by the actions of inward portfolio investors.

In 1914, the major nations in the world were on the gold standard; whereas in 1914 most of America's international obligations were denominated in dollars (sometimes with a gold clause), there were in addition foreign currency obligations, usually in pounds or francs. In 1945, the latter had disappeared; foreign investment obligations in the United States could be satisfied in dollars. In 1914, trade in American securities might be on a number of foreign stock exchanges. In 1945, foreigners who bought American securities (or the agents who acted on their behalf) typically executed the transactions in the United States in dollars. In 1945, foreign portfolio investments in American securities were usually traded ones, traded in dollars on American exchanges; foreign direct investments were in companies incorporated under American law, where the obligations (if the investment were liquidated) would be fulfilled in dollars. There were no more gold clauses. The dollar, not the pound, was the world currency.

In 1914, tax burdens on inward foreign investment were negligible. In 1945, taxes truly mattered. At the start of 1914 government interventions—although far from absent—did not have a dramatic impact on the patterns of inward foreign portfolio and foreign direct investments. In 1945, politics—U.S. and foreign—made a profound difference, and not only in relation to the flows of capital across borders, but everywhere, citizens expected their governments to intervene in all facets of domestic and international economic life. In 1945, inward foreign investors in the United States depended heavily on lawyers and accountants (and other advisers, including in some cases bankers) for knowledge on how the policies of their home authorities and those in Washington would affect their existing stakes and their future plans. This was true of FPI and FDI. At the start of 1914, with the gold standard, foreign exchange fluctuations did not influence most inward foreign investors' strategies. In 1945, foreign governments' plans on exchange availability and rates (including level and stabilization) were critical to foreign investors' decision making—in the case of FPI and FDI.

In 1914, before the outbreak of the war in Europe, the principal inward foreign investors in the United States by nationality were British, German, Dutch, French, and Canadian, ranked in that order, with British investment almost four times that of the Germans. In 1945, in terms of the level of all inward investments into the United States the British remained at the head of the roster, followed by the now second-place Canadians, with the Swiss or Dutch in third rank (probably the former ahead of the latter), and then the French rather far behind. In 1945, there were zero German and Japanese investments in the United States.[119]

In 1914, certain "British" and "Swiss" investments in the United States were beneficially owned by other European nationalities, and there were some limited added pyramided investments. In 1945, international investment patterns were far more complex, and it seems likely that some of the Canadian, a great deal of the Swiss, and a small part of the Dutch investments in the United States were by nationalities other than those listed (i.e., were investments cycled through the nominal source of investment). Then there were the Panamanian investments that were virtually all beneficially owned by other nationalities. In 1914, nearly all foreign investors in the United States came from the private sector (individuals, financial institutions, businesses). In 1945, governments were included among the inward investors.

In 1914, about 75 percent of the inward foreign investment into the United States was of a portfolio nature. In 1945, inward portfolio investments still exceeded direct investments, but there appears to have been a lower ratio of portfolio to direct investment (after a very uneven course between 1914 and 1945). In 1914, foreign investments in federal, state, and municipal bonds were small. In 1945, holdings in government securities remained a minor portion of total inward investment, but because of the large new U.S. federal government bond issues during World War II, more federal government bonds, in both dollar value and relative terms, were held abroad in 1945 than in 1914.[120] In 1914, corporate bonds exceeded equities in the inward portfolio investments. The reverse was true in 1945. In 1914, railroad securities had been the preeminent portfolio investments, but in 1945, industrials and public utilities were the main ones. In 1914, Scottish and English investment trusts were significant investors in America. Investments trusts of other nationalities were also investors. In 1945, these financial intermediaries had a far smaller portion of their portfolios in American investments. In 1914, especially with the Scottish investment trusts, it was often difficult to distinguish mortgage companies and investment trusts. By 1945, the Scottish mortgage companies had been fully transformed into investment trusts.

In 1914, the principal European financial institutions participated in American finance, cooperating with American houses and encouraging the intermediation of foreign investment into the United States. London was the financial center. This was no longer the case in 1945, by which time New York had replaced London. In particular, in 1914, J. P. Morgan & Co. and its London and Paris houses had played a vital role; Barings was still on the American map in 1914, but not in 1945; the house of Rothschild was in the picture in 1914 (although no longer of great significance); it was not in the American story of 1945. In 1945, Morgan, Stanley was the investment banker created after the New Deal banking reforms. After the Glass-Steagall Act, Kuhn Loeb had cast its lot in the securities business, yet it had been far more important vis-à-vis inward foreign investment in 1914 than in 1945. Dillon Read did not exist in 1914. The one European exception to this pattern to the "Americanization" of finance was Lazard Frères, New York, which, interestingly, was probably more American in character in 1914 than in 1945, when the revived French parent played an important role. By 1955, Lazard Frères, New York, would come to rank among the top twenty underwriting firms in the United States.[121] In 1950, the Canadian investment banker Wood Gundy and Co. was the only foreign firm in the top twenty underwriters in the U.S. market.[122] In 1945, the role of foreign financial intermediaries in providing for America's financial requirements was insignificant; they were superfluous.

In 1914, "free-standing companies" were numerous among the inward foreign direct investments in the United States, involved in cattle ranching, mining, meatpacking, breweries, mortgage lending, and a range of other activities. In 1945, "free-standing companies" were in the main absent from the inward FDI group.[123]

In 1914, sixteen British breweries (all free-standing companies and some quite substantial) were in the United States.[124] In 1945, foreign direct investments in brewing in the United States was minimal (and none by free-standing companies). In 1914, the largest producer of flour in the United States, the Pillsbury flour mills, had been owned by a British parent, a free-standing company; this was not the case in 1945, albeit years later Pillsbury would once again become British owned.

In 1914, European-headquartered multinational enterprises such as Michelin, Courtaulds, Ericsson, Pechiney, and Bayer (for example) had direct investments in the United States, manufacturing "high-technology" products. Not one of these five remained in 1945; all would, however, reappear in subsequent years. In 1914, a British subsidiary (Marconi of America) led in U.S. radio communications. In 1945, radio broadcasting was an entirely American proposition (it would be many years before there would be foreign entries once again). In 1914, Merck was a part of a German multinational enterprise; in 1945, Merck was an American company. This is important, for 1914 FDI in the United States was not solely natural resource oriented; it was in traditional and also in new "high-technology" activities.

In 1914, the trade names Philip Morris and Marlboro belonged to a British investor in the United States. In 1945, the successor to that British company, Philip Morris, was still small, but it was a flourishing U.S.-headquartered firm. In 1914, Beecham's had a factory in Brooklyn, and Beecham's pills were advertised and sold well in the American market. In 1945, although Beecham's had U.S. investments, its limited U.S. business was a shadow of what it had once been (it was, moreover, carried on by affiliates of a firm that it had acquired in the United Kingdom); its U.S. business would soon revive.

In 1914, in more than a half dozen U.S. industries, a foreign multinational ranked as the industry leader. In 1945, in only four narrowly defined industries was this so: (1) thread—and in 1945 this was far from an important industry; (2) whiskey, where the Canadian multinational enterprise, Distillers Corporation-Seagrams Ltd. (Seagrams) had the top position; (3) gin, where Gordon's gin, distilled in New Jersey by the Scottish firm Distillers Company Ltd., was the best-seller; and (4) tea, with Lipton Tea the leading brand.[125] Interestingly, three of the four "industrial subsectors" involved beverages—and beer and soft drinks were not included. Thread and tea had been in the top rank in 1914; whiskey and gin came into that category only after the end of Prohibition.

In 1914, twenty foreign banks had licensed agencies in New York.[126] In 1945, there were fewer (eighteen), but in the interim the number had risen sharply and then declined with the takeovers during the war years of the six Japanese and four Italian bank agencies.[127] In 1914, the bank agencies had been principally from London, Toronto, and Montreal; in 1945, that group continued, but there were also the Swiss, Dutch, and French bank agencies. In 1914, the Bank of Montreal was the largest bank in Chicago. By 1945, this was no longer true (years later would it reestablish a sizable Chicago presence).[128] In 1914, the principal accounting firms in the United States had been closely tied to their British origins. Over time, these accounting firms kept their associations with their British houses (and in some cases made new arrangements, as with Peat, Marwick Mitchell in the 1920s), but by 1945 the hierarchy of "British parentage" had been replaced by interlocking partnerships and other affiliations. Whereas it was legitimate to discuss British "parents" in 1914, this was not a valid description in 1945. The American accounting profession had come of age.

In 1914, Americans had been alarmed about British preeminence in cables, radio, and shipping—and about import dependency in dyestuffs, potash, and tin. After U.S. entry into the First World War, there had been anxiety over the damage to American customers should the nation take over German-owned insurance companies. There had also been dismay that U.S. trade was financed in sterling bills, a clear indication of subservience. In 1945, there no longer existed any uneasiness in the United States about foreign "control" over cables or radio (in neither activity did foreign dominance exist or even seem a threat); temporarily U.S. shipping had surpassed that of the British. In 1945, America had no fear of reliance on foreign investors in dyestuffs, for the country had a strong diversified chemical industry. As for potash, the United States had developed adequate domestic supplies—in California and New Mexico (and during World War II there had been the takeover of the German inward direct investments in the mining of that commodity). With tin, the federal government had coped during World War II; there had been no crisis. In 1945, no one looked back or worried about the impact of German influence or the Japanese blockade on this industry; the aid from a Dutch multinational enterprise (NV Billiton) was accepted without hesitation. In 1945, it would have been preposterous had anyone suggested a U.S. need for German insurance companies. Indeed, while the numerous British insurers still conducted extensive business, in relative terms they were less important; America had a healthy domestic insurance sector. As for trade finance, in 1945 international trade was fettered by a range of restrictions; sterling was not an appropriate currency to finance American commerce; the dollar was supreme.

In 1914, Royal Dutch Shell had been a newcomer to investment in the United States; in 1945, it was an integral part of the American oil industry. Neither in 1914 nor in 1945 did the predecessors of British Petroleum, Anglo-Persian and Anglo-Iranian, operate in America, but in 1945 Anglo-Iranian had an office in New York (which Anglo-Persian had not had in 1914). In 1914, Ciba, Sandoz, and SKF had no manufacturing in the United States (Ciba had an independent agent, and Sandoz probably did as well; SKF had a sales subsidiary). In 1945, these three foreign multinationals were well established in this country. In

1914, Lever, Lipton, British American Tobacco, Burroughs Wellcome, Geigy, Hoffmann-La Roche, and Nestlé conducted business in the United States (and had direct investments in manufacturing); their operations were, however, far more substantial in 1945 than in 1914. In 1945, Lipton Tea had its name in fluorescent lights on the New Jersey side of the Hudson River, for all in Manhattan to view.[129]

A predecessor of Electrolux (of Sweden) was in the United States in 1914; had exited by 1920; reentered in 1929; and in 1945 had a minor presence (only to exit in 1968, before an important reentry in 1974). Several foreign multinational enterprises, which had no U.S. operations in 1914 (but had been investors in the United States in prior years), had revived their businesses in America and were once more in evidence in 1945 in the United States: Dunlop is an example. In 1914, NV Philips had a small joint venture; it had little during most of the interwar period but by 1945 was poised to develop substantial U.S. business. In 1914 Saint-Gobain had no presence in the United States (albeit it had a sales office decades earlier). It briefly reentered in the 1920s, then retreated, then reentered in manufacturing in 1933. In 1945, it remained (a minor player).

Then there were the new arrivals, not involved in direct investment in the United States in or prior to 1914. Celanese Corp. of America (and its predecessor), set up by foreign direct investors, would qualify as an important new entry. Undoubtedly, the most conspicuous newcomer in the interwar years that lasted to 1945 was Seagrams (from Canada). Another start-up, with no foreign direct investment in 1914, was J. Henry Schroder Banking Corporation (Schrobanco), established in New York in 1923; it was by 1945 a more important firm than its parent.[130]

In 1914, some Japanese banks, trading companies, shipping firms, and insurers had U.S. direct investments; these grew in number during the First World War and in the interwar years, were taken over during the Second World War, and in 1945 there were no Japanese multinationals in America. In 1914, German direct investments in the United States were extensive; in every state there were nonresident German-owned direct investments. A number returned in the interwar period. Those that did, along with some new German participants, were once more sequestered by the Second World War Alien Property Custodian. In 1945, German multinationals were absent, but many of those that had been in America in 1914 would reappear in the post–World War II years, and in a far stronger manifestation.

Some foreign multinational enterprises, with a trivial U.S. involvement in both 1914 and 1945, had undertaken significant investments in the interwar period from which they withdrew, only to resurface in the post–World War II era, for instance, Rio Tinto, which subsequently became a large investor in the United States, as Rio Tinto-Zinc (RTZ). There were foreign multinational enterprises that were not manufacturing in the United States in 1914, made brief appearances in the interwar years, and had exited by 1945, only to reinvest in post–World War II America: the British Glaxo and the Swiss Brown, Boveri are examples. In 1914, film manufacturing was 100 percent American. Subsequently, three European film makers had become engaged in U.S. manufacturing: Pathé Cinéma in Du Pont Pathe Film Manufacturing Corp. (1924); Agfa, then associated with I. G. Farben, in Agfa-Ansco (in 1928); and Gevaert (in 1941). Two of these foreign investors were gone by 1945, and Gevaert by 1948.[131]

In short, the paths of continuities and discontinuities were highly uneven and idiosyncratic. Just as the foreign multinationals' entries over the years were motivated by an assortment of rationales (from jumping tariff barriers to responding to economic opportunities), so too, the exits, the discontinuities, had no single cause with many reasons (from governmental measures to unsatisfactory performance to changes in corporate priorities). Entries, expansions or contractions, and departures were often associated with a firm's competitive and/or cooperative strategies within a particular industry and intra- and intercorporate solutions as to how particular global product markets should be allocated.

In 1914, foreign affiliates in the United States were frequently extensions of the parent enterprises, barely beginning to shape their own strategies, although a number had already become multiplant and multiproduct establishments (for instance, the operations of J. & P. Coats and English Sewing Cotton's American Thread Company). While there were joint ventures, typically financing for the multinational enterprises (MNEs) had come from abroad. In 1945, by contrast, for those companies that survived, many had long histories, and there were not only far more multiplant and multiproduct businesses, but now there were many multifunctional enterprises (affiliates with manufacturing, distribution, research and development facilities, and so forth). These developed their own product lines and adapted to conditions in the American market. Such foreign-owned firms had come to rely heavily on U.S. advertising agencies, law firms, accounting firms, and other services. Often these affiliates had American managers, who had assumed substantial independence from the parent enterprise. These affiliates had reinvested profits and could borrow in the United States; generally, they did not need to depend on capital flows from the headquarters in the mother country.

What were the impacts abroad of the changing configurations of foreign portfolio and direct investments in America? Global relationships identified with international investments provided a mixture of advantages and vulnerabilities. British assets in the United States had proved helpful to the mother country in the financing of both world wars. Usually, however, during the interwar years, foreign governments around the world had been wary of the outflow of investments (including those that went to the United States), seeing the outflows as alternatives to investment at home and imposing controls. In the 1930s, the German government had, for example, strictly regulated the export of capital, believing that capital exported was that not employed at home. Overall, the financial returns to foreign investors in the United States had not been such as to warrant foreign government support of outward investments, albeit when it looked like the American government would force the divestment of British direct investments prior to U.S. entry into World War II and, possibly, even after the end of the war, the British government had protested that its national interest required the dollar income from such "meager" stakes.

Foreign governments tended to have different views on the home impacts of the outflow of portfolio and direct investments, usually with more fears about and controls on the former than the latter. Foreign concerns over the damage done by capital outflows were general, and often not particular to the flows to the United States (and frequently the attention was focused on short-term more than long-term outflows). At key junctures, however, the concerns were specifically targeted at investment in the United States. For example, in the late 1920s, when the U.S. stock market boom was attracting large amounts of flows from abroad, it seemed necessary to raise interest rates at home (in the United Kingdom, for instance), which it was believed would slow domestic growth. In the 1930s, illegal flight capital to the United States was often interpreted as hurting domestic economies in Europe.

Since foreign direct investments in the United States could be financed in the country and did not require sizable outflows of capital, they seemed to evoke less negative responses on the part of foreign governments. It is not obvious to what extent foreign economies benefited from the technologies transferred out of the United States by foreign multinationals in 1914 to 1945. In the main, foreign multinationals brought technology to America rather than derived knowledge in the United States to carry back home. Yet, over these years, as foreign affiliates had become well established, and as the U.S. economy gained relative stature in the world economy, innovations that originated in the United States could to some extent be returned to European parent firms. Indeed, during World War II, there had been alarm in the United States that this had occurred on a large scale and that American know-how had been extracted by foreign multinationals for their and their parent companies' use. My own reading of the data is that in the years 1914–1945 foreign MNEs introduced more technology into America than they drew from this country, but there was clearly a two-way street in the interchange. By the time of World War II, a number of foreign multinationals had developed research laboratories in the United States, employing American scientists. Initially, these laboratories had been dependent on parent company scientists; in time, Americans took over. So, too, as affiliates of foreign multinationals developed marketing techniques within the United States, in many instances, the parents learned from their offspring (or at least sought to do so). Perhaps most important, the presence of foreign multinationals in the United States gave the parent enterprises a window of information on what was happening in the world's largest economy, and this could only have produced positive feedback for the economies of the parent enterprises. While some of these effects were technological, others related to marketing and advertising expertise; some feedbacks had political and military value, while still others brought immediate specific economic gains. The economic gains were various, for (as examples) foreign affiliates in the United States raised moneys in this country for projects in their home country, helped facilitate international remittances, had positive impacts on their home countries' foreign trade (encouraging imports into the United States), as well as supplying income on the investments.

Probably, one can conclude that the impacts on the United States of the foreign portfolio and direct investments in the years 1914–1945 were greater than on the foreign source nations. The liquidations by foreign investors caused the closing of the New York Stock Exchange at the start of the First World War. Throughout the period 1914–1945, the existence of inward foreign portfolio and direct investment was influential in the maintenance of international economic linkages at times when often other such ties were tenuous. This had its perils as well as its promise. Some have argued, and I am not among them, that the presence of foreign investment in the United States was responsible for (in the extreme) or associated with (in the more moderate rendition) American entry into the First and Second World Wars. Others have attributed the crash of 1929 to foreign withdrawals (and there may well have been linkages here, at least in the timing). But the notion that there would have been no entries into the world wars and no crash had there not been foreign investment in the United States seems impossible to sustain. Perhaps inward foreign investments helped the recovery in the 1930s, and, as noted earlier, I find myself sympathetic to such a view. Undoubtedly, contemporaries were worried lest "hot" money, speculative foreign cash, upset the fragile stock market recoveries in that decade.

The various impacts of foreign portfolio investments on the U.S. economy seem distinct from those of FDI. In the years from 1914 to 1945, the sizable number of European, Canadian, and Japanese MNEs that operated in the United States did have consequences in shaping the contours of some of the industries in which they did business and in a generally positive fashion. There were direct investments in the United States by an important Argentine-based grain trader, a Mexican railroad, a few Chinese banks, an Australian insurance company, and a number of other MNEs from outside of western Europe, Canada, and Japan, but these were exceptional. By contrast, certain inward European MNEs and Canadian and Japanese ones had become during some or all of the years 1914–1945 very much a part of American life.

Overall, in macroeconomic terms, the influence of the foreign MNEs was without question small, owing to the immense size of the American market and the formidable domestic economic contributions. Thus, the brief forays of Rolls Royce and Austin into the American car industry had no lasting effects. That there were foreign makers of crucible steel in this country had little impact on the vast U.S. steel industry. Siemens, Brown, Boveri, and Philips had a role in the U.S. electrical industry, which was dwarfed by the strength of the American giants. Indeed, the U.S. electrical industry came to be dominated by agreements that essentially kept foreign manufacturers at bay. Brown, Boveri's aggressive incursion into the U.S. industry in the 1920s ended in failure. In short, in the big American heavy industries—autos, steel, and electrical—foreign multinationals were inconsequential. The same was true of public utilities, whether for trolleys, light and power, gas, or telephones. There were portfolio investments (and in the Insull companies rather large ones), but no critical unequivocal foreign direct investments. Foreign multinationals were few and far between in the retailing sector, where literally thousands of American firms participated. As for the big retail chains, these were typically domestically owned. Although some foreign-owned retailing existed, foreign MNE's share of the retailing sectors (however narrowly defined) was minor and the impact negligible. And as for American banking, this was domestic. While foreign banks had a presence in New York, and there had been foreign banks elsewhere in the United States, in 1945 no foreign bank had a determining place in U.S. domestic commercial banking. There were thousands of American banks; the large and prominent ones were 100 percent American owned and managed.

All this said, in certain activities foreign multinationals unquestionably made more than casual inroads. In several industries, foreign multinationals had been the innovators in the United States. Courtaulds had been the leader in U.S. rayon output before World War I, and for years foreign companies had continued to dominate this industry that produced the first synthetic textiles. It did not matter that nylon, which came in 1939, superseded rayon, as did the subsequent array of new synthetics, for a time before that happened the contribution of foreign-owned companies in this sector was profound.

Fokker may have had some impact on the course of American airplane manufacture, albeit the FDI was short lived. If Siemens and Philips contributed little to the basic American electrical industry, in the niche area of diagnostic medical technologies, both were in the lead in the United States in developing X-ray equipment. Yet, this was very much on the periphery of American science. More fundamental, Marconi served as the basis for the Radio Corporation of America, but that had occurred by 1919. By contrast, in the chemical and pharmaceutical industries, foreign multinationals assumed a high standing and, in many instances, did so through their direct investments in the United States.

Even though American I. G. Chemical Corporation (and its successor, General Aniline & Film) did not rank at the pinnacle in American dyestuff output, measured by value in 1940 it did hold second spot.[132] The fears of some Americans notwithstanding, this company was, moreover, a conduit for new technologies, with literally thousands of American patents. The innovations were less domestic (i.e., developed in laboratories in the United States) and more based on its international connections, but there was gradual importation of the foreign technologies, and increasingly the products did come to be made and the research come to be done in the United States. This company, established by I. G. Farben in 1929, had a major impact on America's chemistry. Its predecessor firms had introduced Americans to aspirin, a vast collection of dyestuffs, synthetic nitrates, and antisyphilitic medications. World War I had been a temporary interruption, and as I have written elsewhere, through this German affiliate in the interwar years, "from dyestuffs to film, to plastic moldings, malaria drugs (Atabrine), the first sulfa drugs, and petrochemicals (to a lesser extent), I. G. Farben's science and technology was translated into goods and services that played a significant role in the U.S. chemical industry."[133] Although the business of General Aniline & Film was taken over during World War II by the Office of Alien Property Custodian and eventually became Americanized, its considerable contribution to the U.S. chemical and pharmaceutical industry should not be underestimated. Its know-how was diffused.

Other foreign multinationals helped shape the U.S. chemical and pharmaceutical industries. Both giants in the interwar American chemical industry, Du Pont and Allied Chemical & Dye, in attempting to liberate U.S. industry from foreign dependency, were influenced in numerous ways by foreign multinationals. I have documented Du Pont's joint ventures within the United States and its licensing accords, involving foreign MNEs. From its origins in 1920, Allied Chemical had the Belgian Solvay & Cie. as its largest single investor. Solvay & Cie.'s technological offerings to one of Allied Chemical's predecessor companies were more substantial before the First World War than its post-1920 technological interchanges, yet Solvay & Cie. was sufficiently powerful as to be able to oust Allied Chemical's founder (Orlando Weber). Imperial Chemical Industries and its precursor companies had participated in various manners in the U.S. chemical industry; but ICI, although it licensed its patents, had increasingly over the years pulled back as a direct investor, opting for cooperative agreements. After World War II, this would change, and ICI would become a foreign direct investor in the United States.

In cellophane, the French Comptoir de Textiles Artificiels (with its joint venture with Du Pont) and the Belgian Société Industrielle de la Cellulose had been pioneers in the United States. The chemical subsidiary of Shell Union Oil Corporation did advanced work in the United States in the new petrochemical industry. The Swiss enterprises Ciba, Sandoz, and Geigy made the first DDT in America (an innovation that came from the research of Geigy's parent company). The German-owned Schering broke new ground in research in synthetic sex hormones; it supplied Americans with an important sulfa drug, medicines used to cope with arthritis, and an antacid. Like other German firms, although it was taken over during World War II, the research on which it had earlier embarked stayed in the United States and was absorbed by the domestic pharmaceutical industry.[134] Foreign multinationals, from I. G. Farben (through Winthrop Chemical) to Hoffmann-La Roche, offered some of the first contributions in the manufacture of vitamins.[135] Hoffmann-La Roche inaugurated penicillin production in the United States in 1943, under a U.S. government program. Unlike the German firms that did not have a direct continuity into the post-war period, Hoffmann-La Roche's major multibuilding facility at Nutley, New Jersey, was there to participate in the post–World War II pharmaceutical "revolution" in America. Ciba's pharmaceutical group, located since 1937 in Summit, New Jersey, was also creative, particularly in relation to hormone research.[136] So, too, Sandoz's pharmaceutical division in the United States continued into the post–World War II years, partaking in important research on digitalis and on epilepsy treatments. Burroughs Wellcome's affiliate had a major research and production facility in Tuckahoe, New York (in Westchester County); its wide range of pharmaceutical products included painkillers (Empirin) and digitalis preparations. By 1945, a number of foreign MNEs in chemicals and pharmaceuticals, with their U.S. research establishments, were on the frontiers of knowledge. They made high-technology products, taking part in the progress of the U.S. chemical and pharmaceutical industries. There were far more inward technological additions than outflows of technology, and U.S. industry was the beneficiary.

In other industries, if not in first place, foreign multinationals' affiliates ranked in the top four in selected domestic markets. Some branded, well-advertised products introduced by subsidiaries of foreign multinationals had become household names in America. Thus, although Unilever's subsidiary, Lever Brothers Co., was not in first place in soap sales, it was in 1945 a serious competitor to the domestically owned front-runner, Procter & Gamble, and had been so through the interwar and World War II years. Moreover, its 1944 purchase of the Pepsodent Company (with its toothbrush and toothpaste lines) had propelled Lever Brothers into the leading group in that market segment. Pepsodent was an acquired brand, but the others of Lever Brothers' brands (Lux Flakes, Lux Soap, Lifebuoy, for example) had been launched and promoted by the foreign multinational enterprise. The products were, moreover, not simply clones of the parent's offerings. Lifebuoy in the United Kingdom had been a laundry soap; in the United States it was redesigned as a personal hygienic good. Lever also had Spry, which competed with Procter & Gamble's Crisco in the vegetable oil industry.

British American Tobacco Company's subsidiary, Brown & Williamson, was not in the principal three in U.S. cigarette making, but it had achieved fourth rank in the 1930s and early 1940s. Brown & Williamson was important enough that when it offered a cheap cigarette and lowered the price during the early 1930s, the American giants followed suit. And it was Brown & Williamson that introduced the first mentholated cigarettes (Kools) and the first filter-tipped cigarettes (Viceroy). The American subsidiary went beyond its parent's contributions, presenting distinctive new brands. Brown & Williamson had been an acquisition. The parent had taken over the trademark Raleigh. Yet, that aside, the American affiliate assumed an independence—not unlike that of many foreign businesses in the vast U.S. market, meshing BAT's British management with an adaptation to American conditions. Brown & Williamson had not been an important company until it became part of the British multinational enterprise.

By 1945, the Nestlé name in chocolates was well known, and Nescafé instant coffee had been launched in America (in 1939).[137] There were other foreign companies with direct investments in distilling, manufacturing, packing, and marketing in the United States with brand names, all of which were familiar to the 1945 American consumer: for example, Canadian Club (distilled in the United States by Hiram Walker-Gooderham & Worts, a Canadian enterprise); Ovaltine (produced in the Chicago area by the Swiss firm Dr. A. Wander); Crosse & Blackwell (products made by a British firm of the same name); Coleman's Mustard (made by a British enterprise); Salada Tea (marketed by a subsidiary of a Canadian firm); and Tetley Tea (a brand of a British company). Consumer choices were enlarged by the presence of foreign multinationals.[138]

Shell Union Oil Corporation was prominent in chemicals; more significant, it was among the leading enterprises in oil production and distribution within the United States; its Shell Oil brand was by 1945 a visible sight to the domestic consumer. Shell was a major participant in the U.S. oil industry.[139] So, too, the French affiliate, Schlumberger, with its innovative drilling techniques, aided in the development of American oil resources.

In an entirely different sector, the construction industry, while there had been suburban developments in the United States in the 1920s, many had slowed in the 1930s, and when in 1935 the British company Taylor Woodrow moved forward with its housing development in Long Island, New York, complete with garden-style row houses, this set the stage for post–World War II suburbia. The community was a precursor to numerous post–World War II domestic and foreign-owned ventures.

In the grain trade, foreign multinationals had throughout the years 1914–1945 taken on a critical role, dispatching U.S. exports to world markets. They would continue to do so. So, too, in leaf tobacco, foreign-owned multinationals (BAT and Imperial Tobacco) dominated U.S. exports (BAT also led in U.S. cigarette exports). In other products, in the interwar period, Japanese trading firms had been pivotal in American-Japanese commerce, both exports and imports.[140]

Although the American domestically owned insurance industry was large and viable, British insurance companies occupied a well-established position in that sector. British fire and marine insurance companies had started in the U.S. market in the nineteenth century and continued throughout the years 1914–1945, diversifying into broader insurance lines, while retaining their importance in this industry. And, if the American accounting firms had come of age, the British influence had not entirely worn off.

After the passage of the Glass-Steagall Act of 1933, there had been a separation of commercial and investment banking in the United States, and even though there was no marked influence of foreign direct investors on the country's domestic commercial banking activity, there was one of foreign banks on U.S. investment banking, before and after Glass-Steagall. In addition, foreign banks with FDI had a good-sized role in the financing of America's foreign trade and in the handling of America's economic relationships with the rest of the world. Foreign banks provided assistance to nonbanking foreign affiliates in the United States. They also aided U.S. businesses that operated abroad, facilitating transactions. When foreign businesses and governments borrowed in the United States, foreign banks had assisted them in the mechanics of remitting interest payments to the United States. The British J. Henry Schroder Banking Corporation was, for example, in a position to furnish "dollar-based international banking."[141] In 1945 the German and Japanese banks were absent, but they would resume their activities in the post–World War II period to become involved in America as never before in their history.

The foregoing is merely a sampling. What I have sought to indicate is that despite the discontinuities and the many industries where there was minimal or no impact, certain foreign firms in America did have a vital role in this country. Many sustained their operations into the postwar era, as the strong and vigorous U.S. economy emerged after the Second World War. In addition, other companies (such as the German and Japanese ones) would revitalize operations, often in a manner that was so much an extension of the past experience as to almost negate the notion of discontinuity.

In the immediate post–World War II years, contemporaries paid little attention to the continuities in inward foreign portfolio or direct investments—or to their impact or potential impact; that so many of the affiliates had taken on "American" characteristics (including American managers and domestically designed advertising programs) helped obscure their "foreignness." The spotlight was on American business abroad, American lending, and American foreign aid. In 1914, the sizable inward foreign investments had been of consequence in the U.S. economy; in 1945, their importance had become so dimmed that for most observers, the foreign investments were part of the landscape. In that interim period, however, the effects of the presence of foreign investment had not been trivial. In the years between 1914 and 1945, stock market transactions had been greatly transformed as foreign investors had participated. And, probably more important, the knowledge, experience of, and the brands offered by numerous foreign multinational enterprises had been incorporated in the American way of life. To many, it seemed in 1945 that the issues related to inward foreign investment were those of a bygone era. It was not true. There had been exits, but there was also endurance. In 1914, no one predicted the forthcoming breakdown of globalization or the fractured world economy of 1945. So, too, in 1945, it would have been inconceivable to economists that in the late 1980s the United States would again become a debtor nation in world accounts. In 1945, no one forecast the formidable internationalization of the U.S. economy that was to come in the last half of the twentieth century and that existed at the dawn of the twenty-first century. And, in this internationalization process, the role of foreign investment in the United States was profound. This was the case because of the long history, as well as the new waves of investment.

Appendixes

Notes

Bibliography

Index

Appendix 1: Definitions

Acceptance: When a payer on whom a bill is drawn accepts it (i.e., recognizes the bill as an obligation), that bill or draft comes to be known as an acceptance.

Affiliate: An inward foreign direct investment.

Arbitrage: Purchase and sale of a security on different markets with an eye to profit on the price spread.

Billion: One thousand million.

Book value: The value measured from the books of the company.

Capital account: In the balance of payments, international transactions that involve the purchase or sale of assets.

Creditor nation: The level of outward long-term foreign investments exceeds the level of inward long-term foreign investments.

Cross-investments: The coexistence of outward and inward foreign investments.

Current account: In the balance of payments, exports and imports of goods and services, plus unilateral transfers.

Debtor nation: The level of inward long-term foreign investments exceeds the level of outward long-term foreign investments.

Direct investments: *See* Foreign direct investments.

Domestic securities: Securities of American corporations.

Flight capital: Capital seeking a safe haven.

Flows of capital: The flow of capital during a specified period (usually during a particular year).

Foreign: Outside the country.

Foreign direct investment: A foreign investment that carries with it ownership and control (or the potential for control). Today, the U.S. Department of Commerce labels a foreign direct investment as one with a 10 percent or more equity ownership by a single or closely related group of foreign owners. That definition was not consistently used over time. Before 1941, there was no set percentage defining "ownership and control." From 1941 through the period covered by this book (i.e., through 1945) the "ownership and control" was determined in U.S. government data, based on a 25 percent equity interest. These investments were part of the business strategy of the investor; they typically carried with them managerial direction or the potential for managerial direction. *See also* Appendix 2 (f).

Foreign investment: Unless otherwise specified, this refers to nonresident long-term investments, including both foreign direct and foreign portfolio investments.

Foreign portfolio investment: A foreign investment in stocks or bonds, government or corporate, or other long-term financial instruments. Foreign portfolio investments exclude foreign direct investments; in my text, they also exclude short-term investments. These were investments made for financial rather than business-operating purposes. *See also* Appendix 2 (g).

Foreign securities: The term is used in this volume to include dollar-denominated securities designed to provide financing to governments or businesses outside the United States; the term also includes other securities of foreign (not American) governments and businesses. *See also* Appendix 2 (e).

Free-standing company (or free-standing firm): A type of multinational enterprise with a headquarters (but no other operations) in the source of capital country, set up for the purpose of undertaking operations abroad; since it started afresh, initially it had to rely on a cluster of outsiders' competencies.

Gross: *See* Net and gross.

Home country: Place of headquarters of a multinational enterprise. Also called source of capital country.

Host country: Foreign place where the multinational enterprise invests. Also called recipient country.

Inward: Into the United States or into a designated host country.

Level of foreign investment: Foreign investment is often measured by level, that is, position, at year end. The level (or position) at year end is to be distinguished from the flows during a single year.

Long-term: Equities (common and preferred shares) and debt with an original maturity of more than a year. Long-term is defined by the instrument, not by the time the investor retains the investment. Thus, an investor in stocks or bonds could hold these securities for ten minutes, and the holding would still be defined as a long-term investment (flows in the designed period; "level" only if the measure was taken during those ten minutes).

Market value: The value of a security if sold in the market at the time of measurement.

Multinational enterprise: A firm that makes (and/or has) foreign direct investments.

Net and gross: In the literature, the term net is used in two manners: (1) Net flows of capital are the gross flows inward minus the gross flows outward. In this volume, I *never* use such net flows, since my interest is in the size of the inward foreign investments. I do, however, on occasion discuss net levels or net position, which defines creditor or debtor nation status; I always provide the gross figures as well. (2) Net is also used to deal separately with inflows and outflows in a particular period. Thus, with inward liquid foreign portfolio investments in a particular year, these are net of the sales in that period that resulted in repatriations of that inward investment. Inward foreign direct investment flows are net of exits that were followed by withdrawal of the investment (note: a multinational enterprise that reduces its investment in one activity but reinvests in another within the United States would not change the total inward investment but might change the sectoral classification of that inward investment).

Nonresident: Foreign investments are made by investors who are resident outside the country.

Outward: Out from the United States or out from another source of investment country.

Par value: The stated value of a security when issued.

Portfolio investments: *See* Foreign portfolio investments.

Position: *See* Level of foreign investment.

Recipient country: Recipient of inward foreign investments; *see also* Host country.

Short-term: Bank deposits, trade financing, short loans, call loans, notes with a maturity of less than a year. Short-term is defined by the instrument, not by the time the investor holds the investment.

Source of capital country: Place from where capital comes and/or home country.

Subsidiary: An inward foreign direct investment, more than 50 percent owned by the parent firm.

Appendix 2: Notes on the Statistics

(a) The Level of Inward Long-Term Foreign Investments

I have sought to establish the level of inward long-term foreign investments rather than focus on annual flows. My interest has been in the gross inward long-term investments, not net of outward investments. The figures are, however, net of exits and divestments, which is now the conventional way of viewing the data.

For 1914, my data are from Mira Wilkins, *The History of Foreign Investment in the United States to 1914* (Cambridge, Mass.: Harvard University Press, 1989). For 1914–1918, sources for information are provided in the key to Table 1.14. For 1919–1940, my data have been drawn from studies published in the United States. Although I have also consulted many non-U.S. sources, I have found that the most satisfactory series were assembled by Americans. The first work on the "international position" of the United States came with the beginnings of serious balance of payments accounting: Charles J. Bullock, John H. Williams, and Rufus S. Tucker, "The Balance of Trade of the United States," *Review of Economic Statistics*, 1 (July 1919): 213–263. The initial U.S. Department of Commerce's annual balance of payments reports was in 1922; it dealt with flows, but later balance of payments reports came to evaluate position as well. The National Industrial Conference Board, *The International Financial Position of the United States* (New York: National Industrial Conference Board, 1929), was a thorough study, based mainly on data (often unpublished) from the U.S. Department of Commerce. In the 1920s there came to be a differentiation in the monitoring of transactions in stocks and bonds—foreign portfolio investment (FPI)—and foreign direct investment (FDI). In that decade, the Federal Reserve and the U.S. Department of the Treasury began to collect materials on the movements of securities, which data they shared with the U.S. Department of Commerce. In the 1930s, a divide emerged in the studies of FPI and FDI. Thus, in 1934 a Treasury Department regulation required banks, bankers, brokers, and dealers in the United States to report to the Federal Reserve banks all long-term security transactions in which a "foreigner" was a party. These weekly flow data were summarized in Federal Reserve System, Board of Governors, *Banking and Monetary Statistics* (Washington, D.C., 1943); see also Arthur I. Bloomfield, *Capital Imports and the American Balance of Payments 1934–1939* (1950; rpt. New York: Kelley, 1966). Meanwhile, for the most part using very different data, in 1937 the U.S. Department of Commerce published its first survey on foreign investment in the United States, prepared by Amos E. Taylor of the Finance Division of the Bureau of Foreign and Domestic Commerce: U.S. Department of Commerce, Bureau of Foreign and Domestic Commerce, *Foreign Investments in the United States* (Washington, D.C., 1937), often cited in my text as *FIUS–1937;* it contained data on prior estimates, as well as information on the history and growth of foreign investment. Although it included material on FPI, the U.S. Department of Commerce came to concentrate on FDI. The splendid study by Cleona Lewis, *America's Stake in International Investments* (Washington, D.C.: Brookings Institution, 1938), covered outward as well as inward investments, FPI and FDI. There followed, in sequence, an excellent publication of the U.S. Department of Commerce, prepared by Paul D. Dickens: U.S. Department of Commerce, Bureau of Foreign and Domestic Commerce, *Foreign Long-Term Investments in the United States 1937–1939* (Washington, D.C., 1940)—often cited in my text as *FIUS—1940* (it included two sets of 1937 data: mid-1937 and year end 1937; Cleona Lewis, *Debtor and Creditor Countries: 1938, 1944* [Washington, D.C.: Brookings Institution, 1945], used the mid-1937 data for her "1938" figures); William Adams Brown Jr., *The International Gold Standard Reinterpreted 1914–1934,* 2 vols. (New York: National Bureau of Economic Research, 1940); and Hal B. Lary, *The United States in the World Economy* (Washington, D.C., 1943). The material on capital movements in the Lary volume was prepared by Robert L. Sammons of the U.S. Department of Commerce, assisted by Bloomfield of the New York Federal Reserve, who in 1942 had completed a Ph.D. dissertation at the University of Chicago titled "International Capital Movements and the American Balance of Payments: 1929–1940." (Bloomfield substantially revised this dissertation and published it in 1950, as indicated above; in that book when he deals with the level of foreign investment, he repeats figures that first appeared in the Lary volume.)

The Treasury Department census (as of June 14, 1941) on foreign investment in the United States was published in 1945: U.S. Department of the Treasury, *Census of Foreign-Owned Assets in the United States* (Washington, D.C., 1945)—cited herein as *1941 Census.* Robert L. Sammons' figures in "Foreign Investment Aspects of Measuring U.S. National Wealth," National Bureau of Economic Research, *Studies in Income and Wealth* (New York: National Bureau of Economic Research, 1950), 549–586, included his revisions for 1929 and 1939 (as well as new figures for 1946); they took into account the census findings. The *1941 Census* was undertaken after the war in Europe was under way. It was very imperfect (which it acknowledged). It missed, for example, many holders of U.S. government securities; it also missed holders of bearer securities, principally bonds, which securities were physically held abroad. U.S. citizens who resided abroad were included as "foreign" investors. As in prior studies, residence rather than nationality defined foreign investment. Refugees who moved from war-torn Europe and settled elsewhere carried with them their prior holdings of American securities; those refugees who were resident in the United States on June 14, 1941, were not "foreign" investors, although they may have been foreign investors when they acquired the securities. With the cloaking of the 1930s, many foreign-owned securities were held through Switzerland and Panama, for example. Often, the "reported address" was given as Switzerland and Panama, not the country where the investment originated. Germans appear to have held certain U.S. investments through Argentina, although this fails to show up anywhere in the census data; thus, the census indicates that of the $51.4 million in American securities held by "Argentines," merely $1.5 million were by "citizens" of "enemy"—Germany, Italy, Japan, Hungary, Roumania, and Bulgaria—countries (p. 79). These countries were not "enemies" of the United States at the date of the census but had become "enemies" by the time the census was published.

For the war years to year end 1945, I found useful data that was included for comparative purposes in a census of U.S. outward investments: U.S. Department of the Treasury, Office of the Secretary, *Census of American-Owned Assets in Foreign Countries* (Washington, D.C., 1947), chap. 2, esp. p. 9. In 1943, the U.S. Treasury undertook this census of U.S. investments abroad; the report has a chapter (including a table) on the international creditor-debtor position of the United States, 1939, 1945, 1946, which I found particularly helpful for the year end 1945 figures. Despite a 1947 publication date, a note to this table indicated, "Enemy-owned assets in the United States are included as part of the foreign-owned assets, notwithstanding the probability that the major part will be completely vested and value retained by the United

States." The text is full of caveats on the reliability of the data. Note that the census on inward foreign investment *(1941 Census)* was in 1941 and on outward investment in 1943. This created fundamental problems of comparisons, since the benchmark years differed. A second useful source on the war years is U.S. Department of Commerce, Office of Business Economics, *International Transactions of the United States during the War, 1940–1945,* Economic Series No. 65 (Washington, D.C., 1948), 110, 224–225, which contains year end international position data for 1939 to 1945. (This report was prepared under the direction of Sammons.) Unlike the 1943 census report, in this case "the value of enemy property in the United States seized by the Alien Property Custodian has been excluded from foreign assets in this country after vesting." The Federal Reserve System, Board of Governors, *Banking and Monetary Statistics, 1941–1970* (Washington, D.C., 1976), 882, has information on foreign ownership of U.S. government public debt, June and December 1940 through 1945. A separate section on international finance explains that "in July 1942, the reporting basis for liabilities to and claims on foreigners as reported by banks and for securities transactions was changed from weekly to monthly." Banks in all Federal Reserve districts began reporting liabilities to official institutions separately (earlier only some New York banks had made the distinction between liabilities to private and to official institutions). Ibid., 929. This international finance section of the volume has no position data for the war years (although it does have a table on purchases and sales by foreigners of long-term securities, by type, for 1942–1945, and a second table covers the net purchases or sales of U.S. corporate stock by country during 1945). Ibid. 998, 1002.

The U.S. Department of Commerce, Bureau of the Census, *Historical Statistics of the United States, Colonial Times to 1957* (Washington, D.C., 1960), 565, contains figures for inward long-term foreign investments in the United States, separately listing foreign direct investments and "other" investments, for June 1914, and year end 1919, 1924, 1927, 1930, 1931, 1935, 1940, and 1945. (These were reproduced verbatim in the 1975 edition of this work.) I have used this series, gone back to all the sources, and established my own series. In general, the category "other" long-term investments in these historical statistics corresponds to what I have called "portfolio investments."

(b) British Investments in the United States

Since throughout the years covered by my book, British investments in the United States were the largest, I spent time with British (as well as American) measures of this investment. My evaluation of British sources for 1913 and 1914 is incorporated in the data provided in Mira Wilkins, *The History of Foreign Investment in the United States to 1914* (the standard British source for year end 1913 is George Paish, "The Export of Capital and the Cost of Living," *Statist,* suppl., Feb. 14, 1914, i–viii). For the interwar years, British sources are uniformly unsatisfactory in their coverage of British investments in the United States. The Midland Bank (and before that its predecessor, the London Joint City & Midland Bank) regularly collected statistics on the geographic distribution of U.K. "new capital issues." See its *Monthly Review,* 1920 and later. Since British investments in the United States in the interwar years rarely took the form of "new capital issues," the Midland Bank found so little to note in this category that it did not segregate the United States in its geographic designations. The principal collator of statistics on British overseas investment 1929–1939 was Robert M. Kindersley (of Lazard Brothers), who published a series of eleven articles on the subject in the *Economic Journal.* These, as well as Paish's 1914 article, have been reprinted in Mira Wilkins, ed., *British Overseas Investments 1907–1948* (New York: Arno Press, 1977). Kindersley's figures were used in the oft-cited book by the Royal Institute of International Affairs, *The Problem of International Investment* (London: Oxford University Press, 1937). In 1950, the Bank of England adjusted Kindersley's figures for 1938 and updated his material to cover 1938–1948. Bank of England, *United Kingdom Overseas Investments, 1938 to 1948* (London: Bank of England, 1950), also reprinted in Wilkins, *British Overseas Investments.* In his articles, Kindersley complained frequently of his inability to monitor British investments in the United States. The problem was that such investments differed sharply from British stakes in the rest of the world in one fundamental manner: many Britishers acquired American securities traded in New York. A second reason that British figures on their nationals' stakes in the United States were so bad—and this included the Paish data, Midland Bank figures, Kindersley's numbers, and those of the Bank of England—was the absence of good British statistics on FDI. The British literally had no idea of the size of FDI in the United States. Repeatedly, the many British collectors of interwar statistics on foreign investments in the United States (and this includes not only Kindersley but also A. T. K. Grant, the Royal Institute of International Affairs, and the Bank of England) noted that there were British investments in the United States that their figures were not capturing, so contemporaries were well aware of the problems. Three other sources on British overseas investment in the period covered by my book should be noted: (1) A. H. Imlah, *Economic Elements in the Pax Britannica* (Cambridge, Mass.: Harvard University Press, 1958), who looked at balance of payment figures. His figures are not helpful on the level of British investments in the United States. (2) A. R. Conan, "The United Kingdom as a Creditor Country," *Westminster Bank Review,* Aug. 1960, 16–22. He provides only aggregate 1939 figures and then concentrates on the post–World War II years. Charles H. Feinstein, *National Income, Expenditure and Output of the United Kingdom 1855–1965* (Cambridge: Cambridge University Press, 1972), 204–205, T110, gives figures on British overseas assets, *net* of liabilities, based on Imlah and Conan, endorsing Imlah over Conan. And (3) Tom Houston and John H. Dunning, *UK Industry Abroad* (London: Financial Times, 1976), 112, which made estimates of British direct investments in the United States, but since their figures excluded those made by oil companies, banks, and insurance firms, these figures fail to capture the extent of FDI in the United States (and of course exclude FPI entirely). For 1945, see D. F. McCurrach, "Britain's U.S. Dollar Problems, 1939–45," *Economic Journal,* 221 (Sept. 1948): 369. By this time, for political reasons (explained in my text), the British were continuing to undervalue their U.S. assets. Given the difficulties with most of the British figures, I have relied on U.S. figures on British investments in the United States, the general ones of which are indicated in the sources cited in Appendix 2 (a) above.

(c) Canadian Investments in the United States

Canadian figures (in Canadian dollars) have been published in Statistics Canada, *Canada's International Investment Position: Historical Statistics 1926 to 1992* (Ottawa, 1993), which has figures on the level of Canadian direct investments in the United States, 1920–1991 (p. 67); its data on Canadian portfolio investments in the United States are less complete, covering (within the years 1914–1945) only 1926, 1930, 1933, 1939, and 1945 (p. 55)—and this information is described as "weak" (p. 45). See also for earlier definitions and data for 1926, 1930, 1939, and 1945, Dominion Bureau of Statistics, *Canada's International Investment Position, Selected Years, 1926 to 1949* (Ottawa, n.d. [1950]), 39–40. The Canadian figures on FPI and FDI excluded the external assets of Canadian banks and insurance companies, which are discussed separately in ibid., 25–26.

(d) Par, Market, and Book Value

In all the historical measures of FPI and FDI, 1914–1945, there were major inconsistencies in the choices of standards of value. Sometimes, as with the figures of L. F. Loree on railway securities (*Commercial and Financial Chronicle,* Mar. 31, 1917), both par and market values were separately enumerated and provided. The U.S. Department of Commerce and Cleona Lewis usually measured common stock at market (excluding FDI). There were variations in the measures of preferred stock (again excluding FDI), sometimes at par and sometimes at market. The U.S. Department of Commerce in the years covered by this book and Lewis typically measured bonds at par and direct investment at book value. Sammons used market values for all securities, if the securities were publicly traded; the Treasury Department in its *1941 Census* sought a market value, whenever that market value was available—for all securities and for FDI. Market value for an FDI would be available if part of the ownership of an affiliate was traded, as in the case of Shell Union Oil, for example. When the market value was not available, which was the case with most FDI, the Treasury Department followed earlier procedures and used book value figures. The accounts of investors within the United States lacked uniformity in their valuations of their U.S. assets. Canadian statistics on outward FDI used book value in the parent companies' books.

(e) Dollar-Denominated Securities for Foreign Corporations and Governments ("Foreign Securities")

Conceptually, foreign investments in "foreign securities" are difficult to handle. When a Japanese investor bought Anglo-French bonds in New York, do we call this a U.S. investment? When a German bought German bonds in America, was this an "American" investment? In each case, there is capital inflow into the United States to make the purchase (but it was matched by the outward foreign investment of the same face but usually not of the same actual value). The obligation to the purchaser of the securities (to the foreign investor) is *not* an American one, although the transfer agent handling the payment of interest (and the refunding or redemption of the principal) might be in New York. To complicate matters further, foreigners' purchase of a foreign security in New York could have two different consequences: (1) it could be an investment in an existing security, or (2) it could be a repatriation of an earlier foreign issue. The two were never separated in the available statistical data. As I read the Department of Commerce statistics, all nonresident foreign investments in a security offered on the American market would be counted as a foreign investment in the United States (albeit at times I was uncertain whether "foreign" securities were actually included). So, too, the U.S. company that invested abroad or the security that represented a foreign loan would, in turn, be recorded as a U.S. outward investment. Thus, foreign holdings of "foreign securities" can be viewed as inward investments. But this methodology was *not* followed in the *1941 Census,* where in its general tables, the U.S. Department of the Treasury excluded "foreign securities" held by foreigners (the census tabulated such securities separately only if they were reported and held by custodians in the United States on behalf of foreigners). The census report explained that the reason foreign securities were excluded from the general tables was that they were "not basically a part of the American economy, that is, they do not depend for their value upon this country." Weekly flow data (purchases and sales of American securities by foreign investors) from 1935, summarized in Federal Reserve System, Board of Governors, *Banking and Monetary Statistics* (Washington, D.C., 1943), 620–623, 626–629, provided transactions in both domestic and foreign securities, in separate tables. Monthly flow data (purchases and sales of American securities by foreign investors), 1942–1945, are summarized in Federal Reserve System, Board of Governors, *Banking and Monetary Statistics, 1941–1970* (Washington, D.C., 1976), 998, which also provided data on transactions in domestic and foreign securities. Foreign bonds and stock are joined in the 1942 data (and earlier material) and segregated in the 1943–1945 data. None of these data makes it possible to determine whether the purchases of foreign securities represent ongoing holdings or repatriations of prior borrowings, which would wipe the slate clean. To complicate matters even more, if a foreigner sells a "foreign security" to an American, that constitutes an outward American investment; if a foreigner sells a dollar-denominated foreign security to another foreigner (of the same or different nationality), that has no impact on the level of foreign investment in the United States. Some economists argue that the foreign buying of "foreign securities" should never be counted as "investments in the United States," since the underlying assets (and the obligations) are not American.

(f) Foreign Direct Investments (Investments Made by Multinational Enterprises)

In 1937, the U.S. Department of Commerce defined foreign direct investments in the United States to include "all foreign investments in those American corporations or enterprises which are controlled by a person or small group of persons (corporate or natural) domiciled in a foreign country." U.S. Department of Commerce, Bureau of Foreign and Domestic Commerce, *Foreign Investments in the United States* (Washington, D.C., 1937), 31. In its 1940 report the same formulation was retained, but an additional clause was added: "or corporations or enterprises in the management of which such [foreign-resident] person or group of persons has an important voice." U.S. Department of Commerce, Bureau of Foreign and Domestic Commerce, *Foreign Long-Term Investments in the United States 1937–1939* (Washington, D.C., 1940), 4. The Treasury Department for its *1941 Census* adopted the 25 percent or more of equity criteria. U.S. Department of the Treasury, *Census of Foreign-Owned Assets in the United States* (Washington, D.C., 1945), 54. Subsequently, for many years the Commerce Department used that measure for both inward and outward FDI, until in the 1960s it lowered the cutoff to 10 percent for outward U.S. direct investments. Not until the 1974 benchmark survey on FDI in the United States was the cutoff lowered for inward FDI. In U.S. Department of Commerce, *Foreign Direct Investment in the United States,* 9 vols. (Washington, D.C., 1976), I, 4–5, the statement was made that "foreign-owned" and "foreign-controlled" were used to mean a degree of foreign participation of 10 percent or more.

(g) Foreign Portfolio Investments

My definition of foreign portfolio investments is given in Appendix 1—and I have consistently used that definition in this text. Readers should be aware that others have used the phrase differently, and standard sources (such as the International Monetary Fund) have changed their definitions over the years. In this book, my concern has been only with long-term FPI; in some definitions, short-term investments are included (long-term and short-term are defined in Appendix 1). Separate from mine, other definitions of FPI have been narrowly confined to stock holdings of less than 10 percent; still others exclude long-term public sector borrowings.

Appendix 3: Detailed Sources for Tables 2.1, 8.3, and 10.1

Notes to Table 2.1

Columns 1. Based on Cleona Lewis, *America's Stake in International Investments* (Washington, D.C.: Brookings Institution, 1938), 558. The total and portfolio investment figures include common stock at market; bonds and preferred stock are given at par. Portfolio investment includes railroad common stock, preferred stock, and bonds, plus other common stock, preferred stock, and bonds, along with a "miscellaneous category" (1924: $250 million; 1929: $750 million) that is not defined. Lewis provides no separate category for "government" securities or for long-term real estate holdings. Her direct investment figures are at book value. I have adjusted her 1924 figures to cope with an arithmetic error in her table. There is also an arithmetic error in her 1929 figures that I corrected. Lewis provided figures for 1934–1936, which came directly from the U.S. Department of Commerce (see columns 4); I have not repeated them.

Column 2. There is only one entry, which comes from U.S. Department of Commerce, Bureau of Foreign and Domestic Commerce, *The Balance of International Payments of the United States in 1927* (Washington, D.C., 1928), 25: Estimated holdings of American securities by nonresident foreign investors. There is no indication as to whether these holdings are measured at par or at market.

Column 3. U.S. Department of Commerce, Bureau of Foreign and Domestic Commerce, *The Balance of International Payments of the United States in 1931,* Trade Information Bulletin No. 803 (Washington, D.C., 1931), 48, but see the caveat on the absence of "reliable data." Ibid., p. 49.

Columns 4. U.S. Department of Commerce, Bureau of Foreign and Domestic Commerce, *Foreign Investment in the United States* (Washington, D.C., 1937), 14, 16 (the first comprehensive study made by the Commerce Department). The 1927 total is repeated from the column 2 source. The 1929 total is also repeated from an earlier U.S. Department of Commerce estimate: U.S. Department of Commerce, Bureau of Foreign and Domestic Commerce, *The Balance of International Payments of the United States in 1929,* (Washington, D.C., 1930), 32. Ray Hall wrote of the $4.7 billion that it was "assumed to represent the value of the investments—not the actual sums originally tied up here by foreigners in past years nor the par value of securities. In other words, it is the estimated capitalized value of earnings." For 1934–1936, on which the 1937 study concentrated, total and portfolio investment figures give common stock at market; bonds and preferred stock at par; portfolio investments include a mixed group of "other investments" (see p. 13 of the study on what is included; the miscellaneous amount remained at $750 million for each year, 1934–1936). Direct investments were at book value.

Columns 5. U.S. Department of Commerce, Bureau of Foreign and Domestic Commerce, *Foreign Long-Term Investment in the United States, 1937–39* (Washington, D.C., 1940), 2–7. In its revised 1934 figures and its new 1937, 1938, and 1939 figures, bonds were at par value, preferred stock at par value (although market values of preferred stock were provided [p. 7]), and common stock was at market. "Miscellaneous investments"—included under portfolio investments—were given as $750 million in each year and were said to include in 1934 $50 million and in 1937, 1938, and 1939, $100 million in U.S. national, state, and municipal government bonds. The miscellaneous category also covered trust funds on behalf of foreign beneficiaries, real estate mortgages, and unincorporated real estate. Direct investment was given at book value. This same report (pp. 21–22) also gave an alternative *total* of $7,007 million for *mid*-1937—which included the $100 million for government securities. Since columns 5 include year end data, the mid-1937 data are not included herein.

Columns 6. Federal Reserve System, Board of Governors, *Banking and Monetary Statistics* (Washington, D.C., 1943), 637. Figures are from the U.S. Department of Commerce; the definitions are the same as in columns 5. Portfolio investment is divided into "market securities" and "other" (given as $750 million in each year, of which $100 million—in both 1939 and 1940—was in U.S. national, state, and municipal bonds).

Columns 7. Robert L. Sammons, "Foreign Investment Aspects of Measuring U.S. National Wealth," National Bureau of Economic Research, *Studies in Income and Wealth* (New York: National Bureau of Economic Research, 1950), 553. Sammons' "long-term" foreign assets in the

United States had a category "long-term claims" that included bonds, payable in U.S. dollars, other bonds (for which he recorded nothing), and "other long term-claims." The latter were given as $750 million in 1929 (as had Cleona Lewis—see note on columns 1 above), but as $2,015 million in 1939 (compared with $750 million of the U.S. Department Commerce—see notes on columns 5 and 6 above). Sammons' total long-term assets, in addition, included common and preferred shares, direct investments, realty, *and* movable goods. I have eliminated movable goods ($350 million in 1929 and 1939 from his totals). Where securities (stocks and bonds) were publicly traded, Sammons used market values. Sammons' 1929 figures are an adjustment of Lewis'. He kept her $1,400 million as direct investment, to which *I* added his $85 million "realty." His total foreign investment figure (total long-term foreign assets in the United States) for 1929 figure is higher than that of Lewis (column 1) and that of the U.S. Department of Commerce (column 4). For 1939, Sammons adjusted the earlier U.S. Department of Commerce figures (columns 6) to take into account the Treasury census data of 1941 (see notes on columns 8 below). *Because* of the $2,015 million "other long-term claims," his 1939 total and his portfolio investment figure are higher than the Commerce number; if only stocks and bonds were included, it would be lower. Direct investment is much larger than the Commerce figure (and not only because of the $85 million realty addition—the same as included in 1929); this was because of his taking the census into account. Sammons' estimates were designed to be linked with those of the U.S. Treasury (see notes on columns 8 below).

Columns 8. Two sets of 1941 figures are provided, both from the U.S. Department of the Treasury, *Census of Foreign-Owned Assets in the United States* (Washington, D.C., 1945). The census was as of June 14, 1941, and was pursued to aid the "freezing controls" (see Chapter 8 herein). The first set of figures is from ibid., 41. These figures are on long-term foreign investments as defined by the U.S. Treasury. The foreign portfolio investment figure of $5,761 million includes $2,195 million "other assets" ($2,320 million as given in the census minus $125 million in real estate). These "other assets" seem in my view difficult to qualify as long-term portfolio investments. I included them (1) because it is in keeping with the U.S. Treasury definition, and (2) because of its links with column 7. The $5,761 million figure also includes foreign portfolio investments in American securities ($2,699 million) plus those in estates and trusts ($867 million). The foreign direct investment figure of $2,438 million includes foreign-controlled U.S. enterprises ($2,313 million) plus real estate investments ($125 million). The second (alternative) set of 1941 figures is from ibid., 18. The foreign portfolio investment figure of $3,566 million includes foreign portfolio investments in American securities ($2,699 million) plus those in estates and trusts ($867 million); it excludes the $2,195 million "other assets." The foreign direct investment number is identical. The second set of numbers coincides with those given in Table 9.4 (estimate 1, column 1). In the census, the Treasury sought a market value for all foreign-owned assets—whenever that value was available; it found that it was generally not available in the case of foreign direct investment and thus settled on an "estimated or book value" (pp. 56–59).

Notes to Table 8.3

While the *1941 Census* included all foreign investments in the United States, as of June 14, 1941, short-term and long-term, this table is only on long-term investments (it excludes bullion, currency, and deposits, as well as all other short-term assets). The figures also exclude some small amount of long-term assets in insurance policies and annuities. The data are on the basis of "reported address." Two figures are given for each country. The first is the total, and the second is the "country of address," which "covers all assets owned by persons known to be citizens of the country of their reported address" (a subset of the first and accordingly always of a lesser amount). Thus, in the census, a reference to "citizens" of a particular designated country relates to assets belonging to citizens of that country, who were living in that country (p. 78). The difference includes "citizens" (or others) from another country, whose assets were included in the particular country's reported total. Americans who were residing abroad would be included in the total. Elsewhere, the census found that "a substantial part of the Panamanian holdings, and perhaps of the Argentine, was ultimately owned in Europe" (p. 17). This does not seem to be reflected in the data presented in this table. The total value figure for German-controlled enterprise is given in this table as $105 million, of which $96.3 million was by "citizens," albeit elsewhere in the census, the text says, "Of the 171 enterprises tabulated here as owned by Germans with a total value of $105,000,000, 43 with a value of $88,000,000 were reported as held by persons, usually corporations, in Switzerland, the Netherlands, and other non-enemy countries" (p. 30). The two statements cannot be reconciled. In short, the figures provided in this table must be viewed with great skepticism.

a. The totals in this column include the total of securities, controlled enterprises, plus the three categories of miscellaneous investments (real estate, real estate mortgages, and trusts and estates).

b. This column (and the securities that it totals) excludes foreign direct investments in the securities of American companies, which are included under the category "controlled enterprises." The totals by type of domestic security are rounded and will not necessarily add to the component types of securities (they include the same total figures as provided in Table 8.1). In all its general tables, the census excluded "foreign securities" held by foreigners. Separately, the census tabulated reported "securities issued by foreign governments and corporations, and held by custodians in this country on behalf of foreigners"; that total as of June 14, 1941, was $890 million.

c. Control was defined as 25 percent or more of voting stock. "Enterprises" included branches, sole proprietorships, corporations, and other organizations. These are foreign direct investments. The total values by reported address are identical to those in Table 8.2.

d. Because of immigration and marital ties, a number of trusts and estates were set up with the beneficiary abroad. These trusts and estates represented long-term foreign obligations. Of the total $867 million in "trusts and estates," $806 million was in "trusts" and $61 million in "estates." The $867 million total was explained in the census as follows: (1) a large number of wealthy U.S. citizens who resided in France, Italy, and England had their assets in the United States administered through trusts; (2) immigrants left estates and set up trusts for those back home; (3) trusts with English beneficiaries emerged out of marital ties between American women and prominent Englishmen, many of these dating back to 1910 or earlier; (4) some trusts were established by English insurance companies during 1939 and 1940; and (5) "persons in several foreign countries" set up trusts in the United States to evade taxation, avoid double taxation, or "reduce the possibility of seizure by their own and enemy governments." The census found that the percentage of trusts established between 1938 and 1941 was very small in the case of Canadian beneficiaries, a little larger in the case of U.K. and Italian beneficiaries, but substantially higher with German, Dutch, and Swiss beneficiaries (pp. 13–14, 45). From my reading of the evidence, the long-standing investments by British trust companies in the United States would *not* be included under the rubric "trusts and estates." It is not clear, however, whether the census categorized British investments in an American firm such as Commercial Investment Trust Corp. as a British investment in a "trust" or as one in corporate securities (the latter would be more accurate and was probably the way the investment was measured). The trusts established in the United States by NV Philips and Ciba, for example, probably do fit into this category. The census gave only values and no indication of the numbers of trusts and estates. Both appear to have been numerous (especially the estates), at least this is suggested, based on data from the Office of Alien Property Custodian, *Annual Reports.*

e. This U.K. figure included $700 million in assets pledged as collateral for the Reconstruction Finance Corporation (RFC) loan.

f. Less than $50,000.

g. The rest of world total is the difference between the specified country totals and the total of all areas. The totals do not add across because of rounding.

h. The total for all areas includes some bearer securities on which the census did not give country-specific information (these bearer securities are included in the rest of world total, since the latter was derived by subtraction). The bearer securities, primarily bonds, were, "in general, only reported [in the census] when held by custodians and nominees [located in the United States]."

Notes to Table 10.1

The "Foreign investments in the United States" columns (F through J) contain the same information, differently presented, as in "estimate 2," Table 9.4 herein. For this table, I have revised and reordered the figures given in U.S. Department of Commerce, Office of Business Economics, *International Transactions of the United States during the War, 1940–1945,* Economic Series No. 65 (Washington, D.C., 1948), 110, in the following manner: (1) I have omitted short-term obligations (as in Table 9.4 herein); (2) I have subtracted a miscellaneous category of "other long-term" from both U.S. investments abroad and foreign investments in the United States (this figure was subtracted in the second total, estimate 2, Table 9.4 herein); (3) column B is identical to the one given in the source; in contrast, column G, government borrowings (or government obligations), includes *both* $.5 billion of foreign holdings of U.S. federal government bonds and an estimated $.1 billion in state and municipal bonds that the Commerce Department (and Table 9.4 herein) included with private portfolio investments; (4) the private total in column H and the portfolio investments in column I were reduced by $.1 billion (since this was moved into column G); (5) as in the Commerce Department table, columns D and I include investments in securities (stocks and bonds) and also estates and trusts; for column D, estates and trusts totaled $.2 billion; for column I they came to $.6 billion. In short, if estates and trusts were omitted, U.S. portfolio investments abroad in dollar bonds and in securities payable in local currencies would come to $4.0 billion, while foreign investments in the United States in corporate stock and bonds (this excludes $.1 billion in state and municipal bonds and $.5 billion in U.S. government bonds, which are in column G) would come to $3.9 billion (the $3.9 billion differs from the $4.0 billion on Table 9.4 herein, since the latter included the $.1 billion in state and municipal obligations).

Appendix 4: Principal U.S. Federal Legislation Affecting Foreign Investment in the United States, 1914–1945

These were laws that affected inward foreign investment at the time of passage and subsequently. Some had a general impact; others specifically targeted foreign investors. Starred (*) items did not have an immediate impact, but over the years they had profound impacts on inward foreign investment.

1914	Shipping Act
	War Risk Insurance Act
	Clayton Antitrust Act*
	Federal Trade Commission Act*
1915	LaFollette Seamen's Act
1916	Shipping Act
	Emergency Tariff Act
	Revenue Act
1917	Espionage Act
	Trading with the Enemy Act
1918	Revenue Act
	Webb-Pomerene Act
1919	Edge Act
	Volstead Act
1920	Mineral Lands Leasing Act
	Merchant Marine Act (the Jones Act)
	Federal Water Power Act
1921	Emergency Tariff Act
	Kellogg Cable Landing Act
	Knox-Porter Resolution (officially ending World War I)
1922	Fordney-McCumber Tariff Act
1923	Winslow Act
1924	Heroin Prohibition Act

1926	Air Commerce Act
	Air Corps Act
1927	Radio Act
1928	Settlement of War Claims Act
	Jones-White Act
1930	Smoot-Hawley Tariff
1932	Reconstruction Finance Corporation Act*
1933	Congressional Resolution (canceling gold clause)
	Banking Act (Glass-Steagall Act)
	National Industrial Recovery Act
1934	Securities Act (authorizing the Securities and Exchange Commission)
	Gold Reserve Act
	Johnson Act*
	Silver Purchase Act
	Harrison Resolution (on World War I compensation)
	Communications Act
	Reciprocal Trade Agreements Act
	Export-Import Bank Act
1935	Neutrality Act
	Wagner Act
	Federal Alcohol Administration Act
1936	Neutrality Act
	Revenue Act
	Merchant Marine Act
1937	Neutrality Act
	Revenue Act
1938	Civil Aeronautics Act
	Foreign Agents Registration Act*
	Resolution 113 (setting up the Temporary National Economic Committee)
	Robinson-Patman Act
1939	Strategic Materials Act
	Neutrality Act
1941	Lend-Lease Act
	Ship Requisition Act
	War Powers Act
1945	Bretton Woods Agreement Act

Notes

1. The First World War, 1914–1918

1. Editorial, *New York Times,* August 5, 1914 (quotation); Mira Wilkins, *The History of Foreign Investment in the United States to 1914* (Cambridge, Mass.: Harvard University Press, 1989).

2. Barbara W. Tuchman, *The Guns of August* (New York: Macmillan, 1962), and Sidney B. Fay, *The Origins of World War I,* 2nd ed. (New York: Macmillan, 1938). The *New York Times,* July 4, 1914, reported that "Americans" living in Paris—including James Stillman (chairman of National City Bank), Alfred S. Heidelbach (of the American banking firm Heidelbach, Ickelheimer & Co.), and Herman Harjes (of Morgan's Paris house)—would be the "hardest hit" by the new tax. American banks in Paris, receiving investment coupons from their local customers, were deducting 5 percent and handing it to the French Treasury. The law had become effective July 1, and the result had been "hundreds of cablegrams" sent to America ordering that payments (dividends and interest) be held in the United States or diverted to London; such measures "to get around" the tax did not involve divestments, albeit there were also the sales of American securities.

3. J. Lawrence Laughlin, *Credit of Nations* (New York: Charles Scribner's Sons, 1918), 79, on the decline on the Vienna Exchange. *New York Times,* July 14, 15, 1914.

4. *New York Times,* July 20, 21, 22, 23, 24, 25, 1914. Charles J. Bullock, John H. Williams, and Rufus S. Tucker, "The Balance of Trade of the United States," *Review of Economic Statistics,* 1 (July 1919): 240 (gold export point).

5. *New York Times,* July 26, 1914.

6. Ibid. (6 P.M. New York time).

7. Ibid., July 27, 1914.

8. Ibid., July 28, 1914.

9. Ibid., July 29, 1914.

10. Ibid., July 30, 1914.

11. Ibid., July 31, 1914. The *New York Times* contained details on sales of American securities by name of the corporation and the stock price declines since the "war scare." Not only were Europeans selling, but the value of the existing holdings of Europeans was declining. Thomas W. Lamont, *Across World Frontiers* (New York: Harcourt, Brace, 1951), 52.

12. *New York Times,* Aug. 1, 1914. R. S. Sayers, *The Bank of England 1891–1944,* 3 vols. (Cambridge: Cambridge University Press, 1976), III, 346–347 (on the rise in the bank rate). The New York Stock Exchange had closed for a short period in September 1873 after Jay Cooke & Co. suspended operations, and on Saturday, May 11, 1901, because clerks were "worn out" after the May 9, 1901, "panic" in Northern Pacific stock. These were the only two precedents for the stock exchange closing.

13. *New York Times,* Aug. 2, 1914; Sayers, *Bank of England,* III, 347 (British bank rate). The $7.00 was probably a purely nominal rate; there is little evidence of transactions taking place at this price.

14. Frank A. Vanderlip, New York, to Narcissa Vanderlip, Aug. 4, 1914, Vanderlip Papers, Pt. B, Ser. 1, Box 6, Columbia University Library, New York, New York. Aside from the *New York Times,* good sources on the events of July–August 1914 include H. G. S. Noble, *The New York Stock Exchange in the Crisis of 1914* (Garden City, N.Y.: Country Life Press, 1915)—Noble was president of the New York Stock Exchange during the crisis; John J. Arnold, "The American Gold Fund of 1914," *Journal of Political Economy,* 23 (July 1915): 696–706; O. M. W. Sprague, "The Crisis of 1914 in the United States," *American Economic Review* 5 (Sept. 1915): 499–533; Laughlin, *Credit of Nations,* 79–80; Bullock, Williams, and Tucker, "Balance of Trade," 240; William Adams Brown, Jr., *The International Gold Standard Reinterpreted,* 2 vols. (New York: National Bureau of Economic Research, 1940), I, chap. 1. From the British perspective, see Sayers, *Bank of England,* I, 70–74, and Sir Henry Clay, *Lord Norman* (London: Macmillan, 1957), 76–80. The Reichsbank on Aug. 4, 1914, suspended specie payments, as did the Bank of France on Aug. 5, 1914; Brown, *International Gold Standard,* I, 16.

15. Wilkins, *History,* 145 ($7.1 billion). When the First World War came, numerous studies were made to estimate inward foreign investments. Most dealt only with portfolio investments, excluding direct investments; most arrived at a figure substantially lower than $7.1 billion. See ibid., 159–161, 699–709, on how the $7.1 billion figure was determined. Ibid., 625 (nearly 20 percent).

16. Ibid., 188 (minimal holdings). Part of the reason for the lack of recognition of the importance of and size of foreign investment was that the most conspicuous investments have been those related to public finance. By 1914, foreign investments in the United States were not typically in government issues; the New York City obligations were the principal exception, although there were some others.

17. Except when specifically noted, the material in this "setting" section is based on Wilkins, *History.* My interest in that book and herein is exclusively in long-term foreign investments—foreign portfolio and foreign direct investments. See Appendix 1 for definitions.

18. From all the principal railroads to U.S. Steel to American Telephone & Telegraph, America's largest corporations raised money in London and on the European continent. National retailers—Sears, Roebuck, United Cigar, Woolworth, and S. S. Kresge—did so as well. Wilkins, *History,* passim, and 528 (on the retailers). The large enterprises were the most attractive to foreign investors.

19. See, for example, *New York Times,* Mar. 21, 1917, for a list of American railroad bonds put up by the French government as collateral for a loan. The Northern Pacific general lien and land grant 3 percent bonds had a maturity in 2047!

20. Typically bank loans were short- rather than long-term and only became long-term when turned over regularly.

21. Sprague, "Crisis of 1914," 508 (on the unique U.S. position). Ranald C. Michie, *The London and New York Stock Exchanges 1850–1914* (London: Allen & Unwin, 1987), for the interrelationships between the London and New York exchanges. When Russians, for instance, shared with British investors in Russian railroads, often Russians bought

and sold the securities *in* London rather than on the St. Petersburg exchange; when Americans shared with British investors, more often then not the transactions took place in New York. Canadian stock exchanges—the Montreal one founded in 1874 and the Toronto one founded in 1878—were emerging, but activity on them was a shadow of that in New York. As two Canadians write of the era before the First World War, "At the best of times, a few hundred shares dumped on the Montreal or Toronto stock exchanges might break prices sharply." Christopher Armstrong and H. V. Nelles, *Southern Exposure* (Toronto: University of Toronto Press, 1988), 12–23, 127. Although about one-half of Argentine capital in 1913 was said to be foreign owned, while there existed an Argentine Bolsa, it seems that the Argentine stock market did not list the major railroad issues that attracted the large British investments. John H. Coatsworth and Alan M. Taylor, eds., *Latin America and the World Economy since 1800* (Cambridge, Mass.: Harvard University Press, 1998), 141 (size of foreign ownership), 257 (indicates the railroads were not listed in 1929; I feel sure this was also true in 1914). Also see Lance E. Davis and Robert J. Cull, *International Capital Markets and American Economic Growth, 1820–1914* (Cambridge: Cambridge University Press, 1994), who discuss the extent of integration of the London and New York securities markets and explore separate and joint listings. They argue that "a substantial fraction of the American securities traded in London were not even imperfect substitutes for many of the stocks and bonds traded in New York." Ibid., 71. This is a very significant insight. British (and other foreign) investors participated in investing in the United States both through the London (Paris, Amsterdam, etc.) *and* through the New York Stock Market. Cleona Lewis, *America's Stake in International Investments* (Washington, D.C.: Brookings Institution, 1938), 40, found of the British-owned American securities turned over to the American Dollar Securities Committee during the First World War, 18 percent of the railroad securities issued after 1896 had been issued and listed on the American market only.

22. Wilkins, *History*, esp. 621–622.

23. Insurance companies that operated in the United States were governed by state law on what they had to hold against their policy obligations.

24. The lack of attention to foreign exchange matters applies to long-term investors. In trade finance there were opportunities to take advantage of the small fluctuations. C. A. E. Goodhart, *The New York Money Market and the Finance of Trade 1900–1913* (Cambridge, Mass.: Harvard University Press, 1969), 59. For British investors in American securities, British merchant banks took care of foreign exchange matters and paid dividends and interest in pounds; Canadian brokers had connections in New York and handled transactions for their clients.

25. In these cases an investor, in, say, England or Scotland, would buy the shares or debentures in pounds, and the expert (the investment trust) would then invest in American securities.

26. In the Civil War and immediate post–Civil War period, foreign exchange issues had mattered—but in 1914 that was "long ago."

27. Travel and immigration flows also aided the information flows.

28. The proportions are calculated based on the data given on Table 1.2; they are, as indicated in the caption, very rough estimates, and I provide them with great reluctance and hesitation.

29. *New York Times*, July 30, 1914.

30. Sprague, "Crisis of 1914," 510.

31. *Foreign Relations of the United States*, 1914, Supplement, 547–551 (henceforth cited as *FRUS*, 1914, Suppl.). For some of the confusion on what neutrality meant, see Charles Callan Tansill, *America Goes to War* (1938; rpt. Gloucester, Mass.: Peter Smith, 1963), 35–37.

32. Many of the obligations to foreigners were short-term; since my study is of long-term investments, I am not concerned with trade bills except as they were associated with long-term foreign investments.

33. Sprague, "Crisis of 1914," 531–532, traces the steps in the resumption of trading on the New York Stock Exchange; see also Noble, *New York Stock Exchange,* 65, 65–74, and 82–83.

34. Henry F. Grady, *British War Finance* (New York: Columbia University Press, 1927), 19–20. The London Stock Exchange resumed business, January 4, 1915, "under severe restrictions."

35. *New York Times,* Aug. 5, 1914. This would be a conservative estimate of the amounts liquidated. Many of the European-owned securities did not have to be shipped from abroad, since the securities were held in New York by bankers and brokers. And this group was dispatched before British interest rates had soared.

36. Paul Studenski and Herman E. Krooss, *Financial History of the United States,* 2nd ed. (New York: McGraw-Hill, 1963), 282; Alexander Dana Noyes, *The War Period of American Finance* (New York: G. P. Putnam, 1926), 100–102. The Curb and Consolidated Exchanges had closed in the wake of the New York Stock Exchange's closing on July 31, yet brokers continued to deal in securities. Robert Sobel, *The Curbstone Brokers* (New York: Macmillan, 1970), 169–171.

37. The problems of payment, of settlement of obligations, were the same on the short-term and on the long-term obligations; the solutions that followed were designed to cope with both.

38. Sayers, *Bank of England,* I, 75, and III, 347.

39. Thomas W. Lamont, *Henry P. Davison* (New York: Harper & Bros., 1933), 4–5, 172–185; Cyrus Adler, *Jacob H. Schiff,* 2 vols. (Garden City, N.Y.: Doubleday, 1928), II, 241–242.

40. Sprague, "Crisis of 1914," 528.

41. The $80 million figure was determined in September 1914 (after the dollar was firming) by using an exchange rate of $5.035 for pounds and 20 cents for each franc. Lamont, *Henry P. Davison,* 180. Less than a month earlier, on August 21, 1914, J. P. Morgan calculated the amount due and payable in Europe as $84 million. Ibid., 177. Since these obligations were denominated in pounds and francs, the obligation fluctuated with changes in the exchange rate. They could, however, be paid off in gold.

42. Bullock, Williams, and Tucker, "Balance of Trade," 240; Lester Chandler, *Benjamin Strong* (1958; rpt. New York: Arno Press, 1978), 59; Brown *International Gold Standard,* I, 19.

43. Vincent P. Carosso, *Investment Banking in America* (Cambridge, Mass.: Harvard University Press, 1970), 199.

44. On the gold fund, the best source is Arnold, "American Gold Fund of 1914," 696–706. See also Sprague, "Crisis of 1914," 530–531; U.S. Department of the Treasury, *Annual Report 1914,* 17; and Noyes, *War Period,* 84–85. The arrangements that received the approval of the Federal Reserve Board and the Treasury on September 21, 1914, were the first of the "foreign exchange controls" and "controlled gold movements" of the war period. Brown, *International Gold Standard,* I, 19–20.

45. J. P. Morgan, Jr., to Woodrow Wilson, Sept. 4, 1914, in Arthur S. Link, *The Papers of Woodrow Wilson* (Princeton, N.J.: Princeton University Press, 1979), XXX, 483–485. The letter was from J. P. Morgan, Jr., "Jack." The senior J. P. Morgan died March 31, 1913. The Federal Trade Commission Act became law on September 26, 1914, and the Clayton Act, October 15, 1914; a bill that would give the Interstate Commerce Commission power over the issue of railroad stocks and bonds was *not* enacted, because of bankers' opposition and the impact of the war on investment markets. Sidney Ratner called that measure

"the first war casualty of Wilson's domestic reform program." Sidney Ratner, *American Taxation* (New York: W. W. Norton, 1942), 339.

46. Sayers, *Bank of England,* I, 87.

47. James Brown, Benjamin Strong, and A. H. Wiggin to George Paish and Basil Blackett, Oct. 30, 1914, 210.1, Strong Papers, Federal Reserve Bank of New York, New York (henceforth FRBNY). James Brown was with Brown Brothers; Albert H. Wiggin was with Chase National Bank.

48. Sayers, *Bank of England,* I, 88; Kathleen Burk, *Britain, America and the Sinews of War 1914–1918* (Boston: Allen & Unwin, 1985), 56; and Lamont, *Henry P. Davison,* 5.

49. See Frank A. Vanderlip to James Stillman, Dec. 4, 1914, and ibid., Dec. 11, 1914, Vanderlip Papers, Pt. B, Ser. 1, Box 6, and *New York Times,* editorial, Mar. 19, 1915.

50. Lewis, *America's Stake,* 66; Lamont, *Henry P. Davison,* 5, 183; Carosso, *Investment Banking,* 197–199; U.S. Department of the Treasury, *Annual Report 1914,* 17. As the exchange rates moved toward par, the actual amount required to meet the obligation turned out to be $78,167,352. Lamont, *Henry P. Davison,* 183. On the story from New York City's viewpoint, see Edwin R. Lewinson, *John Purroy Mitchel: The Boy Mayor of New York* (New York: Astra Books, 1965), 125–127.

51. Noyes, *War Period,* 90.

52. The law establishing the Federal Reserve System was passed in December 1913. From the start, the New York Federal Reserve Bank was the most involved in international matters. The initial Federal Reserve Board in Washington consisted of Charles S. Hamlin (governor), F. A. Delano, W. P. G. Harding, Paul M. Warburg, and A. C. Miller. Of the Washington board members, Warburg was the most knowledgeable on international transactions. For the role of Secretary of the Treasury McAdoo, see his reminiscences, William G. McAdoo, *Crowded Years* (New York: Houghton Mifflin, 1930), and John J. Broesamle, *William Gibbs McAdoo* (Port Washington, N.Y.: Kennikat Press, 1973).

53. U.S. Ambassador in Great Britain (Walter Hines Page) to Secretary of State (William Jennings Bryan), Aug. 5, 1914, *FRUS,* 1914, Suppl., 215. The definitions were in the 1909 Declaration of London. See also D. T. Jack, *Studies in Economic Warfare* (New York: Chemical Publishing Co., 1941), 69, 74–75, and U.S. Senate, Special Committee Investigating the Munitions Industry, *The Munitions Industry, Hearings,* 74th Cong., 2nd sess. (1936), pt. 27 (Exh. 2503), 8458. These hearings will henceforth be cited as *Nye Committee Hearings.*

54. Jack, *Studies,* 74; Frederic R. Coudert, *A Half Century of International Problems* (New York: Columbia University Press, 1954), 230; Samuel Flagg Bemis, *A Diplomatic History of the United States,* 3rd ed. (New York: Henry Holt, 1950), 596–600.

55. *FRUS,* 1914, Suppl., 221. There were similar problems with other neutral countries as intermediaries. The Swiss People's Bank complained that its telegrams to New York relating to money transfers had not reached their destination owing to British and French interventions. U.S. Minister in Switzerland (Pleasant Alexander Stovall) to Secretary of State, Nov. 5, 1914, *FRUS,* 1914, Suppl., 513–514.

56. National City Bank Vice President (name not included) to Robert Lansing, Oct. 23, 1914, *Nye Committee Hearings,* pt. 25 (Exh. 2045), 7664.

57. Harold van B. Cleveland and Thomas F. Huertas, *Citibank 1812–1970* (Cambridge, Mass.: Harvard University Press, 1985), 44 (Deutsche Bank a correspondent). See, for example, Alien Property Custodian, *Report 1918–1919,* 124, on the Deutsche Bank's activities in the United States on behalf of the German government. This report is henceforth cited as *APC Report.*

58. On the Deutsche Bank's role in moving American securities into German hands, see Wilkins, *History.* That the German government had established in the United States "special military accounts" for "special war necessities" became evident from an

intercepted "Circular" for "German General Headquarters," Nov. 2, 1914. Earl E. Sperry, *German Plots and Intrigues in the United States during the Period of Neutrality* (Washington, D.C.: Committee on Public Information, 1918), 9. Whether the plan was to use the National City Bank account for this purpose is not clear.

59. Late in November 1914, Fred I. Kent of Bankers Trust, New York, had Hugo Schmidt of the Deutsche Bank to lunch to talk over business matters (Kent to Benjamin Strong, Nov. 27, 1914, File C261 England-Bank of England, FRBNY); see also *APC Report,* 43, and *New York Times,* Apr. 8, 1917. The decision to replace Adams had been made by the Deutsche Bank before the outbreak of war—owing to Adams' bad judgment on Western Maryland Railroad securities and his unpopularity among New York bankers. In June 1914, however, Adams did not yet know that he was to be replaced. Benjamin Strong, President of Bankers Trust, Notes on Meeting at Deutsche Bank, June 12, 1914, "Strong's Trip to Europe May–June 1914," Strong Papers 1000.1, FRBNY. According to Lothar Gall et al., *The Deutsche Bank* (London: Weidenfeld & Nicolson, 1995), 154, Hugo Schmidt was sent to New York "to work with . . . Edward Adams." Soon Adams learned that he (Adams) was to be replaced, and Schmidt took charge. Adams had been the Deutsche Bank representative in the United States since 1893. See Wilkins, *History,* 221, 480–482, and 870n.225.

60. On German securities physically held in London, see Wilkins, *History,* 193. After the war was over, in *Direction der Disconto-Gesellschaft v. United States Steel Corporation,* 267 U.S. 22 (1925), the German bank Disconto-Gesellschaft sued U.S. Steel to get back rights to its prewar share ownership. The U.S. Supreme Court ruled that the British government had the right to take over the shares. See Kingman Brewster, *Antitrust and American Business Abroad* (New York: McGraw-Hill, 1958), 342n.105, and Philip C. Jessup, "Introduction," in Coudert, *Half Century,* ix–x.

61. On August 25, 1914, Count Bernstorff, German ambassador to the United States, arrived back from Germany accompanied by Bernhard Dernburg. Reinhard R. Doerries, *Imperial Challenge* (Chapel Hill: University of North Carolina Press, 1989), 39–40 and 259n.10. Dernburg, an experienced German banker, had been employed in earlier years by the Berliner Handels-Gesellschaft; Ladenburg, Thalmann & Co. in New York; the Deutsche Bank; and the Darmstädter Bank. Paul H. Emden, *Money Powers of Europe* (1937; rpt. New York: Garland, 1983), 210, 232–233. He remained in New York until May 1915 (Doerries, *Imperial Challenge,* 47). It would be very surprising if he (along with Hugo Schmidt of the Deutsche Bank) did not participate in the sales of German securities in America. Often—as we will see—the seller of securities did not want or need to remit the proceeds; rather, the proceeds were used for U.S. purchases, which in turn often were exported—with difficulties.

62. Walter E. Sachs Reminiscences (1956), pt. 1, 35–37, Oral History Collection, Columbia University, New York. See also Goodhart, *New York Money Market,* 55–56.

63. *FRUS,* 1914, Suppl., 668. The Radio Act of 1912 had given the president emergency powers. J. Gregory Sidak, *Foreign Investment in American Telecommunications* (Chicago: University of Chicago Press, 1997), 36.

64. Hugh G. J. Aitken, *The Continuous Wave: Technology and American Radio, 1900–1932* (Princeton, N.J.: Princeton University Press, 1985), 284; Manfred Jonas, *The United States and Germany* (Ithaca, N.Y.: Cornell University Press, 1984), 99; and Susan J. Douglas, *Inventing American Broadcasting 1899–1922* (Baltimore: Johns Hopkins University Press, 1987), 270.

65. U.S. Secretary of Navy, *Annual Report 1914,* 23; Aitken, *Continuous Wave,* 285; *FRUS,* 1914, Suppl., 678–679; Wilkins, *History,* 522 (for background). Also, since the station was as yet unlicensed, it could not legally operate; to license either the Germans or the French might be perceived as a violation of U.S. neutrality. See also Douglas,

Inventing American Broadcasting, 270–271. The French wireless company (formed in 1912) was Compagnie Universelle de Téléphonie et Télégraphique sans Fil (CUTT). Homag and Compagnie Générale d'Electricité were CUTT's initial shareholders; in 1913, Marconi's Wireless Telegraph Company, Ltd., London, had secretly acquired the French interest, although in October 1913 Godfrey Isaac (the managing director of the British Marconi) had misinformed his company's shareholders, saying the firm had bought the German portion. All this is according to I. J. Blanken, *The History of Philips Electronics N.V.* (Zaltbommc, The Netherlands: European Library, 1999), III, 142–143. In any case, CUTT was by 1914 already an affiliate of the British Marconi company.

66. *FRUS,* 1914, Suppl., 672, 678; Hugh Barty-King, *Girdle around the World* (London: Heinemann, 1979), 164.

67. E. Rosenbaum and A. J. Sherman, *M. M. Warburg & Co. 1798–1938* (New York: Holmes and Meier, 1979), 113. Did other German banks do the same as Warburg? Were any of the German-owned American securities held by German banks in London physically transferred to Amsterdam? Probably. (Some, however, remained in London to be taken over by the British government.) If radio and cable communications were difficult, mail got through. Priscella M. Roberts, "A Conflict of Loyalties: Kuhn, Loeb and Company and the First World War, 1914–1917," in *Studies in the American Jewish Experience II,* ed. Jacob R. Marcus and Abraham J. Peck (Lanham, Md.: University Press of America, 1984), 171n.29, found a "steady stream" of letters from Max M. Warburg to Kuhn, Loeb's Jacob Schiff. On Telefunken's Sayville, Long Island, facility, see Wilkins, *History,* 522; Aitken, *Continuous Wave,* 285; and Douglas, *Inventing American Broadcasting,* 269–270, 174. Telefunken was a joint venture between two German companies: Siemens & Halske and Allgemeine Elektrizitäts-Gesellschaft.

68. The rules governing U.S. shipping had from 1789 favored U.S.-built, U.S.-owned, U.S.-registered ships. Wilkins, *History,* 44. According to S. G. Sturmey, *British Shipping and World Competition* (London: Athlone Press, 1962), 130, in 1913, U.S.-registered (American-flag) ships handled only 14 percent of U.S. shipping in America's international trade. In 1912, Congress had allowed foreign-built vessels (less than five years old) to be transferred to American registry. Prior to that, a U.S.-registered ship had to be built in the United States. The August 18, 1914, law, removed the five-year limit. Between August 18 and December 23, 1914, 104 ships did change registry—with probably no change in ownership. Ownership and registry were not identical; Standard Oil of New Jersey, United Fruit, and U.S. Steel Products Co., for example, had ships under foreign flags, which after August 18 flew under American flags. On the 1912 and 1914 legislation, see Tansill, *America Goes to War,* 566–567; Thomas R. Heinrich, *Ships for the Seven Seas: Philadelphia Shipbuilding in the Age of Industrial Capitalism* (Baltimore: Johns Hopkins University Press, 1997), 167; Jeffrey J. Safford, *Wilsonian Maritime Diplomacy, 1913–1921* (New Brunswick, N.J.: Rutgers University Press, 1978), 16, 41; Broesamle, *William Gibbs McAdoo,* 196, 214; and J. Russell Smith, *Influence of the Great War upon Shipping* (New York: Oxford University Press, 1919), 187.

69. George Bessell, *Norddeutscher Lloyd 1857–1957* (n.p., n.d.); Ernest R. May, *The World War and American Isolation, 1914–1917* (Cambridge, Mass.: Harvard University Press, 1966), 68.

70. See Safford, *Wilsonian Maritime Diplomacy,* 39–65, esp. 43–47 and 59. Part of the British government's objection was that Americans would pay Germany for its idle merchant fleet, thus providing the enemy with money to carry on the war. May, *World War,* 13–15. See McAdoo, *Crowded Years,* 294ff., and Broesamle, *William Gibbs McAdoo,* 212–215, 217–220 (McAdoo's thinking about U.S. government ownership). I write "nearly all," for see Safford, *Wilsonian Maritime Diplomacy,* 57–60, 64, and May, *World War,* 30–31, 69, on the *Dacia* affair (the *Dacia* was a German merchant vessel—owned by the

Hamburg-American Line—that to avoid capture had at the start of the war docked in Port Arthur, Texas; it *was purchased* by an American, Edward N. Breitung, who claimed he was buying it for purely business reasons; on February 28, 1915, the *Dacia* was captured in the English Channel by a French cruiser). On the German government refusal to give Albert Ballin, head of the Hamburg-American Line, permission to sell ships to Americans, see Bernhard Huldermann, *Albert Ballin* (London: Cassell & Co., 1922), 230.

71. See data in RG 56, Entry 406, National Archives; Burk, *Britain, America,* 56; Safford, *Wilsonian Maritime Diplomacy,* 41, 49, 231; and Broesamle, *William Gibbs McAdoo,* 215–216. William F. Gephart, *Effects of the War upon Insurance* (New York: Oxford University Press, 1918), Appendix A, includes a copy of the War Risk Insurance Act, P.L. 193, 63rd Cong.

72. Wilkins, *History,* 392–394 (on Metz).

73. Memorandum dictated Aug. 12, 1914, by Herman A. Metz, in RG 59, 165.102/2, National Archives. The dictation accounts for the misspellings. There is a note on this memorandum that a telegram was sent to the U.S. Embassy in Berlin on August 20 on this matter. "Leverkusen" was the location of Bayer's plant in Germany. Antipyrine was a fever-reducing and anti-inflammatory drug; 606 was an antisyphilitic drug, also known as Salvarsan.

74. Statement by Metz, Aug. 20, 1914, forwarded by Joseph P. Tumulty (secretary to President Wilson) to Wilbur Carr at the State Department, urging Carr to try to give some assistance, RG 59, 165.102/13. Some aspirin was made in the United States, but much was imported.

75. Metz to Secretary of State, Oct. 3, 1914, RG 59, 165.102/90.

76. See extensive data in RG 59, 165.102.

77. During November 1914, the United States managed to import, chiefly from Germany, coal tar dyes valued at $1.1 million, compared with $520,000 during the same month in 1913. Everyone wanted to stockpile the chemicals. Williams Haynes, *American Chemical Industry,* 6 vols. (New York: Van Nostrand, 1945–1954), II, 27–28, and 29–30, on the November 15, 1914, arrival in New York of the *SS Matanzas,* and two weeks later the *SS American Sun.* See also ibid., III, 212. Data in RG 59, 165.102 are useful on these events; see also Metz's own description of his role in his testimony before the U.S. Senate, Judiciary Committee, *Alleged Dye Monopoly, Hearings,* 67th Cong. (1922), 743–905 (henceforth cited as *1922 Dye Hearings*).

78. Haynes, *American Chemical Industry,* II, 143, 140–150, and *Mineral Industry 1914,* 611ff., on the potash crisis. The British investors were Consolidated Gold Fields of South Africa, Ltd., and Borax Consolidated, Ltd.

79. See correspondence in RG 59, 824.6354, National Archives, especially William C. Redfield, Secretary of Commerce, to William J. Bryan, Secretary of State, Oct. 8, 1914; Ladenburg, Thalmann to William C. Redfield, Oct. 5, 1914; E. F. Sweet, Assistant Secretary, Memorandum for the Secretary of Commerce, Oct. 6, 1914, 824.6354/1; Woodrow Wilson to W. J. Bryan, Oct. 10, 1914, and Robert Lansing to American Minister, La Paz, Bolivia, Oct. 19, 1914, 824.6354/1; John D. O'Rear, American Minister, La Paz, to Secretary of State, Oct. 23, 1914, 824.6354/5; Redfield to Secretary of State, Dec. 5, 1914, 824.6354/10; and Office of Foreign Trade Adviser to Wilbur J. Carr, Feb. 15, 1916, 824.6354/68. Apparently, Bolivian tin entrepreneur Simon Patiño in 1914 shifted his tin trade from Hamburg to Britain, and before decisions were made to smelt Bolivian ores in the United States, he had transferred his smelting from Germany to the United Kingdom. Herbert S. Klein, "The Creation of the Patiño Tin Empire," *Inter-American Economic Affairs,* 19 (Aug. 1965): 11–12. For background on Ladenburg, Thalmann & Co., see Wilkins, *History,* 269, 480, 867.

80. *FRUS,* 1914, Suppl., 372.

81. Wilkins, *History*, chap. 8.

82. *APC Report*, 94; *FRUS*, 1914, Suppl., 338–346, on copper matters. Ibid., 343, suggests that Krupp had houses in Holland, which channeled copper into German arms factories. See also May, *World War*, 29, on U.S. copper that went through the still neutral Italy.

83. Letter from Sir Cecil Spring-Rice to Sir Edward Grey, Oct. 5, 1914, quoted in May, *World War*, 29. Krupp—along with German electrical enterprises—was apparently a large buyer of U.S. copper.

84. Data from Augustus J. Veenendaal and from Charlotte A. van Manen, *De Nederlandsche Overzee Trustmaatschappij*, 8 vols. in 6 parts ('s-Gravenhagen: Martinus Nijhoff, 1935). See also Jack, *Studies*, 109, which notes "the approval of the British government" of the Netherlands Overseas Trust. There were similar problems (and solutions) related to trade with Switzerland, particularly in copper. May, *World War*, 29, and Paul Erdman, *Swiss-American Economic Relations* (Basle: Kyklos, 1959), 38–39.

85. *New York Times*, Feb. 4, 1918, and *APC Report*, 129.

86. *New York Times*, Feb. 5, 1918; see also ibid., Mar. 16, 1918; the *APC Report*, 129, says that Botany Worsted Mills and Forstmann & Huffmann were "not only compensated in money," but rewarded with dyestuffs. Metz would later claim (*1922 Dye Hearings*, 743) that he had full State Department support and was "the go-between" in getting German dyestuffs to American companies. I have been unable to verify Bryan's specific approval of these transactions. See Roberts, "A Conflict of Loyalties," 18, for an interesting discussion of financing German cotton purchases in the fall of 1914.

87. Wilkins, *History*, 224–226 (Grand Trunk), and *FRUS*, 1914, Suppl., 576 (the specific issue). At this time Canadian railways had roughly 7,000 miles of track in the United States (Canadian Pacific, 4,948 miles; the Grand Trunk, 1,868 miles; and the Canadian Northern merely 225 miles, of which 181 were leased). For these 1916 figures, see R. T. Naylor, *The History of Canadian Business, 1867–1914* (Toronto: James Lorimer & Co., 1973), II, 251.

88. Seymour S. Bernfeld, "A Short History of American Metal Climax, Inc.," in American Metal Climax, Inc., *World Atlas* (New York, n.d. 1962?); J. E. Spurr, *Political and Commercial Geology and the World's Mineral Resources* (New York: McGraw-Hill, 1920), 310 ("eliminating alien ownership"). The 16,734 shares in American Metal Co. owned by Henry R. Merton and its British friends were held by British authorities through the war; afterward, the *U.S.* Alien Property Custodian entered into discussions with the British government on the repatriation of these securities. See *APC Report*, 101.

89. Carosso, *Investment Banking*, 210. A vicious attack on Sir Edgar Speyer is in a pamphlet by A. Moreton Mandeville, "The House of Speyer" (London [1915]), 12 (for more on the sad story of Sir Edgar, who was tarred for his German associations, see Emden, *Money Powers*, 275–276). For Speyer & Co.'s prewar German connections, see Wilkins, *History*, 480–482. James Speyer entertained the German ambassador to the United States at his country home in September 1914. Count Bernstorff, *My Three Years in America* (London: Skeffington & Son, n.d. [1922]), 58.

90. On the plans, see Wilkins, *History*, 286–287, 782, and *New York Times*, July 28, 1914. Kendall Beaton, *Enterprise in Oil* (New York: Appleton-Century-Crofts, 1957), 208, indicates that in June 1914, the British group had made an initial payment of $2.5 million; when Weir's British Union Oil Co., Ltd., could not make a second payment, it received 25,000 shares of Union Oil Company of California for the $2.5 million already expended. This represented a minority interest in the California company and became a portfolio investment.

91. Fred C. Foy, *Ovens, Chemicals and Men: Koppers Co.* (New York: Newcomen Society, 1958), 13. This was an important company. It is not clear how Heinrich Koppers

arranged the payment to himself, but he obviously did so. There were some other sales to Americans by German companies. As noted earlier, the Hamburg-American Line (in an exceptional transaction) found a customer for the merchant ship the *Dacia.*

92. Harllee Branch, Jr., *Alabama Power Company and the Southern Company* (New York: Newcomen Society, 1967), 10–11; see also Wilkins, *History,* 554. The parent company was Canadian registered, albeit the funding came from England. What happened here was the start of the process of thoroughly Americanizing the financing of this venture.

93. On Southern Aluminium, see Wilkins, *History,* 283–284, and Paul Fuller to Attorney General of the United States, Aug. 27, 1915, in *U.S. v. Alcoa,* Exhibits, Eq. 85–73 (SDNY 1937–1942), 792 (Exh. 146) and also 793–795 (Exhs. 147, 148, and 149).

94. On the Paish and Blackett mission, see Ron Chernow, *The House of Morgan* (New York: Atlantic Monthly Press, 1990), 186–187, and Burk, *Britain, America,* 55–61.

95. When Paish was in New York on the October–November mission, he urged the reopening of the New York Stock Exchange and suggested to Stock Exchange officials that large U.S. exports of goods would offset the liquidations by foreign owners. Noble, *New York Stock Exchange,* 74.

96. Bernstorff, *My Three Years,* 67–79 (on Heinrich Albert's attempts to organize food and other shipments from the United States to Germany); see also *FRUS,* 1914, Suppl., passim.

97. For Morgan's intimate relationships with the British, see, for example, Chernow, *House of Morgan,* chap. 10. Chernow describes the attitude of J. P. Morgan, Jr.: "For him, the war was a holy cause as well as a business opportunity . . . He inhabited a black-and-white world in which loyalty to England found its equal and opposite emotion in hatred of the Germans." Ibid., 191.

98. Frank A. Vanderlip, San Diego, Calif., to James Stillman, New York, Dec. 30, 1914, Vanderlip Papers, Pt. B, Ser. 1, Box 6.

99. This is my interpretation. The best work on Kuhn, Loeb's partners' viewpoints is Roberts, "A Conflict of Loyalties," 1–32, 169–182. Adler, *Jacob H. Schiff,* I, 229, and II, 181–201, 235–242, 249–254, 259–264, is also particularly good on the dilemmas facing Jacob Schiff, the senior partner in Kuhn, Loeb. In addition, see Stephen Birmingham, *Our Crowd* (New York: Dell Publishing, 1967), 370–377, and Ron Chernow, *The Warburgs* (New York: Random House, 1993), 165–167. The British perceived Kuhn, Loeb as very pro-German. See Tansill, *America Goes to War,* for example, on Paul M. Warburg. Paul Warburg had been a partner at Kuhn, Loeb and in M. M. Warburg, Hamburg, before he joined the new Federal Reserve Board in August 1914. He was married to Nina Loeb. Paul Warburg's brother Felix, who had married Jacob Schiff's daughter, was a partner in Kuhn, Loeb, and when Paul Warburg resigned his partnership in M. M. Warburg, Hamburg, Felix, in addition to remaining a partner in the American firm, also became a partner in the German one (Chernow, *The Warburgs,* 162). Felix nonetheless was said to be pro-Allied (Birmingham, *Our Crowd,* 376), although he would remain a partner in M. M. Warburg, Hamburg, until America entered the war (Rosenbaum and Sherman, *M. M. Warburg,* 117). Max Warburg, a third brother, headed M. M. Warburg, Hamburg, while a fourth brother was also a partner in the Hamburg bank. Otto Kahn, another partner in Kuhn, Loeb, had once worked in the London branch of the Deutsche Bank (Wilkins, *History,* 736). Thus, the firm had very close family ties with Germany. The views of the Kuhn, Loeb partners apparently changed over time. All the partners were undoubtedly more pro-German in the six months after the outbreak of the war than they became as time passed. Roberts, "A Conflict of Loyalties," is especially good in showing the divisions among Kuhn, Loeb partners, the change over the period of neutrality, and the ambivalence.

100. James Speyer, head of Speyer & Co., seems to have been pro-German in these early months of the war. At Goldman, Sachs, while the Sachs brothers were pro-Allied, the older Henry Goldman was very pro-German. For Goldman, Sachs' prewar German connections, see Wilkins, *History,* 480.

101. U.S. Department of the Treasury, *Annual Report 1914,* 1. In the process, a very brief de facto if not, de jure suspension of gold payments had occurred. Brown, *International Gold Standard,* I, 16, 18.

102. It is unclear how great was a decline of foreign investment in the United States, July 1, 1914, to December 31, 1914. All secondary sources concur that there was a decline. Cleona Lewis assumed that the liquidation of railroad securities was at the same rate as during February–July 1915. Lewis, *America's Stake,* 533 (this was a sheer guess). In view of the secondary literature and most contemporary commentary, I was surprised to find that the portfolio of American securities of Shell's British parent was larger in December 1914 than in December 1913 (data in Shell Archives, London); it is not, however, indicated when the increase in the parent Shell's holdings occurred, and this could well have taken place in the first six months of 1914.

103. At the start of the war, the U.S. government had suggested such loans were not appropriate for "neutrals."

104. The chronology on submarine warfare is from Robert Morris and Graham Irwin, eds., *Harper Encyclopaedia of the Modern World* (New York: Harper & Row, 1970), 397–398. Every volume on World War I provides the sequencing.

105. Most of the accusations about foreign investment and U.S. entry into the war related to *outward* U.S. investments (loans to the Allied powers) rather than the inward foreign involvements. Thus, before U.S. entry, American socialists predicted that U.S. participation would be the means by which "Wall Street" would protect its vast investments in war. Chernow, *House of Morgan,* 192, found that in the period of neutrality, J. P. Morgan & Co. received substantial hate mail suggesting that it was (with its efforts on behalf of the British) leading the country inevitably into war. Once America entered the war, the criticism became muted, but during the 1920s and even more during the 1930s it revived with great vigor. Then, as earlier, the thrust of the critics' emphasis was on munitions sales and *outgoing* loans, but there would be attention to inward foreign investment. Some of the specific accusations about inward foreign investment related to the cozy relationships between U.S. bankers and their European counterparts, relationships forged over many years through the intermediation of foreign moneys into America. The international bankers who had brought British capital to America were key, it was argued, in financing pro-British propaganda—which pushed us into war. See, for example, William H. Stuart, *The Twenty Incredible Years* (Chicago: M. A. Donohue & Co., 1935), 32. In Chapter 7, on the 1930s, I will cover the mounting criticism of inward foreign investments, some of which was based on interpretations of the role of that investment in "sucking" Americans into the First World War.

106. The only possible (albeit indirect) influence I find at all plausible related to the press publicity over German "plots" that were often financed by German investments in the United States. The revelations of the plots certainly served to whip up intense hostility to Germany, which made U.S. entry into the war more acceptable. Ernest May would later conclude that the Nye Committee's investigation displayed "beyond a shadow of a doubt the absurdity of the munitions-makers conspiracy theory." May, *World War,* 466. I am equally convinced of the absurdity of the arguments that foreign investment—inward or outward—was material in America's decision to go to war.

107. Financial data from Historical Files, Unilever, London.

108. On this factory, see Wilkins, *History,* 340–342. On the expansion, see W. H. Lever to H. G. Hart, July 29, 1916, Lever Correspondence 8408, Unilever Archives,

London. See also Policy Committee Minutes, Mar. 19, 1917, and May 5, 1917, Unilever, London.

109. Wilkins, *History,* 370–371, for background; D. C. Coleman, *Courtaulds* (Oxford: Oxford University Press, 1969), II, 111, 126, 138–145, 151.

110. Already by 1910, J. & P. Coats had 2,500 employees at Pawtucket; it was a single-site producer only in Rhode Island. It also had major mills in the vicinity of Newark, New Jersey. On Coats history in the United States, see Wilkins, *History,* 361–369, and Dong-Woon Kim, "The British Multinational Enterprise in the United States before 1914: The Case of J. & P. Coats," *Business History Review,* 72 (Winter 1998): 523–551. For 1917 Pawtucket data, see Gary Kulik and Julia C. Bonham, *Rhode Island: An Inventory of Historic Engineering and Industrial Sites* (Washington, D.C.: U.S. Department of Interior, 1978), 139.

111. W. J. Baker, *A History of Marconi Company* (London: Methuen & Co., 1970), 180. In 1919, the New Jersey manufacturing plant was valued at a mere $750,000; nonetheless, that year, a General Electric employee would describe it as a substantial, modern, well-equipped factory. See Aitken, *Continuous Wave,* 378, 381, and also Wilkins, *History,* 520–522.

112. Aitken, *Continuous Wave,* 308, quoting Edward J. Nally to Edwin W. Rice, June 4, 1915.

113. Ibid., 309, 311. See also Wilkins, *History,* 522, 899, and L. S. Howeth, *History of Communications-Electronics in the United States Navy* (Washington, D.C., 1963), 313.

114. Aitken, *Continuous Wave,* 317, 357–358. David Sarnoff, *Looking Ahead* (New York: McGraw-Hill, 1968), 31, 34, 44, writes that in 1915 Sarnoff (then a low-level employee of Marconi of America) had proposed to Nally, head of Marconi of America, "a plan of development which would make radio a 'household utility' in the same sense as the piano or phonograph." Sarnoff's plan was not pursued. This could be attributed to technological conservatism or simply to wartime priorities.

115. For Du Pont's dyestuff developments during World War I, see David Hounshell and John Kenly Smith, *Science and Corporate Strategy: Du Pont R & D 1902–1980* (Cambridge: Cambridge University Press, 1988), 79–91. In 1914, two British dyestuff makers—Levinstein Ltd. and Read Holliday & Sons, Ltd.—had small interests in the United States. The first, Levinstein Ltd. in the 1890s had had close links with the German Bayer and Agfa firms; over the years, these Anglo-German associations had deteriorated, and by 1913–1914 Levinstein was "on bad terms" with the Germans. After the European war had started, the British government had confiscated a manufacturing facility in England built by the German Hoechst, and Levinstein was allowed to purchase that plant. For some years prior to the war, Levinstein had had Edgar Levinstein as its sales representative in Boston (he had never been important in the U.S. market). In 1916, Du Pont and Levinstein Ltd. made an agreement, giving Du Pont exclusive rights to sell Levinstein dyes in the United States; more important, for an annual payment of £25,000 (for ten years), Du Pont would obtain from the British firm its technical know-how, including the knowledge of processes undertaken at the former Hoechst plant in Britain. When, early in 1917, Du Pont started to build its dyestuff plant (a "virtual copy" of the ex-Hoechst British plant), neither Levinstein Ltd. nor Edgar Levinstein had an equity interest in the Du Pont venture. Wilkins, *History,* 824; L. F. Haber, *The Chemical Industry, 1900–1930* (Oxford: Clarendon Press, 1971), 148, 186–187, 190; Hounshell and Smith, *Science and Corporate Strategy,* 83–85; Alfred D. Chandler, Jr., and Stephen Salsbury, *Pierre S. du Pont and the Making of the Modern Corporation* (New York: Harper & Row, 1971), 384; and William J. Reader, *Imperial Chemical Industries: A History* (London: Oxford University Press, 1970), I, 277, 437–438. The U.S. affiliate of the second British dyestuffs producer, Read Holliday & Sons, Ltd., had been (in 1864) the first to synthesize dyes in America.

Its U.S. affiliate had, however, stopped manufacturing in the United States in the 1880s (when it no longer had tariff protection), and at the start of World War I, while Read Holliday maintained a U.S. presence as an importer, like Levinstein, Ltd., it was far from a significant participant in this U.S. industry. In 1915, in the United Kingdom, British Dyes Ltd. acquired Read Holliday & Sons, Ltd. In America, in 1916, the Holliday-Kemp Company was formed by the grandson of Read Holliday; it embarked on dyestuff manufacturing, on a far smaller scale than Du Pont. See Wilkins, *History*, 131, 373, 690, 821–822; Reader, *Imperial Chemical Industries*, I, 271–273, 429, and Haynes, *American Chemical Industry*, III, 237, 471.

116. Wilkins, *History*, 279; Haynes, *American Chemical Industry*, II, 143, 145, 149–150, 159–161, and VI, 393. Muriate of potash, which had sold at $39 a ton before the war, reached $475 a ton in January 1916. It was little wonder that there was incentive for new U.S. production.

117. Mira Wilkins, *The Maturing of Multinational Enterprise: American Business Abroad from 1914 to 1970* (Cambridge, Mass.: Harvard University Press, 1974), 10n; Haynes, *American Chemical Industry*, III, 86–87; National Lead, *Annual Report* 1916, 1917; Klein, "Patiño Tin Empire," 14.

118. Note that the U.S. import substitution was at different parts of the production chain: in dyestuffs, it became the basis for new domestic manufacturing; in potash, for new domestic mining; and in tin, for new domestic processing. In addition, the Belgian-British interests in Semet-Solvay and Solvay Process Company would contribute to dyes and potash production.

119. On the role of these two companies during World War I, see Burk, *Britain, America*, 51–53. For background on these firms, see Stanley Chapman, *Merchant Enterprise* (Cambridge: Cambridge University Press, 1992), 204–208, 211. The British government set up a Wheat Export Company whose English president was G. F. Earle (Earle had spent his career with the Sanday firm) and whose English vice president was H. T. Robson (Robson was a partner in the Smyth firm). On the Wheat Export Company, organized in New York in 1916 as the official wheat-exporting agency for the Allied governments, see U.S. Federal Trade Commission, *Methods and Operations of Grain Exporters*, 2 vols. (Washington, D.C., 1922, 1923), I, 54.

120. Wilkins, *History*, 309–318, esp. 310 (on Morrell).

121. Lawrence Oakley Cheever, *The House of Morrell* (Cedar Rapids, Iowa: Torch Press, 1948), 164–165.

122. "An Outline History of the North American Chemical Co.," typescript 1928, pp. 29, 39A, 40, in Bay City, Michigan, Public Library; see also Wilkins, *History*, 408.

123. See Wilkins, *History*, 443–44; Graham Taylor, "Negotiating Technology Transfers with Multinational Enterprises," *Business History*, 36 (Jan. 1994): 157n.33 (for the sustained stake). See also R. P. T. Davenport-Hines, "Vickers as a Multinational before 1945," in *British Multinationals*, ed. Geoffrey Jones (Aldershot: Gower, 1986), 46, which says Vickers' interest in EBC was to approximately 1918, and 59, which says the direct interest was either liquidated or reduced to a minimum in the 1920s. This direct interest was never revealed in the extensive Nye Committee Hearings. I tried to determine from Vickers Records at Cambridge University Library the details of the financial stake but was unable to do so.

124. Taylor, "Negotiating Technology Transfers," 142, and Tansill, *America Goes to War*, 42–47.

125. Robert Hessen, *Steel Titan: The Life of Charles M. Schwab* (New York: Oxford University Press, 1975), 211–215. In 1915, Henry Carse succeeded Isaac Rice as president of Electric Boat Company. J. D. Scott, *Vickers: A History* (London: Weidenfeld & Nicolson, 1962), 241. Rice in 1899 had been president of the American Siemens company; it was

Rice who had made the initial arrangements between Electric Boat and Vickers. See Wilkins, *History*, 437, 443–444.

126. Burk, *Britain, America*, 118.

127. *Best's Reports, Fire and Marine, 1919*, 308, 412–414, 326–327, 366, and passim.

128. E. Victor Morgan, *Studies in British Financial Policy, 1914–25* (London: Macmillan, 1952), 265.

129. Some British direct investments were liquidated, but no truly viable ones.

130. Wilkins, *History*, 402–406. Haynes, *American Chemical Industry*, III, 46. In 1917, Semet-Solvay would sell its interest in Benzol Products (which it had helped to found) to National Aniline and Chemical Company. Ibid., VI, 368. For Semet-Solvay's vast expansion, see ibid.

131. Ibid., VI, 393, and II, 160–161.

132. To expand in the United States, in 1916 Solvay Process Co. had borrowed from Chicago banks; it issued new stock, half of which was acquired by its "spin-off," Semet-Solvay. As a result of the transactions, the European ownership of SPC was reduced, albeit together the Belgian and British investors held 51.9 percent of SPC shares. The Semet-Solvay Co. was reorganized in 1916. It is not clear what percentage of Semet-Solvay shares the Belgians held; in 1920, Solvay & Cie. owned 20,707 shares in Semet-Solvay, which was a minority interest. Lewis, *America's Stake*, 566, and Reader, *Imperial Chemical Industries*, I, 292 (which indicates that Semet-Solvay was "not controlled from Europe"). Whereas the Belgians and the British shared in ownership in SPC, it seems that it was the Belgians alone who acquired direct interests in Semet-Solvay.

133. For its entry in America, see Wilkins, *History*, 287–292.

134. Beaton, *Enterprise in Oil*, 78–110, 131–170, 752; Reports of the Annual Meetings of The "Shell" Transport and Trading Co. (Ltd)., in *The Times*, London, July 12, 1916, and July 13, 1917; and Royal Dutch Company, *Annual Reports, 1916 and 1917*. In 1915, a group headed by Alexander Mackay (of the Matador Land and Cattle Co.) and R. Leicester Harmsworth (brother of Lord Northcliffe) sold their Oklahoma properties (assets of the Dundee Petroleum Co., the Samoset Petroleum Co., and the Alma Petroleum Co.) to the Royal Dutch Shell Group. Beaton, *Enterprise in Oil*, 136. The transfer was from one foreign owner to another.

135. *Nye Committee Hearings*, pt. 28 (Exhs. 2773–2774), 8972–8973, and Robert T. Swaine, *The Cravath Firm*, 2 vols. (New York: privately printed, 1946, 1948), II, 235–236 (on Kuhn, Loeb's role in the financing).

136. Beaton, *Enterprise in Oil*, 167.

137. 1916: based on figures in Royal Dutch Company, *Annual Reports 1916 and 1917*, and American Petroleum Institute, *Petroleum Facts and Figures* (Washington, D.C.: American Petroleum Institute, 1971), 70 (U.S. crude oil production in 1916, 300,767,000). 1914 percentage in Wilkins, *History*, 291.

138. Charles Wilson, *The History of Unilever*, 3 vols. (New York: Praeger, 1968), II, 183–185.

139. Wilkins, *History*, 514–515, and K. D. Bosch, *Nederlandse Beleggingen in de Verenigde Staten* (Amsterdam: Uitgeversmaatschappij Elsevier, 1948), 440–441.

140. Works Progress Administration, "History of Milltown" (1936), typescript in Milltown, N.J., Public Library; Wilkins, *History*, 422–424.

141. For their earlier history, see Wilkins, *History*, 357–358; for the enlargement of business, see A. P. Thomas, *Woonsocket: Highlights of History, 1800–1976* (East Providence, R.I.: Globe Printing Co., 1976), 108ff.

142. Jin-Mieung Li, "L'Air Liquide," in *Foreign Business in Japan before World War II*, ed. Takeshi Yuzawa and Masaru Udagawa (Tokyo: University of Tokyo Press, 1990), 221–238, and discussion with Li, January 1989. Haynes, *American Chemical Industry*, III,

159, and VI, 5–6, and *Fortune,* 8 (July 1933): 24–29, 108, 117–118 (on Air Reduction Co.). According to information from Patrick Fridenson, June 28, 1995, at origin, L'Air Liquide had a 33 percent interest in Air Reduction Co.

143. Patrick Fridenson, "The Growth of Multinational Activities in the French Motor Industry, 1890–1979," in *Multinationals: Theory and History,* ed. Peter Hertner and Geoffrey Jones (Aldershot: Gower, 1986), 159.

144. Mira Wilkins, "Charles Pathé's American Business," *Entreprises et Histoire,* 6 (1994): 133–144. I knew nothing of this important involvement when I wrote Wilkins, *History. Moody's 1929,* 2739 (for the date of incorporation of Pathé Exchange). Edwin J. Perkins, *Wall Street to Main Street: Charles Merrill and Middle-Class Investors* (Cambridge: Cambridge University Press, 1999), 95, on the role of Merrill, Lynch. Coudert Brothers was a leading American law firm, specializing in international law. It had established a Paris office in 1879 and was frequently retained by French clients. Jessup, "Introduction," in Coudert, *Half Century,* vii, xi.

145. Nestlé & Anglo-Swiss also had an interest in chocolate production in Fulton, New York. For its pre–World War I U.S. business and its separate complex corporate relationships in chocolate with Lamont, Corliss & Co., see Wilkins, *History,* 331–335.

146. U.S. Federal Trade Commission, *Report on Milk and Milk Products, 1914–1918* (Washington, D.C., 1921), 58, 60–61 (Nestlé's Food Company to Federal Trade Commission, July 14, 1919).

147. Hans Conrad Peyer, *Roche; A Company History 1896–1996* (Basle: Editiones Roche, 1996), 69; Haynes, *American Chemical Industry,* III, 305 (Sandoz). Swiss firms in the embroidery industry also expanded their U.S. output.

148. Ragnhild Lundström, "Swedish Multinational Growth before 1930," in *Multinationals,* ed. Hertner and Jones, 148, says manufacture began in 1915. SKF sources give the date as 1916. According to SKF, "The Story of SKF," pamphlet, 1982, 6, SKF in 1916 built its first U.S. plant at Hartford, Connecticut, and later that year acquired control of the Hess-Bright Manufacturing Company of Philadelphia, a well-known bearings producer with patent rights for the German "Conrad type" bearing. Philadelphia subsequently became the headquarters for SKF's U.S. business. See ibid., 3, on its earlier sales subsidiary. A study made during World War II by Jean Pajus provides details on SKF and the Hess-Bright enterprise, which had been founded in 1904 by Americans. In the fall of 1916, SKF acquired the majority, 56 percent, of that company from Fred E. Bright and his associates. Hess-Bright was at that time 44 percent owned by the German Deutsche Waffen-und Munitions Fabriken (DWF), which had acquired the Henry Hess interest in 1912; apparently SKF completed its acquisition when it purchased that German interest on March 12, 1917, shortly before the U.S. entry into the war. Jean Pajus, "Report of A. B. Svenska Kullagerfabriken (SKF)," Prepared for the Foreign Economic Administration, Oct. 1944, RG 169, FEA, Entry 211, Box 1, Folder: SKF Report, National Archives, 119–125, 131–134 (I obtained a copy from Birgit Karlsson, December 2001). In 1912, the Swedish SKF parent had purchased a 50 percent interest in the German Norma Company, which had in 1911 set up an American subsidiary, Norma Company of America, that began to make bearings in the United States in 1913. Initially, in 1913, SKF had hoped to merge its U.S. sales subsidiary with Norma of America, a project that failed. Wilkins, *History,* 427, and Pajus, "Report," 3, 143–144. SKF's American holding company, SKF Administrative Company Inc., New York, was renamed SKF Industries, Dec. 18, 1918. Pajus, "Report," 106.

149. Based on data in *Best's Insurance Reports, Fire and Marine, 1919.* According to information from the files of the U.S. Treasury Department, five Norwegian companies (not three) came in during the eighteen months America was at war. H. W. Nichols,

"Memorandum re: Norwegian Insurance Companies," Oct. 16, 1919, RG 56, Entry 406, Box 10, National Archives.

150. Wilkins, *History,* 531 (for foreign insurance companies, Dec. 31, 1913).

151. Lewis, *America's Stake,* 102; Herbert Marshall, Frank A. Southard, and Kenneth W. Taylor, *Canadian-American Industry* (1936; rpt. New York: Russell & Russell, 1970), 182; *New York Times,* Jan. 12, 1917. In 1938, conclusive evidence was uncovered that the explosion was, in fact, German sabotage (see Swaine, *Cravath Firm,* II, 636–644, esp. 642); before that, German sabotage was only suspected.

152. Marshall, Southard, and Taylor, *Canadian-American Industry,* 182; the Buffalo City Directory of 1916 lists a plant of Canadian Furnace Ltd.

153. This change to foreign flags (and foreign ownership) occurred despite the desire in Washington to build up U.S. shipping. Safford, *Wilsonian Maritime Diplomacy,* 70–73, 128. On the expansion of Japanese shipping, see Tsunehiko Yui and Keiichiro Nakagawa, eds., *Business History of Shipping* (Tokyo: University of Tokyo Press, 1985), xx–xxi, 2, 7–11. Smith, *Influence of the Great War,* 188, writes that reflagging—to the American flag—under the 1914 legislation was now offset. The sale of American ships to foreign owners during 1915–1916 (some 102,479 tons) was greater than the earlier U.S. gains by transfers from foreign flags (83,480 tons).

154. For the 1916 German developments, see Peter Hayes, *Industry and Ideology* (Cambridge: Cambridge University Press, 1987), 11.

155. Haynes, *American Chemical Industry,* VI, 175; *1922 Dye Hearings,* 750; *APC Report,* 40, 50 (on the Century Color Co., which was nominally American owned). The Cassella Color Co. of New York was the sales company of the German Leopold Cassella, GmbH. See Wilkins, *History,* 394.

156. Heinrich Albert reported to Captain Boy-Ed, Apr. 28, 1915, "Our factories [German factories in America] have bound themselves orally and by word of honor to do nothing in the present situation which might help the United States [to create a dyestuffs industry]." A. Mitchell Palmer and Francis P. Garvan, *Aims and Prospects of the Chemical Foundation* (New York, 1919), 53–54.

157. Bernstorff, *My Three Years,* 226–227; Haynes, *American Chemical Industry,* III, 212; *1922 Dye Hearings,* 812. Some authors put the *Deutschland*'s second arrival in October. They are wrong. The submarine docked in the wee hours of the morning of November 1. See *New York Times,* Nov. 1 and 2, 1916. A second German merchant submarine, the *Bremen,* also with a cargo of dyestuffs, was lost at sea. Herman Metz would later describe his role before U.S. entry into the war as "practically the go-between . . . between Secretary of State Bryan and Mr. Lansing, on the one hand, and Count von Bernstorff [the German minister to the United States], on the other, in the matter of facilitating the movement of dyestuffs at that time." *1922 Dye Hearings,* 743. Others saw his role as less benign. He would be accused of being a "German propagandist." Ibid. Aside from the merchant submarine *Deutschland,* U.S. German trade on German vessels had entirely ceased. The best work on the *Deutschland* and the *Bremen* is Dwight R. Messimer, *Merchant U-Boat: Adventures of* Deutschland *1916–1918* (Annapolis, Md.: Naval Institute Press, 1988).

158. In 1917, the imports would have come from Switzerland, England, and France. By 1917, the United States had changed from a net importer to a net exporter of dyestuffs.

159. Haynes, *American Chemical Industry.* III, 314–315, and Tom Mahoney, *The Merchants of Life* (New York: Harper & Row, 1959), 212. In Chapter 2, I will discuss the outcome of the suit.

160. Wilkins, *History,* 391, 821n.50, and *Bayer Co., Inc. v. United Drug Co.,* 272 Fed. 505 (SDNY 1921).

161. U.S. Senate, Committee on Patents, *Salvarsan, Hearings,* 65th Cong., 1st sess. (1917), 3–39. The hearings were held in June 1917. See also Haynes, *American Chemical*

Industry, III, 319. There are variations in the telling of this story. According to *APC Report,* 53, Herman Metz determined on manufacture and sent his brother Gustav to Germany for the necessary permission, which "was refused, but the latter came home [to the United States] with sufficient knowledge to permit the commencement of the work." Haynes writes that the brother, who was a Ph.D. scientist, remained in Germany for eight months of intensive training in the production of Hoechst pharmaceuticals, particularly Salvarsan, which seems strange *if* the permission was refused. Haynes also repeats a story, with the caveat "whether true or not," that Gustav Metz was not permitted to carry notes out of Germany and, therefore, memorized the Salvarsan process piece by piece, making frequent trips to Switzerland, where he wrote up his notes. Clearly, both the Germans and Herman Metz would have preferred not to manufacture in the United States.

162. Herman Metz, President Farbwerke-Hoechst Co., to the Medical Profession, March 1917. Copy in file of Dermatological Research Laboratory at College of Physicians, Philadelphia, Historical Collection. I am indebted to Jonathan Liebenau for this letter.

163. On the expectations for the *Deutschland*'s arrival, see *New York Times,* Jan. 6, 29, 1917, Feb. 1, 1917, and Mar. 7, 1917. Jonathan Liebenau, *Medical Science and Medical Industry* (Baltimore: Johns Hopkins University Press, 1987), 113–121, is very useful on the conflicts between Schamberg and Metz. He errs, however, in assuming that the *Deutschland* arrived in January 1917 (p. 110); it did not. On plans for the third trip and the fate of the *Deutschland* (it was converted into a war boat), see Messimer, *Merchant U-Boat,* 148ff.

164. For basic data on American Nitrogen Co., Ltd., see Du Pont Co. records, Ser. II, Pt. 2, 41–42, Hagley Museum and Library. On Norsk Hydro, see Haber, *Chemical Industry,* 87 (on the Badische interest in it—until 1911); 168–169 (on the French ownership); 88 (on Norsk Hydro's eventual abandonment—in the 1920s—of the arc process in favor of the Haber-Bosch one). See also Harm Schröter, "Risk and Control in Multinational Enterprise: German Businesses in Scandinavia, 1918–1939," *Business History Review,* 62 (Autumn 1988): 425, 433–434.

165. Kuttroff's role in aiding the U.S. war effort was given by his attorney in postwar congressional hearings. See *1922 Dye Hearings,* 188. There were strange goings-on in the Badische organization in America in 1916. Morris R. Poucher, who had been, or perhaps still was, employed by the American Badische unit, in the fall of 1916 became a special consultant to Du Pont. He offered Du Pont "the services of eight of his associates who were skilled in marketing dyestuffs as well as samples of all dyes marketed by Badische." Du Pont promised Poucher the title of dyestuff sales manager should Du Pont become a dyestuff producer. Hounshell and Smith, *Science and Corporate Strategy,* 83. Badische had opened in September 1913 its synthetic ammonia plant at Oppau, Germany, using what came to be known as the Haber-Bosch process. It was the only one of its kind. Haber, *Chemical Industry,* 94, 103, and ibid., 86–95, for the development of the Haber-Bosch process. The U.S. government nitrate plants—built during World War I—did not use the Haber-Bosch process. Graham D. Taylor and Patricia E. Sudnik, *Du Pont and the International Chemical Industry* (Boston: Twayne Publishers, 1984), 55–56.

166. American Metal had no U.S. mining operations in 1914–1916, although it did mine in Mexico. In 1916, its Denver, Colorado, office manager recommended the company take options on molybdenum properties in Colorado (wartime demand had hiked the price of this metal); the company also took an interest in the recovery of potash from Georgia slate. The first of these activities put the company in the molybdenum business; the second proved unsuccessful—at least for many years. American Metal's sales in the half year ending December 31, 1916 ($82.6 million), were greater than in the full year ending July 1, 1914 ($68.8 million), while its profits in that half year ($4.9 million) were almost five times the profits in the entire prewar year ($1.1 million). The big increase in sales and profits had come in 1915–1916. Bernfeld, "A Short History," 7–8, 11, and *APC Report,* 84.

167. *New York Times,* July 19, 1916; there is substantial information on this company in RG 131, Box 212, National Archives.

168. The publication of documents found in Albert's briefcase in August 1915 was a cause célèbre, confirming rumors about German espionage and sabotage. Practically every U.S. diplomatic history covers the dramatic story. The best account is by McAdoo (*Crowded Years,* 321–330), who as secretary of the treasury hired the secret service agent who spirited away the briefcase.

169. Bernstorff, *My Three Years,* 71–80; *APC Report,* 122–125; and Otto Heins, "Military Report—Tying Up Supplies of Munitions for the Enemy," Mar. 30, 1915, copy in Garvan Papers, Box 198, American Heritage Center, University of Wyoming, Laramie, Wyoming (Heins was president of Bosch Magneto Co., New York, a German direct investment in the United States). The first plan was that a representative of the Germans would buy up all the antimony available to make it impossible to fill shrapnel with bullets. McAdoo, *Crowded Years,* 329. The Deutsche Bank seems to have held its American securities in the United States, and these could be sold to finance the schemes. Before the war, the Deutsche Bank had engaged in U.S. lending; repayments could serve wartime goals. For example, an American company, the Kerbaugh-Empire Co., in September 1913 had borrowed 6,740,800 marks (about $1.6 million); when the note came due, it was renewed; partial payments were made; by March 31, 1915, the principal was reduced to 3,216,445 marks. On these transactions, see Appeal of New Orleans, Texas & Mexico Co., 6 Board of Tax Appeals 436 (Mar. 9, 1927). For more on Kerbaugh-Empire Co., see *APC Report,* 149, 326. For additional alleged activities of the Deutsche Bank on behalf of the Imperial Government, see ibid., 42–43. Tauscher of Krupp was accused of having procured large quantities of dynamite and sent his accomplices to blow up the Welland Canal that linked Lakes Erie and Ontario. A. D. McLaren, *Peaceful Penetration* (New York: E. P. Dutton, 1917), 76. For more on Tauscher, see Doerries, *Imperial Challenge,* 179, 336n.240, 337n.244.

170. Hessen, *Steel Titan,* 215–216. Had the Germans made the acquisition, they would of course have stopped the assistance to Britain. The British government got wind of the offer and provided its own financial inducements. See ibid., 216. For the role of Morgan in thwarting the transaction, see Chernow, *House of Morgan,* 189.

171. Wilkins, *History,* 260, 482, 871n.236; Gall et al., *Deutsche Bank,* 154–155; *APC Report,* 42–43.

172. McAdoo, *Crowded Years,* 329.

173. Bernstorff, *My Three Years,* 80–81; Haynes, *American Chemical Industry,* II, 18–20, 130–131; *APC Report,* 43–44; *1922 Dye Hearings,* 814; Palmer and Garvan, *Aims,* 58; and Charles C. Mann and Mark L. Plummer, *The Aspirin Wars* (Boston: Harvard Business School Press, 1991), 39–42. Hounshell and Smith, *Science and Corporate Strategy,* 80, relate an odd story about Morris R. Poucher, who was with the Badische Company in New York and who proposed in December 1915 that Du Pont make certain dye intermediates and export them to England to be turned into finished products; the British plant would then reexport the finished products to America. I could not understand this until I read that the immediate effect would be to cut back on Du Pont's war materiel output—of explosives. Was this plan linked with the German efforts to disrupt U.S. war production? Anyway, Du Pont rejected the proposition.

174. Bernstorff, *My Three Years,* 81–82; see also translation of Hugo Borst, Commercial Manager of the Bosch firm, Stuttgart, to Otto Heins, President Bosch Magneto Co., New York, Aug. 21, 1915, Garvan Papers, Box 198, wherein Borst explained that because of German press attacks, "we cannot give you any confidential drawings of war materials." Other correspondence in the Garvan Papers, Box 198, especially Otto Heins to H. F. Albert, Nov. 30, 1915, shows clearly that Bosch Magneto Co. tried to convince German authorities that it had pursued "an obstruction policy," seeking to withhold from the

Allies certain products, for example, "the much needed special-airplane apparatuses." If Bosch refused to supply the Allies' needs, American competitors would do the manufacturing—which the American Bosch unit sought to prevent. Heins, however, declared *to Albert* "our active interest in the German cause.".

175. Sperry, *German Plots,* 12–15; *APC Report,* 134–136. For more on Rintelen, see Doerries, *Imperial Challenge,* 176–189.

176. *APC Report,* 136.

177. Doerries, *Imperial Challenge,* 53–55, 267n.87. The arrangements were made by Bernstorff, banker Bernhard Dernburg, and Hermann Sielcken of Crossman & Sielcken (a major German-owned coffee importer). On the latter, see Wilkins, *History,* 801n.247.

178. See Paul Fuller to Attorney General of the United States, Aug. 27, 1915, in *U.S. v. Alcoa,* Exhibits, Eq. 85–73 (SDNY 1937–1942), 787–792 (Exh. 146), and also 793–795 (Exhs. 147, 148, and 149); see, in addition, *U.S. v. Alcoa,* Final Judgement, Eq. 85–73 (SDNY 1942), 85. I have always believed that Southern Aluminium Company's inability to find financial aid was a "convenience" to Alcoa, which was delighted to acquire this property. As my text has made clear, other foreign companies found financing in the United States. On Southern Aluminium and Alcoa, see George W. Stocking and Myron W. Watkins, *Cartels in Action* (New York: Twentieth Century Fund, 1947), 243–244.

179. See George David Smith, *From Monopoly to Competition: The Transformations of Alcoa, 1888–1986* (Cambridge: Cambridge University Press, 1988), 110–111 (on Alcoa's use of the facilities); Wilkins, *History,* 283 (on Adrien Badin).

180. On prewar French car production in the United States, see Wilkins, *History,* 419–421. Here the problem was probably less one of finance than one of the cutoff of certain essential parts imported from France.

181. Lewis, *America's Stake,* 562–566.

182. By "shell" enterprises, I mean those that were legal structures with no real operating rationale.

183. *Stock Exchange Official Intelligence 1914,* 1072, and Lewis, *America's Stake,* 562.

184. On the XIT Ranch, see Wilkins, *History,* 301, 305–306; Lewis Nordyke, *Cattle Empire* (New York: William Morrow, 1949), 248n (on the final end to this British investment). According to Nordyke, the British came out well; I am less certain.

185. See data on the Stratton mine in Wilkins, *History,* 242, 757n.35, and Western Range Cattle Industry Study (WRCIS), Reel 72, Acc. 11,092, Library of Congress. British investors, reported to have paid $11 million for the mine in 1899, sold in 1915 what little remained for $325,000 to the Portland Gold Mining Company—a Colorado firm. Marshall Sprague, *Money Mountain: The Story of Cripple Creek Gold* (Boston: Little, Brown, 1953), 314. The returns to investors in the interim had been minimal.

186. This group of railways was associated with the London banking house Emile Erlanger and Co. In 1916, ANOTP sold the New Orleans and Northeastern Railroad to the American-owned and American-controlled Southern Railway. Lewis, *America's Stake,* 104, and Southern Railway Co., *Annual Report for Year-ended June 30, 1917.* On the transformation of ANOTP into Sterling Trust, Ltd., see George Glasgow, *The English Investment Trust Companies* (New York: John Wiley, 1931), 142. On the direct investment aspects of ANOTP, I have used ANOTP, *Directors' Reports.*

187. For free-standing companies in the United States, see Wilkins, *History,* 161–162, and passim. For the general concept, see Mira Wilkins, "The Free-Standing Company, 1870–1914," *Economic History Review,* 2nd ser., 41 (May 1988): 259–282, and Mira Wilkins and Harm Schröter, eds., *The Free-Standing Company in the World Economy* (Oxford: Oxford University Press, 1998). Some free-standing companies probably came to an end because of Britain's wartime taxes; there was no reason to continue the British charter.

188. Wilkins, *History,* 256; Geoffrey Tweedale, *Sheffield Steel and America* (Cambridge: Cambridge University Press, 1987), 120.

189. Tweedale, *Sheffield Steel,* 121 (on its losses); Tweedale indicates that by 1918 the American operation had been absorbed into American Manganese Steel Co. Ibid. The exit was prior to 1918. Tweedale can document the British presence in America in 1910–1913. By 1916, the British firm's facilities in the United States were American owned. See *Moody's 1916,* 855.

190. These mortgage company investments were mainly by free-standing companies, but unlike many free-standing companies, these were conscientiously managed. On the reduction in lending, see Benj. Strong Journal, Mar. 16, 1916, 1000.2 Strong Papers, FRBNY, and Lewis, *America's Stake,* 118. Mortgage loans were in these years typically of three to five years' duration; when they matured, they seem not to have been renewed. See also J. C. Gilbert, *A History of Investment Trusts in Dundee* (London: P. S. King & Son, 1939), 105, which says the mortgage business was affected by the war but not all at once. On British mortgage investments in 1913–1914, see Wilkins, *History,* 509–510.

191. Texas Land and Mortgage Co., Report for Year-ended Mar. 31, 1915, and Report for Year-ended Mar. 31, 1917, Z-G-1, Reels 283 and 284, Bancroft Library, University of California, Berkeley, California. Balfour, Williamson's mortgage and investment company, Pacific Loan and Investment Co., Ltd.—in response to the British government's appeal for dollars—had repatriated its funds as and when they became available, with the result that its American assets by war's end were greatly reduced. Wallis Hunt, *Heirs of Great Adventure,* 2 vols. (London: Balfour, Williamson, 1951, 1960), II, 133. The Pacific Loan and Investment Co. had $4 million in loans at the end of 1913, and $3 million at the end of 1916. Lewis, *America's Stake,* 87n.

192. Haynes, *American Chemical Industry,* III, 361; U.S. Senate, Committee on Military Affairs, Subcommittee on War Mobilization, *Scientific and Technical Mobilization, Hearings,* 78th Cong., 1st and 2nd sess. (1943–1944), pt. 16, 2133 (henceforth cited as *Kilgore Committee Hearings*). Carl Zeiss—with the aid of the Deutsche Bank—sold its $800,000 shareholding and transferred this into 3,933,835 marks on November 8, 1915. Antje Hagen, "Export versus Direct Investment in the German Optical Industry," *Business History,* 38 (October 1996): 19n.46.

193. Mari E. W. Williams, *The Precision Makers* (London: Routledge, 1994), 69.

194. Wilkins, *History,* 409; Roy A. Duffus, Jr., *The Story of M & T Chemicals Inc.* (New York: Cordella Duffus Baker, 1965), 24. The price was $1 million.

195. Wilkins, *History,* 408–409, and Haynes, *American Chemical Industry,* VI, 306–307.

196. Gall et al., *Deutsche Bank,* 155; *APC Report,* 143.

197. The *APC Report,* 56 (dated February 1919), states that prior to U.S. entry into the war, the German 10 percent ownership of the Geigy-Ter-Meer Co. (renamed the Geigy Co.) was sold to the U.S. firm's *Swiss* parent, J. R. Geigy & Co., which was "in good standing with the allied Governments." A World War II report—December 30, 1942—by Charles R. Clark, however, indicates that it was not until May 15, 1917, *after U.S. entry into the war,* that Geigy-Ter-Meer Co. was renamed Geigy Co., Inc., and became 100 percent Swiss owned. See report in File D-63-3, Acc. 65A1063, Box 267, RG 131, U.S. Department of Justice, Washington, D.C. DWF's March 12, 1917, sale to SKF (see this chapter, note 148) can be viewed in this context.

198. *New York Times,* July 1, 7, and 8, 1915; Aitken, *Continuous Wave,* 285; and Howeth, *History of Communications,* 226.

199. Sidak, *Foreign Investment,* 38–39, 41. In April 1915, Atlantic Communication Company—the U.S. subsidiary of the German Telefunken—had "upgraded the Sayville facility." Ibid., 38.

200. Before the July 1915 takeover (in December 1914), Karl Frank had tried to get Philander C. Knox, a former U.S. secretary of state, to be president of the company to disguise its German background. Knox refused. Tansill, *America Goes to War,* 600n. After the takeover came the effort to sell to the Swedes. Aitken, *Continuous Wave,* 285–286. In April 1917, the New York Attorney General's Office would seize the records of Hugo Schmidt, the Deutsche Bank's U.S. representative. These records contained codebooks, and as a consequence federal and state officials could decipher wireless messages flashed back and forth between Sayville, Long Island, and Nauen, Germany. *New York Times,* Nov. 3, 1918.

201. Albert Ballin, as noted earlier, wanted to sell Hamburg-American ships that were stuck in U.S. ports to Americans; he continued to be denied permission by the German government. Huldermann, *Albert Ballin,* 230.

202. Some sales made to neutrals were found to be for cloaking purposes. As early as July 1914, before the outbreak of war in Europe, Heinrich Franck Söhne of Ludwigsburg, Germany, had placed the stock holdings in its U.S. business in the hands of a Swiss company, Internationale Nahrungs und Genussmittel Aktiengesellschaft. The APC saw this as "a mere cover" and seized the stock. *APC Report,* 153–154. See Wilkins, *History,* 337, on this company's U.S. business in chicory. On the other hand, there was no challenge to the transfer of stock in Geigy-Ter-Meer from the German Chemische Fabriken Weiler-Ter-Meer to the Swiss J. R. Geigy, nor DWF to SKF. See notes above.

203. Many of the attempts to disguise German ownership are documented in the *APC Report.* The most common device was "the transfer of their property to their friends or agents in this country without valid consideration or upon consideration to be fixed after the war, and payable out of the business itself at a time when the parties conceived that normal business conditions would be restored" (p. 11). The Alien Property Custodian called these and similar transactions "fake transfers" and would conclude the properties remained "German owned." Ibid., 11–12.

204. Higher wartime corporate and personal income taxes—which included those on alien owners—stimulated tax evasion measures. In 1917, the German-owned Botany Worsted Mills (claiming its bylaws allowed it) paid ten board members $1.6 million and deducted the amount as a business expense. U.S. tax authorities disallowed half that sum; Botany Worsted appealed, and eventually the U.S. Supreme Court ruled against the textile company, maintaining that "the tax payer had not sought [established?] a relationship between the amounts paid and the value and extent of the services rendered." See Bryce M. Stewart and Walter J. Couper, *Profit Sharing and Stock Ownership for Wage Earners and Executives* (New York: Industrial Relations Counselors, 1945), 16n.2. Some of the Swiss holding companies may have been established in order to lower tax obligations.

205. The exceptions to this general decline were based on what appears to have been intra-European securities trade. For example, Dutch, Swedish, and Swiss investors would buy American securities owned by Germans. In net, however, Cleona Lewis believes that not only the British, French, and Germans but the Dutch as well sold many of their portfolio stakes. Lewis, *America's Stake,* 125.

206. Amos J. Peaslee, "Taxing Incomes of Foreign Investors in American Stocks and Bonds," *Columbia Law Review,* 16 (June 1916): 1–2.

207. The price of U.S. Steel shares rose in 1915–1916. S. S. Huebner, "The American Security Market during the War," *Annals of the American Academy of Political and Social Science,* 68 (Nov. 1916): 98, 106. U.S. Steel common was selling at $55.50 on July 31, 1914; its high for 1915 was $89.50; on Sept. 8, 1916, it was selling at $100.75. There was *no* reduction in the number of shares outstanding in U.S. Steel—so the quantity of shares held best reflects the real drop in foreign holdings. Note, however, these figures are probably low, for securities were held in the hands of U.S. nominees.

208. The German portion of the "other foreign" was 2,151 (Mar. 31, 1914); 2,664 (Dec. 31, 1914); 1,178 (Dec. 31, 1915); 628 (Dec. 31, 1916); 628 (Mar. 31, 1917)—i.e., very small relative to the English, Dutch, French, or Canadian holdings. Thus, I did not include a column for the German investments.

209. L. F. Loree's par value figures are undoubtedly low because of the difficulties of determining who held bearer bonds and also the problems of securities in the hands of U.S. nominees. Loree also collected *market* value data—for July 31, 1915 ($1,751.4 million); July 31, 1916 ($1,110.1 million); and January 31, 1917 ($924.5 million). Both sets of figures reveal a decline in foreign investment; the dollar amount of the drop in foreign ownership is greater—July 31, 1915 to January 31, 1917—when measured by par value than by market value, but in both cases it is striking.

210. Railroad securities held by foreigners, measured at market value, were less than the amount when measured at par value. John F. Stover, "Daniel Williard," in *Railroads in the Age of Regulation: Encyclopedia of American Business History and Biography,* ed. Keith Bryant (New York: Facts on File, 1988), 482, on the sorry state of American railroads.

211. *New York Times,* Feb. 27, 1915.

212. See Paul D. Dickens, "The Transition Period in American International Financing: 1897 to 1914," Ph.D. diss., George Washington University, 1933, 261–262, for firms with obligations that matured in 1915. International Harvester, for example, had three-year debenture notes issued in January 1912 that matured in 1915. It did not refinance abroad; it could do so in the United States.

213. See W. R. Lawson, "The British Treasury and the London Stock Exchange," *Annals of the American Academy of Political and Social Science,* 68 (Nov. 1916): 81. The decision to sell American securities and buy British ones involved private sales, albeit it might be argued that they were *government-induced,* as British government policies made *home* investments relatively more attractive.

214. H. P. Davison, London, to J. P. Morgan & Co., New York, June 25, 1915, *Nye Committee Hearings,* pt. 26 (Exh. 2189), 8109.

215. See, for example, J. P. Morgan to H. P. Davison, London, July 9, 1915: "Our investment market exceedingly weak and foreign holdings offered here continue heavy and fast. This morning one broker offered for sale to First National Bank for foreign account in one block $3,500,000 gilt-edge American bonds." *Nye Committee Hearings,* pt. 26 (Exh. 2195), 8114. H. P. Davison, New York, to E. C. Grenfell, July 20, 1915, notes the "continued flow of securities from London." Ibid., pt. 26 (Exh. 2196), 8114. See also George Foster Peabody, William Woodward, and Benjamin Strong to William G. McAdoo, Secretary of the Treasury, Aug. 2, 1915, and other correspondence in File 790, FRBNY.

216. On Fleming's past U.S. involvements, see Wilkins, *History,* passim, and Lazard Frères, New York, to its Paris house, Sept. 16, 1915, *Nye Committee Hearings,* pt. 26 (Exh. 2264), 8136 (Fleming's activities that month).

217. Adler, *Jacob H. Schiff,* II, 248.

218. Lewis, *America's Stakes,* 93, 120, 549–550. A large block sale was that of an unspecified French banking group of 100,000 shares of Utah Copper Co. in September 1915 for $6.6 million. In December 1915, Kuhn, Loeb & Co. bought back almost $25 million of a Central Pacific loan that had been issued in Paris in 1911. For sales in 1916 by French owners of Midwest Refining Co. securities, see Bennett H. Wall and George S. Gibb, *Teagle of Jersey Standard* (New Orleans: Tulane University Press, 1974), 96; on French sales of some portfolio holdings in petroleum, see U.S. Federal Trade Commission, *Report on the Petroleum Industry of Wyoming* (Washington, D.C., 1921), 51.

219. Lewis, *America's Stakes,* 122–123, 534, 536. She estimates (p. 536) that some $300 to $500 million in securities were sold by German investors before U.S. entry into the war. See also Harold G. Moulton and Constantine E. McGuire, *Germany's Capacity to Pay*

(New York: McGraw-Hill, 1923), 279–280. The British came to consider German-held American securities contraband, since receipts furnished the basis for military purchases. Thus, the British claimed that they could seize such securities. Nonetheless, as in 1914, so in 1915, 1916, and early 1917, the Germans figured out numerous ways to realize on their holdings. They often arranged deliveries of the securities through banks in neutral Holland, Switzerland, or a Scandinavian country. Carosso, *Investment Banking,* 213. All during 1915–1916, the British assumed shipments of gold to Holland from America were payments for German liquidations of American securities. Brown, *International Gold Standard,* 233n. It is altogether possible that some of the $100 million in "Dutch" securities said to be liquidated from the outbreak of war to December 1915 (see Table 1.7) were in fact German-owned securities, dispatched through Holland, or alternatively American securities sold to Dutchmen, who in turn resold the securities in the United States. Federal Reserve Bank of New York head, Benjamin Strong, in England in March 1916, learned from Montagu Norman that one way the Germans were realizing on their American securities was to sell them to Dutch bankers, which then sold existing Dutch-held American securities in New York against them. The Dutch bankers made a tidy profit in these transactions. Strong Journal, Mar. 18, 1916, 1000.2 Strong Papers, FRBNY. German-owned securities were apparently frequently sent to the United States on Dutch ships. Early in 1916 the British started searching mail sacks on Dutch ships, taking away all securities found—assuming these were German owned. According to van Manen, in the first five months of 1916, more than $3 million in American securities on board Dutch ships were seized by the British navy. Van Manen, *De Nederlandsche Overzee Trustmaatschappij,* III, 298–330 (I am indebted to A. J. Veenendaal for data from this source); Cleona Lewis writes that in March 1916 alone about $10 million in securities from Holland were seized by British authorities in the belief that they were German owned. Lewis, *America's Stake,* 123. Some of these securities were being forwarded from Scandinavian countries, and the British Foreign Office carefully examined the "stubs" of coupons to see whether in the prior year Scandinavian *owners* (and not Germans) had "clipped" the coupons. *Commercial and Financial Chronicle,* Mar. 18, 1916, 1009. In July 1916, the British government made an agreement with the Nederlandsche Overzee Trustmaatschappij (NOT): securities transported across the Atlantic by the Dutch had to carry Dutch revenue stamps from before January 1, 1915; if the stamps were from after that date, then no German or other enemy stamps could be on the securities. Dutch bankers were required to guarantee in writing that the securities were owned since August 4, 1914, by Dutch citizens (or other neutrals, or citizens of Allied countries). NOT agreed to organize a financial department to assure compliance. Van Manen, *De Nederlandsche Overzee Trustmaatschappij,* III, 298–330, and VII, Appendix 195b, 347–349. The agreement had, however, loopholes; Dutch revenue stamps could be forged, and dates could be altered—and officers and crew members of Dutch ships smuggled packets of securities to the United States and sold them there. Ibid., II, 316–320. These sales of securities through Dutch, Swiss, or Scandinavian banking channels and through Dutch "smuggling" were probably private sales, many of which the German government had no knowledge.

220. August Belmont & Co. to Rothschild Frères, Feb. 7, 1917, Rothschild Papers, AQ, 1074/6472, Archives Nationale, Fontainebleau, France. On August Belmont & Co. and Rothschild Frères, see Wilkins, *History,* 472–476.

221. All figures on the divestments of "Dutch"-held American securities may well include German securities channeled through Holland; all Dutch sales were suspect. The difficulties Dutch investors had with American transactions in 1916–1917 are illustrated by the case of International Mercantile Marine Company (IMM). In the 1916 reorganization of this company, old 4.5 and 5 percent bonds were exchanged for cash and new 6 percent bonds. Two Dutch associations of bondholders held about $18 million in the old

bonds. After consultation with the British government, IMM was able to remit $10 million in cash to the Dutch as partial payment for the old bonds; the rest ($7,949,000) was to be paid in the new 6 percent bonds. A vice-president of New York Trust Co. (the depository for the old bonds) sailed for Europe on November 22, 1916, expecting to hand the new bonds over to Adolph Boissevain in Amsterdam. The transaction was delayed because no NOT declaration had been obtained. The boxes of new bonds were detoured to London for examination and then for more scrutiny to the British legation in the Hague. Finally, on December 16, 1916, the bonds were delivered to the Boissevain firm for distribution to the Dutch bondholders. Van Manen, *De Nederlandsche Overzee Trustmaatschappij,* III, 326–327.

222. Sayers, *Bank of England,* I, 86; Burk, *Britain, America,* is very useful on all the missions.

223. See, for example, James Brown, Benjamin Strong, and A. H. Wiggin to George Paish and Basil Blackett, Oct. 30, 1914, 210.1 Strong Papers, FRBNY.

224. On the Morgan role, see Kathleen Burk, *Morgan Grenfell 1838–1988* (Oxford: Oxford University Press, 1989), 127ff.

225. The house of Morgan had the expertise and connections. The head of Morgan, Grenfell was a director of the Bank of England. The British ambassador to the United States, Cecil Spring-Rice, was a very close friend of J. P. Morgan, Jr. Chernow, *House of Morgan,* 187, 192. In January 1915, Morgan wrote the ambassador that it might be unwise for Morgan to stay at the ambassador's home in Washington, since Morgan wanted the firm's role as commercial agent for the British to be as "inconspicuous as possible." But, the banker invited the ambassador to come and stay with him in New York.

226. H. P. Davison to E. C. Grenfell (of Morgan, Grenfell & Co., London), June 3, 1915, *Nye Committee Hearings,* pt. 26 (Exh. 2186), 8107; see also Davison, London, to J. P. Morgan & Co., June 15, 1915, ibid, pt. 26 (Exh. 2189), 8110. On the depreciating pound, see Burk, *Britain, America,* 62–63, and Davison to J. P. Morgan, June 23, 1915, *Nye Committee Hearings,* pt. 26 (Exh. 2187), 8108, on Davison's conference with the governor of the Bank of England on the exchange situation.

227. Lord Beaverbrook, *Politicians and War* (1925; rpt. London: Archon, 1968), 148, who does not give a date. However, E. C. Grenfell, London, to H. P. Davison, July 22, 1915, *Nye Committee Hearings,* pt. 26 (Exh. 2246), 8131, reported to the Morgan house that the Chancellor of the Exchequer (McKenna) and the governor of the Bank of England (Cunliffe) had that morning met with Prudential Assurance Co. Ltd. executives. See also the cable reply, J. P. Morgan & Co. to Grenfell, July 22, 1915, ibid., pt. 26 (Exh. 2198), 8115, and Burk, *Britain, America,* 63, 236.

228. Stephen McKenna, *Reginald McKenna 1863–1943* (London: Eyre & Spottiswoode, 1948), 237 (quote), and *Report of American Dollar Securities Committee, Parliamentary Papers,* xiii–1, Cmd. 212 (1919), 3 (henceforth cited as *1919 Report of American Dollar Securities Committee*). Sayers, *Bank of England,* I, 91, says the first steps were in June 1915, but this seems highly unlikely, albeit there were *discussions* in June.

229. Burk, *Britain, America,* 64, citing Asquith to the king, Aug. 18, 1915.

230. Burk, *Morgan Grenfell,* 130.

231. The Marquess of Reading, *Rufus Isaacs, First Marquess of Reading, 1914–1935,* 2 vols. (London: Hutchinson, 1942, 1945), II, 31–33, 45, 49; Burk, *Britain, America,* 65, 69, 73–75. The loan turned out to be too large for the American market to absorb—and a sizable portion for a time remained in the hands of the underwriters. Karl Born, *International Banking* (New York: St. Martin's Press, 1983), 202; Carosso, *Investment Banking,* 204–206. Americans eventually ended up selling some of the Anglo-French bonds to the Japanese. Gyoju Odate, *Japan's Financial Relations with the United States* (New York: Columbia University Press, 1922), 98, and data from Paul J. Hauser, Daiwa Securities America, Feb. 1989.

232. Sayers, *Bank of England,* I, 89; since the Anglo-French loan had been so difficult to sell, future borrowings would require collateral. The British government provided a premium to the depositors of securities, as Davison had suggested.

233. Sayers, *Bank of England,* I, 89–90. This measure was the first inkling the British public had that American securities were going to be used as a means of controlling sterling exchange. See Frank L. McVey, *The Financial History of Great Britain, 1914–1918* (New York: Oxford University Press, 1918), 64–65.

234. Sayers, *Bank of England,* I, 91. Sayers does not indicate the amounts of securities that were "borrowed."

235. See *1919 Report of American Dollar Securities Committee,* 3; *London Gazette,* Dec. 17, 1915, 12558–12559; and Morgan, *Studies in British Financial Policy,* 327.

236. "Sir George May," *Dictionary of National Biography, 1941–1950,* 582, for background on May.

237. *1919 Report of American Dollar Securities Committee,* 4–5.

238. Peaslee, "Taxing Incomes," 1; when Peaslee wrote in June 1916, the tax had not yet actually been imposed.

239. Sayers, *Bank of England,* 92. In June 1916, Gaspard Farrer, a director of Baring Brothers & Co., Ltd., wrote his circle of investing friends, advising each one as to which of their American securities they should lend to the British government. He advised lending the minimum amounts acceptable. Heather Gilbert, *End of the Road: The Life of Lord Mount Stephen. Vol. 2, 1891–1921* (Aberdeen: Aberdeen University Press, 1977), 367.

240. Brien Cokayne to Benjamin Strong, June 15, 1916, File C261 (England–Bank of England), FRBNY, and Montagu Norman to Strong, June 21, 1916, 1116.1 Strong Papers, FRBNY. See also Norman to Strong, July 24, 1916, 1116.1 Strong Papers: "Our stream of American securities has been wonderfully long." Norman was at the Bank of England and would become governor in 1920.

241. Sayers, *Bank of England,* 92.

242. Final report upon American Dollar Securities, Sept. 30, 1922, in *Nye Committee Hearings,* pt. 35 (Exh. 4252), 11813 (henceforth cited as *Final Report*).

243. This had been a concern in Britain. See Report of John Maynard Keynes, Feb. 1, 1916, in *The Collected Writings of John Maynard Keynes,* ed. Elizabeth Johnson (London: Macmillan, 1971), XVI, 164, 169–170.

244. Sayers, *Bank of England,* 92. On further resales, see *Final Report,* 11812–11813. By October 1916, Keynes and others at the British Treasury were concerned that "our stock of American securities is much depleted"; *Collected Writings,* XVI, 200.

245. *1919 Report of American Dollar Securities Committee,* 6.

246. Farrer of Barings had earlier lent his American railroad securities. On December 14, 1916, he offered his Great Northern iron ore certificates ($650,000 at current market prices). Gilbert, *End of the Road,* 368. On new British regulations in January 1917, see Grady, *British War Finance,* 50–57, and John Michael Atkin, *British Overseas Investment 1918–1931* (New York: Arno Press, 1977), 26. These were designed to widen the mobilization net.

247. Lamont, *Henry P. Davison,* 202, 205, 210–211, 213–214.

248. Keynes, Memo of Oct. 10, 1916, in *Collected Writings,* XVI, 197–198.

249. Sayers, *Bank of England,* I, 94.

250. Initially some British investment trusts had been reluctant to sell or to turn over their securities to the British government. On September 14, 1915, the governor of the Federal Reserve Bank of New York, Benjamin Strong, inquired by mail of his old friend William Mackenzie of the Alliance Trust Company, Ltd., as to how he and others in his position felt about the sale or loan of American securities to afford the British government means of obtaining larger credit. See Strong to Mackenzie, Sept. 14, 1915, 1112.4 Strong

Papers, FRBNY, and Wilkins, *History,* 498–500, on Mackenzie and the Alliance Trust Company. Mackenzie ignored the question in his reply to Strong (Mackenzie to Strong, Dec. 16, 1915, 1112.5 Strong Papers), but when Strong was in England in March 1916, Mackenzie explained that instead of selling American securities, he and others had borrowed large sums *in the United States* on their American securities and repatriated these borrowings, "paying off the loans gradually out of income liquidation." Mackenzie reported that by this and other means he, his company, and associates had brought to the United Kingdom some £500,000 sterling and would bring more if necessary. Since the Alliance Trust Company was heavily committed to American business, selling their securities and mortgage loans all at once would mean going out of business. See Strong Journal, March 16, 1916, 1000.2 Strong Papers. On the same March 1916 trip, however, Strong learned from another Scot, Alfred Shepherd, that some Scottish investment companies had liquidated "a very considerable amount of their American investments—one of his [Shepherd's] companies, and not a very large one, having recently sold no less than £100,000 sterling. The Scotch companies all along have felt a preference for American securities and invested heavily in them." Ibid., Mar. 15, 1916; on Shepherd, see W. Turrentine Jackson, *The Enterprising Scot* (Edinburgh: Edinburgh University Press, 1968), 270. Historian Jackson writes, "The three Scottish American Trust Companies and the North American Trust of Dundee reported a decrease in the percentage of their investments in the United States during each of the war years." Jackson, *Enterprising Scot,* 278, citing issues of the *Dundee Advertiser,* 1914–1917. The "Scottish American Trust Companies" to which he referred were Robert Fleming's companies. On them, see Wilkins, *History,* 124, 498–500. The historian of the Scottish American Investment Company (not to be confused with the Scottish American Trust Companies) reported that by the end of 1915 that company had deposited (deposited was the equivalent of "lent") £1.6 million worth of American securities with the British government. Ronald Weir, *A History of the Scottish American Investment Company* (Edinburgh: Scottish American Investment Company, 1973), 19. In its directors' report of February 1917, the British Investment Trust noted that it had deposited $7.9 million in American stocks and bonds, while in its report of the same date, the Scottish American Investment Company indicated it had $8 million on deposit. Jackson, *Enterprising Scot,* 277. This is but a sample. To understand the different responses that Strong got from the Alliance Trust Company and from Shepherd, it is important to distinguish the British investment trusts that were exclusively in securities—i.e., in portfolio investments—and those that held American securities and were *also* mortgage lenders. The Alliance Trust Company was in the latter category. In 1914, the mortgage component of its portfolio (virtually all in the United States) was 56 percent, with securities (most but not all of which were American) constituting the rest of its portfolio. In 1914, about 83 percent of its overall investments were in the United States. Many (but far from all) the important Scottish companies combined mortgage lending and investments in securities. See Wilkins, *History,* 494–510. As Youssef Cassis has pointed out, in 1914 both the *Stock Exchange Year Book* and the *Stock Exchange Official Intelligence* had a single section on investment trusts, finance companies, and land and mortgage companies. Youssef Cassis, "The Emergence of a New Financial Institution: Investment Trusts in Britain, 1870–1939," in *Capitalism in a Mature Economy,* ed. J. J. Van Helten and Y. Cassis (Aldershot: Edward Elgar, 1990), 143. Writing in 1976, W. G. Kerr refers to many of the then existing Scottish investment trusts as *originally* mortgage companies. *Scottish Capital on the American Credit Frontier* (Austin: Texas State Historical Association, 1976), 199. The transformation was a gradual one. However, many investment trusts—Scottish and English—had no activity in mortgages and *never* had any.

251. U.S. Department of Commerce, Bureau of Foreign and Domestic Commerce, *British Investment Trusts,* Trade Information Bulletin 88 (Washington, D.C., 1923), 28, 32; Mor-

gan, *Studies in British Financial Policy,* 327; Hunt, *Heirs of Great Adventure,* II, 133. The double taxation of course reduced the return.

252. Wilkins, *History,* 531.

253. State government regulators had stringent rules on "admitted assets." While some states did let British insurance companies substitute British war loans for dollar securities, most of the dollar assets could not be sold and the dollars remitted home; if sold, other dollar assets would need to be purchased.

254. These figures are my own tabulations, based on data in *Best's Insurance Reports, Fire and Marine, 1919.* Some of the British fire and marine insurance companies in America acquired some British war bonds and some of the 1915 Anglo-French loan, but such were only a small part of their U.S. assets.

255. Details on the "Rothschild Frères loan" are given in Lamont, *Henry P. Davison,* 192, and the *Nye Committee Hearings,* pt. 27 (Exhs. 2347A, 2349–2362), 8347–8353. In this case, the securities were denominated in francs and not dollars. In August 1915, Kuhn, Loeb & Co. arranged the conversion of the Pennsylvania Railroad 3¾ percent French franc loan certificates into dollar bonds in order to make feasible their transfer from French to American investment holdings; then Kuhn, Loeb & Co. placed in the United States some $37.5 million of these dollar bonds. Adler, *Jacob H. Schiff,* II, 263–264.

256. Swaine, *Cravath Firm,* II, 234–235. For more on the French government mobilization, see Lewis, *America's Stake,* 120–122 and 551–552. *Federal Reserve Bulletin,* 8 (Oct. 1922): 1181, notes that the French government mobilization produced "indifferent results." See Lewis, *America's Stake,* 121–122, on two "lots" of stocks and bonds (only some of which were American securities) used as collateral for French borrowing. One was $100 to $125 million and the other $100 million. These lots of securities were returned to France after the war. The French had difficulty with collateral in America and turned to the British for aid. Burk, *Britain, America,* 78. On the ineffectiveness of the French mobilization, see ibid., 210. Kuhn, Loeb & Co. became very much involved in aiding the French government, which prompted a July 1916 comment from Montagu Norman: "On the whole things are moving our way on all sides, and I have no doubt the German shoe is beginning to pinch—as indeed one may guess from the strange mixture of Kuhn Loeb & Co., and a French loan!" Norman to Benjamin Strong, July 24, 1916, 1116.1 Strong Papers, FRBNY. The British thought Kuhn, Loeb was very pro-German.

257. Swaine, *Cravath Firm,* II, 235.

258. Carosso, *Investment Banking,* 206–207. This was the American Foreign Securities Company loan. For the role of J. P. Morgan & Co. and France in these years, see Martin Horn, "A Private Bank at War: J. P. Morgan & Co. and France 1914–1918," *Business History Review,* 74 (Spring 2000): 85–112.

259. On the inadequate holdings, see Georges Manchez, *Sociétés de dépot, banques d'affaires* (Paris: Librairie Delagrave, 1918), 58. Another part of the problem was that French taxes on foreign investment had led many French investors in America to conceal their investments. In addition, one should not underestimate "business secrecy." Many Frenchmen just did not want the government to know about their investments.

260. The "cream" of German securities were divested in this period, principally through private sales—albeit there obviously was a German government role in certain of the divestments. Cleona Lewis believes that because German transactions between 1914 and 1917 were under close surveillance by the Allies, there was little opportunity for the German *government* to use her nationals' securities as *collateral.* Not until March 1917 did the German government "resort to the forcible taking over of [borrowing of] foreign securities." Brown, *International Gold Standard,* 61. By then, of course, it was too late to have any impact on German investments in the United States.

261. *New York Times,* Nov. 3, 1918.

262. See Gall et al., *Deutsche Bank,* 154, 820, citing a letter of Dec. 29, 1916. There was probably more success in 1914–1915 than by the end of 1916, when public opinion in the United States was becoming increasingly anti-German. While the British in 1915 felt that Kuhn, Loeb was very pro-German, the Germans were less sure. On September 18, 1915, the German ambassador to America, Count Bernstorff, would write to the Foreign Office, Berlin, probably referring to Kuhn, Loeb: "Our Jewish friends here are . . . 'pussy footing'; they . . . are very anxious to make money . . . *One lesson* we may learn for future reference . . . is that we must not allow ourselves again to be left to the tender mercies of the German-Jewish bankers here. After the war, we must have branches of our large banks in New York just as we have in London." Bernstorff, *My Three Years,* 157–158 (italics in original). The ambassador may not have known that New York state law prohibited German branch banks (indeed, all branch banks). The Deutsche Bank had apparently wanted to establish one early in 1914, before the outbreak of war. Wilkins, *History,* 456. The letter, however, reflects the Germans' dissatisfaction with the bankers in New York who would be the obvious ones to handle the marketing of German bonds. While I am assuming this was a reference to Kuhn, Loeb, it could have been a reference to Speyer & Co. as well.

263. Because of the private sales, all government sales documents—such as the records of the American Dollar Securities Committee—reveal only a part of the liquidation. Atkin, *British Overseas Investment,* 26n, estimated that British private sales "were just as great" as the sales by the British Treasury.

264. Lawson, "British Treasury," 75.

265. My $3.1 billion estimate is based on the following: I accept the $1,550 million given in Table 1.7—for the period from the outbreak of war to December 1915—as reasonable. I am prepared to accept a figure of $350 million in American securities as liquidated in the entire month of July 1914 before the outbreak of war, which brings the total to $1.9 billion divested before December 1915 (since the estimate given in Table 1.7 was published on December 15, it most probably does not include any part of that month). There are records to show that the British *government* sold over $800 million in American securities between January 1, 1916, and March 31, 1917 (see Table 1.8). This brings the total to $2.7 billion. There were by all accounts British government sales in December 1915, and also private British sales as well as French, Dutch, German, and other foreign sales of securities in December 1915, in 1916, and in early 1917. It seems reasonable to estimate those sales at about $400 million, bringing my tentative total to $3.1 billion for the liquidations of foreign securities' holders in the United States (this figure is net of minor purchases of securities that were made in this period).

My estimate is to be compared with the numerous other ones. An oft-quoted number was that "more than $3 billion" in American securities were repatriated from Europe (or in some renditions from Great Britain) between July 1914 and April 1917 (or in other versions between July 1914 and the end of the war). See, for example, Carosso, *Investment Banking,* 212, 213, 216; *The Economist,* Nov. 15, 1930, 896; Lewis, *America's Stake,* 130; and *Nye Committee Hearings,* pt. 28, 8614.

Another set of oft-repeated figures were $2 billion liquidated or more often $2.2 billion—or $2.25 billion between August 1, 1914, and U.S. entry or in some versions "during World War I." Bullock, Williams, and Tucker, "Balance of Trade," 246, 248, 251, estimated a $2 billion figure for 1914–1919, with the bulk of the sales before U.S. entry into the war; Chandler, *Benjamin Strong,* 62, wrote that "foreign customers" resold $2 billion of their holdings of American securities between August 1, 1914, and U.S. entry in the war, April 1917 (this excludes the July sales); Laughlin, *Credit of Nations,* 322, believed "it is fairly within the mark to estimate the total volume of our securities returned to us in the first three years of the war at not less than $2,200,000." George W. Edwards,

International Trade Finance (New York: Henry Holt, 1924), 25, wrote that over $2 billion in American securities were returned to this country during the four years of the war. The $2.2 billion figure (for 1914–1919) was given in the National Industrial Conference Board, *The International Financial Position of the United States* (New York: National Industrial Conference Board, 1929), 49n; U.S. Department of Commerce, Bureau of Foreign and Domestic Commerce, *Foreign Investments in the United States* (Washington, D.C., 1937), 26; and in John T. Madden, Marcus Nadler, and Harry C. Sauvain, *America's Experience as a Creditor Nation* (New York: Prentice-Hall, 1937), 48. I found that the figure first appeared in the Federal Reserve Board, *Annual Report for 1916,* 1–2, which reads, "*from the beginning of the war until the end of December, 1916,* . . . about $2,250,000,000 of securities of American origin . . . have been transferred from foreign to domestic ownership" (my italics). The Federal Reserve estimate of $2.25 billion covered only August 1914 to December 31, 1916 (it excluded July 1914 sales and January through March 1917 sales).

There are substantial methodological problems in determining the appropriate figures because of variations in the market value of the securities, fluctuating exchange rates (important for securities denominated in other than dollars), and the numerous channels by which liquidations occurred. Also, whether July 1 or the date of the "outbreak of war" is the starting point makes a difference.

266. Safford, *Wilsonian Maritime Diplomacy,* 84.

267. Wilkins, *History,* 83–84, 583, 923n.184.

268. Detlev F. Vagts, "The Corporate Alien: Definitional Questions in Federal Restraints on Foreign Enterprise," *Harvard Law Review,* 74 (June 1961): 1495, 1505–1506; Safford, *Wilsonian Maritime Diplomacy,* 92–93; and 36 U.S. Stat. 729–730 (Sept. 7, 1916).

269. For more on the legislation, see Broesamle, *William Gibbs McAdoo,* 235.

270. Wilkins, *History,* 577.

271. U.S. House, Committee on Merchant Marine and Fisheries, *Hearings on HR 19350: A Bill to Regulate Radio Communications,* 64th Cong., 2nd sess. (1917), and Michael Hogan, *Informal Entente* (Columbia: University of Missouri Press, 1977), 130–131. On the provisions in the Radio Act of 1912 related to foreign investment, see Wilkins, *History,* 924n.188.

272. *New York Times,* Apr. 8, 1917.

273. Data in Siemens Archives, Munich.

274. See obituary in *New York Times,* Sept. 30, 1954.

275. *New York Times,* Apr. 8, 1917.

276. Safford, *Wilsonian Maritime Diplomacy,* 96, and René De La Pedraja, *The Rise and Decline of U.S. Merchant Shipping in the Twentieth Century* (New York: Twayne Publishers, 1992), 56. The offices of the Hamburg-American Line in New York had been a center of German propaganda during the period of neutrality, with H. B. Claussen (press agent for the line) and Julius P. Meyer (a director) very much involved. Doerries, *Imperial Challenge,* 41, 53, 259n.12.

277. Aitken, *Continuous Wave,* 286–287. It did so under the authority of the Radio Act of 1912. Sidak, *Foreign Investment,* 44.

278. Both the proclamation and the April 5, 1917, letter from Jesse S. Phillips, Superintendent of Insurance, New York State; Frank H. Harrison, Insurance Commissioner, State of Massachusetts; and Burton Mansfield, Insurance Commissioner, State of Connecticut, are in RG 56, Entry 406, Box 1, National Archives.

279. On all of this, see data in Harry Epstein to R. G. Cholmeley-Jones, Oct. 25, 1920, RG 56, Entry 406, Box 11. A copy of the July 13, 1917, proclamation is published in Gephart, *Effects of the War upon Insurance,* 20–21.

280. Congress approved the Espionage Act, June 15, 1917, which (among its provisions) prohibited the export of coin or bullion, except under regulations to be issued by

the president. An executive order of September 7, 1917, directed that the regulations should be administered by the secretary of the treasury. An executive order of January 26, 1918, transferred to the Federal Reserve Board full authority to regulate foreign exchange dealings and the export of bullion. The aim was to assure that there would be no transfers that would benefit the enemy. The U.S. Treasury carried on separate operations to stabilize exchange rates. The period of "active control" over foreign exchange by the Federal Reserve was February 20, 1918, to June 25, 1919. *Federal Reserve Bulletin,* Dec. 1921, 1400. For further details on the regulations and the full text of the president's order of January 26, 1918, see Federal Reserve Board, *Annual Report 1918.*

281. The best report on the authorizations and activities of the Alien Property Custodian is its own 607-page *Annual Report 1918–1919;* I have been citing this as *APC Report.* (Other APC reports are cited with a date provided.) I have also used material in RG 131, National Archives. An "enemy" was defined by residence in the territory of the enemy. *APC Report,* 7.

282. For a brief biography of Garvan, see Haynes, *American Chemical Industry,* III, 260n.

283. *APC Report,* 156–162.

284. Ibid., 9.

285. After the war was over, in 1923, the Marquise Adele Carcano, who claimed to be an Italian subject, then residing in Paris, filed suit to recover $30,000 worth of Union Pacific Railroad bonds that were purchased on her behalf by the Disconto-Gesellschaft in 1913 and left with Kuhn, Loeb, which mistakenly (according to the marquise) surrendered the bonds to the APC as being enemy owned. See *New York Times,* Jan. 4, 1923. German banks were active in Italy (data from Peter Hertner), and markets in American securities were international; it is not at all implausible that in 1913 Disconto-Gesellschaft might well have put Italians into American railroad securities. (Italy was of course an "ally" in World War I.)

286. According to the *New York Times,* Mar. 16, 1918, there were about 100 volumes containing 40,000 documents in the New York office of the Deutsche Bank. The records provided details on German investments in the United States. See ibid., Nov. 3, 1918. My active efforts notwithstanding, I have failed to locate these documents or uncover what happened to them. I know of no historian who has used these records. I could not find them in RG 131 or in New York State archives. The historians of the Deutsche Bank never used this collection.

287. *APC Report,* 9.

288. Office of Alien Property Custodian, *Annual Report for the Period Mar. 11, 1942 to June 30, 1943,* 94. The amount was always ill-defined. Thus, in the Office of Alien Property Custodian, *Annual Report for the Year-ended June 30, 1944,* 142, the "enemy property" seized by the APC during and immediately after World War I was valued at about $534 million!

289. Federal Reserve Board, *Annual Report 1918,* 51 (this is the first usage in this context that I have seen of the term "cloak," which word came to symbolize the disguises used by foreign, particularly German, investors). There was suspected Dutch cloaking. The Nederlandsche Overzee Trustmaatschappij was called on to verify foreign ownership. Two 1918 transactions (involving Swift & Co. and Gulf States Steel Co.) related to stock dividends issued to holders of the securities in Holland. NOT had to verify that the stock was held by Dutch citizens before the stock dividends could be issued. A third 1918 transaction was associated with a 6 percent ten-year note issue of Union Pacific, sold by a syndicate headed by Kuhn, Loeb & Co. Nederlandsch Administratie en Trustkantoor issued certificates for these notes; the certificates could only be issued after a check by NOT. *Van Oss' Effectenboek 1918/19* and data from A. J. Veenendaal. On Swiss cloaking of German direct investments, see earlier discussion and Mira Wilkins, "Swiss Invest-

ments in the United States 1914–1945," in *La Suisse et les Grandes puissances 1914–1945,* ed. Sébastien Guex (Geneva: Droz, 1999), 101–102, 105.

290. The separation in functions is obvious when one looks at the autobiography and biography of McAdoo (*Crowded Years* and Broesamle, *William Gibbs McAdoo*); neither book has the Alien Property Custodian in its index.

291. *APC Report,* 10.

292. Ibid., 14.

293. See Wilkins, *History,* chap. 16, for the negligible reactions.

294. *APC Report,* 15. The APC spent an immense amount of time making sure that the newly Americanized ventures not only would have access to the technology but also would have rights under the appropriate patents (in some cases, the patents were German owned and had not been assigned to affiliates in the United States); the APC did not want to sell German companies to Americans, "divested of their chief assets," i.e., access to German patented technology. See *APC Report,* 240–241, 181–188. Ibid., 437–471 (for lists of patents and royalties received by the APC).

295. Ibid., 48; *APC Report, 1922,* 87. The actual APC sale was Dec. 12, 1918, *after* the Armistice.

296. *APC Report,* 50–51.

297. Mahoney, *Merchants of Life,* 194.

298. See data on Orenstein–Arthur Koppel Co. in RG 131, National Archives, and *APC Report,* 219. The properties went to the American buyers for $1.3 million.

299. Alfred D. Chandler, Jr., *Scale and Scope* (Cambridge, Mass.: Harvard University Press, 1990), 178, 639; Wilkins, *History,* 426, 836n.73; David T. Beito, "Andrew Mellon," in *Banking and Finance, 1913–1989,* ed. Larry Schweikart (New York: Facts on File, 1990), 272; *APC Report,* 219 (the purchase price was $302,250).

300. As allowed under the president's proclamations of April 6 and July 13, 1917 (see earlier in this section of this chapter).

301. *The Standard,* Boston, Aug. 4, 1917. RG 56, Entry 406, Box 6, contains protests from around the country on the licensing of German insurance companies.

302. See Harry Epstein to R. G. Cholmeley-Jones, Oct. 25, 1920, RG 56, Entry 406, Box 11, which has lists of the companies affected. A copy of the Nov. 26, 1917, announcement is in RG 56, Entry 406, Box 20. Box 8 contains an unsigned memorandum, possibly from Hendon Chubb to the secretary of the treasury, Nov. 15, 1917, indicating that he thought the operations of the German insurers could be discontinued without substantial disruption.

303. *Best's Insurance Reports 1919, Fire and Marine Insurance,* 517–521, 468; *APC Report,* 435; and, most valuable, data in RG 56, Entry 406, esp. Epstein to Cholmeley-Jones, Oct. 25, 1920. "Liquidating licenses" were issued November 27, 1917, by the *secretary of the treasury.* After the Armistice, the licenses were revoked (on November 18, 1918), and the APC took over the assets and continued the liquidation process. Because of "the highly technical character of insurance business and insurance property," the APC appointed two advisory committees, one for fire and marine insurance and the second for life insurance matters, to advise it. The members of the first committee included Jesse S. Phillips, superintendent of insurance for New York State, along with representatives from several American insurance companies; the second committee was made up of executives from American life insurance companies. See *APC Report,* 190–198.

304. *APC Report,* 126–127, 15.

305. The process of APC sales and liquidation of enemy properties had, however, barely begun at the time of the Armistice. Most of the actual disposition of the enemy assets took place after November 1918.

306. On the so-called headquarters effect, where technology remains with the parent, see Edward M. Graham and Paul R. Krugman, *Foreign Direct Investment in the United*

States (Washington, D.C.: Institute for International Economics, 1989), 52–53. See also ibid., chap. 5, on "FDI and National Security in Time of War."

307. *1922 Dye Hearings,* 816. Hoechst had imported the vat dyes that were not made in America.

308. *APC Report,* 134–137.

309. For background, see Wilkins, *History,* 469.

310. Carosso, *Investment Banking,* 220–221. For the plight of the railroads and McAdoo as director-general, see McAdoo, *Crowded Years,* 446–495. Railroad securities that had been deposited with the American Dollar Securities Committee were now sold to the latter.

311. Total foreign ownership of U.S. Steel's common shares dropped from 494,338 (March 31, 1917) to 491,580 (December 31, 1918), or from 9.72 to 9.68 percent. (The English ownership drop in that period was from 188,146 to 172,453 shares; Canadian ownership actually increased from 39,777 shares to 45,613 shares.) *Commercial and Financial Chronicle,* Apr. 21, 1917, 1548, and July 19, 1924, 285–286.

312. In 1917, the purchases of securities by the committee were very heavy and included many securities that had earlier been deposited (i.e., borrowed); the securities were in many cases delivered in New York rather than London. They went directly to J. P. Morgan & Co. *Final Report,* 11814.

313. *1919 Report of American Dollar Securities Committee,* 9. Appendix D (pp. 20–57) lists 1,421 different bonds, while (pp. 57–63) list 389 different shares. While railroads predominated, the second-largest category would be industrials; Cleona Lewis estimated that roughly 10 percent of the securities were those of power and light and telecommunications companies. Lewis, *America's Stake,* 77, 73.

314. The demand loan from Morgan *began in* May 1916 and fluctuated in size. Proceeds from the large publicly issued collateralized loans in September and October 1916 and January 1917 had been used to pay off much of the initial demand loan, but the latter's size had grown before U.S. entry into the war. Kathleen Burk, "Anglo-American Finance during World War I," in *Mobilization for Total War,* ed. W. F. Dreisziger (Waterloo, Ont.: Wilfrid Laurier University Press, 1981), 39–40. U.S. Secretary of the Treasury William G. McAdoo disliked the idea of Britain selling the collateral, for he thought that this would absorb funds that would otherwise go into U.S. liberty bonds. Burk, *Britain, America,* 218. According to Grady, *British War Finance,* 132–134, when the American loan of September 1916 matured in September 1918, $50 million of the amount was paid off by the sale of collateral. Remember, the collateral was made up of securities that the British government had both purchased and borrowed from its nationals. Typically, U.S. *government* lending had no collateral. It was based on the good faith of borrowing governments.

315. Van Manen, *De Nederlandsche Overzee Trustmaatschappij,* VIII, Appendices, 564 and 580, contain figures for 1917–1918 that show a net drop in the nominal value of Dutch holdings of American securities by $7.9 million. For information on the U.S. companies in the Dutch market, I am indebted to A. J. Veenendaal, who derived this information from *Van Oss Effectenbock 1917/18.* All three U.S. companies had tapped European capital markets in the prewar years. In Augustus J. Veenendaal, *Slow Train to Paradise* (Stanford, Calif.: Stanford University Press, 1996), v, he suggests that in 1917–1918, there were large sales of German-held American securities through Amsterdam, which makes the data on "Dutch" investments in American securities extremely unreliable.

316. Federal Reserve Board, *Annual Report 1917,* 18, notes "the continuous return of our securities from Europe" but provides no figures. Foreign exchange transactions in American securities bought from foreigners, February 1918 to December 1918, totaled only $240 million, which was less than the $289 million in foreign exchange transactions relating to American securities sold to foreigners in that period. *Federal Reserve Bulletin,* May 1922, 544. In 1916, the Federal Reserve had estimated that in 1917 $103 million and in 1918 $260

million of "European obligations held in the United States would mature." *Federal Reserve Bulletin,* Nov. 1, 1916, 592. With foreign exchange controls, all transactions were monitored, but there was no interference. Ivar Kreuger's biographer writes of Kreuger's purchases of dollars in 1918 (with Swedish kroner). He held these for about two years (the biographer says nothing on how the dollars were invested in that period); when he sold the dollars, he made huge foreign exchange profits, since the dollar had appreciated vis-à-vis the kroner. Robert Shaplen, *Kreuger* (New York: Alfred A. Knopf, 1960), 51. Were there others who similarly speculated against European currencies? The record is not available, albeit the February 1918 to December 1918 monitoring of foreign exchange transactions in relation to American securities—see earlier discussion—would suggest this. Undoubtedly, the Dutch purchases of American securities in 1918 represented a portion of those purchases (the AT&T issue was $50 million, seven-year, 6 percent convertible gold bonds, offered by Ed. Dentz & Co. and Westendorp & Ten Kate in Amsterdam). The offering, however, was far larger than the securities actually purchased, much less sent to Holland in 1918; those sent, according to van Manen, *De Nederlandsche Overzee Trustmaatschappij,* VIII, 580, totaled a mere £176,885 or about $1.3 million.

317. On Fiat in America, see Wilkins, *History,* 420, 834n.36. On the 1918 sale, see Louis T. Wells, "Automobiles," in *Big Business and the State,* ed. Raymond Vernon (Cambridge, Mass.: Harvard University Press, 1974), 231, 295.

318. Scottish American Mortgage Co., *Annual Report,* Aug. 1, 1915; Gilbert, *History of Investment Trusts,* 106; and Lewis, *America's Stake,* 118–119 (on southern farm loans, including those to cotton farmers).

319. Jackson, *Enterprising Scot,* 278. The Texas Land & Mortgage Co.'s loans on mortgages in Texas were, however, lower at year end, March 31, 1918, than in the prior year (£695,953 v. £752,459), but at the year end March 31, 1919, the amounts were up to £737,233. Texas Land & Mortgage Co., *Reports,* Z-G-1, Reel 284, Bancroft Library, University of California, Berkeley, California.

320. Jackson, *Enterprising Scot,* 279.

321. In 1917 (after Lever acquired A. & F. Pears, Ltd., in Britain), Lever Brothers in America began to manufacture Pears' soap at its Boston Works. Pears' Soap, which had been widely and impressively advertised, had a long and important niche market in America. Wilkins, *History,* 344, 804. The wartime growth of Lever business in the United States was dramatic. Its U.S. sales, which had been $843,466 in 1913, soared to $9,692,743 in 1918. Lever in the United States employed 156 people at year end 1913, 315 at year end 1916, and 740 by year end 1918. "Historical File," Unilever PLC, London.

322. Coleman, *Courtaulds,* II, 140. The first was in Pennsylvania.

323. Ibid., II, 142–143, 152.

324. On Clark Thread Co. and Florida Manufacturing Co. activities, see Minute Books, George A. Clark Bros.–Clark Thread Co., Clark Thread Co. Directors meetings, May 18, 1917, Nov. 5, 1917 (capital raised), Nov. 19, 1917, and July 17, 1918 (Fla. Mfg. Co. dissolved), UGD 199/5/1/1; and on J. & P. Coats, in general, J. & P. Coats, Minute Book 2, July 25, 1917, and Aug. 29, 1917 (decision to sell Fla. Mfg. Co. and quote), UGD 199/1/1/3—both sets of minute books in Archives, University of Glasgow, Glasgow, Scotland. See also Kim, "British Multinational Enterprise," 540, 546–547. According to Kim (ibid., 540, 547), J. & P. Coats acquired its controlling interesting in Florida Manufacturing Co.—a raw cotton supplier, located in Madison, Florida (near the Georgia border)—in 1899 for £192,000. For more on Florida Manufacturing Co., see Wilkins, *History,* 815n.130 (Kim makes it clear that Fine Cotton Spinners' and Doublers' Association's [FCSDA's] investment was tiny compared with that of Coats). Kim writes ("British Multinational Enterprise," 547) that in 1908 J. & P. Coats had purchased (for £10,000) land to grow cotton in Florida and Georgia. It is not clear whether these lands were sold when the

"plant" of Florida Manufacturing Co. was disposed of. According to Kim and my sources as well, the name notwithstanding, Florida Manufacturing Co.'s plant was a facility to process raw cotton—not a textile mill. While the records do not reveal this, my "guess" is that the increased capital of Clark Thread not only reflected the larger business and the rationalization but also was a response to the new tax environment.

325. Chandler, *Scale and Scope,* 640 (it ranked number 128). On its wartime activities, see Haynes, *American Chemical Industry,* III, 46.

326. Haynes, *American Chemical Industry,* III, 48.

327. Tweedale, *Sheffield Steel and America,* 80, 222n, 96.

328. Works Progress Administration, "History of Milltown," 31.

329. Haynes, *American Chemical Industry,* II, 159.

330. Ibid., III, 86–87, and Wilkins, *Maturing,* 10n.

331. Lundström, "Swedish Multinational Growth," 149. This company was an important supplier to SKF, which, as noted, had started U.S. production in 1916.

332. Haynes, *American Chemical Industry,* III, 376. The company made a cellulose acetate coating (called "dope") for the fabric covering the outer skin of airplanes. Its British parent got financial support from the British government to manufacture in Britain (and presumably in the United States as well).

333. U.S. Federal Trade Commission, *Milk and Milk Products,* 56–61; Jean Heer, *World Events 1866–1966: The First Hundred Years of Nestlé* (Rivaz, Switzerland, 1966), 130, 117–119.

334. I am indebted to Himmel Nutrition, Inc., Aug. 28, 1993, for data on Ovaltine's early history in the United States. The product was first brought to America in 1904.

335. Marshall, Southard, and Taylor, *Canadian-American Industry,* 178.

336. For details, see Epstein to Cholmeley-Jones, Oct. 25, 1920, RG 56, Entry 406, Box 11, and other materials in RG 56, Entry 406. Box 11 has a list—as of September 15, 1919—of all foreign companies other than enemy companies licensed to do business in the United States under the Trading with the Enemy Act. The numbers are larger than those given in Table 1.10—as of December 31, 1918. I got the latter from a page-by-page tabulation of data in *Best's Insurance Reports, Fire and Marine,* The lists in RG 56, Entry 406, include foreign insurers other than those in fire and marine. The Chinese and New Zealand companies are included in the U.S. Treasury list under "Great Britain." Box 2 has the application for license forms and the rules. Box 3 has a copy of the executive order of December 7, 1917.

337. The only "exits" were of enemy-owned firms, the thirteen German, the two large Bulgarian, and the one Austrian insurers (and reinsurers). On the substantial gains of British insurance companies in the United States after U.S. entry into the war, see G. Clayton, *British Insurance* (London: Elek Books, 1971), 151.

338. *Best's Insurance Reports, 1919, Fire and Marine.*

339. See H. W. Nichols, "Memorandum re: Norwegian Insurance Companies," Oct. 16, 1919, RG 56, Entry 406, Box 10. I did not find any comparable discussion on the new Danish entries, but these were fewer in number.

340. Nobuo Kawabe, "Japanese Business in the United States before World War II: The Case of Mitsubishi Shoji Kaisha, the San Francisco and Seattle Branches," Ph.D. diss., Ohio State University, 1980, 30–34.

341. Ibid., 74, 97. See also Safford, *Wilsonian Maritime Diplomacy,* 127–137, for the steel embargo and then the release of steel.

342. *Commercial and Financial Chronicle,* Sept. 15, 1917, 1047.

343. U.S.-Japanese relationships were far from harmonious—with tensions arising over shipping matters. Safford, *Wilsonian Maritime Diplomacy,* 127–140. Americans saw the Japanese as taking advantage of wartime conditions to dominate the Pacific commercial trade.

344. These "agencies" were direct investments; New York state law prohibited branches. Taiwan was a Japanese colony, and the Bank of Taiwan was Japanese. On Japanese business in the United States, see Mira Wilkins, "Japanese Multinationals in the United States: Continuity and Change, 1879–1990," *Business History Review,* 64 (Winter 1990): 590–591. RG 131, National Archives, contains the records of the Yokohama Specie Bank's Seattle branch. I am indebted to Professor Y. Homma for information from these records.

345. On the U.S. rules before 1913, see Mira Wilkins, "Foreign Banks and Foreign Investment in the United States," in *International Banking 1870–1914,* ed. Rondo Cameron and V. I. Bovykin (Oxford: Oxford University Press, 1991), 247–248. On the rules and changes in them, Clyde William Phelps, *The Foreign Expansion of American Banks* (New York: Ronald Press, 1927), is excellent.

346. Frederick Huth & Co.'s major involvements in U.S. trade had begun in the 1830s, although it had participated earlier. See Joseph Robert Freedman, "A London Merchant Banker in Anglo-American Trade and Finance, 1835–1850," Ph.D. diss., University of London, 1969, for the extensive early involvements. On its 1917 New York house, see Sayers, *Bank of England,* I, 269n, and Phelps, *Foreign Expansion of American Banks,* 201n.

347. On Baring's early history in America, see Ralph W. Hidy, *The House of Baring in American Trade and Finance 1763–1861* (Cambridge, Mass.: Harvard University Press, 1949). In 1899 Baring Brothers had taken part with Kidder Peabody, Boston, in the presentation in London of securities of the New England Cotton Yarn Company (NECY). Baring Brothers retained a block of shares in this enterprise. NECY was unsuccessful, and by the end of 1917 had sold its physical properties, investing the receipts in securities, often of the spun-off companies. NECY changed its name in 1918 to New England Investment Company. Wilkins, *History,* 360, 811n.64; Vincent P. Carosso, *More Than a Century of Investment Banking: The Kidder, Peabody & Co. Story* (New York: McGraw-Hill, 1979), 58–60; John Orbell, *Baring Brothers & Co. Ltd.* (London: Baring Brothers, 1985), 66–67; and Philip Ziegler, *The Sixth Great Power* (New York: Alfred A. Knopf, 1988), 340.

348. Certain American ships—not government owned—were also authorized to buy previously leased radio transmitters, and, once again, Marconi had no choice but to sell. Aitken, *Continuous Wave,* 286–287.

349. Ibid., 293–300, 312–314.

350. Safford, *Wilsonian Maritime Diplomacy,* 108. On the earlier foreign investment in IMM, see Wilkins, *History,* 518–519.

351. Safford, *Wilsonian Maritime Diplomacy,* 124–127, 136.

352. Beaton, *Enterprise in Oil.*

353. Cheever, *House of Morrell,* 171.

354. Details of the transaction are described in U.S. Department of the Treasury, *Annual Report for Year-ended June 30, 1919,* 66.

355. The Trading with the Enemy Act (1917), Section 5b, gave the president broad powers over international financial transactions in time of war. In 1933, when Franklin Roosevelt declared a national emergency and ordered a bank holiday, he cited as his authority Section 5b of this act. At once, to ratify Roosevelt's action, Congress passed the Emergency Banking Act of 1933, which (retroactively) amended Section 5b to allow the latter to be used by the president in peacetime if he declared a national emergency. Barry E. Carter, *International Economic Sanctions* (Cambridge: Cambridge University Press, 1988), 186.

356. See Wilkins, *History,* 31–36. All the newly issued foreign-acquired U.S. federal government bonds throughout the nineteenth and the twentieth century (up to this point) had been dollar denominated.

357. Within a year, about half of the obligations had been paid off; the rest were paid

off in the next fiscal year. U.S. Department of the Treasury, *Annual Report for Year-ended June 30, 1919,* 66, and *Annual Report for Year-ended June 30, 1920,* 68–69.

358. I first learned of these "peseta bonds" from Robert V. Roosa, September 19, 1987. They were the precedent for the Roosa bonds of 1962. (Roosa used the authority of the 1917 Trading with the Enemy Act.)

359. W. P. G. Harding, "The Results of the European War on America's Financial Position," *Annals of the American Academy of Political and Social Science,* 60 (July 1915): 137. The first governor of the Federal Reserve (Charles Hamlin) served from 1914 to 1916; Harding, on the board in 1914, was governor from 1916 to 1922.

360. The rise of American lending abroad is documented in many places. See, for example, Madden, Nadler, and Sauvain, *America's Experience as a Creditor Nation,* chap. 3. For the expansion of U.S. direct investments, see Wilkins, *Maturing,* chap. 1.

361. The British resident, William Waldorf Astor, for example, had set up in 1916 two trusts (amounting to $25 million in American stocks and bond) for his heirs. The trusts were to avoid the British government mobilization of dollar securities. Virginia Cowles, *The Astors* (London: Weidenfeld & Nicholson, 1979), 170, 189.

362. *Final Report,* 11806.

363. On February 26, 1919, Bankers Trust Co. sent to France part of a shipment of between $100 million and $125 million of securities that had been held as collateral. *Commercial and Financial Chronicle,* Mar. 1, 1919, 822.

364. Burk, "Anglo-American Finance," 39–40. Burk describes American securities as "hostages in the conflict between the British and American treasuries from 1918 to 1923," when Britain finally agreed to a schedule for the repayment of its inter-Allied governmental war debts. Only then (in 1923) were the last of the wartime-held securities finally returned to the British government.

365. The conclusions on the Dutch investors are based on data from Van Oss, *Effectenbock 1918/1919,* assembled for me by A. J. Veenendaal. The conclusions on Swiss investment are the result of my general research. See Record of Benj. Strong trip to Britain, Mar. 18, 1916, 1000.2 Strong Papers, FRBNY, on the transfers; these same securities floated about Europe after the war.

366. Indeed, some foreign investors "hoarded" their American securities. As Benjamin Strong wrote Secretary of the Treasury William G. McAdoo, Aug. 2, 1915, "In the hands of European holders American securities are virtually the same as gold and many holders will hoard them." *Nye Committee Hearings,* pt. 30 (Exh. 3124), 9532. As it turned out, fewer hoarded than Strong expected in 1915, but some did and continued to do so through the war.

367. When foreign direct investors borrowed *in America* or when they reinvested profits, this increased their assets and at the same time the liabilities of the affiliate to its parent, serving to raise the level of the foreign direct investment in the United States.

368. Sturmey, *British Shipping,* 130 (1913 percentage, "shipping in American trades"), 37 (1919: global "shipping tonnage": United Kingdom 16.3 percent; United States 9.8 percent). In global trade, in 1914 the figures were United Kingdom 18.9 percent, Germany 5.1 percent, and United States and Norway each 2.0 percent. Ibid., 37. Richard Sicotte, "Economic Crisis and Political Response: The Political Economy of the Shipping Act," *Journal of Economic History,* 59 (Dec. 1999): 861, is my source for the 1918 figure on American-flag ships.

369. Safford, *Wilsonian Maritime Diplomacy,* 231 (1914 figure).

370. Lewis, *America's Stake,* 136, 558. She did not provide a year end 1918 figure. If common stock is valued at market rather than par, the fall would have been from $4.933 billion to $1.178 billion. In one case the decline was $2.9 billion, and in the second, $2.8 billion. Ibid., 58. Lewis never classified bonds at market.

371. *Commercial and Financial Chronicle,* Oct. 20, 1923, 1740. Foreign holdings of preferred shares of U.S. Steel dropped from 8.7 percent of the total on June 30, 1914, to 4.1 percent on Dec. 31, 1918.

372. See *Federal Reserve Bulletin,* Dec. 1921, 1400, and ibid., May 1922, 533, 547. I got the $1,640,754,000 figure by adding $378,256,000 (American-issued dollar securities held in the United States for the British government), plus $19,433,000 (American-issued sterling securities held in the United States for British government account), plus $1,243,048,000 (American securities held for foreign account, other than that of the British government).

373. Bullock, Williams, and Tucker, "Balance of Trade," 231, 251 (the "interest" as construed by the authors would include "dividends"); Wilkins, *History,* 624 (no major strain before 1914).

2. America's New Role, 1919–1923

1. I use the imprecise dates "late 1980s" for two reasons: one, depending on whether foreign direct investment is measured by historical cost (book value), current cost, or market value, the actual date differs; and two, at various times, the U.S. Department of Commerce has revised its date for the transition. Whatever measure is used (and after the revisions), the transition back to debtor nation occurred in the last half of the 1980s.

2. The phrase "world's financial rentier" is from a New Year's cable, William Harding, Governor of the Federal Reserve Board, to Benjamin Strong, Governor of the Federal Reserve Bank of New York, Dec. 31, 1919, File 790, FRBNY. On the vast U.S. business expansion abroad, see Wilkins, *Maturing.*

3. Brown, *International Gold Standard,* I, 551 and 606; see also Royal Institute of International Affairs, *The Problem of International Investment* (London: Oxford University Press, 1937), 66.

4. See Appendix 2 for more on my sources.

5. On U.S. foreign investment ratios, see Wilkins, *Maturing,* 30, 53–54; these figures exclude U.S. government intergovernmental lending. Cleona Lewis puts these World War I obligations (intergovernmental credits) at $11.7 billion in 1929. Lewis, *America's Stake,* 450. I am indebted to Robert Lipsey for first suggesting to me this difference between inward and outward investment. There was no comparable American obligation to foreign governments, albeit foreign governments did invest in the United States in both government and nongovernment securities.

6. See Appendix 2 (d) on how common and preferred stocks, as well as bonds, were recorded.

7. Although most of America's interwar foreign obligations were denominated in dollars, to use the proceeds after redemption and to obtain income from them, foreigners would have to purchase their own currencies. Accordingly, currency fluctuations affected foreign investors' decisions to buy and sell and thus affected the level of foreign investments in the United States. Also, if one uses foreign—non-U.S.—statistics on foreign investments in the United States, which I did not in Table 2.1, these must be translated into dollars. I have found extremely useful R. L. Bidwell, *Currency Conversion Tables* (London: Rex Collings, 1970).

8. U.S. Department of the Treasury, *Census of Foreign-Owned Assets in the United States* (Washington, D.C., 1945), 41–42 (henceforth cited as *1941 Census*); the federal, state, and local government figure is based on data from Form TFR-300 (the *1941 Census* also gave other estimates); the total and percentage are based on the first set of figures in Table 2.1 for 1941. Of course, information on foreign holdings in 1941 tells us nothing

about such holdings in the 1920s and 1930s; Amos Taylor wrote, "Since the war Government bonds have not formed an important part of foreign investments in this country." U.S. Department of Commerce, Bureau of Foreign and Domestic Commerce, *Foreign Investments in the United States* (1937), 77.

9. See Appendix 2 (e) for how these "foreign" securities were handled in the assembled statistics.

10. American-issued foreign bonds moved "to and fro." Carl Iversen, *Aspects of the Theory of International Capital Movements* (1935; rept. New York: Augustus M. Kelley, 1967), 30. The same was true of American-issued domestic securities. C. H. Feinstein and K. Watson, "Private International Capital Flows in Europe in the Inter-war Period," in *Banking, Currency, and Finance in Europe between the Wars,* ed. Charles H. Feinstein (Oxford: Clarendon Press, 1995), 112–113, note that in the 1920s before the stabilization of French, Belgian, Italian, and other currencies, there was substantial capital flight from these countries; a large "escape" from the French franc occurred in 1924 and 1925, despite the laws forbidding capital exports. In the 1930s, capital flight accelerated. Over the years, a sizable amount of the flight capital went to the United States and was invested in traded securities.

11. Lewis, *America's Stake,* 588, shows that in 1924, foreign-owned stock holdings already exceeded those of bonds; the ratio was 1.33 (with common stock at market and preferred shares and bonds at par). Although shares dropped in value with the stock market crash, this did not make bonds relatively more attractive, since there were also sizable bond defaults.

12. Ibid., 134–140.

13. U.S. Department of Commerce, Bureau of Foreign and Domestic Commerce, *Foreign Long-Term Investments in the United States 1937–1939* (Washington, D.C., 1940), 22, henceforth cited as *FIUS-1940* (I subtracted $117 million from the $3,808 million common and preferred shares to put preferred shares at market; common shares were given at market).

14. Cited in Arthur I. Bloomfield, *Capital Imports and the American Balance of Payments 1934–1939* (1950; rpt. New York: Kelley, 1966), 88n.

15. In 1937 the market value of foreign holdings of common stock of railroads was less than 5 percent of all U.S. foreign investments in common stock. *FIUS-1940,* 27, 70–71. See Chapter 8 for 1941 details.

16. The data that I do have for 1937–1941 are not comparable to the figures of Cleona Lewis, provided in Table 2.2, which is the reason that the table goes only to 1935.

17. On measures of FDI, see Appendix 2 (d) and 2 (f).

18. On the other hand, during 1941, the British wanted to measure British direct investments in the United States by "liquidation" value; the British argued that the liquidation value of these investments, divorced from their parents, was substantially less than their book value. Compilers of the 1941 census (published in 1945) also thought the 1941 book value "might be" more than the market value. *1941 Census,* 59.

19. Column 6, Table 2.1, indicates a rise in FDI in 1939–1940 (and, if we include Column 8, a continuing rise during the first half of 1941). However, comparing Columns 7 and 8 suggests a decline from 1939 to June 1941. I think there was probably a rise in FDI from 1939 to June 1941.

20. I have uncovered many FDIs that the Commerce Department and Cleona Lewis did not know about. The census of 1941 found that the U.S. Department of Commerce had omitted (because it was unaware of them) a large number of direct investments. The Treasury Department's definition used in the census differed from the earlier Commerce Department one, but the larger level of FDI identified lay in discovery, not in definition.

21. Based on Robert Sammons' figures (Column 7, Table 2.1) and my own for 1914, which are provided in Chapter 1. Based on other figures, it never surpassed the 1914 level.

22. The 1914 and 1926 figures are from different series. The comparisons are to give a general picture. A wholesale price index with 1926 as 100 put 1914 at 68.

23. Except for 1918, the figures are those of the U.S. Department of Commerce. Later Table 7.3 shows how mid-1937 differed in the Commerce Department calculations from the December 31, 1937, levels, provided in Table 2.4.

24. The size of British investments in the United States in the interwar period was very differently estimated on the two sides of the Atlantic, with U.S. estimates *always* above the British ones. On British estimates, see Appendix 2 (b).

25. R. C. O. Matthews, C. H. Feinstein, and J. C. Odling-Smee, *British Economic Growth 1856–1973* (Stanford, Calif.: Stanford University Press, 1982), 472.

26. See December 1930 figures in Robert M. Kindersley, "British Overseas Investments," *Economic Journal*, 43 (June 1933): 199–200, but Kindersley always underestimated British investments in the United States. The Royal Institute of International Affairs, *Problem of International Investment* (1937), 84, argued that the British tended to prefer Empire and sterling-bloc borrowers. So, too, students of British direct investment abroad have written that throughout the interwar period there was a notable shift away from U.S. investment toward the Commonwealth; see John M. Stopford, "The Origins of British-Based Multinational Manufacturing Enterprise," *Business History Review*, 48 (Autumn 1974): 326, 333; Geoffrey Jones, *British Multinationals: Origins, Management, and Performance* (Aldershot: Gower, 1986), 17; and Stephen Nicholas, "Location Choice, Performance and the Growth of British Multinational Firms," *Business History*, 31 (July 1989): 127. These conclusions have been made even though there were *no* contemporary British attempts to provide systematic figures on British direct investments. Tom Houston and John H. Dunning, *UK Industry Abroad* (London: Financial Times, 1976), 112, later estimated that excluding oil companies, banks, and insurance firms (which were some of the largest British direct investors overseas), British "direct assets" worldwide at year end 1929 equaled £1,551 million ($7,537 million), of which a mere 2.1 percent (£32.6 million—or $158.4 million) was in the United States. They found 6.1 percent of the total in South Africa, 5.2 percent in Canada, and 4.8 percent in Australia. Their figure for the Indian subcontinent was 9.3 percent. Their U.S. estimate was based on data in the *Economist* and from Kindersley, i.e., British sources. The U.S. Department of Commerce estimated total (FPI plus FDI) British investment in the United States in 1929 was $1.56 billion (see Table 2.4); it gave no separate estimate of British direct investment in the United States in 1929.

27. As an example of the discrepancies between British and American estimates, the Bank of England put the "nominal value" of American securities held by U.K. investors in 1938 at £268 million (ca. $1,240 million)—and gave no figure for FDI. The U.S. Department of Commerce (see Table 2.4) put the long-term British investments in America at year end 1938 at $2,500 million. Cleona Lewis (in her *Debtor and Creditor Countries: 1938, 1944* [Washington, D.C.: Brookings Institution, 1945], 73–74) selected for her "1938 figure" the number that the Commerce Department had given for mid-1937 (see Table 7.3), or $2,743 million. In ibid., she also gave for 1938 U.K. investment in India as $2,725 million, in Canada $2,685 million, in Australia $2,650 million, and in Argentina $1,950 million, which meant the United States as a single country was in first place in her tables. My own reading of the evidence would probably put the United States after India, Canada, and Australia in 1938 as a locale for British investments—but I am uncertain. William Woodruff, *Impact of Western Man* (Washington, D.C.: University Press of America, 1966), 156–157, put the locales of U.K. investment abroad in 1938 as India (including Ceylon and Burma), $3,050 million; United States, $2,750 million (second place); Canada, $2,700 million; Australia, $2,650 million; and Argentina, $1,950. Woodruff, like Lewis, used the Commerce Department's mid-1937 number for year end 1938.

28. The reversal could have been after 1933 rather than 1935. One cannot tell from the figures provided in Tables 2.5 and 2.6. The overall pattern of British diversification away from American securities, 1923–1928, was also apparent in U.S. Securities and Exchange Commission, *Investment Trusts in Great Britain,* H. Doc. 380, 76th Cong., 1st sess. (1939), 48–49, but in the 1920s (according to this source, which relied on the *Economist,* Jan. 1, 1929), the sample of British investment trusts shifted investments not to the British Empire but to central Europe. So, too, data from the *Economist,* Feb. 15, 1930, 347, show that whereas the share of U.S. investments of the twenty-six sampled British investment trusts declined from 17.7 percent in 1923 to 9.9 percent in 1929, those in Europe rose from 4.5 percent to 17.2 percent (this is based on book value of holdings). According to the *Economist,* Nov. 20, 1937, 359, postwar reconstruction had revived British investors' interest in the European continent, an interest that was lost because of "recent experience." All these figures are to be looked at with caution. If the figures are calculated by market value, the percentage held in American securities in 1929, 1933, and 1939 is in each case larger than when measured by book value. *Economist,* Dec. 1, 1934, 8; Aug. 12, 1939, 306; H. Burton and D. C. Corner, *Investment and Unit Trusts in Britain and America* (London: Elek Books, 1968), 84.

29. Based on 1935–1939 data in Federal Reserve System, Board of Governors, *Banking and Monetary Statistics* (Washington, D.C., 1943), 626–629.

30. For the 1875–1914 percentages, see Wilkins, *History,* 157. The 5.4 percent figure for December 1930 is in the Royal Institute of International Affairs, *Problem of International Investment,* 142, based on data in Robert Kindersley, "British Overseas Investments in 1931," *Economic Journal,* 43 (June 1933): 200. The 7.5 percent figure is based on data in Bank of England, *United Kingdom Overseas Investments, 1938 to 1948* (London, 1950), 14. Both probably underestimate the amounts of British investment in the United States. Derek H. Aldcroft, *From Versailles to Wall Street* (Berkeley: University of California Press, 1977), 243, gives an estimate for 1930 of the United States' attracting 5 percent of British foreign investment; his source is the Royal Institute of International Affairs, *Problem of International Investment,* 144 (which rounded the 5.4 percentage provided two pages earlier). Alternative percentages from other sources included that in the *Economist,* Nov. 20, 1937: "By 1929 the proportion of our [British] total investment in the United States (not counting direct purchases through Wall Street) had fallen to less than 3 per cent." *But,* of course, one must count "purchases through Wall Street." I believe this 3 percent figure is far too low. Lewis, in her *Debtor and Creditor Countries,* 74, furnished details on British overseas investment in 1938, indicating that the United States attracted almost 12 percent of the British total. We could add other estimates. None indicates that at any time in the interwar years did the U.S. share of British overseas investment approximate the proportions in 1875–1914.

31. On a strictly *bilateral* basis in relation to the United States, Britain was also a debtor, due mainly to the large World War I U.S. government loans. On Germany as a creditor nation in 1914, see Wilkins, *History,* 159; on Germany's foreign obligations in 1930 compared with other debtor nations, see Royal Institute of International Affairs, *Problem of International Investment,* 233.

32. See Guaranty Trust Co. *The Effect of the War on European Neutrals* (New York: Guaranty Trust Co., 1919), 6–10.

33. See, for example, Lewis, *Debtor and Creditor Countries,* 9; United Nations, *International Capital Movements during the Inter-war Period* (Lake Success, N.Y.: United Nations, 1949), 10, 18, 41; Eugene Staley, *War and the Private Investor* (1935; rpt. New York: Howard Fertig, 1967), 533; the *Midland Bank Monthly Review,* Feb.–Mar. 1938, 5 (estimate that one-third of Dutch wealth took the form of investment abroad); and Kornelis Jacobus Walraven, "International Long-Term Capital Movements of the Netherlands in the Post-

war Period, 1946–1956," Ph.D. diss., Syracuse University, 1959, chap. 3 (historical data). Walraven based his historical work on an unpublished 1952 NBER study by Solomon Fabricant and Conrad G. D. Maarschalk on Dutch international capital movements. Walraven suggests that what was liquidated in U.S. investment seems to have been reinvested in the Dutch East Indies (p. 69).

34. Johan de Vries, *The Netherlands Economy in the Twentieth Century* (Assen: van Gorcum, 1978), 2. Others' figures show the Dutch as a net capital importer in 1930–1938, but if the entire 1919–1939 period is taken into account, the Dutch would remain a creditor nation.

35. I am uneasy about this comparison of very fragile data.

36. Wilkins, *History,* 172 (prewar data); Table 2.4 on Dutch investment in the United States; Lewis, *Debtor and Creditor Countries,* 67. For the heavy Dutch investments in the Netherlands East Indies, see Ben P. A. Gales and Keetie E. Sluyterman, "Dutch Free-Standing Companies, 1870–1940," in *The Free-Standing Company in the World Economy, 1830–1996,* ed. Mira Wilkins and Harm Schröter (Oxford: Oxford University Press, 1996), 293–322.

37. Carlo Zacchia, "International Trade and Capital Movements 1920–1970," in *The Twentieth Century—2, The Fontana Economic History of Europe,* vol. 5, ed. Carlo M. Cipolla (New York: Barnes & Noble, 1977), 577; Staley, *War and the Private Investor,* 527; and Lewis, *Debtor and Creditor Countries,* 10.

38. Sparse data on French interwar investments in American securities are in Royal Institute of International Affairs, *Problem of International Investment,* 204–205, 208, 210–213. On French direct investments in America in these years, see Mira Wilkins, "French Multinationals in the United States: An Historical Perspective," *Entreprises et Histoire,* no. 3 (May 1993): 14–29.

39. See Wilkins, "Swiss Investments," 91–139.

40. Lewis, *Debtor and Creditor Countries,* 72.

41. Wilkins, "Swiss Investments," 117–134.

42. Lewis, *Debtor and Creditor Countries,* 76.

43. All the Canadian economic historians, for example, Gregory Marchildon, Graham Taylor, and Robert Cuff, make this point.

44. Wilkins, *History,* 159 (1914 ranking). Table 2.4 for interwar rankings.

45. It is possible that all the growth was not Canadian and that other nationalities (including U.S. residents) were investing through Canadian intermediaries. A U.S. Treasury Department examination (in 1941) of fifty-seven Canadian investors in the United States "known to be of non-Canadian ownership" found the largest number were owned in the United States, followed by France. *1941 Census,* 26. Of course, 1941 data would *not* by any stretch of the imagination reflect the entire interwar period.

46. The one exception was in alcoholic beverages, in the 1930s, after the end to Prohibition.

47. Marshall, Southard, and Taylor, *Canadian-American Industry,* remains the best study of Canadian direct investments in the United States in the interwar years.

48. Ibid., 175.

49. For example, for much of the war, the dollar-pound exchange rate had been pegged at $4.76. The arrangement ended in March 1919, and the pound fell, so that by February 1920 it was at $3.40; there was a recovery, but the pound stayed under $4.00 until the fall of 1921. During 1922, it fluctuated between $4.40 and $4.50, rising as high as $4.70 in the spring of 1923 and then declining to $4.20 at the start of 1924. A. T. K. Grant, *A Study of the Capital Market in Post-war Britain* (London: Macmillan, 1937), 101.

50. John Maynard Keynes believed that Britain should try to get the United States to agree that all interally governmental debts should be canceled. See his memorandum

of March 1919 in Keynes, *Collected Writings,* XVI, esp. 418. The United States rejected the idea. Ibid., 437ff. (April–May 1919 data).

51. On the general problems of post–World War I Europe, see Charles S. Maier, *Recasting Bourgeois Europe* (Princeton, N.J.: Princeton University Press, 1975), and Dan P. Silverman, *Reconstructing Europe after the Great War* (Cambridge, Mass.: Harvard University Press, 1982). For the German crisis, see Gerald D. Feldman, *The Great Disorder: Politics, Economics, and Society in the German Inflation 1914–1924* (New York: Oxford University Press, 1997).

52. There is controversy as to whether the United States "remained on the gold standard while all other countries abandoned it." See Brown, *International Gold Standard,* I, 27–28, 119. It is true—as Brown argues—that the export of gold was subject to license from September 1917 to June 1919 (ibid., 37); actually it was subject to controls from June 1917. Yet Americans met all their gold obligations during wartime (except those to the enemy, which were not considered as "obligations" any longer). And, as Brown notes (p. 119), "no question ever arose in the public mind that the American gold standard 'in its full integrity' . . . was ever in danger." When the Federal Reserve Board on June 9, announced the removal of licensing restrictions, the American Acceptance Council, *Acceptance Bulletin,* 1 (June 1919): 6, triumphantly reported that the United States was the first country since the war to reestablish a free gold market.

53. Benjamin Strong, "Memo," Aug. 30, 1919, 1000.3 Strong Papers, FRBNY, and his 1919 trip journal, 1000.2 Strong Papers, FRBNY.

54. See export figures in U.S. Department of Commerce, Bureau of the Census, *Historical Statistics of the United States* (Washington, D.C., 1960), 537. Continued U.S. government lending helped pay for the surge in exports. Studenski and Krooss, *Financial History of the United States,* 339.

55. Sturmey, *British Shipping,* 37, 130. U.S. ships, however, handled less than 10 percent of *global* trade.

56. London Joint City and Midland Bank, *Monthly Review,* May 31, 1923, 2, commenting on the transformation.

57. William E. Leuchtenburg, *The Perils of Prosperity 1914–1932* (Chicago: University of Chicago Press, 1958), chap. 4 (on the "red scare").

58. *New York Times,* Mar. 20, 1919, quoted in Thomas N. Guinsburg, *The Pursuit of Isolationism* (New York: Garland, 1982), 31. In his inaugural address, President Harding made it clear that the United States would not join the League of Nations: "A world super-government is contrary to everything we cherish and can have no sanction by our Republic." Francis Russell, *The Shadow of Blooming Grove: Warren G. Harding in His Times* (New York: McGraw-Hill, 1968), 14.

59. There is little controversy now on the depth of America's international economic involvements at the end of World War I. Yet there are those who have argued that although the country was economically bound to the rest of the world, politically it retreated into a cocoon; and the U.S. failure to join the League of Nations was symbolic of this withdrawal. See, for example, Wilkins, *Maturing;* in the same spirit, Derek Aldcroft writes of America's postwar "desire to disengage herself as quickly as possible from inter-Allied organizations." Aldcroft, *From Versailles to Wall Street,* 60. Leuchtenburg, *Perils of Prosperity,* 81, argues that Harding's election "meant . . . an end to internationalism," while Robert K. Murray (in *The Harding Era* [Minneapolis: University of Minnesota Press, 1969], 376), writes of Harding's "strong nationalistic outlook." In the 1980s and 1990s, many scholars countered that in the post-World War I years there was more U.S. political engagement in international affairs than in prior times. See, for instance, Robert Dallek, *American Style of Foreign Policy* (New York: Alfred A. Knopf, 1983); Stephen Randall, *United States Foreign Oil Policy 1919–1948* (Kingston: McGill-Queen's University Press, 1985); and

Walter LaFeber, *The American Age* (New York: W. W. Norton, 1989). Emily S. Rosenberg, *Financial Missionaries to the World: The Politics and Culture of Dollar Diplomacy, 1900–1930* (Cambridge, Mass.: Harvard University Press, 1999), describes a very involved State Department. A balanced appraisal by Jeff Frieden documents the divided U.S. policies, with America's foreign economic policy "torn between insularity and internationalism." See Jeff Frieden, "Sectoral Conflict and U.S. Foreign Economic Policy, 1914–1940," *International Organization,* 42 (Winter 1988): 61, for a fine summary of the debate, as of 1988. The matter of what constitutes internationalism considers, for example, whether U.S. government policies supporting U.S. business abroad are "nationalistic" (insular) or "internationalist." Two works that add a great deal to this controversy are Melvyn P. Leffler, *The Elusive Quest: America's Pursuit of European Stability and French Security, 1919–1933* (Chapel Hill: University of North Carolina Press, 1979), and Guinsburg, *Pursuit of Isolationism.* I agree with the view of Barry Eichengreen and Peter B. Kenen, in Peter B. Kenen, ed., *Managing the World Economy* (Washington, D.C.: Institute for International Economics, 1994), 9, that the U.S. government failed to take responsibility for international economic development.

60. I believe that *using* foreign investors in the United States in order to push advantages for American business abroad is part of a nationalist rather than an internationalist approach.

61. Many portfolio investments by Europeans hoarded during wartime seem to have been liquidated in 1919–1920. Letters from August Belmont & Co. to Rothschild Frères in 1919–1920 documented sales on the New York Stock Exchange "for foreign account." See, for example, letters of Dec. 12, 1919, Aug. 27, 1920, Nov. 19, 1920, Dec. 10, 1920, in Boxes 1076/6474, 1077/6475, AQ 132, Archives Nationale, Fontainebleau. Apparently, many Germans sold securities that they had held before the war to American soldiers who had been stationed abroad. Grosvenor Jones, Chief Financial and Investment Division, Bureau of Foreign and Domestic Commerce to S. H. Cross, Mar. 24, 1934. RG 151, 620 Germany, National Archives.

62. In April 1919 there was the repeal of Defence of the Realm Regulation 41D, which had prohibited Britishers' purchasing securities overseas. Restrictions remained (under Regulation 30F) on new overseas issues until November 1919. Between 1920 and 1923, although the Bank of England "controlled" new issues, there was no "legal force behind this control," which depended on the authority of the Bank. Atkin, *British Overseas Investment,* 28–36, 61, and John Michael Atkin, "Official Regulation of British Overseas Investment, 1914–1931," *Economic History Review,* 2nd ser., 23 (Aug. 1970): 324–330. New issues were not, however, the principal way the British invested in the United States in these years.

63. Rufus Tucker, Acting Chief Financial and Investment Division, Bureau of Foreign and Domestic Commerce, June 13, 1924, in RG 151, 620 UK 1919–1927, National Archives (higher taxes for foreign investors). The secondary source literature is full of complaints about double taxation of income. See, for instance, Cowles, *The Astors,* 189. According to *Le Matin,* Jan. 16, 1923, the U.S. Treasury Department had just announced that securities belonging to nonresident foreigners would not be subject to tax. See article enclosed in George S. Messersmith, American Consulate, Antwerp, to U.S. Secretary of State, Jan. 18, 1923, RG 59, 862.503111/1. Despite substantial effort on my part, I have not been able to locate *any* such U.S. Treasury pronouncement, and as far as I can determine the withholding tax on dividends and interest paid to nonresident foreigners—introduced during World War I—continued. As for the capital gains tax, it was on the books but apparently was unenforceable when applied to foreign residents. The Commerce Department concluded in 1923 that the American income tax was "the most important factor" in British investment trusts' sales of their U.S. investments. U.S. Department of Commerce, Bureau of Foreign and Domestic Commerce, *British Investment Trusts,* 32.

64. U.S. Department of the Treasury, *Annual Report for Year-ended June 30, 1920,* 68–69.

65. U.S. Department of the Treasury, *Annual Report for Year-ended June 30, 1922,* 46–47.

66. New York City, which had sizable foreign obligations at the start of World War I, turned to domestic finance. *Van Oss's Effectenboek,* however, in 1918/19 and in 1925 still listed three long-term New York City bonds (maturing between 1960 and 1963), which would imply some of these securities remained in Holland.

67. The published literature on 1919–1929 contains absolutely nothing on foreign investments in American federal, state, or local government securities, except what was in the Treasury Department *Annual Reports* on the use of U.S. bonds to redeem foreign debt. There were undoubtedly some other investments. In 1923, when the U.S. State Department was protesting *Russian* repudiations of its debt, Frank P. Ward of the Defaulted Bondholders' Syndicate (May 16, 1923) scolded the State Department for not paying attention to the repudiated bonds of Arkansas, North Carolina, South Carolina, Mississippi, and Georgia (these were repudiations of the *1840s* and *1870s*). Presumably heirs of earlier owners still held on these securities. The State Department replied—as it had for many years—that this was a matter for state governments and not for the U.S. federal government. See 1923 correspondence in RG 59, 811.51 State Bonds/—, National Archives.

68. National Industrial Conference Board, *International Financial Position of the United States,* 64.

69. Ibid., 64–66. Carosso, *Investment Banking,* 246; Jackson, *Enterprising Scot,* 280, 366 (on the First Scottish American Trust Company's divestments, based on its *Annual Report,* June 25, 1920). See also August Belmont & Co. to Rothschild Frères, Nov. 21, 1920, and Dec. 10, 1920, Box 1077/6475, AQ 132, Archives Nationale, Fontainebleau.

70. Van Manen, *De Nederlandsche Overzee Trustmaatschappij,* VIII, Appendix 564, p. 859, and Appendix 580, p. 8. The exchange rate fluctuated during 1919. It was 2.36 florins to the dollar in January 1919 and 2.67 florins to the dollar in January 1920. See Bidwell, *Currency Conversion Tables,* 30.

71. *Van Oss' Effectenboek 1925* (I am indebted to A. Veenendaal for this information). On the three funds before the First World War, see Wilkins, *History,* 120, 411. The American law firm, the Cravath firm, that had been very active before the First World War in aiding the inflow of foreign moneys into the United States, now found that "it received fewer retainers from foreign bankers and solicitors than in earlier years," which it attributed to the reversed position of America—now creditor rather than debtor nation. Swaine, *Cravath Firm,* II, 440.

72. William Mackenzie to Benjamin Strong, Aug. 21, 1921, 1112.5 Strong Papers, FRBNY; see also Mackenzie to Strong, Apr. 25, 1921, in ibid.

73. Mackenzie to Strong, Dec. 30, 1924, 1112.4 Strong Papers, FRBNY. William Mackenzie was born in 1847; he began his "brilliant career in investment trust finance" in 1874. He was the architect of the important Alliance Trust Co., formed in 1888, and ran the organization for many years. He seems to have retired from the Alliance Trust Co. by the time of this correspondence. Kerr, *Scottish Capital on the American Credit Frontier,* 168–169, 187. The Alliance Trust Co. reduced its U.S. portfolio from 83 percent of the total in 1914 to 16 percent in 1922. See Table 2.5. (The 16 percent was all in stocks and bonds, while the 83 percent included mortgages.)

74. Gilbert, *End of the Road,* 396. Both Mackenzie's and Lord Mount Stephen's securities were probably lent to the American Dollar Securities Committee and returned after the war. See Wilkins, *History,* for Lord Mount Stephen's huge involvements in U.S. railroad investments. Lord Mount Stephen left an estate of £1,414,000; this ranked him as the fifth most wealthy man in Britain to die in 1921. W. D. Rubinstein, "British Millionaires, 1809–1924," *Bulletin of the Institute of Historical Research,* 47 (1974): 215, 217.

75. Gilbert, *End of the Road,* 396.

76. Letter from Augustus J. Veenendaal to Mira Wilkins, Nov. 9, 1989. In 1922 a new Missouri-Kansas-Texas Railroad emerged with a restructured debt. Veenendaal suggests that Dutch holdings continued on. Veenendaal, *Slow Train to Paradise,* 146–147.

77. Swaine, *Cravath Firm,* II, 225.

78. Ibid., II, 114, 307. It is not clear how much of the New York, New Haven, and Hartford loan was still held in Europe. See Chapter 1 on the French government's efforts to realize on franc denominated American securities.

79. A sample of foreign holdings of railroad *shares* indicates a continued decline in holdings, 1919 through 1920, followed by foreign buying of shares in 1921 and then a leveling off of interest. U.S. Department of Commerce, Bureau of Foreign and Domestic Commerce, *Foreign Investments in the United States* (Washington, D.C., 1937), 74. Cleona Lewis believed the liquidation of foreign holdings of American railroad bonds (as distinct from shares) continued at a steady pace 1919–1923. This would probably relate to bonds reaching maturity and being redeemed. Lewis, *America's Stake,* 136, 558.

80. Important New York–headquartered international banking houses continued to specialize in railroad finance. Kuhn, Loeb & Co. in the 1920s was involved in $2.1 billion in railroad issues (compared with $402 million in industrials and $469 million in foreign issues). Kuhn, Loeb & Co., *International Banking through Four Generations* (New York: Kuhn, Loeb, 1955), 23. The correspondence of the French Rothschild bank from 1919 to 1922 indicates a pattern of divestment, but by 1922 the bank still retained American railroad securities. See esp. Boxes 1078/6476 (1920), 1079/6477 (1922), AQ 132.

81. Lewis, *America's Stake,* 558. She shows both the absolute decline in railroad holdings and the relative decline (relative to other inward foreign investments).

82. *Commercial and Financial Chronicle,* July 19, 1924, 285–286, which contains holdings of both common shares and preferred shares. "Stockholders of record" may *not,* however, reveal the *actual* ownership of nonresident foreigners. The securities could be held by American "nominees." Tax considerations might make this desirable.

83. Ibid.

84. Swaine, *Cravath Firm,* II, 243–244. Despite the large percentage this was by 1919 FPI. For the initial investment and the transformation from FDI to FPI, see Wilkins, *History,* 254. The price appears to have been $13 million; see Lewis, *America's Stake,* 101.

85. Donald F. Davis to Mira Wilkins, May 29, 1981, based on data from Studebaker Corporation papers, Discovery Hall Museum, South Bend.

86. Wilkins, *History,* 448.

87. Studebaker shares were included in *Van Oss' Effectenboek* throughout the period covered by this chapter. Studebaker on other occasions apparently sought—at least indirectly—foreign finance. See T. B. Macaulay to William B. McKinley, Jan. 17, 1923, Macaulay letterbooks (ML), Sun Life Assurance Co. Archives, Toronto. Macaulay was chief executive of the Canadian insurance company. U.S. Senator McKinley, Republican from Illinois, was a partner in J. B. & W. B. McKinley, an Illinois banking house. In this 1923 letter, Macaulay wrote McKinley on the conditions of a proposed $16.5 million loan from Sun Life to "Mr. Studebaker's bankers," which would include "the collateral deposit of the mortgage bonds and debentures of the new (or enlarged) company."

88. Youssef Cassis, "Swiss International Banking," in *Banks as Multinationals,* ed. Geoffrey Jones (London: Routledge, 1990), 168; *Moody's Banks 1928,* 2687.

89. Sun Life Assurance Company, *Annual Reports* and Macaulay letterbooks, Sun Life Assurance Company Archives. By contrast, by July 1922 the French Rothschilds had sold all their large holdings in the common shares of the Interborough Consolidated (the New York subway holding company). Kuhn, Loeb to Rothschild Frères, July 2, 1922, Box 1079/6477, AQ 132.

90. On German capital flight 1919–1922 and the German laws against the transfer of German capital abroad, see Feldman, *Great Disorder,* 134–135, 163–164, 597–599. On the 1920 measure, see data in RG 59, 862.503/4, and for more on German capital flight, George S. Messersmith, American consulate, Antwerp, Belgium, to Secretary of State, Jan. 18, 1923, and attachments, RG 59, 862.503/111/1, National Archives. The end of German inflation in November 1923 did not stop discussions of German capital flight, although it may have cut the actual capital flight. In December 1923, "French authorities" were quoted as estimating that wealthy Germans had invested $1 billion in American securities that were held in New York. Some New York bankers put the sum at $200,000,000. See *Commercial and Financial Chronicle,* Dec. 23, 1923, 2687. These figures were, in my view, far too high. See Feldman, *Great Disorder,* 283, on the Netherlands "as a major repository for German flight capital." Some went through Holland to the United States.

91. Charles E. Lyon, American Trade Commissioner, London, to Director, Bureau of Foreign and Domestic Commerce, Aug. 8, 1923, RG 151, 620 UK 1919–1927, National Archives. Cleveland and Huertas, *Citibank,* 136, show the extensive efforts of the National City Company across the United States in selling bonds; see ibid., 140, on the role of the National City Company in new bond issues in the United States, 1921–1929. Cleveland and Huertas, however, say nothing of the marketing effort in Europe, which was, of course, dwarfed by the National City Company's efforts on behalf of European and other foreign *borrowers.* See ibid., 147–152.

92. Burk, *Morgan Grenfell,* 76, 88.

93. Chernow, *House of Morgan,* 306–307.

94. U.S. Department of Commerce, *The Balance of International Payments of the United States, 1923* (Washington, D.C., 1924), 14.

95. National Industrial Conference Board, *International Financial Position of the United States,* 65–66.

96. Ibid. In this connection, see also Amos Taylor to James Angell, Mar. 22, 1933, in RG 151, 600 U.S. Balance of Payments 1932–1933, National Archives.

97. Rufus S. Tucker, "The Balance of International Payments of the United States in 1923," *Acceptance Bulletin,* 6 (July 31, 1924): 8.

98. Edwards, *International Trade Finance,* 27.

99. Brown, *International Gold Standard,* 308, who gives no figures, suggests that in 1923, British investors began to repurchase American securities sold during the war, encouraged in part by the improvement in sterling. Obviously the value of the dollar made a difference in investors' choices, but more important were the expectations of investors on the future value of the dollar vis-à-vis the investors' own currency. In addition, the point should be made that if the U.S. currency was strong, a foreigner's sale of a security to take advantage of the exchange ratio served to cut off the advantages of a strong dollar to the stream of earnings (that is, of course, if the investor assumed that the dollar would remain strong or would strengthen vis-à-vis the investor's own currency). It seems also that at times, in 1923, U.S. returns were higher than in the United Kingdom. Ibid.

100. See March–June 1922 correspondence in RG 151, 620 General 1919–1925, National Archives. Initially, this turning to Japan struck me as very odd, but see Odate, *Japan's Financial Relations with the United States,* esp. 97–100, 107, for context. Japan emerged from the First World War as a creditor nation in world accounts.

101. See Charles Lyon, American Trade Commissioner, London, to Director, Bureau of Foreign and Domestic Commerce, Aug. 8, 1923, in RG 151, 620 UK 1919–1927, National Archives.

102. National Industrial Conference Board, *International Financial Position,* 64.

103. See Appendix 2 (e) on foreign securities and the special problems related to inward foreign investments in such securities.

104. The author was A. Emil Davies. See A. Emil Davies, *Investments Abroad* (Chicago: A. W. Shaw, 1927), 47.

105. Cleveland and Huertas, *Citibank,* 152.

106. Wilkins, *History,* 339–40, 802n.264, on Philip Morris history. The British firm's first U.S. corporate affiliate was in 1902. What seems to have happened in 1919 is that the small parent firm in the United Kingdom came to an end.

107. Geoffrey Tweedale, "Transatlantic Specialty Steels: Sheffield High-Grade Steel Firms and the USA, 1860–1940," in *British Multinationals,* ed. Geoffrey Jones (Aldershot: Gower, 1986), 79, 83, 87.

108. Thomas R. Navin, *The Whitin Machine Works since 1831* (Cambridge, Mass.: Harvard University Press, 1950), 353.

109. Wilkins, *History,* 411. The subsidiary, set up in 1913, expanded during the First World War and then had overcapacity, which left it in financial difficulty after the war. Haynes, *American Chemical Industry,* IV, 136, 194–195.

110. Wilkins, *History,* 267–268; Jackson, *Enterprising Scot,* chap. 7 and 210; Thomas R. Navin, *Copper Mining and Management* (Tucson: University of Arizona Press, 1978), 232. The Arizona Copper Company owned the ore body that became (after the Phelps Dodge acquisition), the "great Morenci open pit." Ibid., 232n.8.

111. Wilkins, *History,* 267–268, and Haynes, *American Chemical Industry,* IV, 81. I do not know whether the British investors retained any portfolio interests in the reorganized firm.

112. Wilkins, *Maturing,* 10n, 254; Haynes, *American Chemical Industry,* III, 86–87. Others—newly built and not foreign owned—also closed.

113. This was a mortgage company. See Wilkins, *History,* 884n.91; Lewis, *America's Stake,* 86, 563, 574; and Kerr, *Scottish Capital on the American Credit Frontier* 189, 194.

114. Larry A. McFarlane, "British Agricultural Investment in the Dakotas," *Business and Economic History,* 2nd ser., 5 (1976): 114, 118, 120.

115. Balfour, Williamson had a California trading company, Balfour, Guthrie, that was associated with these investments. Hunt, *Heirs to Great Adventure,* II, 133; Wilkins, *History,* 506–507.

116. Wilkins, *History,* 320–323.

117. Charles Byron Kuhlman, *The Development of the Flour Milling Industry in the United States* (Boston: Houghton Mifflin, 1929), 172 (quoting *Northwestern Miller,* July 4, 1923); and John Storck and Walter Dorwin, *Flour for Man's Bread* (Minneapolis: University of Minnesota Press, 1952), 309. For the 1989 acquisition of Pillsbury by Grand Metropolitan, see Grand Metropolitan, *Fact Book, 1990.*

118. *Moody's 1922,* 1714 (the receivership). This company had a modern plant in Brooklyn. J. Emile Pathé, Paris, France, was a vice-president. Interestingly, a director was H. A. Metz, the prewar Hoescht representative in the United States and important in aiding the restoration of German business in America. *Moody's 1920,* 836 (for directors). See also on this company, Wilkins, *History,* 440. *Moody's 1929,* 368, indicates that Pathe Freres Phonograph Co. was reorganized as Pathe Phonograph & Radio Corp. in 1922. That firm, which made phonographs and records in Brooklyn, appears to have had no French connections.

119. See Chapter 1 and Wilkins, "Charles Pathé's American Business," 133–144. Perkins, *Wall Street to Main Street,* 96–98. In 1921 Edmund Lynch had gone to Paris, where he spent three months working out the details of the divestment agreement with the French parent. Perkins describes the transaction "as the boldest" in Merrill, Lynch's history. The purchase price was between $6 and $7 million. Why did Charles Pathé (the principal in Pathé Cinéma) sell out? For some of the reasons see Wilkins, "Charles Pathé's

American Business," 139; in addition, Perkins notes that in 1918–1921 there had been "persistent and unresolvable disagreements" between the management of the Paris parent and that of its U.S. subsidiary. Immediately after Merrill, Lynch's acquisition, the new owners fired Pathe Exchange's president, Paul Brunet, on the grounds of mismanagement and possibly outright fraud.

120. On the 1921 agreement that accompanied the sale to Merrill, Lynch, see *Du Pont v. Pathe Film* (Southern District Court, New York), November 1938 complaint, in Acc. 1410, Box 46, Du Pont Archives, Wilmington, Delaware.

121. Howard Kellogg, Spencer Kellogg and Sons, Inc., Buffalo, N.Y., to Anton Jurgens' Margarine Fabrieken, Feb. 7, 1923; Howard Kellogg to Gerald Fitzgerald (lawyer for Jurgens'), Mar. 22, 1923, and other data in Unilever NV Archives, Rotterdam. I am indebted to A. J. Bannink (Unilever NV) and Geoffrey Jones for xeroxed copies of the documents (Aug. 22, 2002).

122. The best material on this episode of Ericsson's U.S. experience is in Artur Attman et al., *L. M. Ericsson 100 Years* (Stockholm: L. M. Ericsson, [1977?]), 203–207.

123. On the prewar stakes of AB Baltic (Empire Separator Co.) and AB Lux (American Lux Light Co.), see Wilkins, *History*, 432, 838n.105. On AB Baltic's problems of the early 1920s, see Ragnhild Lundström to Mira Wilkins, Oct. 30, 1983; New Jersey corporate records indicate Empire Separator Co. was finally dissolved on May 25, 1923 (New Jersey Department of State to Wilkins, Apr. 3, 1984). New York Department of State to Wilkins, Nov. 17, 1983, certificate for dissolution of American Lux Light Co. Since AB Lux merged with AB Gasaccumulator (Lundström to Wilkins, Oct. 30, 1983), perhaps some of the U.S. manufacturing of AB Lux continued under the aegis of AB Gasaccumulator, which had a U.S. manufacturing subsidiary with a head office in Philadelphia. Wilkins, *History*, 431. AB Electrolux (1919) emerged in Sweden, including part of the old AB Lux. On C. E. Johansson, see Lundström, "Swedish Multinational Growth before 1930," 149. The inventor-founder migrated to the United States and went to work for Ford.

124. *Best's Insurance Reports, Fire and Marine.*

125. Michael Bliss, *A Canadian Millionaire: The Life and Times of Sir Joseph Flavelle, Bart. 1958–1939* (Toronto: Macmillan of Canada, 1978), 330, 389–390, 436–437.

126. T. B. Macaulay, president of Sun Life, would write in November 1923 that prior to the sale of the securities, "we were . . . in control of Illinois Traction Company." Macaulay to George W. Burton, Nov. 29, 1923, Macaulay letterbooks.

127. See Joseph Schull, *The Century of the Sun: The First Hundred Years of Sun Life Assurance Company of Canada* (Toronto: Macmillan of Canada, 1971), 45; Sun Life Assurance Company, *Annual Report 1923*, 27; Macaulay to M. Offer, May 13, 1923, ML, indicates that "tomorrow we expect to be paid Thirty Million dollars in connection with the sale of our Illinois Traction interests, and we are being forced to buy many millions of United States Treasury Notes, yielding only a little over four per cent, to absorb part of this money temporarily." Macaulay soon would be investing on a major scale in other U.S. public utilities—especially Insull-related properties. Based on data in Sun Life Archives. The holding of U.S. Treasury notes appears to have been very short-lived, until investments with a higher return could be identified.

128. Balance Sheets of the Texas Land Mortgage Co., Z-G-1, Reel 284, Bancroft Library, University of California, Berkeley. The Balance Sheet for year end Mar. 31, 1920, had the office building; the next year's one did not.

129. Jackson, *Enterprising Scot*, 279–280.

130. A. Veenendaal compared the listings for such companies in the 1919 and 1925 *Van Oss' Effectenboek.* Using his data, I found that of the eleven Dutch mortgage banks in business in the United States, eight had fewer mortgages outstanding in 1923 than in 1917.

131. Albin Joachim Dahl, "British Investment in California Mining, 1870–1890," Ph.D. diss., University of California, Berkeley, 1961, 258–260.

132. Heer, *World Events 1866–1966,* 130–131, 136, 139. See also *Fortune,* Feb. 1946, 120.

133. Based on *Best's Insurance Reports—Fire and Marine,* for 1919 through 1923. According to Paul J. Best, "Insurance in Imperial Russia," *Journal of European Economic History,* 18 (Spring 1989): 167, in 1925, the New York State Insurance Department took over the branches of the Second Russian Insurance Co., the Russian Reinsurance Company, the Moscow Fire Insurance Co., and the Northern Insurance Co. for liquidation. RG 56, Entry 406, National Archives has information on the Russian insurers in the United States—during and after the war. See data in Box 1, for example, on the Salamandra Insurance Company, its Russian-German connections, and the Danish ones in the war's aftermath.

134. Donald G. Bishop, *The Roosevelt-Litvinov Agreements* (Syracuse, N.Y.: Syracuse University Press, 1965), 182–195 (esp. p. 195, on the "money realized from the Litvinov assignment").

135. After 1933, the process of settlement was tedious, since the Litvinov Assignment of assets was challenged: Were these really "Soviet" assets or the assets of others? Who had control over the assets? Was this a federal government or a state government matter (the insurance companies were state regulated)? The matter went to the Supreme Court: *U.S. v. Belmont,* 301 U.S. 324 (1937), and *U.S. v. Pink,* 315 U.S. 203 (1942). Kermit L. Hall, ed., *Oxford Companion to the Supreme Court of the United States* (Oxford: Oxford University Press, 1992), 267, 776. Eventually, under Public Law 285 (approved Aug. 5, 1955), the U.S. Foreign Claims Settlement was authorized to use some of the "Russian" assets to pay a small portion of American claims, stemming from the Russian Revolution. Wilkins, *Maturing,* 40.

136. On the subsequent investments, see Carl H. McMillan, *Multinationals from the Second World* (New York: St. Martin's Press, 1987), 34, 134–140, and Martin Tolchin and Susan Tolchin, *Buying into America* (New York: Times Books, 1988), chap. 10.

137. Wilkins, *History,* 166; Cowles, *The Astors,* 170, 189. It is not clear how they eventually solved the tax problems, but one can assume they did do so.

138. These are documented in Wilkins, *History.*

139. Ibid. The Otis Steel investment had initially been a direct investment and was before it was divested transformed into a portfolio interest. Some, few, breweries had done well, but they were not typical; most had barely managed to survive.

140. The brewery investments were also ignored because their securities were denominated in sterling, so the sale of the securities could not be used to raise dollars.

141. H. Osborne O'Hagan, *Leaves from My Life,* 2 vols. (London: John Lane, 1929), I, 298.

142. Lewis, *America's Stake,* 98 (she thought the figure was an exaggeration).

143. I discuss this interpretation in Wilkins, *History,* 924n.186.

144. In February 1919 at the Paris Peace Conference, Woodrow Wilson pointed to three concerns in America's global relations: international communication, transportation, and oil. Richard H. K. Vietor uses the phrase "affected with a public interest" to refer to "transportation, telecommunications, energy, and finance" in an entirely different context—as industries that became during the New Deal subject to regulation designed to stabilize competition. Richard H. K. Vietor, "Contrived Competition," *Business History,* 36 (Oct. 1994): 1. In his discussion of the issues of the Harding administration, Murray, *Harding Era,* also singles out these sectors as ones that occupied the nation's attention.

145. Gordon Laxer, in *Open for Business: The Roots of Foreign Ownership in Canada* (Toronto: Oxford University Press, 1989), 141–143, argues the general case that opposition to foreign ownership in late-developing states was often based on "national defense"

issues. See also A. E. Safarian, *Multinational Enterprise and Public Policy* (Aldershot: Elgar, 1993), on how host states protected specific sectors. Both books offer a good, general context for U.S. policy making in this period.

146. The measures taken should be seen as in keeping with nativist, antialien sentiment in the nation that had in wartime resulted in the Espionage Act (1917) and the Sedition Act (1918); the latter in particular had lauded the symbols of 100 percent Americanism. They were also in keeping with new restrictions on immigration and higher tariffs in the early 1920s.

147. The account that follows is based principally on the excellent material in Aitken, *Continuous Wave*, 302–431. I have also used U.S. House, Committee on the Merchant Marine and Fisheries, *Radio Communication Hearings*, 64th Cong., 2d sess. (1917); Gleason Archer, *The History of Radio* (New York: American Historical Society, 1938), chaps. 10 and 11; U.S. Federal Trade Commission, *Report on the Radio Industry* (Washington, D.C., 1923); Howeth, *History of Communications*, chap. 30; and Josephine Young Case and Everett Needham Case, *Owen D. Young and American Enterprise* (Boston: David R. Godine, 1982), chap. 11.

148. Aitken, *Continuous Wave*, 287.

149. Ibid., 391, 330. The prospective French corporate owner of the Tuckerton station in 1914 was Compagnie Universelle de Téléphonie et Télégraphique sans Fil (CUTT). Blanken, *History of Philips Electronics*, III, 142–143. The U.S. government payment was to Compagnie Générale de Télégraphie sans Fil (CSF), formed in 1918. Ibid., 142–143, 174–175, explains the sequential relationship between the two French companies. According to Aitken, using Edward J. Nally as a source, in 1919, the British Marconi company owned half the stock in CSF, and the other half was owned by "French Marconi and allied interests." Aitken, *Continuous Wave*, 391. As for the Sayville station, once war had been declared, the Alien Property Custodian had taken title. Alien Property Custodian, *Annual Report 1918–1919*, 102–107.

150. Before he joined Marconi of America, Nally had had thirty-eight years of experience with Western Union. *Radio Communication, Hearings* (1917), 180.

151. Aitken, *Continuous Wave*, 401.

152. Ibid., 418, 421.

153. Sidak, *Foreign Investment*, 50.

154. Aitken, *Continuous Wave*, 406ff. The State Department as early as January 1916 was seeking to keep wireless communication with Latin America under American ownership. Nonetheless, when Pan American Wireless Co. was formed in 1917, it was three-eighths owned by British Marconi, three-eighths owned by Marconi of America, and two-eighths owned by Federal Telegraph Co. of California. According to Aitken, the Pan American firm never operated, but it became a complication when RCA was created. It passed to RCA control on the latter's formation. In 1921, a cooperative arrangement between RCA, British Marconi, Telefunken, and the French companies was achieved, covering the South American business. On this, see Case and Case, *Owen D. Young*, 821n.38, 222, 226, 822n.47, and 238–242, and Aitken, *Continuous Wave*, 291–292, 406.

155. Brady A. Hughes, "Owen D. Young and American Foreign Policy, 1919–1929," Ph.D. diss., University of Wisconsin, 1969, 92ff. As noted, Nally was an American citizen.

156. Aitken, *Continuous Wave*, 415.

157. Ibid.

158. W. P. Jolly, *Marconi* (New York: Stein and Day, 1972), 231, is the source on the forty trips. Owen Young had met Guglielmo Marconi in 1915. Case and Case, *Owen D. Young*, 174. The two men apparently kept in touch, for Young later recalled being on Marconi's yacht in 1927, and he visited with Marconi in England in 1930. Ibid., 754, 519. Thomas P. Hughes, *American Genesis* (New York: Viking, 1989), 148, has a picture of Marconi in the United States in 1932, posing with inventor Edwin Armstrong. David

Sarnoff stayed in contact with Marconi over the years. For a picture of the two men in 1933, see Margaret Graham, *RCA and the Video Disc: The Business of Research* (Cambridge: Cambridge University Press, 1986), 34, but Graham tells her reader *nothing* about any special relationships between Sarnoff and Marconi in 1919–1937. In 1917, John W. Griggs, then president of Marconi Company of America, told a House committee that although Marconi was an officer of the American Marconi Company, this was an "honorary" position: "he has never taken part in the management of the company." *Radio Communication Hearings* (1917), 169.

159. Sidak, *Foreign Investment,* 33–34, argues that before 1914 Marconi of America clung too long to its spark technology, whereas the future of wireless transmission lay in continuous wave transmission. Yet by the outbreak of World War I, American Marconi was aggressively moving into continuous wave transmission and had attempted to purchase GE's technology. There is no indication that left to its own devices, Marconi would have fallen behind.

160. Norman J. Glickman and Douglas P. Woodward, *The New Competitors* (New York: Basic Books, 1989), 108, made the quoted statement.

161. On Harding's views, see Murray, *Harding Era,* 410.

162. Despite British global preeminence in cables, in 1919 there were important American cable companies. In 1919, radio (wireless) communication was not competitive with cables, which were still the best method of international communication. By 1923, however, the cable companies and the new RCA had identical charges and offered similar services. Case and Case, *Owen D. Young,* 190. The extent of British domination in cables in 1919 was the subject of dispute. British author D. Cameron Watt, *Succeeding John Bull* (Cambridge: Cambridge University Press, 1984), 34, writes of 1919 that "Britain controlled the world's cables," which was the belief of many Americans and the basis for resentment. But the British foreign secretary, Arthur J. Balfour, argued in 1919 in Paris that Britain was being frozen out by "the powerful companies that controlled the landline telegraph systems in the United States." Aitken repeats, without challenge, Balfour's assertion that "the cable [the British] captured from Germany was . . . the *only* one that Britain controlled. Of the thirteen other transatlantic cables, each one was either owned by or leased to an American corporation." Aitken, *Continuous Wave,* 278. Balfour, however, said nothing about *the ownership* of the "American" corporations nor the network of accords. Michael Hogan, in *Informal Entente,* 117, writes that in 1919, American companies owned or operated thirteen of the seventeen transatlantic cables, *but* twelve of these terminated in Ireland or England under landing grants issued by the British Post Office and allowing the British Board of Trade to censor American traffic. Others were linked with the Pender group of companies. On a worldwide basis as distinct from a U.S.-European one, the British did have clear superiority. For more on cables, see Hogan, *Informal Entente,* 116–119; Aitken, *Continuous Wave,* 262–280, and for Britain's submarine cable system and its global supremacy, Barty-King, *Girdle around the World,* 173–179.

163. Hogan, *Informal Entente,* 116; Brewster, *Antitrust and American Business Abroad,* 341n; and Harold Sprout and Margaret Sprout, *Toward a New Order of Sea Power, 1918–1922* (Princeton, N.J.: Princeton University Press, 1940), 66n.37 (on the "Anglo-American struggle for control of electrical communication with South America and the Far East"); see also *Foreign Relations of the United States 1922,* I, 518, 521, 537.

164. Charles Evans Hughes to U.S. Ambassador in France, April 25, 1921, *Foreign Relations of the United States,* II, 154, 158–159. See also ibid., 359, 367, for more on cable policies.

165. Sprout and Sprout, *Toward a New Order,* 53.

166. See Chapter 1 on the Shipping Act of 1916. The best work on U.S. wartime and immediate postwar shipping policies is Safford, *Wilsonian Maritime Diplomacy.* During the war there had been a temporary suspension of the policy relating to *foreign-built*

ships. On the Jones Act, see 41 U.S. Stat. 999 (June 5, 1920). Vagts, "Corporate Alien," 1504–1506, is very valuable.

167. 41 U.S. Stat. 1008 (for the definition of a "citizen"). The 75 percent requirement was not in the 1916 act. Compare the 1920 law with the 1916 one, 39 U.S. Stat. 729 (Sept. 7, 1916).

168. De La Pedraja, *Rise and Decline of U.S. Merchant Shipping,* 62. These additional three provisions of the Jones Act were "allowed to lapse," to the dismay of the senator and Admiral William S. Benson, head of the Shipping Board. Ibid.

169. Beaton, *Enterprise in Oil,* 98.

170. Safford, *Wilsonian Maritime Diplomacy,* 230.

171. Ibid. On maritime insurance, see data on this in RG 56, Entry 406, National Archives. Another related piece of legislation to encourage American shipping was the Ship Mortgage Act of 1920, which was designed to cope with the immediate problems of financing the purchase of ships, consistent with the Jones Act. The Ship Mortgage Act gave "preferred status" to mortgagees who were citizens of the United States. U.S. Department of Commerce, *Foreign Direct Investment in the United States* (Washington, D.C., 1976), VII, K-61–62.

172. N. S. B. Gras and Henrietta M. Larson, *Casebook in American Business History* (New York: Appleton-Century-Crofts, 1939), 566–596, and Wilkins, *History,* 518–519, for background.

173. De La Pedraja, *Rise and Decline of U.S. Merchant Shipping,* 64–66. The White Star Line was owned by IMM. When Lord Pirrie died in 1924, the Royal Mail shipping group bought Harland & Wolff. Franklin had become president of IMM in 1916 (Gras and Larson, *Casebook,* 567, 587). When there was a proposal that the Shipping Board sell vessels to IMM (in 1920), the rhetoric of the opposition was "Don't give up the ships to the British BASTARDS." De La Pedraja, *Rise and Decline of U.S. Merchant Shipping,* 66. When the Harding administration took office, Harding considered appointing Franklin to head the Shipping Board (as the successor to Admiral Benson), but the president quickly dropped Franklin's name when he realized that the Senate probably would not confirm Franklin, owing to his British connections. Murray, *Harding Era,* 282.

174. Safford, *Wilsonian Maritime Diplomacy,* 245. The United States Lines was government owned and operated. De La Pedraja, *Rise and Decline of U.S. Merchant Shipping,* 67, and Lawrence Spinelli, *Dry Diplomacy* (Wilmington, Del.: Scholarly Resources, 1989), 35–37. IMM would acquire controlling interest in United States Lines in December 1931, and eventually United States Lines became *the* operating company, replacing IMM. Gras and Larson, *Casebook,* 567, 589–590. Spinelli, *Dry Diplomacy,* 37–48, is splendid on the problems the U.S. Shipping Board had being competitive, while enforcing U.S. law, i.e. Prohibition. When the attorney general, Harry M. Daugherty, on October 6, 1922, ruled that all American ships were subject to Prohibition and no foreign ship could carry liquor into U.S. waters, IMM and Cunard joined in protesting. Daugherty quickly relaxed the regulations on *foreign* ships (allowing them to bring *sealed* stores into U.S. waters). Travelers switched to foreign ships. Finally, in 1923 the Supreme Court ruled that Prohibition did not extend to American ships beyond the three-mile boundary. Ibid., 44–46.

175. Statement of Representative H. C. Pell (Democrat from New York), quoted in Sprout and Sprout, *Toward a New Order,* 81.

176. For the 1920 role of U.S. shipping and the subsequent economic relapse, see S. G. Sturmey, *British Shipping and World Competition* (London: Athlone Press, 1962), 37, 130; Jeffrey J. Safford, "The United States Merchant Marine in Foreign Trade, 1800–1939," in *Business History of Shipping,* ed. T. Yui and K. Nakagawa (Tokyo: University of Tokyo Press, 1985), 109–111, 115; and Murray, *Harding Era,* 282–293, 395–396, who tells of the Harding administration's frustrations with shipping policies.

177. Just how much actual influence, much less control, the British had over IMM is highly controversial. My reading of the evidence is that the influence declined over time and was by 1919 far less than in the pre-1914 years. The strategy of the Shipping Board was, however, to develop American alternatives to IMM. The Shipping Board never asked for divestment of the foreign-owned holdings of IMM securities, since that was not seen as the basis for the "British" character of the shipping giant. In 1919, in an attempt to be more American, IMM management had proposed the sale of the White Star Line to the Royal Mail group, but IMM's stockholders turned this down. De La Pedraja, *Rise and Decline of U.S. Merchant Shipping,* 65. A Dutch committee participated in the World War I reorganization of IMM, but I have found no other Dutch interventions. In 1917, IMM had sold most of its shares in the Holland-American Lines, thus severing the direct ties that would have heightened the Dutch interest in IMM business operations. Gras and Larson, *Casebook,* 585, 588.

178. There were some concerns about Japanese shipping.

179. Canadian railroads that extended (as FDI) into the United States were never a target of national security concerns. When during the First World War, all U.S. railroads had been put under U.S. government operations, the only problem that seemed to create for the Canadian railroads in the United States related to wage awards given to American workers; the Canadian government required the Canadian railroads to apply such awards to Canadian workers. W. Kaye Lamb, *History of the Canadian Pacific Railway* (New York: Macmillan, 1977), 282–286.

180. It should be noted, however, that in developing national policies, Harding favored new ones toward aviation and government regulation thereof; it was Congress that was slow in acting. Murray, *Harding Era,* 410–411. Had there been legislation, I have no doubt that it would have had a clause relating to foreign involvement—as did the legislation of 1926.

181. There is an immense literature on America's post–World War I oil policy. See, for example, John Ise, *United States Oil Policy* (New Haven, Conn.: Yale University Press, 1926); U.S. Senate, Special Committee Investigating Petroleum Interests in Foreign Countries, *American Petroleum Interests in Foreign Countries,* 79th Cong., 1st sess. (1946), 297–309, 314, 317–319, 322; John DeNovo, "The Movement for an Aggressive American Oil Policy Abroad, 1918–1920," *American Historical Review,* 61 (July 1956): 854–876; Gerald D. Nash, *United States Oil Policy 1890–1964* (Pittsburgh: University of Pittsburgh Press, 1968); Carl Parrini, *Heir to Empire: United States Economic Diplomacy 1916–1923* (Pittsburgh: University of Pittsburgh Press, 1969); Joan Hoff Wilson, *American Business and Foreign Policy, 1921–1933* (Lexington: University of Kentucky Press, 1971); Michael Hogan, "Informal Entente: Public Policy and Private Management in Anglo-American Petroleum Affairs, 1918–1924," *Business History Review,* 48 (Summer 1974): 187–205; Wilkins, *Maturing;* Hogan, *Informal Entente;* Edward W. Chester, *United States Oil Policy and Diplomacy* (Westport, Conn.: Greenwood Press, 1983); Randall, *United States Foreign Oil Policy;* and, from a different perspective, B. S. McBeth, *British Oil Policy 1919–1939* (London: Frank Cass, 1985).

182. For U.S. oil companies' expansion right after the First World War, see Wilkins, *Maturing,* 113ff.

183. "An Act to promote the mining of coal, phosphate, oil, oil shale, gas, and sodium on the public domain." 41 U.S. Stat. 437 (Feb. 25, 1920). Most "minerals"—gold, silver, copper, etc.—were *not* covered by this act. Mining law made the distinction between so-called leasible and locatable minerals. The 1920 law covered only the former. Some authors cite the Mining Law of 1872—which did cover gold, silver, and copper—as having limited alien mining activities. It did not, however, restrict the activities of foreign-owned *companies* that were incorporated in the United States. See Wilkins, *History,* 128–129, 581. Thus, it had never been a barrier to foreign investment in mining or oil production.

184. This 1920 law was not by any means the first use of the reciprocity "stick" in U.S. economic foreign policy. Often treaties of friendship, commerce, and navigation had contained a reciprocity clause. The U.S. State Department had also, long before the Kellogg Cable Act of 1921, insisted on reciprocity when granting foreigners permission to lay cables. Wilkins, *History*, 565. Subsequently, the reciprocity "club" would be used in a variety of contexts. The Fordney-McCumber Tariff of 1922, for example, gave the president authority to retaliate against nations that discriminated against American products. This was a trade rather than investment application, but the goals were identical. See David Lake, *Power, Protection, and Free Trade* (Ithaca, N.Y.: Cornell University Press, 1988), 169. In short, specifically in 1920–1922, in U.S. policies on cables, oil, and tariffs, American law was to be employed to help Americans to be more competitive abroad.

185. For background, see particularly, Randall, *United States Foreign Oil Policy*, 16–17.

186. Harold D. Roberts, *Salt Creek Wyoming* (Denver, Colo.: Midwest Oil Corp., 1956), 145.

187. In 1911, according to a September 1911 memorandum from B. Hopkins to Verner Reed, French investors owned 65 percent, Dutch 10 percent, Belgians 5 percent, and Americans 20 percent of Franco Wyoming. Gene Gressley to Mira Wilkins, June 17, 1991. Franco Wyoming Oil Company was incorporated in Delaware in 1909, but throughout its history it had its "executive offices" in Paris. See correspondence in Charles W. Burdick Papers, Boxes 100–112, American Heritage Center, University of Wyoming, Laramie, Wyoming. I do not know how the ownership changed between 1911 and 1919, but it is clear that the Paris-headquartered firm maintained French-ownership control.

188. See data in Charles W. Burdick Papers. A later audit of Franco Wyoming's 1919 income taxes resulted in a tentative determination of a tax deficiency of $3.5 million. F. W. Mondell to Franco Wyoming Oil Company, Jan. 10, 1927. Burdick Papers, Box 112. I am not clear how this substantial tax obligation related to the cutback in the business involvements in 1919.

189. Data in Box 59, Burdick Papers. Franco Wyoming Oil Co. bought the Dutch stock, which it then resold to Midwest Oil Company. Dutch investors obtained $2.4 million in this sale.

190. Franco Wyoming sold its Salt Creek Producers Association stock, acquired in 1919 as part of its earlier steps toward divestment.

191. Gressley to Wilkins, June 17, 1991, and Cary Reich, *Financier: The Biography of André Meyer* (New York: William Morrow, 1983), 243–246 ("royalty company").

192. Roberts, *Salt Creek Wyoming*, 144–145; *Moody's Industrials 1922*, 1785. In 1922, there were no French names on the board of directors of Midwest Refining Company.

193. As of 1921 the historian of the Wyoming oil industry Harold D. Roberts stops (very abruptly) his discussions on the activities of foreign investors in that state. Roberts' book was published in 1956. He writes that in March 1914, the French stockholders in Midwest Oil Company—also in Wyoming—had sent Henri de Compeigne to America as their personal representative; he returned to France at the outbreak of war to serve as a French officer. Then, in 1919, he came back to America and became a director of Salt Creek Producers, which by then controlled Midwest Oil. The Frenchman remained in the United States until his retirement in 1944. Roberts, *Salt Creek Wyoming*, 108. Paul H. Giddens, *Standard Oil (Indiana)* (New York: Appleton-Century-Crofts, 1955), casts no light on the subsequent role of foreign investors. A 1948 list of French stockholdings in the United States showed very small remaining interests in Standard Oil (Indiana). B63562, Archives Economiques et Financieres, Savigny-le-Temple, France. (Standard Oil [Indiana] was the predecessor of Amoco.) As an aside, H. M. Blackmer, chairman of the board of Midwest Refining (Midwest Oil and Midwest Refining were separate companies), became involved in some dubious behavior vis-à-vis the Teapot Dome Scandal;

by early 1924, he had gone to live in France. Burl Noggle, *Teapot Dome* (New York: W. W. Norton, 1965), 180–182. Undoubtedly, his French connections provided him with French friends.

194. I found no evidence of a direct causal connection between the retreat and the legislation. The principal reasons for the pullback are not, however, clear. Discussion with Gene Gressley, May 21, 1991, Laramie, Wyoming. Gressley believed that part of the explanation lies in the change in "generations"; the foreign participants were getting older, and their interests turned elsewhere. Also, H. M. Blackmer may have told the French that the law might in the future create "one more problem that would afflict the profitability of Salt Creek in coming years." Gressley to Wilkins, June 17, 1991.

195. Wilkins, *History,* 286.

196. Lewis, *America's Stake,* 97.

197. U.S. Federal Trade Commission, *Foreign Ownership in the Petroleum Industry* (Washington, D.C., 1923), 35.

198. At least, I have found no evidence that this was the primary reason. In both Wyoming and Oklahoma, the withdrawals began before the passage of the 1920 legislation, albeit they accelerated after the passage of the law. State law in Oklahoma could, conceivably, have been a partial cause for the French retreat from investment there.

199. Avery D. Andrews, New York, to H. Deterding, Mar. 23, 1923, private and confidential; the letter was directed to the attention of J. B. Aug. Kessler. It is in the Shell Archives, London.

200. J. B. Aug. Kessler, Memo, Feb. 2, 1923, Box C31/4, Pearson Papers, Science Museum, London.

201. Robert P. Skinner to Department of State, Mar. 10, 1920, RG 59, 841.6363/29, National Archives.

202. Ibid. and Skinner to Department of State, Mar. 25, 1920, RG 59, 841.6363/32.

203. For state alien land laws, see Wilkins, *History,* 579–582. Oklahoma had been covered under the federal 1887 Alien Property Act until 1907, when it became a state. Its original constitution had provisions against alien land ownership. Such inclusions were, however, often pro forma and did not imperil a properly structured foreign investment. Oklahoma also passed legislation on alien ownership.

204. John Barton Payne to Secretary of State, May 3, 1920, RG 59, 841.6363/42.

205. A. C. M[illspaugh] to [Wesley] Frost, June 7, 1920, RG 59, 841.6363/42. Millspaugh, the State Department's petroleum adviser, 1920–1921, favored encouraging Anglo-American understanding. Randall, *United States Foreign Oil Policy,* 9–10, 25.

206. Skinner to Secretary of State, Apr. 19, 1920, RG 59, 841.6363/43. See also Skinner to John W. Davis, Apr. 19, 1920, in ibid.

207. John W. Davis to Secretary of State, Apr. 28, 1920, RG 59, 841.6363/45. For more on the debate, see additional data in RG 59, 841.6363. On John W. Davis, see Chernow, *House of Morgan,* 254–255.

208. The secret agreement did not become known to the public at once.

209. Sprout and Sprout, *Toward a New Order,* 76.

210. John B. Payne (Secretary of Interior) to Commissioner, General Land Office, Dec. 10, 1920, and Payne to Secretary of State, Jan. 8, 1921, RG 59, 841.6363/100. A 1914 Canadian ordinance restricting U.S. entries had been revoked in 1920. Laxer, *Open for Business,* 213–214.

211. Andrews to Deterding, Mar. 23, 1923, op. cit.

212. A. C. Geddes to Charles E. Hughes, Apr. 20, 1921, RG 59, 841.6363/143; Avery Andrews to Henry Cabot Lodge, Apr. 27, 1921, RG 59, 841.6363/150.

213. Geoffrey Jones, *The State and the Emergence of the British Oil Industry* (London: Macmillan, 1981), 217.

214. Shell Union Oil Corporation Organization Papers (1922), in Library, Shell Oil Company, London. The principal U.S. assets of the group excluded from the merger were Asiatic Petroleum Company in New York (because it was a supplier of material and oils to Shell companies abroad); the Simplex Refining Co. (which held the Trumble patents used by the group worldwide); the New Orleans Refining Co. (operated by the Asiatic Petroleum Company, New York, and engaged in foreign sales); and the three Shell tankers (whose disposition under the Jones Act was still uncertain). Beaton, *Enterprise in Oil,* 213. The New Orleans refinery had begun operations in May 1920 to process Mexican crude. Ibid., 148. For more on the merger, see Swaine, *Cravath Firm,* II, 296–298.

215. U.S. Federal Trade Commission, *Foreign Ownership in the Petroleum Industry,* 139–140, for balance sheets of constituent companies as of January 2, 1922.

216. The December 1921 recommendation was repeated in Andrews to Deterding, Mar. 23, 1923, op. cit.

217. Anglo-Persian Oil Company was renamed Anglo-Iranian Oil Co. in 1935, and British Petroleum Co. in 1954. It became BP Amoco in 1998. The quotation is in Memorandum from F. M. Dearing, Office of the Assistant Secretary, Department of State, Dec. 23, 1921, RG 59, 841.6363/85. Sir John Cadman had been in charge of the Petroleum Executive of the British government, 1917–1921. Late in 1921, he was appointed technical adviser to Anglo-Persian. R. W. Ferrier, *The History of the British Petroleum Company: Volume 1: The Developing Years 1901–1932* (Cambridge: Cambridge University Press, 1982), 305, 689.

218. Andrews to Deterding, Mar. 23, 1923, op. cit.

219. U.S. Federal Trade Commission, *Foreign Ownership in the Petroleum Industry,* xi,1.

220. Kessler Memo, Feb. 2, 1923, op. cit.

221. Unsigned "Memorandum of Interview held at the Department of Interior, Washington, D.C., on September 19, 1922," p. 2, Box C31/4, Pearson Papers. The memorandum was on the Woodside Permit–Utah and the Lands Leasing Act.

222. Andrews to Deterding, Mar. 23, 1923, op. cit. Indian lands were separately administered from U.S. public lands.

223. Ise, *United States Oil Policy,* 471; Kessler Memo, Feb. 2, 1923, op. cit.

224. For details on the Ferrall bill, see E. DeGolyer, Amerada Petroleum Corporation, to J. B. Body, Feb. 6, 1923, Box C31/4, Pearson Papers.

225. Andrews to Deterding, Mar. 23, 1923, op. cit.

226. Ibid., and Clive Pearson, Whitehall Petroleum Corp. to Board of Trade, Mar. 15, 1923, Box C31/4, Pearson Papers. Shell did not learn of the 1921 Texas legislation until 1923. The law was part of a body of "anti-alien" state laws aimed at resident Asians, particularly Japanese, in California and elsewhere. Dudley O. McGovney, "Anti-Japanese Land Laws of California and Ten Other States," *California Law Review,* 35 (1947): 7–60. The Texas law seemed to apply to British-owned oil companies, although the Shell attorney (Andrews) thought—in 1923—that it was "a dead letter as far as we are concerned." California had passed an alien land law in 1913 and strengthened it in 1920. There is no evidence that the Royal Dutch Shell Group thought it threatening.

227. For Shell's reactions, see Andrews to Deterding, Mar. 23, 1923, op. cit.

228. Ise, *United States Oil Policy,* 473.

229. Andrews to Deterding, Mar. 23, 1923, and Ise, *United States Oil Policy,* 471.

230. On March 15, 1923, Clive Pearson (involved in Amerada Petroleum Corporation) referred to the Oklahoma legislation as "for the moment dead." See his letter to the Board of Trade in Box C31/4 Pearson Papers. Two months later, however, R. Waley Cohen, Anglo-Saxon Petroleum Co., Ltd., wrote the Petroleum Department, Board of Trade, that it had received advice from its New York attorneys (Cravath, Henderson, Leffingwell &

De Gersdorff) that if the Ferrall and Glasser bills were passed, they would be deemed constitutional. Cohen to Director, Petroleum Department, Board of Trade, May 15, 1923, "Secret," in Powe 33/275, Power Ministry, Public Record Office, London.

231. Andrews to Deterding, Mar. 23, 1923, op. cit.

232. See Mira Wilkins, "Multinational Oil Companies in South America in the 1920s," *Business History Review*, 48 (Autumn 1974): 436, 439–440, on how in 1922 the British government acted on behalf of Standard Oil of New Jersey in Peru, at the expense of Royal Dutch Shell.

233. Andrews to Deterding, Mar. 23, 1923, op. cit.

234. Waley Cohen to Board of Trade, May 15, 1923, op. cit., and Ise, *United States Oil Policy*, 471.

235. Waley Cohen to Board of Trade, May 15, 1923, op. cit.

236. Noggle, *Teapot Dome*, 63.

237. Sir G. M. W. Macdonaugh to General Avery D. Andrews, Oct. 4, 1923, Shell Archives, London.

238. It recognized this when it was required to show that it was qualified for leasing public land and withdrew its application for the permit. Data in Shell Archives, London.

239. Jones, *State*, 217.

240. Ibid., 218. Amerada drilled on land in Oklahoma, Kansas, Arkansas, Louisiana, and Texas. On Amerada Petroleum Company and the holding company, Amerada Corporation (incorporated in 1920), see data in Box C31/1, "Amerada Companies," and Box C52/11, "Whitehall Petroleum Corporation—Oil History 1927," in Pearson Papers, Science Museum, London. The U.S. oil properties were acquired in earlier years and placed under Amerada Petroleum Company in 1919. Amerada Corporation, the holding company, had $2.5 million in capital at formation, which was raised to $5 million in 1921 and $6 million in 1922. Data in Box C31/1, Pearson Papers.

241. E. DeGolyer, Amerada Petroleum Company, New York, to J. B. Body, Feb. 6, 1923; Body to De Golyer, Feb. 27, 1923; and Clive Pearson, Chairman, Whitehall Petroleum Corporation, Ltd. to Secretary, Board of Trade, Mar. 15, 1923, all in Box C31/4, Pearson Papers.

242. DeGolyer to Body, Feb. 6, 1923, op. cit.

243. In 1923, in response to Texas legislation toward foreign-controlled firms, the Amerada group formed an American-controlled company, the Rycade Corporation, to acquire from Amerada certain "wildcat" wells. See folder "Whitehall Petroleum Corporation—Oil History 1927," Box C52/11, Pearson Papers.

244. Based on Royal Dutch and Shell, *Annual Reports.*

245. 41 U.S. Stat. 1063, 1065 (June 20, 1920).

246. By "older" I mean the type of formulation that appeared pre-1887. See Wilkins, *History*, 582.

247. See Section 9 of the National Bank Act of 1864.

248. Regulation K governed the operations of Edge Act corporations. The regulations dealt with the transfer of stock in these corporations, to be sure that Edge Act companies would not become foreign controlled. Phelps, *Foreign Expansion of American Banks*, 107; Federal Reserve Board, *Annual Report 1920*, 308; and U.S. Department of Commerce, *Foreign Direct Investment in the United States*, VII, K-177. Edge Act companies remained out-of-bounds for foreign direct investors until the passage of the International Banking Act of 1978.

249. See Wilkins, *History*, for the history of earlier regulations.

250. See Chamber of Commerce of the United States, *Laws and Practices Affecting the Establishment of Foreign Branches of Banks* (Washington, D.C.: Chamber of Commerce of the United States, 1923), 10 (henceforth cited as Chamber of Commerce, *Laws and Prac-*

tices). See also Informal Ruling of the Federal Reserve Board, Apr. 4, 1916, in *Federal Reserve Bulletin,* May 1, 1916, 214.

251. Phelps, *Foreign Expansion of American Banks,* 197–201, and Wilkins, *History,* 456 (New York law). In New York State registered agencies of foreign banks could not take deposits.

252. Phelps, *Foreign Expansion of American Banks,* 207; Chamber of Commerce, *Laws and Practices,* 23. Pierre Jay to Benjamin Strong, Sept. 17, 1920, 320.113 Strong Papers, Federal Reserve Bank of New York. The Chamber of Commerce, *Laws and Practices,* 17–21, contains a discussion of the pros and cons of allowing foreign banks to have branches in the United States and specifically in New York.

253. Chamber of Commerce, *Laws and Practices.* The Illinois act was passed in June 1917, but its requirements did not have to be met until January 1, 1921. F. Cyril James, *The Growth of Chicago Banks* (New York: Harper & Bros, 1938), II, 913–914.

254. Phelps, *Foreign Expansion of American Banks,* 203.

255. Merrill Denison, *Canada's First Bank: A History of the Bank of Montreal* (New York: Dodd, Mead & Co., 1967), II, 353. The branch had been in operation since 1903.

256. This was not an issue that arose in 1919–1923; it would, however, become one in the post–World War II period. It did not arise in these years because foreign banks were not, in the main, involved in *domestic* business. There were, however, already foreign banks with business establishments in more than one state.

Although American "banks" could not branch across state lines, in this period American banks could, through securities affiliates, have out-of-state offices. In 1919, National City Company, an affiliate of National City Bank, had offices in fifty-one cities across the nation. And, of course, even if National City Bank could not branch across the country, it lent money nationally (as well as internationally). Cleveland and Huertas, *Citibank,* 136.

257. There had been a federal anti-alien land law in 1887 that covered foreign investments in the territories. As territories became states, the coverage contracted. Long before the end of the First World War, this act was a dead letter. Wilkins, *History,* 581–582. There had been a wave of state anti-alien laws, 1885–1895, many of which remained on the books in 1919–1923. Ibid., 579–580. My text here has suggested that state anti-alien property measures had some impact on—that is, became a cause for concern for—foreign investors in the oil industry. In 1919 in Mississippi, the Fine Cotton Spinners' and Doublers' Association—a British investor in cotton plantations—was said to have acquired an existing corporation with a broad charter so as to meet that state's alien land ownership rules. Robert L. Brandfon, *Cotton Kingdom of the New South* (Cambridge, Mass.: Harvard University Press, 1967), 129. On the Mississippi law, see Charles H. Sullivan, "Alien Land Laws," *Temple Law Quarterly,* 36 (1962): 19–20, and Justin Miller, "Alien Land Laws," *George Washington Law Review,* 8 (1939): 13. In the early 1920s, a number of states passed new alien property laws, many of which were directed at Japanese resident farmers and had nothing to do with inward FDI. McGovney, "Anti-Japanese Land Laws," 7–8. Laws with this goal were passed in California (1920), Louisiana and Texas (1921), New Mexico (1922), and Idaho, Montana, and Oregon (1923). Anti-alien land laws did affect foreign mortgage companies' right to foreclose, but the decline in mortgage lending does not seem to be the result of any of the post–First World War legislation. In 1923, in four cases, the U.S. Supreme Court upheld the alien property acts of California and Washington. Thomas Reed Powell, "Alien Land Cases in the United States Supreme Court," *California Law Review,* 12 (May 1924): 259.

258. H. W. Nichols, "Memorandum for the Director [Bureau of War Risk Insurance, U.S. Treasury Department]," Aug. 1, 1919, on the federal licensing of foreign insurance companies operating in the United States, in RG 56, Entry 406, Box 23, National Archives. In advocating the continuation of federal government licensing of foreign insurance com-

panies, Nichols wrote that "foreign governments are drafting legislation which discriminates against American insurance companies going abroad. The effect of this legislation may be counteracted by a federal control of insurance permitting insurance treaties between countries, which cannot be effected by the State insurance departments." See also Harry B. Epstein to R. G. Cholmeley-Jones (director of the Bureau of War Risk Insurance), Oct. 25, 1920, RG 56, Entry 406, Box 11, on "whether there is any necessity for continuing the issuance of licenses to foreign insurance companies as provided by the Trading with the Enemy Act" and whether, after the U.S. formally ended the war, it was advisable to continue federal supervision of foreign insurance companies in this country.

259. If foreign "ownership" was not specified, all the foreign investor had to do was to set up a company that was owned from abroad but incorporated domestically.

260. See Bruce M. Russett, *Community and Contention* (Cambridge, Mass.: MIT Press, 1963), 10–12, and Sprout and Sprout, *Toward a New Order,* 66–84. In the main, by 1923, many of the Anglo-American conflicts had been resolved, after the 1923 funding agreements covering war debts (see Lewis, *America's Stake,* 365) and after the Washington Naval Armament Limitation Conference (November 1921–February 1922) covering disputes over the size of the navy. Allied war debts continued, however, as a bone of contention, as did the more general malaise in the United States over perceived British "power."

261. Before the Armistice, only four companies had been sold, the largest of which was Orenstein-Arthur-Koppel. *APC Report;* see also Alien Property Custodian, *Annual Reports,* for subsequent years.

262. See, for example, Rosenbaum and Sherman, *M. M. Warburg,* 124. Some German-Americans could not get passports until 1920. This was the case with Max Stoehr, who was refused a passport in 1919. See *Stoehr v. Miller,* 296 Fed. 414 (Dec. 17, 1923). Others could travel: in 1919 Dr. Franz Hirschland, president of Metal & Thermit Corporation (the renamed Goldschmidt Detinning Co.), made his first postwar trip to Germany. Duffus, *Story of M & T Chemicals.* W. Paul Pickhardt, who was in Paris, June to November 1919, took frequent trips to the Badische factory in Ludwigshafen. See copies of his correspondence from Paris in Francis P. Garvan Papers, Box 44, American Heritage Center, University of Wyoming, Laramie.

263. The Garvan Papers at the American Heritage Center, University of Wyoming, Laramie, provide ample evidence of Garvan's abiding distrust of German business.

264. 41 U.S. Stat. 35–36 (July 11, 1919) and 41 U.S. Stat. 977–980 (June 5, 1920). A number of suits were filed by American and Swiss entities (persons or firms) that felt they were mistakenly deemed enemies.

265. Based on data in Garvan Papers. On Miller's background, see Murray, *Harding Era,* 480.

266. Wilkins, *Maturing,* 23–25 (on American business in Germany during the First World War) and 40–45 (on the Mixed Claims Commission).

267. See data in Garvan Papers, Boxes 24, 46, and 91. Garvan's associates became convinced that in 1921–1922 Attorney General Harry M. Daugherty had surrounded himself with allies of the Germans. Daugherty had selected William J. Burns, a former employee of the Hamburg-American Line, to head the Bureau of Investigation in the Justice Department. He had appointed John W. Crim as assistant attorney general; Crim's law firm, Crim and Wemple, had represented Krupp's Hans Tauscher when the latter "ran afoul" of U.S. neutrality laws. See Chapter 1 and Paul Smith, Memo [undated, ca. Fall 1927] prepared in connection with *U.S. v. Palmer,* in Garvan Papers, Box 91.

268. *New York Times,* Jan. 3, 1923; Alien Property Custodian Report, submitted Jan. 1923; and *New York Times,* Mar. 5, 1923.

269. 42 U.S. Stat., 1511–1516 (Mar. 4, 1923). The Winslow Act amended the Trading with the Enemy Act.

270. Bernfeld, "Short History of American Metal Climax," 11, and Vincent P. Carosso, "A Financial Elite: New York's German-Jewish Investment Bankers," *American Jewish Historical Quarterly,* 66 (Sept. 1976): 85. Even when Palmer and Garvan were APCs, there was no problem in selling German properties to naturalized German-Americans, who expressed loyalty to their adopted country.

271. See Navin, *Copper Mining and Management,* 276, 341–342, and Joseph Borkin, *The Crime and Punishment of I. G. Farben* (New York: Free Press, 1978), 169–178, for slightly different renditions of this oft-told story. Borkin argues that the actual sale of the American shares by Metallgesellschaft to the Swiss company was in November 1919, and the transaction was backdated. Before the war, Richard Merton had been with Henry R. Merton & Co., the London extension of Metallgesellschaft. In 1918, Britain passed an act for the purpose of controlling the nonferrous metal industry, requiring that all persons engaged therein should first obtain a license from the board of trade; Henry R. Merton & Co. was refused a license, and as a result "that company, together with its subsidiary, Merton Metallurgical Co., Ltd., have gone into liquidation." *APC Report,* 93 (report issued in February 1919). After the war, Richard Merton continued to be connected with the successor of Henry R. Merton & Co., the British Metal Corporation. Edward J. Cocks and Bernhardt Walters, *A History of the Zinc Smelting Industry in Britain* (London: George Harrap, 1968), 19, 46, 189. *Moody's Industrials 1929,* 880, identifies Alfred Merton as president of Metallgesellschaft; Richard Merton was chairman of the board of the German company.

272. See data in File D-28-623, Acc. 67A10, Box 1310, RG 131, U.S. Department of Justice, Washington, D.C.

273. In some other cases, there were suggestions of bribery, but not by any means all.

274. Navin, *Copper Mining and Management,* 275–276. Apparently, Vogelstein's own German connections would be revived (see Table 9.2 herein). Central Mining & Securities was his post–World War I company.

275. *APC Report,* 130.

276. *Stoehr v. Wallace et al.,* 255 U.S. 239 (Feb. 28, 1921).

277. *New York Times,* Jan. 25, 1923.

278. The complications of the case are spelled out in the long decision in *Stoehr v. Miller,* 296 Fed. 414 (Dec. 17, 1923).

279. *Moody's Industrials 1929,* 2888.

280. Wilkins, *History,* 356.

281. The founder's grandson, Theodore J. Forstmann, became in 1978 the senior partner in the Wall Street firm Forstmann, Little, & Co. Bryan Burrough and John Helyar, *Barbarians at the Gate* (New York: Harper & Row, 1990), 235–238.

282. National Association of Wool Manufacturers, *Bulletin,* 57 (Oct. 1927): 495–496 (obituary for Christian Bahnsen). With 3,500 employees in 1927, this company became one of the leaders in New Jersey wool production.

283. On the purchase date, see data in RG 131, Box 254, National Archives. See also *Moody's Industrials 1920, 1921, 1922,* and *1923.*

284. National Association of Wool Manufacturers, *Bulletin,* 57 (Oct. 1927): 496. There were, however, other cases—in other industries—where formerly German-owned direct investments passed to Britishers; for example, this was the case with Norma-Hoffmann Bearings Co.

285. Wilkins, *History,* 901n.7, and *Wall Street Journal,* Aug. 1, 1990.

286. In 1922, the U.S. Department of Justice filed a suit, *U.S. v. Palmer,* alleging conspiracy in the sale of Bosch Magneto. The case was finally discontinued, January 31, 1930. See data in Garvan Papers, Box 91. See also American Bosch Corporation, *Annual Report*

1929 and Prospectus for American Bosch Corporation, Oct. 25, 1938, Scudder Collection, Columbia University Library.

287. See Wilkins, *History,* 433–442.

288. Harm Schröter, "A Typical Factor of German International Market Strategy: Agreements between the US and German Electrotechnical Industries up to 1939," in *Multinational Enterprise in Historical Perspective,* ed. Alice Teichova, Maurice Lévy-Leboyer, and Helga Nussbaum (Cambridge: Cambridge University Press, 1986), 162. Schröter identifies a "Herr Lissau" as the AEG representative. It seems that AEG settled for the division of markets with GE (as before the war), whereas Siemens, for a while at least, had a more independent posture. Before the war, Frank had served as the U.S. representative of Telefunken.

289. See letters in Siemens Archives, Munich, cited in Schröter, "Typical Factor," 169, along with other letters in SAA 68/li 262, Siemens Archives.

290. Schröter, "Typical Factor," 162.

291. Ibid., 164.

292. Wilkins, *Maturing,* 65; Stocking and Watkins, *Cartels in Action,* 330. For antitrust reasons, the U.S. company kept itself aloof, as the affiliates abroad joined in alliances.

293. The U.S. Federal Trade Commission, *Electric Power Industry* (Washington, D.C., 1928), 139, says the agreement was on January 1, 1922, as does Frank Costigliola, *Awkward Dominion* (Ithaca, N.Y.: Cornell University Press, 1984), 152, who has seen the actual contract in the Young Papers. Schröter, "Typical Factor," 164, gives the date as 1923. For the 1903 agreement, see Wilkins, *History,* 437–438.

294. U.S. Federal Trade Commission, *Electric Power Industry,* 141.

295. Schröter, "Typical Factor," 165, and Wilkins, *Maturing,* 66. See also Alfred Plummer, *International Combines in Modern Industry,* 2nd ed. (London: Sir Isaac Pitman, 1938), 89–92.

296. K. G. Frank to Reyss, Sept. 18, 1919, SAA 68/li 262, Siemens Archives.

297. See discussion of its incorporation in ibid., and see Frank to Siemens-Schuckertwerke, Apr. 14, 1920, in ibid. for details of the plans. See also Wilfried Feldenkirchen, "Die Anfänge des Siemensgeschäfts in Amerika," in *Wirtschaft Gesellschaft Unternehmen,* ed. Wilfried Feldenkirchen et al. (Stuttgart: Franz Steiner, 1995), 896–897, which covers Siemens' modest U.S. business in this period.

298. See Contract, Oct. 23, 1919, SAA 68/li 262.

299. Frank to Carl F. von Siemens, Oct. 18, 1920, in ibid.

300. Sigfrid von Weiher and Herbert Goetzeler, *The Siemens Company* (Berlin and Munich: Siemens, 1984), 90; on Hugo Stinnes' postwar expansion, see Gras and Larson, *Casebook,* 654–658, and Gerald D. Feldman, *Iron and Steel in the German Inflation 1916–1923* (Princeton, N.J.: Princeton University Press, 1977), 241–244.

301. Stinnes had in December 1919 employed Harvey Allan Miller, a British subject, to be his representative in the United States—to purchase coal, metals, and other commodities for shipment to Europe. Stinnes established a credit line for Miller at the National City Bank (arranged through a Dutch bank, the Rotterdamsche Bankvereeniging). Stinnes claimed to have received approval for such business from the War Trade Section of the U.S. State Department. When in November 1920 Stinnes sued Miller to get an accounting of the latter's profits, the U.S. Justice Department declared no German could do business with the United States while Germany was still the "enemy," and the State Department could *not* authorize such business. Stinnes at once settled with Miller and withdrew his suit. *New York Times,* Nov. 10 and 12, 1920. Meanwhile, in 1920 H. H. Hollesen, had arrived in New York, where he formed H. Hollesen, Inc., which served as "chemical agents for Hugo Stinnes." Haynes, *American Chemical Industry,* V, 127.

302. Frank to Henrich, Mar. 10, 1921, SAA 68li 262.

303. On Adlanco Industrial Products, see Frank to Siemens-Schuckertwerke, Oct. 4, 1921, and Oct. 21, 1921; memos of Nov. 2, 1921, and Nov. 17, 1921; Frank to Siemens-Schuckertwerke, Dec. 31, 1921 (ownership) all in SAA 68/li 261.

304. Siemens-Schukertwerke memo, Feb. 22, 1924, in ibid.

305. Memos, June 25, 1923, and Aug. 21, 1923, in ibid.

306. Harm Schröter to Wilkins, Apr. 12, 1985; *New York Times,* Dec. 15, 1940 (obituary for Karl Frank); and data in SAA 68/li 262.

307. Memo from Lt. Col. Edward Davis, American Mission, Berlin, to Director of Military Intelligence, War Department, Aug. 9, 1920, in RG 165, 2331 B-15, National Archives. I am indebted to Professor Michael Geyer for directing me to this Krupp material. Krupp was Germany's largest company. Before the war, it was an armaments producer (with only 35 percent of its output devoted to civilian markets). By 1918, it had fully converted to making munitions. See the excellent article by Lothar Burchardt, "Between War Profits and War Costs: Krupp in the First World War," in *German Yearbook on Business History 1988,* ed. Hans Pohl and Bernd Rudolph (Berlin: Springer Verlag, 1990), 1–45.

308. Davis to Director Military Intelligence, Aug. 9, 1920, RG 165, 2331 B-15.

309. Memo from Davis to Director Military Intelligence, Oct. 2, 1920, in ibid.

310. See added data in same file.

311. Tauscher would in time become a U.S. citizen. For more on his career, see *New York Times,* Sept. 6, 1941 (obituary); Nov. 27, 1921 (first postwar return to United States); and Oct. 27, 1922 (return to United States on a regular basis).

312. Dornier went to Italy and Switzerland; Heinkel to Sweden; Junkers to the USSR; and Rohrbach to Denmark. Lawrence C. Tombs, *International Organization in European Air Transport* (New York: Columbia University Press, 1936), 10–11.

313. Fokker was born in 1890 in the Dutch East Indies. His first factory was in Germany, where he had manufactured for German military needs. At war's end, he smuggled planes and engines to Holland, organized a Dutch company, and started for the first time Dutch aircraft production that, according to Edward L. Homze, *Arming Lufwaffe: The Reich Air Ministry and the German Aircraft Industry 1919–39* (Lincoln: University of Nebraska Press, 1976), 9, was financed from a secret "Ruhr fund" collected by German industry.

314. Fokker made his first trip to the United States (November 1920–January 1921); he set up a sales company for his Dutch plant. On a second trip in 1922, he announced plans to manufacture in the United States and in 1923 formed the Atlantic Aircraft Corporation, which in 1924 leased factory buildings in New Jersey and started to manufacture there. Marc Dierikx, *Fokker* (Washington, D.C.: Smithsonian Institution, 1997), 108–115; see also Anthony H. G. Fokker and Bruce Gould, *Flying Dutchman: The Life of Anthony Fokker* (New York: Henry Holt & Co., 1931), 9, 15–16, 98–113, 141–148, 215–229, 238–243, 247–250.

315. Lewis, *America's Stake,* 142.

316. Margaret B. W. Graham, "R & D and Competition in England and the United States: The Case of the Aluminum Dirigible," *Business History Review,* 62 (Summer 1988): 265–266.

317. Hugh Allen, *The House of Goodyear* (1943; rpt. New York: Arno Press, 1976), 194.

318. Goodyear obtained in 1924 all the patents and processes of the German Zeppelin works. Allen, *House of Goodyear,* 194. I do not know the size of the German investment (or if it in fact existed); my only source on the investment is Lewis, *America's Stake,* 142. Allen, *House of Goodyear,* 194, writes that a dozen individuals from Zeppelin, headed by Karl Arnstein, came to America to work for Goodyear-Zeppelin. These men took out U.S. citizenship. Allen suggests there was no continuing ongoing relationship with an investing entity in Germany.

319. Margaret Graham to Mira Wilkins, Feb. 20, 1990, and Allen, *House of Goodyear,* 194 (U.S. government initiative).

320. *Moody's Industrials 1928,* 1570.

321. Office of Alien Property Custodian, *Annual Report for Year-ending June 30, 1944,* 79 (the 1920 entry).

322. Richard Sasuly, *I. G. Farben* (New York: Boni & Gaer, 1947), 175. The 1921 agreement is in U.S. Senate, Committee on Military Affairs, *Scientific and Technical Mobilization,* Hearings before the Subcommittee on War Mobilization, 78th Cong., 1st sess. (1943), pt. 16, 2123–2125 (Kilgore Committee Hearings).

323. Rosenbaum and Sherman, *M. M. Warburg,* 124.

324. David Farrer, *The Warburgs* (London: Michael Joseph, 1975), 80.

325. See Chapter 3 for details. A number of sources, including Rosenbaum and Sherman, *M. M. Warburg,* 127n, state that M. M. Warburg & Co. was a founding shareholder. IAB records in the Chase Manhattan Bank Archives, New York, show this was not the case. Despite the fact that Paul Warburg never resumed his prewar partnership in M. M. Warburg & Co., in December 1922 he wrote his brother Max, "I myself have never lost the feeling of belonging to the firm [M. M. Warburg & Co.]." Chernow, *Warburgs,* 161.

326. James P. Warburg, *The Long Road Home* (Garden City, N.Y.: Doubleday, 1964), 52.

327. Testimony of James Speyer, U.S. Senate, Committee on Finance, *Sale of Foreign Bonds, Hearings,* 72nd Cong., 1st sess. (1932), pt. 2, 606–609. See also *Fortune,* Aug. 1931, 79–80, 82.

328. Gwinner retired from the Deutsche Bank in 1920; he died in 1931. Gall et al., *Deutsche Bank,* 88, 184–185. He was, however, an important figure in German banking.

329. Wilkins, *History,* 119; Karl Strasser, *Die Deutschen Banken im Ausland* (Munich: Verlag von Ernst–Reinhart, 1925), 167.

330. *New York Times,* Aug. 8, 1923; see also Strasser, *Deutschen Banken,* 168n, which indicates that its former Leipzig parent house was a creditor to the extent of $2.8 million.

331. "Direction Der Disconto-Gesellschaft," *Bankers Magazine,* New York, 105 (Oct. 1922): 649–652.

332. *New York Times,* Aug. 8, 1923.

333. For his arrest and detainment, see *New York Times,* Apr. 8, 1917, Feb. 4 and Nov. 3, 1918. On his 1921 activities as Deutsche Bank representative in New York, see Gall et al., *Deutsche Bank,* 188; *Moody's Banks, 1928,* 1115, lists him as New York representative of the Deutsche Bank. He retired in 1930. *New York Times,* Sept. 30, 1954 (for his obituary).

334. Sturmey, *British Shipping,* 37.

335. Safford, *Wilsonian Maritime Diplomacy,* 96, 187–188, 194, 203.

336. Rudy Abramson, *Spanning the Century: The Life of W. Averell Harriman 1891–1986* (New York: Morrow & Co., 1992), 115–123.

337. Ibid., 124–130; Safford, *Wilsonian Maritime Diplomacy,* 239–243; Larry I. Bland, "W. Averell Harriman: Businessman and Diplomat 1891–1945," Ph.D. diss., University of Wisconsin, 1972, 35–39; L. U. Scholl, "Shipping in Germany," in Yui and Nakagawa, *Business History of Shipping,* 207. Reading between the lines, it was logical that Harriman would form a link with Hapag. For his father's connections with the Warburgs, see Chernow, *Warburgs,* 48, 88, 184. See ibid., 103–109, for Warburg-Hapag cooperation before the First World War; and ibid., 274, for the postwar relationships (here the sequencing is imprecise, but the associations are conspicuous).

338. Scholl, "Shipping in Germany," 207; see also Norddeutscher Lloyd, *Bericht 1914/1918, 1919, 1920,* and idem., *Bericht 1921.* On the problems of U.S. Mail, see Abramson, *Spanning the Century,* 134–136. The number eleven comes from the North German Lloyd Line Report. Abramson says "thirteen."

339. Bland, "W. Averell Harriman," 47.

340. When in the 1921 downturn, U.S. shipping had virtually collapsed, German problems at home temporarily postponed the rebuilding of German shipping. Nonetheless, in 1921, the German government had provided moneys for the reconstruction of a German merchant marine. Slowly, it began to rise from the ashes of war. Scholl, "Shipping in Germany," 206–207. The 1923 arrangements with Harriman were one step in the process.

341. The new American company that acquired the properties of the onetime German subsidiary went into liquidation in 1929. *Moody's Industrials 1929,* 3127.

342. The American Orenstein-Arthur Koppel Co. was sold to Pressed Steel Car Co., Pittsburgh, for $1.3 million on September 12, 1918. Data in RG 131, Box 212. In 1920, the German parent—acting through its prewar representatives, who had been interned during the war—started to solicit former customers. In 1923, a U.S. circuit court ruled, however, that the American purchaser had "the exclusive right" to carry on the prewar business. *New York Times,* Mar. 25, 1923. On Orenstein & Koppel's post–World War I *European* business, see Harm Schröter, "Continuity and Change," in *The Rise of Multinationals in Continental Europe,* ed. Geoffrey Jones and Harm Schröter (Aldershot: Edward Elgar, 1993), 31.

343. See Chapter 1.

344. On Du Pont's relations with the Nobels, see Wilkins, *History,* 386–389, and Reader, *Imperial Chemical Industries,* I, passim, esp. 395–396 on the 1920 accord.

345. In 1928, Imperial Chemical Industries (ICI), which by then had acquired Nobel Industries, decided to dispose of 5,000 shares of Du Pont stock. Du Pont's treasurer knew nothing of these holdings, since the shares had been acquired by a nominee. Reader, *Imperial Chemical Industries,* II, 50n. ICI's historian does not say when these shares were initially obtained; my *guess* is 1920 would have been a logical time.

346. Chandler and Salsbury, *Pierre S. du Pont* 425–426.

347. See Chapter 1, note 115.

348. A 1924 letterhead of I. Levinstein & Co., Inc., exists in the Garvan Papers, Box 45. It describes the company as having an "American works" at Framingham, Massachusetts, which suggests some manufacturing. Its U.S. warehouses and offices were in Framingham, Chicago, and Boston. Edgar Levinstein was president and treasurer of the American firm.

349. Reader, *Imperial Chemical Industries,* I, 280, 425–436.

350. Du Pont obtained American rights to processes developed by British Dyes (the old Read Holliday), Société Nationale des Matières Colorantes, and the Italian National Dyestuff Company. Haynes, *American Chemical Industry,* III, 244. Wilkins, *History,* 359, 810 (on United Piece Works). Hounshell and Smith, *Science and Corporate Strategy,* 91 (on the Du Pont acquisition of United Piece Works).

351. Haynes, *American Chemical Industry,* III, 245, on the "obscure descriptions" in some of the licensed German chemical patents.

352. Hounshell and Smith, *Science and Corporate Strategy,* 92 (on the losing bid).

353. *APC Report,* 50–51, and Kathryn Steen, "Confiscated Commerce: American Importers of German Synthetic Organic Chemicals, 1914–1929," *History and Technology,* 12 (1995): 269–270, on the Cassella impact on NACC. Also merged into NACC in 1917 was W. Beckers Aniline & Chemical Co., founded in 1912 and headed by the German-born Dr. William Gerard Beckers. Beckers had come to the United States as a color technician for Bayer and then left the German subsidiary to set up his own business. Haynes, *American Chemical Industry,* III, 234–235.

354. Haynes, *American Chemical Industry,* III, 260–262, 482; U.S. Senate, Committee on Judiciary, *Alleged Dye Monopoly, Hearings,* 67th Cong. (1922), 104–105 (henceforth cited as *1922 Dye Hearings).* The 4,500 number is from *APC Report,* 61. The best data on The

Chemical Foundation are in the Garvan Papers at the American Heritage Center, University of Wyoming, Laramie, Wyoming. Box 6 has the foundation's minute books; it contains the certificate of incorporation, Feb. 19, 1919, with a list of the subscribing companies represented. The Chemical Foundation with its patent ownership could control imports into the United States of the patented products. The patents were not only for chemical products but covered all German patents that were in the Alien Property Custodian's possession in February 1919. The difference between the 6,000 and 4,500 numbers relates mainly to the patents that went with Sterling Products' acquisition of Bayer, certain patents that had expired, and other miscellaneous ones.

355. Garvan was au courant on what was happening in Paris. See "Cablegrams," Box 5, Garvan Papers. When Bernard Baruch, with the American delegation in Paris, recommended that The Chemical Foundation send over a dye expert, Garvan's choice was Charles H. Herty, secretary of the War Trade Board (who was passing on licensing imports) and was former president of the American Chemists Society. See dispatch from D. H. Miller, American Mission Paris, Aug. 18, 1919, Box 5, Garvan Papers; for earlier efforts to have Garvan represented, see A. M. Paterson to Clarence M. Woolley, War Trade Board, Apr. 21, 1919, in ibid.

356. As early as April–June 1919, Brunner, Mond officials visited Badische's original Haber-Bosch ammonia plant at Oppau. Reader, *Imperial Chemical Industries,* I, 334–355. See also Haynes, *American Chemical Industry,* III, 506–508, and Borkin, *Crime and Punishment,* 28ff.

357. Mann and Plummer, *Aspirin Wars,* 42, 47–48, and Bericht Herrenbrück, Nordamerika und Kanada, n.d. [ca. 1953], pp. 111–114, Bayer Archives, Leverkusen I/1/6./66. (I am indebted to Elisabeth Glaser-Schmidt for a copy of this document.)

358. Mann and Plummer, *Aspirin Wars,* 53.

359. Erik Verg, *Milestones* (Leverkusen: Bayer, 1988), 208, found an August 14, 1919, cable from Grasselli Chemical Company to the German Bayer, suggesting a meeting with Carl Duisberg. There is no indication as to whether the meeting actually took place.

360. Mann and Plummer, *Aspirin Wars,* 58. Ibid., 50–51, describes Sterling Products as a patent medicine firm. Its founder, Weiss, was, however, a graduate of the Philadelphia College of Pharmacy. Weiss' family had a German background, but as far as I can establish, up until the postwar period he had had no German business connections. For Sterling Products' early history and Weiss' background, see Haynes, *American Chemical Industry,* VI, 406–407.

361. Haynes, *American Chemical Industry,* IV, 235.

362. Haber, *Chemical Industry,* 248–250; Haynes, *American Chemical Industry,* III, 508. The text is in Bernard M. Baruch, *The Making of the Reparation and Economic Sections of the Treaty* (1920; rpt. New York: Howard Fertig, 1970), 167–169.

363. Haynes, *American Chemical Industry,* III, 264. See also cables in Box 5 and correspondence in Box 44, Garvan Papers. The Textile Alliance was an industry-wide association that had cooperated earlier with the National Defense Council and then with the War Industries Board. Haynes, *American Chemical Industry,* III, 264n.

364. For the continuing technical difficulties, see *1922 Dye Hearings,* 816. The textile industry was the largest customer for dyes.

365. See data in Boxes 5 and 44, Garvan Papers.

366. "Morris Richard Poucher," *National Cyclopaedia,* XXXIII, 552. Albert M. Patterson, president of the Textile Alliance, actually introduced Poucher to Garvan in 1918. See Patterson to Garvan, June 14, 1918, Box 44, Garvan Papers.

367. On October 27, 1919, Charles K. Weston, publicity manager, Du Pont, Wilmington, forwarded to Garvan a cable from Poucher, which read, "All conditions here are now wholly favorable proper control entire [dyestuff] shipment through Alliance Stop

Up to you to see that either through Foundation patents or other this plan is not defeated on your side." In Box 5, Garvan Papers.

368. Charles Meade to W. S. Carpenter, Nov. 29, 1919, U.S. Senate, Special Committee Investigating the Munitions Industry, *The Munitions Industry, Hearings,* 74th Cong., 1st sess. (1934), pt. 11, 2571, Exhibit 919 (henceforth cited as *Nye Committee Hearings*).

369. Ibid. Badische officials could not believe "the seizure of patents" by The Chemical Foundation would be upheld in the courts. Nonetheless, they began to make contingency plans. See Paul Pickhardt, Paris, to Adolph Kuttroff, Nov. 7, 1919, in Box 44, Garvan Papers.

370. Eysten Berg to Badische Board of Directors, June 15, 1920, Acc. 1662, Box 34, Du Pont Papers, Wilmington.

371. The draft is in Acc. 1662, Box 34, Du Pont Papers.

372. Reader, *Imperial Chemical Industries,* I, 361 ("no say"). On the foreign ownership of Solvay Process Co., see Wilkins, *History,* 405. On Solvay & Cie.'s ownership interest in Semet-Solvay, see Lewis, *America's Stake,* 566. Solvay & Cie. later would argue that but for its exchange of its large interest in SPC for Allied Chemical & Dye Corporation stock, the latter could not have become an important manufacturer of alkalies, etc.: "A great national industry was . . . organized in the United States with the full support and cooperation of Solvay & Company, for the benefit of American industry and labor." Solvay & Cie. to Orlando Weber, June 24, 1933, circular letter sent Weber and Allied stockholders, in Box 50, Garvan Papers. The latter declaration may, however, have been self-serving.

373. Haynes, *American Chemical Industry,* IV, 86.

374. Reader, *Imperial Chemical Industries,* I, 361. There were rumors that Weber was also negotiating with Badische. See Haynes, *American Chemical Industry,* III, 272n.

375. Eysten Berg to Irénée du Pont et al., Feb. 3, 1920, *Nye Committee Hearings,* pt. 11, 2578–79, Exhibit 925. Of course, Du Pont had everything to do with the difficulties raised against German dyes in America.

376. And, if there were patents held by The Chemical Foundation, the latter expected a royalty payments if there were imports.

377. Mann and Plummer, *Aspirin Wars,* 59–61, 353. I have seen no documentation on the Bayer-Grasselli negotiations of 1920, nor any details on the "arrangements." See, however, Verena Schröter, "Participation in Market Control through Foreign Investment," in Alice Teichova et al., *Multinational Enterprise in Historical Perspective,* 172–173.

378. Mann and Plummer, *Aspirin Wars,* 63, and Wilkins, *Maturing,* 82.

379. See report in Eysten Berg to Irénée du Pont, June 15, 1920, Acc. 1662, Box 34, Du Pont Papers. For more on Poucher, see Metz testimony, *1922 Dye Hearings,* 811.

380. Berg to Badische, June 15, 1920, Acc. 1662, Box 34, Du Pont Papers.

381. Berg to Irénée du Pont, Oct. 25, 1920, Acc. 1662, Box 35, Du Pont Papers.

382. Ibid., and Irénée du Pont to Berg, Mar. 22, 1921, Acc. 1662, Box 35, Du Pont Papers.

383. Enclosure in Berg to Irénée du Pont, Feb. 21, 1921, and Berg to Irénée du Pont, Feb. 24, 1921, Acc. 1662, Box 35, Du Pont Papers.

384. Charles Meade to Irénée du Pont, Mar. 21, 1921, and Irénée du Pont to Berg, Mar. 22, 1921, Acc. 1662, Box 35, Du Pont Papers.

385. Haynes, *American Chemical Industry,* III, 268. The 1916 tariff had raised duties for five years. Steen, "Confiscated Commerce," 267.

386. Reader, *Imperial Chemical Industries,* I, 438.

387. On overcapacity, see Haynes, *American Chemical Industry,* II, 122–123.

388. Ibid., VI, 9.

389. Ibid., VI, 9, and II, 426n (which gives the three names on the board). Wm. J. Matheson, who had represented German Cassella interests in the United States, was also on the

board. Reader, *Imperial Chemical Industries,* I, 292–293, 318–319, 361–362 (for the refusal to cooperate).

390. Reader, *Imperial Chemical Industries,* I, 345, 462 (the agreement would be voided in 1926).

391. Ibid., 318. In 1981 Allied Chemical & Dye Corporation became Allied Corporation, which in 1985 merged with Signal Companies of California to become Allied-Signal. By then it was no longer a chemical company, but in the interwar years it vied with Du Pont for first place in the U.S. chemical industry.

392. Mahoney, *Merchants of Life,* 194. Data on the trustee arrangements are from Louis Galambos, who has had access to Merck & Co. archives.

393. See James M. Gifford to W. W. Wilson (General Counsel Alien Property Custodian), Jan. 22, 1926, Du Pont Papers. This seven-page letter provides much more detail. See also the nine-page chronology entitled "The Roessler & Hasslacher Chemical Co.," Du Pont Papers, showing the changes in the capital structure of Roessler & Hasslacher Chemical Co., 1889–1930.

394. Christopher Kobrak, "Between Nationalism and Internationalism: Schering AG and the Culture of German Capitalism, 1851–1945," Ph.D. diss., Columbia University, 1999, 75–176, 327–333. See also Haynes, *American Chemical Industry,* III, 322, who says Schering & Glatz had American rights to Atophan and began producing it after the war; and ibid., IV, 246n, 255, 536, on Atophan (cinchophen) and Alyco Manufacturing Co. Haynes knew nothing about the German Schering's role.

395. Pierre Cayez to Mira Wilkins, June 26, 1983; Pierre Cayez, *Rhône Poulenc 1895–1975* (Paris: Armand Colin/Masson, 1988), 65, 93–94; and Haynes, *American Chemical Industry,* III, 337, 343, 473, and IV, 253. Before the war, la Société Chimique des Usines du Rhône had had an interest in Fries Brothers. Wilkins, *History,* 399. Fries Bros. survived the war (Haynes, *American Chemical Industry,* III, 470, and VI, 171), but the French company's relations with that firm did not persist. On the continuities from the earlier relationship, see Wilkins, "French Multinationals," 18, 21–22. On Coty, see Lewis, *America's Stake,* 142. Coty Inc. became a "migrating" multinational enterprise, setting up its headquarters in the United States; soon it would be expanding abroad from the U.S. base. For its later history, see Wilkins, *Maturing,* 139.

396. U.S. Senate, Committee on Patents, *Patents, Hearings,* 77th Cong, 2nd sess. (1942), 2061 (henceforth cited as *Bone Committee Hearings*). During the entire period covered by my volume, Ciba, Geigy, and Sandoz remained separate companies. In 1970, after a merger, Ciba-Geigy was formed; then, in 1996, that firm took over Sandoz; the new enterprise was renamed Novartis.

397. For the prewar background, see Wilkins, *History,* 394–395.

398. According to Haynes, *American Chemical Industry,* VI, 362, published in 1949, the Sandoz sales unit was established in 1919. In ibid., III, 305, published in 1954, Haynes writes (based on a company memorandum of 1944 to Haynes), "The Sandoz Chemical Works, American agents of the Swiss dye company, began in 1917 to make medicinal products" in the United States.

399. Ibid., III, 217, and VI, 81, 362, 225. The stock in the Cincinnati Chemical Works was held in the same ratio set out in the 1918 Swiss community of interest agreement: Ciba owned 52 percent, Geigy 24 percent, and Sandoz 24 percent. Wilkins, "Swiss Investments," 104n.51. Ault & Wiborg was an American manufacturer of printing inks, which had started making dyestuff intermediates during wartime. In 1928, it was absorbed into Interchemical Corporation. Haynes, *American Chemical Industry,* III, 102, 217. Before World War I, Ciba had exported to the United States through independent agents. Its shares in Cincinnati Chemical Works appear to have been its first direct investment in the United States. Ibid., VI, 80.

400. Haynes, *America 1 Chemical Industry,* VI, 80, and III, 246n.

401. Alfred Bürgin, *Geschichte des Geigy-Unternehmens von 1758 bis 1939* (Basle: J. R. Geigy, S.A., 1958), 297. Apparently, the Swiss affiliates did employ individuals who had worked for German subsidiaries in America. Thus, according to Haynes, *American Chemical Industry,* IV, 239n, Charles A. Mace, a technical salesman for Badische (1907–1916), joined Ciba in 1919. Although Ciba's first U.S. direct investment appears to have been in 1920, it may well have started hiring technical salesmen in 1919, so this is not inconsistent.

402. On Hoffmann-La Roche, see Haynes, *American Chemical Industry,* VI, 209, and Peyer, *Roche,* 70, 75, 88, 104.

403. Reader, *Imperial Chemical Industries,* I, 229, and Wilkins, *History,* 375, 406–407, on Castner-Kellner's prewar interests. Castner-Kellner Alkali Co. Ltd. had become a wholly owned subsidiary of Brunner, Mond in 1920. Its interest in Mathieson Alkali Works was too small to give it any influence. When in 1922 the capital of the Niagara Electro Chemical Company was raised from $100,000 to $2 million, existing shareholders saw their shareholdings increase; Castner-Kellner's holdings went from 270 shares to 5,400, which represented 27 percent of the outstanding stock. Based on data in the Roessler & Hasslacher Chemical Company files, Du Pont Papers. On Brunner, Mond's control of Castner-Kellner, see Reader, *Imperial Chemical Industries,* I, 329.

404. Haynes, *American Chemical Industry,* VI, 61. In addition, the British-owned Beecham's, which had a prewar factory in Brooklyn, New York, endured as a manufacturer there. In 1920 its U.S. business had $311,000 in sales and $73,000 in profits. It was not—nor would it be in the 1920s—an important factor in the U.S. market. See T. A. B. Corley, "From National to Multinational Enterprise: The Beecham Business 1848–1945," unpublished paper, 1983.

405. Haynes, *American Chemical Industry,* III, 264; *1922 Dye Hearings,* 39, 1422–23, 1428.

406. Translation of I. G. Farben to Reich Ministry of Economics, July 24, 1939, RG 238, T301, Reel 70, NI-8496. This was not exactly what happened: the important Salvarsan, Neo-salvarsan, and Novocaine patents had been licensed to Farbwerke-Hoechst, New York; with the First World War, the latter's licenses were canceled and then reissued to H. A. Metz Laboratories. See Federal Trade Commission, "Report on Administration of Patents," Jan. 28, 1924, published in *Bone Committee Hearings,* pt. 3, 1212–13. From April 10, 1919, to July 2, 1922, H. A. Metz Laboratories paid a licensing fee of $149,953 to the APC and then to the U.S. Treasury for licenses of Salvarsan and Novocaine under the FTC licenses. See "Receipt and Release of the Chemical Foundation," July 22, 1931, Box 103, Garvan Papers. In effect, H. A. Metz—the former German importer—continued to have access to the patents, which was the point of the I. G. Farben official's statement.

407. On the imports and royalties, see data in Box 44, Garvan Papers. Kuttroff, Pickhardt & Co. paid a licensing fee of $4,498.69 for July–September 1922 imports.

408. Haber, *Chemical Industry,* 240, and F. W. Taussig, *The Tariff History of the United States,* 8th rev. ed. (New York: Capricorn Books, 1964).

409. Haynes, *American Chemical Industry,* III, 273–274, 510–511, IV, 240–241. On the price, see Chemical Foundation, Board of Directors Minutes, Apr. 4, 1919, Box 6, Garvan Papers; on Miller's refusal to serve as a director, see ibid., June 21, 1921, Box 6, Garvan Papers. On the suits, see Chemical Foundation, Shareholders' Meeting, Feb. 4, 1924, Box 6, Garvan Papers. Garvan believed that Metz was behind the government suit. See Typed Statement of Francis P. Garvan, July 7, 1922, Box 24, Garvan Paper. The U.S. suit, *U.S. v. The Chemical Foundation,* was filed Sept. 8, 1922.

410. Wilkins, *History,* 392–393.

411. Ibid., 392.

412. Haynes, *American Chemical Industry,* IV, 235.

413. Ibid., IV, 141, and Stocking and Watkins, *Cartels in Action,* 284.

414. Verg, *Milestones,* 221.

415. Verena Schröter located in the Bayer Works archive a copy of the initial agreement between Bayer Leverkusen and Winthrop Chemical Co., Apr. 9, 1923. Schröter, "Participation," 182n.8. On this agreement, see Wilkins, *Maturing,* 82; Mahoney, *Merchants of Life,* 213; Mann and Plummer, *Aspirin Wars,* 69–70; and Corwin Edwards, *Economic and Political Aspects of International Cartels* (1944; Rpt. New York: Arno Press, 1976), 49–50. A half share in the profits of a firm was equivalent to an equity stake. Winthrop Chemical Co. had been incorporated about March 18, 1919, under New York law. See "Strictly Confidential Letter," Proudfoot's Commercial Agency, to National Aniline & Chemical Co., Oct. 2, 1920, Box 108, Garvan Papers.

416. *Bayer Co., Inc. v. United Drug Co.,* 272 Fed. 505 (SDNY 1921).

417. Steen, "Confiscated Commerce," 276, notes that the aspirin business had been kept separate and was not associated with Winthrop Chemical.

418. Bericht Herrenbrück [1953], p. 118.

419. Hounshell and Smith, *Science and Corporate Strategy,* 170–172, 609; George W. Stocking and Willard F. Mueller, "The Cellophane Case and the New Competition," *American Economic Review,* 45 (Mar. 1955): 32–35. Du Pont also had a joint venture with Comptoir des Textiles Artificiels in rayon (see Chapter 3); the viscose method of making rayon was very similar to that used in making cellophane.

420. That the British agreement was vetoed by the Board of Trade president (Sidney Webb) in 1924 is not germane. Reader, *Imperial Chemical Industries,* I, 445–446. What is fundamental is that the linkages were being reestablished.

3. Survival, Expansion, and New Arrivals, 1919–1923

1. This pattern was frequent with U.S.-Canadian companies. British American Tobacco Company, set up in the United Kingdom, came to be controlled from the United Kingdom; I do include it herein, albeit I note that its investments in the United States began when it was U.S. controlled.

2. Some foreign direct investments were excluded from the table because the new entries did not survive until 1934, when the table was prepared. There were no reporting requirements. The Department of Commerce listing, for example, (1) badly understated the distribution investments, (2) may identify as in this period certain manufacturing investments actually made earlier and neglected others, (3) contains no mining investments, which is a mistake, (4) does not include the direct investments in bank agencies, (5) omits other direct investments in banking, and (6) shows no Japanese direct investments, even though most made in this period did last through 1934. There were a number of foreign trade-related investments; some of these companies participated in domestic distribution as well, but the majority did not (such foreign trade–related stakes are clearly understated on this table).

3. For example, Lewis, *America's Stake,* 142, includes as a new British direct investment in these years the Ideal Sewing Company (1920). It was never an important factor in the U.S. sewing machine market, nor did it meet any of my other criteria for importance; thus, I exclude it. Likewise, she lists a 1921 Belgian investment, Belgian American Coke Ovens Corp. (Note Table 3.1 has zero "other Europe" investments for 1921.) I did not discuss it in Chapter 2 when I covered the chemical industry—nor here—because I can find no evidence of its having any consequence. It is possible that Ideal Sewing Machine might be one of the new British manufacturing investments, identified by the U.S. Department of Commerce in 1920.

4. See Lamb, *History of the Canadian Pacific Railroad,* 280–284, 288–299; Graham D. Taylor and Peter A. Baskerville, *A Concise History of Business in Canada* (Toronto: Oxford University Press, 1994), 282–285.

5. See map in Marshall, Southard, and Taylor, *Canadian-American Industry,* 114–115, 263.

6. For background, see Wilkins, *History,* 226. Lewis, *America's Stake,* 106, 546, 558, put Canadian direct investments in U.S. railroads at $99 million in 1919, up from $82 million in 1914, while Mexican direct investments in U.S. railroads were valued by her at $2.5 million in 1919, down from $3.2 million in 1914. She estimated Canadian direct investments in U.S. railroads at $125 million in 1924; she provides no figure for the Mexican direct investments in U.S. railroads in 1924, although she indicates that such investments continued on.

7. In the colonial period, of course, the Virginia Companies had minority interests by the British Crown. I use the word "probably" because there could be some arguments for other contenders, but, for example, neither Anglo-Iranian Oil, which had large British government interests, nor the French government–owned potash mines seems a legitimate contender.

8. Wilkins, *History,* 229–236.

9. On British landownership as a consequence of mortgage defaults, see Jackson, *Enterprising Scot,* 282. The Dutch were having the same experiences.

10. Ivan Wright, *Farm Mortgage Financing* (New York: McGraw-Hill, 1923), 172.

11. Cowles, *The Astors,* 189.

12. See Wilkins, *History,* 512, on when the Dutch held about 15 percent of the best Spokane, Washington, city center properties.

13. See Wilkins, *History,* 351, and Jackson, *Enterprising Scot,* 284, on the problems this company faced in the early 1920s.

14. On the 1911 purchase, see Wilkins, *History,* 351–352. I have reconstructed the FCSDA story with the assistance of Noel Workman, historian of DPLC (conversation June 3, 1999), and Janice Scott Person of DPLC. I thank both for their help. Extremely useful are Lawrence J. Nelson, *King Cotton's Advocate: Oscar G. Johnston and the New Deal* (Knoxville: University of Tennessee Press, 1999), 21–30; *Fortune,* Mar. 1937, 129–130; and Brandfon, *Cotton Kingdom of the New South,* 129–131. In 1919 FCSDA had an interest in three companies: DPLC, Delta Farms, and Empire Farm (the last was folded into DPLC in 1931). Nelson, *King Cotton's Advocate,* 236n.1, says rhetoric notwithstanding, DPLC did *not* have the largest cotton plantation in the United States (a 60,000 acre plantation in Arkansas was larger). Yet the 38,000 acres was unquestionably huge and was the largest in Mississippi.

15. Wilkins, *History,* 302–305.

16. Jackson, *Enterprising Scot,* 134–136.

17. Harmon Ross Mothershead, *The Swan Land and Cattle Company, Ltd.* (Norman: University of Oklahoma Press, 1971), 142–149.

18. For the early history of Riverside Orange, see Wilkins, *History,* 234. Balfour, Guthrie (the Balfour, Williamson firm on the West Coast) retained fruit-growing lands and vineyards in California. On its prewar holdings, see ibid., 318.

19. U.S. Bureau of the Census, *Historical Statistics of the United States* (Washington, D.C., 1975), 497. In 1920, U.S. agricultural exports exceeded imports. By 1922, the balance had changed, and agricultural imports surpassed exports.

20. Wheat and wheat flour (together) were greater than raw cotton exports in 1921 (raw cotton that year exceeded wheat exports, as it did every year); in 1930 (for the one year), machinery exports were larger than raw cotton exports. Ibid. 898.

21. On Balfour, Williamson (and its California partnership, Balfour, Guthrie), see Hunt, *Heirs of Great Adventure,* II, esp. 79–80, 164 (on the flour mill in Portland, Oregon, and Crown Mills). As noted earlier, Balfour, Guthrie also retained interests in fruit lands and vineyards.

22. In both grain and tobacco, there may have been some small holdings by the exporters. In tobacco, these small plots appear to have been for research purposes.

23. Wilkins, *History,* 339.

24. Mira Wilkins, *The Emergence of Multinational Enterprise. American Business abroad from the Colonial Era to 1914* (Cambridge, Mass.: Harvard University Press, 1970), 92–93. After 1911, Americans remained as managing directors of BAT branches where American Tobacco had been well established (as in China); English directors managed branches where Imperial had the long history. See Sherman Cochran, *Big Business in China* (Cambridge, Mass.: Harvard University Press, 1980), 13. The story of British American Tobacco is recounted in Howard Cox, *The Global Cigarette: Origins and Evolution of British American Tobacco, 1880–1945* (Oxford: Oxford University Press, 2000).

25. At least according to Howard Cox, "Growth and Ownership in the International Tobacco Industry: BAT 1902–1927," *Business History,* 31 (Jan. 1989): 55–57, and Howard Cox, "The Global Cigarette," Ph.D. diss., University of London, 1990, 125. In March 1915, of the 10 million registered shares, 7 million were reported as held in Great Britain. Ibid., 133. In Cox, *Global Cigarette,* 6, Cox states that already in 1912 Imperial Tobacco Company was the leading minority shareholder; he does not, however, provide figures on James B. Duke's personal shareholdings. In December 1918, BAT had nine directors of American nationality (three with U.S. addresses, five with British addresses, and one with a Shanghai address) and eight of British nationality, all with U.K. addresses. Ibid., 141.

26. On the relationship between BAT and Imperial Tobacco, see *B.A.T. Industries, Facts and Figures 1991,* 14th ed. (London: B.A.T. Industries PLC, May 1991), 21, and Cox, *Global Cigarette,* passim. In 1913, BAT had moved to a new, prestigious head office location at Westminister House, Millbank, London, next door to the Houses of Parliament. It did not share this head office with Imperial Tobacco.

27. R. T. Davenport-Hines, "Sir Hugo Cunliffe-Owen," *Dictionary of Business Biography,* I, 865. Cox, "Growth," 47, 57; Cox, "Global Cigarette," 127; and Cox, *Global Cigarette,* passim. Cunliffe-Owen was a founding director of British American Tobacco Company and remained a director until February 1945. Ibid., 95. Ibid., 124, says Duke had decided to transfer Cunliffe-Owen to New York in *1910.* He had apparently gone for a year, returned home, and then after the Supreme Court decision and the dissolution of American Tobacco become BAT's New York representative.

28. Cox, "Growth," 57–58. Howard Cox, "Learning to Do Business in China: The Evolution of BAT's Cigarette Distribution Network, 1902–41," *Business History,* 39 (July 1997): 49ff., for the rise of London control over the huge Chinese business.

29. Cox, "Growth," 58–59, and Cox, *Global Cigarette,* passim, are very convincing on the control moving to London. Yet in certain overseas markets, China, for example, American control or at least influence was still very much in evidence. Compare Cochran, *Big Business in China,* 124–126, with Cox, "Learning to Do Business." Cox, *Global Cigarette,* 126, 135, on the factories in Richmond and Petersburg, Virginia. See also ibid., 10, 137–138, on how BAT shifted its source of cigarette exports to China from Great Britain to the United States during the war years. The cigarette factory in Richmond, Virginia, was actually owned by BAT's subsidiary, Export Leaf Tobacco Co., reflecting the linkage between leaf and cigarette exports. Ibid., 249n.19. See ibid., 249, for BAT's manufacturing facilities in the United States.

30. On Duke's stepping down, see Cox, *Global Cigarette,* 242–248, and Reavis Cox, *Competition in the American Tobacco Industry 1911–1932* (New York: Columbia University Press, 1933), 73, 297. See also Cochran, *Big Business in China,* 164.

31. In connection with this joint venture (which is not mentioned in Cox, *Global Cigarette*), BAT agreed to purchase a "substantial amount" of its foil and waxed paper needs from U.S. Foil. Nannie M. Tilley, *The R. J. Reynolds Tobacco Company* (Chapel Hill: University of North Carolina Press, 1985), 349, 651–652. U.S. Foil Co. was the parent to Reynolds Metals, formed in 1928. See William G. Reynolds, Jr., letter in *Wall Street Journal,* Aug. 31, 1992. In 1917, BAT had bought the Smith Paper Company of Lee, Massachusetts, and during the war, it set up the Garland Steamship Corporation. It held on to the Smith Paper Co. at least through the 1920s; the steamship company was divested in the 1920s. Cox, *Global Cigarette,* 249n.31, 264n.74. Cox sees the latter investments as an attempt by BAT's American office to engage in "some degree of vertical integration." Ibid.

32. Lewis, *America's Stake,* 562, identified as "British-owned" a firm formed in 1907 and called United States Lumber and Cotton Co. I have not been able to establish foreign equity ownership. There was, however, foreign involvement in a $2 million bond issue (March 1910). The company paid its last dividend in 1915; it stopped paying interest on the debt in 1917. It sold some 8,000 acres in Mississippi in 1919 and applied most of the proceeds to retiring a large part of the bond issue. In the early 1920s, it owned about 93,000 acres of timberland in southwestern Alabama. The company "suspended operations" in 1927. *Moody's Industrials 1929,* 1509, and *Moody's Industrials 1933,* 629. This was a case where cotton and timber lands were combined, and there were others. Also, some paper and pulp producers and some mining companies owned timberland.

33. Marshall, Southard, and Taylor, *Canadian-American Industry,* 178.

34. The Kellner Partington Co. Ltd. had built the Borregaard mills *in Norway* in partnership with Norwegian businessmen; it had a paper mill in Britain and another in Austria. In 1917, control of the British Kellner Partington passed to A/S Borregaard—a case of a migrating multinational enterprise. By the early 1920s, the Norwegian firm had plants in Norway, Sweden, Austria, and Great Britain, as well as the United States. Letter from Even Lange to Mira Wilkins, Apr. 5, 1988; Jorma Ahvenainen and Even Lange, "Foreign and Domestic Capital in the Growth of the North European Timber Industries, 1860–1920," unpublished paper, given at Campinas, Brazil, 1989; *Stock Exchange Year Book 1929,* 2904; and Haber, *Chemical Industry,* 167.

35. Since long before the First World War, N. S. Stowell & Co., Dixfield, Maine, was the principal supplier of spools for the J. & P. Coats mills at Pawtucket, while John MacGregor provided the Clark Thread Company's requirements from his mill in South Lincoln, Maine. Both the Stowell and MacGregor's mills exported to fill certain needs of the Scottish parent Coats company. Stowell had been able to expand with the financial aid of the Coats firm. It is not clear whether MacGregor got financing from the Coats organization, but he depended on the Coats-Clark companies for his business. See David Keir, "The Coats Story," unpublished typescript, 1964 (access granted by Coats), III, 154. On BAT's investment in the paper company, see this chapter, note 31.

36. Agnes H. Hicks, *The Story of the Forestal* (London: The Forestal Land, Timber & Railway Co., 1956), 21, and Wilkins, *History,* 817n.179. The Brooklyn subsidiary was called the New York Quebracho Extract Co., a name that was "later" (n.d.—probably in the early 1920s) changed to the Tannin Co. The Forestal Land, Timber & Railway Co. did not own timberland in the United States.

37. Kawabe, "Japanese Business," 74, 120. Mitsubishi Goshi Kaisha established in 1918 MSK, which took over its trade department, including the Seattle branch. Ibid., 33.

38. Spurr, *Political and Commercial Geology,* 479.

39. See Wilkins, *History,* 241, 861; Tomboy Gold Mines, Ltd., Reel 73, Roll 44, Western

Range Cattle Industry Study, Library of Congress, Acc. 11,092. The Tomboy Gold Mines was wound up in 1929.

40. William Kilbourn, *The Elements Combined: A History of the Steel Company of Canada* (Toronto: Clarke, Irwin, 1960), 103.

41. On Loncala Phosphate Co., see Mira Wilkins, *New Foreign Enterprise in Florida* (Miami, 1980), 12; in the late *1970s* this company was one of the five largest foreign-owned holders of "agricultural land" in Florida. Data on its history come from Harry McGhin, Agricultural Stabilization and Conservation Service, Gainesville, Florida. On Andrew Weir, see Wilkins, *History,* 286–287, and Chapter 1 herein. Loncala Phosphate Co. had in the early 1920s crushing, drying, and storage facilities essential to the hard rock phosphate mining industry. Jesse W. Markham, *The Fertilizer Industry* (Nashville, Tenn.: Vanderbilt University Press, 1958), 51.

42. There had been German and Austrian investments in the pre–World War I American phosphate industry, which ended with the war. RG 131, Box 161, National Archives, has considerable data on International Agricultural Corporation and the "enemy" investment. In the postwar years there may have been some Belgian investment. Mirko Lamer, *The World Fertilizer Economy* (Stanford, Calif.: Stanford University Press, 1957), 191, suggests a Belgian connection with the firm J. Buttgenbach & Co. There appears to have been more British investment than that in Loncala, and it is possible that some of the prewar French investment may have survived beyond the First World War years, albeit most of the latter seems to have been divested as alternative high-grade deposits of phosphate discovered in Morocco turned French attention to the nearer North African resources. See Arch Fredric Blakey, *The Florida Phosphate Industry* (Cambridge, Mass.: Harvard University Press, 1973), 59.

43. On Consolidated Goldfields' prewar interests in American gold mining, see Wilkins, *History,* 241. This was Cecil Rhodes' company, which had begun in South Africa, but by 1909 was diversifying and in 1919 had less than 50 percent of its investments in South Africa. At war's end, it planned a huge U.S. expansion, setting up a new firm called New Consolidated Goldfields with that in mind. Robert Vicat Turrell and Jean Jacques Van-Helten, "The Investment Group," *Economic History Review,* 2nd ser., 40 (May 1987): 270n.20, and Paul Johnson, *Consolidated Gold Fields* (New York: St. Martin's Press, 1987), 40. On Consolidated Goldfields' subsidiary, Gold Fields American Development Company (1911–1950), see Film Z-G1, Reel 33, Bancroft Library Archives, University of California, Berkeley. Before the First World War, in connection with its diversification, Consolidated Goldfields of South Africa had also gotten involved in the U.S. potash industry. Wilkins, *History,* 279. It was this potash production, through its subsidiary American Trona, that it had expanded during the First World War (see Chapter 1). Haynes, *American Chemical Industry,* II, 159 (by the end of First World War, American Trona was "by long odds the biggest American potash enterprise"; Haynes clearly defined "American" by place of mining potash rather than by ownership).

44. George W. Stocking, *The Potash Industry* (New York: Richard R. Smith, 1931), 148.

45. Haynes, *American Chemical Industry,* II, 170–180, and IV, 323.

46. Ibid., II, 244–246.

47. According to a "Searles Valley [California] Timeline," American Trona introduced in 1919 its Three Elephant brand name for borax to indicate strength relative to the competing 20-Mule Team brand. See www.maturango.org/SearlesTime.html (accessed Nov. 2, 2002). Pacific Coast Borax, under the control of Borax Consolidated, had substituted a railroad spur for the twenty-mule teams that hauled their ore from the mines, but it kept the brand identification. Haynes, *American Chemical Industry,* II, 245.

48. The country (and specifically Pacific Borax) may have exported some borax, but basically production was for domestic consumption.

49. On this firm, see Cheever, *House of Morrell.*

50. Wilkins, *History,* 335–336 (on the prewar activities); Geo. W. Crutchley, *John Mackintosh* (London: Hodder & Stoughton, 1921), 127 (founder's death); H. A. Thomson, ed., *By Faith and Work: The Autobiography of the 1st Viscount Mackintosh of Halifax* (London: Hutchinson & Co., 1966), 66 (1922 investment).

51. Geoffrey Jones, "The Chocolate Multinationals: Cadbury, Fry and Rowntree 1918–1939," in *British Multinationals: Origins, Management and Performance,* ed. Geoffrey Jones (Aldershot: Gower, 1986), 101 (on Rowntree: this seems to be a reference to Mackintosh). On the other hand, Mackintosh apparently persisted. Thomson, *By Faith and Work,* 66.

52. On Nestlé's troubled milk business, see Chapter 2. According to historian Jean Heer, the chocolate factory and premises at Fulton, New York, had "come into the possession" of Lamont, Corliss in 1917; the Swiss chocolate firm Peter, Cailler, and Kohler had an interest in Lamont, Corliss; in turn, Nestlé & Anglo-Swiss had an interest in Peter, Cailler, and Kohler. Heer, *World Events 1866–1966,* 105, 106, 144, 218. It seems that in this period, the success of the Swiss in the U.S. chocolate business was based on the activities of the American firm Lamont, Corliss.

53. Peter Mathias, *Retailing Revolution* (London: Longmans, Green, 1967), 343, and "History Outline" on Thomas J. Lipton, Inc., Hoboken, N.J., Dec. 2, 1947, in Unilever Archives, London.

54. Data from the files of John H. Dunning, Reading, England (henceforth cited as Dunning data).

55. *Fortune,* 8 (Aug. 1933): 35.

56. Harrison & Crosfield in the United States joined with two U.S. importers in 1914 and in 1924 to form in 1924 Irwin-Harrisons-Whitney Inc. Geoffrey Jones and Judith Wale, "Merchants as Business Groups: British Trading Companies in Asia before 1945," *Business History Review* 72 (Autumn 1998): 378, 390 (on Harrison & Crosfield), 373 (Finlay and Anglo-American). Geoffrey Jones, *Merchants to Multinationals: British Trading Companies in the Nineteenth and Twentieth Centuries* (Oxford: Oxford University Press, 2000), 58 (on Dodwells). See ibid., 271–273, for more on the tea traders' U.S. business.

57. For an overview, see Wilson, *History of Unilever,* I, 285–287.

58. William H. Lever to C. W. Barnish, Dec. 21, 1921, L. Corr. 8536, Unilever Archives.

59. Lever to F. A. Countway, Sept. 19, 1922, L. Corr. 1482, Unilever Archives.

60. Rinso was first made by Lever in Britain in 1910. Wilson, *History of Unilever,* I, 121. Countway inaugurated a selling campaign for Rinso soap powder in 1919. U.S. sales rose from 84,000 cases that year to 550,000 cases in 1923. Ibid. In 1917 in the United States, Lever had begun to manufacture Pears' Soap at its Cambridge plant. Pears' Soap had been marketed for thirty-six years in the United States by Walter Janvier. In 1920, Lever Brothers took over the marketing of this soap, which was sold through *drugstores.* Lever Brothers organized a separate sales force to sell this product. See "Lever Golden Jubilee–USA, 1895–1945," booklet, 5. Lever never seems to have developed the potential of Pears' Soap. It was not one of the firm's main products.

61. Lever to Special Committee, Apr. 13, 1923, L. Corr. 162, Unilever Archives.

62. Lever to Ernest Walls, Aug. 13, 1923, L. Corr. 7894, Unilever Archives.

63. Wilkins, *History,* 342, and Wilson, *History of Unilever,* I, 286.

64. Lever to C. E. Tatlow, Aug. 7, 1923, L. Corr. 7823, Unilever Archives.

65. Lars Hassbring, *The International Development of Swedish Match Company, 1917–1924* (Stockholm: LiberFörlag, 1979), 78.

66. For background on Kreuger and his companies, see Shaplen, *Kreuger,* 1–51; ibid., 57 (American Krueger & Toll; its $6 million capital was ostensibly based on Swedish Match Co. shares); ibid., 58 (U.S. businesses).

67. Håkan Lindgren, *Corporate Growth: The Swedish Match Industry in Its Global Setting* (Stockholm: LiberFörlag, 1979), 304, 419n.5; Karl-Gustaf Hildebrand, *Expansion Crisis Reconstruction* (Stockholm: LiberFörlag, 1985), 152, 439n.82; see also Hassbring, *International Development,* 298, and Shaplen, *Kreuger,* 58.

68. Lindgren, *Corporate Growth,* 70. Safety matches had been introduced as early as the 1840s, but they were very expensive and not regarded as practical. Numerous modifications had to be made before a demand arose. Safety matches used a type of phosphorus with none of the highly poisonous side effects typical of yellow phosphorus. The matches could only be ignited when struck against a match box (or match folder) surface. Hildebrand, *Expansion Crisis Reconstruction,* 20–21.

69. Lindgren, *Corporate Growth,* 102, 296, and Hassbring, *International Development,* 86.

70. Lindgren, *Corporate Growth,* 297; Hassbring, *International Development,* 91, 175; Wilkins, *Maturing,* 153.

71. Hassbring, *International Development,* 113.

72. Shaplen, *Kreuger,* 74.

73. Lindgren, *Corporate Growth,* 300. See also Swaine, *Cravath Firm,* II, 510–511; Shaplen, *Kreuger,* 74–77.

74. Hildebrand, *Expansion Crisis Reconstruction,* 152.

75. Ibid.; Hassbring, *International Development,* 253, 298; Lindgren, *Corporate Growth,* 420.

76. Shaplen, *Kreuger,* 73–74.

77. See Wilkins, *History,* 352–369, and Chapter 1 of the present volume.

78. On Coats in Rhode Island, see Kulik and Bonham, *Rhode Island,* 138–139, and Rhode Island Historical Preservation Commission, Historical Preservation Commission Report, Pawtucket, R.I., P-PA-7 (Oct. 1978), 17–18. On Coats in general, the three new mills in Pawtucket, and the Bloomfield, New Jersey, plant, see Keir, "Coats Story," III, 146.

79. Thomas, *Woonsocket,* chap. 11.

80. Ibid., 114–116.

81. Ibid., 109.

82. Ibid., 113; I include it here rather than in a later chapter because it was part of the cluster of French participants.

83. Wilkins, *History,* 359; "Note du Professeur P. Cayez," Jan. 4, 1983, in files of Mira Wilkins; and *Silk Association Bulletin.*

84. "Note du Professeur P. Cayez," Jan. 4, 1983.

85. The U.S. company was Vaucanson Silk Mills, Inc. Pierre Vernus, "The Export Policy of Lyon Silk Firm Bianchini Férier (1890s–1970)," in *Transnational Companies,* ed. Hubert Bonin et al. (Paris: Éditions P.L.A.G.E., n.d. [2002]), 143, 145, 152n.22.

86. On the pre–World War I Schwarzenbach activities, see Wilkins, *History,* 359–360. In 1910, AGUT, headquartered in Thalwil in Switzerland, became the parent. The American business was started in West Hoboken, New Jersey. Schwarzenbach, Huber, & Co. was formed in 1888; by 1914, in addition to its West Hoboken facility, the U.S. affiliate had mills in Altoona, Pa. (1893); Bayonne, N.Y. (1902); Stirling, N.J. (1909); Hackensack, N.J. (1910); Juniata, Pa. (1912); Front Royal, Va. (1913); Norwich, Conn. (1913); and Columbia, Pa. (1914). Harm Schröter to Mira Wilkins, Sept. 6, 1996. The chain of silk plants was still in existence in 1926. Silk Association of America, *Annual Report 1926.*

87. Data from Harm Schröter.

88. On the start, see Wilkins, *History,* 355. See also Dunning data. Bradford Dyers' Association was a major British enterprise. Alfred Chandler (in *Scale and Scope,* 668), ranked it thirty-one (in market value of its shares) on his 1919 list of leading British

industrials. In 1922, E. B. Clegg, of another large British firm, Calico Printers' Association, visited the United States and wrote a report, favoring his company's making an investment there. Clegg concluded that the only way to cash in on the American market was to set up a works there, using the present glut of American money "to capitalise our name and experience." Nothing seems to have come of his plan. Anthony Howe to Mira Wilkins, May 1, 1986, based on a thirty-five-page report in the CPA Secretary's Correspondence, 1922–1928, File 95, Manchester Central Library, England.

89. On all these companies, see Dunning data.

90. Ranked by assets in 1917, Chandler put American Thread (the affiliate of English Sewing Cotton) as number 160, among the top U.S. industrials. By 1930, however, it was not in the top 200 U.S. companies. Chandler, *Scale and Scope,* 639, 645. The Coats-Clark group in the United States was larger in sales than American Thread and probably larger in assets as well, but since it was not publicly traded, it was not included on Chandler's lists. By contrast the *parents* of a number of the British textile firms in the United States were on Chandler's 1919 British list of giant companies (the ranking was by market value of the shares): J. & P. Coat (2), Bradford Dyers (31), English Sewing Cotton (37), Linen Thread (44), Winterbottom Book Cloth (162), and Sir Titus Salt (191). All these companies (except Sir Titus Salt)—with the ranking changed—remained on Chandler's 1930 list. Ibid., 668–669 and 675. On specialty producers in the United States, see Philip Scranton, *Endless Novelty: Specialty Production and American Industrialization, 1865–1925* (Princeton, N.J.: Princeton University Press, 1997). Apparently, some Japanese silk manufacturers opened offices in New York and engaged in direct export sales. Mitsui & Co., Ltd., *The 100 Year History of Mitsui & Co., Ltd., 1876–1976* (Tokyo: Mitsui & Co., Ltd., 1977), 92. As far as I can gather, there were no Japanese investments in silk manufacturing in the United States in this period.

91. Coleman, *Courtaulds,* II, 255, 289–303. The American subsidiary of Courtaulds was founded in 1910 as American Viscose Co; it became The Viscose Co. in 1915. In 1922, American Viscose Corp. was founded. The American affiliate, however, continued to use the name The Viscose Co. until 1937. See ibid., 302–303. On the adoption of the name rayon to describe the new product, see Mois H. Avram, *The Rayon Industry,* 2nd ed. (New York: Van Nostrand, 1929), 16.

92. On the processes, see Jesse W. Markham, *Competition in the Rayon Industry* (Cambridge, Mass.: Harvard University Press, 1952), 16–17; on the expiration of Courtaulds' patents in the United States, see ibid., 16, and Coleman, *Courtaulds.* II, 191.

93. Hounshell and Smith, *Science and Corporate Strategy,* 162–163, 608; Ferdinand Schultz, *The Technical Division of the Rayon Department, 1920–1951* (Wilmington, Del.: Du Pont, 1952), 3, 5–6; Pierre Cayez to Mira Wilkins, Jan. 5, 1983, and Wilkins, *History,* 359, 810 (on Gillet).

94. Avram, *Rayon Industry,* 146.

95. According to Williams Haynes, the Industrial Fibre Corporation was the successor to the American Borvisk Company, a subsidiary of Borvisk Kunstseiden, Hertzberg, Germany, started in 1916. Haynes writes that American Borvisk interests had in 1920 joined with Snia Viscosa in the new Industrial Fibre Corporation. Haynes, *American Chemical Industry,* IV, 379; see also Avram, *Rayon Industry,* 56.

96. Coleman, *Courtaulds,* II, 290–291.

97. Avram, *Rayon Industry,* 45.

98. J. Heim, President, Bally Inc., to Mira Wilkins, Apr. 5, 1983.

99. Lewis, *America's Stake,* 142.

100. A. H. John, *A Liverpool Merchant House, Being the History of Alfred Booth & Co. 1863–1958* (London: George Allen & Unwin, 1959), 86, 113–118, 122–128.

101. The Mercedes plant had burned in 1913 and was not rebuilt. Wilkins, *History,*

420. The French companies assembling in the United States did not continue after the war. Fiat's Poughkeepsie plant was sold in 1918 (see Chapter 1). On Renault's postwar sales outlet, see Fridenson, "Growth," 161.

102. Fridenson, "Growth," 160.

103. Wilkins, *History,* 420 (on the tariff).

104. Ian Lloyd, *Rolls Royce: The Years of Endeavor* (London: Macmillan, 1978), 23–55.

105. Alfred P. Sloan, Jr., *My Years with General Motors* (Garden City, N.Y.: Doubleday & Co., 1964), 14.

106. Alfred D. Chandler, Jr., ed., *Giant Enterprise* (New York: Harcourt, Brace & World, 1964), 3. Ford that year sold 664,482 units. Ibid.

107. For the Du Pont–British Nobels relationship, see Chapter 2.

108. Chandler, *Giant Enterprise,* 70.

109. Ibid., 71.

110. Reader, *Imperial Chemical Industries,* I, 320, 385. In addition, the British Nobels were also party to having the Canadian Explosives Ltd., their Canadian joint-venture company with Du Pont, assist in the GM financing. Chandler and Salsbury, *Pierre S. Du Pont,* 479, 505, and Reader, *Imperial Chemical Industries,* I, 385.

111. Chandler and Salsbury, *Pierre S. Du Pont,* 479 and 500 inset (for 1921 GM board); ibid., 564, inset, has the 1924 board with McGowan but not Chamberlain, who had by then left Nobel Industries. Reader, *Imperial Chemical Industries,* I, 393.

112. Sloan, *My Years with General Motors,* passim.

113. The increase was through the British Nobels' acquisition of the shares in GM that had temporarily been held by the British Nobels' affiliate, Canadian Explosives Ltd. See Reader, *Imperial Chemical Industries,* I, 385, and the preceding Note 110.

114. Reader, *Imperial Chemical Industries,* I, 384.

115. Geoffrey Jones, "The Multinational Expansion of Dunlop 1890–1939," in Jones, *British Multinationals,* 30, and Geoffrey Jones, "The Growth and Performance of British Multinational Firms before 1939: The Case of Dunlop," *Economic History Review,* 2nd ser., 37 (Feb. 1984): 42–43.

116. Chandler and Salsbury, *Pierre S. Du Pont,* 464.

117. Bernard A. Weisberger, *The Dream Maker* (Boston: Little, Brown, 1979), 240–241; Mira Wilkins and Frank Ernest Hill, *American Business Abroad: Ford on Six Continents* (Detroit: Wayne State University Press, 1964), 101–102.

118. Simon Reich, *Fruits of Fascism* (Ithaca, N.Y.: Cornell University Press, 1990), 208 (on GM's interest in Austin), 205 (on the Dunlop-Austin connection). See also R. J. Wyatt, *The Austin, 1905–1952* (Newton Abbot: David & Charles, 1981), 57–59, and Roy Church, *Herbert Austin* (London: Europa, 1979), 59–60. Austin also turned to McGowan for financial aid. Ibid., 59.

119. Weisberger, *Dream Maker,* 242, and Chandler and Salsbury, *Pierre S. Du Pont,* 464, on the GM investment in "Dunlop." The GM investment appears to have been in the *parent* Dunlop Rubber Company and not in the U.S. affiliate. I am indebted to Ms. Marjorie G. McNinch of the Hagley Museum and Library, Wilmington, Delaware, for her help in deciphering the story that is in my text.

120. Letter from F. C. Walcott to Pierre du Pont, July 27, 1920, in Longwood Mss., Group 10 Series A, File 784, Hagley Museum and Library. This letter refers to the 1919 activities.

121. Minutes of a Special Meeting of the Board of Directors of Dunlop America, Ltd., Aug. 13, 1920, in Longwood Mss., Group 10 Series A, File 784, Hagley Museum and Library. Utica is over 100 miles from Buffalo, so this seems a strange "location" decision.

122. Chandler and Salsbury, *Pierre S. Du Pont,* 464. On the date of Pierre du Pont's election to the board, see the Minutes of a Special Meeting of the Board of Directors of

Dunlop America, Ltd., Aug. 13, 1920, op. cit. Pierre du Pont joined the board of the *American* company. I have not been able to locate any evidence of a GM investment in the American affiliate; rather, the GM investment was apparently in the parent company.

123. Minutes of a Special Meeting of the Board of Directors of Dunlop America, Ltd., Aug. 13, 1920, op. cit. For details of the progress in construction, see Walcott to du Pont, July 27, 1920, op. cit.

124. Cable, Sir Harry McGowan to Pierre du Pont, Dec. 11, 1920, in Longwood Mss., Group 10 Series A, File 784, Hagley Museum and Library.

125. Pierre du Pont to McGowan, Dec. 11, 1920, in Longwood Mss., Group 10 Series A, File 784, Hagley Museum and Library.

126. See Robert Sobel, *The Life and Times of Dillon Read* (New York: Truman Talley Books, 1991), 60–68 (on Goodyear's problems).

127. Jones, "Growth," 45.

128. Wilkins, *History.* 421–422.

129. Michael French, "Structural Change and Competition in the United States Tire Industry, 1920–1937," *Business History Review,* 60 (Spring 1986): 30, 33.

130. Jones, "Growth," 45. The exchange rate at the start of 1924 was £1 = $4.20.

131. Data in Longwood Mss., Group 10 Series A, File 784, Hagley Museum and Library, show that in 1923 the American Dunlop was doing a good business with GM. See Jones, "Multinational," 34 (on the limits of GM's support for Dunlop).

132. See Clayton Lindsay Smith, *The History of Trade Marks* (n.p., 1923), 43. See also Works Progress Administration, "History of Milltown," 1936 typescript in Milltown Public Library, Milltown, New Jersey, p. 31, and H. Rodney Luery, *The Story of Milltown* (South Brunswick, N.J.: A. S. Barnes, 1971), 100.

133. The top five in 1926 were all domestic: Goodyear, Firestone, B. F. Goodrich, U.S. Rubber, and Fisk (this would be the same group in 1923 and 1924, although the order might be different). Dunlop, with .8 percent of U.S. tire sales in 1926, was classified by Michael French as an important "third-rank" firm. French, "Structural Change," 31–32. French has no sales data for Michelin, but scattered evidence that I have collected would put Michelin ahead of Dunlop in U.S. sales in 1923 and 1924 and probably a second-rank rather than third-rank firm. By my calculations, in the mid-1920s, Michelin sales were greater than those of General Tire and Rubber Company, which French classified as a "medium-sized firm." The placing of these foreign-owned tire producers in the "top ten" is my own estimate.

134. Claude Ph. Beaud, "The Schneider Group," in *Multinational Enterprise in Historical Perspective,* ed. Alice Teichova, Maurice Lévy-Leboyer, and Helga Nussbaum (Cambridge: Cambridge University Press, 1986), 98.

135. *Moody's Industrials 1929,* 1030.

136. For the pre–World War I investments, see Wilkins, *History,* 254–256; on the exit of Edgar Allen Manganese Steel, see Chapter 1.

137. Tweedale, *Sheffield Steel and America,* 96, 121–124, 126, and Tweedale, "Transatlantic Specialty Steels," 88–89.

138. Dunning data.

139. Ibid. The acquisition was by Cambridge & Paul Instrument Co., Ltd., which two years later was renamed Cambridge Instrument Co. The British company bought a U.S. manufacturer of electrocardiographs. Williams, *Precision Makers,* 113, 150, 153.

140. On Norma Company of America, see data in RG 131, Box 200, National Archives. This box contains details on the 1922 arrangements.

141. See Chapter 1 on its U.S. beginnings. Indiana-born William L. Batt, who became president of SKF's U.S. business in 1923, had joined SKF in 1916 when the Swedish firm took over Hess-Bright Manufacturing Company (Batt had been employed at Hess-Bright

since 1907). *Who's Who in America 1948–1949,* 154, and Charles Higham, *Trading with the Enemy* (New York: Delacorte Press, 1983), 117–118. The parent Swedish SKF had prewar and postwar interests in the *German* Norma company. Ibid., 251, and SKF, "The Story of SKF," pamphlet, 1982, 5.

142. On the Canadian company's prewar activities in the United States, see Wilkins, *History,* 418–419. In 1917, the Canadian firm raised its interest in the Johnston Harvester Company, Batavia, New York, to 100 percent and renamed that company Massey-Harris Harvester Company, Inc.; on this and on the impact of the 1920–1921 downturn, see Merrill Denison, *Harvest Triumphant* (Toronto: Collins, 1949), 197–198, 253.

143. See Wilkins, *Maturing,* 75, and passim.

144. Ibid., passim.

145. Wilkins, *History,* 844n.205, and Marshall, Southard, and Taylor, *Canadian-American Industry,* 179. Not all of his U.S. investments were in book publishing and printing.

146. On the Moore enterprises, I have used *Moody's Industrials;* Marshall, Southard, and Taylor, *Canadian-American Industry,* 179–180; and Joseph Schull and J. Douglas Gibson, *The Scotiabank Story* (Toronto: Macmillan of Canada, 1982), 111–114.

147. For background, see Wilkins, *History,* 536–546.

148. Paul J. Miranti, *Accountancy Comes of Age: The Development of an American Profession, 1886–1946* (Chapel Hill: University of North Carolina Press, 1990), 113.

149. Ibid., 123.

150. Geoffrey Jones has influenced my thinking. See Jones, *Merchants to Multinationals,* and Geoffrey Jones, ed., *Multinational Traders* (London: Routledge, 1998). See also Shin'ichi Yonekawa and Hideki Yoshihara, eds., *Business History of General Trading Companies* (Tokyo: University of Tokyo Press, 1987), and Philippe Chalmin, *Négociants et Chargeurs* (Paris: Economica, 1985).

151. One reason that information about the trading companies has been so slow to be incorporated in the general business history literature is that many persisted for generations as secretive family firms. Also complicating matters were changing partnerships with different names. It is often very hard to decipher the varying relationships over time.

152. See U.S. Federal Trade Commission, *Methods and Operations of Grain Exporters,* 2 vols. (Washington, D.C., 1922, 1923), I, 42–56 (henceforth cited as FTC, *Methods*).

153. Wilkins, *History,* 319; Dan Morgan, *Merchants of Grain* (New York: Penguin Books, 1980), 113.

154. *New York Times,* July 19, 22, 1919; Morgan, *Merchants of Grain,* 72, 114; Chalmin, *Négociants et Chargeurs,* 26, 204. On P. N. Gray & Co., see Richard Roberts, *Schroders* (Houndmills: Macmillan, 1992), 217, and FTC, *Methods,* I, 44.

155. Ricardo Sidicaro, *Note sur le Conglomerat Bunge et Born* (Paris: Institut National de La Recherche Agronomique, 1975), 2. The Bunge brothers had started a family trading firm for hides and spices in Amsterdam in 1817; the headquarters moved to Antwerp in 1850, and the firm expanded into grain, wool, cotton, and coffee. The Antwerp company was known as Bunge & Co. In 1884, Ernesto Bunge, with his brother-in-law Jorge Born, formed a partnership in Argentina, known as Bunge & Born. Jorge Schvarzer, *Bunge & Born* (Buenos Aires: CISEA, 1989), and Richard Robinson, *Business History of the World* (Westport, Conn.: Greenwood Press, 1993), 209. By the 1920s, the closely allied Bunge & Co. and Bunge & Born were grain traders par excellence. The American affiliate Bunge Corporation was also a grain trader. Bunge & Co. remained based in Antwerp, while Bunge & Born was in Buenos Aires. In the early 1920s, Edouard Bunge ran the Antwerp part of the business; his brother Ernesto Bunge was president of the Buenos Aires firm. In the late 1920s, however, the Bunge family would die out, and the direction of the firm increasingly shifted to Argentina. Alfredo Hirsch (who had been with Bunge & Born, Buenos Aires, since the late nineteenth century) became president of

Bunge & Born and the principal figure in the trading company. Morgan, *Merchants of Grain,* passim, and Schvarzer, *Bunge & Born,* 9, 13, 15, 18, 69–70, 76.

156. Morgan, *Merchants of Grain,* 102, 109.

157. FTC, *Methods,* I, 42.

158. On these, see Wilkins, *History.* 516–517. Included were the Japan Cotton Trading Company, which had a subsidiary in Fort Worth, Texas, and the Gōshō Company, with one in San Antonio, Texas.

159. These New York offices usually handled exports from the United States, but they might handle imports of related products, such as chemicals used in the mining business. They also dealt in metal imports, when appropriate. British Metal Corporation (BMC) was formed in London in November 1918 by Vivian, Younger, & Bond; C. Tennant, Sons, & Co; Cookson & Co.; British Aluminium Co; Morgan Grenfell & Co.; and the largest stockholders in Rio Tinto. BMC took over the Merton interests (i.e., the British interests of the Metallgesellschaft group). The Glasgow firm C. Tennant, Sons, & Co., traders in ores, concentrates, and metal products (and also involved in chemicals), had a New York office; BMC acquired an interest in this New York business. On BMC, consult Spurr, *Political and Commercial Geology,* 286 (for the founders); Godfrey Harrison, *V.Y.B.* (London: Vivian, Younger, and Bond, 1959), 46–48 (for the VYB connection); Burk, *Morgan Grenfell,* 98 (for Morgan, Grenfell); Cocks and Walters, *History of the Zinc Smelting Industry,* 46–47; Chandler, *Scale and Scope,* 562–563 (for the German connections); Dunning data (on C. Tennant, Sons, & Co., New York). Another metal trader set up in New York (in 1921) was the French-owned firm International Ores and Metals Selling Corp. David Stanley McClain, "Foreign Investment in United States Manufacturing and the Theory of Direct Investment," Ph.D. diss., MIT, 1974.

160. Robert G. Greenhill, "Investment Group, Free-Standing Company, or Multinational: Brazilian Warrant, 1909–1952," *Business History,* 37 (Jan. 1995): 96, 99.

161. Silk Association of America, *Annual Reports;* Jones, *Merchants to Multinationals,* 103 (on Jardine Matheson in New York); ibid., 57 (on the history of the relationship between Matheson & Co. and Jardine Matheson; the Matheson investment group had earlier separate U.S. investments of various sorts, in particular in California mining, in the Mountain Copper Company, Ltd.).

162. For example, the East Asiatic Company (Denmark), which had an office in New York and rubber plantations in Malaya. See James P. Warburg, London, to F. Abbot Goodhue, Oct. 14, 1921, James P. Warburg Papers, Box 1, Kennedy Library, and Chalmin, *Négociants et Chargeurs,* 62. The EAC was also involved in teak production in Thailand and the teak trade. Jones, *Merchants to Multinationals,* 48.

163. E. R. Kenzel to William P. G. Harding (Governor, Federal Reserve Board), Dec. 18, 1920, File 790, FRBNY. Balfour, Williamson & Co.'s main business—through Balfour, Guthrie—was on the West Coast. See Hunt, *Heirs of Great Adventure.* Geoffrey Jones writes that Balfour, Guthrie opened a New York office in 1889, and in 1918 the "New York partnership" had become a separate one, for tax reasons (relating to British, not American, taxes). Jones, *Merchants to Multinationals,* 168, 198. The firm's New York office letterhead in 1921 (in File 790, FRBNY) reads Balfour, Williamson & Co. (not Balfour, Guthrie). Antony Gibbs & Co. had opened a branch office in New York in 1912; in 1920, it established an American subsidiary, Antony Gibbs & Co. (Inc.), with a capital of $1 million. Antony Gibbs & Sons, Ltd., *Merchants and Bankers 1880–1958* (London: Antony Gibbs & Sons, Ltd., 1958), 102–103.

164. See Letter from Bertram A. Blyth, Balfour, Williamson & Co., March 29, 1921, File 790, FRBNY.

165. Professor Y. Homma has pointed out to me that in the 1920s bread and grain-based products were not part of the typical Japanese diet.

166. See Wilkins, *History*, 516–517, 894n.193, on its early history in the United States. Information on Mitsui & Co.'s U.S. staff in 1919 is in a paper by Sherman Cochran, "Three Roads to Shanghai's Market," typescript, 1988, 55.

167. Cochran, "Three Roads." The value of Mitsui & Co.'s trade handled by its New York office was larger than that of its Shanghai, Hong Kong, Dalian, Hankow, and Taipei branches combined.

168. See Kawabe, "Japanese Business," 34.

169. Yasuaki Nagasawa, "The Overseas Branches of Mitsubishi Limited during the First World War," *Japanese Yearbook on Business History*, 6 (1989): 141–142. Its imports into the United States far exceeded its exports to Japan from the United States.

170. Kawabe, "Japanese Business," 34, 36, 77–78.

171. A major—and unsuccessful—effort of *Americans* to get involved in general trading on a global scale was that of W. R. Grace & Co. See Lawrence A. Clayton, *Grace: W. R. Grace & Co.: The Formative Years 1850–1930* (Ottawa, Ill.: Jameson Books, 1985), 173–274, 303–306.

172. See Sturmey, *British Shipping*, 130–131. As noted, in 1913 only 14 percent of the ships in American foreign trade were under an American flag; in 1920, the share was 50.8 percent; but, by 1929, the figure was down to 37.6 percent. After the 1920–1921 recession, American sponsorship of a domestic merchant shipping fleet waned. "Flag" and "ownership" are not identical, but in this period "flag" did still reflect changes in ownership. These figures are those of Sturmey. The ones given in Sicotte, "Economic Crisis and Political Response," 861, 864, are slightly different (1914: barely 10 percent; 1918: more than 40 percent, peaking in 1920 at about 45 percent, and then decline). Both sets of figures reveal the same trends and the resurgence of the role of foreign shipping, after the early 1920s.

173. See Chapter 2 on the rules.

174. State law regulated insurance activities, but typically any single insurance company, whether domestic or foreign owned, was registered to do business in a number of states.

175. *Best's Insurance Reports* were published annually. There were separate volumes for (1) fire and marine; (2) casualty, surety, miscellaneous; and (3) life insurance. They are an invaluable source on the companies, domestic and foreign, that did business in the United States. Unless otherwise noted, what follows is based on data in these volumes.

176. On the U.K. merger, Harold E. Raynes, *History of British Insurance* (London: Isaac Pittman, 1950), 380, and H. A. L. Cockerell and Edwin Green, *The British Insurance Business* (London: Heinemann, 1976), 94.

177. Wilkins, *History*, 78, 134.

178. In the United Kingdom, Prudential Assurance handled life insurance; it did not provide such coverage in the United States.

179. *Best's Insurance Reports, Fire & Marine, 1930.* 138. The Oslo company did fire reinsurance in the United States.

180. For this suggestion, see Fritz Hodne, "The Multinational Companies of Norway," in *The Rise of Multinationals in Continental Europe*, ed. Geoffrey Jones and Harm Schröter (Aldershot: Edward Elgar, 1993), 128. Norway was in political union with Denmark, 1450–1814, and dynastic union with Sweden, 1814–1905.

181. On some of the difficulties in the 1920s, see Press Release from the U.S. State Department on the Hannevig Case, Mar. 28, 1940, FO 371/24255, Public Record Office, London.

182. The North China Insurance Co., Shanghai, started in the United Kingdom in 1863; then it was reestablished in China by the same British interests in 1903; it first entered the United States in 1912 to do marine business. In March 1919, it was licensed by the

New York Insurance Department to write fire insurance. It would be reincorporated in 1928 under Hong Kong law. The second Chinese insurance company was the Yang-Tsze Insurance Association, Shanghai.

183. As noted earlier, all through the interwar years *Best's Insurance Reports* separated the predominantly fire and marine companies from the casualty, surety, and other non–life insurers. Many British companies did both with separate subsidiaries set up in the United States for non-fire and marine and non-life activities.

184. Eagle Indemnity Co. (incorporated in New York in 1922) and Royal Indemnity Co. (incorporated in New York in 1910) were owned by Royal Insurance Co., while Commercial Union Assurance Co. had Ocean Accident and Guarantee Corp. Ltd. and Columbia Casualty Co. as affiliates.

185. On the prewar arrangements by United States Trust and Guarantee, for example, see Wilkins, *History*, 496–497; for the Scottish American Investment Co., see ibid. 499; by British Assets, see Ranald C. Michie, "Crisis and Opportunity: The Formation and Operation of the British Assets Trust 1897–1914," *Business History*, 25 (July 1983): 138–139. These same arrangements persisted in the postwar years.

186. On prewar British mortgage lending, see Wilkins, *History*, 501–510. In some cases, firms used independent agents. In others, they had their own employees on the spot. On the process of change from mortgage company to investment trust, see Jackson, *Enterprising Scot*, 280, 283; George Glasgow, *The Scottish Investment Trust Companies* (London: Eyre & Spottiswoode, 1932); and Gilbert, *History of Investment Trusts.* In 1918, for example, the Alliance Trust, Dundee, took over the management of the Western and Hawaiian Investment Co. (WHIC), which had 81.8 percent of its portfolio in American land mortgages. In 1923 WHIC became the Second Alliance Trust. It moved out of American land loans to stocks and bonds and diversified away from U.S. business–following the pattern of its parent. See Jackson, *Enterprising Scot*, 283, and Gilbert, *History of Investment Trusts*, 105.

187. There were others, but these were the principal ones. See Kerr, *Scottish Capital on the American Credit Frontier*, 190, and Jackson, *Enterprising Scot*, 279–283. All of the firms mentioned were Scottish. The Texas Land and Mortgage Co. was registered in London but run by Scots. In the Archives, Bancroft Library, University of California, Berkeley, are British registration records of all these companies. The Texas Land and Mortgage Co. records are on Film Z-G1, Reels 282–285; the others are on Film Z-G2, Reels 74–76 (Alliance Trust), Reels 53–56 (Scottish American Mortgage Co., Ltd), and Reels 30–31 (Oregon Mortgage Co., Ltd.). McFarlane, "British Agricultural Investments in the Dakotas," 120, notes that the English firms Iowa Land Company (1884–1940) and Trust and Mortgage Company of Iowa Ltd. (1889–1940) were still lending in South Dakota. The business of these two firms was managed by the firm C. W. Benson & Co., with a U.S. head office in St. Paul, Minn. Ibid., 120. The latter was closely associated with the Robert Benson & Co. group of investment trusts. On the relationship *before* 1914, see Wilkins, *History*, 749–750, which information was heavily based on a *1922* publication. On the Robert Benson & Co. trusts in the interwar years, see Jehanne Wake, *Kleinwort Benson* (Oxford: Oxford University Press, 1997), 299. Wake has nothing on the post–World War I history of the Iowa companies.

188. John Fahey, "When the Dutch Owned Spokane," *Pacific Northwest Quarterly*, 71 (Jan. 1981): 10 (on post–World War I activities of the Northwestern and Pacific Hypotheekbank.).

189. Herman E. Krooss and Martin R. Blyn, *A History of Financial Intermediaries* (New York: Random House, 1971), 155; Phelps, *Foreign Expansion of American Banks;* Paul Philip Abrahams, *The Foreign Expansion of American Finance . . . 1907–1921* (New York: Arno Press, 1976), chaps. 5–7; and Cleveland and Huertas, *Citibank*, 91–112, 119–127.

190. It is bizarre that Table 3.1 shows only three direct investments in banking, 1919–1923.

191. Chernow, *House of Morgan,* on the new generation; see also Burk, *Morgan Grenfell.* The name of the Paris house, Morgan, Harjes et Cie., was changed to Morgan et Compagnie in 1926. Chernow, *House of Morgan,* 286, 450.

192. Wilkins, *History,* documented the close earlier connections between Sir Ernest Cassel and Jacob Schiff.

193. Correspondence in the French Rothschild Papers, AQ 132, Archives Nationale, Fontainbleau, France; Carosso, "Financial Elite," 86, indicates that the firm August Belmont & Co. lingered on until the beginning of the 1930s, when it was dissolved; by then, it was a ghost. See also Sobel, *Life and Times of Dillon Read,* 229–230. The first August Belmont—the original representative of the Rothschilds—died in 1890; his son August Belmont lived from 1853 to 1924. His grandson August died in 1919, and for a while the latter's brother, Morgan Belmont, headed August Belmont & Co. The founder's great-grandson August Belmont IV (the son of the August Belmont who died in 1919) was born in 1908; he went to work in the late 1920s for Bonbright & Co. and later joined Dillon, Read. He made the decision not to continue August Belmont & Co.

194. Lord Rothschild's brothers, Alfred and Leopold, who had not been active in the business, died before the end of the war. Niall Ferguson puts the matter of discontinuity in more general terms: "Between the death of Alphonse [de Rothschild, who was "a formidable force in French finance"] in 1905 and that of Alfred in 1918, the generation which had dominated Rothschild finance since around 1875 disappeared." Niall Ferguson, *The House of Rothschild: The World's Banker 1849–1999* (New York: Viking, 1999), 441, 220 (on Alphonse).

195. On Lee Higginson's earlier relationships with the British Rothschilds, see Wilkins, *History,* 474; data in the Rothschild Archives London II/53OB and II/327; and in the Henry Lee Higginson Papers, Harvard Business School, Boston, Mass. Ferguson, *House of Rothschild,* 466, notes that in 1929, N. M. Rothschilds would join Lee, Higginson & Co. in the share issue for Kreuger's empire, but this was hardly indicative of an ongoing arrangement.

196. The Belmont & Co. correspondence with the Paris Rothschild Bank, AQ 132, Archives Nationale, Fontainbleau, as noted, goes to 1926 and shows that the U.S. firm that had long been the Rothschild representatives in America provided information on what was happening in the United States and handled certain securities transactions. The British Rothschilds were founding shareholders in the International Acceptance Bank, New York. Evelyn de Rothschild (born in 1931), the grandson of Leopold Rothschild and in 1988 chairman of N. M. Rothschild & Sons, was that year (1988) quoted as saying, "We never seized the initiative in America and that was one of the mistakes my family made." *New York Times Magazine,* Dec. 4, 1988. It became legend that the Rothschilds had done little in America, which was far from true–at least before 1914. The "legend" took shape in the interwar era. By the time of the birth of Evelyn de Rothschild, the family firm was of no importance in the United States. The legend is repeated in Ferguson, *House of Rothschilds,* 457–458, who asks "why did the Rothschilds fail to capitalise on the financial opportunities of the First World War?" He answered that "it was J. P. Morgan who succeeded N. M. Rothschild as the linchpin of war finance—confirming what a strategic error it had been not to establish a Rothschild house on the other side of the Atlantic." In ibid., 456–458, Ferguson traces with acumen and sophistication the "relative decline" of the Rothschilds, 1918–1945; he does note some of their American business in the 1920s, including their participation with the Warburgs in the International Acceptance Bank.

197. Sir Edgar Speyer, who had made Speyer Brothers, London, a leading British merchant bank, had been subject to sharp criticism during the war, based on his German family firm's associations. After Sir Edgar moved to America, he became a New York

resident; he rejoined (as a partner) Speyer & Co., New York, but was not active (when he lived in London before the First World War, he had been a partner of the New York house). He died in 1932. Emden, *Money Powers,* 275–277. On Sir Edgar's style of life in America in 1929, see John Brooks, *Once in Golgonda* (New York: Harper & Row, 1969), 117–118 (Brooks is mistaken when he calls Sir Edgar "an important Wall Streeter"; there is no evidence of that). For a while, Gordon Leith & Co. had represented Speyer & Co. in England. (Leith had been with Speyer Brothers for many years). By contrast, Eduard Beit von Speyer in Germany remained head of the well-connected private Lazard Speyer-Ellissen, Frankfurt, until his death in 1933; Beit von Speyer did play a prominent role in aiding Speyer & Co., New York, in its substantial international business. Emden, *Money Powers,* 276–277; on Leith, see *New York Times,* Apr. 3, 1941, and Ioanna Pepelasis Minoglou, "Between Informal Networks and Formal Contracts: International Investment in Greece during the 1920s," *Business History,* 44 (Apr. 2002): 55.

198. See Chapter 2 for the rules.

199. These "agencies" were direct investments. They were licensed by the New York State Banking Department, which each year in its annual report listed the licensed agencies. These reports were my basic source. I specify "out-of-country" because "foreign" in state government parlance can mean "out-of-state."

200. The reason that there were nine rather than ten London overseas bank agencies was the absence of the African Banking Corporation (its business was absorbed by the Standard Bank of South Africa, which had a licensed New York agency). In 1923, the London and Brazilian Bank, London, and the London and River Plate Bank, London, merged to form the Bank of London and South America (BOLSA). Geoffrey Jones, *British Multinational Banking 1830–1990* (Oxford: Oxford University Press, 1993), 141, 404–405, 409. This was *not* yet reflected in the New York State Banking Reports and thus is not indicated on Table 3.4.

201. *Bankers Magazine,* New York, 105 (Oct. 1922): 645, and 104 (Mar. 1922): 521.

202. Ibid., 104 (June 1922): 1056, and 105 (Nov. 1922): 810. On the establishment in China of modern banks, 1917–1923, see Noel H. Pugach, *Same Bed, Different Dreams: A History of the Chinese American Bank of Commerce, 1919–1937* (Hong Kong: Centre of Asian Studies, University of Hong Kong, 1997), 27ff.

203. While I am able to establish linkages between Japanese service companies (trading, shipping, and insurance) and the banks, there do not appear to be similar network connections in the Chinese case. Thus, I cannot establish a tie-in between the Chinese insurance company present in the United States and the Chinese banks. The British Hongkong & Shanghai Banking Corporation was another matter, with all kinds of interconnections with various clusters of services.

204. The longevity is documented in the New York State, Banking Department, *Annual Reports,* 1917–1941. On the Mitsubishi Bank, see Nagasawa, "Overseas Branches of Mitsubishi Limited," 138. RG 131, National Archives contains data on all six Japanese banks. The latter indicates that the Mitsui Bank began operations in 1922. (I have taken the 1921 date from the New York State Bank Superintendent's Annual Report.) I have included the two colonial banks, the Bank of Taiwan and the Bank of Chosen, as Japanese, since they were Japanese controlled and Japanese run.

205. On the prewar foreign influences on the Italian banks, see Peter Hertner, "Foreign Capital in the Italian Banking Sector," in *International Banking* 1870–1914, ed. Rondo Cameron and V. I. Bovykin (Oxford: Oxford University Press, 1990), 347–348; on the Italian banks' expansion in South America, see Giandomenico Piluso, "Le banche miste italiane in Sud America . . . (1906–1933)," LIUC Papers, VII (1994).

206. On the history of the Belgian entry, the Banque Belge pour l'Etranger (BBE), Brussels, which was controlled by Société Générale de Belgique, see Herman Van der Wee and Mon-

ique Verbreyt, *The Generale Bank 1822–1997* (Tielt, Belgium: Lanno Publishers, 1997), 103, 112–114, 130, 153, 155–159, 192, 217, 326. The BBE had British origins and operated all during World War I from a London base. It had set up a New York office in 1917 (see ibid., 158). After the war, it remained in London, and the New York office became the licensed New York agency in 1921; this agency—although listed in State Banking Reports as headquartered in Brussels—was an extension of the "London subsidiary bank's office" (ibid., p. 326).

207. Krooss and Blyn, *History*, 154.

208. J. R. Jones, "Historical Data" from Hongkong & Shanghai Banking Corp. Archives, J4. My thanks go to S. W. Muirhead, July 2, 1984, for this material.

209. W. A. Scott to J. E. Crane, Oct. 11, 1920, File 792, FRBNY.

210. J. E. Crane to Jacobsen, Oct. 18, 1920, File 792, FRBNY.

211. Report of the Federal Reserve Board Economic Liaison Committee, Oct. 27, 1920 (St. 1538). Typescript. File 792, FRBNY.

212. E. R. Kenzel, "Memorandum of Conversation with Sir Frederick Huth Jackson," Dec. 15, 1920, File 790, FRBNY.

213. On the shift to dollars in Latin American trade, see Jones, *British Multinational Banking*, 192.

214. A. S. J. Baster, *The Imperial Banks* (London: P. S. King, 1929), 236–237. It would be taken over by Barclays Bank (Dominion, Colonial and Overseas) in 1925. See also Jones, *British Multinational Banking*, 149.

215. There were only three exits (see Table 3.4), all of which involved takeovers by banks that already had New York representation.

216. See Wilkins, *History*, 878–879, on this form.

217. Banca Commerciale Italiana, Board of Directors Minutes, Feb. 23 and May 18, 1922 (I am indebted to Dr. Giandomenico Piluso for this information.) See Chapter 5 for its 1924 trust company.

218. Gretchen Marlatt, State of New York, Banking Department, to Mira Wilkins, Aug. 1, 1983 (date of authorization of Italian Discount and Trust Company); *Stock Exchange Year Book 1919*, 2415; and New York State Banking Department, *Annual Report 1921*, 6. It had been a joint-venture with Guaranty Trust, which, sold its 50 percent interest in the Italian Discount and Trust Co. in 1921, *before* the collapse of Banca Italiana di Sconto. Giandomenico Piluso to Mira Wilkins, Dec. 15, 1993.

219. Marlatt to Wilkins, Aug. 1, 1983 (date of authorization); *Stock Exchange Year Book 1929*, 3463; David Joslin, *A Century of Banking in Latin America* (London: Oxford University Press, 1963), 259–260. Joslin is wrong in his statement that the agency was converted into the trust company; both coexisted, with the identical management. The reason for the trust company was fear of "technical conflict" with New York law, since credits temporarily established for international clients might be construed as deposits. The president of the Anglo-South American Trust Co. assured the deputy governor of the Federal Reserve Bank of New York that it was not their intention to compete with American banks for deposits, either local or foreign. E. R. Kenzel, Deputy Governor, to F. J. Zurlinden, Deputy Governor, Federal Reserve Bank of Cleveland, Feb. 4, 1924, Alpha File "J. Henry Schroeder," FRBNY.

220. The Westminster Bank's New York representative was C. M. Parker: see *Bankers Magazine*, New York, 107 (Oct. 1923): 637. The French bank's representative was Aimé Dumaine. Ibid., 105 (Oct. 1922): 627. Disconto-Gesellschaft's representative was Adolf Koehn. Ibid., 105 (Oct. 1922): 639.

221. The earliest of these New York State–authorized international banking organizations had been established before the passage of the Edge Act in December 1919.

222. See Federal Reserve Board, *Annual Report 1918*, 59; Phelps, *Foreign Expansion of American Banks*, 32, 36, 156, 153; Abrahams, *Foreign Expansion of American Finance*, 51, 131.

By year end 1919, the American Foreign Banking Corporation had nine foreign branches. Federal Reserve Board, *Annual Report 1919,* 54.

223. Phelps, *Foreign Expansion of American Banks,* 156–157; Abrahams, *Foreign Expansion of American Finance,* 174. Pugach, *Same Bed,* 33, 42, indicates that Chase National had organized and led American Foreign Banking Corporation from the start.

224. Phelps, *Foreign Expansion of American Banks,* 7, 32; ownership and the foreign branches are given in Federal Reserve Board, *Annual Report 1919,* 54. Union Bank of Canada apparently had interlocking directors with Lloyd's Bank of London. Parrini, *Heir to Empire,* 115.

225. On the end to Park-Union Foreign Banking Corporation, see Phelps, *Foreign Expansion of American Banks,* 158, and Abrahams, *Foreign Expansion of American Finance,* 175–176. The Asia Banking Corporation, founded in 1918, went into voluntary liquidation in 1924. Phelps, *Foreign Expansion of American Banks,* 157–158. The Union Bank of Canada last appears with a New York agency in New York State, Banking Department, *Annual Report 1924.*

226. Phelps, *Foreign Expansion of American Banks,* 201n. Date of establishment from Kevin Cook, State of New York, Banking Department, to Mira Wilkins, July 18, 1983. This bank carried on an acceptance business. Phelps, *Foreign Expansion of American Banks,* 174. Details on ownership are in the Federal Reserve Board, *Annual Report 1919,* 53–54. See also Abrahams, *Foreign Expansion of American Finance,* 129–130. Excellent material on the French American Banking Corporation is in the Alpha file, C440, FRBNY. See *Bankers Magazine,* 105 (Oct. 1922): 623 (for the advertisement).

227. Abrahams, *Foreign Expansion of American Finance,* 129–130.

228. Statement from the First National Bank of Boston, Apr. 30, 1919, in French American Banking Corp., Alpha File, C440, FRBNY.

229. On the International Acceptance Bank, I have used IAB records in the Chase Manhattan Bank Archives (CMBA), New York; Phelps, *Foreign Expansion of American Banks;* Rosenbaum and Sherman, *M. M. Warburg & Co.;* Farrer, *The Warburgs,* 90–91; Abrahams, *Foreign Expansion of American Finance,* 193–194; Warburg, *Long Road Home,* 56–57 (James P. Warburg—son of Paul M.—joined IAB in the fall of 1921); Swaine, *Cravath Firm,* II, 307. I have also used data in the James P. Warburg Papers, John F. Kennedy Library, Boston, Mass., and the James P. Warburg Reminiscences, Oral History Collection, Columbia University Library, New York. A good brief history of the IAB is in its 1924 confidential *Annual Report* (Jan. 20, 1925) in the Strong Papers, 120.0, FRBNY; this *Annual Report* is also in the CMBA.

230. Benjamin J. Klebaner, "Paul M. Warburg," in *Banking and Finance, 1913–1989,* ed. Larry E. Schweikart (New York: Buccoli, Clark, 1990), 447–449.

231. On First National Bank of Boston and American International Corporation as stockholders, see Report of the Examination of International Acceptance Bank by the Federal Reserve Board, Washington, as of Sept. 26, 1922, in Merged Banks—Bank of the Manhattan Company—International Acceptance Bank, RG 3, CMBA. American International Corporation was also set up (in 1916) under New York State law to handle international business. On AIC, see Wilkins, *Maturing,* 20–22, 52; Cleveland and Huertas, *Citibank,* 91–94, 367–368 (Citibank was an important participant in the organization of AIC); and *Moody's Banks 1928,* 1363 (for New York incorporation; this statement indicates that AIC participated in the formation of IAB and was an original shareholder).

232. The relationships in foreign lending between Kuhn, Loeb, IAB, and "our mutual friends, Messrs. M. M. Warburg & Co., Hamburg," are spelled out in an exchange of correspondence, Paul M. Warburg to Kuhn, Loeb & Co., May 3, 1922, and Kuhn, Loeb & Co. to Paul M. Warburg, May 4, 1922, in "Merged Banks—Bank of the Manhattan Co.—International Acceptance Bank, "Foreign Loan Agreement w/Kuhn Loeb," RG 3, CMBA.

233. This list of foreign stockholders, as of Sept. 26, 1922, is in Report of the Examination of International Acceptance Bank by the Federal Reserve Board, Washington, in Merged Banks—Bank of the Manhattan Company—International Acceptance Bank, RG 3, CMBA. According to a history of the Swiss Bank Corporation, that bank took part in the formation of the "United States Foreign Commerce Banking Corporation (USFCBC)." Hans Bauer, *Swiss Bank Corporation, 1872–1972* (Basle: Swiss Bank Corp., 1972), 236. I have not been able to locate any information on the USFCBC. I feel certain that the USFCBC, described by Bauer, was the IAB (and that the description of it as an organization to encourage U.S. foreign commerce got mistranslated as the name of the bank). It was apparently a prestigious matter to be included in IAB. When James P. Warburg was in London (in November 1921), a representative of Barclay's Bank expressed "hurt" that Barclay's had not been asked to be a stockholder bank. The Warburgs were, however, committed to an association with Sir Felix Schuster of National Provincial and Union Bank. James Warburg recommended to his father: "I think we ought to get Schuster to let them [Barclay's] in." James P. Warburg, London, to Paul Warburg, Nov. 3, 1921, in Warburg Papers, Box 1. On Schuster, see Emden, *Money Powers,* 343–348. Barclay's was never included. Stockholder lists in RG 3, CMBA. The list of stockholders also contained "stockholder banks and firms in the United States," as of Sept. 26, 1922.

234. Phelps, *Foreign Expansion of American Banks,* 23.

235. IAB, *Annual Report 1924.*

236. James P. Warburg, Stockholm, to F. Abbot Goodhue, Sept. 14, 1921, Warburg Papers, Box 1. Brown Bros. had a long-standing international business in financing trade.

237. James P. Warburg, London, to F. Abbot Goodhue, Oct. 14, 1921, Warburg Papers, Box 1. Mark Clark and Henry Nielsen, "Crossed Wires and Missing Connections," *Business History Review,* 65 (Spring 1995): 10, describe the East Asiatic Company as one of Denmark's few international businesses. See also Jones, *Merchants to Multinationals,* 75, on the importance of EAC.

238. James P. Warburg, Hamburg, to F. Abbot Goodhue, Oct. 19, 1921, Warburg Papers, Box 1.

239. Swaine, *Cravath Firm,* 307.

240. See Roberts, *Schroders.* I have followed Roberts on the umlauts in the bank titles. See also Stanley Chapman, *The Rise of Merchant Banking* (London: Allen & Unwin, 1984), 11, 55, 105, 120–121, and passim (on the British house), and Wilkins, *History,* 103, 112, 268, 476, 862n.175 on Schroder's nineteenth-century and early twentieth-century U.S. business. Roberts indicates that Schroders contemplated becoming a shareholder bank in International Acceptance Bank, but after a "change of heart" decided to go ahead on its own. Roberts, *Schroders,* 215.

241. E. R. Kenzel, Deputy Governor, Federal Reserve Bank of New York, to F. J. Zurlinden, Deputy Governor, Federal Reserve Bank of Cleveland, Feb. 4, 1924, Alpha File, "J. Henry Schroeder," FRBNY.

242. Roberts, *Schroders,* 152, on the issue of a naturalization certificate to Baron Bruno on August 7, 1914 (war was declared August 4) to avoid sequestration of the firm.

243. Roberts, *Schroders,* 188 (on the baron's brother). See also Interrogation of Kurt Freiherr von Schröder, Nov. 7, 1945, NI-226, p. 4; Nov. 8, 1945, NI-227, p. 1; Nov. 13, 1945, NI-231, p. 1; and Nov. 23, 1945, NI-240, p. 2, all in RG 238 (T301, Reel 3), National Archives.

244. Sayers, *Bank of England,* I, 151; II, 635, 648n.1.

245. Ibid., I; 175, 176n II, 507.

246. Roberts, *Schroders,* 537 (assets). Kenzel to Zurlinden, Feb. 4, 1924, as cited earlier (quote). When the head of the New York Federal Reserve Bank, Benjamin Strong, had desired to provide his son experience at a London firm, he had in the early 1920s chosen

Schroders in London. Data in Strong Papers, FRBNY. The J. Henry Schroder Banking Corporation was incorporated in New York in September 1923. Benjamin Haggott Beckhart, *The New York Money Market,* vols. II and III (New York: Columbia University Press, 1932), III, 303. Roberts, *Schroder,* 218, gives the reasons behind the use of the particular form of operation: the model was Warburg's International Acceptance Bank. On the organization of the banking corporation and its stockholders, see ibid., 215–221. Among the minority stockholders were Schröder Gebrüder, Hamburg, and J. H. Stein, Cologne. Also involved were two other German private banks, Gebrüder Bethmann and Deichmann & Co.; two Austrian banks, Boden-Credit Anstalt and Bankhaus Johann Liebig & Co.; the Swiss Banque Privée de Glaris; and the Buenos Aires merchant house Staudt & Cia. Ibid., 221. The British Schroders were, of course, the key investors.

247. Sayers, *Bank of England,* I, 268–269 (background on Frederick Huth & Co.); E. R. Kenzel, Deputy Governor, Federal Reserve Bank of New York, "Memoranda of Conversation with Sir Frederick Huth Jackson," Dec. 15, 1920, File 790, FRBNY, described Frederick Huth Jackson as "chairman of the association of accepting bankers of London." The memo contained data on the firm's New York house, which was expected to transact dollar business, especially in respect to South America. Huth & Co., New York, Financial Statement, Dec. 31, 1920, "Customer Statements," Box IE7, RG 3, CMBA, provides information on the assets of the New York business.

248. Sayers, *Bank of England,* I, 268–270. There are financial data on Huth & Co., New York, in RG 3, CMBA. The material therein gives Huth & Co., New York, financial statements for Dec. 31, 1920, and Aug. 31, 1924 (in a miscellaneous file—"Customers Statements"—for the International Acceptance Bank); these files also show that Huth & Co., New York, was a shareholder in the IAB in 1922 and in 1925, but not in 1928; it was listed as one of the many "customers" of IAB in a 1927 list. Roberts, *Schroders,* 215, writes that Frederick Huth & Co. (along with the Schroders) had contemplated becoming founding shareholders in IAB. Although Schroders did not participate, Roberts seems unaware that Huth & Co., New York, was included on the IAB list of "stockholder banks and firms in the United States" as of September 26, 1922 (this list is in RG 3, CMBA). It seems the New York house, Huth & Co., not the British parent, was the participant.

249. *Bankers Magazine,* 105 (Oct. 1922): 617.

250. Phelps, *Foreign Expansion of American Banks,* 203; Bank of Nova Scotia, *Bank of Nova Scotia 1832–1932* (Toronto: privately printed, 1932), 164. The Bank of Nova Scotia's Boston branch had financed the Boston-headquartered United Fruit Company's business in Jamaica. It lost this major account in 1914 to the British overseas bank The Colonial Bank. Neil C. Quigley, "The Bank of Nova Scotia in the Caribbean," *Business History Review,* 63 (Winter 1989): 811–812. The Colonial Bank—long active in the Caribbean—had a New York agency (see Table 3.4).

251. See Kidder, Peabody to Baring Brothers, Ltd., Apr. 14, 1922, Letterbook No. 9, Kidder, Peabody Papers, Harvard Business School, Boston; Carosso, *More Than a Century,* 58–60; Ziegler, *Sixth Great Power,* 340; and Orbell, *Baring Brothers,* 78.

252. Phelps, *Foreign Expansion of American Banks,* 174; Beckhart, *New York Money Market,* III, 303–305.

253. On the Wall Street address, see Carosso, *More Than a Century,* 148 (since 1891), and ibid., 51–52, on the decision in the 1920s to keep Kidder, Peabody's head office in Boston despite the rise of New York as the nation's principal financial center.

254. On the Bank of Montreal, see Denison, *Canada's First Bank;* on the Bank of Nova Scotia, see Phelps, *Foreign Expansion of American Banks,* 203; on the Banco di Napoli, see James, *Growth of Chicago Banks,* II, 1171.

255. Until its 1918 merger with the Bank of British North America (BBNA), the Bank of Montreal had had no presence in San Francisco. When California state banking author-

ities refused to transfer the branch charter of the BBNA to the Bank of Montreal, the BBNA branch in San Francisco was incorporated as the British American Bank, capital $1 million; then, when the merger took place, the Bank of Montreal acquired the capital stock of the British American Bank. Subsequently, the Bank of Montreal opened a San Francisco agency along with maintaining the British American Bank. Denison, *Canada's First Bank,* II, 332, 353. The Bank of Montreal's branch at Spokane had been set up in 1903 before the passage of the 1919 legislation (see Chapter 2). In 1924, the Bank of Montreal closed the Spokane branch and transferred its local business and fixed assets to the American-owned Old National Bank of Spokane. Ibid., II, 353.

256. Victor Ross, *A History of the Canadian Bank of Commerce,* 2 vols. (Toronto: Oxford University Press, 1920, 1922), II, 558. The San Francisco and Seattle branches were set up before the laws were passed disallowing such branches; Oregon law continued to allow foreign branches.

257. J. R. Jones, "History of the Bank in California," HSBC Archives, Hong Kong (data from S. W. Muirhead, July 2, 1984).

258. Superintendent of Banks (California), *Annual Report 1919,* 700.

259. Date of Seattle branch opening is from RG 131, National Archives, inventory.

260. Ira Cross, *Financing an Empire* (Chicago: S. J. Clarke, 1927), II, 764 (San Francisco). Odate, *Japan's Financial Relations with the United States,* 81, 84 (Seattle). The Seattle bank had three Americans among its five directors to comply with Washington law, but Odate describes it as, in effect, a "branch" of the Sumitomo bank, Osaka.

261. Cross, *Financing an Empire,* III, 266.

262. This is, of course, the argument in Chandler, *Scale and Scope.*

263. Thread had once been a critical industry, but by the 1920s there was little innovative about this industry; moreover, the rise of ready-made (off-the-rack) clothing meant a decline in consumers' thread purchases. Potash and borax were "niche" industries—important but not in terms of the entire economy.

4. Prosperity, 1924–1929

1. See George Soule, *Prosperity Decade* (New York: Holt, Rinehart and Winston, 1947); Leuchtenburg, *Perils of Prosperity.*

2. League of Nations, *Industrialization and Foreign Trade* (Geneva: League of Nations, 1945), 13 (42.2 percent).

3. Every economic history of the 1920s covers the expansion of American lending. Lewis, *America's Stake;* Aldcroft, *From Versailles to Wall Street;* Barry Eichengreen, *Golden Fetters* (New York: Oxford University Press, 1992); and Feinstein, *Banking, Currency, and Finance,* are particularly useful. For the diplomacy of U.S. lending, see Leffler, *Elusive Quest,* and Rosenberg, *Financial Missionaries to the World.*

4. The expansion of American business abroad was coincidental with the expansion of American lending but quite separate. See Wilkins, *Maturing,* chaps. 3–7, and Frank A. Southard, Jr., *American Industry in Europe* (Boston: Houghton Mifflin, 1931).

5. The $11.7 billion (in Column B) was all World War I–related loans and all intergovernmental. The 1929 figure is larger than the year end 1918 one because it includes added Allied debts incurred under the Liberty Loan Act plus some additional Allied credits. Lewis, *America's Stake,* 360–366 (Allied war debts), 450 (the $11.7 billion); these were foreign government obligations to the United States government. Typically, the late 1920s loans to foreign governments (included in Column D) were bonds issued by bankers and sold to U.S. private investors; these were private American portfolio investments abroad, with foreign governments the borrowers.

6. The holdings of the British government in American securities during the First World War appear to have ended after 1923—with the borrowed securities returned to private ownership and the remaining owned securities ultimately sold.

7. See U.S. Department of the Treasury, *Annual Report for Year-ended June 30, 1923*, 261–262 (the funding agreement); ibid., *1925*, 22–23, and ibid., *1930*, 26. Even before the funding agreement, this procedure had been followed in certain repayments, ibid., *1922*, 46–47.

8. This is based on data I found in the archives of the Federal Reserve Bank of New York (FRBNY).

9. Most government-owned companies (worldwide) were national rather than multinational enterprises. And, in the 1920s, there were not that many government-owned enterprises. Amtorg, the Russian trading agency, was one government entity with a presence in the United States, but the size of its U.S. stakes was tiny. So, too, the French government-owned potash mines had a small investment in marketing in the United States.

10. Sources on these figures disagree. The $414 million and $979 million are from Royal Institute of International Affairs, *Problem of International Investment*, 309. The other pair of figures ($330 million and $982 million) are from U.S. Department of Commerce, Bureau of the Census, *Historical Statistics of the United States* (Washington, D.C., 1975), II, 864.

11. The British maintained certain restrictions on foreign issues but not on trading in foreign securities, which was how British nationals typically made foreign portfolio investments in America.

12. James Foreman-Peck, *A History of the World Economy*, 2nd ed. (New York: Harvester/Wheatsheaf, 1995), 211.

13. U.S. Department of the Treasury, *Annual Report for the Year-ended June 30, 1927*, 68.

14. The best discussion of this is in Hermann Janssen and Wilhelm Kiesselbach, *Das Amerikanische Freigabe-Gesetz vom 10 Marz 1928 (Settlement of War Claims Act of 1928)* (Mannheim: J. Bensheimer, 1928). See also Norddeutscher Lloyd, *Bericht 1927* (Mar. 26, 1928); idem, *Bericht 1928* (Mar. 29, 1929); and idem, *Bericht 1929* (Mar. 25, 1930). I have found useful on Mellon's views, U.S. Department of the Treasury, *Annual Reports*, for example, for year-ended June 30, 1926, 15–17, 266–274, and ibid., *1927*, 67–70. Eventually (in June 1930), the War Claims Arbitrator entered tentative awards in favor of German nationals for ninety-four merchant ships for $74,252,933. U.S. Department of the Treasury, *Annual Report for Year-ended June 30, 1931*, 91.

15. See, for example, Maier, *Recasting Bourgeois Europe;* W. Arthur Lewis, *Economic Survey 1919–1939* (New York: Harper Torchbooks, 1949), chap. 3; and Paul Einzig, *World Finance 1914–1935* (New York: Macmillan, 1935), 147–148 (for the "false feeling of security and stability").

16. On this I have found Charles R. Geisst, *Entrepôt Capitalism: Foreign Investment and the American Dream in the Twentieth Century* (New York: Praeger, 1992) stimulating.

17. My study is confined to long-term investments. There were also sizable short-term investments in the United States. The short-term moneys were very much part of the entrepôt that New York had become. See Beckhart, *New York Money Market*, vols. II and III, esp. III, 184–192. On definitions of long-term and short-term, see Appendix 1 herein.

18. Davies, *Investments Abroad*, chap. 11; Edwin R. A. Seligman, *Double Taxation and International Fiscal Cooperation* (New York: Macmillan, 1928); U.S. Department of the Treasury, *Annual Report for Year-ended June 30, 1929*, 26–28; and Paul Deperon, *International Double Taxation* (New York: Committee on International Economic Policy, 1945), 14–16.

The first concerns by the U.S. government had been to relieve the tax burden on U.S. business abroad, and with this in mind the United States enacted its initial foreign tax credit provisions in the Revenue Act of 1918. Other countries, principally in Europe, took steps to exempt foreign-source income from home-country taxation, but to the extent that this had the effect of substantially reducing revenues collected, it met obstacles. In the 1920s, it became apparent that agreements between governments would be desirable, and the League of Nations undertook studies of double taxation and developed model tax treaties. See Cym H. Lowell and Jack P. Governale, *U.S. International Taxation* (Boston: Warren, Gorham & Lamont, 1997), chap. 9, par. 9.01 [1]. Out of the First World War, and in the 1920s, in the United States and Europe, there emerged what W. Elliot Brownlee has called "democratic-statist tax regimes." See his *Federal Taxation in America* (Cambridge: Cambridge University Press, 1996), 48; Brownlee describes how in the United States Republican administrations lowered taxes during the 1920s, but there was no return to the tax regime of pre–World War I America. Archival records on investors in the United States in the late 1920s are full of concerns over how to handle matters related to taxes.

19. Davies, *Investments Abroad*, chap. 12.

20. "Kreuger III," *Fortune*, 8 (July 1933): 74. See also Einzig, *World Finance*, 155, and U.S. Senate, Committee on Banking and Currency, *Stock Exchange Practices, Report*, 73rd Cong., 2nd sess. (1934), 323–327.

21. Harold James, *The German Slump* (Oxford: Clarendon Press, 1986), 132, writes of Germany that "tax evasion and capital flight came to be built into the Weimar system." Large companies in Britain arranged to use tax havens to minimize their tax burdens (based on my own archival research). The existence of a 2 percent stamp tax in Britain on bearer bonds was probably a "strong disincentive to foreign lending" done from the United Kingdom. Alec Cairncross, *Control of Long-Term International Capital Movements* (Washington, D.C.: Brookings, 1973), 56.

22. George David Smith and Richard Sylla, "The Transformation of Financial Capitalism: An Essay on the History of American Capital Markets," *Financial Markets, Institutions and Instruments*, 2 (May 1993): 28–29. The best work on the public utilities holding companies is James C. Bonbright and Gardiner C. Means, *The Holding Company* (New York: McGraw-Hill, 1932).

23. Foreigners did continue to hold and to purchase some sterling- and franc-denominated bonds issued in pre–World War I years and still outstanding, but the amounts appear to be insignificant.

24. The 54 percent figure is from Lewis, *America's Stake*, 558. Note that by year end 1929, stock *values* were 68 percent of the September 30, 1929 values. Charles P. Kindleberger, *The World in Depression* (Berkeley: University of California Press, 1973), 111. This gives a hint at the difficulties of measuring the "level" of such common stock investments. In the 1920s, Sun Life Assurance Co., Canada, a giant investor in marketable American securities, published three columns of figures on its U.S. (and Canadian) investments: (1) par value of securities; (2) "ledger value" (the price at which the company acquired the securities); and (3) market value. Sun Life Assurance Co., *Annual Reports 1919–1929*.

25. On the problems of using "book value" figures, see Robert Eisner and Paul J. Pieper, "Real Foreign Investment in Perspective," *The Annals*, 516 (July 1991): 22–35. More serious than the underestimate caused by using "book value" figures was the underestimate through ignorance on the extent of the involvements. I have not raised the figure, since I do not know how much to increase the sum. A revision would only add to the messy numerical series already available.

26. For 1914 figure, see Chapter 1 herein and Wilkins, *History*, 145. Both figures are in current dollars.

27. Ibid., 625.

28. $5.8 billion foreign investment divided by $103.1 billion gross national product equals .056. The GNP figure—in current dollars—is from U.S. Department of Commerce, Bureau of the Census, *Historical Statistics of the United States,* I, 224.

29. If we use the 1929 income figures in Royal Institute of International Affairs, *Problem of International Investment,* 309 ($414 million on inward investment and $979 on outward investment), and put in the denominator the figures given in Columns F and C in Table 4.1, we get a return on investment in the United States that is higher than the return on investment abroad: 7.1 percent versus 6.3 percent. If, however, the amount of foreign investment in the United States is larger than the $5.8 billion, that would bring down the difference (if smaller, it would increase the difference), and if we use other income figures, the return on inward investment is lower than that on outward investment. All these figures are suspect, so I am only dealing with "perceptions," which is what motivates investors. And I am dealing with the entire period 1924–1929, where it seems likely that investors considered that the return in the United States was lower than elsewhere.

30. In Mira Wilkins, "Cosmopolitan Finance in the 1920s: New York's Emergence as an International Financial Centre," in *The State, the Financial System, and Economic Modernization: Comparative Historical Perspectives,* ed. Richard Sylla, Richard Tilly, and G. Tortella (Cambridge: Cambridge University Press, 1999), 271–291, I make the point that New York was very new to its role as a financial entrepôt. The newness created special conditions. I also make the point that while certain of the outward international activities of the 1919–1923 period had not lasted, the capital exports had persisted.

31. As indicated in Chapter 3, I have been excluding such inward foreign direct investments from my discussion, if I can establish that the Canadian firm was U.S. controlled. I include this here only to show the complex web.

32. See letters from T. B. Macaulay to G. D. Finlayson, Sept. 20, 1927; Sept. 24, 1927; Nov. 30, 1927; and to W. L. Mackenzie King, May 30, 1928, all in Macaulay letterbooks, Sun Life Assurance Co. Archives, Toronto, Canada.

33. Americans did the same thing in purely domestic transactions, often borrowing and using stocks as collateral. See Charles R. Geisst, *Wall Street: A History* (New York: Oxford University Press, 1997), 176–177.

34. Wilkins, *History,* 466; Wilkins, "Japanese Multinationals," 591. In Chapter 3, I gave an example, of the Chinese Merchants Bank, which hoped to help U.S. business *in Chinese* investments.

35. Shaplen, *Kreuger,* passim.

36. As noted in Chapter 3, Price Waterhouse (in its 1932 investigation) could find no evidence that Krueger ever had the interest.

37. Lindgren, *Corporate Growth,* 305, 357.

38. Shaplen, *Kreuger,* 96; U.S. Senate, Committee on Banking and Currency, *Stock Exchange Practices, Hearings,* 72nd Cong., 1st sess. (1933), pt. 4, 1153. Shaplen says $18 million, but this was the total offering, not that placed in the United States.

39. *Moody's Industrials 1929,* 2824; Shaplen, *Kreuger,* 80, 122–123.

40. *Stock Exchange Practices, Hearings,* pt. 4, 1154.

41. Ibid., 1152–1153.

42. This is clear from all contemporary reports and data that I have seen in corporate and U.S. government archives.

43. Kreuger securities offered in the United States, which were all sold, in this period equaled $210.2 million—some of which were bought by foreign investors. The $210.2 million is from documents provided by Donald Durant, a partner in Lee, Higginson & Co., Kreuger's lead banker. *Stock Exchange Practices, Hearings,* pt. 4, 1152–1154.

44. Office of Alien Property Custodian, *Annual Report for the Year-ending June 30, 1944,* 76–78.

45. Sobel, *Life and Times of Dillon Read,* 102–103, 111. A copy of the statement prepared by Dillon, Read & Co. for the 1926 bond flotation for United Steel Works is in U.S. Senate, Committee on Military Affairs, Subcommittee on War Mobilization, *Scientific and Technical Mobilization, Hearings* 78th Cong., 1st and 2nd sess. (1943–1944), pt. 16, 2264 (Exhibit 528). These hearings are henceforth cited as *Kilgore Committee Hearings.*

46. Roberts, *Schroders,* 233. See also for this firm's participation in other German loans. In the 1926 bond prospectus for United Steel Works there was the statement that "bondholders may at their option, collect principal and interest in London in Pounds Sterling at the buying rate for sight exchange in New York on the date of presentation for collection." *Kilgore Committee Hearings,* pt. 16, 2264 (Exhibit 528).

47. *Moody's Industrials 1929,* 1030–1031.

48. Wilkins, *Maturing,* 106, and Klein, "Patiño Tin Empire," 16. I am indebted to Jean-François Hennart for pointing out to me the similarity between Patiño's behavior and that of Kreuger, the Stinnes family, and Schneider-Creusot. Each was making an investment in the United States for capital exports to projects outside the United States.

49. Luciano Segreto to Mira Wilkins, Sept. 28, 1993, and *Moody's Public Utilities 1929,* 908–1000. To show how complicated and pyramided matters could become, 50 percent of the shares in Italian Superpower were acquired by American Superpower in January 1929; then United Corporation, later in 1929, acquired control of American Superpower. William J. Hausman and John Neufeld, "U.S. Foreign Direct Investment in Electrical Utilities in the 1920s," in *The Free-Standing Company in the World Economy, 1830–1996,* ed. Mira Wilkins and Harm Schröter (Oxford: Oxford University Press, 1998). 374.

50. U.S. Securities and Exchange Commission, *Investment Trusts and Investment Companies,* H. Doc. 279, 76th Cong., 1st sess. (1940), pt. 3, 3. Henceforth cited as SEC, *Investment Trusts,* pt. 3.

51. See favorable discussion of British investment trusts—as the models—in U.S. Department of Commerce, Bureau of Foreign and Domestic Commerce, *British Investment Trusts.* On the proliferation of such companies in the United States and their British antecedents, see Theodore J. Grayson, *Investment Trusts* (New York: John Wiley, 1928). For a less sympathetic rendition, see the four-part U.S. Securities and Exchange Commission, *Report on Study of Investment Trusts,* 75th–77th Cong. (1939–1942), cited as SEC, *Investment Trusts,* by part number. (The title of each part varied slightly.)

52. Hugh Bullock, *The Story of Investment Companies* (New York: Columbia University Press, 1959), 62–67.

53. See wonderful material in Edgar Higgins Collection (Mss 793), Baker Library, Harvard Business School, Boston, Box 3. Higgins was an "investment trust consultant."

54. John Kenneth Galbraith, *The Great Crash 1929* (Boston: Houghton Mifflin, 1961), 68–69. On the Swiss holding company's ownership of Solvay American at origin, see SEC, *Investment Trusts,* pt. 4, 152. Solvay American was large. Of the fourteen management investment companies and investment holding companies in the United States with assets over $100 million in December 1929, Solvay American ranked ninth, with assets of $165 million. Bullock, *Story of Investment Companies,* 40 (based on SEC data). Of the fourteen listed, only Solvay American was foreign controlled, although some of the others had attracted foreign investments.

55. In his glossary, Bullock, *Story of Investment Companies,* 184, distinguished investment companies (which aimed to buy securities as an investment) from holding companies (which aimed to control or influence the management of the companies in which they invested). In the late 1920s, the distinction was often obscure.

56. On Hamburg American Insurance Co., see *Best's Insurance Reports, Fire and Marine, 1930.* On New York Hamburg Corp., see *Moody's Banks 1929,* 975. For wonderful material on the pre-1914 activities of H. Mutzenbecher, Jr., in the United States, see Hartwell Cabell, Report to Alien Property Custodian. Sept. 23, 1918, RG 56, Entry 406, Box 1, National Archives.

57. Cassis, "Swiss International Banking," 168.

58. Youssef Cassis to Mira Wilkins, Feb. 7, 1990.

59. *Moody's Banks 1928,* 2687. M. Georges Aubert wrote a book on *La Finance Américaine,* published in 1910. On Hentsch and Lombard, Odier & Co., see index to Wilkins, *History.* On the Pictets and Lullins, as well as the Lombards and Hentsches, see Nicholas Faith, *Safety in Numbers* (New York: Viking Press, 1982), 22, 24, 287. For some details on Pictet & Cie. trade in American securities at a later date, see Memorandum, Dec. 17, 1941, on Pictet & Cie., Geneva, FO 115/441, Public Record Office, London.

60. Cassis, "Swiss International Banking," 168.

61. *Moody's Banks 1928,* 2687.

62. On Loewenstein, see William Norris, *The Man Who Fell from the Sky* (New York: Viking, 1987); Armstrong and Nelles, *Southern Exposure,* 256–265; and Interrogation of Kurt Freiherr von Schroeder, Nov. 23, 1945, RG 238, T301, Reel 3, NI-240, National Archives.

63. Armstrong and Nelles, *Southern Exposure,* 262, and Orbell, *Baring Brothers,* 82.

64. Norris, *Man Who Fell from the Sky,* 115. On Hydro-Electric Securities Corporation, see Bullock, *Story of Investment Companies,* 121–123.

65. Interrogation of von Schroeder; see also Roberts, *Schroders,* for the relationships between Loewenstein and the Schroeders.

66. Norris, *Man,* 163. Norris gives a company by the name of Middlewest Standard Gas Co. I cannot identify such a firm and have included two logical substitutes. Roberts, *Schroders,* 237, shows Loewenstein acquired major interests in Standard Gas and Electric (Stangas) during this U.S. trip. See also ibid., 290–291, on Stangas.

67. At least that is the way I interpret Norris, *Man Who Fell from the Sky,* 231.

68. *Economist,* Aug. 10, 1929, 282. *The Economist* did not mention the Belgian stockholdings. Hydro-Electric Securities Corp.(HESC) was organized in Canada under a tax designation known as "4K"; it paid only a nominal Canadian tax and was prohibited from deriving income from or from owning property in Canada. Bullock, *Story of Investment Companies,* 123. In the 1920s, companies such as HESC, set up in Canada, were often used as financial intermediaries by out-of-Canada investors to invest in the United States and elsewhere abroad. HESC was huge. Bullock, *Story of Investment Companies,* 221–222, lists the 1929 "size" of about fifty Canadian investment companies; HESC, with assets (at "cost price") of $61.6 million, was by far the largest. In second place was Power Corporation of Canada, formed in 1925, with its 1929 assets (based on "market price") of $47.0 million.

69. See data in RG 3, Chase Manhattan Bank Archives.

70. Rosenbaum and Sherman, *M. M. Warburg,* 140.

71. On U.S. investment banking in the 1920s, see Carosso, *Investment Banking,* chaps. 13 and 14. On the foreign lending of National City Company (the securities affiliate of National City Bank), see Cleveland and Huertas, *Citibank,* 145–153. On Chase Securities (the securities affiliate of Chase National), see John D. Wilson, *The Chase: The Chase Manhattan Bank N.A. 1945–1985* (Boston: Harvard Business School Press, 1986), 13.

72. The interactions were numerous. Thus, Dillon, Read & Co.'s United States & Foreign Securities Corporation (set up in 1924) invested in the American & Continental Corp., which had been set up by the International Acceptance Bank (IAB). Sobel, *Life and Times of Dillon Read,* 87, 89. J. Henry Schroder Banking Corp., which was British

owned, formed with Lee, Higginson in 1925, the European Mortgage and Investment Corporation to raise funds in the United States for central European lending. Roberts, *Schroders.* 233.

73. Nevertheless, I was very surprised to find comprehensive Federal Reserve examiners' reports for 1927, 1928, and 1929 for the International Acceptance Bank in the Chase Manhattan Bank Archives, RG 1. The 1927 report involved ninety-seven days of scrutiny.

74. U.S. Department of Commerce, Bureau of Foreign and Domestic Commerce, *The Balance of International Payments of the United States in 1929* (Washington, D.C., 1930), 32. This did not mean that taxes did not matter. They did. But the new corporate architecture set up for tax purposes seemed at this point to be accomplishing its purpose.

75. Bank secrecy was "deeply rooted" in long-established Swiss banking practices. Sébastien Guex, "The Origins of the Swiss Banking Secrecy Law and Its Repercussions for Swiss Federal Policy," *Business History Review,* 74 (Summer 2000): 237–243.

76. On the lax monitoring, see Armstrong and Nelles, *Southern Exposure.* For more on the use of Canadian intermediates to reduce taxes, see *Stock Exchange Practices, Report,* 323–327 and Albert Broder, "The Multinationalisation of the French Electrical Industry 1880–1914," in *Multinationals: Theory and History,* ed. Peter Hertner and Geoffrey Jones (Aldershot: Gower, 1986), 191n. The work of Canadian business historians has made it clear that the Toronto and Montreal business communities had different characteristics.

77. It was little wonder that the U.S. Department of Commerce expressed concern over its failure to develop satisfactory measures of the complex investment patterns. See, for example, U.S. Department of Commerce, Bureau of Foreign and Domestic Commerce, *The Balance of International Payments of the United States in 1927* (Washington, D.C., 1928), 42–47.

78. The figures are to be viewed with caution and skepticism. They cannot be reconciled with ones later presented by Hal Lary, nor do they mesh with statistics in Raymond Goldsmith, *A Study of Savings* (Princeton, N.J.: Princeton University Press, 1955), 1082, which gives only net figures and relies on Lary's work. Nonetheless, these figures suggest a substantial trade in securities and show a rise in inward investments based on foreign purchases of securities.

79. Cleona Lewis' totals are provided in column 1, Table 2.1 herein. Other authors offer different figures: Goldsmith, *Study of Savings,* 1089, did not give 1924 figures; his 1929 ones are from Robert L. Sammons, "Foreign Investment Aspects of Measuring U.S. National Wealth," National Bureau of Economic Research, *Studies in Income and Wealth* (New York: National Bureau of Economic Research, 1950), 553, 566 (Sammons used the term "portfolio investments" to cover only equities; in Table 2.1, Column 7, where I reproduced Sammons' 1929 figures, I got the $4,320 million total by adding his recorded investments in stocks to his figure for long-term claims, which included bonds and "other long-term claims"). Lewis' and Sammons' figures seem to deal with domestic securities and ignore foreign investments in foreign securities.

80. See Table 4.6, adding common stock in railroads with other common stock.

81. See Robert Sobel, *The Great Bull Market: Wall Street in the 1920s* (New York: W. W. Norton, 1968).

82. When a foreign investor acquired a dollar-denominated "foreign" security, the *obligation* was that of the foreign issuer, *but* the dividends or interest were payable in dollars.

83. National Industrial Conference Board, *International Financial Position of the United States,* 65, 67n.2.

84. Ibid., 65.

85. Albert Fishlow, "Debt: Lessons from the Past," *International Organization,* 39 (Summer 1985): 418–419, was struck by the magnitude of public borrowing in the international investments of the late 1920s.

86. Sammons, "Foreign Investment Aspects," 566, estimated the amount in 1929 as a mere $125 million, a figure accepted by Goldsmith, *Study of Savings,* 1089.

87. Corporation of Foreign Bondholders, London, *Annual Reports,* 1920–1929, especially 1920, pp. 27–18 (on the settlement and Mississippi). This will be the last mention in my book of the Corporation of Foreign Bondholders (CFB), although it continued on a regular basis to complain (in vain) about the perfidy of these southern states, up until the very end of the CFB, in 1989. Barry Eichengreen, "Historical Research on International Lending and Debt," *Journal of Economic Perspectives,* 5 (Spring 1991): 162n.20.

88. See *Best's Insurance Manual, Fire and Marine* for the 1920s.

89. J. P. Morgan & Co. told a Senate committee in 1933 that of its domestic issues in the late 1920s, bonds of railroad companies represented the largest single category. It generally shared its issues with its London (Morgan, Grenfell) and Paris (Morgan et Cie. after 1926) houses. *Stock Exchange Practices, Hearings,* pt. 2, 879–880. Kuhn, Loeb also had large railroad issues. In the spring of 1929, stockholders in the Pennsylvania Railroad were offered the opportunity to buy Pennroad Corporation shares. British investors could pay for the shares in this holding company at Midland Bank, Ltd., in London. Ibid., pt. 3, 1242. Foreign banks and companies remained on Kuhn, Loeb's syndicate list for its new railroad issues. See ibid., pt. 3, 1262–1267.

90. *Commercial and Financial Chronicle,* Feb. 4, 1928, 664, has the year end 1927 figures.

91. In 1927, *Iron Age* was noting the lack of in-house innovation at U.S. Steel Corporation. Janet T. Knoedler, "Market Structure, Industrial Research, and Consumers of Innovation," *Business History Review,* 67 (Spring 1993): 109.

92. See *American Magazine,* 98 (Oct. 1924): 90, advertisement, reprinted in Roland Marchand, "The Corporation Nobody Knew," *Business History Review,* 65 (Winter 1991): 849.

93. Sobel, *Life and Times of Dillon Read,* 130–131.

94. Soule, *Prosperity Decade,* 184.

95. Wilkins, *History,* 472, 483, 523–524.

96. *Stock Exchange Practices, Hearings,* pt. 2, 370, 372, 503. A much smaller allotment went to the Stockholm Enskilda Bank. Ibid., 371.

97. See, for example, Sun Life Assurance Co., *Annual Report 1929.*

98. Forrest McDonald, *Insull* (Chicago: University of Chicago Press, 1962), 71–73, 95, 144, 145n, 239–240, 277. On the "Robert Benson" and "Fleming" groups of investment trusts, see U.S. Department of Commerce, Bureau of Foreign and Domestic Commerce, *British Investment Trusts,* Trade Information Bulletin 88 (Washington, 1923), 33–34, and U.S. Securities and Exchange Commission, *Investment Trusts in Great Britain,* House Doc. 380, 76th Cong., 1st sess. (1939), 17–18. Wake, *Kleinwort Benson,* 301, writes that "Flemings" and "Bensons" in the late 1920s were regarded on Wall Street as the leaders in the investment trust movement. When Robert Fleming died in 1933, the press noted that his Investment Trust Corporation was "loaded up" with Insull securities. *Fortune,* 8 (Sept. 1933): 15. And that was only one of the numerous Flemings' investment trusts. Wake, Kleinwort Benson, 294, writes that in the 1920s, Insull sold many of his concerns' shares to Bensons' investment trusts.

99. McDonald, *Insull,* 299; Wilkins, *History,* 554–555; Schull, *Century of the Sun;* data in Sun Life Archives.

100. T. B. Macaulay to Samuel Insull, Apr. 15, 1924, Macaulay letterbooks, Sun Life Archives. On April 23, 1925, Macaulay gave instructions that Sun Life buy Commonwealth Edison common stock (Commonwealth Edison was an Insull company). Macaulay wanted to increase Sun Life's holdings by 10,000 shares. J. W. Brown to E. A. MacNutt, Apr. 23, 1925, Box 138, 116/3, Sun Life Archives.

101. Wilkins, *History,* 552.

102. *Moody's Public Utilities 1929,* 1217.

103. See Sun Life Assurance Co., *Annual Report 1929,* for example, which had more than $10 million invested in each of these, except for Standard Gas and Electric, the securities of which I found in the portfolios of other foreign investors.

104. Bonbright and Means, *Holding Company.*

105. Donald Moggridge, *British Monetary Policy* (Cambridge: Cambridge University Press, 1972), 212. I found confirmation of this pattern in the 1933 *Stock Exchange Practices, Hearings.*

106. I am indebted to Stephen A. Schuker for this insight (Schuker to Wilkins, Aug. 7, 1994), although the interpretation is my own.

107. Moggridge, *British Monetary Policy,* 211–212.

108. Ibid., 212 (the New York broker was not specified).

109. Ibid., 214.

110. Kathleen Burk, "Money and Power," in *Finance and Financiers in European History, 1880–1960,* ed. Youssef Cassis (Cambridge: Cambridge University Press, 1992), 364.

111. This point is made in Davies, *Investments Abroad,* 44–45.

112. Stephen A. Schuker, *American "Reparations" to Germany, 1919–33: Implications for the Third World Debt Crisis* (Princeton, N.J.: Princeton Studies in International Finance, 1988), 116–117.

113. Edward M. Lamont, *The Ambassador from Wall Street: The Story of Thomas W. Lamont* (Lanham, Md.: Madison Books, 1994), 209.

114. Moggridge, *British Monetary Policy,* 215.

115. Geisst, *Entrepôt Capitalism,* 12, suggests there was substantial interexchange trading, which meant there were opportunities for arbitrage.

116. Michael Bliss, *Northern Enterprise* (Toronto: McClelland & Stewart, 1987), 406. There are some Canadian statistics for year end 1926 on the level of Canadian investments in U.S. stocks and bonds, but the data are described as "weak." Statistics Canada, *Canada's International Investment Position: Historical Statistics 1926 to 1992* (Ottawa, 1993), 45, 55. Also, all evidence shows a sizable increase in investments in 1926–1929.

117. Geisst, *Entrepôt Capitalism,* 13.

118. Cleveland and Huertas, *Citibank,* 152.

119. Bliss, *Northern Enterprise,* 405, and Bullock, *Story of Investment Companies,* 118, 123.

120. Avram, *Rayon Industry,* 149. The Belgian electrical power and rayon industries were joined through the activities of Alfred Loewenstein. On Dominion Securities involvement in foreign public utilities, see Bliss, *Northern Enterprise,* 394. It also participated in Dillon, Read's United States & Foreign Securities Corp. *Stock Exchange Practices, Hearings,* pt. 4, 1611.

121. Armstrong and Nelles, *Southern Exposure,* 251; Taylor and Baskerville, *Concise History,* 257.

122. Bullock, *Story of Investment Companies,* 119.

123. Ibid., 10. On A. Iselin & Co.'s British, Swiss, and French connections, see Wilkins, *History,* 466, 511, 666, 672, 893. By 1929, the Royal Bank of Canada had surpassed the Bank of Montreal to become Canada's largest. Holt was very much involved in international business, including Latin American (as well as Canadian) utilities. Taylor and Baskerville, *Concise History,* 252–253, and Armstrong and Nelles, *Southern Exposure,* 123, 142–143, 262–269.

124. Bullock, *Story of Investment Companies,* 122.

125. A *1936* study found that ninety-two Canadian investment trusts held American securities. Marshall, Southard, and Taylor, *Canadian-American Industry,* 175. The number in 1929 would probably be in the same range.

126. T. B. Macaulay to D. J. Scott, Nov. 22, 1926, Macaulay letterbook, Sun Life Archives.

127. [V. B.] Van Art to [J. W.] Brown, Feb. 4, 1929, Investment Correspondence, Box 19, 11/14, Sun Life Archives (for American investments), and Sun Life Assurance Co., *Annual Report 1928,* for total.

128. See Statistical Section to [J. W.] Brown, May 7, 1929, re: Industries Represented in Sun Life's Security Holdings, Investment Correspondence, Box 19, 11/14, Sun Life Archives.

129. *Economist,* Feb. 15, 1930, 347. In 1923, based on balance sheets of twenty-six companies, the U.S. attracted almost 18 percent of the portfolio and continental Europe 4.5 percent; by 1929, only 10 percent of their portfolio was in the United States, while over 17 percent was invested in continental Europe.

130. Moggridge, *British Monetary Policy,* 215. Data on English holdings in U.S. Steel common shares, at year end 1924 and 1925, reveal a sharp drop in 1925 from 100,689 to 26,217 shares (*Commercial and Financial Chronicle,* Feb. 4, 1928, 664), which is *not* inconsistent with Moggridge's findings; it is likely that before the British went back to gold, Britishers (early in 1925) sold the American holdings. Subsequently, they began to rebuild their American interests, albeit not necessarily in U.S. Steel shares.

131. Moggridge, *British Monetary Policy,* 215n.

132. Grant, *Capital Market in Post-war Britain.*

133. What may very well have happened is that the older investment trusts as they divested their railroad securities reinvested more often in the United Kingdom rather than in the new industrials and public utilities in the United States. U.S. Securities and Exchange Commission, *Investment Trusts in Great Britain,* H. Doc. 380, 76th Cong., 1st sess. (1939), 50 (on old and new British investment trusts). By 1929, most had greater investments in the United Kingdom and continental Europe than in the United States.

134. Wake, *Kleinwort Benson,* 294–302. Robert Fleming & Co. acted "as an operating corporation for a number of leading [English and Scottish] investments trusts," including Investment Trust Corporation, Ltd., founded by Fleming in 1888. This 1928 quotation is from Grayson, *Investment Trusts,* 191. On Fleming companies, see U.S. Department of Commerce, Bureau of Foreign and Domestic Commerce, *British Investment Trusts,* 33. For the Scottish investment trusts associated with the Fleming group, see Glasgow, *Scottish Investment Trust Companies,* 68, 86, 88 (for example). Glasgow wrote (p. 13) that Robert Fleming companies never published lists of investments. Since it is apparent that the Fleming group of companies continued to make sizable U.S. investments, it is possible that published lists may underestimate the British trust companies' U.S. activities in the late 1920s.

135. This was as of April 1925, the date when Britain returned to the gold standard. See Weir, *History of the Scottish American Investment Company,* 21.

136. Ibid., 22–23.

137. Reader, *Imperial Chemical Industries,* II, 14–15.

138. *Fortune,* 8 (Sept. 1933): 127.

139. Maxwell boasted of his near relatives: the duke of Norfolk, the duke of Buccleuch, and Montagu Collet Norman (governor of the Bank of England). Ibid., 127, 130. John T. Pratt, a partner in G. M.-P. Murphy & Co., New York, was a director in 1925 of the International Acceptance Bank. See *Who's Who, 1924–1925,* and International Acceptance Bank, *Annual Report* (Jan. 1925).

140. *Fortune,* 8 (Sept. 1933): 127, for the list. See also Ranald C. Michie, *The London Stock Exchange: A History* (Oxford: Oxford University Press, 1999), 218–220, 243.

141. *Stock Exchange Practices, Hearings,* pt. 3, 958, 1320. The companies were American Investment & General Trust, Ltd.; English & Caledonian Investment Co., Ltd.; Foreign,

American & General Trust Co., Ltd.; Foreign & Colonial Investment Trust Co., Ltd.; London Border & General Trust Ltd.; London Prudential Investment Trust Company; National Mutual Life Assurance Society; Scottish Stockholders Investment Trust Ltd.; Southern Stockholders Investment Trust, Ltd.; Underground Electric Rys. Co. of London; and European Merchant Banking Co., Ltd. For more on Leith, see *New York Times,* Apr. 3, 1941.

142. On this company, see Samuel Insull, "Memoirs" (1934–1935), 202, Samuel Insull Papers, Box 17, Archives, Loyola University, Chicago.

143. Samuel Insull to Insull, Son & Co., Ltd., London, Aug. 5, 1929, Samuel Insull Papers, Box 1, Folder 2.

144. See Wilkins, *History,* passim. Hallgarten & Co. had a prewar London office, which it reestablished in 1919. "Draft History of Hallgarten & Co.," typescript, copy from Jon Bulkley, Moseley, Hallgarten, Estabrook & Weeden Holding Company, New York.

145. *Fortune,* 8 (Sept. 1933): 130. Louis F. Rothschild (who was *not* related to the European Rothschild family) had founded L. F. Rothschild & Co. in 1899. Paul Hoffman, *The Dealmakers* (Garden City, N.Y.: Doubleday, 1984).

146. *Fortune,* 8 (Sept. 1933): 120.

147. U.S. Department of Commerce, Bureau of Foreign and Domestic Commerce, *Balance of International Payments of the United States in 1927,* 24–25.

148. *Fortune,* 8 (Sept. 1933): 124 (dealing with 1929 trading).

149. Swaine, *Cravath Firm,* II, 440.

150. William J. Reader, *A House in the City: A Study of the City and of the Stock Exchange Based on the Records of Foster and Braithwaite, 1825–1975* (London: B. T. Batsford, 1979), 142.

151. Even before the First World War, "Woolworth . . . had become so familiar to European ears as to almost lose [its] . . . American identity." Southard, *American Industry in Europe,* xiv, 109, 149. On the British Courtaulds' gross income, 46 percent in 1927, 47 percent in 1928, and 56 percent in 1929 came from its American business. Coleman, *Courtaulds,* II, 255, 315.

152. Einzig, *World Finance,* 211. Discussing British participation in the U.S. stock market, July 1928 to September 1929, Heywood W. Fleisig, *Long Term Capital Flows and the Great Depression: The Role of the United States 1927–1933* (New York: Arno Press, 1975), 36, writes, "Great Britain possessed one of the largest pools of liquid investible capital in the world. However, the British stock market was steady rather than strongly bullish. To the extent that foreign participation in the New York stock markets was a function of the size of the foreigner's liquid assets and his alternative domestic investment opportunities, it is likely that a considerable portion of foreign transactions in outstanding securities originated in Britain."

153. On Winston Churchill's investments (made with the advice of stockbroker E. F. Hutton), see Lamont, *Ambassador from Wall Street,* 265.

154. "Draft History of Hallgarten & Co.," 8–10. On the other hand, a Dutch banking directory, Historische Bedrijfsarchiven, *Bankwezen* (Amsterdam: NEHA, 1992), 87, suggests that Pierson & Co. was the successor to A. Boissevain.

155. *Stock Exchange Practices, Hearings,* pt. 3 (Kuhn, Loeb), 959. Felix Warburg, a partner in Kuhn, Loeb, was the brother of Max Warburg, head of M. M. Warburg, Hamburg.

156. These figures are given in Amos Taylor to Hague Office, U.S. Department of Commerce, Mar. 22, 1932, in RG 151, 600 U.S. Balance of Payments 1932–1933, National Archives. The $450 million is $50 million more than the published figures for 1929 in U.S. Department of Commerce, Bureau of Foreign and Domestic Commerce, *Balance of International Payments of the United States in 1929,* 12, as given in Table 2.4.

157. U.S. Department of Commerce, Bureau of Foreign and Domestic Commerce, *Balance of International Payments of the United States in 1927,* 24–25.

158. See *Van Oss' Effectenboek.* I am indebted to A. Veenendaal for this information.

159. Royal Institute of International Affairs, *Problem of International Investment,* 213.

160. Schuker, *American "Reparations,"* 116–117.

161. Emden, *Money Powers,* 268, 276; Fritz Seidenzahl, *100 Jahr Deutsche Bank* (Frankfurt: Deutsche Bank, 1970), 289; *Moody's Banks 1929,* 2308 (Deutsche Bank Board). For Konrad Adenauer's "speculation" in these rayon companies' securities, see Hans-Peter Schwarz, *Konrad Adenauer,* vol. 1 (Providence, R.I.: Berghahn Books, 1995), 210–212. The story told here is a splendid example of how Germans were attracted to "American" securities.

162. *Foreign Relations of the United States: Current Economic Developments, 1945–1954, Current Economic Developments,* 52 (June 17, 1946), 2. We do not, of course, know whether the Swedes acquired these securities in the 1920s or if they acquired them later.

163. Cross, *Financing an Empire,* III, 266. My thanks go to Professor Hidemaga Morikawa (who was the first to point out to me the connection between Fujimoto Bill Broker Bank, Fujimoto Securities, and its successor Daiwa Securities), and to Paul J. Hauser of Daiwa Securities America Inc., who filled me in on the important details (Hauser to Wilkins, Feb. 22, 1989). Daiwa records indicate that the New York office of Fujimoto Securities opened in 1924. When Gyoju Odate wrote his *Japan's Financial Relations with the United States,* in 1922, he relied heavily on information from "Fujimoto Bill Broking Bank, Osaka" (p. 10). Ibid., 107, refers to a September 1919 agreement between the New York private banker Bonbright & Co. and "Fujimoto Bill Broking [*sic*] Bank" on the mutual introduction of bonds and stocks in the American and Japanese market. Bonbright & Co. was particularly active in public utility securities.

164. It was the recipient of a $1 million broker's loan from Kuhn, Loeb & Co. in January 1927, which it repaid in April 1927. The loan had as collateral Japanese, South American, and other bonds. See *Stock Exchange Practices, Hearings,* pt. 3 (Kuhn, Loeb), 1404–1405.

165. Nomura Securities Co., Osaka, was formed in 1925 to underwrite and to distribute "government bonds, corporate bonds, and stock" and to trade in such securities. It, along with the Osaka Nomura Bank (formed in 1918 and the precursor to the Daiwa Bank), was part of a newly formed *zaibatsu* controlled by the Nomura Co. By the late 1920s, Nomura Securities had eight domestic offices along with its New York office. Samuel L. Hayes and Philip M. Hubbard, *Investment Banking* (Boston: Harvard Business School Press, 1990), 145, 185, 266–267.

166. Historical data from Nomura Securities International, Inc., June 29, 1988. Hayes and Hubbard, *Investment Banking,* 167, indicate that the firm dealt in dollar-denominated Japanese government securities.

167. On Japanese dollar loans in the 1920s, see William W. Lockwood, *The Economic Development of Japan* (Princeton, N.J.: Princeton University Press, 1954), 259.

168. Historical data from Nomura Securities International.

169. Japan had a negative balance on merchandise trade, 1920–1929. Lockwood, *Economic Development of Japan,* 157.

170. Gustav Cassel, *Foreign Investments* (Chicago: University of Chicago Press, 1928), 212, discusses bank deposits; the investments were more than bank deposits. Other data show the investments in American securities.

171. Rufus Tucker to Walter Tower, June 13, 1924, RG 151 620 UK 1919–1927, National Archives.

172. Chandler, *Benjamin Strong,* passim., discusses the rationale behind U.S. monetary policies from 1924 to 1928. Gold flows were, of course, considered; so was the encouragement of U.S. capital exports; but foreigners' purchases of U.S. securities (at least until June 1928) were not a consideration in domestic monetary policy. Chandler (p. 456) writes that "between June 1928 and October 1929," they became a concern.

173. Eichengreen, *Golden Fetters,* 12, argues for the first reason. Charles P. Kindleberger, *Manias, Panics, and Crashes* (New York: Basic Books, 1978), 137, believes that for-

eign lending came to a halt when the U.S. stock market started to rise. See also Fleisig, *Long Term Capital Flows,* 8.

174. Eichengreen, *Golden Fetters,* 13–14.

175. Roberts, *Schroders,* 238.

176. The New York affiliate of the British Schroders, for example, greatly increased its provision of call loans to brokers who were prepared to pay extremely high rates. Ibid.

5. The Foreign Multinationals, 1924–1929

1. Southard, *American Industry in Europe,* 199–200. On preemptive investments, see Edward M. Graham, "Oligopolistic Imitation and European Direct Investment in the United States," D.B.A. diss., Harvard Business School, 1975. Thus, Agfa responded to Eastman Kodak's entry into Germany; American Tobacco responded to British American Tobacco's U.S. entry.

2. Since there were *no* reporting requirements on foreign investments, the Department of Commerce could easily miss new investments. The table's data, like the earlier part of this Commerce Department tabulation (shown in Table 3.1), should be used with the greatest caution. It is included, as was Table 3.1, as providing a bare minimum of the new activity. The Department of Commerce provided no 1920s inward foreign direct investment figures by nationality or industry.

3. During the brief interlude that it was foreign owned and controlled Edison General Electric had 6,000 employees. Wilkins, *History,* 435. J. & P. Coats' prewar multiplant business in the United States had about 6,000 employees. Ibid. 363.

4. See Clive Trebilcock, *Phoenix Assurance and the Development of British Insurance—Vol. II* (Cambridge: Cambridge University Press, 1998), 464–466, for the experience of London Guarantee & Accident with its Chicago building.

5. Soule, *Prosperity Decade,* 155, 172, on soaring real estate prices at decade's end.

6. Louis Dreyfus & Co. was run by members of the Louis-Dreyfus family, which used the hyphenated name. In this period, it was variously referred to as the Dreyfus or the Louis Dreyfus firm. The partners in the 1920s were Louis Louis-Dreyfus and Charles Louis-Dreyfus. See Federal Trade Commission, *Methods and Operations of Grain Exporters* 2 vols. (Washington, 1922–1923), I, 43 (for Louis Dreyfus & Co. as of 1921); this is henceforth cited as FTC, *Methods.* See also "Assets in the US of America of Messrs. Louis Dreyfus & Co.," Memo from F. A. Strass, Louis Dreyfus & Co., London, n.d., ca. Aug. 19, 1940, FO 371/24263, Public Record Office, on Louis Louis-Dreyfus and his family. On the foreign-owned grain traders' move into the interior in the late 1920s, see Wayne G. Broehl, Jr., *Cargill: Trading the World's Grain* (Hanover, N.H.: University Press of New England, 1992), 281, 334–335, 429–430, 588–589, and Dan Morgan, *Merchants of Grain,* 110, 123 (Fribourg quote).

7. The histories of the most prominent foreign-owned family grain traders are difficult to document. Wayne Broehl's study of the American firm Cargill has some data on its competitors. Morgan, *Merchants of Grain,* is helpful. Schvarzer, *Bunge & Born,* is good on Bunge & Co. in Antwerp and Bunge & Born in Argentina and the other parts of South America, but it has virtually nothing on Bunge in the United States. FTC, *Methods,* I, is excellent on foreign grain traders in 1921, but none of the subsequent Federal Trade Commission reports on the grain trade gives information on the changes in the activities of the foreign grain traders during the 1920s.

8. Samuel Sanday & Co.'s American branch operated as Sanday & Co. and was by far the largest wheat exporter from the United States in 1921, with 15 percent of the total. That year, Louis Dreyfus was in second place with 10.7 percent, followed by P. N. Gray & Co. (the affiliate of the Bunge group) with 5.5 percent. FTC, *Methods,* I, 42.

9. Sanday was important in 1921, Ross T. Smyth less important. In 1921, Paul, Robson, & Co., New York, was the foreign partnership operating in the United States as a flour-buying agency for Ross T. Smyth & Co., Liverpool. The partners in Paul, Robson & Co. were all British: Edward Paul (from Liverpool) and Hugh R. Rathbone and Herbert T. Robson (both from London). On Ross T. Smyth & Co.'s role in 1921, see FTC, *Methods,* I, 54. In the early 1930s, when Cargill began to develop "listening posts" in Europe, the Smyth firm acted as "informal British representative for Cargill." Cargill had a very friendly relationship with that firm over several decades. Broehl, *Cargill,* 587, 772, 794. Morgan, *Merchants of Grain,* 114n, states that among the reasons that British traders were "losing out" in the 1920s in the international grain trade might be British tax laws and currency controls that made it difficult for these firms to survive in the competitive fluid grain market.

10. Hunt, *Heirs of Great Adventure,* II, 164. In 1921, Balfour, Guthrie & Co. exported some 1.7 percent of U.S. wheat exports. FTC, *Methods,* I, 42.

11. Hunt, *Heirs of Great Adventure,* II, 189. California Packing Corp., which used the Del Monte brand name, was a 1916 merger of local canning companies. It built up a sizable domestic marketing organization and also was a large exporter (through Balfour, Guthrie). On its domestic activities, see Alfred Chandler, *Visible Hand* (Cambridge, Mass.: Harvard University Press, 1977), 349. On its exports, see Thomas Horst, *At Home Abroad* (Cambridge, Mass.: Ballinger, 1974), 42.

12. N. Kawabe, "Development of Overseas Operations by General Trading Companies, 1868–1945," in *Business History of General Trading Companies,* ed. Shin'ichi Yonekawa and Hideki Yoshihara (Tokyo: University of Tokyo Press, 1987), 82. The wheat exports of Mitsui & Co. (some .6 percent of the U.S. total) and of Mitsubishi (some .3 percent) for 1921 are given in FTC, *Methods,* I, 42.

13. W. A. Meneight, *A History of United Molasses Co., Ltd.* (Liverpool: privately printed, 1977), 3, 28, 39, 42–45.

14. The story of Fine Cotton Spinners' and Doublers' Mississippi cotton plantations in the 1920s is provided in Nelson, *King Cotton's Advocate,* 30–42 (Oscar Johnston became the new CEO); see also *Fortune,* Mar. 1937, 131–132.

15. Jackson, *Enterprising Scot,* 284, 293. The Alliance Trust Co., Dundee, held a large interest in the Deltic Investment Co.

16. In the decree that resulted from the Supreme Court decision in the 1911 American Tobacco case, Imperial Tobacco and British American Tobacco were permanently enjoined from using a common leaf-buying agent in the United States. Thus, although Imperial Tobacco was in the late 1920s the largest single shareholder in BAT, the buying organizations of the two companies in the United States remained separate. In a 1920 report, the U.S. Federal Trade Commission had charged that the two British firms had been cooperating in violation of the decree; yet the U.S. Department of Justice took no action, believing that the practices complained of had been corrected. Cox, *Competition in the American Tobacco Industry,* 161–165.

17. Maurice Corina, *Trust in Tobacco* (London: Michael Joseph, 1975), 142–143, 157.

18. Jackson, *Enterprising Scot,* 136–137.

19. Mothershead, *Swan Land and Cattle Company,* 151, 153.

20. Brompton Pulp and Paper Company, for example, in 1924, acquired 140,000 acres of freehold timberland in Maine. Marshall, Southard, and Taylor, *Canadian-American Industry.* 178. The Deltic Investment Company (whose main investments were in cotton-growing lands) had timberlands.

21. Donald Mackay, *Empire of Wood: The MacMillan Bloedel Story* (Vancouver: Douglas & McIntyre, 1982), 24, 105–107. Seaboard Lumber Sales was the second key British Columbia firm with a New York office. Ibid., 107.

22. Kawabe, "Overseas Operations," 82.

23. Hunt, *Heirs of Great Adventure,* II, 52, 189.

24. The Canadian Pacific holdings were in Cambridge Collieries in Ohio; according to one source, the Steel Company of Canada's interests to the south of the border in iron ore properties had been acquired in 1917, 1924, and 1926; its U.S. coal interests were obtained in 1918. See Marshall, Southard, and Taylor, *Canadian-American Industry,* 185. Kilbourn, *Elements Combined,* 103, says the steel company acquired the ore mines in the Mesabi range in 1918–1919; he includes nothing on subsequent acquisitions.

25. On the ownership and control, see Marshall, Southard, and Taylor, *Canadian-American Industry,* 57. Its U.S. mines were acquired before the First World War. Duncan McDowall, *Steel at the Sault* (Toronto: University of Toronto Press, 1984), provides details on Algoma Steel. On the acquisition of the U.S. coal mines (Cannelton Coal Co. of West Virginia and Lake Superior Coal Co.) and of the limestone quarries, see ibid., 52, 61. On U.S. control of Algoma 1918–1927, and then the British control, see ibid., 66, 130, and passim.

26. Marshall, Southard, and Taylor, *Canadian-American Industry,* 185. Sterling Coal Co., Ltd., for example, owned coal mines in Ohio and West Virginia.

27. Tweedale, *Sheffield Steel and America,* 96–97, 168, 227n.47. The U.S. firm was Wolf-Tongue Mining Co., located in Colorado. William P. Rawles, *The Nationality of Commercial Control of World Minerals* (New York: American Institute of Mining and Metallurgical Engineers, 1933), 40, notes that the United States (in 1930) produced 3.7 percent of world tungsten; he indicated that the control of U.S. tungsten output was domestic. China and Burma were the main producers of tungsten.

28. Foreign interests in gold mining were not substantial. Consolidated Gold Field's U.S. subsidiary was Gold Fields American Development Co. Ltd. (which was managed by "New Consolidated Gold Fields, Ltd., London," another subsidiary of Consolidated Goldfields). Johnson, *Consolidated Gold Fields,* discusses the creation of New Consolidated Gold Fields in the aftermath of the First World War but then gives no indication at all of its activities. Gold Fields American Development Co., Ltd., maintained a New York office. *Moody's Industrials 1929,* 864–865. The office was apparently mainly involved in problems related to potash rather than gold mining activities. Film Z-G1, Reel 33, Bancroft Library, University of California, Berkeley, has data on directors and stockholders of Gold Fields American Development Co. but nothing on its U.S. operations in the 1920s. On Camp Bird Ltd., see Wilkins, *History,* 242–243, 757. For its activities in the 1920s, see *Moody's Industrials 1929,* 863–864, and data on Film Z-G1, Reels 80F-82F, Bancroft Library, University of California, Berkeley. Reel 82F has the Camp Bird Ltd. *Annual Report 1929* (Dec. 9, 1929) that discloses the arrangements between Camp Bird Ltd. and New Consolidated Gold Fields Ltd.: certain directors of New Consolidated joined the board of Camp Bird Ltd., which company would participate in certain business undertaken by New Consolidated. Anne T. Ostrye, *Foreign Investment in the American and Canadian West 1870–1914* (Metuchen, N.J.: Scarecrow Press, 1986), 129–159, has a list of British companies, some of which were in gold or silver mining that persisted through the 1920s.

29. Rawles, *Nationality,* 32. In 1929, the United States produced 23.4 percent of the world's silver output.

30. The British-owned Mountain Copper Co. Ltd., formed in 1896, had been at the turn of the century one of the ten largest copper mines, producing 2.19 percent of world output at its mine in California. Navin, *Copper Mining and Management,* 396. It had a smelter in Martinez, California, completed in 1905. The firm stopped production in 1914, resumed it in 1916, closed down again in 1920, and reopened in 1923. It produced copper, pyrites, sulfurous ore, and other minerals; it also got involved in fertilizer production. As its better-grade ores were depleted, it began to manufacture sulfuric acid extracted

from its high-sulfur pyrites. Dahl, "British Investment in California Mining," 250, 257–260, 266, and Lewis, *America's Stake,* 92.

31. U.S. Federal Trade Commission, *Report on the Copper Industry* (Washington, D.C., 1947), 207.

32. Chandler, *Scale and Scope,* 563.

33. See Chapter 3, note 159, on British Metal Corporation, Ltd. In 1924, C. Tennant Sons, New York, started to manufacture wire strapping at a small plant in Warren, Ohio. Based on undated brochure of C. Tennant, Sons, New York, in Dunning data.

34. In 1923, Hans Bernstorff (a onetime employee of Metallgesellschaft), head of the Ore & Chemical Department of American Metal Company, organized the separate Ore & Chemical Corporation (OCC), a trading company. Three years later, Bernstorff asked the Germans for financial help, and Metallgesellschaft bought stock in OCC through a Dutch intermediary, Montaan Metaal NV. ("Ore & Chemical Corp., Statement of Alfred Merton and [his son] Wilhelm Merton," Mar. 12, 1942, and other data in file D-28-623, Acc. 67A10, Box 1310, RG 131, U.S. Department of Justice, Washington, D.C.) OCC began as and always was a trading company. However, according to Lamer, *World Fertilizer Economy,* 191, by 1929 it had also become an important producer of phosphates in Florida. Under a 1929 contract, Metallgesellschaft—possibly through OCC—established (jointly with Coronet Phosphate Co.) a phosphorous blast furnace in Pembroke, Florida, near the phosphate mines of Coronet Phosphate Co. Based on June 1, 1938 report in file F-28-2624, Acc. 67A10, Box 850, RG 131, U.S. Department of Justice, Washington, D.C., and Haynes, *American Chemical Industry,* V, 124. Coronet Phosphate Co. was a large Florida phosphate producer, having acquired in 1913 major holdings once owned by French investors. Wilkins, *History,* 176. Markham, *Fertilizer Industry,* 41, reports that in 1927 Metallgesellschaft made a contract with Coronet to handle the latter's *European* sales. On Davison and Southern Phosphate, see Haynes, *American Chemical Industry,* IV, 98–99. Not only did Metallgesellschaft resume associations with the postwar British Metal Corporation, but the largest stockholders in Rio Tinto had participated in BMC's founding; in 1929 Rio Tinto itself acquired an interest in BMC. Spurr, *Political and Commercial Geology,* 286 (founders); Charles Harvey, *The Rio Tinto Company, 1873–1954* (Penzance, Cornwall: Alison Hodge, 1981), 214; and Cocks and Walters, *History of the Zinc Smelting Industry,* 46–47.

35. Rawles, *Nationality,* 30.

36. The ownership of PIC is not clear, but it was certainly German controlled. On potash, 1923–1924: Haynes, *American Chemical Industry,* IV, 323; Joseph Brandes, *Herbert Hoover and Economic Diplomacy* (Pittsburgh: University of Pittsburgh Press, 1962), 40, 138. According to Stocking, *Potash Industry,* 282, the August 1924 agreement divided the U.S. market between the German and French industries, 67.5 percent to the former and 32.5 percent to the latter; the August 1924 accord was then followed by a broader one, in May 1925, divvying up the world.

37. Given U.S. objections, on December 2, 1925, Lee, Higginson, the lead banker in the loan negotiations, decided to turn to European sources for funding. The potash syndicate raised the money in London. On views within the U.S. government on this foreign lending proposal, see *Foreign Relations of the United States, 1926,* II, 205–213; Iversen, *International Capital Movements,* 125; Herbert Feis, *The Diplomacy of the Dollar 1919–1932* (New York: W. W. Norton, 1950), 32; Fishlow, "Debt," 422; and Harm Schröter, "The International Potash Syndicate," in *International Cartels Revisited,* ed. Dominique Barjot (Caen, France: Editions Diffusion du Lyes, 1994), 89 (for a wonderful quotation from Commerce Secretary Herbert Hoover, Nov. 28, 1925).

38. Brandes, *Herbert Hoover,* 140, and Haynes, *American Chemical Industry,* IV, 323.

39. Harm Schröter, *Die Internationale Kaliwirtschaft 1918 bis 1939* (Kassel, Germany:

Kali und Salz, 1985), 40. Haynes, *American Chemical Industry,* IV, 323, suggests that NV Potash Export was formed before the indictment, which seems to be incorrect.

40. Office of the Economic Adviser, Department of State, "Memorandum," Mar. 14, 1929, RG 59, 862.6373/115, National Archives (I am indebted to Harm Schröter for a copy of this memorandum). See also Schröter, "International Potash Syndicate," 89.

41. Brewster, *Antitrust and American Business Abroad,* 45; *U.S. v. Deutsches Kalisyndikat Gesellschaft et al.,* 31 F. 2d 199 (SDNY 1929); Haynes, *American Chemical Industry,* IV, 323.

42. Brewster, *Antitrust and American Business Abroad,* 230ff (on characteristics of consent decrees); Brandes, *Herbert Hoover,* 144 (Concannon).

43. "Memorandum," Mar. 14, 1929.

44. Haynes, *American Chemical Industry,* IV, 323–324, and Office of Alien Property Custodian, *Annual Report for Year-ending June 30, 1944,* 65–66. I find it implausible that the top U.S. management could be so innocent. In fact, I uncovered clear contemporary circumstantial evidence of the German connection. Throughout the 1930s, the Consolidated Gold Fields of South Africa, London, through its various subsidiaries (together with the parent known as the Congold group), continued its long-standing association with American Potash & Chemical. Count Louis Antoin Gaston Dru, a naturalized British subject of French birth, had been a director of American Trona, living in New York City, when in 1923 he also became a director of Gold Fields American Development Co., part of the Congold group. That year Count Dru became chairman of Gold Fields' advisory committee in America. When, in 1926, American Potash & Chemical replaced American Trona, Count Dru stayed on as a director and became the new president of American Potash & Chemical. In 1931 and 1932, he was elevated to the position of chairman of American Potash & Chemical and listed his address as *Berlin.* In 1933, still chairman of American Potash & Chemical, he was back in London and still on the board of Gold Fields. The Congold group had to know about the German connections. All this is from material on Gold Fields American Development, Film Z-G1, Reel 33, Bancroft Library, University of California, Berkeley. Dru died in 1945.

45. Haynes, *American Chemical Industry,* IV, 144–145; *Chemical Age,* London, Feb. 23, 1929, 185. Borax Consolidated in the late 1920s retained the U.S. law firm Cravath, Henderson & de Gersdorff to help it with a proposed consolidation of all borax producers that would have resulted in practically a worldwide monopoly. The law firm advised its client, however, that the proposal would so clearly violate U.S. antitrust laws that it was not worth pursuing; Borax Consolidated followed the attorney's advice, and there was no merger. Swaine, *Cravath Firm,* II, 435.

46. *Moody's Industrials 1929,* 868.

47. For a number of years, Lord Cowdray (through Whitehall Petroleum Corp., which was formed in June 1919) had controlled 60 percent of the shares in Amerada. In January 1926, before Lord Cowdray's death, Dillon, Read & Co. had purchased 40 percent of Amerada, and there was a U.S. public offering. See 1928 data in Box C31/1, S. Pearson & Son Papers, Library, Science Museum, London. On Whitehall Petroleum Corp., see Box C52/4,6, Pearson Papers. See also Lewis, *America's Stake,* 142. In the late 1920s, the British holdings appear to have become purely financial (portfolio) ones. The minority interest was maintained by the Pearson family until the Second World War. Jones, *State,* 218.

48. The Canadian ones, said to number seven or eight, included British American Oil Co., Ltd. (which had oil wells in Texas and Oklahoma), and Atlantic Keystone Petroleum Co., Ltd. (with drilling subsidiaries in Wyoming and Texas). Four other Canadian ones—Ajax, Acme, Bethel, and Alberta Pacific—had wells in Oklahoma, Texas, and Montana. Marshall, Southard, and Taylor, *Canadian-American Industry,* 185–186. Interestingly, Marshall, Southard, and Taylor do not mention the Vancouver Midway Oil Co.

(see Chapter 2). Ostrye, *Foreign Investment*, 130–151, lists nine pre–World War I British incorporated oil companies in California, Wyoming, Oklahoma, and Texas that lingered on into and through the late 1920s; her list does not include Amerada, which was not in existence before 1914. Franco Wyoming Oil Co., formed in 1909, continued to have French investors involved.

49. I am indebted to Geoffrey Bowker for his help on Schlumberger history and for data from the Schlumberger Archives, Paris. On the 1921 engagements in the United States, see "Travaux Effectues par la Société de Prospection Electrique pour Diverses Compagnies [1920–1927]," in Schlumberger Archives. Geoffrey C. Bowker, *Science on the Run* (Cambridge, Mass.: MIT Press, 1994), 9, for background.

50. "Travaux Effectues," op. cit., and Louis A. Allaud and Maurice H. Martin, *Schlumberger* (New York: John Wiley, 1977), 67.

51. Allaud and Martin, *Schlumberger*, 70–72.

52. On its New York headquarters, ibid., 73. Address given in data from Schlumberger Archives; location of Shell Union Oil is from 1927 letterhead in Shell Archives, London. In the 1920s, Standard Oil of New Jersey's head office was at 26 Broadway. Henrietta M. Larson, Evelyn H. Knowlton, and Charles S. Popple, *New Horizons 1927–1950* (New York: Harper & Row, 1971), 23.

53. Allaud and Martin, *Schlumberger*, 77, 150.

54. Marshall, Southard, and Taylor, *Canadian-American Industry*, 177–179.

55. See Chapter 3 and *Stock Exchange Year Book 1929*, London, 2904.

56. *Moody's Industrials 1928*.

57. Marshall, Southard, and Taylor, *Canadian-American Industry*, 179. In 1928, in Canada, Canadian entrepreneur Samuel J. Moore formed the Moore Corporation to acquire three companies in which he already was interested. The first was the American Sales Book Company, which had plants in Niagara Falls and Elmira, New York. The second was Gilman-Fanfold Corp., Ltd. with plants in Niagara Falls and Brooklyn, New York. The third was Pacific-Manifolding Book Co., Ltd., with factories in Emeryville and Los Angeles, California, and Seattle, Washington. Together the three subsidiaries (in 1927 before the formation of the Moore Corporation) had assets of $11.5 million principally in the United States. Moore's U.S. business was larger than his Canadian operations. *Moody's Industrials 1929*, 2222–2224. In 1927 Moore had become president of the Bank of Nova Scotia. Schull and Gibson, *Scotiabank Story*, 112–114, 138. In addition, outside the Moore Corporation, Moore himself had other investments in the United States in souvenir silver and paper boxes. Marshall, Southard, and Taylor, *Canadian-American Industry*, 179–180.

58. Cheever, *House of Morrell*, esp. 206 (on the U.S. company's becoming the parent). On migrating multinationals, see Jones, *British Multinationals*, 7.

59. Dunning data.

60. Wilkins, *History*, 343 (on Reckitt's early U.S. business); Basil N. Reckitt, *The History of Reckitt and Sons, Ltd.* (London: A. Brown & Sons, 1952), 52, 77–78, 101, 103; and Derek F. Channon, *The Strategy and Structure of British Enterprise* (Boston: Harvard Business School Press, 1973), 191.

61. Both British companies, packagers and distributors in the United States, were longtime direct investors in this country.

62. *Fortune*, Aug. 1931, 46, 120.

63. Managing Directors Conference 151, June 14, 1928, Unilever Archives (UA), London, on its heavy advertising budget. Its U.S. competitors had, however, even larger budgets for advertising. *Fortune*, Dec. 1931, 94.

64. Data from Historical File, Unilever PLC, London; from "Chronicle of Lever Brothers in the U.S., 1895–1948," prepared by Lever Brothers, Boston, Feb. 1948, in UA; from

Wilson, *History of Unilever,* I, 309–310; from Managing Directors Conference 48 and 49, Feb. 21 and Mar. 7, 1929, UA (on the purchase of the site at Hammond, Indiana, and the plans to start production in 1930), and from booklet (ca. 1952) on research and development, UA. Its rank in 1930 (which seems to have been the same as in 1929) is given in *Fortune,* Dec. 1931, 94. Procter & Gamble also expanded greatly in the 1920s, adding in 1926 Camay soap to its mainstay, Ivory. In 1929, P & G began negotiations with the German Henkel company, with "the objective of obtaining their new U.S. patents, the first of which was granted this year, in order to help fill out" its product line. Procter & Gamble, *Into a Second Century with Procter & Gamble* (Cincinnati: privately printed, 1944), 46–47. Colgate & Co. merged with Palmolive-Peet Co. in 1928 to become Colgate-Palmolive-Peet Co. On its outward international business, see Wilkins, *Maturing,* 83; the merger date is from a Colgate-Palmolive-Peet Company prospectus.

65. "Chronicle of Lever Brothers in the United States, 1895–1948," Feb. 1948, UA.

66. Wilson, *History of Unilever,* II, 306–307, on Unilever and the dual ownership structure, and ibid., 353, for the importance of the U.S. subsidiary in Unilever business. The merger resulted in two separate parent companies with identical boards of directors (Ltd., based in London, and NV, in Rotterdam). All operating companies sent dividends to one or the other. Lever in the United States remitted dividends to Britain until 1937, when the U.S. firm "technically" became Dutch owned.

67. Dunning data.

68. Marshall, Southard, and Taylor, *Canadian-American Industry,* 184, and *Moody's Industrials 1929,* 1745.

69. *Fortune,* Aug. 1933, 35. Like its British counterparts, it appears to have done packaging in the United States.

70. *Fortune,* Aug. 1931, 46, 120. See Hal Morgan, *Symbols of America* (New York: Penguin Books, 1986), 120, for Canada Dry's 1921 advertising.

71. Margarine Unie, before its merger into Unilever, had small margarine interests in the United States, although Anton Jurgens' joint venture in Buffalo had ended in 1923. Dutch cocoa companies seem to have had representatives in New York and may have done some packaging.

72. Heer, *World Events 1866–1966,* 140. The problems were based on the overexpansion in the aftermath of the First World War (see Chapter 2 herein).

73. *Forward with Fulton,* May 30–June 3, 1962, 5.

74. Heer, *World Events 1866–1966,* 144, 218. In effect, Nestlé & Anglo Swiss, which had had an indirect interest in Lamont, Corliss, now obtained a direct one. Not until 1949–1951 did the U.S. chocolate business "revert entirely to Nestlé." Ibid., 105 (1951), 218 (1949).

75. On the entry of Wander into U.S. production in 1917, see Chapter 1 herein. The Wander company became an important Swiss multinational enterprise. It not only was active in promoting its product in the United States but also had begun manufacturing outside London (England) in 1919; Ovaltine became established as "the leading proprietary milk food drink in interwar Britain." Geoffrey Jones, "Multinational Cross-Investment between Switzerland and Britain 1914–1945." in *La Suisse et les Grandes Puissances 1914–1945,* ed. Sébastien Guex (Geneva: Droz, 1999), 436.

76. Lindgren, *Corporate Growth,* 305, 357.

77. Cox, *Global Cigarette,* 249, 85. BAT's first factory at Petersburg came in 1903 when BAT acquired David Dunlop Inc.; further production facilities were added in 1904 in Petersburg and Richmond when BAT acquired the business of the Cameron group of companies. Then BAT built a new factory in Richmond, which came into operations in 1916. By the mid-1920s, BAT had other investments as well (e.g., a paper mill in Lee, Massachusetts).

78. Cox, *Global Cigarette,* 272–273. Its Chinese sales were far greater than Indian and Malayan ones combined; on the growth in Latin America, see ibid., 250–259.

79. For the problems in China, see Cochran, *Big Business in China,* chap. 7. For the purchase of Brown & Williamson, see Cox, *Global Cigarette,* 262–263. In June 1927, a meeting was held between BAT and Imperial Tobacco. BAT agreed not to import cigarettes into the United Kingdom or sell in that market, retaining that aspect of the 1902 agreement. For the important arrangements made at this meeting, see ibid., 262n. The 1902 agreement had barred BAT from the U.S. market as well, leaving that to American Tobacco. BAT considered that part of the agreement null and void, hence the purchase of Brown & Williamson. On American Tobacco's response and the effect on competition in the United Kingdom, see ibid., 263, 267. Since American Tobacco's invasion of the British market affected Imperial Tobacco (and not BAT), the outcome "seems to have been to fracture relations between BAT Co. and Imperial," so that by the 1930s the chairmen of BAT and Imperial Tobacco "were scarcely on speaking terms with one another" (ibid., 267)—and this while Imperial Tobacco continued to be the largest single stockholder in BAT.

80. On the new factory, the brand, and the market share, see Cox, *Global Cigarette,* 263, 297. See also Dunning data on the Louisville plant. In March 1929, the BAT Co. established in Delaware the Pocahontas Corporation, a holding company for almost all its various U.S.-based businesses. This provided BAT the opportunity to offset the initial substantial losses incurred by Brown & Williamson with the profits of its various other operations. Cox, *Global Cigarette,* 264.

81. Dunning data. Both J. & P. Coats and American Thread Company were multiplant companies. In 1929, all of the Coats-Clark group of plants were still in the North. For Coats' activities in the United States in the 1920s, see David Keir, "The Coats Story," typescript 1964 (access granted by Coats), vol. III, 146–151, which shows that the Coats group was in the 1920s considering a new southern plant. At the start of 1928, American Thread operated five plants in the North: in Willimantic and Stonington, Connecticut; Fall River and Holyoke, Massachusetts; and Milo, Maine, as well as its new mill in Dalton, Georgia. In March 1928, it sold its so-called Hadley plant in Holyoke, Massachusetts. *Moody's Industrials 1929,* 1104.

82. Dunning data.

83. *National Association of Wool Manufacturers Bulletin,* 57 (Oct. 1927): 496.

84. *New York Times,* July 22, 1941.

85. Marshall, Southard, and Taylor, *Canadian-American Industry,* 184.

86. The U.S. Department of Commerce, Bureau of Foreign and Domestic Commerce, *Foreign Investments in the United States* (Washington, D.C., 1937), 32, identified for 1934 French investments of $6.7 million in textiles (most of which were in wool, albeit there were some in silk) and Swiss investments of $3.4 million in textiles (most of which would be in silk and embroidery); the French and Swiss investments were larger in 1929 than in 1934.

87. John, *Liverpool Merchant House,* 122, 124. Booth also had other investments in the United States, aside from the tanneries.

88. See General Meeting, Forestal Land, Timber & Railway Co., *Times* (London), May 28, 1927 (on the sale of New York—Brooklyn—properties). On the late 1920s corporate restructuring and the Wilmington plant, see Hicks, *Story of the Forestal,* 21–22. The continuation of Forestal "control" is evident from testimony and documents provided in the U.S. Senate, Committee on Military Affairs, Subcommittee on War Mobilization, *Scientific and Technical Mobilization, Hearings,* 78th Cong., 1st sess., 1943, pt. 9, esp. 1047–49, 1051, 1053, 1054 (letter from Ely, President of Tannin Corp., Dec. 23, 1941), 1087 (Tannin Corp. to Emile B. d'Erlanger, Dec. 16, 1938). These hearings on scientific and technical mobiliza-

tion are henceforth cited as *Kilgore Committee Hearings.* On the "New York Tannin Corporation," see General Meeting, Forestal Land, Timber & Railway Co., *Times* (London), June 12, 1925, and ibid., June 24, 1926.

89. Marshall, Southard, and Taylor, *Canadian-American Industry,* 184.

90. At least this is my conclusion. In 1941, in connection with the British obtaining lend lease, British investors "pledged" 300,000 shares of common stock of Congoleum-Nairn (see Chapter 8). Although I do not know for certain that all or a sizable part of this stock was owned by the Scottish Nairn company or the family, it seems highly likely.

91. For the early history of Nairn in the United States, see Wilkins, *History,* 354. For later data, *Moody's 1925,* 538; Augustus Muir, *Nairns of Kirkcaldy* (Cambridge: W. Heffer & Sons, 1956), esp. 112–113; and Great Britain, Monopolies and Restrictive Practices Commission, *Report on the Supply of Linoleum* (1956), 5–6. The company history says nothing about the 1924 financial arrangements; the *Report on the Supply of Linoleum,* which is not entirely accurate in other details, says that between *1929* and 1953, Nairn obtained a small share in Congoleum-Nairn, which in turn in 1956 had an interest in the Scottish Nairn. Ibid., 6. My "hunch" is that in the 1924 merger, the Scottish Nairn would have obtained an interest in Congoleum-Nairn and that between 1929 and 1953 that minority interest fluctuated. The *Report on the Supply of Linoleum* indicates that when Congoleum-Nairn Inc. was founded, the Scottish Nairn acquired *British Congoleum, Ltd.* This suggests a division of markets, with Congoleum-Nairn Inc. handling the American business and Nairn, the British trade. Could there have been an exchange of equity in 1924?

92. Muir, *Nairns of Kirkcaldy,* 113. Congoleum Inc. before the merger had assets of $18.4 million (December 31, 1923); after the merger, Congoleum-Nairn, Inc., had assets of $33.6 million (December 31, 1924). Based on *Moody's 1924* and *Moody's 1925.* In 1930 Barry and Staines Linoleum Ltd. became a holding company in the United Kingdom, controlling five subsidiaries, one of which was Barry and Staines Inc., New York. The latter appears to have been a marketing company. Great Britain, Board of Trade, *Survey of International and Internal Cartels* 2 vols. (London, 1944, 1946), I, 169. In contrast with Congoleum-Nairn, Barry and Staines was insignificant in the U.S. market.

93. The first southern rayon plant was that of The Viscose Company in Virginia in 1916. Subsequently, Du Pont's joint venture built a plant some forty miles from Nashville, Tennessee.

94. Hounshell and Smith, *Science and Corporate Strategy,* 162.

95. Ibid., 608. Lammot du Pont to Edmond Gillet, May 21, 1929, Acc. 1662, Box 8, Du Pont Papers, Hagley Museum and Library, Wilmington, Delaware. On the French company's minority shareholdings in Du Pont, see Joseph Frazier Wall, *Alfred I. Du Pont* (New York: Oxford University Press, 1990), 584. Du Pont's assets in 1930 were $617.6 million. Chandler, *Scale and Scope,* 646.

96. See Table 5.2. For more on Du Pont Rayon Company, see Haynes, *American Chemical Industry,* IV, 547; Markham, *Competition in the Rayon Industry,* 15–16; and Schultz, *Technical Division,* 49, 56.

97. On the arrangements, Cayez, *Rhône-Poulenc,* 105–107; Avram, *Rayon Industry,* 562; Haynes, *American Chemical Industry,* IV, 383; and Schultz, *Technical Division,* 56. The Société pour la Soie "Rhodiaceta," Paris, was formed in 1922 by Comptoir des Textiles Artificiels (CTA) and Société Chimique des Usines du Rhône (SCUR). Avram, *Rayon Industry,* 90, 562, and Coleman, *Courtaulds,* II, 184.

98. See Table 5.2; Markham, *Competition,* 8; Avram, *Rayon Industry,* 53, 138, 147 (Avram notes that the firm was very profitable).

99. Avram, *Rayon Industry,* 146. The company ended its royalty agreement with the Belgian-headquartered firm and instead purchased the rights to the Belgian patents and processes. By 1928, there were no Belgian officers or directors of the U.S. company. Ibid.,

138–149. Yet included among the directors was "E. R. Wood, President of Dominion Securities Corporation, Ltd., Toronto, Canada." Wood had long been associated in various ventures with the Belgian entrepreneur Alfred Loewenstein, and by 1920 Loewenstein had acquired control of the Tubize firm in Belgium. On Wood, see Armstrong and Nelles, *Southern Exposure,* 7, 10, 88, 94, 164, 171, 269; on Loewenstein and the Belgian Tubize company, see Norris, *Man Who Fell from the Sky,* 84. The presence of Wood on the board may indicate Canadian portfolio investments in this company, but Loewenstein often invested in the United States through Canadian intermediaries (Loewenstein died in 1928).

100. Haynes, *American Chemical Industry,* IV, 379. The Italian owners included not only Snia Viscosa but also Unione Italiana Fabrica Viscosa and Banca Agricola Italiana. Over time, the foreign holdings were purchased by Americans. Markham, *Competition,* 17. At decade's end, Industrial Rayon Corporation was building new viscose plants. Avram, *Rayon Industry,* 177. Snia Viscosa helped it become a successful firm. Ibid., 354. In 1927, Courtaulds acquired a controlling interest in Snia Viscosa. Geoffrey Jones, "Courtaulds in Continental Europe 1920–1945," in *British Multinationals: Origins, Management, and Performance,* ed. Geoffrey Jones (Aldershot: Gower, 1986), 120, 123.

101. Jones, "Courtaulds," 123, explains Courtaulds' interest in Snia Viscosa in 1927 as an attempt to curb the latter's *U.S.* expansion.

102. By the mid-1920s, the nitrocellulose process was considered inferior to the viscose one, and no new entries used it.

103. For a brief history of British Celanese, see Coleman, *Courtaulds,* II, 180–184; also read Norris, *Man Who Fell from the Sky,* 71–90.

104. Haynes, *American Chemical Industry,* III, 376 (1921 production).

105. Ibid., VI, 15, 76 (commercial production of rayon in 1925). In 1927, when Celanese Corporation of America was formed, it went to the public for financing, selling common and preferred shares. The financing was arranged through J. P. Morgan & Co. (along with Bankers Trust Co. and National City Bank, New York, and Robert Fleming & Co., London). Americans acquired an interest, yet it seems appropriate to call British Celanese the "parent." The British and American enterprises were run by two Swiss-born brothers, Henri and Camille Dreyfus. The former managed the British "parent," while the latter had charge of the U.S. business. Henri Dreyfus was a director of the Celanese Corporation of America until his death in 1944. Together, by 1927, Henri and Camille Dreyfus had "control" over the "parent," British Celanese. On this, see Coleman, *Courtaulds,* II, 184n.1, 271; Haynes, *American Chemical Industry,* III, 375n. Avram, *Rayon Industry,* 71, writes that British Celanese "controlled" the American enterprise. See also "Swiss Family Dreyfus," *Fortune,* Oct. 1933, 51–55, 139–144, and Norris, *Man Who Fell from the Sky,* 71–90, 181. When in the 1990s John Cantwell studied the patent behavior of European multinationals in the United States in the interwar years, he treated the Celanese Corporation of America as an "affiliate" of British Celanese. John Cantwell and Pilar Barrera, "The Localisation of Corporate Technological Trajectories in the Interwar Cartels," *Economics of Innovation and New Technology,* 6 (1998): 265.

106. Haynes, *American Chemical Industry,* IV, 547; on the Meadville plant, see Coleman, *Courtaulds,* II, 290, 308–310; Coleman says "effective commercial production" did not begin until 1930. Ibid., 310.

107. Avram, *Rayon Industry,* 53, 57.

108. Jones, "Courtaulds," 121–122, writes that in April 1925, Fritz Blüthgen, described as "chairman of VGF [Vereinigte Glanzstoff-Fabriken]," suggested that his company and Courtaulds establish a joint venture in America. Courtaulds was open to the idea of a joint venture *in Germany,* but not in the United States. VGF then decided to go it alone in the United States—in competition with Courtaulds.

109. According to Avram, *Rayon Industry,* 20, in Germany, the prohibitions on munitions manufacture after the First World War had provided a stimulus for the rayon industry; it was a way to keep factories employed.

110. The president of American Bamburg, Dr. Arthur Mothwurf, had been active in the Bayer operation at Rensselaer, New York, and had been interned during the First World War. On Mothwurf, see Berick Herrenbrück [1953?], Nordamerika und Kanada, pp. 113–114, Bayer Archives, Leverkusen (my thanks go to Elisabeth Glaser-Schmidt for this document).

111. *Associated Rayon Corporation Prospectus,* Nov. 27, 1928, Scudder Collection, Business School Library, Columbia University Libraries, New York; Johnson City, *Staff-News,* Oct. 29, 1926; Markham, *Competition,* 17–18. On Fritz Blüthgen's (of VGF) "selling of" American Bemberg and American Glanzstoff shares in Germany, see Schwarz, *Konrad Adenauer,* I, 211.

112. They also had serious labor problems. See *Journal of Commerce,* May 6, 1929, *Daily News Record,* May 17, 1929, and Thomas D. Clark and Albert D. Kirwan, *The South since Appomattox* (New York: Oxford University Press, 1967), 232–233, which gives employment at 5,000 and documents the conditions of labor.

113. Markham, *Competition,* 18. This was a $24 million venture, financed almost entirely in Europe. Avram, *Rayon Industry,* 134. It is not included in Table 5.2, since it had not begun production in 1928.

114. *Associated Rayon Corporation Prospectus,* Nov. 27, 1928. See also Schwarz, *Konrad Adenauer,* I, 211 (on the exchange of American Bemberg and American Glanzstoff shares for Associated Rayon shares and the raising of new moneys in the process).

115. On the formation of AKU, see John M. Stopford, *Directory of Multinationals* (New York: Stockton Press, 1992), I, 32, and Gall et al., *Deutsche Bank,* 316. The quotation is from Robert Liefmann, *Cartels, Concerns, and Trusts* (London: Methuen, 1932), 267; for a similar interpretation, see James, *German Slump,* 131, 137, which makes the general point that for tax reasons many German firms used foreign subsidiaries to purchase shares of the parent companies. AKU was at origin controlled by VGF, although a diagram of corporate structure would suggest that AKU "controlled" VGF.

116. Markham, *Competition,* 18. When AKU was organized, Courtaulds' management learned that the Germans would definitely control it. As it turned out, the Dutch Enka group had considerable influence. Coleman, *Courtaulds,* II, 376. For more on AKU, see James Stewart Martin, *All Honorable Men* (Boston: Little, Brown, 1950), 131–136, and RG 238, T301, Reel 3, Interrogation of Kurt Freiherr von Schroder, Nov. 21, 1945, NI-239, National Archives. The leading figure in AKU was Frederik H. Fentener van Vlissingen, a Dutch coal trader with close German associations. Fentener van Vlissingen served on the "Aufsichtsrat" of the most important German steel company, Vereinigte Stahlwerke, AG. See its *Annual Report, 1938/1939* in RG 238, T301, Reel 29, NI-4067, and Martin, *All Honorable Men,* 100. Harold James, in Gall et al., *Deutsche Bank,* 315–316, describes the formation of AKU as "bank inspired," combining "the dynamic but highly indebted" VGF with the technologically lagging Dutch enterprise. In the United States the two plants using German technology were in Elizabethport, Tennessee, while the one using Dutch technology was near Asheville, North Carolina. Thus, despite a common overall management in the United States, there seems, in fact, to have been a somewhat separate course. To make life more complicated, Courtaulds, in the course of its European expansion, had acquired shares in VGF (worth in 1928 £950,000). Accordingly, when AKU was formed, Courtaulds obtained an interest (its AKU shares were valued at £1,250,000 in 1930). For the relationships, see Jones, "Courtaulds," 129. Courtaulds viewed the Dutch Enka as a price cutter and tried to get VGF to control Enka.

117. It is not included in Table 5.2 because it was brand-new. On it, see Haynes, *American Chemical Industry,* IV, 381, 547, and Avram, *Rayon Industry,* 174–175. The Italian par-

ent committed itself to sending men to supervise operations for seven years. Ibid., 174–175, 563.

118. For example, the Delaware Rayon Corporation used a viscose yarn-making process owned by the French Allegre-Mondon Company, which provided the technical staff and saw the Delaware Rayon Corporation as "really a branch of the French company." Another example was Skenandoa Rayon Corporation, which got technical advice from French "Strasbourg interests." See Markham, *Competition,* 18–19; Haynes, *American Chemical Industry,* IV, 547, for their 100 percent U.S. ownership *in 1929* (100 percent in 1929 was not necessarily 100 percent at their origins in 1927 and 1928, respectively, and also this could be inaccurate). See also Avram, *Rayon Industry,* 57–61, on other small American companies.

119. Coleman, *Courtaulds,* II, 398.

120. Ibid., 296.

121. Markham, *Competition,* 32.

122. *Johnson City Chronicle,* Sept. 2, 1928. American Glanzstoff Corp. also expanded in 1929. See *Moody's Industrials 1937,* 2026.

123. The parent company Courtaulds was "a party" to price agreements with VGF and Snia Viscosa. Louis Domeratsky of the U.S. Department of Commerce reported there was an international "convention" on prices. Coleman, *Courtaulds,* II, 283, 392–393.

124. Coleman, *Courtaulds,* II, 291, 305.

125. Based on Table 5.2. Coleman, *Courtaulds,* II, 299 (says over 60 percent). Fifty-five or 60 or over 60 percent does not matter. The Viscose Company was clearly far out front.

126. Coleman, *Courtaulds,* II, 165 and 456: for 1915 (2,000) and the late 1930s (20,000). Avram, *Rayon Industry,* 607, gives the figure 15,000 *before* the large expansion of 1928–1929.

127. Coleman, *Courtaulds,* II, 305. This would rank it about number sixty-eight among U.S. companies in assets. See Chandler, *Scale and Scope,* 644–650, for comparisons (it is not included on Chandler's list).

128. Avram, *Rayon Industry,* 607.

129. On the industry as a whole, see Haynes, *American Chemical Industry,* IV, 547, and Avram, *Rayon Industry,* 353–354.

130. Jean-Pierre Daviet, *Un Destin International: La Compagnie de Saint-Gobain de 1830 à 1939* (Paris: Éditions des Archives Contemporaines, 1988), 414, 417–419.

131. The best book on I. G. Farben is Hayes, *Industry and Ideology;* the best work on ICI and its predecessors is Reader, *Imperial Chemical Industries..*

132. Stocking and Watkins, *Cartels in Action,* 473. On Winthrop Chemical's acquisition of H. A. Metz Laboratories, see Memorandum by August von Knieriem, May 9, 1939, BAL 9/A1 Amerika Geschaft. I received this document that came from the Bayer Archives in Leverkusen from Elisabeth Glaser-Schmidt. See also Mahoney, *Merchants of Life,* 213–214, which gives no date for the acquisition of Metz Laboratories, and Haynes, *American Chemical Industry,* V, 259, which gives 1935 as the date; I have trusted the information from the Bayer Archives; the acquisition seems to have been in 1926, *after* the formation of I. G. Farben. H. A. Metz Laboratories had been set up by Metz personally to preserve Hoechst interests in the United States during the war years.

133. Schröter, "Participation in Market Control," 173; see also Sasuly, *I. G. Farben,* 181.

134. The German Bayer, however, appears to have had an equity interest in Grasselli Dyestuff from the start, as well as a share in the profits; Steen, "Confiscated Commerce," 276, explains that the Alien Property Custodian had never insisted that Grasselli not sell stock to former German owners.

135. Haynes, *American Chemical Industry,* IV, 233; VI, 183.

136. I. G. Farben to Reich Ministry of Economics, July 24, 1939, RG 238, T301, Reel 70, NI-8496. An advertisement in the *National Association of Wool Manufacturers Bulletin,*

in 1925, described General Dyestuff Corporation as the "successor to Dyestuff Department of H. A. Metz & Co., Inc."

137. On the Metz and Ludwig businesses, see Haynes, *American Chemical Industry,* IV, 233. H. A. Metz Laboratories, Inc., does not seem to have been included, since it was apparently folded into Winthrop Chemical in 1926. Ludwig had been with National Aniline & Chemical Co. (NACC), as of 1920 a subsidiary of Allied Chemical & Dye Corporation; it is not clear whether he ever left NACC; by the 1930s he was the operating head of NACC. Mira Wilkins, "German Chemical Firms in the United States from the Late 19th Century to Post–World War II," in *The German Chemical Industry in the 20th Century,* ed. John Leisch (Dordrecht, Netherlands: Kluwer, 2000), 307n.74. On the Bayer and Badische sales agencies, see Haynes, *American Chemical Industry,* IV, 234.

138. Haynes, *American Chemical Industry,* IV, 234n. Metz, too, was reimbursed. See I. G. Farben to Reich Ministry of Economics, July 24, 1939. GDC was set up by Americans and "technically" was American. It is not clear how the stock was allocated in 1926.

139. Haynes, *American Chemical Industry,* IV, 235; see also Interrogation of Hermann Schmitz, Oct. 29, 1945, RG 238, T301, Reel 8, NI-711, p. 43. Both Metz and Kuttroff were American citizens. The only manufacturing brought into GDC was that of Metz's small Hoechst companies, which seem to have been linked with Metz's business and thus were acquired with the sales activities.

140. Translation of Draft Report from I. G. Farben to the German Ministry of Economics, Sept. 26, 1940, RG 238, T301, Reel 20, NI-2746. In this 1940 document, I. G. Farben explained to the German ministry the background on I. G. Farben's predecessors' foreign sales network.

141. GDC is usually discussed as an I. G. Farben company—for example, Fred Aftalion, *A History of the International Chemical Industry* (Philadelphia: University of Pennsylvania Press, 1991), 187.

142. Reader, *Imperial Chemical Industries,* II, 47.

143. Haynes, *American Chemical Industry,* IV, 317.

144. Reader, *Imperial Chemical Industries,* II, 47–48.

145. Hounshell and Smith, *Science and Corporate Strategy,* 186–187.

146. Haynes, *American Chemical Industry,* IV, 317.

147. Haber, *Chemical Industry,* 296. This was to be part of a never-to-be-consummated larger scheme wherein Allied Chemical, Brunner Mond, British Dyestuffs Corporation, Solvay & Cie., and I. G. Farben would be linked by an exchange of shares and technology. Ibid.

148. F. C. Protto and Fred G. Singer to W. F. Harrington, May 30, 1928, in U.S. Senate, Committee on Patents, *Patent Hearings,* 77th Cong., 2nd sess. (1942), pt. 5, 2258–2259. These hearings are henceforth cited as *Bone Committee Hearings.*

149. See data in Francis P. Garvan Papers, American Heritage Center, University of Wyoming, Laramie, Wyoming, Box 47.

150. Wilkins, *Maturing,* 81; Hayes, *Industry and Ideology,* 37; Larson, Knowlton, and Popple, *New Horizons,* 154–155; Wall and Gibb, *Teagle of Jersey Standard,* 299–302; and Frank A. Howard, *Buna Rubber* (New York: Van Nostrand, 1947), 16–27.

151. Stocking and Watkins, *Cartels in Action,* 389–390.

152. The initial agreement (March 19, 1928) between Agfa-Ansco and I. G. Farben defined their relationship; it showed I. G. Farben's subscription to stock in Agfa-Ansco and is published in full in *Kilgore Committee Hearings,* pt. 10 (Monopoly and Cartel Practices: The Hormone Cartel), 1180–1183 (even though this had nothing to do with hormones). I. G. Farben had controlling interest in Agfa-Ansco. See also Francis Garvan to Charles H. Herty, Aug. 28, 1929, Garvan Papers, Box 76; *Moody's 1928;* Lutz Alt, "The Photochemical Industry," Ph.D. diss., MIT, 1986, 52–53; Haynes, *American Chemical In-*

dustry, VI, 176; Schröter, "Participation in Market Control," 174–175, 178–179; Southard, *American Industry in Europe,* 104 (Kodak in Germany); *Journal of Commerce,* Sept. 16, 1928 (employment). On Ansco's "considerable difficulties" before the merger, see C. E. K. Mees, Eastman Kodak, to William W. Buffum, Chemical Foundation, May 22, 1929, Garvan Papers, Box 76. Ansco's predecessor companies went back to the early nineteenth century; it was a 1901 merger: Anthony and Scovill Company, renamed in 1907 Ansco.

153. In July 1925, the German interest in Grasselli Dyestuff had been increased from 50 to 65 percent. Sasuly, *I. G. Farben,* 181. Haynes, *American Chemical Industry,* IV, 234; VI, 175–176, on the further increase.

154. See I. G. Farben, *Annual Report 1928* (English translation, prepared for I. G. Farben annual meeting, June 11, 1929). A copy is in the Garvan Papers, Box 76. The place of incorporation is given in *Moody's Industrials 1929,* 2821. Before American I. G. acquired its own head office, its staff was located at the New York office of the I. G. Farben's affiliate, Synthetic Nitrogen Corporation. Statement of Gustav Frank-Fahle, June 4, 1945, RG 238, T301, Reel 12, NI-1183.

155. *Moody's Industrials 1929,* 2820–2822 (on American I. G.'s affiliation with I. G. Farben). On I. G. Chemie, 1928–1929, see Wilkins, "Swiss Investments," 109–111. I. G. Chemie (Internationale Gesellschaft für Chemische Unternehmungen, AG) was formed in Basle, Switzerland, in June 1928, as a holding company for certain of I. G. Farben's international assets. The original principal rationale seems to have been tax related. German companies (and individuals), for tax reasons, often held shares of foreign enterprises through foreign holding companies. Eventually, I. G. Chemie came to hold I. G. Farben's interest in American I. G. Chemical Corporation. It is not exactly certain when this happened, but it does not matter. Later every facet of I. G. Chemie's relationships with American I. G. came under intense scrutiny. For one of the first such scrutinies and its frustrations, see U.S. Securities and Exchange Commission, *Investment Trusts and Investment Companies,* H. Doc. 279, 77th Cong., 1st sess. (1942), 135–151 (the coverage of this SEC document goes back into the 1930s). In the present book, I am interested in showing the basic business relationships; it would waste my reader's time (and try his or her patience) to detail all the complex changing legal, corporate interconnections; instead, I will try to cut through the corporate veils and decipher the core story line. The bottom line was that American I. G. was established by and controlled by I. G. Farben.

156. For a list of board membership and officers, see U.S. Senate, Committee on Finance, *Sale of Foreign Bonds, Hearings,* 72nd Cong., 1st sess. (1932), pt. 2, 603; Haynes, *American Chemical Industry,* IV, 236; *Moody's Industrials 1929,* 2820, and ibid., 1930, 2149. The 1929 *Moody's* listed only three I. G. Farben directors (Bosch, Schmitz, and Greif), making the board look overwhelmingly American; the 1930 *Moody's* listed the additional I. G. Farben men as given in my text. Walter Duisberg was the son of Carl Duisberg, who with Carl Bosch had been a principal figure in the foundation of I. G. Farben. Borkin, *Crime and Punishment of I. G. Farben,* 186–187, on the relationship. The I. G. Farben *Annual Report 1928* listed only the American directors of American I. G.

157. Hermann Schmitz had gone to work for Carl Bosch in 1919 at Badische. As head of I. G. Farben's Central Finance Office from 1925 to 1935, he was the key person in dealing with the financial policies of I. G. Farben. He made trips to the United States, but he resided in Germany. RG 238, T301, esp. Reel 7, NI-710, and Hayes, *Industry and Ideology,* 25–26. Greif was German born, German educated, and represented I. G. Farben in the United States. *New York Times,* Oct. 30, 1937 (his obituary), and Statement of G. Frank-Fahle, June 4, 1945, p. 3, RG 238, T301, Reel 12, NI-1183.

158. *Moody's Industrials 1929,* 2821.

159. Wilkins and Hill, *American Business Abroad,* 195–196, and Edsel Ford to Creighton R. Coleman (Special Attorney, U.S. Department of Justice), Nov. 6, 1940, Acc. 6, Ford

Archives, Henry Ford Museum, Dearborn, Michigan. Elisabeth Glaser-Schmidt came across in the Minutes of the Arbeitsausschuss, Jan. 13, 1928, located in the Bayer Archives, data to suggest that I. G. Farben sought a "working alliance" with Ford in order to develop nitrocellulose lacquer production. She was not, however, able to establish the consummation of any such relationship and learned, in fact, that I. G. Farben's plan for lacquer production in the United States was abandoned. Elisabeth Glaser-Schmidt to Mira Wilkins, June 9, 1994. I found nothing on this in the Ford Archives.

160. There has been a lot written on these agreements. See, for example, Stocking and Watkins, *Cartels in Action,* 92–93; Wilkins, *Maturing,* 81; Edwards, *Economic and Political Aspects of International Cartels;* Larson, Knowlton, and Popple, *New Horizons,* 156; Borkin, *Crime and Punishment of I. G. Farben,* 51; Howard, *Buna Rubber,* 27–30; Wall and Gibb, *Teagle of Jersey Standards,* 302. I have consulted the actual agreements, which are printed, out of sequence, in the *Bone Committee Hearings.*

161. *Bone Committee Hearings,* pt. 7, 3451–3457. The "four parties" were I. G. Farben, "S.I.G." (later named Standard-I. G. Company), Standard Oil Company (New Jersey), and Standard Oil Co. of New Jersey. The last two "parties" were referred to in the agreement as "Standard." (See Larson, Knowlton, and Popple, *New Horizons,* 13, for these two: the first was a holding company; the other its subsidiary.)

162. *Bone Committee Hearings,* pt. 7, 3444–3445 (division of fields agreement), 3461–3467 (German oil market), 3467–3468 (agreement on "future eventualities").

163. This is based on Wilkins, *Maturing,* 81; Larson, Knowlton, and Popple, *New Horizons,* 156; Borkin, *Crime and Punishment of I. G. Farben,* 185; Howard, *Buna Rubber,* 23, 27–28, as well as the *Bone Committee Hearings.* Apparently for tax reasons these shares were never held directly by I. G. Farben. In the September 12, 1945, interrogation of Hermann Schmitz (RG 238, T301, Reel 8, NI-711, pp. 13, 18), Schmitz, who was I. G. Farben's financial mastermind and the signer for I. G. Farben of these 1929 agreements, reported that in 1929, Standard Oil shares "may have been in the name of [Swiss banker Eduard] Greutert [as trustee] and might have belonged to I. G. Chemie [I. G. Farben's Swiss holding company]." Later, Schmitz indicated that "to support" American I. G., he transferred the SONJ shares to it. Such international transfers of shares were not uncommon in the late 1920s and early 1930s; Ivar Kreuger, of course, was in the vanguard of such shuffling, but he was far from alone. As I read Exhibit 9, dated Nov. 19, 1929, *Bone Committee Hearings,* pt. 7, 3460–3461, the shares went to I. G. Chemie.

164. On August 31, 1928, Bosch had described the negotiations between SONJ and I. G. Farben as leading to a "marriage." *Bone Committee Hearings,* pt. 7, 3326, 3429.

165. Wall and Gibb, *Teagle of Jersey Standard,* 300.

166. American I. G. did not hold all the shares in these firms. Agfa-Ansco Corporation's preferred shares, for example, continued to be listed and traded on the New York Curb Exchange. *New York Times,* Dec. 4, 1929.

167. According to *U.S. v. Bayer Co. Inc., et al.,* 135 F. Supp. at 67 (SDNY 1955), I. G. Farben transferred its Winthrop stock to American I. G. in 1929; Sterling Products' founder, W. E. Weiss, was on the American I. G. Board. "The genuine beneficial ownership [of the 50 percent] never left the German I. G. Farbenindustrie," was the view of Edwin M. Cage and H. E. Dreman, "Confidential Report on Investigation of I. G. Farbenindustrie (Bayer Division)," Sept. 18, 1945, p. 12, RG 238, T301, Reel 13, NI-1305.

168. Hounshell and Smith, *Science and Corporate Strategy,* 205–206.

169. For the 1927–1929 negotiations, see *Bone Committee Hearings,* pt. 5, 2071, 2247–2261. Stocking and Watkins, *Cartels in Action,* 91 ("singularly independent"). This is evident in Hounshell and Smith, *Science and Corporate Strategy,* as well.

170. Hounshell and Smith, *Science and Corporate Strategy,* 447, 701; Haynes, *American Chemical Industry* IV, 343; Du Pont, *Annual Report 1928.*

171. In 1934 (a date for which we have information), Du Pont held shares in both I. G. Farben and I. G. Chemie. W. Arthur Murphy to J. E. Crane, June 26, 1934, Acc. 1231, Box 4, Du Pont Archives. I do not know when these shares were acquired, but 1929 seems very plausible.

172. The size of the German operations of I. G. Farben was awesome. Peter Hayes writes that the "core" firm alone employed almost 120,000 people in 1929. Hayes, *Industry and Ideology,* 17. By way of comparison, Standard Oil Company of New Jersey worldwide had 129,817 employees in 1929, of which only 57,865 were in the United States. Larson, Knowlton, and Popple, *New Horizons,* 819. I do not know the size of employment of I. G. Farben affiliates in the United States in 1929.

173. This is important, for the corporate structures related to I. G. Farben's U.S. holdings were complex and changed over time. In the 1920s, as taxes had risen, I. G. Farben had sought to minimize its tax obligations. It would later explain that "camouflaging" (or elaborate corporate architecture) was done to avoid host country taxes. See Draft Report from I. G. Farben to the German Ministry of Economics, Sept. 26, 1940, RG 238, T301, Reel 20, NI-2246. It is possible that one motive for American I. G. could have been to offset the strength of I. G. Farben's dyestuff business with the losses from its film business, and thus minimize U.S. taxes. (BAT's Pocahontas Corp., incorporated just one month before American I. G., and also in Delaware, had that as a motive.) More critical, American I. G. was a fine way to raise money in the United States. For especially large investments, I. G. Farben sought to hold them through Swiss and Dutch intermediaries—in the 1920s for tax reasons, typically related to German taxes. The tax considerations were obvious when in February 1929, I. G. Farben concluded a "dividend guarantee agreement with I. G. Chemie, Basel, whereby the distribution . . . of a dividend on that company's common stock is guaranteed at the same rate as that of the dividend distributed by ourselves [I. G. Farben] in Goldmarks on our own common stock for the same fiscal year *without deduction of dividend tax.*" I. G. Farben, *Annual Report 1928* (my italics). I perceive the I. G. Chemie–American I. G. relationship as similar in some respects to the AKU–Associated Rayon structures, described in the section on rayon.

174. See Wilkins, *Maturing,* 81n, and *Bone Committee Hearings,* pt. 7, 3328, 3440 (Mar. 21, 1929 statement).

175. There was some speculation that Bosch's anger over Allied Chemical's subsidiary NACC's invasion of European markets had prompted his push into the United States. Protto and Singer to Harrington, May 30, 1928, *Bone Committee Hearings,* pt. 5, 2258–2259.

176. Memo of the meeting of I. G. Farben and SONJ, Mar. 21, 1929, *Bone Committee Hearings,* pt. 7, 3328, 3440. This was in keeping with its German domestic strategies as well. It deliberately stayed away from certain chemicals. Aftalion, *History of the International Chemical Industry,* 187.

177. On April 27, 1929, in the very same month that American I. G. was organized, I. G. Farben entered into a major set of cartel agreements with Swiss and French dyestuff producers. Harm Schröter, "Cartels as a Form of Concentration." in *German Yearbook on Business History 1988,* ed. Hans Pohl and Bernd Rudolph (Berlin: Springer-Verlag, 1990), 128. I. G. Farben was developing a broad new approach to its international business, that combined cooperation and innovative activities.

178. See Chapter 4 on the GM investment.

179. "Outline History of the North American Chemical Company," typescript, 1928, Bay City, Michigan, Library; Haynes, *American Chemical Industry,* IV, 130.

180. Reader, *Imperial Chemical Industries,* I, 438–439; Haynes, *American Chemical Industry,* IV, 236; and Stocking and Watkins, *Cartels in Action,* 452. DCA's 1924 letterhead has its headquarters at 281–285 Franklin Street, Boston, which was the head office of I. Levinstein & Co., Inc.; the letterhead describes DCA as the "trading successor to I. Lev-

instein & Co. and Read Holiday & Sons Ltd." Dyestuffs Corporation of America to Chemical Foundation, May 23, 1924, Garvan Papers, Box 45.

181. Reader, *Imperial Chemical Industries,* II, 15.

182. Ibid., I, 462–463.

183. In 1920, Brunner, Mond acquired Castner-Kellner Alkali Co. Ltd. and with it an interest in Niagara Electro Chemical Company; Roessler & Hasslacher Chemical (R & H) purchased Niagara Electro Chemical Co. in 1925. Brunner, Mond/Castner-Kellner, in turn, got an interest in R & H. "The Roessler & Hasslacher Chemical Company," Du Pont Papers.

184. Reader, *Imperial Chemical Industries,* II, 48.

185. All during the 1920s, antitrust concerns shaped the strategies of large U.S. enterprises. Also, and perhaps as important, Du Pont did not want ICI to have any reason to share technology (its own or Du Pont's) with Allied Chemical.

186. Reader, *Imperial Chemical Industries,* II, 49–50.

187. Ibid., II, 50n, and "The Roessler & Hasslacher Chemical Company."

188. Stocking and Watkins, *Cartels in Action,* 452.

189. Reader, *Imperial Chemical Industries,* II, 50–54; Wilkins, *Maturing,* 79–80; Hounshell and Smith, *Science and Corporate Strategy,* 191–194. The July 1, 1929, agreement is printed in *Bone Committee Hearings,* pt. 2, 783–792.

190. The agreement did not say that, in deference to U.S. antitrust law. It did, however, deal with where technology (and patents) could be used, and the result was tantamount to a division of markets.

191. Robert W. Dunn, *American Foreign Investment* (1926; rpt. New York: Arno Press, 1976), 36. The 1924 bond issue was to redeem and retire an earlier issue, which appears to have been floated in 1920. See Solvay & Cie. to Orlando Weber, June 24, 1933, Garvan Papers, Box 50.

192. SAIC was organized through Solvay & Cie.'s wholly owned Swiss subsidiary, Gesellschaft für Beteiligungen der Chemischen Industrie. U.S. Securities and Exchange Commission, *Investment Trusts,* pt. 4, 152. After a 1930 merger, the name Libbey Owens Ford was adopted by the American glass company. Haynes, *American Chemical Industry,* VI, 245.

193. For Libbey-Owens' international business, see Wilkins, *Maturing,* 498n.39, and Francesca Bova, "American Direct Investment in the Italian Manufacturing Sectors, 1900–1940," paper presented at Business History Conference meetings, Ft. Lauderdale, Florida, Mar. 1995.

194. Daviet, *Destin International,* 419.

195. *Moody's Banks 1928,* 2800–2801.

196. Reader, *Imperial Chemical Industries,* II, 50. The addition of 366,480 and 105,600 would bring the total to 472,080—but this is not the figure Reader provides. The difference is not material. What is important is that Solvay & Cie.'s interest was substantial.

197. *Moody's Industrials, 1929,* 753.

198. This had been true even before Solvay & Cie. bought ICI's holdings. U.S. Securities and Exchange Commission, *Investment Trusts,* pt. 4, 153.

199. *Moody's Banks 1931,* 1773. A later Solvay & Cie. statement would explain that the $25 million was used to purchase 100,000 shares of Allied Chemical from ICI. Solvay & Cie. to Orlando Weber, June 24, 1933, p. 5, Garvan Papers, Box 50. The purchase was made, according to ICI records, in November 1928, but it was paid for out of the August 1929 Solvay American stock offering.

200. Haynes, *American Chemical Industry,* IV, 89; VI, 380–383. Beaton, *Enterprise in Oil,* 517, 521, and 502–524, for background. There had been a predecessor to the 1928 Shell Development Co., organized in 1927. Ibid., 517.

201. Beaton, *Enterprise in Oil,* 514n.

202. Reader, *Imperial Chemical Industries,* II, 167–168. Du Pont worried lest ICI share with Shell knowledge obtained from and also knowledge shared with Du Pont; moreover, Du Pont did not want ICI in the American market *in any role.*

203. Ibid., II, 167. See Ervin Hexner, *International Cartels* (Chapel Hill: University of North Carolina Press, 1946), 315, for the connections between ICI, Royal Dutch Shell, and I. G. Farben in the International Bergin Company, a firm set up in Holland to develop the hydrogenation process under patents of the German Friedrich Bergius.

204. And, on February 25, 1930, I. G. Farben and ICI made a global agreement (excluding North America) on ammonia production. Ibid., II, 113. The interrelations between all these firms were intricate—and often different, depending on the particular product line.

205. See Wilkins, *History,* on Degussa. According to Hexner, *International Cartels,* 222, Degussa was by 1938 represented in the United States by "its subsidiary" Metal & Thermit Corporation, New York.

206. Haynes, *American Chemical Industry,* IV, 417 (on its founding; this suggests it was entirely American); ibid., III, 499 (on its use of German patents); Office of Alien Property Custodian, *Annual Report 1942–1943,* 38, 54, 100; and data in Acc. 67A10, Box 2579, RG 131, U.S. Department of Justice, Washington, D.C. (on the German involvements).

207. Sheldon Hochheiser, *Rohm and Haas* (Philadelphia: University of Pennsylvania Press, 1986), 25, 31, 36, 41–45.

208. Haynes, *American Chemical Industry,* IV, 297n, 299; Wilkins, *History,* 399 (Schimmel/Fritzsche Brothers); Wilkins, *History,* 399–400; Haynes, *American Chemical Industry,* III, 324; IV, 253–254; and VI, 207 (Heyden). Martin, *All Honorable Men,* 212, however (in 1950), would describe the Heyden Chemical Corporation in 1925 as an American subsidiary of the Chemische Fabrik von Heyden AG of Radebeul near Dresden.

209. Haynes, *American Chemical Industry,* IV, 109, 130–131.

210. Harvey, *Rio Tinto Company,* 211–214; Haynes, *American Chemical Industry,* III, 405; IV, 327–328.

211. Haynes, *American Chemical Industry,* V, 290, VI, 17, 237–238; and Dunning data. The two companies would merge in 1930 to form Kay Fries Chemicals, Inc., which built a modern plant in West Haverstraw, New York (north of West Nyack). These activities appear to be separate from the Tennant group's New York City metal trading office, C. Tennant Sons & Co.

212. Hounshell and Smith, *Science and Corporate Strategy,* 172, 608; Stocking and Mueller, "Cellophane Case," 35–36.

213. The company sent Gillet monthly résumés of what took place. Wall, *Alfred I. Du Pont,* 585. Gillet died in 1931.

214. Wilkins, "Charles Pathé's American Business," 139–141. For more details, see Du Pont complaint against the Pathe Film Corporation in the Southern District Court of New York, Nov. 1938, Acc. 1410, Box 46, Du Pont Public Affairs Files, Du Pont Papers; V. B. Sease, "Brief History of Du Pont Film Plant at Parlin, New Jersey," Aug. 4, 1944, Acc. 1410, Box 42. Hounshell and Smith, *Science and Corporate Strategy,* 206 (on Du Pont and Agfa discussions). On the February 3, 1925, seventy-five-year "assignment of option from Pathé Cinéma S.A. covering right to manufacture moving picture film, limiting license and use of information to North America and certain other territories," see *Bone Committee Hearings,* Exhibits, pt. 2, 803, and pt. 5, 2313. See Alt, "Photochemical Industry," 51, 257 (the tariff), 256 (Pathé's expertise) and 257 (Kodak's response to Du Pont's entry into film manufacture). In 1928–1929, the American-controlled Pathe Exchange sold its 49 percent interest in DPF, retaining the right to repurchase that stake (later it would do so; in 1941, Pathe Exchange finally sold out completely). Du Pont Pathe Film

Manufacturing Corporation (DPF) was renamed Du Pont Film Manufacturing Corporation in 1931. Hounshell and Smith, *Science and Corporate Strategy,* 604. Note that the usually reliable and superb book by Hounshell and Smith got the Pathe story a bit wrong, since they mixed up Pathé Cinéma (the French company) and Pathe Exchange. On the Pathé business in France, see Alan Williams, *Republic of Images: A History of French Filmmaking* (Cambridge, Mass.: Harvard University Press, 1992), 52–53, and Charles Pathé, "De Pathé Frères à Pathé Cinéma," *Premier Plan,* no. 55, 1970. Eastman Kodak apparently was far more worried about Du Pont's activities in film in the United States than about the Agfa-Ansco venture. Pathé in France had close ties with the Gillet family businesses, and it seems obvious that the Du Pont–CTA connections provided the initial link between the French Pathé and Du Pont. See Pathé, "De Pathé Frères," 90.

215. Hounshell and Smith, *Science and Corporate Strategy,* 184–186; data from Patrick Fridenson, June 28, 1995, on L'Air Liquide's getting an interest in Du Pont with the sale. Unlike CTA, L'Air Liquide did not get representation on the Du Pont board of directors.

216. Air Reduction Co. is listed under "subsidiaries and affiliates" of L'Air Liquide in *Moody's Industrials 1930,* 1084. For the vastness of L'Air Liquide's international business, see Li, "L'Air Liquide," 221–238, and unpublished manuscript by Alain Jemain on L'Air Liquide.

217. Société Chimique des Usines du Rhône merged with Poulenc Frères in 1928 in France to form Rhône-Poulenc. On Rhodia Chemical, see Cayez, *Rhône-Poulenc 1895–1975,* 94, and Haynes, *American Chemical Industry,* IV, 253. On Du Pont/Newport, Hounshell and Smith, *Science and Corporate Strategy,* 158, 610. Newport Chemical Co. had a strong position in dyestuffs. Du Pont would have preferred to buy I. G. Farben's American operations, but since this was impossible, it bought Newport. Ibid.

218. Hounshell and Smith, *Science and Corporate Strategy,* 176–177; Haynes, *American Chemical Industry,* IV, 353; VI, 417; and Stocking and Mueller, "Cellophane Case," 34–35, 39. The 1929 rise in duties was based on a reclassification. The Smoot-Hawley Act of 1930 would set the duty at 45 percent ad valorem. Ibid., 35, a rare case where the Smoot-Hawley Act had the effect of lowering a tariff.

219. Greta Devos, "Agfa-Gevaert and Belgian Multinational Enterprise," in *The Rise of Multinationals in Continental Europe,* ed. Geoffrey Jones and Harm G. Schröter (Aldershot: Edward Elgar 1993), 207.

220. When in 1920 the Swiss dye makers had acquired the Cincinnati Chemical Works, the U.S. hope had been to avoid German involvements. In the late 1920s, however, the Swiss parent firms had resumed their close associations with the Germans. Schröter, "Cartels," 125, 128. When I discuss the Swiss role, I am talking about industrial operations, not the holding company structures.

221. Haynes, *American Chemical Industry,* III, 515; IV, 297n, 301–302, 305.

222. Haynes, *American Chemical Industry,* III, 152; IV, 182–183; VI, 376. Testimony of Irving Lipkowitz, *Bone Committee Hearings,* pt. 3, 1364–1365.

223. Also impeding imports was the vigilance of The Chemical Foundation, which monitored imports of goods made under its license.

224. On the U.S. business abroad, see Wilkins, *Maturing.*

225. Hounshell and Smith, *Science and Corporate Strategy,* 91, 449.

226. Mahoney, *Merchants of Life,* 3.

227. For the relationships between Winthrop Chemical and I. G. Farben in the United States (in products and processes for "activating or irradiating ergosterol and its derivatives as an anti-rachitic"), see Agreement of November 10, 1928, in *Kilgore Committee Hearings,* pt. 6 (Monopoly and Cartel Practices: Vitamin D), 933–934. In 1929, Winthrop Chemical Company was totally dependent on Germany for advanced technology. Winthrop Chemical Company's manufacturing was at Rensselaer, New York (the old Bayer

facility). Mann and Plummer, *Aspirin Wars,* 53, 69. Sterling Products had not put aspirin into Winthrop Chemical Company; at the start, however, Winthrop Chemical handled sixty-three other medications formerly sold by Bayer. Ibid., 52. On the German chemist as plant manager (and another who followed) and on Drug Inc., see Mahoney, *Merchants of Life,* 214. Winthrop Chemical Company got American rights for I. G. Farben pharmaceuticals. Accordingly, in 1926, it had obtained sole rights to the first synthetic antimalarial drug, Plasmochin, a substitute for quinine, which had been developed in Germany in 1924. Haynes, *American Chemical Industry,* IV, 286.

228. On Ciba, Geigy, Sandoz, and Hoffmann-La Roche in America, see Mahoney, *Merchants of Life,* chap. 15. The best work on Hoffmann-La Roche is Peyer, *Roche,* 88 (1922 and 1926 employment), 108–109 (on the move to Nutley). See also Haynes, *American Chemical Industry,* IV, 289–290; VI, 209.

229. Haynes, *American Chemical Industry,* IV, 290.

230. Wilkins, *Maturing,* 82, 499n.53.

231. Prior to 1929, certain Schering products had been imported into the United States by Schering & Glatz, Inc. ("manufacturers of medicinal chemicals and pharmaceuticals"); the latter had established Alyco Manufacturing Co., in which the Germans had a secret interest. Schering & Glatz, which apparently had no nonresident German ownership in 1914, survived World War I, after which it paid license fees to The Chemical Foundation to import Hormonal and Hegonon; it was in litigation with The Chemical Foundation for some ten years on trademark and patent issues. Discontent with its distributor resulted in Schering-Kahlbaum establishing Schering Corporation. In 1930, Schering & Glatz would be acquired by William R. Warner & Co., a U.S. company. That year Alyco was dissolved. Kobrak, "Between Nationalism and Internationalism," 328–333; Wilkins, *History,* 397; Schering & Glatz to The Chemical Foundation, June 16, 1925, and Feb. 11, 1929, Garvan Papers, Box 45; Hans Hollander, *Geschichte de Schering AG* (Berlin: Schering, 1955), 96–97 (products); Haynes, *American Chemical Industry,* III, 322; V, 259; VI, 470. Schering in Germany merged with Kahlbaum in 1927 to become Schering-Kahlbaum.

232. Haynes, *American Chemical Industry,* IV, 290; VI, 61; Mahoney, *Merchants of Life,* 113, 99; Fred A. Coe, Jr., *Burroughs Wellcome Co. 1880–1980* (New York: Newcomen Society, 1980), 12. Roy Church has a history of Burroughs Wellcome in process. In 1884 the firm had registered "Tabloid" as a trademark.

233. I did not mention either in my *History.* For background on A. J. White Ltd., makers of "Mother Seigel's Syrup," see T. A. B. Corley to Mira Wilkins, Sept. 15, 1983. The 1927 arrangement appears to have related to the British market. See "Twice upon a Time . . . The Story of A. J. White Ltd. and Menley & James," n.d. I thank Corley for sending me (July 14, 1994) this undated excerpt from a house journal, which he obtained from Smith Kline & French's immediate successor, SmithKline Beckman. Menley & James Ltd. sold "Iodex," an ointment prepared from iodine. Both A. J. White Ltd. and Menley & James Ltd. were in business in the United States throughout the interwar period. The British parents would be taken over by the U.S. company Smith Kline & French in 1956.

234. Haynes, *American Chemical Industry,* III, 303. Earlier, in December 1914, the United States had put controls on the sales of chemical derivatives of opium. Ibid., III, 300, 303.

235. Ibid., III, 303, and Peyer, *Roche,* 95. Hoffmann-La Roche and Sandoz were the Swiss firms most affected. The former in 1923–1924 had turned to quinine and other products to compensate for declining sales of opiates. Ibid., 95–99.

236. Wilkins, *History,* for its prewar activities; T. A. B. Corley to Wilkins, June 27, 1982, for the situation in the 1920s.

237. Corley to Wilkins, June 27, 1982; Corley, "From National to Multinational Enterprise"; according to the *Stock Exchange Year Book 1929,* 2388, Beecham's Pills, Ltd., was registered to acquire the pill business of Beecham Estate and Pills Ltd. The new firm

was said to "own" a works at Niagara Falls, New York; Corley writes that the Niagara Fall plant was leased.

238. *Moody's Industrials, 1929,* 895. International Proprietaries also acquired a company called Genotherm Corporation in New York. I have no idea when Eno Ltd. acquired or built the Buffalo plant.

239. H. G. Lazell, *From Pills to Penicillin: The Beecham Story* (London: Heinemann, 1975), 114.

240. Discussions with T. A. B. Corley and Lazell, *From Pills to Penicillin.* Beecham's was the predecessor to SmithKline Beecham, formed in 1989, as a merger of SmithKline Beckman and Beecham's. Stopford, *Directory of Multinationals,* II, 1242. In January 2000, Glaxo Wellcome and SmithKline Beecham announced a proposed $74 billion merger of the two British companies to form GlaxoSmithKline, thus dropping both the Beecham and Wellcome names. Glaxo Wellcome was the 1995 combination of Glaxo Holdings and Wellcome PLC (as of 1985 the corporate parent of the Wellcome group that included Burroughs Wellcome in the United States). Information from Glaxo Wellcome. The merger took place in December 2000, with the formation of GlaxoSmithKline. *Financial Times,* Dec. 27, 2000.

241. Denison, *Harvest Triumphant,* 252–253, and E. P. Neufeld, *A Global Corporation: A History of the International Development of Massey-Ferguson, Ltd.* (Toronto: University of Toronto Press, 1969), 22, 30.

242. Denison, *Harvest Triumphant,* 250–254; Neufeld, *Global Corporation,* 24, 29, 184; Wilkins, *History,* 418 (1914 employment).

243. Marshall, Southard, and Taylor, *Canadian-American Industry,* 182.

244. Chandler, *Scale and Scope,* 649 (assets of International Harvester). In 1930, Deere & Co. had assets of $118.7 million. With assets of $12.5 million, the U.S. subsidiary of Massey-Harris would not rank among America's top 200 companies. Ibid., 644–650.

245. Simon N. Whitney, *Antitrust Policies,* 2 vols. (New York: Twentieth Century Fund, 1958), II, 235.

246. Neufeld, *Global Corporation,* 29.

247. My thanks to the late Gunnar Hedlund for referring me to Gustaf Bondeson, "The Growth of a Global Enterprise: Alfa-Laval 100 Years" (n.p.: Alfa-Laval, n.d. [1983?]), 44–45, 60, 74. The group was renamed Alfa-Laval AB in 1963. Ibid., 52. On De Laval Separator Co., see also *Moody's Industrials 1929,* 910.

248. Chandler, *Giant Enterprise,* 4, 7.

249. Lloyd, *Rolls-Royce,* 54–70, 79–82; *Moody's Industrials 1928,* 2334.

250. George Edward Domer, "The History of the American Austin and Bantam," *Automobile Quarterly,* 14 (1976): 406; see also Church, *Herbert Austin,* 95–96.

251. Domer, "History of the American Austin and Bantam," 406–407.

252. U.S. Department of Commerce, Bureau of the Census, *Historical Statistics of the United States* (Washington, D.C., 1975), 895, for the tiny imports. Wilkins, *Maturing,* and Wilkins and Hill, *American Business Abroad,* on the worldwide expansion of American car companies.

253. American Bosch Magneto Corp., *Annual Report 1929,* and Prospectus, American Bosch Corp., Oct. 25, 1938, both in Scudder Collection, Columbia University Library. According to Gerard Aalders and Cees Wiebes, "Stockholms Enskilda Bank, German Bosch, and I. G. Farben," *Scandinavian Economic History Review,* 33 (1985): 26, it was the stock market crash of 1929 that gave the German Bosch the opportunity to reacquire its ex-subsidiary in America.

254. The best source on Fokker in America is Dierikx, *Fokker,* 113–136 (for his role in this period). See also Fokker and Gould, *Flying Dutchman,* 14, 248–251; *Van Oss' Effectenboek 1934* (on the 1929 Dutch issue of Fokker Aircraft Corporation of America securities);

John B. Rae, *Climb to Greatness* (Cambridge, Mass.: MIT Press, 1968), 44; Sloan, *My Years with General Motors,* 362–364; U.S. Federal Trade Commission, *Report on Motor Vehicles* (Washington, D.C., 1939), 482.

255. Luery, *Story of Milltown,* 99 (quote); Works Progress Administration, "History of Milltown." By way of comparison, Goodyear, the industry leader, had a daily capacity of 54,000 tires in 1926 and 89,500 tires in 1929. French, "Structural Change," 39.

256. In 1924–1925, General Motors had renewed its earlier (1919–1920) efforts to buy Austin Motor Car Co. in Britain; instead, it bought Vauxhall Motors. On the 1924–1925 plans, see Sloan, *My Years with General Motors,* 318–320; see Reich, *Fruits of Fascism,* on both GM attempts to buy Austin. Whereas Austin had special ties with Dunlop in the United Kingdom, Vauxhall did not. Pierre du Pont's board membership is indicated in *Moody's Industrials 1929,* 1043.

257. In 1924, Lee, Higginson & Co. was recommending to Pierre du Pont, Dunlop Tire & Rubber Corporation 7 percent bonds, due 1942, at 94, to yield 7.6 percent, as "taxable securities with a high return." See W. W. Corlaran (?), Lee, Higginson & Co., to Frank A. McHugh, Feb. 27, 1924, Longwood Mss 10/A/File 229, Box 7, P. S. du Pont Papers.

258. French, "Structural Change," 31.

259. Jones, "Growth," 46.

260. Michael French, *The U.S. Tire Industry* (Boston: Twayne, 1991), 58 (Du Pont and U.S. Rubber).

261. French, "Structural Change," 30, 33; Jones, "Growth," 45.

262. Jones, "Growth," 46. Jones gives data from 1926 and 1929 that shows that Dunlop's sales in the original equipment market steadily declined in those years. As noted, Pierre S. Du Pont remained on the board of Dunlop Tire & Rubber Corp (see *Moody's Industrials 1929,* 1043), but this did not help Dunlop sell to GM.

263. Wilkins, *Maturing,* 98–102.

264. Tweedale, *Sheffield Steel and America,* 96–97, 168, 227n.47.

265. Krupp's American "partners" are listed in W. P. Ehrenberg, Essen, to Gustav von Bohlen, Mar. 17, 1930, RG 238, T301, Reel 10, NI-1040.

266. Martin, *All Honorable Men,* 92.

267. *Bone Committee Hearings,* pt. 1, 38–520 (on tungsten carbide), esp. 51–53, 169.

268. External Security Coordinating Committee, "Report on Krupp," n.d. [1945], Secret, RG 238, T301, Reel 36, NI-R907; and M. Louis, Krupp AG, Essen, to F. Redies, Sept. 2, 1940, RG 238, T301, Reel 36, NI-4900.

269. Wilkins, *History,* 260; U.S. Senate, Committee on Military Affairs, Subcommittee on War Mobilization, *Elimination of German Resources for War,* 79th Cong., 1st sess. (1945–1946), pt. 4, 588 (henceforth cited as *Kilgore Committee Hearings II*). Graef & Schmidt seems eventually to have done more than sell cutlery. It became a manufacturer in the United States of scissors, knives, and manicure instruments. Office of Alien Property Custodian, *Annual Report 1943–1944,* 48.

270. The German giant Vereinigte Stahlwerke, AG (United Steel Works Corporation), which in 1926–1927 was raising moneys in the U.S. bond market, did have an indirect interest in two New York sales companies, Steel Piling Inc. (organized in March 1926) and Steel Union Inc. (set up in June 1927). The two would be merged in 1935 and become Steel Union–Sheet Piling Inc.; in 1935 the owner of record was Dutch. *Kilgore Committee Hearings,* pt. 16 (Cartel Practices and National Security), 2048–2049. Canada Foundries and Forgings, Ltd. had a subsidiary, Delaney Forge & Iron Corp., Buffalo, New York. *Moody's Manual 1929,* 891. These investments and some others were far from significant.

271. Dunning data.

272. Ben P. A. Gales and Keetie E. Sluyterman, "Outward Bound: The Rise of Dutch Multinationals," in Jones and Schröter, eds., *Rise of Multinationals,* 68, 75.

273. Leon E. Hotz, president, Sauer Textile Machinery Group, to Mira Wilkins, Oct. 2, 1987, writes that Feldmühle Rorschach and Sauer Inc., New York, discontinued their U.S. operations in 1929/1930. The former was associated with SASTIG (the Schweizerisch-Amerikanischen Stickerei-Industrie-Gesellschaft), which made embroidery in the United States.

274. Based on information from Ragnhild Lundström and her "Swedish Multinational Growth before 1930," 138, 150.

275. Wilkins, *Maturing,* passim. There were undoubtedly more sales outlets for foreign machinery and some foreign machinery made in the United States. I do not know whether Sulzer Brothers, Switzerland, for example, retained its prewar U.S. investments. See Wilkins, *History,* 432. J. M. Lehmann Co., Inc. (prewar German-owned importers of chocolate and cocoa-producing machinery) was sold after the First World War to U.S. citizens and then in 1921 was resold to Germans. *Kilgore Committee Hearings II,* 588. It was vested during World War II and described as a maker of "machines tools" in the United States; a more detailed report had it producing marine auxiliaries and capstan winches for cargo vessels, as well as optical grinding and polishing machines. Office of Alien Property Custodian, *Annual Report 1942–1943,* 54, and ibid., *1943–1944,* 48. Perhaps, this industrial sector ought to include the forms-handling and printing equipment made in the United States by the Canadian-owned Moore Corporation.

276. Cambridge Instrument Co.'s entry into the United States had come in 1922. At the end of the decade, it manufactured scientific instruments, at Ossining, New York; it also opened an office in New York City. Williams, *Precision Makers,* 150, 153.

277. Before the First World War the company made, sold, and exported from the United States very specialized surgical instruments, including dissecting and microscopic instruments. Wilkins, *History,* 428, 836n.80. For the post–First World War revival, see *Kilgore Committee Hearings II,* 588.

278. Hagen, "Export versus Direct Investment," 9, 19n.61; *Kilgore Committee Hearings,* pt. 16, 2118; and Office of Alien Property Custodian, *Annual Report 1943–1944,* 79–80.

279. For details, see exhibits in *Kilgore Committee Hearings,* pt. 16, 2117–2166; on the competition in certain products, see particularly 1935 correspondence, in ibid., 2166–2167; for lack of competition in other product lines, see ibid., 2119 (*U.S. v. Bausch & Lomb Optical Co.,* Civil Action No. 9-404 [SDNY 1940]).

280. The histories of the German steel and electrical enterprises would henceforth be separate.

281. In steel, Vereinigte Stahlwerke, AG, had also raised moneys in the United States, for the same reason.

282. Internal memo, Siemens & Halske, Apr. 10, 1929, SAA 68/li262, Siemens Archives, Munich.

283. Southard, *American Industry in Europe,* 27, and Wilkins, *Maturing,* 66–69. When Carl Köttgen of Siemens visited New York in September 1929, he did so to take part in discussions with General Electric. Karl Frank to Reyss, Oct. 1, 1929, SAA 68/li262.

284. They could not compete for two reasons: (1) the division-of-market agreements and (2) they had no advantage over their American counterparts.

285. Gales and Sluyterman, "Outward Bound," 74; International General Electric, *Annual Report 1929;* and text of *U.S. v. General Electric, et al.,* Civil Action No. 1364 (DNJ, 1949). I used copy reprinted in U.S. Senate, Committee on the Judiciary, Subcommittee on Antitrust and Monopoly, *International Aspects of Antitrust, Hearings,* 89th Cong., 2nd sess. (1966), pt. 2, 949–950, 837, 897, 899, 901–902. NV Philips had been founded in 1891; in 1912 it had participated in a U.S. joint venture, Laco-Philips; see A. Heerding, *The History of N.V. Philips' Gloeilampenfabrieken,* 2 vols. (Cambridge: Cambridge University Press, 1986, 1988), II, 181–184, 302–305, 343–344. (Its partner in 1912 was Lamont, Corliss & Co.) See

Blanken, *History of Philips Electronics,* III, 6 (1919 GE-Philips agreement, 20 percent equity, and board representation), and passim (international relations in the European lamp industry). In radios, on July 22, 1925, Philips made a contract with RCA, which divided markets. Ibid., 214–217, and, passim, for Philips' international business in radios.

286. *New York Times,* Sept. 24, 1925; see also British Electrical & Allied Manufacturers' Association, *Combines and Trusts in the Electrical Industry* (London: BEAMA, 1927), 47. The *New York Times,* Sept. 29, 1925, contained a huge advertisement, entitled "Introducing a Significant Name to American Industry . . . BROWN, BOVERI."

287. Sidney Pollard and Paul Robertson, *The British Shipbuilding Industry* (Cambridge, Mass.: Harvard University Press, 1979), 128; *New York Times,* Oct. 5, 1925. For New York Shipbuilding Corporation's facilities, see Heinrich, *Ships for the Seven Seas,* chaps. 6 and 7, and 213–215.

288. *New York Times,* Apr. 4, 1924, and Aug. 22, 1925. See also Heinrich, *Ships for the Seven Seas,* 215–216.

289. *New York Times,* Mar. 3, 1925; Aug. 22, 1925; Sept. 28, 1925. See also advertisement in ibid., Sept. 29, 1925. Section 37 of the 1916 Shipping Act required the U.S. secretary of commerce to give prior approval for any transfer of shipbuilding facilities to foreign ownership. See U.S. Department of Commerce, *Foreign Direct Investment in the United States* (Washington, D.C., 1976), VIII, K-59 (henceforth cited as *FDIUS–1976).* I can find no evidence that such approval was requested, given, or denied. The rule seems to have been ignored.

290. American Brown Boveri, *Annual Report 1927.*

291. *New York Times,* Oct. 5, 7, 9, 1925.

292. Ibid., Nov. 25, 1925.

293. Lewis, *America's Stake,* 143.

294. American Brown Boveri, *Annual Report 1926.*

295. Ibid. (The 1926 annual report came out in the summer of 1927.)

296. American Brown Boveri, *Annual Report 1927.*

297. Ibid. For the situation at the Camden Shipyards, see Heinrich, *Ships for the Seven Seas,* 216–217.

298. British Electrical & Allied Manufacturers' Association, *Combines and Trusts,* 130.

299. *Moody's 1928,* 3114.

300. Wilkins, *Maturing,* 65–68, on GE's strategy.

301. Mira Wilkins interviews with W. R. Herod, Feb. 24 and Mar. 11, 1964; Great Britain, Board of Trade, *Survey of International and Internal Cartels,* I, 41.

302. Wilkins interview with Herod, Mar. 11, 1964.

303. It is hard to understand why Brown, Boveri had *believed* it could triumph in the American market. See R. P. T. Davenport-Hines, "Vickers and Schneider," in *Historical Studies in International Corporate Business,* ed. Alice Teichova, Maurice Lévy-Leboyer, and Helga Nussbaum (Cambridge: Cambridge University Press, 1989), 127, for Brown, Boveri's difficulties in the early 1920s.

304. Wilkins, *History,* 842n.167, and R. M. Morgan, *Callender's 1882–1945* (Prescott, Merseyside: BICC, 1982), 78–81.

305. Geoffrey Jones, in "The Gramophone Company: A British Multinational," *Business History Review,* 59 (Spring 1985): 97, writes that in 1923, an English syndicate purchased the Columbia Graphophone Company, Ltd., and "shortly thereafter" the British Columbia Graphophone acquired its U.S. parent; by early 1926 Columbia Graphophone Co. Ltd. had twelve foreign factories, including the one in the United States. See also Oliver Read and Walter L. Welch, *From Tin Foil to Stereo* (Indianapolis: Howard W. Sams & Co., 1959), 402–403, 406–407. Southard, *American Industry in Europe,* 107, gives the 1925 date for the purchase by British Columbia of its U.S. parent, a date also sug-

gested in Read and Welch. Southard (ibid., 108) reports that by April 1930, three-quarters of the stock of the British Columbia company was held in the United States. In 1931, the Electrical and Musical Industries Ltd. (EMI) came into being, a British-based multinational; it absorbed the British Columbia company; soon, EMI disposed of the shares it had acquired in the American Columbia company. Jones, "Gramophone Company," 98.

306. On Electrolux history and its international business, see Jan Glete, "Swedish Managerial Capitalism," *Business History*, 35 (Apr. 1993). 106, Lundström, "Swedish Multinational Growth before 1930," 138, 150; and Klaus Wohlert, "Multinational Enterprise—Financing, Trade, Diplomacy: The Swedish Case," in *Historical Studies*, ed. Teichova, Lévy-Leboyer, and Nussbaum, 80 (Electrolux had twenty foreign subsidiaries in 1930).

307. Stockholm office of U.S. Bureau of Foreign and Domestic Commerce to Finance Department, Nov. 5, 1936, RG 151 620 General 1936, National Archives, citing data from a Swedish stockholders' yearbook.

308. *Economist*, Dec. 21, 1929, 1213, and Wilkins, *History*, 448. Its plant was in Detroit, Michigan.

309. Its plant was in Jamestown, New York. Dunning data.

310. Oxford University Press, *Oxford Publishing since 1478* (London: Oxford University Press, 1966), 6–10.

311. Swaine, *Cravath Firm*, II, 297, and Beaton, *Enterprise in Oil*, 360.

312. J. C. Eck to Henri Deterding, Jan. 16, 1924; General Land Office, Washington, D.C., to Register, Vernal, Utah, Jan. 1924; G. Legh-Jones to J. C. van Eck, Jan. 22, 1924; J. C. van Eck to Henri Deterding, Mar. 28, 1924; and G. Legh-Jones to Henri Deterding, Dec. 19, 1925, all in Shell Archives, London.

313. G. Legh-Jones to Henri Deterding, Dec. 19, 1925, Shell Archives.

314. Adrian Corbett for J. B. Aug. Kessler to J. C. van Eck, Jan. 24, 1927, Shell Archives (general situation); Randall, *United States Foreign Oil Policy*, 35 ("to tranquilize," quoting a Mar. 30, 1927, Foreign Office minute).

315. Kessler to van Eck, Nov. 23, 1927, Shell Archives.

316. Van Eck to Kessler, Dec. 30, 1927, Shell Archives.

317. Kessler to F. de Kok, Jan. 27, 1928, Shell Archives.

318. Wilkins, *Maturing*, 88.

319. Undated memo, Andrew Agnew to H. W. Cole, Shell Archives.

320. Van Eck to Deterding, Feb. 25, 1929 (telegram), Shell Archives.

321. Deterding to van Eck, Feb. 27, 1929 (telegram), Shell Archives.

322. Kessler to Deterding, Mar. 25, 1929 (telegram), Shell Archives. On Gulf Oil plans and problems, see Wilkins, *Maturing*, 119–120, and Daniel Yergin, *The Prize* (New York: Simon & Schuster, 1991), 282–283, 292–295.

323. Andrew Agnew to H. W. Cole, May 7, 1929, quoted in McBeth, *British Oil Policy*, 121–122.

324. W. C. Teagle to Deterding, June 20, 1929; see also van Eck to Deterding, July 17, 1929; and R. Jacobson to F. Godber, July 18, 1929, Shell Archives.

325. Royal Dutch Company, *Annual Report 1929*, 25.

326. Beaton, *Enterprise in Oil*, 698. (At this time there were forty-eight states; Alaska and Hawaii did not become states until 1959.)

327. Royal Dutch Company, *Annual Report 1929*, 25. This supplemented other earlier financing in New York markets. See Beaton, *Enterprise in Oil*, 360.

328. The 1930 figures are in Chandler, *Scale and Scope*, 646. For the four American companies, these asset figures probably include at least some of their international business. For Shell Union, the stated assets were exclusively those in the United States.

329. As my third volume will show, the 1920 legislation—still on the books—would be invoked against Kuwait Petroleum Company's U.S. affiliate in 1982. Then it would take a mere three years before the decision was reversed and Kuwait Petroleum Company's affiliate, Santa Fe International Corp., would be permitted to lease public lands. Leroy D. Laney, "The Impact of U.S. Laws on Foreign Direct Investment," *The Annals,* 516 (July 1991): 146n.4. Periodically, in the interim, issues related to the 1920 law would arise, but not until the Santa Fe International Corp. case did the restrictions again assume major significance. See U.S. House, Committee on Government Operations, Subcommittee on Commerce, Consumer and Monetary Affairs, *Federal Response to OPEC Country Investments* (pt. 2), 97th Cong., 1st sess. (1982), 536–545.

330. Henri Deterding, *An International Oilman* (London: Harper & Bros., 1934), 72. The two men first met in 1907. Between that time and 1928, there had been far from peace and harmony between Standard Oil of New Jersey and Royal Dutch Shell.

331. *Moody's 1929,* 809, on the *Toronto* refineries; Bliss, *Northern Enterprise,* 519 (on the U.S. ones).

332. Marshall, Southard, and Taylor, *Canadian-American Industry,* 180–182; see confirmatory material in *Moody's 1929,* 809.

333. In 1927, the Canadian firm Clear Vision Pump Company changed its name to Service Station Equipment Ltd. (SSEL); the next year, it acquired the large Bennett Pump Corporation, Muskegon, Michigan, and also the Delaware-incorporated sales firm Service Station Equipment Co. In 1929, British American and SSEL shared the same president (A. L. Ellsworth); British American was said to be "interested in" this supplier of service station gasoline pumps and other equipment. Marshall, Southard, and Taylor, *Canadian-American Industry,* 180–181; *Moody's 1929,* 809, 1743. (Ellsworth founded British American in 1906; Bliss, *Northern Enterprise,* 516.)

334. Swaine, *Cravath Firm,* II, 433; Giddens, *Standard Oil Company (Indiana),* 240–244, 246, 248.

335. J. H. Bamberg, *The History of the British Petroleum Co., Vol. 2: The Anglo-Iranian Years, 1928–1954* (Cambridge: Cambridge University Press, 1994), 273, 113.

336. Ferrier, *History of the British Petroleum Co.,* I, 549.

337. I would emphasize the oil companies already in the United States and the management of Anglo-Persian's reluctance to compete. Diane Olien has suggested to me (March 1995) that the anti-British sentiment in the United States might be a more valid reason. For a perceptive study of American "anglophobia" that covers the 1920s, see John E. Moser, *Twisting the Lion's Tail: American Anglophobia between the World Wars* (New York: New York University Press, 1999). Moser, like others, points to the ebbs and flows and the ambiguities in U.S.-British relationships. As I read the material, anglophobia was quite subdued and "latent" in the late 1920s.

338. Bamberg, *History of the British Petroleum Co.,* II, 215.

339. In 1929 U.S. oil production was just over 1 billion barrels; Venezuela, in second place, produced 137.5 million barrels; the Soviet Union was in third place with 100.6 million barrels. American Petroleum Institute, *Petroleum Facts and Figures,* 548–556.

340. Virtually all the very sizable inward foreign investments were portfolio ones. Foreign individuals and institutions (investment trusts, holding companies, insurance companies, for example) acquired major holdings in individual public utilities; their interests were, however, passive, financial ones; they did not seek to operate the utility, to staff it, to sell equipment to it, or to link it up with other networks. Often, however, the portfolio investors did have special expertise in utilities investments. By contrast, American public utilities were participants in huge outward FDI. On U.S. electric power enterprises abroad, see Hausman and Neufeld, "U.S. Foreign Direct Investment in Electrical

Utilities," 361–390, and Wilkins, *Maturing,* 129–134. On telephone services, International Telephone and Telegraph had major outward FDI.

341. Mark Evan Mason, "The Development of United States Enterprise in Japan," Ph.D. diss., Harvard University, 1988, 170–171 (on Morimura Brothers and IBM).

342. Bliss, *Northern Enterprise,* 405; Bliss, *Canadian Millionaire,* 437; and Marshall, Southard, and Taylor, *Canadian-American Industry,* 186, 215 (Loblaw); Marshall, Southard, and Taylor, *Canadian-American Industry,* 184, 215–216, and Bliss, *Northern Enterprise,* 405 (Honey Dew and Laura Secord).

343. *Rubber Age,* 27 (Sept. 10, 1930): 602; Thomas J. Bata, *Bata* (Toronto: Stoddart, 1990), 144, dates the U.S. shoe stores to "the early 1930s"; it is possible, but doubtful, that the first Bata store was opened in the United States in 1930; I think they dated from the late 1920s. Office of Alien Property Custodian, *Annual Report 1943–1944,* 83–84 (on Yamanaka and Co.)

344. Wilkins, "Charles Pathé's American Business," 139–144. After 1921, Pathé Cinéma's role in America had been minimal; after 1929, it was nonexistent.

345. Howard T. Lewis, *The Motion Picture Industry* (New York: D. Van Nostrand, 1933), 423, 403. At the end of 1929, Gaumont-British Corporation was reported to have come under American control. *New York Times,* Dec. 8, 1929.

346. Wilkins, *History,* 536–546.

347. Ibid., 544, 907; T. A. Wise, *Peat, Marwick, Mitchell & Co. 85 Years* (n.p.: Peat, Marwick, Mitchell & Co., 1982), 14–15.

348. Compare Tables 1.10 and 5.3.

349. An exception was Prudential Assurance, whose American subsidiary in December 1923 had cut back its capital; it did only fire reinsurance in America.

350. According to Clayton, *British Insurance,* 155, the most profitable market for British insurers of automobiles was the United States.

351. Based on *Best's Insurance Reports, Fire and Marine, 1930* and *Best's Insurance Reports, Casualty, Surety, Miscellaneous, 1930/31.* As an example of the surge of activities, "Phoenix nearly doubled its commitment to the US market between the three-year periods 1922–1924 and 1925–1927"; in 1927, its U.S. business represented 58 percent of the entire group's business; in 1928, Phoenix Assurance's U.S. subsidiaries employed 1,300 individuals. Trebilcock, *Phoenix Assurance,* 570–571, 724, 641. Although in 1919 there had been "the fusion of the capital stock" of Royal Insurance Co., Ltd. (Liverpool) and Liverpool & London & Globe (Liverpool), each company had continued to operate independently in the United States. Effective October 1, 1929, their U.S. branches had been placed under joint management. *Best's Insurance Reports, Fire and Marine, 1930,* 390.

352. *Best's Insurance Reports, Fire and Marine, 1930,* 1169–1170.

353. At origin the Hamburg American Insurance Company had four directors from the firm H. Mutzenbecher, Jr., Hamburg. By 1929, its directors included a representative from J. Henry Schroder Banking Corp., a partner of Hallgarten & Co. (the American securities broker, long connected in German business), and Julius P. Meyer (of the Hamburg-American shipping line). *Best's Insurance Reports, Fire and Marine, 1929,* 303–304.

354. On Munich Reinsurance's pre–World War I business, see Wilkins, *History,* 534. It was the most important German insurance company in the United States in 1914.

355. *Best's Insurance Reports, Fire and Marine, 1930,* 573–574, revealed that the stock of Pilot Reinsurance was "very closely held," that Schreiner was "well known" (and his prewar management of the U.S. branch of Munich Reinsurance), and gave the background of Vice-President A. F. Sadler (who prior to the war was with the Munich Reinsurance at its London Office and then in Hartford, Connecticut) and of G. Aschermann (vice-president and treasurer, who before the First World War was secretary of the U.S.

branch of the Hamburg-Bremen Insurance Co.). On Schreiner's birthplace as Germany, see Office of Alien Property Custodian, *Annual Report for Year-ending June 30, 1945,* 93–96. I excluded Pilot Reinsurance from Table 5.3 because nothing in *Best's Insurance Reports* confirmed foreign ownership, and the table was based on those reports. For the 1925 ownership, see Carl Schreiner to Wilhelm Kisskalt, Mar. 24, 1925, and Schreiner to Kisskalt, Apr. 21, 1925, A-2.3, 1fd, Nr. 164, Munich Reinsurance Company Archives, Munich. I am indebted to Gerald Feldman for these documents. (Kisskalt was general director of Munich Reinsurance Co. at the time of the correspondence.) Munich Reinsurance and Allianz were associated companies; Munich Reinsurance had founded Union Reinsurance in 1923; Assicurazioni Generali often participated with Munich Reinsurance in joint ventures. Gerald Feldman, *Allianz* (Cambridge: Cambridge University Press, 2001), esp. 281, 431.

356. *Best's Insurance Reports, Fire and Marine, 1930.*

357. French premiums were down, with fewer French participants. Canadian premiums dropped because one large company, British American Assurance Company, Toronto, Canada, passed from Canadian to U.S. control. *Best's Insurance Reports, Fire and Marine, 1930,* 93 (in 1926 Crum & Foster acquired a substantial interest in this company). I do not think including Pilot Reinsurance and others that might be neglected would make a substantial difference in these conclusions.

358. Trebilcock points out that the term "accident" in Britain was the same as "casualty" in the United States. Trebilcock, *Phoenix Assurance,* 444. For the bad experiences that Phoenix had with London Guarantee and Accident in the United States in the 1920s, see ibid., 442–444, 459–468. Trebilcock writes that "the acquisition of London Guarantee & Accident (LGA) in 1922 was one of the worst things to happen to the Phoenix in the twentieth century." Ibid., 442. The main business of LGA was in the United States.

359. Clayton, *British Insurance,* 153, makes the point that diversification by the large British insurers made them better able to handle risks. The diversification was in different branches of insurance as well as geographic. The experiences related by Trebilcock on Phoenix do not seem to conform to this generalization.

360. *Best's Insurance Reports, Casualty, 1930/31,* 533, 614.

361. *Best's Insurance Reports, Life Insurance.*

362. T. B. Macaulay to G. D. Finlayson, Nov. 30, 1927, Macaulay letterbooks, Sun Life Archives.

363. Safford, "The United States Merchant Marine in Foreign Trade," 110–111; Sturmey, *British Shipping,* 130; and De La Pedraja, *The Rise and Decline of U.S. Merchant Shipping,* 68.

364. Sturmey, *British Shipping,* 130–131.

365. Count Bernstorff, *Memoirs* (New York: Random House, 1936), 101.

366. G. R. S. Harris, *Germany's Foreign Indebtedness* (London: Oxford University Press, 1935), 117.

367. Abramson, *Spanning the Century,* 138.

368. See Norddeutscher Lloyd, *Bericht* 1923–1929, and Harris, *Germany's Foreign Indebtedness.* 118.

369. Norddeutscher Lloyd, *Bericht* 1927, 1928, 1929.

370. Keiichiro Nakagawa, "Japanese Shipping," in *Business History of Shipping,* ed. Tsunehiko Yui and Keiichiro Nakagawa (Tokyo: University of Tokyo Press, 1985), 9–15.

371. New York State, Banking Department, *Annual Reports 1923–1929;* on the problems of the Union Bank of Canada, see Denison, *Canada's First Bank,* II, 348.

372. Beckhart, *New York Money Market,* III, 189–191. "Short loans" were loans not exceeding thirty days.

373. According to Duncan McDowall, historian of the Royal Bank of Canada, Mar. 22, 1991. On the relative size of the Royal Bank (as measured by domestic assets),

see James L. Dairoch, "Global Competitiveness," *Business History*, 34 (July 1992): 158. In 1925, the Royal Bank of Canada acquired from the U.S.-owned Bank of Central and South America (formed in 1922) most of the latter's branches in Colombia, Venezuela, Costa Rica, and Peru, which it converted into branches of the Royal Bank of Canada. Phelps, *Foreign Expansion of American Banks*, 159–160.

374. Quigley, "Bank of Nova Scotia," 797–838.

375. The best work on all these banks is Jones, *British Multinational Banking*.

376. On the Bank of Canton, see Frank M. Tamagna, *Banking and Finance in China* (New York: Institute of Pacific Relations, 1942), 41.

377. P. L. Cottrell with C. J. Stone, "Credits, and Deposits to Finance Credits," in *European Industry and Banking Between the Wars*, ed. P. L. Cottrell, Håkan Lindgren, and Alice Teichova (Leicester: Leicester University Press, 1992), 66. The Brussels, London, and Paris branches of the Belgian-headquartered bank also had dollar-denominated deposits with the Vienna bank. The Banque Belge pour l'Etranger, Brussels, was a subsidiary of Société Générale de Belgique. Van der Wee and Verbreyt, *Generale Bank*, 103, 113, 130, 153–160, 192, 217.

378. *Moody's Banks 1929*, 2333.

379. Phelps, *Foreign Expansion of American Banks*, 201. The dates when the trust companies were established are from Gretchen Marlatt, Banking Department, Albany, N.Y., to Wilkins, Aug. 1, 1983; http://banking.state.ny.us/histba.txt indicates that Banco di Sicilia Trust Co., New York, which in June 1927 acquired the Security State Bank and in August 1928 the Windsor State Bank, changed its name in September 1929 to the Bank of Sicily Trust Co.

380. See 1932 list in Gianni Toniolo, *One Hundred Years, 1894–1994: A Short History of the Banca Commerciale Italiana* (Milan: BCI, 1994), 62 (I feel certain these offices would have been opened by 1929).

381. *Moody's Public Utilities 1929*, 998–999; Toniolo, *One Hundred Years*, 61, has a picture of a BCI business delegation to the United States in 1928; this was probably in connection with the Italian Superpower issue. See ibid., 70.

382. Avram, *Rayon Industry*, 175; for BCI's associations in Italy with Chatillon, see Toniolo, *One Hundred Years*, 57.

383. *Moody's Banks 1931*, 1190. The trust company's assets at year end 1929 were $2.7 million. Richard Roberts, *Schroders*, 228, writes that the subsidiary received "a commercial banking charter from the state of New York and became a member of the Federal Reserve System. The trust company was able to take deposits and offered services such as chequing accounts and trusteeships, stock transfer agencies, registrarships and escrows, as well as conducting investment accounts for individuals."

384. Roberts, *Schroders*, 213, 221–238, 129 (for background on Czarnikow-Rionda).

385. *Moody's Banks 1929*, 2331. The other New York correspondents of the State Bank of the U.S.S.R. listed in *Moody's* were Equitable Trust Co., Chase National Bank, Irving Trust Co., and National City Bank, all American banking institutions.

386. I use "quasi-foreign" for want of a better term. By quasi-foreign I mean firms (financial institutions) that had some, but not controlling, foreign ownership, others that had foreign-based partners, and still others partially "controlled" from abroad (i.e., with close interrelationships with a foreign firm).

387. Marshall, Southard, and Taylor, *Canadian-American Industry*, 175 (this is as of 1935, but I am sure these offices existed in 1929). According to the Royal Bank of Canada website (accessed Aug. 6, 2003). Dominion Securities Corporation, New York, was incorporated in April 1929.

388. *Fortune*, Aug. 1931, 79, 82, and testimony of James Speyer, U.S. Senate, Committee on Finance, *Sale of Foreign Bonds, Hearings*, 72nd Cong., 1st sess. (1932), pt. 2, 605–606. It is not clear when in the 1920s the Germans resumed their partnership in the American

firm. In March 1925, the J. Henry Schroder Banking Corporation had moved its offices to 27 Pine Street, which its historian describes as a "very convenient location for calling on friends: the International Acceptance Bank was at 29–31; Speyer & Co. at 24–26." Roberts, *Schroders*, 225. This cluster of bankers (located in the Wall Street vicinity) worked closely together in lending to Germany and other central European countries. All had foreign participation in the American firms.

389. The American Lazard Frères had its start in 1847, founded by three brothers who had emigrated to the United States from France. Ultimately three Lazard banks emerged—New York (Lazard Frères), Paris (Lazard Frères et Cie.), and London (Lazard Brothers & Co.); the three worked in tandem. Wilkins, *History*, 850n.43. By the eve of the First World War, each bank had evolved into an "independently managed entity," linked by "a common ownership." During the war that common ownership was partially severed when "the Bank of England forced Lazard [New York] to sell the London bank to British interests," to the Cowdray group. J. A. Spender, *Weetman Pearson* (London: Cassell & Co., 1930), 249, reports that Lord Cowdray interests acquired an *equal* stake with the French house in Lazard Brothers & Co.; Sir Robert Kindersley, representing the Cowdray group, took over the management. On the other hand, the common ownership of Lazard New York and Paris continued. By 1925, the main bridge between the New York and Paris houses was David David-Weill, who had been raised in the United States but had moved to Paris to run the Paris bank. The latter bank was a vibrant entity, considered in the mid-1920s by fellow bankers to be "the most capable exchange people on the continent." David David-Weill's son, Pierre David-Weill, followed his father as a principal in the French firm. From 1926 through 1939, he visited the United States for at least one or two months a year. During this period (and indeed since 1916), the New York Lazard Frères was run by Frank Altschul, the son of a longtime Lazard Frères (U.S.) employee. The New York bank was a bond house, handling new foreign issues and other matters in cooperation with the French bank. It appears that Frank Altschul in the many years that he ran the New York house never had "voting control." Altschul's son believed that "the power had always remained in the hands of the David-Weill family—as the sole blood relations of the Lazards still in the banking empire"; it is not clear whether this retrospective view of Altshul's son is accurate. In the 1920s, in the United States Frank Altschul seems to have had a great deal of independence within the New York house; also in the 1920s there were still Lazards active in the French bank. Reich, *Financier*, 27–28, 210, 37–41, and Stephen A. Schuker, *The End of French Predominance in Europe* (Chapel Hill: University of North Carolina Press, 1976), 104–105, 113–114, 130.

390. Fujimoto Securities Co. was an affiliate of Fujimoto Bill Broker Bank, Osaka.

391. Ownership material is based on IAB shareholder records in the Chase Manhattan Bank Archives. Klebaner, "Paul M. Warburg," 448 (gives the profits).

392. IAB, in turn, controlled a trust company, International Acceptance Trust Co., New York, formed March 9, 1926. *Moody's Banks 1929*, 1297. I did not include this in the six trust companies listed earlier in this chapter, since that group included only those trust companies wholly foreign owned by a foreign bank or financial institution.

393. "Strictly Confidential": International Acceptance Bank, Annual Report, Jan. 20, 1925, 11, in 120.0, Strong Papers, FRBNY; see also Swaine, *Cravath Firm*, II, 307, and Sobel, *Life and Times of Dillon Read*, 89.

394. P. L. Cottrell, "Aspects of Western Equity Investment in the Banking Systems of East Central Europe," in *International Business and Central Europe 1918–1939*, ed. Alice Teichova and P. L. Cottrell (New York: St. Martin's Press, 1983), 324, and Roberts, *Schroders*, 233, 235.

395. Alice Teichova found data on this in the National Archives, Paris, Min. Fin. f30627 (letter of May 28, 1929). Teichova to Wilkins, June 22, 1981. Harriman developed many

associations in central European finance. Abramson, *Spanning the Century,* chaps. 5, 6, and 8.

396. *Moody's Banks 1928,* 2720; Abramson, *Spanning the Century,* 139; James P. Warburg, Oral History Reminiscences, p. 394, Oral History Collection, Columbia University Library. The American Warburgs were involved in Kuhn, Loeb, the banker for E. H. Harriman (Averell's father, who died in 1909); in Germany, Max Warburg had in 1920–1923 aided Harriman in his earlier arrangements with the Hamburg-American Line.

397. Denison, *Canada's First Bank,* II, 351.

398. On all these institutions, see Beckhart, *New York Money Market,* III, 302–305. On IAB's acceptance business, see Klebaner, "Paul M. Warburg," 448; on Schroder's, see Roberts, *Schroders,* 221, 225–229; on Kidder Peabody Acceptance, see Carosso, *More Than a Century,* 60–61, 63. On the New York agency of Yokohama Specie Bank, see Hiroaki Yamazaki, "The Yokohama Specie Bank," in *Finance and Financiers in European History,* ed. Youssef Cassis (Cambridge: Cambridge University Press, 1992), 394. See also American Acceptance Council, *Acceptance Bulletin,* Jan. 1930, 16–17.

399. American Acceptance Council, *Acceptance Bulletin,* Mar. 1930, 7–9, has wonderful figures on foreign short-term holdings in the United States.

400. Federal Reserve Board, Examiners Report on International Acceptance Bank, as of June 11, 1927, in Merged Banks—Bank of the Manhattan Co.—International Acceptance Bank, RG 3, Chase Manhattan Bank Archives (CMBA), New York.

401. Federal Reserve Board, Examiners Report on International Acceptance Bank, as of June 16, 1928, in ibid.

402. *Moody's Banks 1929,* 2308. Hugo Schmidt, on his release from jail after the Armistice, once again had taken up his position as the Deutsche Bank's man in New York, and during the 1920s he continued to serve in that role. See Gall et al., *Deutsche Bank,* 226.

403. See interrogation of Carl Goetz, Jan. 10, 1946, NI-836, RG 238, T301, Reel 8, National Archives. On Henry Nathan of Dresdner Bank, see Harold James, "Banks and Bankers," in Cassis, ed., *Finance and Financiers,* 266 (James describes him as one of the leading Weimar bankers).

404. Data from Arnhold and S. Bleichroeder, Inc., New York, Nov. 9, 1992. See also Emden, *Money Powers,* 254. The Arnhold firm would in Germany in 1931 for all practical purposes merge with S. Bleichroeder, Berlin.

405. *Moody's Banks 1929,* 2307; U.S. Senate, Committee on Banking and Currency, *Stock Exchange Practices, Hearings,* 73rd Cong., 1st sess. (1933), pt. 3, 1015. The Dreyfus representative was Fernand Leval. Both the bank and the grain trading house were controlled by the Louis-Dreyfus family. On the bank, see J. S. G. Wilson, *French Banking Structure and Credit Policy* (Cambridge, Mass.: Harvard University Press, 1957), 143; on the relationship between the two at a much later date, see Peter Newman, *The Bronfman Dynasty* (Toronto: McClelland & Stewart, 1978), 172, and also 1940 data in "Assets in the US of America of Messrs Louis Dreyfus & Co." FO 371/24263, Public Record Office, London.

406. A. S. J. Baster, *The International Banks* (1935; rpt. New York: Arno Press, 1977), 22. He was writing in 1934, but this was equally true in the late 1920s.

407. *Moody's Banks 1929,* 2310 (Dresdner), 2310 (Disconto-Gesellschaft), 1239 (Danat Bank); Wilkins, *History,* 480 (Hallgarten-Darmstädter Bank connections). In October 1929 the Deutsche Bank and the Disconto-Gesellschaft would merge (in Germany). *Moody's Banks—1931,* 2092. On the merger, see Gall et al., *Deutsche Bank,* 234–235.

408. Based on my own tabulations of data in *Moody's Banks 1929.*

409. *Moody's Banks 1929,* 1209–1287, 2281–2347.

410. The assets of the Bank of the Manhattan Company at year end 1928 were $538 million compared with $133 million of IAB. But the larger bank had in 1928 net profits of $3.4 million compared with IAB's net profits of $2.1 million. Ibid., 1296–1297.

411. The transaction was complicated. In 1929, the Bank of the Manhattan Company took over the assets of IAB. See data in Merged Banks—Bank of the Manhattan Co.—International Acceptance Bank, RG 3, CMBA. For the plan that would be consummated, see Paul M. Warburg and F. Abbot Goodhue, IAB, to Holders of "Special Stock" in IAB, Dec. 21, 1928, James P. Warburg Papers, Box 1, John F. Kennedy Library, Boston. For the reasons behind the merger, I have found helpful Warburg, *Long Road Home,* 87–88, and Rosenbaum and Sherman, *M. M. Warburg,* 140, as well as data in the various archives that I have used.

412. Data in CMBA; *Moody's Banks 1929,* 1295–1297, 2873. The International Manhattan Co. was formed in March 1929.

413. James P. Warburg to Stephen Baker and J. Stewart Baker, Dec. 18, 1928, Warburg Papers, Box 1. See Chapter 3 on the names of the foreign banks involved in 1922. The foreign stock-holding banks were not identical through the years. Thus, M. M. Warburg & Co., Hamburg, did not become a shareholder until 1925. By the end of the 1920s, there were two Austrian banks involved (both from Vienna): S. M. von Rothschild and Österreichische Creditanstalt für Handel & Gewerbe; neither was a shareholder in 1922. The Bank of Montreal, a stockholder in 1922, was no longer one in the late 1920s. Number and percentage based on complete IAB shareholder records, as of December 31, 1928, in CMBA.

414. Paul M. Warburg and F. Abbot Goodhue, International Acceptance Bank, to Holders of "Special Stock" in IAB, Dec. 21, 1928, Warburg Papers, Box 1; see also complete data on these transactions in Corporate Documentation, Letters of Assent, Bank of the Manhattan Company, RG 1, CMBA.

415. *Moody's Banks 1931,* 1210–1211, on the transactions; see also Bauer, *Swiss Bank Corporation, 1872–1972,* 248.

416. The Manhattan Company became the holding company that would own the stock in the constituent companies. Klebaner, "Paul M. Warburg," 449, gives December 10, 1929, as the date Warburg became chairman of The Manhattan Company. Another publication suggests a date in November for the restructuring. The domestic bank (the operations of the old Bank of the Manhattan Company) became The Bank of the Manhattan Trust Co., with Stephen Baker as chairman of the board and his son J. Stewart Baker as president; the other subsidiaries were the International Acceptance Bank and the International Manhattan Co. Manhattan Co., *"Manna-Hatin" The Story of New York* (New York: Manhattan Co., 1929), 269.

417. The Bank of the Manhattan Company had been chartered under New York State law in 1799. For its earlier international connections, see Wilkins, *History,* 62, 84, 655n.95 (on the Marquis of Carmarthan in the 1830s); 58, 650n.50, 75 (with the Rothschilds); 665n.229 (1853 data); and 848 (London City and Midland Bank linkage in 1909). These were scattered and of little consequence. The Bank of the Manhattan Company's forte was domestic, and Wilson, *Chase,* 59, emphasizes how in the 1920s the Manhattan Bank had expanded in New York City, branching into all five boroughs and acquiring in the process many existing banks. For its numerous domestic acquisitions, see *Moody's Banks 1929,* 1295–1296, and data in CMBA. With its merger with IAB, its London Rothschild connection was briefly revived (N. M. Rothschild was one of the many shareholder banks in IAB that became a shareholder in The Manhattan Company).

418. Carosso, *Investment Banking,* 316. In September 1929, Kidder, Peabody's New York office employed 300, while its "main" office in Boston had only 170 employees. Ibid.

419. Carosso, *More Than a Century,* 61.

420. Schull and Gibson, *Scotiabank Story,* 310.

421. *Moody's Banks 1929,* 1214.

422. See Table 5 in Giandomenico Piluso, "The Major Italian Banks in South America: Strategies, Markets, and Organization," unpublished paper, 1993, and Toniolo, *One Hun-*

dred Years, 64–65. The bonds of Italian Superpower Corporation were listed on the Boston Stock Exchange. See *Moody's Public Utilities 1929,* 999.

423. *Rand McNally's Bank Directory 1929,* 361. The Chicago branch of the Bank of Montreal was the continuation of the branch opened in 1871, while the Chicago branch of the Bank of Nova Scotia had opened in 1892. The Banco di Napoli had been set up in Chicago in 1920. James, *Growth of Chicago Banks,* II, 1171, 1173.

424. The only one mentioned in Chapter 3 as in San Francisco that is not included here was the Commercial Bank of Spanish America, which lasted on the West Coast until 1926, when its parent was absorbed by the Anglo–South American Bank Ltd. See Superintendent of Banks (California), *Annual Report 1926,* where it is included, and the 1927 report, where it was not included. L. S. Pressnell and John Orbell, *A Guide to the Historical Records of British Banking* (New York: St. Martin's Press, 1985), 30 (on Anglo–South American's role). The Bank of Montreal had closed its Spokane branch in 1924. Phelps, *Foreign Expansion of American Banks,* 202, lists the Canton Bank, San Francisco, as controlled by the Oriental Commercial Bank, Ltd., Hong Kong. This appears to be a mistake. The Canton Bank was established by *resident* Chinese in San Francisco in 1907. (The Canton Bank is not to be confused with the Bank of Canton, San Francisco, with which it was not connected and which was owned by its namesake in Hong Kong.) The Canton Bank served for almost two decades as the principal banking house for about 100,000 Chinese residents of the United States and Mexico. On July 19, 1926, it was closed by the California superintendent of banks on account of losses incurred in its foreign exchange operations. The Oriental Commercial Bank, Ltd., Hong Kong, upon which the Canton Bank wrote its exchange, had failed on June 10, 1926. On the Canton Bank and its failure, see Cross, *Financing an Empire,* II, 696, and Superintendent of Banks (California), *Annual Report 1927,* xxxvii. A. P. Giannini's Bank of Italy (the predecessor to the Bank of America) was an American bank, the name notwithstanding.

425. A. St. L. Trigge, *A History of the Canadian Bank of Commerce, Vol. 3 (1919–1930* (Toronto: Canadian Bank of Commerce, 1934), 405.

426. Superintendent of Banks (California), *Annual Reports.*

427. Frank H. H. King, *The Hongkong Bank between the Wars and the Bank Interned, 1919–1945. The History of the Hongkong and Shanghai Banking Corporation-Vol. III* (Cambridge: Cambridge University Press, 1988), 81.

428. Cross, *Financing an Empire,* III, 266–267.

429. *Van Oss' Effectenboek 1929; Van Oss' Effectenboek 1934;* Fahey, "When the Dutch Owned Spokane," 2–10, on the Dutch in pre–World War I Spokane, and ibid., 10, on the Northwestern & Pacific Hypotheekbank in Spokane in the interwar years. The urban lending in Spokane was exceptional; most of these banks lent in rural communities. In the 1920s, the Spokane lending was ongoing, and there were no significant new foreign investments, yet the relative importance of Spokane is indicated in Table 5.7. Four of the eight mortgage banks had Spokane as their American "center."

430. See data on Films Z-G2, Reel 55 (SAMC) and Z-G1, Reel 284 (TLMC), Bancroft Library Archives, University of California, Berkeley. The Texas Land and Mortgage Company was London based, but Scottish owned and controlled.

431. Annual Reports, Film Z-G2, Reel 55, Bancroft Library. The disbursements indicated a direct payment to run the American business.

432. Jackson, *Enterprising Scot,* 282.

433. Gilbert, *History of Investment Trusts,* 108.

434. Jackson, *Enterprising Scot,* 282–283.

435. Glasgow, *Scottish Investment Trust Companies,* 60. British Assets Trust, Ltd., Edinburgh, owned 95 percent of the Second British Assets Trust. Ibid., 80. In 1975, this company would be renamed Edinburgh American Assets, reflecting the renewed interest in

American investments. John Scott and Michael Hughes, *The Anatomy of Scottish Capital* (London: Croom Helm, 1980), 181. For more on the Edinburgh American Land Mortgage Co. Ltd. and the Second British Assets Trust, see data in UGD 228 9/1/1 and 3/1/1, University of Glasgow Library, Glasgow. This archives contains substantial material on Scottish mortgage lenders in the United States. See, for example, its collection (UGD 228 5/1/75ff) on Investors Mortgage Security Co. Ltd., which company in the mid-1920s had agencies to provide mortgages in Texas (Paris, San Antonio, Fort Worth, Waco, and Dallas); in Missouri (Kansas City); in Georgia (Macon and Augusta); and in Oregon (Portland). It also invested in American securities and had decided to change over to a pure investment trust business (Glasgow, *Scottish Investment Trust Companies,* 96, says this decision was made in 1922.) In 1928, the Scottish Realisation Trust Ltd. was established (UGD 228 7/1/1). It purchased from Investors Mortgage Security Co. Ltd. the latter's U.S. and (far smaller Canadian) mortgage and real estate holdings and set out to liquidate them. Investors Mortgage Security Co. remained involved in American securities, as an investment trust.

436. Jackson, *Enterprising Scot,* 280.

437. McFarlane, "British Agricultural Investments in the Dakotas," 120, and Larry A. McFarlane, "British Investment in Midwestern farm Mortgages and Land, 1875–1900: Iowa and Kansas," *Agricultural History,* 47 (Jan. 1974): 190. The American "agent" seems to have supervised the U.S. business. The "Iowa" name was part of history; by the 1920s, the firm did little or no mortgage lending in Iowa. Wake, *Kleinwort Benson,* has nothing on the Benson's Iowa business in the post–World War I years. In the 1920s, Robert Benson & Co. was involved in investment trusts and American securities and was still considered in its "traditional role" as an "Anglo-American" house (see Wake, *Kleinwort Benson,* 291). Robert ("Robin") Benson, who in the 1880s had been enthusiastic about Iowa land, died on April 4, 1929; historian Wake writes that with his death, "the firm finally turned its back on the nineteenth century to face the twentieth." Ibid., 169 (for Robin and Iowa land) and 285 (for the quotation).

438. RG 131, in the National Archives, which contains the records of the APC for the First World War, covers the period 1917 (from the APC's foundation) to 1957. Even after the APC came to an end in 1934, there remained unsettled issues. The Francis Garvan Papers, in Laramie, Wyoming, contain substantial material on the litigation during the 1920s. The litigation over The Chemical Foundation came to a close in 1926.

439. *Bankers Magazine,* 108 (Mar. 1924): 346–347 (lack of hospitality). Phelps, *Foreign Expansion of American Banks,* 208, wrote in 1927 that "the opposition to bills seeking to ameliorate the condition of agencies of foreign banks in New York seems to come primarily from the numerous small bankers who fear an invasion of great foreign banks. . . . It would seem that the [domestic] banking organizations of New York and California are strongly enough developed to look with composure upon the competition of fully empowered branches of foreign banks, especially if such branches were limited to the cities of New York, San Francisco, and Los Angeles. And, as far as the safeguarding of the interests of American depositors is concerned, the branches of foreign banks may be so regulated and supervised as to leave no greater risk of loss than is present in the case of American banking establishments." But no such "hospitable" bills were passed in the 1920s.

440. *Bankers Magazine,* 108 (Mar. 1924): 346–347, and Phelps, *Foreign Expansion of American Banks,* 208, for discussion of "reciprocity" considerations.

441. For Phoenix Assurance officials' experience with American state regulations in the late 1920s, see Trebilcock, *Phoenix Assurance,* 461–462, 466, 579–580. In 1927, Massachusetts introduced compulsory liability insurance for all drivers. This denied insurers the ability to select for quality. By 1928, as a consequence, the British Phoenix Assurance

got out of this business. But the measure did not discriminate against out-of-country companies; it applied to American as well as non-American insurers—as did a mass of other regulations. See ibid., 679, for the effect on Phoenix Assurance.

442. The Air Commerce Act is 44 Stat. 568 (May 20, 1926). See also Vagts, "Corporate Alien," 1519–1520.

443. U.S. Department of Commerce, *Foreign Direct Investment in the United States* 9 vols. (Washington, D.C., 1976), VII, K-44, K-272 (henceforth cited as *FDIUS–1976*). Vagts, "Corporate Alien," 1497–1508, and De la Pedraja, *Rise and Decline of U.S. Merchant Shipping*, 98, 110–111.

444. William A. M. Burden, *The Struggle for Airways in Latin America* (New York: Council on Foreign Relations, 1943), 22–27.

445. 44 U.S. Stat. 780, 787 (July 2, 1926); U.S. House, Committee on Military Affairs, HR 1395, 69th Cong., 1st sess. (June 7, 1926), and *FDIUS–1976*, VII, K-25–27.

446. In a *New York Times* section on aviation, Dec. 16, 1928, Fokker (described as "Designer, Fokker Aircraft Corp.") wrote that two years earlier he had resolved to become a U.S. citizen and devote "the remainder of my career to the advancement of the aeronautical industry here." Fokker, however, kept his Dutch factory and by 1931 had not yet become a naturalized American. *New York Times*, June 20, 1931. See also Dierikx, *Fokker*, 117, 126–127. Clearly, Fokker's 1926 plan to become a U.S. citizen was based on this legislation. His holdings in the sequence of Fokker companies do not seem to have exceeded the 25 percent level. Fokker was not on the board of directors of Fokker Aircraft Corp.

447. 44 U.S. Stat. 1162, 1167 (Feb. 23, 1927). An excellent discussion of the foreign ownership restrictions in the Radio Act of 1927 is in Sidak, *Foreign Investment*, 60–65.

448. Letter of the Secretary of Navy, Mar. 22, 1932, included in *FDIUS–1976*, VII, K-101, K-301n.13. This law was a change from the prewar legislation. See Wilkins, *History*, 924n.188, on the Radio Act of 1912. Nothing in the 1912 act had dealt with ownership of corporations set up in the United States. C. Joseph Pusateri, *A History of American Business*, 2nd ed. (Arlington Heights, Ill.: Harland Davidson, 1988), 272, notes that in April 1927, the Columbia Phonograph Broadcasting System (later renamed Columbia Broadcasting System [CBS]) was formed, with "primary financial support from the Columbia [Phonograph] Record Company." Pusateri continues, "the next year, for unexplained reasons" the Columbia Phonograph company pulled out, and William S. Paley became the principal sponsor. Undoubtedly, the reason lay in the explicit statement in the Radio Act of 1927 on foreign ownership and the fact that Columbia Phonograph company was at that time British controlled.

449. Similar legislation by Canadians (and other nationalities) to regulate foreign-owned broadcasting was frequently designed to protect national "culture." Safarian, *Multinational Enterprise and Public Policy*, 114, 125, 134, 141.

450. *Oliver American Trading Co. v. Government of Mexico*, 5 F. 2d 659 (CCA, 1924).

451. See *U.S. v. Deutsches Kalisyndikat Gesellschaft*, 31 F.2d 199 (SDNY 1929) and Brewster, *Antitrust and American Business Abroad*, 23.

452. U.S. Department of Commerce, Bureau of Foreign and Domestic Commerce, *The Balance of International Payments of the United States in 1927*, iii, 22–25, 41–45.

453. There were other circumstances in the 1920s where the percentage issue came into play; for example, U.S. government awards of contracts to build planes: the recipient company had to be 75 percent American owned. Edge Act banks had to be majority owned by U.S. citizens.

454. The U.S. Department of Commerce defined a foreign investor as a nonresident.

455. Vagts, "Corporate Alien," 1533–1534. As Vagts points out, this enabled owners to be able, for example, to let their estates pass to chosen heirs—even if the heirs were not Americans; to stop such a transfer reduced the value of the assets.

456. Vagts, "Corporate Alien," 1532. Royal Dutch Shell became eligible to lease land because Holland was called a reciprocating nation. British shareholders in the American subsidiaries persisted; Britain, however, was not yet a reciprocating country. Not until 1936 did the United States accept Great Britain as a reciprocating country.

457. Avram, *Rayon Industry,* 176.

458. While overall anticartel views were not key to the policy agenda in the late 1920s, they were evident. See, for example, U.S. Department of Commerce, Bureau of Foreign and Domestic Commerce, *The International Cartel Movement,* by Louis Domeratzky. Trade Information Bulletin 556 (Washington, D.C., 1928). Such studies got press coverage.

459. Wilkins, *History,* 579, on alien land laws. Moser, *Twisting the Lion's Tail,* 193, writes of these years, "The denunciations of British policy so commonly made by Irish- and German-Americans, northern liberals and socialists, southern populists, and midwestern progressives were directed as much toward Wall Street and Big Business as they were at the British."

460. Avery Andrews to J. B. Aug. Kessler, Feb. 26, 1926, Shell Archives, suggests the Americanization of Amerada was based on Texas alien land laws. I found nothing in the Pearson Papers to explain the 1926 divestiture. Andrews' explanation may *not* be legitimate; Lord Cowdray had earlier (in 1923) spun off the Texas business to meet Texas law; Amerada's main production was in Oklahoma. See data in Box C31, Pearson Papers. Diane Olien, an expert on the Texas oil industry, believes that anti-British sentiment continued to be strong in Texas in the late 1920s (discussion with Ms. Olien, Mar. 1995).

461. Clark and Kirwan, *The South since Appomattox,* 232–233.

462. Based on local newspaper reports.

463. See Garvan Papers, esp. material in Box 76.

464. See *New York Times,* May 5, 1929, and *Chemical Markets,* 24 (June 1929): 586, for example.

465. This was not for want of effort on the part of Garvan. See, for example, Dr. S. Isermann to F. P. Garvan, Nov. 22, 1929, Garvan Papers, Box 76.

466. Draft of letter from Francis Garvan to Charles Mitchell, W. C. Teagle, Edsel Ford, Paul M. Warburg, May, 1929, Garvan Papers, Box 76.

467. On the retention of Ivy Lee, see data on Max Ilgner, Oct. 23, 1945, in RG 238, T301, Reel 8, NI-712, p. 4, and statement of Max Ilgner, Apr. 25, 1947, in T301, Reel 51, NI-6702, pp. 1–2.

468. On Ivy Lee, see *Fortune,* Dec. 1931, 52. For a sample of Lee's writings, see Ivy Lee, "The Black Legend: Europe Indicts America," *Atlantic Monthly* 143 (May 1929): 577–588, wherein he described European criticisms of America's smug, self-centered material progress. The article called out for more responsible international involvement by the United States. Lee served in the 1920s as a publicity consultant for J. P. Morgan & Co. Chernow, *House of Morgan,* 283, 191. He would later by retained by Dillon, Read. Sobel, *Life and Times of Dillon Read,* 179–180. He provided public relations programs for Bethlehem Steel. Hessen, *Steel Titan.*

6. A Time of Anguish, October 1929–March 1933

1. *Journal of Commerce,* Aug. 13, 1929. For the enthusiasm about American securities in June and July 1929, see David Kynaston, *The City of London, vol. 3, Illusions of Gold 1914–1945* (London: Chatto & Windus, 1999), 183.

2. *New York Times,* Aug. 19, 29, 1929; Eichengreen, *Golden Fetters,* 227.

3. Recounted in *Fortune,* 8 (Sept. 1933): 32. Nancy Lisagor and Frank Lipsius, *A Law unto Itself: The Untold Story of the Law Firm Sullivan and Cromwell* (New York: William Morrow and Co., 1988), 104–105 (on the Blue Ridge Corporation). In July 1929, the board

of the Scottish American Investment Co. (a large participant in American securities) decided yields had dropped too low and started to sell American securities. Weir, *History of the Scottish American Investment Company,* 22.

4. Some of the literature suggests that the more sophisticated British investors had retreated from American securities in the summer and early fall of 1929, but Heywood Fleisig in a careful study found that from mid-1928 and in the first three quarters of 1929 there was movement of foreign moneys *to* the New York Stock Market to take advantage of the rising prices and the hope of further appreciation in values. Fleisig, *Long Term Capital Flows,* 8, 25. A historian of an experienced British firm writes that in the late summer of 1929, the partners in Kleinworts dispatched a partner to New York to liquidate their American position. He was caught in the "buy, buy, buy" atmosphere—and instead of selling he purchased added securities on behalf of the firm. Wake, *Kleinwort Benson,* 241–242.

5. On Hatry see David Fanning, "Clarence Charles Hatry," *Dictionary of Business Biography,* III, 110–114; Steven Tolliday, *Business, Banking, and Politics* (Cambridge, Mass.: Harvard University Press, 1987), 190–191, 202; and William J. Reader, *A House in the City* (London: B. T. Batsford, 1979), 146–156.

6. *Fortune,* 8 (Sept. 1933): 32. This was also the view of officials of the London Stock Exchange. See Michie, *London Stock Exchange,* 263, citing a May 15, 1930, document.

7. On the rationale for the rise in the Bank Rate, see Moggridge, *British Monetary Policy,* 137–139. For the impact, see the Federal Reserve Board, *Annual Report for 1929,* 9; Irving Fisher, *The Stock Market Crash—and After* (New York: Macmillan, 1930), 4, 229–230, 263; Francis W. Hirst, *Wall Street and Lombard Street* (New York: Macmillan, 1931), 8–9.

8. Sayers, *Bank of England,* I, 229. Moggridge put it slightly differently: he believed the Hatry collapse left Norman (governor of the Bank of England) "politically free" to raise the Bank Rate. Moggridge, *British Monetary Policy,* 138.

9. Barrie A. Wigmore, *The Crash and Its Aftermath* (Westport, Conn.: Greenwood Press, 1985), 10, describes the "pandemonium" in London on "Black Thursday," October 24, 1929; p. 13 describes the heavy foreign withdrawals on Monday, October 28, 1929; p. 15 deals with the massive Dutch and German selling on October 29. For contemporary views, see the *Washington Star,* Oct. 27, 1929, which editorialized that the stock market crash of the previous week was precipitated primarily by foreign liquidation of American securities. The *New York Times,* Tuesday, Oct. 29, 1929, had a front-page headline, "Stock Prices Slump $14,000,000,000." A subheadline read "Selling by Europeans and 'Mob Psychology' Big Factors in Second Big Break."

10. *Fortune,* 8 (Sept. 1933): 32. In a memorandum sent to Franklin Delano Roosevelt in March 1933, Morgan partner Thomas Lamont wrote, "The notorious, fraudulent Hatry failure in London was the beginning of the end of the great boom in 1929." Thomas W. Lamont to Franklin Delano Roosevelt, Mar. 27, 1933, Thomas Lamont Papers, Harvard Business School, Boston. Writing in 1935, Paul Einzig, *World Finance,* 212, agreed: "Even though the amount of British funds withdrawn was only a small percentage of the total engaged in Wall Street speculation, the shock was sufficient to bring about the long overdue slump."

11. Sayers, *Bank of England,* I, 229n (the comment was on Oct. 30, 1929).

12. The liquidation of "foreign holdings" involved the sale of "long-term" foreign investments in the United States and also the withdrawal of short-term loans extended by foreigners to New York brokers and dealers in securities. Milton Friedman and Anna Jacobson Schwartz, *A Monetary History of the United States* (Princeton, N.J.: Princeton University Press, 1963), 305n, indicates that in the two weeks before October 23, loans to brokers for the account of "others" dropped $120 million, largely as a result of

withdrawals of funds by foreigners. See also Beckhart, *New York Money Market*, III, 162, 164–165, 168–169, 185–192. Short-term funds in Treasury certificates were also pulled out. Ibid., 187.

13. Federal Reserve Board, *Annual Report for 1929*, 13.

14. Horace G. White, "Foreign Trading in American Stock Exchange Securities," *Journal of Political Economy*, 48 (Oct. 1940): 670n.14. This figure is to be taken with a great deal of reservation.

15. See, for example, Fisher, *Stock Market Crash*, 31–32; Hirst, *Wall Street and Lombard Street*, 6, 8–9; James Harvey Rogers, *America Weighs Her Gold* (New Haven, Conn.: Yale University Press, 1931), 26; and Einzig, *World Finance*, 212.

16. Kindleberger, *World in Depression*, 118; Kindleberger, *Manias, Panics, and Crashes*, 84. George Soule, *Prosperity Decade*, 306, suggested that "several influences started the decline," but—following Fisher—he begins with the Hatry scandal and the raising of the British rediscount rate.

17. Fleisig, *Long Term Capital Flows*, 85, 17; Michie, *London Stock Exchange*, 263, shares the skepticism.

18. Galbraith, *Great Crash 1929*, 96–97.

19. Fleisig, *Long Term Capital Flows*, 86; Bloomfield, *Capital Imports*, 99n. A 1929 U.S. Department of Commerce questionnaire on margin buying received inconclusive responses. The department, however, for balance of payments purposes, calculated that the cash margins deposited with brokers by foreigners in 1929 averaged the "high level" of 35 percent. U.S. Department of Commerce, Bureau of Foreign and Domestic Commerce, *The Balance of International Payments of the United States in 1929* (Washington, D.C., 1930), 54. Henceforth cited as *Commerce Report 1930*. American buyers often had much lower cash margins, albeit no comparable average for U.S. buyers is provided in this report.

20. The Commerce Department "averages" may not be meaningful. On the buying on margin by foreigners, see National Industrial Conference Board, *International Financial Position of the United States*, 65. Charles Geisst, *Entrepôt Capitalism*, 12, believes "U.S. brokers regularly advanced margin money to foreign accounts, usually at slightly higher rates than for domestic investors." There is, for example, archival evidence that Sir James Dunn, whose American securities were "largely bought 'on margin,'" was not atypical, albeit we do not know the size of the cash margins. See McDowall, *Steel at the Sault*, 125. It was, in fact, *Canadian* transactions that prompted the Commerce Department to ask questions about "foreigners" in general and their purchases on margin. *Commerce Report 1930*, 54.

21. Fleisig, *Long Term Capital Flows*, 86 (my italics).

22. Wigmore, *The Crash and Its Aftermath*, 15, suggests that by Monday, October 28, 1929, the end of the 1929 boom "was clearer to foreign investors." I have my doubts. I am not sure why this would be the case.

23. Einzig, *World Finance*, 213.

24. *Congressional Record*, vol. 72, pt. 2, 1243–1244 (Jan. 8, 1930); ibid., pt. 3, 2417, 2423 (Jan. 27, 1930).

25. Ibid., pt. 2, 1243 (Jan. 8, 1930); ibid., pt. 3, 2427 (Jan. 27, 1930).

26. Wilkins, *History*, 566–585, and sentiments described earlier in the present book. Wheeler's antipathy was reciprocated: Samuel Salvage, the chief executive of the Courtaulds' subsidiary, American Viscose Co., denounced Wheeler as "a Bolshevik Senator from the West." Coleman, *Courtaulds*, II, 395. There was no love lost.

27. *Congressional Record*, vol. 72, pt. 3, 2429, 2441 (Jan. 27, 1930).

28. Du Pont had in 1929 bought out its French partner, and Du Pont Rayon in early 1930 was 100 percent American.

29. *Congressional Record,* vol. 72, pt. 3, 2429 (Jan. 27, 1930). The reader will recall that the Dutch-German American Enka Corporation had set up a plant in Asheville, North Carolina, in 1929 to manufacture rayon.

30. Simmons, a five-term senator, had been cosponsor of the 1913 Underwood-Simmons tariff that had *lowered* duties. He had, however, opposed Democratic candidate Alfred Smith (on the Prohibition issue) in 1928 and supported Hoover that year.

31. On the opposition to higher tariffs from farm senators, see Wayne S. Cole, *Senator Gerald P. Nye and American Foreign Relations* (Minneapolis: University of Minnesota Press, 1962), 64. The tariff discussion was full of nuances. The *American* chemical industry wanted continued protection. On the lobbying see, for example, S. Isermann to F. P. Garvan, Nov. 22, 1929, Francis P. Garvan Papers, Box 76, American Heritage Center, University of Wyoming, Laramie. I. G. Farben in America would benefit, and Garvan was strongly opposed to I. G. Farben's setting itself up in America. But Garvan thought that I. G. Farben's business would be larger were it not for the high tariffs.

32. Joseph M. Jones, *Tariff Retaliation* (Philadelphia: University of Pennsylvania Press, 1934).

33. Quotation in Guinsburg, *Pursuit of Isolationism,* 282.

34. For a textbook rendition of the controversy, as of the late 1980s and early 1990s, see Robert C. Puth, *American Economic History,* 2nd ed. (Chicago: Dryden Press, 1988), 475–484, and Puth, *American Economic History,* 3rd ed. (Chicago: Dryden Press, 1993), 533–542. See also Michael A. Bernstein, *The Great Depression: Delayed Recovery and Economic Change in America, 1929–1939* (Cambridge: Cambridge University Press, 1987), 4–20. Ben S. Bernanke, *Essays on the Great Depression* (Princeton, N.J.: Princeton University Press, 2000), maintained that the principal cause of the Depression lay in monetary factors, along with the adherence to the gold standard. Nobel Prize winner Robert Mundell has gone so far as to declare, "Had the price of gold been raised in the late 1920's, or alternatively had the major central banks pursued policies of price stability instead of adhering to the gold standard, there would have been no Great Depression, no Nazi revolution, and no World War II." Robert Mundell, "A Reconsideration of the Twentieth Century," *American Economic Review,* 90 (June 2000): 331. In such an analysis, the behavior of foreign investors in the United States seems entirely irrelevant.

35. Gottfried Haberler, *The World Economy, Money, and the Great Depression 1919–1939* (Washington, D.C.: American Enterprise Institute, 1976), 7, 33.

36. *Commerce Report 1930,* 33.

37. Peter Temin, *Did Monetary Forces Cause the Great Depression?* (New York: W. W. Norton, 1976), 153.

38. This was particularly true of foreign portfolio investments; foreign direct investment that was made based on the higher tariff was probably a bit greater than U.S. domestic investment that would not have been made without protection.

39. Domestic (American) investors, who were engaged in international transactions, were affected by many of the same considerations, but the international environment undoubtedly had far more impact on foreign investors in the United States than on Americans' domestic investment strategies. Because of different information and different transaction costs, an open economy analysis cannot assume foreign and domestic investors will make identical choices. Markets are (and were) imperfect.

40. The U.S. Securities and Exchange Commission, *Investment Trusts in Great Britain,* H. Doc. 380, 76th Cong., 1st sess. (1939), 50 (this document is henceforth cited as *SEC Report 1939*), shows major systematic differences in the purchases and sales of American securities, 1929–1933, of British investment trusts established before the First World War *and* those established after the war. This seems to have related both to the acquisition dates of securities and to the experiences of investment managers.

41. There is very little evidence on this matter of taxes. There was clearly substantial tax evasion—and it is not clear that there is any way of measuring the effects of different tax regimes (and the changes) on the *pace* of foreign portfolio investments in the United States in this period.

42. McDonald, *Insull,* 289.

43. I am indebted to Professor Luciano Segreto for his help on this. See Bank für Elektrische Unternehmungen, Zurich, *Geschaftsbericht 1 Juli 1930 bis 30 Juni 1931,* 4.

44. Ibid., 26. Compare the list in the Elektrobank annual report with Bonbright and Means, *Holding Company,* 94.

45. Leland B. Yeager, *International Monetary Relations* (New York: Harper & Row, 1966), 295.

46. For a fascinating background on the genesis of the moratorium, see June 1931 data in Box 98, folder 18, Lamont Papers, Harvard Business School, Boston. See also Diane B. Kunz, *The Battle for Britain's Gold Standard* (London: Croom Helm, 1987), 53–63. German reparations were mainly due to Britain and France, albeit arrangements had been made in the 1920s and in the Debt Funding Agreement of June 23, 1930, for a share of the reparation payments to go to the United States to liquidate the obligations of Germany to U.S. bondholders. The Germans interpreted the one-year moratorium to cover these "reparation" payments as well, although the Hoover Moratorium had exempted "private obligations." See Edwin Borchard, "Reprisals on Private Property," *American Journal of International Law,* 30 (Jan. 1936): 109–111, and U.S. Secretary of the Treasury, *Annual Report for Year end 1934,* Exhibit 37, 247, and 252.

47. The figure is as of 1929 and given in Table 4.1.

48. Britain made some subsequent token payments; the British Exchequer never repudiated its obligation. It simply followed the view that war debts were "a dead issue." Walter A. Morton, *British Finance 1930–1940* (Madison: University of Wisconsin Press, 1943), 281–282. These occurrences had substantial effect on outward U.S. foreign investment, as legislation was passed in the 1930s to bar loans to defaulting countries. The United States and Britain had very different views on the inter-Allied obligations. Britain, and even more so France, felt that these obligations should not exist and were moreover linked with reparations. Most Americans felt the debts were owed, entirely separate from reparations.

49. The events are well told in Yeager, *International Monetary Relations,* 296. See also Schuker, *American "Reparations,"* 52–61, esp. 58–59 on the capital flight. On the breakdown of the German financial system, see James, *German Slump,* 285. (The German government would merge the Danat Bank into the Dresdner Bank.) It was both German *and* foreign capital in Germany that sought to flee Germany. The German government put restrictions on foreign travel to prevent Germans "on their way to cures in Swiss sanatoria taking suitcases stuffed with Marks with them." Ibid., 301.

50. As with all "flight capital" movements, it is impossible to determine the exact amounts involved. I have not, however, found evidence that the rise in German investment in the United States was substantial. Also, there is the problem of the blending of the short-term and long-term capital exodus.

51. The Bank of England correspondence with the Federal Reserve Bank of New York details the efforts to support the pound. Federal Reserve Bank of New York Archives, New York (henceforth cited as FRBNY).

52. Atkin, *British Overseas Investment,* 306–317.

53. On its sale of U.S. Treasury bonds, see cables, Bank of England to Federal Reserve Bank New York (confidential for Sproul), Aug. 24, 1931; Harrison to Bank of England, Aug. 24, 1931; and Bank of England to Federal Reserve Bank, all in C261 England–Bank of England, FRBNY. In Rogers, *America Weighs Her Gold,* which has an August 27, 1931,

date on the preface, the Yale economist wrote (p. 148) that "the huge British holdings of foreign securities provide now, as at the beginning of the Great War, an emergency reserve of high value. Their mobilization could probably be accomplished should catastrophe become imminent," i.e. if Britain could not cope with the "extraordinary gold situation."

54. *New York Times,* Aug. 31, 1931.

55. Ibid., Sept. 1, 1931. I went through the Lamont Papers and found nothing on the mobilization of foreign securities. Likewise, I found nothing in the Federal Reserve Bank of New York Archives to indicate that the mobilization of British subjects' holdings of American securities was ever seriously contemplated by the British government. The best work on the British defense of sterling is Kunz, *Battle for Britain's Gold Standard;* she shows that mobilization of foreign holdings in the United States was not a consideration in the extension of the credit. Ibid., 115–117. Kynaston, *City of London,* III, 223–245, covers the events leading up to Britain's going off gold; in this connection, he does not discuss the mobilization of foreign holdings in the United States.

56. Philip Snowden, *Parliamentary Debates,* vol. 256, Sept. 21, 1931, 1296. See also Atkin, *British Overseas Investment,* 306–315, who stresses (p. 310) the matter of "time." Yet the British had been able to act rapidly when in the summer of 1915 Reginald McKenna had called in Prudential Assurance Company executives. Also, the repudiated *New York Times* story of August 31 suggests that Prudential Assurance was once more prepared to come to the rescue. Sir George May, who had been secretary of Prudential Assurance in 1915 and manager in World War I of the American Dollar Securities Committee, was in 1931 either still secretary of Prudential Assurance (Wake, *Kleinwort Benson,* 303) or "recently retired" (Kynaston, *City of London,* III, 215, says that May had "recently retired" from Prudential Assurance, when he took on the task of heading the "May Committee," which committee on August 1, 1931, issued a report on the budget deficit and its dangers). May was very much a participant in the discussions before Britain went off gold. See David Dimbleby and David Reynolds, *An Ocean Apart: The Relationship between Britain and the United States in the Twentieth Century* (New York: Random House, 1988), 97. Morton, *British Finance,* 49 and 276n, suggests that the proposal to mobilize foreign investments had come from the Trades Union Congress General Council (affiliated with the Labour Party) and was considered and rejected. Morton's obiter dictum was "It was evidently believed [by the government] that such an effort to maintain the gold standard was not worth while." Lord Reading, who was familiar with the World War I securities mobilization, suggested to Snowden on September 11 that the Treasury analyze the possible mobilization of foreign securities. Kunz, *Battle for Britain's Gold Standard,* 129. Atkin, *British Overseas Investment,* 312, refers to an undated Treasury memorandum prepared after the devaluation of sterling; it dealt with mobilization of foreign securities and, perhaps, was the result of Lord Reading's suggestion. By the time Lord Reading made his proposal, the die had probably been cast. Kunz, *Battle for Britain's Gold Standards,* 147–150. Remember, however, many thought the suspension was for a short time only. The National Government stated that it anticipated that "once the trade account was balanced," the country would "return to the gold standard," while Montagu Norman, governor of the Bank of England, wrote in September 1931 of the need to work to "restore and maintain an international Gold Standard." If there was little support for such views from the Treasury and if John Maynard Keynes was "jubilant," there were still men who expected the nation to go back to gold. Kynaston, *City of London,* III, 246 and 362.

57. *New York Times,* Sept. 21, 1931 (two articles), and Sept. 23, 1931 (which did not indicate whether it was growing to or beyond the $1.5 billion). In Britain, it was commonly accepted that during the First World War, "Britain [had] sacrificed practically all its Stock Exchange holdings in the United States." See, for example, Hirst, *Wall Street*

and Lombard Street, 112 (published in London in April 1931). Yet there had been a renewal of investments in securities in the 1920s, and certain investors had retained their prewar holdings (there had also been liquidations in late 1929 to 1930).

58. Sayers, *Bank of England,* II, 419ff.

59. *New York Times,* Sept. 22, 1931.

60. Ibid., Sept. 24, 1931; *Financial Times,* Sept. 23, 1931.

61. Ratner, *American Taxation,* 444; Weir, *History of the Scottish American Investment Company,* 23; *Fortune,* 8 (Sept. 1933): 33.

62. Brooks, *Once in Golgonda,* 139. See also *New York Times,* Oct. 8, 1931.

63. Charles W. Calomiris, *U.S. Bank Deregulation in Historical Perspective* (Cambridge: Cambridge University Press, 2000), 187; U.S. Department of the Treasury, *Annual Report for Year-ended June 30, 1932,* 4. With the gold outflow, banking reserves fell. There was "acute credit contraction." Bank failures multiplied. The NCC would be replaced by the Reconstruction Finance Corporation, which came into being on January 22, 1932. Walter F. Todd, "History of and Rationales for the Reconstruction Finance Corporation," *Economic Review* (Federal Reserve Bank of Cleveland), 28, no. 4 (1992): 24.

64. In addition, after the devaluation of sterling, the Bank of France and the National Bank of Belgium began to convert dollars to gold. Stuart Bruchey, *Enterprise* (Cambridge, Mass.: Harvard University Press, 1990), 435; Kindleberger, *World in Depression,* 167–169; and Friedman and Schwartz, *Monetary History of the United States,* 315–317.

65. On its defense of the gold standard, see Eichengreen, *Golden Fetters,* 289.

66. The $8.3 billion figure that the *New York Times* gave was obviously bizarre. Also it is difficult to decipher the differences between "short-term" and "long-term" holdings. The latter, if in traded stock market securities, were as liquid as the former.

67. This assumes not only that the result was bad Federal Reserve policy but also that the continuing decline in stock values reduced all investors' wealth and was demoralizing.

68. Kindleberger, *World in Depression,* 111.

69. Federal Reserve Bank of New York, "Confidential Memorandum for Secretary of Treasury, Nov. 30, 1932, in C261, England–United Kingdom, FRBNY, referring to the first half of 1932. See also Geisst, *Wall Street,* 207–210, for the presence of the "conspiracy theory": European capitalists had organized a bear market to force America off gold.

70. Lindgren, *Corporate Growth,* 304.

71. Ibid., 306, 421.

72. U.S. Senate, Committee on Banking and Currency, *Stock Exchange Practices, Hearings,* 72nd Cong., 1st sess. (1933), pt. 4, 1154 (henceforth cited as *Stock Exchange Practices, Hearings*).

73. Shaplen, *Kreuger,* 5–6 and 224ff. for the events of March–April 1932. Earlier plans to investigate stock market activities accelerated. On April 11, 1932, the Senate Committee on Banking and Currency began hearings on stock exchange practices; later, this committee would investigate the Kreuger scandal.

74. Statement of Donald Durant, *Stock Exchange Practices, Hearings,* pt. 4, 1233.

75. Testimony of George O. May in ibid., 1271.

76. McDonald, *Insull,* 162–167, 204, 239–240, 289.

77. Ibid., 299, 301; Samuel Insull, "Memoirs," 228, Samuel Insull Papers, Box 17, Loyola University, Archives, Chicago. William Hausman, an expert on the U.S. power and light industry, believes that Forrest McDonald exaggerated. E-mail to Mira Wilkins, Feb. 25, 2002.

78. McDonald, *Insull,* 304.

79. Insull, "Memoirs, 83. These were written in 1934–1935.

80. *Fortune,* 8 (Sept. 1933): 125.

81. In 1932, for example, John Maynard Keynes made his first investments on Wall Street, buying preferred shares in giant American public utility holding companies, which he believed were "now hopelessly out of fashion with American investors and heavily depressed below their real value." Robert Skidelsky, *John Maynard Keynes* (New York: Penguin Books, 1992), II, 524–525.

82. Federal Reserve Bank of New York, "Confidential Memorandum for Secretary of Treasury," Nov. 30, 1932, C261, England–United Kingdom, FRBNY; and Barrie A. Wigmore, "Was the Bank Holiday of 1933 Caused by a Run on the Dollar?" *Journal of Economic History,* 47 (Sept. 1987): 742, citing undated data from the Bank of England. See also Lamont, *Ambassador from Wall Street,* 330–331.

83. George Harrison Memorandum, "Guaranty Trust Company Requests for and Custody of Gold for Account of Customers," Feb. 9, 1933, Harrison Papers 1550.2 (b), FRBNY.

84. Michie, *London Stock Exchange,* 175–184.

85. Ibid., 220–221, 241. see Chapter 4 on the ones present in the late 1920s; one of the exits was Pynchon & Co., which failed in 1931. Geisst, *Wall Street,* 212. Fenner & Beane, the renamed Fenner, Beane, & Ungerleider, merged with Merrill, Lynch in 1941. Perkins, *Wall Street to Main Street,* 167–168.

86. Wilkins, *History,* 216–218.

87. Because in the immediate postwar years and through much of the 1920s foreign investments had become more complicated than had been the case in the almost universal gold standard years before 1914, increasingly it was only the large or sophisticated investor (or well-connected individuals) who could deal with the complexities. Banks, investment trusts, insurance companies with access to information, with financial expertise, could spread risks and were more prepared than the small saver to handle foreign securities in general and American ones in particular. Iversen, *International Capital Movements,* 111. In the 1920s, virtually all America's obligations to foreigners (inward foreign investment) were dollar denominated and thus for the foreign investor involved dealing with foreign exchange.

88. Families would invest in American securities through financial trusts, in the Kleinwort family case, for example, through the Moonhill Trust. This trust handled the family's personal holdings as distinct from the Kleinwort firm holdings. Wake, *Kleinwort Benson,* 242. Experienced fund managers, such as Helbert, Wagg & Co., set up investment trusts for groups of investors. Thus, in April 1931 Helbert, Wagg formed and would manage the Westpool Investment Trust, which entered the American securities market before the devaluation of sterling and when American security prices were very low; it was able to take advantage of the market recovery. The capital of Westpool Investment Trust was subscribed by British investors: one-third by the road transport firm Thomas Tilling, one-third by the retailer Lewis', and the rest by insurance companies. Roberts, *Schroders,* 382.

89. Bliss, *Northern Enterprise,* 413.

90. Orbell, *Baring Brothers,* 79.

91. Carosso, *More Than a Century,* 65–76.

92. Ziegler, *Sixth Great Power,* 340.

93. Beckhart, *New York Money Market,* III, 303.

94. Harvey, *Rio Tinto Company,* 219, 221, and 227n.73.

95. On the general decline of the London Rothschilds, see Richard Davis, *The English Rothschilds* (Chapel Hill: University of North Carolina Press, 1983), 245, and Chernow, *The Warburgs,* 326. In 1929, the London Rothschilds had joined with Lee, Higginson & Co. to issue shares for Kreuger. Lee, Higginson & Co. collapsed; the London Rothschilds survived, albeit damaged in the process. Ferguson, *House of Rothschild,* 466.

96. Based on data in AQ 132, Rothschild Papers, Archives Nationale, Fontainebleau, France. Herbert R. Lottman, *The French Rothschilds* (New York: Crown Publishers, 1995), 170–171, suggests that at the time of the Wall Street crash, the French Rothschilds may still have retained, based on pre–World War I investments, some securities of the Interborough Rapid Transit (the IRT) obtained through August Belmont (the IRT went into bankruptcy in August 1932 and in June 1940 was acquired by New York City).

97. Wake, *Kleinwort Benson*, 301.

98. Ibid., 298–302.

99. *Economist*, Dec. 1, 1934, 8 (based on market value). These data on fourteen trusts may not reflect the overall pattern of British investment trusts vis-à-vis American securities; the market value fluctuated in both 1929 and 1933, so the different dates when the portfolio of each investment trust was measured matter (and there was no consistency in when the measurement was made). Table 2.6, based on book rather than market value, shows a greater decline in investment trusts' American involvements from 1929 to 1933 (yet this, too, reflects apples and oranges—1929, twenty-six companies; 1933, twenty companies), while data on book value for twenty companies, 1929, 1933, in the *Economist*, Dec. 1, 1934, 8, indicate the opposite: a rise in the U.S. share from 7.3 to 7.6 percent of portfolio. All the evidence demonstrates a shift away from continental European investments.

100. *Economist*, Dec. 1, 1934. Again, the month that the translation was made into pound sterling matters, and this was not provided in the data, nor was it apparently consistent.

101. *Fortune*, 8 (Sept. 1933): 33. For the events of June 1932, see Kunz, *Battle for Britain's Gold Standard*, 166.

102. Weir, *History of the Scottish American Investment Company*, 20 (Apr. 1925), 24 (Dec. 1931, Dec. 1932).

103. Emden, *Money Powers*, 276–277. Speyer & Co., New York, would shut down in June 1939. Carosso, "Financial Elite," 86.

104. J. P. Warburg, "European Problem," June 11, 1932, and L. S. Chandler, Jr., to James P. Warburg, July 7, 1932, in James P. Warburg Papers, Box 5, John F. Kennedy Library, Boston.

105. Felix Warburg was "semiretired" and would die in 1937. Chernow, *The Warburgs*, 445, 455.

106. Roberts, *Schroders*, 222, 226, 238–242, 248, 256, for the Schroder house's experiences, 1929–1933.

107. *Van Oss' Effectenboek 1934*, courtesy of Augustus Veenendaal. The 1909 figures are from Wilkins, *History*, 730n.58. The once sizable Dutch holdings in The Missouri, Kansas & Texas are not included in Table 6.2: Dutch common stock holdings in this railroad were said to be $15.7 million in 1918 but only $3.1 million in 1934. Veenendaal, *Slow Train to Paradise*, 147.

108. Bank für Elektrische Unternehmungen, Zurich, *Geschaftsbericht*, 1930–1931, 1931–1932, 1932–1933. Insull's Middle West Utilities was among the ten American securities listed in 1930–1931 in Elektrobank's annual report; it was dropped in 1931–1932; however in 1932–1933 (each year ends 30 June), there were two new additions to the 1930–1931 list of holdings. I am indebted to L. Segretto for insights into these investments and for copies of the annual reports.

109. Mitsui & Co., *100 Year History*, 113–114.

110. Yamazaki, "Yokohama Specie Bank," 382–386, esp. Table 20.6.

111. Data from "Nomura Co. History," p. 48, obtained from Nomura Securities International Inc., June 29, 1988.

112. Einzig, *World Finance*, 234.

113. Data from "Nomura Co. History," p. 48.

114. Data from Paul J. Hauser, Daiwa Securities America Inc., Feb. 22, 1989.

115. *Fortune,* Mar. 1937, 132, and Nelson, *King Cotton's Advocate,* 41–42. On low cattle prices and the losses of the Matador Land and Cattle Co., see Jackson, *Enterprising Scot,* 136.

116. Cox, *Global Cigarette,* 294. Imperial Tobacco's 51 percent interest in Gallaher (acquired in 1932) would be reduced to 42.5 percent in 1946 and sold off entirely in 1968 when American Brands (the successor to American Tobacco) bought Gallaher. By a twist of fate, in 1932, American Tobacco, irritated by BAT's advances in the U.S. market, had threatened to take over Gallaher in Britain, which was what provoked Imperial Tobacco to counter and acquire control of Gallaher. Channon, *Strategy and Structure of British Enterprise,* 102.

117. Dahl, "British Investment in California Mining," 260–262, 268.

118. American-born Alfred Chester Beatty was a graduate of the Columbia School of Mines. In 1913 he moved to London and from there had become a leader in developing the Copper Belt in Northern Rhodesia (now Zambia). A. J. Wilson, *The Life and Times of Sir Alfred Chester Beatty* (London: Cadogan Publications, 1985); Navin, *Copper Mining and Management,* 29, 357; Wilkins, *History,* 547. Wilson, *Life and Times,* 212, gives the 25 percent figure.

119. Beatty's motive was to obtain *U.S.* capital to develop his Northern Rhodesia properties. American Metal Company undertook to raise $10 million to complete the construction at the Roan Antelope and Mufilira mines. Wilson, *Life and Times,* 212. On the issue of $20 million gold notes (April 1, 1930), see *Moody's Manual 1931,* 1009. See also Navin, *Copper Mining,* 277; Selection Trust would remain the largest single stockholder in American Metal until 1975. Ibid., 284.

120. Haynes, *American Chemical Industry,* VI, 448–451.

121. New Consolidated Gold Fields, *Annual Reports, 1930, 1931, 1932.* Microfilm Z-G1, Reel 116, Bancroft Library, University of California, Berkeley. Even though American Potash & Chemical was German controlled, Consolidated Gold Fields remained involved.

122. Data from the files of John H. Dunning, University of Reading, England (henceforth cited as Dunning data). See Hexner, *International Cartels,* 236, on the cartel in platinum (Oct. 21, 1931) and Johnson, Matthey & Co.'s role.

123. Wigmore, *The Crash and Its Aftermath,* 163 (Shell Union was not wholly owned by the Royal Dutch Shell Group).

124. Royal Dutch Company, *Annual Report 1930,* 8–9, 24, 34–35; ibid., *1931,* 24–25, 27.

125. Beaton, *Enterprise in Oil,* 783. It lost $5.1 million in 1930, $27.0 million in 1931, and $4.2 million in 1933; its $660,000 profit in 1932 did little to offset these large losses.

126. Royal Dutch Company, *Annual Report 1931,* 11–12.

127. Ibid., *1932,* 23, 14.

128. Yergin, *Prize,* 266; Bamberg, *History of the British Petroleum Company,* 112; Wilkins, *Maturing,* 233–234; U.S. Federal Trade Commission, *The International Petroleum Cartel* (Washington, D.C., 1952), chap. 8.

129. This is the impression that comes out of the Royal Dutch annual reports: Royal Dutch Company, *Annual Report 1930,* 35–36; ibid., *1931,* 26; ibid., *1932,* 26. Beaton, *Enterprise in Oil,* 364–369, suggests "retrenchment," reductions in personnel, and major cutbacks.

130. Basil Jackson to John Cadman, Jan. 20, 1933, quoted in Bamberg, *History of the British Petroleum Company,* 114. While Standard Oil Co. (Indiana) was very large in the United States, it was not one of the key *global* players. In 1932, it had sold its principal foreign business to Standard Oil of New Jersey. Wilkins, *Maturing,* 209–210. But the price of crude oil was a world price.

131. Heer, *World Events 1866–1966,* 158–159.

132. For Lipton's leading position in the U.S. market, see *Fortune,* 8 (Aug. 1933): 35. On Lord Inverforth as president, see *Herald Tribune* (New York), May 20, 1937. For a general background on Andrew Weir & Co. and Andrew Weir (1865–1955, as of 1919 Lord Inverforth), see *Dictionary of Business Biography,* V, 719–720, which regrettably gives nothing on the man's extensive U.S. business activities.

133. Reckitt and Colman (through their investment in R. T. French, in mustard), the Canadian-owned Salada Tea, and the British-owned Tetley Tea, as well as the Swiss-owned Ovaltine company, would be included among the few. *Fortune,* 8 (Aug. 1933): 35, which identified Lipton Tea as the leader in tea sales, indicated that its rivals were Salada Tea Co. and, in third place, Tetley Tea.

134. *Fortune,* Dec. 1931, 93.

135. Wilson, *History of Unilever,* II, 355, and "Chronicle of Lever Brothers in US, 1895–1948," prepared in Boston, Feb. 1948, in Historical File, Unilever Archives, London; Minutes Managing Directors Conference, June 19, 1930, and Oct. 30, 1930, Unilever Archives.

136. Minutes Managing Directors Conferences, Oct. 30, 1930, Unilever Archives.

137. "Chronicle of Lever Brothers in US, 1895–1948."

138. Minutes Managing Directors Conference, Mar. 20, 1930; Oct. 30, 1930; Dec. 11, 1930; and Apr. 7, 1931, Unilever Archives.

139. *Fortune,* Dec. 1931, 94.

140. Joint Directors Minutes, Apr. 2/3, 1930, BB46 Unilever Archives. See also Executive Committee Minutes, Apr. 16, 1930, in ibid. In 1930, the Dutch firm's margarine trade in the United States was negligible. Once Jurgens' had divested its interests in Kellogg Products, Inc., in 1923, it had paid little attention to the U.S. margarine trade.

141. Special Committee Minutes, Apr. 8, 1931; Joint Directors Minutes, Apr. 10, 1931, BB46 Unilever Archives; Wilson, *History of Unilever,* II, 355; and "Chronicle of Lever Brothers in US, 1895–1948." In *1923* Lever Brothers, with "a vision of the future," had "secured waterside premises at Edgewater, N.Y. [actually New Jersey] because they could be bought at a reasonable price." W. H. Lever to C. E. Tatlow, Aug. 7, 1923, L. Corr. 7823, Unilever Archives.

142. See sales and profit data, Unilever PLC, London. The parent company thought Lever Brothers was gaining ground on both Procter & Gamble and Colgate-Palmolive. Managing Directors' Conference Minutes, Jan. 21, 1932, Unilever Archives. See also report of G. Heyworth, H. F. Poulson and Mark Hardy, Sept./Oct. 1932, BB43 Unilever Archives.

143. Cox, *Global Cigarette,* 297; ibid., 10, shows that exports of cigarettes from the United States in 1929 were 8.5 billion sticks; in 1930, 4.9 billion; in 1931, 3.0 billion; and in 1932, 2.5 billion sticks. It is not clear what percentage of these exports were from BAT factories in the United States, but it probably was a substantial portion of the total.

144. Ibid., 289, 264, and Cox, "Global Cigarette," 226–228; Cox, *Competition in the American Tobacco Industry,* 73–77; Corina, *Trust in Tobacco,* 152, 236.

145. Cox, *Global Cigarette,* 300, 263, 298. Figures on the percentage of total U.S. production of Brown & Williamson (not of BAT) are given in *American Tobacco, et al. v. U.S.,* 328 U.S. 781 (1946) at 794 (these production figures are not identical to the BAT U.S. sales figures given in Table 6.6 that Howard Cox found in the BAT archives and included in his Ph.D. dissertation; the difference does not seem to be exports, which do not appear to be in the Brown & Williamson figures; the figures correspond very closely to figures that Cox provides from non-BAT sources in Cox, *Global Cigarette,* 299).

146. Cox, "Global Cigarette," 377.

147. David Keir, "The Coats Story," typescript, 1964, vol. III (access granted by Coats), 149 (1922 plans), 150 (1929 plans), 153 (Clarksdale), 153, 155 (cutback in New Jersey);

UGD 199 1/1/5, J. & P. Coats Minute Book, July 11, 1929 (plans for the southern plant), June 12, 1930 (approval to erect mill in the South). The Scots did approve the sale of four East Newark, New Jersey, mills that had been built in 1885–1888 (1), 1889 (2), and 1922 (1), yet it retained its principal plant in Newark. The sale of the mills would be at less than the original cost. J. & P. Coats Minute Book, Dec. 11, 1930. The minute books are in the Archives of the University of Glasgow. Keir, "Coats Story," 153, writes that equipment from East Newark was moved to the main Newark mill, but that it took until 1935 to dispose of these East Newark buildings. In addition, in 1933, Coats' old Chadwick Greenville mill in New Jersey was sold. Ibid., 155. Throughout the 1930s, the company retained operations in New Jersey and in Rhode Island, but the retreat from New Jersey had begun. On Coats see also Dunning data. Historically, the Clark (Clark Thread Co.) and Coats (J. & P. Coats [Rhode Island] Inc.) operations in the United States had been separately run, with the Clark operations in New Jersey and now in the American South as well and the Coats operations in Rhode Island. The parents of both were joined in Glasgow, and increasingly in the United States the group was run as one.

148. Keir, "Coats Story," III, 152–155; IV, 73. There had been various earlier New York offices. In 1931, it was John B. Clark and his assistants who moved to the Empire State Building.

149. Leon E. Hotz, Sauer Textile Machinery Group, Greenville, S.C., to Mira Wilkins, Oct. 2, 1987 (on Swiss embroidery companies). The U.S. Department of Commerce, Bureau of Foreign and Domestic Commerce, *Foreign Investments in the United States* (Washington, D.C., 1937), 32, put Swiss direct investments in textiles and textile products at year end 1934 at only $3.4 million (henceforth this document is cited as *FIUS—1937*). See also Wilkins, "Swiss Investments," 108–109n.65. Swiss direct investments in the United States in "silk and textiles" included the interests of Schwarzenbach, Huber & Co. (a silk maker with a long history in the United States) and Stoffel & Co. (in fashion fabrics, especially "organdy"). Mauro Cerutti, "Le Blocage des Avoirs Suisses aux États-Unis en 1941," in *La Suisse et les Grandes Puissances, 1914–1945,* ed. Sébastien Guex (Geneva: Droz, 1999), 187. I am indebted to Mr. Patrick Stoffel, Patrick Stoffel Collections, for background on Stoffel & Co.: E-mails to Mira Wilkins, Sept. 29, 2000, and Oct. 2, 2000. Patrick Stoffel recalled that his father established a New York office of Stoffel & Co. in the late 1920s. Stoffel & Co. imported fine fabrics from Switzerland (fabrics not made in the United States) and had relationships with individual American companies, not owned by Stoffel & Co., for printing on other fabrics, to Stoffel & Co. designs.

150. Stanley Pigott, *Hollins* (Nottingham: William Hollins & Co., 1949), 124–125.

151. J. Heim, President Bally Inc., to Mira Wilkins, Apr. 5, 1983.

152. Bata had in the early 1920s bought a small shoe factory in Lynn, Massachusetts; the venture was a failure. Subsequently, it had appointed a representative for the U.S. market; it opened retail shops. In 1930 it set up Bata Shoe Co., New York. At the peak point (and it is unclear when that was), Bata had seventy stores in the United States, mainly in the Chicago area. With the Smoot-Hawley Tariff and threats of even higher tariffs, the firm decided to manufacture in the United States. *Rubber Age,* 26 (Sept. 10, 1930): 602 (mention of Bata stores); Anthony Cekota, *Entrepreneur Extraordinary: The Biography of Tomas Bata* (Rome: E.I.S., 1968), 149–150 (Lynn shoe factory), 240–248 (retail stores, exports to U.S.), 382–383 (foreign affiliates); Thomas J. Bata, *Bata* (Toronto: Stoddart Publishing, 1990), 144 (Lynn shoe factory), 144–145 (retail stores), 146–147 (the land purchase, the reasons for manufacturing, and the postponed decision).

153. U.S. domestic production of rayon (measured by weight) rose from 97.9 million pounds in 1928 to 130.3 million pounds in 1930; imports fell from 12.7 million pounds in 1928 to 5.8 million pounds in 1930. Silk Association of America, *Annual Report 1930–31,* 85.

154. Markham, *Competition,* 17; Coleman, *Courtaulds,* II, 191. The merged firm was producing by the nitrocellulose, viscose, and acetate processes. *Fortune,* Oct. 1933, 143.

155. Coleman, *Courtaulds,* 385–386, 390, 401–408.

156. There was also the large interest in thread and other stakes as well. The figures are as of year end 1934, but I see no reason to believe this would not be true of 1933 as well. *FIUS—1937,* 32.

157. Daviet, *Destin International,* 419–420.

158. Ibid., 404, 420, on American Securit and its involvement in these arrangements.

159. Stocking and Watkins, *Cartels in Action,* 452.

160. Quoted in Plummer, *International Combines,* 59. See also Reader, *Imperial Chemical Industries,* II, passim.

161. *Fortune,* 8 (Sept. 1933): 125, reported that McGowan's business interests had brought him to the United States forty-five times.

162. The best material on the International Nitrogen Cartel is in Stocking and Watkins, *Cartels in Action,* 143–154; see also Annex 2 to Interrogation of Hermann Schmitz, RG 238, T301, Reel 6, NI-570, National Archives, Washington, D.C.

163. The plant was built by Allied's subsidiary the Atmospheric Nitrogen Corp. Haynes, *American Chemical Industry,* VI, 394. On its size and importance, see ibid., IV, 40; VI, 394, and U.S. Department of Agriculture, *Survey of the Fertilizer Industry,* Circular No. 129 (Washington, D.C., 1931), 19–21. See Lisagor and Lipsius, *Law unto Itself,* 124, on its exports, and Reader, *Imperial Chemical Industries,* II, 145ff., on overcapacity in the industry.

164. Allied Chemical's subsidiary, National Aniline & Chemical Co. (NACC) seems to have been involved in a separate set of international agreements with I. G. Farben and ICI. Akiro Kudo, "Dominance through Cooperation: I. G. Farben's Japan Strategy," in *The German Chemical Industry in the Twentieth Century,* ed. John E. Lesch (Dordrecht, Netherlands: Kluwer, 2000), 265, 267, on two 1931 agreements on dyestuff and indigo exports to China. Agreements in this era were numerous and product specific, so lack of conformity in one case did not establish a general pattern. Kudo says that Du Pont was also drawn into these two 1931 agreements on exports to China.

165. U.S. Department of Agriculture, *Survey of the Fertilizer Industry,* 20; Haynes, *American Chemical Industry,* VI, 380; Beaton, *Enterprise in Oil,* 521–527.

166. Haynes, *American Chemical Industry,* VI, 380–385; Beaton, *Enterprise in Oil,* 521–527, 532–534.

167. Schröter, "Participation in Market Control," 179. *Moody's Industrials 1935,* 853; see also Interrogation of Hermann Schmitz, Sept. 12, 1945, RG 238, T301, Reel 8, NI-711, 13, 18.

168. Schröter, "Participation in Market Control," 179–180; Verena Schröter, *Die Deutsche Industrie auf dem Weltmarkt 1929 bis 1933* (Frankfurt: Peter Lang, 1984), 477. American I. G. Chemical Corporation embarked on new products in these years. Its subsidiary, Unyte Corporation, for example, started to produce plastic moldings in 1932. Haynes, *American Chemical Industry,* V, 336.

169. Schröter, *Deutsche Industrie,* 475 (change in ratios). In these years, new top management took charge at General Dyestuff Corporation and General Aniline. Adolf Kuttroff, chairman of GDC, died in 1930; Herman Metz became chairman, and E. K. Halbach replaced Metz as president. Haynes, *American Chemical Industry,* VI, 184. Kuttroff's death ended a long-standing relationship. Metz, too, had been associated with the German interests in the United States since he was a teenager (he was born in 1867). Metz was a director of the Bank of United States, New York, and when it failed in December 1930, he found himself in personal financial difficulties and sold his shares in GDC to Dietrich A. Schmitz (the brother of Hermann Schmitz). Halbach took leadership at GDC. Metz

was president of General Aniline in 1930 and 1931; Rudolf Hütz replaced him at General Aniline in 1932, probably when Metz turned sixty-five. Statement of E. K. Halbach, May 7, 1941, in U.S. Senate, Committee on Patents, *Patents, Hearings,* 77th Cong., 2nd sess. (1942), pt. 5, 2238 (hearings henceforth cited as *Bone Committee Hearings*); American I. G. Chemical Corporation, *Annual Reports* (issued Mar. 31, 1930, and Mar. 31, 1931); and Seward Davis to William W. Buffum, Oct. 4, 1932, Box 199, Francis P. Garvan Papers, Laramie, Wyoming.

170. So close had the relationship between Bayer and Winthrop Chemical become that a later historian referring to December 1933 would call Winthrop Chemical Company a foreign agency of Bayer's pharmaceutical division. Hayes, *Industry and Ideology,* 107.

171. For example, John H. Dessauer (born in 1905), a German chemical engineer, migrated to the United States in 1929 and went to work in 1930 for Agfa-Ansco in Binghamton, New York. Six years later he moved to Rochester, left the American I. G. group, and became one of the innovators in the development of xerography. *New York Times,* Aug. 14, 1993 (his obituary), and John H. Dessauer, *My Years with Xerox* (Garden City, N.Y.: Doubleday, 1971), 8–9.

172. Larson, Knowlton, and Popple, *New Horizons,* 156.

173. Howard, *Buna Rubber,* 34–35. It is unclear how I. G. Farben paid its part of the expenses (it could easily have done so through technical assistance transfers).

174. Procter & Gamble, *Into the Second Century,* 25, 47.

175. Aftalion, *History of the International Chemical Industry,* 147, indicates that as early as 1910 Bayer had taken out patents for synthetic rubber; during the First World War there had in fact been some synthetic rubber produced in Germany, and then the interest had collapsed with the 1920–1921 fall in crude rubber prices. With the cartel in the mid-1920s pushing up rubber prices, the interest once again revived.

176. Larson, Knowlton, and Popple, *New Horizons,* 157–158 (Baton Rouge developments).

177. Specific data on the formation of the United States & Transatlantic Service Corporation and Chemnyco came from the Department of State, Albany, New York, Nov. 9, and Dec. 10, 1990. Most important, see the Memorandum of Agreement between the U.S. & Transatlantic Service Corporation and I. G. Farben, Nov. 7, 1930; the sworn statement of Max Braune (secretary-treasurer of Chemnyco), July 3, 1941; and other data in File D-28-517, Acc. 67A10, Box 1303, RG 131 (Dept.-Justice). Data for 1933 in RG 238, T301, Reel 12 NI-1187, described Chemnyco as an outgrowth of an earlier "office of Dr. Wilfrid Greif" (of the American I. G. Chemical Corporation) and of the later U.S. & Transatlantic Service Corporation. See also statement of G. Frank-Fahle, June 4, 1945, RG 238, T301, Reel 12, NI-1183. Chemnyco probably stood for Chemicals–New York–Company. The retainer fee was included in the 1930 agreement; on it see Statement of Frank-Fahle and Statement of Max Ilgner, June 21, 1945, pp. 13–14, RG 238, T301, Reel 13, NI-1293, as well as data in File D-29-517, Acc. 67A10, Box 1303, RG 131 (Dept.-Justice). There is added material on Chemnyco in Interrogation of Hermann Schmitz, Oct. 29, 1945, p. 47, RG 238, T301, Reel 8, NI-711. An extensive sample of correspondence from Chemnyco files is provided in the *Bone Committee Hearings,* pts. 3, 4, 5, and 6. Robert M. Hunter, special assistant to the attorney general, Antitrust Division, Department of Justice, noted that when one Justice Department official (John R. Jacobs) went into "the vault of Chemnyco after the Treasury Department had taken it over . . . he had never imagined there could be such a complete file of information concerning the American chemical industry as he saw there." *Bone Committee Hearings,* pt. 6, 2624. RG 131 (Dept.-Justice) contains a number of large boxes on Chemnyco. These are the files that were once in the possession of the World War II Office of Alien Property Custodian. For insights on (and the importance of) the patent-gathering functions of American firms, see Naomi R. Lamoreaux

and Kenneth L. Sokoloff, "Inventors, Firms and the Market for Technology," in *Learning by Doing,* ed. Naomi R. Lamoreaux, Daniel M. G. Raff, and Peter Temin (Chicago: University of Chicago Press, 1999), 19–57, which deals with patents; it does not mention Chemnyco. One of Chemnyco's functions was to gather U.S. patent information and forward it to Germany. Kathryn Steen, "German Chemicals and American Politics," in Lesch, *The German Chemical Industry in the Twentieth Century,* 339–344 (on the Settlement of War Claims Act of 1928 and specifically the final decision granting I. G. Farben the award).

178. *The Times* (London), June 24, 1930.

179. In 1931, the shares in International Bergin Co. had come to be owned by International Hydrogenation Patents Co., a firm that after April 1931 was owned by Standard Oil of New Jersey, Shell, and ICI. On IHP, see Hexner, *International Cartels,* 314–319, and Reader, *Imperial Chemical Industries,* 169–170. In March 1931, Standard-I. G. had transferred its rights with reference to all countries except the United States and Germany to the IHP. Hexner, *International Cartels,* 317.

180. *Bone Committee Hearings,* pt. 3, 1374–1375, 1377–1378, 1432 (Exhibit 6, Ludwig to Weber-Andreae, et al., Aug. 4, 1930; and Exhibit 7, I. G. [Nitrogen Division] to Hochschwender [Chemnyco], June 28, 1932). I. G. Farben also wanted to be certain that the output was not exported from the United States. See also letterhead, Herman Metz, Advance Solvents & Chemical Corporation, to Chemical Foundation, Sept. 6, 1933, Garvan Papers, Box 45.

181. Metz to Chemical Foundation, Sept. 6, 1933. No reply exists in the Garvan Papers. The letter contained the standard assurances required by The Chemical Foundation when imports under the foundation's patents were desired.

182. *Bone Committee Hearings,* pt. 3, 1432–1433 (Exhibit 8, Report by W. P. Pickhardt, July 31, 1933, on July 26, 1933, meeting between vom Rath and J. G. Davidson of Union Carbide). Union Carbide was the leading producer in the United States of acetylene and acetylene products. *Bone Committee Hearings,* pt. 3, 1377.

183. I am *not* implying that The Chemical Foundation was "cozy" with the I. G. Farben–Metz U.S. organization. Francis Garvan, president of The Chemical Foundation, always saw Metz as an adversary. What was "cozy" was that I. G. Farben kept interested parties in the U.S. chemical industry well informed about who was doing what.

184. Haynes, *American Chemical Industry,* IV, 332; Schröter, "Participation in Market Control," 176. For Pennsylvania Salt Manufacturing Co.'s pre–World War I German connections, see Wilkins, *History,* 409.

185. On I. G. Farben in magnesium, see Stocking and Watkins, *Cartels in Action,* 284–296; Schröter, "Participation in Market Control," 176–178, 183; Smith, *From Monopoly to Competition,* 230; I. G. Farben, *Annual Report 1931* (probably issued in May 1932), in Garvan Papers, Box 76; report on I. G. Farben's American Business, July 1933, p. 12, RG 238, T30l, Reel 12, NI-1187, and I. G. Farben to Col. Thomas, Oct. 29, 1936, RG 238, T301, Reel 7, NI-622. American Magnesium Co. (AMC) had been a producing company but had ceased production in 1927; Dow Chemical had become the supplier to AMC (which did "processing") and, in turn, supplied Alcoa. In June 1933, Alcoa and Dow agreed to continued this relationship. AMC was the largest magnesium *processing* company in the United States.

186. See data on the travels of Max Ilgner (Oct. 23, 1945), RG 238, T301, Reel 8, NI-712, p. 5.

187. On the visit, see biographical data on Hermann Schmitz, May 2, 1947, RG 238, T301, Reel 50, NI-6539; for the February 1931 date, data on Max Ilner, Oct. 23, 1945, RG 238, T301, Reel 8, NI-712; President Hoover's engagement calendar indicates that at noon on February 25, 1931, Schmitz was presented to the president by the German ambassador. The Hoover Library, West Branch, Iowa, has the engagement calendar, which indi-

cates that there were thirty minutes until the next appointment. A later "composite" suggests, however, that the meeting was scheduled for merely fifteen minutes. I am indebted to Archivist Dwight M. Miller for this information.

188. For the context, see Schuker, *American "Reparations,"* 56.

189. My efforts to determine what happened at the meeting have been in vain. In a biographical sketch on Schmitz, printed in U.S. Senate, Committee on Military Affairs, Subcommittee on War Mobilization, *Elimination of German Resources for War, Hearings,* 79th Cong., 1st sess. (1945), pt. 5, 869, he was described as "a reparations expert." He obviously wore more than "one hat," albeit there is a logic in this, since German dyestuffs were a key issue in the earlier reparation discussions. Also, this was the time when I. G. Farben still expected reimbursement for World War I losses, under the War Settlements Act, so it was a very interested party in reparation financing.

190. Office of Alien Property Custodian, *Annual Report 1944,* 28.

191. See book published in Berlin in 1932 and underlined translation in Garvan Papers, Box 76. Presumably, Garvan was the reader.

192. Haber, *Chemical Industry,* 288; Martin, *All Honorable Men,* 116; and Haynes, *American Chemical Industry,* V, 287.

193. Procter & Gamble, *Into the Twentieth Century,* 25, 27, 18.

194. Haynes, *American Chemical Industry,* V, 290, VI, 237–238; and Dunning data.

195. Harvey, *Rio Tinto Company,* 221–222, and Haynes, *American Chemical Industry,* V, 309–310, 321n. The largest part of the Rio Tinto investment had been in Davison Chemical Company. Rio Tinto may have retained a small interest in British Metal Corporation (acquired in 1929) and through it some minor interests in the United States. Harvey, *Rio Tinto Company,* 214. Likewise, its subsidiary, the Pyrites Co., Inc., remained in existence.

196. Du Pont, *Annual Report 1931,* 18 (on his death).

197. U.S. firms participated, albeit they did so with great care. Even though antitrust enforcement was in abeyance in the late 1920s and early 1930s, the word "cartel" remained a pejorative one. There continued to be concern lest arrangements violate the provisions of the Sherman Antitrust Act that forbade agreements in restraint of trade. Often accords were structured so as nominally to exclude the United States, or they dealt with technological exchanges, assuming that the interchange of technology justified territorial restrictions on competition (later the courts would find this not to be legitimate).

198. Wilkins, *Maturing,* 82, 252. Most of the companies involved in Drug Inc. handled over-the-counter products. Sterling Products, with its Winthrop Chemical, was unique in its role in the research-oriented, science-based pharmaceutical business.

199. Kobrak, "Between Nationalism and Internationalism," 334–339. During most of the 1920s, Alyco Manufacturing Co. (the secret joint venture between Schering Berlin and Schering & Glatz, Bloomfield, New Jersey) had operated in the United States. Kobrak explains Schering Berlin's dissatisfaction with the venture and how after the new Schering company was formed, it would become the basis for the German firm's further expansion. Alyco came to an end in early 1930, with its assets divided between the shareholders. Ibid., 328–333. That year Schering & Glatz was acquired by William R. Warner & Co. Mahoney, *Merchants of Life,* 254, and Haynes, *American Chemical Industry,* VI, 470.

200. Elmer Bobst, president of Hoffmann-La Roche, Inc., made it a success story. Mahoney, *Merchants of Life,* 223–224, and Peyer, *Roche,* 103–104, 108–109, 141.

201. Neufeld, *Global Corporation,* 29–30.

202. Bondeson, "Growth of a Global Enterprise," 38.

203. Lloyd, *Rolls Royce,* 70, 66, 71–82; *Moody's Industrials 1935,* 1807.

204. On the American Austin, see Domer, "History of the American Austin and Bantam," 407–414.

205. A. J. Barnard, Detroit Office, to Automotive Division, Bureau of Foreign and Domestic Commerce, Apr. 21, 1930 (80 percent American ownership), and Julian E. Gillespie, Commercial Attache Istanbul, to Director, Bureau of Foreign and Domestic Commerce, May 13, 1930 (close cooperation), both in RG 151, 451 American Austin Co. 1930–1936, National Archives.

206. Domer, "History of the American Austin and Bantam," 408, 414. On E. E. C. Mathis and the Mathis car, see Wilkins and Hill, *American Business Abroad,* 112, 248.

207. It would have consisted of what remained of the 100,000 shares marketed in London in 1929; these shares were probably pretty nearly worthless in 1932–1933.

208. Domer, "History of the American Austin and Bantam," 414–423. Sir Herbert Austin and the Austin Motor Co. apparently never took up an option they had to purchase 50,000 shares. Wyatt, *The Austin,* 131.

209. On sales and share-of-market figures, see Chandler, *Giant Enterprise,* 3.

210. Dierikx, *Fokker,* 138–144, 153, 222n.44; *New York Times,* July 13, 1931 (Fokker announces plans to start a new corporation to build planes in the United States); I do not know what happened with the GM-Dornier connection, but there does not appear to have been any FDI on Dornier's part (merely a licensing arrangement), and Dornier never reappears as a direct investor in the United States. In 1933, General Aviation merged with North American Aviation. Dierikx, *Fokker,* 145. With the laws on foreign involvement in U.S. aviation, Fokker had decided to become an American citizen; but he failed to do so in the 1920s, since with his American investors he apparently had been able to conform to the U.S. rules without pursuing his citizenship application. In 1931, completely expelled from his old company and planning to start up on his own, he told the press that he had taken out "his first [citizenship] papers several years ago," and thus he now could file a petition for citizenship. *New York Times,* June 20, 1931, and July 13, 20, 1931. Like Rupert Murdoch in the 1980s in broadcasting, Fokker was aware that for business reasons he needed to be an American citizen; and just as Murdoch's principal company, News Corporation, remained Australian, so too Fokker's Amsterdam manufacturing venture continued on as Dutch. Murdoch became an important figure in American broadcasting; Fokker's ambitious plans of 1931 never came to pass. On Murdoch, see William Shawcross, *Murdoch* (New York: Touchstone, 1994), passim.

211. *Milltown Review,* Apr. 25, 1930; ibid., Sept. 11, 1930.

212. Jones, "Growth," 45–47 (Dunlop's chain stores); French, *The U.S. Tire Industry,* 57, 62 (number of Dunlop stores compared with the principal U.S. tire makers), 47 (market shares of the top companies). In 1929, 4.4 percent of replacement tires had been sold through manufacturers' stores; in 1933, 11 percent were. See Pamela Pennock, "The National Recovery Administration and the Rubber Tire Industry," *Business History Review,* 71 (Winter 1997): 549. Dunlop, in integrating forward into retailing, was following the example of the majors.

213. Martin Kenney and Richard Florida, *Beyond Mass Production* (New York: Oxford University Press, 1993), 193.

214. SKF made automobile (and other kinds of) bearings; I have excluded it here because it had a more general market.

215. For the pre-merger expansion of American Bosch Magneto Corporation, see its *Annual Reports,* 1920–1929, in Scudder Collection, Business School Library, Columbia University Libraries, New York. For the activities of 1929 to 1933, see American Bosch Corporation, *Prospectus,* Oct. 15, 1938, in Scudder Collection. UABC would be renamed American Bosch Corporation in 1938. I have no accounts for UABC for 1930–1933, but as of December 31, 1929, American Bosch Magneto had an "earned surplus" of $2.2 million; UABC as of December 31, 1935, had an "earned surplus" of merely $50,000.

216. Allis-Chalmers Manufacturing Co., *Prospectus,* Nov. 6, 1935, Scudder Collection. The Camden shipyards had resumed (in 1928) their earlier name, New York Shipbuilding Corp. Heinrich, *Ships for the Seven Seas,* 217 (on the name change). In the exit process, Brown, Boveri obtained a small minority interest in Allis-Chalmers. On Brown, Boveri & Co., see *Geschaftsbericht 1930–1931* (I am indebted to Luciano Segreto for data from this 1931 report).

217. Wilkins, *Maturing;* "General Electric," Harvard Business School Case BH81RI, 55–62; Wilfried Feldenkirchen, "Siemens in the US," in *Foreign Multinationals in the United States: Management and Performance,* ed. Geoffrey Jones and Lina Gálvez-Muñoz, (London: Routledge, 2002), 92.

218. Jones, "Gramophone Company, 98; and Channon, *Strategy and Structure of British Enterprise,* 137. The American Columbia company, which had become nearly entirely American owned in 1929, was now completely U.S. owned.

219. R. Lundström to M. Wilkins, July 1, 1991.

220. Sandvik Conveyor Manufacturing Co. to Chemical Foundation, Sept. 10, 1932, Garvan Papers, Box 45. By 1934, its U.S. company was Sandvik Steel Inc. Sandvik Steel Inc. to Chemical Foundation, May 10, 1934. For background on Sandvik, see Stopford, *Directory of Multinationals,* II, 1184; see also Stockholm Office, to Finance Division, U.S. Bureau of Domestic and Foreign Commerce, Nov. 5, 1936, RG 151, 620 General 1936, National Archives, which reported that Sandrikens Jernverks, Aktb, Sandviken, had an investment in Sandvik Saw and Tool Corp., Minneapolis, Minnesota.

221. Chandler, *Scale and Scope,* 644–650.

222. Coleman, *Courtaulds,* II, provides ample evidence that The Viscose Company should be included in Chandler's top 100, measured by assets (the reason for the exclusion was that The Viscose Company was a wholly owned subsidiary). Chandler's 1930 list had 200 companies: number 125 was American I. G. Chemical Corporation, and number 177 was Davison Chemical Co., both of which were in 1930 FDIs. Number 190 was Celanese Corp. of America, which in 1930 would qualify as a FDI. Absent from Chandler's list of 200 were several foreign subsidiaries, Brown & Williamson, Lever Brothers, and Dunlop. I do not think any one of these three foreign-owned manufacturers would rank in the top 100, but Brown & Williamson by 1933 had *sales* greater than P. Lorillard, which ranked 73; Lever was probably not that much below Colgate-Palmolive, which ranked 117; and Dunlop was surely not that much smaller than Fisk Rubber Co., which ranked 137. It is doubtful (but possible) that Nestlé was large enough in 1930 to rank in the top 200.

223. Marshall, Southard, and Taylor, *Canadian-American Industry,* 186.

224. U.S. Department of Commerce, Bureau of the Census, *Historical Statistics of the United States* (Washington, D.C., 1960), 537.

225. Hunt, *Heirs of Great Adventure,* II, 189.

226. Meneight, *History of the United Molasses Co.,* 49, 42, 56, 58.

227. Jones, *Merchants to Multinationals,* 94, 102 (Gibbs), 104, 267 (Dodwell), 103, 172, 217 (Jardine Matheson). For the sad state of the U.S. silk market, see Silk Association, *Annual Reports, 1929–1933.*

228. Wilkins, "Japanese Multinationals," 594–595.

229. Morgan, *Merchants of Grain,* 123.

230. I tried to figure out whether the Japanese trading companies improved their position vis-à-vis raw cotton purchases in the same fashion as Continental Grain was doing vis-à-vis grain. They do not seem to have been able to do so. Cotton prices were at a nadir, but the Japanese do not seem to have been able to take advantage of this. Japanese companies appear, however, to have dominated the transpacific raw cotton trade.

231. The point is made by many authors. See in particular Sturmey, *British Shipping,* 61, for the decline in British shipping.

232. In June 1930, the War Claims Arbitrator had set tentative awards for ninety-four merchant ships for $74,252,933. In July 1930, about 27 percent of the tentative award was paid. See U.S. Department of the Treasury, *Annual Report for Year-ended June 30, 1931,* 91. The North German Lloyd Line as late as 1933 still expected to be fully paid. See Norddéutscher Lloyd, *Bericht 1932* (July 27, 1933). The complex matter of these claims and the U.S. side of the story can be followed in the U.S. Department of the Treasury, *Annual Reports.* On the plight of German shipping, see Sturmey, *British Shipping,* 115.

233. Sturmey, *British Shipping,* 129–130.

234. Nakagawa, "Japanese Shipping," 13–17.

235. Sturmey, *British Shipping,* 130. The U.S. contribution (36.8 percent) remained the largest, but it was down slightly from its 1929 share of 37.6 percent; foreign shipping as a whole continued in the dominant position.

236. Krooss and Blyn, *History,* 207–208 (general conditions); Barry Supple, *Royal Exchange Assurance* (Cambridge: Cambridge University Press, 1970), 478–480; and *Best's Insurance Reports.*

237. Schull, *Century of the Sun,* 65–66.

238. Ibid., 66. The Canadian superintendent of insurance recorded that the declines in the New York Stock Market on Friday September 18, 1931, had the effect of reducing the market value of the assets of Sun Life below the value of its liabilities. Memo to R. B. Bennett, Sept. 19, 1931, cited in Bliss, *Northern Enterprise,* 416–417. (Note that Britain went off the gold standard on Monday, September 21, 1931.) Sun Life took steps to bring its assets into line with its liabilities.

239. Schull, *Century of the Sun,* 66.

240. The Queensland Insurance, Sydney, Australia, and Reinsurance Company Salamandra, Copenhagen, were the "exits." See *Best's Insurance Reports, Fire and Marine, 1942,* 1091.

241. Control of Metropolitan Fire Insurance Co., which had been in the hands of Assecuranz-Union of 1865, passed in 1930 to Société Anonyme de Reassurances Contre l'Incendie, Paris, through Transatlantic Securities (see *Moody's Banks 1931,* 1967) and the license of Hamburg American Insurance Co., New York, was suspended in July 1932, when that firm failed to conform with New York Insurance Department regulations (see *Best's Insurance Reports, Fire and Marine, 1942,* 1090).

242. In 1932, for the first time, a man with a German address, Dr. Wilhelm Kisskalt, Munich, was listed as on the board of Pilot Reinsurance (*Moody's Banks 1932,* 1534; *Best Insurance Reports, Fire and Marine, 1932,* and prior volumes). Kisskalt, who had been involved in the founding of Pilot Reinsurance, was general director of the Munich Reinsurance Company, 1922–1937, and a member of the supervisory board of Allianz, 1922–1945. Gerald Feldman, *Allianz* (Cambridge: Cambridge University Press, 2001), 288.

243. *Best's Insurance Reports, Casualty, Surety, Miscellaneous, 1933/1934.*

244. *FIUS-1937,* 32.

245. New York State, Banking Department, *Annual Reports 1929, 1933.* The Banco National de Mexico was not on the 1929 list, but it was on the 1933 one. Data on the Web site of the Banking Department of New York (http://banking.state.ny.us/histba.txt), posted July 5, 2000, indicate that the Mexican bank was licensed July 11, 1929. Thomas Cook & Sons, the British counterpart of American Express, handled travelers' needs and was licensed in New York as a foreign bank agency.

246. Data on Hellenic Bank Trust Company from Adrian Tschoegl, Aug. 3, 2000, the Atlantic Bank Web site, and the New York State Banking Department Web site (http://banking.state.ny.us/histh.txt).

247. Anglo-South American Bank's problem was its heavy dependence on nitrates, Jones, *British Multinational Banking,* 160–162, 240–242. On the poor performance of the Bank of London and South America, in 1930–1931, see ibid., 167, 241.

248. Roberto di Quirico, "The Initial Phases of Italian Banks' Expansion Abroad," *Financial History Review*, 6 (Apr. 1999): 18n (Banco di Napoli Trust Co., New York). James, *Growth of Chicago Banks*, 1171, and *Moody's Banks 1939*, 269 (Banco di Napoli Trust Co. of Chicago).

249. Carosso, *More Than a Century*, 65–66.

250. Between 1929 and 1932, "The Manhattan Company" was a holding company: its subsidiaries were the domestic bank (the activities of the old Bank of the Manhattan Company, restyled The Bank of the Manhattan Trust Co.), the International Acceptance Bank (IAB), and the International Manhattan Co. This holding company structure was dismantled in 1932; the Bank of the Manhattan Company resumed its old title. On November 22, 1932, the business of the IAB was taken over by the Bank of the Manhattan Company, and IAB ceased to exist, since its activities were folded into the parent bank. The International Manhattan Co., the securities subsidiary that had been formed in 1929, was liquidated. *Moody's Banks 1935*, 6; Wilson, *The Chase*, 60; and data in CMBA.

251. James P. Warburg served as vice-chairman of the Bank of the Manhattan Co., 1932–1935, and continued as a director to 1947. See biographical data in James P. Warburg Papers, and data on his resignation in those papers, Box 46, Kennedy Library. A large part of the income from Paul Warburg's "shrunken estate was invested in Bank of Manhattan shares," which motivated his son to stay on with the bank (once the son had been an active participant in IAB). Warburg, *Long Road Home*, 111.

252. On the conditions of foreign banks in 1929–1933 in Europe, see Feinstein, *Banking, Currency, and Finance*, passim. In the United States there were a few foreign-owned deposit-taking institutions, aside from the trust companies, but they were exceptional (some of the foreign banks in California did take deposits).

253. Calomiris, *U.S. Bank Deregulation*, 15, 18–19.

254. Gilbert, *History of Investment Trusts*, 108, 131.

255. Eugene White, "Banking and Finance in the Twentieth Century," in *Cambridge Economic History of the United States*, vol. 3, *The Twentieth Century*, ed. Stanley L. Engerman and Robert E. Gallman (Cambridge: Cambridge University Press, 2000), 763, notes that twenty-five states enacted foreclosure moratorium laws between 1932 and 1934.

256. Lewis, *America's Stake*, 558, and Table 2.1, Column 1.

257. Ibid., 558, and *FIUS–1937*, 14. See also Table 2.1, Columns 1 and 4 on FDI. This makes the FDI total suspect, for there were some substantial FDI inflows, March 1933–December 1934.

258. There is a problem not only with Lewis' figures but also with the mixing of market and book value figures. The difficulties with these figures make comparisons likely to be flawed.

7. A World at Risk, 1933–1939

1. Yeager, *International Monetary Relations*, 304–309; Studenski and Krooss, *Financial History of the United States*, 383–390; John Morton Blum, *From the Morgenthau Diaries, Years of Crisis, 1928–1938* (Boston: Houghton Mifflin, 1959), I, 61–75, 120–134; Friedman and Anna Jacobson Schwartz, *Monetary History of the United States*, 462ff.; Eichengreen, *Golden Fetters*.

2. For the long-standing U.S. commitment to exchange stabilization, see Rosenberg, *Financial Missionaries to the World*.

3. Originally, the United States would sell gold only to foreign countries on the gold standard; after 1936, it was to any central bank or government. Blum, *From the Morgenthau Diaries*, I, esp. 179. Henry Morgenthau was Roosevelt's secretary of the treasury.

4. Kindleberger, *World in Depression*.

5. Over the years, scholars (and others) have come to look more favorably on Roosevelt's devaluation of dollar, seeing it in positive terms, and they may wonder at my use of the word "despite" the devaluation of the dollar. At the time, investors tended to share the views of Winthrop Aldrich (chairman of Chase National Bank), perceiving the devaluation as "an act of economic destruction of fearful magnitude." Aldrich soon became a proponent of the New Deal, and the "act of economic destruction" seemed hardly that. Charles H. Feinstein, Peter Temin, and Gianni Toniolo, "International Economic Organization," in *Banking, Currency, and Finance in Europe between the Wars,* ed. Charles H. Feinstein (Oxford: Clarendon Press, 1995), 48.

6. *New York Times,* Nov. 14, 1936 (my italics).

7. At least according to Cleona Lewis' estimates. If not the largest debtor, the United States was clearly among the largest. Cleona Lewis, *Debtor and Creditor Countries,* made a valiant effort to determine the level of outward and inward foreign investments, on an international basis as of 1938. In Table 7.2 I reorganized her figures to conform to the patterns that I put forth in Table 1.1. Her figures are interesting in another respect: as of 1938, she has the United Kingdom far above the United States as a creditor nation worldwide. Of that $22.9 billion, she indicated that more than half ($11.6 billion) was placed within the British Empire, with the U.K. investment in the United States at $2.7 billion. Ibid., 48, 74 (the $2.7 billion is the figure given in my Table 7.3, and is from the U.S. Department of Commerce, for mid-1937, not 1938).

8. Arthur Feiler, "International Movements of Capital," *American Economic Review,* supplement, 25 (Mar. 1935): 63–73; Marco Fanno, *Normal and Abnormal Capital Transfers* (Minneapolis: University of Minnesota Press, 1939), 9, 29–32, 114–115; Bloomfield, *Capital Imports,* esp. viii–ix, 30–32 (the "normal" pattern was that which existed in the pre–World War I years). Cleona Lewis' figures on the level of investments in 1938 (Table 7.2) do not effectively capture the accumulated debtor-to-creditor flows on which Feiler commented. The problem was that no one knew the exact dimensions of the flows.

9. Frank D. Graham and Charles R. Whittlesey, *The Golden Avalanche* (1939; rpt. New York: Arno Press, 1978). File C261.3 Bank of England, Federal Reserve Bank of New York Archives, deals with the gold flows to New York in the context of the possibilities of war (henceforth this archive is cited as FRBNY). See also White, "Foreign Trading," 655.

10. For the inwardness of Americans' views, see William L. Langer and S. Everett Gleason, *The Challenge to Isolation 1937–1940* (New York: Harper Brothers, 1952), 13–15.

11. Bloomfield, *Capital Imports,* 86; see also White, "Foreign Trading," 655–702.

12. U.S. Senate, Committee on Banking and Currency, *Stock Exchange Practices, Hearings,* 73rd Cong., 1st sess. (1933), pt. 2, 530–531, and ibid., pt. 1, 177.

13. Yeager, *International Monetary Relations,* 305. Because foreign investors had been "burned" when America had issued paper currency during the Civil War, thereafter they had often insisted on "gold clauses" in bonds. Veenendaal, *Slow Train to Paradise,* 32. U.S. government paper held abroad in 1933—from the Liberty Loans of World War I onward—had the stipulation "The principal and interest hereof are payable in United States gold coin of the present standard of value." This was what was repudiated. For a futile Swiss government protest—March 22, 1935—see material in AF, E 2001 (c) 4/147, Swiss Federal Archives, Bern. I am indebted to Antoine Fleury for this reference. See also Michael D. Bordo, Christopher M. Meissner, and Angela Redish, "How 'Original Sin' Was Overcome: The Evolution of External Debt Denominated in Domestic Currencies in the United States and the British Dominions 1800–2000," paper presented at conference at Harvard University, July 2002.

14. Friedman and Schwartz, *Monetary History of the United States,* 474; Graham and Whittlesey, *Golden Avalanche,* 59; and Bloomfield, *Capital Imports,* passim.

15. On the court decision, see Madden, Nadler, and Sauvain, *America's Experience as a Creditor Nation,* 33. Franklin D. Roosevelt's message to Congress on war debts, June 1, 1934, in U.S. Department of the Treasury, *Annual Report for Year-ended June 30, 1934,* 243–244, on the "sacredness of the obligation." That American states as well as foreigners had bonds in default was part of the 1930s rhetoric. Max Winkler, *Foreign Bonds: An Autopsy* (Philadelphia: Roland Swain, 1933), 203, 264–286. How could Americans criticize Europeans for defaults when they themselves had such a bad record?

16. Editorial, *New York Times,* Nov. 25, 1936; see also ibid., Nov. 14, 1936.

17. On U.S. silver policy, see Broadus Mitchell, *Depression Decade* (New York: Holt, Rinehart & Winston, 1964), 146–150, and Akira Iriye, *The Globalizing of America, 1913–1945* (Cambridge: Cambridge University Press, 1993), 142.

18. Hiram Johnson to Harold Ickes, Oct. 17, 1933, quoted in Guinsburg, *Pursuit of Isolationism,* 150.

19. Carosso, *Investment Banking,* chaps. 16 and 17.

20. See the questioning at the July 11, 1934, hearings of U.S. House, Special Committee on Un-American Activities, *Investigation of Nazi Propaganda Activities and Investigation of Certain Other Propaganda Activities,* 73rd Cong., 2nd sess. (1934), vol. 7, p. 208 (henceforth cited as *McCormack Committee Hearings*); Senator Arthur Vandenberg (Republican from Michigan) on Sept. 2, 1936, wrote U.S. Secretary of the Treasury Morgenthau, complaining that Europeans were selling gold in the United States (which the U.S. government bought) and buying American securities at the same time as European governments were in default on their debts; it was not right. Blum, *From the Morgenthau Diaries,* I, 167.

21. Chernow, *House of Morgan,* 381–382, 399, the committee hearings, and data in the Thomas Lamont Papers, Harvard Business School, Baker Library, Boston, esp. Boxes 213–217.

22. Leffingwell to Thomas Lamont, Dec. 16, 1935, Leffingwell Papers, Yale University, quoted by W. Elliot Brownlee, in *Journal of American History,* 77 (Sept. 1990): 706.

23. Guinsburg, *Pursuit of Isolationism,* 192; Stuart, *Twenty Incredible Years,* 512; Frank Freidel, *America in the Twentieth Century* (New York: Alfred A. Knopf, 1960), 369–371.

24. Blum, *From the Morgenthau Diaries,* I, 330.

25. White, "Foreign Trading," 681n.23.

26. Ibid., 657, 692–697.

27. It had always been difficult to distinguish between "investment holdings" and "speculative holdings" in securities, try as many had done. Many people believed (and believe) the distinction had little validity. Others decided it was "only a matter of estimate and impression." The quotation is from an unsigned memo headed "Sir Frederick Phillips [Treasury] *Foreign Investments in the United States*" in T177/27, folder entitled "Foreign Investments in the U.S.-1936," Public Record, Office, This memorandum represented a British view but one shared by Americans. On similar, earlier concerns over speculative foreign holdings, see Wilkins, *History,* 566, 594.

28. Blum, *From the Morgenthau Diaries,* I, 359.

29. For details on the 1936 law, see Roy G. Blakey and Gladys C. Blakey, "The Revenue Act of 1936," *American Economic Review,* 26 (Sept. 1936): 468–470; Roy G. Blakey and Gladys C. Blakey, "The Revenue Act of 1937," *American Economic Review,* 27 (Dec. 1937): 703; and U.S. Department of the Treasury, *Annual Report for Year-ended June 30, 1938,* 26–27.

30. White, "Foreign Trading," 694–695. By contrast, it was easy to collect the withholding tax on dividends and interest. Ibid., 693–694.

31. Blum, *From the Morgenthau Diaries,* I, 331.

32. White, "Foreign Trading," 657.

33. Blum, *From the Morgenthau Diaries,* I, 337; Blakey and Blakey, "Revenue Act of 1937," 698–704; Mark H. Leff, *The Limits of Symbolic Reform: The New Deal and Taxation* (Cambridge: Cambridge University Press, 1984), 202.

34. U.S. Department of the Treasury, *Annual Report for Year-ended June 30, 1938,* 27. Double-taxation treaties involving the United States were very few: the first one was with France, signed in Paris on April 27, 1932, which came into force January 1, 1936. League of Nations, *Treaty Series,* CLXIV, p. 211, No. 3795 (this treaty would be superseded by another signed July 25, 1939). The second treaty was with Canada, signed December 30, 1936, and effective January 31, 1938. Ibid., CLXXXIV, p. 473, No. 4268. The third was with Sweden and covered not only double taxation but also rules on "administrative assistance in the case of income and other taxes." It was signed March 23, 1939, and came into force January 1, 1940. Ibid., CXCIX, p. 17, No. 4661. Paul Deperon, *International Double Taxation,* confirms that the United States was party in the 1930s to only these three double-taxation treaties. Even before the tax treaty with Canada became effective, under the 1936 Revenue Act, taxes withheld from dividend payments to Canadians were 5 percent, compared with 10 percent for all other foreign investors. U.S. Department of Commerce, Bureau of Foreign and Domestic Commerce, *Foreign Long-Term Investments in the United States 1937–1939* (Washington, D.C., 1940), 48n, 58 (henceforth cited as *FIUS—1940*).

35. White, "Foreign Trading," 681n.23, 694–696.

36. Interest on state and local bonds had been exempted from federal income tax from the start (since 1913). In the 1920s, Secretary of the Treasury Andrew Mellon was vigorously opposed to tax-exempt securities and sought in vain for repeal. The Roosevelt administration also favored the end to tax-exempt securities, but Congress retained them as a means of aiding states and local governments to raise revenues. John F. Witte, *The Politics and Development of the Federal Income Tax* (Madison: University of Wisconsin Press, 1985), 78, 89–90. The tax exemption meant interest rates on state and local securities would be lower, making such securities less attractive to foreign investors who apparently could not take full advantage of the tax benefits. However, there may have been more investment in these securities than we know about because of unreliable information. On the absence of information, see U.S. Department of the Treasury, Office of the Secretary, *Census of Foreign-Owned Assets in the United States* (Washington, D.C., 1945), 42 (henceforth cited as *1941 Census*).

37. The volatility concerns existed throughout the 1930s. Thus, in July 1933, George Harrison at the New York Federal Reserve was extremely worried that foreigners would dump American securities. He discussed possible controls with Richard Whitney, president of the New York Stock Exchange and with Dean Acheson (then undersecretary of the treasury). Acheson brought the matter to Roosevelt's attention. At the end of 1933, Henry Clay at the Bank of England would write of the movement of capital from New York to London, "But we have no idea how big it is." See George L. Harrison, Memo, July 11, 1933, Harrison Papers, 2680.0; Harrison, Memo, July 14, 1933, Harrison Papers, 2013.2 (b); and Henry Clay to J. E. Crane, Dec. 21, 1933, C261 England–Bank of England, all in FRBNY.

38. "Roosevelt Begins Inquiry on Alien Funds in Market: Fears Quick Withdrawal," *New York Times,* Nov. 14, 1936, and *Financial Times,* Nov. 27, 1936; see also data in "Foreign Investments in the U.S.-1936," T 177/27, Public Record Office.

39. The weekly transaction data were collected by the Federal Reserve to monitor the volatility. Figure 7.1 is only on "domestic" securities. We have similar data on "foreign" securities. Note that Roosevelt's concerns arose not long after the sharp influx of moneys in the week ending November 11, 1936.

40. Blum, *From the Morgenthau Diaries,* I, 360–366, 376–378, and Studenski and Krooss, *Financial History of the United States,* 394. Sterilization of gold inflows (when they were not nearly so alarming) had been a part of *1920s* monetary policy (Eichengreen, *Golden Fetters,* 165, 205–206, and Haberler, *World Economy,* 6), so this was not a new policy approach.

41. Blum, *From the Morgenthau Diaries,* I, 376–378, 393, 405–406, 418–419, 422, 425–426, and Studenski and Krooss, *Financial History of the United States,* 395, 399.

42. William O. Douglas (Chairman of the Securities and Exchange Commission) to Herbert Feis (Adviser on International Economic Affairs, State Department), Jan. 29, 1938, RG 151, 620 General/1937, National Archives, Washington, D.C.

43. On the definition of "long-term," see Appendix 1. For the fears, see, for example, George Harrison, Memorandum, Apr. 10, 1939, Harrison Papers 2012.8, FRBNY.

44. Marriner Eccles to Herbert Feis, Feb. 12, 1938, RG 151, 620 General/1938, National Archives.

45. Francis P. Garvan, *"Hot Money" vs Frozen Funds* (New York: The Chemical Foundation, 1937), unpaged Foreword. This pamphlet was published the year Garvan died.

46. James Powers to David I. Walsh, June 16, 1937, with enclosure, in RG 151, 620 General/1937, National Archives.

47. Christina Romer, "What Ended the Great Depression?" *Journal of Economic History,* 52 (Dec. 1992): 781.

48. *McCormack Committee Hearings,* vol. 7, 176, 183ff. Actually, by 1933–1934, there had also come to be confusion within I. G. Farben's management on how politics and business could be (or should be) mixed.

49. Borchard, "Reprisals on Private Property," 111, 113. By Executive Order No. 6694, dated May 1, 1934, the remaining functions of the Alien Property Custodian in relation to property seized during the First World War were transferred as of March 2, 1934, to the Department of Justice, and the World War I Alien Property Custodian office (opened in 1917) came to an end. See Office of Alien Property Custodian, *Annual Report for the Period March 11, 1942 to June 30, 1943,* 7.

50. *Homer S. Cummings, Attorney General of the United States, and W. A. Julian, as Treasurer of the United States, v. Deutsche Bank und Disconto-Gesellschaft,* 300 U.S. 115 (1937), and *American Journal of International Law,* 31 (July 1937): 532–537, on the Supreme Court decision. A later estimate was that "up to 80 percent of the value of vested enemy properties was paid to former owners" after World War I. U.S. Department of Commerce, Office of Business Economics, *International Transactions of the United States during the War, 1940–45,* Economic Series No. 65 (Washington, D.C., 1948), 100. That figure may be high.

51. 48 U.S. Stat. 1064 (June 19, 1934). The restrictions are on p. 1086. A radio license could not be granted to or held by foreign governments, companies organized under foreign law, or any corporation of which any officer or director was an alien or of which more than one-fifth of the stock was owned by aliens or their representatives (this repeated the stipulations in the Radio Act of 1927). The additions over and above those in the 1927 act related to pyramided ownership. Any corporation that was directly or indirectly controlled by another corporation that had an officer or more than one-fourth of the directors as an alien or whose voting stock was more than one-fourth owned by aliens or their representatives was now in the excluded category, but the text of the act had a qualification—"if the Commission finds that the public interest will be served by the refusal or revocation of such license." Many years later this clause would be interpreted as providing the FCC with leeway in enforcement. Apparently, the clause was inserted so as to avoid a possible application of the law to the U.S.-headquartered multinational enterprise International Telephone & Telegraph Corporation, which had attracted inward foreign portfolio interests. Although the 1934 Communications Act regu-

lated telephones, it contained nothing on foreign ownership in the American telephone industry. All the provisions on foreign ownership related specifically to radio broadcasting, that is, to wireless communication. Sidak, *Foreign Investment in American Telecommunications* 69–73.

52. *Central Vermont Transportation Co. v. Durning,* 294 U.S. 33 (1935) at 37–38 (Durning was the customs officer), and U.S. Department of Commerce, *Foreign Direct Investment in the United States,* 9 vols. (Washington, D.C., 1976), VII, K-46–47, K-275n.29 (exceptions granted by the ICC to certain Canadian rail lines were found not to apply in the *Central Vermont* case); henceforth cited as *FDIUS—1976.* De La Pedraja, *Rise and Decline of U.S. Merchant Shipping,* 114–115, 126 (1936 Shipping Act). On the 1938 Civil Aeronautics Act and predecessor, 52 U.S. Stat. 973; 44 U.S. Stat. 568; and *FDIUS—1976,* VII, K-65–67.

53. William O. Douglas to Herbert Feis, Jan. 29, 1938, RG 151, 620 General/1937, National Archives.

54. On the subsequent importance of this act vis-à-vis FDI, see Martin Tolchin and Susan Tolchin, *Buying into America* (New York: Times Books, 1988), 18, 26, and U.S. House, Committee of the Judiciary, Subcommittee on Administrative Law and Governmental Relations, *Foreign Agents Registration Act of 1938, Hearings,* 102nd Cong., 1st sess. (1991).

55. For example, on the British multinational enterprise Courtaulds, see Coleman, *Courtaulds,* II, 409–411. On the experiences of the Canadian multinational Seagrams, see data later in this chapter. For the management of J. & P. Coats' concern with the rising New Deal taxes, see David Keir, "The Coats Story," typescript 1964 (access granted by Coats), III, 156.

56. For a useful discussion of the 1936 Revenue Act and its treatment of foreign banks and insurance companies, see R. C. Lindsay, British Embassy, Washington, to Foreign Office, London, Apr. 2, 1936; Lindsay to Secretary Anthony Eden, July 14, 1936; and other data in FO 115/3410, Public Record Office.

57. For example, Kobrak, "Between Nationalism and Internationalism," 597–598, provides, based on records in the German Schering archives, data from the correspondence of Schering's U.S. tax counsel on the 1937 impact of the 1936 U.S. tax law. Schering's lawyer noted that the 1936 U.S. law had a "provision severely penalizing what are loosely termed improper accumulations of surplus by corporations. A heavy tax, in addition to all other taxes, is imposed if a corporation allows profits to accumulate beyond the reasonable needs of the business instead of being distributed." For the foreign-owned multinational enterprise, it became important to structure ownership in a way that protected the declared dividend.

58. Frequently, foreign companies in the United States imported inputs for their U.S. producing units. If foreign companies had only sales organizations in the United States, the imports would be the finished products. In each case, higher tariffs raised the price to the final consumer and made the offerings of the foreign companies less competitive.

59. Minutes of I. G. Farben Commercial Committee, Aug. 20, 1937, RG 238, T301, Reel 36, NI-4927.

60. For the U.S. Treasury in the 1930s, this interest in foreign multinationals was at a relatively low level in the policy-making bureaucracy, far subordinate to the U.S. Treasury's concerns over the heavy influx of FPI. Most dumping matters were, moreover, not considered in the context of FDI. For a fascinating background on the policies of the U.S. Treasury and the U.S. State Department vis-à-vis German dumping, see Alfred E. Eckes, *Opening America's Market* (Chapel Hill: University of North Carolina Press, 1995), 266. Under 1921 U.S. antidumping legislation (and until 1979), the secretary of the treasury had "broad discretionary power to conduct investigations and to impose duties offsetting the injurious effects of dumping." The State Department in the 1930s was nervous that imposing antidumping duties on German imports would be contrary to Ameri-

ca's attempt to increase international trade and "its whole international trade program." Ibid., 261, 266.

61. Earlier the Dutch had been designated a reciprocating nation, but not the British. Both Chester, *United States Oil Policy,* 55, and McBeth, *British Oil Policy,* 126, discuss the 1934–1935 British legislation and the U.S. decision. Neither seems to have understood the position of Standard Oil of New Jersey's affiliate and the bargaining chips involved. My phrase "rather reluctantly" comes from my reading of the rationale for the solicitor's opinion that Britain was "a reciprocal country," which Harold Ickes, U.S. secretary of the interior, received. "Solicitor's Opinion," April 2, 1936, and the accompanying explanation from the solicitor, Nathan R. Margold, to Ickes, April 2, 1936, were reprinted in U.S. House, Committee on Government Operations, Subcommittee on Commerce, Consumer and Monetary Affairs, *Federal Response to OPEC Country Investments* (pt. 2), 97th Cong., 1st sess. (1982), 538–545. See also ibid., 536, for 38 Op. Att'y Gen. 476 (1936), wherein the U.S. attorney general, following the solicitor's opinion, found Great Britain to be a reciprocating nation. Eugene Staley, *Raw Materials in Peace and War* (1937; rpt. New York: Arno Press, 1976), 162, notes that after 1931, following the principles in the 1920 legislation, in the "newer commercial treaties" the United States inserted a special reciprocity clause covering the rights and privileges "accorded the nationals of any other States with respect to the mining of coal, phosphate, oil, oil shale, gas, and sodium, on the public domain of the other."

62. Ellis W. Hawley, *The New Deal and the Problem of Monopoly* (Princeton, N.J.: Princeton University Press, 1966), 15, 19ff., and Bernstein, *Great Depression,* 202, who writes on the "relaxation (indeed abrogation) of the antitrust law" under the National Recovery Administration in the early New Deal years.

63. On the TNEC and its twelve members, three from the Senate, three from the House, and one each from the Departments of Justice, Treasury, Labor, and Commerce, the Securities Exchange Commission, and the Federal Trade Commission, see Robert Franklin Maddox, *The War within World War II: The United States and International Cartels* (Westport, Conn.: Praeger, 2001), 3. For an overview of New Deal policies, see Hawley, *New Deal and the Problem of Monopoly.* Thurman Arnold, head of the Antitrust Division of the Justice Department, announced that during the year ending June 30, 1939, there had been 1,375 "complaints involving alleged violations of anti-trust laws," with more than forty industries involved. The Antitrust Division of the Justice Department had 213 cases pending in the courts and "investigations pending in 185 other cases." *New York Times,* July 18, 1939. This was only the beginning.

64. LaFeber, *American Age,* 365.

65. Nelson, *King Cotton's Advocate;* Morgan, *Merchants of Grain,* 128–129.

66. U.S. Department of the Treasury, *Annual Report for Year-ended June 30, 1935,* 170–171, and *Annual Report for Year-ended June 30, 1936,* 205; *Federal Reserve Bulletin,* Dec. 1934, 780; ibid., May 1937, 394ff. The best source for these data on the inward flows is Federal Reserve System, *Banking and Monetary Statistics.* In the 1930s, whereas banks, brokers, and dealers were required to report long-term securities transactions that involved foreign investors, there was no formal reporting requirement for foreign-owned companies on their intracompany international capital flows (or, for that matter, on intracompany international trade transactions).

67. White, "Foreign Trading," 667n.6, cites U.S. Securities and Exchange Commission, *Selected Statistics on Securities and on Exchange Markets,* Aug. 1939, 59–61, on foreign trading, 1935–1938.

68. U.S. Department of Commerce, Bureau of Foreign and Domestic Commerce, *Foreign Investments in the United States* (Washington, D.C., 1937) (henceforth cited as *FIUS—1937*). *FIUS—1940.*

69. Grosvenor Jones to Alexander V. Dye, Jan. 15, 1938, RG 151, 620 General/1937, National Archives. Interestingly, Jones mentioned only the Federal Reserve and the SEC and *not* Treasury (I added the latter); the reason undoubtedly was that the Federal Reserve banks compiled the figures for the Treasury.

70. When, for example, the U.S. Temporary National Economic Committee (*The Distribution of Ownership in the 200 Largest Financial Corporations,* Monograph No. 29 [Washington, D.C., 1940], chap. 8) considered foreign holdings in the 200 largest American companies, its study used IRS Form 1042 (dividends paid to foreigners) to determine the stock holdings.

71. Lewis, *America's Stake.*

72. Marshall, Southard, and Taylor, *Canadian-American Industry.*

73. The interest was in both outward and inward investments; much of the new interest in foreign investment in the 1930s was related to the defaults on the *outward* portfolio investments. Inward and outward investments were often looked at together, but at other times the two were studied separately. Thus, for example, U.S. Commerce Department benchmark reports on the level of outward foreign investments and inward ones were prepared in different years, so that the best year end comparisons on the level of investment were always asymmetrical. Also, the Federal Reserve–Treasury figures were assembled as *flow* data (with the assumption—later found to be a false one—that accumulated flows would add up to the level of the investment). The Commerce Department also studied flows (for its balance of payments accounts), but it had started to undertake benchmark studies on the level of investment. It found its flow figures did not coincide with its benchmark findings. Mira Wilkins, "Flows Do Not Stock Make," unpublished paper, 1986, summarizes some of the many reasons why adding international capital flows do not result in appropriate "level of investment" figures.

74. Economists considered why a nation might be both an exporter and importer of capital. See, for example, Iversen, *International Capital Movements,* esp. 107–112 (the first edition was published in 1935). In keeping with the balance of payments approach, those researchers who studied international finance and particularly FPI considered that the large capital inflows into the United States were "abnormal," since the United States continued to be a net exporter of goods; thus, capital "should be" flowing out as a "balance—to finance the export of goods." Moreover, as a rich country vis-à-vis the rest of the world, many economists argued, the United States should have capital going outward to capital-short countries where the returns would be higher. Contemporary economists, in their attempt to explain the "abnormal" flows to the United States, did take into account risks in the source of capital country versus the United States. To the best of my knowledge, however, none suggested that the returns might be higher in the United States than in other countries *because* of more advanced technology, scale economies, or skilled labor inputs that enhanced the returns to capital as well as labor. Students of foreign direct investments in the 1930s described the behavior of firms and saw nothing odd in the cross-investments that they were documenting. Already there was a difference in analysis between students of FPI and FDI.

75. The only exception was in the revolutionary and immediate post-revolutionary period. See Wilkins, *History,* 31.

76. British investment in the United States was estimated at 39 percent of the total inward foreign investment in 1934, 39 percent in 1937, 38 percent in 1939 (Table 2.4 contains year end dollar values on the level of investment; Table 7.3 has the identical 39 percent for midyear 1937). Compare this with the 60 percent in 1914. Wilkins, *History,* 159. These are figures for all inward long-term British investment, FPI and FDI, and are based on American data.

77. *Fortune,* 8 (Sept. 1933): 33. See Roberts, *Schroders,* 245–246, on marketing American securities in England in May and June 1933.

78. Grant, *Capital Market in Post-war Britain,* 263, 263n.1, 171, and 179.

79. See Robert M. Kindersley's papers in the *Economic Journal,* 1934–1939, reprinted in Wilkins, ed. *British Overseas Investments.*

80. White, "Foreign Trading," 680–681, has an interesting discussion on the concerns of New York Stock Exchange and Securities and Exchange Commission officials when transactions were executed in London (or Amsterdam).

81. Michie, *London Stock Exchange,* 274, 175; the 1939 figure is as of March 24. If the 1933 nominal value figure was before the devaluation (Michie gives no month), the nominal dollar assets translated into pounds would at once be reduced.

82. Ibid., 143. These "dollar securities" could be "foreign" or "domestic" securities—that is, dollar-denominated foreign bonds or dollar-dominated domestic stocks and bonds.

83. Figure 7.2 indicates that the net cumulative British purchases January 2, 1935 to August 30, 1939, came to $433.5 million, or 37 percent of the total foreign purchases of $1,177.5 million (based on G. Gokkent's tabulations).

84. The net cumulative purchases by foreigners, 1935–1939, of "foreign" securities came to $657.8, of which the British bought $127.4 million (or 19 percent). Figures from G. Gokkent's work with data from Federal Reserve System, *Banking and Monetary Statistics,* 626–629.

85. White, "Foreign Trading," 655.

86. Robert M. Kindersley, "British Overseas Investments in 1933 and 1934," *Economic Journal,* 45 (Sept. 1935): 452–453, and subsequent Kindersley articles, reprinted in Wilkins, ed. *British Overseas Investments.* Some large British corporations and individuals held American securities. In 1936–1937, Imperial Chemical Industries still owned 390,100 shares of General Motors stock (practically all acquired in the 1920s) and 120,000 shares of International Nickel (when, on January 1, 1929, Mond Nickel Company, Ltd., merged with International Nickel Company, there had been an exchange of shares—John F. Thompson and Norman Beasley, *For the Years to Come* [New York: G. P. Putnam's, 1960], 205; my guess is that ICI acquired these holdings in International Nickel through Brunner, Mond, a predecessor company of ICI, which had interests in Mond Nickel Company). In addition to corporate investments, wealthy and knowledgeable individuals had sizable U.S. holdings. Thus, 6,500 shares of General Motors stock were held by ICI head, Sir Harry McGowan, and his relatives in April 1937; McGowan also owned 16,800 shares of International Nickel. McGowan's personal holdings seem to have been acquired in the late 1920s or the 1930s; they had a combined value in April 1937 of £300,000. Reader, *Imperial Chemical Industries,* II, 239, 242. John Maynard Keynes, who became involved in American securities for the first time as late as 1932, by 1936 had 40 percent of his personal portfolio in "dollar shares." Skidelsky, *John Maynard Keynes,* II, 524. (This is rather curious, for a man who was urging his fellow countrymen to invest at home.) Keynes' position in American securities was still "huge" in early 1938, but he seems to have made substantial sales in the last two weeks of March 1938. Robert Skidelsky, *John Maynard Keynes* (New York: Viking Penguin, 2001), III, 15.

87. My own research confirms the statement of Amos Taylor (of the U.S. Commerce Department) to Sir Robert Kindersley, Oct. 12, 1937, RG 151, 620 General/1937, National Archives: "We have been unable to find any evidence that British investment trusts or any other group of institutions have important holdings in United States bonds." This was in response to Kindersley's comments on the comparatively small amount of British investments in bonds in the United States. The context seems to deal with corporate bonds, not U.S. government bonds.

88. The 1938 estimate is in Burton and Corner, *Investment and Unit Trusts,* 84, and comes from a summary in the *Economist.* Apr. 11, 1953 (sample said to be "one-eighth of the industry's investments"). The *Economist,* Aug. 12, 1939, 306, has the 1939 figure.

That the percentage in 1938 was larger than in 1939 is not meaningful, since the samples appear to have been different. On some of the groups of investment trusts, see U.S. Securities and Exchange Commission, *Investment Trusts in Great Britain,* H. Doc. 380, 76th Cong., 1st sess. (1939), 17. The so-called Layton-Bennett group was another one that continued to be involved in U.S. business; it was associated with Layton-Bennett, Chiene & Tait, Edinburgh, chartered accountants; this group included the Scottish Investment Trust Co., Ltd., and the Second Scottish Investment Trust Co., Ltd.

89. "Lethargic" holdings were not uncommon; investors just did not sell. American securities held in the United Kingdom, such as U.S. Steel, AT&T, and Cities Service, were long-standing favorites.

90. Stakes in Allis-Chalmers, Amerada, Radio Corporation of America, and John Morrell & Co. are examples.

91. For example, United Shoe Machinery, Westinghouse Air Brakes, Singer Manufacturing Co., and Eastman Kodak.

92. The best work on the British overseas banks is Jones, *British Multinational Banking.*

93. Theo Barker, "Pilkington," in *British Multinationals: Origins, Management and Performance,* ed. Geoffrey Jones (Aldershot: Gower, 1986), 185.

94. *1941 Census,* 29. Virtually all of these 600 were already in existence in 1939.

95. Canadian investment in the United States was estimated at 22 percent of the total inward foreign investment in 1934; 17 percent in 1937; 17 percent in 1939. See Tables 2.4 and 7.3 for the dollar values. These are figures for all inward Canadian investment in the United States, FPI and FDI.

96. Dominion Bureau of Statistics, *The Canadian Balance of International Payments* (Ottawa, 1939), 135.

97. Dominion Bureau of Statistics, *Canada's International Investment Position, Selected Years 1926 to 1949* (Ottawa, n.d. [1950]), 24; see also Dominion Bureau of Statistics, *Canada's International Investment Position, 1926–1954* (Ottawa, 1956), 51. Trade in foreign securities (as explained in Chapter 4) was a very complicated matter. A number of American-owned companies set up in Canada probably fit under the Federal Reserve rubric of foreign securities. These were traded in New York and passed easily between Americans and Canadians. Some of the transactions in foreign securities could be related to sorting out the partial exodus of Canadian capital from direct investments in U.S. railroads. Some could be linked with the more complex story of Europeans' trading through Canadian intermediaries in American foreign securities.

98. Dominion Bureau of Statistics, *Canada's International Investment Position . . . to 1949,* 24.

99. The best source on Canadian direct investment in the United States in the 1930s is Marshall, Southard, and Taylor, *Canadian-American Industry.* See also Dominion Bureau of Statistics, *Canada's International Investment Position . . . to 1949,* 22–23, 25, 40 (report prepared by Herbert Marshall, "Dominion Statistician").

100. More precisely 21.5 percent and 26.2 percent of the total. See Table 2.4 for the actual figures; mid-1937 data are in Table 7.3.

101. Recently, Dutch scholar Joost Jonker found substantial arbitrage between New York, Amsterdam, and London in the 1930s by such Dutch firms as Pierson & Co. and Labouchère, Oyens & Co. Discussion with M. Wilkins, Odense, Denmark, Mar. 31, 2001. See also Veenendaal, *Slow Train to Paradise,* 18. Article 47 of the Swiss Banking Act of 1934 was on bank secrecy. See Guex, "Origins of the Swiss Banking Secrecy Law," 237–266; Guex insists that bank secrecy was part of Swiss history and that this legislation merely reinforced existing policies.

102. On Swiss capital flows to the United States in the 1930s, see Erdman, *Swiss-American Economic Relations,* 26, 65–82, and Wilkins, "Swiss Investments," 91–139, esp. 117–124.

103. U.S. Department of Commerce, Special Circular, No. 417, June 5, 1936, in RG 151, Box 24 (Genl. Corr. Alexander V. Dye), National Archives. See also Veenendaal, *Slow Train to Paradise,* on Dutch investments in American railroads before 1914 and the Dutch propensity to hold on to the securities. Whereas Michie found that in the case of London, the transactions in American securities by 1938 were mainly done in New York, the suggestion here is that this was not the case with Amsterdam. On Dillon Read, see Sobel, *Life and Times of Dillon Read,* 209. Interestingly, it was Dillon Read's Paris office (which had always done a sizable amount of *German* business) that was making the arrangements for the Amsterdam listings in December 1937. See also F. Y. Steiner to Dillon, Nov. 17, 1937, cited in ibid., 208. *Midland Bank Monthly Review,* Feb.–Mar. 1938, 7, and Bosch, *Nederlandse Beleggingen,* 389, contain useful information on Dutch interests in the United States.

104. I am indebted to Augustus Veenendaal for 1930s data from *Van Oss' Effectenboek, 1940.* In 1933, the Rotterdamsch Beleggings Consortium NV (subsequently called Robeco) was established. By 1938, more than 37 percent of its investments were in American securities. Similarly, in 1938, NV Internationale Beleggings Unie "Interunie" was organized; it had almost one-third of its portfolio in American stocks and bonds in the late 1930s. There were traded in Amsterdam in the 1930s a collection of new investment funds heavily involved in American shares. By contrast, some of the older Dutch holding companies that had invested exclusively in U.S. railroads were finally being liquidated (e.g., Vereenigd Bezit van Amerikaansche Hypothecaire Spoorweg-Obligatiën in 1939). A May 1940 letter from Arthur Purvis (who headed the British purchasing in America) discussed the forty or fifty Dutch investment institutions, known as "Administratie Kantoren," which acted as trustees, holding American securities in safes located in Holland; he explained that these Administratie Kantoren then issued bearer certificates to Dutch investors. As of May 1940, his estimate was that some $600 million (at that date's market value) of American securities were physically held in Holland. See Arthur Purvis to Jean Monnet, May 11, 1940, FO 115/3787, Public Record Office.

105. Data from Augustus Veenendaal. Arbitrage in corporate and other American securities between New York, London, and Amsterdam was routine for Dutch banking (brokerage) houses.

106. Erdman, *Swiss-American Economic Relations,* 77–80; Federal Reserve Bank, *Banking and Monetary Statistics,* 602–629; Bank für Elektrische Unternehmungen, Zurich, *Geschäftsbericht,* 1933–1939. No values were given in the reports. I am indebted to Luciano Segreto for providing me with copies of the Elektrobank reports.

107. The reasons why Unilever's subsidiary in the United States, Lever Brothers Co., became Dutch owned in 1937 involved tax considerations and the equalization of dividends to the British and Dutch parts of the business. J. D. Keir to Sir David Orr, Apr. 21, 1981 (copy provided to Mira Wilkins by J. D. Keir, Unilever, London, in 1981). See also Managing Directors Conference, Feb. 10, 1938, BB46, Unilever Archives, London (on Lipton and Mavibel NV). Geoffrey Jones, "Control, Performance, and Knowledge Transfers in Large Multinationals: Unilever in the United States, 1945–1980," *Business History Review,* 76 (Autumn 2002): 436, writes that the 100 percent Dutch ownership of Unilever's U.S. operations continued until 1987, when the British company got a 25 percent shareholding.

108. The 95 percent figure for the first two companies only is given in Ben P. A. Gales and Keetie E. Sluyterman, "Outward Bound: The Rise of Dutch Multinationals" in *The Rise of Multinationals in Continental Europe,* ed. Geoffrey Jones and Harm Schröter (Aldershot: Elgar, 1993), 66. On NV Philips, see Blanken, *History of Philips Electronics,* IV.

109. Calculations based on figures in Table 2.4 (for the general year end 1934–1939) and Table 7.3 (for mid-1937, which indicate 81 percent for foreign investment in general and 82 percent for FDI).

110. Morgan & Cie. served both Americans in Paris and the French community. Ron Chernow describes its vaults "brimming with securities owned by Americans and Frenchmen." Chernow, *House of Morgan,* 450. Presumably these securities were principally dollar-denominated ones. Some scholars have assumed a less active role for the House of Morgan in France after Herman Harjes died in 1926 and Morgan, Harjes was replaced by Morgan & Cie. (see Horn, "Private Bank at War," 110–112). My own research indicates substantial continuity.

111. Bloomfield, *Capital Imports,* 9; Roberts, *Schroders,* 245–247, 272, 281, 283.

112. Yeager, *International Monetary Relations,* 313–317; Blum, *From the Morgenthau Diaries,* I, 134; Federal Reserve System, *Banking and Monetary Statistics,* 620–629. The French had laws that required its nationals to declare capital held abroad (Yeager, *International Monetary Relations,* 317), but there is good evidence of noncompliance. By December 1937, Pierre Fournier, deputy governor of the Banque of France, was insisting that "a large portion of French capital was now abroad . . . about a third being in the United States and half Britain." December 8, 1937, Unsigned Note in Bank of England archives, cited by Harold James, *The End of Globalization: Lessons from the Great Depression* (Cambridge, Mass.: Harvard University Press, 2001), 193–194, 252n.22.

113. Wilkins, "French Multinationals," 13–14.

114. In October 1936, the Belgian holding company Sofina acquired a substantial share holding in Middle West Corp. (this was the reorganized Middle West Utilities Co.). See *Moody's Utilities 1937,* 788, 613; ibid., *1938,* 920; ibid., *1939,* 1741; and ibid., *1940,* 617. There continued to be important Belgian stakes in cellophane; there were also direct investments by the Belgian firm Gevaert in selling film. These investments seem to have gone directly from Belgium to the United States. Much of Belgian business in the United States was conducted through London. Van der Wee and Verbreyt, *Generale Bank,* 326. Roberts, *Schroders,* 291, writes of the Loewenstein investment trusts with U.S. interests in the late 1930s; these probably involved Canadians and Belgian investors intermixed, since many of Loewenstein's investment trust activities had gone through Canadian intermediaries.

115. Based on data in Federal Reserve System, *Banking and Monetary Statistics,* 620–629. On repatriations of dollar-denominated bonds, see Lewis, *America's Stake,* 416, 495, and Adam Klug, *The German Buybacks, 1932–1939: A Cure for Overhang* (Princeton, N.J.: Princeton Studies in International Finance, 1993), 12–16, which explains the reasons for the "buybacks." After Hitler came to power, the German government made annual demands on all German businesses involved in foreign trade to supply foreign exchange for which they would be reimbursed in marks. German firms that had U.S. affiliates and a U.S. presence had dollar profits and often dollar revenues from royalties. They would buy in New York discounted *German* dollar bonds and use them to meet their foreign exchange quotas. On this I have found useful Charles R. Clark Report, Foreign Funds Control, Dec. 26, 1942, file D-63-1, Acc. 65A1063, Box 267, RG 131 (Dept.-Justice.), and also Kobrak, "Between Nationalism and Internationalism," 528–533, on Schering's experiences. Klug, *German Buybacks,* 15, points out that "buyers [of the German dollar bonds] exploited the differences between the prices on the New York and Berlin stock exchanges," that is, participated in straightforward arbitrage exchanges. Klug insists that the buybacks were more than "a covert export subsidy"; they were an attempt by the German government to encourage reduction of dollar debts.

116. Based on *FIUS—1940,* 10; alternatively, see Table 2.4 herein.

117. Royal Institute of International Affairs, *Problem of International Investment,* 83n.1. See also Office of Alien Property Custodian, *Annual Report 1943–44,* 28–29, on the 1936 stiffening of restrictions.

118. When German firms argued that the overseas businesses should not be sold because they provided foreign exchange, the German Economics Ministry (January 1938)

allowed that this might be the case but insisted that all profits be repatriated, German exports be increased, and the overseas businesses be "purged of Jews." Hayes, *Industry and Ideology,* 196. On German "investments" in return for patents and technical services, see Office of Alien Property Custodian, *Annual Report 1942–1943,* 98.

119. Swedish direct investment exceeded portfolio investments. With the Italians it was the other way around. See Table 7.3. In 1938, J. P. Morgan & Co. partners provided advice to the Vatican (through Morgan's Italian representative, Giovanni Fummi) on American securities purchases. Chernow, *House of Morgan,* 487.

120. Barbara Stallings, *Banker to the Third World* (Berkeley: University of California Press, 1986), 333, and 323–325 (on her sources); see also Lewis, *America's Stake,* 495.

121. It would make a nice exercise for an expert on Western Hemisphere capital flows to compare the data on Figures 7.4 and 7.7, both of which deal with trade in "foreign" securities. Whereas the Canadians were net sellers of such securities, Latin Americans (investors resident in Latin America) were net buyers, with the heavy buying in the last half of 1937 (were these in response to earlier Canadian divestments of dollar-denominated Latin American debt?); were these repatriation of debt? It is possible that part of the trade in Latin American holdings of foreign (and domestic) securities may have been the result of European purchases and sales through Latin American intermediaries. *FIUS—1940,* 9, suggests this for *later* Latin American investments. Some transactions involved arbitrage. See Chapter 8 on Panamanian companies. See also Roberts, *Schroders,* 286–287, on the Schroder bank in Argentina and in the rest of Latin America.

122. On the politics, see Blum, *From the Morgenthau Diaries,* I, 183–228. On Chinese silver exports, see ibid., 196, 204–220; King, *The Hongkong Bank between the Wars,* 406–407. See also Sterling Seagrave, *The Soong Dynasty* (New York: Harper & Row, 1985), 96, 325, 307. The silver exports were what ultimately forced China off the silver standard.

123. Siegfried Stern, *The United States in International Banking* (New York: Columbia University Press, 1951), 319.

124. Seagrave, *Soong Dynasty.*

125. Wilkins, "Japanese Multinationals," 588–599.

126. Keetie E. Sluyterman and Hélène J. M. Winkelman, "The Dutch Family Firm," *Business History,* 35 (Oct. 1993): 152–183.

127. Wilkins, "French Multinationals," 23.

128. The term "production joint ventures" became very popular in the late 1980s and early 1990s; it occurs when two existing firms join together in joint venture production. See, for example, Carl Shapiro and Robert D. Willig, "On the Antitrust Treatment of Production Joint Ventures," *Journal of Economic Perspectives,* 4 (Summer 1990): 113–130. In such discussions, there was little awareness of how common such practices were in the interwar years. A few joint production ventures involved more than two existing firms (e.g., Ciba, Geigy, and Sandoz in Cincinnati Chemical Works).

129. *1941 Census,* 28.

130. The date of formation is given in U.S. Securities and Exchange Commission, *Investment Trusts and Investment Companies,* H. Doc. 707, 75th Cong., 3rd sess., 1939, 146.

131. For background on Murnane and his relations with Dulles, see Lisagor and Lipsius, *Law unto Itself,* 111–113, 147, and Ronald W. Pruessen, *John Foster Dulles* (New York: Free Press, 1982), 119, 130. See also George Murnane to Frederick Flick, Feb. 1, 1938, RG 238, T301, Reel 24, NI-3242 (for the address of Murnane's firm).

132. RG 238, T301, Reels 9, 24, 25, 26, 38, 39, and 41 contain an immense amount on the Petschek properties in Germany. There were two Petschek family groups, those of Ignaz Petschek and of Julius Petschek. As far as I can tell, Murnane represented only the latter.

133. Otto Steinbrinck, File Note, Jan. 29, 1938, RG 238, T301, Reel 25, NI-3450. What Flick did not tell Murnane was that I. G. Farben also wanted the Petschek properties

(see Otto Steinbrinck statement, Jan. 27, 1947, RG 238, T301, Reel 25, NI-3500) *and* that I. G. Farben would have never agreed to such a swap. Murnane represented the Solvay & Cie. interests on the Allied Chemical board.

134. Murnane to Roseborough, May 16, 1938, RG 238, T301, Reel 26, NI-3572. Flick believed that UCC was a dummy company acting for the Petscheks. See Otto Steinbrinck, File Note, Jan. 28, 1938, RG 238, T301, Reel 25, NI-3245; see also unsigned "Memo," May 24, 1938, RG 238, T301, Reel 41, NI-5326.

135. See RG 238, T301, Reel 24, NI-3236 (contract of May 21, 1938), NI-3320 (approval by Goering, May 25, 1938), NI-3233 (foreign exchange approvals, June 8, 1938). According to Walter Bauer, Berlin, Apr. 11, 1946, RG 238, T301, Reel 25, NI-3415, the banking firm Petschek & Co., Prague, owned 33⅓ percent of UCC. The properties of the Julius Petschek group were sold before the Munich agreement of September 1938 and the German occupation of the Sudetenland and in March 1939 the remaining Czech lands.

136. I do not know when they moved, probably after the Germans expanded into Czechoslovakia in 1938. In 1946 Paul Petschek was living in Toronto, while Walter and Hans Petschek were in New York. See June 19, 1946, data, RG 238, T301, Reel 25, NI-3449.

137. Royal Institute of International Affairs, *Problem of International Investment,* 305 (40 percent figure). Klug, *German Buybacks,* deals with the German repatriations, 1932–1939; the figures in *Banking and Monetary Statistics* indicate that while between January 2, 1935 and August 30, 1939, German cumulative net purchases of foreign securities were $36.4 million, total cumulative purchases came to $657.8 million; thus, the monitored (disclosed) German ones were only 5.5 percent of the total. Look, however, at Figure 7.7 on Latin American net purchases: these came to 27.2 percent of the total. (I suspect these related mainly to Latin American debt and not German debt.)

138. *FIUS—1940,* 5–6. The volatility of fall 1936 through spring 1937, shown on Figure 7.1, seems to have coincided with the aftermath of the Tripartite Monetary Agreement; Kynaston, *City of London,* III, 400, and Charles P. Kindleberger, *A Financial History of Western Europe,* 2nd ed. (New York: Oxford University Press, 1993), 387–389.

139. Yeager, *International Monetary Relations,* 317, 318, 332.

140. *FIUS—1940,* 6.

141. Ibid., 43.

142. *FIUS—1937,* 11, 14, and *FIUS—1940,* 43 (the Commerce Department treated the holdings of insurance companies as FDI and did not separately consider their assets). Canadian statisticians excluded the external assets of Canadian insurance companies from the totals of Canadian investments abroad, since "these assets must be considered in relation to the external liabilities of the same concerns arising from their business outside of Canada." Dominion Bureau of Statistics, *Canada's International Investment Position . . . to 1949,* 25. *Best's Insurance Reports* gives the foreign insurance companies' reserves and shows holdings in U.S. government securities, by foreign insurance company and by year. *FIUS—1940,* 43, on holdings of short-term U.S. government issues by foreign banks; the holdings were not only short-term issues. Thus, for example, the British-controlled J. Henry Schroder Banking Corporation, New York, had 49 percent of its total assets, 1936–1949, in "highly marketable US Government securities." Roberts, *Schroders,* 292. One has to be careful of double counting with all such investments.

143. Since there was no withholding tax on interest paid on U.S. government bonds, foreign investors did not have to report their holdings. According to a Swiss source, in 1935 Swiss residents held $1,392,450 in U.S. government bonds (acquired before June 1933). Antoine Fleury, "Les Discussions américano-suisses autour de la clause-or au début des années 1930," in Guex, *La Suisse et les Grandes Puissances,* 150–154. The Commerce Department found total Swiss investment in the United States at year end 1934

to be $380 million (see Table 2.4 herein). Thus, the $1.4 million in U.S. government bonds would be a very small fraction of the total.

144. *FIUS—1937,* 11, 14.

145. *FIUS—1940,* 1.

146. I have found useful the research summaries on network approaches in John H. Dunning, *Multinational Enterprise and the Global Economy* (Wokingham, England: Addison-Wesley, 1993), 207–208; the quotations are from ibid., 207.

147. The more complete mid 1937 data remain very incomplete, covering only 1,172 companies. In the 1941 Census, the U.S. Treasury Department identified 2,816 affiliates (*1941 Census,* 29); there was some increase in the number of FDIs in the years 1937–1941, but surely not as many as 1,644. The year end 1934 and mid-1937 details on inward FDI are the first such available from the Commerce Department. There was nothing comparable for earlier years.

148. Lamb, *History of the Canadian Pacific Railway,* 334–336.

149. On DPLC in the 1930s, see *Fortune,* Mar. 1937, 125–132, 156, 158, 160, and Nelson, *King Cotton's Advocate.* The *Fortune* article is excellent on labor conditions on the plantations; it also gives a breakdown on company revenues. See ibid., 158 (hedging), 160 (Washington contacts), 125 (plowing under benefits), and even better Nelson, *King Cotton's Advocate,* on Johnston, DPLC, and the Washington positions. Nelson shows how Johnston took low-yield lands out of production and got higher yields on the best land. He actually increased output. On comments by Michigan's Republican senator Arthur H. Vandenberg about the British corporate interests, see ibid., 159–160, 169. On DPLC's scientific accomplishments, see Clark and Kirwan, *The South Since Appomatox,* 101–102.

150. However, during the 1930s, U.S. agricultural exports were a shadow of times past. In 1919, American farmers received nearly $4 billion for exported products that required 55 million acres of land for their production; in 1932, they took in $590 million for the output of 34 million acres; in 1936, they got $750 million (as prices improved from their nadir), although the farmland in production was 20 million acres. U.S. Department of Agriculture, *1940 Yearbook of Agriculture* (Washington, D.C., 1940), 104–105.

151. Dahl, "British Investment in California Mining," 261–162, and Film Z-G1, Bancroft Library, University of California, Reels 33 (on Gold Fields American Development Co.), 81F-82F (Camp Bird), and 116–117 (New Consolidated Gold Fields).

152. On Metallgesellschaft's business activities in phosphates in the United States, see File F-28-2624, Acc. 67A10, Box 850, and File D-28-623, Acc. 67A10, Box 1310, RG 131 (Dept.-Justice). See also Haynes, *American Chemical Industry,* V, 124, and Richard Threlfall, *The Story of 100 Years of Phosphorous Making* (Oldbury: Albright & Wilson, 1951), 265. In 1937, Metallgesellschaft was forced by the Nazis to go through the process of "Aryanization," and in Germany there was a complete managerial change. "Memo," Nov. 6, 1937, in RG 238, T301, Reel 17, NI-1843. Richard Merton was put in a concentration camp in 1938 from which he escaped (data in File D-28–623). The complexities of the corporate ownership structure of Ore & Chemical Corporation and Pembroke Chemical Corporation, as of 1938, are shown in the previously cited data in RG 131 (Dept.-Justice). Ore & Chemical Corporation was also involved in lead and zinc reclamation from mining dumps in Colorado. Office of Alien Property Custodian, *Annual Report 1943–1944,* 48.

153. *Mineral Industry 1939,* 469.

154. *FIUS—1940,* 34, shows Belgian investment in mining, which were probably in phosphates in Florida; at least that is my guess.

155. Jorge Niosi, *Canadian Multinationals* (Toronto: Between the Lines, 1985), 119. On the history of Cominco, see ibid., 118–120, and Lamb, *History of the Canadian Pacific Railway,* 207, 259–260, 396–398. Lamb says nothing about Cominco's 1930s phosphate mining

investment in Montana, nor have I found anything elsewhere other than in Niosi. Lamb does note a lead mine stake in Montana (but does not give a date for the investment).

156. See Reich Minister for Economics to Mitteldeutsche Stahlwerke AG, June 8, 1938, RG 238, T301, Reel 24, NI-3233.

157. Haynes, *American Chemical Industry,* VI, 450.

158. Ibid., V, 128–132; VI, 450.

159. Markham, *Fertilizer Industry,* 95, indicates that APCC's after-tax returns on its investment for 1936–1938 ranged from 11.7 to 14.7 percent, whereas U.S. Potash had returns in the same years from 25.5 to 39.5 percent.

160. Ibid., 92–93.

161. *Mineral Industry 1939,* 534. An antitrust case in borax came later than the one in potash. For the dominance, see, however, abstract of August 16, 1945, consent decree in *U.S. v. Borax Consolidated Ltd., et al.,* Civil No. 23690 G (DND Calif.), in Talbot S. Lindstrom and Kevin P. Tighe, *Antitrust Consent Decrees,* 2 vols. (Rochester, N.Y.: Lawyers' Cooperative, 1974), I, 371–375 (Abstract 212).

162. For its diverse activities in the United States, one needs to consult Film Z-G1, Bancroft Library, University of California, data on Reels 33 (on Gold Fields American Development Co.), 81F–82F (Camp Bird), and 116–117 (New Consolidated Gold Fields). These reels reflect the British-headquartered Consolidated Gold Fields' continued interest in American Potash & Chemical Corp., in Missouri Mining Co., and in Tri-State Zinc, Inc., as well as in Camp Bird (gold mining) and in a new gold and silver mining property in California (Golden Queen Mining Co.). New Consolidated Gold Fields had a New York office, with an "American Advisory Committee." The interest of Gold Fields American Development Co. in American Potash & Chemical Corp. meant Gold Fields would later be a defendant in the U.S. antitrust suit covering the borax industry. For Gold Fields' September 28, 1945, compliance in the August 16, 1945, consent decree, see *U.S. v. Borax Consolidated Ltd., et al.,* Civil No. 23690 G (DND Calif.), in Lindstrom and Tighe, *Antitrust Consent Decrees,* I, 375. In the mining industry joint production was common; Gold Fields and American Potash were separate companies but closely associated. (Gold Fields does not seem, however, to have been charged in the 1939 potash antitrust litigation.)

163. At year end 1937, Selection Trust held nearly 24 percent of the common stock of American Metal Company. U.S. Temporary National Economic Committee, *Distribution of Ownership,* 142. On American Metal Company's U.S. smelters and refineries, see Navin, *Copper Mining and Management,* 273–276. American Metal also had operations in Mexico.

164. Data from the files of John H. Dunning, University of Reading, England (henceforth cited as Dunning data), and Stopford, "Origins of British-Based Multinational Manufacturing Enterprises," 327.

165. There were separate annual reports for Royal Dutch and Shell. Royal Dutch's reports gave full details: See Royal Dutch Company, *Annual Report 1933,* 26–27; ibid., *1934,* 20–21; ibid., *1935,* 24; ibid., *1936,* 25–27; ibid., *1937,* 20–23. See also Beaton, *Enterprise in Oil,* 405–406 (for the developments in aviation).

166. Royal Dutch Company, *Annual Report 1933,* 26–27; ibid., *1934,* 19–20; ibid., *1935,* 21–23; ibid., *1936,* 25; ibid., *1937,* 20–27; and ibid., *1938,* 20–21.

167. Beaton, *Enterprise in Oil,* 783.

168. Ibid., 698, 429–430, 458–459, 757. According to Tyler Priest, "Managing Shell's Business in the United States," in *Foreign Multinationals in the United States: Management and Performance,* ed. Geoffrey Jones and Lina Gálvez-Muñoz (London: Routledge, 2002), 191, in 1933–1939 Royal Dutch Shell's American operations were still divided into two separate organizations, one east and one west of the Rocky Mountains. Not until 1949 did the formal centralization of the management of the American enterprise occur, with a head office in New York. The steps to rationalize the business in the 1930s were, how-

ever, a move in that direction. Beaton indicates that Shell Oil Company Inc. was formed in 1939 to unify the firm's U.S. oil business; the New York central office opened in the fall of 1940; in 1949 Shell Union Oil Corporation, on absorbing Shell Oil Company Inc., would adopt the name Shell Oil Company. Beaton, *Enterprise in Oil,* 760, 757; R. J. Forbes, *A Chronology of Oil,* 2nd rev. ed. (n.p.: Shell, 1965), 75.

169. Bamberg, *History of the British Petroleum Co.,* II, 190, 273.

170. Bowker, *Science on the Run,* 67, 100–103, 108. See data in Schlumberger's Archives, Paris, for Schlumberger's New York and Houston offices.

171. Dunning data.

172. Heer, *World Events 1866–1966,* and *Fortune,* Feb. 1946, 116ff.

173. Heer, *World Events 1866–1966,* 155, 160, 164–165, 182; *Fortune,* Feb. 1946, 122.

174. The Swiss company was the Wander Co. Data on it from Himmel Nutrition, Inc., Aug. 28, 1993. On the incorporation by the Wander Co., Chicago, of vitamin D in Ovaltine, see U.S. Senate, Committee on Military Affairs, Subcommittee on War Mobilization, *Scientific and Technical Mobilization, Hearings,* 78th Cong., 1st and 2nd sess. (1943–1944), 774 (henceforth cited as *Kilgore Committee Hearings*).

175. "History Outline on Thomas J. Lipton Inc.," Dec. 2, 1947, Unilever Archives, London; Minutes of Managing Directors Conference, Oct. 8, 1936; Nov. 11, 1936; Jan. 21, 1937; May 7, 1937; July 8, 1937; Jan. 20, 1938; Feb. 10, 1938; June 16, 1938; Sept. 15, 1938; Dec. 8, 1938; Jan. 12, 1939; Feb. 23, 1939; Mar. 2, 1939, BB46 Unilever Archives, for Unilever's role. See also Mathias, *Retailing Revolution,* 344.

176. In the United States Lipton had begun as early as 1920 to provide tea bags for restaurant and hotel distribution; in 1929, it introduced gauze tea bags for home use; in the 1930s, the paper tea bag as it is known today was sold for the first time. Data from Geoffrey Jones, "Unilever and Tea," unpublished paper, 2000.

177. *Red Book of Commerce, 1938,* 152.

178. *FIUS—1940,* 36–37.

179. The Federal Alcohol Control Administration administered the code for the liquor industry, under the provisions of the National Industrial Recovery Act. Robert F. Burk, *The Corporate State and the Broker State* (Cambridge, Mass.: Harvard University Press, 1990), 120; K. Austin Kerr, "Distilled Spirits," in *Manufacturing,* ed. David O. Whitten (New York: Greenwood Press, 1990), 59; and Blum, *From the Morgenthau Diaries,* I, 113.

180. Blum, *From the Morgenthau Diaries,* I, 112–113.

181. The best material on the Scottish DCL's association with Bronfman in Canada is in Ronald Weir, *The History of the Distillers Company* (Oxford: Oxford University Press, 1995), 260–267; see also Newman, *Bronfman Dynasty,* 62–63, 105–108.

182. Newman, *Bronfman Dynasty,* 134. Weir argues that the Bronfmans should not have been surprised, for DCL never even considered extending its Canadian associations into the U.S. market. Weir, *History of the Distillers Company,* 269.

183. Newman, *Bronfman Dynasty,* 134. Not until the 1970s was the Canadian parent company's *name* changed from DC-SL to The Seagram Company, Ltd.

184. Ibid., 134; Marshall, Southard, and Taylor, *Canadian-American Industry,* 183.

185. Newman, *Bronfman Dynasty,* 135.

186. Samuel Bronfman, ". . . from little acorns . . ," in Distillers Corporation-Seagrams Ltd., *Annual Report 1970,* 65.

187. Ibid., 67; Newman, *Bronfman Dynasty,* 137n.

188. Blum, *From the Morgenthau Diaries,* I, 118.

189. Bronfman, ". . . from little acorns," 68.

190. Clair Wilcox, *Public Policies toward Business,* 3rd ed. (Homewood, Ill.: Richard D. Irwin, 1966), 706–708. The purpose of fair trade laws was to protect the small retailer against the giant price cutters. See also Blum, *From the Morgenthau Diaries,* I, 111. After

the NRA code provisions were thrown out by the U.S. Supreme Court, Congress passed (on August 24, 1935), the Federal Alcohol Administration Act. This act had no provisions on price maintenance. Kerr, "Distilled Spirits," 60.

191. Newman, *Bronfman Dynasty,* 137. The plaintiff, Old Dearborn Distributing Co., owned four retail liquor stores and sold at both wholesale and retail.

192. *Old Dearborn Distributing Co. v. Seagram Distillers Corp.,* 299 U.S. 183 (1936). Seagram Distillers Corp. seems to have been a marketing subsidiary in the Seagram group. The Canadian parent corporation was Distillers Corp.–Seagrams. Ibid., 299 U.S. at 194 (the judge's comments). As U.S. antitrust policy stiffened in the late 1930s, there was a coincident attempt to protect "small" retailers from the big chains. Retail price maintenance was seen not as antagonistic to but as a complement to a strong antitrust policy. The Robinson-Patman Act of 1938 reflected congressional endorsement of this sentiment.

193. Newman, *Bronfman Dynasty,* 135, 137.

194. Samuel Bronfman later claimed that as early as 1928 he had become convinced that "repeal" was inevitable and had increased Canadian inventories so as to be able to ship to America—and penetrate the market before U.S. production resumed. Bronfman, ". . . from little acorns," 64.

195. The U.S.-owned Schenley Distillers Company held first place in total sales until 1937, when it was surpassed by Seagrams. Newman, *Bronfman Dynasty,* 134, and Bronfman, ". . . from little acorns," 67.

196. On the Canadian histories of these Canadian firms, see Newman, *Bronfman Dynasty,* 29n, 24–25n, and 32n. On their U.S. business, see "List of Foreign-Controlled Manufacturers of Whiskey in the United States," Nov. 7, 1939, RG 151, 620 General/1939, National Archives. See also Bliss, *Northern Enterprise,* 399–400, 405 (on Harry Hatch).

197. Kerr, "Distilled Spirits," 59. Seagrams, Schenley, and National Distillers Products Corporation (the successor to the old Distillers Trust) were the other three.

198. Marshall, Southard, and Taylor, *Canadian-American Industry,* 183, 224–225; William L. Downard, *Dictionary of the History of the American Brewing and Distilling Industry* (Westport, Conn.: Greenwood Press, 1980), 205.

199. *D.C.L. Gazette,* Spring 1959, 7, indicates that DCD's establishment was reported to the DCL board in October 1932. See also Weir, *History of the Distillers Company,* 275.

200. Weir, *History of the Distillers Company,* 275, 269. On National Distillers Products Corporation, see Kerr, "Distilled Spirits," 58–59.

201. Weir, *History of the Distillers Company,* 269, notes that Herd's trip was *before* the Bronfman brothers' one to Edinburgh in 1933. However, DCD was established on recommendations from the Canadian affiliate. See *D.C.L. Gazette,* Spring 1959, 6.

202. Dunning data and data from Nicholas Morgan, Archivist, United Distillers, July 2, 1993. In the United Kingdom, DCL had acquired Tanqueray Gordon & Co. in 1922 and the appropriate trade names. For background, see Weir, *History of the Distillers Company,* 276–280.

203. Weir, *History of the Distillers Company,* 277–282, shows the unrealized plans of DCL to invest in National Distillers Products Corporation. DCL would invest £441,000 in Schenley Distillers Company shares in 1936, but Weir calls this a "portfolio investment." Ibid., 280. Weir says nothing more on this investment, and when the Bank of England later asked DCL to provide it with a list of foreign securities that it owned, it did nothing to try to maintain this particular holding (in fact, it seems likely that this was then repatriated; see Chapter 8 of the present book).

204. *Financial Times,* Oct. 23, 1961.

205. Downard, *Dictionary,* 129.

206. *Miami Herald,* Apr. 24, 1988, on the early history of the Bacardi Company.

207. Walter J. Donnelly, Havana, to Finance Division, Bureau of Foreign and Domestic Commerce, Nov. 24, 1936, RG 151, 620 General/1936, National Archives.

208. Wilkins, *History,* and Chapter 2 of the present volume.

209. Some of the formerly British-owned firms survived Prohibition, but as far as I can tell, most had shed British ownership. See Downard, *Dictionary.* The British-owned Denver United Breweries Ltd. lingered on after the end of Prohibition as a corporate shell, seeking to sell its assets. It never resumed production. See 1926–1945 data on Denver United Breweries, Ltd., on Film Z-G1, Reel 295, Bancroft Library, University of California, Berkeley. Stanley Baron, *Brewed in America* (1962; rpt. New York: Arno Press, 1972), 326, gives the top six brewery companies in the United States in 1940 as Anheuser Busch, Schlitz, Pabst, Ballantine, Schaefer, and Ruppert. All were American owned. Ballantine Scotch and Ballantine beer were entirely separate businesses.

210. *The Stock Exchange Official Intelligence, 1914,* 447, indicates that F. W. Cook Brewing Co., Ltd., registered January 1, 1892, acquired the capital stock of F. W. Cook Brewing Co., Evansville, Indiana. This was a profitable company before the First World War. With Prohibition this facility stopped making beer. In 1939, F. W. Cook Co., Evansville, Indiana, was included, *followed by a question mark,* on a list of foreign-controlled manufacturers of *whiskey* in the United States, prepared by the Finance Department of the Bureau of Foreign and Domestic Commerce, Nov. 7, 1939, list in RG 151, 620 General/1939, National Archives. (This seems to be an error: it was a foreign-owned brewery, not a distillery.) When in 1941 the Reconstruction Finance Corporation loan was collateralized in part by British-owned direct investments in the United States, F. W. Cook was on the schedule of corporations in which "the shares in British ownership are substantial." See Agreement between the Government of the United Kingdom of Great Britain and Northern Ireland and Reconstruction Finance Corporation, July 21, 1941, London 1941, Cmd. 6295, 3, 18, in "Loans: RFC," FO 115/341, Public Record Office. Downard, *Dictionary,* 52, indicates that the Evansville brewery reopened after the repeal of Prohibition.

211. Marshall, Southard, and Taylor, *Canadian-American Industry,* 183; on Carling, see Baron, *Brewed in America,* 341–342, and Bliss, *Northern Enterprise,* 441. Carling of London, Ontario, was by 1933 a subsidiary of Brewing Corporation of Canada, which in 1937 became Canadian Breweries, Ltd.

212. Office of Alien Property Custodian, *Annual Report 1944–1945,* 88.

213. Downard, *Dictionary,* 243.

214. Testimony of a U.S. Department of Commerce representative at U.S. Temporary National Economic Committee, *Hearings,* 76th Cong., 3rd sess. (1940), pt. 25, 13307. Another estimate was that "from 35 to 50 percent of the production of distilled liquors in this country in 1937 was in the plants of Canadian-owned companies." *1941 Census,* 28.

215. As for wine, there may have been some small foreign investments in California vineyards; certain foreign-controlled importers handled French and other foreign wines. There was, however, no consequential foreign investment story to be told about wine.

216. Howard Cox, "Global Cigarette," 228, and Cox, *Global Cigarette,* 299.

217. *American Tobacco, et al. v. U.S.,* 328 U.S. 781 at 794 (1946). The "Brown & Williamson production" figures do not appear to include BAT's cigarette export output from the United States; they (and the total) seem to include only cigarette production for the domestic market.

218. Corina, *Trust in Tobacco,* 236; Cox, *Global Cigarette,* 300.

219. Cox, *Global Cigarette,* 299.

220. The percentages and the cigarette production figures from which they were derived are from *American Tobacco, et al. v. U.S.,* 328 U.S. 781 at 794 (1946).

221. Cox, "Global Cigarette," 377–378.

222. Cox, *Global Cigarette,* 10, provides for the 1930s U.K. and U.S. cigarette exports; he does not give BAT's cigarette exports but suggests that they were probably a large percentage of both the U.K. and U.S. totals.

223. Sales and profit data from Unilever, London.

224. Minutes of Directors Management Conference, June 15, 1933, and July 13, 1933, Unilever Archives, London, and Report of Harold Greenhalgh, Albert Van den Bergh, Nov. 1933, BB43 Unilever Archives.

225. Wilson, *History of Unilever*, II, 357.

226. Ibid. II, 354. Wilson does not give 1939 sales in Europe, but reading between the lines, it seems evident that Unilever's U.K. soap sales (and certainly European sales, including the United Kingdom) continued to be larger than its U.S. sales. Nicholas Faith, *The Infiltrators: The European Business Invasion of America*, (London: Hamish Hamilton, 1971), 61 (market shares in U.S. laundry soap).

227. The important FDI position, indicated in Table 6.1, came to an end. Lindgren, *Corporate Growth*, 308–309, and Hildebrand, *Expansion Crisis Reconstruction*, 370.

228. There were stakes in other textiles as well. Thus, *FIUS—1940*, 6, refers to some in "silk textile" manufacture. These would have included the Swiss Schwarzenbach, Huber & Co. and Stoffel & Co. The French firm Bianchini Férier had a silk weaving mill in Port Jervis, New York, 1921–1958. Vernus, "Export Policy," 143, 147, 149. There were also a number of long-standing specialized British textile producers in America.

229. Dunning data. American Thread in Dalton, Georgia, ran a company town. See Douglas Flamming, *Creating the Modern South* (Chapel Hill: University of North Carolina Press, 1992), 150. On Coats, see Keir, "Coats Story," III, 153, 158–160. In addition to its new textile production in the South, in 1936 Coats bought control of Crown Fasteners Corp. and started to make zippers in Rhode Island. Ibid. 155. The Coats affiliate Clark Thread Co. had serious labor problems in Newark, New Jersey, which encouraged Coats' move to the South. Ibid., 159–160. The company's historian does not indicate that its rural Georgia plants faced major labor difficulties in the 1930s. There was, however, from 1934, substantial labor unrest at American Thread's Dalton, Georgia, plant, which was in a different part of the state and had been in existence longer. In 1937, mill hands at American Thread's Dalton plant signed a union contract with the company. Contract aside, all was not peace and harmony in Dalton. Flamming, *Creating the Modern South*, 199, 210, 213.

230. On their labor problems see Kulik and Bonham, *Rhode Island*, 273, who describe the organization of the International Textile Union (later known as the Industrial Trades' Union) in 1931, which drew on the "tradition of French and Belgian syndicalism and presaged the CIO's mass organization drives of the mid-1930s." They write that in the 1930s this union grew to "impressive strength" in the Woonsocket area.

231. In 1928, it represented 55 percent of the 98 million pounds of rayon produced in the United States; in 1929, it had over 50 percent of the 121 million pounds of output; by 1940, it had 25 percent of the U.S. output of 390 million pounds. Haynes, *American Chemical Industry*, V, 372–373. Du Pont was in second place.

232. The total direct investment in Shell, partly British (and the rest Dutch), was larger.

233. *Fortune*, July 1937, 110. Aside from American Viscose and Du Pont, the charged companies were Industrial Rayon, Tubize Chatillon (a 1930 merger of two companies with Belgian and Italian ownership), American Glanzstoff, American Enka, Belamose, Skenandoa Rayon, Delaware Rayon, and Acme Rayon. Du Pont and the last three small firms were the only ones that were 100 percent American owned. On the case and its disposition, see Haynes, *American Chemical Industry*, V, 376–377 and Coleman, *Courtaulds*, II, 400ff.

234. Coleman, *Courtaulds*, II, 409–411.

235. Annette C. Wright, "Spencer Love and Burlington Mills," *Business History Review*, 69 (Spring 1995): 71n.44. At one time, the U.S. affiliate had been a highly innovative enterprise.

236. Markham, *Competition,* 32; Haynes, *American Chemical Industry,* V, 369–380, esp. 377n.

237. The Celanese Corporation of America (otherwise known as American Celanese and an affiliate of British Celanese) became after 1933 one of the "Big Three" rayon producers in America. Markham, *Competition,* 17, and Haynes, *American Chemical Industry,* V, 372–373. It was not included in the 1934 antitrust suit, since it was not in viscose production; it produced acetate yarn; the two industry leaders, American Viscose and Du Pont, made both viscose and acetate yarn. In terms of innovative activities, British Celanese (and American Celanese) filed 1,438 U.S. patents in 1930–1939, which would rank the parent and its affiliate among the most innovative in the American "chemical" industry. Cantwell and Barrera, "Localisation of Corporate Technological Trajectories," 269.

238. Gall et al., *Deutsche Bank,* 316–317, 841; *Moody's 1937,* 86, and *Moody's 1940,* 2024.

239. Marie Tedesco, Johnson City, Tennessee, to Mira Wilkins, Aug. 8, 1988, and *Moody's 1940,* 1190.

240. *Moody's 1940,* 652, 1190, 1806 (directors); on Stauss, see Gall et al., *Deutsche Bank,* 308–318, which says (p. 317) that the German members of the "AKU Delegates Committee, including Stauss," resigned in 1939. This probably would have been true of the U.S. boards as well, but it was not reflected in *Moody's 1940;* however, Stauss was not listed in *Moody's 1941* as a director of the U.S. rayon companies.

241. Verg, *Milestones,* 291, 337; Hounshell and Smith, *Science and Corporate Strategy,* 207; J. E. Crane to Fritz Ter Meer, Apr. 18, 1941, Acc. 1231, Box 4, Du Pont Papers, Hagley Museum and Library, Wilmington, Delaware. Cayez, *Rhône Poulenc,* 135; Aftalion, *History of the International Chemical Industry,* 282.

242. Hounshell and Smith, *Science and Corporate Strategy,* 384–385.

243. *FIUS—1940,* 37.

244. See earlier chapters in this volume and Hexner, *International Cartels,* 296–349.

245. For their impact on U.S. business abroad, see Wilkins, *Maturing,* 78–82.

246. Appended to the Du Pont–ICI agreements of July 1, 1929, and June 30, 1939, were lists of existing patent licensing agreements. U.S. Senate, Committee on Patents, *Patents, Hearings,* 77th Cong., 2nd sess. (1942), pt. 2, 783–792, 794–811 (henceforth cited as *Bone Committee Hearings*).

247. Dunning, *Multinational Enterprise,* 256, suggests that cartels tend to flourish "where technology is static." In the 1930s, this was not the case in the chemical industry, where technological progress was alive and well. I find myself in complete agreement with Cantwell and Barrera, "Localisation of Corporate Technological Trajectories," 285, who concluded that "technological cooperation seems to have strengthened the focus of technological specialisation of the cartelised firms. In the chemical industry, such cooperation seems to have been associated with an active coordination of localised but closely complementary learning processes, with the result that firms became more similar to one another in terms of their broader patterns of specialisation." I would add that frontier chemistry came in large part to be shared.

248. Raymond Vernon, "Where Are the Multinationals Headed?" in *Foreign Direct Investment,* ed. Kenneth A. Froot (Chicago: University of Chicago Press, 1992), 64.

249. Reader, *Imperial Chemical Industries,* II, 325.

250. Ibid., II, 413, 419–420.

251. Ibid., II, 420. There apparently, however, was a paper trail. See ibid., II, 420–421. The paper trail was unraveled as antitrust investigations multiplied.

252. Review of Du Pont–ICI Agreement (n.d., late 1938?), in *Bone Committee Hearings,* Exhibits, pt. 5, 2400–2401.

253. Reader, *Imperial Chemical Industries,* II, 420–421.

254. Robert Sobel, *The Big Board* (New York: Free Press, 1965), 284. See also May 24, 1933, data in Francis P. Garvan Papers, Box 50, American Heritage Center, Laramie, Wyoming.

255. Solvay & Cie. to Orlando F. Weber, June 24, 1933, in Garvan Papers, Box 50. Francis P. Garvan got into the controversy, denouncing Solvay & Cie.'s exercise of "the power to attempt destruction of the Allied Chemical Company." Statement of Francis P. Garvan, n.d., Garvan Papers, Box 47. Solvay & Cie. apparently retained Ivy Lee as a public relations consultant to help it out. Ray Eldon Hiebert, "Courier to the Crowd: Ivy Lee and the Development of Public Relations in America," Ph.D. thesis, University of Maryland, 1962, 260, 280. As noted earlier, Ivy Lee served as a public relations consultant for I. G. Farben, American I. G. Chemical Corporation, and Standard Oil of New Jersey.

256. On Solvay & Cie., Sullivan and Cromwell, Atherton, and the cartel, see Lisagor and Lipsius, *Law unto Itself,* 113, 124–125. On Solvay & Cie's *unsuccessful* efforts to oust Weber *in 1933,* see Pruessen, *John Foster Dulles,* 130, who based his account on stories in the *New York Times.* In June 1933, Solvay & Cie. denied that it favored the removal of Weber as president. Solvay & Cie. to Weber, June 24, 1933, Garvan Papers, Box 50. See Haynes, *American Chemical Industry,* V, 36 (for more on Atherton); ibid., IV, 40 (Weber was born in 1878). George Murnane was elected a director of Allied Chemical in April 1936 and became the conduit for Allied Chemical's communications with Solvay & Cie. Pruessen, *John Foster Dulles,* 130–131. *Fortune,* Oct. 1939, 45ff., ran an article on Allied Chemical suggesting that "so far as the destiny of Allied was concerned," Weber's retirement "was incidental," and that "Allied is a reflection of Mr. Weber's personality" (pp. 150, 152). Why, then, did Weber give up the titles? I think *Fortune*—although it mentions (in a footnote) the "biggest single shareholder Solvay American Corporation"—did not understand Solvay & Cie.'s significance in the cartelization process and in the "forced" resignation of Weber. There was also an additional noteworthy Allied Chemical international connection. All during the 1930s, B. A. Ludwig was the operating head of National Aniline & Chemical Company (NACC), the dyestuff group within Allied Chemical. Ludwig had close and long-standing German ties. See Chapter 5 and Wilkins, "German Chemical Firms," 307n.74. Solvay & Cie. and I. G. Farben had various European cartel relationships, and it seems that Allied's NACC was expected to comply.

257. *Moody's Banks 1935,* 1399, and U.S. Temporary National Economic Committee, *Distribution of Ownership,* 143. *Moody's Banks, 1939,* 696 (SAIC name change). As of December 31, 1937, Allied Chemical had 2,214,099 shares outstanding, which would mean that Solvay & Cie.'s 500,000 shares would equal 22.6 percent of the equity. *Moody's Industrials 1939,* 2736 (on Allied Chemical's shares outstanding).

258. As of March 31, 1938, the Solvay holding company held 20,305 shares of Union Carbide stock (compared with the 500,000 in Allied Chemical). U.S. Temporary National Economic Committee, *Distribution of Ownership,* 143. On the expansion of Union Carbide in the 1930s, see Haynes, *American Chemical Industry,* V, 35–36. I have no evidence that Solvay & Cie. had much, if any, influence on Union Carbide's management. There does not seem to have been a similar effort to get Union Carbide to conform to cartel restrictions, perhaps because of the differences in product lines.

259. In RG 238, T301, Reel 12, NI-1187, there is a July 1933 chart accompanied by a sixteen-page explanation on I. G. Farben's numerous connections in the United States and Canada. For the 2,000 figure, see U.S. Senate, Committee on Military Affairs, Subcommittee on War Mobilization, *Elimination of German Resources for War,* 78th and 79th Cong. (1945), pt. 7, 943.

260. Long before Hitler took office, Francis P. Garvan had predicted that I. G. Farben would withhold "the fundamental secrets of German processes." See his May 1929 draft letter, quoted at length in Chapter 5.

261. See George von Schnitzler, Frankfurt, to Edwin Selck, Berlin, Aug. 28, 1933, in RG 238, T301, Reel 7, NI-697. On Ilgner's 1933 trips, see Oct. 23, 1945, data in RG 238, T301, Reel 8, NI-712, and Apr. 25, 1947, data in RG 238, T301, Reel 51, NI-6702. In RG 238, T301, Reel 51, NI-6702, Max Ilgner (in a statement dated April 25, 1947) explained that when, in the spring of 1933, there were attacks on National Socialism and on I. G. Farben in the U.S. press, he had invited Ivy Lee to visit Europe, arranged an interview with Hitler, and mapped out a public relations campaign. Lee, who had been working for the American affiliate of I. G. Farben since 1929, was after Hitler came to power retained by the parent as well. See Hayes, *Industry and Ideology,* 105; Hiebert, "Courier to the Crowd," 275, 278–290, and Lee's 1934 testimony at the *McCormack Committee Hearings,* vol. 7, 175–193, which gives his point of view. Lee died November 9, 1934. Hiebert, "Courier to the Crowd," 291. His testimony was given on May 19, 1934, at an executive session of the House Committee on Un-American Activities; it was included in the public record on July 11, 1934.

262. On his return from the United States, at a meeting of the Zentralausschuss of I. G. Farben, von Schnitzler gave an evaluation of the impact of the "boycott movement" on I. G. Farben's U.S. business. See Minutes of Meeting, Nov. 9, 1933, RG 238, T301, Reel 18, NI-1941. The *New York Times* during 1933 offers a good guide to the boycotts. The boycotts appear to be the initial reason for I. G. Farben's hiring Lee (and having him try to vindicate National Socialism in America). *McCormack Committee Hearings,* vol. 7, 179, 182.

263. Legal Committee, Minutes, Mar. 17, 1939, RG 238, T301, Reel 20, NI-2796. In RG 238, T301, Reel 11, NI-1084, is an eight-page document dated March 1, 1934, in which a Dr. Küpper provides detailed legal advice on the camouflaging of I. G. Farben sales offices in foreign countries; there were no country identifications; the United States was not specifically mentioned; the strategy was general.

264. Borkin, *Crime and Punishment of I. G. Farben,* 185–186.

265. See RG 238, T301, Reel 7, NI-684, for basic information on Schmitz (not dated, but probably 1945).

266. Walter Carpenter to Jasper Crane, Oct. 23, 1935, 5, cited in Chandler, *Scale and Scope,* 827.

267. Francis P. Garvan, President, The Chemical Foundation, sent a long letter to the SEC, Oct. 11, 1935, Garvan Papers, Box 76, analyzing the defects of American I. G.'s initial filing. On its subsequent filings, see letter from W. H. vom Rath to all present and past directors of General Aniline & Film Corp., Sept. 3, 1941, in Acc. 6, Ford Archives, Dearborn, Michigan. See also Borkin, *Crime and Punishment of I. G. Farben,* 186–188.

268. See, for example, statement of Max Ilgner, June 21, 1945, p. 12, RG 238, T301, Reel 13, NI-1293; evidence of Lawrence Linville in interrogation of Hermann Schmitz, Sept. 12, 1945, p. 7, RG 238, T301, Reel 8, NI-711; Confidential Report on Investigation of I. G. Farben Industrie (Bayer Division), Sept. 18, 1945, Section II, RG 238, T301, Reel 13, NI-1305; Wilhelm Mann and Max Brüggemann, "Report on Negotiations in New York from March 9 to 21, 1939," RG 238, T301, Reel 8, NI-780. I use the word "affiliates" because the ultimate beneficial ownership (or at least the ultimate beneficial control) was clearly that of the German I. G. Farben. The details of the process of disguises were very intricate, and the investigations into the arcane relationships have been numerous. In this book, I hope to provide the fundamentals of the story (and not bog my reader down in a forest of minutiae).

269. Borkin, *Crime and Punishment of I. G. Farben,* 186. Although he took over Hermann Schmitz's title, Dietrich Schmitz actually replaced I. G. Farben's Wilfried Greif as "headman at the American company." See interrogation of Hermann Schmitz, Oct. 29, 1945, p. 46, RG 238, T301, Reel 8, NI-711. Greif became ill in 1935, returned to Germany, and

died in 1937. See obituary, *New York Times,* Oct. 30, 1937. Greif had been the I. G. Farben man in charge of the American affiliate.

270. Borkin, *Crime and Punishment of I. G. Farben,* 186–187. On Walter Duisberg as patent attorney, see statement of G. Frank-Fahle, RG 238, T301, Reel 12, NI-1183, and Life History of Max Ilgner, RG 238, T301, Reel 8, NI-712. There is a fascinating copy of an unsigned confidential memorandum, dated Oct. 7, *1926,* in the Garvan Papers, Box 76, which reports that Carl Bosch was then in the United States, accompanied by "an understudy, the son of Dr [Carl] Duisberg, who is to be trained to take personal charge of the American business. The young man is to return to Germany and then come back to the United States and become an American citizen." As noted in the text, Carl Duisberg's son, Walter, became a U.S. citizen in 1933.

271. Hütz had come to the United States in 1909 to manage Bayer's Boston office and had been associated with the American business from that point on; he had been interned during the closing months of World War I but after the war had become a U.S. citizen. Hütz had replaced Herman Metz as president of GAW in 1932. Seward Davis to William W. Buffum, Oct. 4, 1932, Garvan Papers, Box 199 (Hütz as president GAW). Haynes, *American Chemical Industry,* IV, 235n, says Hütz became president of GAW in 1935 (I have relied on the contemporary source). On Hütz's arrest for espionage on August 21, 1918, his internment, and his subsequent naturalization, see John Boylan, *Sequel to the Apocalyse* (New York: Booktab, 1942), 43, and *New York Times,* Aug. 22 and 23, 1918.

272. Edwards, *Economic and Political Aspects of International Cartels,* 9 (for Dietrich Schmitz's role). See interrogation of Hermann Schmitz, Oct. 29, 1945, RG 238, T301, Reel 8, NI-711, pp. 43–45, for a very confused discussion on the ownership of GDC. It seems the "American" ownership from the start was German financed. A 1933 report in I. G. Farben files describes GDC as 100 percent I. G. Farben—and then had, in parentheses, "Konsortial" (a word not in my German dictionaries but with obvious connotations): for the report, see RG 238, T301, Reel 12, NI-1187. For more on ownership and "options" granted to I. G. Farben and Halbach's relationship to I. G. Farben, see statement by E. K. Halbach, May 7, 1941, published in *Bone Committee Hearings,* pt. 5, 2238, 2236–2239. Borkin, *Crime and Punishment of I. G. Farben,* 195, writes that in August 1939, just before the outbreak of war, "I. G. Farben sold the controlling interest in GDC to Halbach." Haynes, *American Chemical Industry,* VI, 184 (on Halbach). On the mid-1930s GDC imports from I. G. Farben and I. G. Farben's representative (Gustav Frank-Fahle) in the United States in February 1935, see Frank-Fahle, Statement, June 4, 1945, p. 13, in RG 238, T301, Reel 12, NI-1183, who indicates that the large dyestuff exports to the United States were at the request of the German government in order to provide foreign exchange for the German import of oil. I. G. Farben would explain to the German government that these exports were undertaken, "although considerable difficulties might have arisen for us by reason of the American tariff and dumping regulations." I. G. Farben, "Report on Exports with Losses in Order to Obtain Foreign Currency for Germany," Oct. 1937, RG 238, T301, Reel 33, NI-4453. That these were intracompany (within a German multinational enterprise) transactions made them possible.

273. Their important share of the U.S. dyestuff market in 1938–1939 is given in Schröter, "Cartels as a Form of Concentration," 118, and Stocking and Watkins, *Cartels in Action,* 508. Absent from the I. G. Farben's American management were two "old-timers," Adolf Kuttroff and Herman Metz; the first died in 1930, and the second in 1934.

274. See Chapter 6 on the establishment of Chemnyco. The best material on Chemnyco and its functions is in File D-28-517, Acc. 67A10, Box 1303, RG 131 (Dept.-Justice.). Other files in RG 131 (Dept.-Justice) also have material from the New York office of Chemnyco. See also Sasuly, *I. G. Farben,* 101–102. Additional useful materials include statement of Frank-Fahle, June 4, 1945, pp. 5–6, RG 238, T301, Reel 12, NI-1183, who notes that German

foreign exchange authorities created difficulties, seeking to prevent I. G. Farben's payment of large retainer fees to Chemnyco (apparently, however, they were paid); July 1933 document on I. G. Farben's American relationships, p. 17, RG 238, T301, Reel 12, NI-1187; statements of Max Ilgner, June 21, 1945, pp. 13 and 14, RG 238, T301, Reel 13, NI-1293, and Apr. 25, 1947, p. 4, RG 238, T301, Reel 51, NI-6699. When, for example, I. G. Farben entered into a cross-licensing agreement with Rohm & Haas, Philadelphia, Chemnyco acted for I. G. Farben. *Bone Committee Hearings,* 670–673. Substantial data presented in evidence at the Bone Committee Hearings came from Chemnyco files. Rudolf Ilgner had come to the United States in 1923 to work for Kuttroff, Pickhardt & Co. and became a naturalized American in 1930. Chemnyco, "Essential Facts & Information," by T. M. Robertson, Sept. 23, 1942, in File D-28-517, Acc. 67A10, Box 1303, RG 131 (Dept.-Justice). Chemnyco was a legal entity; its personnel overlapped with that of American I. G. Chemical.

275. Haynes, *American Chemical Industry,* V, 336; VI, 246–247. On I. G. Farben's interest in Plaskon, see data in RG 238, T301, Reel 45, NI-6058.

276. Haynes, *American Chemical Industry,* VI, 176, and Alt, "Photochemical Industry," 53.

277. Haynes, *American Chemical Industry,* VI, 407, and Mahoney, *Merchants of Life,* 206.

278. According to Mahoney, *Merchants of Life,* 214. Verg, *Milestones,* 275 (says it was Prontylin that saved the life of the president's son). Gerhard Domagk's discovery in Germany in 1935 of sulfonamides revolutionized medical therapy. Ibid., 272–276, and Henry E. Sigerist, *Civilization and Disease* (Ithaca, N.Y.: Cornell University Press, 1943), 176. For data on the complex U.S.-German financial relations vis-à-vis Winthrop Chemical Co., see Wilhelm Mann and Max Brüggemann, "Report on Negotiations in New York from March 9 to 21, 1939," RG 238, T301, Reel 8, NI-780. On p. 16 of this report these I. G. Farben representatives noted that "the dependency of the American I. G. on the European decisions conspicuous during the negotiations of American I. G. [the German side] with the American side [Dr. W. E. Weiss and Sterling Drug, the joint venture partner in Winthrop Chemical] will greatly endanger" the view that I. G. Farben had been fostering that American I. G. was not German controlled. (In this internal document, American I. G. rather than Chemnyco is referred to as basic in the interconnections.)

279. Interrogation of Heinrich Hörlein, May 2, 1947, RG 238, T301, Reel 52, NI-6787, on his four trips to the United States between 1927 and 1938 in connection with sulfa drugs and Atabrine. For background on Hörlein, see Verg, *Milestone,* 219 (in 1910, he had taken charge of Bayer's pharmaceutical department) and 197 (in 1912, he developed Luminal, a soporific and antiepileptic drug). It was Hörlein who recruited Domagk to I. G. Farben in 1927 and encouraged his research in that firm's laboratories on sulfonamides. Ibid., 272ff.

280. On cartel relations in nitrogen, see Stocking and Watkins, *Cartels in Action,* 142–154. On Synthetic Nitrogen Products Corporation, interrogation of Hermann Schmitz, Oct. 29, 1945, pp. 46–47, RG 238, T301, Reel 8, NI-711; July 1933 Statement on I. G. Farben's North American Holdings, RG 238, T301, Reel 12, NI-1187; and Haynes, *American Chemical Industry,* V, 336n; IV, 313, 317. Du Pont had started construction of the Belle, West Virginia, plant in 1925. Hounshell and Smith, *Science and Corporate Strategy,* 186. The ICI and Solvay & Cie. role in nitrogen has been referred to earlier in this chapter.

281. *Bone Committee Hearings,* pt. 5, 1437, and letter from Hochschwender (Chemnyco) to I. G. Farben, Apr. 25, 1934, in ibid., pt. 5, 1439.

282. Minutes of Meeting, Sept. 2, 1935, RG 238, T301, Reel 18, NI-1941.

283. Haynes, *American Chemical Industry,* V, 219–220.

284. W. Arthur Murphy to J. E. Crane, June 26, 1934, Acc. 1231, Box 4, Du Pont Archives.

285. J. K. Jenney to J. E. Crane, Dec. 9, 1936, Acc. 1231, Box 4, Du Pont Archives, indicates that Du Pont had "substantial investments in I. G. Farbenindustrie, Dynamit A. G., and Deutsche Gold-und Silber Scheideanstalt."

286. As of March 31, 1938, American I. G. Chemical Corporation owned 6,500 shares of Du Pont stock. U.S. Temporary National Economic Committee, *Distribution of Ownership,* 143.

287. In July 1933, I. G. Farben owned 120 common shares of Atlas Powder and 1,080 common and 76 preferred shares of Hercules Powder Co. In December 1937, I. G. Farben had the same holdings in Atlas Powder; its interests in Hercules Power were 2,376 common and 11 preferred shares. Data in RG 238, T301, Reel 12, NI-1187, and Reel 45, NI-6058. On these two firms and their relations with Du Pont, see Chandler and Salisbury, *Pierre S. Du Pont,* 293, 296–299, 567–569.

288. "Report on Investigation of Patents and Processes Situation Respecting du Pont and I. G. Farben," Mar. 18, 1936, *Bone Committee Hearings,* pt. 5, 2074, 2263–2266.

289. Ibid., 2266.

290. As noted, in May 1939 (May 23), Du Pont signed a licensing agreement with I. G. Farben to share with the latter its new nylon technology. There were other agreements between Du Pont and I. G. Farben in the late 1930s, including a monovinylacetylene (September 14, 1938) and a styrene (November 22, 1938) agreement. See J. E. Crane to Fritz Ter Meer, Apr. 18, 1941, Acc. 1231, Box 4, Du Pont Archives, and Hounshell and Smith, *Science and Corporate Strategy,* 207.

291. See data in RG 238, T301, Reel 4, NI-306, and Reel 9, NI-882; *Bone Committee Hearings,* pt. 6, 2666. For a brief summary of I. G. Farben's predecessors and I. G. Farben's early work on synthetic rubber, see Peter Morris, "I. G. Farben and the Third Reich," in *I. G. Farben Study Group, Newsletter No. 2* (n.d. Oct. 1990), 13. See also Interrogation of Carl Krauch, Sept. 20, 1945, RG 238, T301, Reel 52, NI-6768.

292. Davis R. B. Ross, "Patents and Bureaucrats: U.S. Synthetic Rubber Developments before Pearl Harbor," in *Business and Government,* ed. Joseph Frese and Jacob Judd (Tarrytown, N.Y.: Sleepy Hollow Restorations, 1985), 119–155, emphasizes the importance of low crude rubber prices in deterring American research efforts. On the history of synthetic rubber and Du Pont's development of DuPrene (later called Neoprene), see the March 20, 1934, memorandum that Du Pont prepared for forwarding to Herbert Feis, economic adviser, Department of State. Du Pont wrote that it had been producing DuPrene on a commercial scale since May 1932. "Our production cost is at present considerably in excess of our selling price which is $1.00 a pound. At this price DuPrene is obviously used only for purposes for which it is superior to natural rubber. Our experience to date indicates that DuPrene is superior to natural rubber for many industrial purposes and is the equal of natural rubber for practically all important industrial uses." The difficulty was the high cost of production. Du Pont explained, "If our supplies of natural rubber should be shut off and the rubber industry should have to depend to a large measure on DuPrene, we believe . . . that the requisite quantity of DuPrene could be supplied quite promptly but if that should happen it would probably take several years for the rubber industry to learn to adapt DuPrene to . . . tires." It was not currently used for tires because of its high cost. Memorandum enclosed in E. G. Robinson, Du Pont, to F. P. Garvan, Mar. 23, 1934, Garvan Papers, Box 66. For more on Du Pont's work on synthetic rubber, see Hounshell and Smith, *Science and Corporate Strategy,* 234–236, 251–257, and Peter J. T. Morris, *The American Synthetic Rubber Research Program* (Philadelphia: University of Pennsylvania Press, 1989), 7. One of Du Pont's principal rubber technologists, Oliver M. Hayden, would visit I. G. Farben's rubber plants in 1936. O. M. Hayden, "Trip to Europe, Jan. 3–Mar. 14, 1936," Acc. 1850, Du Pont records, cited in Hounshell and Smith, *Science and Corporate Strategy,* 665n.28. On Standard Oil of New

Jersey's rubber program, see Howard, *Buna Rubber,* and Larson, Knowlton, and Popple, *New Horizons,* 170–173. As for the tire companies, in the spring of 1934, General Tire Co., Akron, Ohio, tested I. G. Farben's Buna N rubber and made a negative appraisal. Morris, *American Synthetic Rubber,* 7–8. Ibid., 8, suggests more interest on the part of Goodrich and Goodyear in the 1930s than most of the other literature. He notes trips of their executives to Germany in 1937–1938 to visit with I. G. Farben officials on Buna S developments. To obtain butadiene (a key raw material), Goodrich cooperated with Phillips Petroleum and Goodyear with Shell Development Co. and Dow Chemical. Shell, of course, was linked with I. G. Farben and Standard Oil of New Jersey in accords on hydrogenation. See also Howard, *Buna Rubber,* 63–64, 70, on the tire companies' interest. Mansel G. Blackford and K. Austin Kerr, *BF Goodrich* (Columbus: Ohio State University Press, 1996), 153–154, on Goodrich and synthetic rubber in the 1930s. Practically all of part 6 of the *Bone Committee Hearings* is on synthetic rubber and the roles of I. G. Farben, Du Pont, Standard Oil Company of New Jersey, and the American tire companies in U.S. developments. See also Stocking and Watkins, *Cartels in Action,* 96–101.

293. In September 1935, I. G. Farben had established an Army Liaison Office (the Vermittlungsstelle) in Berlin to deal with German government military restrictions on its business. As one I. G. Farben official put it, "If we wanted to give experiences, valuable and technical experiences," to anyone abroad, "we had to ask . . . the government." The Vermittlungsstelle dealt with what could and could not be transferred to Americans. Hayes, *Industry and Ideology,* 142, and interrogation of August von Knieriem, Aug. 21, 1945, p. 3, RG 238, T301, Reel 13, NI-1320.

294. *Bone Committee Hearings.* See, for example, testimony of Robert Hunter of the Antitrust Division of the Justice Department. See also Wall and Gibb, *Teagle of Jersey Standard,* 308–314.

295. Stocking and Watkins, *Cartels in Action,* 284–303.

296. For the 1936 rules, see Office of Alien Property Custodian, *Annual Report 1943–1944,* 28–29, and Royal Institute of International Affairs, *Problem of International Investment,* 83n.1.

297. Küpper, Legal Division, to von Schnitzler et al., June 8, 1939, which encloses the Minutes of the Legal Committee, Mar. 17, 1939, RG 238, T301, Reel 20, NI-2796. See also I. G. Farben to Reich Ministry of Economics, June 26, 1939, RG 238, T301, Reel 43, NI-5769. In addition, see Report on Negotiations in New York, Mar. 9–21, 1939 (by Wilhelm Mann and Max Brüggemann), re: I. G. Farben's U.S. pharmaceutical interests, RG 238, T301, Reel 8, NI-780.

298. Memorandum on "Security Measures in the Event of War" from I. G. Farben Legal Department—Dyes, July 22, 1939, RG 238, T301, Reel 12, NI-1191. For other plans, see I. G. Farben to Reich Ministry of Economics, July 14, 1939, RG 238, T301, Reel 70, NI-8496, and I. G. Farben to Reich Ministry of Economics, Aug. 15, 1939, RG 238, T301, Reel 55, NI-7078.

299. Haynes, *American Chemical Industry,* V, 108, 209–211, 307; VI, 381, 383–384; Morris, *American Synthetic Rubber,* 8, 40; Beaton, *Enterprise in Oil,* 527–553, 560, 592; Haynes, *American Chemical Industry,* V, 218, says the gasoline shipment was to the War Department (the Army Air Corps. was within the War Department, so there is no inconsistency).

300. Letter from I. G. Farben to Chemnyco, Jan. 31, 1938, in *Bone Committee Hearings,* pt. 3, 1444. The other "very important field" was not specified. The emphasis was in the original.

301. On CRA see Larson, Knowlton, and Popple, *New Horizons,* 169–170; Howard, *Buna Rubber,* 77; Beaton, *Enterprise in Oil,* 572. Universal Oil Products Co. was a patent holding company, with the main ownership by Shell Union and Standard Oil (California). See *Kilgore Committee Hearings,* 155.

302. Schröter, "Cartels as a Form of Concentration," 118–119. The parents and their affiliates took out 653 U.S. patents between 1930 and 1939. Cantwell and Barrera, "Localisation of Corporate Technological Trajectories," 269.

303. Haynes, *American Chemical Industry,* VI, 80.

304. On Ciba in pharmaceuticals. see Mahoney, *Merchants of Life,* 233–234; "Die Chemische Industrie der Schweiz," RG 238, T301, Reel 14, NI-1406; Haynes, *American Chemical Industry,* V, 278; and Foreign Fund Control Report, by Charles R. Clark, Dec. 26, 1942, File D-63-1, Acc. 65A1063, Box 267, RG 131 (Dept.-Justice.).

305. On Sandoz history, see Mahoney, *Merchants of Life,* 229–232 (on the New York headquarters and manufacturing); Haynes, *American Chemical Industry,* III, 305; and Foreign Fund Control Report, by Charles R. Clark, Dec. 26, 1942, File D-63-1, Acc. 65A1063, Box 267, RG 131 (Dept.-Justice). A letter from George F. Handel, New York, attorney for Sandoz Chemical Works, New York, to Ernest Probst, Sandoz AG, Basle, Nov. 14, 1940, in ibid., refers to a Sandoz factory in Paterson, New Jersey. In New York it seems to have made tablets and the like. In New Jersey, the line seems to have been heavily dependent on imports and related to textile processing.

306. Bürgin, *Geschichte des Geigy-Unternehmens,* 298; Haynes, *American Chemical Industry,* V, 176.

307. Haynes, *American Chemical Industry,* VI, 209–210; Mahoney, *Merchants of Life,* 225; Peyer, *Roche,* 126, 133, 141–144.

308. Haynes, *American Chemical Industry,* V, 276; Mahoney, *Merchants of Life,* 223; Peyer, *Roche,* 143; Gales and Sluyterman, "Outward Bound," in Jones and Schröter, *Rise of Multinationals in Continental Europe,* 95n.45; Hexner, *International Cartels,* 312–313; *Kilgore Committee Hearings,* pt. 10, 1131.

309. "Die Chemische Industrie der Schweiz," pp. 59–60, RG 238, T301, Reel 14, NI-1406; Haynes, *American Chemical Industry,* V, 285, 292.

310. Mahoney, *Merchants of Life,* 95–96, 112, 114–115; Haynes, *American Chemical Industry,* V, 277; VI, 62–63.

311. The Glaxo story is complicated. The merchant firm of Joseph Nathan had begun business in New Zealand; eventually, the parent company, Joseph Nathan & Co. (JN & Co.), became headquartered in London. In 1935 Glaxo Laboratories was formed; it would buy out its parent JN & Co. in 1947. Before all that happened, in 1934, JN & Co. made an agreement with Ayerst, McKenna & Harrison, Ltd., Montreal, to form a joint venture, Ayerst, McKenna & Harrison (United States), which was incorporated in New York, to sell pharmaceuticals and other products made by the Canadian firm under license from the British one. By June 1935 the U.S. affiliate had "a sales team working New England, Chicago, Detroit, Boston and New York." Information from Richard P. T. Davenport-Hines, Aug. 6, 1985, and Sept. 26, 1985, and Richard P. T. Davenport-Hines, "Glaxo as a Multinational before 1963," in *British Multinationals,* ed. Geoffrey Jones (Aldershot: Gower, 1986), 139–140, 150. The U.S. Justice Department found a patent licensing agreement between the Wisconsin Alumni Research Foundation (WARF) and Joseph Nathan & Co. of Great Britain that prohibited the latter from exporting certain products to the United States. Ayerst, McKenna & Harrison (U.S.), Ltd., Rouses Point, New York, had a license from WARF for the "incorporation of ergosterol in glucose D (a food product)." *Kilgore Committee Hearings,* pt. 6, 745, 746, 774. No date is given on the licensing agreement, but from the context it would have been in the 1930s. (WARF will be familiar to the reader because of its involvement in the stem cell research controversies of 2001.)

312. Corley, "From National to Multinational Enterprise"; Lazell, *From Pills to Penicillin,* 28, 33, 36, 114–115; and Beecham Group Ltd., "Beecham Group in the Western Hemisphere," 1952/1953 (sent to me by T. A. B. Corley, June 27, 1982).

313. Acc. 61A109, Box 681, RG 131 (Dept.-Justice) has excellent data on the relationships between Schering Corp. and its German parent, on Chepha, and on Julius Weltzien, who told Americans that his mother was Jewish (Eugene H. Clay, Memo, Jan. 22, 1942, in ibid.). Mahoney, *Merchants of Life,* 254–255, is the source of the Jewish "great-grandparent." On Weltzien's role in the parent firm see Holländer, *Geschichte der Schering,* 46, 104, and Kobrak, "Between Nationalism and Internationalism," passim. Kobrak writes that Weltzien "was only half Jewish; both his brother and sister survived the war [in Germany] relatively unmolested"; his mother committed suicide after the war started. Ibid., 575. Important data from the Clay memorandum of Jan. 22, 1942, are in Charles R. Clark Report, Dec. 26, 1942, in File D-63-1, Acc. 65A1063, Box 267, RG 131 (Dept.-Justice.). See also Office of Alien Property Custodian, *Annual Report 1943–1944,* 73. The royalty agreement with Schering AG was published in full in *Kilgore Committee Hearings,* pt. 10, 1141–1155. On the complicated Stockholms Enskilda Bank's involvements, see statement of Rolf Calissendorff, a director of the bank, Nov. 14, 1945, in Acc. 61A109, Box 681, RG 131 (Dept.-Justice.). Kobrak, "Between Nationalism and Internationalism," 606–607, cites a January 18, 1939, letter in the Schering Archives on the German government investigation of Schering's U.S. camouflages.

314. *New York Times,* Dec. 18, 1941. Later, the Office of Alien Property Custodian would vest 100 percent of the shares in Rare Chemicals, deciding that it was "German owned." Office of Alien Property Custodian, *Annual Report 1943–1944,* 51. C. F. Boehringer, Mannheim, had a joint venture in Rare Chemicals with Pyridium Corp., with which it shared a plant at Nepara Park, near Yonkers, New York. Pyridium Corp. sold its 50 percent interest in Rare Chemicals in 1939. Apparently, the son of the president of C. F. Boehringer then acquired the 100 percent interest. Haynes, *American Chemical Industry,* VI, 347, and E. T. Fritzsching Memorandum, Mar. 29, 1939, on the need to have an American citizen own the Boehringer shares, *Kilgore Committee Hearings,* pt. 10, 1159.

315. Martin, *All Honorable Men,* 212; data from Harm Schröter, Oct. 1988 (the German interest); Haynes, *American Chemical Industry,* IV, 253–254; V, 258, 485, 523; VI, 207–208 (on the American firm). I can find no evidence that Heyden Chemical Co. was vested by the Alien Property Custodian in World War II. By the 1930s, Merck & Co. also had reestablished "amicable" associations with its former parent; in the case of Merck, there was clearly no transatlantic ownership or control relationship. Merck between 1922 and 1932 had agreements with E. Merck, Darmstadt, on particular products and the use of the Merck name. On November 17, 1932, it signed a general agreement with E. Merck on the use of the name, an agreement that also provided for profit sharing on the manufacture of certain specialties. For details see George W. Perkins, Executive Vice President, Merck & Co. to C. D. Blauvelt, Foreign Funds Control Division, Federal Reserve Bank of New York, Mar. 21, 1942, in Acc. 61A109, Box 681, Foreign Funds Control Files, RG 131 (Dept.-Justice.).

316. The British companies included A. J. White and Menley & James. The British firm Albright & Wilson had interests in Oldbury Electro-Chemical and Pembroke Chemical (on the former's product line and its activities at its plant in Niagara Falls, see Haynes, *American Chemical Industry,* VI, 314). The British-controlled Kay-Fries became in 1938 the third-largest producer of formaldehyde in America. Synthite Ltd., another firm in the Tennant group, had perfected a new process of formaldehyde manufacture that Kay-Fries adopted. Haynes, *American Chemical Industry,* VI, 238, and Dunning data. As for Belgian involvements, a subsidiary of the Belgian enterprise Société Industrielle de la Cellulose (SIDAC), Sylvania Industrial Corporation, manufactured Sylphrap at a plant in Virginia, which product captured roughly 24 percent of the U.S. cellophane market. Haynes, *American Chemical Industry,* IV, 353; VI, 417–418; Hounshell and Smith, *Science*

and Corporate Strategy, 176–178; and Stocking and Mueller, "Cellophane Case," 41–44. The Belgian film manufacturer Gevaert had sales offices, and in 1939, with war threatening in Europe, it made plans to manufacture in the United States. Devos, "Agfa-Gevaert and Belgian Multinational Enterprise," 208, and Alt, "Photochemical Industry," 92, 98. The French L'Air Liquide held a minority stake in Air Reduction Company. Data from Patrick Fridenson, June 28, 1995, based on unpublished history of L'Air Liquide by Alain Jemain. There were German (and possibly Swiss) direct investments in Buffalo Electro-Chemical Company, the largest manufacturer of hydrogen peroxide in the United States. Office of Alien Property Custodian, *Annual Report 1942–1943,* 38. So, too, Rohm and Haas, an innovator in Plexiglas production, had minority German ownership. Hochheiser, *Rohm and Haas,* 58–62, 81, and Office of Alien Property Custodian, *Annual Report 1943–1944,* 101. For other German-owned (or partly German-owned) chemical companies, which would be vested during World War II, see Office of Alien Property Custodian, *Annual Report 1943–1944,* 44.

317. The German-Swiss dyestuff cartel (April 19, 1929) was to run to December 31, 1968. Schröter, "Cartels as a Form of Concentration," 128. French interests became involved in this cartel, as in 1932 did ICI.

318. *Kilgore Committee Hearings,* pt. 10. Specifically on the May 26, 1937, agreement of the parent companies, see Hexner, *International Cartels,* 312–313.

319. Stocking and Mueller, "Cellophane Case."

320. Tweedale, *Sheffield Steel and America,* 96–97.

321. On the important stainless steel patents of Krupp-Nirosta, see M. Louis to F. Redies, Sept. 2, 1940, RG 238, T301, Reel 36, NI-4900. The president of Krupp-Nirosta was Emil Schill, who for many years had represented Krupp (and Thyssen interests as well) in the United States.

322. Martin, *All Honorable Men,* 92–93, and *Kilgore Committee Hearings,* pt. 16, 2082–2083. After the First World War, Disconto-Gesellschaft had acquired an interest in H. Albert de Bary & Co., Amsterdam. *Bankers Magazine,* New York, 105 (Oct. 1922): 652, and *Moody's Banks 1929,* 2309. The German connections were maintained after the merger of Deutsche Bank and the Disconto-Gesellschaft in 1929. *Moody's Banks 1939,* 781. See also Nederlandsch Economisch-Historisch Archief, *Bankwezen* (Amsterdam: NEHA, 1992), 38–39, 63. In 1936 H. Albert Bary & Co., Amsterdam, was a subsidiary of the Deutsche Bank; that year, the Deutsche Bank tried to camouflage its ownership of the Dutch bank by transferring the stock "to nominally Dutch hands." Gall et al., *Deutsche Bank,* 329.

323. Report on a telephone call from Ewald Loeser, Krupp, Essen, to Carl Goetz (of the Dresdner Bank), Sept. 28, 1938, RG 238, T301, Reel 13, NI-1286. Martin, *All Honorable Men,* 93; see also RG 238, T301, Reel 36, NI-4907, and *Kilgore Committee Hearings,* pt. 16, 2083.

324. For list see RG 238, T301, Reel 27, NI-3748.

325. Graef & Schmidt was later found to be 100 percent owned by J. A. Henckels. On its activities see Office of Alien Property Custodian, *Annual Report 1944–1945,* 174, and ibid., *1945–1946,* 49. On the 100 percent ownership of these two subsidiaries, see U.S. Senate, Committee on Military Affairs, Subcommittee on War Mobilization, *Elimination of German Resources for War, Hearings* 79th Cong., 1st sess. (1945), II, 588. Wilkins, *History,* 171, 260, 766n.151 (on J. A. Henckels' pre–World War I activities). After the First World War, the affiliate had been acquired by its American agent, Hermann Kind; when the latter died, the properties went back to German ownership.

326. Data from *U.S. v. Norma-Hoffmann Bearings Corp.,* Civil Action No. 24216. 1953 Trade Case (ND Ohio 1953). See also *New York Times,* Mar. 27, 1941. The British parent of Norma-Hoffmann Bearings was Hoffmann Manufacturing Co., Ltd., Chelmsford, Essex.

327. The best description of the firm's business in 1933–1937 is in American Bosch Corporation, Prospectus, Oct. 25, 1938, Scudder Collection, Business School Library, Columbia University Libraries. The firm operated at a loss in 1936 and an even larger one in the first six months of 1938. For the ownership structures and the cloaking, see Gerald Aalders and Cees Wiebes, "Stockholms Enskilda Bank," *Scandinavian Economic History Review,* 33 (1985): 26–27, 30–31, and Aalders and Wiebes, *The Art of Cloaking Ownership,* (Amsterdam: Amsterdam University Press, 1996), 37–42. (Mendelssohn & Co., Amsterdam, for all practical purposes came to an end with Mannheimer's suicide.) On Mendelssohn and its relation to H. Albert de Bary & Co. and the Deutsche Bank, see Nederlandsch Economisch-Historich Archief, *Bankwesen,* 38–39. The Mendelssohn Bank, Berlin, was a long-standing German private bank that by the late 1930s was being "Aryanized."

328. From 1920 to 1936, Massey-Harris's U.S. business had suffered losses in fourteen out of sixteen years. By 1935, so heavy were its U.S. losses that the Canadian firm's board decided to end the U.S. business. The board, however, changed its mind and, with new management, resolved to revive its U.S. operations. Neufeld, *Global Corporation,* 29–35. In 1937 in farm machinery, Massey-Harris had a 1 percent U.S. market share, down from its 1.7 percent share in 1929. Whitney, *Antitrust Policies,* II, 235.

329. On AGA (AB Gasaccumulator), AGA, *The Aga Saga* (Cleveland: AGA Gas, n.d. 1986?), booklet with no pages. There were other Swedish machinery producers, for example, Sandvik Saw and Tool Corp.

330. However, among the "enemy assets" that the Office of Alien Property Custodian vested during World War II were those of "Fiat S.A. and of its Detroit branch." Was this a machinery purchasing unit? See Vesting Order No. 180 (Fed. Reg. Citation 7:88814), Office of Alien Property Custodian, *Annual Report 1942–1943,* 102, and ibid., *1943–1944,* 57. Fiat and Renault would both have had the "nearly dormant" sales subsidiaries.

331. Jones, "Growth," 45, 47. Dunlop's British operations in the 1930s were run by an American, John Collyer, who had been hired by the American Dunlop company in 1923 and joined the parent in 1929. In 1939 Collyer was recruited to run Goodrich. Blackford and Kerr, *BF Goodrich,* 148.

332. On these companies, see Office of Alien Property Custodian, *Annual Report 1942–1943,* 99–101 (Vesting orders nos. 28, 35, and 102). It is not clear when Adlanco became Adlanco X-Ray Corp., but it probably was in the 1930s. The Siemens-Westinghouse patents agreement of 1924 was renewed in 1934 for another decade. As the Siemens historian has written, under the terms of this agreement, "the American market remained largely inaccessible to Siemens." See Feldenkirchen, "Anfänge des Siemensgeschäfts in Amerika," 898–899, and Wilfried Feldenkirchen, *Siemens,* (Munich: Piper, 2000), 293 (quotation).

333. On Metal & Thermit Co. in the interwar years, see Duffus, *Story of M & T Chemicals.* On beryllium in particular, see Thurman Arnold testimony in *Bone Committee Hearings,* 640–661. The quotation is from an undated letter from V. Englehardt of Siemens & Halske to Dr. F. H. Hirschland of Metal & Thermit Co., printed in ibid., 641. See also Hexner, *International Cartels,* 222.

334. Stockholm office of U.S. Bureau of Foreign and Domestic Commerce to Finance Department, Nov. 5, 1936, RG 151, 620 General 1936, NA, citing data from a Swedish stockholder's yearbook.

335. Faith, *Infiltrators,* 81, and Robinson, *Business History of the World,* 297 (1934). In lamps and radios, NV Philips was party to international agreements that left the U.S. market to Americans (General Electric and RCA). X-ray tubes and equipment were not covered by any agreements, however, and in the summer of 1933, NV Philips decided to introduce its tubes and equipment into the U.S. market and to manufacture X-ray tubes in America. In 1933, Philips' products had been boycotted in the United States on

the assumption that Philips was under German influence; finally, in December 1933, the management convinced buyers that Philips was truly Dutch. Its factory, in Mount Vernon, New York, was opened in 1934. The U.S. affiliate was Philips Metalix Corporation. Blanken, *History of Philips Electronics,* IV, 62–65.

336. *Moody's Industrials 1935,* 1075, and ibid., *1941,* 753–54, 3157. See also Kynaston, *City of London,* III, 417, and Robinson, *Business History of the World,* 319, both of which got the name of the American company wrong and did not exactly understand the complexity of the "Brunswick" record story, which can be deciphered through a reading of these volumes, along with *Moody's.*

337. Office of Alien Property Custodian, *Annual Report 1943–1944,* 79. On the international relationships between Carl Zeiss, Jena, Germany, and Bausch & Lomb Optical Co., Rochester, from 1907 through the First World War and in the interwar years, see testimony of Wendell Berge, Assistant Attorney General of the United States, Sept. 7, 1944, and documents in *Kilgore Committee Hearings,* pt. 16, 1981–1982, 1987–2167. The German Zeiss firm had had a 25 percent interest in Bausch and Lomb in 1914 (see Wilkins, *History,* 446). Zeiss had sold to "members of the Bausch & Lomb families" its equity interest in Bausch & Lomb before American entry into the First World War. Associations resumed after the war, but there was no renewal of investment by the German Zeiss in Bausch & Lomb Optical Co. The Germans set up their own subsidiary, Carl Zeiss, Inc.

338. Office of Alien Property Custodian, *Annual Report 1942–1943,* 54.

339. Eckes, *Opening America's Market,* 147–148, citing State Department correspondence of March 1939.

340. Marc Linder, *Projecting Capitalism: A History of the Internationalization of the Construction Industry* (Westport, Conn.: Greenwood Press, 1994), 93; *Miami Herald,* Mar. 21, 1978. Some four decades later, in the late 1970s, Taylor Woodrow would be the largest British developer in Florida. Mira Wilkins, *Foreign Enterprise in Florida* (Miami: University Presses of Florida, 1979), 27.

341. Morgan, *Merchants of Grain,* 128; Sébastien Guex, "Development of Swiss Trading Companies," in *The Multinational Traders,* ed. Geoffrey Jones (London: Routledge, 1998), 160.

342. Morgan, *Merchants of Grain,* 128–129.

343. Ibid., 133; Broehl, *Cargill,* 466, 552, 568–570.

344. Broehl, *Cargill,* 554, writes that Cargill's two "arch rivals" in 1935 were Continental Grain and Louis Dreyfus.

345. There were a number of other foreign grain traders, but none achieved "Big Five" global status. Archer-Daniels-Midland (ADM) emerged much later as a significant American contender in this trade. Morgan, *Merchants of Grain,* 310, published in 1979, refers to the latter as a "competitor" to the "Big Five." Balfour, Williamson (Balfour, Guthrie) was not in this league.

346. In the 1941 U.S. antitrust suit, two leaf tobacco exporters were charged, Export Leaf Tobacco Co. (a subsidiary of British American Tobacco) and Imperial Tobacco. Whitney, *Antitrust Policies,* II, 55.

347. Whitney, *Antitrust Policies,* II, 36, describes Imperial Tobacco as the biggest buyer in the United States of flue-cured tobacco, all for export. On the coordination from London of British American Tobacco's leaf buying in the United States, see Cox, *Global Cigarette,* 309.

348. In this decade, the three principal Japanese traders in raw cotton were Nihon Menka (Japan Cotton Company), Tōyō Menka (which had been spun off from Mitsui in 1920), and Gōshō. All three had direct investments in Texas offices to buy American raw cotton for export, operations that had begun before the First World War. Nihon Menka (Japan Cotton Company) was in Fort Worth; Tōyō Menka (as Southern Cotton

Co.) was in Dallas; and Gōshō (as Crawford Gōshō) was in San Antonio. Based on Tetsuya Kuwahara, "Comment," in *Business History of General Trading Companies,* ed. Shin'ichi Yonekawa and Hideki Yoshihara (Tokyo: University of Tokyo Press, 1987), 268–269; Kawabe, "Overseas Operations," 81; J. R. Killick, "The Atlantic Cotton Trade," in Yonekawa and Yoshihara, *Business History,* 254 (on Japan Cotton Company); Mitsui & Co., Ltd., *100 Year History,* 88, A34, A35; and inventory of the records of Southern Cotton Co., RG 131, National Archives. On German cotton imports, barter arrangements, and the activities after 1937 of Lentz & Hirschfeld, Bremen, Germany, and its agent (affiliate) in the United States, Adam T. Schildge, Inc., see *Kilgore Committee Hearings,* pt. 16, 2046, 2062–2074, and exhibits, 2288–2339. Sébastien Guex writes that in the 1920s and 1930s the New York subsidiary of the Swiss Volkart group was "one of the most important participants in the US cotton market." Guex, "Development of Swiss Trading Companies," 164. The key U.S. raw cotton exporters—Anderson, Clayton (by far the leader) and the McFaddens—were American. Some foreign grain traders, Ralli Brothers, Bunge & Born, for example, also handled raw cotton. Killick, "Atlantic Cotton Trade," 250–261, and P. Chalmin, "International Commodity Trade," in Yonekawa and Yoshihara, *Business History,* 285, which says the Liverpool-based Ralli Brothers moved from grain to cotton trading "before 1939." Another grain trader was the French Weil frères; Killick writes of the important Alabama-headquartered cotton trader, Weil Brothers; I do not know the relationship between these French and U.S. Weil firms, each carrying the same name. See Chalmin, "International Commodity Trade," 285, and Killick, "Atlantic Cotton Trade," 254, 257–261, 266. Certain of the foreign raw cotton exporters also imported into the United States cotton textiles; this would be true of the Japanese trading companies (and their affiliates) and may well have been the case with the Swiss Volkart group, which had a network of subsidiaries in India, Japan, elsewhere in Asia, and in Europe.

349. Meneight, *History of United Molasses Co.,* 59, 44, 79, 159–161; Chalmin, *Négociants et Chargeurs,* 138, 147, 227.

350. Jones, *Merchants to Multinationals,* 105, 204, 273.

351. Ibid., 93.

352. Wilkins, "Japanese Multinationals," 594–596; U.S. Department of Commerce, Bureau of the Census, *Historical Statistics of the United States* (Washington, D.C., 1975), 903.

353. RG 131, National Archives, has a substantial collection on Japanese trading companies' activities in the United States, including records of the Asahi Corporation (1929–1941, principally dealing with silk matters); Ataka and Co., Ltd., New York (1930–1941); Z. Horikoshi and Co., Inc., General Correspondence (1911–1943) and Chicago office (1911–1943); Mitsubishi Shoji Kaisha, San Francisco, Los Angeles, Seattle (1919–1941); Mitsui & Co., San Francisco, Los Angeles, Seattle (1913–1941); Okura and Co. (1900–1942); and Southern Cotton Co., Dallas office (1912–1941) and New York office (1935–1941). For a short description of the activities of Mitsubishi Shoji Kaisha's U.S. branches, see Office of Alien Property Custodian, *Annual Report 1943–1944,* 81; for more details, see Kawabe, "Japanese Business in the United States before World War II: The Case of Mitsubishi Shoji Kaisha," 26.

354. Stern, *United States in International Banking,* 327.

355. Sturmey, *British Shipping,* 130. Sturmey's measures seem to be based on "flag tonnage," which was not identical to ownership. In the hostility to foreigners in the 1930s, U.S. steamship lines that owned foreign flag ships were seen as unpatriotic. In fact, from the late 1920s, International Mercantile Marine had been disposing of its foreign-flag ships. Thus, in the years 1933–1938, in the U.S. case, ownership and flag may well have become more coincident. It continued, however, not to be exact (American multinationals, oil and fruit companies, apparently often used Panamanian flags in the 1930s to

avoid U.S. "red tape"). No matter, the decline in the share of U.S. shipping was real. De La Pedraja, *The Rise and Decline of U.S. Merchant Shipping,* 126, 137, and chap. 7.

356. Marshall, Southard, and Taylor, *Canadian-American Industry,* 197.

357. Raynes, *History of British Insurance,* 173. The five groups together in 1937 collected $77.5 million in premiums in the United States.

358. One estimate was that in mid-1937 three-quarters of the $351 million in FDI in insurance in the United States was British (or $263 million); with the level of British FDI at that time given as $833 million, that would mean that almost a third of British FDI that year was in insurance. I think those figures may underestimate the amounts. The figures are based on data in *FIUS—1940,* 34–37.

359. Wilkins, "Japanese Multinationals," 593n.23.

360. Alois Alzheimer, Aktennote, Feb. 9, 1939; MR an Atlas (Stockholm), Apr. 3, 1939; and Duchtetmann (?) an Walther Meuschel, Oct. 10, 1950 (Betrifft: Pilot Swenska Veritas), all in A-2.3, 1fd, Nr. 164, Munich Reinsurance Company Archives, Munich. See also Office of Alien Property Custodian, *Annual Report 1944–1945,* 93–96, which says that "after January 1, 1939," the German companies that owned shares of stock in Pilot Reinsurance Company "transferred most of their shares to companies in Holland, Sweden, and Switzerland."

361. These figures are to be accepted with a great deal of reservations; for the problems of valuing foreign-owned insurance branches and affiliates, see *1941 Census,* 30–31.

362. The material on foreign (out-of-country) banks with licensed agencies is based on New York State, Banking Department, *Annual Reports,* 1933–1939. Anglo-South American went into voluntary liquidation in 1936. Jones, *British Multinational Banking,* 404.

363. New York State, Banking Department Web site, http://banking.state.ny.us/hista.txt on Bank of Montreal Trust Co.

364. New York State, Banking Department, *Annual Reports,* 1933–1939.

365. Tamagna, *Banking and Finance in China,* 126, 146. The Bank of China was a "semigovernment" bank. Set up in China in 1912 and headquartered in Peking, it had moved to Shanghai in 1928 and was granted a new charter to transact foreign exchange. It then began a reorganization from a principally state-owned bank into one principally owned by individual shareholders. On March 28, 1935, with the flight of silver from China, the Chinese government "seized majority control of the bank's board of directors," ending the bank's autonomy from the government. Wen-Hsin Yeh, "Corporate Space, Communal Time: Everyday Life in Shanghai's Bank of China," *American Historical Review,* 100 (Feb. 1995): 102–106, 119. On the Chinese currency reform of November 1935, see King, *Hongkong Bank between the Wars,* 412–443. The Bank of China was one of the managers of the stabilization fund to maintain the market value of the new inconvertible paper currency, after China abandoned the silver standard. Stern, *United States in International Banking,* 317.

366. According to Eduard Kubu, "Behaviour and Fate of Companies with Foreign Capital in the Czech Lands 1938–1945," unpublished paper, 2001, and conversation with Kubu, March 2001, after the Munich agreement, Jewish shareholders in the Anglo Prague Credit Bank (also known as the Anglo-Czechoslovak and Prague Credit Bank) sold their shares and used the newly established New York agency of the bank to transfer their moneys to the United States. Zbigniew Landau and Wojciech Morawski, "Polish Banking in the Inter-war Period," in *Banking, Currency, and Finance in Europe between the Wars,* ed. Charles H. Feinstein (Oxford: Clarendon Press, 1995), 366, describe the Bank Polska Kasa Opieki SA as state owned and founded at the end of 1929, with the aim to "take care of the savings of Polish economic emigrants"; they have nothing on the Paris (or the New York) locale. In 1921 and 1920, Czech and Polish banks had opened New York agencies, which had been closed in 1924 and 1926, respectively (see Tables 3.4 and 5.5); these were not the same banks that set up New York agencies in the late 1930s.

367. The July date for the Swiss Bank Corporation is from the New York State Banking Department Web site: http:/banking.state.ny.us/hists.txt; see also Bauer, *Swiss Bank Corporation,* 282, and *New York Times,* July 8, 28, 30, 1939, Aug. 5, 1939, and Oct. 15, 1939.

368. For its long participation, see Wilkins, *History,* 483.

369. *New York Times Times,* Nov. 22, 1939.

370. A 1936 letter from the British embassy says "forbidden to take deposits from *residents in New York State*" (my italics). R. C. Lindsay to Anthony Eden, July 14, 1936, FO 115/3410, Public Record Office. I wonder if this was the way the banks had come *to interpret* the legislation, which would allow them to hold money of their nationals and other foreigners who were resident abroad, or have temporary deposits so as to carry on transactions. As noted in earlier chapters, some foreign banks organized trust companies in New York, as deposit-taking institutions, to cope with the prohibition against the licensed agencies' taking deposits. The *1941 Census,* 31, discussing the "Business of Foreign Banks in the United States," seems to suggest that the agencies were holding "foreign deposits." The law, however, forbade the taking of deposits.

371. The Bank of Nova Scotia was technically headquartered in Halifax, but regular directors meetings were held in Toronto from 1929 onward, and the key executives had run the bank from Toronto since about 1900. Schull and Gibson, *Scotiabank Story,* 142.

372. Canadian businesses had major Latin American interests. Apparently the Bank of Montreal took over (and renamed) the Anglo-South American Trust Co.; the history of the Bank of Montreal contains nothing on this (our source is the New York State Banking Department).

373. When the British embassy in Washington heard that under the U.S. Revenue Act of 1936, foreign banks were subject to a 22 percent tax on income while domestic banks were taxed at a 15 percent rate, the financial adviser to the embassy discussed this with representatives of certain British banks in New York and learned that the "British banks in New York are not disposed to take the matter seriously, partly because their earnings are insufficient to make this a matter of practical importance, and partly because they are forbidden by New York State law to compete with domestic banks in many ways (e.g. they may not take deposits from residents in New York State) and consequently they feel that there may be some justice in treating them on the same lines as other foreign corporations rather than on the same lines as domestic banks." R. C. Lindsay to Anthony Eden, July 14, 1936, FO 115/3410, Public Record Office. Much more important was the matter of the insurance companies. And it was moot, for foreign and domestic insurance companies were treated alike, taxed at a 15 percent rate. Ibid. (The difference clearly related to the "form" of—the legal structure of—operations.)

374. Professor Y. Homma has looked at some of the records of the six Japanese banks with New York agencies that are located in RG 131, National Archives; he made available to me the brief inventories of these records that reveal the activities of the banks. As an indication of the diversity of their business, there is one set of records (1910–1941) that deals with correspondence, customs documents, and letters of credit issued to South American firms by the Yokohama Specie Bank (YSB). Another set contains correspondence between the New York agency of YSB and its London branch regarding the repayment of Japanese government bonds and sterling loans. These records are clearly invaluable for any student of Japanese-American business relationships in the 1930s.

375. Comptoir National d'Escompte de Paris had a representative in New York during the entire interwar years, albeit not a licensed agency; its representative was Maurice Silvester; see Memo from First National Bank of Boston, Apr. 30, 1919, in French American Banking Corporation file, 1919–1950, C440, FRBNY; *Moody's 1929,* 2307; and Stern, *United States in International Banking,* 195. Stern notes other French banks with representatives in New York, presumably by the 1930s: Maurice Mercadier for Banque Nationale

Française du Commerce and Maurice Boyer for the Banque de Paris et des Pays-Bas. None of these banks had licensed New York agencies.

376. *Moody's Banks 1939,* 933.

377. Ibid., 124. The reasons for the divestment were undoubtedly the absence of profitability and the political situation in Europe.

378. See data in French American Banking Corporation file, 1919–1950, C440, FRBNY.

379. Roberts, *Schroders,* 244–248, 281–291. Avery Rockefeller was the grandson of the brother of John D. Rockefeller (William Rockefeller). Ibid., 583n.20.

380. Reich, *Financier,* 39–41, writes that Lazard Frères, New York, was French controlled throughout the 1930s, albeit run by its longtime leader, Frank Altschul. On its choice of the investment banking route, see ibid., 38.

381. Cassis, "Swiss International Banking," 166. Walter Adolf Jöhr, *Schweizerische Kreditanstalt 1856–1956* (Zurich: Schweizerische Kreditanstalt, 1956), 514, 564; and R. Tirana to McKeon, Mar. 4, 1940, Swiss American Corporation file, FRBNY.

382. I tried, in vain, to trace the foreign banks' ownership in the Chase Manhattan Bank archives (in 1955 Bank of the Manhattan Company would merge with Chase National Bank to become Chase Manhattan). James P. Warburg, who remained associated with the Bank of the Manhattan Company, does not seem to have played the active role that he had when the International Acceptance Bank was in existence. He had, however, broad international contacts, and the Bank of the Manhattan Company took part in some international business. I found a letter from Robert Kaeppeli, Finance Manager, Ciba-Basle, to William Howard Schubart, vice-president of the Bank of the Manhattan Company, March 26, 1936, wherein Kaeppeli wrote, "I take once more the liberty of availing myself of your offer to give me your assistance in the handling of important matters relating to our American business." This was in connection with Ciba-Basle's plans to establish a manufacturing plant for its pharmaceutical products in the United States. The letter is in File D-631-1, Acc. 65A1063, Box 267, RG 131 (Dept.-Justice.), together with other information on an ongoing relationship between Ciba in the United States and the Bank of the Manhattan Co. A May 13, 1940, letter in the files of the Federal Reserve indicates the use by National Provincial Bank Ltd. and Nederlandsche Handel-Maatschappij (two of the original shareholder banks in IAB) of the services of the Bank of the Manhattan Company. Bolton (Bank of England) to Federal Reserve Bank of New York, May 13, 1940, C261 England–Bank of England, FRBNY. I found nothing on a Bank of the Manhattan Company's role in aiding refugee capital transfers to the United States, albeit I would be surprised if that had not occurred.

383. The Bank of Canton, Ltd., Hong Kong, founded in 1912 by American and Hong Kong Chinese, had opened an agency in New York City in 1922 and a branch in San Francisco in 1924. Tamagna, *Banking and Finance in China,* 41, 172; New York State, Banking Department, *Annual Report 1922;* Superintendent of Banks (California), *Annual Report 1925.* In 1931, the bank's New York agency was shut, and in 1935 the Bank of Canton suspended business in Hong Kong. At this point it was "saved" by T. V. Soong and reopened in Hong Kong with its savior as chairman of the board. In San Francisco, the earlier branch (established in 1924) was reorganized in 1937 as the Bank of Canton, San Francisco, a commercial and savings bank. T. V. Soong's brother was chairman of the board of the California bank. New York State, Banking Department, *Annual Report 1930,* and ibid., *1931;* Seagrave, *Soong Dynasty,* 326; Superintendent of Banks (California), *Annual Report 1937,* and ibid., *1941.* The New York agency did not reopen (the "Soong" bank in New York was the agency of the Bank of China).

384. On the Banco di Napoli Trust Co. of Chicago, see *Moody's Banks 1939,* 269.

385. See *Moody's Banks, 1938,* 82; *Moody's Banks, 1939,* 54.

386. Michele D'Alessandro, "Managing Multinational Banking Networks: The Case of Two Leading Italian Banks (1910s–1930s)," and Carlo Brambilla, "Italian Multinational Banking," in Bonin et al., *Transnational Companies,* 436n.46, and 447n.44. The three BCI trust companies were thus closed down in sequence, Boston, Philadelphia, and New York.

387. George Glasgow, *Glasgow's Guide to Investment Trust Companies (1935)* (London: Eyre and Spottiswoode, 1935), includes it as an "investment trust." Note that in 1933 its total securities owned far exceeded its mortgages and real estate in America.

388. Based on data in the company's annual reports, which for this period are located on Film Z-G2, Reel 55, Bancroft Library Archives, University of California, Berkeley.

389. Gilbert, *History of Investment Trusts,* 108, 131, 121.

390. See Annual Financial Statements, as of 31 March, on Film Z-G1, Reels 283–285, Bancroft Library. The balance sheet changes 1933–1934 also show a sharp rise in "investments at cost" and foreclosures.

391. Veenendaal, *Slow Train to Paradise,* 153. Three years later (as of June 14, 1941), the census would identify only $100,000 in Dutch holdings of real estate mortgages in the United States. *1941 Census,* 84. This is not inconsistent because there would have been a drop from 1938 to 1941. See also Gales and Sluyterman, "Dutch Free-Standing Companies," 316 (for the decline of Dutch mortgage lending in the 1930s).

392. I have not systematically discussed FPI by sector, except to note the clear trends away from railroad securities; there were some studies by the Department of Commerce of industry distributions, but they were all inconclusive.

393. Although there are no figures for March 1933 (when Roosevelt took office) compared with September 1939 (when war broke out in Europe), year end 1933 and year end 1939 figures show a clear increase. Table 2.1 provided three different estimates for year end 1939; all are higher than the one year end estimate for 1933. In the late 1930s, refugees often came with capital or followed capital flight. Some of the transfers related to FPI and fewer to FDI. Whether or not these investors were considered "nonresident" foreign investors was often ambiguous in the statistics. If their capital transfers preceded immigration, then these would be foreign investments; when refugees became U.S. residents, their investments were no longer foreign.

8. War Abroad, 1939–1941

1. Bemis, *Diplomatic History,* 838.

2. U.S. Department of the Treasury, *Census of Foreign-Owned Assets in the United States* (Washington, D.C., 1945). The census was as of June 14, 1941. It is henceforth cited as *1941 Census.*

3. Israel B. Oseas, "Antitrust Prosecutions of International Business," *Cornell Law Review,* 30 (1944): 61.

4. Table 8.1 excludes $890 million identified as "foreign securities" held by custodians in the United States on behalf of foreigners. *1941 Census,* 50–51. The margin would become larger if foreign holdings of "foreign securities" are included. For the reasons why the U.S. Treasury excluded "foreign securities," see Appendix 2 (e).

5. Thus, Americans who were residing abroad were included on the first line, the foreign investment total, but not in the second figure provided; the difference, however, was far from solely that of Americans, since other nationalities were also included on the first line.

6. See Appendix 3, Notes to Table 8.3 (note d) for details.

7. *New York Times,* Sept. 1, 1939; Michie, *London Stock Exchange,* 288.

8. *New York Times*, Sept. 2, 1939.

9. John Morton Blum, *From the Morgenthau Diaries* Vol. 2, *Years of Urgency, 1938–1941* (Boston: Houghton Mifflin, 1965), 88.

10. Ibid., II, 88–89, for the discussion. See also the twelve-page, George L. Harrison, Memorandum, Apr. 20, 1939, Harrison Papers 2012.8, Federal Reserve Bank of New York (FRBNY).

11. For details of the British controls of August 26, 1939, see Burton and Corner, *Investment and Unit Trusts; Financial Times*, Aug. 28, 1939; and D. F. McCurrach, "Britain's U.S. Dollar Problems, 1939–45," *Economic Journal*, 221 (Sept. 1948): 357. See also *New York Times*, Sept. 4, 5, 1939, and Blum, *From the Morgenthau Diaries*, II, 93.

12. *New York Times*, Sept. 2, 3, 5, 6, 1939.

13. W. N. Medlicott, *The Economic Blockade*, vol. 1 (London: Longman's Green. 1952), 1, shows the British had been making plans for economic warfare since *1936*. On the Dutch government's national defense preparations, after the failure of the London international disarmament conference *in 1935*, see Blanken, *History of Philips Electronics*, 102ff.

14. Sayers, *Bank of England*, II, 571–573.

15. *Financial Times*, Aug. 25, 1939.

16. George L. Harrison, Memo, Aug. 24, 1939, Harrison Papers 2013.2, FRBNY, wherein Harrison records his telephone conversation with John W. Hanes, undersecretary of the treasury, on his plans for the foreign exchange committee. In a telephone conversation between L. W. Knoke of the New York Federal Reserve Board and G. L. F. Bolton of the Bank of England, Knoke told Bolton about the formation of the foreign exchange committee. L. W. Knoke, Memorandum of Telephone Conversation, Sept. 1, 1939, C261.3 England–Bank of England, FRBNY. See also Allan Sproul, Memo, Apr. 9, 1940, and Harrison, Memo, Apr. 10, 1940, Harrison Papers 2012.8, FRBNY; and Allan Sproul, Memo, June 28, 1940, Harrison Papers 2550.2, FRBNY. Robert F. Loree of Guaranty Trust Company chaired the foreign exchange committee, which also included representatives from National City Bank, Chase National Bank, The Central Hanover Bank & Trust Co., Bankers Trust, J. P. Morgan & Co., Brown Bros. Harriman & Co., and Goldman Sachs. C. J. Stephenson was probably chosen as the one foreign banker, since he was a well-known figure; he had been with the Canadian Bank of Commerce's New York agency since 1926.

17. *Financial Times*, Aug. 28, 1939; Burton and Corner, *Investment and Unit Trusts*, 71; and Sayers, *Bank of England*, II, 590.

18. L. W. Knoke, Memorandum of Telephone Conversation, Sept. 1, 1939, C261.3 England–Bank of England, FRBNY.

19. Sayers, *Bank of England*, II, 572–573.

20. Harrison, Memo, Aug. 24, 1939, Harrison Papers 2013.2, FRBNY.

21. Since 1933, Americans had no obligations to pay off debts in gold. Foreign *governments* could, however, exchange dollars for gold, but with abundant gold that seemed to be no problem.

22. Michie, *London Stock Exchange*, 288.

23. Du Pont Press Release, Sept. 12, 1939, Francis P. Garvan Papers, Box 66, American Heritage Center, University of Wyoming, Laramie, Wyoming, contains Lammot du Pont's speech. For example, when the war started in Europe in September 1939, U.S. imports of German-made dyes accounted for only 3 percent of all dyes consumed in the United States; in 1914, U.S. imports principally of German-made dyes had been 75 percent of U.S. consumption. Haynes, *American Chemical Industry*, VI, 185 (1939); U.S. Tariff Commission data provided in Table 1.3 in the present book (1914).

24. Wilkins, *Maturing*, 253–255, for its impact on American business abroad.

25. On tin, NV Billiton, and the Longhorn Tin Smelter in Texas City, Texas, see "Tin Smelting," The Handbook of Texas Online <http:/www.tsha.utexas.edu/handbook/

online/articles/view/TT/dkt1.html> (accessed July 14, 2001). Both Jean-François Hennart (who has written on international tin transactions) and Dutch business historian Keetie Sluyterman, using histories of Billiton written in Dutch, confirmed for me the role of that enterprise. Billiton's Johannes van den Broek was in the Netherlands East Indies when the Germans invaded Holland; he went to the United States and participated in the construction of the smelter. Other Billiton employees were in Switzerland at that time and managed to get to the United States. NV Billiton had expertise in both mining and smelting of tin. See D. W. Fryer, *World Economic Development* (New York: McGraw Hill, 1965), 420, on the new techniques in metal recovery and more economical uses of tin that developed during World War II.

26. Gary Clyde Hufbauer, Jeffrey J. Schott, and Kimberly Ann Elliott, *Economic Sanctions Reconsidered: Supplemental Case Histories,* 2nd ed. (Washington, D.C.: Institute for International Economics, 1990), 45, and Medlicott, *Economic Blockade.*

27. *New York Times,* Sept. 12, 1939.

28. I have used P. N. Davies, "British Shipping and World Trade," in *Business History of Shipping,* ed. Tsunehiko Yui and Keiichiro Nakagawa (Tokyo: University of Tokyo Press, 1985), 78, for 1913 and 1914 figures; his 1939 ones are 27.9 percent for the British and 16.6 percent for the U.S. fleet. I have taken my 1939 figures from U.S. Department of Commerce, Office of Business Economics, *International Transactions of the United States during the War, 1940–1945,* Economic Series No. 65 (Washington, D.C., 1948), 49–50, so as to be able to make comparisons in Chapter 9 with 1945. Davies does not give 1945 figures. If we look at shipping in America's foreign trade (as distinct from world trade), according to Sturmey, *British Shipping,* 130, in 1913, Americans handled 14.0 percent and in 1938, 26.6 percent, while in 1913 the British handled 51.7 percent and in 1938, 27.5 percent.

29. H. Duncan Hall, *North American Supply* (London: Longmans, Green, 1955), 53–54. For the subterfuges used to get around this legislation in shipping, see De La Pedraja, *Rise and Decline of U.S. Merchant Shipping,* 134–141.

30. Ratner, *American Taxation,* 462. The figures are in current dollars. The trend was the same when measured as a percentage of gross national product: 1919, 32.3 percent; 1930, 18.6 percent; 1940, 43 percent. The GNP figures are from U.S. Department of Commerce, Bureau of the Census, *Historical Statistics of the United States* (Washington, D.C., 1960), 139. I did the arithmetic.

31. Ratner, *American Taxation,* 462.

32. Later the topic of internal versus external debt would become a matter that economists debated at length. See, for example, P. A. Diamond, "National Debt in a Neoclassical Growth Model," *American Economic Review,* 55 (Dec. 1965): 1126–1150, and G. O. Bierwag et al., "National Debt in a Neo-classical Growth Model: Comment," *American Economic Review,* 59 (Mar. 1969): 205–210. Much later, in a totally different world (when 22 percent of U.S. Treasury securities were held abroad), the International Monetary Fund would examine (in the context of a short-lived U.S. budget surplus) the financial implications of a shrinking supply of U.S. Treasury securities. *IMF Survey,* Apr. 2, 2001, 110–113.

33. *1941 Census,* 18. The census also uncovered another $93 million in state and municipal obligations. Ibid. Yet the report stated, "Data available with respect to foreign holdings of United States national, state and municipal bonds have never been complete or reliable." The census might well have missed foreign holders of such securities. Ibid., 42.

34. Carter, *International Economic Sanctions,* 186.

35. U.S. Department of the Treasury, *Documents Pertaining to Foreign Funds Control* (Washington, D.C., 1945); and Bank of International Settlements, Monetary and Eco-

nomic Department, *United States Regulations Relating to Foreign Funds Control,* 4th ed. (Basle: Bank of International Settlements, Feb. 1944).

36. *New York Times,* May 19, 1940.

37. Notes of talk with FDR, Sun. May 19, 1940, 127–24, Thomas Lamont Papers, Harvard Business School, Baker Library, Boston. Interestingly, data collected by the Federal Reserve do show British selling in the week ending May 15, 1940.

38. *New York Times,* May 19, 1940. Data from the Federal Reserve confirm this.

39. George L. Harrison, Memo, Nov. 27, 1940, Harrison Papers 2500.3, FRBNY. Blum, *From the Morgenthau Diaries,* II, 331, for Secretary of the Treasury Henry Morgenthau's advocacy of extending the freeze in November 1940. The attachment of assets was to meet certain claims.

40. According to the *1941 Census,* 4, there was substantial reduction in German, Italian, and Japanese "liquid" assets, April 10, 1941, to June 11, 1941. Morgenthau had long wanted to extend the freeze to Germany and Italy (as well as Poland and Czechoslovakia). Secretary of State Cordell Hull had reservations and did not agree until June 12, 1941, two days before Executive Order 8785. On the Morgenthau-Hull controversy, see Blum, *From the Morgenthau Diaries,* II, 327–343. There was a similar controversy over Japanese and Chinese assets. In 1940 China's T. V. Soong had suggested the freezing of Japanese and Chinese assets; Morgenthau concurred; Hull objected, fearing that extending the control would only serve to provoke Japan. Ibid., 368–369. U.S. Treasury, *Documents,* 3–5, 85.

41. U.S. Treasury, *Documents,* 85; the same phrase was used in relation to Finland, Portugal, Spain, and the USSR. Cerutti, "Le blocage of avoirs suisses," 185–235, is excellent on the blockage of Swiss assets in the United States.

42. *1941 Census,* 5.

43. U.S. Treasury, *Documents,* 35–64 (for general licenses), 85–91 (press releases on general licenses).

44. On June 24, 1941, a press release was issued, explaining that "a general license under the freezing control order was issued today with respect to transactions of the Union of Soviet Socialist Republics and its nationals. The State Department requested, and the Treasury Department and the Department of Justice approved, the issuance of the license without the requirement of the formal assurances which have been requested of European neutral nations affected by the freezing order . . . Recent events concerning the Union of Soviet Socialist Republics have made such assurances unnecessary." U.S. Treasury, *Documents,* 85–86 (the press release), 51 (General License No. 51). For all practical purposes, the small Soviet assets in the United States were unfrozen. Bishop, *Roosevelt-Litvinov Agreements,* 244.

45. This was the first (and only) World War II–related extension of the Foreign Funds Control concept to the Far East. The motives were identical to those in the earlier European freeze. For its context in relation to other U.S. economic sanctions against Japan, see Mira Wilkins, "The Role of U.S. Business," in *Pearl Harbor as History,* ed. Dorothy Borg and Shumpei Okamoto (New York: Columbia University Press, 1973), 373.

46. According to the *New York Times,* June 15, 1941.

47. "Foreign Funds Control Report," submitted to the president, Dec. 18, 1941, Morgenthau Diaries, vol. 474, p. 112, Franklin D. Roosevelt Library, Hyde Park, New York (more than $7 billion). The "almost $8 billion" estimate, published in 1945, is in *1941 Census,* vii, and included long- and short-term assets, gold, and foreign securities.

48. On the "Proclaimed List," see U.S. Treasury, *Documents,* 10–11 (Proclamation, July 17, 1941), 86–87 (press release issued July 17, 1941). On Treasury Department licenses, "Foreign Funds Control Report," 112. If one compares this 2,500 figure to the 2,816 total number of foreign-controlled enterprises in the United States in June 14, 1941

(as given in Table 8.2), there is obviously a disparity, since, for example, no Canadian or Newfoundland (241) or U.K. enterprises (623) needed a license. Or, put another way, 2,816 minus 2,500 leaves only 318 enterprises not subject to blockage.

49. The "freeze order," covering Danish and Norwegian assets, was April 10, 1940. The Danish and Norwegian situations were different, since Norway was considered a belligerent nation on the Allied side, and the British took over her merchant marine. Information from Hans Ch. Johansen, Jan. 29, 1999, and Feb. 15, 1999 (e-mails).

50. Johansen e-mail, Jan. 28, 1999, and De La Pedraja, *Rise and Decline of U.S. Merchant Shipping,* 135.

51. De La Pedraja, *Rise and Decline of U.S. Merchant Shipping,* 180.

52. 55 *U.S. Stat.,* 242–245 (June 6, 1941). The law authorized the takeover with compensation of any ship "lying idle" in U.S. waters. The executive order (see Office of Alien Property Custodian, *Annual Report 1942–1943,* 148, and *Federal Register,* 6 [June 7, 1941]: 2759) was the result of the passage of the June 6, 1941, Ship Requisition Act. Johansen e-mail, Jan. 28, 1999, on the Danish ships.

53. Hall, *North American Supply,* 318, 312.

54. *Financial Times,* July 28, 1941, and Dean Acheson, *Present at the Creation* (New York: Signet, 1970), 51–53. Japanese ships got permission to leave; no Japanese ships were seized after Pearl Harbor.

55. U.S. Treasury, *Documents,* 10–11, 86–87. On July 2, 1940, Congress had given the president authority to subject U.S. exports to a licensing system whenever national defense was in jeopardy (54 U.S. *Stat.* 712, sec. 6, at 714). For details, see Wilkins, *Maturing,* 258, and Acheson, *Present at the Creation,* 42, for the role of the State Department. The July 17, 1941, press release indicated that the Proclaimed List was the "result of long and intensive investigations and studies by the interested governmental agencies [the Departments of State, Treasury, and Commerce, the attorney general, the Administrator of Export Control, and the Coordinator of Commercial and Cultural Relations between the American Republics]." U.S. Treasury, *Documents,* 86.

56. Blum, *From the Morgenthau Diaries,* II, 337.

57. Beaton, *Enterprise in Oil,* 556; Michael B. Stoff, *Oil, War, and American Security* (New Haven, Conn.: Yale University Press, 1980), 17–21.

58. Wilkins, *Maturing,* 258, and Acheson, *Present at the Creation,* 46.

59. U.S. Senate, Special Committee Investigating the National Defense Program, *Hearings,* 77th Cong., 1st sess. (1941). The TNEC issued its final report and recommendations on March 31, 1941, just before the Truman Committee hearings began. The TNEC influence washed over onto the subsequent general investigations. Maddox, *War within World War II,* 5, 9n.10.

60. Based on data in RG 131, U.S. Justice Department, Washington, D.C.—henceforth cited as RG 131 (Dept.-Justice). See also Acheson, *Present at the Creation,* 48. Justice and Treasury both had had representatives on the TNEC. Maddox, *War within World War II,* 3.

61. Office of Alien Property Custodian, *Annual Report, Mar. 11, 1942–June 30, 1943,* 1, 9, 25.

62. This is evident from Acheson, *Present at the Creation,* and Wilkins, *Maturing,* 259. The State Department addressed in particular German influences in Latin America and German businesses in the United States that were exporting to Latin America. Mann and Plummer, *Aspirin Wars,* 360, 362, used State as well as Justice Department records in their study of the I. G. Farben–Sterling Products connections.

63. See, for example, J. Edgar Hoover to Assistant Attorney-General Francis M. Shea, Oct. 28, 1941, which contains special agents reports dating back to Oct. 1940, in File D-63–4, Acc. 67A10, Box 2572, RG 131 (Dept.-Justice), and Mann and Plummer, *Aspirin Wars,* 360n.104.

64. U.S. Securities and Exchange Commission, *Report on Study of Investment Trusts and Investment Holding Companies,* 75th–77th Cong. (1939–1942), pts. I–IV, esp. pt. IV, presented to Congress, June 9, 1941.

65. For this strictly covert activity during the period when the United States was "neutral," see the remarkable story in William Stevenson, *A Man Called Intrepid* (New York: Harcourt Brace Jovanovich, 1976), 171–177, 267–303, esp. 288, and passim.

66. Arnold at U.S. Senate, Committee on Patents, *Patents, Hearings,* 77th Cong., 2nd sess. (1942), 627 (henceforth cited as *Bone Committee Hearings*).

67. Ibid., 640.

68. *New York Times,* Jan. 13, 1941.

69. Ibid., Jan. 4, 1941. Alton Frye, *Nazi Germany and the American Hemisphere 1933–1941* (New Haven, Conn.: Yale University Press, 1967), esp. 96–97 and 121, shows how Germans provided fuel to U.S. isolationism, with an eye to keeping America out of the war.

70. Reader, *Imperial Chemical Industries,* 421, and Lamer, *World Fertilizer Economy,* 180.

71. *U.S. v. Allied Chemical & Dye Corp., et al.,* Civil No. 14-320 (SDNY 1941), abstract in Lindstrom and Tighe, *Antitrust Consent Decrees,* I, 265–268; Stocking and Watkins, *Cartels in Action,* 153. Consent decree in *U.S. v. Synthetic Nitrogen Products Corp.,* Civil No. 15-36 (SDNY 1941), in Lindstrom and Tighe, *Antitrust Consent Decrees,* I, 282–284; Oseas, "Antitrust Prosecutions," 60. The case filed against ICI, *U.S. v. Imperial Chemical Industries,* Civil No. 17-282 (SDNY 1942), would not be settled until after the United States entered the war.

72. *U.S. v. American Potash and Chemical Corp. et al.,* SDNY Civil Action 8-498, Complaint filed May 15, 1940; order of dismissal, May 21, 1940. See also Markham, *Fertilizer Industry,* 92–93.

73. *U.S. v. Bausch and Lomb Optical Co., et al.,* Civil No. 9-404 (SDNY 1940), in Lindstrom and Tighe, *Antitrust Consent Decrees,* I, 222. The full complaint and consent decree are in U.S. Senate, Committee on Military Affairs, Subcommittee on War Mobilization, *Scientific and Technical Mobilization, Hearings,* 78th Cong., 1st and 2nd sess. (1943–1944), pt. 16, 2117–2131 (henceforth cited as *Kilgore Committee Hearings*). The German company Carl Zeiss was a defendant in the case. Jurisdiction over Zeiss, Jena, was through its sales subsidiary in New York: allegations in the complaint were "deemed to mean" acts of Zeiss in Germany or Carl Zeiss, Inc., New York. Neither the German Zeiss nor its American affiliate, Carl Zeiss, Inc., New York, was a party to the consent decree, which governed the future transactions of Bausch and Lomb.

74. See *Bone Committee Hearings,* 43 and 156ff., for the actual indictment. *U.S. v. General Electric, Fried. Krupp AG, et al.,* Criminal No. 108-172 (SDNY 1940). For a second indictment, *U.S. v. General Electric et al.,* Criminal No. 110-442 (SDNY 1941). See also M. Louis Friedr. Krupp, Essen, to F. Redies, I. G. Farben, Sept. 7, 1940, RG 238, T301, Reel 36, NI-4900, National Archives (Krupp read about the indictment in the newspapers.)

75. *U.S. v. General Electric Co et al.,* Civil No. 1364 (DNJ 1949) for the history of the proceedings. As of January 13, 1941, GE held at least 9 percent of the equity of NV Philips' Gloeilampenfabrieken. Blanken, *History of Philips Electronics,* IV, 156 (ownership).

76. Stocking and Watkins, *Cartels in Action,* 302; *New York Times,* Jan. 31 and Feb. 7, 1941; Smith, *From Monopoly to Competition,* 232.

77. *New York Times,* Apr. 11, 1941. The next day the *New York Times* reported that General Aniline & Film "stated" its records had *not* been subpoenaed. On the April 1941 antitrust "investigation" of Schering, see Paul M. Greene and Donald P. McHugh, Memorandum, Jan. 11, 1944, in Acc. 61A109, Box 681, RG 131 (Dept.-Justice).

78. Consent decree in *U.S. v. Alba Pharmaceutical Co., et al.,* Civil No. 15-363 (SDNY 1941), in Lindstrom and Tighe, *Antitrust Consent Decrees,* I, 278–279. Alba Pharmaceutical

Co. (formed in 1940) was an affiliate of Winthrop Chemical Co. See Arthur D. Little, Report on Winthrop Chemical, July 8, 1942, in File D-63–4, Acc. 65A1063, Box 267, RG 131 (Dept.-Justice).

79. Consent decree in *U.S. v. Bayer Co., Inc.,* Civil No. 15-364 (SDNY 1941), in Lindstrom and Tighe, *Antitrust Consent Decrees,* I, 280–281. The Bayer Co. was a subsidiary of Sterling Products. In 1919, Sterling Products had two subsidiaries, the Bayer Co. for aspirin and Winthrop Chemical Co. for other medications. Mann and Plummer, *Aspirin Wars,* 52. The Germans never resumed an interest in Bayer Co., Inc., but there were market allocation agreements.

80. Larson, Knowlton, and Popple, *New Horizons,* 419, 428.

81. On some of the criminal cases naming foreign defendants, 1940–1941, see Oseas, "Antitrust Prosecutions," 56n.40.

82. Tilley, *R. J. Reynolds Tobacco Company,* 416, 413–426, 663–664.

83. Whitney, *Antitrust Policies,* II, 30–31, 36, 55–56.

84. Beaton, *Enterprise in Oil,* 485–486; Larson, Knowlton, and Popple, *New Horizons,* 427–428.

85. The case was *U.S. v. American Petroleum Institute,* Civil No. 8524 (DDC 1940). On the relaxation in late 1941, see Stoff, *Oil, War, and American Security,* 21.

86. *New York Times,* Dec. 11, 1941.

87. According to Martin, *All Honorable Men,* 19–20. The conclusions were in the context of strong anti-German feelings. It is curious: Did the German government promise to reimburse the insurer for its liabilities? Did insurance contracts have war-risk exemptions? Martin, whose book was based on U.S. Justice Department wartime inquiries, never explains the insurers' "conflict of interest."

88. *New York Times,* Jan. 22, 1941. These same charges, related to 1941, would resurface in 1944. Maddox found a June 9, 1944, document in Justice Department files that claimed "German and Japanese insurance companies were able to get complete plans and engineering reports on every industrial plant in the United States that carried fire insurance." Maddox, *War within World War II,* 20, 35n.42.

89. "Top Secret Dispatch on the Safeguarding of Foreign Assets," from Gustav Schlotterer of the German Economics Ministry, Sept. 9, 1939, RG 238, T301, Reel 4, NI-300.

90. Martin, *All Honorable Men,* 77–80; Office of Alien Property Custodian, *Annual Report 1944–1945,* 178–179; Larson, Knowlton, and Popple, *New Horizons,* 405–407; *Standard Oil Co (New Jersey) et al. v. Markham,* 64 F. Supp. 656 (SDNY 1945); Stocking and Watkins, *Cartels in Action,* 101–103; Edwards, *Economic and Political Aspects of International Cartels,* 69–70.

91. See letter from W. H. vom Rath to all present and past directors of General Aniline & Film Corp., Sept. 3, 1941, in Ford Archives, Acc. 6, Henry Ford Museum, Dearborn Michigan.

92. I. G. Farben to Reich Ministry of Economics, July 24, 1939, RG 238, T301, Reel 70, NI-8496.

93. I. G. Farben to Reich Ministry of Economics, Aug. 15, 1939, RG 238, T301, Reel 55, NI-7078.

94. Hayes, *Industry and Ideology,* 355. After the war, Hermann Schmitz provided a "calculation" on the beneficial ownership of I. G. Chemie, Basle, showing there was *no* I. G. Farben interest in the Swiss firm. See data, Sept. 30, 1945, from Schmitz, RG 238, T301, Reel 6, NI-572. The best contemporary discussion of what I. G. Farben intended is in I. G. Farben (Kurt Kreuger and I. von Henze) to the Reich Economics Ministry, May 15, 1940, RG 238, T301, Reel 43, NI-5768; and I. G. Farben to Reich Ministry, June 11, 1940, RG 238, T301, Reel 43, NI-5772. See also Deutsche Länderbank to Reich Ministry

of Finance, Aug. 7, 1940, RG 238, T301, Reel 43, NI-5767; and *Bone Committee Hearings,* pt. 5, 2435.

95. Walter Germann, managing director, Internationale Industrie und Handelsbeteiligungen AG, Basle (the postwar successor to I. G. Chemie), to Mirko Lamer, Sept. 5, 1953, cited in Lamer, *World Fertilizer Economy,* 179, 197n.30.

96. Borkin, *Crime and Punishment of I. G. Farben,* 190. *Bone Committee Hearings,* pt. 5, 2109, contains a list of directors of General Aniline & Film (and its predecessor, American I. G.): Hermann Schmitz is listed as a director from 1929 to 1939. He had resigned as president of American I. G. in 1935.

97. RG 238, T301, Reel 11, NI-1127. In February 1929, I. G. Farben and I. G. Chemie had made "a dividend guarantee agreement . . . whereby the distribution from time to time of a dividend" on I. G. Chemie's common stock was guaranteed at the same rate as I. G. Farben dividends. I. G. Farben, *Annual Report 1928* (presented at the June 1929 annual meeting). This 1929 agreement was canceled in June 1940, as part of the divorce of the German and Swiss firms.

98. Statement of Orville Harden, Standard Oil Co. (New Jersey), Dec. 2, 1940, printed in *Bone Committee Hearings,* Exhibits, pt. 5, 2462–2463. The proposed "trade" was not unlike that suggested in January 1938 by George Murnane, who hoped Allied Chemical would acquire GAF (see Chapter 7).

99. Stocking and Watkins, *Cartels in Action,* 474; Interrogation of F. H. Ter Meer, Sept. 25, 1945, RG 238, T301, Reel 38, NI-5185; for background and plans, see Harold Mediger to August von Knieriem, Oct. 11, 1939, RG 238, T301, Reel 43, NI-5774. Haynes, *American Chemical Industry,* VI, 177. Even earlier, it had sold its shares in Pen-Chlor Inc. to GAF. See I. G. Farben to Foreign Exchange Department of Reichshauptbank, Nov. 17, 1939, RG 238, T301, Reel 43, NI-5770. The patents I. G. Farben sold to GAF were a different set from the ones covered by I. G. Farben's Standard Oil of New Jersey arrangements.

100. Blum, *From the Morgenthau Diaries,* III, 6.

101. In April 1943, Libbey-Owens-Ford would acquire the balance. Haynes, *American Chemical Industry,* VI, 246–247. On I. G. Farben's interest in Plaskon, see data in RG 238, T301, Reel 45, NI-6058. To add to the complexity, my reader will recall that the Belgian Solvay & Cie. had years earlier acquired interests in Libbey-Owens-Ford.

102. See Special Agent Report, Oct. 21, 1940, included in J. Edgar Hoover to Assistant Attorney General, Francis M. Shea, Oct. 28, 1941, File D-63–4, Acc. 67A10, Box 2572, RG 131 (Dept.-Justice).

103. Letter, Mar. 20, 1941, RG 238, T301, Reel 11, NI-1126.

104. *New York Times,* Feb. 7, 1941; *Bone Committee Hearings,* pt. 5 2434–2435; Thurman Arnold to Kenneth Payne, Aug. 2, 1941, in Gene M. Greesley, ed., *Voltaire and the Cowboy: The Letters of Thurman Arnold* (Boulder: Colorado Associated University Press, 1977), 325.

105. U.S. Securities and Exchange Commission, *Investment Trusts and Investment Companies,* H. Doc. 246, 77th Cong., 1st sess. (1942), 135–151. Although dated 1942, this document was referred to the Committee on Interstate and Foreign Commerce and ordered to be printed June 9, 1941 (see cover page and *New York Times,* June 11, 1941). It deals with the SEC pursuit of ownership information in earlier years. It refers to a lengthy statement made by D. A. Schmitz, president of General Aniline & Film, Dec. 4, 1940, titled "The History of Ownership of Securities of General Aniline and Film Corp."

106. Letter from W. H. Vom Rath to all present and past directors of General Aniline & Film Corp., Sept. 3, 1941, in Ford Archives, Acc. 6.

107. Ibid. and other data in the Ford Archives. U.S. Securities and Exchange Commission, *Investment Trusts and Investment Companies,* 139, 146–148, contains an interview with Walter Teagle, who eventually conceded, "I took it for granted that they [I. G. Farben] were the owners of it [American I. G. in 1929]." It is not clear when Teagle was inter-

viewed, but he insisted that throughout his tenure as a director, he did not know who controlled American I. G.

108. *New York Times,* Jan. 14, 1942.

109. Hayes, *Industry and Ideology,* 335.

110. Edsel Ford to William C. Breed, May 27, 1941, and Edsel Ford to D. A. Schmitz, president General Aniline & Film, May 27, 1941, Ford Archives.

111. *Time,* July 28, 1941, says Teagle had stepped down in 1940.

112. Borkin, *Crime and Punishment of I. G. Farben,* 195–196. Ford also had sizable blocked German assets; I found no evidence in the Ford Archives that Ford had sought to trade these assets for GAF.

113. *Time,* July 28, 1941.

114. Ibid. Auditors' reports on GAF for year end 1940 and 1941 are in File D-63-4, Acc. 65A1063, Box 267, RG 131 (Dept.-Justice). The earnings figures that *Time* reported for 1940 were accurate.

115. The German affiliate had always combined domestic production with imports, imports of intermediate and end products.

116. *Time,* July 28, 1941 (*Time* got W. H. Vom Rath's first name wrong; I have made the correction. On Walther Vom Rath (the father), see Hayes, *Industry and Ideology,* 27–28. Walther Vom Rath was vice-chairman of the I. G. Farben board of directors (1925–1940); see data in File D-28-517, Acc. 67A10, Box 1302, RG 131 (Dept.-Justice).

117. All the relationships were given in U.S. Securities and Exchange Commission, *Investment Trusts and Investment Companies,* 147–148; the SEC report was full of misspellings.

118. I have pieced together the story of what happened in these months from Affidavit of John E. Mack, Dec. 8, 1941, printed in *Bone Committee Hearings,* pt. 5, 2426–2441; Homer Cummings to the directors of General Aniline & Film, Oct. 8, 1941, printed in ibid., pt. 5, 2448–2451; Borkin, *Crime and Punishment of I. G. Farben,* 196–198; *New York Times,* esp. Oct. 3, 1941, Dec. 6, 13, 16, 20 (on the directors' decision to elect Bullitt as chairman), 1941; ibid., Jan. 14, 1942; and German Consul, Basle, to German Foreign Office, Jan. 30, 1942, RG 238, T301, Reel 11, NI-1125. Bullitt's biography in *Who's Who in America 1948* says nothing about his role in General Aniline & Film, but it does document his ambassadorial appointments.

119. Blum, *From the Morgenthau Diaries,* III, 7; Treasury Secretary Morgenthau was far from enthusiastic about Mack and Bullitt. Roosevelt had suggested Mack as GAF president; Mack had then brought in Bullitt; Bullitt's role was short-lived; he resigned as GAF chairman in February 1942.

120. Clearly the preparatory work had been done before the war. The actual indictments are printed in the *Bone Committee Hearings,* pt. 5, 2602–2619. See also *New York Times,* Dec. 20, 1941.

121. Blum, *From the Morgenthau Diaries,* III, 6 (more than 6,000); *New York Times,* Mar. 11, 1942 (says 8,000 employees).

122. This might explain the 1940 domestic sales, including imports, of GAF, since GAF and GDC worked in tandem.

123. Special Agent Report, Oct. 21, 1940, included in J. Edgar Hoover to Assistant Attorney General, Francis M. Shea, Oct. 28, 1941, File D-63-4, Acc. 67A10, Box 2572, RG 131 (Dept.-Justice); E. K. Halbach Statement, May 7, 1941, printed in *Bone Committee Hearings,* pt. 5, 2236; and Edwards, *Economic and Political Aspects of International Cartels,* 9, 70. See also 1953 testimony of Halbach, at U.S. Senate, Committee on the Judiciary, Subcommittee to Investigate the Administration of the Trading with the Enemy Act, *Administration of the Trading with the Enemy Act, Hearings,* 83rd Cong., 1st sess., (1954), 668–669, 672–673.

124. At the early stages of the war, to avoid the British blockade, I. G. Farben arranged to ship intermediates to Winthrop Chemical over the Trans-Siberian Railway and by ship across the Pacific. Mann and Plummer, *Aspirin Wars,* 100. Winthrop Chemical sent a company representative to meet with Germans in Florence, Italy, to obtain technical data and to work out appropriate arrangements, given the war in Europe; the meeting took place on February 6, 1940. Ibid., 100–101.

125. See the excellent Arthur D. Little Report on Winthrop Chemical Company, July 8, 1942, File D-63–4, Acc. 65A1063, Box 267, RG 131 (Dept.-Justice).

126. Wilkins, *Maturing,* 252, 259; Haynes, *American Chemical Industry,* VI, 409; Mann and Plummer, *Aspirin Wars,* 97–119. Edward S. Rogers was Sterling's trademark lawyer in its contract negotiations with I. G. Farben. Ibid., 117.

127. *New York Times,* June 17, 1941, and Report of Gustav Frank-Fahl to I. G. Farben, Commercial Committee Meeting, July 8, 1941, RG 238, T301, Reel 45, NI-6086. Oseas, "Antitrust Prosecutions," 58, has an interesting discussion on how the Justice Department got foreign defendants to respond to American charges: in the Magnesium Case, for example, the Justice Department issued a writ of *distringas,* seizing I. G. Farben's funds. The procedure worked. "The foreign defendant filed a notice of appearance."

128. I. G. Farben to Reich Ministry of Economics, July 21, 1941, RG 238, T301, Reel 34, NI-4615. The phrase "our American patents" is significant, this despite the "transfer" of the patents to Standard Oil of New Jersey and General Aniline & Film.

129. Larson, Knowlton, and Popple, *New Horizons,* 413–415; Edwards, *Economic and Political Aspects of International Cartels,* 59–60; and *Kilgore Committee Hearings,* pt. 1, 48 (which says that "Goodyear was notified of the possibility of a similar suit").

130. J. E. Crane to Fritz ter Meer, Apr. 18, 1941, and Fritz ter Meer to Crane, June 25, 1941, Acc. 1231, Box 4, Du Pont Papers, Hagley Museum and Library, Wilmington, Delaware.

131. See "State of Relations with Basler Farbenfabriken" (Zurich Conference, Oct. 8, 1940), I. G. Farben, Minutes of Dyestuffs Committee, Dec. 17, 1940, and ibid., Apr. 17, 1941, RG 238, T301, Reel 36, N.I.-4852 and NI-4847. The "general business routine" had been established by the German-Swiss dyestuff cartel of April 1929. Schröter, "Cartels as a Form of Concentration," 128. There was considerable variety in the degree to which the Swiss companies were ready to follow I. G. Farben's bidding. Ciba's management was *very* alarmed when Felix Iselin, president of I. G. Chemie and also of the Schweizerische Treuhandgesellschaft in Basle, got involved in General Aniline in the United States. Ciba-Basle's president called General Aniline "our biggest competitor" and thought Iselin's role untenable. James Brodbeck (Ciba-Basle) to A. F. Liechtenstein, Ciba, N.Y., Jan. 9, 1941, in Charles R. Clark, Report, Dec. 26, 1942, File D-63–1, Acc. 65A1063, Box 267, RG 131 (Dept.-Justice).

132. For the German side of the story, see Gall et al., *Deutsche Bank,* 317–318.

133. Edwards, *Economic and Political Aspects of International Cartels,* 14; Mahoney, *Merchants of Life,* 255; Office of Alien Property Custodian, *Annual Report 1943–1944,* 74–75. Kobrak, "Between Nationalism and Internationalism," 586n.113, found in Schering archives a memorandum of March 16, 1940, indicating that Schering AG should not correspond on matters concerning Chepha, Atlantis SA, and Forinvent to avoid problems for the U.S. operations. On Forinvent, see ibid., 601–605, and historical data in Paul M. Greene and Donald P. McHugh, Memo, Jan. 11, 1944, Acc. 61A109, Box 681, RG 131 (Dept.-Justice).

134. Rolf Calissendorf, Stockholms Enskilda Bank, to Paul Oberer, chairman, Chepha, May 28, 1940, Acc. 61A109, Box 681, RG 131 (Dept.-Justice); Paul Oberer, Memo, Feb. 14, 1940, and Memo of Conference on Chepha, Feb. 17, 1940 (attended by Julius Weltzein, Schering Corp; J. J. Brodbeck, Ciba-N.J.; Armand Dreyfus and others from Swiss Bank

Corp.), in Charles R. Clark, Report, Dec. 26, 1942, File D-63–1, Acc. 65A1063, Box 267, RG 131 (Dept.-Justice).

135. James Brodbeck-Sandreuler to J. J. Brodbeck, Dec. 5, 1941, included in Clark Report (note 134) and ibid., for the Swiss Bank Corp. holdings.

136. This oversimplifies a very complicated story. See Aalders and Wiebes, "Stockholms Enskilda Bank," 30–35, and Aalders and Wiebes, *Art of Cloaking,* 37–42. See also announcement in *New York Times,* May 21, 1940. On Batt's election as director, September 6, 1938, see American Bosch Corporation, Prospectus, Oct. 25, 1938, Scudder Collection, Business School Library Columbia University Libraries, New York.

137. Martin, *All Honorable Men,* 93, and data in RG 238, T301, Reel 36, NI-4907. See also "Strictly Confidential Report . . . on Investigation into Foreign Currency Operations of Friedrich Krupp A.G.," Jan. 12, 1940, RG 238, T301, Reel 15, NI-1496. This report by the Foreign Currency Control Officer, Düsseldorf, contains a list of Krupp's foreign affiliates, including Krupp-Nirosta Co., Inc. (capital $120,000). At the end of 1939, Krupp was seeking to capitalize the royalties it received from GE's subsidiary, Carboloy. It sought to sell GE exclusive rights to the patent(s) for a set period, for a lump sum. H. B. Pearce, International General Electric Co., Berlin, to Zay Jeffries, Dec. 11, 1939, *Bone Committee Hearings,* Exhibits, pt. 1, 220–221. For more on the transactions and the Swiss companies involved, from the German standpoint, September 25, 1939 through October 2, 1940, see data in RG 238, T301, Reel 43, NI-5816 and NI-5815. Krupp's main problem was how to avoid the loss of revenues from its licensing of patents in the United States, should war between the United States and Germany occur. More on the Krupp-Nirosta story is in the *Kilgore Committee Hearings,* pt. 16, 2084 and 2362–2363.

138. Martin, *All Honorable Men,* 116. Henkel, like many German companies, had used Swiss holding companies for years (in Henkel's case since 1931). See Susanne Hilger, "The Internationalization of a Family Firm: The Case of the German Chemical Producer Henkel," in *Transnational Companies,* ed. Hubert Bonin, et al. (Paris: Éditions P.L.A.G.E., n.d. [2002]), 880–881.

139. The story of the pyramided relationships can in part be deciphered from data in File D-28–623, Acc. 67A10, Box 1310, RG 131 (Dept.-Justice). Rotopulsor, AG, the Swiss holding company, had been set up by Metallgesellshaft, probably in the late 1930s. According to data in this file, NV Hollandsche Koopmansbank was substantially owned by Berliner Handelsgesellschaft, Berlin. (Aalders and Wiebes, "Stockholms Enskilda Bank," 41, tell a more tangled tale on the ownership of Hollandsche Koopmansbank.)

140. There are literally thousands of boxes in RG 131 (Dept.-Justice) with materials documenting these complexities; so, too, many other sources are available on these holding companies. Examples proliferate.

141. Guex, "Origins of the Swiss Banking Secrecy Law," 257.

142. See August 1940 correspondence in *Bone Committee Hearings,* pt. 7, 4162. On the developments in fluid catalytic cracking, see ibid., pt. 7, 4134–4163, and Larson, Knowlton, and Popple, *New Horizons,* 166–169, 410–412. On Anglo-Iranian's New York office, see Bamberg, *History of the British Petroleum Company . . . 1928–1954,* 602 (Basil Jackson was the firm's New York representative 1929–1934 and 1939–1948).

143. F. A. Howard's remarks at a Jersey Standard Technical Committee Meeting, sent by H. W. Fisher to R. C. Wilson, Nov. 14, 1939, *Bone Committee Hearings,* pt. 7, 4135–4136; see also Wilkins, *Maturing,* 246.

144. See, for example, the discussion on how polyurethanes developed in German laboratories compared with those of Du Pont, recorded in the September 25, *1941* Minutes of the Vorstand of I. G. Farben. The presentation was technical; there was *no* consideration in this instance of the impact of World War II. Minutes in RG 238, T301, Reel 43, NI-5813. Many contracts were temporarily suspended. See, for example, Dr. Scheuing

(German legal adviser to Rohm & Haas), Stuttgart, to Rohm & Haas, Philadelphia, July 30, 1940, in Thurman Arnold Papers, Box 21, American Heritage Center, University of Wyoming, Laramie, wherein Scheuing commented on the "interruption of exchange of information" between Darmstadt and Philadelphia. A satisfactory situation would be reestablished "as soon as normal conditions" resumed.

145. Edwards, *Economic and Political Aspects of International Cartels,* 63.

146. *Bone Committee Hearings,* pt. 3, 1405–1407, 1514–1517.

147. Daniel Macmillan, chairman, Macmillan & Co. Ltd., to Foreign Office, May 29, 1940 and Marquess of Lothian (Washington) cable to Foreign Office, May 27, 1940, FO 371/24258, Public Record Office; the problem was that the parent company had used the stock as collateral to borrow from Westminister Bank, London, which physically held the securities.

148. *Moody's Industrial 1941,* 3157; interestingly, E. R. Lewis, described in Kynaston, *City of London,* III, 230, as a broker who was instrumental in floating Decca Record Co. Ltd., in 1929, stayed on as chairman of Decca Records Inc., New York, even though the British parent had disposed of its equity interest.

149. Hall, *North American Supply,* 104, 149, 198, 288, 290–292. The British government bought the French government's interest in Tennessee Powder Company in June 1940 for $8 million. Ibid., 149. In June 1940, the complete designs of the British Rolls-Royce Merlin Engine went to the U.S. government, leaving "the rights" of and payments to the Rolls Royce and Hanley Page companies to be determined later. A team of Rolls Royce engineers was sent over to help the Packard Co. produce the engines. Ibid., 191, 37–38. On the British government's expenditures on plants in the United States, see also Skidelsky, *John Maynard Keynes,* III, 94.

150. Beaton, *Enterprise in Oil,* 569–575, 592–593, 599–600.

151. Mahoney, *Merchants of Life,* 107, 111, 113; Haynes, *American Chemical Industry,* V, 277; VI, 60–63; and data from G. A. Burchett, Corporate Archivist, Glaxo Wellcome, Research Triangle Park, North Carolina, Mar. 1999.

152. *New York Times Book Review,* Apr. 30, 1989.

153. Roberts, *Schroders,* 292–293. Indicative of its connections is a seating list for a 1937 luncheon at the German-American Chamber of Commerce, which was complete with representatives from Krupp-Nirosta, North German Lloyd, American I. G. Chemical Corp., Chemnyco, and American Bemberg; it also included the Schroeder Bank. *Kilgore Committee Hearings,* pt. 16, 2073.

154. A. F. W. Plumptre, *Mobilizing Canada's Resources for War* (Toronto: Macmillan, 1941), 183–192 (foreign exchange controls). Canadian net purchases of American domestic securities January 9, 1935 to August 30, 1939, came to $13 million, while the net sales of foreign securities came to $41.5 million. Canadian net sales, August 30, 1939, to December 31, 1941, of American domestic securities came to $57.7 million, while the net purchases of foreign securities were $76.9 million. Based on data from the Federal Reserve System, *Banking and Monetary Statistics* (Washington, D.C., 1943), 620–623, 626–629. I am indebted to G. Gokkent for his preparation of charts and these tabulations.

155. Dominion Bureau of Statistics, *Canada's International Investment Position, Selected Years, 1926 to 1949* (Ottawa, n.d. [1950]), 24–25, deals with Canadian portfolio investments in the United States, 1939 and 1949. This report does not specifically deal with the 1939–1941 Canadian purchases in the United States of non-American ("foreign") securities; from its vantage point, the term "foreign securities" included U.S. domestic ones. The purchases of "foreign securities" by Canadians recorded by the Federal Reserve were not trivial; they not only were larger than Canadian sales of American domestic securities, 1939–1941, but also were larger than Canadian sales of foreign securities, 1935–1939. While the Canadian report is suggestive, the transactions recorded by the

Federal Reserve are not explained. I also consulted Dominion Bureau of Statistics, *Canada's International Investment Position, 1926–1954* (Ottawa, 1956). The British government insisted on the sales of certain of its nationals' assets in Canada and the United States to finance British wartime purchases; I wonder whether some of the permitted "switching and trading" might have involved Canadians in transactions involving these formerly British-held securities, which may in some cases have met the Federal Reserve definition of "foreign securities."

156. The British firm Glaxo's joint venture in the United States with the Canadian firm Ayerst, McKenna & Harrison Ltd. came to an end; the U.S. affiliate became a wholly owned subsidiary of the Canadian AMH. R. P. T. Davenport-Hines, "Glaxo as a Multinational before 1963," in *British Multinationals: Origins, Management and Performance,* ed. Geoffrey Jones (Aldershot: Gower, 1986), 150.

157. *1941 Census,* 28–29. On Massey-Harris, see Neufeld, *Global Corporation,* 35, 44. In the 1930s, the firm had virtually decided to close its loss-generating American operations but then changed its mind. Finally, by 1939–1940, with new products and "war orders," the Canadian owners had a new confidence in the future of the company in the United States.

158. If we use *Canadian-citizen* ownership of securities, see Table 8.3. This is not the case if we use reported address (Tables 8.1, 8.2, and total Canada line on Table 8.3). Canadian data show at year end 1939 portfolio investment in the United States was greater than direct investment, whereas the opposite was true as of year end 1945. There are no Canadian data for 1941. Dominion Bureau of Statistics, *Canada's International Investment Position, Selected Years, 1926 to 1949,* 39.

159. By contrast, U.S. businesses in Canada were very much involved in these complex relationships. Also, it was often Canadians who represented "British" interests in America during wartime. In addition, on occasion, "Canadian trusts" were used "to protect" foreign investors' U.S. assets. Thus, Canadian holding companies sometimes served third-country investors in the United States (and while there were suspicions of German cloaks, there seems to have been little behind such suspicions).

160. The Dutch were net purchasers of American domestic securities, September 1939–December 1941, to the extent of $16.1 million, practically all concentrated in the period September 1939 to May 1940. Based on data from Board of Governors, Federal Reserve System, *Banking and Monetary Statistics,* 620–623.

161. NV Philips' small U.S. business was governed by its agreements with International General Electric Company. Southard, *American Industry in Europe,* 31, 166–167, 211; *U.S. v. General Electric et al.,* Civil No. 1364 (DNJ 1949), on incandescent lamps; and Ben P. A. Gales and Keetie E. Sluyterman, "Outward Bound: The Rise of Dutch Multinationals," in *The Rise of Multinationals in Continental Europe,* ed. Geoffrey Jones and Harm G. Schröter (Aldershot: Edward Elgar, 1993), 74. NV Philips also had agreements with Radio Corporation of America. Edwards, *Economic and Political Aspects of International Cartels,* 20 (on the 1925 agreement on radio equipment that was still in force in 1939). According to Cantwell and Barrera, "Localisation of Corporate Technological Trajectories," 268, Philips had been very active in patenting its inventions in the United States, 1925–1939; by 1935–1939, its patenting activity in the United States in electrical equipment was third among European firms, after the German AEG and Siemens. The best material on Philips is in Blanken, *History of Philips Electronics,* IV.

162. Edwards, *Economic and Political Aspects of International Cartels,* 70; Faith, *Infiltrators,* 81. On April 29, 1940, Maynard T. Hazen of Hartford National Bank and Trust Co. and P. T. Utermöhlen of NV Philips, who was "temporarily" in New York, told officials of the New York Federal Reserve about the "elaborate trust arrangements" that had been made earlier to enable the Dutch firm to continue to do business in the event that Holland

was overrun by Germany. L. W. Knoke, Memo, Apr. 29, 1940, File 765.41 Genl. Corresp., FRBNY. On the "American Trust" and Bezit (Gemeenschappelijk Bezit van Aandelen Philips' Gloeilampenfabrieken, NV), see Blanken, *History of Philips Electronics,* IV, 120 ("The American Trust came into effect on 25 August 1939"); 337 (the structure of the Philips group, including the Bezit holding company, before the invasion of the Netherlands); 338 (the structure on June 1, 1940). After the invasion of Holland, the voting provisions of the trust were activated, and Philips' units in the United States came to be held by the American Trust, Hartford National Bank and Trust Co. For the Dutch parent's problems in 1940 and 1941, see ibid., 150–171. Important Philips directors had moved to London when the Germans invaded, and at the end of May 1940 they decided that the group headquarters should be transferred to New York. Ibid., 144–145. Discussions with I. J. Blanken, Philips, Odense, Denmark, Mar. 29–30, 2001.

163. "A Short History of the Royal Dutch/Shell Group of Companies" (London, 1970), 7, and Gales and Sluyterman, "Outward Bound," 78. *1941 Census,* 30. Note "place of business" and "administration of" (direction of) business were different.

164. *New York Times,* Dec. 18, 1941. The Dutch parent had Jewish management, so there was a different imperative in play with this firm. Gales and Sluyterman, "Outward Bound," 95n.45.

165. Keetie E. Sluyterman, "From Licensor to Multinational Enterprise," *Business History,* 34 (Apr. 1992): 38–39.

166. Data from Unilever PLC. Wilson, *History of Unilever,* II, 374–375, writes that after the invasion of Holland, in May 1940, relations between the London and Rotterdam Unilever head offices were severed. "Technically," the Netherlands government in exile in London "expropriated all Dutch property" outside Holland, which included Lever Brothers Co., and appointed Unilever Ltd., London, administrator of those assets.

167. On its acquisition of Continental Foods, see "History Outline on Thomas J. Lipton Inc.," Dec. 2, 1947, Unilever Archives, London. Lipton Inc. was associated with Unilever from 1937 (see Chapter 7). The subsequent ownership relationships between Unilever and Lipton were very complicated, and it was not until September 1946 that the Unilever group completed its acquisition of the controlling interest in Lipton Inc. Wilson, *History of Unilever,* II, 377.

168. In the case of Shell, the Hague may have been more involved in the U.S. business than Rotterdam was in the U.S. business of Unilever, but often the *Dutch* executives worked out of London in the case of Shell's multinational business. In the United States in the fall of 1940, Shell set up a new central office in New York City. The Shell Oil Company Inc. became the principal unit in the American business. Forbes, *Chronology of Oil,* 75.

169. Telephone conversations, L. W. Knoke and Bank of England, May 13, 1940, May 22, 1940, and cable Bolton, Bank of England to Federal Reserve Bank of New York, C261 England–Bank of England, FRBNY, and New York State, Banking Department, *Annual Report 1941.* The agency opened on January 31, 1941 (New York State Banking Dept. Web site: http:/banking.state.NY.US/histn.txt). For the experiences of other Dutch trading companies in the United States in this period, see Joost Jonker and Keetie Sluyterman, *At Home on the World Markets: Dutch International Trading Companies from the 16th Century until the Present* (The Hague: Sdu Uitgevers, 2000), 253, 258, 260 (on Ceteco, Internatio, and Hagemeyer). Nederlandsche Handel-Maatschappij NV was one of the predecessor banks to ABN-AMRO.

170. *Moody's Public Utilities 1937,* 788, says Sofina acquired 89,000 shares; ibid., 1938, 920, says it owned 39,500 shares, whereas ibid., 1940, 61, says had "an interest." See ibid., 1937, 613, on Middle West Corporation. In ibid., 1940, 706, under the subhead "control," the entry on Middle West Corporation reads: "Company disclaims affiliation with any party or parties. As of Mar. 11, 1940, holders of record of more than 10% of the common

stock included 557,546 shares (16.96%) registered in the name of Bankers Trust Co., New York, and 497,252 shares (15.13%) registered in the name of First National Bank, Chicago." Some of these bank holdings might have been on behalf of the Belgians or other foreign investors.

171. On the transfers, see German Military Commander in Belgium and Northern France to Karl Rasche, Dresdner Bank, Feb. 3, 1941, RG 238, T301, Reel 51, NI-6695. On Heineman and Sofina's relations to Crédit Suisse, see Armstrong and Nelles, *Southern Exposure,* 258–259, and *Fortune,* July 1931, 42. Also on Heineman, see Van der Wee and Verbreyt, *Generale Bank,* 167.

172. Van der Wee and Verbreyt, *Generale Bank,* 103, 112–114, 130, 153, 155–158, 192, 217, 326–327. L. W. Knoke, Telephone Conversation with Bank of England, May 13, 1940, and May 22, 1940, C261 Bank of England, FRBNY.

173. Gall et al., *Deutsche Bank,* 330–331.

174. New York State, Banking Department, *Annual Report 1941.* On this Belgian bank, formed in 1934, see Van der Wee and Verbreyt, *Generale Bank,* 355.

175. Alt, "Photochemical Industry," 111n.73.

176. Devos, "Agfa-Gevaert and Belgian Multinational Enterprise," 207–208. The plant operated during the war years.

177. The *1941 Census,* 25, looked at 110 Panamanian corporations that were found to have U.S. investments: 43 were owned in Switzerland, 20 in the United States, and 47 in twenty-three additional countries (only 9 of the 47 could not be traced beyond Panama).

178. *Fortune,* Feb. 1946, 170, 172, 175, and Heer, *World Events 1866–1966,* 166–167, 170, 178.

179. Heer, *World Events 1866–1966,* 164–165, 182.

180. Ibid., 215, 70–71. Wilkins, *History,* 336.

181. Peyer, *Roche,* 150, 152. The American operations were run by Maryland-born Elmer H. Bobst, who had been put in charge in 1920 and granted a share in the profits (at a time when the affiliate was unprofitable). Bobst had turned the business around and put it on a path to success. The incentive system had worked miracles. Ibid., 103–104, 108–109.

182. Sapac had been formed (for tax purposes) in 1927 as a Liechtenstein holding company. It was moved to Panama in 1938. Ibid., 112, 114, 143. See also Mahoney, *Merchants of Life,* 223.

183. For details, see data in Acc. 61A109, Box 681, and Report by Charles R. Clark for U.S. Treasury Foreign Funds Control, Dec. 26, 1942, in File D-63–1, Acc. 65A1063, Box 267, both boxes in RG 131 (Dept.-Justice). Actually, for other purposes, Ciba did use a Panamanian intermediary. At one point, Paciba, SA (Panama), which Ciba controlled, owned 49 percent of Chepha (the Swiss company that owned Schering Corp. of Bloomfield, New Jersey). Based on other data in File D-63–1, Acc. 65A1063, Box 267, RG 131 (Dept.-Justice) and Acc. 61A109, Box 681, RG 131 (Dept.-Justice).

184. In fact, the management of Sandoz and Geigy believed Ciba's trusts violated the three companies' 1918 Basle IG agreement. Sandoz and Geigy instituted proceedings against Ciba *in Switzerland* on January 10, 1941. On this, see wonderful data in Report by Clark, Dec. 26, 1942, in the prior note. Sandoz and Geigy did dispatch representatives from their Basle headquarters to the United States and took certain steps to Americanize their U.S. boards of directors so as to appear less foreign. Ibid.

185. Charles R. Clark, Report, Dec. 16, 1942, in File D-631–1, Acc. 65A1063, Box 167, RG 131 (Dept.-Justice).

186. E-mails from Patrick Stoffel to Mira Wilkins, Sept. 29 and Oct. 2, 2000.

187. The license to do business in New York was granted to the Swiss Bank Corp. on July 28, 1939 (New York State Banking Dept. Web site); the opening came October 16;

Bauer, *Swiss Bank Corporation 1872–1972,* 282; New York State, Banking Department, *Annual Reports 1939;* R. G. Rouse, "Swiss Bank Corporation," Nov. 15, 1939, FRBNY. Crédit Suisse applied for permission from the New York State Banking Department to open a New York agency, March 11, 1940, Swiss American Corporation file, FRBNY. See also Jöhr, *Schweizerische Kreditanstalt,* 421, 514, 564. Cassis, "Swiss International Banking," 166; and R. Tirana to McKeon, Mar. 4, 1940, Swiss American Corporation file, FRBNY.

188. Cassis, "Swiss International Banking," 169.

189. Its portfolio of securities (which included U.S. Treasury bonds, public utility and railroad bonds, some common shares of public utilities, railroads, and industrials, and New York Title and Mortgage Company guaranteed first mortgages) was transferred to the New York Federal Reserve from the New York agency of Crédit Suisse and from the Bank of the Manhattan Company, Guaranty Trust Co., J. P. Morgan & Co., and Irving Trust Co. Banque Nationale Suisse, Berne, to Federal Reserve Bank of New York, Sept. 18, 1940, in C261, Switzerland-Banque Nationale Suisse, FRBNY.

190. *New York Times,* June 15, 1941. R. Tirana of the New York Federal Reserve Bank believed Dutch interests were probably involved in the Swiss American Corporation. Tirana to McKeon, Mar. 4, 1940, Swiss American Corporation file, FRBNY. It was not only German and Dutch investors that used Swiss intermediaries; French investors often did so, as did those of many other nationalities. The *1941 Census* would, however, find that only 28 percent of the long-term Swiss assets in the United States were not from "citizens" (based on data on Table 8.3 herein); this percentage is highly suspect; it was probably much larger. Guex, "Origins of the Swiss Banking Secrecy Law," 240–252, shows how in the early 1930s the Swiss protected French investors. When, in 1943, Americans pushed the Swiss to identify the origins of all frozen assets in the United States, the Union Bank of Switzerland responded that for Swiss banks to do so "would ruin the entire private banking business." Ibid., 259. In short, the U.S. Census of 1941 had only Swiss reports and no way of verifying their accuracy.

191. *1941 Census,* 15, 87. This total does not equal $1.2 billion for I have excluded some other "miscellaneous" short-term assets.

192. See Cerutti, "Le blocage of avoirs suisses," 186–187 (Cerutti does not mention Ciba representatives, but I would be surprised if they were not there).

193. Wilkins, *History,* 95, 205–206, 484–485, 672n.23 (on Lombard, Odier); Faith, *Safety in Numbers,* 22–23, on Pictet and Lombard, Odier; members of the Lombard and Pictet families were involved in the American European Securities Company in the 1920s. British intelligence, monitoring international transactions, intercepted a letter dated May 27, 1941, from Pictet & Cie., Geneva, to the brokerage house Dominick & Dominick, New York, which authorized the sale of various American securities deposited with the Dominick firm in Pictet's name but which were actually the property of Pictet's French clients (resident in France). French assets in the U.S. at that time were frozen, while Swiss assets were not yet blocked (thus, the sale affecting French assets circumvented U.S. Foreign Funds Control rules). Pictet had and managed (from Geneva) "many" Panamanian holding companies, the most important of which was the Fiduciary Custodian Corp. The Panamanian companies were used to hold securities on behalf of the French clients. On the intercepted letter and the analysis, see Memorandum, Dec. 17, 1941, on Pictet & Cie., FO115/4141, Public Record Office. Different Swiss financial intermediaries chose to leave their French and other European clients in American securities. The brokerage house Dominick & Dominick, New York, apparently was used in French-Swiss-German transactions. Thus, on July 9, 1940 (after French assets were frozen but before Swiss assets were), Emil Schill, president of Krupp-Nirosta, now renamed Nirosta Corp., in response to a State Department inquiry on Nirosta's Swiss ownership (51 percent), noted that 49 percent of Nirosta shares were held in the United States. Schill stated, "A few shares

out of the 49 percent were originally in the name of a Frenchman, [Jean-Marcel ?] Aubert, but have in the meantime been transferred from Aubert to [Felix?] Iselin and later on from Iselin to Dominick & Dominick. Dominick & Dominick appear on the books of Nirosta as the owners of the stock originally held by Aubert." Emil Schill, Memorandum of Telephone Conversation . . . with L. C. Tubbs, United States Department of State, 3:30 P.M., July 9, 1940, published in *Kilgore Committee Hearings,* pt. 16, 2362.

194. These figures are based on weekly data published by the Board of Governors, Federal Reserve System, *Banking and Monetary Statistics* (1943), 620–623. As noted earlier, the Dutch had also been net purchasers of American securities (to the extent of $16.1 million).

195. Birgit Karlsson, "Fascism and Production of Ball-Bearings: SKF, Germany and the Soviet Union, 1942–1952," unpublished paper delivered in Odense, Denmark, Mar. 30, 2001; Martin, *All Honorable Men,* 253–254; Ulf Olsson, "Securing the Markets: Swedish Multinationals in a Historical Perspective," in Jones and Schröter, *Rise of Multinationals in Continental Europe,* 105–106; and Jean Pajus, "Report of A. B. Svenska Kullagerfabriken (SKF)," 94, 113, 156, RG 169, Foreign Economic Administration, Entry 211, Box 1, Folder: SKF Report, National Archives. It is useful to compare the voting trust set up by NV Philips, which was activated with the German invasion of Holland, with the arrangements made by SKF-Sweden (Sweden remained neutral during the war). In 1940 SKF-Sweden had made plans (which were not necessary to carry out) that would have come into effect only if Sweden had been invaded. Discussion with I. J. Blanken (Philips) and Birgit Karlsson, Odense, Denmark, Mar. 29–30, 2001. Ms. Karlsson found material on SKF's Panamanian holding company, Panrope Corp. SA, in SKF Board Minutes, May 22, 1940; see also Pajus, "Report," 113–115.

196. Aalders and Wiebes, *Art of Cloaking,* deals with the role of the Swedes, particularly the Stockholms Enskilda Bank, in cloaking German assets and acting on behalf of German clients. Aalders and Wiebes found, for example, that in the period June 1940 to May 1941 (before the U.S. freezing of Swedish assets), the Enskilda Bank was active in "assisting" Germans in repatriating their bonded debt "in neutral ownership." This meant buying foreign bonds in the United States. The Enskilda Bank (which had an account with Brown Brothers, Harriman in New York) in October 1940, for example, transferred Siemens & Halske debentures from New York to an Enskilda account with Banco Hispano Americano, Madrid. Ibid., 95–97. It also used Credito Italiano, which had an agency in New York. Ibid., 97. For Enskilda's transactions on behalf of the German Otto Wolff, October 1940–January 1941, see ibid., 99. The State Department would find evidence of Enskilda's activities in getting around the earlier "freeze" of Dutch assets in the United States, for the benefit of German interests. Ibid., 99.

197. *New York Times,* Nov. 4, 11, 22, and 25, 1939.

198. The FABC was a banking corporation, not a New York State–licensed agency. On it, see C440, French American Banking Corp., 1919–1950, FRBNY.

199. According to Hall, *North American Supply,* 278, $1.6 billion was the value given in the 1941 lend-lease hearings. Evidence on French investments is far smaller than on, say, Swiss or Swedish or German ones, for the French were less often suspected of sheltering enemy assets and thus not as subject to intense subsequent scrutiny. After the war (February 19, 1948), L'Office des Changes in the French Ministry of Finance compiled a list of American securities owned by Frenchmen at that time and held in France, Belgium, Canada, the United States, Switzerland, and elsewhere. The market price at "requisition" by the French government (mainly in 1946) was $91,771,082. As of February 10, 1948, the market price was $83,678,538. List is in file B63562, Archives Economiques et Financieres, Savigny-le-Temple, France. This incomplete list is valuable because it offers the names of the securities. It is *not,* however, indicative of what was held from 1939 to

1941. The tabulation is to be compared with another source on French holdings in the United States, the figures in Table 8.3, which indicate the value of American securities held in France, as of June 14, 1941 (note that not only the dates but also the definition of what was "French" are different; in addition, the 1948 list excluded French-owned U.S. government bonds).

200. Wilkins, "French Multinationals," 24, using *1941 Census,* 29, 64. The term "persons" includes corporate entities. Of the two-thirds, $32.5 million was in the industrial group labeled "public utility and transportation" (up from $1.5 million identified by the U.S. Department of Commerce in mid-1937); these investments remain a mystery. Historian Pierre Lanthier has been very helpful to me in trying to cast additional light on this matter, but he and other French economic historians have been unable to do so. One thought, not included in my *Entreprises et Histoire* article, is that the activities of the French grain traders in shipping and storing grain might be labeled as stakes in "transportation," although the U.S. Treasury did have a category for foreign direct investment in "trade." A "controlled enterprise" was defined as 25 percent or more foreign owned. French public utilities had interests in American securities, but I have not been able to identify any U.S. public utility in which they controlled 25 percent or more of the equity. Could Franco Wyoming (which was French controlled) be classified under "public utility and transportation"? It is possible. Another thought is that this might be linked with some remaining French connections of the d'Erlanger group's investments in U.S. railroads (if so, this would not be a French FDI, census tabulations notwithstanding).

201. See Table 8.1.

202. The census identified less than $50,000 "in bullion," which should cover the gold holdings. *1941 Census,* 82. Hall, *North American Supply,* 278, suggests that after the Germans moved into France the British government took over French war contracts in the United States "without benefit of the French gold and dollar resources on which the contracts had been based"; but see ibid, 149–155, on British-French transactions. The only explanation for the sharp drop is French payments for the supplies.

203. Morgan, *Merchants of Grain,* 132–133; Chalmin, *Négociants et chargeurs,* 199.

204. The Louis Dreyfus Co. in America became Leval & Co., and not until 1955 did the Dreyfus name resurfaced in American trade. Swiss-born Fernand Leval had long been the Louis-Dreyfus representative in New York. Morgan, *Merchants of Grain,* 113, 133. On the family's U.S. holdings, see Memorandum from F. A. Strass, Louis Dreyfus & Co., London, n.d., ca. Aug. 19, 1940, Assets in the US of America of Messrs. Louis Dreyfus & Co., FO 371/24263 Public Record Office. This memorandum has an excellent description of the Louis Dreyfus group. Strass claimed that the family of Louis Louis-Dreyfus, Paris, were all anti-Nazi and would want to fight for the Allied cause. Strass asked for the aid of the British Foreign Office to get the release of the firm's frozen U.S. assets to pay certain British liabilities. The Foreign Office decided not to support any application for release of blocked funds, writing the British ambassador in the United States: "We are informed that Mr. Maxim Levy, who was the administrative head of Louis Dreyfus, is being allowed out by the Germans to proceed to New York. We presume he will endeavor to get credits placed at the disposal of Germany." Foreign Office to Lord Lothian, Washington, Oct. 1, 1940, in ibid. All this seems a bit strange, given that the Louis Dreyfus family was a prominent Jewish family whose members would move to New York for the duration of the war.

205. U.S. Senate, Committee on Military Affairs, Subcommittee on War Mobilization, *Elimination of German Resources for War, Hearings,* 79th Cong., 1st and 2nd sess. (1945–46), pts. 1–10 (henceforth cited as *Kilgore Committee Hearings II*), pt. 3, 484.

206. Ferguson, *House of Rothschild,* 474. See also Joseph Wechsberg, *The Merchant Bankers* (Boston: Little, Brown, 1966), 361, and Reich, *Financier,* 37.

207. Reich, *Financier,* 34–37, 39, 41.

208. Based on data provided by Geoffrey Bowker from Schlumberger Archives, Paris, and Allaud and Martin, *Schlumberger,* viii. Members of the Schlumberger family came to the United States to take command. *Kilgore Committee Hearings II,* pt. 3, 336.

209. *Kilgore Committee Hearings II,* pt. 3, 336. On Charles Tiberghien in Woonsocket during the war, see Thomas, *Woonsocket: Highlights as History,* 112. Members of the Lepoutres family also came to manage the family woolen mills in Woonsocket during the war; ibid., 112, 117. In each of these cases the business in France continued during the war years.

210. *Kilgore Committee Hearings II,* pt. 3, 336, on both the Schlumberger and Tiberghien families.

211. 246 of these were subsidiaries, 114 were branches. *1941 Census,* 29. After the war began, there were the takeovers of all Japanese enterprises in the United States (as properties of an enemy). Thus, there was close attention to the numbers (the census, albeit dated as of June 14, 1941, was not published until 1945 and clearly took into account the subsequent sequestrations by the Office of Alien Property Custodian, thus improving the census coverage).

212. The key exceptions were the Japanese cotton traders in Texas and the important retailer Yamanaka and Co., which had "corporations" in Massachusetts, Illinois, and New York and "branches" in Florida and Rhode Island (its principal store was in New York City); the numbers also appear to include Japanese investments in the "Territory of Hawaii" (Hawaii did not become a state until 1959).

213. On Japanese investments in the United States at this time, see Mira Wilkins, "American-Japanese Direct Foreign Investment Relationships, 1930–1952," *Business History Review,* 56 (Winter 1982): 504–510, and Wilkins, "Japanese Multinationals," 588–599, as well as data from the Office of Alien Property Custodian, *Annual Reports 1942–1946* and from RG 131. The inventories of RG 131 provide substantial details on Japanese business in the United States.

214. Office of Alien Property Custodian, *Annual Report 1943–1944,* 58.

215. Bata, *Bata,* 144–153, 256 (Bata in the United States), and 39, 48–76 (the Canadian story). The book says nothing about a requirement for a license for Bata after June 1941. Bata's U.S. business was owned through a Swiss holding company; ibid., 125, 156. The Czech business continued all during the war. The widow of the founder, who had left for Canada with her son just before the outbreak of war in Europe, returned to maintain the wartime operations of Bata's Zlin (Czechoslovakia) factory. Cekota, *Entrepreneur Extraordinary,* 98–99. The brother of the founder claimed that he would (did) not speak out against the Germans because he wanted to safeguard the properties (and the lives of employees) in Zlin. Bata, *Bata,* 149.

216. For the list of countries with blocked assets, see Table 8.4. No Western Hemisphere assets were blocked (thus, for example, Cuban, Panamanian, and Argentine assets in the United States were not blocked). There was attention to Panamanian assets, in particular, since holding companies there were used by investors from countries with blocked assets. The Treasury Department in its blocking regulations often ignored the corporate intermediaries and blocked those assumed to be of a particular nationality.

217. In my research for this book, I sought archival data at the New York Federal Reserve on these transactions. I found nothing. However, in 1992, I did find substantial data on Foreign Funds Control in RG 131 (Dept.-Justice). The latter records, at the time I used them, were under the custody of the Justice Department (I obtained access under the Freedom of Information Act); the records reflected the combined Treasury Department, Office of Alien Property Custodian, and Justice Department's handling of foreign "enemy" or "possible enemy" assets, from 1940 onward. The records went to the Justice

Department because of its post–World War II role as the custodial successor of the Office of Alien Property Custodian.

218. It is not clear whether they just did so or did so with any kind of formal (or informal) U.S. government permission.

219. Taylor and Baskerville, *Concise History,* 397; Hall, *North American Supply,* 228–235.

220. As noted earlier, for the entire period September 1939 to December 1941, Canadians' net sales of American domestic securities were more than offset by their net purchases of American "foreign securities."

221. Taylor and Baskerville, *Concise History.* 398–399. The Hyde Park Agreement (or Declaration) is discussed in every book on Canadian-American relations in this period. It represented an important commitment to U.S.-Canadian economic cooperation. See, for example, R. D. Cuff and J. L. Granatstein, *Ties That Bind,* 2nd ed. (Toronto: Samuel Stevens, 1977), chap. 4. On the *British* views, see ibid., 79. A copy of the agreement is included in ibid., 165–166. See also Hall, *North American Supply,* 235–239.

222. Cypher telegram from the Foreign Office (drafted by E. Rowe-Dutton, Treasury) to Lord Lothian, Mar. 15, 1940, in Financial Arrangements with the US—Australian Secret, FO 371/24254, Public Record Office. It seems that as in the case of other dollar-denominated bonds ("foreign securities") issued in the United States, some ownership was held outside the country. The British government put Australian insurance companies in a separate category (as it did with their U.K. counterparts).

223. *The Times* (London), Aug. 28, 1939; Sayers, *Bank of England,* II, 589–590. Another estimate (as of October 1939) was that the British held $600 million in securities.

224. Blum, *From the Morgenthau Diaries,* II, 93; Burton and Corner, *Investment and Unit Trusts,* 71.

225. Blum, *From the Morgenthau Diaries,* II, 103.

226. Ibid., 103–104. This, of course, was appreciated by Americans, for there were fears that British sales would upset the stock market.

227. Chernow, *House of Morgan,* 442. Another company, the Scottish American Investment Trust Co. (not to be confused with the Scottish Investment Trust Co.) reduced its U.S. investments from 53 percent of its total investments in 1939 to 27.5 percent in 1940, paying over to the British government $7 million. Burton and Corner, *Investment and Unit Trusts,* 72. The Scottish American Investment Trust Co. continued to cut back its U.S. investments, so that in 1941 they represented a mere 9 percent of its portfolio. Weir, *History of the Scottish American Investment Company,* 25.

228. Jackson, *Enterprising Scot,* 292; Scottish American Mortgage Co., *Annual Report 1941,* Film Z-G2, Reel 55, Bancroft Library, University of California, Berkeley.

229. The result was curious, for by the end of May 1940, Scottish American Mortgage Co. once more (as in most of the 1930s) had more moneys invested in U.S. mortgages and real estate than in American securities; the reduction in American securities owned occurred faster than the reduction in mortgages and real estate holdings, but both were reduced. Similarly, the Texas Land and Mortgage Co., Ltd., which had been cutting back on its loans on mortgages all during the 1930s, continued to do so. See *Annual Reports,* Film Z-G-1, Reel 285, Bancroft Library.

230. T. J. Carlyle Gifford, *Letters from America 1939–1941* (Edinburgh: privately printed, 1969), foreword; Blum, *From the Morgenthau Diaries,* II, 105. The Neutrality Act of 1939 passed the Senate on October 27 and the House on November 2; it was signed by the president and became law November 4, 1939. See also Sayers, *Bank of England,* II, 590.

231. On Whigham and the Fleming group of companies: Sayers, *Bank of England,* II, 432, 590; Burton and Corner, *Investment and Unit Trusts,* 71; Wake, *Kleinwort Benson,* 301;

and *New York Times,* Aug. 16, 1948 (Whigham obituary); U.S. Securities and Exchange Commission, *Investment Trusts in Great Britain* H. Doc. 380, 76th Cong., 1st sess., 1939, 18.

232. Gifford, *Letters from America,* 1–6; Blum, *From the Morgenthau Diaries,* II, 105–106; George Harrison, Memo, Nov. 24, 1939, Harrison Papers 3110.0, FRBNY; Minutes of Meeting of the Board of Governors, Federal Reserve System, Dec. 1, 1939, C261 England–United Kingdom, FRBNY; and L. W. Knoke, Memo, Dec. 4, 1939, C261 England–Bank of England, FRBNY.

233. Blum, *From the Morgenthau Diaries,* II, 105–106. The gold holdings were disposed of early, since they brought in no income. U.S. Department of Commerce, Office of Business Economics, *International Transactions of the United States during the War, 1940–1945,* 101.

234. Gifford, *Letters from America.* Gifford worked closely with the better-known representatives of the British government, Arthur Purvis, Sir Edward Peacock, and Sir Frederick Phillips.

235. Roosevelt "was particularly opposed to any revival of the British connection with Morgan or any other American bank." Langer and Gleason, *Challenge to Isolation,* 289. What emerges very vividly in Gifford, *Letters from America,* is his close friendship with the Morgan partners but, at the same time, the insistence from Washington that the British deal directly with the U.S. *government.* Gifford was told by the British ambassador that "I must have a separate office not at the Morgans." The U.S. Secretary of the Treasury Henry Morgenthau stressed to Gifford the "point of being independent and not using M[organs] solely." Ibid., in particular, 20, 21, 68. In September 1939, Thomas W. Lamont, the principal partner in J. P. Morgan & Co., had proposed that the Morgan bank act as a depository and disbursing agent for the British government's U.S. purchasing program and also that the bank was ready to handle all the sales of American securities on behalf of the British. On October 31, 1939, the British ambassador to the United States, Lord Lothian, had written to Lamont that the British would use the New York Federal Reserve Bank as their depository, but J. P. Morgan & Co. would be involved in handling the sales in New York of British-owned American securities to pay for the purchases. Subsequently, the French government also looked to J. P. Morgan & Co. as well. Lamont, *Ambassador from Wall Street,* 443, 468, on the Morgan role. An item in Blum, *From the Morgenthau Diaries,* II, 104, reads: "Though the British believed they could best protect their interests by working through the House of Morgan, they hesitated to do so because of Roosevelt's opinion [that discussions about 'English securities take place in Washington'] and because of the danger of public criticism."

236. Blum, *From the Morgenthau Diaries,* II, 107–109; Hall, *North American Supply,* 102. On these vesting orders, see McCurrach, "Britain's U.S. Dollar Problems," 358, 360, and Gifford, *Letters from America,* 17ff. As an example of how this worked, the Kleinwort family in England had a large portfolio of American securities (in excess of £500,000) held by the Moonhill Trust. In 1940, the holdings were "sequestered" by the British Treasury. Wake, *Kleinwort Benson,* 242, 322.

237. U.S. Department of Commerce, Office of Business Economics, *International Transactions of the United States During the War, 1940–1945,* 101.

238. Jackson, *Enterprising Scot,* 292. When in 1940 the British Treasury "sequestered" Kleinworts' substantial dollar assets, the British merchant bank had asked if £500,000 could be retained in order to form a New York branch. The Kleinwort partners discussed taking a direct interest in Goldman Sachs. Nothing came of these 1940 plans, albeit after the war the Bank of England was prepared to allow Kleinworts the use of the dollar assets that suggests they were not "vested" but rather "pledged," that is, borrowed by the British government. It is, of course, possible (or even likely) that the British Treasury

sold the dollar-denominated securities in 1940 (or later) and when the British were ready to release dollars to Kleinworts in 1945, the dollars came from a different source. Wake, *Kleinwort Benson,* 322–323, is not clear on this.

239. Cable, Bank of England to the Federal Reserve Bank of New York, May 31, 1940, C261 England–Bank of England, FRBNY.

240. Hall, *North American Supply,* 78. Whether the Dutch moneys were in fact used is not known. See also Arthur Purvis, New York, to Jean Monnet, May 11, 1940, and Foreign Office to British Consulate General, New York, May 12, 1940, FO115/3787, Public Record Office.

241. Jackson, *Enterprising Scot,* 253–254, 274–276, 284, 293. The far larger Mississippi properties of the Delta and Pine Land Co. and its affiliated Delta Planting Co. (controlled by Fine Cotton Spinners' and Doublers' Association) were *not* sold.

242. Jackson, *Enterprising Scot,* 293.

243. Gifford, *Letters from America,* 35, 37, and Chernow, *House of Morgan,* 442.

244. *New York Times,* Nov. 22, 1939.

245. For the complicated story, see Hall, *North American Supply,* 146–155, and 278. It is not at all clear how much in the way of dollar resources was actually obtained.

246. Skidelsky, *John Maynard Keynes,* III, 94 (quoting Winston Churchill).

247. Swaine, *Cravath Firm,* II, 673.

248. Figure 8.1, which compares British sales with all foreign divestments of domestic securities, shows the influence of British sales. The purchases during the first week of September 1939 were Swiss and Dutch; Italian purchases in the week ending June 5, 1940, pushed that peak. The July–August 1940 sales were not confined to any particular nationality. These findings are based on data from Board of Governors, Federal Reserve System, *Banking and Monetary Statistics* (1943). Negative figures in the caption indicate sales rather than purchases. Cumulative British purchases of domestic securities had come to only $433.5 million during the period January 2, 1935 to August 30, 1939 (see Figure 7.2); the reader should not worry about the sales being larger than the purchases, for there were earlier purchases (prior to 1935), but, more important, there was the appreciation in value of existing securities.

249. Sayers, *Bank of England,* II, 635; Gifford, *Letters from America,* 70ff.

250. Orbell, *Baring Brothers,* 82–83. Peacock had been a director of the Bank of England from 1921 to 1924, but he had to step down on joining Barings, since no single firm was allowed more than one Bank of England director. Sayers, *Bank of England,* II, 596n. In the 1931 defense of the pound, before Britain abandoned the gold standard, Peacock had been very much involved. Kunz, *Battle for Britain's Gold Standard,* passim, esp. 94–95 (in the summer of 1931, Morgan partner Edward Grenfell called Peacock the "most important man in the City").

251. Reported in *New York Times,* Jan. 30, 1941. The British Treasury had made an estimate of $600 million in October 1940. Hall, *North American Supply,* 273. The problem was, there was no independent market for these investments.

252. Gifford, *Letters from America,* 84. The use of the word "my" was in the context of all British stock exchange investments in the United States ("my" in the sense of "my familiar" securities).

253. Unlike the 1930s British collectors of statistics on outward foreign investment, the U.S. Department of Commerce had been assembling information on inward FDI, including British direct investment.

254. Arthur D. Purvis (1890–1941) was the one British government representative who knew a great deal about British multinational enterprise. He was a Scot who had been employed by British Nobel Industries in South America, South Africa, and the United States; he had run Nobel Industries' joint venture with Du Pont in Canada, Canadian

Explosives, Ltd. (CXL), which became in 1927 Canadian Industries Ltd. (CIL) after the British Nobel firm was folded into Imperial Chemical Industries. When CIL came into existence in 1927, Purvis had already been president of CXL for two years. He had been an aggressive manager of that subsidiary, and at the time of his appointment in 1939 as head of the British government purchasing group in New York, he was considered *Canada's* leading industrialist. He died in a plane crash on August 14, 1941. On Purvis, see Reader, *Imperial Chemical Industries,* II, 212–214, and Hall, *North American Supply,* 72–74.

255. Blum, *From the Morgenthau Diaries,* II, 170; *New York Times,* Feb. 13, 1941, and Mar. 23, 1941 ($900 million). I put quotation marks around "British-owned," for at the time the ownership of Lever Brothers was Dutch, and Shell was British-Dutch. According to *Moody's 1940,* 2050, as of December 31, 1939, almost 65 percent (64.35) of Shell Union shares were owned by a Dutch firm, which was, in turn, owned 60 percent by Royal Dutch and 40 percent by the British Shell. The rest of the shares outstanding in Shell Union were traded on several stock exchanges and held by Americans, Britishers, and other nationalities.

256. Freidel, *America in the Twentieth Century,* 381.

257. David Reynolds, *The Creation of the Anglo-American Alliance 1937–1941* (Chapel Hill: University of North Carolina Press, 1981), 159, 162. By political clout, I mean that the key officials in the British insurance industry were often advisers to the British Treasury or the Bank of England.

258. Hall, *North American Supply,* 273; McCurrach, "Britain's U.S. Dollar Problems," 357; for a similar view, a bit earlier, see also G. L. F. Bolton to S. Tink, Feb. 17, 1941, quoted in Roberts, *Schroders,* 294. Skidelsky, *John Maynard Keynes,* III, 97.

259. Reynolds, *Creation of the Anglo-American Alliance,* 164.

260. *New York Times,* Feb. 13, 1941.

261. Trebilcock, *Phoenix Assurance,* II, 835. There did not seem to be anything comparable among industrial enterprises.

262. Roberts, *Schroders,* 294, found in the Bank of England files a review of British companies in the United States for possible sale.

263. Blum, *From the Morgenthau Diaries,* II, 236.

264. Warren F. Kimball, *The Most Unsordid Act: Lend-Lease, 1939–1941* (Baltimore: Johns Hopkins University Press, 1969), 254, 185.

265. Sir Edward Peacock letter to Gifford of February 15, 1941, quoted in Coleman, *Courtaulds,* II, 466–467. See also Blum, *From the Morgenthau Diaries,* II, 236.

266. Coleman, *Courtaulds,* II, 467–468; Blum, *From the Morgenthau Diaries,* II, 237; Gifford, *Letters from America,* 91.

267. Reynolds, *Creation of the Anglo-American Alliance,* 162.

268. *New York Times,* Mar. 16, 1941.

269. Coleman, *Courtaulds,* II, 469; Chernow, *House of Morgan,* 462. For the best insider details, see Gifford, *Letters from America,* 91–94 (letter of March 16, 1941) on how the plans were made and consummated in several days. The arrangements were made with the Morgan partners. Dillon, Read & Co. was brought in for "political reasons," that is, to keep up the appearance that everything did not go through the Morgans.

270. Gifford, *Letters from America,* 93.

271. *New York Times,* Mar. 17, 1941.

272. Coleman, *Courtaulds,* II, chap. 15.

273. Reader, *Imperial Chemical Industries,* II, 375.

274. Hall, *North American Supply,* 273.

275. Gifford, *Letters from America,* 92. Gifford was intimately involved in the sale of AVC. He even cabled London "to warn them against any indiscreet statement by Sam Courtaulds." Ibid., 93–95. By contrast, there seems to have been special care taken by

the British government to keep the insurance companies' interests intact. See Trebilcock, *Phoenix Assurance,* II, 835.

276. Skidelsky, *John Maynard Keynes,* III, 113–114; Coleman, *Courtaulds,* II, 473–489.

277. This is my interpretation. At the end, even Purvis, who knew a great deal about multinationals, was convinced that the British had to comply with American demands. Hall, *North American Supply,* 274.

278. *New York Times,* Mar. 18, 1941. The statement about British insurance companies' representing about one-half of British direct investment in the United States is doubtful, although insurance companies were important. (According to the *1941 Census,* 65, taken as of June 14, 1941, "finance," which included insurance, banking, and other financial institutions, represented $247.5 million of the total interests of $711.5 million in U.K.-controlled enterprises in the United States.) See also *New York Times,* Mar. 23, 1941. Yet the worry over British insurance companies had been Phillips' concern in December 1940. The editorial in the *New York Times* seems to echo what had become the British mantra. See, for example, McCurrach, "Britain's U.S. Dollar Problems," 357, and Skidelsky, *John Maynard Keynes,* III, 97, 104.

279. Reynolds, *Creation of the Anglo-American Alliance,* 165, who relied on British Treasury documents, is convinced that "the British Treasury did all it could to avoid selling off Britain's securities and direct investments in the U.S.A."

280. Freidel, *America in the Twentieth Century,* 382.

281. The top three in the U.S. cigarette industry (R. J. Reynolds, American Tobacco, and Liggett & Myers) were all American owned.

282. At its annual meeting in January 1941, Sir Hugo Cunliffe-Owen told the stockholders that BAT had paid taxes amounting to £2 million in advance of the due date to help the British government provide funds for war purposes. *New York Times,* Jan. 21, 1941.

283. Gifford, *Letters from America,* 98.

284. Blum, *From the Morgenthau Diaries,* II, 239; Coleman, *Courtaulds,* II, 476.

285. The *New York Times,* Jan. 9, 1942, noted that of the $40 million RFC loan, $25 million "was taken over by the British Government to pay for war supplies and the balance was used for debt retirement."

286. The management of American Viscose belatedly, ineffectively, and in vain tried to reverse its company's sale to the bankers and follow this pattern; it was too late. Blum, *From the Morgenthau Diaries,* II, 239; Coleman, *Courtaulds,* II, 476–478; Hall, *North American Supply,* 275n.1; Gifford, *Letters from America,* 107. Reynolds, *Creation of the Anglo-American Alliance,* 166, notes that Peacock had much earlier suggested this approach. Skidelsky, *John Maynard Keynes,* III, 104, suggests that the RFC involvement was Arthur Purvis' idea and that Keynes had endorsed it as early as March 19.

287. Blum, *From the Morgenthau Diaries,* II, 239, 244–245; Skidelsky, *John Maynard Keynes,* III, 106–114 (on his trip).

288. The April 17 RFC loan was to BAT's U.S. subsidiary. BAT had *then* arranged for the resulting dollars to go to the British Treasury. See *Financial Times,* July 26, 1941. Only with the June 1941 congressional authorization to the RFC was the more general solution possible. Earlier, U.S. neutrality legislation would have forbade such a loan.

289. *New York Times,* June 26, 1941; *1941 Census,* 16 ($700 million). The value of the collateral was variously estimated. For some of the background, see Gifford, *Letters from America,* 109–143. In New York, Gifford met with key British insurers on June 5 to clear up details, and on June 16 he talked with Sir James Henderson of J. & P. Coats on that firm's subsidiaries. Sir James was "waxing hot and contemptuous about American ways of doing business." Ibid., 110, 115.

290. Agreement between the United Kingdom of Great Britain and Northern Ireland and Reconstruction Finance Corporation, July 21, 1941, London 1941, Cmd. 6295, "Loans:

RFC," FO 115/3431, Public Record Office (henceforth cited as *RFC Agreement*). *New York Times,* Dec. 3, 1941, on disbursements.

291. *RFC Agreement.* Schedules B and C detail the collateral: B-1 has the subsidiaries of the insurance companies; B-2 (a) has U.S. affiliates where ownership was "controlling"; B-2 (b) has U.S. companies where ownership was "substantial"; B-3 has securities of U.S. companies held in the United Kingdom; and C lists branches of insurance companies.

292. Trebilcock, *Phoenix Assurance,* II, 836.

293. Unlike those securities in the direct investments, given in Table 8.7, the securities listed on Schedule B-3 (and in Table 8.10) were traded, and at any point in time a market price could be determined.

294. The division between parts 1 and 2 in Table 8.10 (vested and pledged securities) was confirmed in the later U.S. Senate, Committee on Banking and Currency, *Anglo-American Financial Agreement, Hearings,* 79th Cong., 2nd sess. (1946), 72–73.

295. *New York Times,* July 22, 1941.

296. Meneight, *History of United Molasses Co.,* 80.

297. *New York Times,* July 26, 1941. In point of fact, not all the income was remitted; some British affiliates in the United States were allowed to reinvest their earnings.

298. Measures of the size of insurance companies' investments are always difficult, and the size of the assets does not indicate the investment value. The $805 million "assets" is based on figures in the *Financial Times,* July 24, 1941, for fifty-three branches and subsidiaries (see Table 8.9 herein for the branches and subsidiaries given). As noted, this list includes only fifty-three branches and subsidiaries, compared with the eighty-two listed on the schedules and in Table 8.8. However, according to the *1941 Census,* 65, taken as of June 14, 1941, "finance"—which comprised insurance, banking, and other financial institutions—represented a British direct investment of merely $247.5 million. The authors of the *1941 Census* report (on p. 16) estimated that the total collateral put up at the time of the loan was $700 million.

299. *1941 Census,* 29 (623). The 46 on Table 8.6 plus the 82 on Table 8.7 comes to 128 total.

300. Imperial Tobacco's U.S. assets were in its purchasing organization and probably were not very substantial.

301. The British Ministry of Economic Warfare had special dealings with Borax Consolidated on U.S. borax, which might explain the omission. See Medlicott, *Economic Blockade,* I, 685.

302. See Roberts, *Schroders,* 293–294, on purposeful exclusion.

303. Macmillan & Co., Ltd., London, had used the stock of its U.S. affiliate as collateral to borrow from Westminster Bank, London. Daniel Macmillan, chairman, Macmillan & Co. Ltd. to Foreign Office, May 29, 1940, FO 371/24258, Public Record Office.

304. Celanese Corporation of America (CCA) was a firm whose securities were traded, but where there is considerable evidence of continuing British direct investment. John Cantwell and Pilar Barrara include CCA as "an affiliate of British Celanese" (see their "Localisation of Corporate Technological Trajectories," 267). CCA was not on the list of direct investments (see Table 8.7); it is, however, on the list of nonvested securities (Table 8.10, part 2). Alfred Chester Beatty's sizable Selection Trust investments in American Metal Co. are not included as direct investments. Initially, I wondered whether there had been some "special arrangement" made, perhaps a favor returned. In December 1939, the U.S. Treasury Department had learned that the Russians were buying large quantities of American molybdenum (utilized to manufacture high-speed tools and steel armor plate) and were probably reexporting it to Germany. Treasury Secretary Henry Morgenthau had turned to his old friend Harold Hochschild, president of American Metal Co. and secretary of the affiliated Climax Molybdenum Co.—the largest U.S.

molybdenum producer. Hochschild shared with Morgenthau a telegram from "one of his big English stockholders" (undoubtedly Beatty), who said he would be "'willing to forgo his dividends' if his company would stop selling molybdenum to Russia." Hochschild mobilized other U.S. sellers to cancel their Russian contracts. All molybdenum shipments to Germany and Japan were also ended. Morgenthau received congratulations from Roosevelt. Blum, *From the Morgenthau Diaries,* II, 126–127. Although American Metal is not on Table 8.10, Climax Molybdenum is—and it is conceivable that Selection Trust at this time had all or a large part of its holdings in Climax Molybdenum rather than American Metal. The listing is on part 2 of Table 8.10 (the holdings in Climax Molybdenum were not vested).

305. McCurrach, "Britain's U.S. Dollar Problems," 357, 369. The British-owned Burroughs, Wellcome, for example, was not on the collateral list. Perhaps it would have fit into this category. McCurrach, writing in 1948, thought Americans *and* British had overestimated the value of British direct investments, for he believed that the value of such investments had to be judged by what they would bring were they converted to dollars (i.e., "sold") at any particular point in time. Among the many British-owned companies in the United States that were not included on the collateral lists were Bradford Dyeing Association (USA), with a plant in Rhode Island; Cambridge Instrument Co. Inc., with a small factory at Ossining-on-Hudson, New York; J. & J. Cash, manufacturers of woven name tapes in South Norwalk, Connecticut; Crosse & Blackwell Ltd., with a factory in Baltimore, Maryland; R & J. Dick, with plants in New Jersey and Iowa making industrial belting; Hope's Windows, Inc., maker of metal windows in Jamestown, New York; International Paint Co., with plants in Brooklyn, New York, Union, New Jersey, and San Francisco; and J. Bishop & Co., a subsidiary of Johnson Mattheys Co. Ltd., with a platinum works in Malvern, Pennsylvania, used in stainless steel needles. See data in the files of John Dunning, University of Reading; Dunning, in his 1959–1960 research, found that all these British-owned companies manufactured in the United States in 1941.

306. The Great Northern Railway securities were vested (i.e., were sold to the British government); 70,000 Great Northern Iron Ore Properties certificates of beneficial interest were also on the list, as "pledged." These were a railroad-related investment. Before the First World War, the Great Northern (James Hill's railroad) had attracted sizable British investments. Wilkins, *History,* 213–215. Great Northern Iron Ore certificates were lent by Gaspard Farrer of Barings to the American Dollar Securities Committee during World War I (in 1916)–see Chapter 1.

307. Swaine, *Cravath Firm,* II, 673.

308. The *1941 Census,* 13, noted that historically foreigners had held railroad *bonds;* as of June 1941, such investments were "relatively unimportant." The U.S. Temporary National Economic Committee, *The Distribution of Ownership in the 200 Largest Nonfinancial Corporations,* Monograph No. 29 (Washington, D.C., 1940), 137, found that 17 U.S. companies in the top 200 in 1937 paid more than 10 percent of their dividends to foreigners (nationality unspecified). That list contained three railroads, the Kansas City Southern (40.3 percent), the Great Northern Railway (12.3 percent), and the Union Pacific (10.2 percent). The Kansas City Southern and the Union Pacific had sizable Dutch investments, which might account for the large holdings and the omission of the British stakes in 1941. Robert Benson & Co. had been involved in the Illinois Central in its earlier days and in this connection had in 1898 acquired stock in The Clearing Industrial District Inc. (CID were owners of stockyards alongside the Illinois Central). The CID securities were in the Benson family portfolio as late as 1971. Wake, *Kleinwort Benson,* 189. It is not clear what happened to them during 1939–1941, but then, they were not "railroad securities," and there is no indication that the Bensons retained into the post–World War II years

any Illinois Central shares or, for that matter, any other American railroad securities. The absence of CID stock on any of the lists confirms my point that the collateral lists did not represent all British assets in America. The 10,000 shares of General American Transportation Corp., a business involved in railroad *cars,* also would have had their genesis in earlier railroad investment. See *Moody's Manual 1941,* 2831 (on General American Transportation Corp.).

309. It seems clear that (and I am assuming that) there was some small amount remaining.

310. Based on data on Table 8.1 herein.

311. Why did the shift occur? Was taxation a consideration? It is not clear. Stocks could appreciate. Bonds, once thought of as a more stable investment, had proved subject to default; they were no longer "gold" backed; interest rates were low. Stocks offered more possibility of gain. Table 8.6 on Scottish American Mortgage Co.'s securities portfolio reflects the trend.

312. Commercial Investment Trust Corp. was founded in 1908 as Commercial Credit and Investment Co.; the name was changed to Commercial Investment Trust Corp. in 1915 (it went public in 1924); later, as the renamed C.I.T. Financial Corp., it became a giant in commercial finance and leasing. The U.S. and International Securities Corp. was formed under the sponsorship of Dillon, Read & Co. in August 1928 (a subsidiary of their first investment trust), while the Tri-Continental Corp. had been established by J. & W. Seligman & Co. in January 1929. Foreign investments in these three were associated with the wave of investments in the late 1920s in American financial intermediaries. Dividends Shares was created later; it came into being in 1932, as part of the Bullock group of companies (but many of the latter had been organized in the late 1920s and had attracted substantial British investments). *Moody's Manuals;* U.S. Securities and Exchange Commission, *Investment Trusts and Investment Companies,* H. Doc. 279, 76th Cong., 1st sess. (1940), pt. 1 of pt. 3, 8, and H. Doc. 707, 75th Cong., 3rd sess. (1939), pt. 1, 108; Bullock, *Story of Investment Companies,* 36, 39, 72, 156–159, 240, 251–252, 268; and Web site of The CIT Group (http://www.citgroup.com), useful on the history of Commercial Investment Trust Corp. Note that the British investments in Commercial Investment Trust Corp. and Tri-Continental Corp. were vested, whereas those in U.S. and International Securities Corp. and Dividend Shares were pledged. I am not sure of the significance of this, but it may relate to the relationships between Dillon, Read and between the Bullocks and their British clients.

313. On Allis-Chalmer, see Wilkins, *History,* 430. W. R. Grace was founded in Peru by an Irishman; it always had strong British connections. See Marquis James, *The Story of W. R. Grace: Merchant Adventurer* (Wilmington, Del.: SR Books, 1993). On Amerada, Radio Corporation of America, Standard Oil (Ind.), and John Morrell, see the index of the present volume.

314. It is likely that these represented ongoing British direct investments. See the index of the present volume on Celanese of America and Congoleum-Nairn. I derived the percentages from *Moody's Manual 1940,* 3095, 2971. On Celanese of America, the 50,000 shares were 30.3 percent of the prior preferred, while the 40,000 shares were 27 percent of the 7 percent cum shares outstanding.

315. The 900,000 vested common shares in Shell Union Oil Corp. represented only 6.9 percent of the common shares outstanding of this firm that was part of the Royal Dutch Shell Group. They were part of the roughly 36 percent of the shares of Shell Union not owned by the group; share holdings could have been spread among a number of British owners. So, too, there were probably multiple British owners of the General Motors stock as well, but did the large block of these shares (the 434,000 shares) include the holdings of Imperial Chemical Industries? Reader, *Imperial Chemical Industries,* II, 239, indicates

that as of July 1936, ICI still held 390,100 shares of GM stock; Reader says nothing about what happened to those securities from 1936 to 1952, when his book ends. My guess is that ICI and other holders of GM stock sold these securities to the British government, as part of the vesting program. The Temporary National Economic Committee found that International Paper & Power Company and Singer Manufacturing Company had substantial "foreign" (not necessarily British) ownership in 1937. U.S. Temporary National Economic Committee, *Distribution of Ownership,* 137 and 270. Both are on Table 8.10, part 2. In 1929, Britishers had found U.S. Steel, American Telephone & Telegraph, and Pennsylvania Railroad popular stocks (see Chapter 4). The first two are in Table 8.10, part 1; the last is missing along with the general absence of railroads.

316. See Table 8.3, but consider the big British stakes in U.S. "trusts and estates." On the latter, see material earlier in this chapter and Appendix 3, Notes to Table 8.3 (note d).

317. The collateral for the RFC loan was supposed to be "secret." A British White Paper issued on July 22, 1941, gave details of the agreement but did not list the collateral. Federal Loan Administrator Jesse Jones disclosed the information, much to Gifford's displeasure. Gifford wrote at the time (July 22, 1941) in a letter home that this "might cause some trouble in London." Gifford, *Letters from America,* 137. I am not exactly sure why, although it might relate to the exclusions from the list and the differences between vested and pledged securities. It certainly revealed that, protests notwithstanding, the British still had American assets.

318. Hall, *North American Supply,* 287–292.

319. *1941 Census,* 3; this estimate was made when the census was published in 1945; this excludes British sales of gold, which amounted to $2.5 billion. Ibid. Compare this estimate to the one in Hall, *North American Supply,* 278 (published in 1955): he estimated that $820 million of American securities and investments were sold by the British prior to the lend-lease agreement.

320. *1941 Census,* 7.

321. The 1853 survey—U.S. Senate, *Report of the Secretary of the Treasury in Answer to a Resolution of the Senate Calling for the Amount of American Securities Held in Europe and Other Foreign Countries, on the 30th June 1853,* Executive Doc. 42, 33rd Cong., 1st sess. (1854)—is reprinted in full in Mira Wilkins, ed., *Foreign Investments in the United States: Department of Commerce and Department of Treasury Estimates* (New York: Arno Press, 1977), and is discussed in Wilkins, *History.*

9. World War II, 1941–1945

1. Blum, *From the Morgenthau Diaries,* II, 342–343. Data from the records of Foreign Funds Control, RG 131, U.S. Department of Justice, Washington, D.C.; this record collection is henceforth cited as RG 131 (Dept.-Justice). "Foreign Funds Control Report," Dec. 18, 1941, Morgenthau Diaries, vol. 474, pp. 105–119, Franklin D. Roosevelt Library, Hyde Park, New York; henceforth cited as Foreign Funds Control Report (Dec. 18, 1941).

2. New York State, Banking Department, *Annual Report 1941,* 74. The Japanese bank agencies taken over in New York were those of the Bank of Chosen, Chosen; the Bank of Taiwan, Taiwan; the Mitsubishi Bank, Tokyo; the Mitsui Bank, Tokyo; the Sumitomo Bank, Osaka; and the Yokohama Specie Bank, Yokohama. The last was the largest of the group.

3. U.S. Department of the Treasury, *Documents Pertaining to Foreign Funds Control* (Washington, D.C., 1945), 91; the order was very broad: it said, "No Japanese national now has the status of a generally licensed national." For later modifications of this blanket order, see press releases Dec. 13, 15, and 20, 1941, ibid., 92.

4. The largest of the group, with U.S. assets of about $8 million, was Tokyo Marine and Fire Insurance. *New York Times,* Dec. 11, 1941.

5. Tate M. Robertson, "Chemnyco: Essential Facts and Information," Sept. 23, 1942, Acc. 67A10, Box 1303, RG 131 (Dept.-Justice).

6. As in the case of the Japanese bank agencies, this was done in conjunction with the New York banking authorities. New York State, Banking Department, *Annual Report 1941,* 74. The Banco di Napoli Trust Company of New York and the Banco di Napoli Trust Company, Chicago, had been operating under general licenses. Their general licenses were revoked on December 11, 1941. U.S. Treasury, *Documents,* 49.

7. *New York Times,* Dec. 13 and 20, 1941.

8. Elizabeth F. Washburn to Mira Wilkins, Jan. 27, 1993; see also John Morton Blum, *From the Morgenthau Diaries, vol. 3, Years of War, 1941–1945* (Boston: Houghton Mifflin, 1967), 6.

9. Office of Alien Property Custodian, *Annual Report 1944–1945,* 88 (henceforth reports coming from that office will be cited as OAPC, *AR 1944–1945,* or with the appropriate dates).

10. Eugene H. Clay, "Memo," Jan. 22, 1942, Foreign Funds Control File, Acc. 61A109, Box 681, RG 131 (Dept.-Justice).

11. Aalders and Wiebes, *Art of Cloaking,* 47; they write that on December 15, "The U.S. Treasury blocked the ABC shares as being of German origin." That cannot be right: the assets had already been "blocked" under the June 14, 1941, order; what was new was that the Treasury was taking charge.

12. Foreign Funds Control Report (Dec. 18, 1941). From the looks of the report, it must have been weeks in preparation, but its presentation was clearly made more crucial and accelerated with U.S. entry into the war. The unpublished report had a covering letter, Henry Morgenthau to Henry Wallace, Dec. 18, 1941.

13. Foreign Funds Control Report (Dec. 18, 1941).

14. *New York Times,* Jan. 14, 1942; Blum, *From the Morgenthau Diaries,* III, 6. See ibid., 7, for General Aniline & Film president John Mack's response.

15. Blum, *From the Morgenthau Diaries,* III, 6.

16. *New York Times,* Jan. 30, 1942.

17. Blum, *From the Morgenthau Diaries,* III, 7; Aalders and Wiebes, *Art of Cloaking,* 61.

18. Blum, *From the Morgenthau Diaries,* III, 4 (this has to be by spring 1942, although it is not dated).

19. As indicated in Chapter 8, the Proclaimed List had been established on July 17, 1941; additional firms had subsequently been added to the list.

20. U.S. Treasury, *Documents,* 97–98.

21. *New York Times,* Apr. 24, and Apr. 25, 1942.

22. Interrogation of Hermann Schmitz, Sept. 12, 1945, RG 238, Microfilm T301, Reel 8, NI-711, p. 18, National Archives.

23. U.S. Temporary National Economic Committee, *The Distribution of Ownership in the 200 Largest Non Financial Corporations,* Monograph 29 (Washington, D.C., 1940), 143.

24. *New York Times,* Apr. 24, 1942.

25. OAPC, *AR 1943–1944,* 68; OAPC, *AR 1942–1943,* 7. Over the war years, the remaining $18 million debt would be retired. It amounted to $12 million on June 30, 1944, and $10 million on June 30, 1945; this $10 million would be called in for redemption on November 1, 1945. OAPC, *AR 1944–1945,* 71; OAPC, *AR 1945–1947,* 72. This debt had been guaranteed by I. G. Farben, so its elimination served to sever the last formal link between I. G. Farben and GAF.

26. There were four hormone criminal cases: (1) *U.S. v. Schering Corporation, Jules Weltzein, Ciba Pharmaceutical Products, Vincent A. Burgher, Roche-Organon, Elmer H. Bobst,*

Rare Chemicals, and E. T. Fritzsching, Criminal No. 550; (2) *U.S. v. Ciba Pharmaceutical Products, Vincent A. Burgher, Schering Corporation, Gregory Stragnell, Roche-Organon, and Elmer H. Bobst,* Criminal No. 551; (3) *U.S. v. Julius Weltzien and Schering Corporation,* Criminal No. 552; and (4) *U.S. v. Roche-Organon, Inc. and Elmer H. Bobst,* Criminal No. 553—all in the District Court of New Jersey on December 17, 1941. The cases were *not* reported in standard sources, but data on them are available in the National Archives, Northeast Region (New York). Some are listed in Oseas, "Antitrust Prosecutions," 63–65; see also data in RG 131, File D-63-3, Acc. 65A1063 (Dept.-Justice), and U.S. Senate, Committee on Military Affairs, Subcommittee on War Mobilization, *Scientific and Technical Mobilization, Hearings,* 78th Cong., 1st sess. (1943), pt. 10, 1117 (henceforth cited as *Kilgore Committee Hearings*).

27. This case was *U.S. v. Schering Corp. et al.,* Civil No. 1919 (DNJ 1941). For details, see Eugene H. Clay, "Memo," Feb. 13, 1942, and Paul M. Greene and Donald P. McHugh, "Memo," Jan. 11, 1944, in Acc. 61A109, Box 681, RG 131 (Dept.-Justice). Whereas the other hormone cases were criminal cases, this was a civil case. The consent decree is abstracted in Lindstrom and Tighe, *Antitrust Consent Decrees,* I, 298–300. See also *Kilgore Committee Hearings,* pt. 10, 1117.

28. See *U.S. v. Swiss Bank Corp.,* Civil No. 1920 (DNJ 1941). The consent decree is abstracted in Lindstrom and Tighe, *Antitrust Consent Decrees,* 301.

29. The first case was *U.S. v. General Dyestuff Corp., General Aniline & Film Corp., I. G. Farben Industrie, AG., Hermann Schmitz, Dietrich A. Schmitz, E. K. Halbach, and Hans W. Aickelin,* Criminal No. 111-135 (SDNY 1941); the second, *U.S. v. General Aniline & Film, I. G. Farbenindustrie, Hermann Schmitz, Dietrich A. Schmitz, Ernst Schwartz,* Criminal No. 111-136 (SDNY 1941); the third, *U.S. v. Dietrich A. Schmitz, General Aniline & Film, F. William von Meister, and William H. vom Rath,* Criminal No. 111-137 (SDNY 1941). See U.S. Senate, Committee on Patents, *Patents, Hearings,* 77th Cong., 2nd sess. (1942) pt. 5, 2611–2619, 2607–2610, 2602–2607 (henceforth cited as *Bone Committee Hearings*); and *New York Times,* Dec. 20, 1941. All of these cases, filed after war broke out, had been long in preparation.

30. These were "New York" cases, since they were filed in the Southern District Court of New York. The actual indictments are included in *Bone Committee Hearings,* pt. 5, 2602–2619; see also *New York Times,* Dec. 20, 1941. An Office of Alien Property Custodian report that discusses this matter does not state that there was a formal postponement, but it seems likely; see OAPC, *AR 1943–1944,* 72, for that suggestion. Since the German I. G. Farben was a defendant in two of the three cases, there was no way the litigation could be pursued during the war years, unless the German company was excluded in some manner, which was not what the Justice Department desired. Wyatt Wells writes that the Justice Department "could not bring itself to drop the matter. Its suit dragged on for years." Wyatt Wells, *Antitrust and the Formation of the Postwar World* (New York: Columbia University Press, 2002), 72.

31. Edwards, *Economic and Political Aspects of International Cartels,* 60; see also Larson, Knowlton, and Popple, *New Horizons,* 507; Blackford and Kerr, *BF Goodrich,* 160; and Morris, *American Synthetic Rubber,* 9.

32. The consent decree of February 18, 1942, in *U.S. v. Imperial Chemical Industries,* Civil No. 17-282 (SDNY 1942), is abstracted in Lindstrom and Tighe, *Antitrust Consent Decrees,* I, 313–314. Other litigation remained unresolved. See also Reader, *Imperial Chemical Industries,* II, 420–421.

33. Larson, Knowlton, and Popple, *New Horizons,* 431. *U.S. v. Standard Oil Company of New Jersey, et al.,* Civil No. 2091 (DNJ 1942); Lindstrom and Tighe, *Antitrust Consent Decrees,* 318–322, contains an abstract of the decree; the entire decree is printed in the *Bone Committee Hearings,* pt. 6, 2862–2873; on April 7, 1943, a supplement judgment was entered to clarify the compulsory licensing of catalytic refining patents.

34. Larson, Knowlton, and Popple, *New Horizons*, 428.

35. *Bone Committee Hearings*, pt. 1, 654. See abstract of the decree in *U.S. v. Aluminum Company of America, et al.*, Civil No. 18-31 (SDNY 1942), in Lindstrom and Tighe, *Antitrust Consent Decrees*, 323–325.

36. *Bone Committee Hearings*, pt. 1 642.

37. Corwin Edwards, "Thurman Arnold and the Antitrust Laws," *Political Science Quarterly*, 58 (Sept. 1943): 351–352, on Arnold's reluctance to postpone these cases. Wells, *Antitrust and the Formation of the Postwar World*, 70ff., is excellent on Arnold's frustrations.

38. The case was *U.S. v. General Electric et al.*, Civil No. 1364; its history was given in the case report DNJ, Jan. 19, 1949; certain defendants in this case did settle with consent decrees: Westinghouse Electric & Manufacturing did so on April 10, 1942; the trial against GE, Philips, and others would resume after the war.

39. The trial date had been set for June 15, 1942; the secretary of war asked for a postponement; the attorney general replied that he understood the defendants were no longer engaged in the restrictive practices charged in the indictment and indicated the Justice Department would apply for an appropriate adjournment. *Bone Committee Hearings*, pt. 5, 2020–2021. There were a number of cases against General Electric, which were either settled or postponed.

40. For details, see OAPC, *AR 1945–1946*, 70. The case was *U.S. v. Allied Chemical & Dye Corp.*, Criminal No. 753c, DNJ, filed May 1942; see *Bone Committee Hearings*, pt. 5, 2589–2601.

41. See Edwards, "Thurman Arnold," 352, on the postponements.

42. Hochheiser, *Rohm and Haas*, 75–79; there were two cases, involving acrylic products and acrylic dentures: *U.S. v. Rohm & Haas Co.*, Criminal No. 877 and Criminal No. 878 (DNJ 1942). See also Simon N. Whitney, *Antitrust Policies* (New York: Twentieth Century Fund, 1958), I, 207–208. This survey of ours of the antitrust cases taken up by the Justice Department involving inward foreign investment issues is by no means complete. Thus, for example, on June 24, 1942, the Justice Department charged the Tannin Corporation and its British parent, Forestal Land, Timber & Railways Ltd., with antitrust violations (involving a "monopoly" in U.S. quebracho imports). The Tannin Corporation entered a plea of nolo contendere and was fined; a nolle prosequi (a stay of proceedings) was entered as to the case against the British company, since it was seen as outside the jurisdiction of the court. The case was *U.S. v. Tannin Corporation, et al.* Criminal No. 18-31 (SDNY 1942). See also *Kilgore Committee Hearings*, pt. 9, 1047–1048.

43. This issue would surface in many different settings. I have come across the issues in the context of antitrust cases so different as those involving Forestal Land, Timber & Railways Ltd. (see previous note), I. G. Farben, Imperial Chemical Industries, NV Philips, and the Swedish SKF. Often the foreign parent firm claimed to be out of the U.S. court's jurisdiction (with affiliates stoutly maintaining that they were "independent," or alternatively, as in the case of Imperial Chemical Industries, that it did not do business in the United States and thus should not be subject to U.S. prosecution).

44. Maddox, *War within World War II*, 14–15.

45. OAPC, *AR 1942–1943*, 7, 25; Blum, *From the Morgenthau Diaries*, III, 4–9.

46. Foreign Funds Control Report (Dec. 18, 1941), 117–118.

47. OAPC, *AR 1942–1943*, 8.

48. Ibid., 9, 79, 155 (Executive Order 9095; Mar. 11, 1942). In the first years of the New Deal, Crowley had been head of the Federal Deposit Insurance Corporation and had been in constant conflict with the Treasury Department and the Federal Reserve. Blum, *From the Morgenthau Diaries*, III, 4–10. Roosevelt, however, thought Crowley "one of the best administrators inside or outside the government." Acheson, *Present at the Creation*, 77.

49. OAPC, *AR 1942–1943,* 7, 24–25.

50. OAPC, *AR 1943–1944,* 144, and OAPC, *AR 1942–1943,* 11. Once OAPC had taken over enemy properties, anyone with a complaint sued OAPC. The suits were numerous and various. Lists exist within the reports of the Office of Alien Property Custodian.

51. Executive Order 9193 (July 6, 1942) in OAPC, *AR 1942–1943,* 11, 155–158.

52. On the early clashes (December 1941–March 1942) between Treasury and Justice, and the continuance of the OAPC-Treasury discord, see, for example, "Minute Sheet," Mar. 2, 1943, "Secret," in "Custodian of Enemy Property," FO 115/3998, Public Record Office, London. Indeed, at times there was talk in Washington about whether the Office of Alien Property Custodian and Treasury were "duplicating each other's work." See report in British government records, in ibid.

53. OAPC, *AR 1942–1943,* 99 (vesting order no. 4); for details, see OAPC, *AR 1943–1944,* 73–75.

54. OAPC, *AR 1943–1944,* 68, and OAPC, *AR 1942–1943,* 99 (vesting order no. 5) on General Aniline & Film. OAPC, *AR 1943–1944,* 70, and OAPC, *AR 1942–1943,* 99 (vesting order no. 33) on General Dyestuff.

55. OAPC, *AR 1942–1943,* 99 (vesting order no. 2)

56. Ibid., 99 (vesting order no. 9); OAPC, *AR 1943–1944,* 63; Aalders and Wiebes, *Art of Cloaking,* 47–49.

57. Hochheiser, *Rohm and Haas,* 81–82; OAPC, *AR 1942–1943,* 101 (vesting order no. 131).

58. OAPC, *AR 1942–1943,* 104 (vesting order no. 249), and OAPC, *AR 1945–1946,* 64.

59. Markham, *Competition,* 212; this must have been under a supervisory order or special order, since these companies were not vested until after the end of World War II.

60. OAPC, *AR 1942–1943,* 23, 28.

61. See later statement of James E. Markham, Alien Property Custodian, June 28, 1945, U.S. Senate, Committee on Military Affairs, Subcommittee on War Mobilization, *Elimination of German Resources for War, Hearings,* 79th Cong., 1st sess. (1945), II, 580–595 (henceforth cited as *Kilgore Committee Hearings II*). In this statement Markham discusses the reasons for and techniques of "cloaking." The attention to cloaked properties was from the earliest vesting. Thus, when 99.9 percent of the outstanding common stock of Schering Corp. was vested in 1942, the OAPC explained that the vesting was because the shares "were held for the benefit of Schering A. G., of Germany . . . At the time of vesting they were held of record in the names of American nominees of Swiss companies. The Swiss companies were found by the Custodian to be acting as cloaks for the German beneficial owners." OAPC, *AR 1943–1944,* 74. Although this detailed information was in the 1943–1944 report, the vesting itself was at the very start of the OAPC's existence.

62. OAPC, *AR 1942–1943,* 1–2.

63. Ibid., 2–3.

64. Ibid., 3 (1,792 and estimated value). A list of 1,757 is given in ibid., 99–131, with no values included (it is not clear why 35 were omitted). Table 1, in ibid., 34, shows 1,792 vesting orders, classified by principal type of property (and nationality); the 361 business enterprises come from that table (177 were German, 148 Japanese, 32 Italian, and 4 were of "other" unspecified nationalities). A later table, on p. 35, indicates that these 361 vesting orders resulted in the OAPC acquiring title to the former enemy ownership in 318 separate businesses. All vested "branches" of a foreign affiliate were considered as a single enterprise; thus, the 50 percent interest in Winthrop Chemical by General Aniline & Film was not listed under a separate vesting order (it was included in the vesting order for General Aniline & Film). Ibid., 36. A 25 percent or greater ownership of outstanding stock of a company was the defining criteria for "control." "Enemy" was the beneficial owner—as perceived by the OAPC—not the nominal "cloaking" owner.

65. Ibid., 38, and OAPC, *AR 1943–1944,* 70. The assets and the book value of the shares vested did not correspond—and not all the shares in GAF were vested. OAPC, *AR 1943–1944,* 70, indicates that as of March 31, 1942, the book value of GAF shares vested was $36.4 million, whereas the book value of the shares not vested came to $3.8 million. Shares not vested were those determined to be owned by Americans with no "enemy" associations.

66. In OAPC, *AR 1943–1944,* 62–89, these particular firms, which were noted in OAPC, *AR 1942–1943* as vested in 1942, were singled out for detailed discussion.

67. OAPC, *AR 1942–1943,* 3, 19, 50–52; no separate list of supervisory orders was provided in any of the OAPC Annual Reports.

68. Ibid., 3–4, 28, 40 (5 percent), 40–45 (numbers of patents vested by industrial sectors). There were large German interests in the U.S. chemical industry, but very limited FDI in the electrical industry. On the other hand, the German electrical companies, Allgemeine Elektrizitäts-Gesellschaft (AEG) and Siemens had over the years taken out many U.S. patents. Cantwell and Barrera, "Localisation of Corporate Technological Trajectories," 268. These now were vested. Five percent does not seem especially large, but the patents were probably more critical than revealed by the percentage.

69. OAPC, *AR 1942–1943,* 48. There is no mention of any Japanese ships' being seized.

70. Exhibit E, in ibid., 139–146, has a list of "court cases in which the Office of Alien Property Custodian is interested." Its interest was in cases involving the enemy property it had vested. Shipping cases included those pending against the Hamburg-American Line, North German Lloyd on everything from ticket refunds to freight damage claims. The Japanese trading company Mitsubishi Shoji Kaisha, Ltd., which was vested, was involved in a number of cases where it had been the plaintiff, suing for relief for failure of a shipping company to deliver cargo and damages to cargo. OAPC now became party to these prewar suits.

71. OAPC, *AR 1942–1943,* 3. There were certain sizable Italian banking assets. Some were already in liquidation when OAPC assumed authority. OAPC did, for example, vest 98 percent of the common stock of Banco di Napoli Trust Co., New York. Ibid., 103. For other Italian firms vested, see, for example, vesting orders (number proceeds description) in ibid., 102 (no. 180, Fiat branch in Detroit; this seems to have been a purchasing outlet, buying machines tool and perhaps parts); 103 (no. 218, New York branch of the insurance company Assicurazioni Generali di Trieste & Venezia; Generali was an important Italian multinational enterprise); and 104 (no. 274, American branch of Italian Tobacco Regie; this was the Italian state tobacco monopoly).

72. Ibid., 3, 54.

73. Ibid., 4–5; all royalty payments due on the vested patents were collected by the OAPC.

74. OAPC, *AR 1945–1946,* 3, for the policy change.

75. Table 9.1 is based on four OAPC annual reports; the first and shortest was 166 pages; each of the next three was more than 250 pages; with the report for year end 1945, running 273 pages. These reports have been conveniently republished as U.S. Office of Alien Property Custodian, *Annual Reports, 1942–1946* (New York: Arno Press, 1977). The last of the reports was prepared by the Office of Alien Property within the Justice Department, since the functions of the Office of Alien Property Custodian were transferred to the Office of Alien Property on October 14, 1946; see OAPC, *AR 1945–1946,* iv. On Crowley and Markham, see OAPC, *AR 1943–1944,* 152; Crowley's appointment as head of the Foreign Economic Administration in September 1943 appears to have overlapped with his position as Alien Property Custodian. James Markham served as Deputy Alien Property Custodian from March 19, 1942, that is, he was appointed as Crowley's deputy eight days after the establishment of the OAPC.

76. OAPC, *AR 1944–1945,* 37.

77. Ibid., 11; OAPC *AR 1945–1946,* 35.

78. Markham's roster is in *Kilgore Committee Hearings II,* pt. 4, 588–589, and reproduced as Table 9.2 herein. Winthrop Chemical Co. is not visible on the list; it is there under the Bayer, General Aniline & Film sequence; Berlin Aniline was commonly known as AGFA; Badische is known today as BASF. On Barth, see Alien Property Custodian, *Report 1918-1919,* 296.

79. On the Hamburg-American Line and the North German Lloyd Line, earlier discussion in text; on the Haarmann & Reimer interests in Haarmann–de Laire, see Wilkins, *History,* 400. Table 9.2 herein records that the German interest in Haarmann–de Laire–Schaefer was absorbed by Maywood Chemical Works. Haynes, *American Chemical Industry,* I, 329, indicates that Maywood Chemical Works had German backing before the First World War; it was the source for that statement in Wilkins, *History,* 399.

80. OAPC, *AR 1943–1944,* 51–52 (the list of eleven sold by year end June 30, 1944 is on p. 51); OAPC, *AR 1944–1945,* 46, has the list of nineteen sold between March 11, 1942, and June 30, 1945, and includes the sales price. The sales were of a miscellaneous collection of small vested enemy properties. The largest sum obtained ($632,000) was for 29.2 percent of the stock of American Platinum Works, Newark, New Jersey (a refiner of precious metals and manufacturer of precious metal products); the purchaser was American Platinum Works. The custodian's report explained that the vested shares of this company had "limited market appeal." Under its contract with the former German owner of the vested securities, American Platinum Works had held first purchase rights on these shares. Rather than challenge this and have a public auction, the OAPC in a private sale allowed American Platinum Works to buy back its own securities. Ibid., 45–46. Another sale in this set of nineteen was that of the pharmaceutical plant of Rare Chemicals Inc. and Boehringer Corp. in Flemington, New Jersey; the buyer was an American company, National Oil Products Co., in August 1943, after a bid by that firm of $125,000; the final sales price turned out to be merely $40,683. See OAPC, *AR 1942–1943,* 66–67; OAPC, *AR 1944–1945,* 46; and Haynes, *American Chemical Industry,* VI, 310. The plant manufactured anesthetics, physiological and nutritional deficiency correctives, vitamins, and hormones. The plant at Flemington, New Jersey, appears to have been built in 1940. A January 1941 letter is addressed to Rare Chemicals Inc. at Flemington, New Jersey. *Kilgore Committee Hearings,* 1251. Earlier, this joint venture between the two German affiliates had manufactured near Yonkers, New York.

81. Haynes, *American Chemical Industry,* VI, 408; OAPC, *AR 1944–1945,* 68–69. The OAPC reinvested the proceeds of the sale of Winthrop stock in U.S. government securities, which became part of the assets of General Aniline & Film; see ibid., 70–71. GAF properties had been vested and the title to most of its securities remained in the hands of the OAPC.

82. William Erhard Weiss, the founder of Sterling Products, who had been expelled from Sterling management in late August 1941, died in car crash at the age of sixty-three in 1942. Mann and Plummer, *Aspirin Wars,* 119. On Sterling during the war years, see Haynes, *American Chemical Industry,* VI, 408. Ultimately, all these efforts to cut the German connections proved not to work: in 1988, Eastman Kodak acquired Sterling Drug; subsequently, SmithKline Beecham PLC purchased Sterling Drug's Winthrop unit; and, in 1994, the German Bayer bought back the Bayer aspirin line that Sterling Products had acquired at the close of World War I. Wilkins, "German Chemical Firms," 319n.100.

83. OAPC, *AR 1945–1946,* 47, 64; the eight sold July 1, 1945, to June 30, 1946—*after* the end of the war in Europe—are listed in ibid., 48. American Potash & Chemical was the only company listed that sold for more than $1 million.

84. OAPC, *AR 1943–1944,* iii.

85. OAPC, *AR 1944–1945,* 49; OAPC, *AR 1943–1944,* iii–iv.
86. OAPC, *AR 1945–1946,* 85–86.
87. Wilkins, "American-Japanese Direct Foreign Investment Relationships," 442–445.
88. OAPC, *AR 1943–1944,* iv.
89. OAPC, *AR 1945–1946,* 95; see the classification by nationality, ibid., 96.
90. OAPC, *AR 1943–1944,* v.
91. Ibid., 63; Aalders and Wiebes, *Art of Cloaking,* 49–50; and *U.S. v. American Bosch Corp., et al.,* Civil No. 20-164 (SDNY 1942), abstract of consent decree in Lindstrom and Tighe, *Antitrust Consent Decrees,* I, 352–357.
92. *Kilgore Committee Hearings,* pt. 7, 960.
93. David M. Hart, *Forged Consensus: Science, Technology, and Economic Policy in the United States, 1921–1953* (Princeton, N.J.: Princeton University Press, 1998), 95–96.
94. OAPC, *AR 1943–1944,* 76–79; OAPC, *AR 1944–1945,* 77–80; OAPC, *AR 1945–1946,* 79–82; the custodian followed the policy of vesting securities "on the books" of foreign-controlled domestic corporations; not only did these securities cover foreign properties, but often the certificates were not in the United States. OAPC, *AR 1945–1946,* 13–14.
95. Not the least of the difficulties involved the determination of what was an enemy property and what was not. Not only did the Treasury continue to snipe at the activities of the OAPC, but the latter's performance was subject to British criticism as well. R. J. Stopford, at the British embassy in Washington, sent a dispatch to J. M. Toutbeck, Ministry of Economic Warfare, London, February 22, 1943, to the effect that when the Alien Property Custodian was appointed, "it was laid down that he should follow the English system of only vesting when this was necessary for a particular reason and not the Canadian system of automatic vesting of enemy assets." (I found no such distinctions in the U.S. discussions, and this seems to be a British interpretation.) Stopford went on that in fact APC's procedure was now (in early 1943) to take "title to or supervision over foreign or enemy property in order to prevent it from being useful to the enemy and *in order to administer it in the interest of the United States*" (emphasis added by Stopford). Stopford was wary. See R. J. Stopford to J. M. Toutbeck, Feb. 22, 1943, Custodian of Enemy Property, FO 115/3998, Public Record Office. The British saw this as an extension of American "power" and did not like it at all.
96. See Edwards, "Thurman Arnold," 344–345; Israel Oseas starts his article "Antitrust Prosecutions," 42, making this very point; see also Tony Freyer, *Regulating Big Business: Antitrust in Great Britain and America 1880–1990* (Cambridge: Cambridge University Press, 1992), 223–229.
97. Martin, *All Honorable Men,* 9–12. See also data in RG 131 (Dept.-Justice). The OAPC found a scale model of the Fiat plant in Turin, Italy, among the assets of Fiat's small branch in Detroit. The Italian Fiat made planes for the Axis. The "find" was turned over to U.S. Army Intelligence, which used it in bombing the plant. OAPC, *AR 1943–1944,* 57.
98. G. L. F. Bolton, Bank of England, to G. C. Gibbs, Enemy Transactions, Ministry of Economic Warfare, Mar. 8, 1943, Proposed Disclosure of Customers, FO115/3986, Public Record Office.
99. R. J. Stopford, British Embassy, Washington, to Geoffrey Gibbs, Apr. 9, 1943, in Proposed Disclosure of Customers, FO115/3986, Public Record Office.
100. See, for example, Foreign Funds Control data on Ciba/Geigy/Sandoz in RG 131 (Dept.-Justice). The Swiss consul general in New York denounced the investigations as an "inquisition." See his April 9, 1943, comments, cited in Cerutti, "Le blocage des avoirs suisses," 199. The Swiss view was that Treasury Department officials were "Blokierungs fanatiker"—that is, fanatics, taking their jobs in Foreign Funds Control well beyond the bounds of rational behavior. Ibid., 200.

101. It was Foreign Funds Control, Department of the Treasury, that in May and June 1944 pursued a major investigation of the Swedish company SKF and its U.S. affiliates. Jean Pajus, "Report of A. B. Svenska Kullagerfabriken (SKF)," prepared for the Foreign Economic Administration, Oct. 1944, RG 169, FEA, Entry 211, Box 1, Folder: SKF Report, National Archives, 137, 157 (I obtained a copy from Birgit Karlsson, December 2001)—henceforth cited as *Pajus 1944 Report*. See also Aalders and Wiebes, *Art of Cloaking*, chap. 5.

102. Olsson, "Securing the Markets," 105–106. Compare his rendition with that of Charles Higham, *Trading with the Enemy* (New York: Delacorte Press, 1983), 116–129, 250–253, and Aalders and Wiebes, *Art of Cloaking*, 76–91. Authors of these last two volumes were convinced of the terrible wartime activities of the Swedish *and* American SKF. They took their point of departure from many contemporary views. Thus, Vice-President Henry Wallace thought that Batt was a "front" for "German-dominated international cartels." Randall Bennett Woods, *A Changing of the Guard: Anglo-American Relations, 1941–1946* (Chapel Hill: University of North Carolina Press, 1990), 127. It did not help that Batt had been a director of American Bosch since 1938 and had been appointed president of that "German-controlled" company in 1940. The most exhaustive inquiries on SKF were undertaken by Jean Pajus. See especially *Pajus 1944 Report*.

103. Aalders and Wiebes, *Art of Cloaking*, 97.

104. In 1942 Milo Perkins, executive director of the Board of Economic Warfare, had written the attorney general requesting reports on the business links between U.S. firms and those companies in enemy territory. Martin, *All Honorable Men*, 9. On FEA investigations, see Aalders and Wiebes, *Art of Cloaking*, 165ns.38, 43, and 172n.1, citing reports on Bosch and SKF that came out of the FEA investigations; Acheson, *Present at the Creation*, 85, and *Kilgore Committee Hearings II*, pt. 2, 36. The *Pajus 1944 Report*, based on May and June 1944 Foreign Funds Control inquiries, had an FEA imprint.

105. Blum, *From the Morgenthau Diaries*, III, 132; the executive order establishing the FEA was September 25, 1943. There seems to have been a period when Crowley was both Alien Property Custodian and head of the FEA. The OAPC, *AR 1943–1944*, 152, says Crowley was APC until February 11, 1944. According to *Who's Who in America, 1948–49*, 559, Crowley was Alien Property Custodian in 1942 and 1943; he was appointed foreign economic administrator and served in that position from October 1943 to October 1945.

106. See F. W. McCombe to E. H. Coleman, Dec. 10, 1943, FO115/3998, Public Record Office.

107. Birgit Karlsson, "Fascism and Production of Ball-Bearings: SKF, Germany, and the Soviet Union 1942–1952," unpublished paper presented in Odense, Denmark, April 2001.

108. I have written the story of SKF, using the material of the many critics but also depending heavily on the work of Martin Fritz and Birgit Karlsson, who assembled in *SKF i stormaktspolitikens Kraftfält: Kullagerexporten 1943–1945* (Göteborg: Novum Grafiska, 1998), 102 documents relating to SKF in the war period. Many of the documents were in Swedish, and I have had help from Ms. Karlsson in translations. In the document collection, Fritz and Karlsson also reproduced a sequence of correspondence in English from *Foreign Relations of the United States* (which compiles U.S. State Department records). So, too, I have used British materials from the Ministry of Economic Warfare, located in the Public Record Office. Ms. Karlsson sent me a copy of Pajus' 200-page October 1944 report, *Pajus 1944 Report*. Aalders and Wiebes, *Art of Cloaking*, 76–91, has much to say on SKF. On the U.S. pressures on the Swedish SKF through its U.S. subsidiary, see Acheson, *Present at the Creation*, 85. Karlsson, "Fascism and Production of Ball-Bearings," shows that in December 1943, as the Allies were pressing the Swedish SKF to reduce

Swedish exports of ball-bearings to Germany, the company "compensated diminished offers of ball bearings with increasing offers of ball-bearing steel and ball-bearing machines."

109. U.S. Senate, Special Committee Investigating the National Defense Program, *Investigation of the National Defense Program, Hearings,* 77th Cong., 1st sess.—79th Cong. 2nd sess., 1941–1947 (Truman Committee 1941—June 1944). Truman left the chairmanship in June 1944. David McCullough, *Truman* (New York: Simon and Schuster, 1992), 271, has the summary of its activities.

110. June 15, 1942, broadcast quoted in McCullough, *Truman,* 266–267.

111. *Bone Committee Hearings*, pt. 1, 11, 14, 643.

112. The subcommittee hearings were divided into two sets. The first set had sixteen parts: U.S. Senate, Committee on Military Affairs, Subcommittee on War Mobilization, *Scientific and Technical Mobilization, Hearings,* 78th Cong., 1st and 2nd sess. (1943–1944), cited herein as *Kilgore Committee Hearings.* The second set was also relevant. Its subject was *Elimination of German Resources for War,* 79th Cong., 1st sess. (1945). These hearings began on June 22, 1945, after V-E Day, but before V-J Day. I am citing and have cited them as *Kilgore Committee Hearings II.* At both sets of hearings, documents were produced from investigations of corporate records that dealt with the behavior of foreign business in the United States before and during World War II.

113. I found these same hearings relevant when I studied American business abroad; see Wilkins, *Maturing,* 263–267. There was substantial overlapping evidence presented in the various hearings. Thus, part 4 of the *Kilgore Committee Hearings* was devoted to the testimony of Senator Bone.

114. There is wonderful material on the cartels in hormones and vitamin D, for example.

115. Boylan, *Sequel to the Apocalyse;* that same year Guenther Reimann published *Patents for Hitler* (New York: Vanguard Press, 1942); other similar books would follow, for example, Howard W. Ambruster, *Treason's Peace* (New York: Beechhurst Press, 1947); Sasuly, *I. G. Farben* (1947). Then came Martin, *All Honorable Men* (1950). And, in the 1970s and 1980s, but of the identical genre, Borkin, *Crime and Punishment of I. G. Farben,* (1978) and Higham, *Trading with the Enemy* (1983). On Ambruster's background see Mann and Plummer, *Aspirin Wars,* 94–96, 109, 111. During wartime, Martin was chief of the Economic Warfare Section in the Department of Justice. In 1945, Borkin was an economist in the Justice Department's antitrust division. *Kilgore Committee Hearings II,* pt. 4, 565 (on Borkin). By contrast, Higham is best known for his biographies of Hollywood celebrities; he got into "Nazi chasing" after writing a popular and much criticized biography of the actor Errol Flynn, claiming the latter was a Nazi spy. See Contemporary Authors Online, The Gale Group, 2001 (accessed Sept. 4, 2001).

116. The files of Francis Garvan are at the American Heritage Center, Laramie, Wyoming. On the Chemical Foundations' role in the book's publication, see Charles R. Clark, "Report on Geigy," Dec. 30, 1942, File D-63–3, Acc. 65A1063, Box 267, RG 131 (Dept.-Justice). In Stevenson, *Man Called Intrepid,* 280–283, credit for *Sequel to the Apocalyse* goes to British spies—the "British Security Coordination" New York office—with help from Nelson Rockefeller. The Chemical Foundation's role is not mentioned.

117. Edwards, *Economic and Political Aspects of International Cartels,* vi. This preface was despite a disclaimer (on p. v) that the report was for the committee's consideration and did not express its opinions or that of any member.

118. Ibid., 8.

119. Ibid., 71–72. Edwards' monograph, published in February 1944, did not include a document dated November 7, 1944, reporting on an August 10, 1944, meeting of German industrialists in Strasbourg to discuss postwar plans: the Germans *believed* that "patents

for stainless steel [that] belonged to the Chemical Foundation, Inc., New York, and the Krupp Co. of Germany, jointly" meant that American steel companies, including U.S. Steel, were "under an obligation to work with the Krupp concern." See document in *Kilgore Committee Hearings II,* pt. 2 (June 25, 1945), 30. Francis Garvan would have turned over in his grave.

120. Its protests are documented by the historian of NV Philips, Blanken, *History of Philips Electronics,* IV, 307–308. According to Blanken, after representations by the Dutch ambassador, the Kilgore Committee "halted distribution of the [Edwards] monograph and promised to make necessary corrections in any future edition." The monograph, however, had already been distributed, and no future edition was put out by the Kilgore Committee. Philips' management in the United States received a communication from the committee (Feb. 25, 1944) that indicated "withdrawal of the existing copies was not thought to be a good idea as it would attract further publicity."

121. I did not know about the refutation until I read the Blanken volume. Blanken says the company issued a "'white book' in which all of Edwards' accusations [in relation to Philips] were rebutted." Ibid., 308. It is true that Senator Kilgore was more tempered when he spoke at his committee's hearings on August 29, 1944, stating, "There is no intention to impugn the patriotism of any particular American corporation which may have been a member of an international cartel." (NV Philips' "American company" was the North American Philips Company.) Kilgore was interested in I. G. Farben, "German aggression," and "our national security." See *Kilgore Committee Hearings,* pt. 16, 1965.

122. Edwards noted that the word "cartel" had for Americans a "foreign flavor." The Justice Department under Thurman Arnold used it to indicate any international arrangement in restraint of trade; Edwards added that "although Arnold occasionally spoke of 'domestic cartels,' usually he did not employ the term to cover domestic restraint of trade." Edwards, "Thurman Arnold," 344.

123. Freyer, *Regulating Big Business,* 211. McGowan's 1943 comments to William Benton, when published in *Life* magazine, created a stir. Senator Kilgore referred to them disapprovingly in his hearings. *Kilgore Committee Hearings,* pt. 7 (Nov. 3, 1943), 961. Freyer (*Regulating Big Business,* 227) points out that the National Foreign Trade Council advocated changes in U.S. law that would allow reasonable business agreements, but the NFTC never adopted a vocabulary that could be interpreted as favoring "cartels." More important, see ibid., 257–261, esp. 259, for British reactions. The British embassy in 1944 held the view that U.S. attitudes were "more emotional than rational." The British woke up very slowly to the fact that on the U.S. side of the Atlantic, a "cartel" was seen as "un-American." Comments on business cooperation were, of course, nothing new for ICI's McGowan. Other large European businesses shared McGowan's views.

124. For the U.S. corporate defense, see, for example, the statement by W. S. Farish of Standard Oil (New Jersey) before the Kilgore Committee, *Kilgore Committee Hearings,* pt. 4 (June 4, 1943), 686–700. For the traumatic experience of the wartime accusations for the oil company, see Wall and Gibb, *Teagle of Jersey Standard,* 310–315.

125. For the comparable attacks on the banks, see Carosso, *Investment Banking,* 408ff.

126. In addition, Arnold's appointment to the U.S. Court of Appeals did not silence him. It was as "former" assistant attorney general that he was the opening witness at the Kilgore Committee hearings, March 30, 1943. *Kilgore Committee Hearings,* pt. 1. As assistant attorney general for the Antitrust Division, Arnold was replaced by Tom Clark, who held that position for about five months; then on August 28, 1943, the post went to Wendell Berge (Tom Clark became assistant attorney general for the Criminal Division). See *New York Times,* Mar. 17, 1943 (Clark nominated as Arnold's successor); Mar. 30, 1943 (Clark took the oath of office yesterday); and Aug. 29, 1943 (Berge's and Clark's new appointments). Reader, *Imperial Chemical Industries,* III, 424, on Francis Biddle's Janu-

ary 1944 views. See also testimony of Biddle, Sept. 7, 1944, *Kilgore Committee Hearings,* pt. 16, 1966–1979. Biddle was attorney general from 1941 to 1945.

127. Testimony of Wendell Berge, Oct. 21, 1943, and Nov. 4, 1943, *Kilgore Committee Hearings,* pt. 6, 745, and pt. 7, 960, 978. Later research indicates I. G. Farben had literally hundreds of additional agreements that had no (or only indirect or remote) impact on American business. A 1945 estimate was 2,000 agreements in all.

128. *Kilgore Committee Hearings,* pt. 7, 960.

129. Reader, *Imperial Chemical Industries,* II, 428–431; *U.S. v. Imperial Chemical Industries,* 100 F. Supp. 504 (SDNY 1951); *U.S. v. Imperial Chemical Industries,* 105 F. Supp. 251 (SDNY 1952).

130. The 1942 acrylic case against Rohm and Haas was "reopened" in September 1944. Hochheiser, *Rohm and Haas,* 79. This case involved Du Pont. There was also *U.S. v. Borax Consolidated Ltd.,* Criminal No. 28900-S and Civil No. 23690-G (DND Calif. 1945). See U.S. House, Committee of the Judiciary, Subcommittee on Study of Monopoly Power, *Study of Monopoly Power, Hearings,* 81st Cong., 2nd sess. (1950), 29. The criminal indictment, charging antitrust violations, was returned by a federal grand jury in San Francisco on September 14, 1944. In addition to Borax Consolidated and its U.S. affiliate Pacific Coast Borax Company, American Potash & Chemical Corporation and its subsidiary Three Elephant Borax Corporation were defendants. The civil suit of the same day was to enjoin the continuation of the alleged violations. Both suits were settled August 16, 1945. In the criminal suit the defendants pleaded nolo contendere and were fined. The civil suit ended with a consent decree. See OAPC, *AR 1943–1944,* 66, and OAPC, *AR 1944–1945,* 62–63; an abstract of the consent decree in *U.S. v. Borax Consolidated Ltd., et al.,* Civil No. 23690-G (DND Calif. 1945) is in Lindstrom and Tighe, *Antitrust Consent Decrees,* I, 371–375.

131. Fritz and Karlsson, *SKF,* 343 (Doc. 98, Telegram dated Dec. 26, 1944) and Karlsson, "Fascism and Production of Ball-Bearings"; the first contains a report from the Swedish embassy in Washington, and the second has comments on the report. Pajus's October 1944 report contained a substantial amount on cartels in the bearings industry *(Pajus 1944 Report).*

132. On this commitment see Susan Aaronson, *Trade and the American Dream: A Social History of Postwar Trade Policy* (Louisville: University of Kentucky Press, 1996); Thomas W. Zeiler, *Free Trade, Free World: The Advent of GATT* (Chapel Hill: University of North Carolina Press, 1999); and Harley Notter, *Postwar Foreign Policy Preparation* (Washington, D.C., 1949).

133. Freyer, *Regulating Big Business,* 260; see ibid., 261–263, for the discussions of cartels in the context of the plans for the International Trade Organization. The State Department may have seemed more flexible than the Justice Department in British *perceptions,* but read the State Department document, prepared before V-E Day, and presented and published in the *Kilgore Committee Hearings II,* pt. 2, 56–57 (June 25, 1945): "the so-called normal operation of cartel arrangements has had undesirable and dangerous economic consequences . . . We hope to achieve the concurrence of other governments in an agreement prohibiting participation of commercial enterprises in contracts and combinations which restrain international trade, restrict access to international markets, or foster monopolistic control in international trade." This was what the State Department hoped to achieve with the proposed International Trade Organization.

134. The distinction was never well delineated, although the State Department often referred specifically to agreements among "commercial enterprises" or *private* restrictive agreements, while at the same time it was prepared to accept and to have the United States participate in certain commodity agreements. In contrast, the German government sponsorship of cartels was always absolutely bad from the U.S. perspective.

135. Freidel, *America in the Twentieth Century,* 411–412. According to U.S. Department of Commerce, Office of Business Economics, *International Transactions of the United States during the War, 1940–1945,* Economic Series No. 65 (Washington, 1948), 80 (henceforth cited as *Commerce Study 1940–1945*), the average withholding tax applied to income paid to nonresident aliens not engaged in trade or business in the United States increased from about 12.3 percent in 1940 to about 26.1 percent in 1945. The U.S. withholding tax rate applicable to most types of income payments to foreigners (except for those foreign investors residing in Canada and Sweden, for which countries tax treaties established special rates) was 10 percent at the start of 1940, rose to 16 percent by the end of that year, reached 27 percent in 1941, and increased to 30 percent in 1942, a rate that held for the rest of the war years. The *Commerce Study 1940–1945* says nothing about the French tax treaty. With France an occupied country, all dividends and interest were subject to Treasury Department controls, and there were no remittances to France. The percentages just given (both from the same source) do not appear to correspond to one another, probably because one relates to "nonresident aliens not engaged in trade or business in the United States" and the other covers all income payments to foreign investors (except those from Canada and Sweden). Both sets of figures show sharp wartime increases in taxes.

136. Freidel, *America in the Twentieth Century,* 411–412; Federal Reserve System, *Banking and Monetary Statistics, 1941–1970* (Washington, D.C., 1976), 882 (figures show a more than fourfold increase in national debt). Freidel's figures suggest an increase of more than fivefold.

137. Blum, *From the Morgenthau Diaries,* III, 103–104; U.S. Department of the Treasury, Office of the Secretary, *Census of Foreign-Owned Assets in the United States* (Washington, D.C., 1945), 39 (henceforth cited as *1941 Census*).

138. On the large Canadian official dollar balances in the United States in 1945, see Dominion Bureau of Statistics, *Canada's International Investment Position, Selected Years, 1926 to 1949* (Ottawa, n.d. [1950]), 39. On the Latin American portfolio investments flows to the United States, see Stallings, *Banker to the Third World,* 333.

139. Roberts, *Schroders,* 293–295. Roberts gives the assets of J. Henry Schroder Banking Corp. 1941–1945, as rising from $37.8 million (year end 1941) to $65.6 million (year end 1945). Ibid., 537–538. Another U.S. affiliate of the London Schroder firm—Schroder, Rockefeller & Co.—in May 1944 became a dealer in U.S. government securities. Ibid., 290–291. It is very possible that the J. Henry Schroder Banking Corp. (and Schroder, Rockefeller & Co.) marketed U.S. government issues to Latin American investors, since the Schroder firms had substantial contacts in Latin America.

140. Trebilcock, *Phoenix Assurance,* II, 861–862. Although Trebilcock is not specific, these holdings have to be a reference to those of Phoenix's branches and subsidiaries in the United States and not to the parent company. I was a bit surprised that as much as 17 percent was still in railroad bonds in 1943, after the findings presented in Chapter 8 herein. Note that for the Reconstruction Finance Corporation loan, the insurance companies themselves constituted the collateral, not the holdings of these companies.

141. *Commerce Study 1940–1945,* 100 (quotation), 110, 218. Over the post–World War II period, especially after the end to the Bretton Woods agreement, U.S. Treasury securities came to comprise a large part of other nations' foreign exchange reserve holdings. *IMF Survey* 30 (Apr. 2, 2001): 111. The practice of foreign governments' (or central banks') buying dollar securities for currency stabilization purposes seems to have had its genesis in the 1930s.

142. Ratner, *American Taxation,* 462. The Commerce Department study implies that the U.S. government did not start to monitor foreign purchases and sales of U.S. government long-term securities until 1943. *Commerce Study 1940–1945,* 218. I have (consistent

with my approach throughout this volume) dealt only with long-term securities, those with maturities over a year. Ibid. gave two different figures on foreign investments in short-term U.S. government securities at year end 1945, $1.8 billion (p. 81) and $3 billion (p. 110), while "Flow of Funds" data, compiled by the Federal Reserve, indicated year end 1945 foreign investment in "U.S. government securities" (including both short-term and long-term government obligations) was $2.6 billion. U.S. Department of Commerce, Bureau of the Census, *Historical Statistics of the United States* (Washington, D.C., 1975), II, 984, Series X305. Still another source indicates that foreign ownership of "U.S. government public debt" rose from $200 million at the end of June 1941, to $400 million year end 1941, to $2.4 billion at year end 1945; with the "total gross debt" given as $64.3 billion at year end 1941 and $278.7 billion at year end 1945, foreign ownership would have increased from 0.6 percent to 0.9 percent of national debt in that interval—thus remaining less than 1 percent of the national debt. Federal Reserve System, *Banking and Monetary Statistics, 1941–1970,* 882. This same source shows a net rise in foreign purchases of "marketable U.S. government bonds and notes" and corporate bonds 1942–1945, of $326 million. Ibid., 998, 1001 (explanation).

143. OAPC, *AR 1942–1943,* 55. Once vested, firms were no longer "technically" foreign owned. Because OAPC ignored corporate veils, I use the phrases "presumed to be" or "assumed to be."

144. With Hoffmann-La Roche and Lazard Frères, European management replaced the American top official. With Nestlé, Swiss and American management worked together, but with a newly enhanced role of the men from Geneva. With Philips, where there had been very little U.S. business, the Europeans began to build a whole new organization in America.

145. Michie, *The City,* 164 (on the successful business of British insurance companies in America in these years).

146. OAPC, *AR 1942–1943,* 54; OAPC, *AR 1943–1944,* 47–49.

147. OAPC, *AR 1942–1943,* 63; OAPC, *AR 1943–1944,* 101.

148. Haynes, *American Chemical Industry,* VI, 296.

149. OAPC, *AR 1942–1943,* iii, iv, and see a list of selected sample of companies, Table 9.3 herein.

150. OAPC, *AR 1942–1943,* 80 (Zeiss); OAPC, *AR 1944–1945,* 48, 174; and OAPC *AR 1945–1946,* 49 (Henckels).

151. OAPC, *AR 1943–1944,* 48; on the earlier development of its U.S. research and clinical presence, see Christopher Kobrak, "Between Nationalism and Internationalism: Schering AG and the Culture of German Capitalism, 1851–1945," Ph.D. diss., Columbia University, 1999, 690.

152. OAPC, *AR 1943–1944,* 65–69; OAPC, *AR 1944–1945,* 59–70; details of what they produced for war purposes are provided in these reports.

153. *Kilgore Committee Hearings II,* pt. 5, 888.

154. *Moody's 1941,* 532–533. Subsequently, these plants seem to have operated under an OAPC supervisory arrangement.

155. *Moody's 1945,* 1379; *Moody's 1942,* 753 (1940 employment); I do not have World War II employment figures for North American Rayon or American Bemberg, both of which continued to manufacture in Elizabethton, Tennessee; in 1940–1941, North American Rayon, employed about 2,800 individuals (see *Moody's 1941,* 532, and *Moody's 1942,* 839).

156. OAPC, *AR 1943–1944,* 68. "The patents standing of record in the United States Patent Office in the name of General Aniline & Film Corporation had originated with I. G. Farbenindustrie or one of the eleven German companies which were its predecessors or subsidiaries. The patents had been transferred to General Aniline & Film Corporation

by various contracts. . . . The Alien Property Custodian vested all right [*sic*], title and interest of the German firms in *all* of the patents and patent applications recorded in the United States Patent Office in the name of General Aniline & Film Corporation." (This was "in order to cut off any possible implicit reversionary interest which the German companies might assert.") OAPC, *AR 1944–1945,* 65.

157. OAPC, *AR 1944–1945,* 114, has a list of vested business enterprises and the "patents and patent applications owned by [these] vested business enterprises, as of June 30, 1945." General Aniline & Film had by far the largest number. The 3,909 patents and 382 pending patent applications (total, 4,291) included only those patents where General Aniline & Film had title and, as with other vested enterprises, did not include patents "under which the companies have merely licenses." Ibid., 113. Cantwell and Barrera, "Localisation of Corporate Technological Trajectories" 269, found that I. G. Farben (and its U.S. affiliates, broadly defined) had taken out 917 U.S. patents in 1920–1929 and 4,620 U.S. patents in the period 1930–1939. Not all of these patents would have been transferred to General Aniline & Film. Remember the transfers of the "rights to" some 2,000 patents to Standard Oil of New Jersey with the Hague Agreement.

158. OAPC, *AR 1942–1943,* 4–5; all royalty payments set out under existing arrangements at the start of the war and due on the vested patents were collected by the OAPC. Table 9.1 in the present book gives the total numbers of vested patents and licenses issued. Note my use of the word "perceived," for the evidence casts doubt on whether the diffusion of technological accomplishments was in fact retarded by the existence of the interwar licensing relationships.

159. OAPC, *AR 1943–1944,* 103–104.

160. Haynes, *American Chemical Industry,* V, 390.

161. Jordan A. Schwarz, *The Speculator: Bernard M. Baruch in Washington 1917–1965* (Chapel Hill: University of North Carolina Press, 1981), 390–391 (analogy with nitrates); Hayes, *Industry and Ideology,* 355 (analogy with dyes). An enormous amount has been written on the U.S. synthetic rubber program. For a start, see Howard, *Buna Rubber;* William M. Tuttle Jr., "The Birth of an Industry: The Synthetic Rubber 'Mess' in World War II," *Technology and Culture,* 22 (Jan. 1981): 35–67; and Morris, *American Synthetic Rubber.*

162. Ross, "Patents and Bureaucrats," 122, 126–135, for example.

163. OAPC, *AR 1944–1945,* 70.

164. Haynes, *American Chemical Industry,* VI, 381.

165. On Seagrams, see Bronfman, ". . . from little acorns . . ." in Distillers Corporation-Seagrams Ltd., *Annual Report 1970,* 70–71, and Distillers Corporation-Seagrams Ltd. *Annual Report 1971,* 31–32.

166. Wilkins, *Maturing,* 255, on Goodyear, Firestone, and U.S. Rubber's synthetic rubber production. Blackford and Kerr, *BF Goodrich,* 153–159 (on Goodrich synthetic rubber program from 1936 on). The indirect influence of FDI was on Goodrich, first through a path that evolved from the activities of the British War Mission during World War I and second through the related hiring of John L. Collyer, an executive trained in the Dunlop organization: (1) In the last year of World War I, at the start of 1918, the British War Mission and the U.S. Air Service had purchased the Commercial and Majestic whiskey distilleries in Terre Haute, Indiana, to make acetone by the so-called Weizmann process. The War Mission and Air Service formed Commercial Solvents Corp. *of New York* to manage this venture. At that time, in England, Chaim Weizmann had been making butyl alcohol in an attempt to develop synthetic rubber. When the First World War was over, in 1919 an American group that included David Goodrich (son of the founder of the BF Goodrich Co.) purchased the Terre Haute distilleries and obtained exclusive rights under the Weizmann patents (exit the brief involvement of the British War Mission and the

U.S. Air Service). The *American* acquirers in 1919 founded the Commercial Solvents Corp. *of Maryland.* There was no foreign investment involved. In 1928, David Goodrich became chairman of BF Goodrich. (2) In the summer of 1939, it was David Goodrich who recruited Collyer to head the Goodrich company. Collyer—an American—had begun his career in the tire industry in 1923 with the British-owned Dunlop in Buffalo, New York, had joined Dunlop in England in 1929, and by 1939 was a "joint managing director." When Collyer came to Goodrich, the latter was already deeply involved in synthetic rubber research—through the influence of David Goodrich. This story line is developed from Weir, *History of the Distillers Company,* 149, 156; Haynes, *American Chemical Industries,* VI, 85–86; Blackford and Kerr, *BF Goodrich,* 90, 148, 153–154; and data in Cornell University Library manuscript collection on John L. Collyer. Collyer brought to Goodrich experience in the rubber tire business. Dunlop—in Buffalo—was not one of the leading U.S. tire companies and was *not* involved in the wartime synthetic rubber program.

167. Bronfman, ". . . from little acorns," 71.

168. Stoff, *Oil, War, and American Security,* 21–22.

169. Ibid., 26. Harold Ickes first invited Jackson to attend the FOC on March 19, 1942. Ibid., 96n.

170. Ibid., 97.

171. Ibid.; Wilkins, *Maturing,* chaps. 10 and 11.

172. Stoff, *Oil, War and American Security,* 96, 98, 107.

173. Ibid., 104, quoting Sir Frederick Godber of Shell. The oil companies and the British government were particularly uneasy, since the U.S. government was considering developing oil in the Middle East. See, for example, ibid., 98, 108, and passim, and Wilkins, *Maturing,* chap. 11.

174. On Shell's formidable contributions to the war effort, see Beaton, *Enterprise in Oil,* 554ff., 575. In 1942, it was the leading U.S. producer of 100-octane gasoline.

175. Fritz and Karlsson, *SKF,* 210–211 (Doc. no. 60, May 19, 1944, containing the May 16, 1944, statement in full). For the press reports in early May that triggered this statement, see Higham, *Trading with the Enemy,* 126–127.

176. Acc. 61A109, Box 681, and File D-63–1, Acc. 65A1063, Box 267, RG 131 (Dept.-Justice); and Wilkins, "Swiss Investments," 137.

177. Peyer, *Roche,* 132, 150, 152.

178. Ibid., 103–104 (Bobst put in charge and incentive program); 152 (wartime activity; employment figures). According to Peyer, the Swiss executives, Emil Barrell and others, wanted Bobst to deal "only with the American side of the business, leaving research, production and international relations" and general corporate strategies to the Swiss owners. That was unacceptable to Bobst, who had run the U.S. affiliate on his own for years and had overseen its success. Ibid., 152–153. See also Mahoney, *Merchants of Life,* 40, 224.

179. Peyer, *Roche,* 143.

180. G. A. Burchett, Corporate Archivist, GlaxoWellcome, Research Triangle Park, North Carolina, in March 1998, provided me with the following: (1) "1942–1943 Price List of Fine Products" (1941), which has a picture of the Wellcome Building in New York City, which describes the company's products, and from which source the quotation on "Tabloid" comes; (2) The Wellcome Foundation, Ltd., "Post-war Plans," June 1944, typescript, which on p. 5 discusses the New York and Tuckahoe enterprise; and (3) *Wellcome News,* I:1 (Jan. 1944), an internal company publication, which boasts of the Army-Navy "E" flag. On Burroughs Wellcome & Co., I have also used data in the files of John Dunning, University of Reading (henceforth cited as Dunning data). Mahoney, *Merchants of Life,* 111, 113, says Burroughs Wellcome's first U.S. research laboratory was established in Tuckahoe, New York, in 1928. Burroughs Wellcome's sizable U.S. business was *not*

put up as collateral for the RFC loan, probably because the value of these properties divorced from the parent was completely indeterminable. Another reason may have been associated with the British ownership structure: the Wellcome Foundation, a charitable foundation, that also owned the British parent operations, was by World War II the sole owner of Burroughs Wellcome & Co., USA. The Wellcome Foundation, Ltd., "Post-war Plans," 5, 24–25.

181. Haynes, *American Chemical Industry,* VI, 28. On the location, see *Kilgore Committee Hearings,* pt. 6, 774. Also on AMH and Glucose-D, see ibid., pt. 6, 746, 794. Between 1934 and 1941, the U.S. subsidiary of Ayerst, McKenna & Harrison Ltd. had been a joint venture between the Canadian AMH and Glaxo Laboratories (in the United Kingdom), which sold its shares in the U.S. affiliate to the Canadian AMH in 1941 for $224,350. R. P. T. Davenport-Hines, "Glaxo as a Multinational before 1963," in *British Multinationals: Origins, Management and Performance,* ed. Geoffrey Jones (Aldershot: Gower, 1986), 150. The Rouses Point, New York, address, which seems to go back to the 1930s, puzzled me. Why set up a "manufacturing" venture in that location? My "guess" is that this might be related to tariffs; adding extra value across the border would have reduced the value of the product imported into the United States and accordingly lowered the duties paid.

182. Haynes, *American Chemical Industry,* VI, 81; Mahoney, *Merchants of Life,* 227–228 (In 1948 Dr. Paul Müller received a Nobel Prize in medicine for DDT.) The U.S. federal government also produced DDT under license from Geigy, as did Du Pont and some dozen other American companies. Hounshell and Smith, *Science and Corporate Strategy,* 453, 702n.38.

183. Haynes, *American Chemical Industry,* VI, 80–81; data in File D-63–1, Acc. 65A1063, Box 267, RG 131 (Dept.-Justice).

184. Prior to 1941, the National Aniline Division (then called National Aniline & Chemical Co.) had been a subsidiary of Allied Chemical & Dye Corp. Haynes, *American Chemical Industry,* VI, 292. On the dyes for khaki made by the National Aniline Division–Allied Chemical and its other wartime contributions to organic chemistry, see ibid., 296; on the contributions of Allied Chemical's subsidiary Solvay Process Co., ibid., 394–395; Solvay Process Co. became a division of Allied Chemical in 1948, ibid., 391; for the important wartime contributions of the Semet-Solvay Co., also a subsidiary of Allied Chemical, ibid., 370.

185. Wells, *Antitrust and the Formation of the Postwar World,* 212.

186. *Fortune,* Feb. 1946, 122, 172, 175.

187. Selection Trust (Alfred Chester Beatty's investment holding company) had a large interest in American Metal (or possibly Climax Molybdenum); Seymour Bernfeld, "A Short History of American Metal Climax, Inc." in American Metal Climax, Inc., *World Atlas* (New York, n.d. [1962]), 12 (on the awards).

188. Dunning data on Coats' 1943 new plant in Pelham, Georgia, and American Thread's new plant in Clovis, South Carolina (bought in 1945).

189. Flamming, *Creating the Modern South,* 236, 242–245. American Thread, still a subsidiary of English Sewing Cotton, Ltd., in 1945, had five plants in the United States. Dunning data.

190. Dunlop in Buffalo was an authorized "war industrial facility." U.S. Civilian Production Administration, *War Industrial Facilities Authorized, July 1940–August 1945. Listed Alphabetically by Company and Plant Location* (Washington, D.C., 1946). In this report, the "source of public funds and sponsor" for Dunlop was given as "British." On blimps, see *Buffalo Courier Express,* July 25, 1943.

191. U.S. Civilian Production Administration, *War Industrial Facilities,* lists these two companies and indicates that they were involved in war production.

192. Cox, *Global Cigarette,* 326.

193. "Chronicle of Lever Brothers in the United States, 1895–1948," Typescript 1948, "Historical File," Unilever, PLC. For after-tax profits of Lever Brothers Co., Boston, see data from Unilever archives. Gordon Boyce and Simon Ville, *The Development of Modern Business* (New York: Palgrave, 2002), 218–219 (1944 Lux soap advertisements).

194. The best material on NV Philips, the trust agreement, and the Dutch firm's U.S. business during World War II is in Blanken, *History of Philips Electronics,* IV.

195. Ibid., IV, 301–303, 305, 310, 312–314. The practical reasons were not simply antitrust related; the parent of NV Philips was in Nazi-occupied Europe. Interchanges with that parent were not "practical."

196. Ibid., IV, 305. The managing trustees also reduced intracompany loans to Philips' South American and Canadian affiliates, reallocating the funds to the U.S. business operations.

197. Taylor and Baskerville, *Concise History,* 399–400, on the close ties between the two nations.

198. OAPC, *Annual Reports,* passim.

199. Frank H. H. King, *The Hongkong Bank in the Period of Development and Nationalism, 1941–1984, vol. 4, The History of the Hongkong and Shanghai Banking Corporation* (Cambridge: Cambridge University Press, 1991), 27, 937n.4. Before the First World War, A. G. Kellogg, an American citizen, had joined the Hongkong Bank as a local staff person in New York; later he had served the bank in Kobe, Yokohama, Darien, Manila, and Tokyo, returning to New York in 1930. He had become manager of the New York agency in 1937 and would retire in 1948.

200. For example, Dutch bankers informed the OAPC on the cloaked ownership of the American Potash & Chemical Corp. See testimony at U.S. House, Committee on the Judiciary, Subcommittee on Study of Monopoly Power, *Study of Monopoly Power,* Hearings, 81st Cong., 2nd sess., 1950, pt. 5, 36, 84.

201. See Eugene W. Stetson to Allan Sproul, Jan. 6, 1948, French American Banking Corporation, Alpha File, C440, Federal Reserve Bank of New York (FRBNY).

202. French American Banking Corporation, New York, "Memorandum," Mar. 17, 1942, in French American Banking Corporation, Alpha File, C440, FRBNY.

203. Stern, *United States in International Banking,* 195.

204. Reich, *Financier,* 37–42. In the fall of 1944, André Meyer hired George Murnane, whose name is familiar to the reader of this book (as a partner in Monnet & Murnane, as a representative of Solvay & Cie. interests, and as a director of Allied Chemical & Dye, for example) to help rejuvenate Lazard Frères; Murnane would bring the Solvay family account to Lazard Frères, along with other important business. Ibid., 42–43.

205. Roberts, *Schroders,* 295. Roberts writes that in 1930 the London firm represented 62 percent of the combined book value of the New York and London houses, while in 1946, the London house represented merely 34 percent of the combined value. For much of the 1930s and 1940s (as well as the 1950s), the London house had only continued "because of the willingness of the family to support the firm with funds secured on their interest in the New York firm." Ibid., 353.

206. Schull and Gibson, *Scotiabank Story,* 310.

207. The Bank of Montreal would close its Chicago branch in 1952. Denison, *Canada's First Bank,* II, 400. King, *Hongkong Bank,* IV, 489.

208. See OAPC, *AR 1944–1945,* 93–96.

209. *Best's Insurance Reports.*

210. The American merchant marine was by 1945 more than four times its 1939 size. *Commerce Study 1940–1945,* 49. In June 1939, the U.S. fleet accounted for 14.4 percent of the *world's* gross tonnage of ocean shipping, while Britain accounted for 31.0 percent.

As of June 1945, the figures were 52.2 percent for the U.S. fleet and 22.8 for that of Britain. Ibid., 50. For the quoted passage and conclusions, see De La Pedraja, *Rise and Decline of U.S. Merchant Shipping,* 141–153. In 1938, in America's international trade, more British flag ships had cleared American ports than did U.S. flag ships. Symbolically, Morgan's old company, the International Mercantile Marine Co., which over the years had been "not quite American," which had been identified with British (and Dutch) interests, and which had shed its foreign flag ships from the late 1920s onward, finally, on May 21, 1943, gave up its old name, and its subsidiary the United States Lines (which had been its main operating company since 1937) became the replacement. De La Pedraja, *Rise and Decline of U.S. Merchant Shipping,* 128–129.

211. Richard N. Gardner, *Sterling-Dollar Diplomacy in Current Perspective: The Origins and the Prospects of Our International Economic Order,* rev. ed. (New York: McGraw-Hill, 1980), 54.

212. In February 1943, the War Production Board, for example, queried the U.S. Department of Commerce on British long-term investments in the United States. See reply from Hal Lary, Feb. 12, 1943, RG 151 620 UK 1942–, National Archives, Washington, D.C. On the discussions, see Woods, *Changing of the Guard,* 90ff, and Hall, *North American Supply,* 276.

213. McCurrach, "Britain's U.S. Dollar Problems," 362; on the time by which the British had drawn this sum, see Hal B. Lary to Charles O'Donnel, Feb. 12, 1943, RG 151 620 UK 1942–, National Archives.

214. McCurrach, "Britain's U.S. Dollar Problems," 357.

215. The State Department tended to agree; Morgenthau in Treasury was a bit more wary; see Acheson, *Present at the Creation,* 54, for the controversy.

216. Woods, *Changing of the Guard,* 97 (1943 quote); ibid., 95–100; and McCurrach, "Britain's U.S. Dollar Problems," 366 (on the rise of British gold and dollar reserves). Continuing exports, new gold from South Africa, and by late 1943, "out-of-pocket" spending by American troops were the main way the "rot in our [British] reserve position" was stopped. McCurrach, "Britain's U.S. Dollar Problems," 366.

217. Notter, *Postwar Foreign Policy Preparation,* 239; Stoff, *Oil, War, and American Security,* passim.

218. Scottish American Mortgage Co., *Annual Reports,* 1942–1945, Film Z-G2, Reel 56, Bancroft Library, University of California, Berkeley.

219. Ibid. The company's portfolio of securities had the latter listed at market value, and it is likely that this rise reflected, in the main, the appreciation in stock values rather than new purchases.

220. Based on The Texas Land and Mortgage Company, Ltd., *Annual Reports,* 1942–1945, which are on Film Z-G-1, Reel 285, Bancroft Library, University of California, Berkeley.

221. McFarlane, "British Investment in Iowa and Kansas," 190; and Larry A. McFarlane, "British Investment and the Land: Nebraska, 1877–1946," *Business History Review,* 57 (Summer 1983): 266–268.

222. John, *Liverpool Merchant House,* 116, 123, 125.

223. Hicks, *Story of the Forestal,* 22n.

224. *Kilgore Committee Hearings,* pt. 9 (Nov. 14, 1943), 1053, which indicates the complex corporate structure: "Through St. Helen's Ltd., a Canadian corporation, Forestal of England owns substantially all of the stock of Tannin Products Corporation, a Delaware corporation, which in turn owns all the capital stock of Tannin Corporation, a New York corporation."

225. Wilkins, *History,* 256 (the start); Tweedale, *Sheffield Steel and America,* 96, on the ups and downs of this investment in the interwar years and the passive nature of the

investment by 1944. According to Tweedale, the proceeds of the sale ("expected" to be about $1.7 million) were to be invested in Firth Brown Steels in Canada. Ibid., 96, 227n.48.

226. Jones and Wale, "Merchants as Business Groups," 373.

227. Jones, *Merchants to Multinationals,* 101–102 (on the sale of Crown Mills).

228. On Delta and Pine Land Company, see Nelson, *King Cotton's Advocate,* passim. On Delta Planting Company—Delta Farms before 1934—see ibid., 28, 37, 42, 162, 207 (which indicates its sale at the end of World War II). Delta Planting Company in 1937 had an outstanding debt, owned in Holland, see *Fortune,* Mar. 1937, 160, and Wilkins, *History,* 805n.6; it is not clear what happened to this debt when the British sold out their interest.

229. There is some suggestion that with firms that were put up for collateral, the reinvested earnings were part of keeping "the collateral" healthy. Also, since foreign direct investment was measured by book value, appreciation in values was not reflected in the numbers that we have available. On the appreciation in value see Hall, *North American Supply,* 276.

230. Harold James, *International Monetary Cooperation since Bretton Woods* (New York: Oxford University Press, 1996), 53 (forty-five nations).

231. Aalders and Wiebes, *Art of Cloaking,* 121. Resolution VI at Bretton Woods sought to get neutral countries to take steps to prevent the enemy from concealing within their territory valuable enemy assets. See *Foreign Relations of the United States,* 1945, pt. 2, 852, and ibid., 852–933. Resolution VI used the term "enemy" (as there were still "enemies" in 1944). In 1945, the Swiss ambassador objected, emphasizing its neutrality during the entire war; the term enemy was not applicable in the Swiss context. Minister in Switzerland (Harrison) to Secretary of State, Mar. 6, 1945, in ibid., pt. 2, 861. Yet ultimately the Swiss endorsed the "Safehaven Program." Resolution VI is printed in full in *Kilgore Committee Hearings II,* pt. 2, 135–136; see also ibid., pt. 1, 7; pt. 2, 47–56; and pt. 3, 469–492. It is also available in United Nations Monetary and Financial Conference, *Proceedings and Documents of the United Nations Monetary and Financial Conference, Bretton Woods, New Hampshire, July 1–22, 1944* (Washington, D.C., 1948), I, 939.

232. James, *International Monetary Cooperation since Bretton Woods,* passim. See also Mira Wilkins, "Two Literatures, Two Story-Lines: Is a General Paradigm of Foreign Portfolio and Foreign Direct Investment Feasible?" *Transnational Corporations,* 8 (Apr. 1999): 76–77, on the views at Bretton Woods on capital controls.

233. Blum, *From the Morgenthau Diaries,* III, 308, on Churchill's saying in 1944 "England was broke." Woods, *Changing of the Guard,* 155, quoting Churchill in 1944; ibid., 340, on economist John Maynard Keynes and Lord Halifax (the British ambassador to the United States) on the same subject in 1945.

234. McCurrach, "Britain's U.S. Dollar Problems," 367.

235. Blum, *From the Morgenthau Diaries,* III, 269.

236. *Commerce Study 1940–1945,* 214–215. A number of the Canadian issues involved refunding, the redemption of outstanding issues prior to maturity, as Canadian "debtors took advantage of favorable money-market conditions to reduce interest charges and extend maturity." Ibid., 98.

237. Ibid., 189, and 98–99; on the monitoring, see Robert Bothwell, Ian Drummond, and John English, *Canada, 1900–1945* (Toronto: University of Toronto Press, 1987), 364, 366. See also Dominion Bureau of Statistics, *Canada's International Investment Position, Selected Years, 1926 to 1949* (Ottawa, n.d. [1950]); henceforth cited as *Statistics Canada 1950.* The relevant "selected years" were 1939 and 1945.

238. *Commerce Study 1940–1945,* 100.

239. According to Canadian statistics, Canadian portfolio investments in bonds and stocks (excluding Canadian government holdings) in the United States were lower at

year end 1945 than at year end 1939 (year end 1941 figures are not available for private portfolio investments). The same data on Canadian assets in the United States, 1939, 1945 are given in *Statistics Canada 1950,* 39, and Statistics Canada, *Canada's International Investment Position: Historical Statistics 1926 to 1992* (Ottawa, 1993), 55 (henceforth cited as *Statistics Canada 1993*), albeit the 1950 report refers to "official balances in U.S. dollars" and the second to "international reserve assets." (Note balances in dollars would not have been kept in currency form; they were probably invested in U.S. government bonds and notes.) *Statistics Canada 1993,* 67, gives Canadian direct investments in the United States at each year end 1939–1945. These data (in Canadian dollars) give Canadian portfolio investments in the United States as $501 million at year end 1939 and $409 million at year end 1945; Canadian direct investment in the United States $412 million at year end 1939, $414 million at year end 1941, and $455 million at year end 1945. At year end 1939, 51 percent of Canadian direct investment in the United States was in railroads and utilities (with the vast bulk in railroads); at year end 1945 that figure was 47 percent. At year end 1945, the Canadian government's international reserve assets in the United States ("official balances in U.S. dollars") exceeded the total Canadian direct investment and portfolio investment in the United States ($1.3 billion versus $864 million in Canadian dollars). Note that all the Canadian portfolio and direct investment figures exclude the external assets of Canadian banks and insurance companies. Direct investment figures are book value ones and do include reinvested earnings. *Statistics Canada 1950,* 22–23, 25, 40; *Statistics Canada 1993,* 41.

240. *Commerce Study 1940–1945,* 71.

241. The "home bias" literature that helps explain imperfect information in international transactions is useful in understanding this. See Wilkins, "Two Literatures," 83, 87, 99. I say "might have slightly lower returns," for by the 1940s those foreign investors who remained involved in international investments were often highly sophisticated, with excellent financial advisers. The *Commerce Study 1940–1945,* 82, had a different explanation for the slightly lower returns: "The lower yield to foreigners was to be expected since some preferred stocks were included among the issues held by foreigners and because foreign investors have generally preferred high-grade stocks."

242. *Commerce Study 1940–1945,* 71, 224 (definitions).

243. Ibid., 80, points out that "little is known about such reinvested earnings during the war years." Obviously, a better ratio measure, which is not available, would be income to book value rather than outward payments to book value. Other explanations sometimes do, and sometimes do not, relate to performance. There are explanations associated with accounting asymmetries, that is, with noncomparable numbers involved in the comparisons. Also, the book value figures on foreign investments in the United States were always very problematic. Ibid., 81–82.

244. Ibid., 82.

245. In estimate one, the 1941 numbers are the second set of estimates on Table 2.1. For more details on sources, see Appendix 2 (a).

246. The category "other" includes real estate and mortgages as well as a range of "other miscellaneous capital assets." *Commerce Study 1940–1945,* 170. But see how small the "Mortgages and Real Estate" portion was in the *1941 Census* (estimate one); thus mortgages and real estate were not the largest portion of the "other" category. Since I found many of these "miscellaneous investments" did not fit well into my definition of long-term assets, I favored subtracting the "other" category from estimate two to get more realistic numbers.

247. There were no Treasury, Federal Reserve, or Commerce Department figures that included all nationalities for the period December 1941 to December 1945. It is not clear that *in net* there was a substantial decline during 1942–1945 in British holdings of U.S.

securities (because the ones that continued to be held appreciated in value, and this in part offset the divestments). I have good evidence on a drop in real estate mortgages, which the updated section in the Treasury Department report *(1941 Census)* ignored, but the British total in real estate mortgages—according to the census—in June 1941 was merely $9.8 million (see Table 8.3). As for British direct investments, from the start of 1942 through 1945, the few divestments appear to have been offset by increases, based mainly on reinvested earnings. Everyone agrees that by the time of Pearl Harbor, the British "liquidation" process had been virtually completed. *Commerce Study 1940–1945,* 115, and Chapter 8 herein.

248. Barbara Stallings' figures indicate that earlier portfolio investment "outflows" from Latin America to the United States continued, 1941–1945. Stallings, *Banker to the Third World,* 333, and 323–325 (on her sources). She points out that her actual figures for the "negative net lending" in these years may well lack reliability; nonetheless there was clearly "flight capital" from Latin America to the security of the United States and also further repatriation of "foreign debt." *Commerce Study 1940–1945,* 141.

249. See *Commerce Study 1940–1945,* 100, for the rise in inward portfolio investments; see also, ibid., 217–218 (for further details). The Dow Jones industrial average rose 52 points, or 42 percent from December 1941 to August 1945. Data from Dow Jones. The Dow Jones continued to rise from August to December 1945, so the figures I am giving are not symmetrical. Other figures from the Federal Reserve System, *Banking and Monetary Statistics, 1941–1970,* 998, 1001 (explanations) show net foreign purchases of marketable U.S. government bonds and notes and corporate bonds 1942–1945 ($326 million), but net foreign sales of U.S. corporate equities, 1942–1945 ($154 million), netting out to $172 million in foreign purchases of domestic securities. In addition, Federal Reserve data show $118 million in foreign purchases of "foreign securities"—bonds and shares. If these are counted as inflow, there would have been a net increase in foreign portfolio investments of $290 million.

250. I have not been able to locate any overall estimates by nationality on the level of inward foreign investment into the United States for 1945 or 1946. For 1946, I have found figures on "Foreign holdings of United States Corporate Stock, by Selected Countries," in Samuel Pizer and Frederick Cutler, "Record Growth of Foreign Investments," *Survey of Current Business,* Aug. 1957, 29, with the source given as "U.S. Department of Commerce, Office of Business Economics." Widely divergent estimates are available for long-term British investments in the United States at year end 1945 in U.S. Senate, Committee on Banking and Currency, *Anglo-American Financial Agreement, Hearings,* 79th Cong., 2nd sess. (1946), 74 (submitted by Secretary of Treasury Fred M. Vinson) and in McCurrach, "Britain's U.S. Dollar Problems," 369–370. For year end 1945, Vinson put the total British long-term investments as $1,515 million, while McCurrach's estimate was $850 million. See *Statistics Canada 1993,* 55 (levels of foreign direct and portfolio investments in the United States for 1945).

251. In 1941 figures had Dutch stakes larger than Swiss ones (see Table 8.3). The 1950 figures only for foreign direct investment gave the Swiss ones as larger than the Dutch. U.S. Department of Commerce, Office of Business Economics, *Foreign Business Investments in the United States, A Supplement to the Survey of Current Business,* by Samuel Pizer and Zalie V. Warner (Washington, D.C., 1962), 36. And, 1946 figures for Swiss holdings in U.S. corporate stock also put the Swiss ahead of the Dutch. Pizer and Cutler, "Record Growth of Foreign Investments," 29. I use the phrase "at least nominally," for in 1946 Swiss holding companies might be "a front" for other nationalities.

252. Reordering the figures that Vinson gave at the *Anglo-American Financial Agreement, Hearings,* 74, puts British portfolio investments in the United States at $575 million and British direct investments at $940 million at year end 1945. *Statistics Canada 1993,*

55, has (in Canadian dollars) private Canadian portfolio investment in the United States at $409 million and Canadian direct investment at $455 million. (At year end December 1945, the official rate was 90.9 cents per Canadian dollar, while the free rate was 90.7 cents.) Federal Reserve System, *Banking and Monetary Statistics, 1941–1970,* 1036.

10. American Hegemony

1. For a brief review of government controls over long-term capital exports in the 1930s and also the multiplication of exchange controls, see United Nations, *International Capital Movements,* 53–55, 68–70. A good brief summary of British capital controls, 1914 to 1945, is in Cairncross, *Control of Long-term International Capital Movements,* 56–58.

2. Arthur I. Bloomfield "Postwar Control of International Capital Movements" *American Economic Review,* Papers and Proceedings Issue, 36 (May 1946): 687 (italics in original).

3. Quoted in ibid. The Robinson statement came from Joan Robinson, "The United States in the World Economy," *Economic Journal,* 54 (1944): 435–436.

4. Bloomfield, "Postwar Control," 687.

5. I discuss this in Wilkins, "Two Literatures," 76–77. In 2000, economist Stanley Fischer was arguing on the "impossible trinity": (1) stable exchange rates, (2) national monetary policy, and (3) free capital flows. See extracts from his July 26, 2000, address, in *IMF Survey,* 29:15 (July 31, 2000): 241. The Bretton Woods system would incorporate the first two; economists pointed out that the gold standard of 1914 had stable rates and free capital flows, leaving national monetary policy ineffective.

6. U.S. Department of Commerce, Office of Business Economics, *Foreign Business Investments in the United States, A Supplement to the Survey of Current Business,* by Samuel Pizer and Zalie V. Warner (Washington, D.C., 1962), 1.

7. The 1970 percentage figure is based on the $48.7 billion figure on "long-term foreign investments in the United States," given in U.S. Department of Commerce, Bureau of the Census, *Historical Statistics of the United States: Colonial Times to 1970,* Washington, D.C., II 868–869, divided by the GNP, as provided in Series F1, in ibid., I, 224, which gives GNP in 1970 at current prices as $977.1 billion.

8. The contemporary literature on general international economic problems has virtually nothing on foreign investment in the United States. See, for example, Lloyd A. Metzler, Robert Triffin, and Gottfried Haberler, *International Monetary Policies* (Washington, D.C.: Board of Governors of the Federal Reserve System, 1947).

9. See U.S. Senate, Committee on Banking and Currency, *Anglo-American Financial Agreement, Hearings,* 79th Cong., 2nd sess. (1946).

10. McCurrach, "Britain's U.S. Dollar Problems," 364–365; Woods, *Changing of the Guard,* chaps. 10–13.

11. McCurrach, "Britain's U.S. Dollar Problems," 368, reflects this point of view. See also Woods, *Changing of the Guard,* chaps. 8–13; and U.S. Senate, Committee on Banking and Currency, *Anglo-American Financial Agreement, Hearings.*

12. McCurrach, "Britain's U.S. Dollar Problems," 367, had predicted the loan would be satisfied in 1953. Clayton, *British Insurance,* 186 (on the repayment). The RFC itself came to an end in July 1953. Jonathan J. Bean, *Big Government and Affirmative Action: The Scandalous History of the Small Business Administration* (Lexington: University of Kentucky Press, 2001), 9.

13. *Financial Times,* Dec. 6, 1956.

14. In February 1948, the U.S. National Advisory Council on International Monetary and Financial Problems stated that it would not be the policy of the federal government, as a condition for Marshall Plan aid, to force the liquidation of assets in the United States

belonging to foreign nationals. John W. Snyder, Press Release, February 2, 1948, copy in B63562, Archives Economiques et Financieres, Savigny-le-Temple, France. See also Stern, *United States in International Banking,* 86.

15. See, for example, discussions on the International Monetary Fund, the World Bank, the International Trade Organization, the General Agreement on Tariffs and Trade, and the Marshall Plan, in James, *International Monetary Cooperation since Bretton Woods;* Aaronson, *Trade and the American Dream;* Zeiler, *Free Trade, Free World;* and Michael J. Hogan, *The Marshall Plan* (Cambridge: Cambridge University Press, 1987).

16. Mothershead, *Swan Land and Cattle Company,* 154–159.

17. W. M. Pearce, *The Matador Land and Cattle Company* (Norman: University of Oklahoma Press, 1964); Jackson, *Enterprising Scot,* 133–137; John H. Dunning, "British Investment in U.S. Industry," *Moorgate and Wall Street,* Autumn 1961, 12; Reich, *Financier,* 56–59. Robert Fleming, the Scottish founder of the investment trust movement, had taken part in the Matador enterprise in the 1880s. Wilkins, *History,* 301. According to W. G. Kerr, "Scotland and the Texas Mortgage Business," *Economic History Review,* 2nd ser., 16 (Aug. 1963): 103, at the time he was writing, no oil had yet been found on the Matador land.

18. See data on Reel 285, Z-G1, Bancroft Library, University of California, Berkeley. Kerr, writing in the early 1960s, indicated that the London and Aberdeen Investment Trust still did some business in Texas. It had a small office in Midland, Texas, which handled "mineral rights and royalties." Kerr, "Scotland and the Texas Mortgage Business," 103. According to historian Larry McFarlane, the English company Trust and Mortgage Company of Iowa, Ltd. (and its subsidiary Iowa Land Company), "after an erratic career in the Plains states . . . retired its last American investments in 1946." McFarlane, "British Investment in Midwestern Farm Mortgages and Land, 1875–1900: Iowa and Kansas," 190; and McFarlane, "British Investment and the Land," 266–268.

19. On its initial investments, see Wilkins, *History,* 368–369. Linen Thread Co. sold all its shares of its wholly owned U.S. subsidiary, the Linen Thread Co., Inc., to Indian Mills of New York in January 1959. See material in the files of John H. Dunning, University of Reading, Reading, England (henceforth cited as Dunning data); *Financial Times,* Jan. 19, 1959; and *Business Week,* Jan. 31, 1959.

20. Dunning data; Kulik and Bonham, *Rhode Island,* 250 (sold out "about 1961"). The Rhode Island plant at war's end had been one of the largest commission dyeing and finishing works in the United States. Robert L. Tignor, *Egyptian Textiles and British Capital 1930–1956* (Cairo: American University Press, 1989), 70, 142 (based on data from the parent company's annual reports).

21. Burton and Corner, *Investment and Unit Trusts,* 84; Burton and Corner got their figures from a diagram in the *Economist,* Apr. 11, 1953. For figures from the *Economist,* Aug. 12, 1939, based on a sample of sixty-one companies, see Table 2.6 herein; this shows that based on book value, these companies had 14 percent of their portfolio in the United States in 1939. Different samples and measures brought forth different percentages. It is the general range that is significant.

22. Jackson, *Enterprising Scot,* 294. On British interest in American securities in the late 1940s and 1950s and the difficulties in coping with the premium on the dollar-pound exchange rate, see Michie, *London Stock Exchange,* 351, 381, 399, 401 (American brokers in London bought and sold on behalf of British clients in New York).

23. The Labour government was in power from July 1945 to October 1951; the Conservatives won the election of October 25, 1951, and remained in office until the election of October 15, 1964, when the second postwar Labour government won the election. Distribution of investments of Alliance Trust Co., Ltd., "based on valuation," January 31, 1959, is from Bullock, *Story of Investment Companies,* 260; this compared with 17 percent in

1938. On the other hand, in 1914, 83 percent of Alliance Trust Co., Ltd.'s, investments were in the United States (the 83 percent included both mortgages and securities). Wilkins, *History*, 500. The 1959 investments were all in securities. Some of the other continuities were quite extraordinary. The *Financial Times*, Mar. 15, 1996, noted that the Fleming American Investment Trust (the successor to the 1881 Alabama, New Orleans, Texas and Pacific Junction Railways Co., and then to the 1917 Sterling Trust Ltd.) was being charged by the U.S. Environmental Protection Agency for pollution of a site in Slidell, Louisiana. The pollution had occurred in 1882–1902, when the railway company had operated a creosote factory for treating ties (the wooden beams used for holding the rails in place). The original Robert Fleming's investment trusts had been involved in American investments from the 1870s. See Wilkins, *History*, 498.

24. Included among the immediate postwar British discontinuities was that by the British trading company, Alfred Booth, which in 1946 sold its shipping company that provided services between the United States, Britain, and northern Brazil. Jones, *Merchants to Multinationals*, 146. In 1950, Alfred Booth & Co. still had some 600 employees in the United States. Dunning data. Within the next decade, however, it sold its Surpass Leather Company's Philadelphia factory and its Densten Felt and Hair Company and "reverted to its former occupation as suppliers of leather and raw-stock for the American light leather industry." By 1960 it was a small company in America with some 60 employees. John, *Liverpool Merchant House*, 185, and Dunning data (collected July 21, 1961). Another British retreat was the Ferguson-Sherman Mfg. Corp.; it had entered business in the United States in 1939 as a distributor of Ford tractors, Ferguson system. It was not a manufacturer during wartime (Ford Motor Company made the tractors). In 1946–1947, Ford canceled its relationship with the renamed Harry Ferguson Inc. In the spring of 1948, the British-owned Harry Ferguson Inc. found financing within the United States, built a plant to produce tractors in Detroit, and began manufacturing in October 1948. Meanwhile, Harry Ferguson and Harry Ferguson Inc. sued Ford for violating the 1939 agreement and for patent infringement, a case concluded in 1952, in an out-of-court settlement, when Ford paid $9.25 million to Ferguson. In 1953, the Canadian multinational enterprise Massey-Harris purchased the parent tractor company of Harry Ferguson, including Ferguson's U.S. business, so this remained a foreign investment in the United States, but a Canadian one. For the pre-1952 story, see extensive data in *Harry Ferguson and Harry Ferguson, Inc. v. Ford Motor Company, et al.*, in the Ford Archives, esp. Acc. 375, Box 3, and Acc. 536, Box 40, Ford Archives, Dearborn, Michigan. On the Massey-Harris takeover of Ferguson, see Bliss, *Northern Enterprise*, 467.

25. Statistics Canada, *Canada's International Investment Position: Historical Statistics 1926 to 1992* (Ottawa, 1993), 53, 55 (I calculated the percentages).

26. Practically all the "blocked assets" fit into the categories of neutral country assets, assets of enemy-occupied territories, and enemy country assets. One exception was the trivial amount of Russian assets in the United States that had been blocked on June 14, 1941; a general license had been issued on June 24, 1941, two days after Germany invaded Russia, and remained in effect after U.S. entry into the war. For all practical purposes, the limited Russian assets had been deblocked as lend lease had been provided to the Russians and the United States became an ally of the Soviet Union. A Department of Justice press release of June 27, 1953, dealing with the status of foreign assets subject to "Executive Order 8389, as amended" (see Table 8.4 for what was covered under Executive Order 8389, as amended), ignored assets of the USSR. Presumably, the general license of June 24, 1941, "unblocked" these negligible USSR assets.

27. U.S. Senate, Committee on Military Affairs, Subcommittee on War Mobilization, *Elimination of German Resources for War, Hearings*, 79th Cong., 1st and 2nd sess. (1945–1946), pts. 1–10, 55 (henceforth cited as *Kilgore Committee Hearings II*).

28. On the Washington Accord, or Washington Agreement, see *Foreign Relations of the United States: Current Economic Developments 1945–1954, Current Economic Developments,* 49 (May 27, 1946), 4–5 (henceforth cited as CED).

29. CED, 57 (July 22, 1946), 2–3.

30. This point is made by Guex, "The Origins of the Swiss Banking Secrecy Law," 263. For background, see Faith, *Safety in Numbers,* 130–144. The pressure on Swiss banks for disclosure had begun during wartime. See Stern, *United States in International Banking,* 78–79, who does not indicate that the United States finally gave in.

31. Cerutti, "Le blocage des avoirs suisses," 222.

32. On the sale, see AGA, *The AGA Saga.*

33. Cerutti, "Le blocage des avoirs suisses," 225n. I have had conversations with several Swedish economic and business historians on the documents available in Sweden. Fritz and Karlsson, *SKF,* published 102 documents, covering the period from September 26, 1942, to October 6, 1945. In hearings of the U.S. Senate, Committee on the Judiciary, Subcommittee to Investigate the Administration of the Trading with the Enemy Act, *Administration of the Trading with the Enemy Act, Hearings,* 83rd Cong., 1st sess. (1954), 652, an attorney in the Justice Department noted that under a court order, the Swiss corporate successor to I. G. Chemie inspected some 20,000 documents that the Justice Department thought relevant to the determination as to whether the successor was really Swiss. (The hearings are henceforth cited as *Trading with the Enemy Act Hearings*). Higham, *Trading with the Enemy,* 120, who dealt with the reports by Jean Pajus on the alleged German involvements with the Swedish-owned SKF-US, included nothing after the end of 1945. Birgit Karlsson e-mail to Wilkins, Nov. 26, 2001, confirmed that the prior U.S. accusations against SKF-US and the Swedish parent did not impede the unblocking of the assets. On Swedish cloaking before, during, and after the war, see Aalders and Wiebes, *Art of Cloaking* vi–vii (for the many records that they consulted on Swedish "cloaks").

34. Stern, *United States in International Banking,* 84; Stern was writing about blocked bank deposits and also about "custodial securities" held by banks. Custodial securities were foreign-owned securities held by a bank in custody for the foreign investor.

35. On the sale of shares in Air Reduction, which were initially acquired in 1915 by L'Air Liquide and now were a mere 7 percent interest, see Aftalion, *History of the International Chemical Industry,* 267, 290, and data from Patrick Fridenson, June 28, 1995, based on Alain Jemain's as yet unpublished business history of L'Air Liquide. On the Du Pont stock, see note 215 in Chapter 5.

36. The text of General License 95 is in 10 FR 15414 (Dec. 29, 1945), effective for France, Oct. 5, 1945. In B63562 and B63562/1, Archives Economiques et Financieres (henceforth cited as AEF), Savigny-le-Temple, France, there are more than a thousand documents related to the deblocking of the French assets in the United States from 1945 to 1953. My text is based on that material. Especially useful were Guillame Guindey, French Ministry of Finance, to U.S. secretary of the treasury (Fred M. Vinson), Sept. 17, 1945 (on the draft "General License" and confirmation of agreement); conversation held at the [French] Ministry of Finance, June 24, 1946, with [Winthrop] Aldrich, president of Chase National Bank (U.S. banks would provide credit of two to three years at a low rate of interest, guaranteed by French-held American securities so the French could obtain dollars and not have to sell the securities all at once); John W. Snyder, secretary of the Treasury, to Henri Bonnet, French ambassador to the United States, Oct. 30, 1946 (Snyder explained that U.S. Census data are collected on a confidential basis and cannot be released to the French; he realizes that this creates problems on the certification of assets and the unblocking of French properties in the United States); H. Sherwood, acting commissioner of the IRS, to Christian Valensi, financial counsellor of the French embassy,

Feb. 17, 1948 (on the U.S. tax consequence of the July 26, 1946, French decree requisitioning American securities); Office des Changes, Service des Avoir Étrangers to M. Celier, inspecteur des finances, Mar. 11, 1947 (in connection with blocked assets, they have gone through more than 11,000 "dossiers," of which 1,272 were still blocked as of Feb. 23, 1947; few of the latter seem tainted with enemy associations). On February 19, 1948, Littaye, director general de l'Office des Changes, sent to the financial attaché at the French embassy, Washington, a list of more than 500 American securities in which there was French ownership. The securities were those of well-known American companies, and the dollar amounts were small; there were only three securities where the total holdings exceeded $100,000: General Electric ($188,991), Kennecott Copper ($104,687), and Standard Oil of New Jersey ($131,201). Owners were not identified. The archives does not contain a comparable list on FDI (the 1941 census indicated 250 French enterprises in the United States). Likewise, there is no list of holders of U.S., state, or municipal securities, albeit one letter refers to such as "forthcoming." I am deeply indebted to Archivist Laurent Dupuy for his assistance in my use of these French archival materials.

37. Copy of letter, Ministry of Finance to secretary of the treasury, Sept. 17, 1945, in B63562, AEF. The letter continued that "the sequestration measures imposed during the German occupation of France on property rights and interests belonging to nationals of the United States have been removed in all important particulars and any that still remain will be terminated immediately." The fingerprints of American policy makers in these comments are obvious—and, indeed, documents in B63562 show this.

38. Wilkins, "French Multinationals in the United States," 25; Thomas, *Woonsocket: Highlights of History*, chap. 11; and Kulik and Bonham, *Rhode Island*, 24–25, 273–274. It was said (*Kilgore Committee Hearings II*, 319, 336) that the French woolen makers collaborated with the Nazis as a means of preserving family interests and of making profits. The wool makers were family enterprises. The Lefebvre, Prouvost, and Tiberghien families, all of which had business in Rhode Island, apparently diversified internationally (South America, South Africa, Australia, Morocco) to safeguard their assets.

39. *Moody's Manual (Banking) 1950*, 830; data in the Charles Burdick Papers, American Heritage Center, Laramie, Wyoming; and Reich, *Financier*, 243–246, and passim.

40. See L. W. Knoke to Allan Sproul, Dec. 15, 1947, in French American Banking Corporation, 1919–1950, Alpha file, C440, Federal Reserve Bank of New York (henceforth cited as FRBNY), and M. Henri Bonnet (French ambassador to Washington) to Georges Bidault, Ministry of Foreign Affairs, Paris, Feb. 26, 1945, in B63562, AEF, for the French American Banking Corporation's activities on behalf of the French government. This February 26, 1945, letter was written while French assets were still blocked, but the banking corporation operated under a general license, as it had during the war period.

41. Knoke to Sproul, Dec. 15, 1947; Sproul to files, Dec. 17, 1947, in French American Banking Corporation, 1919–1950, Alpha file, C440, FRBNY. Other correspondence in this folder casts light on the activities of the French American Banking Corporation.

42. Conversation held at [French] Ministry of Finance, June 24, 1946, with [Winthrop] Aldrich, president of Chase National Bank, B63562, AEF. Aldrich told the French that Chase, J. P. Morgan, and National City Bank were assisting the Dutch government in the liquidation of American securities.

43. Blanken, *History of Philips Electronics*, IV, 119, 314.

44. Ibid., 314n. There appears to have been some small remaining railroad securities involved. In 1939, Algemeene Trust Maatschappiji still held 118,500 common shares of Chesapeake & Ohio stock. The latter was not dropped from price lists in Amsterdam until 1982. At war's end, some Dutch holdings in the Chicago, Burlington, & Quincy seem to have persisted. Veenendaal found a number of other American railroads were still quoted in Amsterdam in 1939 (and if that was the case, it was likely that there were

Dutch holdings at the time of the German move into Holland in 1940). The Chicago, Rock Island & Pacific redeemed Rock Island, Arkansas & Louisiana bonds in 1952. The Southern Pacific redeemed bonds of the Central Pacific in 1954. Veenendaal suggests that when this occurred there were Dutch holdings to be redeemed. The last Dutch-held share in the Texas & Pacific was sold in 1955. Veenendaal, *Slow Train to Paradise,* 207–267. All in all, however, these remnants of Dutch holdings in U.S. railroad securities did not amount to a great deal. Nonetheless, it is by no means clear that the Dutch government injunction to sell American securities was fulfilled. (Moreover, these railroad securities would have brought very small returns in 1946–1947.)

45. Maxwell's land sales went on until 1963; that year, the name of the company was changed to Maxwell Petroleum Holding NV, which company held stock in one of the Royal Dutch Shell affiliates as well as mineral rights to the 200,000 acres owned by others. Augustus J. Veenendaal, "'Dutch' Towns in the United States of America," in *The Low Countries and Beyond,* ed. Robert S. Kirsner (Lanham, Md.: University Press of America, 1993), 315–321.

46. Wilson, *History of Unilever,* III, 375–377; Beaton, *Enterprise in Oil.*

47. Great Britain, Foreign and Commonwealth Office, History Notes, "British Policy towards Enemy Property during and after the Second World War," *Historians, LRD* no. 13 (Apr. 1998): 23 (www.enemyproperty.gov.UK, accessed in 1999; henceforth cited as "British Policy"). The pagination given here is as of 1999, when I first used the material.

48. "Chronicle of Lever Brothers in the United States, 1895–1948," Typescript 1948, Historical Files, Unilever, PLC. When Lever Brothers in 1944 acquired Pepsodent, with that acquisition came Charles Luckman, who became head of the Pepsodent division of Lever Brothers Co.; on July 1, 1946, he became president of Lever Brothers Co., replacing the retired, longtime, extraordinarily successful Francis A. Countway. In 1946, with Unilever's full ownership and control, the ownership of Lipton in the United States became 100 percent "Dutch." By the late 1930s, Unilever (London) was already playing a role in the management of Thomas J. Lipton Inc. When, in January 1939, Sir George Ernest Schuster had resigned from the board of Thomas J. Lipton Inc., Unilever (London) had been involved in installing new management; that management was clearly American. The Unilever Minutes of the Managing Directors Conference, Jan. 12, 1939, noted that Countway had the matter in hand. Minutes, BB46, Unilever Archives, London. In September 1940, Thomas J. Lipton, Inc. had acquired 100 percent ownership of the American company Continental Foods, Inc., a manufacturer and seller of dried soups. Lipton dismantled Continental Foods' Chicago plant and moved the operations to the Lipton factory and main operations in New Jersey; Continental Foods in March 1942 had purchased the plant and equipment of Thomas J. Sweet Company, Albion, New York, for use in manufacturing dehydrated foods, principally the soup lines—Lipton Noodle Soup and Lipton Tomato Vegetable Soup Mix. "History Outline on Thomas J. Lipton, Inc., Hoboken, New Jersey," Dec. 2, 1947, Unilever Archives.

49. See Priest, "The 'Americanization' of Shell Oil," 192.

50. Data on Lever and Lipton from Unilever Archives, with assistance from Geoffrey Jones, who is writing a history of Unilever. Although Lord Inverforth (1931–1937) and then Schuster (1937–1939) had been presidents of Lipton Inc., the company had long been run by Americans. On Shell, see Priest, "'Americanization' of Shell Oil," 188.

51. See Department of Justice press release, June 27, 1953, which reported that "the Attorney General, Herbert Brownell, today announced the removal of all remaining World War 2 freezing controls" for the thirteen European countries and Japan. It indicated that still subject to controls, under Executive Order 8389, as amended, were Bulgaria, Hungary, Roumania, Yugoslavia, Czechoslovakia, Poland, Estonia, Latvia, and Lithuania, as well as eastern Germany.

52. Mahvash Alerassool, *Freezing Assets* (New York: St. Martin's Press, 1993), 11, 13. See also 47 FR 12339 (Mar. 23, 1982), in 31 CFR 520.103 (1993); certain Eastern European assets would be unblocked under the International Claims Settlement Act of 1949 (and its amendments), including some (or all) of the assets of Yugoslavia (1954, 1969), Bulgaria, Hungary, and Roumania (1959), and Poland (1966). U.S. Comptroller General, Report to Congress, "Treasury Should Keep Better Track of Foreign Assets" (Washington, D.C., Nov. 14, 1980), 61.

53. Stern, *United States in International Banking,* 273, and Department of Justice press release, June 27, 1953.

54. Office of Alien Property Custodian, *Annual Report 1944–1945,* 7 (henceforth cited as OAPC, *AR 1944–45* or with the appropriate dates). Vesting of Austrian properties had been formally discontinued by 1944–1945, except if it was found that the Austrians acted on behalf of the enemy.

55. Wilkins, "Japanese Multinationals," 599–600.

56. U.S. Senate, Committee on Military Affairs, Subcommittee on War Mobilization, *Scientific and Technical Mobilization, Hearings,* 78th Cong., 1st and 2nd sess. (1943–1944), pt. 16 (Aug. 29, 1944), 1967 (henceforth cited as *Kilgore Committee Hearings*).

57. Testimony of William L. Clayton, Assistant Secretary of State, June 25, 1945, *Kilgore Committee Hearings II,* pt. 2, 47–49; Faith, *Safety in Numbers,* 125ff.

58. June 22, 1945, Statement of Elbert D. Thomas, Utah, Chairman of the Committee on Military Affairs, providing the mandate for the second round of Kilgore Committee Hearings, *Kilgore Committee Hearings II,* pt. 1, 1.

59. OAPC, *AR 1945–1946,* 13–14; John Gimbel, *Science, Technology, and Reparations: Exploitation and Plunder in Postwar Germany* (Stanford, Calif.: Stanford University Press, 1990), on German "technological assets."

60. Kindleberger, *Financial History of Western Europe,* 409.

61. The agreement is in *American Journal of International Law, Supplement* 40, no. 4 (1946): 117–134; Article 6A is on p. 122. The whole complicated reparation issue and how it was handled in this basic agreement is discussed in Henry P. DeVries, "The International Responsibility of the United States for Vested German Assets," *American Journal of International Law,* 51, no. 1 (Jan. 1957): 18–28; ibid., 21n.13 (specifically on Article 6C).

62. The transfer was pursuant to Executive Order 9788; see OAPC, *AR 1945–1946,* iv; on the expanded vesting, ibid., 15–16.

63. Ibid., 1–2.

64. When the British embassy in 1953 inquired about how much property had been released under this act, the U.S. government responded, according to a British report, that the sum was $12.5 million of the $388 million vested. "British Policy," 33–34.

65. "History," in National Archives and Records Administration (NARA) description of the Records of the Office of Foreign Assets Control, RG 265.

66. On Morgenthau's resignation a few months after the April 12, 1945, death of President Roosevelt, see his "personal note," in Blum, *From the Morgenthau Diaries,* I, xvi, and Blum, *From the Morgenthau Diaries,* I, xvi, and Blum, *From the Morgenthau Diaries,* III, 421–476. See also McCullough, *Truman,* 404, 507.

67. In December 1992, I used the voluminous Record Group 131 documents at the Justice Department, Washington, D.C., made available under the Freedom of Information Act, which included the activities of this Office of Alien Property; I found in this collection many records and investigations undertaken earlier by the Treasury Department's Foreign Funds Control Department; clearly, the Justice Department used this material in its further investigations. Hans-Dieter Kreikamp, *Deutsches Vermögen in den Vereinigten Staaten* (Stuttgart: Deutsche Verlags-Anstalt, 1979), 38 (more vesting orders: 7,906 versus 11,200 vesting orders). Executive Order 9989, 13 FR 4891 (Aug. 20, 1948), indicated

that the remaining blocked assets were transferred to Office of Alien Property, Department of Justice; see also Lyle J. Holverstott and Fred L. Miller, "Preliminary Inventory of the Records of the Foreign Funds Control (Record Group 265)," Washington, D.C., 1962 (on the sequencing from Foreign Funds Control, Department of Treasury, to the Office of Alien Property, Department of Justice). When the new wave of blocking began in December 1950 of Chinese and North Korean assets (associated with the Korean war), these were handled by a *newly created* Division of Foreign Assets Control, Office of International Finance, in the Treasury Department (this office existed from 1950 to 1962, to be followed by the Office of Foreign Assets Control, Treasury Department). U.S. Department of the Treasury, *Foreign Assets Control: Regulations and Related Documents* (Washington, D.C., 1954), and "History," NARA description.

68. See Article 14, 2 (I). The treaty was signed September 8, 1951, effective April 28, 1952. The text is published in the *American Journal of International Law, Suppl.,* 46, no. 3 (July 1952): 71–86, with the relevant article on p. 77; see also U.S. Department of State, *United States Treaties and Other International Agreements* (Washington, D.C., 1952), III, pt., 3, 3180–3183. Aaron Forsberg, *America and the Japanese Miracle: The Cold War Context of Japan's Postwar Economic Revival, 1950–1960* (Chapel Hill: University of North Carolina Press, 2000), 57–58, 70–71 (on the reparations program as it affected Japan and the treaty considerations).

69. The Superintendent of Banks (California), *Annual Report for 1953,* reported on the liquidation of prewar Japanese banks in that state, while admitting the same banks (or their successors) to post–World War II business in the state. Wilkins, "Japanese Multinationals," 602.

70. Aalders and Wiebes, *Art of Cloaking,* 119–121, 150–152; OAPC, *AR 1945–1946,* 62. On the Swedish-Soviet-U.S. issues involved, see Aalders and Wiebes, *Art of Cloaking,* 107–117, 142–150, and, more specifically, Aalders and Wiebes, "Stockholms Enskilda Bank," 25–26, 49–50. The board of Enskilda decided to accept the settlement offer on April 27, 1950, before the outbreak of the Korean War. According to Aalders and Wiebes, *Art of Cloaking,* 152, in the sale of the shares more than the settlement sum had been obtained, and the extra went to the U.S. War Claims Commission to be included in the general pool of assets available to satisfy war claims. For the performance of the War Claims Commission and the war claims arising out of World War II, see U.S. House, *War Claims Arising Out of World War II,* H. Doc. 67, 83rd Cong., 1st sess. (Jan. 16, 1953). On July 16, 1945, three Swedish companies, Atlas, Svenska Veritas, and Atlantica, filed claims with the Alien Property Custodian, asserting that they, not Munich Reinsurance, were owners of the shares of Pilot Reinsurance Company at the time of the vesting. OAPC, *AR 1945–46,* 85, 205.

71. *Kilgore Committee Hearings II,* pt. 5, 888. In Germany, in connection with the Nuremberg trials of Nazi industrialists, there was a full month of questioning of Kurt Freiherr von Schroeder (Nov. 7, 1945 to Dec. 3, 1945), who had joined the board of AKU in 1938 or 1939; he discussed with the investigators (one of whom was Jean Pajus, who was so important in the SKF inquiries) the relationship of the German rayon company Vereinigte Glanzstoff-Fabriken and AKU and the latter's American subsidiaries; see in particular the interrogations on Nov. 21, 1945, RG 238, T301, NI-239, Reel 3, pp. 5–18, and on Nov. 23, 1945, RG 238, T301, NI-240, Reel 3, pp. 1–2. On AKU and its U.S. subsidiaries, see also Haynes, *American Chemical Industry,* VI, 16, 311, and Markham, *Competition,* 212. For the Harold James quotation, see Gall et al., *Deutsche Bank,* 381.

72. OAPC, *AR 1945–1946,* 78n. Decision in *Heyden Chemical Corporation v. Clark, Attorney General,* 85 F. Supp. 949 (SDNY Oct. 23, 1948). Mahoney, *Merchants of Life,* 259. The March 6, 1952, sale was made to a group consisting of (1) Merrill Lynch, Pierce, Fenner and Beane; (2) Kidder, Peabody & Co.; and (3) Drexel & Co. These firms took Schering

public, with an offering of 1,760,000 shares. Schering Corporation employees acquired shares at this time. Julius Weltzien, the prewar head of Schering Corporation, died in 1953. Schering's historian, Christopher Kobrak, "Between Nationalism and Internationalism," 702, does not tell us whether Weltzien acquired shares in Schering Corporation in the public offering.

73. Stopford, *Directory of Multinationals,* II, 1195–1196. Not until 1988 was the German parent able to reacquire rights to the Schering name in the United States.

74. Wilkins, *History,* 384, 399–400; Chapter 1 of the present volume; James E. Markham did not include it as a company that had reverted to German ownership (see Table 9.2 herein).

75. See OAPC, *AR 1945–1946,* 79–81.

76. See Peyton Ford, Assistant to the Attorney General, to C. Murray Bernhardt, General Counsel, Subcommittee on Study of Monopoly Power, Oct. 11, 1949, in U.S. House, Committee on the Judiciary, Subcommittee on Study of Monopoly Power, *Study of Monopoly Power, Hearings,* 81st Cong., 1st sess. (1950), Serial No. 14, Part 2-B, 1457–1459.

77. See Larson, Knowlton, and Popple, *New Horizons,* 560–561, and Bennett Wall, *Growth in a Changing Environment* (New York: McGraw-Hill, 1988), xliii (Wall says "most of the patents" were returned, but some 2,000 patents were affected by the Hague Agreement, and the tabulation in Larson, Knowlton, and Popple, *New Horizons,* 561, does not seem to fit under the rubric "most").

78. DeVries, "International Responsibility of the United States for Vested German Assets," 18–21; Charles Wesley Harris, "International Relations and the Disposition of Alien Enemy Property Seized by the United States during World War II: A Case Study on German Properties," *Journal of Politics,* 23 (Nov. 1961): 641–666; and Kreikamp, *Deutsches Vermögen in den Vereinigten Staaten,* passim; Kreikamp's excellent 315-page volume is on 1952–1962 discussions of prewar and wartime German assets in the United States. See also *Trading with the Enemy Act Hearings.*

79. The U.S. government appointed the management of the company. In November 1945, the large 1929 bond issue of the company was called in and redeemed. The company continued to operate, meeting its general obligations. There is a vast amount of material on this case in RG 131 (Dept.-Justice) and elsewhere. The writings on the postwar litigation are extensive, much of it before the resolution: for the late 1950s and early 1960s status, see, for example, Erdman, *Swiss-American Economic Relations,* 158–167, and Harris, "International Relations and the Disposition of Alien Enemy Property," 656–662. General Dyestuff Corp. went through a separate litigation process, until 1953 when the Department of Justice merged it into GAF. See *New York Times,* Nov. 6, 1953 (on the merger).

80. Raymond Stokes, *Divide and Prosper* (Berkeley: University of California Press, 1988).

81. H.G., "Settlement of the Interhandel Case," *American Journal of International Law,* 59, no. 1 (Jan. 1965): 97–98, a lawyer's description of the steps in the sixteen-year litigation, referring back to the many articles in the *American Journal of International Law* that dealt with the twists and turns in the case. See also Kreikamp, *Deutsches Vermögen in den Vereinigten Staaten,* passim; Faith, *Safety in Numbers,* 158–177; and Joseph Borkin, *The Crime and Punishment of I. G. Farben,* 206ff. Over the years, GAF would fall in rank in the U.S. chemical industry; in 1978, it divested its photo, dyes, and felt division and sold to BASF Wyandotte Corporation (now BASF Corporation) the original Bayer—General Aniline Works—in Rensselaer, New York. Richard Leader, "113 Years of Dyes in Rensselaer," *Chemical Heritage,* 12 (Summer 1995): 23. Thus, a successor to I. G. Farben did in time regain a part of the lost properties. But long before 1978, indeed before 1965, BASF, Bayer, and Hoechst would be establishing new beginnings in the United States.

82. With the 1965 settlement, from a *U.S.* standpoint, the matter of Interhandel was over. For the Swiss side of the story and the subsequent (and earlier) history of Interhandel, see Mario König, *Interhandel. Die Schweizerische Holding der IG Farben und ihre Metamorphosen–eine Affäre um Eigentum und Interessen (1910–1999),* Independent Commission of Experts Switzerland, vol. 2 (Zurich: Chronos, 2001). After the war, I. G. Farben had remained as a paper company ("in dissolution") to handle residual liquidation matters and to cope with any legal proceedings connected with the old firm. In time, however, in a rather extraordinary twist, the liquidators of I. G. Farben sought to share in Interhandel's proceeds from the GAF securities sale. König writes that in 2000 a crucial 1946 Swiss report on Interhandel was still classified and that legal proceedings involving the German-Swiss connections were still continuing. Historian Harm Schröter told Mira Wilkins (July 2002) that after German unification occurred in 1990, I. G. Farben liquidators made claims for certain East German properties (claims that were either turned down or withdrawn); it was the interest in those assets that had encouraged I. G. Farben to go after the possible assets in Switzerland, that is, those of Interhandel.

83. With the Korean War, the new wave of freezes (including Chinese and North Korean assets) had been handled first by the newly created Division of Foreign Assets Control, Office of International Finance, Treasury Department (1950–1962), and then by its successor, the Office of Foreign Assets Control, Treasury Department. It was the Office of Foreign Assets Control, Treasury Department, that after 1966 had authority over the assets (mainly Eastern European ones) that had not yet been unfrozen from 1940–1941 blockages. The Comptroller General Report to the Congress, "Treasury Should Keep Better Track of Blocked Foreign Assets," Nov. 14, 1980, 5, says that the Foreign Funds Control Department, Treasury Department, was the "forerunner" to the Office of Foreign Assets Control, which was the case, *but with the interim agencies in between.* The early part of the historical sequence on the agencies is provided in the National Archives description of RG 265, in Holverstott and Miller, "Preliminary Inventory," and confirmed by the U.S. Department of the Treasury, *Foreign Assets Control.* Within the Justice Department, a small office remained that would handle certain residual litigation in connection with World War I and World War II activities; I dealt with that "skeleton" office in 1992 when I wanted access to documents in RG 131, National Archives, that were still in the "legal custody" of the Department of Justice.

84. Alerassool, *Freezing Assets,* 11.

85. See executive order in 60 FR 3,725 (1995).

86. The new group of blocked assets arose out of the political environment in post–World War II America—the Korean War, Castro's takeover in Cuba, and so forth.

87. In 1948 alone, Attorney General Tom Clark filed antitrust suits against almost half of the nation's largest 100 corporations. Freyer, *Regulating Big Business,* 230. Foreign-owned firms were included as defendants in a large number of cases.

88. Wilkins, *Maturing,* 292–300.

89. On the extension in 1946 of the SKF voting trust for antitrust reasons, see Karlsson, "Fascism and Production of Ball-bearings."

90. There were similar questions about subpoenas directed at Imperial Chemical Industries. On Philips, I have had (in the spring of 2001) useful discussions with I. J. Blanken, historian of NV Philips. In the case of the Swedish company SKF, no board member of the parent company was allowed to travel to the United States for a period of time, so as to avoid the accusation that the parent "maintained activity with the USA." Karlsson, "Fascism and the Production of Ball-Bearings." For the legal issues, see David G. Gill, "Problems of Foreign Discovery," in Kingman Brewster, Jr., *Antitrust and American Business Abroad* (New York: McGraw-Hill, 1958), 474–488, esp. 482 (on general questions, affecting both outward *and* inward foreign direct investments). Yergin, *Prize,* 473–474,

has excellent material on the Justice Department's interest in going after Shell, Anglo-Iranian, and the French company CFP; the British government ordered Anglo-Iranian and Shell not to cooperate with the Justice Department's "Witch-hunt." The Dutch and the French governments also protested. The quotation in the text is from ibid., 473. Gill's piece deals with Swiss government secrecy rules, as well as those of the other governments.

91. Wilkins, *History,* 289–292 (on Shell); Cox, *Global Cigarette, passim.*

92. See Wilkins, *History,* 283–284, and Chapter 1 of the present volume.

93. For the consequences, see Hart, *Forged Consensus,* 95–96, and Alfred D. Chandler Jr., *Inventing the Electronic Century* (New York: Free Press, 2001), 34.

94. As taxes rose in the United States and abroad, the tax evasion policy concerns were numerous and diffuse. Sometimes the U.S. ones related to Americans going through foreign shells and then making inward "foreign" investments in the United States; other times, they were associated with the mysteries of "flight capital" and the awareness that nominal and beneficial ownership were far from identical; still other times, foreign investors seemed able to escape the tax penalties that could be imposed on domestic investors. The rise of tax haven countries in the interwar period contributed to the disquiet.

95. State and municipal bonds often carried low interest rates because the interest was tax deductible; this benefit was more advantageous for Americans than for foreign investors. It has been argued that this was reason there was so little inward FPI in state and municipal securities. Here tax made a difference for FPI, but not for FDI.

96. Some of the blockages of foreign assets in the United States, for example, were resolved within a year. As for the long-standing state alien landownership laws, these typically did not cover corporate ownership, so all a foreign investor needed to do was to set up a corporation in an American state; the foreign investor could own all the shares in the corporation, which in turn acquired the land. When Shell Oil wanted to build a refinery in the state of Washington (in 1953), it was successful in lobbying for an amendment to the state constitution, which dropped the prohibition against alien landownership. Priest, "'Americanization' of Shell Oil," 197. Although the matter of state laws and constitutional provisions against alien landownership arose periodically, and concerned investors and their lawyers, and there is an enormous literature on alien land laws, I know of no instance during the years 1914 to 1945 where such laws or constitutional requirements actually prevented foreign direct (or portfolio) investments in the United States. There were no federal alien property laws, 1914–1945, unless one includes the Mineral Lands Leasing Act.

97. For example, foreign banks could not have branches in New York, only agencies. Eventually, however, as First National City Bank and Chase Manhattan were pushing their own banking abroad, they encountered complaints that foreign banks could not branch in New York, so why let the American banks branch in Japan or in Latin America? Reciprocity had seemed a necessity; the large New York banks campaigned successfully for a law to permit foreign banks to have branches in New York. The New York State legislature complied, and the legislation took effect in 1961. Francis A. Lees, *Foreign Banking and Investment in the United States* (London: Macmillan, 1976), 12; and Adrian E. Tschoegl, "Foreign Banks in the United States since World War II," in Jones and Gálvez-Muñoz, *Foreign Multinationals in the United States,* 155.

98. There were, of course, restrictions on the allocation of earnings of firms put up for collateral under the RFC loan, but they came to an end when the loan was paid off.

99. For example, Romer, "What Ended the Great Depression" 757–784, and Barry Eichengreen, "U.S. Foreign Financial Relations in the Twentieth Century," in *Cambridge Economic History,* ed. Stanley Engerman and Robert Gallman (Cambridge: Cambridge

University Press, 2000), 488. In this discussion, I have been influenced by Fishlow, "Debt," 383–439, who stressed the importance of the "use that borrowing countries made of international finance."

100. This point was emphasized in the very influential Stephen Hymer, *The International Operations of National Firms: A Study of Direct Foreign Investment* (Cambridge, Mass.: MIT Press, 1976), chap. 1. (This was Hymer's 1960 Ph.D. dissertation, which was published after his death.) Hymer did allow that there could be cross-investments with portfolio investments, when risk, uncertainty and barriers to movement were introduced, but he did not devote time to discussing these imperfections of capital markets; rather, he insisted FDI was different and that cross-investments were typical of FDI.

101. Indeed, in 1789, more than one-fifth of America's federal government debt had been denominated in foreign currencies. This "foreign debt" (as it was called by contemporaries) was entirely paid off by 1810. Wilkins, *History*, 31–32, 35.

102. Bordo, Meissner, and Redish, "How 'Original Sin' was Overcome."

103. I added "virtually" no exceptions, because there just might have been some leftover securities (from the pre–World War I era) denominated in a foreign currency, since some railroad bonds had maturities that went into the late twentieth and twenty-first centuries; but these were unquestionably rarities.

104. I have profited greatly from the insights of Michael Bordo.

105. Hymer, *International Operations of National Firms*, 22–23, on symmetries in industries. He does not discuss textiles. On machinery he gives Moore Business Forms as an example of inward U.S. FDI, but its main business was not that of *machinery*, although it did as a sideline make some printing equipment. By contrast, with the work of Hymer, John Dunning found major asymmetry in the bilateral cross-FDIs between the United States and the United Kingdom. In his studies of American investment in the United Kingdom and British investment in the United States, which were roughly coincidental in time with those of Hymer's findings (late 1950s), Dunning discovered that "the industrial composition of U.K. direct investment in U.S. was very different from that of U.S. direct investment in the U.K." See his retrospect: John H. Dunning, "Perspectives on International Business Research: A Professional Autobiography," *Journal of International Business Studies*, 33 (2002); 820. For U.S. outward FDI, see Wilkins, *Maturing*.

106. The complex and diverse interrelationships between FPI and FDI appear not to be confined to U.S. inward (and outward) investments but are part of a global story. As I have written elsewhere on the more general issue, "On the sequence of FDI and FPI: I am not satisfied that there is any discernible sequence in global FDI and FPI over the past decades, much less century (centuries). The two types of foreign investment have long existed side by side, albeit in different ratios in different countries and different periods. Whether we are measuring inward or outward investment, there seem to have been variations in sequencing, proportions, and inward/outward ratios over time." Wilkins. "Two Literatures," 102.

107. America's new postwar leadership role and new outward foreign investments spurred such inquiries. The Library of Congress collected materials on the British role in the nineteenth-century development of the American West, including (casually) the investments of other nationalities. The best bibliography, including the various microfilm collections and their location, is in Ostrye, *Foreign Investment;* see also Wilkins, *History*.

108. Some of the earliest postwar writings with this theme were H. O. Brayer, "The Influence of British Capital on the Western Range Cattle Industry," *Journal of Economic History, Supplement*, 9 (1949): 85–98; and Leland Jenks, "Britain and American Railway Development," *Journal of Economic History*, 11 (Autumn 1951): 375–88.

109. Dominion Bureau of Statistics, *Canada's International Investment Position, Selected Years, 1926 to 1949* (Ottawa, n.d. [1950]), 22–23, 40 (important direct investments in rail-

roads). In 1999, the two principal Canadian railroads (the Canadian Pacific and the Canadian National) ranked among the top ten nonfinancial Canadian businesses. In 1998, the Canadian National bought the Illinois Central Railroad. In 1999, the Canadian Pacific and the Canadian National each had in excess of $3 billion in U.S. assets. Graham D. Taylor, "Canadian Companies in the United States," in Jones and Gálvez-Muñoz, *Foreign Multinationals in the United States,* 72, 75.

110. Similarly, Dutch mortgage lending seems to have come to a close. Gales and Sluyterman, "Dutch Free-Standing Companies," 310–311, 316, where they show a decline in the Dutch mortgage banks' lending in the years after 1917. Yet mortgage lending by foreign investors did not disappear. It would, in fact, resurface.

111. For example, see Clark Spence, *British Investments in the American Mining Frontier, 1860–1901* (Ithaca, N.Y.: Cornell University Press, 1958). The British Mountain Copper Co., Ltd., in California (formed December 1, 1896, but not included in the Spence volume), did mine copper at Iron Mountain and in the vicinity until about 1930; it also mined other minerals as well: pyrite, gold, silver, and zinc. It closed down as late as 1963. See Dahl, "British Investment in California Mining, 1870–1890," 250, 257–264 (the title of this dissertation notwithstanding, it did cover the twentieth-century operations of Mountain Copper Co. Ltd.); and U.S. Environmental Protection Agency, Region 9, News Release, "U.S., California Announce Long-Term Settlement for Iron Mountain Mine," Oct. 19, 2000 (site history). In 1962, when briefly recounting the history of foreign direct investments in the United States, the Commerce Department included "mining (especially copper)" as part of the no longer existing interests of times long in the past. U.S. Department of Commerce, Office of Business Economics, *Foreign Business Investments in the United States* (1962), 7. See also Wilkins, *History,* 267–269, and Chapter 2 of the present book. There were continuities in potash and borax. One continuity in the mineral industries—from 1930 (thus, not part of the frontier investments) into the immediate postwar years—was that of Alfred Chester Beatty's interest in American Metal/Climax Molydenum: in the mid-1970s, his family's Selection Trust held 12 percent of the stock in American Metal Climax and was the largest single stockholder; his son sat on the board of AMAX. Navin, *Copper Mining and Management,* 277n.

112. Delta Pine and Land Company continued as British owned until 1978, when its U.S. management purchased the British interests. Data from the company, May 26, 1999. Another sizable property, acquired in 1920, some 29,600 acres, in northern Florida (owned by Andrew Weir & Co.), also remained in British hands in the post–World War II years. Wilkins, *New Foreign Enterprise in Florida,* 12.

113. Yet far more than in mortgage lending, in the second half of the twentieth century foreign direct investors would once again participate in a significant manner in copper mining in the American West; there was a thread of continuity in these cases, since the investments were made by foreign multinational enterprises (such as RTZ) whose predecessor companies had had U.S. direct investments.

114. John Dunning, "Revisiting UK FDI in US Manufacturing and Extractive Industries in 1960," in Jones and Gálvez-Muñoz, *Foreign Multinationals in the United States,* 56. According to Dunning, J. & P. Coats had 5,568 employees in the United States in 1960 (compared with more than 6,200 in 1950), while English Sewing Company's American Thread Co. had 4,940 employees in the United States in 1960 (compared with 5,500 in 1950). Ibid., and Dunning data. By contrast, Shell Oil, the leader among foreign investors in U.S. employment, had 31,000 employees by 1952 and 35,600 employees in 1960 in the United States. Priest, "'Americanization' of Shell Oil," 193, provides the 1952 figure; Dunning, "Revisiting," 56, gives the 1960 employment.

115. David Keir, "The Coats Story," Typescript 1964, vol. 4, 74 (access granted by Coats). Keir indicates that the research was on cotton, silk, rayon, nylon, Saran, Orlon,

Fibre V, and other synthetics. Already in the pre–World War II years, a Coats affiliate (Clark Thread Company) had set up a thread fellowship at Mellon Institute in Pittsburgh to facilitate research on the product; after the war, it provided funding for three fellowships at MIT, hoping to encourage textile research.

116. Nelson, *King Cotton's Advocate,* 157.

117. Wilkins, *History,* 607.

118. I thought perhaps, in 1945, Canada might be a larger recipient of inward foreign investment than the United States; it would be the only possible rival. Yet, if in 1945 inward long-term foreign investment in the United States was $7.9 billion (see Table 10.1) and inward long-term foreign investment in Canada was $7.0 billion (Canadian dollars), the United States was in first place (the Canadian figures are from Statistics Canada, *Canada's International Investment Position: Historical Statistics 1926 to 1992,* 54, and include both inward direct and portfolio investments). If "other debt" and "other liabilities" are added to the Canadian total, the amount comes to $8.1 billion (Canadian dollars), which at the then current rate of exchange would be $7.3 billion (U.S. dollars), so even that would be a lesser sum. If we consider only FDI, using the same sources, the U.S. inward FDI was estimated at $2.7 billion, while the Canadian inward FDI was $2.8 billion (Canadian dollars), which translates to $2.5 billion (U.S. dollars). Thus, assuming the accuracy of these figures, in 1945 the United States was a larger host than Canada to inward FDI as well as to overall inward long-term foreign investment.

119. They begin to reappear in the early 1950s.

120. This can be seen by comparing Tables 1.14 and 10.1. Column G in each of these tables is on "government borrowings." The increase is all in federal government issues, not state and local government bonds.

121. Reich, *Financier,* passim. André Meyer, who had been with the French house before the war and had come to America during the war, emigrated, became a U.S. citizen, and sustained the firm's close relationship with the French house. Ibid., 218, 54. Pierre David-Weill, from the French firm, who had also spent the war years in the United States, returned to France after the war. Ibid., 39, 41, 311. In 1950, Lazard Frères, New York, did not rank among the top twenty underwriting firms in the United States; it would achieve that rank after 1955. Samuel L. Hayes III, A. Michael Spence, and David Van Praag Marks, *Competition in the Investment Banking Industry* (Cambridge, Mass.: Harvard University Press, 1983), 118.

122. It ranked sixteen among the top twenty underwriting firms in the *U.S.* market in 1950. Hayes, Spence, and Marks, *Competition in the Investment Banking Industry,* 119.

123. Part of this was because of the tax laws and part was because free-standing companies no longer served a needed function, since America was a capital-rich country. For more on free-standing companies, see Wilkins, "Free-Standing Company," 259–282, and Wilkins and Schröter, *Free-Standing Company in the World Economy.*

124. Wilkins, *History,* 330.

125. Ibid., 621, gives the industries for 1914. Chandler, *Scale and Scope,* 651, ranks Schenley Industries (no. 37) ahead of Joseph E. Seagram & Sons, Inc. (no. 45) in assets in 1948; my data indicate that Seagrams had larger U.S. whiskey *sales* in 1945 than Schenley.

126. Wilkins, *History,* 464–465.

127. Based on data from New York State, Banking Department, *Annual Reports,* and the Web site of the New York State Banking Department. The number had reached a peak of thirty-eight at year end 1923.

128. Wilkins, *History,* 457–458; in 1952 it would close its Chicago branch, substituting a representative office. Denison, *Canada's First Bank,* II, 400. Later, under a 1973 Illinois law, it would reopen its branch. By the spring of 2002, the Bank of Montreal was in the midst of a major expansion in Chicago, enlarging its presence to 200 branches. *Miami Herald,* July 12, 2002.

129. See the Lipton sign in the upper-left-hand corner of an undated picture (probably taken in the very early 1950s) in Howard Rock and Deborah Dash Moore, *Cityscapes: A History of New York in Images* (New York: Columbia University Press, 2001), 346. The sign had been there since 1919. See Chapter 3 herein and Mathias, *Retailing Revolution,* 343.

130. Roberts, *Schroders,* 282.

131. The Gevaert plant, closed in 1948, was ultimately sold to Remington Rand. Devos, "Agfa-Gevaert and Belgian Multinational Enterprise," 207–208; Alt, "Photochemical Industry," 98–99.

132. See Table 8.5 herein. In 1940 its domestic sales of dyestuff, including imports (excluding exports), measured by value were actually in first place.

133. Wilkins, "German Chemical Firms," 314.

134. Ibid., 314; see Chapter 7; and Kobrak, "Between Nationalism and Internationalism" (on Schering).

135. Peyer, *Roche,* 126, on the production in Nutley, New Jersey, of vitamins.

136. Mahoney, *Merchants of Life,* 233.

137. For details on the complex story of Nestlé's chocolate business in the United States, see Heer, *World Events 1866–1966,* 105, 144, 218.

138. Interestingly, in 1959, the category "food, tobacco, beverages" ranked in first place in inward foreign direct investments in U.S. manufacturing. U.S. Department of Commerce, Office of Business Economics, *Foreign Business Investments in the United States* (1962), 8. Obviously, this was part of the 1914–1945 legacy.

139. Hal Morgan, *Symbols of America* (New York: Penguin Books, 1986), 171.

140. On the importance, see Wilkins, "American-Japanese Direct Foreign Investment Relationships," 508–510.

141. Roberts, *Schroder,* 297.

Bibliography

Primary Materials: Collections Consulted

In a number of cases, archivists, librarians, and academicians have mailed me copies of unpublished data from these collections; in some cases, I have used microfilms obtained on interlibrary loan or purchased by a library distant from the locale of the original records.

Canada

Toronto. Sun Life Assurance Co. Archives. Macaulay letterbooks and other records.

England and Scotland

Cambridge. University Library. Vickers Papers.

Kew. Public Record Office. Board of Trade (BT), Foreign Office (FO), Power Ministry (Powe), Treasury (T), Treasury: Papers of Sir Frederick Phillips (T 177).

London. Rothschild Archives.

London. Science Museum Library. S. Pearson & Son Papers.

London. Shell Oil Company, Archives and Library.

London. Unilever PLC, Archives. Historical Files; T. J. Lipton, Inc. Papers; Lever Correspondence; Committee Minutes.

Glasgow. Coats (a member of the Coats Viyella Group). David Keir, "The Coats Story," typescript, 1964 (Coats permitted access to this unpublished typescript).

Glasgow. University of Glasgow Library. J.&P. Coats Papers. Minute books of George A. Clark Bros.–Clark Thread Co.; Clark Thread Co. directors meetings; Minute books of Clark Thread Company; Minute books of J.&P. Coats.

Glasgow. University of Glasgow Library. Records of Edinburgh American Land Mortgage Co. Ltd., the Second British Assets Trust, Investors Mortgage Security Co. Ltd., Scottish Realisation Trust Ltd.

Manchester. Manchester Central Library. Thirty-five-page report in the British Calico Printers Association secretary's correspondence, 1922–1928, File 95. Information provided to me in Anthony Howe to Mira Wilkins, May 1, 1986.

Reading. University of Reading. Files of John H. Dunning. British business in the United States. Data collected in the late 1950s and early 1960s. This material is cited throughout my book as Dunning data.

France

Fontainebleau. Archives Nationale. Rothschild Papers, "New York–Belmont" and other Correspondence. AQ 132.

Paris. Archives Nationale. Rothschild Papers.

Paris. Schlumberger Archives. I am indebted to Geoffrey Bowker for his providing me data from this archives.

Savigny-le-Temple. Centre des Archives Economiques et Financieres. "Blocage et deblocage des avoirs français, 1940–1960," B63562, and "Relations économique et financieres franco-americaines–avoirs américaine en France," B63562/1. (The documents in B63562 and B63562/1 have been reclassified from their earlier B33919-B33921 designations, which were described in French inventories as containing data on French blockages in the United States 1943–1945 and French properties in the United States 1940–1948.)

Germany

Leverkusen. Bayer Archives. Bericht Herrenbrück, Nordamerika und Kanada, n.d. [ca. 1953], pp. 111–114, I/1/6./66. I am indebted to Elisabeth Glaser-Schmidt for a copy of this document.

Munich. Munich Reinsurance Company Archives. I am indebted to Gerald Feldman for material on Pilot Reinsurance Company that comes from this archives.

Munich. Siemens Archives. My thanks go to Harm Schröter, who guided me as I consulted these archives, and to Wilfried Feldenkirchen, who has written on Siemens in America)

Hong Kong

Hong Kong. Hongkong and Shanghai Banking Corporation Archives. J. R. Jones, "Historical Data." My thanks go to S. W. Muirhead, July 2, 1984, for this material.

The Netherlands

Rotterdam. Unilever NV Archives. A. J. Bannink provided documents on Jurgens' U.S. operations. My thanks go to Geoffrey Jones for the arrangements.

Switzerland

Bern. Swiss Federal Archives. I am indebted to Antoine Fleury for material from AF, E 2001 (c) 4/147.

United States

Albany, New York. State of New York. Banking Department. I am indebted to Gretchen Marlatt and Kevin Cook for information on various banks regulated by the state.

Albany, New York. State of New York. Department of State. Incorporation information.

Bay City, Michigan. Public Library. "An Outline History of the North American Chemical Co." Typescript, 1928.

Berkeley, California. University of California. Bancroft Library. Microfilmed records on British companies in the United States from Companies Registration Office (London), Companies Registration Office (Edinburgh), U.K. Public Record Office, and Board of Trade Dissolved Company files. This a huge and invaluable collection, with hundreds of microfilm reels, classified under Films Z-G1, Z-G2, and Z-G3. (It is superior to the material available in the United Kingdom, since the latter was "pruned" after the filming was done.) This collection is, however, more satisfactory on British companies in the American West than in the South, for the goal was to document British investments on the western frontier. The filming was done in the early 1950s, and the documents go to 1951. The Bancroft Library's inventory of the collection is excellent. An incomplete (but useful) index to the films in Z-G1 and Z-G2 is in Anne T. Ostrye, *Foreign Investment in the American and Canadian West, 1870–1914: An Annotated Bibliography* (Metuchen, N.J.: Scarecrow Press, 1986), 129–167. Ostrye's book does not, however, contain an index of the films in Z-G3; her index goes beyond 1914 but does not cover British companies started after 1914.

Boston. Massachusetts. Harvard Business School. Baker Library. Edgar Higgins Collection; Henry Lee Higginson Papers; Kidder, Peabody Papers; Thomas Lamont Papers.

Boston. John F. Kennedy Library. James P. Warburg Papers.

Buffalo, New York. Buffalo and Erie Country Public Library. Access to Buffalo City Directory, through Barbara M. Soper, librarian.

Chicago. Loyola University. Archives. Samuel Insull Papers.

College Park, Maryland. National Archives. See Washington, D.C.

Dearborn, Michigan. Henry Ford Museum. Ford Archives, Acc. 6; Acc. 375; Acc. 536.

Fulton, New York. Fulton Public Library. Data on Nestlé plant from Ellen I. Morin, librarian.

Gainsville, Florida. Agricultural Stabilization and Conservation Service. Harry McGhin provided me with information on Loncala Phosphate.

Hyde Park, New York. Franklin D. Roosevelt Library. Morgenthau Diaries, vol. 474.

Ithaca, New York. Cornell University Library. John L. Collyer Manuscripts.

Laramie, Wyoming. American Heritage Center, University of Wyoming. Thurman Arnold Papers; Charles W. Burdick Papers; Francis P. Garvan Papers.

Milltown, New Jersey. Milltown Public Library. Data on Michelin Tire Company; Works Progress Administration, "History of Milltown" typescript, 1936.

New York. Arnhold and S. Bleichroeder, Inc. Historical data.

New York. Chase Manhattan Bank Archives. International Acceptance Bank Records; Huth & Co., New York, Financial Statement, Dec. 31, 1920.

New York. Columbia University Libraries. Business School Library. Scudder Collection.

New York. Columbia University Libraries. Special Collections. Oral History Collection. Walter E. Sachs Reminiscences; James P. Warburg Reminiscences.

New York. Columbia University Libraries. Special Collections. Vanderlip Papers.

New York. Daiwa Securities America Inc. Historical data on Fujimoto Securities. From Paul J. Hauser.

New York. Federal Reserve Bank of New York. File C261: England–Bank of England; General Files (Files 790, 792, and others); Alpha files on particular foreign banks; Harrison Papers; Strong Papers.

New York. Moseley, Hallgarten, Estabrook & Weeden Holding Company. "Draft History of Hallgarten & Co.," typescript, Apr. 28, 1950, copy from Jon Bulkley (sent Dec. 15, 1983).

New York. National Archives, Northeast Region. Court cases not reported in standard sources.

New York. Nomura Securities International, Inc. Historical data.

Philadelphia. Dermatological Research Laboratory at College of Physicians, Historical Collection. I am indebted to Jonathan Liebenau for material from this collection.

South Bend, Indiana. Discovery Hall Museum, Studebaker Corporation papers. I am indebted to Donald F. Davis for information from these papers.

Trenton, New Jersey. New Jersey Department of State. Corporate records.

Washington, D.C. Library of Congress. Manuscript Division. Western Range Cattle Industry Study. Acc. 11,092. 75 reels of microfilm. Contains materials on mining as well as cattle companies.

Washington, D.C. National Archives. Over the years, I used some of these documents (and inventories of the collections) in Washington, D.C., in Suitland, Md., and at the National Archives II at College Park, Md.; it is my understanding that the documents are now (as of 2002), in the main, in College Park, Md.: Record Groups 40 (Department of Commerce); 56, Entry 406 (Treasury, Bureau of War Risk Insurance); 59 (Department of State); 122 (Federal Trade Commission); 131 (Alien Property Custodian; Office of Alien Property Custodian); 151 (Bureau of Foreign and Domestic Commerce, Department of Commerce); 165 (War Department); 169 (Foreign Economic Administration, SKF Report); 238/T301 (Occupation Records for the Nuremberg Trial—Nazi Industrialists); 265 ("History" and Lyle J. Holverstott and Fred L. Miller, "Preliminary Inventory of the Records of the Foreign Funds Control [Record Group 265]"; the title of the inventory notwithstanding, the collection has no records of Foreign Funds Control, as applied to foreign assets in the United States).

Washington, D.C. U.S. Department of Justice. Substantial material on German and Swiss investments in the United States during World War II are in Record Group 131, National Archives. When I used the material in 1992, many of the documents in RG 131 were in the physical possession of the National Archives (and classified as part of RG 131) but were under the legal custody of the Office of Foreign Litigation of the U.S. Department of Justice. Documents in this category were made available to me through the U.S. Department of Justice and the Freedom of Information Act. They are cited as RG 131, U.S. Department of Justice or RG 131 (Dept.-Justice). For other data in RG 131, see Washington, D.C., National Archives.

Wilmington, Delaware. Hagley Museum and Library. Du Pont records.

West Branch, Iowa. Hoover Library. Herbert Hoover Papers.

Court Cases

American Tobacco, et al. v. U.S., 328 U.S. 781 (1946).

Bayer Co., Inc. v. United Drug Co., 272 Fed. 505 (SDNY 1921).

Central Vermont Transportation Co. v. Durning, 294 U.S. 33 (1935).

Direction der Disconto-Gesellschaft v. United States Steel Corporation, 267 U.S. 22 (1925).

Du Pont v. Pathe Film, Complaint (SDNY 1938).

Heyden Chemical Corporation v. Clark, Attorney General, 85 F. Supp. 949 (SDNY 1948).

Homer S. Cummings, et al. v. Deutsche Bank und Disconto-Gesellschaft, 300 U.S. 115 (1937).

Old Dearborn Distributing Co. v. Seagram Distillers Corp., 299 U.S. 183 (1936)

Oliver American Trading Co. v. Government of Mexico, 5 F. 2d 659 (CCA 1924).

Standard Oil Co (New Jersey), et al. v. Markham, 64 F. Supp. 656 (SDNY 1945).

Stoehr v. Miller, 296 Fed. 414 (1923).

Stoehr v. Wallace et al., 255 U.S. 239 (1921).

U.S. v. Alba Pharmaceutical Co., et al., Civil No. 15-363 (SDNY 1941).

U.S. v. Alcoa, Eq. 85–73 (SDNY 1937–1942).

U.S. v. Allied Chemical & Dye Corp., Civil No. 14-320 (SDNY 1941).

U.S. v. Allied Chemical & Dye Corp., Criminal No. 753c (DNJ 1942).

U.S. v. Aluminum Company of America, et al., Civil No. 18-31 (SDNY 1942).

U.S. v. American Bosch Corp., et al., Civil No. 20-164 (SDNY 1942).

U.S. v. American Petroleum Institute, Civil No. 8524 (DDC 1940).

U.S. v. American Potash and Chemical Corp., et al., Civil No. 8-498 (SDNY 1940).

U.S. v. Bausch & Lomb Optical Co., et al., Civil No. 9-404 (SDNY 1940).

U.S. v. Bayer Co., Inc., Civil No. 15-364 (SDNY 1941).

U.S. v. Bayer Co. Inc., et al., 135 F. Supp. 65 (SDNY 1955).

U.S. v. Belmont, 301 U.S. 324 (1937).

U.S. v. Borax Consolidated Ltd., et al., Civil No. 23690-G (DND Calif. 1945).

U.S. v. Borax Consolidated Ltd., Criminal No. 28900-S (DND Calif. 1945).

U.S. v, Chemical Foundation, 294 Fed. 300 (DCD 1924).
U.S. v. Chemical Foundation, 5 F.2d 191 (1925).
U.S. v. Chemical Foundation, 272 U.S. 1 (1926).
U.S. v. Ciba Pharmaceutical Products, Vincent A. Burgher, Schering Corporation, Gregory Stragnell, Roche-Organon, and Elmer H. Bobst, Criminal No. 551 (DNJ 1941).
U.S. v. Deutsches Kalisyndikat Gesellschaft, et al., 31 F. 2d 199 (SDNY 1929).
U.S. v. Dietrich A. Schmitz, General Aniline & Film, F. William von Meister, and William H. vom Rath, Criminal No. 111-137 (SDNY 1941).
U.S. v. General Aniline & Film, I.G. Farbenindustrie, Hermann Schmitz, Dietrich A. Schmitz, Ernst Schwartz, Criminal No. 111-136 (SDNY 1941).
U.S. v. General Dyestuff Corp., General Aniline & Film Corp., I. G. Farben Industrie, AG, Hermann Schmitz, Dietrich A. Schmitz, E. K. Halbach, and Hans W. Aickelin, Criminal No. 111-135 (SDNY 1941).
U.S. v. General Electric et al., Criminal No. 110-442 (SDNY 1941).
U.S. v. General Electric, et al., Civil No. 1364 (DNJ 1949).
U.S. v. General Electric, Fried. Krupp AG, et al., Criminal No. 108–172 (SDNY 1940).
U.S. v. Imperial Chemical Industries, Civil No. 17-282 (SDNY 1942).
U.S. v. Imperial Chemical Industries, 100 F. Supp. 504 (SDNY 1951).
U.S. v. Imperial Chemical Industries, 105 F. Supp. 251 (SDNY 1952).
U.S. v. Imperial Chemical Industries, Civil No. 24-13 (SDNY 1954–1966).
U.S. v. Julius Weltzien and Schering Corporation, Criminal No. 552 (DNJ 1941).
U.S. v. Norma-Hoffmann Bearings Corp., Civil No. 24216, 1953 Trade Case (ND Ohio 1953).
U.S. v. Pink, 315 U.S. 203 (1942).
U.S. v. Roche-Organon, Inc. and Elmer H. Bobst, Criminal No. 553 (DNJ 1941)
U.S. v. Rohm & Haas Co., Criminal No. 877 and Criminal No. 878 (DNJ 1942).
U.S. v. Schering Corp. et al., Civil No. 1919 (DNJ 1941).
U.S. v. Schering Corporation, Jules Weltzein, Ciba Pharmaceutical Products, Vincent A. Burgher, Roche-Organon, Elmer H. Bobst, Rare Chemicals, and E. T. Fritzsching, Criminal No. 550 (DNJ 1941).
U.S. v. Standard Oil Company of New Jersey, et al., Civil No. 2091 (DNJ 1942).
U.S. v. Swiss Bank Corp., Civil No. 1920 (DNJ 1941).
U.S. v. Synthetic Nitrogen Products Corp., Civil No. 15-36 (SDNY 1941).
U.S. v. Tannin Corporation, et al., Criminal No. 18-31 (SDNY 1942).

Books, Articles, Dissertations, Public Documents, Annual Reports

Aalders, Gerald, and Cees Wiebes. *The Art of Cloaking Ownership.* Amsterdam: Amsterdam University Press, 1996.
———. "Stockholms Enskilda Bank, German Bosch, and I. G. Farben." *Scandinavian Economic History Review,* 33 (1985): 25–50.
Aaronson, Susan. *Trade and the American Dream: A Social History of Postwar Trade Policy.* Louisville: University of Kentucky Press, 1996.
Abrahams, Paul Philip. *The Foreign Expansion of American Finance . . . 1907–1921.* 1967 Ph.D. diss. New York: Arno Press, 1976.
Abramson, Rudy. *Spanning the Century: The Life of W. Averell Harriman 1891–1986.* New York: Morrow & Co., 1992.
Acheson, Dean. *Present at the Creation.* New York: Signet, 1970.
Adler, Cyrus. *Jacob H. Schiff.* 2 vols. Garden City, N.Y.: Doubleday, 1928.
Aftalion, Fred. *A History of the International Chemical Industry.* Philadelphia: University of Pennsylvania Press, 1991.
AGA. *The AGA Saga.* Cleveland: AGA Gas, n.d. [1986?].

Ahvenainen, Jorma, and Even Lange. "Foreign and Domestic Capital in the Growth of the North European Timber Industries, 1860–1920." Unpublished paper, Campinas, Brazil, 1989.

Aitken, Hugh G. J. *The Continuous Wave: Technology and American Radio, 1900–1932.* Princeton, N.J.: Princeton University Press, 1985.

Aldcroft, Derek H. *From Versailles to Wall Street.* Berkeley: University of California Press, 1977.

Alerassool, Mahvash. *Freezing Assets.* New York: St. Martin's Press, 1993.

Allaud, Louis A., and Maurice H. Martin. *Schlumberger.* New York: John Wiley, 1977.

Allen, Hugh. *The House of Goodyear.* 1943. Rpt. New York: Arno Press, 1976.

Alt, Lutz. "The Photochemical Industry." Ph.D. diss., MIT, 1986.

Ambruster, Howard W. *Treason's Peace.* New York: Beechhurst Press, 1947.

American Bosch Corporation. *Annual Reports.*

American Brown Boveri. *Annual Reports.*

American I. G. Chemical Corporation. *Annual Reports.*

American Petroleum Institute. *Petroleum Facts and Figures.* Washington, D.C.: American Petroleum Institute, 1971.

Anderson, Gordon Blythe. "The Effects of the War on New Security Issues in the United States." *Annals,* 67 (Nov. 1916): 118–130.

Antony Gibbs & Sons, Ltd. *Merchants and Bankers 1880–1958.* London: Antony Gibbs & Sons, Ltd., 1958.

Archer, Gleason. *The History of Radio.* New York: American Historical Society, 1938.

Armstrong, Christopher, and H. V. Nelles. *Southern Exposure.* Toronto: University of Toronto Press, 1988.

Arnold, John J. "The American Gold Fund of 1914." *Journal of Political Economy,* 23 (July 1915): 696–706.

Atkin, John Michael. *British Overseas Investment 1918–1931.* New York: Arno Press, 1977.

———. "Official Regulation of British Overseas Investment, 1914–1931." *Economic History Review,* 2nd ser., 23 (Aug. 1970): 324–335.

Attman, Artur, et al. *L. M. Ericsson 100 Years.* Stockholm: L. M. Ericsson [1977?].

Aubert, M. Georges. *La Financé Américaine.* Paris: Ernest Flammarion, 1910.

Avram, Mois H. *The Rayon Industry.* 2nd ed. New York: Van Nostrand, 1929.

Bailey, Thomas A. *A Diplomatic History of the American People.* 6th ed. New York: Appleton-Century-Crofts, 1958.

———. "The United States and the Blacklist during the Great War." *Journal of Modern History,* 6 (1934): 14–35.

Baker, W. J. *A History of Marconi Company.* London: Methuen & Co., 1970.

Balogh, Thomas. *Studies in Financial Organization.* Cambridge: Cambridge University Press, 1950.

Bamberg, J. H. *The History of the British Petroleum Co., Vol. 2: The Anglo-Iranian Years, 1928–1954.* Cambridge: Cambridge University Press, 1994.

Bank für Elektrische Unternehmungen, Zurich. *Geschäftsberichts.*

Bank of England. *United Kingdom Overseas Investments, 1938 to 1948.* London: Bank of England, 1950.

Bank of International Settlements, Monetary and Economic Department. *United States Regulations Relating to Foreign Funds Control.* 4th ed. Basle: Bank of International Settlements, 1944.

Bank of Nova Scotia. *Bank of Nova Scotia 1832–1932.* Toronto: privately printed, 1932.

Baron, Stanley. *Brewed in America.* 1962. Rpt. New York: Arno Press, 1972.

Barty-King, Hugh. *Girdle around the World.* London: Heinemann, 1979.

Baruch, Bernard M. *The Making of the Reparation and Economic Sections of the Treaty.* 1920. Rpt. New York: Howard Fertig, 1970.

Baster, A. S. J. *The Imperial Banks.* London: P. S. King, 1929.
———. *The International Banks.* 1935. Rpt. New York: Arno Press, 1977.
Bata, Thomas J. *Bata.* Toronto: Stoddart, 1990.
Bauer, Hans. *Swiss Bank Corporation, 1872–1972.* Basle: Swiss Bank Corp., 1972.
Bean, Jonathan. *Big Government and Affirmative Action: The Scandalous History of the Small Business Administration.* Lexington: University of Kentucky Press, 2001.
Beaton, Kendall. *Enterprise in Oil.* New York: Appleton-Century-Crofts, 1957.
Beaud, Claude Ph. "The Schneider Group." In Alice Teichova, Maurice Lévy-Leboyer, and Helga Nussbaum, eds., *Multinational Enterprise in Historical Perspective,* pp. 87–102. Cambridge: Cambridge University Press, 1986.
Beaverbrook, Lord. *Politicians and War.* 1925. Rpt. London: Archon, 1968.
Beckhart, Benjamin Haggott. *The New York Money Market.* Vols. 2 and 3. New York: Columbia University Press, 1932.
Beito, David T. "Andrew Mellon." In Larry Schweikart, ed., *Banking and Finance, 1913–1989,* pp. 267–282. New York: Facts on File, 1990.
Bemis, Samuel Flagg. *A Diplomatic History of the United States.* 3rd ed. New York: Henry Holt, 1950.
Bernanke, Ben S. *Essays on the Great Depression.* Princeton, N.J.: Princeton University Press, 2000.
Bernfeld, Seymour S. "A Short History of American Metal Climax, Inc." In American Metal Climax, Inc., *World Atlas.* New York, n.d. [1962?]
Bernstein, Michael A. *The Great Depression: Delayed Recovery and Economic Change in America, 1929–1939.* Cambridge: Cambridge University Press, 1987.
Bernstorff, Count. *Memoirs.* New York: Random House, 1936.
———. *My Three Years in America.* London: Skeffington & Son, n.d. [1922].
Bessell, George. *Norddeutscher Lloyd 1857–1957.* N.p., n.d.
Best, Paul J. "Insurance in Imperial Russia." *Journal of European Economic History,* 18 (Spring 1989): 139–170.
Bhagwati, Jagdish N. "The Capital Myth." *Foreign Affairs,* 77 (May/June 1998): 7–16.
Bidwell, R. L. *Currency Conversion Tables.* London: Rex Collings, 1970.
Bierwag, G. O., et al. "National Debt in a Neo-Classical Growth Model: Comment." *American Economic Review,* 59 (Mar. 1969): 205–210.
Birmingham, Stephen. *Our Crowd.* New York: Dell Publishing, 1967.
Bishop, Donald G. *The Roosevelt-Litvinov Agreements.* Syracuse, N.Y.: Syracuse University Press, 1965.
Blackford, Mansel G., and K. Austin Kerr, *BF Goodrich.* Columbus: Ohio State University Press, 1996.
Blakey, Arch Fredric. *The Florida Phosphate Industry.* Cambridge, Mass.: Harvard University Press, 1973.
Blakey, Roy G., and Gladys C. Blakey. "The Revenue Act of 1936." *American Economic Review,* 26 (Sept. 1936): 466–482.
———. "The Revenue Act of 1937." *American Economic Review,* 27 (Dec. 1937): 698–704.
Bland, Larry I. "W. Averell Harriman: Businessman and Diplomat 1891–1945." Ph.D. diss., University of Wisconsin, 1972.
Blanken, I. J. *The History of Philips Electronics N.V.* Vols. 3 and 4. Zaltbomme, Netherlands: European Library, 1999.
Bliss, Michael. *A Canadian Millionaire: The Life and Times of Sir Joseph Flavelle, Bart. 1958–1939.* Toronto: Macmillan of Canada, 1978.
———. *Northern Enterprise.* Toronto: McClelland & Stewart, 1987.
Bloomfield, Arthur I. *Capital Imports and the American Balance of Payments 1934–1939.* 1950. Rpt. New York: Kelley, 1966.

———. "International Capital Movements and the American Balance of Payments: 1929–1940." Ph.D., diss. University of Chicago, 1942.

———. "Postwar Control of International Capital Movements." *American Economic Review,* Papers and Proceedings Issue, 36 (May 1946): 687–709.

Blum, John Morton. *From the Morgenthau Diaries: Years of Crisis, 1928–1938* Vol. 1. Boston: Houghton Mifflin, 1959.

———. *From the Morgenthau Diaries: Years of Urgency, 1938–1941* Vol. 2. Boston: Houghton Mifflin, 1965.

———. *From the Morgenthau Diaries: Years of War, 1941–1945* Vol. 3. Boston: Houghton Mifflin, 1967.

Bonbright, James C., and Gardiner C. Means. *The Holding Company.* New York: McGraw-Hill, 1932.

Bondeson, Gustaf. "The Growth of a Global Enterprise: Alfa-Laval 100 Years." N.p.: Alfa-Laval, n.d. [1983?].

Bonin, Hubert, et al., eds. *Transnational Companies.* Paris: Éditions P.L.A.G.E., n.d. [2002].

Borchard, Edwin. "Reprisals on Private Property." *American Journal of International Law,* 30 (Jan. 1936): 108–113.

Bordo, Michael D., Christopher M. Meissner, and Angela Redish. "How 'Original Sin' Was Overcome: The Evolution of External Debt Denominated in Domestic Currencies in the United States and the British Dominions 1800–2000." paper for conference at Harvard University, July 2002.

Borkin, Joseph. *The Crime and Punishment of I. G. Farben.* New York: Free Press, 1978.

Born, Karl. *International Banking.* New York: St. Martin's Press, 1983.

Bosch, K. D. *Nederlandse Beleggingen in de Verenigde Staten.* Amsterdam: Uitgeversmaatschappij Elsevier, 1948.

Bothwell, Robert, Ian Drummond, and John English. *Canada, 1900–1945.* Toronto: University of Toronto Press, 1987.

Bova, Francesca. "American Direct Investment in the Italian Manufacturing Sectors, 1900–1940." Paper at Business History Conference meetings, Ft. Lauderdale, Florida, March 1995.

Bowker, Geoffrey C. *Science on the Run.* Cambridge, Mass.: MIT Press, 1994.

Boyce, Gordon, and Simon Ville. *The Development of Modern Business.* New York: Palgrave, 2002.

Boylan, John. *Sequel to the Apocalyse: The Uncensored Story: How Your Dimes and Quarters Helped Pay for Hitler's War.* New York: Booktab, 1942.

Branch, Harllee, Jr. *Alabama Power Company and the Southern Company.* New York: Newcomen Society, 1967.

Brandes, Joseph. *Herbert Hoover and Economic Diplomacy.* Pittsburgh: University of Pittsburgh Press, 1962.

Brandfon, Robert L. *Cotton Kingdom of the New South.* Cambridge, Mass.: Harvard University Press, 1967.

Brayer, H. O. "The Influence of British Capital on the Western Range Cattle Industry." *Journal of Economic History,* Supplement, 9 (1949): 85–98.

Brewster, Kingman. *Antitrust and American Business Abroad.* New York: McGraw-Hill, 1958.

British Electrical & Allied Manufacturers' Association. *Combines and Trusts in the Electrical Industry.* London: BEAMA, 1927.

Broehl, Wayne G., Jr. *Cargill: Trading the World's Grain.* Hanover, N.H.: University Press of New England, 1992.

Broesamle, John J. *William Gibbs McAdoo.* Port Washington, N.Y.: Kennikat Press, 1973.

Bronfman, Samuel. ". . . from little acorns . . . ." In Distillers Corporation-Seagrams Ltd., *Annual Report 1970.*

Brooks, John. *Once in Golgonda.* New York: Harper & Row, 1969.
Brown, William Adams, Jr. *The International Gold Standard Reinterpreted.* 2 vols. New York: National Bureau of Economic Research, 1940.
Brownlee, W. Elliot. *Federal Taxation in America.* Cambridge: Cambridge University Press, 1996.
Bruchey, Stuart. *Enterprise.* Cambridge, Mass.: Harvard University Press, 1990.
Bullock, Charles J., John H. Williams, and Rufus S. Tucker. "The Balance of Trade of the United States." *Review of Economic Statistics,* 1 (July 1919): 213–263.
Bullock, Hugh. *The Story of Investment Companies.* New York: Columbia University Press, 1959.
Burchardt, Lothar. "Between War Profits and War Costs: Krupp in the First World War." In Hans Pohl and Bernd Rudolph, eds., *German Yearbook on Business History 1988,* pp. 1–45. Berlin: Springer Verlag, 1990.
Burden, William A. M. *The Struggle for Airways in Latin America.* New York: Council on Foreign Relations, 1943.
Bürgin, Alfred. *Geschichte des Geigy-Unternehmens von 1758 bis 1939.* Basle: J. R. Geigy, 1958.
Burk, Kathleen. "Anglo-American Finance during World War I." In W. F. Dreisziger, ed., *Mobilization for Total War,* pp. 23–42. Waterloo, Ont.: Wilfrid Laurier University Press, 1981.
———. *Britain, America and the Sinews of War 1914–1918.* Boston: Allen & Unwin, 1985.
———. "Money and Power." In Youssef Cassis, ed., *Finance and Financiers in European History, 1880–1960,* pp. 359–369. Cambridge: Cambridge University Press, 1992.
———. *Morgan Grenfell 1838–1988.* Oxford: Oxford University Press, 1989.
Burk, Robert F. *The Corporate State and the Broker State.* Cambridge, Mass.: Harvard University Press, 1990.
Burrough, Bryan, and John Helyar. *Barbarians at the Gate.* New York: Harper & Row, 1990.
Burton, H., and D. C. Corner. *Investment and Unit Trusts in Britain and America.* London: Elek Books, 1968.
Cairncross, Alec. *Control of Long-Term International Capital Movements.* Washington, D.C.: Brookings, 1973.
Calomiris, Charles W. *U.S. Bank Deregulation in Historical Perspective.* Cambridge: Cambridge University Press, 2000.
Canada. Dominion Bureau of Statistics. *The Canadian Balance of International Payments.* Ottawa, 1939.
———. *Canada's International Investment Position, Selected Years, 1926 to 1949.* Ottawa, n.d. [1950].
———. *Canada's International Investment Position, 1926–1954.* Ottawa, 1956.
Canada. Statistics Canada. *Canada's International Investment Position: Historical Statistics 1926 to 1992.* Ottawa, 1993.
Cantwell, John, and Pilar Barrera. "The Localisation of Corporate Technological Trajectories in the Interwar Cartels." *Economics of Innovation and New Technology,* 6 (1998): 257–290.
Carosso, Vincent P. "A Financial Elite: New York's German-Jewish Investment Bankers." *American Jewish Historical Quarterly,* 66 (Sept. 1976): 67–88.
———. *Investment Banking in America.* Cambridge, Mass.: Harvard University Press, 1970.
———. *More Than a Century of Investment Banking: The Kidder, Peabody & Co. Story.* New York: McGraw-Hill, 1979.
Carter, Barry E. *International Economic Sanctions,* Cambridge: Cambridge University Press, 1988.

Case, Josephine Young, and Everett Needham Case. *Owen D. Young and American Enterprise.* Boston: David R. Godine, 1982.

Cassel, Gustav. *Foreign Investments.* Chicago: University of Chicago Press, 1928.

Cassis, Youssef. "The Emergence of a New Financial Institution: Investment Trusts in Britain, 1870–1939." In J. J. Van Helten and Y. Cassis, eds., *Capitalism in a Mature Economy,* pp. 139–158. Aldershot: Edward Elgar, 1990.

———. "Swiss International Banking." In Geoffrey Jones, ed., *Banks as Multinationals,* pp. 160–172. London: Routledge, 1990.

Cayez, Pierre. *Rhône-Poulenc 1895–1975.* Paris: Armand Colin/Masson, 1988.

Cekota, Anthony. *Entrepreneur Extraordinary: The Biography of Tomas Bata.* Rome: E.I.S., 1968.

Cerutti, Mauro. "Le blocage des avoirs suisses." In Sébastien Guex, ed., *La Suisse et les Grande Puissances, 1914–1945,* pp. 185–235. Geneva: Droz, 1999.

Chalmin, Philippe. *Négociants et chargeurs.* Paris: Economica, 1985.

Chamber of Commerce of the United States. *Laws and Practices Affecting the Establishment of Foreign Branches of Banks.* Washington, D.C.: Chamber of Commerce of the United States, 1923.

Chandler, Alfred D., Jr. *Inventing the Electronic Century.* New York: Free Press, 2001.

———. *Scale and Scope.* Cambridge, Mass.: Harvard University Press, 1990.

———. *Strategy and Structure.* Cambridge, Mass.: MIT Press, 1962.

———. *Visible Hand.* Cambridge, Mass.: Harvard University Press, 1977.

———, ed. *Giant Enterprise.* New York: Harcourt, Brace & World, 1964.

Chandler, Alfred D., Jr., and Stephen Salsbury. *Pierre S. du Pont and the Making of the Modern Corporation.* New York: Harper & Row, 1971.

Chandler, Lester. *Benjamin Strong.* 1958. Rpt. New York: Arno Press, 1978.

Channon, Derek F. *The Strategy and Structure of British Enterprise.* Boston: Harvard Business School Press, 1973.

Chapman, Stanley. *Merchant Enterprise.* Cambridge: Cambridge University Press, 1992.

———. *The Rise of Merchant Banking.* London: Allen & Unwin, 1984.

Cheever, Lawrence Oakley. *The House of Morrell.* Cedar Rapids, Iowa: Torch Press, 1948.

Chernow, Ron. *The House of Morgan.* New York: Atlantic Monthly Press, 1990.

———. *The Warburgs.* New York: Random House, 1993.

Chester, Edward W. *United States Oil Policy and Diplomacy.* Westport, Conn.: Greenwood Press, 1983.

Church, Roy. *Herbert Austin.* London: Europa, 1979.

Clark, Thomas D., and Albert D. Kirwan. *The South since Appomattox.* New York: Oxford University Press, 1967.

Clay, Sir Henry. *Lord Norman.* London: Macmillan, 1957.

Clayton, G. *British Insurance.* London: Elek Books, 1971.

Clayton, Lawrence A. *Grace: W. R. Grace & Co.: The Formative Years 1850–1930.* Ottawa, Ill.: Jameson Books, 1985.

Cleveland, Harold van B., and Thomas F. Huertas. *Citibank 1812–1970.* Cambridge, Mass.: Harvard University Press, 1985.

Coatsworth, John H., and Alan M. Taylor, eds. *Latin America and the World Economy since 1800.* Cambridge, Mass.: Harvard University Press, 1998.

Cochran, Sherman. *Big Business in China.* Cambridge, Mass.: Harvard University Press, 1980.

———. "Three Roads to Shanghai's Market." Typescript, 1988.

Cockerell, H. A. L., and Edwin Green. *The British Insurance Business.* London: Heinemann, 1976.

Cocks, Edward J., and Bernhardt Walters. *A History of the Zinc Smelting Industry in Britain.* London: George Harrap, 1968.

Coe, Fred A., Jr. *Burroughs Wellcome Co. 1880–1980.* New York: Newcomen Society, 1980.

Cole, Wayne S. *Senator Gerald P. Nye and American Foreign Relations.* Minneapolis: University of Minnesota Press, 1962.

Coleman, D. C. *Courtaulds.* Vol. 2. Oxford: Oxford University Press, 1969.

Conan, A. R. "The United Kingdom as a Creditor Country." *Westminster Bank Review,* Aug. 1960, 16–22.

Corina, Maurice. *Trust in Tobacco,* London: Michael Joseph, 1975.

Corley, T. A. B. "From National to Multinational Enterprise: The Beecham Business, 1848–1945." Unpublished paper, 1983.

Corporation of Foreign Bondholders, London. *Annual Reports.*

Costigliola, Frank. *Awkward Dominion.* Ithaca, N.Y.: Cornell University Press, 1984.

Cottrell, P. L. "Aspects of Western Equity Investment in the Banking Systems of East Central Europe." In Alice Teichova and P. L. Cottrell, eds., *International Business and Central Europe 1918–1939,* pp. 309–347 New York: St. Martin's Press, 1983.

Cottrell, P. L., with C. J. Stone. "Credits, and Deposits to Finance Credits." In P. L. Cottrell, Håkan Lindgren, and Alice Teichova, eds., *European Industry and Banking between the Wars,* pp. 43–78. Leicester: Leicester University Press, 1992.

Coudert, Frederic R. *A Half Century of International Problems.* New York: Columbia University Press, 1954.

Cowles, Virginia. *The Astors.* London: Weidenfeld & Nicholson, 1979.

Cox, Howard. "The Global Cigarette." Ph.D. diss., University of London, 1990.

———. *The Global Cigarette: Origins and Evolution of British American Tobacco, 1880–1945.* Oxford: Oxford University Press, 2000.

———. "Growth and Ownership in the International Tobacco Industry: BAT 1902–1927." *Business History,* 31 (Jan. 1989): 44–67.

———. "Learning to Do Business in China: The Evolution of BAT's Cigarette Distribution Network, 1902–41." *Business History,* 39 (July 1997): 30–64.

Cox, Reavis. *Competition in the American Tobacco Industry 1911–1932.* New York: Columbia University Press, 1933.

Cross, Ira. *Financing an Empire.* 4 vols. Chicago: S. J. Clarke, 1927.

Crutchley, Geo. W. *John Mackintosh.* London: Hodder & Stoughton, 1921.

Cuff, R. D., and J. L. Granatstein. *Ties That Bind.* 2nd ed. Toronto: Samuel Stevens, 1977.

Dahl, Albin Joachim. "British Investment in California Mining, 1870–1890." Ph.D. diss., University of California, Berkeley, 1961.

Dairoch, James L. "Global Competitiveness." *Business History,* 34 (July 1992): 153–175.

Dallek, Robert. *American Style of Foreign Policy.* New York: Alfred A. Knopf, 1983.

Davenport-Hines, R. P. T. "Glaxo as a Multinational before 1963." In Geoffrey Jones, ed., *British Multinationals: Origins, Management and Performance,* pp. 137–163. Aldershot: Gower, 1986.

———. "Vickers and Schneider." In Alice Teichova, Maurice Lévy-Leboyer, and Helga Nussbaum, eds. *Historical Studies in International Corporate Business,* pp. 123–134. Cambridge: Cambridge University Press, 1989.

———. "Vickers as a Multinational before 1945." In Geoffrey Jones, ed., *British Multinationals,* pp. 43–74. Aldershot: Gower, 1986.

Davies, A. Emil. *Investments Abroad.* Chicago: A. W. Shaw, 1927.

Davies, P. N. "British Shipping and World Trade." In Tsunehiko Yui and Keiichiro Nakagawa, eds., *Business History of Shipping,* pp. 39–85. Tokyo: University of Tokyo Press, 1985.

Daviet, Jean-Pierre. *Un Destin International: La Compagnie de Saint-Gobain de 1830 à 1939.* Paris: Éditions des Archives Contemporaines, 1988.

Davis, Lance E., and Robert J. Cull. *International Capital Markets and American Economic Growth, 1820–1914.* Cambridge: Cambridge University Press, 1994.

Davis, Lance E., and Robert E. Gallman, *Evolving Financial Markets and International Capital Flows: Britain, the Americas, and Australia 1865–1914.* Cambridge: Cambridge University Press, 2001.

Davis, Richard. *The English Rothschilds.* Chapel Hill: University of North Carolina Press, 1983.

De La Pedraja, René. *The Rise and Decline of U.S. Merchant Shipping in the Twentieth Century.* New York: Twayne Publishers, 1992.

Denison, Merrill. *Canada's First Bank: A History of the Bank of Montreal.* 2 vols. New York: Dodd, Mead & Co., 1966, 1967.

———. *Harvest Triumphant.* Toronto: Collins, 1949.

DeNovo, John. "The Movement for an Aggressive American Oil Policy Abroad, 1918–1920." *American Historical Review,* 61 (July 1956): 854–876.

Deperon, Paul. *International Double Taxation.* New York: Committee on International Economic Policy, 1945.

Dessauer, John H. *My Years with Xerox.* Garden City, N.Y.: Doubleday, 1971.

Deterding, Henri. *An International Oilman.* London: Harper & Bros., 1934.

Devos, Greta. "Agfa-Gevaert and Belgian Multinational Enterprise." In Geoffrey Jones and Harm G. Schröter, eds., *The Rise of Multinationals in Continental Europe,* pp. 201–212. Aldershot: Edward Elgar, 1993.

DeVries, Henry P. "The International Responsibility of the United States for Vested German Assets." *American Journal of International Law,* 51:1 (Jan. 1957): 18–28.

Diamond, P. A. "National Debt in a Neo-classical Growth Model." *American Economic Review,* 55 (Dec. 1965): 1126–1150.

Dickens, Paul D. "The Transition Period in American International Financing: 1897 to 1914." Ph.D. diss., George Washington University, 1933.

Dierikx, Marc. *Fokker.* Washington, D.C.: Smithsonian Institution, 1997.

Dimbleby, David, and David Reynolds. *An Ocean Apart: The Relationship between Britain and the United States in the Twentieth Century.* New York: Random House, 1988.

Doerries, Reinhard R. *Imperial Challenge.* Chapel Hill: University of North Carolina Press, 1989.

Domer, George Edward. "The History of the American Austin and Bantam." *Automobile Quarterly,* 14 (1976): 407–414.

Douglas, Susan J. *Inventing American Broadcasting 1899–1922.* Baltimore: Johns Hopkins University Press, 1987.

Downard, William L. *Dictionary of the History of the American Brewing and Distilling Industry.* Westport, Conn.: Greenwood Press, 1980.

Duffus, Roy A., Jr. *The Story of M & T Chemicals Inc.* New York: Cordella Duffus Baker, 1965.

Dunn, Robert W. *American Foreign Investment.* 1926. Rpt. New York: Arno Press, 1976.

Dunning, John H. "British Investment in U.S. Industry." *Moorgate and Wall Street,* Autumn 1961: 5–23.

———. *Multinational Enterprise and the Global Economy.* Wokingham, Eng.: Addison-Wesley, 1993.

———. "Perspectives on International Business Research: A Professional Autobiography." *Journal of International Business Studies,* 33 (2002): 817–835.

Eckes, Alfred E. *Opening America's Market.* Chapel Hill: University of North Carolina Press, 1995.

Edwards, Corwin. *Economic and Political Aspects of International Cartels.* 1944. Rpt. New York: Arno Press, 1976.

———. "Thurman Arnold and the Antitrust Laws." *Political Science Quarterly,* 58 (Sept. 1943): 338–355.

Edwards, George W. *International Trade Finance.* New York: Henry Holt, 1924.

Eichengreen, Barry. *Golden Fetters.* New York: Oxford University Press, 1992.

———. "Historical Research on International Lending and Debt." *Journal of Economic Perspectives,* 5 (Spring 1991): 149–169.

———. "U.S. Foreign Financial Relations in the Twentieth Century." In Stanley Engerman and Robert Gallman, eds., *Cambridge Economic History,* pp. 463–504. Cambridge: Cambridge University Press, 2000.

Einzig, Paul. *World Finance 1914–1935.* New York: Macmillan, 1935.

Eisner, Robert, and Paul J. Pieper. "Real Foreign Investment in Perspective." *The Annals,* 516 (July 1991): 22–35.

Ekelund, Robert B., Jr., and Robert F. Hébert. *A History of Economic Theory and Method.* 3rd ed. New York: McGraw-Hill, 1990.

Emden, Paul H. *Money Powers of Europe.* 1937. Rpt. New York: Garland, 1983.

Erdman, Paul. *Swiss-American Economic Relations.* Basle: Kyklos, 1959.

Fahey, John. "When the Dutch Owned Spokane." *Pacific Northwest Quarterly,* 71 (Jan. 1981): 2–10.

Faith, Nicholas. *The Infiltrators: The European Business Invasion of America.* London: Hamish Hamilton, 1971.

———. *Safety in Numbers.* New York: Viking Press, 1982.

Fanno, Marco. *Normal and Abnormal Capital Transfers.* Minneapolis: University of Minnesota Press, 1939.

Farrer, David. *The Warburgs.* London: Michael Joseph, 1975.

Fay, Sidney B. *The Origins of World War I.* 2nd ed. New York: Macmillan, 1938.

Federal Reserve Board. *Annual Reports.*

Federal Reserve System, Board of Governors. *Banking and Monetary Statistics.* Washington, D.C., 1943.

———. *Banking and Monetary Statistics, 1941–1970.* (Washington, D.C., 1976.

Feiler, Arthur. "International Movements of Capital." *American Economic Review,* Suppl., 25 (Mar. 1935): 63–74.

Feinstein, Charles H. *National Income, Expenditure and Output of the United Kingdom 1855–1965.* Cambridge: Cambridge University Press, 1972.

———, ed. *Banking, Currency, and Finance in Europe between the Wars.* Oxford: Clarendon Press, 1995.

Feinstein, Charles H., and Katherine Watson. "Private International Capital Flows in Europe in the Inter-war Period." In Charles H. Feinstein, ed., *Banking, Currency, and Finance in Europe between the Wars,* pp. 94–130. Oxford: Clarendon Press, 1995.

Feis, Herbert. *The Diplomacy of the Dollar 1919–1932.* New York: W. W. Norton, 1950.

Feldenkirchen, Wilfried. "Die Anfänge des Siemensgeschäfts in Amerika." In Wilfried Feldenkirchen et al., eds., *Wirtschaft Gesellschaft Unternehmen,* pp. 876–900. Stuttgart: Franz Steiner, 1995.

———. *Siemens.* Munich: Piper, 2000.

———. "Siemens in the US." In Geoffrey Jones and Lina Gálvez-Muñoz, eds., *Foreign Multinationals in the United States: Management and Performance,* pp. 89–105. London: Routledge, 2002.

Feldman, Gerald D. *Allianz.* Cambridge: Cambridge University Press, 2001.

———. *The Great Disorder: Politics, Economics, and Society in the German Inflation 1914–1924.* New York: Oxford University Press, 1997.

———. *Iron and Steel in the German Inflation 1916–1923.* Princeton, N.J.: Princeton University Press, 1977.

Feldstein, Martin, ed. *The United States in the World Economy.* Chicago: University of Chicago Press, 1988.

Ferguson, Niall. *The House of Rothschild: The World's Banker 1849–1999.* New York: Viking, 1999.

Ferrier, R. W. *The History of the British Petroleum Company: Volume 1: The Developing Years 1901–1932.* Cambridge: Cambridge University Press, 1982.

Fisher, Irving. *The Stock Market Crash—and After.* New York: Macmillan, 1930.

Fishlow, Albert. "Debt: Lessons from the Past." *International Organization,* 39 (Summer 1985): 383–439.

Flamming, Douglas. *Creating the Modern South.* Chapel Hill: University of North Carolina Press, 1992.

Fleisig, Heywood W. *Long Term Capital Flows and the Great Depression: The Role of the United States 1927–1933.* 1969 diss. New York: Arno Press, 1975.

Fleury, Antoine. "Les Discussions américano-suisses autour de la clause-or au début des années 1930." In Sébastien Guex, ed., *La Suisse et les Grandes Puissances, 1914–1945,* pp. 141–154. Geneva: Droz, 1999.

Fokker, Anthony H. G., and Bruce Gould. *Flying Dutchman: The Life of Anthony Fokker.* New York: Henry Holt & Co., 1931.

Forbes, R. J. *A Chronology of Oil.* 2nd rev. ed. N.p., Shell, 1965.

Foreman-Peck, James. *A History of the World Economy.* 2nd ed. New York: Harvester/Wheatsheaf, 1995.

Forsberg, Aaron. *America and the Japanese Miracle: The Cold War Context of Japan's Postwar Economic Revival, 1950–1960.* Chapel Hill: University of North Carolina Press, 2000.

Foy, Fred C. *Ovens, Chemicals and Men: Koppers Co.* New York: Newcomen Society, 1958.

Freedman, Joseph Robert. "A London Merchant Banker in Anglo-American Trade and Finance, 1835–1850." Ph.D. diss., University of London, 1969.

Freidel, Frank. *America in the Twentieth Century.* New York: Alfred A. Knopf, 1960.

French, Michael. "Structural Change and Competition in the United States Tire Industry, 1920–1937." *Business History Review,* 60 (Spring 1986): 28–54.

———. *The U.S. Tire Industry.* Boston: Twayne, 1991.

Freyer, Tony. *Regulating Big Business: Antitrust in Great Britain and America 1880–1990.* Cambridge: Cambridge University Press, 1992.

Fridenson, Patrick. "The Growth of Multinational Activities in the French Motor Industry, 1890–1979." In Peter Hertner and Geoffrey Jones, eds., *Multinationals: Theory and History,* pp. 157–168. Aldershot: Gower, 1986.

Frieden, Jeff. "Sectoral Conflict and U.S. Foreign Economic Policy, 1914–1940." *International Organization,* 42 (Winter 1988): 59–90.

Friedman, Milton, and Anna Jacobson Schwartz. *A Monetary History of the United States.* Princeton, N.J.: Princeton University Press, 1963.

Fritz, Martin, and Birgit Karlsson. *SKF i stormaktspolitikens Kraftfält: Kullagerexporten 1943–1945.* Göteborg: Novum Grafiska, 1998.

Frye, Alton. *Nazi Germany and the American Hemisphere 1933–1941.* New Haven, Conn.: Yale University Press, 1967.

Fryer, D. W. *World Economic Development.* New York: McGraw-Hill, 1965.

Galbraith, John Kenneth. *The Great Crash 1929.* Boston: Houghton Mifflin, 1961.

Gales, Ben P. A., and Keetie E. Sluyterman. "Dutch Free-Standing Companies, 1870–1940." In Mira Wilkins and Harm Schröter, eds., *The Free-Standing Company in the World Economy, 1830–1996,* pp. 293–322. Oxford: Oxford University Press, 1996.

———. "Outward Bound: The Rise of Dutch Multinationals." In Geoffrey Jones and Harm Schröter, eds., *The Rise of Multinationals in Continental Europe,* pp. 65–98. Aldershot: Elgar, 1993.

Gall, Lothar, et al. *The Deutsche Bank.* London: Weidenfeld & Nicolson, 1995.

Gardner, Richard N. *Sterling-Dollar Diplomacy in Current Perspective: The Origins and Prospects of Our International Economic Order.* Rev. ed. New York: Columbia University Press, 1980. The 1st ed. was in 1956.

Garvan, Francis P. *"Hot Money" vs. Frozen Funds.* New York: The Chemical Foundation, 1937.

Geisst, Charles R. *Entrepôt Capitalism: Foreign Investment and the American Dream in the Twentieth Century.* New York: Praeger, 1992.

———. *Wall Street: A History.* New York: Oxford University Press, 1997.

"General Electric." Harvard Business School Case BH81RI.

Gephart, William F. *Effects of the War upon Insurance.* New York: Oxford University Press, 1918.

Giddens, Paul H. *Standard Oil Company (Indiana).* New York: Appleton-Century-Crofts, 1955.

Gifford, T. J. Carlyle. *Letters from America 1939–1941.* Edinburgh: privately printed, 1969.

Gilbert, Heather. *End of the Road: The Life of Lord Mount Stephen.* Vol. 2, *1891–1921.* Aberdeen: Aberdeen University Press, 1977.

Gilbert, J. C. *A History of Investment Trusts in Dundee.* London: P. S. King & Son, 1939.

Gill, David G. "Problems of Foreign Discovery." In Kingman Brewster Jr., *Antitrust and American Business Abroad,* pp. 474–488. New York: McGraw-Hill, 1958.

Gimbel, John. *Science, Technology, and Reparations: Exploitation and Plunder in Postwar Germany.* Stanford, Calif.: Stanford University Press, 1990.

Gini, Corraco. *Report on Problem of Raw Materials and Foodstuffs.* Geneva: League of Nations, 1921.

Glasgow, George. *The English Investment Trust Companies.* New York: John Wiley, 1931.

———. *Glasgow's Guide to Investment Trust Companies (1935).* London: Eyre and Spottiswoode, 1935.

———. *The Scottish Investment Trust Companies.* London: Eyre and Spottiswoode, 1932.

Glete, Jan. "Swedish Managerial Capitalism." *Business History,* 35 (Apr. 1993): 99–110.

Glickman, Norman J., and Douglas P. Woodward. *The New Competitors.* New York: Basic Books, 1989.

Gokkent, Giyas. "Theory of Foreign Portfolio Investment." Ph.D. diss., Florida International University, 1997.

Goldsmith, Raymond. *A Study of Savings.* Princeton, N.J.: Princeton University Press, 1955.

Goodhart, C. A. E. *The New York Money Market and the Finance of Trade 1900–1913.* Cambridge, Mass.: Harvard University Press, 1969.

Grady, Henry F. *British War Finance.* New York: Columbia University Press, 1927.

Graham, Edward M. "Oligopolistic Imitation and European Direct Investment in the United States." D.B.A. diss., Harvard Business School, 1975.

Graham, Edward M., and Paul R. Krugman. *Foreign Direct Investment in the United States.* Washington, D.C.: Institute for International Economics, 1989.

Graham, Frank D., and Charles R. Whittlesey. *The Golden Avalanche.* 1939. Rpt. New York: Arno Press, 1978.

Graham, Margaret. "R & D and Competition in England and the United States: The Case of the Aluminum Dirigible." *Business History Review,* 62 (Summer 1988): 261–285.

———. *RCA and the Video Disc: The Business of Research.* Cambridge: Cambridge University Press, 1986.

Grant, A. T. K. *A Study of the Capital Market in Post-war Britain.* London: Macmillan, 1937.

Gras, N. S. B., and Henrietta M. Larson. *Casebook in American Business History.* New York: Appleton-Century-Crofts, 1939.

Grayson, Theodore J. *Investment Trusts.* New York: John Wiley, 1928.

Great Britain. Board of Trade. *Survey of International and Internal Cartels.* 2 vols. London, 1944, 1946.

Great Britain. Foreign and Commonwealth Office. History notes, "British Policy towards Enemy Property during and after the Second World War." *Historians, LRD,* no. 13 (Apr. 1998). www.enemyproperty. gov.UK (accessed in 1999 and 2000).

Great Britain. Monopolies and Restrictive Practices Commission. *Report on the Supply of Linoleum.* 1956.

Great Britain. Parliamentary Papers. *Report of American Dollar Securities Committee.* XIII-1, Cmd. 212. 1919.

Greenhill, Robert G. "Investment Group, Free-Standing Company, or Multinational: Brazilian Warrant, 1909–1952." *Business History,* 37 (Jan. 1995): 86–111.

Greesley, Gene M., ed. *Voltaire and the Cowboy: The Letters of Thurman Arnold.* Boulder: Colorado Associated University Press, 1977.

Guaranty Trust Co. *The Effect of the War on European Neutrals.* New York: Guaranty Trust Co., 1919.

Guex, Sébastien. "The Origins of the Swiss Banking Secrecy Law and Its Repercussions for Swiss Federal Policy." *Business History Review,* 74 (Summer 2000): 237–266.

———, ed. *La Suisse et les grandes puissances, 1914–1945.* Geneva: Droz, 1999.

Guinsburg, Thomas N. *The Pursuit of Isolationism.* New York: Garland, 1982.

Haber, L. F. *The Chemical Industry, 1900–1930.* Oxford: Clarendon Press, 1971.

Haberler, Gottfried. *The World Economy, Money, and the Great Depression 1919–1939.* Washington, D.C.: American Enterprise Institute, 1976.

Hagen, Antje. "Export versus Direct Investment in the German Optical Industry." *Business History,* 38 (Oct. 1996): 1–20.

Hall, H. Duncan. *North American Supply.* London: Longmans, Green, 1955.

Hall, Kermit L., ed. *Oxford Companion to the Supreme Court of the United States.* Oxford: Oxford University Press, 1992.

Harding, W. P. G. "The Results of the European War on America's Financial Position." *Annals of the American Academy of Political and Social Science,* 60 (July 1915): 113–118.

Harris, Charles Wesley. "International Relations and the Disposition of Alien Enemy Property Seized by the United States during World War II: A Case Study on German Properties." *Journal of Politics,* 23 (Nov. 1961): 641–666.

Harris, G. R. S. *Germany's Foreign Indebtedness.* London: Oxford University Press, 1935.

Harrison, Godfrey. *V.Y.B.* London: Vivian, Younger, and Bond, 1959.

Hart, David M. *Forged Consensus: Science, Technology, and Economic Policy in the United States, 1921–1953.* Princeton, N.J.: Princeton University Press, 1998.

Harvey, Charles. *The Rio Tinto Company, 1873–1954.* Penzance, Cornwall: Alison Hodge, 1981.

Hassbring, Lars. *The International Development of Swedish Match Company, 1917–1924.* Stockholm: LiberFörlag, 1979.

Hausman, William J., and John Neufeld. "U.S. Foreign Direct Investment in Electrical Utilities." In Mira Wilkins and Harm Schröter, eds., *The Free-Standing Company in the World Economy, 1830–1996,* pp. 361–390. Oxford: Oxford University Press, 1998.

Hawley, Ellis W. *The New Deal and the Problem of Monopoly.* Princeton, N.J.: Princeton University Press, 1966.

Hayes, Peter. *Industry and Ideology.* Cambridge: Cambridge University Press, 1987.

Hayes, Samuel L., III, and Philip M. Hubbard. *Investment Banking.* Boston: Harvard Business School Press, 1990.

Hayes, Samuel L., III, A. Michael Spence, and David Van Praag Marks. *Competition in the Investment Banking Industry.* Cambridge, Mass.: Harvard University Press, 1983.

Haynes, Williams. *American Chemical Industry.* 6 vols. New York: Van Nostrand, 1945–1954.

Heer, Jean. *World Events 1866–1966: The First Hundred Years of Nestlé.* Rivaz, Switzerland, 1966.

Heerding, A. *The History of N. V. Philips' Gloeilampenfabrieken.* 2 vols. Cambridge: Cambridge University Press, 1986, 1988.

Heinrich, Thomas R. *Ships for the Seven Seas: Philadelphia Shipbuilding in the Age of Industrial Capitalism.* Baltimore: Johns Hopkins University Press, 1997.

Hertner, Peter, and Geoffrey Jones, eds. *Multinationals: Theory and History.* Aldershot: Gower, 1986.

Hessen, Robert. *Steel Titan: The Life of Charles M. Schwab.* New York: Oxford University Press, 1975.

Hexner, Ervin. *International Cartels.* Chapel Hill: University of North Carolina Press, 1946.

H. G. "Settlement of the Interhandel Case." *American Journal of International Law,* 59:1 (Jan. 1965): 97–98.

Hicks, Agnes H. *The Story of the Forestal.* London: The Forestal Land, Timber & Railway Co., 1956.

Hidy, Ralph W. *The House of Baring in American Trade and Finance 1763–1861.* Cambridge, Mass.: Harvard University Press, 1949.

Hiebert, Ray Eldon. "Courier to the Crowd: Ivy Lee and the Development of Public Relations in America." Ph.D. diss., University of Maryland, 1962.

Higham, Charles. *Trading with the Enemy.* New York: Delacorte Press, 1983.

Hildebrand, Karl-Gustaf. *Expansion Crisis Reconstruction.* Stockholm: LiberFörlag, 1985.

Hilger, Susanne. "The Internationalization of a Family Firm: The Case of the German Chemical Producer Henkel." In Hubert Bonin, et al., eds., *Transnational Companies,* pp. 879–895. Paris: Éditions P.L.A.G.E., n.d. [2002].

Hirst, Francis W. *Wall Street and Lombard Street.* New York: Macmillan, 1931.

Historische Bedrijfsarchiven. *Bankwezen.* Amsterdam: NEHA, 1992.

Hochheiser, Sheldon. *Rohm and Haas.* Philadelphia: University of Pennsylvania Press, 1986.

Hoffman, Paul. *The Dealmakers.* Garden City, N.Y.: Doubleday, 1984.

Hogan, Michael. *Informal Entente.* Columbia: University of Missouri Press, 1977.

———. "Informal Entente: Public Policy and Private Management in Anglo-American Petroleum Affairs, 1918–1924." *Business History Review,* 48 (Summer 1974): 187–205.

———. *The Marshall Plan.* Cambridge: Cambridge University Press, 1987.

Hollander, Hans. *Geschichte de Schering AG.* Berlin: Schering, 1955.

Homze, Edward L. *Arming Lufwaffe: The Reich Air Ministry and the German Aircraft Industry 1919–39.* Lincoln: University of Nebraska Press, 1976.

Hooper, Peter, and J. David Richardson. *International Economic Transactions: Issues in Measurement and Empirical Research.* Chicago: University of Chicago Press, 1991.

Horn, Martin. "A Private Bank at War: J. P. Morgan & Co. and France 1914–1918." *Business History Review,* 74 (Spring 2000): 85–112.

Horst, Thomas. *At Home Abroad.* Cambridge, Mass.: Ballinger, 1974.

Hounshell, David, and John Kenly Smith. *Science and Corporate Strategy: Du Pont R & D 1902–1980.* Cambridge: Cambridge University Press, 1988.

Houston, Tom, and John H. Dunning. *UK Industry Abroad.* London: Financial Times, 1976.

Howard, Frank A. *Buna Rubber.* New York: Van Nostrand, 1947.

Howeth, L. S. *History of Communications—Electronics in the United States Navy.* Washington, D.C., 1963.

Huebner, Solomon S. "The American Security Market during the War." *Annals,* 68 (Nov. 1916): 93–117.

Hufbauer, Gary Clyde, Jeffrey J. Schott, and Kimberly Ann Elliott. *Economic Sanctions Reconsidered: Supplemental Case Histories.* 2nd ed. Washington, D.C.: Institute for International Economics, 1990.

Hughes, Brady A. "Owen D. Young and American Foreign Policy, 1919–1929." Ph.D. diss., University of Wisconsin, 1969.

Hughes, Thomas P. *American Genesis.* New York: Viking, 1989.

Huldermann, Bernhard. *Albert Ballin.* London: Cassell & Co., 1922.

Hunt, Wallis. *Heirs of Great Adventure.* 2 vols. London: Balfour, Williamson, 1951, 1960.

Hymer, Stephen. *The International Operations of National Firms: A Study of Direct Foreign Investment.* 1960 diss. Cambridge, Mass.: MIT Press, 1976.

I. G. Farben. *Annual Reports.*

Imlah, A. H. *Economic Elements in the Pax Britannica.* Cambridge, Mass.: Harvard University Press, 1958.

International Acceptance Bank. *Annual Reports.*

International General Electric. *Annual Reports.*

Iriye, Akira. *The Globalizing of America, 1913–1945.* Cambridge: Cambridge University Press, 1993.

Ise, John. *United States Oil Policy.* New Haven, Conn.: Yale University Press, 1926.

Iversen, Carl. *Aspects of the Theory of International Capital Movements.* 1935. Rpt. New York: Augustus M. Kelley, 1967.

Jack, D. T. *Studies in Economic Warfare.* New York: Chemical Publishing Co., 1941.

Jackson, W. Turrentine. *The Enterprising Scot.* Edinburgh: Edinburgh University Press, 1968.

James, F. Cyril. *The Growth of Chicago Banks.* 2 vols. New York: Harper & Bros., 1938.

James, Harold. "Banks and Bankers." In Youssef Cassis, ed., *Finance and Financiers in European History.* Cambridge: Cambridge University Press, 1992.

———. *The End of Globalization: Lessons from the Great Depression.* Cambridge, Mass.: Harvard University Press, 2001.

———. *The German Slump.* Oxford: Clarendon Press, 1986.

———. *International Monetary Cooperation since Bretton Woods.* New York: Oxford University Press, 1996.

James, Marquis. *The Story of W. R. Grace: Merchant Adventurer.* Wilmington, Del.: SR Books, 1993.

Janssen, Hermann, and Wilhelm Kiesselbach. *Das Amerikanische Freigabe-Gesetz vom 10 Marz 1928 (Settlement of War Claims Act of 1928).* Mannheim: J. Bensheimer, 1928.

Jenks, Leland. "Britain and American Railway Development." *Journal of Economic History,* 11 (Autumn 1951): 375–388.

John, A. H. *A Liverpool Merchant House, Being the History of Alfred Booth & Co. 1863–1958.* London: George Allen & Unwin, 1959.

Johnson, Paul. *Consolidated Gold Fields.* New York: St. Martin's Press, 1987.

Jöhr, Walter Adolf. *Schweizerische Kreditanstalt 1856–1956.* Zurich: Schweizerische Kreditanstalt, 1956.

Jolly, W. P. *Marconi.* New York: Stein and Day, 1972.

Jonas, Manfred. *The United States and Germany.* Ithaca, N.Y.: Cornell University Press, 1984.

Jones, Geoffrey. *British Multinational Banking 1830–1990.* Oxford: Oxford University Press, 1993.

———. "The Chocolate Multinationals: Cadbury, Fry and Rowntree 1918–1939." In Geoffrey Jones, ed., *British Multinationals: Origins, Management and Performance,* pp. 96–118. Aldershot: Gower, 1986.

———. "Control, Performance, and Knowledge Transfers in Large Multinationals: Unilever in the United States, 1945–1980." *Business History Review,* 76 (Autumn 2002): 435–478.

———. "Courtaulds in Continental Europe 1920–1945." In Geoffrey Jones, ed., *British Multinationals: Origins, Management and Performance,* pp. 119–136. Aldershot: Gower, 1986.

———. "The Gramophone Company: A British Multinational." *Business History Review,* 59 (Spring 1985): 76–100.

———. "The Growth and Performance of British Multinational Firms before 1939: The Case of Dunlop." *Economic History Review,* 2nd ser., 37 (Feb. 1984): 35–53.

———. *Merchants to Multinationals: British Trading Companies in the Nineteenth and Twentieth Centuries.* Oxford: Oxford University Press, 2000.

———. "Multinational Cross-Investment between Switzerland and Britain 1914–1945." In Sébastien Guex, ed., *La Suisse et les grandes puissances 1914–1945,* pp. 427–459. Geneva: Droz, 1999.

———. "The Multinational Expansion of Dunlop 1890–1939." In Geoffrey Jones, ed., *British Multinationals: Origins, Management and Performance,* pp. 24–42. Aldershot: Gower, 1986.

———. *The State and the Emergence of the British Oil Industry.* London: Macmillan, 1981.

———, ed. *British Multinationals: Origins, Management and Performance.* Aldershot: Gower, 1986.

———. *Multinational Traders.* London: Routledge, 1998.

Jones, Geoffrey, and Lina Gálvez-Muñoz, eds. *Foreign Multinationals in the United States: Management and Performance.* London: Routledge, 2002.

Jones, Geoffrey, and Harm G. Schröter, eds. *The Rise of Multinationals in Continental Europe.* Aldershot: Edward Elgar, 1993.

Jones, Geoffrey, and Judith Wale. "Merchants as Business Groups: British Trading Companies in Asia before 1945." *Business History Review* 72 (Autumn 1998): 367–408.

Jones, Joseph M. *Tariff Retaliation.* Philadelphia: University of Pennsylvania Press, 1934.

Jonker, Joost, and Keetie Sluyterman. *At Home on the World Markets: Dutch International Trading Companies from the 16th Century until the Present.* The Hague: Sdu Uitgevers, 2000.

Joslin, David. *A Century of Banking in Latin America.* London: Oxford University Press, 1963.

Karlsson, Birgit. "Fascism and Production of Ball-Bearings: SKF, Germany, and the Soviet Union, 1942–1952." Unpublished paper delivered in Odense, Denmark, Mar. 30, 2001.

Kawabe, Nobuo. "Development of Overseas Operations by General Trading Companies, 1868–1945." In Shin'ichi Yonekawa and Hideki Yoshihara, eds., *Business History of General Trading Companies,* pp. 71–103. Tokyo: University of Tokyo Press, 1987.

———. "Japanese Business in the United States before World War II: The Case of Mitsubishi Shoji Kaisha, the San Francisco and Seattle Branches." Ph.D. diss., Ohio State University, 1980.

Kenen, Peter B., ed. *Managing the World Economy.* Washington, D.C.: Institute for International Economics, 1994.

Kenney, Martin, and Richard Florida. *Beyond Mass Production.* New York: Oxford University Press, 1993.

Kerr, K. Austin. "Distilled Spirits." In David O. Whitten, ed., *Manufacturing,* pp. 56–62. New York: Greenwood Press, 1990.

Kerr, W. G. "Scotland and the Texas Mortgage Business." *Economic History Review,* 2nd ser., 16 (Aug. 1963): 91–103.

———. *Scottish Capital on the American Credit Frontier.* Austin: Texas State Historical Association, 1976.

Keynes, John Maynard. *The Collected Writings of John Maynard Keynes.* Ed. Elizabeth Johnson. Vol. 16. London: Macmillan, 1971.

Kilbourn, William. *The Elements Combined: A History of the Steel Company of Canada.* Toronto: Clarke, Irwin, 1960.

Kim, Dong-Woon. "The British Multinational Enterprise in the United States before 1914: The Case of J. & P. Coats." *Business History Review,* 72 (Winter 1998): 523–551.

Kimball, Warren F. *The Most Unsordid Act: Lend-Lease, 1939–1941.* Baltimore: Johns Hopkins University Press, 1969.

Kindersley, Robert M. See Mira Wilkins, ed., *British Overseas Investments 1907–1948* (New York: Arno Press, 1977), for eleven articles by Kindersley, published 1929–1938, on British foreign investments.

Kindleberger, Charles P. *A Financial History of Western Europe.* 2nd ed. Oxford: Oxford University Press, 1993.

———. *Manias, Panics, and Crashes.* New York: Basic Books, 1978.

———. *The World in Depression.* Berkeley: University of California Press, 1973.

King, Frank H. H. *The Hongkong Bank between the Wars and the Bank Interned, 1919–1945. The History of the Hongkong and Shanghai Banking Corporation,* vol. 3. Cambridge: Cambridge University Press, 1988.

———. *The Hongkong Bank in the Period of Development and Nationalism, 1941–1984. The History of the Hongkong and Shanghai Banking Corporation,* vol. 4. Cambridge: Cambridge University Press, 1991.

Klebaner, Benjamin J. "Paul M. Warburg." In Larry E. Schweikart, ed., *Banking and Finance, 1913–1989,* pp. 447–449. New York: Buccoli, Clark, 1990.

Klein, Herbert S. "The Creation of the Patiño Tin Empire." *Inter-American Economic Affairs,* 19 (Aug. 1965): 3–23.

Klug, Adam. *The German Buybacks, 1932–1939: A Cure for Overhang.* Princeton, N.J.: Princeton Studies in International Finance, 1993.

Kobrak, Christopher. "Between Nationalism and Internationalism: Schering AG and the Culture of German Capitalism, 1851–1945." Ph.D. diss., Columbia University, 1999.

König, Mario. *Interhandel. Die Schweizerische Holding der IG Farben und ihre Metamorphosen–eine Affäre um Eigentum und Interessen (1910–1999).* Independent Commission of Experts Switzerland, vol. 2. Zurich: Chronos, 2001.

Kreikamp, Hans-Dieter. *Deutsches Vermögen in den Vereinigten Staaten.* Stuttgart: Deutsche Verlags-Anstalt, 1979.

Krooss, Herman E., and Martin R. Blyn. *A History of Financial Intermediaries.* New York: Random House, 1971.

Kubu, Eduard. "Behaviour and Fate of Companies with Foreign Capital in the Czech Lands 1938–1945." Unpublished paper, 2001.

Kudo, Akiro. "Dominance through Cooperation: I. G. Farben's Japan Strategy." In John E. Lesch ed., *The German Chemical Industry in the Twentieth Century,* pp. 243–283. Dordrecht, Netherlands: Kluwer, 2000.

Kuhlman, Charles Byron. *The Development of the Flour Milling Industry in the United States.* Boston: Houghton Mifflin, 1929.

Kuhn, Loeb & Co. *Investment Banking through Four Generations.* New York: Kuhn, Loeb, 1955.

Kulik, Gary, and Julia C. Bonham. *Rhode Island: An Inventory of Historic Engineering and Industrial Sites.* Washington, D.C.: U.S. Department of the Interior, 1978.

Kunz, Diane B. *The Battle for Britain's Gold Standard.* London: Croom Helm, 1987.

Kynaston, David. *The City of London: Vol. 3. Illusions of Gold 1914–1945.* London: Chatto & Windus, 1999.

LaFeber, Walter. *The American Age.* New York: W. W. Norton, 1989.

Lake, David. *Power, Protection, and Free Trade.* Ithaca, N.Y.: Cornell University Press, 1988.

Lamb, W. Kaye. *History of the Canadian Pacific Railroad.* New York: Macmillan, 1977.

Lamer, Mirko. *The World Fertilizer Economy.* Stanford, Calif.: Stanford University Press, 1957.

Lamont, Edward M. *The Ambassador from Wall Street: The Story of Thomas W. Lamont.* Lanham, Md.: Madison Books, 1994.

Lamont, Thomas W. *Across World Frontiers.* New York: Harcourt, Brace, 1951.

———. *Henry P. Davison.* New York: Harper & Bros., 1933.

Lamoreaux, Naomi R., and Kenneth L. Sokoloff. "Inventors, Firms and the Market for Technology." In Naomi R. Lamoreaux, Daniel M. G. Raff, and Peter Temin, eds. *Learning by Doing,* pp. 19–57. Chicago: University of Chicago Press, 1999.

Landau, Zbigniew, and Wojciech Morawski. "Polish Banking in the Inter-war Period." In Charles H. Feinstein, ed., *Banking, Currency, and Finance in Europe between the Wars,* pp. 358–373. Oxford: Clarendon Press, 1995.

Laney, Leroy D. "The Impact of U.S. Laws on Foreign Direct Investment." *Annals,* 516 (July 1991): 144–153.

Langer, William L., and S. Everett Gleason. *The Challenge to Isolation 1937–1940.* New York: Harper Brothers, 1952.

Larson, Henrietta M., Evelyn H. Knowlton, and Charles S. Popple. *New Horizons 1927–1950.* New York: Harper & Row, 1971.

Lary, Hal B. *The United States in the World Economy.* Washington, D.C., 1943.

Laughlin, J. Lawrence. *Credit of Nations.* New York: Charles Scribner's Sons, 1918.

Lawson, W. R. "The British Treasury and the London Stock Exchange," in *The Annals,* 68 (Nov. 1916): 71–92.

Laxer, Gordon. *Open for Business: The Roots of Foreign Ownership in Canada.* Toronto: Oxford University Press, 1989.

Lazell, H. G. *From Pills to Penicillin: The Beecham Story.* London: Heinemann, 1975.

Leader, Richard. "113 Years of Dyes in Rensselaer." *Chemical Heritage,* 12 (Summer 1995).

League of Nations. *Industrialization and Foreign Trade.* Geneva: League of Nations, 1945.

———. *Treaty Series.*

Lee, Ivy. "The Black Legend: Europe Indicts America." *Atlantic Monthly* 143 (May 1929): 577–588.

Lees, Francis A. *Foreign Banking and Investment in the United States.* London: Macmillan, 1976.

Leff, Mark H. *The Limits of Symbolic Reform: The New Deal and Taxation.* Cambridge: Cambridge University Press, 1984.

Leffler, Melvyn P. *The Elusive Quest: America's Pursuit of European Stability and French Security, 1919–1933.* Chapel Hill: University of North Carolina Press, 1979.

Leuchtenburg, William E. *The Perils of Prosperity 1914–1932.* Chicago: University of Chicago Press, 1958.

Lewinson, Edwin R. *John Purroy Mitchel: The Boy Mayor of New York.* New York: Astra Books, 1965.

Lewis, Cleona. *America's Stake in International Investments.* Washington, D.C.: Brookings Institution, 1938.

———. *Debtor and Creditor Countries: 1938, 1944.* Washington, D.C.: Brookings Institution, 1945.

Lewis, Howard T. *The Motion Picture Industry.* New York: D. Van Nostrand, 1933.

Lewis, W. Arthur. *Economic Survey 1919–1939.* New York: Harper Torchbooks, 1949.

Li, Jin-Mieung. "L'Air Liquide." In Takeshi Yuzawa and Masaru Udagawa, eds., *Foreign Business in Japan before World War II,* pp. 221–238. Tokyo: University of Tokyo Press, 1990.

Liebenau, Jonathan. *Medical Science and Medical Industry.* Baltimore: Johns Hopkins University Press, 1987.

Liefmann, Robert. *Cartels, Concerns, and Trusts.* London: Methuen, 1932.

Linder, Marc. *Projecting Capitalism: A History of the Internationalization of the Construction Industry.* Westport, Conn.: Greenwood Press, 1994.

Lindgren, Håkan. *Corporate Growth: The Swedish Match Industry in Its Global Setting.* Stockholm: LiberFörlag, 1979.

Lindstrom, Talbot S., and Kevin P. Tighe. *Antitrust Consent Decrees.* 2 vols. Rochester, N.Y.: Lawyers' Cooperative, 1974.

Link, Arthur S., ed. *The Papers of Woodrow Wilson.* Vol. 30. Princeton, N.J.: Princeton University Press, 1979.

Lipsey, Robert E. "Changing Patterns of International Investment in and by the United States." In Martin Feldstein, ed., *The United States in the World Economy,* pp. 475–545. Chicago: University of Chicago Press, 1988.

Lisagor, Nancy, and Frank Lipsius. *A Law unto Itself: The Untold Story of the Law Firm Sullivan and Cromwell.* New York: William Morrow and Co., 1988.

Lloyd, Ian. *Rolls Royce: The Years of Endeavor.* London: Macmillan, 1978.

Lockwood, William W. *The Economic Development of Japan.* Princeton, N.J.: Princeton University Press, 1954.

Lottman, Herbert R. *The French Rothschilds.* New York: Crown Publishers, 1995.

Lowell, Cym H., and Jack P. Governale. *U.S. International Taxation.* Boston: Warren, Gorham & Lamont, 1997.

Luery, H. Rodney. *The Story of Milltown.* South Brunswick, N.J.: A. S. Barnes, 1971.

Lundström, Ragnhild. "Swedish Multinational Growth before 1930." In Peter Hertner and Geoffrey Jones, eds., *Multinationals: Theory and History,* pp. 135–156. Aldershot: Gower, 1986.

Mackay, Donald. *Empire of Wood: The MacMillan Bloedel Story.* Vancouver: Douglas & McIntyre, 1982.

Madden, John T., Marcus Nadler, and Harry C. Sauvain. *America's Experience as a Creditor Nation.* New York: Prentice-Hall, 1937.

Maddox, Robert Franklin. *The War within World War II: The United States and International Cartels.* Westport, Conn.: Praeger, 2001.

Mahon, James E., Jr. *Mobile Capital and Latin American Development.* University Park: Pennsylvania State University Press, 1996.

Mahoney, Tom. *The Merchants of Life.* New York: Harper & Row, 1959.

Maier, Charles S. *Recasting Bourgeois Europe.* Princeton, N.J.: Princeton University Press, 1975.

Manchez, Georges. *Sociétés de dépot, banques d'affaires.* Paris: Librairie Delagrave, 1918.

Mandeville, A. Moreton. "The House of Speyer." London [1915].

Manhattan Co. *"Manna-Hatin" The Story of New York.* New York: Manhattan Co., 1929.

Mann, Charles C., and Mark L. Plummer. *The Aspirin Wars.* Boston: Harvard Business School Press, 1991.

Marans, J. Eugene, Peter C. Williams, and Joseph P. Griffin, eds. *Foreign Investment in the United States 1980: Legal Issues and Techniques.* Washington, D.C.: District of Columbia Bar, 1980.

Markham, Jesse W. *Competition in the Rayon Industry.* Cambridge, Mass.: Harvard University Press, 1952.

———. *The Fertilizer Industry.* Nashville, Tenn.: Vanderbilt University Press, 1958.

Marshall, Herbert, Frank A. Southard, and Kenneth W. Taylor. *Canadian-American Industry.* 1936. Rpt. New York: Russell & Russell, 1970.

Martin, James Stewart. *All Honorable Men.* Boston: Little, Brown, 1950.

Mason, Mark. "The Development of United States Enterprise in Japan." Ph.D. diss., Harvard University, 1988.

Mastel, Greg. *Antidumping Laws and the U.S. Economy.* Armonk, N.Y.: M. E. Sharpe, 1998.

Mathias, Peter. *Retailing Revolution.* London: Longmans, Green, 1967.

Matthews, R. C. O., C. H. Feinstein, and J. C. Odling-Smee. *British Economic Growth 1856–1973.* Stanford, Calif.: Stanford University Press, 1982.

May, Ernest R. *The World War and American Isolation, 1914–1917.* Cambridge, Mass.: Harvard University Press, 1966.

McAdoo, William G. *Crowded Years.* New York: Houghton Mifflin, 1930.

McBeth, B. S. *British Oil Policy 1919–1939.* London: Frank Cass, 1985.

McClain, David Stanley. "Foreign Investment in United States Manufacturing and the Theory of Direct Investment." Ph.D. diss., MIT, 1974.

McCullough, David. *Truman.* New York: Simon and Schuster, 1992.

McCurrach, D. F. "Britain's U.S. Dollar Problems, 1939–45." *Economic Journal*, 221 (Sept. 1948): 356–372.

McDonald, Forrest. *Insull.* Chicago: University of Chicago Press, 1962.

McDowall, Duncan. *Steel at the Sault.* Toronto: University of Toronto Press, 1984.

McFarlane, Larry A. "British Agricultural Investment in the Dakotas." *Business and Economic History*, 2nd ser., 5 (1976): 112–126.

———. "British Investment and the Land: Nebraska, 1877–1946." *Business History Review*, 57 (Summer 1983): 258–272.

———. "British Investment in Midwestern Farm Mortgages and Land, 1875–1900: Iowa and Kansas." *Agricultural History*, 47 (Jan. 1974): 179–198.

McGovney, Dudley O. "Anti-Japanese Land Laws of California and Ten Other States." *California Law Review*, 35 (1947): 7–60.

McKenna, Stephen. *Reginald McKenna 1863–1943.* London: Eyre & Spottiswoode, 1948.

McLaren, A. D. *Peaceful Penetration.* New York: E. P. Dutton, 1917.

McMillan, Carl H. *Multinationals from the Second World.* New York: St. Martin's Press, 1987.

McVey, Frank L. *The Financial History of Great Britain, 1914–1918.* New York: Oxford University Press, 1918.

Medlicott, W. N. *The Economic Blockade.* Vol. 1. London: Longmans Green, 1952.

Meneight, W. A. *A History of United Molasses Co., Ltd.* Liverpool: privately printed, 1977.

Messimer, Dwight R. *Merchant U-Boat: Adventures of* Deutschland *1916–1918.* Annapolis, Md.: Naval Institute Press, 1988.

Metzler, Lloyd A., Robert Triffin, and Gottfried Haberler. *International Monetary Policies.* Washington, D.C.: Board of Governors of the Federal Reserve System, 1947.

Michie, Ranald C. "Crisis and Opportunity: The Formation and Operation of the British Assets Trust 1897–1914." *Business History*, 25 (July 1983): 125–147.

———. *The London and New York Stock Exchanges 1850–1914.* London: Allen & Unwin, 1987.

———. *The London Stock Exchange: A History.* Oxford: Oxford University Press, 1999.

Miller, Justin. "Alien Land Laws." *George Washington Law Review*, 8 (1939): 1–20.

Minoglou, Ioanna Pepelasis. "Between Informal Networks and Formal Contracts: International Investment in Greece during the 1920s." *Business History*, 44 (Apr. 2002): 40–64.

Miranti, Paul J. *Accountancy Comes of Age: The Development of an American Profession, 1886–1946.* Chapel Hill: University of North Carolina Press, 1990.

Mitchell, Broadus. *Depression Decade.* New York: Holt, Rinehart & Winston, 1964.

Mitsui & Co., Ltd. *The 100 Year History of Mitsui & Co., Ltd., 1876–1976.* Tokyo: Mitsui & Co., Ltd., 1977.

Moggridge, Donald. *British Monetary Policy.* Cambridge: Cambridge University Press, 1972.

Morgan, Dan. *Merchants of Grain.* New York: Penguin Books, 1980.

Morgan, E. Victor. *Studies in British Financial Policy, 1914–25.* London: Macmillan, 1952.

Morgan, Hal. *Symbols of America.* New York: Penguin Books, 1986.

Morgan, R. M. *Callender's 1882–1945.* Prescott, Merseyside: BICC, 1982.

Morris, Peter J. T. *The American Synthetic Rubber Research Program.* Philadelphia: University of Pennsylvania Press, 1989.

Morton, Walter A. *British Finance 1930–1940.* Madison: University of Wisconsin Press, 1943.

Moser, John E. *Twisting the Lion's Tail: American Anglophobia between the World Wars.* New York: New York University Press, 1999.

Mothershead, Harmon Ross. *The Swan Land and Cattle Company, Ltd.* Norman: University of Oklahoma Press, 1971.

Moulton, Harold G., and Constantine E. McGuire. *Germany's Capacity to Pay.* New York: McGraw-Hill, 1923.

Muir, Augustus. *Nairns of Kirkcaldy.* Cambridge: W. Heffer & Sons, 1956.

Mundell, Robert. "A Reconsideration of the Twentieth Century." *American Economic Review,* 90 (June 2000): 327–340.

Murray, Robert K. *The Harding Era.* Minneapolis: University of Minnesota Press, 1969.

Nagasawa, Yasuaki. "The Overseas Branches of Mitsubishi Limited during the First World War." *Japanese Yearbook on Business History,* 6 (1989): 115–146.

Nakagawa, Keiichiro. "Japanese Shipping." In Tsunehiko Yui and Keiichiro Nakagawa, eds., *Business History of Shipping,* pp. 1–33. Tokyo: University of Tokyo Press, 1985.

Nash, Gerald D. *United States Oil Policy 1890–1964.* Pittsburgh: University of Pittsburgh Press, 1968.

National Industrial Conference Board. *The International Financial Position of the United States.* New York: National Industrial Conference Board, 1929.

National Lead. *Annual Reports.*

Navin, Thomas R. *Copper Mining and Management.* Tucson: University of Arizona Press, 1978.

———. *The Whitin Machine Works since 1831.* Cambridge, Mass.: Harvard University Press, 1950.

Naylor, R. T. *The History of Canadian Business, 1867–1914.* 2 vols. Toronto: James Lorimer & Co., 1973.

Nederlandsch Economisch-Historisch Archief, *Bankwezen.* Amsterdam: NEHA, 1992.

Nelson, Lawrence J. *King Cotton's Advocate: Oscar G. Johnston and the New Deal.* Knoxville: University of Tennessee Press, 1999.

Neufeld, E. P. *A Global Corporation: A History of the International Development of Massey-Ferguson, Ltd.* Toronto: University of Toronto Press, 1969.

Nevins, Allan, and Frank Ernest Hill. *Ford: Decline and Rebirth.* New York: Scribner's 1962.

New York State, Banking Department. *Annual Reports.*

Newman, Peter. *Bronfman Dynasty.* Toronto: McClelland & Stewart, 1978.

Nicholas, Stephen. "Location Choice, Performance and the Growth of British Multinational Firms." *Business History,* 31 (July 1989): 122–141.

Niosi, Jorge. *Canadian Multinationals.* Toronto: Between the Lines, 1985.

Noble, H. G. S. *The New York Stock Exchange in the Crisis of 1914.* Garden City, N.Y.: Country Life Press, 1915.

Noggle, Burl. *Teapot Dome.* New York: W. W. Norton, 1965.

Norddeutscher Lloyd. *Berichte.*

Nordyke, James W. *International Finance and New York.* New York: Arno Press, 1976.

Nordyke, Lewis. *Cattle Empire.* New York: William Morrow, 1949.

Norris, William. *Man Who Fell from the Sky.* New York: Viking, 1987.

Notter, Harley. *Postwar Foreign Policy Preparation.* Washington, D.C., 1949.

Noyes, Alexander Dana. *The War Period of American Finance.* New York: G. P. Putnam, 1926.

Odate, Gyoju. *Japan's Financial Relations with the United States.* New York: Columbia University Press, 1922.

O'Hagan, H. Osborne. *Leaves From My Life.* 2 vols. London: John Lane, 1929.

Olsson, Ulf. "Securing the Markets: Swedish Multinationals in a Historical Perspective." In Geoffrey Jones and Harm G. Schröter, eds., *The Rise of Multinationals in Continental Europe,* pp. 99–127. Aldershot: Edward Elgar, 1993.

Orbell, John. *Baring Brothers & Co. Ltd.* London: Baring Brothers, 1985.

Oseas, Israel B. "Antitrust Prosecutions of International Business." *Cornell Law Review,* 30 (1944): 42–65.

Ostrye, Anne T. *Foreign Investment in the American and Canadian West 1870–1914.* Metuchen, N.J.: Scarecrow Press, 1986.
Oxford University Press. *Oxford Publishing Since 1478.* London: Oxford University Press, 1966.
Palmer, A. Mitchell, and Francis P. Garvan. *Aims and Prospects of the Chemical Foundation.* New York, 1919.
Parrini, Carl. *Heir to Empire: United States Economic Diplomacy 1916–1923.* Pittsburgh: University of Pittsburgh Press, 1969.
Pathé, Charles. "De Pathé Frères à Pathé Cinéma." *Premier Plan,* no. 55 (1970).
Pearce, W. M. *The Matador Land and Cattle Company.* Norman: University of Oklahoma Press, 1964.
Peaslee, Amos J. "Taxing Incomes of Foreign Investors in American Stocks and Bonds." *Columbia Law Review,* 16 (June 1916): 1–15.
Pennock, Pamela. "The National Recovery Administration and the Rubber Tire Industry," *Business History Review,* 71 (Winter 1997): 543–568.
Perkins, Edwin J. *Wall Street to Main Street: Charles Merrill and Middle-Class Investors.* Cambridge: Cambridge University Press, 1999.
Peyer, Hans Conrad. *Roche: A Company History 1896–1996.* Basle: Editiones Roche, 1996.
Phelps, Clyde William. *The Foreign Expansion of American Banks.* New York: Ronald Press, 1927.
Pigott, Stanley. *Hollins.* Nottingham: William Hollins & Co., 1949.
Piluso, Giandomenico. "The Major Italian Banks in South America: Strategies, Markets, and Organization." Unpublished Paper, 1993.
Plummer, Alfred. *International Combines in Modern Industry.* 2nd ed. London: Sir Isaac Pitman, 1938.
Plumptre, A. F. W. *Mobilizing Canada's Resources for War.* Toronto: Macmillan, 1941.
Pollard, Sidney, and Paul Robertson. *The British Shipbuilding Industry.* Cambridge, Mass.: Harvard University Press, 1979.
Posner, Richard. *Economic Analysis of Law.* 3rd ed. Boston: Little, Brown, 1986.
Powell, Thomas Reed. "Alien Land Cases in the United States Supreme Court." *California Law Review,* 12 (May 1924): 259–282.
Pressnell, L. S., and John Orbell. *A Guide to the Historical Records of British Banking.* New York: St. Martin's Press, 1985.
Priest, Tyler. "The 'Americanization' of Shell Oil" In Geoffrey Jones and Lina Gálvez-Muñoz, eds., *Foreign Multinationals in the United States: Management and Performance,* pp. 188–206. London: Routledge, 2002.
Procter & Gamble. *Into the Second Century with Procter & Gamble.* Cincinnati: privately printed, 1944.
Pruessen, Ronald W. *John Foster Dulles.* New York: Free Press, 1982.
Pugach, Noel H. *Same Bed, Different Dreams: A History of the Chinese American Bank of Commerce, 1919–1937.* Hong Kong: Centre of Asian Studies, University of Hong Kong, 1997.
Pusateri, C. Joseph. *A History of American Business.* 2nd ed. Arlington Heights, Ill.: Harland Davidson, 1988.
Puth, Robert C. *American Economic History.* 2nd and 3rd eds. Chicago: Dryden Press, 1988, 1993.
Quigley, Neil C. "The Bank of Nova Scotia in the Caribbean." *Business History Review,* 63 (Winter 1989): 797–838.
Quirico, Roberto di. "The Initial Phases of Italian Banks' Expansion Abroad." *Financial History Review,* 6 (Apr. 1999): 7–24.
Rae, John B. *Climb to Greatness.* Cambridge, Mass.: MIT Press, 1968.
Randall, Stephen. *United States Foreign Oil Policy 1919–1948.* Kingston: McGill-Queen's University Press, 1985.

Ratner, Sidney. *American Taxation.* New York: W. W. Norton, 1942.

Rawles, William P. *The Nationality of Commercial Control of World Minerals.* New York: American Institute of Mining and Metallurgical Engineers, 1933.

Raynes, Harold E. *History of British Insurance.* London: Isaac Pittman, 1950.

Read, Oliver, and Walter L. Welch. *From Tin Foil to Stereo.* Indianapolis: Howard W. Sams & Co., 1959.

Reader, William J. *Bowater.* Cambridge: Cambridge University Press, 1981.

———. *A House in the City: A Study of the City and of the Stock Exchange Based on the Records of Foster and Braithwaite, 1825–1975.* London: B. T. Batsford, 1979.

———. *Imperial Chemical Industries: A History.* 2 vols. London: Oxford University Press, 1970, 1975.

Reading, the Marquess of. *Rufus Isaacs, First Marquess of Reading, 1914–1935.* 2 vols. London: Hutchinson, 1942, 1945.

Reckitt, Basil N. *The History of Reckitt and Sons, Ltd.* London: A. Brown & Sons, 1952.

Reich, Cary. *Financier: The Biography of André Meyer.* New York: William Morrow, 1983.

Reich, Simon. *Fruits of Fascism.* Ithaca, N.Y.: Cornell University Press, 1990.

Reimann, Guenther. *Patents for Hitler.* New York: Vanguard Press, 1942.

Reynolds, David. *The Creation of the Anglo-American Alliance 1937–1941.* Chapel Hill: University of North Carolina Press, 1981.

Rhode Island Historical Preservation Commission. "Historical Preservation Commission Report." Pawtucket, R.I., P-PA-7, October 1978.

Roberts, Harold D. *Salt Creek Wyoming.* Denver, Colo.: Midwest Oil Corp., 1956.

Roberts, Priscella. "A Conflict of Loyalties: Kuhn, Loeb and Company and the First World War, 1914–1917." In Jacob R. Marcus and Abraham J. Peck, eds., *Studies in the American Jewish Experience II,* pp. 1–32, 169–182. Lanham, Md.: University Press of America, 1984.

———. "Willard D. Straight and the Diplomacy of International Finance during the First World War." *Business History Review,* 40 (July 1988): 16–47.

Roberts, Richard. *Schroders.* Houndmills: Macmillan, 1992.

Robinson, Richard. *Business History of the World.* Westport, Conn.: Greenwood Press, 1993.

Rock, Howard, and Deborah Dash Moore. *Cityscapes: A History of New York in Images.* New York: Columbia University Press, 2001.

Rogers, James Harvey. *America Weighs Her Gold.* New Haven, Conn.: Yale University Press, 1931.

Romer, Christina. "What Ended the Great Depression?" *Journal of Economic History,* 52 (Dec. 1992): 757–784.

Rosenbaum, E., and A. J. Sherman. *M. M. Warburg & Co. 1798–1938.* New York: Holmes and Meier, 1979.

Rosenberg, Emily S. *Financial Missionaries to the World: The Politics and Culture of Dollar Diplomacy, 1900–1930.* Cambridge, Mass.: Harvard University Press, 1999.

Ross, Davis R. B. "Patents and Bureaucrats: U.S. Synthetic Rubber Developments before Pearl Harbor." In Joseph Frese and Jacob Judd, eds., *Business and Government,* pp. 119–155. Tarrytown, N.Y.: Sleepy Hollow Restorations, 1985.

Ross, Dorothy. *The Origins of American Social Science.* Cambridge: Cambridge University Press, 1991.

Ross, Victor. *A History of the Canadian Bank of Commerce.* 2 vols. Toronto: Oxford University Press, 1920, 1922.

Royal Institute of International Affairs. *The Problem of International Investment.* London: Oxford University Press, 1937.

Royal Dutch Company. *Annual Reports.*

Rubinstein, W. D. "British Millionaires, 1809–1924." *Bulletin of the Institute of Historical Research,* 47 (1974): 205–223.

Russell, Francis. *The Shadow of Blooming Grove: Warren G. Harding in His Times.* New York: McGraw-Hill, 1968.
Russett, Bruce M. *Community and Contention.* Cambridge, Mass.: MIT Press, 1963.
Safarian, A. E. *Multinational Enterprise and Public Policy.* Aldershot: Elgar, 1993.
Safford, Jeffrey J. "The United States Merchant Marine in Foreign Trade, 1800–1939." In T. Yui and K. Nakagawa, eds., *Business History of Shipping,* pp. 91–118. Tokyo: University of Tokyo Press, 1985.
———. *Wilsonian Maritime Diplomacy, 1913–1921.* New Brunswick, N.J.: Rutgers University Press, 1978.
Sammons, Robert L. "Foreign Investment Aspects of Measuring U.S. National Wealth." National Bureau of Economic Research. *Studies in Income and Wealth,* pp. 549–586. New York: National Bureau of Economic Research, 1950.
Sarnoff, David. *Looking Ahead.* New York: McGraw-Hill, 1968.
Sasuly, Richard. *I. G. Farben.* New York: Boni & Gaer, 1947.
Sayers, R. S. *The Bank of England 1891–1944.* 3 vols. Cambridge: Cambridge University Press, 1976.
Scholl, L. U. "Shipping in Germany." In Tsunehiko Yui and Keiichiro Nakagawa, eds., *Business History of Shipping,* pp. 185–213. Tokyo: University of Tokyo Press, 1985.
Schröter, Harm. "Cartels as a Form of Concentration." In Hans Pohl and Bernd Rudolph, eds., *German Yearbook on Business History 1988,* pp. 113–144. Berlin: Springer-Verlag, 1990.
———. *Die Internationale Kaliwirtschaft 1918 bis 1939.* Kassel, Germany: Kali und Salz, 1985.
———. "The International Potash Syndicate." In Dominique Barjot, ed., *International Cartels Revisited,* pp. 75–92. Caen, France: Editions Diffusion du Lyes, 1994.
———. "Risk and Control in Multinational Enterprise: German Businesses in Scandinavia, 1918–1939." *Business History Review,* 62 (Autumn 1988): 420–443.
———. "A Typical Factor of German International Market Strategy: Agreements between the US and German Electrotechnical Industries up to 1939." In Alice Teichova, Maurice Lévy-Leboyer, and Helga Nussbaum, eds., *Multinational Enterprise in Historical Perspective,* pp. 160–170. Cambridge: Cambridge University Press, 1986.
Schröter, Verena. *Die Deutsche Industrie auf dem Weltmarkt 1929 bis 1933.* Frankfurt: Peter Lang, 1984.
———. "Participation in Market Control through Foreign Investment." In Alice Teichova, Maurice Lévy-Leboyer, and Helga Nussbaum, eds., *Multinational Enterprise in Historical Perspective,* pp. 171–184. Cambridge: Cambridge University Press, 1986.
Schuker, Stephen A. *American "Reparations" to Germany, 1919–33: Implications for the Third World Debt Crisis.* Princeton, N.J.: Princeton Studies in International Finance, 1988.
———. *The End of French Predominance in Europe.* Chapel Hill: University of North Carolina Press, 1976.
Schull, Joseph. *The Century of the Sun: The First Hundred Years of Sun Life Assurance Company of Canada* Toronto: Macmillan of Canada, 1971.
Schull, Joseph, and J. Douglas Gibson. *The Scotiabank Story.* Toronto: Macmillan of Canada, 1982.
Schultz, Ferdinand. *The Technical Division of the Rayon Department, 1920–1951.* Wilmington, Del.: Du Pont, 1952.
Schvarzer, Jorge. *Bunge & Born.* Buenos Aires: CISEA, 1989.
Schwarz, Hans-Peter. *Konrad Adenauer.* Vol. 1. Providence, R.I.: Berghahn Books, 1995.
Schwarz, Jordan A. *The Speculator: Bernard M. Baruch in Washington 1917–1965.* Chapel Hill: University of North Carolina Press, 1981.
Scott, J. D. *Vickers: A History.* London: Weidenfeld & Nicolson, 1962.
Scott, John, and Michael Hughes. *The Anatomy of Scottish Capital.* London: Croom Helm, 1980.

Scranton, Philip. *Endless Novelty: Specialty Production and American Industrialization, 1865–1925.* Princeton, N.J.: Princeton University Press, 1997.

Seagrave, Sterling. *The Soong Dynasty.* New York: Harper & Row, 1985.

Seidenzahl, Fritz. *100 Jahr Deutsche Bank.* Frankfurt: Deutsche Bank, 1970.

Seligman, Edwin R. A. *Double Taxation and International Fiscal Cooperation.* New York: Macmillan, 1928.

Shapiro, Carl, and Robert D. Willig. "On the Antitrust Treatment of Production Joint Ventures." *Journal of Economic Perspectives,* 4 (Summer 1990): 113–130.

Shaplen, Robert. *Kreuger.* New York: Alfred A. Knopf, 1960.

Shawcross, William. *Murdoch.* New York: Touchstone, 1994.

"Shell" Transport and Trading Co. (Ltd). *Annual Reports.*

Sicotte, Richard. "Economic Crisis and Political Response: The Political Economy of the Shipping Act." *Journal of Economic History,* 59 (Dec. 1999): 861–884.

Sidak, J. Gregory. *Foreign Investment in American Telecommunications.* Chicago: University of Chicago Press, 1997.

Sidicaro, Ricardo. *Note sur le conglomerat Bunge et Born.* Paris: Institut National de La Recherche Agronomique, 1975.

Sigerist, Henry E. *Civilization and Disease.* Ithaca, N.Y.: Cornell University Press, 1943.

Silk Association of America. *Annual Reports.*

Silverman, Dan P. *Reconstructing Europe after the Great War.* Cambridge, Mass.: Harvard University Press, 1982.

SKF. "The Story of SKF." Pamphlet, 1982.

Skidelsky, Robert. *John Maynard Keynes.* Vol. 2. New York: Penguin Books, 1992.

———. *John Maynard Keynes.* Vol. 3. New York: Viking Penguin, 2001.

Sloan, Alfred P., Jr. *My Years with General Motors.* Garden City, N.Y.: Doubleday & Co., 1964.

Sluyterman, Keetie E. "From Licensor to Multinational Enterprise." *Business History,* 34 (Apr. 1992): 28–49.

Sluyterman, Keetie E., and Hélène J. M. Winkelman. "The Dutch Family Firm." *Business History,* 35 (Oct. 1993): 152–183.

Smith, Clayton Lindsay. *The History of Trade Marks.* N.p., 1923.

Smith, George David. *From Monopoly to Competition: The Transformations of Alcoa, 1888–1986.* Cambridge: Cambridge University Press, 1988.

Smith, George David, and Richard Sylla. "The Transformation of Financial Capitalism: An Essay on the History of American Capital Markets." *Financial Markets, Institutions and Instruments,* 2 (May 1993): 1–62.

Smith, J. Russell. *Influence of the Great War upon Shipping.* New York: Oxford University Press, 1919.

Sobel, Robert. *The Big Board.* New York: Free Press, 1965.

———. *The Curbstone Brokers.* New York: Macmillan, 1970.

———. *The Great Bull Market: Wall Street in the 1920s.* New York: W. W. Norton, 1968.

———. *The Life and Times of Dillon Read.* New York: Truman Talley Books, 1991.

Soule, George. *Prosperity Decade.* New York: Holt, Rinehart and Winston, 1947.

Southard, Frank A., Jr. *American Industry in Europe.* Boston: Houghton, Mifflin, 1931.

Southern Railway Co. *Annual Reports.*

Spence, Clark. *British Investments in the American Mining Frontier, 1860–1901.* Ithaca, N.Y.: Cornell University Press, 1958.

Spender, J. A. *Weetman Pearson.* London: Cassell & Co., 1930.

Sperry, Earl E. *German Plots and Intrigues in the United States during the Period of Neutrality.* Washington, D.C.: Committee on Public Information, 1918.

Spinelli, Lawrence. *Dry Diplomacy.* Wilmington, Del.: Scholarly Resources, 1989.

Sprague, Marshall. *Money Mountain: The Story of Cripple Creek Gold.* Boston: Little, Brown, 1953.

Sprague, O. M. W. "The Crisis of 1914 in the United States." *American Economic Review* 5 (Sept. 1915): 499–533.

Sprout, Harold, and Margaret Sprout. *Toward a New Order of Sea Power, 1918–1922.* Princeton, N.J.: Princeton University Press, 1940.

Spurr, J. E. *Political and Commercial Geology and the World's Mineral Resources.* New York: McGraw-Hill, 1920.

Staley, Eugene. *Raw Materials in Peace and War.* 1937. Rpt. New York: Arno Press, 1976.

———. *War and the Private Investor.* 1935. Rpt. New York: Howard Fertig, 1967.

Stallings, Barbara. *Banker to the Third World.* Berkeley: University of California Press, 1986.

Steen, Kathryn. "Confiscated Commerce: American Importers of German Synthetic Organic Chemicals, 1914–1929." *History and Technology,* 12 (1995): 261–284.

———. "German Chemicals and American Politics." In J. E. Lesch, ed., *The German Chemical Industry in the Twentieth Century,* pp. 323–346. Dordrecht, Netherlands: Kluwer, 2000.

Stern, Siegfried. *The United States in International Banking.* New York: Columbia University Press, 1951.

Stevenson, William. *A Man Called Intrepid.* New York: Harcourt Brace Jovanovich, 1976.

Stewart, Bryce M., and Walter J. Couper. *Profit Sharing and Stock Ownership for Wage Earners and Executives.* New York: Industrial Relations Counselors, 1945.

Stocking, George W. *The Potash Industry.* New York: Richard R. Smith, 1931.

Stocking, George W., and Willard F. Mueller. "The Cellophane Case and the New Competition." *American Economic Review,* 45 (Mar. 1955): 29–63.

Stocking, George W., and Myron W. Watkins. *Cartels in Action.* New York: Twentieth Century Fund, 1947.

Stoff, Michael B. *Oil, War, and American Security.* New Haven, Conn.: Yale University Press, 1980.

Stokes, Raymond. *Divide and Prosper.* Berkeley: University of California Press, 1988.

Stopford, John M. *Directory of Multinationals.* 2 vols. New York: Stockton Press, 1992.

———. "The Origins of British-Based Multinational Manufacturing Enterprise." *Business History Review,* 48 (Autumn 1974): 303–335.

Storck, John, and Walter Dorwin. *Flour for Man's Bread.* Minneapolis: University of Minnesota Press, 1952.

Strasser, Karl. *Die Deutschen Banken im Ausland.* Munich: Verlag von Ernst–Reinhart, 1925.

Stuart, William H. *The Twenty Incredible Years.* Chicago: M. A. Donohue & Co., 1935.

Studenski, Paul, and Herman E. Krooss. *Financial History of the United States.* 2nd ed. New York: McGraw-Hill, 1963.

Sturmey, S. G. *British Shipping and World Competition.* London: Athlone Press, 1962.

Sullivan, Charles H. "Alien Land Laws." *Temple Law Quarterly,* 36 (1962): 15–53.

Sun Life Assurance Co. *Annual Reports.*

Superintendent of Banks (California). *Annual Reports.*

Supple, Barry. *Royal Exchange Assurance.* Cambridge: Cambridge University Press, 1970.

Swaine, Robert T. *The Cravath Firm.* 2 vols. New York: privately printed, 1946, 1948.

Tamagna, Frank M. *Banking and Finance in China.* New York: Institute of Pacific Relations, 1942.

Tansill, Charles Callan. *America Goes to War.* 1938. Rpt. Gloucester, Mass.: Peter Smith, 1963.

Taussig, F. W. *The Tariff History of the United States.* 8th rev. ed. New York: Capricorn Books, 1964.

Taylor, A. J. P. *Beaverbrook.* New York: Simon & Schuster, 1952.

Taylor, Graham D. "Negotiating Technology Transfers with Multinational Enterprises." *Business History,* 36 (Jan. 1994): 127–158.

Taylor, Graham D., and Peter A. Baskerville. *A Concise History of Business in Canada.* Toronto: Oxford University Press, 1994.

Taylor, Graham D., and Patricia E. Sudnik. *Du Pont and the International Chemical Industry.* Boston: Twayne Publishers, 1984.

Teichova, Alice, Maurice Lévy-Leboyer, and Helga Nussbaum, eds. *Historical Studies in International Corporate Business.* Cambridge: Cambridge University Press, 1989.

———. Maurice Lévy-Leboyer, and Helga Nussbaum, eds. *Multinational Enterprise in Historical Perspective.* Cambridge: Cambridge University Press, 1986.

Temin, Peter. *Did Monetary Forces Cause the Great Depression?* New York: W. W. Norton, 1976.

Thomas, A. P. *Woonsocket: Highlights of History, 1800–1976.* East Providence, R.I.: Globe Printing Co., 1976.

Thompson, John F., and Norman Beasley. *For the Years to Come.* New York: G. P. Putnam's 1960.

Thomson, H. A., ed. *By Faith and Work: The Autobiography of the 1st Viscount Mackintosh of Halifax.* London: Hutchinson & Co., 1966.

Threlfall, Richard. *The Story of 100 Years of Phosphorous Making.* Oldbury: Albright & Wilson, 1951.

Tignor, Robert L. *Egyptian Textile and British Capital 1930–1956.* Cairo: American University Press, 1989.

Tilley, Nannie M. *The R. J. Reynolds Tobacco Company.* Chapel Hill: University of North Carolina Press, 1985.

Todd, Walter F. "History of and Rationales for the Reconstruction Finance Corporation." *Economic Review,* 28, no. 4 (1992).

Tolchin, Martin, and Susan Tolchin. *Buying into America.* New York: Times Books, 1988.

Tolliday, Steven. *Business, Banking, and Politics.* Cambridge, Mass.: Harvard University Press, 1987.

Tombs, Lawrence C. *International Organization in European Air Transport.* New York: Columbia University Press, 1936.

Toniolo, Gianni. *One Hundred Years, 1894–1994: A Short History of the Banca Commerciale Italiana.* Milan: BCI, 1994.

Trebilcock, Clive. *Phoenix Assurance and the Development of British Insurance.* Vol. 2. Cambridge: Cambridge University Press, 1998.

Trigge, A. St. L. *A History of the Canadian Bank of Commerce, 1919–1930.* Vol. 3. Toronto: Canadian Bank of Commerce, 1934.

Tuchman, Barbara W. *The Guns of August.* New York: Macmillan, 1962.

Turrell, Robert Vicat, and Jean Jacques Van-Helten. "The Investment Group." *Economic History Review,* 2nd ser., 40 (May 1987): 267–274.

Tuttle, William M., Jr. "The Birth of an Industry: The Synthetic Rubber 'Mess' in World War II." *Technology and Culture,* 22 (Jan. 1981): 35–67.

Tweedale, Geoffrey. *Sheffield Steel and America.* Cambridge: Cambridge University Press, 1987.

———. "Transatlantic Specialty Steels: Sheffield High-Grade Steel Firms and the USA, 1860–1940." In Geoffrey Jones, ed., *British Multinationals: Origins, Management and Performance,* pp. 75–95. Aldershot: Gower, 1986.

United Nations. *International Capital Movements during the Inter-war Period.* Lake Success, N.Y.: United Nations, 1949.

United Nations Monetary and Financial Conference. *Proceedings and Documents of the United Nations Monetary and Financial Conference, Bretton Woods, New Hampshire, July 1–22, 1944.* Washington, D.C., 1948.

U.S. Alien Property Custodian. *Annual Reports 1918–1934.*

———. *Report 1918–1919.* New York: Arno Press, 1977.

U.S. Civilian Production Administration. *War Industrial Facilities Authorized, July 1940–August 1945. Listed Alphabetically by Company and Plant Location.* 1946.

U.S. Comptroller General. Report to Congress. "Treasury Should Keep Better Track of Foreign Assets." 1980.

U.S. Congress. House. *War Claims Arising Out of World War II.* H. Doc. 67, 83rd Cong., 1st sess., 1953.

———. Committee of the Judiciary, Subcommittee on Administrative Law and Governmental Relations. *Foreign Agents Registration Act of 1938, Hearings.* 102nd Cong., 1st sess., 1991.

———. Committee of the Judiciary, Subcommittee on Study of Monopoly Power. *Study of Monopoly Power, Hearings.* 81st Cong., 2nd sess., 1950.

———. Committee on Government Operations, Subcommittee on Commerce, Consumer and Monetary Affairs. *Federal Response to OPEC Country Investments.* Pt. 2. 97th Cong., 1st sess., 1982.

———. Committee on Merchant Marine and Fisheries. *Hearings on HR 19350: A Bill to Regulate Radio Communications.* 64th Cong., 2nd sess., 1917. Radio Communication Hearings.

———. Committee on Military Affairs. *Hearings on HR 1395.* 69th Cong., 1st sess., 1926.

———. Special Committee on Un-American Activities. *Investigation of Nazi Propaganda Activities and Investigation of Certain Other Propaganda Activities.* 73rd Cong., 2nd sess., 1934. McCormack Committee Hearings.

U.S. Congress. Senate. *Report of the Secretary of the Treasury in Answer to a Resolution of the Senate Calling for the Amount of American Securities Held in Europe and Other Foreign Countries, on the 30th June 1853.* Exec. Doc. 42, 33rd Cong., 1st sess., 1854.

———. Committee on Banking and Currency. *Anglo-American Financial Agreement, Hearings.* 79th Cong., 2nd sess., 1946. Loan Hearings.

———. Committee on Banking and Currency. *Stock Exchange Practices, Hearings.* 72nd Cong., 1st sess., 1932–1933—7 pts. in 6 vols.; 72nd and 73rd Cong., 1933–1934—20 pts. in 9 vols. In January 1933, Ferdinand Pecora was retained as counsel to the committee; thereafter these were referred to as the Pecora Committee Hearings.

———. Committee on Banking and Currency. *Stock Exchange Practices, Report.* 73rd Cong., 2nd sess., 1934.

———. Committee on Finance. *Sale of Foreign Bonds, Hearings.* 72nd Cong., 1st sess., 1932.

———. Committee on the Judiciary. *Alleged Dye Monopoly, Hearings.* 67th Cong. 1922. 1922 Dye Hearings.

———. Committee on the Judiciary, Subcommittee on Antitrust and Monopoly. *International Aspects of Antitrust, Hearings.* 89th Cong., 2nd sess., 1966.

———. Committee on the Judiciary, Subcommittee to Investigate the Administration of the Trading with the Enemy Act. *Administration of the Trading with the Enemy Act, Hearings.* 83rd Cong., 1st sess., 1954.

———. Committee on Military Affairs, Subcommittee on War Mobilization. *Elimination of German Resources for War, Hearings.* 79th Cong., 1st sess., pts. 1–10. 1945–1946. Kilgore Committee Hearings II.

———. Committee on Military Affairs, Subcommittee on War Mobilization. *Scientific and Technical Mobilization, Hearings.* 78th Cong., 1st and 2nd sess., pts. 1–16. 1943–1944.
Kilgore Committee Hearings.

———. Committee on Patents. *Patents, Hearings.* 77th Cong, 2nd sess., 1942. Bone Committee Hearings.

———. Committee on Patents. *Salvarsan, Hearings.* 65th Cong., 1st sess., 1917.

———. Special Committee Investigating the Munitions Industry. *The Munitions Industry, Hearings.* 74th Cong., 1st and 2nd sess., 1934–1936. Nye Committee Hearings.

———. Special Committee Investigating the National Defense Program. *Investigation of the National Defense Program, Hearings.* 77th Cong., 1st sess.–79th Cong., 2nd sess., 1941–1947. Truman Committee Hearings, 1941–June 1944.

———. Special Committee Investigating Petroleum Interests in Foreign Countries. *American Petroleum Interests in Foreign Countries.* 79th Cong., 1st sess., 1946.

U.S. Department of Agriculture. *Survey of the Fertilizer Industry*. Circular No. 129. 1931.
———. *1940 Yearbook of Agriculture*. 1940.
U.S. Department of Commerce. *The Balance of International Payments of the United States, 1923*. 1924.
———. *Foreign Direct Investment in the United States*. 9 vols. 1976. *FDIUS—1976*.
———. *Long-Term Economic Growth 1860–1965*. 1966.
U.S. Department of Commerce, Bureau of the Census. *Historical Statistics of the United States*. 1960.
———. *Historical Statistics of the United States: Colonial Times to 1970*. 2 vols. 1975.
U.S. Department of Commerce, Bureau of Foreign and Domestic Commerce. *The Balance of International Payments of the United States in 1927*. 1928.
———. *The Balance of International Payments of the United States in 1929*. 1930.
———. *The Balance of International Payments of the United States in 1931*. 1931.
———. *British Investment Trusts*. Trade Information Bulletin No. 88. 1923.
———. *Foreign Investments in the United States*. 1937. *FIUS—1937*.
———. *Foreign Long-Term Investments in the United States 1937–1939*. 1940. *FIUS—1940*.
———. *The International Cartel Movement*, by Louis Domeratzky. Trade Information Bulletin No. 556. 1928.
U.S. Department of Commerce, Office of Business Economics. *Foreign Business Investments in the United States, A Supplement to the Survey of Current Business*, by Samuel Pizer and Zalie V. Warner. 1962.
———. *International Transactions of the United States during the War, 1940–1945*. Economic Series No. 65. 1948. *Commerce Study 1940–1945*.
[U.S. Department of Commerce and U.S. Department of Treasury]. *Estimates of United States Direct Foreign Investment, 1929–1943 and 1947*. New York: Arno Press, 1976.
U.S. Department of the Navy. *Annual Reports of the Secretary*.
U.S. Department of State. *Foreign Relations of the United States*.
———. *United States Treaties and Other International Agreements*. 1952.
U.S. Department of the Treasury. *Annual Reports*.
———. *Census of Foreign-Owned Assets in the United States*. 1945. *1941 Census*.
———. *Documents Pertaining to Foreign Funds Control*. 1945.
———. *Foreign Assets Control: Regulations and Related Documents*. 1954.
U.S. Department of the Treasury, Office of the Secretary. *Census of American-Owned Assets in Foreign Countries* (1947).
U.S. Federal Trade Commission. *Electric Power Industry*. 1928.
———. *Foreign Ownership in the Petroleum Industry*. 1923.
———. *The International Petroleum Cartel*. 1952.
———. *Methods and Operations of Grain Exporters*. 2 vols. 1922, 1923.
———. *Report on the Copper Industry*. 1947.
———. *Report on Milk and Milk Products, 1914–1918*. 1921.
———. *Report on Motor Vehicles*. 1939.
———. *Report on the Petroleum Industry of Wyoming*. 1921.
———. *Report on the Radio Industry*. 1923.
U.S. Office of Alien Property Custodian. *Annual Reports 1942–1946*. New York: Arno Press, 1977.
U.S. Securities and Exchange Commission. *Investment Trusts and Investment Companies*. H. Doc. 707, 75th Cong., 3rd sess., 1939.
———. *Investment Trusts and Investment Companies*. H. Doc. 279, 76th Cong., 1st sess., 1940.
———. *Investment Trusts and Investment Companies*. H. Doc. 246, 77th Cong., 1st sess., 1942.
———. *Investment Trusts in Great Britain*. H. Doc. 380, 76th Cong., 1st sess., 1939.

———. *Report on Study of Investment Trusts and Investment Holding Companies.* 75th–77th Cong., 1939–1942. (4 pts., with the title of each part varying slightly.)

U.S. Temporary National Economic Committee. *The Distribution of Ownership in the 200 Largest Financial Corporations.* Monograph 29. 1940.

———. *Hearings.* 76th Cong., 3rd sess., 1940.

U.S. Works Progress Administration. "History of Milltown," 1936 Typescript in Milltown Public Library, Milltown, New Jersey.

Vagts, Detlev F. "The Corporate Alien: Definitional Questions in Federal Restraints on Foreign Enterprise." *Harvard Law Review* 74 (June 1961): 1489–1551.

Van der Wee, Herman, and Monique Verbreyt. *The Generale Bank 1822–1997.* Tielt, Belgium: Lanno Publishers, 1997.

Van der Zee, Jacob. *The British in Iowa.* Iowa City: State Historical Society of Iowa, 1922.

Van Manen, Charlotte A. *De Nederlandsche Overzee Trustmaatschappij.* 8 vols. in 6 parts. 's-Gravenhagen: Martinus Nijhoff, 1935.

Vatter, Harold G. *The U.S. Economy in World War II.* New York: Columbia University Press, 1985.

Veenendaal, Augustus J. "'Dutch' Towns in the United States of America." In Robert S. Kirsner, ed., *The Low Countries and Beyond,* pp. 315–321. Lanham, Md.: University Press of America, 1993.

———. *Slow Train to Paradise.* Stanford, Calif.: Stanford University Press, 1996.

Verg, Erik. *Milestones.* Leverkusen: Bayer, 1988.

Vernon, Raymond. "Where Are the Multinationals Headed?" In Kenneth A. Froot, ed., *Foreign Direct Investment,* pp. 57–83. Chicago: University of Chicago Press, 1992.

Vernus, Pierre. "The Export Policy of Lyon Silk Firm Bianchini Férier (1890s–1970s)." In Hubert Bonin et al., eds., *Transnational Companies,* pp. 139–152. Paris: Éditions P.L.A.G.E., n.d. [2002].

Vietor, Richard H. K. "Contrived Competition." *Business History,* 36 (Oct. 1994): 1–32.

Vries, Johan de. *The Netherlands Economy in the Twentieth Century.* Assen: van Gorcum, 1978.

Wake, Jehanne. *Kleinwort Benson.* Oxford: Oxford University Press, 1997.

Wall, Bennett H., *Growth in a Changing Environment.* New York: McGraw-Hill, 1988.

Wall, Bennett H., and George S. Gibb. *Teagle of Jersey Standard.* New Orleans: Tulane University Press, 1974.

Wall, Joseph Frazier. *Alfred I. Du Pont.* New York: Oxford University Press, 1990.

Walraven, Kornelis Jacobus. "International Long-Term Capital Movements of the Netherlands in the Post-war Period, 1946–1956." Ph.D. diss., Syracuse University, 1959.

Warburg, James P. *The Long Road Home.* Garden City, N.Y.: Doubleday, 1964.

Watt, D. Cameron. *Succeeding John Bull.* Cambridge: Cambridge University Press, 1984.

Wechsberg, Joseph. *The Merchant Bankers.* Boston: Little, Brown, 1966.

Weiher, Sigfrid von, and Herbert Goetzeler. *The Siemens Company.* Berlin and Munich: Siemens, 1984.

Weir, Ronald. *The History of the Distillers Company.* Oxford: Oxford University Press, 1995.

———. *A History of the Scottish American Investment Company.* Ltd., 1873–1973. Edinburgh: Scottish American Investment Company, 1973.

Weisberger, Bernard A. *The Dream Maker.* Boston: Little, Brown, 1979.

Wells, Louis T., Jr., "Automobiles." In Raymond Vernon, ed., *Big Business and the State,* pp. 229–254, 295–298. Cambridge, Mass.: Harvard University Press, 1974.

Wells, Wyatt. *Antitrust and the Formation of the Postwar World.* New York: Columbia University Press, 2002.

White, Eugene. "Banking and Finance in the Twentieth Century." In Stanley L. Engerman and Robert E. Gallman, eds., *Cambridge Economic History of the United States. The Twentieth Century,* Vol. 3, pp. 743–802. Cambridge: Cambridge University Press, 2000.

White, Horace G. "Foreign Trading in American Stock Exchange Securities." *Journal of Political Economy,* 48 (Oct. 1940): 655–702.

Whitney, Simon N. *Antitrust Policies.* 2 vols. New York: Twentieth Century Fund, 1958.

Wigmore, Barrie A. *The Crash and Its Aftermath.* Westport, Conn.: Greenwood Press, 1985.

———. "Was the Bank Holiday of 1933 Caused by a Run on the Dollar?" *Journal of Economic History,* 47 (Sept. 1987): 739–755.

Wilcox, Clair. *Public Policies toward Business.* 3rd ed. Homewood, Ill.: Richard D. Irwin, 1966.

Wilkins, Mira. "American-Japanese Direct Foreign Investment Relationships, 1930–1952." *Business History Review,* 56 (Winter 1982): 497–518.

———. "Charles Pathé's American Business." *Entreprises et Histoire,* no. 6 (Sept. 1994): 133–144.

———. "Cosmopolitan Finance in the 1920s: New York's Emergence as an International Financial Centre." In Richard Sylla, Richard Tilly, and G. Tortella, eds., *The State, the Financial System, and Economic Modernization: Comparative Historical Perspectives,* pp. 271–291. Cambridge: Cambridge University Press, 1999.

———. *The Emergence of Multinational Enterprise: American Business Abroad from the Colonial Era to 1914.* Cambridge, Mass.: Harvard University Press, 1970.

———. "Foreign Banks and Foreign Investment in the United States." In Rondo Cameron and V. I. Bovykin, eds., *International Banking 1870–1914,* pp. 233–252. Oxford: Oxford University Press, 1991.

———. *Foreign Enterprise in Florida.* Miami: University Presses of Florida, 1979.

———. "The Free-Standing Company, 1870–1914." *Economic History Review,* 2nd ser., 41 (May 1988): 259–282.

———. "French Multinationals in the United States: An Historical Perspective." *Entreprises et Histoire,* no. 3 (May 1993): 14–29.

———. "German Chemical Firms in the United States from the late 19th Century to Post–World War II." In John Leisch, ed., *The German Chemical Industry in the 20th Century,* pp. 285–321. Dordrecht, Netherlands: Kluwer, 2000.

———. *The History of Foreign Investment in the United States to 1914.* Cambridge, Mass.: Harvard University Press, 1989.

———. "Japanese Multinationals in the United States: Continuity and Change, 1879–1990." *Business History Review,* 64 (Winter 1990): 585–629.

———. *The Maturing of Multinational Enterprise: American Business Abroad from 1914 to 1970.* Cambridge, Mass.: Harvard University Press, 1974.

———. "Multinational Oil Companies in South America in the 1920s." *Business History Review,* 48 (Autumn 1974): 414–446.

———. *New Foreign Enterprise in Florida.* Miami, 1980.

———. "The Role of U.S. Business." In Dorothy Borg and Shumpei Okamoto, eds., *Pearl Harbor as History,* pp. 341–376, 681–690. New York: Columbia University Press, 1973.

———. "Swiss Investments in the United States, 1914–1945." In Sébastien Guex, ed., *La Suisse et les Grandes puissances 1914–1945,* pp. 91–139. Geneva: Droz, 1999.

———. "Two Literatures, Two Story-Lines: Is a General Paradigm of Foreign Portfolio and Foreign Direct Investment Feasible?" *Transnational Corporations,* 8 (Apr. 1999): 53–116.

———, ed. *British Overseas Investments 1907–1948.* New York: Arno Press, 1977.

———, *Foreign Investments in the United States: Department of Commerce and Department of Treasury Estimates.* New York: Arno Press, 1977.

Wilkins, Mira, and Frank Ernest Hill. *American Business Abroad: Ford on Six Continents.* Detroit: Wayne State University Press, 1964.

Wilkins, Mira, and Harm Schröter, eds. *The Free-Standing Company in the World Economy.* Oxford: Oxford University Press, 1998.

Williams, Alan. *Republic of Images: A History of French Filmmaking.* Cambridge, Mass.: Harvard University Press, 1992.

Williams, Mari E. W. *The Precision Makers.* London: Routledge, 1994.

Wilson, A. J. *The Life and Times of Sir Alfred Chester Beatty.* London: Cadogan Publications, 1985.

Wilson, Charles. *The History of Unilever.* 3 vols. New York: Praeger, 1968.

Wilson, J. S. G. *French Banking Structure and Credit Policy.* Cambridge, Mass.: Harvard University Press, 1957.

Wilson, Joan Hoff. *American Business and Foreign Policy, 1921–1933.* Lexington: University of Kentucky Press, 1971.

Wilson, John D. *The Chase: The Chase Manhattan Bank N.A. 1945–1985.* Boston: Harvard Business School Press, 1986.

Winkler, Max. *Foreign Bonds: An Autopsy.* Philadelphia: Roland Swain, 1933.

Wise, T. A. *Peat, Marwick, Mitchell & Co. 85 Years.* N.p.: Peat, Marwick, Mitchell & Co., 1982.

Witte, John F. *The Politics and Development of the Federal Income Tax* (Madison: University of Wisconsin Press, 1985).

Wohlert, Klaus. "Multinational Enterprise—Financing Trade, Diplomacy: The Swedish Case. In Alice Teichova, Maurice Lévy-Leboyer, and Helga Nussbaum, eds., *Historical Studies in International Corporate Business,* pp. 77–85. Cambridge: Cambridge University Press, 1989.

Woodruff, William. *Impact of Western Man.* Washington, D.C.; University Press of America, 1966.

Woods, Randall Bennett. *A Changing of the Guard: Anglo-American Relations, 1941–1946.* Chapel Hill: University of North Carolina Press, 1990.

Wright, Annette C. "Spencer Love and Burlington Mills." *Business History Review,* 69 (Spring 1995): 42–79.

Wright, Ivan. *Farm Mortgage Financing.* New York: McGraw-Hill, 1923.

Wyatt, R. J. *The Austin, 1905–1952.* Newton Abbot: David & Charles, 1981.

Yamazaki, Hiroaki. "The Yokohama Specie Bank." In Youssef Cassis, ed., *Finance and Financiers in European History,* pp. 371–403. Cambridge: Cambridge University Press, 1992.

Yeager, Leland B. *International Monetary Relations.* New York: Harper & Row, 1966.

Yeh, Wen-Hsin. "Corporate Space, Communal Time: Everyday Life in Shanghai's Bank of China." *American Historical Review,* 100 (Feb. 1995): 97–122.

Yergin, Daniel. *The Prize.* New York: Simon & Schuster, 1991.

Yonekawa, Shin'ichi, and Hideki Yoshihara, eds. *Business History of General Trading Companies.* Tokyo: University of Tokyo Press, 1987.

Yui, Tsunehiko, and Keiichiro Nakagawa, eds. *Business History of Shipping.* Tokyo: University of Tokyo Press, 1985.

Zacchia, Carlo. "International Trade and Capital Movements 1920–1970." In Carlo M. Cipolla, ed., *The Twentieth Century—2, The Fontana Economic History of Europe,* Vol. 5, pp. 509–602. New York: Barnes & Noble, 1977.

Zeiler, Thomas W. *Free Trade, Free World: The Advent of GATT.* Chapel Hill: University of North Carolina Press, 1999.

Ziegler, Philip. *The Sixth Great Power.* New York: Alfred A. Knopf, 1988.

Newspapers, Journals, Directories, Bulletins, Encyclopedias

Acceptance Bulletin
American Journal of International Law
Annalist

Bankers Magazine
B.A.T. Industries, Facts and Figures
Best's Insurance Reports, Casualty, Surety, Miscellaneous
Best's Insurance Reports, Fire and Marine
Best's Insurance Reports, Life Insurance
Chemical Age
Chemical Markets
Commercial and Financial Chronicle
Congressional Record
Dictionary of Business Biography
Dictionary of National Biography
Economist
Encyclopedia of American Business History and Biography
Federal Register
Federal Reserve Bulletin
Financial Times
Fortune
Grand Metropolitan Fact Book
Handbook of Texas
Harper Encyclopaedia of the Modern World
Herald Tribune (New York)
IMF Survey
Journal of Commerce
London Gazette
Miami Herald
Midland Bank Monthly Review (and predecessor)
Mineral Industry
Moody's Industrial Manual (title varies)
Moody's Manual Banks (title varies)
Moody's Manual of Public Utilities (title varies)
National Association of Wool Manufacturers Bulletin
National Cyclopaedia
New York Times
Petroleum Facts and Figures
Rand McNally's Bank Directory
Red Book of Commerce
Silk Association Bulletin
Stock Exchange Official Intelligence
Stock Exchange Year Book
Survey of Current Business
The Times (London)
Van Oss' Effectenboek
Wall Street Journal
Who's Who in America

Index

Harvard Studies in Business History

1. John Jacob Astor, Business Man, *by Kenneth Wiggins Porter*
2. Jay Cooke, Private Banker, *by Henrietta M. Larson*
3. The Jacksons and the Lees: Two Generations of Massachusetts Merchants, 1765–1844, *by Kenneth Wiggins Porter*
4. The Massachusetts–First National Bank of Boston, 1784–1934, *by N. S. B. Gras*
5. The History of an Advertising Agency: N. W. Ayer & Son at Work, 1869–1949, *revised edition, by Ralph M. Hower*
6. Marketing Life Insurance: Its History in America, *by J. Owen Stalson*
7. History of Macy's of New York, 1858–1919: Chapters in the Evolution of the Department Store, *by Ralph M. Hower*
8. The Whitesmiths of Taunton: A History of Reed & Barton, 1824–1943, *by George Sweet Gibb*
9. Development of Two Bank Groups in the Central Northwest: A Study in Bank Policy and Organization, *by Charles Sterling Popple*
10. The House of Hancock: Business in Boston, 1724–1775, *by W. T. Baxter*
11. Timing a Century: History of the Waltham Watch Company, *by C. W. Moore*
12. Guide to Business History: Materials for the Study of American Business and Suggestions for Their Use, *by Henrietta M. Larson*
13. Pepperell's Progress: History of a Cotton Textile Company, 1844–1945, *by Evelyn H. Knowlton*
14. The House of Baring in American Trade and Finance: English Merchant Bankers at Work, 1763–1861, *by Ralph W. Hidy*
15. The Whitin Machine Works since 1831: A Textile Machinery Company in an Industrial Village, *by Thomas R. Navin*
16. The Saco-Lowell Shops: Textile Machinery Building in New England, 1813–1949, *by George Sweet Gibb*
17. Broadlooms and Businessmen: A History of the Bigelow-Sanford Carpet Company, 1825–1953, *by John S. Ewing and Nancy P. Norton*
18. Nathan Trotter: Philadelphia Merchant, 1787–1853, *by Elva Tooker*
19. A History of the Massachusetts Hospital Life Insurance Company, *by Gerald T. White*
20. The Charles Ilfeld Company: A Study of the Rise and Decline of Mercantile Capitalism in New Mexico, *by William J. Parish*
21. The Rise and Decline of the Medici Bank, 1397–1494, *by Raymond de Roover*
22. Isaac Hicks: New York Merchant and Quaker, 1767–1820, *by Robert A. Davison*
23. Boston Capitalists and Western Railroads: A Study in the Nineteenth-Century Railroad Investment Process, *by Arthur M. Johnson and Barry E. Supple*

24. Petroleum Pipelines and Public Policy, 1906–1959, *by Arthur M. Johnson*

25. Investment Banking in America: A History, *by Vincent P. Carosso*

26. Merchant Prince of Boston: Colonel T. H. Perkins, 1764–1854, *by Carl Seaburg and Stanley Paterson*

27. The Maturing of Multinational Enterprise: American Business Abroad from 1914 to 1970, *by Mira Wilkins*

28. Financing Anglo-American Trade: The House of Brown, *by Edwin J. Perkins*

29. British Mercantile Houses in Buenos Aires, 1810–1880, *by Vera Blinn Reber*

30. The British Shipbuilding Industry, 1870–1914, *by Sidney Pollard and Paul Robertson*

31. Moving the Masses: The Evolution of Urban Public Transit in New York, Boston, and Philadelphia, 1880–1912, *by Charles W. Cheape*

32. Managerial Hierarchies: Comparative Perspectives on the Rise of Modern Industrial Enterprise, *edited by Alfred D. Chandler Jr. and Herman Daems*

33. Big Business in China: Sino-Foreign Rivalry in the Cigarette Industry, 1890–1930, *by Sherman Cochran*

34. The Emergence of Multinational Enterprise: American Business Abroad from the Colonial Era to 1914, *by Mira Wilkins*

35. Kikkoman: Company, Clan, and Community, *by W. Mark Fruin*

36. Family Firm to Modern Multinational: Norton Company, a New England Enterprise, *by Charles W. Cheape*

37. Citibank, 1812–1970, *by Harold van B. Cleveland and Thomas F. Huertas*

38. The Morgans: Private International Bankers, 1854–1913, *by Vincent P. Carosso*

39. Business, Banking, and Politics: The Case of British Steel, 1918–1939, *by Steven Tolliday*

40. Enterprising Elite: The Boston Associates and the World They Made, *by Robert F. Dalzell Jr.*

41. The History of Foreign Investment in the United States to 1914, *by Mira Wilkins*

42. News over the Wires: The Telegraph and the Flow of Public Information in America, 1844–1897, *by Menahem Blondheim*

43. The History of Foreign Investment in the United States, 1914–1945, *by Mira Wilkins*